For Reference

Not to be taken from this room

CONGRESS
A to Z

CONGRESS A TO Z

FIFTH EDITION

CQ PRESS

A Division of Congressional Quarterly Inc.
Washington, D.C.

CQ Press
2300 N Street, NW, Suite 800
Washington, DC 20037

Phone: 202-729-1900; toll-free, 1-866-4CQ-PRESS (1-866-427-7737)

Web: www.cqpress.com

CQ Press gratefully acknowledges the permission to use the photo on page 500 granted by the United States Holocaust Memorial Museum. The views or opinions expressed in this book and the context in which the images are used, do not necessarily reflect the views or policy of, nor imply approval or endorsement by the United States Holocaust Memorial Museum.

Composition: Auburn Associates, Inc.
Cover design: Auburn Associates, Inc.
Cover photos: Clockwise from top, Photodisc, Architect of the Capitol, AP Images

∞ The paper used in this publication exceeds the requirements of the American National Standard for Information Sciences—Permanence of Paper for Printed Library Materials, ANSI Z39.48-1992.

Printed and bound in the United States of America

12 11 10 09 08   1 2 3 4 5

Library of Congress Cataloging-in-Publication Data
Congress A to Z.—5th ed.
    p. cm.
 "CQ Press, a Division of Congressional Quarterly Inc."
 Includes bibliographical references and index.
 ISBN 978-0-87289-558-4 (alk. paper)
 1. United States. Congress—Dictionaries. I. Congressional Quarterly, Inc.
 JK1021.C554 2008
 328.73003—dc22

                    2008011284

CQ PRESS
AMERICAN GOVERNMENT A TO Z SERIES

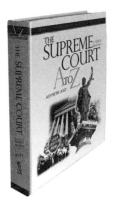

The Supreme Court A to Z, 4th Edition

This is the definitive source for information on the Court, its justices, and its impact on American democracy.

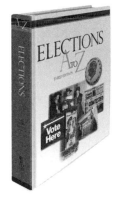

Elections A to Z, 3rd Edition

This single, convenient volume explores vital aspects of campaigns and elections, from voting rights to the current state of House, Senate, and presidential elections.

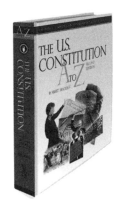

The U.S. Constitution A to Z, 2nd Edition

This is an ideal resource for anyone who wants reliable information on the U.S. Constitution and its impact on U.S. government and politics.

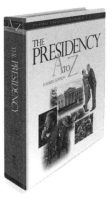

The Presidency A to Z, 4th Edition

This is an invaluable quick-information guide to the executive branch and its responses to the challenges facing the nation over time.

Contents

REFERENCE MATERIAL

Tables and Figures

About the Book

Congress A to Z is part of CQ Press's five-volume American Government A to Z series, which provides essential information about the history, powers, and operations of the three branches of government, the election of members of Congress and the president, and the nation's most important document, the Constitution. In these volumes, CQ Press's writers and editors present engaging insight and analysis about U.S. government in a comprehensive, ready-reference encyclopedia format. The series is useful to anyone who has an interest in national government and politics.

Congress A to Z offers accessible information about the inner workings of the legislative branch, including biographies of influential members; discussions of congressional relations with the president, the bureaucracy, interest groups, the media, political parties, and the public; and explanations of the concepts and powers related to Congress, including the committee system, the federal budget process, and congressional investigations. The entries are arranged alphabetically and are extensively cross-referenced to related information. This volume includes a detailed index, useful reference materials, and a bibliography.

The fifth edition of *Congress A to Z* has been thoroughly updated to cover contemporary events, including the 2006 midterm elections that shifted party control in the House and Senate to the Democrats for the first time in twelve years. The volume contains new entries on the Capitol Visitor Center, C-SPAN, earmarks, electronic voting, line-item vetoes, and the newly formed House Select Committee on Energy Independence and Global Warming. Short biographies profile significant figures in today's Congress, including Nancy Pelosi and Harry Reid. Presented in a new and engaging design, this edition contains a wealth of stimulating sidebar material, such as memorable quotations and numerous features inviting the reader to explore issues in further depth.

Preface

In the five years since *Congress A to Z* was last published in 2003, control of Congress—the central institution of the Founders' plan for the new nation's federal government—changed hands once again, illustrating both the ferment and the intractability of divided power in Washington, D.C. In the 2006 midterm elections, the Democrats swept their Republican counterparts out of the Senate and House to take full control of Congress for the first time in twelve years.

The Democratic ascendancy in 2006 was attributed—more than any other single factor—to voter concern about the conduct of the U.S.-led war in Iraq, which President George W. Bush launched in 2003 to topple dictator Saddam Hussein, who was believed to be harboring chemical and biological weapons and developing nuclear weapons. Republicans compounded their problems with a series of high-profile scandals in the House that allowed Democrats to argue it was time for a change. In fact, the significant switch in the fortunes of House Democrats was due to electoral wins in normally Republican-leaning districts, most of which had gone comfortably for President Bush in 2004. Whether Democrats maintain their majority is likely to depend on the outcome of contests for those seats in 2008 and later elections.

Democratic gains in 2006 were substantial in the House but narrow in the Senate. At the start of the 110th Congress in 2007, with President Bush in office for his final two years, Washington once again returned to the divided government that has characterized much of the period since 1947.

The first year of the 110th Congress demonstrated how little the relationship between the legislative and executive branches has changed since the advent of a more powerful modern presidency, often attributed to Franklin D. Roosevelt's tenure as chief executive from 1933 to 1945. For example, Congress remains ill equipped to influence directly and immediately the conduct of foreign policy and military matters. The Democrats in 2006 pledged they would bring U.S. troops home swiftly if they won the midterm elections; by the end of 2007, however, American forces in Iraq had actually increased in number as Bush had deployed more soldiers in an effort to reduce growing violence, much of it between Iraqi sects. Congress can influence executive conduct of foreign policy over longer periods, but the limits of its influence in the short term were evident in 2007.

Domestic policy was more amenable to congressional influence in 2007 because legislators had the power to enact new programs and to fund them. Yet even in domestic matters, the president retained the upper hand through his power to veto legislation—as long as his party attracted enough votes in one of the chambers to prevent a two-thirds majority vote to override, a task easily accomplished in the Senate given the presence of forty-nine Republican senators. By the end of the year, Bush had indeed vetoed several bills, and only one of those—a massive spending measure (critics called it pork-barrel legislation) that benefited a vast majority of members of both parties—had been overridden as of February 2008.

Although 2007 brought the drama of a Republican White House pitted against a Democratic Congress, the accompanying divisiveness and partisanship had become all too familiar over the previous twelve years. In the fall 1994 elections, Republicans captured control of Congress for the first time since the 1952 elections gave them a two-year majority. Partisanship is never far away from daily activity in Congress, but the period starting with GOP control in 1995 was defined by a deep divide between the two parties over not only legislative priorities but also basic philosophies of government and fundamental political agendas. The differences existed before, but Republicans had been unable to assert their beliefs against the long-standing Democratic majority, other than through the actions of the GOP presidents who controlled the White House for much of the period from 1952 to 1992.

Differences were exacerbated in the late 1990s by Republican hostility, principally in the House, toward Democratic president Bill Clinton. An unsuccessful House effort to remove Clinton from office through impeachment presaged the bitterness of the 2000 election, when Bush won the White House after recounts of disputed vote tallies in Florida were halted by the Supreme Court's 5–4 decision. Partisanship deepened over the next six years as Republicans, in control of both chambers much of that time, moved aggressively, and largely successfully, to enact their legislative agenda, often via heavy-handed use of rules and political muscle. Republicans showed little interest in aggressive oversight of the executive branch, preferring to give mostly solid support to White House actions. Democrats protested vigorously but, being in the minority, had no leverage. Only after gaining the majority in the 2006 elections were the Democrats—particularly in the House— able to exercise aggressive oversight in 2007 through a number of congressional committees.

With the parties' roles reversed, Republicans in 2007 began singing much the same refrain as had Democrats, protesting that they were not allowed meaningful participation in legislative decisions. On some occasions Bush and members of both parties came together to attempt significant legislative accomplishments, most notably on reform of national immigration policy. They failed, however, on that issue and others, at least by halftime in the 110th Congress.

This new edition of *Congress A to Z* marks the twentieth anniversary of the first edition published by Congressional Quarterly in 1988. In updating the text for the fifth edition, editors noted—as they had during previous revisions—how much did *not* change in the operation, procedures, structure, and even fundamental attitudes of members, despite the partisanship and the raucous differences over the issues of the day. Political parties vied for supremacy, legislation was passed, vast sums of money were appropriated, scandals occurred, and the public's view of Congress—if the polls were to be believed—remained low.

Congress A to Z is designed to help students, activists, interested citizens, and anyone concerned about the vitality of self-government in the United States understand better the ways in which the most representative institution of the federal government operates. Although only the president is elected by all the voters, Congress is selected by a vast array of voter subsets that arguably are as close a reflection of the views and concerns of citizens as can be obtained in a representative government. How this institution understands, reflects, and responds to these citizen concerns is of vital importance.

The original edition of *Congress A to Z* was planned and in large part written by Mary Cohn, for many years a senior editor at Congressional Quarterly. Significant portions of her work are continued in this edition. Subsequent editions were updated by many CQ reporters and editors, most recently by David R. Tarr, former executive editor at CQ Press, and Ann O'Connor, a former CQ editor and director of the book publishing operations. This edition was updated under the supervision of CQ Press acquiring editor Doug Goldenberg-Hart. Anna S. Baker and Tim Arnquist ably shepherded it through the editorial process. The text was edited by Jon Preimesberger, who made endless improvements in the language and focus of the entries and who also handled the book's production, under the guidance of managing editor Joan Gossett.

The entries in *Congress A to Z* and its companion volumes on the presidency, the Supreme Court, elections, and the Constitution are arranged alphabetically and are extensively cross-referenced to guide readers to related information elsewhere in each book. Each volume also has a detailed index.

The core of the Congress volume is a series of essays that provide overviews of major topics such as the House and the Senate, legislation, leadership, power of the purse, and war powers. Supporting the essays are shorter entries covering items mentioned in them and specific items related to Congress and legislation. Brief biographies of important congressional figures are included. An extensive appendix includes a variety of tables and other reference material for quick reference about facts and figures. A bibliography is arranged by subject.

Readers who need more extensive, in-depth explanations of Congress as an institution may wish to consult CQ Press's *Guide to Congress*, Sixth Edition, after reading the appropriate entries in *Congress A to Z*.

We hope that this volume, and the others that make up the American Government A to Z series, will achieve the simple goal underpinning all the books: to provide readers with easily understood, accurate information about Congress, the presidency, the Supreme Court, the elections that so dramatically influence these institutions, and the Constitution of the United States.

CQ Press Editors
March 2008

Historic Milestones

The history of Congress is studded with events that have helped to shape the legislative branch and define its relations with the nation as a whole. Some of these milestones in congressional history are listed here.

1787

Delegates to the Constitutional Convention agree to establish a national legislature consisting of two chambers: a HOUSE OF REPRESENTATIVES to be chosen by direct popular vote and a SENATE to be chosen by the state legislatures. Under the terms of the "Great Compromise" between the large and small states, representation in the House would be proportional to a state's population; in the Senate each state would have two votes.

1789

The First Congress is scheduled to convene on March 4 in New York City's Federal Hall. The House does not muster a quorum to do business until April 1, and the Senate takes until April 6. Congress continues to meet in New York until August 1790. President George Washington appears twice in the Senate to consult about an American Indian treaty. His presence during Senate proceedings creates such tension that later presidents never participate directly in congressional floor proceedings.

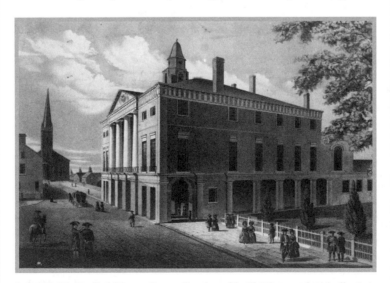

Federal Hall in New York City was the meeting place of the First Congress from April 1789 to August 1790.
Source: Library of Congress

1790

Congress moves to Philadelphia, where it meets in Congress Hall from December 1790 to May 1800.

1800

Congress formally convenes in Washington, D.C., on November 17. Both houses meet in the north wing of the Capitol, the only part of the building that has been completed.

1801

In its first use of contingent election procedures established by the Constitution, the House of Representatives chooses Thomas Jefferson as president. The election is thrown into the House when Democratic-Republican electors inadvertently cast equal numbers of votes for Jefferson and Aaron Burr, their candidates for president and vice president, respectively. The Twelfth Amendment to the Constitution, requiring separate votes for president and vice president, will be ratified in time for the next presidential election in 1804. (See ELECTING THE PRESIDENT; CONSTITUTIONAL AMENDMENTS.)

1803

The Supreme Court, in the case of *Marbury v. Madison,* establishes its right of judicial review over legislation passed by Congress.

In 1814 British troops raided Washington, D.C., and burned several buildings, including the Capitol.
Source: The Granger Collection, New York

1812

Using its WAR POWERS for the first time, Congress declares war against Great Britain, which has seized U.S. ships and impressed American sailors.

1814

British troops raid Washington, D.C., on August 24, setting fire to the CAPITOL BUILDING, the White House, and other buildings. Congress meets in makeshift quarters until it can return to the Capitol in December 1819.

1820

House Speaker Henry CLAY negotiates settlement of a bitter sectional dispute over the extension of slavery. Known as the Missouri Compromise, Clay's plan preserves the balance between slave and free states and bars slavery in any future state north of 36°30′ north latitude.

1825

The House settles the 1824 presidential election when none of the four major contenders for the office receives a majority of the electoral vote. Although Andrew Jackson leads in both the popular and the electoral vote, the House elects John Quincy ADAMS on the first ballot.

1830

The doctrine of nullification sparks one of the most famous debates in Senate history. As articulated by Vice President John C. CALHOUN of South Carolina, the doctrine asserts the right of states to nullify federal laws they consider unconstitutional. In a stirring Senate speech, a fellow South Carolinian, Sen. Robert Y. HAYNE, defends the doctrine and urges the West to ally with the South against the North. Massachusetts Whig Daniel WEBSTER responds with a passionate plea for preservation of the Union.

1834

The Senate adopts a resolution censuring President Andrew Jackson for his removal of deposits from the Bank of the United States and his refusal to hand over communications to his cabinet on that issue. (The censure resolution is expunged from the Senate *Journal* in 1837 after Jacksonian Democrats gain control of the Senate.)

1846

The House passes the Wilmot Proviso, which would bar slavery in territories to be acquired from Mexico in settlement of the Mexican War. Southerners, led by Calhoun, defeat the measure in the Senate. The proviso—named for its sponsor, Rep. David Wilmot of Pennsylvania—deepens the sectional split in Congress over extension of slavery.

1850

The Compromise of 1850, Clay's final attempt to keep the South from seceding from the Union, brings together Webster, Clay, and Calhoun for their last joint appearance in the Senate. Ill and near death, Calhoun drags himself into the chamber to hear his speech read by a colleague. Clay, in a speech that extends over two days, urges acceptance of his proposals, which exact concessions from both the North and

Henry Clay's last great effort to hold the Union together was known as the Compromise of 1850. Visitors packed the galleries during this debate, which marked the last joint appearance in the Senate of Clay, Daniel Webster, and John C. Calhoun.
Source: Library of Congress

South. The compromise package clears the way for California to be admitted to the Union as a free state, permits residents of the New Mexico and Utah territories to decide in the future whether they will permit slavery there, abolishes the slave trade in the District of Columbia, and establishes a strong fugitive slave law.

1854

Congress passes the Kansas-Nebraska Act, repealing the Missouri Compromise of 1820 and permitting settlers in the Kansas and Nebraska territories to decide whether they want slavery. Opponents of the new law establish the Republican Party. Conflict over slavery in Kansas leads to violence in the territories—and in Congress.

Abraham Lincoln rose to national prominence during his 1858 debates with Sen. Stephen A. Douglas.
Source: The Granger Collection, New York

1856

During debate on the Kansas statehood bill, two South Carolina representatives attack Sen. Charles SUMNER at his desk in the Senate chamber. They beat him so severely that the Massachusetts senator is unable to resume his seat until 1859.

1858

Abraham Lincoln, Republican candidate for the Senate from Illinois, challenges Sen. Stephen A. DOUGLAS, his Democratic opponent, to a series of debates on the slavery issue. Lincoln loses the election, but his moderate views recommend him for the presidential nomination two years later.

1859

The Thirty-sixth Congress convenes on December 5, its members inflamed by the execution of abolitionist John Brown only days before. The House takes two months and forty-four ballots to elect a Speaker; its choice is William Pennington of New Jersey, a new member of the House and a political unknown. The session is marked by verbal duels and threats of secession. Pistols are carried openly in the House and Senate chambers.

1860

South Carolina secedes from the Union in the wake of Lincoln's election to the presidency. Ten other southern states follow. The Civil War and its aftermath exclude the South from representation in Congress until 1869.

1861

Congress establishes a Joint Committee on the Conduct of the War. The committee, a vehicle for Radical Republicans opposed to President Lincoln, uses its far-ranging inquiries to criticize Lincoln's conduct of the war.

1863–1865

The Radicals, opposed to Lincoln's mild policies for postwar Reconstruction of the South, pass a bill placing all Reconstruction authority under the direct control of Congress. Lincoln pocket-vetoes the bill after Congress adjourns in 1864. Radicals issue the Wade-Davis Manifesto, asserting that "the authority of Congress is paramount and must be respected." They put their harsh Reconstruction policies into effect when Democrat Andrew Johnson becomes president after Lincoln's assassination in 1865. (See RECONSTRUCTION ERA.)

1868

The House votes to impeach Johnson for dismissing Secretary of War Edwin M. Stanton in violation of the Tenure of Office Act. In the ensuing Senate trial, Johnson wins acquittal by a one-vote margin. (See JOHNSON IMPEACHMENT TRIAL.)

A bulletin published by the Charleston Mercury *announces South Carolina's decision to secede from the Union, December 1860.*
Source: The Granger Collection, New York

1870

The first black members take their seats in Congress, representing newly readmitted southern states. The Mississippi legislature chooses Hiram R. Revels to fill the Senate seat once occupied by Confederate president Jefferson Davis. Joseph H. Rainey of South Carolina and Jefferson F. Long of Georgia enter the House. All are Republicans. (See BLACKS IN CONGRESS.)

1873

Several prominent members of Congress are implicated in the Crédit Mobilier scandal. A congressional investigating committee clears House Speaker James G. BLAINE, but two other representatives are censured for accepting bribes from Crédit Mobilier of America, a company involved in construction of the transcontinental railroad. (See INVESTIGATIONS.)

1877

Disputed electoral votes from several states force Congress for the first time to rule on the outcome of a presidential election. Congress determines that Republican Rutherford B. Hayes has been elected president over Democrat Samuel J. Tilden by the margin of one electoral vote. Tilden leads in the popular vote count by more than a quarter of a million votes, but Hayes wins the electoral vote, 185–184. He is sworn into office on March 4.

1881

The Supreme Court, in the case of *Kilbourn v. Thompson,* for the first time asserts its authority to review the propriety of congressional investigations.

1890

Republican Speaker Thomas Brackett REED puts an end to Democrats' obstructionist tactics, which have paralyzed the House. The "Reed Rules" are adopted by the House after bitter debate. (See SPEAKER OF THE HOUSE.)

Called upon to settle the disputed 1876 presidential election, Congress declared Republican Rutherford B. Hayes the winner by a one-vote electoral college margin. This print shows a campaign banner for the winning ticket of Hayes and running mate William A. Wheeler.

Source: Library of Congress

1910

The House revolts against the autocratic rule of Speaker Joseph G. CANNON and strips him of much of his authority. The power of the Speaker goes into a decline that lasts nearly fifteen years.

1913

Ratification of the Seventeenth Amendment to the Constitution ends the practice of letting state legislatures elect senators. Senators, like representatives, now will be chosen by direct popular election. The change is part of the Progressive movement toward more democratic control of government. (See DIRECT ELECTION OF SENATORS.) Also in 1913, President Woodrow Wilson revives the practice of addressing Congress in joint session. The last president to do so was John Adams in 1800.

1916

Although it will be four more years before women win the franchise, the first woman is elected to Congress: Jeannette RANKIN, a Montana Republican. (See WOMEN IN CONGRESS; WOMEN'S SUFFRAGE.)

1917

A Senate FILIBUSTER kills the Wilson administration's bill to arm merchant ships in the closing days of the Sixty-fourth Congress. "The Senate of the United States is the only legislative body in the world which cannot act when its majority is ready for action," Wilson rails. "A little group of willful men, representing no opinion but their own, have rendered the great government of the United States helpless and contemptible." The Senate quickly responds by adopting restrictions on debate through a process known as cloture.

> **"The Senate of the United States is the only legislative body in the world which cannot act when its majority is ready for action."**
>
> **—President Woodrow Wilson** in response to a 1917 Senate filibuster

1919

The Senate refuses to ratify the Versailles Treaty ending World War I. Senate opposition is aimed mainly at the Covenant of the League of Nations, which forms an integral part of the treaty. During consideration of the treaty, the Senate uses its cloture rule for the first time to cut off debate. (See TREATY-MAKING POWER.)

1922–1923

A Senate investigation of the TEAPOT DOME oil-leasing scandal exposes bribery and corruption in the administration of President Warren G. Harding. His interior secretary, Albert B. Fall, ultimately is convicted of bribery and sent to prison.

1933

Franklin D. Roosevelt assumes the presidency in the depths of the Great Depression and promptly calls Congress into special session. In this session, known as the "Hundred Days," lawmakers are asked to pass, almost sight unseen, several emergency economic measures. Roosevelt's NEW DEAL establishes Democrats as the majority party in Congress for most of the next sixty years.

President Franklin D. Roosevelt instituted hundreds of "New Deal" programs in the 1930s to help pull the nation out of the Great Depression.
Source: U.S. Senate Historical Office

1934

For the first time Congress opens its session on January 3, as required by the Twentieth Amendment to the Constitution. The amendment, ratified in 1933, also fixes January 20 as the date on which presidential terms will begin every four years; that change will take effect in 1937 at the beginning of Roosevelt's second term.

1937

Roosevelt calls on Congress to increase the membership of the Supreme Court, setting off a great public uproar. The Court has ruled unconstitutional many New Deal programs, and critics claim the president wants to "pack" the Court with justices who will support his views. The plan eventually dies in the Senate. In the 1938 elections, Roosevelt tries unsuccessfully to "purge" Democratic members of Congress who opposed the plan. (See COURTS AND CONGRESS.)

1938

The House establishes the Dies Committee, one in a succession of special committees on "un-American activities." The committee is given a broad mandate to investigate subversion. The committee chair, Texas Democrat Martin Dies, is avowedly anticommunist and anti–New Deal.

1941

The Senate sets up a Special Committee to Investigate the National Defense Program. The committee, chaired by Missouri Democrat Harry S. TRUMAN, earns President Roosevelt's gratitude for serving as a "friendly watchdog" over defense spending without embarrassing the president. Truman will become Roosevelt's vice presidential running mate in 1944 and succeed to the presidency upon Roosevelt's death the following year.

1946

Congress approves a sweeping legislative reform measure. The most important provisions of the

The House Un-American Activities Committee investigated State Department official Alger Hiss in 1948 for allegedly being a communist spy.
Source: AP Images

Legislative Reorganization Act of 1946 aim to streamline committee structure, redistribute the congressional workload, and improve staff assistance. Provisions to strengthen congressional review of the federal budget soon prove unworkable and are dropped. A section on regulation of lobbying has little effect. (See REFORM, CONGRESSIONAL.)

1948

The House Un-American Activities Committee launches an investigation of State Department official Alger Hiss. Its hearings, and Hiss's later conviction for perjury, establish communism as a leading political issue and the committee as an important political force. The case against Hiss is developed by a young member of the committee, California Republican Richard NIXON.

1953

Sen. Joseph R. MCCARTHY, a Wisconsin Republican, conducts widely publicized national investigations of communism during his two-year reign as chair of the Permanent Investigations Subcommittee of the Senate Government Operations Committee. His investigation of the armed services culminates in the 1954 Army-McCarthy hearings and McCarthy's censure by the Senate that year. (See INVESTIGATIONS.)

1957

South Carolina senator Strom THURMOND sets a record for the longest speech in the history of the Senate. During a filibuster on a civil rights bill, Thurmond, a Democrat who later switches to the Republican Party, speaks for twenty-four hours and eighteen minutes.

1963

President John F. KENNEDY is assassinated, and Vice President Lyndon B. JOHNSON succeeds him. Johnson is elected president in his own right in 1964. Using political skills he honed as Senate majority leader (1955–1961), Johnson wins congressional approval of a broad array of social programs, which he labels the GREAT SOCIETY. Mounting opposition to his Vietnam War policy leads to his retirement in 1968.

1964

Congress adopts the Tonkin Gulf Resolution, giving the president broad authority for use of U.S. forces in Southeast Asia. The resolution becomes the primary legal justification for the Johnson administration's prosecution of the Vietnam War. (Congress repeals the resolution in 1970.)

The Supreme Court, in the case of *Wesberry v. Sanders,* rules that congressional districts must be substantially equal in population. Court action is necessary because Congress has failed to act legislatively on behalf of heavily populated but underrepresented areas. (See REAPPORTIONMENT AND REDISTRICTING.)

1967

The House votes to exclude veteran representative Adam Clayton POWELL Jr. from sitting in the Ninetieth Congress. Powell, a black Democrat from New York's Harlem district, has been charged with misuse of public funds; he ascribes his downfall to racism. Later, in 1969, the Supreme Court rules that the House improperly excluded Powell, a duly elected representative who met the constitutional requirements for citizenship. Powell is reelected to the House in 1968 but rarely occupies his seat. (See DISCIPLINING MEMBERS.)

In 1968 Shirley Chisholm became the first black woman to be elected to the House of Representatives.
Source: Library of Congress

1968

New York Democrat Shirley Chisholm is the first black woman to be elected to the House of Representatives. Born in Brooklyn in 1924, she worked as a nursery school teacher and director and headed a child-care center before being elected to the state assembly in 1964.

1970

Congress passes the first substantial reform of congressional procedures since 1946. The Legislative Reorganization Act of 1970 opens Congress to closer public scrutiny and curbs the power of committee chairs. Among other things, the act changes House voting procedures to allow for recorded floor votes on amendments, requires that all recorded committee votes be publicly disclosed, authorizes radio and television coverage of committee hearings, encourages more open committee sessions, and requires committees to have written rules. (See VOTING IN CONGRESS.)

1971

Congress passes the Federal Election Campaign Act of 1971, which limits spending for media advertising by candidates for federal office and requires full disclosure of campaign contributions and expenditures. It is the first of three major campaign laws to be enacted during the 1970s; major amendments are enacted in 1974 and 1976. (See CAMPAIGN FINANCING.)

1973

The Senate establishes a select committee to investigate White House involvement in a break-in the previous year at Democratic National Committee headquarters in the Watergate office building in Washington, D.C. The committee hearings draw a picture of political sabotage that goes far beyond the original break-in. (See WATERGATE SCANDAL.)

In its first use of powers granted by the Twenty-fifth Amendment to the Constitution, Congress confirms President Nixon's nomination of House minority leader Gerald R. FORD to be vice president. Ford succeeds Spiro T. Agnew, who has resigned facing criminal charges.

Congress passes the War Powers Resolution over Nixon's veto. The resolution restricts the president's powers to commit U.S. forces abroad without congressional approval.

1974

The House Judiciary Committee recommends Nixon's impeachment and removal from office for his role in the Watergate scandal. Nixon resigns to avoid almost certain removal. Ford succeeds to the presidency; Congress confirms Nelson A. Rockefeller, his choice as vice president. (See JUDICIARY COMMITTEE, HOUSE; NIXON IMPEACHMENT EFFORT.)

Seeking better control over government purse strings, Congress passes the Congressional Budget and Impoundment Control Act. The new law requires legislators to set overall budget levels and then make their individual taxing and spending decisions fit within those levels. (See BUDGET PROCESS.)

1975

The House Democratic Caucus elects committee chairs for the first time and unseats three incumbent chairs. It thus serves notice that seniority, or length of service, will no longer be the sole factor in selecting chairs. The chairs' defeat is one of the most dramatic manifestations of the reform wave that sweeps Congress in the 1970s. (See SENIORITY SYSTEM.)

1977

The House and Senate adopt their first formal codes of ETHICS, setting guidelines for members' behavior. Personal finances must be disclosed, income earned outside Congress is restricted, and use of public funds is monitored.

1979

The House begins live radio and television coverage of its floor proceedings. The Senate will not begin gavel-to-gavel broadcasts until 1986.

1983

The Supreme Court invalidates the LEGISLATIVE VETO, a device Congress has used for half a century to review and overturn executive branch decisions carrying out laws. In the case of *Immigration and Naturalization Service v. Chadha,* the Court rules that the legislative veto violates the constitutional SEPARATION OF POWERS.

1987

Senate and House committees hold joint hearings on the IRAN-CONTRA AFFAIR, investigating undercover U.S. arms sales to Iran and the diversion of profits from those sales to "Contra" guerrillas in Nicaragua. The committees conclude that President Ronald Reagan allowed a "cabal of zealots" to take over key aspects of U.S. foreign policy.

Brian Lamb of C-SPAN interviews former Oklahoma representative Dave McCurdy. When C-SPAN first aired in March 1979, with the mission of providing live coverage of congressional proceedings, the network had four employees, a $450,000 budget, and one telephone line.
Source: AP Images/C-SPAN

1989

House Speaker Jim WRIGHT resigns as Speaker, amid questions about the ethics of the Texas Democrat's financial dealings. It is the first time in history that a House Speaker has been forced by scandal to leave the office in the middle of his term.

1991

A sharply divided Congress votes to authorize the president to go to war against Iraq if that country does not end its occupation of Kuwait. Although this is not a formal declaration of war, it marks the first time since World War II that Congress has confronted the issue of sending large numbers of American troops into combat.

"No law, varying the compensation for the services of the senators and representatives, shall take effect, until an election of representatives shall have intervened."

—Twenty-seventh Amendment, as first proposed by James Madison in 1789 and ratified by the states in 1992

1992

Ratification of a constitutional amendment prohibiting midterm pay raises for members of Congress is completed more than two centuries after the amendment was first proposed. The amendment, proposed by James MADISON, was approved by the First Congress in 1789.

Democrat Carol Moseley-Braun of Illinois is the first black woman elected to the Senate.

1994

The 1994 elections usher in a Republican-controlled House and Senate for the first time since 1953. No Republican incumbents are defeated at the polls. Newt GINGRICH of Georgia is in line to become the first Republican Speaker of the House from the South. For the first time since the end of Reconstruction in the 1870s, Republicans win a majority of the congressional districts in the South.

Another record intact since the Civil War is broken: Thomas S. FOLEY of Washington becomes the first sitting Speaker to lose reelection since Galusha A. Grow of Pennsylvania was defeated in 1862.

1995

The Republicans' willingness to close the government fails to force President Bill Clinton to accept their plan to balance the federal budget in seven years while providing major tax cuts. The result is two partial federal government shutdowns from December 1995 to January 1996.

1996

For the first time ever, voters reelect a Democratic president and simultaneously entrust both chambers of Congress to the Republican Party.

1997

The House votes to reprimand Speaker Gingrich and impose a $300,000 penalty for violating House rules. It is the first time in history that the House reprimands a sitting Speaker.

1998

The federal government records a budget surplus for the first time since 1969. In the congressional elections the Democrats gain five seats, marking the first time since 1934 that the party in control of the White House gains House seats in a midterm election.

Independent Counsel Kenneth W. Starr charges President Clinton with possible impeachable offenses in his effort to cover up an extramarital affair. After House Judiciary Committee hearings on the Starr referral, a lame-duck House votes two articles of impeachment against Clinton, charging him with perjury and obstruction of justice. Clinton becomes only the second president in history to be impeached.

1999

For the second time in U.S. history, the Senate acquits a president impeached by the House. The Senate vote to acquit President Clinton on two articles of impeachment falls mostly along partisan lines. (See CLINTON IMPEACHMENT TRIAL.)

2001

As the 107th Congress begins, Republicans control both chambers of Congress and the White House for the first time since 1953, at the beginning of President Dwight D. Eisenhower's administration. The Senate is evenly divided with fifty Democrats and fifty Republicans, but control goes to the GOP because the Republican vice president, Richard B. CHENEY, can cast a tie-breaking vote. Recognizing the potential for deadlock, Senate leaders of the two parties negotiate a power-sharing arrangement, unprecedented in Senate history, which gives the two parties equal representation on committees.

But control of the Senate switches from the Republicans to the Democrats six months into the session when a Republican senator from Vermont, James M. Jeffords, becomes an Independent and caucuses with the Democrats. As a result of Jeffords's switch, Democrats take control of committees and the legislative agenda.

Following the September 11 attacks on the World Trade Center in New York and the Pentagon outside Washington, the Capitol is temporarily evacuated. Urgent debates over national security dominate the rest of the session. In October fears of bioterrorism arise as packages containing the deadly toxin anthrax are mailed to Majority Leader Tom DASCHLE, D-S.D., and others. The Hart building, where half of all senators have offices, is closed for ninety-six days.

2002

Congress authorizes President George W. Bush to attack Iraq.

In the 2002 elections, Republicans break historic trends to win back Congress. For the third time in a century, the party in control of the White House wins seats in a midterm election, and for the first time, Republicans controlling the White House win back the Senate.

2004

George W. Bush wins reelection as president, and Republicans increase their strength in Congress, allowing the GOP in 2005 to push through important parts of their agenda, including an industry-oriented energy package, changes in tort law that Republicans said were needed to stem frivolous antibusiness lawsuits, and a major rewriting of the bankruptcy laws.

2006

Republicans are rocked by a series of scandals ranging from influence-peddling, to bribery, to inappropriate sexual advances toward some male House pages by a Florida representative. Democrats charge back from the wilderness to take control of Congress, winning a net of thirty seats in the House and six in the Senate. Democrats pick up seats in all four national regions. In the Northeast only one Republican survives. Republicans, still in control of Congress until 2007, leave much of the legislative agenda unfinished, passing only two of eleven appropriations bills for fiscal 2007.

"In a few moments, I'll have the high privilege of handing the gavel of the House of Representatives to a woman for the first time in American history. Whether you're a Republican, a Democrat, or an independent, this is a cause for celebration."

—Republican minority leader John A. Boehner of Ohio, introducing Democrat Nancy Pelosi of California as Speaker of the House

2007

Democrats become the majority in both the Senate and House and organize Congress for the first time since 1994. Rep. Nancy Pelosi, D-Calif., is elected House Speaker, the first time a woman has held that position. She thus becomes the highest-ranking woman in the government and second in line for the presidency.

2008

Three U.S. senators emerge as leading candidates for the presidential nomination of their parties. Republican John McCain of Arizona has all but locked up the GOP position by March. Two Democrats, Hillary Clinton of New York and Barack Obama of Illinois, are in a nearly dead heat for the Democratic nomination going into the final round of primaries in March and beyond. The match-ups mean that for the first time since 1960, when John F. Kennedy defeated Richard Nixon, a sitting senator will most likely move into the White House.

By March 2008 three sitting senators were top contenders in that year's presidential race: Hillary Rodham Clinton, D-N.Y., Barack Obama, D-Ill., and John McCain, R-Ariz.
Source: Reuters/Brian Snyder

A

Adams, John

The second U.S. president, John Adams also established many precedents as the first president of the Senate.
Source: Library of Congress

John Adams (1735–1826) is most famous for being the nation's second president, succeeding George Washington, and for losing his reelection to Thomas Jefferson, which essentially ended the role of the Federalists in the new government and ushered in the long run of the Jeffersonian party known by various names but usually called Democratic-Republicans.

But Adams also was Washington's vice president (1789–1797, which made him under the new Constitution the Senate's first president. It was a role for which he was not well suited. Adams was a contentious man, given to outspoken comments and vigorous debates. He even allowed, as titular head of the Senate, that he was more "accustomed to take a share in . . . debates, than to preside in . . . deliberations," by his own description. But his Senate role was to preside, a task he found particularly difficult. In the words of a later senator, Robert Dole of Kansas: "Time after time, he rushed into action, only to be forced to check himself. Time after time, he tried in vain to hold his tongue. As the first Senate labored to establish precedents of protocol and conduct, Adams was vociferous as he campaigned endlessly for elaborate titles and ceremonies."

As Washington's vice president, Adams spent eight years in a job for which even he admitted was not designed for him. But he did exercise one constitutional power aggressively: the right to break tie votes. As vice president Adams cast twenty-nine tie-breaking votes, a record that remained unbroken in 2007.

Adams was the father of a later president, John Quincy Adams (see below).

Adams, John Quincy

John Quincy Adams served seventeen years in the House of Representatives after leaving the White House.
Source: Library of Congress

John Quincy Adams (1767–1848), the sixth president of the United States, represented Massachusetts in both the Senate and House of Representatives during his long career in public life.

The son of John Adams (see above), the nation's second president, John Quincy Adams was a man of uncompromising rectitude and inflexible purpose. Adams entered the Senate in 1803 as a Federalist, but he soon ran into trouble for supporting Jeffersonian policies. He resigned his Senate seat in 1808. After holding various diplomatic posts, he served with distinction from 1817 to 1825 as President James Monroe's secretary of state. He was chiefly responsible for the Monroe Doctrine, which barred colonization in the Western Hemisphere by European nations. He also is known as one of the few presidents to serve a full term without issuing any vetoes of legislation. Another was his father.

Adams ran for president in 1824, in an inconclusive four-way race that ultimately had to be decided by the House of Representatives. Although Andrew Jackson was the leading candidate in both the popular and the electoral votes, the House chose Adams.

Lacking political or popular support, Adams was not a successful president; Jackson defeated him in 1828.

In 1830 Adams was elected to the House of Representatives, where he served for seventeen years until his death. Known as "Old Man Eloquent," he conducted an almost single-handed attack on so-called gag rules that prevented discussion of antislavery proposals. The House repealed the rules in 1844.

On February 21, 1848, the eighty-year-old Adams was stricken ill at his desk in the House chamber. He was carried to the Speaker's room, where he died two days later.

Adams was one of two presidents to serve in Congress after leaving the White House. Andrew Johnson, also a former senator, returned to the Senate for five months before his death in 1875. (See ELECTING THE PRESIDENT.)

Adjournment

Adjournment is the action of Congress in bringing its meetings to a close. In the congressional context the word has several different meanings.

⊙ CLOSER LOOK

John Quincy Adams was one of two presidents to serve in Congress after leaving the White House. The other was Andrew Johnson.

The terms of Congress run in two-year cycles, and Congress must hold a regular series of meetings, called a session, each year.

At the end of a year's session, the Senate and House adjourn *sine die* (a Latin phrase meaning "without a day"). This means that the lawmakers do not intend to meet again in that particular session. Adjournment of the second session is generally the final action of a term of Congress. The president has authority under the Constitution to convene special sessions of Congress. Members frequently authorize their leaders to call them back into session as well. Unless called back, Congress will meet next on the constitutionally fixed date for a new session, January 3 of the next year. The Constitution gives the president power to adjourn Congress when the houses cannot agree about the time of adjournment, but this has never happened.

Within a session Congress may adjourn for holiday observances, vacations, or other brief periods. This practice is known as adjournment to a day certain. Lawmakers set a date for the session to reconvene. By constitutional directive neither chamber may adjourn for more than three days without the consent of the other.

In the House of Representatives daily sessions almost always end in daily adjournment. The Senate may also adjourn, but it is far more likely to recess. By recessing, it continues the same legislative day into the next calendar day, an arrangement that offers certain procedural benefits under Senate rules. A single legislative day may go on for weeks and does not end until the Senate next adjourns.

> **More on this topic:**
>
> *Legislative Day, p. 344*
>
> *Terms and Sessions of Congress, p. 556*

Advice and Consent

This is the power the Constitution grants to the Senate, but not the House, to approve or reject certain actions by the president. These are nominations of most high-ranking and many lesser persons in the executive branch and independent agencies and consenting to the ratification of treaties submitted by the president. Nominations require a simply majority; treaties require a two-thirds majority. See APPOINTMENT POWER.

Aging Committee, Senate

The Senate Special Committee on Aging has served as an effective platform for advocates of the elderly for many years. Although the panel is barred by congressional rules from handling legislation, its hearings, investigations, and reports give the problems of the elderly increased visibility. As the first of 77 million baby boomers approach retirement, the panel is actively publicizing such issues as the quality of nursing home care, Medicare funding issues, and difficulties associated with Social Security.

The Senate Aging Committee was set up as a temporary panel in 1961. In 1977 a proposal to kill the committee received the votes of only four senators after a vigorous campaign by the senior citizens' lobby to keep the panel alive. The Senate instead made it a permanent special committee.

The House had its Aging Committee from 1975 until 1993. Rep. Claude Pepper, a Florida Democrat, served as chair of the House Select Committee on Aging from 1977 to 1983 and made the panel an influential voice in Congress for the elderly. Even after moving to chair another House committee in 1983, Pepper kept issues concerning the elderly and the Aging committee in high profile. Many ideas he championed, such as curbs on mandatory retirement, eventually became law. But after Pepper's death in 1989, no member of his stature pressed for support for the elderly, and the House committee began to lose influence.

In 1993 pressure to cut costs throughout the federal government, driven by efforts to reduce the federal budget deficit, prompted legislators to kill a number of special committees in the House, including Aging. The Senate, however, rejected proposals to terminate its special committees. In 2007 Herb Kohl, D-Wis., chaired the Senate panel.

Agriculture Committee, House

The chief responsibility of the House Agriculture Committee, like its Senate counterpart, is to oversee the federal government's many programs of support and assistance to farmers. Committee members, who mostly represent heavily rural areas, are the leading advocates in the House for the interests of farmers.

The most important element of the committee's jurisdiction has historically been farm price supports. Through a variety of mechanisms, such as government loans and direct cash payments, these federal programs have determined the minimum prices farmers would receive for their wheat, corn, cotton, and other crops. The goal of these programs, which had their origins in the farmland devastation of the Great Depression in the 1930s, was to provide farmers with some protection against wide swings in market prices for farm products. In addition, the committee is responsible for other agricultural issues, such as the federal law regulating use of pesticides. Also under the committee's authority is the federal food stamp program, which helps poor people buy food.

By the 110th Congress, which began in 2007, the old verities were under attack from new forces and interest groups that in the past did not exist or had little political clout. The old farm coalition, dominated by a handful of major commodity trade groups and the primary umbrella groups, the American Farm Bureau Federation and the National Farmers Union, was facing not only international developments in a globalized world, but newly active domestic groups arguing that nutrition, health, environment, and even transportation should be part of farm policy decisions.

Some of these groups bringing their views to the committee, and its Senate counterpart, were not new players at all. The American Farmland Trust, a twenty-six-year-old organization seeking

> "Historically, we have not had to fight activist groups from their ivory towers about defining what they think rural life should be about."
>
> *—Brent Gattis,* farm lobbyist and former longtime Agriculture Committee staff member

to preserve farm and grazing lands and rural communities, by 2007 was in alliance with the National Association of State Departments of Agriculture and other groups to promote public health issues including nutrition programs as part of the 2007 farm bill. The American Cancer Society and the American Heart Association backed the push to make nutrition part of farm policy. Oxfam American, an antihunger organization, argued for restructuring farm subsidies that it said encouraged overproduction of U.S. crops, which it contended were "dumped" overseas in ways that impeded growth of new agricultural markets and depressed world prices. Environmental groups such as the Nature Conservancy and hunting and fishing groups such as Ducks Unlimited were arguing for wider inclusion of farmland in federal conservation programs. Even the trucking industry was pushing for a trust fund for rural road maintenance and tax credits for other transportation expenses related to agriculture.

This was an entire new world for the traditional "iron triangle" of major commodity groups. As one farm lobbyist, Brent Gattis, a longtime Agriculture Committee staffer, told a reporter: "Historically, we have not had to fight activist groups from their ivory towers about defining what they think rural life should be about."

In addition to new groups demanding a place at the farm policy table, U.S. agriculture by 2007 was increasingly buffeted by international trade law pressures. Other nations, many of them important U.S. trade partners, were charging that American law violated World Trade Organization (WTO) rules by allowing the federal government to spend too much on farm subsidies. The WTO already ruled, in 2005, that the U.S. cotton program violated global trade rules. Developing countries, in particular, claimed American farm and trade and tariff policies were hurting their ability to sell in the United States.

Although the committee works on legislation in every session of Congress, its principal work comes in years when it must report a comprehensive "farm bill," establishing the overall shape of farm programs for the next five or six years. The year in which the farm bill comes up for renewal is a time of intense activity for committee members. Congress passed a major farm bill in 2002, with one scheduled for 2007—just as international pressures were building and new groups were muscling for a voice in the debate—and another in about 2012 or 2013.

Traditionally, members of the Agriculture Committee come from states in the South and Midwest, where farm issues are a prime concern. Some of the members were farmers themselves or came from districts where farming was an important part of the local economy. Few members came from big cities or industrial regions. While this remained true in 2007 as Congress was preparing for a major farm law overhaul, national population were changing the face of agricultural support. The number of rural House districts began to decline in the 1960s. By 2005, only 14 percent of the districts met common definitions of rural, some 42 percent fewer than forty years earlier.

Politically and traditionally, the most important aspect of the Agriculture Committee's work has been the "farm coalition" of the five major commodity producers: corn, wheat, cotton, rice, and soybeans, plus dairy producers. This coalition was essential because no single crop is important everywhere in the United States. In the Midwest wheat and corn crops dominate, and farmers there are most concerned with preserving federal assistance to those products. In the South farmers mostly grow cotton and rice, and they care much more about price supports for these crops than about assistance for wheat or corn.

By sticking loyally to the farm coalition, Agriculture Committee members were able for many years to win House approval of legislation providing increased federal support for their crops. If opposition developed to price sup-

The House and Senate Agriculture committees represent farmers' interest in Congress. Their efforts depend on a coalition of members from the Midwest, where wheat, corn, and alfalfa (shown here) are the leading crops, and the South, where cotton, rice, and soybeans predominate.
Source: Loren R. and Yvonne Notsch, Stearns County, Minnesota

ports for any one crop, committee members usually were able to overcome it by offering to increase federal aid to other crops as well. In this way they won over enough members to obtain a majority. Generous funding for the federal food stamp program, which was a pilot program in 1961 and expanded nationwide in 1974, brought liberal, urban Democrats into the coalition supporting farm legislation.

But by the 1970s and 1980s various factors began to undermine the strength of the farm coalition in the House. One was the declining political importance of farmers as fewer districts remained rural, the suburbs grew rapidly, and many cities saw a new in-migration of young professionals. The continuing decrease in the number of people living in rural areas meant that fewer

More on this topic:

Agriculture, Nutrition, and Forestry Committee, Senate, p. 6

House members were primarily concerned with farm interests. Moreover, the spiraling cost of federal farm programs increased opposition to the farm coalition and to Agriculture Committee legislation, as the government continued to run large budget deficits.

In the 1970s federal farm programs typically cost about $3 billion a year. By the 1980s the amount had swollen to more than $20 billion annually. As a result, Agriculture Committee members found themselves under heavy pressure from other House members to hold down the cost of farm programs. In 1995 the Republican-controlled Congress included a major overhaul of federal farm programs in its larger plan to balance the budget. After a highly emotional debate, Congress in 1996 passed the Freedom to Farm Act, which did away with the decades-old policy of issuing subsidies when market prices dropped and requiring farmers to plant the same commodities every year. Instead, the new law guaranteed farmers fixed, declining federal payments through 2002 regardless of market prices.

But soon, as the rural economy went into a deep slump, the new law began to look increasingly irrelevant. Although the law had been intended to encourage farmers to reduce dependence on government supports, a collapse in commodity prices sent farmers back to Congress for a series of emergency farm aid packages totaling $30.5 billion between 1998 and 2001.

Congress wrote a new farm law in 2002 that revived the commodity-based support policies of the past. It reversed the 1996 law's policy of limiting federal price supports but also renewed the fixed annual payments that had been instituted in 1996 in hopes of weaning farmers off the subsidies. In a compromise, conferees agreed to give farmers higher support prices during the first two years. After that, support prices were to decline and fixed federal payments to farmers not tied to commodity prices were to rise.

CLOSER LOOK

Historically, the Senate and House agriculture committees have been closely identified with the "farm coalition" comprised of the five major commodity producers: corn, wheat, cotton, rice, and soybeans, plus dairy producers. This coalition was essential because no single crop is important everywhere in the United States. In the Midwest wheat and corn crops dominate, and farmers there are most concerned with preserving federal assistance to those products. In the South farmers mostly grow cotton and rice, and they care much more about price supports for these crops than about assistance for wheat or corn.

Agriculture, Nutrition, and Forestry Committee, Senate

The Senate Agriculture Committee shares with its House counterpart jurisdiction over federal farm programs. Historically, the amount of economic help the federal government provided to farmers depended in large part on the decisions made in the committee and on the skill of committee members in guiding their legislation through the full Senate. The committee is formally known as the Agriculture, Nutrition, and Forestry Committee.

As is true of the House Agriculture Committee, the main work of the Senate agriculture committee takes place only every five or six years, when Congress considers renewal of legislation authorizing federal farm price supports, food stamps, and related programs. In between, the committee considers a variety of legislation responding to changes in the agricultural economy, from help for farmers hit by droughts or floods to emergency assistance for the banks that provide operating loans to farmers.

In many respects, the political situation of the Senate Agriculture Committee is similar to that of its House counterpart. Both panels are dominated by members from states where agriculture is a key factor in the local economy. Senate committee members also share with their House colleagues the primary goal of protecting the interests of farmers in the competition for federal resources. Furthermore, the Senate committee, like the House committee, traditionally has depended on the farm coalition, in which advocates of various crops band together for mutual political support.

By 2007, the Senate committee—like its counterpart—faced the same set of new challenges from international globalization, including pressure from the World Trade Organization (WTO) to change farm subsidies, and the arrival on the farm policy scene of a raft of new players seeking to make nutrition, health, conservation, environment, and other issues part of the debate.

It was a stunning change for the traditional farm lobby coalition of the American Farm Bureau Federation and the National Farmers Union plus the producers of the major U.S. commodities: corn, wheat, cotton, rice, and soybeans, plus dairy products. Key players in the traditional coalition were fully aware that past ways of doing farm business were threatened by competition from nontraditional groups. Mary Kay Thatcher, director of public policy with the Farm Bureau, told a reporter in 2007: "It causes us to come together even more. We're circling the wagons."

> ### "It causes us to come together even more. We're circling the wagons."
>
> **—Mary Kay Thatcher,** American Farm Bureau on farm policy demands from nontraditional farm groups

However, the farm coalition on the Senate Agriculture Committee has tended to be more powerful politically than its House counterpart because of the differences in representation in the two chambers. In the 435-member House, sparsely populated farm states, such as North Dakota, have very little voting strength. But the same states each have two votes in the 100-member Senate, giving them far more power and making farm issues considerably more important.

For many years, the Senate panel's work consisted largely of tallying up the requests of various special interest lobbies, and so fashioning farm programs to cover each group's particular desires. The farm coalition on the committee came under increasing pressure in the 1980s as the rapidly growing costs of farm programs collided with the spiraling federal budget deficit. The strain on the coalition, within the committee and in the full Senate, was shown clearly by action over the 1985 farm bill. The bill sparked bitter debates over the efforts of President Ronald Reagan to hold down the cost of farm programs. But the measure achieved its purpose, nursing the nation's farmers back to health and at the same time reducing federal payments in the future. The 1990 farm bill included only modest revisions over the 1985 act.

In 1996, however, Congress passed the Freedom to Farm Act, ending the New Deal–era policy of federal subsidies for heavily regulated crop production. The legislation allowed farmers to plant whatever they wanted in exchange for fixed but declining payments through 2002.

However, soon after the 1996 bill became law, members of both parties called for revisions. The law had been designed to wean farmers off government price supports, but when commodity prices plummeted, lawmakers responded by increasing the very federal payments that were supposed to decline under the 1996 act. Farmers received emergency farm aid totaling $30.5 billion between 1998 and 2001.

Congress wrote a new farm law in 2002 that revived the commodity-based support policies of the past. The six-year law gave farmers higher support prices for two years, and

CLOSER LOOK

New Players at the Table

Historically, formation of farm policy has been the province of the American Farm Bureau Federation and the National Farmers Union in league with trade groups representing growers of corn, wheat, cotton, soybeans, and rice. By 2007 they were being challenged by new groups:

- **Specialty Crop Farm Bill Alliance.** Representing fruit, nut, vegetable, and wine producers; seeking multibillion program of conservation and grants for marketing and research.
- **American Farmland Trust.** With similar groups, seeking funds for conservation, particularly to pay farmers to retire farmland from production.
- **Renewable Fuels Association.** Alternative energy advocates seek research grants and government procurement mandates.
- **Oxfam American.** Antihunger organization wants farm subsidy changes that critics say cause overproduction of U.S. crops that are then sent abroad, harming new agricultural markets in developing countries and depressing world prices.
- **Vaccine makers.** Drug companies urge the government to stockpile avian flu vaccines and diagnostic tools to test livestock for animal diseases.
- **American Trucking Association.** U.S. truckers seek to include in farm policy a trust fund for rural road maintenance and tax credits to pay for truck security upgrades and trucking facilities.

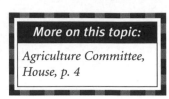

More on this topic:

Agriculture Committee, House, p. 4

then the support prices were to decline while fixed federal payments not tied to commodity prices rose.

At the insistence of the Senate, the law also increased spending for conservation. It renewed a number of existing conservation programs and created a new program that paid farmers to implement conservation methods on working lands.

Albert, Carl B.

Carl B. Albert (1908–2000) was a Democratic member of the House for thirty years and its Speaker for six. An Oklahoma lawyer and former Rhodes scholar, Albert entered the House in 1947.

On the day of his arrival, legend has it, the tiny (five feet, four inches) newcomer was mistaken for a congressional page by a veteran representative who called him over and directed, "Son, take these papers over to my office."

During his career in the House, Albert traveled a careful political road along which he made few enemies. He was a protégé of Speaker Sam RAYBURN, who chose him to become majority whip in 1955. Albert moved on up the Democratic leadership ladder to become majority leader in 1962 and Speaker in 1971. He was acceptable to most factions of the party and won election as Speaker with only token opposition.

Because of his low-key style, Albert did little either to help or to impede liberal reform efforts of the early 1970s, and his passive manner soon drew criticism. Some freshman Democrats talked openly of removing him after the House in 1975 upheld Republican president Gerald R. Ford's veto of a Democratic-backed bill to control strip mining. No effort was made to oust Albert, however, and criticism subsided by 1976. He did not run for reelection that year.

On two occasions during Albert's tenure as Speaker, the nation was without a vice president and Albert was in line to succeed the president. That was true following the resignation of Vice President Spiro T. Agnew in 1973 and when Vice President Ford succeeded President Richard Nixon in 1974.

Aldrich, Nelson W.

Nelson W. Aldrich (1841–1915) was arguably the most influential member of the Senate from the 1890s until his retirement in 1911. A staunch conservative, he allied himself with other like-minded Republican senators to control the first powerful party leadership organization in the Senate.

Aldrich was elected to the House of Representatives from Rhode Island in 1879. In 1881 he resigned from the House to fill a vacant Senate seat, which he held for the next thirty years. A successful financier, Aldrich conformed to the contemporary stereotype of the Senate as a "millionaires' club." Wealth, however, was not his only claim to the job. He was accomplished at parliamentary tactics and had a strong interest in the economic affairs of the country.

Until the 1890s members of the Senate had only experimented with leadership by political party. In the last decade of the nineteenth century, a group of Republican senators led by Aldrich and William B. ALLISON of Iowa pooled influence so that they might control the Senate. Calling themselves the School of Philosophy Club, members of the group cemented their ties during after-hours poker games. With the help of his friends, and through force of personality, Aldrich wielded tremendous power even though he held no leadership position until 1899, when he became chair of the Finance Committee.

With Allison, Aldrich effectively controlled committee assignments, the scheduling of legislation, and the business of standing committees. Loyalty to Aldrich and his group was rewarded by good committee assignments and timely consideration of legislation. Rebellious Republicans were punished with the opposite treatment. The Aldrich "machine" was so effective that it was able to hinder the enactment of President Theodore Roosevelt's progressive policies and to force concessions from Roosevelt.

A champion of commercial interests, Aldrich opposed any substantive regulation of business and was able to temper restrictions imposed by the Interstate Commerce Act of 1887 and the Sherman Antitrust Act. He supported protective tariffs and clashed with Roosevelt over tariff reform. A protectionist tariff bill sponsored by the Aldrich party machine proved so unpopular with the public that it contributed to Republican defeats in the 1910 elections, and the backlash gave impetus to the formation of the Bull Moose or Progressive Party. (See POLITICAL PARTIES.)

Four powerful Republican senators at the beginning of the twentieth century, left to right, Orville H. Platt, John C. Spooner, William B. Allison, and Nelson Aldrich meet in 1903 at Aldrich's estate in Newport, Rhode Island, the summer playground of that era's elite.
Source: Senate Historical Office

Allison, William B.

William B. Allison (1829–1908) represented Iowa in both the House of Representatives and the Senate. He was counted among the most influential senators of his day.

Allison entered the House of Representatives in 1863 and continued there until 1871. As a representative he served on the Ways and Means Committee and championed the interests of the nation's railroads. He served in the Senate from 1873 until 1908.

During his thirty-five years in the Senate, Allison was known more as a power broker than as a legislator. With Nelson W. ALDRICH of Rhode Island, Allison was a leader of the conservative Republicans who controlled the Senate around the turn of the twentieth century. Allison's influence and authority originally derived from his position as chair of the Appropriations Committee. In 1897, as the most senior Republican in the Senate, he became chair of the Republican Caucus. He was the first to realize that the position might be a useful tool in building and consolidating power.

He believed that "both in the committees and in the offices, we should use the machinery for our own benefit and not let other men have it." Acting on that belief, he took control of the Republican Steering Committee. Through the steering committee he took over the scheduling of legislation and the proceedings on the floor of the Senate. His authority over the Committee on Committees allowed him to fill committee vacancies to punish or reward fellow Republicans.

Under the leadership of Allison and Aldrich, conservative Republicans were transformed into a cohesive political force that scored many victories over the more progressive Republican president, Theodore Roosevelt. On occasion Roosevelt was able to split the two senators, but for the most part Allison and Aldrich worked successfully with each other and their supporters to challenge Roosevelt's policies.

Amendments

Amendments are proposals to alter or rewrite legislation being considered by Congress. The amending process provides a way to shape bills into a form acceptable to a majority in both the Senate and House of Representatives.

The process of amending legislation has three aspects. First, it is one of the chief functions of the legislative committees of Congress. Second, it is at the heart of floor debate in both chambers. Third, it is vital to working out compromises on bills during House-Senate conference negotiations. (See LEGISLATIVE PROCESS.)

Amendments have many objectives. Members may introduce amendments to dramatize their stands on issues, even if there is little chance that their proposals will be adopted. Some amendments are introduced at the request of the executive branch, a member's constituents, or special interests. Some become tools for gauging sentiment for or against a bill. Some may be used as "sweeteners" to broaden support for the underlying measure. Others are used to stall action on or to defeat legislation. In the House, where debate is strictly limited, amendments may be used to buy time; a member may offer a pro forma amendment, later withdrawn, solely to gain a few additional minutes to speak on an issue.

Amendments themselves are frequently the targets of other amendments offered by members having different points of view. The amending process becomes the arena for a struggle among these diverse viewpoints. At times, amendments become the most controversial elements in a bill.

Some amendments take on an identity of their own, regardless of the legislation to which they are attached. The Hyde amendment, a proposal to ban federal funding for abortions, is a classic example. Its sponsor, Rep. Henry J. Hyde, an Illinois Republican, touched off an emotional battle when he first offered his amendment in the 1970s. The amendment became widely known and variations of it were still being attached to legislation decades later.

In Committee

Legislation comes under its sharpest congressional scrutiny at the committee stage. Typically a bill first undergoes section-by-section review and amendment by a specialized subcommittee, a process known as "marking up" the measure. Occasionally the subcommittee may approve the legislation unaltered, but it is more likely to amend the bill or even to substitute an entirely new version. The legislation then goes to the full committee, where the process may be repeated. The committee may accept the subcommittee amendments with little or no change, or it may make additional amendments.

If the changes are substantial and the legislation is complicated, the committee may introduce a "clean bill" incorporating the proposed amendments. The original bill is then put aside and the clean bill, with a new bill number, is reported to the full chamber. If committee amendments are not extensive, the original bill is "reported

○ CLOSER LOOK

There are several types of amendments:

- **Basic.** A formal proposal to alter the text of a bill, resolution, amendment, motion, or some other text. It may strike out (eliminate) part of a text, insert new text, or strike out and insert—that is replace all or part of the text with new text.
- **In the nature of a substitute.** Usually, an amendment to replace the entire text of a measure.
- **Amendment tree.** A diagram showing the number and types of amendments that the rules and practices of either house permit to be offered to a measure before any of the amendment is voted on.
- **Amendments between the houses.** The basic method for reconciling House and Senate differences on a measure, by passing it back and forth between the two chambers until both have agreed to identical language.
- **Amendments in disagreement.** Amendments in dispute between the houses. A conference committee is required to deal only with these amendments, and its conference report may contain recommendations concerning only those amendments on which it has reached agreement.
- **Amendments in technical disagreement.** Amendments on which conferees have agreed but are not included in the conference because they violate the rules of one or both houses, and therefore are subject to a point of order. Each house considers the conference report recommendations on these technical disagreements one at a time. After 1995, when Republicans took control of the House, this problem was more often avoided by issuing special rules that blocked points of order.

with amendments." Later, when the bill comes up on the floor, the House or Senate must approve, alter, or reject the committee amendments before the bill itself can be put to a vote.

On the Floor

During floor action members may seek to change the intent, conditions, or requirements of a bill; modify, delete, or introduce provisions; or replace a section or the entire text of a bill with a different version. A member may offer an amendment that is entirely unrelated to the bill under consideration. Such an amendment, called a rider, is much more common in the Senate than in the House.

All these attempts to alter legislative proposals involve one of three basic types of amendments: those that seek to add text, those that seek to substitute alternative language for some or all of the existing text, and those that seek to delete some or all of the existing text.

Amendments that seek to revise or modify parts of bills or other amendments are called perfecting amendments. Substitute amendments aim to replace previously introduced, or pending, amendments with alternatives. A variation of the substitute, referred to as an "amendment in the nature of a substitute," seeks to replace the pending bill with an entirely new version.

Although the rules are interpreted somewhat differently in the House and Senate, both chambers prohibit the offering of amendments past the "second degree." An amendment offered to the text of a bill is a first degree amendment. An amendment to that amendment is a second-degree amendment and is also in order. But an amendment to an amendment to an amendment—a third-degree amendment—is not permissible. The rule, simply laid out in *Jefferson's Manual* in the late 1700s, is more complex than it sounds because the two chambers differ in how they interpret first- and second-degree amendments. While there are usually only four amendments pending at the same time in the House, there can be more in the Senate.

Generally speaking, bills in the House are considered section by section, with floor amendments in order only to the section of the bill then being considered. In the Senate amendments usually are in order to any section at any time, unless such practices are prohibited by unanimous consent. It is a basic concept of the amending process that once an amendment has been rejected, it may not be offered again in precisely the same form (although sometimes another vote can be forced on the same amendment).

Committee amendments—those made by the committee that reported the bill—normally are considered before amendments introduced from the floor. However, committee amendments themselves are subject to floor amendments. Both chambers vote on second-degree amendments before voting on first-degree amendments, although the precise order varies from House to Senate because of their differing interpretations of the rules.

In Conference

Legislation cannot go to the president for signature until both chambers of Congress approve it in identical form. Differences between House and Senate versions of a bill—called "amendments in disagreement"—can be resolved in one of three ways: one chamber may simply accept the other chamber's amendments; amendments may move back and forth between the two chambers until both agree; or a conference committee may be convened.

When a bill goes to conference, the compromises that are reached are incorporated in a conference report, on which each chamber votes as a whole. But sometimes House and Senate conferees are unable to reach agreement on every difference in a bill sent to conference. Amendments still in disagreement must be resolved separately in each chamber once the conference report itself has been adopted. The bill will fail unless the two chambers reach compromises on all amendments in disagreement or agree to drop them altogether.

Conferees generally are able to reach agreement, and Congress approves the bill. On occasion there are irreconcilable disagreements over content, but the more typical disagreement is a technical one. This occurs when conferees reach agreement on their differences but the rules of one chamber—usually the House—prohibit its conferees from accepting certain provisions added by the other chamber. This frequently occurs when the Senate adds unrelated, or nongermane, amendments to legislation passed by the House; when legislative provisions are added to appropriations bills; or when entirely new provisions are added by conferees. Such amendments are reported in "technical disagreement." In the past, these amendments would not be included in the body of the conference report and the House would vote on them separately. But after the Republicans took control of Congress in 1995, the House leadership worked to avoid the problem altogether by having the Rules Committee issue rules that waived points of order, or challenges, raised against such amendments, which were now included in the report itself. In 2007 Senate rules were changed to allow members to raise points of order on provisions added during a conference committee but not previously approved by either chamber. Such items could be struck individually on points of order that, if successful, would require sending the bill back to the House for approval of the changes.

Anthrax Attack

Biohazard workers rinse off after leaving the Hart Senate Office Building in 2001. The building, two blocks from the Capitol, was closed for cleaning after an anthrax-laden letter was opened in the office of Senate Majority Leader Tom Daschle.
Source: CQ Photo/Scott J. Ferrell

Barely one month after the September 11, 2001, terrorist attacks on New York and Washington, Congress confronted terrorism first-hand when a sample of potentially deadly anthrax bacteria was mailed to Senate Majority Leader Tom DASCHLE, D-S.D. Anthrax already had been sent through the U.S. mail to several media organizations, and one man had died. The series of attacks ultimately would kill five people, including postal workers who handled the letters. No one on Capitol Hill was infected by anthrax, although a number tested positive for exposure. As of fall 2007, the source of the anthrax and the person or group that sent the substance to Capitol Hill remained unknown.

On October 15, 2001, an intern opening Daschle's constituent mail in the lawmaker's Hart Senate Office Building suite sliced open a small envelope hand addressed in block letters and postmarked Trenton, N.J. The same post office had handled a widely reported envelope containing anthrax sent to NBC News. When a puff of fine, white dust flew out, the woman alerted her supervisor, who then contacted the Capitol Police and federal authorities. A comprehensive search for anthrax ensued throughout the Capitol complex. Mail delivery to all congressional offices was stopped and tours of the Capitol were temporarily halted. Investigators later found among quarantined pieces of mail a similar letter addressed to Senate Judiciary Committee Chair Patrick J. Leahy, D-Vt. That letter was opened in a sealed and controlled environment to avoid releasing deadly anthrax spores into the air.

Authorities later estimated the Daschle letter contained two grams of a highly potent form of anthrax. All staffers and lawmakers in the vicinity of the office were offered doses of the antibiotic Cipro by the Office of the Attending Physician and public health officials to prevent anthrax infections. Initially, twenty-two Senate staffers and six Capitol Police officers tested positive for exposure to what scientists measured as 3,000 times the lethal dose of anthrax. More than 3,900 people were tested for exposure and in the end nearly 1,200, including seventy Senate aides, were put on sixty-day courses of Cipro. As an extra precaution, forty-eight of the aides later received additional medication.

Congress's initial response was confused. House leaders told members and aides to go home October 17, believing that their Senate counterparts were doing likewise. But Senate leaders faced a rebellion within their ranks at the idea of leaving town and instead announced that the Senate would remain at work. That left the House leadership having to absorb the grumbling derision of House members and senators alike. It was the first time in history that the House had postponed its deliberations in the face of danger.

After lawmakers returned to Washington on October 23, Congress tried to retain its regular schedule to create an air of normalcy and reassure the public that its government was continuing to operate. Still, many found themselves in the uncomfortable position of legislating at a crime scene, evidenced by the addition of a hundred national guardsmen patrolling the perimeter of the Capitol complex to augment Capitol Police. All offices were off-limits while federal agents searched for additional anthrax. Traces of the finely milled substance turned up elsewhere in the Hart building, in the Dirksen Senate Office Building mailroom that handled the Daschle letter, in several members' offices in the Longworth House Office Building, and in a mail processing center in the Ford House Office Building.

Most of the congressional office buildings were closed only temporarily, but it would be ninety-six days before the Hart building reopened. Authorities undertook an aggressive decontamination plan in that building, where half of the senators maintain offices and where anthrax was found in at least four places. Chlorine dioxide gas—most commonly used to kill bacteria in drinking water—was pumped through portions of the building's 10 million cubic feet. Because the fumigation killed every living thing it touched, anxious senators were allowed to draw up manifests of special items—such as pet fish, artwork, or antique furniture—for the Environmental Protection Agency (EPA) to decontaminate separately. Antibacterial foam and spray were used during an eighteen-day cleanup in the Longworth building, where only trace amounts were found in four suites. The EPA estimated the cost of the cleanup totaled $41.7 million.

Congress responded to the attack by purchasing special equipment to irradiate all congressional mail and kill off any bacterial contamination. The mail also was subjected to a second off-site screening before being sent to members' offices. Use of e-mail surged during the attack and cleanup and increasingly became a preferred means of communications due to delays in mail delivery.

The anthrax attack spurred House and Senate lawmakers to boost funding for security at the Capitol complex beginning in fiscal 2003. The increased funding covered extra pay for Capitol Police with special duties, such as those who served with the bomb squad or who protected members and visiting dignitaries, as well as a 9.1 percent pay raise for officers. Work on a new Capitol visitor center was accelerated as well in the aftermath of the 2001 terrorist attacks. The center, estimated to cost about $600 million, was scheduled to open in summer 2008.

CLOSER LOOK

The deadly anthrax bacteria were contained in a letter addressed to Senate Majority Leader Tom Daschle, D-S.D., that was opened in the Hart Senate Office Building. Traces of anthrax also were found in other congressional office buildings, all of which were closed temporarily, but the Hart building remained closed for decontamination for ninety-six days.

More on this topic:

Capitol Building, p. 76

Capitol Visitor Center, p. 83

Security: Capitol Building, p. 491

Appeal

In both the Senate and House of Representatives, a member may challenge a parliamentary ruling of the PRESIDING OFFICER if he or she believes it violates the chamber's rules. Such a challenge is known as an appeal.

A senator appeals to fellow senators to overturn the presiding officer's decision, which can be done by majority vote. In the House, the ruling of the Speaker traditionally has been final, and members are seldom asked to reverse the Speaker's stand. To appeal a ruling is considered an attack on the Speaker. The Senate is more likely to overturn the rulings of its chair, often on political grounds that have little to do with the parliamentary situation.

Appointment Power

The Constitution gives the Senate the right to confirm or reject presidential appointments to many government positions. Senators sometimes use this "advice and consent" power to press for their political beliefs and to assert Congress's independence from the executive branch.

Like the authority to approve or reject treaties, the right to review presidents' choices for jobs within the government is given only to the Senate. The House does not vote on presidential nominations, and representatives rarely have much influence in decisions about which people the president will appoint.

Senators participate in the selection of Supreme Court justices, cabinet officers, ambassadors, and other high-level government officials. Only the president has the formal right to select someone to fill one of those positions. But the Senate has used its power to reject presidential appointments and pressure the president into selecting people more to its liking. In some cases, such as certain federal judgeships, senators traditionally have dictated the selection of nominees.

In the vast majority of cases, however, the Senate's power over appointments is little more than a bureaucratic chore. The Senate typically receives tens of thousands of nominations a year, most of which are routine military and civilian appointments and promotions. Routine appointments include those to the Foreign Service and Public Health Service. In the 105th Congress (1997–1999), for example, the Senate received 46,290 nominations, of which 45,878 were confirmed. By the 109th Congress (2005–2006) the nominations totaled 55,841, with 53,820 confirmed.

The president's nominations even for high-level positions normally are approved by the Senate with little debate or objection. During the first two years of President George W. Bush's administration, the Senate confirmed 419 of 501 nominees to cabinet and subcabinet positions, according to the Brookings Institution's Presidential Appointee Initiative. Most senators believe that the president has a right to pick his cabinet officers, unless one of his choices has committed some illegal or unethical action or holds beliefs that are repugnant to most Americans. Since Congress first convened, the Senate has rejected only nine nominees for cabinet positions, although others were withdrawn when unfavorable information emerged.

A similar argument often is made about Supreme Court nominations: that the president, who was endorsed by the people in the last election, has the right to name a justice who agrees with the president's legal philosophy. That argument has less force, however, because Supreme Court justices serve for life rather than just for the term of the incumbent president. Twenty-nine Supreme Court nominations (including one person who was nominated twice) have been rejected or dropped as a result of Senate opposition. A similar argument developed about lower courts, especially the circuit courts of appeal, in the latter decades of the twentieth century and into the twenty-first as liberal and conservative interest groups fought tenaciously over the philosophical orientation of the entire federal judiciary.

The effect of the Senate's power is seen most clearly in the small number of cases in which a nominee for a court seat or an executive branch position encounters real opposition. Such opposition may crystallize during committee hearings on a nomination. In many instances presidents or the nominees themselves withdraw an appointment when it becomes clear that many senators are prepared to vote against it. Less often, presidents continue to press an appointment in the face of possible defeat on the Senate floor. An outright rejection of an important nomination usually represents a major political setback for a president.

Usually the opposition will come from the political party that does not hold the White House, but on rare occasions internal rifts in the president's party have the same effect. Perhaps the most dramatic modern example came in 2005 when President Bush had an opening on the Supreme Court to fill. He initially nominated his White House counsel Harriet Miers, to the great consternation of conservatives and their Senate Republican allies—as well as right-wing critics on television and radio talk shows. Miers had no national recognition and no judicial record to assuage conservatives that she would faithfully back their judicial philosophy. With the nomination in deep trouble, Bush withdrew it.

More typically, the Senate rejects presidential appointments for several reasons. Partisan political considerations play a role, as do concerns about the personal conduct and ethics of a nominee. Interest groups and the press also influence the confirmation process.

In the 1990s, when Bill Clinton was president and Republicans controlled the Senate, Democrats complained that many of Clinton's nominees never came to votes in the Judiciary Committee or on the Senate floor. Many of those who were confirmed languished for years before they saw action, Democrats contended.

The acrimony over judicial nominations continued when the White House changed hands in the 2000 elections as Republicans similarly charged that Democrats delayed or scuttled President Bush's nominations. Bush during his first term from 2001 to 2005 enjoyed considerable success, nevertheless. By the end of the four years he had filled 203 lifetime seats on the federal trial and circuit appeals courts, or 24 percent of the total. His executive branch nominations also were largely successful.

Still, the statistics belied the intense partisanship and rancor over the makeup of the courts, which had been building for at least twenty years. Democrats in the 108th Congress from 2003 to 2005, then in the minority in the Senate, mounted the first coordinated filibusters against judicial nominations in more than a quarter-century. The impasse nearly led to a fundamental change in the Senate's cherished filibuster rule that would have wiped out the right to unlimited debate, at least on nominations and by implication other issues. That was averted, however, and both sides backed away from serious further confrontation in Bush's second term. As a result, all but Bush's most controversial judicial nominations were confirmed, and he won approval of two new Supreme Court justices, as of 2007.

The President . . . shall nominate, and by and with the Advice and Consent of the Senate, shall appoint Ambassadors, other public Ministers and Consuls, Judges of the supreme Court, and all other Officers of the United States, whose Appointments are not herein otherwise provided for, and which shall be established by Law; but the Congress may by Law vest the Appointment of such inferior Officers, as they think proper, in the President alone, in the Courts of Law, or in the Heads of Departments.

The President shall have Power to fill up all Vacancies that may happen during the Recess of the Senate, by granting Commissions which shall expire at the End of their next Session.

—Article II, section 2, of the Constitution

History

Senatorial confirmation of executive appointments is a distinctly American practice. It was included in the Constitution as the result of a compromise. Some delegates to the Constitutional Convention favored giving the Senate the exclusive right to select people to fill important non-elected offices. Others argued that the president should have complete control of appointments. The compromise gave the president the power to choose nominees, subject to the approval of the

SENATE REJECTIONS OF CABINET NOMINATIONS

Nominee	Position	President	Date	Vote
Roger B. Taney	Secretary of Treasury	Jackson	June 23, 1834	18–28
Caleb Cushing	Secretary of Treasury	Tyler	March 3, 1843	19–27
Caleb Cushing	Secretary of Treasury	Tyler	March 3, 1843	10–27
Caleb Cushing	Secretary of Treasury	Tyler	March 3, 1843	2–29
David Henshaw	Secretary of Navy	Tyler	January 15, 1844	6–34
James M. Porter	Secretary of War	Tyler	January 30, 1844	3–38
James S. Green	Secretary of Treasury	Tyler	June 15, 1844	not recorded
Henry Stanbery	Attorney General	Johnson	June 2, 1868	11–29
Charles B. Warren	Attorney General	Coolidge	March 10, 1925	39–41
Charles B. Warren	Attorney General	Coolidge	March 16, 1925	39–46
Lewis L. Strauss	Secretary of Commerce	Eisenhower	June 19, 1959	46–49
John Tower	Secretary of Defense	G.H.W. Bush	March 9, 1989	47–53

SOURCE: Adapted from George H. Hayes, *The Senate of the United States: Its History and Practice.* 2 vols. (Boston: Houghton Mifflin, 1938).

Senate. The president "shall nominate, and by and with the Advice and Consent of the Senate, shall appoint" officials, the Constitution states.

The framers disagreed on the consequences of the compromise. Alexander Hamilton thought it was not especially important, because the Senate would have no power to select officeholders independent of the president. But John Adams thought that the Senate's power would inevitably be used for partisan political purposes. Adams was quickly proved correct, during his term as president from 1797 to 1801. By 1800 it was clear that Senate approval of nominations would depend on political considerations.

Virtually every president since then has faced difficult confirmation battles with the Senate. Presidents with solid political support in the Senate generally fared better than those who had to contend with a hostile Senate. But even strong chief executives sometimes were subjected to embarrassing defeats of their nominees.

In many cases the confirmation battles of the past seem trivial, even if their political consequences were significant. In the 1880s, for example, Senate Republican leader Roscoe CONKLING resigned from the Senate as a result of a dispute with President James A. Garfield over appointments for the port of New York. Other confirmation battles have been events of lasting importance to the nation. The long and bitter fight that led to the confirmation of Louis D. Brandeis as a Supreme Court justice in 1916 marked a crucial turning point in the direction of legal philosophy in the twentieth century.

The details of most confirmation disputes have faded with time, but two long-term trends stand out. One is the rise and decline of the president's control over relatively minor but well-paying government positions. The other is the development of senators' power to control nominations that concern their states.

Spoils System

By 1820 the so-called spoils system was solidly established in the awarding of government jobs. The term comes from the expression "to the victor belong the spoils." This tradition held that the party that had won the last presidential election had a right to put its people in government offices, regardless of whether or not the previous officeholders were doing a good job. That rule still

SUPREME COURT NOMINATIONS NOT CONFIRMED BY THE SENATE

In the more than two centuries from 1789 to January 2008, the Senate has confirmed 122 presidential nominees for the Supreme Court. Of these, 115 served and seven declined to serve—no one has declined since 1882. The Senate rejected twelve nominees outright, took no action on ten others, and postponed action on three more, effectively killing their nominations. In addition, eleven nominees were withdrawn, according to figures compiled by the Senate historian. Some nominations were withdrawn or were postponed by the Senate but were later confirmed. Following are nominees who did not get confirmed.

Nominee	President	Date of nomination	Senate action	Date of Senate action
William Paterson[1]	Washington	February 27, 1793	Withdrawn	
John Rutledge[2]	Washington	December 10, 1795	Rejected (10–14)	December 15, 1795
Alexander Wolcott	Madison	February 4, 1811	Rejected (9–24)	February 13, 1811
John J. Crittenden	John Quincy Adams	December 17, 1828	Postponed	February 12, 1829
Roger Brooke Taney[3]	Jackson	January 15, 1835	Postponed (24–21)	March 3, 1835
John C. Spencer	Tyler	January 9, 1844	Rejected (21–26)	January 31, 1844
Reuben H. Walworth	Tyler	March 13, 1844	Withdrawn	
Edward King	Tyler	June 5, 1844	Postponed (29–18)	June 15, 1844
John C. Spencer	Tyler	June 17, 1844	Withdrawn	
Reuben Walworth	Tyler	June 17, 1844	Not acted upon	
Edward King	Tyler	December 4, 1844	Withdrawn	
Reuben Walworth	Tyler	December 4, 1844	Withdrawn	
John M. Read	Tyler	February 7, 1845	Not acted upon	
George W. Woodward	Polk	December 23, 1845	Rejected (20–29)	January 22, 1846
Edward A. Bradford	Fillmore	August 16, 1852	Not acted upon	
George E. Badger	Fillmore	January 3, 1853	Withdrawn	
William C. Micou	Fillmore	February 14, 1853	Not acted upon	
Jeremiah S. Black	Buchanan	February 5, 1861	Rejected (25–26)	February 21, 1861
Henry Stanbery	Andrew Johnson	April 16, 1866	Not acted upon	
Ebenezer R. Hoar	Grant	December 14, 1869	Rejected (24–33)	February 3, 1870
George H. Williams[2]	Grant	December 1, 1873	Withdrawn	
Caleb Cushing[2]	Grant	January 9, 1874	Withdrawn	
Stanley Matthews[1]	Hayes	January 26, 1881	Not acted upon	
William B. Hornblower	Cleveland	September 19, 1893	Rejected (24–30)	January 15, 1894
William B. Hornblower	Cleveland	December 5, 1893	Rejected (32–41)	February 16, 1894
Wheeler H. Peckham	Cleveland	January 22, 1894	Rejected (39–41)	
John J. Parker	Hoover	March 21, 1930	Withdrawn	May 7, 1930
Abe Fortas[2]	Lyndon Johnson	June 26, 1968	Not acted upon	
Homer Thornberry	Lyndon Johnson	June 26, 1968	Withdrawn	
Clement F. Haynsworth Jr.	Nixon	August 21, 1969	Rejected (45–55)	November 21, 1969
G. Harrold Carswell	Nixon	January 19, 1970	Rejected (45–51)	April 8, 1970
Robert H. Bork	Reagan	July 1, 1987	Rejected (42–58)	October 23, 1987
Harriet E. Miers	George W. Bush	October 7, 2005	Withdrawn	
John G. Roberts Jr.[3]	George W. Bush	July 29, 2005	Withdrawn	

SOURCE: U.S. Senate Historical Office

NOTES: 1. Later nominated and confirmed. 2. Nominated for chief justice. John Rutledge offered to serve as a replacement for John Jay, the chief justice who was about to retire. President Washington gave him a temporary commission because the Senate was in recess. But the Senate, when it reconvened in December, rejected the nomination, making Rutledge the first rejected Court nominee and the only recess appointed justice not to be subsequently confirmed. Abe Fortas was a sitting justice who was nominated to be chief justice. 3. Later nominated for chief justice and confirmed.

holds for top-level government offices, such as members of the cabinet and their ranking subordinates. But in the nation's early days the principle of party control of government jobs extended to lesser positions. Jobs such as postmaster and collector of import duties at a port were eagerly sought after, and victorious political candidates rewarded their supporters with them.

The Senate soon moved to take over its share of the PATRONAGE bonanza. In 1820 it enacted a law limiting the terms of federal officials to four years. That ensured constant turnover, allowing senators to give many more jobs to friends and relatives. The period from 1837 to 1877 marked the high point of Senate efforts to control executive appointments. During this period the spoils system reached its peak, and all presidents were subject to intense pressure for patronage appointments.

The excesses of the spoils system eventually became so serious that Congress reacted against political patronage. President Rutherford B. Hayes began to fight against the system in 1877, and in 1883 Congress established a civil service system to award most government jobs on the basis of merit.

Senatorial Courtesy

A key element of the Senate's confirmation power was the notion of senatorial courtesy. This custom, initiated in the 1780s, provided that the Senate would refuse to confirm a nomination within a particular state unless the nominee had been approved by the senators from that state who belonged to the president's party. In practice, this meant that senators usually could select many officeholders directly—a power that enhanced their political strength at home. When neither of the senators from a state was of the president's party, the right of senatorial courtesy often was given to House party members or to local party officials. The tradition of senatorial courtesy declined in importance as patronage declined and more government jobs moved into the civil service system. But senators still exert a strong influence over certain federal judgeships and other offices within their states.

Senators sometimes use their confirmation power as a political bargaining chip by placing a "hold"—or temporarily delaying action—on a nomination. When Republicans controlled the Senate for periods during the 1980s and 1990s, Jesse Helms of North Carolina repeatedly held up nominations because he found them politically unacceptable or because he wished to force political opponents to compromise on policy issues. A different example of the use of holds to pressure an administration on issues of interest to Congress came in 2007 when Sen. Ron Wyden, D-Ore., said he would block a high-level Bush administration nomination to the Department of Homeland Security because the department had failed to implement an emergency response program that Wyden had proposed almost six years earlier and which Wyden claimed the department had promised to set up. The hold was placed on a person nominated to run an immigration enforcement agency that had little to do with Wyden's program.

Politics, Ethics, and Credentials

In the latter decades of the twentieth century confirmation debates shifted from the issue of patronage to questions about the political beliefs and ethics of nominees. Far more than in earlier years, nominees became subject to searching inquiries—by the press and interest groups as well as the Senate.

The inquiries could focus, for example, on a nominee's views on such controversial issues as abortion or affirmative action programs to help boost the position of women and minorities. Sometimes questions were raised about financial dealings that might be illegal or pose a conflict of interest for the potential officeholder. For some confirmations, questions were raised about aspects of personal conduct never before discussed so openly. Nominees to high posts faced allegations ranging from marijuana use and alcohol abuse to sexual harassment.

Much more rarely, and usually only with judicial nominees, a nomination will draw opposition because of doubts about a person's credentials for a position. This unusual event occurred in 2005 when President Bush nominated his White House counsel, Miers, to a vacant Supreme Court seat before withdrawing it in the face of withering criticism from his base of conservative supporters. Although seen as a competent lawyer with an impressive resume of a woman succeeding in an often male-dominated environment, she had no judicial experience or constitutional law background, and was thought not to be as strong a candidate for the high court as the president might have selected.

Political Views

Confirmation debates that centered on political opinions often involved appointments to independent boards, commissions, and agencies, such as the Federal Communications Commission and the Environmental Protection Agency. Most of these agencies were created by acts of Congress and were not subordinate to any executive department. Thus, members of Congress tended to see these agencies as arms of Congress and expected to play a larger role in appointments to them.

Arguments over political views also cropped up in relation to appointments to major cabinet offices and the federal judiciary, especially the Supreme Court. Between 1933 and 1945 several of President Franklin D. Roosevelt's cabinet nominees faced vocal opposition because of their allegedly radical views, although all were confirmed. Roosevelt also won confirmation of Hugo L. Black as a Supreme Court justice in 1937, despite charges linking Black, an Alabama senator, to the Ku Klux Klan.

Robert H. Bork, who was nominated to the Supreme Court in 1987 by President Ronald Reagan, lost his confirmation battle at least in part because a majority of senators believed that his judicial views on subjects such as civil rights and privacy were so conservative as to be outside the mainstream of American legal philosophy.

The tables were turned in 1993, when President Bill Clinton's nomination of Lani Guinier to head the Justice Department's civil rights division came under attack from conservatives, who accused her of holding dangerously radical views on minority rights. Clinton ultimately withdrew the nomination. Some observers saw the Guinier fight as payback for Bork's defeat.

In 1997 National Security Adviser Anthony Lake withdrew as Clinton's nominee for director of the Central Intelligence Agency (CIA), complaining of what he and his supporters saw as "endless" delays and the politicizing of the confirmation process. Opponents had raised questions about Lake's stewardship of the National Security Council and the potential for political interference at the CIA.

In 2001 President Bush's first nominee to be labor secretary, Linda Chavez, drew fire from labor and civil rights groups for her opposition to the minimum wage and affirmative action. Before her nomination could be acted on, Chavez withdrew following reports she had given shelter in the early 1990s to an illegal immigrant from Guatemala who did household chores for her and received spending money in return.

The authority to pick candidates for federal district courts and courts of appeal is one of the most enduring powers presidents enjoy, allowing them to

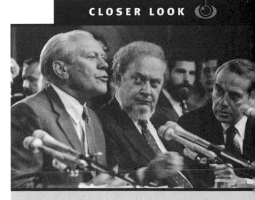

CLOSER LOOK

Former president Gerald R. Ford (left) and Sen. Robert Dole (right) present the case for Supreme Court nominee Robert H. Bork at Senate confirmation hearings in 1987.
Source: AP Images/Charles Tasnadi

One particularly virulent debate over a Supreme Court nomination brought a new word into the common political lexicon: Borked. The term, generally attributed to conservative commentators, derived from Robert H. Bork, who President Ronald Reagan nominated to fill a Supreme Court seat in 1987. Bork, a legal scholar widely admired for intellectual strengths, was strongly opposed by civil and women's right groups for his conservative views and refusal to concede a constitutional right to privacy, the keystone of abortion rights. A vigorous attack by these and other groups, virtually unprecedented in modern times, convinced the Senate that his views were so conservative as to be outside the mainstream of American legal philosophy. He was rejected by the Senate 42–58, the last time as of early 2008 that the Senate voted against a Court nomination.

Thereafter, conservatives often applied the term "Borked" to liberal attacks on conservative judicial nominees and often on executive branch officials. But even liberal groups were known to use the term, or its verb form "to bork," to indicate a vigorous opposition to a nominee.

influence the law long after their tenure in the White House is over. The highly politicized and acrimonious battles over judicial nominees in the Clinton and Bush administrations provided dramatic proof of just how potent that power was.

Personal Ethics

As the standards for government service in high positions evolved in the decades after World War II, the issue of conflict of interest became a frequent topic of concern. By the end of the twentieth century nominees were expected to avoid all situations in which their official decisions could benefit their personal interests or in which they received money from people who stood to benefit from their actions. Financial dealings that appeared shady often caused serious trouble for a nominee. One well-known example is the case of Abe Fortas, the Supreme Court justice nominated to the post of chief justice by President Lyndon B. Johnson in 1968. Critics blocked the nomination, partly on the grounds that Fortas had accepted money from past business associates, creating a conflict of interest or at least the appearance of conflict.

But some neutral observers not involved in any particular nomination fight often noted that many prominent and successful men and women who, with their backgrounds, would be legitimate candidates to serve the nation were also likely to have complex and extensive financial interests that opponents could use to block the confirmation or make the task so arduous that the individuals would decline even being nominated.

Nevertheless, personal conduct and history plagued more than a few presidential nominations over the years. President Richard Nixon's appointment of Clement F. Haynsworth Jr. to the Supreme Court was defeated because of charges that Haynsworth had failed to show sensitivity to ethical questions and the appearance of a conflict of interest—even though critics conceded that he was not personally dishonest. And President Reagan's nominee for attorney general, Edwin Meese III, endured a thirteen-month delay before he was confirmed because of concern over the legality and propriety of his financial dealings.

A nominee's personal behavior also comes under scrutiny. In 1987 Douglas Ginsburg was selected by Reagan for a seat on the Supreme Court, but his name was withdrawn before the nomination was officially submitted to the Senate after the press reported that he had smoked marijuana some years before.

U.S. Supreme Court nominee Clarence Thomas testifies during his hearing before the Senate Judiciary Committee on October 11, 1991. The Senate has the constitutional power to confirm the president's nominees to the Supreme Court, the cabinet, and other high-ranking federal positions.
Source: CQ Photo/Michael Jenkins

Personal ethics and conduct were at issue again in 1989 when the Senate rejected President George H. W. Bush's nomination of former Republican senator John Tower of Texas as secretary of defense—the first rejection of a cabinet nominee since 1959 and only the ninth cabinet-level nominee ever turned down. Although knowledgeable about defense issues from years in Congress, Democratic opponents of the nomination questioned Tower's fitness for office, citing allegations of alcohol abuse and womanizing. Tower's work as a consultant for defense contractors also was questioned as a possible conflict of interest. Republicans countered that the allegations were unfounded and that the Democrats simply wanted to eliminate a strong advocate for policies they opposed.

Bush watched another intense confirmation battle unfold two years later, when he nominated

Judge Clarence Thomas to the Supreme Court. Thomas, chosen to succeed Thurgood Marshall as the only black on the Court, won confirmation but only after an unprecedented airing of allegations of sexual harassment leveled against him by Anita F. Hill, a law professor who previously had worked for Thomas at two federal agencies. The bitter and divisive battle was complicated by the belief of many members of the Democratic-controlled Congress that Thomas was too conservative in his judicial philosophy.

In 1993 personal conduct took a different twist when Clinton had to drop his first two choices for attorney general—corporate attorney Zoë Baird and federal judge Kimba M. Wood—after questions arose over their use of illegal immigrants as domestic workers.

Recess Appointments

Presidents have one way to get around the Senate confirmation process, although it works only temporarily. But used aggressively, it can inflame partisan divisions. The Constitution allows the president to fill vacant positions during recesses in the middle of a session or between sessions of Congress, when the Senate is not meeting. These "recess appointments" are allowed to stand until the completion of the Senate's next session. Such appointments—a remnant of early days when senators could be away and out of touch with Washington for months—were traditionally limited to noncontroversial nominees, but that tradition took a beating after President Bush's election in 2000.

Earlier, tempers flared in 1997 when it appeared the Clinton administration was going to use a recess appointment to install a nominee for a high-ranking Justice Department post. The nomination of Bill Lann Lee to be assistant attorney general had been blocked in committee, caught up in a battle between Democrats and Republicans over affirmative action programs. The controversy was defused for a time when President Clinton named Lee an "acting" assistant attorney general. But when the Senate again refused to act on Lee's nomination after it was resubmitted in 1999, Clinton in 2000 finally gave Lee a recess appointment.

Presidents often go around an unreceptive Senate by giving a recess appointment to controversial nominees, as President George W. Bush did when he made John L. Bolton UN ambassador in 2005.
Source: CQ Photo/Michael Jenkins

In 2002, during a congressional recess, President Bush appointed Otto J. Reich as assistant secretary of state for western hemispheric affairs. Reich and Sen. Christopher J. Dodd, D-Conn., had clashed for two decades over policy toward Latin America, and Dodd, then chair of a Senate Foreign Relations Committee subcommittee on western hemispheric affairs, refused to hold a confirmation hearing. When Reich's temporary appointment expired, Bush named him a special envoy for western hemisphere initiatives.

Later, in 2005, Bush gave a recess appointment to John L. Bolton as United Nations ambassador. Bolton was an aggressive, confrontational, and controversial State Department official who Democrats said displayed all the wrong approaches to U.S. diplomacy and would be especially offensive at the UN. Democrats blocked confirmation, but Bush gave him a recess appointment nevertheless. Bolton resigned the job before the 110th Congress, controlled by Democrats, convened.

Tensions between a White House controlled by one party and a Senate by the other were illustrated even more in 2007 with President Bush using recess appointments to fill various jobs that Senate Democrats opposed and were determined not to confirm. The conflict was exacerbated by a provision of

More on this topic:

Courts and Congress,
p. 146

Holds, p. 260

Patronage, p. 408

Senatorial Courtesy,
p. 505

a 2006 antiterrorism law that allowed the U.S. attorney general to appoint ostensibly temporary U.S. attorneys who could serve indefinitely without Senate confirmation. The power took on special prominence after the Bush administration in 2006 fired eight U.S. attorneys. Although all U.S. attorneys, the chief law enforcement officers in federal judicial districts, serve at the pleasure of the president—that is, they can be dismissed at any time—the reasons for the firings quickly became muddled in countercharges. Republicans said the firings were performance-related, but indications started to emerge that some were fired for lack of aggressive prosecution of cases of interest to White House political operatives and some Republicans in Congress. If true, that would involve meddling in ongoing criminal investigations.

Apportionment

This is an action, taken after each decennial census, of allocating the number of seats in the House to each state. The size of the House is fixed by law, as of 2007, at 435 members. The number of seats a state gets is based on its proportion of the nation's total population. All states, under the Constitution, have at least one representative, no matter the size of its population. The remainder are distributed under a mathematical formula called the method of equal proportions. Each decennial census has been a traumatic moment for many states, at least for those—such as in the Midwest or the Northeast—that have been losing population to the South and Southwest. That population shift meant that some states would lose seats, and thereby clout, in Congress for the next decade. (See REAPPORTIONMENT AND REDISTRICTING.)

Appropriations Bills

One of Congress's most important duties each year is to pass bills appropriating money to operate government agencies and programs. The Constitution says money cannot be drawn from the U.S. Treasury except "in consequence of appropriations made by law." If Congress did not provide money in appropriations bills, the government would have to shut down. Brief shutdowns occur from time to time when Congress fails to appropriate funds in time, usually as a result of policy disputes with the president.

Appropriations bills provide legal authority to spend money previously approved in authorization bills, but they need not provide all of the money authorized and usually do not. This has often been a source of tension between authorizing committees and special interest groups, which take pride in creating new government programs, and appropriators, who historically have seen themselves as guardians of the Treasury and frequently acted to limit the scope of programs by not fully funding them.

By custom, the House acts first on appropriations bills; the Senate revises the House version, although on occasion it has written its own separate measure.

CLOSER LOOK

Each year, Congress must pass twelve general appropriations bills to fund various parts of the federal government, although the number has varied somewhat in recent years and for several decades totaled thirteen. About one-half of federal spending each year is funded through this process. The other half is funded automatically, by the authority granted by laws governing entitlement and other mandatory programs.

The twelve regular appropriations bills are:

- Agriculture, Rural Development, Food and Drug Administration
- Commerce, Justice, Science
- Defense
- Energy and Water Development
- Financial Services and General Government
- Homeland Security
- Interior, Environment
- Labor, Health and Human Services, Education
- Legislative Branch
- Military Construction, Veterans Administration
- State, Foreign Operations
- Transportation, Housing, and Urban Development

Each year Congress must pass twelve regular appropriations bills by October 1 to fund the various parts of the federal government. About one-half of federal spending each year is funded through this process. The other half is funded automatically, by the authority granted by laws governing entitlements and other mandatory programs, including interest on the national debt. Each of the regular appropriations bills covers one or more governmental functions—one bill covers defense, for example, while another covers labor, health and human services, and education. (See list, p. 22)

In addition to regular appropriations bills, Congress usually passes one or more supplemental appropriations bills annually to provide funds for unbudgeted programs or events, or—more rarely—for ongoing events of special importance. By 2007, the most important example of the latter was the war in Iraq, begun in 2003, and on a larger scale the George W. Bush administration's self-proclaimed "war on terror." The fiscal 2007 defense appropriations bill, one of only two on which Congress completed action by the end of 2006, included $70 billion in emergency supplemental funds, most of it for the wars in Iraq and Afghanistan. The Congressional Research Service reported that the $70 billion pushed total supplemental appropriations for the "war on terrorism" to about $500 billion since September 11, 2001.

Other notable examples include supplemental appropriations to fund the Persian Gulf War in 1991, for emergency urban aid after the Los Angeles riots in 1992, for farmers after severe crop and weather damage in the late 1990s, and for relief and rebuilding from devastation in many southern states, especially Louisiana, following Hurricane Katrina in 2005. Supplementals were used extensively to fund the Iraq war that President Bush launched in 2003.

If one or more of the regular appropriations bills have not been enacted by October 1, Congress typically passes a continuing resolution to keep agencies operating temporarily. The continuing resolution may last only a few days or up to an entire fiscal year. It can cover one function or the whole government in an omnibus bill. A dramatic example occurred in 2007 when Democrats, who had just taken back control of Congress from Republicans after the 2006 elections, decided to fund most of the government for fiscal 2007, which would end at the end of September that year, through a continuing resolution. Only two regular bills for that year had cleared, one of them for defense and the other for homeland security. Democrats, newly in control, decided it was better to start with a fresh approach to appropriations by focusing on the fiscal 2008 bills rather than revisit the many conflicts and controversies in the unfinished 2007 bills.

More on this topic:

Authorization Bills, p. 22

Budget Process, p. 54

Continuing Resolution, p. 145

Entitlements, p. 192

Omnibus Bills, p. 401

CLOSER LOOK ◉

An earmark is a way of setting aside funds for a specific purpose, use, or recipient. Virtually all appropriations bills are earmarked in some way, as are certain revenue sources that are credited to trust funds, such as gasoline taxes for highway construction. But by 2006 the term had taken on a darker hue that produced front-page headlines about dozens and even hundreds of earmarked funds inserted in appropriation bills by members of Congress to benefit constituents and, increasingly, special interest groups. In common usage, these earmark funds fell under a long-accepted category of directing money to research and demonstration projects, parks, academic areas, and contracts in specific congressional districts or states— usually to the political benefit of House members or senators. An earmark thereby short-circuits usual government procedures that involve department evaluations of spending proposals and other standards to measure government outlays. By 2007 the public outcry against use of these directed spending provisions was so loud that both the Senate and House changed their rules to require disclosure of earmarks in bills and the names of their sponsors.

Appropriations Committee, House

The House Appropriations Committee is traditionally the largest standing committee in Congress, and one of the most powerful as well. Its members play a crucial role in the annual process by which Congress determines funding levels for government agencies and programs. In early 2007 the committee numbered sixty-six members, thirty-seven of whom were Democrats and twenty-nine Republicans. It is the third-largest House committee.

David Obey, D-Wisc., chairs the House Appropriations Committee during markup of fiscal 2007 supplemental appropriation bill.
Source: CQ Photo/Scott J. Ferrell

By custom, all spending bills begin in the House of Representatives. The job of the Appropriations Committee is to write the first versions of the regular APPROPRIATIONS BILLS each year, as well as any emergency funding measures that may be required. In some years long budget battles have caused the Senate to take the lead on a few spending bills.

The full Appropriations Committee looks to its subcommittees to make most of the important decisions. The recommendations of the subcommittees—one for each of the twelve annual spending bills—are generally accepted by the full committee without substantial change.

The real work of the Appropriations Committee is done in the subcommittees. Subcommittee members each year listen to many hours of testimony from government officials, who come to explain the dollar amounts requested for their agencies in the federal government's budget as prepared by the president. Subcommittee members and staff then meet to go over programs line by line and decide the exact dollar amounts to be given to each.

Subcommittee members follow closely the activities of the agencies under their jurisdiction, year after year. As a result they often acquire a great deal of knowledge about and power over government programs. For example, Jamie L. Whitten, a Democratic representative from Mississippi, became chair of the full Appropriations Committee in 1979 but remained chair as well of the panel's agriculture subcommittee, which he had headed since 1949. He was often referred to as "the permanent secretary of agriculture," because his influence went on and on while the real secretaries of agriculture came and went.

The Appropriations Committee lost some of its influence after the 1970s. The congressional budget process limited the freedom of the Appropriations Committee to set spending levels. Annual spending caps set by budget legislation in the 1990s placed further, if temporary, restrictions on the Appropriations Committee's flexibility. A more significant and lasting limitation on the Appropriations Committee was the existence of entitlement programs, such as Social Security. An increasing share of the federal budget is consumed by such programs, which the government is legally required to pay for completely. The Appropriations Committee has little or no ability to alter the amounts required for entitlements.

One development in the 1980s was used to shore up the committee's power to make decisions. This was the practice of bundling appropriations for most or all federal agencies into a single omnibus bill, known as a continuing resolution. These comprehensive spending bills usually were passed toward the end of a congressional session in an atmosphere of haste and pressure, hiding many of the committee's funding decisions. Inclusion of authorizing measures in these packages also increased the clout of appropriators at the expense of the authorizing committees. In the early 1990s, after criticism from presidents Ronald Reagan and George H. W. Bush, Congress backed away from using the continuing resolution as a permanent appropriations measure and instead put it to its more typical use of continuing funding primarily for short periods of time. But when the Republican-controlled Congress and the Democratic White House of Bill Clinton began waging heated battles over spending in the mid-1990s, Congress increasingly turned to omnibus bills to package together at least some of the annual appropriations bills. In early 2003 Congress once again relied on a continuing resolution as the vehicle for eleven appropriations bills the previous Congress had failed to clear.

Just a few years later, in early 2007, Congress approved a continuing resolution to finance nearly the entire government through the remainder of that fiscal year, which ended on September 30. The previous Congress, the 109th, had passed only two appropriations bills before quitting at the end of 2006. In 2007 Democrats—newly in charge of both chambers—decided not to revisit the left-over battles of appropriations from the previous year to focus instead on the fiscal 2008 bills for the year that would begin October 1, 2007. But that required a long continuing resolution for the remainder of fiscal 2007; it was the fourth approved 2007 to keep the government running between September 1, 2006, and September 30, 2007.

Service on the Appropriations Committee was always one of the most sought-after positions for House members. Representatives would lobby vigorously to be appointed to the committee, and only those with either the backing of important House leaders or strong regional support were likely to gain a seat there. Members who win a spot on the panel give up their chance to participate in the shaping of new government activities, because the Appropriations Committee does not have the power to prepare legislation establishing government programs. Instead, members have the opportunity to steer funds to activities that are important to them or their constituents.

Turnover on the Appropriations Committee normally is low. In 1993, however, nineteen members left the committee due to retirements and defeats. The turnover set the stage for a new era in the committee's history, which continued changing after the Republicans took control of the House in 1995. Under term limit rules changes that the Republicans adopted, committee and subcommittee chairs cannot hold their positions for more than six years. As a result, six Appropriations subcommittee chairs, known as "cardinals," were forced to leave their posts at the start of the 107th Congress in January 2001. However, the cardinals largely traded positions with each other. The Democrats kept this rule change when they took back control in 2007.

History

Until the Civil War, spending matters were considered along with tax legislation in the House Ways and Means Committee. Overseeing both revenues and spending became too large a task for one committee, however, so in 1865 the Appropriations Committee was established.

The spending panel quickly became a powerful committee. Under the leadership of Democrat Samuel J. Randall of Pennsylvania, the Appropriations Committee became the object of hostility from other members, who thought it was too tightfisted. That resentment gave rise to a move to curb the committee's power. House members voted to take away the panel's jurisdiction over several government programs, including defense, river and harbor projects, agriculture, and the Post Office. By 1885 the committee had lost control over half the federal budget.

But dispersal of spending power to several different committees frustrated efforts to establish control over government budget policy. To centralize spending power, the House in 1920 restored to the Appropriations Committee the exclusive right to approve appropriations bills.

Appropriations Committee members gained more power and independence in the following decades. Committee members often won reelection easily year after year. Because of their long years of service the seniority system placed them in positions of power as chairs of the committee and key subcommittees, where they became politically entrenched. They were thus able to pursue their own goals with little interference from the House leadership.

> **"Not one cent for scenery."**
>
> —*Rep. Joseph G. Cannon,* House Speaker, 1903–1911, denying a request for a federal conservation expenditure. Quoted in Blair Bolles, *Tyrant from Illinois* (1951).

> **"Well, today we are repealing Cannon's law. We are declaring a new doctrine of conservation."**
>
> —*President Lyndon B. Johnson* in 1965 quoting Cannon as he signed legislation establishing the Assateague Island National Seashore on the Atlantic coast of Maryland and Virginia

Committee meetings were almost always held in secret, and even the records of hearings were usually withheld from outsiders until shortly before the appropriations bill came to the floor. Consequently, few members who were not on the subcommittee were in a position to challenge the bill. Two of the most powerful committee chairs were Clarence CANNON of Missouri, chair for most of the period between 1949 and 1964, and George H. Mahon of Texas, who held the post from 1964 to 1979.

In the 1970s House leaders began to curb the autonomy of the Appropriations Committee. The Legislative Reorganization Act of 1970 caused most Appropriations subcommittee hearings to be opened to the public, although many bill-drafting sessions remained closed. In 1971 the seniority system was attacked and changed by many younger, newer House members, who wanted to share in the power then concentrated in the hands of their more senior colleagues. One major change allowed committee and subcommittee chairs to be selected without regard to seniority.

In 1975 the Democrats, who were in the majority, emphasized the importance of the Appropriations subcommittees by requiring that the chairs of those panels, like the chairs of full committees, be elected by a secret vote of all House Democrats. This raised the threat that senior chairs might be voted out by colleagues. It tended to make chairs more responsive to the needs and interests of other House members, including the elected party leadership. Another Democratic Party action that year also was aimed at Appropriations: a rule barring members from serving on more than two subcommittees. The rule was intended to prevent senior Appropriations Committee members from monopolizing key positions.

After the Republican takeover of the House in 1995, the power to select the subcommittee chairs initially was given to the Appropriations Committee chair alone. But when the budget process broke down in the House in 2002, conservative Republicans railed against what they perceived to be an arrogant and maverick group of top appropriators who were too eager to spend money. They pushed their more fiscally conservative party leadership to rein in the subcommittee chairs, and they won. Beginning in the 108th Congress (2003–2005), the subcommittee chairs were to be selected by the leadership-backed House Republican Steering Committee. The new rule adopted by the House Republican Conference clearly was intended to send a strong message about the desire for greater party loyalty on spending issues. Under the Democrats in 2007, the ranking party member on most subcommittees became the chair.

More on this topic:
Appropriations Committee, Senate, p. 26
Authorization Bills p. 33
Budget Committees, pp. 49, 51
Budget Process, p. 54
Continuing Resolution, p. 145
Entitlements, p. 192
Omnibus Bills, p. 401
Reform, Congressional, p. 470
Seniority System, p. 505

Appropriations Committee, Senate

The Senate Appropriations Committee is one of the largest committees in the Senate and one of the most important. But traditionally its role in the Senate has been considered less significant than that played by its counterpart in the House. In early 2007 the committee had twenty-nine members—fifteen Democrats and fourteen Republicans.

Like the House panel, the Senate committee is responsible for preparing the annual bills that provide money for federal government agencies. The committee reviews the spending proposals of the executive branch and can recommend to the full Senate changes in the amounts requested for various programs. For decades the Senate Appropriations Committee existed in the shadow of its more powerful House counterpart, because an unwritten rule in Congress requires that the House be the first chamber to act on these annual spending bills (called appropriations bills).

But beginning in the 1980s Senate committee members sought to strengthen their role. Members worked to unite their committee and to establish a more unified stance in negotiations with the House in conference committees. The committee gained a new focus when former Senate majority leader Robert C. BYRD, a West Virginia Democrat known for upholding congressional prerogatives, served as chair from 1989 to 1995. When Byrd regained the gavel in 2001, it was at his insistence that all thirteen fiscal 2002 spending bills became law as separate measures. Republican Ted Stevens of Alaska—another passionate defender of congressional spending prerogatives but

also a party loyalist—succeeded Byrd as chair in 2003. Byrd came back into the chair in the 110th Congress at the beginning of 2007 after Democrats recaptured Senate control in the 2006 elections.

The Senate Appropriations Committee normally takes up a spending bill only after it has passed the House, although preliminary subcommittee work on the bills begins earlier. During protracted budget battles in the 1980s, the Senate Appropriations Committee acted on some spending bills before its House counterpart, but still the full Senate did not take up the bills on the floor before the House acted. For the most part, Senate committee members find themselves in the position of reacting to a completed bill that has already been approved by the House. As a result, Senate members are likely to allow much of the House bill

Senate Appropriations Transportation Subcommittee chair Patty Murray, D-Wash., and ranking member Christopher S. Bond, R-Mo., confer on a fiscal year 2008 transportation appropriation bill.
Source: CQ Photo/Scott J. Ferrell

to go through unchanged, while focusing their attention on increasing or reducing funding for a few highly visible programs.

For many years the Senate committee operated largely as a "court of appeals." Supporters of programs whose funding had been cut by the House would try to lobby Senate committee members to restore some or all of the money. Senators frequently sought to increase funding levels approved by the House, and they rarely proposed funding reductions. After a 1990 budget agreement between Congress and President George H. W. Bush, the Senate Appropriations Committee several times scaled back House proposals, bringing them closer to the president's position.

The heavy and diverse workloads of senators put the Senate Appropriations Committee at a disadvantage in dealing with the House spending panel. Senate committee members serve on one or two other major committees in addition to Appropriations, while House Appropriations Committee members generally serve only on that committee. As a result senators often have less time than House committee members to master the details of spending bills.

More on this topic:

Appropriations Bills, p. 22

Appropriations Committee, House, p. 23

Conference Committees, p. 123

Architect of the Capitol

The post of architect of the Capitol has existed as a permanent position since 1876, when Congress transferred to the architect the functions performed previously by the commissioner for public

Capitol, 1907.
Source: Library of Congress

buildings and grounds. However, beginning with William Thornton in 1793, nine presidential appointees have had the architect's responsibility for construction and maintenance of the Capitol.

The architect of the Capitol need not be a professional architect, for the position today is largely an administrative one. The architect is charged with the structural and mechanical care of the following buildings: the Capitol and two hundred acres of grounds, the Senate and House office buildings, the Library of Congress buildings and grounds, the U.S. Supreme Court buildings and grounds, the Senate garage, the Thurgood Marshal Federal Judiciary Building; the Capitol Police headquarters; the Robert A. Taft Memorial, and the Capitol Power Plant, which heats and cools some buildings in addition to the Capitol complex. The architect also is charged with the operation of the U.S. Botanic Garden and the Senate restaurants.

The architect performs these tasks under the direction of the Speaker of the House, the Senate Committee on Rules and Administration, the House Office Building Commission, and the Joint Committee on the Library. Employees working for the architect of the Capitol include tree surgeons, stone inspectors, nurses, subway car and elevator operators, electricians, garage workers, and flag clerks. Services provided for congressional committees and members of Congress by the architect's office include work-space design, furniture acquisition and delivery, housekeeping, painting, and catering.

A 1989 law established an appointment process and a ten-year term, with eligibility for reappointment. A congressional commission recommends three names to the president who makes the appointment, which is subject to Senate confirmation. At the beginning of 2007 the architect's annual salary was $163,700. The architect since 1997, Alan M. Hantman, retired in early 2007. A new architect had not been named as of early 2008.

◎ CLOSER LOOK

Following is a list of persons who have been appointed by the president to serve as architect of the Capitol, although under other titles in the early years:

1793–1794 William Thornton
1803–1811, 1815–1817 Benjamin Henry Latrobe
1818–1829 Charles Bulfinch
1851–1865 Thomas Ustick Walter
1865–1902 Edward Clark
1902–1923 Elliott Woods
1923–1954 David Lynn
1954–1970 J. George Stewart
1971–1997 George M. White
1997–2007 Alan M. Hantman
2007– Stephen T. Ayers (acting)

Armed Services Committee, House

The House Armed Services Committee has jurisdiction over most aspects of U.S. national defense. Along with its Senate counterpart, the House committee each year prepares the legislation that sets the upper limits on how much the Defense Department can spend for weapons, troops, and military facilities.

With increased defense outlays connected to wars in Afghanistan and Iraq, the committee—and its Senate counterpart—authorized vast amounts. Congress agreed to authorize $532.8 billion for defense in fiscal 2007, up from $393 billion just four years earlier. That fiscal 2003 sum was the largest increase in military spending since Ronald Reagan's presidency in the 1980s. The enormous size of the defense budget makes Armed Services one of the most important and powerful committees in the House.

Committee members spend much of their time reviewing requests for funding of new and existing weapons programs submitted by military and civilian officials in the Pentagon. The committee largely determines the size, strength, and fighting ability of the

Congressional oversight of the armed forces extends beyond the approval of a budget. Rep. Duncan Hunter, chair of the House Armed Services Committee, is escorted by Commander of Troops Col. Robert Pricone, U.S. Army, as he inspects the joint services honor guard at the Pentagon in September 2005.
Source: Department of Defense, R. D. Ward

nation's armed forces. The committee does not, however, have complete control over spending for defense. The Budget Committee sets an overall limit on the amount of money available for defense each year, and the Appropriations Committee determines the exact dollar amounts for individual defense programs. But the Armed Services Committee plays the most important role in determining how the money will be spent.

The committee is also a significant arena for debate over issues of strategic defense. Committee members have been deeply involved in controversies over nuclear arms control, as well as proposals for new nuclear missiles and an antimissile defense program. The committee took the lead in the House in shaping the U.S. defense program following the disintegration of the Soviet Union in the early 1990s. During George W. Bush's administration, the panel addressed questions about the war in Afghanistan and concerns about Iraq's possession of weapons of mass destruction, even before the administration invaded Iraq in 2003 to topple its dictator, Saddam Hussein.

The members of Armed Services traditionally have been conservative and strongly prodefense. Both Democratic and Republican members have worked closely over the years with Pentagon officials and supported their budget requests, sometimes at levels considerably higher than those favored by a majority of the House. The committee's strong tradition of bipartisanship was rocked somewhat in the early 1990s when Democrats solidified their control of the committee and began forcing through more partisan bills. But after a few years of liberal chairs, Republicans took control of the House in 1995, and the panel tilted back toward the right.

With Democrats back in control in 2007, the panel's agenda shifted once again, with oversight of the Iraq war a top item, and a refocusing on the conflict in Afghanistan. The new chair, Ike Skelton, D-Mo., widely viewed as a leading congressional voice on military matters, initially supported the war in Iraq but by 2007 said he favored a phased withdrawal of troops.

History

The origin of the Armed Services Committee goes back to the creation of the Military and Naval Affairs committees in 1822. The modern history of the committee began in the years after World War II, about the time the unified Department of Defense was created. The actual committee was created by the Legislative Reorganization Act of 1946 out of the combination of the Military and Naval Affairs committees.

For more than three decades the committee was dominated by a solid core of conservative southern Democrats and Republicans, who ensured that the annual defense bills closely followed Pentagon recommendations. The committee was chaired by a succession of powerful southern Democrats, who ran it with an iron hand.

The first of the autocratic chairs was Carl Vinson, a Georgia Democrat who controlled the committee from 1949 to 1965, except for the years from 1953 to 1955, when Republican Dewey Short of Missouri was chair. Next came South Carolina Democrat L. Mendel Rivers (1965–1971), who was frequently accused of running the committee as his personal domain, dictating its agenda and rarely allowing junior members to have much of a voice. Rivers worked hard to steer Pentagon spending projects, such as military bases and defense contracts, to South Carolina. Cynics said he was so successful that the entire state would sink into the ocean if another military base were established there. Rivers's strenuous efforts to bring job-creating military bases and contracts to his home state were typical of the concerns of many committee members during this period.

Major changes in the committee began to occur in the 1970s. One new factor was the arrival on the committee of a small number of liberal Democrats. These Democrats, who were strongly opposed to U.S. military involvement in Vietnam, soon became vocal critics of the committee's prodefense majority. Members such as Les Aspin of Wisconsin and Patricia Schroeder of Colorado used their committee positions to highlight their attacks on what they saw as wasteful and excessive military spending. But they were overwhelmingly outnumbered on the committee and rarely had the strength to influence committee decisions.

Another factor that began to affect the committee in the 1970s was the House attack on the seniority system. Reform-minded Democrats sought to replace the existing method of selecting committee chairs according to length of service with a method based on elections within the House Democratic Caucus. The Armed Services chair at the time, F. Edward Hébert of Louisiana, was one of the prime targets of reformers. The House Democratic Caucus, the organization of party members, deposed Hébert in 1975, replacing him with seventy-year-old Melvin Price of Illinois.

For the next ten years Price chaired the committee, which in the early 1980s prepared legislation authorizing the massive military buildup sought by President Reagan. But Price was not a strong chair, and many of his colleagues saw him as too aged and infirm to manage the committee effectively. A major turning point for the committee came in 1985, when Aspin challenged Price for the leadership position. Although Price was supported strongly by the Democratic leaders of the House, in a highly unusual move the Democratic Caucus selected Aspin as the new chair.

Although Aspin was sometimes at odds with his party's liberal-dominated caucus, particularly when he supported some of the White House's key defense proposals, he emerged as the Democrats' savvy and politically influential spokesperson on defense. In 1991, for example, Aspin was instrumental in lining up the majorities that voted to go to war with Iraq after that nation invaded neighboring Kuwait. With the disintegration of the Soviet Union, House Democrats looked to him to articulate a Democratic defense program for the post–cold war era.

In 1993 the chair passed to California Democrat Ronald V. Dellums, a self-described socialist who regularly had denounced Pentagon budgets. Although ironic that Dellums should chair the committee responsible for spending billions on defense, his political finesse and commitment to the deliberative process won him the high regard of many conservatives in Congress.

More on this topic:

Armed Services
Committee, Senate,
p. 31

Seniority System, p. 505

Two years later in 1995, with the Republican Party ascending to majority status, South Carolina's Floyd Spence became chair. Tight budgets, overseas troop deployments, and the lack of a strong leader at the top of the committee made defense budget negotiations with the Democratic White House much more difficult. Arguments with the Clinton administration over the size and scope of the budget delayed the completion of defense budgets so much that the appropriations panel sometimes set defense spending priorities.

But tensions between the legislative and executive branches were eased after President Bush took office in 2001, particularly in the wake of the terrorist attacks on the country on September 11 of that year. There was some speculation that the panel would take on a more ambitious agenda when Duncan W. Hunter, R-Calif., took over the chair in 2003. Hunter had objected to Bush's past and projected defense budgets, calling them too small to fund military operations and new weaponry. As expected, Hunter consistently backed increased defense budgets and more advanced weapons. He also sided with the Bush administration on rules governing the treatment of military detainees and interrogation methods, both of which came under increasingly scathing criticism from Democrats and many moderate Republicans.

Armed Services Committee, Senate

Like its House counterpart, the Senate Armed Services Committee has responsibility for most aspects of U.S. national defense. Because it has authority over the vast array of Defense Department programs, the committee usually is considered to be among the most influential committees in the Senate.

The work of the Armed Services Committee revolves around the annual Defense Department authorization bill. This measure must be reported and passed each year to give the Defense Department authority to spend money. Once it has been passed, Congress may approve appropriations bills for purchase of weapons, military operations, and construction of military facilities.

The Senate committee resembles the House Armed Services panel in many ways. Their jurisdictions are basically the same, with the exception of the Senate panel's jurisdiction over defense-related executive nominations. The two committees also have a similar political approach to defense issues. The Senate committee historically has had a prodefense majority, which has tended to give strong support to Pentagon requests for funding of proposed new weapons systems.

Senate Armed Services has faced challenges to its authority over defense spending similar to those that have confronted the House committee at least since the early 1990s. The development of the congressional budget process and a newly assertive attitude on the part of the Appropriations Committee posed threats to the Armed Services panel's control over the amount of money available for defense spending.

The Senate Armed Services Committee for the most part did not face the kind of political problems that often plagued its House counterpart during the 1970s and 1980s. Senate committee members generally proposed defense policies and spending levels that enjoyed broad support in the Senate. This was in marked contrast to the House, where Armed Services Committee proposals often were opposed by a majority of Democrats in the whole House. But with the demise of the Soviet Union in the early 1990s, even the Senate committee felt increased pressure from Democrats to make deep cuts in the defense budget. A decade later, however, defense budgets jumped dramatically as fears about terrorism took root after the September 11, 2001, attacks on New York and Washington and the twin wars in Afghanistan and—particularly—Iraq absorbed vast financial and human resources.

History

Since its creation by the Legislative Reorganization Act of 1946, the Senate Armed Services Committee has frequently been controlled by a strong chair who has put a personal imprint on Senate defense policy. The first and most powerful of these was Richard B. RUSSELL, a Georgia Democrat who ran the committee for a total of sixteen years, from 1951 to 1953 and then again from 1955 to 1969.

Russell, whose Senate career had begun in 1933, was one of the most powerful senators of his day. He was a dominant force on defense policy for nearly two decades. He towered over Senate debates on defense bills because of both his mastery of defense issues and the immense respect his colleagues had for him. He was rarely challenged, either in the committee or on the Senate floor. His control of defense topics became even more entrenched in the 1960s, when he also became chair of the Defense Subcommittee of the Appropriations Committee.

Russell's successor, Mississippi Democrat John C. STENNIS, chaired the committee from 1969 to 1981. He also wielded considerable influence because he chaired both Armed Services and the defense spending subcommittee. Despite the personal admiration many senators felt for him, however, Stennis did not dominate defense debates the way Russell had. Another committee member, Washington Democrat Henry M. Jackson, was widely viewed as the Democrats' defense expert. His knowledge of defense issues and advocacy of a strong defense posture made him a major force in the Senate and a leader among the section of the Democratic Party that favored a tough stance toward the Soviet Union.

The Republican takeover of the Senate in 1981 put Texan John Tower in the Armed Services chair. Tower, a strong-willed negotiator who favored a hard line toward the Soviet Union, guided President Ronald Reagan's massive defense buildup through the Senate in the early 1980s. Later, when enthusiasm for defense increases cooled, Tower was a key force in protecting Pentagon spending requests from budget cuts. He was followed for two years (1985–1987) by Arizona Republican Barry M. Goldwater, a blunt-spoken conservative who had been his party's nominee for president in 1964.

With the Democrats back in power in 1987, Sam Nunn became chair in the Russell tradition. Nunn, also from Georgia, was universally recognized as the most knowledgeable senator on defense issues. His expertise on both broad strategic questions and technical defense matters made him the Senate's dominant force on defense. For example, in 1987 Nunn stopped Reagan's effort to reinterpret a 1972 U.S.-Soviet treaty so it would not conflict with the president's proposed antimissile defense system. In 1989 he spearheaded the Democratic defeat of the nomination of former senator Tower to be President George H. W. Bush's secretary of defense. The chair successfully resisted Democratic pressure to slash the post–cold war defense budget in the early 1990s. Some observers believed that Nunn lost clout in 1991 when he voted against U.S. involvement in the Persian Gulf War. But others disagreed and felt, as one of his Senate colleagues put it, that Nunn was "still the man to beat" on defense issues.

When Republicans gained control of the committee in 1995, Strom Thurmond of South Carolina assumed the chair. Despite questions about his age (he was in his nineties), Thurmond and his Republican counterpart in the House, Floyd Spence, fought long, hard battles with the administration of President Bill Clinton and with their colleagues in Congress to ensure their committees' continued primacy in defense issues.

In 1999 Thurmond voluntarily relinquished the chair to fellow Republican John Warner, a senator from Virginia since 1979 who had also served as Secretary of the Navy from 1972 to 1974. Warner established a reputation for innovative thinking during his tenure for two and a half years before the Democrats gained control in 2001. Democrat Carl Levin of Michigan served as chair in 2001–2003. A liberal, often dovish lawmaker, Levin had to alter his legislative priorities to adjust to the new realities of a War Congress in the wake of the 2001 terrorist attacks. Yet Levin—in his trademark legislative style of a dogged but genial negotiator—still sparred with the Republican administration over some defense issues.

Warner returned to the committee's chair in 2003, when the GOP again controlled the Senate but Levin was back in the chair in 2007 when Democrats regained power in the 2006 elections. The committee in 2007 was seen as a ministage for presidential contenders in 2008 including ranking Republican John McCain, R-Ariz., and Hillary Rodham Clinton, D-N.Y.

But the focus remained on Levin, who was a dogged adversary of President George W. Bush, especially on the war in Iraq. Before the war began Levin pushed the administration to seek congressional and UN approval before invading Iraq, and he voted in October 2002 against the congressional resolution authorizing force. Levin said it constituted a "blank check" approval of a unilateral operation. He also had charged that the administration manipulated intelligence about Iraq to justify the war, a claim that an increasing amount of evidence by 2007 suggested was plausible. Levin in early 2007 remained a war critic but—unlike some other senators and many in the House—did not advocate an immediate withdrawal of U.S. troops.

More on this topic:
Appropriations Committee, Senate, p. 26
Armed Services Committee, House, p. 29
Budget Process, p. 54

Army-McCarthy Hearings   *See* MCCARTHY, JOSEPH R.

At-Large Representative   *See* HOUSE OF REPRESENTATIVES.

Authorization Bills

Congress passes authorization bills to determine which programs and agencies the federal government is allowed to operate. Authorization bills may create legal authority for new programs or continue the operation of existing ones, either indefinitely or for one or several years. These bills set policy and procedures for government programs. Some authorizations set a ceiling on the amount of money that may be appropriated for the programs; others are open-ended, simply permitting the appropriation of "such sums as may be necessary."

Authorization bills do not themselves provide money; that requires separate action through the appropriations process. In fact, historically members of appropriations committees—seeing themselves as guardians of the Treasury and many carrying a conservative philosophy about government spending—have provided less, sometimes much less, for programs than the authorizing legislation allowed. Congressional rules state that programs must be authorized before money can be appropriated for them, but the requirement is often waived. Members of authorizing committees resist this waiver but have little power to prevent it, because they believe it diminishes their role in overseeing and guiding programs. In 2006 Congress cleared a $532.8 billion defense authorization for fiscal 2007. However, for the fifth consecutive year, lawmakers did not clear the authorization until after the defense appropriations bill had been enacted. This was a trend that Armed Services Committee members, who write the authorizing legislation, saw as diminishing their relevance and clout. (See APPROPRIATIONS BILLS).

B

Backdoor Spending

Normally, the authority to spend federal tax dollars is attained through the appropriations process when the appropriations committees in the Senate and House and then the chambers themselves vote on funding legislation. Backdoor spending refers to the authority to incur obligations that evades the normal appropriations process because it is provided in legislation other than appropriations acts. The most common legislative forms of backdoor spending are borrowing authority, contract authority, and entitlement authority. Many members of Congress, especially the senators and representatives charged with handling the appropriations legislation, dislike backdoor spending authority because it removes spending decisions from their control. Fiscal conservatives often denounce backdoor spending because they believe it requires government spending far into the future without the normal oversight of the regular appropriations process. This lack of oversight is especially true with entitlements, such as Social Security or Medicare, that require payments if a person meets legal requirements. However, the Congressional Budget Act of 1974 gave the appropriations committees some control over new borrowing and contract authority. (See PURSE, POWER OF.)

Baker, Howard H., Jr.

Howard H. Baker Jr. (1925–) of Tennessee was first elected to the Senate in 1966 and served until his retirement in 1985. From 1981 to 1985 he was majority leader.

Defeated in his first campaign for the Senate in 1964, Baker ran again and won in 1966, becoming the first popularly elected Republican senator from Tennessee. Baker had strong roots in

*Sens. Howard H. Baker Jr., R-Tenn. (right), and Samuel Ervin,
D-N.C., of the Senate Watergate Committee in 1974. Baker summa-
rized the committee's investigation succinctly with his question,
"What did the president know, and when did he know it?"*
Source: The Granger Collection, New York

Congress: both of his parents served in the House of Representatives, and his father-in-law, Everett McKinley DIRKSEN, was minority leader of the Senate.

Baker gained national prominence in 1973 for his participation in Senate hearings on the Watergate scandal. Disclosure of administration efforts to cover up political sabotage in the Watergate affair ultimately drove President Richard Nixon out of office. As vice chair of the Select Committee on Presidential Campaign Activities, Baker impressed his colleagues and the country at large with his calm and measured approach in investigating the president of his own party. The question he posed to witnesses, "What did the president know, and when did he know it?" entered the language.

In 1977, after a last-minute campaign and by a slim margin, Baker was elected Senate minority leader. He became majority leader in 1981, after Ronald Reagan was elected president and Republicans won control of the Senate. Despite philosophical differences with the president, Baker decided that he would become, in his own words, Reagan's "spear-carrier in the Senate." It was a role he filled faithfully during his four years as majority leader.

Baker's style was relaxed and effective. Under his leadership the Republicans in the Senate became a voting bloc that handed Reagan significant victories on taxation and budget issues. As majority leader, Baker also played a large part in the Senate's decision to allow television coverage of Senate floor proceedings.

In 1984, saying that "eighteen years is enough," Baker announced that he would retire from the Senate to practice law. He had run unsuccessfully for the Republican presidential nomination in 1980 and was widely expected to try again in 1988. But in February 1987, under pressure in the Iran-contra affair, Reagan asked Baker to become White House chief of staff. By accepting the appointment, Baker removed himself from the 1988 presidential contest.

In early 2001 President George W. Bush named Baker to be ambassador to Japan. Baker replaced former House Speaker Thomas S. FOLEY, who had been named to the position by President Bill Clinton. Baker left the post in 2005 and was replaced by J. Thomas Schieffer, the former ambassador to Australia and a long-time business associate of President Bush.

> **More on this topic:**
>
> *Iran-contra Affair, p. 301*
>
> *Watergate Scandal,
> p. 596*

Baker v. Carr

Baker v. Carr was the first in a series of Supreme Court cases, largely decided in the 1960s, that fundamentally changed the way voters were represented in state legislatures and, later, the U.S. Congress. The cases led to the now-famous declaration of "one person, one vote."

The *Baker* decision arose out of a challenge in Tennessee from state residents who argued that rural areas were vastly overrepresented in the legislature compared to city and suburban areas. The

Tennessee legislature, controlled by representatives from rural districts, had refused to reapportion itself since 1901 despite a state constitutional requirement to do so every ten years. A group of urban residents led by Charles W. Baker, chairman of the Shelby County (Memphis) government body, sued Tennessee's secretary of state, Joe Carr, in federal court to force the legislature to comply with the requirement.

During previous decades the Supreme Court had refused to get involved in congressional districting disputes, grounded in the belief that the judicial branch should not be ruling on political questions. In 1962, however, the Court ruled, 6–2, that federal courts could hear such a case. But the Court did not decide the merits of the Tennessee's plaintiff's claim.

> **"Legislators represent people, not trees, or acres."**
>
> —U.S. Supreme Court, *Reynolds v. Sims*

The issues raised in the Tennessee case played out in decisions over the next several years. In 1963 the Court in *Gray v. Sanders* struck down an unusual system used in Georgia that gave an advantage to numerous rural counties at the expense of urban areas. In its decision the Court said that political equality "can mean only one thing—one person, one vote."

The following year the Court applied the same principle to congressional districts in another case from Georgia, *Westberry v. Sanders.* Later in 1964 the Court also required districts of equal population for both houses of bicameral state legislatures. In that decision, *Reynolds v. Sims,* the Court said: "Legislators represent people, not trees or acres."

In subsequent decisions the Court handed down decisions that required mathematical equality between districts at all levels. In later years, however, the Court backed away from that as applied to state legislatures, but the requirement of strict numerical equality for congressional districts within a state remained intact. (See REAPPORTIONMENT AND REDISTRICTING.)

Balanced Budget and Emergency Deficit Control Act of 1985 *See* GRAMM-RUDMAN-HOLLINGS ACT.

Banking, Housing and Urban Affairs Committee, Senate

Watching over the nation's banking and financial institutions is the chief responsibility of the Senate Committee on Banking, Housing and Urban Affairs. The Federal Reserve System, the comptroller of the currency, and the Federal Deposit Insurance Corporation fall within its purview. The banking committee also shares oversight of international economic policy, including foreign trade.

Although the panel also has jurisdiction over housing and urban issues, financial issues have been at the top of the committee's agenda in recent decades. A bailout of failed savings and loan institutions and banking regulation were the two issues that dominated lawmakers' attention in the 1980s and 1990s. Corporate fraud and accountability moved to center stage early in the next decade. By the mid-2000s, however, banking again became the focus after a meltdown in the mortgage industry.

Interest in a seat on the committee tends to rise and fall with the issues before it. Liberals were attracted to it when urban redevelopment was a hot issue. Its popularity waned during the savings and loan debacle and an accompanying scandal involving a group of senators. However, as the panel tackled the politically potent issues of corporate scandals and banking regulation, interest returned.

The senator who was probably the best known for drafting banking legislation was Virginia Democrat Carter Glass. Glass was coauthor of one of the major banking laws of 1933, the Glass-Steagall Act, which prohibited banks in the Federal Reserve System from selling stocks and bonds. Glass, who chaired a key Senate banking subcommittee, also played a major role in the creation of the Securities and Exchange Commission in 1934. A senator from 1920 until his death in 1946, Glass had previously served in the House; as chair of the House banking committee, he had helped establish the Federal Reserve System in 1913. In that same year the Senate set up its Banking and Currency Committee.

The Senate changed its banking committee's name in the 1970s to reflect its role in housing and urban affairs. William Proxmire, an independent-minded Wisconsin Democrat, chaired the committee from 1975 to 1981 and from 1987 to 1989. Utah Republican Jake Garn held the post during the intervening years, when Republicans controlled the Senate.

After Proxmire retired, Donald W. Riegle Jr., a Michigan Democrat, took over the committee in 1989, just as the savings and loan bailout, bank troubles, and the resulting congressional scandal became public knowledge. Under Riegle's direction, the panel crafted legislation that overhauled the savings and loan industry and provided $50 billion in cleanup costs. Additional money was approved in following years as bailout demands grew. Thousands of savings and loan institutions had gone bankrupt under the weight of failed loans, a national recession, and the collapse of the commercial real estate market. The federal government was left to pay off depositors.

At the same time Riegle and Alan Cranston of California, the number-two committee Democrat, were charged with using their positions to influence federal regulators' oversight of a savings and loan owned by Charles H. Keating Jr., a political contributor. Riegle was rebuked for showing poor judgment, while Cranston received a more serious reprimand. (See SCANDALS, CONGRESSIONAL.)

New York's colorful Alfonse M. D'Amato took control of the committee in 1995 and promptly got the committee involved in the complicated investigation of President Bill Clinton's role in a convoluted land deal known as Whitewater. After seemingly endless hearings, the committee wrapped up its probe having found no evidence that the president had committed a crime. D'Amato was defeated in the 1998 elections.

Sen. Christopher J. Dodd, D-Conn. chairs the Senate Banking, Housing and Urban Affairs Committee during committee hearings in January 2007.
Source: CQ Photo/Scott J. Ferrell

In 1999 Republican Phil Gramm of Texas became chair of the committee and shepherded through the Senate an overhaul of the Glass-Steagall Act. Gramm had filibustered to death a House overhaul bill the previous year. In the end, and under pressure from his party's leadership and the industry, he made the concessions necessary to win final passage and White House approval.

When the Democrats took control of the Senate in 2001, Gramm turned the committee over to Paul S. Sarbanes, a Democrat from Maryland. The new chair oversaw the Senate's response to corporate accounting scandals. Momentum for legislation began building after the December 2001 bankruptcy of Enron Corp. The Houston-based energy giant earlier had disclosed that it would revise some of its previous financial statements, reducing its net income over those years by $569 million. Arthur Anderson LLP, the accounting firm that audited Enron's books, also was implicated. The subsequent news that WorldCom Inc., the telecommunications giant, had improperly booked $3.9 billion of its overhead as capital expenditures made the legislation unstoppable. The new law, which largely reflected Sarbanes's work, imposed new rules on the accounting industry and increased criminal penalties for securities fraud.

The Senate returned to Republican control in 2003. Richard C. Shelby of Alabama, taking over the helm of the committee at the start of the 108th Congress, made protecting the privacy of consumers' financial information as one of his top priorities.

With Democrats back in Senate control in 2007, the chair went to Christopher J. Dodd, D-Conn. His elevation did not change the overall tone or agenda of the committee because members generally worked across party lines in recent decades. Dodd, however, represented a shift from Sarbanes, the last Democratic chair who had retired from Congress in 2006. Sarbanes was often suspicious of financial industry motivations, giving special attention to consumer and investor concerns. Dodd was more sympathetic to business concerns. He was especially concerned about the insurance industry, which had a major presence in Connecticut.

Barkley, Alben W.

As majority leader of the Senate from 1937 to 1947, Alben W. Barkley (1877–1956) played an important role in the passage of President Franklin D. Roosevelt's NEW DEAL legislation. Barkley was a supporter of Roosevelt, but not blindly loyal to him and on occasion differed strongly and publicly from the president.

Barkley began his career in Congress in 1912, when he was elected as a Democrat to represent

Even though he was the majority leader in the Democratic Senate, Alben Barkley was highly critical of President Franklin D. Roosevelt's veto of a tax bill in 1944. Barkley also served as vice president from 1949 to 1953 before being reelected to the Senate.
Source: Library of Congress

Kentucky's First District. After seven terms in the House of Representatives, he was elected to the Senate in 1926, where he spent the remainder of his congressional career.

In 1937, upon the death of Majority Leader Joseph T. Robinson of Arkansas, Barkley waged a hard-fought campaign to succeed him. He defeated his rival for the post, Pat Harrison of Mississippi, by a narrow margin—just one vote. His success was attributed to a perception that Roosevelt favored his candidacy. The contest brought to the surface deep rifts in the party between conservative southerners and New Deal Democrats. Once revealed, the division among the Senate Democrats contributed to the defeat of some of Roosevelt's domestic initiatives—most notably, his attempt to increase the number of justices on the Supreme Court, which became known as the Court-packing scheme to reverse many decisions that had gone against New Deal legislation.

As majority leader, Barkley loyally supported Roosevelt's policies and served as a spokesperson for the president in his relations with Congress. In fall 1938, at Roosevelt's request, Barkley agreed to punish senators who worked to defeat the president's Court-packing scheme.

Barkley, however, forcefully opposed Roosevelt's unprecedented veto of a tax bill in 1944. He spoke against the president on the floor of the Senate, calling the veto "a calculated and deliberate assault upon the legislative integrity of every member of Congress." He said, "Other members of Congress may do as they please, but as for me, I do not propose to take this unjustifiable assault lying down. . . . I dare say that during the last seven years of tenure as majority leader, I have carried the flag over rougher territory than ever traversed by any previous majority leader. Sometimes I have carried it with little help from the other end of Pennsylvania Avenue." Barkley promptly resigned as majority leader and was just as promptly reelected by a unanimous vote of the Senate Democrats.

In 1948 President Harry S. Truman persuaded Barkley to leave the Senate and run for election as his vice president. The ticket won, and Barkley became a popular public figure, known affectionately as "the Veep." After completing one term as vice president, Barkley was reelected to the Senate in 1954. A campaigner to the end, he died while making a political speech in 1956.

Bells, Legislative

Business on Capitol Hill is often interrupted by the jarring noise of bells that signal a floor vote in the House or Senate. Committee hearings and bill-drafting sessions stop while representatives and senators listen to the signal.

Each chamber has its own legislative call system consisting of bells (House) or buzzers (Senate), as well as lights. New members quickly learn that two rings have a different meaning from three or five. The sound of five bells means members have only a few minutes to get to the floor to vote. Fast walkers may ignore the first warning and wait until the last minute to leave their office building for a vote, but others respond immediately. Slow-moving legislators need every minute to reach the Capitol, even with special subways to speed their trip. When five bells ring, members race for the floor. Every police officer, door attendant, and elevator operator helps clear the way for senators and representatives on their way to vote.

The system of legislative bells has been operating in Congress for decades; wiring for buzzers was installed as early as 1912. The House administrative officer has now supplemented the buzzers with wireless email pagers. Lawmakers also use beepers and portable telephones.

The longest signal is twelve rings rung at two-second intervals. It is the same in both chambers and signifies a civil defense warning.

Benton, Thomas Hart

Sen. Thomas Hart Benton of Missouri opposed the expansion of slavery into the western territories.
Source: Library of Congress

Thomas Hart Benton (1782–1858) served as one of Missouri's first senators upon its admission to the Union. A man of strongly held opinions and a colorful past, Benton represented western agrarian interests and championed equality of opportunity at a time when western expansion and the issue of slavery preoccupied the Senate. He was involved in nearly every major issue of the years he spent in Congress.

Benton was editor of the St. Louis *Enquirer* when he was elected to the Senate as a Democrat in 1821. An advocate of popular democracy, he supported western expansion and the availability of cheap land. He led the fight in the Senate against rechartering the Bank of the United States; the bank, a private corporation, engaged in commercial banking activities as well as issuing currency and serving as the official depository for federal funds. He opposed the use of paper currency and thereby acquired the nickname "Old Bullion."

Benton supported Andrew Jackson's unsuccessful bid for the presidency in 1824 even though he and Jackson had a falling out years earlier. Benton had served on Jackson's staff during the War of 1812, but their friendship ended in a brawl in which Jackson attacked Benton with a horsewhip and was himself shot in the shoulder. When Jackson won the presidency in 1828, however, Benton became one of his most valuable supporters in the Senate. Jackson's withdrawal of government funds from the Bank of the United States led the Senate to censure him in 1834; Benton led a successful fight to expunge the censure resolution from the Senate *Journal*.

Although Benton himself owned slaves, he believed that economic influences, aided by the country's geographic expansion, would ultimately destroy the system. To this end he supported new western states' constitutions barring slavery. During the heated debate on the floor of the Senate over the Compromise of 1850, which brought California into the Union as a free state, Benton so enraged Sen. Henry S. Foote of Mississippi that Foote threatened him with a cocked pistol.

Benton's belief that slavery had reached its geographic limits, coupled with the expansion of business interests in Missouri that were unsympathetic to his populist ideals, caused him to lose his Senate seat in 1851. He later served one term in the House (1853–1855) but was defeated for reelection over his opposition to the Kansas-Nebraska bill, which allowed settlers in those territories to decide whether or not they wanted slavery there.

In retirement he wrote a three-volume memoir of his three decades in the Senate, titled *Thirty Years View*. He already was suffering from cancer when the first volume appeared in 1854. His third volume appeared two years later. Although bedridden by then he turned to his final work, a sixteen-volume *Abridgment of the Debates of Congress,* which he finished in 1858 shortly before he died.

Beveridge, Albert J.

Albert J. Beveridge (1862–1927), an Indiana Republican, was elected to the Senate in 1899. As a freshman senator, he pledged his support to the ruling Republican clique led by Nelson W. ALDRICH of Rhode Island and William B. ALLISON of Iowa. Soon, however, Beveridge became one of a small group of Republicans who supported the policies of President Theodore Roosevelt and opposed the more conservative views espoused by powerful Senate Republicans.

Upon joining the Senate Beveridge sent Allison, who had absolute control over committee assignments, a list of preferred committees with a statement of loyalty: "I feel that the greatest single point is gained in the possession of your friendship. I will labor very hard, strive very earnestly to deserve your consideration." That loyalty was short-lived. When Roosevelt became president in 1901, Beveridge found a Republican leader more to his liking. Against the pressure of the majority of his Republican colleagues, Beveridge became an enthusiastic and vocal advocate of a strong federal government and progressive domestic policies.

Beveridge failed to win reelection in 1910. In 1912 he served as chair and keynote speaker at the national convention of the Progressive Party, which nominated Roosevelt as its presidential candidate. Beveridge ran unsuccessfully for governor of Indiana and twice again for his Senate seat. He received the Pulitzer Prize in 1920 for his *Life of John Marshall*.

Bill

This is the term used for the primary method, or vehicle, that Congress uses to enact laws. Bills that start their lives in the House are labeled H.R. and those from the Senate use the letter S, followed by a number assigned in the order in which they are introduced. The numbers proceed sequentially over the two-year life of a Congress. A bill becomes a law if passed in identical form by each house and signed by the president, or passed over a president's veto. (See LEGISLATION.)

Blacks in Congress

Black Americans were excluded from Congress for long periods of its history. But since the civil rights movement of the 1960s, they have made important gains in congressional elections. As of January 2008, 116 black Americans had served in Congress, five in the Senate and 111 in the House.

At the beginning of the 110th Congress (2007–2009), there were forty-one black members, the same number as in the 109th Congress. One was a Democratic senator. The other forty were House Democrats. Two other blacks served as nonvoting DELEGATES in the House.

Despite their electoral gains, African Americans remained numerically underrepresented in Congress. In 2007 blacks made up about 13 percent of the population according to Census Bureau projections, but they constituted just 9 percent of the House and 1 percent of the Senate.

Background

The first black member of Congress, Mississippi Republican Hiram R. Revels, entered the Senate in 1870. Another black, Republican John W. Menard, had been elected in 1868, but his election in Louisiana was disputed and the House had denied him a seat.

From 1870 through January 2008, five black senators and 111 black representatives served in Congress. Twenty-two of these served in the nineteenth century, all of them belonging to the party of Abraham Lincoln, the Republican Party. In the twentieth century almost all black legislators were Democrats. (See list of blacks who have served, p. 44; total for each Congress, above.)

The key to election of blacks after the Civil War was that southern states were not allowed to reenter the Union until they had enfranchised black voters. The Fifteenth

BLACKS IN CONGRESS, 1947–2007

Congress	Senate	House
80th (1947–1949)	0	2
81st (1949–1951)	0	2
82nd (1951–1953)	0	2
83rd (1953–1955)	0	2
84th (1955–1957)	0	3
85th (1957–1959)	0	4
86th (1959–1961)	0	4
87th (1961–1963)	0	4
88th (1963–1965)	0	5
89th (1965–1967)	0	6
90th (1967–1969)	1	5
91st (1969–1971)	1	9
92nd (1971–1973)	1	12
93rd (1973–1975)	1	15
94th (1975–1977)	1	16
95th (1977–1979)	1	16
96th (1979–1981)	0	16
97th (1981–1983)	0	17
98th (1983–1985)	0	20
99th (1985–1987)	0	20
100th (1987–1989)	0	22
101st (1989–1991)	0	24
102nd (1991–1993)	0	26
103rd (1993–1995)	1	39
104th (1995–1997)	1	38
105th (1997–1999)	1	37
106th (1999–2001)	0	37
107th (2001–2003)	0	36
108th (2003–2005)	0	39
109th (2005–2007)	1	40
110th (2007–2009)	1	40

NOTE: House totals reflect the number of members at the start of each Congress and exclude nonvoting delegates. Figures for the 110th Congress are as of January 2007.

Amendment to the Constitution, adopted in 1870, barred states from denying voting rights on the basis of race. Sixteen of the twenty-two blacks who served in Congress during the nineteenth century were elected in the 1870s—all from the South, where most black Americans lived.

As federal troops were withdrawn, southern states began to erode the voting rights of black citizens. By the end of the century, literacy tests, poll taxes, and other devices designed primarily to prevent blacks from voting had been established. Between 1901 and 1929 no blacks sat in Congress.

The long period without a black American in Congress ended when Chicago's south side sent Republican Oscar De Priest to the House in 1929. That same Chicago area con-

The first black members of Congress were not elected until 1870. The key to elections of blacks after the Civil War was that southern states were not allowed to reenter the Union until they had enfranchised black voters. This Currier and Ives lithograph shows the first black senator and six representatives holding seats in the Forty-first and Forty-second Congresses.
Source: Library of Congress

tinued to provide Congress with its sole black legislator—De Priest and two successors—until 1945, when the black representative from Chicago was joined by Democrat Adam Clayton POWELL Jr. of Harlem in New York City.

Another watershed came in 1965, when Congress approved the Voting Rights Act, an aggressive move to end literacy tests and other requirements that kept African Americans off voter registration lists in the South. The year before, the Supreme Court had boosted black influence by endorsing the principle of "one person, one vote." That decision eventually put an end to the practice in southern states of diluting black voting power by drawing district lines to break up black communities. Another step toward increased black voting was ratification in 1964 of the Twenty-fourth Amendment, which outlawed payment of any poll tax or other tax as a voter qualification in federal elections. As black voter turnouts increased so did black representation in Congress.

Along with that increased representation came a number of milestones. In 1968 Shirley Chisholm, a New York Democrat, became the first black woman to be elected to the House. Southern voters, who had last elected a black American in 1899, broke the long dry spell in 1972. In that year Democrats Barbara Jordan of Texas and Andrew Young of Georgia won seats in the House. Both Georgia and Texas later sent other black representatives, who were joined by black House members from Tennessee, Mississippi, and Louisiana.

The 1992 elections included several firsts for black Americans. Carol Moseley-Braun of Illinois became the first black woman ever elected to the Senate, and the first African American to serve in the Senate since Edward W. Brooke, a Massachusetts Republican, left in 1979. For the first time since the Reconstruction era, the House delegations from Alabama, Florida, North Carolina, South Carolina, and Virginia included black members.

The dramatic gains for African Americans in 1992 were largely a result of judicial interpretations of the Voting Rights Act requiring that minorities be given maximum opportunity to send members of their own racial or ethnic group to Congress. After the 1990 census, maps in thirteen

BLACK MEMBERS OF CONGRESS, 1870–2007

As of January 2008, 116 black Americans had served in Congress; five in the Senate and 111 in the House. Following is a list of the black members, their political affiliations and states, and the years in which they served. In addition, John W. Menard, R-La., won a disputed election in 1868 but was not permitted to take his seat in Congress. In addition to those listed below, Walter E. Fauntroy, D-D.C. (1971–1991), Eleanor Holmes Norton, D-D.C. (1991–), and Donna M. C. Christensen, D-V.I. (1997–) served as delegates.

Senate

Hiram R. Revels, R-Miss.	1870–1871	Carol Moseley-Braun, D-Ill.	1993–1999
Blanche K. Bruce, R-Miss.	1875–1881	Barack Obama, D-Ill.	2005–
Edward W. Brooke III, R-Mass.	1967–1979		

House

Joseph H. Rainey, R-S.C.	1870–1879	Yvonne B. Burke, D-Calif.	1973–1979
Jefferson F. Long, R-Ga.	1870–1871	Cardiss Collins, D-Ill.	1973–1997
Robert C. De Large, R-S.C.	1871–1873	Barbara C. Jordan, D-Texas	1973–1979
Robert B. Elliott, R-S.C.	1871–1874	Andrew J. Young Jr., D-Ga.	1973–1977
Benjamin S. Turner, R-Ala.	1871–1873	Harold E. Ford, D-Tenn.	1975–1997
Josiah T. Walls, R-Fla.	1871–1876	Julian C. Dixon, D-Calif.	1979–2000
Richard H. Cain, R-S.C.	1873–1875; 1877–1879	William H. Gray III, D-Pa.	1979–1991
John R. Lynch, R-Miss.	1873–1877; 1882–1883	George T. Leland, D-Texas	1979–1989
Alonzo J. Ransier, R-S.C.	1873–1875	Bennett McVey Stewart, D-Ill.	1979–1981
James T. Rapier, R-Ala.	1873–1875	George W. Crockett Jr., D-Mich.	1980–1991
Jeremiah Haralson, R-Ala.	1875–1877	Mervyn M. Dymally, D-Calif.	1981–1993
John A. Hyman, R-N.C.	1875–1877	Gus Savage, D-Ill.	1981–1993
Charles E. Nash, R-La.	1875–1877	Harold Washington, D-Ill.	1981–1993
Robert Smalls, R-S.C.	1875–1879; 1882–1883; 1884–1887	Katie B. Hall, D-Ind.	1982–1985
		Charles A. Hayes, D-Ill.	1983–1993
James E. O'Hara, R-N.C.	1883–1887	Major R. Owens, D-N.Y.	1983–2007
Henry P. Cheatham, R-N.C.	1889–1893	Edolphus Towns, D-N.Y.	1983–
John M. Langston, R-Va.	1890–1891	Alan D. Wheat, D-Mo.	1983–1995
Thomas E. Miller, R-S.C.	1890–1891	Alton R. Waldon Jr., D-N.Y.	1986–1987
George W. Murray, R-S.C.	1893–1895; 1896–1897	Mike Espy, D-Miss.	1987–1993
George H. White, R-N.C.	1897–1901	Floyd H. Flake, D-N.Y.	1987–1997
Oscar S. De Priest, R-Ill.	1929–1935	John Lewis, D-Ga.	1987–
Arthur W. Mitchell, D-Ill.	1935–1943	Kweisi Mfume, D-Md.	1987–1996
William L. Dawson, D-Ill.	1943–1970	Donald M. Payne, D-N.J.	1989–
Adam Clayton Powell Jr., D-N.Y.	1945–1967; 1969–1971	Craig A. Washington, D-Texas	1990–1995
Charles C. Diggs Jr., D-Mich.	1955–1980	Barbara-Rose Collins, D-Mich.	1991–1997
Robert N. C. Nix, D-Pa.	1958–1979	Gary A. Franks, R-Conn.	1991–1997
Augustus F. Hawkins, D-Calif.	1963–1991	William J. Jefferson, D-La.	1991–
John Conyers Jr., D-Mich.	1965–	Maxine Waters, D-Calif.	1991–
Shirley A. Chisholm, D-N.Y.	1969–1983	Lucien E. Blackwell, D-Pa	1991–1995
William L. Clay, D-Mo.	1969–2001	Eva Clayton, D-N.C.	1992–2003
Louis Stokes, D-Ohio	1969–1999	Sanford D. Bishop Jr., D-Ga.	1993–
George W. Collins, D-Ill.	1970–1972	Corrine Brown, D-Fla.	1993–
Ronald V. Dellums, D-Calif.	1971–1998	James E. Clyburn, D-S.C.	1993–
Ralph H. Metcalfe, D-Ill.	1971–1978	Cleo Fields, D-La.	1993–1997
Parren J. Mitchell, D-Md.	1971–1987	Alcee L. Hastings, D-Fla.	1993–
Charles B. Rangel, D-N.Y.	1971–	Earl F. Hilliard, D-Ala.	1993–2003

BLACK MEMBERS OF CONGRESS, 1870–2007 (CONTINUED)

House

Eddie Bernice Johnson, D-Texas	1993–	Carolyn Cheeks Kilpatrick, D-Mich.	1997–
Cynthia McKinney, D-Ga.	1993–2003; 2005–2007	Barbara Lee, D-Calif.	1998–
Carrie P. Meek, D-Fla.	1993–2003	Gregory W. Meeks, D-N.Y.	1998–
Melvin J. Reynolds, D-Ill.	1993–1995	Stephanie Tubbs Jones, D-Ohio	1999–
Bobby L. Rush, D-Ill.	1993–	William Lacy Clay, D-Mo.	2001–
Robert C. Scott, D-Va.	1993–	Diane Watson, D-Calif.	2001–
Bennie Thompson, D-Miss.	1993–	Frank W. Ballance Jr., D-N.C.	2003–2004
Walter R. Tucker III, D-Calif.	1993–1995	Artur Davis, D-Ala.	2003–
Melvin Watt, D-N.C.	1993–	Denise L. Majette, D-Ga.	2003–2005
Albert R. Wynn, D-Md.	1993–	Kendrick B. Meek, D-Fla.	2003–
Chaka Fattah, D-Pa.	1995–	David Scott, D-Ga.	2003–
Jesse Jackson Jr., D-Ill.	1995–	G. K. Butterfield Jr., D-N.C.	2004–
Sheila Jackson-Lee, D-Texas	1995–	Emanuel Cleaver II, D-Mo.	2005
J. C. Watts Jr., R-Okla.	1995–2003	Al Green, D-Texas	2005–
Elijah E. Cummings, D-Md.	1996–	Gwen Moore, D-Wis.	2005–
Juanita Millender-McDonald, D-Calif.	1996–2007	Yvette D. Clarke, D-N.Y.	2007–
Julia Carson, D-Ind.	1997–2007	Keith Ellison, D-Minn.	2007–
Danny K. Davis, D-Ill.	1997–	Hank Johnson, D-Ga.	2007–
Harold E. Ford Jr., D-Tenn.	1997–	Laura B. Richardson, D-Calif.	2007–

SOURCE: Maurine Christopher, *America's Black Congressmen* (Crowell, 1971); *Biographical Directory of the American Congress, 1774–1996* (Alexandria, Va.: CQ Staff Directories, 1997); *CQ Weekly*, selected issues.

states were redrawn to increase the number of so-called majority-minority districts, where minorities made up the majority of voters. However, this device came under increasing attack in the courts as the decade wore on.

As the number of black Americans continued to increase in the House, those elected earlier gained seniority and, in some instances, committee chairmanships or ranking positions on committees. In the Democrat-controlled 103rd Congress (1993–1995), for example, Ronald V. Dellums of California chaired the House Armed Services Committee, John Conyers Jr. of Michigan headed the House Government Operations Committee, and William L. Clay of Missouri chaired the House Post Office and Civil Service Committee. Dellums had entered the House in 1971, Conyers in 1965, and Clay in 1969. At the beginning of the 110th Congress in 2007, blacks held the chairs of two of the most influential House committee. Charles B. Rangel, D-N.Y., headed the Ways and Means Committee, and Conyers was chair of the Judiciary Committee. In addition, Bennie Thompson, D-Miss., headed the Homeland Security Committee, and Juanita Millender-McDonald, D-Calif., was chair of the House Administration Committee; she died from cancer a few months into the new session.

African Americans also won positions in the House leadership. In 1989 Democrat William H. Gray III of Pennsylvania became the highest-ranking black leader in the history of the House, when he was elected to the No. 3 job, majority whip. He held the post until he left Congress in 1991. The next African American to be elected to a high ranking position was Republican J. C. Watts Jr. of Oklahoma. Watts served as chair of the House Republican Conference from 1999 until he retired from Congress in 2003. In 2007 James E. Clyburn, D-S.C., was the majority whip for Democrats, and John Lewis, D-Ga., was the senior chief deputy whip.

More on this topic:

Hispanics in Congress,
p. 259

Reapportionment and
Redistricting, p. 456

Women in Congress,
p. 606

The new generation of African Americans elected to Congress since 1992 reflected the changes begun during the civil rights era. Many came to Congress with considerable experience in state legislatures and other local government positions. For example, of the five African American freshmen in the 108th Congress, all of whom were elected from southern states, three had served in their state legislatures; the other two served in judicial system positions.

Black Caucus

The formal organization of black members of Congress is the Congressional Black Caucus, founded in the early 1970s when only a handful of African Americans had been elected. The caucus worked for passage of legislation endorsed by its members and took positions that sometimes were at odds with those of the majority of Democrats, as when it opposed the Persian Gulf War in 1991. Although it was sometimes confrontational, the caucus also sought a role in the House power structure, lobbying to win seats for blacks on key committees.

When the Republicans took control of the House in 1995, they eliminated funding for the House's twenty-eight legislative service organizations, including the Black Caucus. Members of the caucus kept it going by contributing staff and resources.

Blaine, James G.

James G. Blaine's congressional service included three terms as Speaker of the House. He also served twice as secretary of state and ran unsuccessfully for president.
Source: Library of Congress

James G. Blaine (1830–1893), a Maine Republican, had a long and varied career in public life. As an influential newspaper editor he helped establish the Republican Party in Maine. His congressional service, from 1863 to 1881, included three terms as Speaker of the House. Blaine was the unsuccessful Republican candidate for president in 1884; he twice served as secretary of state.

As Speaker (1869–1875), Blaine reorganized committees to advance his party's legislative priorities. A powerful and effective leader, he urged committee chairs who were grateful to him for their positions to pass Republican legislation favorable to the railroads and business in general.

During Blaine's tenure as Speaker, a corruption scandal came to light in the House of Representatives that cast a shadow over his later career. Blaine was accused of having received bribes from Crédit Mobilier of America and the company for which it was building railroad lines, the Union Pacific Railroad. Blaine was implicated in the scandal by letters indicating that he had done legislative favors for railroads in return for gifts of stock. On the floor of the House, Blaine forestalled a move to censure him by reading (but refusing to show) excerpts from the letters.

In July 1876 Blaine left the House to fill an unexpired Senate term. He was later elected to a full term but relinquished his seat in 1881 to become secretary of state for the newly elected president, James A. Garfield. He left the cabinet post after Garfield's assassination the same year.

In 1884 the Republicans chose Blaine as their presidential candidate. The campaign against Democrat Grover Cleveland was characterized by ill feeling and bitter rhetoric. Blaine's involvement in the railroad bribery scandal hurt his candidacy. Cleveland supporters chanted, "Blaine, Blaine, James G. Blaine! Continental liar from the state of Maine." Blaine lost the election but later reentered public life to serve as an able and effective secretary of state under Benjamin Harrison (1889–1892).

Blue Dog Democrats

Blue Dog Democrats, who formally call themselves the Blue Dog Coalition, are a group of House members who consider themselves moderate or conservative members of the party. The organization was formed in the 104th Congress (1995–1997) and takes its name from the longtime description of a southern "Yellow Dog" Democrat, meaning any person who would vote for a yellow dog so long as it was a Democrat. The organization claims it took Blue Dog as a name because it felt moderate to conservative views had been "choked blue" by party leaders leading up to the 1994 elections when Democrats lost control of the House for the first time in forty years.

In the following years, Blue Dog Democrats became a force to contend with in House battles, particularly over taxing and spending legislation. In 2007 they numbered forty-three members, a bloc large enough to be courted by others who sought their support on closely divided issues.

The organization, which had original roots primarily among southern Democrats, included by 2007 members from most parts of the nation. Most of the members come from moderate to conservative districts and states that are competitive in many elections.

Bolling, Richard

Richard Bolling (1916–1991), a Democrat from Missouri, became one of the most powerful members of the House of Representatives. Although he never became Speaker, as he had hoped to do, Bolling may have influenced the House more than any other member of his generation. He assembled coalitions to pass major domestic programs and was the guiding spirit behind the reform movement that changed the institution in the 1970s. (See REFORM, CONGRESSIONAL.)

Bolling was a master parliamentarian and had a practical grasp of intricate House rules. He wrote several books on the workings of the House and led a bold but unsuccessful move in the early 1970s to restructure the jurisdictions of the House standing committees. He was a principal architect of the congressional BUDGET PROCESS.

Bolling was first elected to the House in 1948. A protégé of Speaker Sam RAYBURN, he joined the Rules Committee in 1955. There, as a loyal lieutenant to Rayburn, he plotted strategy against the Republicans and conservative Democrats who had effective control of the committee. In 1961 Bolling and fellow liberals talked Rayburn into enlarging the Rules Committee and adding more Democratic members to help outvote the old conservatives. Bolling became chair in 1979, by which time the committee stood firmly with the Democratic leadership. (See RULES COMMITTEE, HOUSE.)

Bolling failed to win leadership elections in 1962, when Carl ALBERT defeated him for majority leader, and in 1976, when he fell three votes short in a contest eventually won by Jim WRIGHT. He was excluded from the Democratic center of power while John W. MCCORMACK was Speaker (1962–1971) but returned to the inner circle when Albert became Speaker in 1971. Bolling was a close adviser to Speaker Thomas P. O'NEILL Jr., who succeeded Albert in 1977. Bolling retired in 1983.

Borah, William E.

William E. Borah (1865–1940) was a Republican senator from Idaho for thirty-three years. He is best known for his efforts in 1919 to prevent the United States from signing the Versailles Treaty after World War I and to keep it from joining the League of Nations and the World Court. A man of strong principles, Borah was not so much an isolationist as one opposed to international treaties enforced by anything more concrete than moral sanctions.

Borah, a Boise lawyer, was elected to the Senate by the Idaho legislature in 1907. Later he was a strong supporter of the Seventeenth Amendment to the Constitution, which provided for the DI-RECT ELECTION OF SENATORS. During his first term Borah sponsored legislation to establish the Department of Labor. He also strongly supported ratification of the Sixteenth Amendment, which cleared the way for the imposition of an income tax.

Although Borah supported President Woodrow Wilson during World War I, he vigorously opposed Wilson's peace proposals. He was one of the group of "irreconcilables" or "bitterenders" who objected to the treaty. The irreconcilables feared that Article Ten of the League Covenant, which stated that League members would support each other against external aggression, would involve the United States in armed conflicts not central to its interests. Borah also viewed the League Covenant as a "scheme which either directly or indirectly, greatly modifies our governmental powers."

Sen. William E. Borah, left, chair of the Senate Foreign Relations Committee, with Secretary of State Frank Kellog, 1927.
Source: Library of Congress

Borah was the author of a resolution calling for the Washington Conference on the Limitation of Armament, convened in 1921–1922 to discuss naval disarmament. He served as chair of the Senate Foreign Relations Committee from 1924 until 1933. He endorsed the Kellogg-Briand Pact of 1928, which sought to outlaw war, and supported U.S. recognition of the Soviet Union. He died in office on the eve of World War II.

Buckley v. Valeo

This Supreme Court decision is one of a collection of cases in the latter decades of the twentieth century that addressed the extent to which Congress could regulate political speech. The 1976 decision in *Buckley,* struck down limits on campaign spending and on the amount of money that candidates could contribute to their own campaign. Citing the government's interest in preventing corruption, the ruling upheld certain limits on campaign contributions but also stated that the limit did not apply to a candidate's expenditures from personal funds. The Court also upheld public subsidies for presidential campaigns and spending limits imposed on candidates who accepted public funds. However, this restriction had become all but moot by 2007 as the cost of presidential campaigning soared and all major candidates declined public financing. (See CAMPAIGN FINANCING.)

Budget Act

The budget act is the common name for the Congressional Budget and Impoundment Control Act of 1974, which established the basic procedures of the congressional budget process. It created the House and Senate budget committees and enacted procedures for reconciliation, deferrals, and rescissions. It also created the Congressional Budget Office. The budget act was extensively amended by the Balanced Budget and Emergency Deficit Control Act of 1985, better known as the Gramm-Rudman-Hollings law. (See BUDGET PROCESS.)

Budget and Accounting Act of 1921

For the first time, in 1921, Congress passed a law that authorized the president to submit to Congress an annual budget for the entire federal government. Previously, most federal agencies sent their budget requests to the appropriate congressional committees without review by the president, which meant there was no overall review or control of expenditures. The act also established a Bureau of the Budget (renamed the Office of Management and Budget—OMB—in 1970 to assist the president in preparing a budget. It also created the General Accounting Office, headed by the comptroller general of the United States, to act as the principal auditing agency of the federal government. (See BUDGET PROCESS.)

Budget Committee, House

Of all House committees, the Budget Committee is the one most concerned with broad questions about the overall shape of federal spending and taxation. Established by the Congressional Budget and Impoundment Control Act of 1974, the committee has responsibility for ensuring that the House complies with the budget-planning process created by the same law. Like its Senate counterpart, the House Budget Committee does not have authority to approve substantive legislation or spending bills directly. Instead its task is to set out guidelines and goals for bills approved by other committees. To do that, the Budget Committee has two main duties. One is to propose an annual budget resolution, which establishes targets for total federal spending and revenue, and the amounts that can be spent on broad categories of federal programs, such as defense or welfare. The other duty is to try to make other committees and the whole House comply with those spending targets.

The committee is also the first House committee to examine the president's proposed budget each year. It thus influences the tenor of the budget debate for the whole year. In addition, the committee may prepare instructions, included in the annual budget resolution, that require other committees to cut programs to meet budget targets. The committee cannot tell other committees how to comply with savings

Office of Management and Budget director Rob Portman in July 2007 defends the White House's fiscal 2008 budget proposal before the House Budget Committee chaired by John M. Spratt Jr., D-S.C.
Source: CQ Photo/Scott J. Ferrell

instructions, but sometimes there are few options for meeting the targets. This procedure is known as reconciliation.

Although they have much the same jurisdiction, several factors put the House Budget panel at something of a disadvantage with its Senate counterpart. One of these was the way the House panel was constituted. To allow more members the opportunity to serve on the panel, the rules of the House limited the tenure of members to eight years in six consecutive Congresses. The Democrats set an even more stringent limit of six years on their members. As a result, House committee members usually did not have a chance to build up experience and knowledge of budget issues to match that of Senate Budget Committee members, who had no such limit. The rules of the House also required that five members each would come from the Appropriations and Ways and Means panels and one member each from the House majority and minority leadership. In 2007 the committee consisted of thirty-nine members, twenty-two Democrats and seventeen Republicans.

The combination of a rotating membership and a core group of members whose allegiance lay with other committees worked against committee cohesion. Further complicating things were the deep partisan divisions between Democratic and Republican members. Unlike the Senate committee, where bipartisanship was more prevalent, House committee members of the two parties rarely were able to agree on anything. The budget resolutions produced by the House committee largely were written by the committee's majority, with little minority participation. On the floor they usually were protected from specific amendments; the minority could offer only complete substitutes.

History

The short-term nature of service on the Budget Committee, along with other factors, made it more difficult for Budget Committee chairs to assert their influence in the budget process.

More on this topic:

Budget Committee, Senate, p. 51

Budget Process, p. 54

Purse, Power of, p. 446

The first chair was a Washington Democrat, Brock Adams, who served for only two years before resigning in 1977 to become President Jimmy Carter's secretary of transportation. Adams steered a policy of accommodating other committees and avoiding confrontation over spending limits.

The next chair, Robert N. Giaimo, a Connecticut Democrat, more frequently found himself at odds with other House members. Particularly in the Ninety-sixth Congress (1979–1981), Giaimo had the difficult task of developing controls on the rapid growth of federal spending, while at the same time putting together a coalition that could command a majority of the House.

The tenure of Oklahoma Democrat James R. Jones was even stormier. Jones had the misfortune of becoming the Budget Committee chair in the wake of Ronald Reagan's presidential victory and heavy losses by House Democrats in the 1980 elections. The new president demanded drastic spending cuts in domestic social programs. In response Jones tried to put together a coalition of moderates from both parties. However, he was overwhelmed by an alliance of conservative Republicans and "Boll Weevil" southern Democrats, backed by Reagan's great popularity.

By his second term (1983–1985) Jones was able to establish an effective relationship with House Democratic leaders to regain control of the budget process. The pattern was continued by William H. Gray III, a Pennsylvania Democrat. The first black chair of the committee, Gray was successful in guiding budget resolutions through the House, although less so in fashioning workable budget agreements with the Senate.

In 1989 one of Congress's most respected budget experts, California Democrat Leon Panetta, became chair. Panetta's training for the job included a six-year term as a member of the Budget Committee from 1979 to 1985. Still, during Panetta's tenure in the 102nd Congress (1991–1993), the House Budget Committee lost much of its power to shape budget policy, at least temporarily.

The deficit reduction agreement—$500 billion over five years—negotiated by Congress and President George H. W. Bush in 1990 set spending limits, defined pay-as-you-go rules for mandatory spending, and allowed the deficit to keep growing. In effect it stripped the Budget Committee of its power to make decisions about the budget. During this period, however, the House Budget Committee continued to draft budget resolutions that stated the committee's priorities.

Panetta in 1993 became President Bill Clinton's director of the Office of Management and Budget. He was succeeded as committee chair by Martin O. Sabo, a Minnesota Democrat, who held the post for one Congress. During his tenure, he was instrumental in building the case for Clinton's controversial plan to raise taxes and cut the deficit, which was hailed as laying the groundwork for future budget surpluses.

John R. Kasich of Ohio became chair in 1995 when the Republicans took control of the House. Republicans used the committee to advance proposals to slash the budgets of some federal departments, cut taxes and social spending, and increase defense spending. The Republican leadership engaged in protracted budget negotiations on these topics with President Clinton from 1995 to 1996. During the frequently bitter discussions, parts of the federal government shut down and Congress received much of the blame.

After two years of such warfare, Congress and Clinton came together on a balanced budget agreement in 1997—a historic achievement. In 1998, however, internal dispute among Republicans over what should be in a budget resulted in no agreement—for the first time since the 1974 budget law Congress did not adopt a budget resolution. Ironically, in fiscal 1998, a strong economy helped the government post a $70 billion surplus, the first surplus in twenty-nine years.

Kasich's conservative views were carried on by his successor, Jim Nussle of Iowa. However, unlike Kasich who offered the minority party practically no input on the legislation and budget resolutions written during his tenure, Nussle—although considered a loyalist of President George W. Bush—created a bit more room for Democrats on the panel to influence the committee's work early in his tenure.

The tone and activity of the committee changed in the 110th Congress after Democrats won the 2006 election and took control in 2007. This put John M. Spratt Jr., D-S.C., in the committee's chair. Spratt was a moderate who had pushed in the past for a summit among both parties to discuss ways to slow growth of the multitrillion federal debt. Republicans rebuffed the effort.

Under Republicans the committee was guided by conservatives who capped discretionary spending—allowing little year-to-year growth—while permitting additional tax cuts. However, Appropriation Committees often worked around those caps in various ways, angering fiscal conservatives.

Budget Committee, Senate

Ever since its creation by the Congressional Budget and Impoundment Control Act of 1974, the Senate Budget Committee has been an important player in the Senate spending debate.

Like its House counterpart, the Senate Budget Committee faces an exceptionally difficult task each year. The committee must prepare a budget resolution setting out goals for spending and revenues in the next fiscal year and must struggle to resist the many changes proposed as amendments on the Senate floor.

The committee's task is even harder in times of budgetary stress, when the federal government takes in less money than it spends. These conditions defined budget debates in the 1980s, early 1990s, and again in the early years of the twenty-first century, putting the committee under conflicting pressures.

The committee has only limited power to make and enforce its spending decisions. Still, the Senate committee has been far more successful in its history than has the House Budget Committee. The Senate Budget Committee has played a greater role in shaping spending decisions and has more power to make other committees accept its views.

There are several reasons for the Senate committee's greater influence. One is that committee members serve continuously and so build up considerable experience and knowledge about budget issues. This is not true in the House, where that chamber's rules limit the number of years committee members may serve.

Unlike the House Budget Committee, the Senate committee has had a strong tradition of bipartisan cooperation. The Senate committee chair and ranking minority member usually have cooperated to form a consensus on issues, which typically would win the backing of the full Senate. The committee also has had a tradition of strong leaders deeply committed to the budget process. In early 2007 the committee had twenty-three members, twelve Democrats (including one independent) and eleven Republicans.

The Senate committee has sought to establish its influence by focusing on broad budget issues, while avoiding specific policies that are under the jurisdiction of the authorizing committees. Instead of going over the budget line by line, as the House committee typically does, the Senate committee concentrates on the overall shape of the budget and the long-term implications of budget policy.

Although it cannot propose substantive legislation to the Senate on its own, the Budget Committee has several ways to try to enforce the fiscal policies embodied in the budget resolution each year. One is a process known as reconciliation, under which spending programs are altered through legislation to reduce their costs. The Budget Committee can direct other committees to approve legislation to reduce spending under their jurisdiction by a certain amount, although it cannot tell the committees exactly how to achieve those savings.

Senate Budget Committee members have successfully challenged spending proposals on the Senate floor. Under the 1974 Budget Act, legislation that calls for spending more than the amounts set by the budget resolution is subject to a point of order, or parliamentary challenge. Senate Budget Committee leaders have used this tactic frequently and have usually had the floor votes to make the spending limits stick.

History

In its early years the Budget Committee was shaped by its first chair, Maine Democrat Edmund S. Muskie. A veteran senator and one-time Democratic vice-presidential candidate, Muskie was a major figure in the Senate. His decision to devote much of his energy and influence to the committee was an important factor in establishing its importance. Muskie was greatly aided in his efforts by his alliance with ranking minority member Henry S. Bellmon, a conservative Republican from Oklahoma.

The committee's role was easier in the early years because there was less pressure to cut spending. Instead of having to make painful choices about which programs to cut, the committee tried to accommodate the spending needs of most federal programs. But Muskie and Bellmon tried to ensure that Congress stuck with its budget, by challenging proposals that exceeded its limits. The committee had less success, however, in making sure that tax bills written by the Finance Committee complied with the budget.

The Budget Committee became more prominent in the late 1970s and early 1980s, as Congress confronted the growing deficit and significant inflation. First in 1980 and again in 1981 the committee used the reconciliation process to direct other committees to recommend savings in politically popular programs. The 1981 bill, written by the committee's new Republican majority, embodied the Reagan administration's plan for major cutbacks in federal social programs for the poor.

In the years that followed, chair Pete V. Domenici, a New Mexico Republican, and colleagues struggled to keep the budget process alive. Each year they had to overcome seemingly insurmountable political obstacles to have a budget approved at last, even if months after the official deadline. One of Domenici's most dramatic victories came in 1985, when he and the new majority leader, Kansas Republican Robert DOLE, produced a budget that passed only after an ailing Republican senator was brought from the hospital by ambulance in the middle of the night to cast the deciding vote.

Florida Democrat Lawton Chiles became Budget chair in 1987 when the Democrats regained the Senate. He and Domenici were able to force closer adherence to spending targets in appropriations bills by staging parliamentary attacks on them on the Senate floor on the grounds that they exceeded the spending targets of the budget resolution.

Senate Budget chair Kent Conrad, D-N.D., meets with reporters in the Senate Daily Press Gallery in May 2007 to discuss the Senate and House's agreement on the fiscal 2008 budget.
Source: CQ Photo/Scott J. Ferrell

In 1989 Jim Sasser, a Tennessee Democrat, became chair of the Budget Committee after Chiles left the Senate, partly out of frustration over the budget. After a 1990 deficit reduction agreement stole much of the power from the budget committees in both the House and Senate, Sasser and Domenici crafted budget resolutions that had a limited impact on policy but served to keep the budget process on the minds of members.

In 1995 the Republicans came back in power and Domenici regained control of the committee. In the budget battles that erupted in 1995 and 1996 leading to several government shutdowns, Domenici found himself caught between the more aggressive House Republicans, led by John R. Kasich of Ohio, and the Clinton White House. But the Senate chair played a leading role in the balanced budget agreement of 1997, a bill that held out hope of future budget surpluses. The battle then switched to the other top Republican priority of cutting taxes, with Domenici playing his traditionally cautious role. However, in 2001, Domenici had little choice but to support President George W. Bush's $1.4 trillion tax cut.

The budget process is not always smooth even when one party controls both houses. In 1998, for the first time since the modern budget process was created in 1974, the Republican Congress failed to adopt a budget resolution after the House and Senate approved drastically different versions of the budget. This occurred again in 2002 when Democrat Kent Conrad of North Dakota was at the helm of the Senate Budget Committee while the House remained under GOP control.

When Republican Don Nickles of Oklahoma became chair in 2003, many expected the panel to take a more partisan turn. While Domenici had regularly communicated across the aisle to write budget resolutions both parties could support, Nickles was a conservative Reagan Republican at heart, with a far sharper partisan edge. The new chair also had a bigger appetite for tax cuts than Domenici had. Even with Republicans back in control of both houses the budget process remained frayed as Congress in 2004 and 2006 could not produce a budget resolution.

When the Democrats retook control in 2007, Conrad returned to the chair. After railing for years against a growing "wall of debt" under GOP leadership, Conrad was eager to return to pay-as-you-go budget rules that required new tax cuts and new entitlement spending to be offset to block adding to the federal deficit. The legislators did exactly that as the 110th Congress got underway that year. Conrad also had backed caps on discretionary spending and bipartisan negotiations to restrain the costs of entitlement programs.

Budget Process

Since the mid-1970s Congress has used a budget process to determine government spending requirements, decide how to pay for them, and examine the relationship between spending and revenues. The process requires legislators to set overall goals for government spending and revenues—and then to tailor their actions to meet those goals. Congress makes many of its most difficult policy decisions during this exercise.

The budget process is a cyclical activity that starts early each year when the president sends budget proposals to Capitol Hill. The president's budget lays out priorities for the fiscal year that will begin October 1. Before Congress adjourns for the year, the Senate and House of Representatives will have created their own budget and provided the money needed to carry it out. Negotiations with the White House may narrow the differences between the two plans, but the congressional budget is likely to differ in important respects from that proposed by the president.

Lawmakers set their own priorities, deciding how much the government should spend and on what, whom to tax and by how much, and what gap should be allowed between spending and revenues. These decisions often bring Congress into sharp conflict with the president.

Beginnings

Through most of its history Congress acted piecemeal on tax bills and spending bills; it had no way of assessing their impact on the federal budget as a whole. Although the Constitution entrusted Congress with the power of the purse, primary control over budget policy passed to the executive branch.

Congress first conferred budget-making authority on the president in passing the BUDGET AND ACCOUNTING ACT OF 1921. That law required the president to submit to Congress each year a budget detailing actual spending and revenues in the previous fiscal year, estimates for the year in progress, and the administration's proposals for the year ahead. The law also created a Bureau of the Budget (renamed the Office of Management and Budget in 1970) to assist the president.

Congress was not bound by the president's recommendations. It could provide more or less money for particular programs than the president requested, and it could change tax laws to draw in more or less revenue. But half a century went by before lawmakers began drawing up their own comprehensive budget plans.

Budget Act of 1974

The congressional budget process grew out of fights over spending control in the 1970s. Angered by President Richard Nixon's refusal to spend money it had appropriated—a practice known as impoundment of funds—Congress decided to set up its own budget system. The Congressional Budget and Impoundment Control Act of 1974 established a budget committee in each chamber to analyze the president's budget proposals and to recommend a congressional budget policy. The Congressional Budget Office was created to provide data and analyses to help Congress make its budget decisions.

The law required Congress each year to adopt a budget resolution setting overall targets for spending and revenues and establishing congressional spending priorities. (Originally, two budget resolutions were required, but the requirement for the second was eventually dropped.) Budget resolutions did not require the president's approval—but the president retained veto power over legislation to carry out the congressional plans.

Once a budget resolution was in place, Congress was required to pass legislation making any changes in law needed to ensure that spending and taxing guidelines were met. These changes were made through the appropriations process and through reconciliation, a procedure under which individual committees were required to adjust revenues or cut the cost of entitlement programs within their jurisdictions to meet assigned spending limits. Appropriation bills were required to conform to limits established in the budget resolution. The 1974 act set a timetable for action to be completed before the start of the fiscal year on October 1.

Changes in Law

The process seldom worked as intended. Deadlines were rarely met, Congress's budgetary restraint was weak, and federal deficits ballooned to more than $200 billion annually. In 1985 reformers pushed through a drastic change in the procedure. The Balanced Budget and Emergency Deficit Control Act of 1985—known as the Gramm-Rudman-Hollings Act for its congressional sponsors—established annual deficit reduction requirements that were designed to lead to a balanced budget by fiscal 1991. The law invented a new weapon, called sequestration, to make automatic the tough decisions on spending reduction that members were unwilling to face. It accelerated the budget timetable and strengthened procedures to make Congress meet its schedule.

Like the 1974 act, the Gramm-Rudman-Hollings Act did not work as intended, and Congress voted a further revision in 1987. The new measure promised a balanced budget by fiscal 1993, two years later than required in Gramm-Rudman-Hollings. It also revised the procedures for automatic spending cuts to meet objections the Supreme Court had raised the previous year.

Congress overhauled its budget procedures once again in 1990. The revised law allowed Congress to pay less attention to the deficit. Any increases in the budget deficit that were the result of either economic conditions or spending required for new people eligible for entitlement programs would not be subject to the automatic spending cuts. Congress had only to abide by new discretionary spending limits and pay-as-you-go rules requiring revenue increases to cover any changes in the law that resulted in mandatory spending on new or expanded entitlement programs or tax cuts. The measure abandoned the idea of a balanced budget deadline.

The idea of amending the Constitution to require a balanced budget had been raised frequently since the early 1980s. Support built gradually as frustration mounted over the seemingly permanent budget deficit and the ever-growing national debt—the accumulation of those annual deficits. Over the years, the text of the constitutional amendment was crafted and massaged by

CLOSER LOOK

The budget timetable can be summarized as follows:

First Monday in February: President submits budget request and the executive branch's economic forecast to Congress for the fiscal year beginning October 1.

February 15: Congressional Budget Office (CBO) submits its budget and economic outlook for the next ten years to Congress (usually occurs in January).

Six weeks after president submits budget: All legislative committees submit their "views and estimates" of spending under their jurisdiction for the coming fiscal year to the Budget committees.

April 1: Senate Budget Committee reports its budget resolution to the Senate floor (no comparable deadline for the House Budget Committee).

April 15: Congress completes action on its budget resolution.

May 15: Annual appropriations may be considered on the House floor, even if there is no adopted budget resolution.

June 10: House Appropriations Committee reports the last annual appropriations bill to the floor.

June 15: Congress completes action on reconciliation bill, if it is required by the budget resolution (unless the budget resolution sets a different deadline).

June 30: House completes action on last annual appropriations bill.

July 15: President submits executive branch's midsession review of the budget to Congress.

Mid-August: CBO submits an updated version of its budget and economic outlook to Congress.

October 1: Fiscal year begins.

members of both chambers and both parties. But supporters were not able to muster the two-thirds vote required in both houses to adopt it and send it to the states to be ratified.

When the Republican Party took control of Congress in 1995, the centerpiece of the House Republicans' ambitious agenda was adoption of a balanced budget amendment. The House passed a balanced budget measure in 1995, but the Senate failed in 1995 and 1996. In the next Congress, the Senate again rejected a constitutional amendment to balance the budget. The House declined to push for a floor vote, expecting certain defeat.

Another proposal to change the budget-writing process captured the attention of Congress for two years in the late 1990s, but it was rejected by the House in 2000. The proposal was born from complaints that the existing system forced Congress to spend too much time and energy on budgeting and appropriations but too little effort on program oversight and authorization. Critics also had complained about the growth of emergency and supplemental spending measures. The bill sparked a territorial war between its sponsors and the appropriators, who saw it as an assault on their power.

The bill would have created an annual reserve fund for emergencies, designed to limit nonbudgeted supplemental spending. The annual budget resolution would have been changed from a concurrent resolution, which does not require the president's signature, to a joint resolution, which has the force of law upon enactment. It would have eased pay-as-you-go budget rules to allow surpluses not generated by Social Security to be used for tax cuts or new entitlement spending and weakened the Senate rule that required sixty votes to amend budget-reconciliation bills with nongermane provisions.

The White House was relieved when the House rejected the measure. The Clinton administration had objected to the bill. Its alternative, which also was defeated, would have created a two-year budget cycle, with passage of a budget resolution and appropriations bills during the first year of each session. The following election year would have been reserved for program authorization and oversight.

The statutory spending caps on appropriations and pay-as-you-go rules that had been first enacted in 1990 and subsequently extended expired in 2002, when Congress was unable to agree on a vehicle to extend them. Congress had routinely evaded spending caps by ignoring them in session-ending budget deals and had averted cuts by simply adopting language each year wiping the pay-as-you-go scorecard clean. Still, budget hawks said the rules had had a restraining effect on Congress, and they vowed to revisit the issue in the next Congress. When the Democrats regained control of Congress in 2007 following the 2006 elections they resurrected the pay-go rules in both the Senate and House.

Competition for Dollars

In the early years of the process, congressional budget-making was largely a process of accommodation. House and Senate leaders, anxious to keep the process going, proposed budget resolutions that left room for new programs and additional spending. As long as Congress remained in an expansive mood, the House and Senate were able to construct budgets that satisfied the particular interests of various committees and groups.

When Congress tried to shift to more austere budgets in the 1980s, it encountered much rougher going. While acknowledging the need to hold down spending, members sought to avoid cuts in programs important to their constituents. That became increasingly difficult as the competition for federal dollars increased.

"A billion here, a billion there. Pretty soon you are talking about real money."

—Attributed to Sen. Everett McKinley Dirksen, R-Ill., by a long-time confidant, although the statement does not appear in any formal address or Dirksen's papers

Budget battles with the White House consumed Congress during the administration of President Ronald Reagan. Upon taking office in 1981 Reagan used the congressional budget machinery to carry out sweeping cuts in spending and taxes, as he had promised in his election campaign. In later years Congress routinely dismissed Reagan's budgets, but it had trouble developing plans of its own that also were acceptable to the president. Each year witnessed the two branches battling over the federal deficit, which more than doubled during Reagan's first term.

The stalemate between Congress and the president led to a new form of budget negotiations in the late 1980s, called summits. An October 1987 crash in the stock market propelled a

In recent years, deficit spending has been the norm for the federal government, except for a four-year period from 1998 to 2001 when surpluses occurred. In 2004 a record $412 billion deficit was posted.
Source: AP Images/Dennis Cook

reluctant President Reagan into a budget summit with congressional leaders of both parties. Congress approved their work—a deficit reduction package of $76 billion over two years—but the experience did not make the summits popular. Many senators and representatives felt they had been excluded from the most important decisions of the session. "You work all year in your committees and then end up with three-quarters of the government run by a half-dozen people locked up in a room for three or four weeks," said Rep. Marvin Leath, a Texas Democrat. "I resent that."

Despite the anger over the 1987 budget summit, in 1990 President George H. W. Bush and Congress attempted to use a budget summit to negotiate a massive deficit reduction package. Again, the summit alienated many members of Congress who were excluded from the negotiations. For ten days the negotiators met in seclusion at Andrews Air Force Base in suburban Maryland, but they failed to reach agreement. As a last resort, a "hyper-summit" of only eight White House and congressional leaders drafted a deficit reduction plan. But the alienated members had their say, soundly defeating the plan and embarrassing the president. Congress finally passed a compromise $500 billion plan that was drafted by the Senate Finance Committee and House Ways and Means Committee.

> **"You work all year in committees and then end up with three-quarters of the government run by a half-dozen people locked up in a room for three or four weeks. I resent that."**
>
> —*Rep. Marvin Leath,* D-Texas, complaining about "summit" meetings in the late 1980s between high executive branch officials and senior legislators at which most crucial spending matters were decided

The 1990 agreement limited Congress's ability to change spending priorities for a five-year period. The bill set spending limits for discretionary spending in three categories—domestic, defense, and international spending—for 1991 to 1993. For 1994 and 1995, the legislation set overall limits for discretionary spending. The agreement also included the pay-as-you-go rules to offset legislation that resulted in decreased revenues or increased spending for entitlement programs.

Building on a strong economy and two earlier rounds of deficit reduction, President Bill Clinton and the Republican majority in Congress struck a historic agreement in 1997 to balance

More on this topic:

Appropriations Bills, p. 22

Budget Committee, House, p. 49

Budget Committee, Senate, p. 51

Congressional Budget Office, p. 133

Gramm-Rudman-Hollings Act, p. 250

Impoundment of Funds, p. 285

Purse, Power of, p. 446

the federal budget in five years, while cutting taxes and increasing spending in selected administration priorities in areas such as children's health care. It was almost immediately translated into a congressional budget resolution that formally set Congress's budget guidelines.

Angry Democrats denounced the closed-door negotiations and objected to their second-class status as Clinton and the Republicans made their final compromise. In the end, pro-business, conservative, and moderate Democrats were pleased with the budget agreement, while their more liberal, blue-collar counterparts viewed the package as tilted against the poor and the tax cuts as stacked in favor of the rich.

In fiscal 1998 the government posted a $70 billion surplus, the first surplus in twenty-nine years. A strong economy had boosted tax receipts, while the series of budget agreements over the previous years had constrained spending increases. The surpluses continued for four straight years, until fiscal 2001.

But, more ominously, for the first time since the modern congressional budget process was established in 1974, Congress in 1998 failed to agree on a budget resolution for the coming fiscal year. The House and Senate passed dramatically different versions and never even began formal negotiations to work out the differences, which principally involved the size of a proposed tax cut and the consequent spending cuts needed to offset the revenue loss. An upward surge in projections for a budget surplus only served to deepen the differences. It was a harbinger of things to come: three times in fives years—2002, 2004, and 2006—Congress did not produce a budget. In 2007 Democrats—newly back in power in both chambers—passed a budget resolution early in the year.

The era of budget surpluses was brief. A recession, a decline in the stock market, and President George W. Bush's $1.4 trillion tax cut in 2001 forced a decline in revenues that had been soaring. At the same time, spending increased after the September 11, 2001, terrorist attacks and the Afghanistan military campaign.

In fiscal 2001, the year Bush took office, the government showed a surplus of $128.2 billion. That swung to a deficit of $157.8 billion the following year and to $277.6 billion in fiscal 2003. It hit a whopping $412.7 billion in deficit in fiscal 2004. The sea of red ink subsided slightly thereafter but still stood at $248.2 billion for fiscal 2006 and an estimated $244.2 billion for fiscal 2007.

During that time, the appropriations process was divisive and difficult as the White House sought to limit domestic spending while proposing additional tax cuts and defense spending. The result was an appropriations logjam and a series of continuing resolutions to fund the government. This same pattern continued in the following years. By 2006, Congress passed only two regular fiscal 2007 appropriations bills and left the rest to the incoming Democratic majority in 2007. Rather than deal with all the issues in the unpassed bills, the Democrats funded all the rest of the government for fiscal 2007 with a single massive continuing resolution. They then turned their attention in early 2007 to funding the government in fiscal 2008.

One other attribute of the George W. Bush years that troubled congressional appropriators and budget hawks in and out of Congress was the method legislators used at the president's behest to finance the wars in Iraq and Afghanistan. Instead of including money for those military actions in regular appropriations bills, Bush requested emergency supplemental spending every year. This was important because it meant that war spending did not count toward deficit projections, even though it did show up on the bottom line of the amounts spent each year. As a result, there was no pressure to reduce other spending or to raise taxes to prevent the projected deficit from widening. It was only after the fact that the true volume of red ink was evident. Democrats vigorously protested the practice and vowed to end it once back in control of Congress in 2007.

Budget Terms

Appropriations

Acts of Congress that provide actual funding for programs within limits established by authorizations. Appropriations usually cover one fiscal year, but they may run for a definite or indefinite number of years. More than half of all federal spending—for programs such as Social Security and interest payments on the federal debt—has permanent appropriations, which do not have to go through the annual appropriations process. (See APPROPRIATIONS BILLS.)

Authorizations

Acts of Congress that establish discretionary government programs or entitlements, or that continue or change such programs. Authorizations specify program goals and, for a discretionary program, set the maximum amount that may be spent. For entitlement programs, an authorization sets or changes eligibility standards and benefits that must be provided by the program. (See AUTHORIZATION BILLS.)

Budget

A financial plan for the U.S. government prepared annually by the executive branch. The budget sets out in fine print how government funds have been raised and spent and what the president plans for the country in the fiscal year ahead. It is sent to Congress each year in early February. The budget provides for both discretionary and mandatory expenditures. Discretionary funds are appropriated by Congress each year. Congressional appropriations bills are not required to follow the guidelines specified in the president's budget. Mandatory spending is for entitlement programs such as Medicare and veterans' pensions. An entitlement can be changed only by a separate authorizing bill.

Budget Authority

Legal authority to enter into obligations that will result in immediate or future government spending, called outlays. Budget authority is provided by Congress through appropriations bills.

Budget Resolution

A congressional spending plan that does not require the president's signature. A budget resolution sets binding totals for broad categories of spending—expressed in budget authority and outlays—and for revenues. Authorization and appropriations bills must then observe these totals. The resolution assumes that certain changes will be made in existing law, primarily to achieve savings assumed in the spending totals. These savings are legislated in appropriations bills and sometimes in reconciliation bills. Each year Congress is supposed to complete action by April 15 on a budget resolution for the fiscal year that will begin October 1. From 1974 through early 2007, Congress had failed to adopt a budget resolution four times: 1998, 2002, 2004, and 2006. (See BUDGET PROCESS.)

Congressional Budget and Impoundment Control Act

The 1974 law that established the congressional budget process and created the CONGRESSIONAL BUDGET OFFICE.

Deficit

The excess of spending over revenues. A surplus exists if revenues are greater than spending. From fiscal 1969, when a small surplus occurred, through fiscal 1997, the budget was always in deficit. Surpluses were recorded the following four fiscal years and then plunged back into deficit from fiscal 2002 through fiscal 2008. Budget analysts projected the deficits to continue into the near-term future.

Entitlement

A program that must provide specified benefits to all eligible persons who seek them. Social Security, Medicare, and Medicaid are examples of entitlements. Generally, these programs are permanently authorized and are not subject to annual appropriations. (See ENTITLEMENTS.)

Fiscal Year

The federal government's accounting period. The fiscal year begins on October 1 and ends on September 30 of the following year. A fiscal year (FY) is designated by the calendar year in which it ends; for example, FY 2008 began on October 1, 2007, and was to end on September 30, 2008. (See FISCAL YEAR.)

Gramm-Rudman-Hollings Act

Sen. Phil Gramm, R-Texas, was one of three cosponsors of the Gramm-Rudman-Hollings Act.
Source: CQ Photo/Scott J. Ferrell

A 1985 act of Congress that set a timetable for achieving a balanced budget and specified a procedure designed to accomplish that goal through mandatory automatic spending cuts. Originally, the act called for achieving a balanced budget by 1991. The timetable was amended in 1987 and again in 1990, at which time the size of the deficit was downplayed and a balanced budget target date was deleted. The act is properly called the Balanced Budget and Emergency Deficit Control Act of 1985. It quickly became known by the names of its three Senate sponsors: Phil Gramm of Texas and Warren B. Rudman of New Hampshire, both Republicans, and Ernest F. Hollings, a South Carolina Democrat.

Impoundment

A president's refusal to spend money appropriated by Congress. The Congressional Budget and Impoundment Control Act of 1974 established procedures for congressional approval or disapproval of presidential impoundments. (See IMPOUNDMENT OF FUNDS.)

Outlays

Actual cash expenditures made by the government. In passing appropriations bills, Congress does not directly vote on the level of outlays. Each year's outlays derive in part from budget authority provided in previous years. Outlays also include net lending—the difference between what the government lends and what borrowers repay—such as payments on student loans.

PAY-GO

The term stands for pay-as-you-go. It was, for a period, an important part of the effort to control ballooning federal spending and deficits. The PAY-GO law, enacted in 1990, theoretically triggered across-the-board spending reductions if tax cuts or new entitlement spending were not offset by revenue increases or entitlement cuts. The PAY-GO rules were often avoided by various budget tricks commonly used in Congress. But budget hawks said the rules were a restraining effect on Congress. They warned that without the rules it would be easier for members to approve spending that worsened the deficit. The rules expired in 2002, and the hawks were proven correct as tax cuts combined with significant new spending sent the deficit soaring. In 2007 Democrats, newly in control of both houses, reinstated the rules. The House approved PAY-GO rules in January, and the Senate followed suit in May in the fiscal 2008 budget resolution.

Receipts (Revenues)

Government income from taxes and other sources, such as import duties, user fees, and sales of federal assets.

Reconciliation

Legislation that revises program authorizations to achieve levels of spending required by the budget resolution. Reconciliation bills usually also include revenue increases. The bills are based on instructions in the budget resolution that require authorizing committees to draft legislation specifying revenue adjustments or cost-cutting changes in programs under their jurisdiction.

Sequestration

An automatic procedure for making spending cuts required by the Gramm-Rudman-Hollings law if Congress and the president fail to make them legislatively. Under the Gramm-Rudman-Hollings law, as revised by subsequent laws, the president's Office of Management and Budget (OMB) determines whether spending will fall within the range set by law. If the legal limit is exceeded, OMB determines how much needs to be cut, or sequestered, from the budget. The Congressional Budget Office plays an advisory role. About two-thirds of federal spending is exempt in some way from the automatic cuts. If cuts are needed, they are imposed fifteen days after Congress adjourns. This procedure has expired and is no longer is use.

Byrd, Robert C.

On June 12, 2006, Robert C. Byrd (1917–) became the longest-serving senator in American history: serving more than forty-seven years. He surpassed the previous record holder, Sen. Strom Thurmond, R-S.C., who served forty-seven years and a little more than five months. If Byrd completes the six-year term he was serving at the beginning of 2007, he would become the long-serving member of Congress ever.

During his long career Byrd held the post of Democratic floor leader of the Senate, PRESIDENT PRO TEMPORE, and chair of the powerful Senate Appropriations Committee. Throughout, he performed his duties with his trademark old-fashioned courtesy and consummate parliamentary skills and became known for his fierce defense of congressional, particularly Senate, prerogatives. (See MEMBERS OF CONGRESS: CHARACTERISTICS.)

Byrd held the post of Democratic floor leader of the Senate from 1977 to 1989. After a productive 100th Congress, Byrd did not seek reelection to the LEADERSHIP post. Instead the West Virginia senator in 1989 became president pro tempore as the most senior member of the majority party. He retained much power in the chamber by taking over as chair of the

In June 2006 Sen. Robert C. Byrd, D-W.V., became the longest-serving senator in the history of the Senate. During his half-century tenure in Congress he has held several leadership positions including Senate majority leader, Senate minority leader, and president pro tempore.
Source: CQ Photo/Scott J. Ferrell

Appropriations Committee, a position he held from 1989 to 1995 and again from 2001 to 2003. Byrd used the position to channel federal spending to his state. He once declared, "I want to be West Virginia's billion dollar industry," and he certainly surpassed that goal.

Byrd began his legislative career in 1946, when he won election to the West Virginia state legislature. He was elected to the House of Representatives in 1952. His campaign had been threatened by disclosure that he had joined the Ku Klux Klan when he was twenty-four. Byrd explained the membership as a youthful indiscretion committed because of his alarm over communism. Elected to the Senate in 1958, Byrd combined his Senate duties with law school, finally earning a degree in 1963. In 1967 he won his first leadership post, secretary of the Democratic Conference.

In 1971 Byrd became majority whip, replacing Massachusetts Democrat Edward M. KENNEDY. Byrd had assiduously courted his colleagues by arranging schedules to suit their convenience, sharing campaign funds, even sending birthday cards. "My role will be that of a legislative tactician," he said. "I don't want to thrust an ideological position on anyone."

By the time majority leader Mike MANSFIELD retired in 1977, Byrd had made himself indispensable to colleagues, and he had the votes to succeed the Montana Democrat.

With President Jimmy Carter in the White House, Byrd found himself cast as the experienced insider. His legislative skills several times saved Carter's programs, particularly his energy bills and, in 1978, the Panama Canal treaties.

When Ronald Reagan assumed the presidency in 1981, Republicans won control of the Senate and Byrd became minority leader. He tried to unite Democrats by holding weekly meetings and weekend retreats, and he became more aggressive in responding to Reagan.

In 1987 when Democrats regained control of the Senate, Byrd became majority leader for the 100th Congress. After giving up the leadership post, he enlarged the office of president pro tempore and became the most assertive Appropriations chair in many years. His prime role was as guardian of Senate traditions and powers. Beginning in 1981 he gave a series of addresses tracing the history of the Senate that were published in 1989–1990 and became an authoritative reference work.

Calendar

A list of business awaiting floor action by Congress is called a calendar. The House of Representatives has an elaborate system of calendars to help schedule its work. In the smaller Senate, the scheduling system is more flexible. The House operates with five calendars, the Senate with two.

After a bill is reported from a House committee and before it is scheduled for floor action, it goes on one of three legislative calendars: the Union Calendar, House Calendar, or Private Calendar. Bills already on the Union or House calendars may also be placed on a Corrections Calendar. Another calendar, the Discharge Calendar, is used only for motions to free bills that are bottled up in a committee. All of these calendars are collected in one document entitled *Calendars of the United States House of Representatives and History of Legislation*. The document, a valuable tool for congressional researchers, is published daily when the House is in session and is accessible on the Library of Congress's Thomas Web site (http://www.thomas.loc.gov). The first issue of the week lists all House and most Senate measures that have been reported by committees, with a capsule history of congressional action on each. It also includes a general index. Midweek issues deal only with that week's action.

The House calendars split up bills by broad category. The CLERK OF THE HOUSE assigns bills to one of the calendars when they are reported from committee. They are listed in the order in which they are reported, although they are not necessarily called up for floor action in that order. In fact, some never come to the floor at all.

Bills that have any effect on the Treasury—revenue bills, general appropriations bills, and authorization bills—go on the Union Calendar. Most other major bills, which generally deal with administrative or procedural matters, go on the House Calendar. If all these bills had to be taken up in the order in which they are listed on the calendars, as was the practice in the early nineteenth century,

Calendars in Congress

House Calendars

Union Calendar: Legislation dealing with raising or spending money.

House Calendar: Legislation not dealing directly with money, plus matters internal to the House.

Private Calendar: Bills dealing with individuals, or groups, on matters such as immigration.

Corrections Calendar: Noncontroversial legislation to alter or repeal overly burdensome, costly, or unnecessary laws or government regulations. Seldom used after the 1990s.

Discharge Calendar: A motion to take legislation away from a committee for further action. A controversial procedure, it is seldom used.

Senate Calendars

Calendar of Business: All regular legislative business.

Executive Calendar: Used for nominations and treaties.

many would not reach the House floor before Congress adjourned. Instead, most major legislation reaches the floor by being granted a special rule that allows it to be considered out of order.

Bills involving private matters are referred to the Private Calendar. They cover a range of purposes, from claims against the government to waivers of immigration requirements. Under House procedures, the Speaker must call up private bills on the first Tuesday of each month, unless the House dispenses with the call of the calendar, which it often does. The Speaker may call up private bills on the third Tuesday as well.

Noncontroversial bills were placed on what was known as the Consent Calendar beginning in 1909. But by the 1990s that calendar was no longer being used, as leaders opted to use unanimous consent and suspension of the rules process instead to deal with noncontroversial measures. When the Republicans took control of the House in 1995, they abolished the Consent Calendar and replaced it with a new Corrections Calendar. Bills may be placed on the Corrections Calendar by the Speaker if they are considered noncontroversial and deal with "correcting," or eliminating, overly burdensome, costly, or unnecessary laws or government regulations. The Corrections Calendar may be called on the second and fourth Tuesdays of each month, if desired by the Speaker. A three-fifths vote is needed for passage, which effectively prevents the Speaker from using it for consideration of controversial matters. After an initial flurry of partisan activity in 1995, the Corrections Calendar was used infrequently. Twenty-two bills were considered under this procedure in the calendar's first year, but just six years later, in the 107th Congress, the number had declined to a single bill.

The final House calendar, the Discharge Calendar, is rarely used. It comes into play only when a majority of the total House membership (218 representatives, if there are no vacancies) sign a petition to take a bill away from the committee that is holding it. This practice, known as discharging a committee, makes it possible for the full House to act on measures that otherwise would remain buried in a hostile committee. Discharge measures may be considered on the second and fourth Mondays of each month, except during the last six days of a session.

In the Senate, all bills are placed on a single legislative calendar, called the Calendar of Business. In addition, the chamber has an Executive Calendar listing treaties and nominations, which require the Senate's advice and consent. Schedules for floor action in the Senate are worked out informally, and bills need not be taken up in calendar order.

More on this topic:

Appropriations Bills, p. 22

Authorization Bills, p. 33

Discharge a Committee, p. 157

Legislative Process, p. 344

Suspension of the Rules, p. 549

Unanimous Consent, p. 565

Calendar Wednesday

House rules provide a way for committee chairs to force House debate on bills that have been reported by their committees but not scheduled for floor action by the Rules Committee. (See RULES COMMITTEE, HOUSE.) Under the procedure, known as Calendar Wednesday, bills (except those that are "privileged," or have priority over other bills, such as a general appropriations bill or a budget resolution) may be brought directly to the floor on Wednesdays as the Speaker calls each committee in alphabetical order. (See PRIVILEGE.) General debate is limited to two hours, and action must be completed in the same legislative day. The procedure is vulnerable to delaying action and is seldom used. It is not observed during the last two weeks of a session and may be omitted at other times by a two-thirds vote. In practice the House almost always dispenses with Calendar Wednesday by unanimous consent.

The procedure was adopted in 1909 in protest against the autocratic rule of Speaker Joseph G. CANNON, an Illinois Republican who maintained tight control over the House agenda.

Calhoun, John C.

A brilliant philosopher and an eloquent champion of states' rights, John C. Calhoun (1782–1850) was the foremost spokesperson for the South in the troubled period leading to the Civil War. As lawyer, state legislator, U.S. representative, senator, secretary of war, secretary of state, and vice president, he played a critical role in the course of U.S. foreign and domestic policy in the first half of the nineteenth century.

Calhoun entered the House of Representatives in 1811. During his six years in the House he was a nationalist, supporting efforts to strengthen the central government. With Speaker Henry CLAY, he was one of a group known as the War Hawks who helped push the nation into the War of 1812.

Calhoun left Congress in 1817 to become President James Monroe's secretary of war. In 1824 he was elected vice president under John Quincy ADAMS, a position that made him presiding officer of the Senate. More loyal to Andrew Jackson than to Adams, Calhoun assigned supporters of Jackson to key committee posts. The Senate, which had only recently extended the assignment power to the presiding officer, quickly took back that power.

John C. Calhoun (above), along with Speaker Henry Clay, was one of a group known as the War Hawks who helped push the nation into the War of 1812.
Source: Library of Congress

Calhoun was reelected to the vice presidency in 1828, this time under Jackson, but he and Jackson soon were at odds. Jackson believed in a strong central government, while Calhoun had become an advocate of states' rights. Angered by high protective tariffs, Calhoun became an eloquent advocate of the doctrine of nullification, which held that individual states had the right to annul federal laws they considered illegal.

Calhoun resigned as vice president in 1832 and returned to the Senate, where he defended states' rights in a succession of dramatic debates with Daniel WEBSTER. He became an apologist for slavery and fought efforts to prohibit slavery in new states and territories. Except for a brief period (1844–1845) as secretary of state under John Tyler, Calhoun remained a senator for the rest of his life.

Shortly before his death in 1850, Calhoun dragged himself into the Senate chamber to hear a colleague read his final speech in what has been called the greatest debate in the Senate's history. It marked the final appearance in the Senate chamber of the "great triumvirate": Calhoun, Webster, and Clay. Calhoun in that speech attacked northern opponents of slavery and opposed Clay's final attempt to forestall the South's secession from the Union. Clay's proposals included, among others, a measure clearing the way for California's admission as a free state. They were subsequently adopted and became known as the Compromise of 1850.

Campaign Committees *See* LEADERSHIP.

Campaign Financing

Being elected to Congress requires money. Most candidates for House and Senate seats raise a great deal of money to pay for campaign staff salaries, travel costs, mailings, print advertising, radio and television commercials, Web sites, political consultants, and many other expenses of campaigning.

Perhaps no other aspect of the American political system has aroused so much concern in recent decades as the financing of political campaigns. Debate on this subject involves basic issues of representative democracy and the integrity of Congress. As one reform advocate put it, "There are no fights like campaign finance fights because they are battles about the essence of politics and power."

Over the years, congressional candidates have raised money from businesses, labor unions, individuals, and political organizations. The candidates themselves have been important sources of funds at different times during the history of Congress. Today businesses and unions are barred from contributing directly to campaigns, but they participate by forming and operating separate funds called political action committees (PACs). Other organizations, such as ideological and issue groups, also have PACs. PACs and individuals are the major sources of campaign funds for congressional candidates.

Spending by political parties, although still small when compared to PAC and individual spending, rose sharply in the 1990s. Creative use of massive amounts of "soft money"—contributions to party committees that were ostensibly for nonfederal activities and therefore largely unrestricted at that time by federal campaign finance law—as well as more federally regulated "hard" dollars increased the clout of party committees dramatically. Party leaders feared loss of their new-found influence in the wake of a ban on national party use of soft money enacted in 2002. However, they soon discovered that independent expenditures—spending that is not coordinated with a campaign—gave them a significant tool for moving large sums of money to competitive races especially late in a campaign.

The enormous expense of modern campaigns has made the ability to raise funds crucial to political strength. Congressional candidates in the 2005–2006 election cycle spent almost double what had been spent a decade earlier—$1.4 billion compared with $765 million. House candidates spent nearly $855 million in the 2006 campaign and Senate candidates about $563 million.

The ability to raise money often is a key factor in measuring a candidate's chances of being elected. This is particularly true for challengers, who must work hard to raise enough money to pay for the political advertising needed to make their names familiar to the voters. Incumbents almost always have an easier time raising money. Particularly if they hold positions of influence in Congress, most incumbents can count on ample contributions from organized interest groups. Incumbents sometimes raise so much money in advance of an election that potential challengers decide not to run against them.

The campaign finance system depends on the willingness of individuals and organizations to make donations. People and groups give to candidates for many reasons. Ideally, contributions are made because the giver agrees with the candidate on important issues and thinks the candidate would do a good job of governing. Viewed this way, political contributions offer a constructive way for citizens to participate in political life.

But critics of the current system of financing campaigns worry that many members of Congress have become captives of special interests that pour money into campaign treasuries in return for favorable treatment on Capitol Hill. Some critics complain that contributors are buying votes. While other observers would not go that far, few would deny that donors are buying access. Members are more likely to meet with donors or return their phone calls, thereby giving contributors an opportunity to argue their position on legislative issues. Members of Congress, of course, may vote against the interests of their major contributors, but they place themselves at risk of losing that financial support in the next election.

Politicians themselves are frustrated by the current system, which can force them into a constant and demeaning quest for contributions, sometimes at the expense of their congressional responsibilities. Even some donors are becoming disenchanted with the system, complaining of multiple invitations to members' fundraisers and of "shakedowns" by money-hungry campaigns.

Major reforms in the campaign finance system were enacted in the 1970s. But dissatisfaction with the campaign finance system grew during the next several decades, as loopholes in the law were increasingly exploited and scandals unfolded. After numerous attempts by Congress, laws to close what critics saw as several of the more egregious loopholes in the system were enacted in 2000 and 2002. The controversy surrounding money and politics, however, was far from resolved.

> **More on this topic:**
>
> *Direct Election of Senators, p. 154*
>
> *Financial Disclosure, p. 220*
>
> *Patronage, p. 408*
>
> *Political Action Committees, p. 417*
>
> *Watergate Scandal, p. 596*

History

Campaign financing was rarely controversial during Congress's first century. Fund raising at that time was completely unregulated. Most candidates paid their campaign expenses or relied on a few wealthy backers.

By the 1860s federal workers had become the chief source of campaign money. The party that held the White House and controlled federal patronage was able to persuade or require government workers to contribute to its campaign coffers. In the 1868 election, for example, about three-quarters of the Republican Congressional Committee's campaign money was said to have come from federal employees.

The pressure on federal workers to contribute became one of the most unpopular aspects of the "spoils system," under which the party in power was entitled to distribute jobs and contracts to its supporters. As early as 1867 Congress passed a law to protect workers in federal shipyards from having to make political contributions to keep their jobs. Agitation against the spoils system continued until 1883, when Congress passed the Civil Service Reform Act, which barred mandatory political contributions for federal workers and made it a crime for a federal employee to solicit campaign funds from another federal employee.

Political campaign managers next turned for funds to wealthy individuals and to corporations. Large companies had begun to exert increasing control over the economy in the last decades of the nineteenth century. In the 1896 campaign, financier Mark Hanna raised an estimated $3.5 million in corporate donations, a staggering amount for the time, to finance the successful campaign of Republican presidential candidate William McKinley.

The unrestrained spending by big business on behalf of favored candidates became a chief target of the reformist Progressive movement, which sought to end corruption and increase public involvement in political life. With the backing of President Theodore Roosevelt, Congress in 1907

Presidential Election, 1896. American cartoon by Louis Dalrymple on businessman Mark Hanna dividing the spoils of the presidency with newly elected Republican William McKinley.

Source: The Granger Collection, New York

passed the Tillman Act, which prohibited any corporation or national bank from making contributions to candidates for federal office.

In 1910 came the first Federal Corrupt Practices Act, which established the first requirement that political committees backing candidates for the House disclose their total receipts and expenditures, as well as the names of their contributors of $100 or more and recipients of $10 or more. But the reports were not due until thirty days after the election. The following year reporting requirements were extended to committees influencing Senate elections and to House and Senate candidates as well. The 1911 law also required preelection reports, extended coverage to party primaries and nominating conventions, and set the first limits on the amounts that candidates could spend on their campaigns: no more than $10,000 for Senate candidates and $5,000 for House candidates, or the maximum amount permitted in their states, whichever was less. (The process for electing senators was also undergoing change at this time. The Seventeenth Amendment was ratified in 1913 requiring direct election of senators by the voters instead of by the state legislatures.)

The federal law governing campaign finance was further overhauled in 1925, when Congress passed a new Federal Corrupt Practices Act in the wake of the TEAPOT DOME scandal. That law, which formed the basis of federal campaign law for nearly half a century, limited the amounts that candidates could spend in the general election. (The Supreme Court had ruled in 1921 that Congress did not have jurisdiction over primary elections and nomination activities.) The new limits were $25,000 for Senate candidates and $5,000 for House candidates, unless a state law set a smaller amount. The act continued the existing prohibitions on corporate contributions and solicitation of federal employees and extended the reporting requirements for campaign funds.

Laws enacted in the following decades expanded the scope of the 1925 act but left its basic structure intact. One change was the extension of reporting requirements and spending limits to primary campaigns, a move that was upheld by the Supreme Court in 1941. Another made it unlawful for anyone to contribute more than $5,000 to a federal candidate or political committee in a single year, but contributions made through state or local party committees were exempt. Another made labor unions subject to the ban on political contributions that already applied to businesses.

The 1925 law and the other changes had little impact on the practices of congressional candidates. Spending limits and reporting requirements were widely violated over the years, but no one was ever prosecuted under the act. Candidates soon learned that they could ignore the law, raising and spending money freely with only token efforts to comply. Indeed, there were so many ways for candidates to get around the statute that it was said to be more loophole than law.

Contributors and candidates developed a variety of ways to evade the law. The reporting requirement for contributions of $100 or more, for example, encouraged givers to make multiple contributions to candidates of $99.99. To get around the $5,000 limit on what an individual could give, wealthy people channeled much larger sums to candidates through family members and friends, each of whom was allowed to contribute up to $5,000 per committee. They also contributed to multiple committees set up to support the candidate and additional committees established in the District of Columbia. Corporations were able to make contributions by awarding special bonuses to executives, who in turn gave the money to candidates.

For candidates, another loophole was the provision of the law that applied the spending and reporting requirements only to financial activity made with the "knowledge and consent" of the candidate. As a result, candidates could receive and spend as much as they wanted simply by maintaining the legal fiction that they did not know the transactions were taking place. Frequently, candidates who conducted expensive campaigns reported that they had received and spent little or nothing. Candidates also could evade the limits by creating multiple committees, each with its own spending ceiling.

1970s Reforms

By the beginning of the 1970s television advertising was having a growing impact on political campaigns. This, together with the weakness of the existing law, convinced Congress that new campaign finance legislation was needed. Within the next few years Congress passed major laws changing the way both presidential and congressional campaigns were financed and conducted.

The first major change in campaign law since 1925 was the Federal Election Campaign Act of 1971. That legislation combined two different approaches to reform. One part of the law set strict limits on the amounts that federal candidates could spend on communications media. The law essentially limited spending on electronic and print media advertising by House and Senate candidates to $50,000 or ten cents for each voting-age person in the congressional district (or state, for Senate candidates), whichever was greater. In addition, no more than 60 percent of the total media amount was allowed to go for television and radio advertising.

The other part of the law tightened the reporting requirements for contributions to candidates. Backers of the law hoped that full financial disclosure would reduce the likelihood of corruption and unfair advantage for large donors. All the ineffective spending and contribution limits were repealed, except the ban on corporate and labor contributions.

The 1971 law was praised by many reformers for improving disclosure of campaign finances and limiting media spending. The law did little, however, to prevent widespread illegal campaign finance activities. A pattern of such activities was revealed by investigation of the Watergate scandal. Although most of those abuses involved the 1972 reelection campaign of President Richard NIXON, public outrage over the revelations led to pressure for further reforms in congressional as well as presidential campaigns.

The result was the federal election law of 1974, which was technically a set of amendments to the 1971 law but in reality the most comprehensive such legislation ever enacted. It overhauled the existing system for financing federal elections and established the Federal Election Commission (FEC), a six-member body responsible for overseeing campaign finance activities. The law imposed limits on the amounts that could be given to candidates in an election. Individuals were limited to a gift of $1,000 to a candidate per election (primary, runoff, special, and general elections were each counted as a separate election with a separate limit), with an overall annual contribution limit of $25,000; political committees could give no more than $5,000 to any one candidate per election but were not limited in the total amount they could give. In addition, the law tightened reporting requirements and established a system of optional public financing of presidential elections.

The 1974 law repealed the media spending limits adopted in 1971 and replaced them with overall spending limits for Senate and House candidates. A candidate for the House could spend no more than $140,000: $70,000 in a primary race and $70,000 in the general election. A Senate candidate could spend no more than $250,000: $100,000, or eight cents per eligible voter, whichever was greater, in a primary campaign and $150,000 or twelve cents per eligible voter, whichever was greater, in the general election.

The Supreme Court in 1976 overturned the candidates' spending limits in the landmark case of *BUCKLEY V. VALEO*. Both liberal and conservative plaintiffs in the case had argued that the law represented an unconstitutional restraint on the free expression of citizens and political candidates. Although the Court struck down the limits on the amounts that candidates could spend on campaigns (except for presidential candidates who accepted public funding), it upheld provisions of the law limiting the amounts that individuals and political committees could contribute to specific candidates, as well as the reporting and disclosure requirements. The Court also held that the composition of the FEC violated the separation of power principles because the law provided for Congress to appoint some of the commission's members.

Congress amended the campaign finance law in 1976 to bring it into line with *Buckley*. The amendments included a restructuring of the FEC so that its members would be appointed by the president and confirmed by the Senate, and new limits on the amounts that individuals could contribute to PACs and national political parties, and that PACs could contribute to national political parties. The law also set down rules for fundraising by labor and corporate PACs. Further amendments to the campaign finance law enacted in 1979 reduced the paperwork involved in complying with the law, but compliance remained complex and time-consuming.

Soft Money Growth

The 1979 amendments also codified a Federal Election Commission ruling that encouraged political party activity. Party leaders had complained that the post-Watergate reforms had stifled state and local party activity. The 1979 legislation permitted those parties to use unlimited amounts of hard dollars to purchase grassroots campaign materials and conduct certain voter registration and get-out-the-vote drives, without the money counting as a contribution even if the activities indirectly aided a federal candidate.

Also in the late 1970s the Federal Election Commission issued a ruling allowing political parties to use money raised outside the federal campaign finance law—direct contributions from corporations and unions, in this case—to defray a portion of their administrative costs and the costs of voter drives, as long as the federal share of these costs was paid in hard dollars. Prior to that time all the costs would have been paid in hard dollars. This cost-sharing had the effect of freeing up a substantial amount of hard dollars for the national parties to contribute to federal candidates. Plus, federal candidates benefited indirectly from any money spent on voter drives, no matter what formula of soft money versus hard money was used.

The combination of the 1979 amendments and the commission ruling prompted an influx of soft money into the 1980 elections, as the national parties raised millions of dollars from wealthy individuals, corporations, and unions.

Soft money contributions grew steadily, despite an outcry from reform advocates. But the commission did not revisit the issue until 1990, when, under pressure from a court case, it required that soft money contributions and disbursements be reported, beginning in 1991. It also set specific formulas for allocating the federal-state split of costs, but placed no further restrictions on soft money.

Reform Stalemate

After the wave of campaign finance overhaul efforts in the 1970s, momentum on the issue seemed to come to a halt. Disagreements between and within the parties, as well as between the House and Senate, blocked repeated attempts to change the system.

Congressional reform efforts were driven largely by the desire to find a way to limit spending without violating the mandates of the *Buckley* decision. With the ceiling on expenditures removed, campaign costs grew apace during the next decade, and candidates became increasingly dependent on raising money from PACs.

Because the Supreme Court in *Buckley* had upheld public funds for presidential candidates who agreed to abide by spending limits, reform advocates pushed for the same for congressional campaigns. Backers argued that it would reduce the influence of special interests. They contended that public financing had cleaned up the previously corrupt campaign finance system for presidential candidates.

Source: Cagle Cartoons

Opponents of public financing responded that it would give too great an advantage to incumbents. If challengers were blocked by law from outspending the incumbent, opponents argued, they would have little chance against the advantages of incumbency, such as free mailings under the congressional FRANKING PRIVILEGE and greater recognition among voters.

Most Democrats endorsed the idea of public funding to replace the loss of funds from private sources, but the idea was still controversial even among Democrats, and proponents differed on exactly where the money was to come from. Republicans asserted that the problem with the existing system of campaign finance lay with tainted sources of money, not with the amounts contributed. Instead of spending limits, which they feared would help lock in a Democratic majority in Congress, they proposed curbs on specific sources of funds, such as PACs. But Democrats were reluctant to give up PAC money.

Advocates of campaign finance reform made little headway for more than a decade. In 1992 congressional Democrats managed to push through the most extensive legislation on campaign finance since the 1974 law, but they could not muster the votes to override the veto of Republican president George H. W. Bush. The bill would have, among other things, provided partial public funding for congressional candidates who accepted limits on campaign spending. Pressure for reform had built up in the wake of the savings and loan scandals that had tarnished Congress, most notably the Keating Five scandal. Televised hearings in 1990–1991 revealed how a wealthy businessman, Charles H. Keating Jr., used campaign donations to further his interests on Capitol Hill. Revelations about mismanagement of the House's internal post office and bank added fuel to the fire of voter outrage. (See SCANDALS, CONGRESSIONAL.)

Proponents of campaign finance reform were encouraged by the election in 1992 of a Democratic president, Bill Clinton, who during his campaign had endorsed reforms even more stringent than those included in the measure vetoed by Bush. But the stalemate continued. Legislation passed both chambers in 1993 but never made it to conference. In 1996 legislation was defeated in the Republican House and stymied by a GOP filibuster in the Senate.

In the meantime, massive amounts of money moved through the system, another campaign finance scandal erupted, and loopholes in the law widened.

Campaign Finance Scandal

The Clinton administration's aggressive solicitation of soft money contributions to the Democratic Party in the 1996 presidential campaign triggered investigations by the Republican majority in the Senate and House. Republicans had hoped to showcase what they saw as egregious abuses of campaign finance laws by the Democrats during the 1996 elections. Beyond the numerous stories of bent or broken campaign regulation, Republicans believed they had a particularly explosive mix that included allegations of a conspiracy by the Chinese communist government to try to influence U.S. elections; the virtual sale of the White House and high-level access by Clinton, Vice President Al GORE, and the Democratic National Committee; and the spectacle of a variety of Asian and Asian American fundraisers contravening U.S. laws by funneling foreign cash into Democratic campaigns.

Although congressional investigators produced story after story of embarrassing behavior by Democratic fundraisers and painted a portrait of a White House and a Democratic Party desperate for reelection cash, there was no direct proof of a Chinese government conspiracy, no proof that the White House ever knowingly accepted foreign money, and no proof that the Clinton administration ever changed policy in return for campaign contributions. Moreover, Democrats managed to reveal that Republicans had in one instance been just as lax about fundraisers letting foreign money infiltrate their political organizations.

But other investigations into 1996 election activities continued for several years. Various requests were made for the appointment of an independent counsel to investigate Clinton and Gore, but the Democratic attorney general found no grounds for such an appointment. A Justice Department task force looked into allegations of illegal fundraising, and ultimately a number of Democratic fundraisers and donors were convicted of campaign law violations that included making illegal foreign contributions and contributions in the name of another. The FEC leveled civil penalties against individuals and corporations, as well as the Democratic National Committee and a Clinton/Gore campaign committee.

New Issues, New Laws

The emergence of what many regarded as new loopholes in the system recast the campaign finance debate in the 1990s. Since the 1970s, proposals for change had focused on public financing, limits on campaign spending, and a limit or ban on PACs. But those issues were increasingly overshadowed by the millions of dollars of soft money contributions to the national parties.

One major concern of reform advocates was the use of soft money for "issue advocacy" advertising. These ads fell outside federal regulation because they did not expressly advocate the election or defeat of a particular candidate. But reform advocates scoffed at the distinction some attempted to draw between an ad during an election campaign that praised or criticized a member's stand on an issue and an ad that asked people to vote for or against that person.

Parties gained additional clout when the Supreme Court ruled in 1996 that they could spend as much hard money as they wanted on independent expenditures on behalf of federal candidates.

All of this contributed to unlimited amounts of money moving through the electoral system and sent reform advocates back to the drawing board.

The House passed legislation restricting soft money and issue ads in 1998 and again in 1999, but action on Senate proposals in the 105th and 106th Congresses was stymied by filibusters. Members, however, did agree in 2000 to require disclosure of contributors to and spending by a growing number of secret political groups known as "Section 527 groups" after the section of the tax code that governed their existence. Sen. John McCain, R-Ariz., a leader on this issue as well as broader campaign finance overhaul, had been targeted by a Section 527 group during his unsuccessful bid for the Republican presidential nomination in 2000. Two backers of Texas governor George W. Bush had formed a group called Republicans for Clean Air, which ran about $2.5 million worth of television ads attacking McCain's environmental record.

Major campaign finance legislation was finally enacted in 2002. McCain, along with Wisconsin Democrat Russ D. Feingold in the Senate, and Connecticut Republican Christopher Shays and Massachusetts Democrat Martin T. Meehan in the House, led the effort.

The new law—the Bipartisan Campaign Reform Act of 2002—banned the national parties and federal candidates from raising and spending soft money. It also broadened the definition of issue ads to include any ad that referred to a specific federal candidate sixty days before a general election and

Congressional supporters of campaign finance reform (from left to right) Rep. Christopher Shays, R-Conn., Rep. Martin T. Meehan, D-Mass., Sen. Russ D. Feingold, D-Wis., Sen. James M. Jeffords, I-Vt., and Sen. John McCain, R-Ariz., were responsible for a bipartisan bill that banned national parties and federal candidates from raising and spending soft money. Here they speak at a news conference on the Bipartisan Campaign Reform Act of 2002.
Source: CQ Photo/Scott J. Ferrell

thirty days before a primary. It barred the use of corporate or union money for such ads and required that the names of major backers of the ads be disclosed.

The legislation made a number of other changes. The limit on individual contributions to a federal candidate was raised from $1,000 to $2,000 per election, with an overall two-year-election-cycle limit of $37,500 for contributions to candidates and $57,500 for contributions to other committees, up from an aggregate annual limit of $25,000. The new limits were to be indexed for inflation. Political parties were barred from making independent expenditures on behalf of a candidate if they made coordinated expenditures for that candidate.

As soon as the law was signed, opponents—including lead plaintiff Mitch McConnell, a Republican senator from Kentucky—went to court to challenge various provisions as an infringement of their First Amendment right to free speech.

Sponsors of the law soon were unhappy as well. They sharply attacked the Federal Election Commission's regulations for implementing the law as weak and loophole-ridden and launched challenges in federal court and in Congress.

In a 5–4 decision in *McConnell v. Federal Election Commission,* the Supreme Court in 2003 upheld the major provisions of the 2002 law, including its ban on soft money and its restrictions on issue advertising. The Court, however, struck down the provision that had barred political parties from making both independent and coordinated expenditures on behalf of a candidate.

It was not long before another lawsuit was brought to the courts. While the Court in *McConnell* had ruled that the issue ad provision was not on its face overbroad and unconstitutional, this time the provision was challenged as it applied to a specific set of ads a Wisconsin nonprofit corporation had wanted to run before the 2004 election. In 2007 the Court—with several new justices on the bench—ruled 5–4 in *Federal Election Commission v. Wisconsin Right to Life, Inc.,* that three of the issue ads constituted "grassroots lobbying advertisements" and therefore the law's restrictions as applied to those ads were unconstitutional. Opponents of the ad provision saw the decision as a victory for the First Amendment right to free speech, while those on the other side said it opened a loophole blurring the line between grassroots issue advocacy and political campaigning.

It soon was apparent that, like issue ads, the problem of unregulated money had not been resolved either. Once the political parties were put out of the soft money business, there was a dramatic increase in the flow of unregulated money from wealthy individuals, unions, and corporations to Section 527 groups. After those groups spent more than $400 million in the 2004 elections, some members of Congress called for legislation to bring them under the same limits and restrictions that applied to party committees, political campaigns, and PACs. None of the proposals had been enacted by mid-2007.

Even if Section 527 groups were brought under campaign law restrictions, experts predicted that big money would find another outlet, and it would most likely be tax-exempt entities organized under Section 501(c) of the tax code. Those groups were already involved in election-related activities such as voter registration, get-out-the-vote drives, and issue advertising.

The System in Operation

As members of Congress debated ways to further reform campaign financing, spending on congressional campaigns grew at a steady pace. Candidates for House and Senate seats spent $115.5 million in the 1976 election cycle. By 2006, the total had risen to more than $1.4 billion.

A breakdown of the total receipts of congressional candidates in the 2006 election cycle gives some idea of the advantage of incumbency. House and Senate incumbents together received about $792 million, while challengers received $375 million. Candidates for open seats (where no incumbent was running) received nearly $254 million. Individual contributors provided about 60 percent of the total receipts of both House and Senate candidates. PAC money accounted for about 32 percent of House candidates' receipts but only about 12 percent of Senate candidates.

How that money is spent varies from one campaign to another. The needs of a challenger differ from those of an incumbent. A Senate candidate in a large state runs a different campaign than does a candidate in a small state. Campaigns for the House depend on the character of the district—whether it is urban, suburban, or rural—and on the candidates' personal styles. Senate campaigns, because they cover an entire state, usually rely heavily on media advertising. House races more often feature personal campaigning.

Even when inflation is taken into account, the cost of congressional campaigns has increased dramatically since the 1960s. Population growth has contributed to this trend; as the electorate expands, so does the cost of reaching voters. But more important, campaigning has become a sophisticated enterprise. Campaigns that once featured volunteers stuffing envelopes and canvassing voters now rely on computerized mass mailings, web-based fundraising, slick radio and television ads, and well-paid political consultants. All of that takes money.

Cannon, Clarence

During his four decades in the House of Representatives, Missouri Democrat Clarence Cannon (1879–1964) earned a reputation as a tough Appropriations Committee chair and as the House's foremost authority on parliamentary procedure. He was the author of *Cannon's Procedure* and *Cannon's Precedents*, both still used by Congress.

Cannon arrived in Washington in 1911, three years after receiving his law degree, to work as confidential secretary to House Speaker James B. "Champ" CLARK, also a Missouri Democrat. After Clark died in 1921, Cannon ran for his seat and won election to the House in 1922. He remained in the House until his death in 1964.

Cannon was chair of the Appropriations Committee from 1941 to 1964, except for two brief periods (1947–1949, 1953–1955) when Republicans controlled the chamber. In 1950 he was one of the chief proponents of a move to lump all regular appropriations for government agencies into a single bill. The experiment was unsuccessful, and in 1951 Congress returned to the practice of passing separate appropriations measures.

Cannon was a stickler for what he viewed as the prerogatives of the House. He reacted angrily in 1962 when the chair of the Senate Appropriations Committee, Arizona Democrat Carl HAYDEN, demanded equal status in the appropriations process—an area in which the House traditionally had claimed primacy. The feud between the two, both of whom were in their eighties, held up action on spending bills for much of the 1962 session.

Cannon, Joseph G.

Joseph G. Cannon (1836–1926), a conservative Republican from Illinois, was the last in a succession of autocratic Speakers who dominated the House of Representatives during the late nineteenth century and the first decade of the twentieth.

Cannon was the most powerful Speaker in history from 1903 until 1910, when Republicans and Democrats revolted against his arbitrary rule. He was stripped of most of his power by new rules that prohibited the Speaker from naming members or serving on the Rules Committee, through which Cannon had controlled the shape and fate of many bills; removed the authority to make committee assignments; and reduced the power to deny recognition to members during House floor debate. (See RULES COMMITTEE, HOUSE; SPEAKER OF THE HOUSE.)

"Uncle Joe" Cannon served in the House for half a century, from 1873 until 1923, with two short breaks (1891–1893, 1913–1915). He was never associated with any particular piece of legislation or cause, although he opposed the progressive policies of President Theodore Roosevelt. His seniority made him chair of the Appropriations Committee in 1897, and he became Speaker six years later.

Cannon fully exploited the authority established by his predecessors. As Speaker, he was chair of the Rules Committee, and he used this position to prevent legislation from coming to the House floor. He also took full advantage of his power over committee assignments: members loyal to Cannon could be confident of good committees, while dissidents were banished to unpopular ones. Using his power of recognition, Cannon arbitrarily determined which members could speak on the floor. His counting of voice votes was suspect. "The Ayes make the most noise, but the Nays have it," he once ruled.

Republican Joseph G. Cannon thwarted many an opponent during his powerful reign as Speaker in the early 1900s.
Source: Library of Congress

In 1909 the House rejected a resolution to curtail the Speaker's powers. The resolution was introduced by James B. "Champ" CLARK, who succeeded Cannon in the post two years later. Nebraska Republican George W. NORRIS introduced another such resolution in 1910. Although Cannon tried to prohibit debate on the measure, the House overruled him and adopted it after twenty-nine hours of debate. Cannon then offered to resign as Speaker. Because he was well liked by many, the

House refused to consider his resignation, and he remained Speaker until the Sixty-first Congress ended the following year.

Capitol Building

It was a "pity to burn anything so beautiful," a British officer reportedly said before setting fire to the U.S. Capitol during the War of 1812. Even at so early a date, the seat of Congress was the most striking public building in Washington, D.C. It remains so to this day.

This illustration depicts the original Capitol in 1800. During the war of 1812 the British forces burned down this building.
Source: Library of Congress

"A pity to burn anything so beautiful."

—Attributed to a British officer before setting fire to the Capitol during the War of 1812

Although it may appear to the first-time visitor as a unified whole, the Capitol is not one structure but several. There have been many additions to the original building over its more than two centuries of existence, and the process has by no means ended. A three-year-long restoration of the Capitol's West Front—the side that faces the Washington Monument midway down the Mall—was completed in November 1987. Construction of a center to welcome—and screen—the millions of tourists who visit the Capitol each year was begun in 2002.

The Capitol is constructed of sandstone and marble in the classic style. It rests on an elevated site chosen by George Washington in consultation with Major Pierre L'Enfant, a French engineer and city planner. In 1792 a competition was held to choose an architect; William Thornton gained the president's approval with a plan submitted after the deadline. Washington praised Thornton's design for its "grandeur, simplicity, and beauty of the exterior." In 1793 the president set the cornerstone, with Masonic rites, and the building was begun.

The north, or Senate, wing of the Capitol was finished in 1800. In October of that year records, archives, and furniture arrived by ship from Philadelphia, the former seat of the federal government. Congress convened in the Capitol for the first time on November 21, 1800. President John Adams addressed the members the next day, congratulating them "on the prospect of a residence not to be changed." The Senate then consisted of thirty-two members from sixteen states, while the House of Representatives numbered 105.

All three branches of the national government have had close association with the Capitol. For 134 years the building was the home of the Supreme Court. Starting with Thomas Jefferson in 1801, most presidents have taken the inaugural oath of office in the Capitol or on its grounds. Also, the Capitol long housed the Library of Congress, which now occupies three nearby buildings.

> **"If the people see the Capitol going on, it is a sign that we intend the Union shall go on."**
>
> **—President Abraham Lincoln** in 1863 in response to persons who said construction was an extravagance as the Civil War was being fought

Fire and Reconstruction

A British expeditionary force set fire to the Capitol on the night of August 24, 1814. Only the exterior walls were left standing. The damage might have been still greater if a violent thunderstorm, typical weather for that time of year in Washington, had not extinguished the flames.

Restoration work began in 1815 under the direction of Benjamin H. Latrobe, who had been appointed twelve years earlier as surveyor of public buildings. The central portion of the Capitol, with a low dome designed by Latrobe's successor, Charles Bulfinch, was completed in 1827.

After Bulfinch's appointment ended in 1829, his position remained vacant until 1851, when President Millard Fillmore appointed Thomas U. Walter to oversee an urgently needed enlargement of the building. By that time sixty-two senators and 232 House members were jammed into space designed to accommodate a much smaller number. Besides new Senate and House wings, Walter suggested the addition of a larger dome to replace the original one of copper-sheathed wood.

The new House chamber was occupied December 16, 1857. About a year later, on January 4, 1859, the Senate moved into its new quarters. The Supreme Court took over

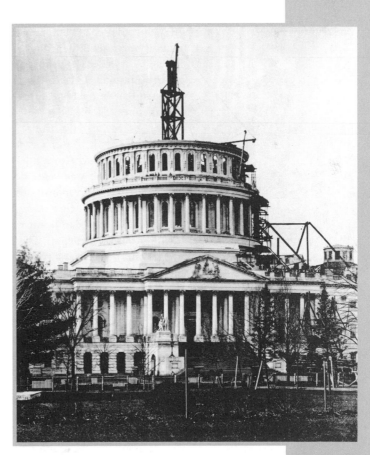

President Abraham Lincoln ordered construction of the Capitol dome to continue during the Civil War as "a sign that we intend the Union shall go on."
Source: Library of Congress

Statue of Freedom
Source: Architect of the Capitol

The bronze Statue of Freedom by Thomas Crawford is the crowning feature of the dome of the United States Capitol. The statue is a classical female figure of Freedom wearing flowing draperies. Her right hand rests upon the hilt of a sheathed sword; her left holds a laurel wreath of victory and the shield of the United States with thirteen stripes. Her helmet is encircled by stars and features a crest composed of an eagle's head, feathers, and talons, a reference to the costume of Native Americans. A brooch inscribed "U.S." secures her fringed robes. She stands on a cast-iron globe encircled with the national motto, E Pluribus Unum. The lower part of the base is decorated with fasces and wreaths. Ten bronze points tipped with platinum are attached to her headdress, shoulders, and shield for protection from lightning. The bronze statue stands 19 feet 6 inches tall and weighs approximately 15,000 pounds. Her crest rises 288 feet above the east front plaza.

the former Senate chamber the following year, and in 1864 the old House chamber became Statuary Hall by act of Congress.

Even after the outbreak of the Civil War, work continued on the Capitol dome. "If the people see the Capitol going on," President Abraham Lincoln said, "it is a sign that we intend the Union shall go on." On December 2, 1863, a great crowd gathered to watch Thomas Crawford's sculpture—the Statue of Freedom placed atop the dome, fulfilling Lincoln's vision.

Ironically, the final bronze casting of the Freedom statue had been overseen by a slave. Philip Reid, a slave working at the foundry where the casting was being done, reportedly had been given the responsibility when his boss went on strike for higher wages. Slave labor, in fact, had played a significant role throughout the Capitol's construction. The workforce had been composed in large part of black slaves hired out by their masters in the District of Columbia and neighboring Maryland and Virginia, as was then a common custom. Slaves did everything from clear land and haul building materials to the more skilled jobs of carpentry, stonecutting, and bricklaying. Public records indicated owners being paid $5 per month for a slave's work.

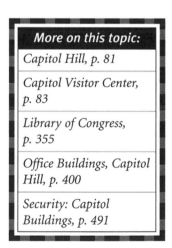

More on this topic:
Capitol Hill, p. 81
Capitol Visitor Center, p. 83
Library of Congress, p. 355
Office Buildings, Capitol Hill, p. 400
Security: Capitol Buildings, p. 491

The Capitol Today

The Capitol has undergone several major structural changes since the 1860s. Under provisions of the Legislative Appropriations Act of 1956, a new marble East Front was erected, faithfully reproducing the design of the old sandstone facade. The new front was placed 32 feet east of the original walls, which were retained to serve as interior walls. Work on the extension began in 1958 and was completed four years later, adding 102 rooms and 100,000 square feet of space to the Capitol's five floors at a total cost of $11.4 million.

A visit to the opulent Speaker's Lobby in the Capitol's interior provides a chance to follow the footsteps of thousands of past and present members of Congress.
Source: Architect of the Capitol

Visitors' Information

Public tours of the Capitol are offered at no charge between 9:00 a.m. and 4:30 p.m., Monday through Saturday, except for Thanksgiving and Christmas, when the Capitol is closed. The tours are about thirty minutes and are timed and ticketed. As of 2007, tickets are free and available beginning at 9 a.m. at a ticket kiosk on First Street, S.W., across from the U.S. Botanical Garden. This arrangement will change when the visitors center is completed (slated for late 2008). Recorded information is available at 202-225-6827. Groups and individuals may gain admission to the public galleries of the Senate and House of Representa-

tives from the members of Congress representing their state or locality. Senate and House gallery passes are not interchangeable, nor do they admit the bearer to special events or to joint sessions of Congress.

Visitor access in the Capitol building has been tightened since the September 11, 2001, terrorist attacks. All visitors entering the building must pass through enhanced security screening and may be subject to several searches. Visitors must be chaperoned at all times, either by uniformed tour guides or by congressional staffers. (See SECURITY: CAPITOL BUILDING.)

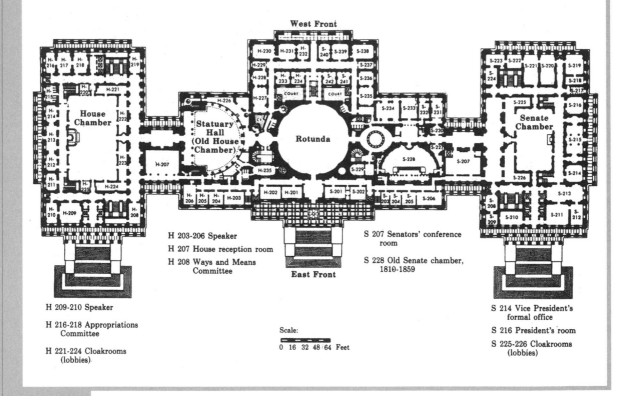

H 203-206 Speaker

H 207 House reception room

H 208 Ways and Means Committee

S 207 Senators' conference room

S 228 Old Senate chamber, 1810-1859

H 209-210 Speaker

H 216-218 Appropriations Committee

H 221-224 Cloakrooms (lobbies)

Scale:
0 16 32 48 64 Feet

S 214 Vice President's formal office

S 216 President's room

S 225-226 Cloakrooms (lobbies)

For the next two decades controversy raged over a proposed extension of the Capitol's West Front. In 1983 Congress voted instead to restore the West Front, which includes the last remaining portions of the Capitol's original exterior. Unlike most other federally funded construction projects in the nation's capital, the West Front restoration was completed well ahead of time and under budget. The refurbished building, said the architect of the Capitol, George M. White, "will look exactly [as] it did when it was new, but it will be structurally sound for the foreseeable future."

In 2000 ground was broken for a visitors center under the East Front of the Capitol. The new center was to provide educational facilities and amenities for tourists, while also enhancing security for the more than 20,000 lawmakers and staff who work in the Capitol complex.

The center had first been conceived in the 1970s as a way to improve the comfort and education of tourists. But after the 1998 killing of two Capitol Police officers on the Capitol's ground floor, members of Congress began talking about the long-stalled project's security benefits as much as its tourist benefits. The center would ensure that all tourists would face security screening several hundred feet from the Capitol itself. Work was accelerated and plans for the center expanded to include new congressional office space in the aftermath of the September 11, 2001, terrorist attacks and the ANTHRAX ATTACK on Capitol Hill a month later. Major construction work began in mid-2002 and the center was scheduled to be completed in late 2004. It was later pushed to 2007 and then 2008. Its total cost was estimated at $374 million as of early 2003 but by 2007 was expected to be double that.

The public may take a tour of several important rooms in the Capitol. These include the Rotunda, situated under the dome and decorated with statues and large-scale historical paintings, and Statuary Hall, which contains a collection of bronze and marble statues presented by the various states to commemorate distinguished citizens.

The bodies of many celebrated Americans have lain in state in the Rotunda. The list includes eleven presidents: Lincoln, Garfield, McKinley, Harding, Taft, Kennedy, Hoover, Eisenhower, Lyndon B. Johnson, Reagan, and Ford.

The Capitol is 751 feet, 4 inches long and 350 feet wide. It contains sixteen acres of floor space, an area slightly smaller than the White House grounds. The building's height at its tallest point, the top of the Freedom statue, is 287 feet, 5½ inches. The Senate and House occupy opposite ends of the building; the Senate chamber is in the north wing, the House in the south. The Capitol also includes committee chambers, offices, restaurants, repair shops, and other rooms. Tunnels and subways link the Capitol to Senate and House office buildings nearby.

Atop the dome are twelve columns around a lantern, which is lit when one or both houses are in session. The lit lantern tradition—it is not a legal requirement—dates from the mid-nineteen century when many members lived in boarding houses and hotels in the vicinity of the Capitol. A flag flies over either chamber when it is in session. Flags also fly over the east and west fronts twenty-four hours a day, a tradition that dates from World War I.

Raising the Flags

Since 1937 employees of the flag office of the architect of the Capitol have raised and lowered thousands of American flags each year over the roof of the Capitol. Having flown over the Capitol, the flags are then shipped to citizens or organizations that request one in writing from their member of Congress. On average, 300 flags a day—more than 100,000 a year—are run up a flagpole set aside for the purpose and lowered almost instantly. When mailed, each flag is accompanied by a certificate of authenticity. The recipient is charged a fee according to the type of fabric used, cotton or nylon. Senators and House members may forward to the flag office as many constituent requests as they wish.

Capitol Hill

When Pierre L'Enfant laid out the streets of Washington in the 1790s, he called the hill on the eastern end of town a "pedestal waiting for a monument." L'Enfant placed the Capitol Building there,

September 11 Attack Thwarted

Of the four commercial airliners hijacked on September 11, 2001, three were flown into their intended targets: the World Trade Center's twin towers in New York City and the Pentagon just outside Washington, D.C., killing nearly 3,000 people, destroying the towers, and severely damaging the Pentagon. The fourth plane crashed in a field in rural Pennsylvania after passengers—realizing what had happened earlier with the other airliners—attacked their hijackers but were unable to prevent the plane's destruction. Although definitive evidence had not been uncovered in the years immediately following September 11, that plane was widely believed headed into the U.S. Capitol.

MAP OF CAPITOL HILL BUILDINGS

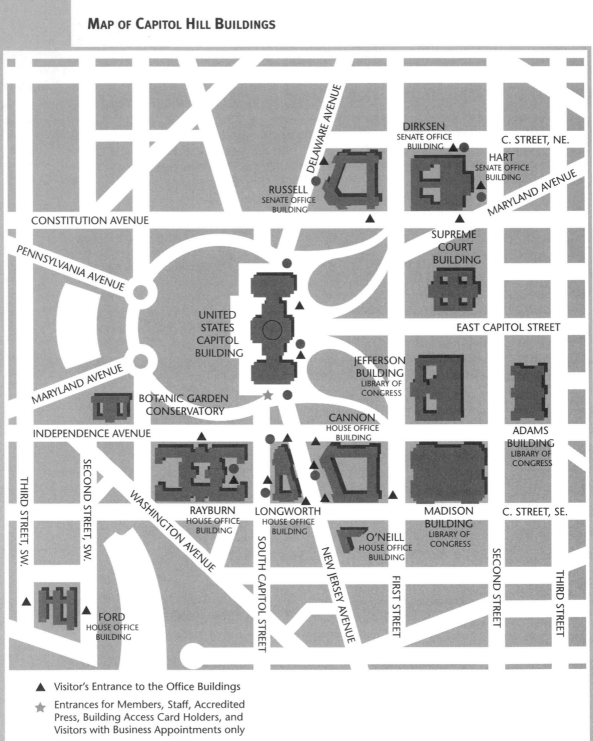

▲ Visitor's Entrance to the Office Buildings

★ Entrances for Members, Staff, Accredited Press, Building Access Card Holders, and Visitors with Business Appointments only

● Barrier-Free Entrances for Handicapped

housing the legislative and judicial branches. It stood a mile from the White House, which he located at the other end of Pennsylvania Avenue.

Known then as Jenkins Hill, the site had a sweeping view to the west of swampy land and the Tiber Creek, a finger of the Potomac first straightened into a canal and then captured in pipes and buried. Now Capitol Hill overlooks a formal panorama: the tree-lined lawn of the Mall, surrounded by museums and punctuated by the Washington Monument in the distance. Congress guaranteed its view in 1901, when it banned buildings higher than the Capitol dome—the equivalent of about thirteen stories.

The Capitol itself stands alone on a city block, its grounds a combination of gardens and parking lots. The grounds still reflect the design created in the 1870s by noted landscape architect Frederick Law Olmsted. Flanked on the north by Senate office buildings and on the south by House office buildings, the Capitol has on its eastern side the Supreme Court and the Library of Congress. Collectively, these buildings make up the area referred to as Capitol Hill.

> **More on this topic:**
>
> *Capitol Building, p. 76*
>
> *Office Buildings, Capitol Hill, p. 400*

Capitol Hill is also the name for the neighborhood of homes and commercial establishments radiating eastward of the congressional enclave. Developed to serve legislators and their families early in the nineteenth century, the village-like community serves the same function today. Restaurants and shops are filled at lunchtime with congressional employees. Many senators and representatives live in the restored townhouses common in the area. Three lines of the Washington subway system serve the community.

As a neighbor, Congress has not always been popular. In the mid-1970s, plans to build a fourth House office building where homes already existed prompted an outcry from residents. The plans were modified. Since then schemes for expanding Congress have been replaced by concerns about controlling staff size and the legislative budget.

This pre–Civil War illustration shows the view down Pennsylvania Avenue to the Capitol building atop Capitol Hill.
Source: Library of Congress

This area is a focal point, but just one part, of the larger federal enclave known as the District of Columbia. The Constitution in Article 1 provided for states to cede land up to ten square miles for a seat of government. Maryland and Virginia did so, and in 1790 President George Washington selected the area on the Potomac River that became the District of Columbia. The Virginia land was returned to the state in 1846.

Capitol Visitor Center

In 2000 ground was broken for a visitor center under the East Front of the Capitol. The new center was to provide educational facilities and amenities for tourists, while also enhancing security for the more than 20,000 lawmakers and staff who work in the Capitol complex.

While some called it a boondoggle for being too ornate and over budget, the new Capitol Visitor Center, scheduled to open in 2008, will provide added security and comfort to Capitol Hill visitors and members of Congress.
Source: CQ Photo/Scott J. Ferrell

The center had first been conceived in the 1970s as a way to improve the comfort and education of tourists. But after the 1998 killing of two Capitol Police officers on the Capitol's ground floor, members of Congress began talking about the long-stalled project's security benefits as much as its tourist benefits. The center would ensure that all tourists would face security screening several hundred feet from the Capitol itself. Work was accelerated and plans for the center expanded to include new congressional office space in the aftermath of the September 11, 2001, terrorist attacks and the ANTHRAX ATTACK on Capitol Hill a month later. The original budget estimate in 1999 was $265 million. Major construction work began in mid-2002, and the center was scheduled to be completed in late 2004. It was later pushed to 2007 and then late 2008. Its total cost was estimated at $374 million as of early 2003. The architect of the Capitol put the overall project budget at $522 in early 2007. But news reports said the government auditors believed the project would reach about $600 million.

The project was grandiose in every respect. It was built on three levels entirely underground on the east side of the Capitol with long gracefully curved walkways approaching the entrance. The structure includes 580,000 square feet and includes 170,000 square feet for House and Senate expansion space. The area in total is about three-quarters the size of the entire Capitol.

In the space, the "great hall" includes information and ticketing desks and a spacious area— large enough to hold 8,000 people—with two huge skylights through which the Capitol dome can be seen. The center also included an exhibition gallery, detailed congressional history, and two orientation theaters, a dining area for 550 people, two gifts shops and twenty-six rest rooms.

Although the architect's Web site does not detail the materials used, news reports said there were to be cast bronze handrails, dark cherry wood paneling, and thousands of square feet of pink marble, gray granite, and lush sandstone.

The project became increasingly controversial as the costs went up and the delays kept pushing the completion date back. The architect's office and center advocates defended the cost overruns and delays as necessary because of continually changing security requirements for the structure, which they said added around $150 million to the project's cost. But other matters added to costs also, including construction of congressional offices and hearing rooms—originally planned for later—and a major TV-radio studio on the Senate side. Many members of Congress were impressed by the center as it progressed but others were sharply critical of the expenses. Rep. Debbie Wasserman-Schultz, a Florida Democrat who in 2007 chaired the legislative appropriations subcommittee, told a *Washington Post* reporter: "I've never seen a bigger boondoggle in my life. It's like they're playing with Monopoly money."

Caucuses, Party

Party caucuses are the formal organizations of Democratic and Republican members within the House and Senate. Every two years as members organize for a new Congress, representatives and senators vote in their party caucuses on party leadership, committee chairs (or ranking minority member posts), and committee assignments. Contests for House Speaker, Senate majority leader, and other top posts can be controversial, but many other caucus votes simply endorse the leaders' recommendations.

Only one of the four party caucuses in Congress—House Democrats—actually calls itself a caucus; the others officially call themselves conferences. The Senate Democratic Conference and Senate Republican Conference meet weekly for luncheons to discuss scheduling and strategy when Congress is in session. The House Republican Conference and the House Democratic Caucus also gather weekly. Caucus sessions are closed to the public.

Within each caucus are committees that recommend party positions on bills, help schedule legislation, and make committee assignments. These groups handle most caucus business. Each caucus also has a campaign committee that raises and distributes money and provides other assistance to candidates for congressional office.

Changing Caucus Role

From 1800 to 1824 party caucuses in the House doubled as the national organizations for the major parties, choosing the nominees for president and vice president. By the 1830s national party conventions had begun to select presidential nominees, and the importance of both major parties' caucuses had diminished.

In the 1890s the caucuses were revived as forums for discussion of legislative strategy. But they were soon overshadowed by strong Speakers. Speaker Thomas Brackett REED, a Republican from Maine, and his successor, Joseph G. CANNON, an Illinois Republican, used the caucus primarily to get their party's stamp of approval on decisions they had already made.

The caucus gained new life after the 1910–1911 revolt against Cannon's autocratic rule. The House took away from the Speaker authority to name the floor leader, select committee chairs, and make committee assignments. Those duties were shifted to the political parties. Democrats, when they gained the majority in 1911, used their caucus to solidify control of the House.

The House caucuses were also used as a way to secure votes on legislative issues. At that time a two-thirds vote of the caucus could bind members to vote a certain way on legislation. House Republicans quickly abandoned this type of caucus; they even renamed their group a conference to clarify its role. Democrats used the binding rule during the first terms of presidents Woodrow Wilson and Franklin D. Roosevelt but later invoked it only on procedural or party issues.

The Democratic caucus was particularly strong during Wilson's first term (1913–1917). Wilson, a student of Congress, saw the caucus as an "antidote to the committees," providing unity and cohesion to counter committee independence.

The committees grew even more independent as the unwritten SENIORITY SYSTEM became entrenched, beginning in the 1920s. The post of committee chair went automatically to the majority member with the longest record of service on a committee. The party leadership and the caucus were rarely involved and, as a result, were less able to hold the chairs accountable.

The Democratic caucus was also one step removed from another set of decisions: committee assignments. As part of the revolt against Cannon, that responsibility had been given to Democrats on the House WAYS AND MEANS COMMITTEE. Republicans used a Committee on Committees, which included party leaders, to make assignments.

As the committees gained in power, the authority of the party caucus diminished. Party unity among Democrats also suffered because of political differences within party ranks that had conservative southern Democrats often voting with Republicans.

The development of party caucuses in the Senate paralleled their course in the House. In 1846 the caucuses won the power to make committee assignments. During the Civil War and Reconstruction, Republicans used their caucus to discuss and adopt party positions on legislation. Republican leaders used the caucus extensively in the 1890s to maintain party discipline.

Senate Democratic leaders adopted a binding caucus rule in 1903 and used it effectively in 1913–1914 in support of Wilson's legislative objectives. Twenty years later, charged with enacting Franklin D. Roosevelt's New Deal, Senate Democrats readopted the rule. It was not employed, but frequent nonbinding caucuses were held to mobilize support. Since that time neither party has seriously considered using caucus votes to enforce party loyalty on legislative issues.

Activist House Caucuses

A dramatic revitalization of party caucuses in the House took place in the latter decades of the twentieth century.

House Democratic Caucus

Liberal Democrats campaigned in the late 1960s and early 1970s to revive the House Democratic Caucus. They then used the reborn caucus to make dramatic reforms in House procedures, including a sweeping assault on the seniority system.

Nancy Pelosi of California, Steny H. Hoyer of Maryland, and James E. Clyburn of South Carolina raise their joined hands in celebration after the Democrats retook control of the House in 2007. Pelosi became the first female Speaker of the House in history.
Source: CQ Photo/Scott J. Ferrell

Their first step was to get Speaker John W. MCCORMACK, a Massachusetts Democrat, to agree in 1969 to hold regular monthly meetings of the caucus. Then in the early 1970s a wave of liberal Democrats was elected to the House. The newcomers added to the ranks of those sitting members who were frustrated with the rigid seniority system, which kept members of longest standing, who often were out of step with party politics, in top positions. The larger bloc of reformers made changes possible.

The caucus voted to give responsibility for nominating committee chairs to a new panel, the Steering and Policy Committee, headed by the Speaker. The panel, an arm of the leadership, also proposed committee assignments, a job previously handled by Democrats on the Ways and Means Committee. (Republicans in 1917 gave that role to a Committee on Committees, renamed the Steering Committee in 1995. In the Senate, similar policy groups within each party recommended committee posts.)

The caucus also decided to vote, by secret ballot, on nominations for committee chairs and for chairs of subcommittees of the Appropriations Committee. (Beginning in 1991, subcommittee chairs of the Ways and Means Committee also were elected by the party caucus.) The caucus agreed to have Democrats on each committee, instead of the chair, choose subcommittee chairs. Worried that the rule on binding votes might be resurrected after years of disuse, the caucus repealed it.

The reforms—and the new authority of the caucus—were dramatically used in 1975, when the House Democratic Caucus unseated three incumbent chairs. Two years later the caucus for the first time voted to oust a sitting subcommittee chair from the Appropriations Committee. The caucus replaced another full committee chair in 1985, two more in 1991, and one in 1993.

Although the Democratic Caucus focused primarily on procedural reforms in the 1970s, it also gave some attention to substantive issues. Caucus votes occasionally were used as a tool when a large bloc of the caucus was unhappy with the leadership and wished to express its discontent on controversial issues, such as the Vietnam War. These votes were divisive, however, and party leaders tried to avoid them.

A proposal in the 1970s to have the Democratic Caucus instruct committee members on legislative matters died quickly, as did an attempt in 1993 to discipline subcommittee chairs who had voted against a Democratic budget bill.

More on this topic:
Caucuses, Special, p. 88
Conservative Coalition, p. 138
Leadership, p. 325
Reform, Congressional, p. 470
Speaker of the House, p. 516

House Republican Conference

The House Republican Conference had rarely served as a policy-setting body. During his tenure as minority leader from 1981 to 1995, Robert H. Michel of Illinois used the conference as a sounding board to determine the party's position on substantive matters and to communicate the viewpoint of House Republicans to the Republican administration.

When the Republicans took control of the House in 1995, the Republican Conference assumed an aggressive posture. Revitalized by Speaker Newt GINGRICH of Georgia, the conference often served as the vehicle pressing the Republican leadership to implement the "Contract with America," the Republicans' 1994 campaign manifesto, and other items on the party's legislative agenda. There were frequent policy discussions and votes on strategy. For example, a conference majority urged continuation of the controversial government shutdown at the end of the 1995 session, when Congress and the White House failed to reconcile their differences over spending bills.

Led by House Speaker Newt Gingrich, the Republican caucus was revitalized after Republicans took control of the House in 1995.
Source: CQ Photo: Scott J. Ferrell

Gingrich also summoned members to conference meetings to explain votes at variance with party policy, such as when defections resulted in the defeat in 1997 of a committee funding resolution. Later that year senior members of the Republican leadership were forced to explain to the conference their knowledge of and roles in a celebrated and unsuccessful effort to replace Gingrich as Speaker.

Gingrich almost fell victim to the resurgent conference in 1997, when House Republicans, disgruntled with his ethics problems and erratic leadership, only narrowly reelected him Speaker. But he was not as lucky in the wake of Republican losses in the 1998 elections. Faced with eroding support from his party, Gingrich decided not to run for another term as Speaker and resigned from Congress. In 1999 at the start of the 106th Congress, the conference selected J. Dennis HASTERT of

Illinois to succeed him. Hastert regularly took the pulse of his members through conference meetings held in the basement of the Capitol.

Caucuses, Special

The many regional, cultural, economic, and ethnic differences that mark American society are also reflected in special caucuses in Congress. These informal member groups are unofficial organizations that allow members of Congress to pursue common interests important to them and their constituents. Many are small, some little more than luncheon groups. The Congressional Research Service (CRS) counted at least 417 informal groups in the 109th Congress from 2005 through 2006. Of these, 282 were registered as congressional member organizations (CMOs) with the House Administration Committee, which meant that they consisted of members from the House or from both chambers who shared official resources. Representatives and senators also are automatically members of their party caucus or conference.

Until the Republican takeover of the House in 1995, the most prominent of the caucuses were known as legislative service organizations (LSOs). Under 1981 rules these groups could not accept funding from outside sources, and some left Capitol Hill rather than operate under the restrictions. Most accepted the restrictions to gain an LSO designation, which allowed them to receive donations of unused official expense allowance funds from House members to support their activities. However, many of these more than two dozen organizations, such as the Congressional Black Caucus, were active in pursuing Democratic goals. The Republicans in 1995 eliminated the $4 million yearly funding for the LSOs, forcing the organizations to lay off staff and shut down offices. This forced the privatization of a few of the LSOs, such as the Democratic Study Group, which issued analyses of proposed legislation.

Many of the former LSOs continued to operate but now were known as CMOs. The major difference was that, like the more minor caucuses, they were run out of members' offices without special staff. "That's our whole point: They could continue to function," said Republican representative Pat Roberts of Kansas who led the fight to eliminate the funding. "To have them taxpayer-funded was not necessary."

A common denominator of some kind draws members to each informal caucus. The link may be ethnic background (the Congressional Hispanic Caucus) or geographic location (the Long Island Sound Caucus). It may be a shared interest, whether narrowly focused (the House Footwear Caucus, the Senate Jewelry Task Force) or broad in scope (Congressional Coalition on Population and Development). It may be concern over an issue, from abortion (the Pro-Life Caucus) to tourism (the Congressional Travel and Tourism Caucus).

Many CMOs focus on a single issue while others are as varied as nanotechnology, shellfish, small brewers, and the Silk Road. These are primarily House organizations, although senators can be members so long as at least one person is a representative. Caucuses are less prominent in the Senate. That chamber has only one officially recognized group: the Caucus on International Narcotics Congress, which was established by law in 1985. The CRS survey turned up twenty-nine Senate organizations including the narcotics control group.

Although informal groups have always existed in Congress, their formal regulation dates from the 1995 Republican changes in the rules. As of 2007, CMOs had to register with the House Administration Committee and had no legal or corporate identity. They could not use the free congressional mailing privilege (the frank), could not have their own web site, and could not accept financial support from outside Congress. They were limited to office space made available by a member of Congress.

Some caucuses can wield considerable clout. In 1998 the Conservative Action Team—a group of about forty conservative House Republicans—lobbied top leaders to pass a tax cut worth hundreds of billions of dollars. Although the lobbying failed at the time, the effort helped lay the groundwork for a greater emphasis on tax cuts the following year. Renamed the Republican Study Committee, the group subsequently argued against increased deficit spending, warning GOP lawmakers to promote more fiscal discipline. On the other side, the Tuesday Group, a loose-knit organization of about fifty moderate Republicans, worked to scale back plans to cut taxes and government regulations while urging increased domestic spending.

With Congress closely divided between the two political parties in the late 1990s and early 2000s, the caucuses found themselves with increasing leverage. Republicans had to win the support of members of both moderate and conservative caucuses in order to muster a floor majority. For their part, Democrats worked hard to hold the support of one of the most prominent caucuses, the BLUE DOG DEMOCRATS, a moderate group that sided with Republicans on some fiscal issues.

Some caucuses have only a handful of members, others more than a hundred. Membership is rarely selective. However, some caucuses have criteria for membership, such as the caucus set up at the beginning of each Congress by new House members, or the caucuses with party affiliations. Even a few state delegations have evolved into well-organized caucuses overseen by selected staff in members' offices.

Caucuses have thrived in the House, where many members feel isolated and anonymous, even within their parties. Many caucuses function almost as internal interest groups, lobbying committees and individuals for a particular cause. Caucuses sometimes send representatives to testify at hearings, and some draft specific legislative proposals.

Unlike legislative committees and the official party groups, which often have to mute conflict to build compromises, caucuses can endorse even the most controversial points of view. In 1987 the staff director of the House Republican Study Committee, a conservatively oriented caucus, praised the cohesiveness of that group: "I've got a core group of people it would be hard to offend no matter how conservative I got." In contrast, the Republican Conference, the party's official caucus, is constrained by the need to satisfy the wide range of political views represented in its membership.

Party Groups

Legislators have always formed alliances, but the modern special caucus dates from 1959, when liberal members of the House, frustrated by the successes of conservatives, revamped their own loosely knit group into a formal organization, the Democratic Study Group. With about a hundred members, a formal title, and annual dues (at that time, $25), the Democratic Study Group was the prototype for dozens of partisan and bipartisan caucuses organized for the next thirty-five years.

Dissatisfied, narrowly focused groups within a party have used caucuses to draw attention to their demands. Conservative Republicans created the Conservative Opportunity Society in the 1980s; their relationship with House Democrats was more confrontational than the approach favored by Republican Party leaders. A group of conservative Democrats organized the Conservative Democratic Forum, which was known informally as the Boll Weevils.

Some political caucuses are little more than a label for a loose coalition. The Gypsy Moths, also known as the Northeast-Midwest Republican Coalition, mobilized to fight budget cuts by the Reagan administration in the early 1980s. Another Republican-based caucus, the 92 Group, focused on winning a Republican majority in 1992.

Minority Caucuses

Ethnic and minority groups have often banded together when Congress considered issues particularly important to them. Italian Americans, Polish Americans, Irish Americans, and others have periodically spoken in unison. African Americans, Hispanics, and women are also represented by organized caucuses.

Among the most effective of all caucuses has been the Congressional Black Caucus, which includes every black Democratic legislator. When black members first began to meet in 1969, there were only nine of them and they had little role in the congressional power structure. The group became known as the Congressional Black Caucus in 1971. By 2007 the Black Caucus had forty-one members, including one senator and forty representatives. At times, the caucus drew support from across the aisle, although the only black Republican in the House in the late 1990s and early 2000s, J. C. Watts of Oklahoma, refused to participate. He retired from Congress in 2003. (See BLACKS IN CONGRESS.)

In the 1980s the caucus successfully pressured the Democratic leadership to have black members appointed to powerful House committees. For example, William H. Gray III, a black Democrat from Pennsylvania, served as chair of the Budget Committee and then as Democratic Party whip before retiring from Congress in 1991 to head the United Negro College Fund. A major victory for the caucus was passage in 1986 of legislation imposing economic sanctions against South Africa. Among the House's most liberal lawmakers, members of the Black Caucus denounced Republican cuts to poverty programs in the 1990s and emerged as some of President Bill Clinton's most passionate defenders during the impeachment proceedings in 1998–1999. The Black Caucus's agenda gained increased prominence after Sen. Trent Lott of Mississippi resigned as the Republican majority leader before the start of the 108th Congress after making remarks that appeared to tacitly endorse segregation. Lott and other Republicans reached out to black colleagues, in part to avoid the perception among swing voters that the GOP was against civil rights.

Chair of the Congressional Hispanic Caucus Rep. Joe Baca, D-Calif. (center), and fellow caucus members Henry Cuellar, D-Texas (left), and Ciro D. Rodriguez, D-Texas, hold a news conference on the minimum wage bill being considered by the House in 2007.
Source: CQ Photo/Scott J. Ferrell

The cohesiveness of the Black Caucus contrasted with the caucus of Hispanic members, which rarely took a unanimous position. Legislators in the Congressional Hispanic Caucus ranged from conservative to liberal, which led to disagreements over such issues as whether to lift an embargo on sales of food to Cuba. On occasions, personal disputes have rocked the Hispanic Caucus. In 2007 two members—Reps Linda T. Sanchez and Loretta Sanchez, the only sisters in the House and both from California—quit the organization. Loretta Sanchez quit early in the year after claiming that the caucus chair, Joe Baca, another California representative, had insulted her by referring to her with a derogatory term that impugned her virtue. Two months later her sister "suspended" her membership, she said, until the caucus overhauled its leadership structure. The Sanchez sisters were Democrats, as was Baca.

Women in the House formed a caucus in 1977. In 1981 they reorganized the group as the Congressional Caucus on Women's Issues and opened it to male members. In 1995, the group reorganized and reverted to an all-female organization. Among other activities, the bipartisan caucus supported legislation to improve the economic status of women. (See WOMEN IN CONGRESS.)

Other Alliances

Energy shortages in the 1970s intensified economic conflicts between southern and western states in the Sun Belt and the older industrialized areas of the Northeast and Midwest. Forming a caucus was a simple, direct way to recognize these complex problems, and accordingly the Congressional Sun Belt Caucus and the Northeast-Midwest Congressional Coalition were established.

Industries such as steel, textiles, and automobiles have firm allies in their lobbying efforts: caucuses specifically to promote each industry. Primarily composed of legislators whose districts depend on a particular industry, the caucuses have focused on limiting imports and removing trade barriers to U.S. products abroad.

Censure   *See* DISCIPLINING MEMBERS.

Chadha Decision   *See* LEGISLATIVE VETO.

Chaplain

Both the Senate and the House of Representatives have a chaplain, who is responsible for opening each daily session with a prayer. The chaplain also serves generally as spiritual counselor to members, their families, and their staffs. The chaplains are officers of the House and Senate. At the beginning of 2007, the House chaplain had an annual salary of $163,700, and the Senate chaplain, $143,000.

The official chaplain does not offer the opening prayer every day. That honor occasionally goes to guest chaplains, who are often from members' home districts. In 1983 the Supreme Court ruled that the practice of a legislature (Nebraska's, in this case) opening sessions with a prayer did not violate the ban on establishment of religion contained in the First Amendment to the Constitution. The Court noted that the practice dated back to the First Congress of the United States, the Congress that adopted the First Amendment. "The practice of opening legislative sessions with prayer has become part of the fabric of our society," the Court said.

The Senate elected its first chaplain on April 25, 1789, and the House followed suit five days later. Each was paid $500 a year, comparable to the $6 received by members of Congress for each day of attendance. On June 27, 2003, the Senate elected its first black and first Seventh-Day Adventist chaplain: Dr. Barry C. Black, a rear admiral and former chief of chaplains for the Navy. He replaced Dr. Lloyd Ogilvie, a Presbyterian minister, who had resigned in March 2003.

Senate Majority Leader Bill Frist, R-Tenn., welcomes Rear Admiral Barry C. Black, left, in June 2003. Black became the first African American and first military chaplain to hold the job of Senate chaplain. The Senate's business day begins with the chaplain reciting an opening prayer.
Source: AP Images/Stephen J. Boitano

The House chaplain's position became the object of a major controversy in 2000, when House Republican leaders rejected a bipartisan committee's recommendation of Rev. Timothy J. O'Brien, a priest, as chaplain and instead chose a Presbyterian minister. The move continued a tradition of selecting Protestant chaplains since the House was established, but the decision triggered charges of anti-Catholic bias and questions about whether one religious figure could legitimately minister to 435 lawmakers. After the minister withdrew amid the uproar, a Catholic—Rev. Daniel Coughlin, vicar of priests for the Chicago Archdiocese—was selected for the post by Speaker J. Dennis Hastert, R-Ill.

Both Black and Coughlin remained as chaplains at the beginning of the 110th Congress in 2007.

Cheney, Richard B.

Vice President Richard B. Cheney leaves the Capitol after meeting with the Senate Republicans in November 2007. As of that month Cheney had cast seven tie-breaking votes in the Senate since taking office in 2001.

Source: CQ Photo/Scott J. Ferrell

One of the most influential vice presidents in history, Richard B. Cheney (1941–) enjoyed a wide-ranging career that included service in the White House as President Gerald R. Ford's chief of staff, in the House as representative for Wyoming, in the cabinet as secretary of defense, and again in the White House as the vice president for George W. Bush.

In his role as vice president, Cheney's stature overshadowed that of the president's early in the administration, and he was quickly assigned many of the most difficult tasks facing the White House in 2001. Cheney oversaw a task force that wrote the administration's controversial energy policy in May 2001. After terrorist attacks shocked the nation in September 2001, Cheney turned to his experience as defense secretary from 1989 to 1993 under Bush's father, President George H. W. Bush. He contributed heavily to plans to launch a military campaign in Afghanistan. The following year, Cheney was one of the most adamant members of the administration in insisting that Iraqi president Saddam Hussein should be removed from power. Cheney served as one of Bush's most trusted advisors.

He began his political career as an administration aide in the early 1970s. He replaced Donald Rumsfeld, his mentor and later George W. Bush's secretary of defense, as White House chief of staff in 1975. He was elected in 1978 as the sole House member from the sparsely populated state Wyoming. In Congress he enjoyed a reputation as a moderate in his personal style but had a staunchly conservative voting record. He served in the House until he joined the George H. W. Bush administration in 1989 as secretary of defense. In that position, he oversaw the 1991 Persian Gulf War that was praised as a success despite the continued hold on Iraq by Hussein. After the elder Bush was defeated by President Bill Clinton in 1992, Cheney joined the private sector. He made millions as the chairman and chief executive officer of Halliburton Co., a worldwide engineering and construction company for the petroleum industry. He served as an advisor for the campaign of the younger Bush and led a search for Bush's running mate before being offered the job himself.

The vice president, as the constitutional presiding officer of the Senate, can cast a vote if a roll call has resulted in a tie. As of May 2007 Cheney had cast seven tie-breaking votes since taking office in 2001.

Christmas Tree Bill

Few sessions of Congress have gone by without passage of a "Christmas tree bill," so called because it was adorned with amendments like baubles on a holiday tree.

The traditional Christmas tree bill was a minor measure passed by the House, on which the Senate hung a variety of unrelated amendments providing benefits for special interests. The amendments most often involved tax or trade treatment. Enactment of these bills often came as Congress was preparing to adjourn for the winter holidays.

Russell B. LONG, chair of the Senate Finance Committee from 1965 to 1981, claimed to be the originator of the Christmas tree bill. The prototype was a measure passed in 1966, in the Louisiana Democrat's second year as committee chair. The original purpose of the bill was to help the United States solve its balance-of-payments difficulties. But Long's committee transformed it into a gem of legislative vote trading and congressional accommodation that aided, among others, presidential candidates, the mineral ore industry, large investors, hearse owners, and Scotch whisky importers.

The Christmas tree bill in its traditional form became less common beginning in the 1980s. Members of Congress preferred to tuck special-interest amendments into huge OMNIBUS BILLS where their presence was unlikely to be noticed. Emergency funding measures, called continuing resolutions, became magnets for unrelated amendments because they had to be passed quickly to keep government agencies from shutting down. (See CONTINUING RESOLUTION.)

Clark, James B. "Champ"

James B. "Champ" Clark (1850–1921), a Democrat from Missouri, was a member of the House of Representatives from 1893 until 1921, except for one two-year period (1895–1897). From 1911 to 1919 he was Speaker of the House, succeeding Joseph G. CANNON, whose removal he had helped engineer. In 1912 Clark was a candidate for the Democratic presidential nomination but lost to Woodrow Wilson after forty-six ballots.

Clark was elected Democratic minority leader in the Republican-controlled House in 1907. Opposed to Cannon's iron rule as Speaker, Clark proposed a resolution in 1909 to curtail the Speaker's powers. Although Clark's resolution was defeated, a measure based on his proposal won approval the following year.

In 1911, when the Democrats gained a majority in the House, Clark became Speaker, but without the sweeping powers Cannon had enjoyed. Oscar W. UNDERWOOD of Alabama was elected majority leader and chair of the Ways and Means Committee. The Democratic Caucus decided that the party's members on Ways and Means would make up the Committee

When he was minority leader in the House, "Champ" Clark opposed the amount of power Speaker Joseph Cannon had amassed. He was active in trying to curtail the Speaker's powers.
Source: Library of Congress

on Committees with responsibility for making committee assignments—a power previously exercised by the Speaker. As a result Underwood, not Clark, functioned as the leader of House Democrats, and the power of the Speaker went into a fifteen-year decline.

Clay, Henry

Henry Clay was known as the "Great Compromiser" for his efforts to resolve sectional disputes over slavery.
Source: Library of Congress

Henry Clay (1777–1852) of Kentucky was one of the giants of Congress during the first half of the nineteenth century. Gifted with charm and eloquence, Clay was called "the Great Compromiser" for his efforts to resolve sectional disputes over slavery. His initiatives included two plans to curb the expansion of slave territory: the Missouri Compromise of 1820 and the Compromise of 1850.

A spokesperson for western expansion, Clay proposed an "American System" for economic development that featured a federally financed transportation network and high tariffs to protect American industry. Clay ran unsuccessfully for president as a Democratic-Republican in 1824, as a National Republican in 1832, and as a Whig in 1844. (See POLITICAL PARTIES.)

Clay began his congressional career with two brief stints in the Senate, where he filled unexpired terms in 1806–1807 and 1810–1811. In 1810 he was elected to the House of Representatives, where he served for most of the next fifteen years. In the House he quickly joined other young War Hawks in pushing the nation into the War of 1812 against England.

Clay was chosen as Speaker on the day he took office in 1811, and he remained Speaker as long as he was in the House. Although he resigned his seat twice—in 1814, to help negotiate an end to the War of 1812, and again in 1820—he was reelected Speaker as soon as he returned to the House in 1815 and 1823. A formidable presiding officer and an accomplished debater, Clay kept firm control over the House until he left the chamber for good in 1825.

Running for president in 1824, Clay wound up last in a four-way race that had to be decided by the House of Representatives. There Clay threw his support to John Quincy ADAMS, ensuring Adams's election. When the new president made Clay his secretary of state, critics charged that Clay was being paid off for his election support. (See ELECTING THE PRESIDENT.)

In 1830 Clay was elected to the Senate, where he played a leading role in the debates over slavery that preceded the Civil War. He left the Senate in 1842 but returned in 1849 and served until his death in 1852.

Clay's final effort to prevent the breakup of the Union, known as the Compromise of 1850, attempted to calm rising passions between slaveholding and free states. Among other measures the Compromise of 1850 permitted California to be admitted to the Union as a free state and strengthened the federal law governing capture and return of runaway slaves.

Clay's proposals prompted a debate that has often been called the greatest in the Senate's history. It marked the last appearance in the Senate chamber of the "great triumvirate": Daniel

WEBSTER of Massachusetts, an apostle of national unity; John C. CALHOUN of South Carolina, the South's foremost defender of slavery and states' rights; and Clay himself. Calhoun, who was fatally ill, sat in the chamber while his final speech was read by a colleague.

Clerk of the House

The clerk of the House runs the day-to-day operations of the House of Representatives. The Senate counterpart is known as the SECRETARY OF THE SENATE. The clerk's wide-ranging responsibilities include providing stationery supplies; attesting and fixing the seal of the House to subpoenas; recording and printing bills and reports; reporting debates and keeping the official House *Journal;* certifying passage of bills; compiling lobby registration information; and preparing a variety of periodic reports. At one time the clerk was also responsible for providing electrical and mechanical equipment and office furniture, and paying salaries of House employees. These responsibilities now lie with the chief administrative officer (see HOUSE CHIEF ADMINISTRATIVE OFFICER). The job pays about $160,000 annually.

Lorraine C. Miller became the House clerk on February 15, 2007, after Democrats regained control of the chamber. She previously was an advisor to Rep. Nancy Pelosi, D-Calif., who became Speaker in 2007. Earlier Miller had worked for two other Speakers, Jim Wright of Texas and Tom Foley of Washington, both Democrats. She was the thirty-fifth clerk of the U.S. House of Representatives.

The clerk is elected by the majority party in the House and typically remains in the job until that party loses control of the chamber. But the clerk may be removed by the Speaker.

In 1967, however, the House replaced Ralph R. Roberts, who had served in the post of clerk since 1949. Roberts had been criticized for using the chauffeur and limousine that went with his job for trips to his home in Indiana and to racetracks. In 1998 Robin H. Carle resigned as clerk amid press reports of allegations by the House inspector general of her personal use of a House credit card. The official version of the inspector general's report and letter to House leaders recommended changes to prevent the misuse of credit cards in the clerk's office but gave no details of any problems. Carle had been clerk since the Republican takeover of Congress in 1995.

Clinton, Hillary Rodham

Hillary Rodham Clinton was elected to the Senate in 2000 from New York. Even before that she was a prominent political figure on the national scene as the wife of President Bill Clinton (1993–2001). With her 2000 victory, she became the first first lady to be elected to the Senate, or to any other public office.

She was raised in the Chicago suburb of Park Ridge by parents whose strong support for education and self-reliance were important factors in her growth and development. She attended public high school in Chicago and then went to Wellesley College, where her intelligence and skills as a mediator won praise, and her political views became more liberal.

After her graduation from Yale Law School in 1973, Hillary worked at the Children's Defense Fund for a brief time and then, in January 1974, joined the U.S. House of Representatives Judiciary Committee's Impeachment Inquiry staff, which was grappling with legal questions surrounding the possible impeachment of President Richard Nixon. Her work with the committee led to several prestigious job offers after Nixon's resignation, but she decided to join Bill Clinton, whom she met at Yale, in Arkansas where they married. She taught law at the University of Arkansas in Fayetteville.

In Arkansas she carved out a successful legal career while her husband was first elected attorney general and then governor. Although he lost his first reelection bid he rebounded in 1982 to win

First Lady Hillary Rodham Clinton and Vice President Al Gore pose for photos in the Old Senate Chamber after Clinton's swearing in on January 3, 2001. Clinton was the first first lady to be elected to the U.S. Senate. After her 2006 re-election, she announced her intention to run for president.

Source: CQ Photo/Scott J. Ferrell

back the position, which he held for the next decade. In the meantime, she spearheaded education reform by serving as the chair of the Arkansas Education Standards Committee. She also served as an adviser to her husband, evincing political skills good enough to earn her mention as a gubernatorial candidate in her own right.

In the 1992 presidential campaign, her intelligence and proven abilities, which sometimes led the campaign to claim the public would be getting "two for the price of one" in a Clinton presidency, proved to be a double-edged sword. It won many supporters, some of whom thought her better qualified than her husband to be president; but it also left her open to attacks from political opponents, particularly the Republican right, who claimed that she had too much influence with her husband and that her views were "antifamily."

Once the Clintons were in the White House, Hillary Clinton quickly became the most high-profile and openly powerful first lady ever. She maintained an office in the West Wing, which no first lady had previously done, and chaired staff meetings herself. She publicly served as one of her husband's most important advisers on almost every topic; "Ask Hillary" was the watchword in the White House. Most significantly, President Clinton appointed her to head a task force established to create a health care reform program. When after eight months the commission produced a plan, Hillary Clinton became its foremost advocate, lobbying behind the scenes and testifying before five different congressional committees to explain and defend it. Nevertheless, in the face of aggressive lobbying by medical interests, including the pharmaceutical industry, the plan was not enacted, a major setback for the Clintons.

As in her roles in Arkansas, controversy followed her at almost every step, including her role in the 1993 firing of the White House Travel Office staff and in the handling of the Clintons' Whitewater real estate venture in Arkansas. In the latter case, she responded to questions from a Senate investigation committee and, in February 1996, became the first sitting first lady to be subpoenaed by, and to testify before, a grand jury. In March 2002 a special prosecutor's final report found insufficient evidence to charge her with any wrongdoing in the case.

Revelations in January 1998 about President Clinton's extramarital relationship with a White House intern created a political and personal crisis for Hillary Clinton. She nevertheless mounted a spirited defense of the president in the face of Republican efforts to impeach and remove him from office, an effort that failed. (See CLINTON IMPEACHMENT TRIAL.)

Although always involved in politics, she had never held an elected office. As the Clinton administration drew to a close, she decided to seek the New York Senate seat being vacated by Democrat Daniel Patrick Moynihan. In 1999 the Clintons bought a house in Chappaqua, New York, to establish residency in the state. She entered the Senate race and handily won the election in 2000.

Hillary Clinton was an unusual freshman senator; she already was extremely well known and was seen as a possible candidate for national office. Her Senate committee assignments included Armed Services, Environment and Public Works, and Health, Education, Labor and Pensions. But the former first lady succeeded in learning the ropes and forging alliances while maintaining a lower profile than some had expected. During her first year in the Senate, she fought for money for New York in the wake of the terrorist attacks of September 11, 2001; the state received $20 billion in emergency aid.

In the 108th Congress, Hillary Clinton took on a leadership role as chair of the Steering and Coordination Committee, which coordinates between Senate Democrats and other Democratic political leaders around the country. As the 2004 presidential election drew closer, she remained in the spotlight as a potential White House aspirant, but she chose not to run for president that year.

She achieved an easy reelection to the Senate in the 2006 midterm elections. On January 20, 2007, she announced her bid for the 2008 Democratic presidential nomination.

Clinton Impeachment Trial

For only the second time in U.S. history, the Senate in 1999 sat in judgment of a president—Bill Clinton—to determine whether he should be removed from office. Unlike the first president to face an impeachment trial—Andrew Johnson, who in 1868 escaped removal by a single Senate vote—the outcome of Clinton's fate was never seriously in doubt. In fact, at the end of the five-week trial presided over by the Supreme Court's chief justice William Rehnquist, the Senate could not muster even a simple majority to convict Clinton when it voted on the two articles of impeachment.

Under the Constitution, a supermajority of two-thirds of all senators present is necessary to convict and remove a president. In the present Senate this amounts to sixty-seven senators. The Republican-controlled Senate's failure to get any Democrats to vote to convict their party's popular president was foreshadowed by the bitterly partisan impeachment hearings and vote in the House of Representatives, which adopted the articles against Clinton on December 19, 1998, with the support of only a handful of Democrats. The impeachment effort begun against Richard NIXON in 1974 was considered to have been much more likely to succeed because it had broad bipartisan support. Nixon resigned before the House could impeach him for his role in the Watergate crimes and cover-up.

Independent Counsel

The impeachment of President Clinton arose out of the findings of an independent counsel—Kenneth W. Starr, a former Republican U.S. solicitor general. Starr was appointed in 1994 to investigate Whitewater, a tangled web of political and financial relationships involving an Arkansas land investment by then-governor Clinton and his wife, Hillary Rodham CLINTON, in the 1970s and 1980s. The investigation subsequently widened to cover the 1993 firing of White House Travel Office employees and the White House's requests in 1993 and 1994 for hundreds of Federal Bureau of Investigation (FBI) files on former Republican administration officials. Then, in January 1998, Starr received authorization to broaden his probe to include allegations that Clinton had had an extramarital affair with then-twenty-two-year-old White House intern Monica S. Lewinsky, lied about it under oath, and urged her to lie about it under oath. When the allegations became public that month, Clinton quickly and vehemently denied all charges.

Clinton had said he did not have a sexual relationship with Lewinsky in a January 1998 civil deposition in a sexual harassment lawsuit brought against him by former Arkansas state employee Paula Corbin Jones. Lewinsky had signed an affidavit in that

A sight rarely seen in Congress, Chief Justice William Rehnquist administers an oath of impartiality to the Senate at the start of President Bill Clinton's impeachment trial in January 1999.
Source: U.S. Senate

case, also denying a sexual relationship with Clinton. The Supreme Court in *Clinton v. Jones* had allowed that case to go forward when it decided in May 1997 that a sitting president could face civil charges. Starr used Clinton's deposition in his investigation, even though the judge in the Jones case deemed the Lewinsky portion of it immaterial and eventually dismissed the civil suit.

Starr's office took grand jury testimony and issued numerous subpoenas that the Clinton administration challenged in court. Federal district court rulings in May 1998 prevented Clinton from invoking EXECUTIVE PRIVILEGE or attorney-client privilege to keep his aides from testifying before Starr's grand jury and from establishing a "protective function" privilege to keep Secret Service agents from giving testimony. Avoiding comparisons to Nixon during the WATERGATE SCANDAL, the White House did not appeal these decisions to the Supreme Court—including the constitutionality of Starr's subpoena for Clinton, himself, to appear before the grand jury.

On August 17, 1998, in videotaped testimony at the White House, Clinton directly answered the prosecutor's questions. That evening in a nationally televised address, Clinton admitted that he had had a relationship with Lewinsky that was "not appropriate" and that he had "misled" the public about it. He insisted that his deposition in the Jones case was "legally accurate." He claimed the definition of "sexual relations" put forth by the lawyers in the case did not cover the kind of activity he had engaged in with Lewinsky. Clinton also said that he did not ask anyone to lie or to destroy evidence.

In a public display at the steps of the Capitol on September 9, Starr's deputies delivered his summary report and dozens of boxes of accompanying evidence. Quickly and widely disseminated—even over the Internet—the Starr report contained numerous details about Clinton's sexual relationship with Lewinsky but nothing about Whitewater, the travel office firings, or the FBI files. Starr leveled eleven specific charges of wrongdoing against Clinton, including lying under oath, obstruction of justice in working with Lewinsky to conceal their relationship, witness tampering in attempting to improperly influence the testimony of his personal secretary, and abusing the power of his office in an effort to cover up his extramarital affair.

House Judiciary Committee

As the House Judiciary Committee sifted through the mountainous amount of evidence that accompanied the Starr report, in an unprecedented move Republicans on the committee voted to release to the public videotape of Clinton's secret grand jury testimony. As with the Starr report, the testimony seemed to have no profound impact on the president's popular standing.

On October 5 the committee's Republican majority found that there was "substantial and credible evidence" to recommend that the House begin an open-ended impeachment investigation of the president. The full House assented October 8, with thirty-one Democrats joining all 227 Republicans in voting "aye."

As the 1998 congressional elections approached, House Speaker Newt GINGRICH and the Republican Party tried to capitalize on the scandal with a multimillion-dollar advertising campaign in key congressional races. On election day, however, Democrats upset the prognosticators by winning five seats in the House and losing none in the Senate. Facing an insurrection among Republicans in the wake of the disappointing election results, Gingrich announced that he would resign from Congress.

House Judiciary Committee Chair Henry J. Hyde of Illinois pledged shortly afterward that he would limit the impeachment inquiry and call only Starr as a witness. That same week, lawyers for the president and for Jones reached an out-of-court settlement ending the Jones sexual harassment case, which Jones was appealing. Clinton agreed to pay Jones $850,000 but would not apologize to her—a stumbling block to an earlier settlement.

Making a dramatic twelve-hour appearance before the House Judiciary Committee on November 19, Starr expressed his belief that any violation of the law by a president, even if not in his official capacity, is a potential impeachable offense. Committee Democrats called Starr's tactics high-handed and his investigation partisan. Starr exonerated Clinton on the White House Travel Office firings and the FBI file matters and also conceded that he still lacked sufficient evidence to recommend impeachment on Whitewater-related charges.

The following day Starr's ethics adviser, Samuel Dash, the Democratic counsel to the Senate Judiciary Committee during Watergate, resigned. Dash said that Starr had "no right or authority under the law … to advocate for a particular position" on impeaching Clinton.

In late November Clinton provided legalistic responses to eighty-one questions submitted to him by the committee. He reiterated that his testimony in the Lewinsky matter was "not false and misleading." Energized by Clinton's refusal to admit illegal wrongdoing of any sort, the Republicans pressed on with the inquiry.

Hyde, although respected on both sides of the aisle, had difficulty controlling the often rancorous, bitterly split committee. Republicans were unwavering in their push for impeachment; Hyde called Clinton's action's "an assault on the rule of law." Committee Democrats, acknowl-

House Judiciary Committee chair Henry J. Hyde had difficulty controlling a sharply divided committee during the Clinton impeachment hearings.
Source: CQ Photo/Scott J. Ferrell

edging that Clinton's deeds were deplorable, argued that impeachment should be reserved for high crimes, not for vague statements under oath about an extramarital affair. Some advocated censure—a rarely used mechanism that Republicans saw as meaningless.

In Clinton's defense the president's lawyers presented alternative interpretations of the alleged facts and brought in experts on prosecutorial standards and the Constitution. They argued that Clinton's alleged offenses were trivial and, even if true, did not rise to the high level of impeachment. The defense's arguments were to no avail as the Judiciary Committee voted along strict party lines to recommend to the full House four articles of impeachment against President Clinton.

House Votes to Impeach

Speaker Newt Gingrich called the House of Representatives back into a lame-duck session to consider the impeachment articles. However, on the eve of the scheduled debate on the articles,

President Clinton announced in a nationally televised address that he had ordered a series of military strikes against Iraq. Congressional Democrats advocated postponing the impeachment vote until the cessation of military action. The Republican leadership, skeptical of Clinton's timing of the strikes, put off the debate for only one day.

The House was further shaken by the admission of Speaker-designate Robert L. Livingston that he had had several extramarital affairs. During the impeachment debate, the Louisiana Republican announced that he would not run for Speaker and would resign his seat in Congress. Over the course of the impeachment inquiry, the past indiscretions of several members of Congress, including Hyde, had come under public scrutiny.

On December 19, with U.S. military forces engaged overseas and Livingston having just announced that he would resign, the lame-duck session of the 105th Congress impeached Clinton. Despite continued public opposition and with the concurrence of only a handful of Democrats, the House adopted two of the four articles against Clinton. Article I, perjury before a grand jury, was adopted 228–206; Article II, perjury in his deposition in the Paula Jones case, was rejected 205–229; Article III, obstruction of justice, was adopted 221–212; and Article IV, abuse of power, was rejected 148–285.

Before the vote, the Democratic caucus staged a brief protest by walking out of the House chamber en masse. Democrats were upset because the Republican majority would not allow a floor vote on an alternative presidential censure resolution.

Senate Trial

In a solemn ceremony on January 7, 1999, Chief Justice Rehnquist swore the 100-member Senate to an oath of impartiality. The Constitution mandates that the chief justice preside over the impeachment trial of the president. Dire predictions of a lengthy, tumultuous Senate trial did not turn out to be true. Devoid of the hostile partisanship that characterized the proceedings in the House, the Senate conducted an abbreviated and decorous trial.

Led by Hyde, the thirteen Republican House managers (of the House Judiciary Committee) presented their arguments of Clinton wrongdoing in exhaustive detail. In rebuttal, Clinton's defense lawyers, led by Charles Ruff and David E. Kendall, methodically poked enough factual holes in the prosecution's case to raise doubts about the strength of the managers' conclusions.

On January 27 the Senate rejected a motion by elder Democratic statesman Robert C. BYRD of West Virginia to dismiss the case entirely. The 44–56 vote revealed solid Democratic support and showed that Clinton was unlikely to be removed from office since sixty-seven votes were required for conviction.

The Senate then moved swiftly to wrap up the trial. Rejecting the call for live testimony, the Senate took videotaped depositions from only three witnesses: Lewinsky, Clinton friend and Washington attorney Vernon Jordan, and White House adviser Sidney Blumenthal. Excerpts of the tapes were introduced as evidence during the closing arguments. Lewinsky's long-awaited testimony was ambiguous enough to provide arguing points for both sides.

For three days senators conducted their final deliberations in private. A few moderate Republicans came forward to announce that they would not vote to convict. Republican James M. Jeffords of Vermont said that although Clinton committed shameful acts and "misled the American people.... his actions in this case do not reach the high standard of impeachment."

The Senate acquitted President Clinton on both impeachment articles on February 12, 1999. Article I, accusing the president of perjury, was rejected 45–55, with ten Republicans joining all forty-five Democrats in voting "not guilty." The obstruction of justice article, now called Article II, failed 50–50, with five Republicans joining the forty-five Democrats in voting to acquit.

On the day of his acquittal Clinton appeared in the White House's Rose Garden to issue his most humble apology yet for "what I said and did to trigger these events and the great burden they have imposed on the Congress and on the American people."

The conclusion of the trial left many wondering how the constitutional ordeal had come about. Unlike the 1868 impeachment of Johnson that was tied up with how the nation would conduct the RECONSTRUCTION of the South, or the congressional effort against Nixon in the 1970s that dealt with a grave abuse of executive power, Clinton's scandal involved misconduct in his personal life.

Was Clinton's impeachment the culmination of what had become known as the "politics of destruction"—the intense partisanship and attack politics that had begun in the 1980s? Democrats saw it that way. While readily admitting that the president had committed moral misdeeds, they saw the whole affair as a political witch hunt intent on the acute embarrassment of Clinton. But Republicans blamed it on the president himself, saying it was his character flaws, not politics, that brought this on the nation. They argued that lying under oath, even in a civil lawsuit, and obstruction of justice were serious enough for impeachment and saw the case against Clinton as a test of whether the "rule of law" applied to the president.

Protesters rally at the West Front of the Capitol against the proposed impeachment of President Bill Clinton.
Source: CQ Photo/Douglas Graham

Thus the partisan divisions that had formed early during the House impeachment hearings remained unshakable to the end. Just as unshakable, however, was the opposition of the American people to the impeachment and removal of President Clinton. Public opinion polls repeatedly showed that, while they disapproved of Clinton's behavior, a majority of Americans wanted him to continue in office.

Clinton sought to put the matter behind him as he entered private life. On January 19, 2001, his last full day as president, he agreed to a settlement in which he avoided the possibility of indictment in exchange for acknowledging that he gave false testimony under oath. He also agreed to pay a fine and surrender his law license for five years.

The final report of the independent counsel's office, which was issued in March 2002, found that there was insufficient evidence to show that Clinton and his wife, who by then was a U.S. senator from New York, were involved in criminal wrongdoing in the Whitewater real estate venture. The report—which was issued by prosecutor Robert Ray, who succeeded Starr—said that "some of the statements given by both the president and the first lady during official investigations were factually inaccurate," but there was not enough evidence to show that either of the Clintons engaged in deliberate lying.

More on this topic:

Impeachment Power,
p. 280

Johnson Impeachment
Trial, p. 307

Nixon Impeachment
Effort, p. 396

Cloakrooms

The locker rooms of the House and Senate are the cloakrooms, narrow L-shaped rooms along the sides and rear of the two chambers. Originally designed to hold coats, the hideaways now feature well-worn leather chairs, refrigerators stocked with soda and candy, and televisions. When a series of votes is taking place on the floor, legislators congregate in the cloakrooms, where they are able to relax while remaining only steps from the chamber.

Cloakrooms are Democratic or Republican; each party oversees the cloakroom on its side of the chamber. Employees assigned to the cloakrooms prepare messages several times a day describing floor action and floor schedules. These recorded updates are available by telephone.

In addition to the cloakrooms, both chambers maintain special lounges for women members and the wives of male members. The Senate Ladies' Lounge underwent renovation in 1998. The comparable facility on the House side of the Capitol is the Lindy Claiborne Boggs Congressional Women's Reading Room. Boggs was a Democrat from Louisiana who served in the House from 1973 to 1991.

Closed Rule

A closed rule is a special rule devised by the House Rules Committee that prohibits amendments to a bill that the House will debate and vote on. A closed rule may permit amendments by the committee that reported the legislation. Nearly all major legislation that is brought to the full House is under some type of rule that governs the way the legislation is considered. By contrast, an open rule from the Rules Committee permits members to offer as many floor amendments as members wish, so long as the amendments are germane to the bill and do not violate other House rules. Open rules can lead to lengthy debate and voting on major legislation. But closed rules are controversial because the minority party in the House can charge that the majority—which dictates the terms of any rule—is not allowing them meaningful participation in forming legislation. (See LEGISLATIVE PROCESS, RULES COMMITTEE, HOUSE.)

Cloture   *See* FILIBUSTER.

Commerce Power

The Constitution gives Congress the power to regulate commerce with foreign nations and among the states.

Under its authority to control foreign commerce, Congress authorizes the federal government to regulate international trade, shipping, aviation, and communications. Congress promotes exchange with some countries while imposing tariffs and embargoes to inhibit trade with others. This power is an important aspect of U.S. foreign policy and has never been questioned.

The other part of the commerce power—authority to regulate commerce among the states—has been much more problematic as it evolved from its initial narrow focus to the basis for a vast array of federal laws that govern how Americans behave and do business.

For many years the Supreme Court resisted a broad use of the interstate commerce power, considering it an intrusion on states' rights and private property rights. But in the late 1930s, under pressure from President Franklin D. Roosevelt, the Court relented and the interstate commerce power eventually grew to match the federal government's authority to oversee foreign commerce.

Since the Roosevelt era, Congress has continued to expand the federal government's regulation of interstate commerce. The long list of areas covered includes such issues as farming, banking, labor practices, food and drugs, consumer products, and pollution.

The interstate commerce power seemed to have few legal restraints remaining on its use. But in several decisions since the mid-1990s the Supreme Court has ruled that Congress overstepped its authority under the commerce clause in new laws it had written. These rulings had some observers questioning whether the power was as limitless as was once believed.

Regulation v. Deregulation

The need for specific regulations has been hotly debated in the political arena for some time. In the 1970s and 1980s, Democratic president Jimmy Carter convinced Congress to "deregulate" the transportation industry to increase economic competition. The strict federal rules on rates and fares that had controlled the airlines since 1938 were lifted in 1978. Substantial deregulation of the trucking and railroad industries followed in 1980.

The next president, Republican Ronald Reagan, promised to get the federal government "off the people's backs." One aspect of Reagan's antigovernment agenda was his campaign to curtail the growing number of federal regulations covering areas such as worker safety and the environment—regulations that often drew complaints from businesses.

During Reagan's two terms there was less federal regulatory activity. His successor, Republican president George H. W. Bush, also criticized federal regulations for hampering businesses. Bush outraged environmental and consumer activists by setting up a Council on Competitiveness, headed by Vice President Dan Quayle, to review proposed regulations, specifically for their possible effects on business and economic competitiveness in general.

When the Democrats regained the White House, one of Bill Clinton's first acts as president in 1993 was to disband Bush's Council on Competitiveness. Clinton attempted a middle approach: he advocated easing the regulatory burden on industry with less red tape and costly federal mandates, while at the same time "keeping the regulatory cop on the beat."

The push for deregulation gained greater momentum after the Republican Party took control of Congress in 1995. Although sweeping proposals to change the way federal agencies developed regulations and to make it harder to impose new regulations on business and property owners failed, Republicans scored some notable victories when they scaled back their deregulatory ambitions enough to forge a consensus with the Democrats. Laws enacted, such as an overhaul of the New Deal–era Communications Act and revisions of pesticide and safe drinking water acts, required new approaches to regulation. The legislation called for increased flexibility, more analysis of the costs and benefits of regulations, and more information for consumers. Republicans also used oversight hearings and carefully worded missives to pressure agency bureaucrats to be more restrained in their regulatory activities.

Deregulation forces gained further clout when Republican George W. Bush moved into the White House in 2001. Early in his administration

Commerce: An "Alphabet Soup" of Agencies

Most modern federal regulatory agencies owe their existence to the Constitution's interstate commerce clause. A look at a few specific agencies shows how broadly the clause has been applied to create an array of agencies, from the FTC to the NRC. Most of these agencies are commonly known by the acronyms formed from their names, creating an "alphabet soup" of agencies.

Among the oldest regulatory groups are the Federal Trade Commission (FTC, 1914) and Food and Drug Administration (FDA, 1927). The New Deal era saw a rapid expansion of the federal government and the establishment of many new agencies. Among them were the Securities and Exchange Commission (SEC, 1933), the Federal Deposit Insurance Corporation (FDIC, 1933), the Federal Communications Commission (FCC, 1934), and the National Labor Relations Board (NLRB, 1938).

Still operating under its commerce power and the duty to protect the general welfare, Congress has since added other agencies. These include the Occupational Safety and Health Administration (OSHA, 1970), the Environmental Protection Agency (EPA, 1970), and the Consumer Product Safety Commission (CPSC, 1972).

Sometimes Congress abolishes an agency, but it almost always creates a new one in its place. For example, in 1974 Congress abolished the Atomic Energy Commission (AEC, 1946) and authorized the Nuclear Regulatory Commission (NRC) to assume its regulatory functions. The nation's oldest independent regulatory agency, the Interstate Commerce Commission (ICC, 1887), was disbanded in 1995, but many tasks still deemed necessary were transferred to a new board within the Transportation Department.

President Bush signaled his intention to reverse or revise certain Clinton-era regulations. One of the first bills he signed into law was a congressional resolution repealing a Clinton ergonomics rule opposed by many major business groups as too costly to implement. Environmentalists and consumer activists were fearful that the alliance of industry officials, the White House, and GOP committee chairs would leave them out of the rule-making equation.

Origins

The Articles of Confederation, adopted in 1777, set up a weak Congress that had little power over the states. The result was conflict and disorder, as the states printed their own money, taxed the goods of other states, and disagreed over how the economy should function. To rectify that situation, the framers of the new Constitution wrote a broad "commerce clause" giving Congress the power to "regulate Commerce with foreign Nations, and among the several States, and with the Indian Tribes."

The framers of the Constitution left it to the courts to decide just how broad the commerce clause should be. The Supreme Court first defined congressional power to regulate interstate commerce in the landmark case of *Gibbons v. Ogden* (1824). The case involved a dispute over steamboat navigation rights. On behalf of the Court, Chief Justice John Marshall emphatically asserted the supremacy of federal control over commerce with foreign countries and between the states. More than a century passed, however, before the Court gave full approval to Marshall's expansive interpretation.

Congress too moved only gradually toward a broad application of the commerce clause. In the first part of the nineteenth century, as new frontiers opened up, Henry CLAY envisioned a strong federal role in the development of roads and canals, which he called an "American System." Although Clay won support for this plan in Congress, President James MADISON vetoed the legislation in 1817. Madison's successor, James Monroe, similarly argued that authority over interstate commerce was limited and did not give Congress the power to establish roads and canals.

Within Congress the federal role was hotly debated. Southerners anxious to maintain slavery argued against broad federal power and in favor of states' rights. The opposition was led by John RANDOLPH, an acerbic Virginia representative who opposed Clay's American System. "If the Congress can do that," he argued, "it can emancipate the slaves."

Congress tried to get around the controversy by purchasing stock in private companies that were building roads and canals and by giving land grants to states. But even that approach was unacceptable to President Andrew Jackson, who in 1830 vetoed the purchase of stock in the Maysville Road, a Kentucky turnpike. He argued that the road was local, not national. Congress was forced to draw back from road building, and the coalition behind the American System fell apart.

Jackson's 1830 veto came just as the nation's railroads were being built. That same year the Baltimore & Ohio Railroad opened. The nation's transportation, and the focus of interstate commerce, shifted from canals and turnpikes to rails. Congress did not become actively involved in highway building again until 1916.

Regulation Begins

Railroad expansion led Congress to assume new power under the commerce clause. At first the legislators simply promoted the transportation system, giving generous land grants and government credit to the railroad companies.

A network of tracks eventually crisscrossed the nation, but not without controversy. Railroad rate structures favored certain companies and regions over others, and rebates and price fixing were common. Farmers protested loudly, arguing that these practices put them at an economic disadvantage. The states tried to regulate the railroads, with only limited success.

In 1886 the Supreme Court severely limited the states' regulatory authority. The Court said states could not regulate an enterprise engaged in interstate commerce, even if it passed through the states, because interstate matters were a federal concern. Since most railroad companies by then operated in more than one state, this decision ended most state regulation of the railroads.

Congress responded to the need for federal oversight of the railroads by passing the Interstate Commerce Act of 1887. With the new law, Congress began a decades-long expansion of federal regulation of interstate commerce. The Interstate Commerce Commission (ICC), established to carry out the regulation, was the prototype for later regulatory commissions. The ICC was weak, however, and the Supreme Court within a decade weakened it further.

Under the commerce clause, Congress became actively involved in regulating railroad expansion.
Source: Library of Congress

Congress found the Court equally reluctant to allow congressional regulation of huge corporations. The anger against the railroads among farmers, consumers, and small-business owners in the late 1800s was matched by their outrage at the growing power of the trusts that controlled industries such as steel, oil, sugar, and meat packing. The trusts thwarted competition by combining smaller companies into huge corporations and by controlling manufacturing and distribution as well as production of raw materials.

In an attempt to break up the trusts and to "protect commerce against unlawful restraints and monopolies," Congress passed the Sherman Antitrust Act of 1890. But within five years the Supreme Court narrowly limited application of the antitrust law, again reflecting the justices' conservative outlook. Congress did not fully address antitrust law again until 1914, when it passed both the Clayton Act and the Federal Trade Commission Act. That same year the Supreme Court upheld the ICC's authority to set railroad rates. The commerce power had finally become a useful, if controversial, tool for Congress.

As it endorsed an expansion of federal authority over railroads and corporations, Congress also began to experiment with broader federal "police power," to protect public health, safety, and even morals. This responsibility traditionally had been left to the states. Here again, the commerce power was the means for expanding congressional authority.

At first Congress focused on the railroads. It required that safety devices be installed on all railroad cars used in interstate commerce to protect workers from smashing their hands while coupling the cars. Another safety measure limited the number of hours that railroad employees could work at a stretch.

Congress did not stop with railroads. In 1895, concerned about the spread of gambling, Congress used its police power to outlaw the transport of lottery tickets across state lines. That expansion of federal police power ended up before the Supreme Court, as had so many other acts based on the commerce clause. In 1903 the Court agreed with Congress that lottery tickets were commerce, thus upholding the federal government's power to regulate transport of the tickets.

The "Stream of Commerce"

Gradually, the Supreme Court accepted a broader view of the commerce clause. The landmark decision in *Swift & Co. v. United States* (1905) introduced the term *stream of commerce*. Justice Oliver Wendell Holmes Jr. wrote that Congress had authority over the production, marketing, or purchase of a product even if this took place entirely within one state, because it was part of the overall stream of commerce.

After that decision, Congress moved into new areas, enacting laws that prohibited the interstate transportation of explosives, diseased livestock, insect pests, falsely stamped gold and silver articles, narcotics, and prostitutes.

An important new realm, protection of the consumer's health and safety, was opened to federal control in 1906. In that year Congress passed the Pure Food and Drug Act, which banned all harmful substances from food and provided penalties for false labeling. Congress went on to require inspection of red meat being shipped across state lines and, in 1910, to authorize federal action against misbranded or dangerous poisons, such as insecticides. In 1914 deceptive advertising came under the federal regulatory umbrella. In each case, Congress depended on the commerce clause.

The new and broader interpretation of the commerce power took Congress back into highway building, an area it had largely avoided since the Maysville Road veto of 1830. The 1916 Federal Road Aid Act provided federal money to states to help build highways. After passing that law, Congress steadily expanded its financial commitment, eventually paying for 90 percent of the nationwide interstate highway system.

New Deal Expansion

The commerce power had never been extended so broadly or rapidly as it was by President Franklin D. Roosevelt. The nation's economy was in a shambles when he took office in 1933. Roosevelt promptly launched a bold attack on the Great Depression. Spurred by the president, Congress invoked its commerce power and other authority to undergird his NEW DEAL programs.

Roosevelt's efforts were hampered by the Supreme Court. By mid-1936 the Court had found eight of ten New Deal laws unconstitutional. "We have been relegated to the horse-and-buggy definition of interstate commerce," Roosevelt complained. His running battle with the Court eventually ended with victory for the president. From 1937 on, the Court consented to an unprecedented expansion of federal authority. The first step was its ruling in favor of the 1935 National Labor Relations Act, which gave workers the right under federal law to organize and bargain collectively. The Court had made a major shift since its earlier ruling that unions violated antitrust laws.

Civil Rights

The commerce clause played a special role in congressional battles over civil rights legislation in the 1960s. The Fourteenth Amendment had been added to the Constitution after the Civil War to clarify individual rights, but its scope was limited. Supreme Court decisions had restricted its application to actions carried out by states, and not to those by individuals and private organizations.

To close that gap Congress turned to the commerce clause. The Supreme Court had already used the clause to restrict segregation. In 1946, for example, the Court upheld a black woman's refusal to give up her bus seat to a white. Such rules burdened interstate commerce, the Court ruled.

President John F. KENNEDY used the commerce clause as the basis for his 1963 legislation to end discrimination in restaurants, hotels, and other public accommodations. It seemed the best legal route for requiring those outside of government to end racial discrimination. Use of the commerce clause was also a way to outwit southern opponents of the proposed civil rights law in Congress. Because of its wording, Kennedy's bill was sent to the Senate Commerce Committee; it thus bypassed the chair of the Judiciary Committee, a southerner who had buried many civil rights bills. The Commerce Committee acted quickly on the measure, and its members served as key supporters on the floor. After various compromises, Congress passed the sweeping Civil Rights Act of 1964.

The Constitution's commerce clause played an important role in congressional battles over civil rights legislation in the 1960s. A landmark 1964 civil rights law was rooted in the interstate commerce clause.
Source: Library of Congress

Challenges to the law were quickly filed, but Supreme Court decisions upheld its application even to local enterprises. The classic case involved a Birmingham, Alabama, restaurant that claimed not to be covered by the law because its clientele was strictly local. The federal government successfully argued that 46 percent of the food served had been supplied through interstate commerce, and the restaurant's refusal to serve blacks was declared illegal.

New Limits

After the civil rights decisions of the 1960s, federal authority under the commerce clause appeared to be nearly limitless.

However, the Supreme Court issued a surprising ruling in 1995 in which it narrowed the definition of what activity constituted commerce. Striking down a law that prohibited people from carrying guns near local schools, the Court—with a one-vote majority—declined to defer as much to Congress as it had in the past, saying that federal lawmakers had overstepped their authority to intervene in local affairs.

What the 1995 opinion meant in the long term for Congress's exercise of its commerce power was the subject of much debate. Some observers downplayed its significance, while others viewed it as the beginning of a new era.

The debate was renewed in 2000 when the Supreme Court again drew sharp limits around Congress's use of the commerce power. By another 5–4 ruling, the Court held that Congress had exceeded its authority in a section of a 1994 law that allowed women who were victims of gender-motivated violence, such as rape, to sue their attackers in federal court. In writing the law, Congress had relied on its authority to regulate interstate commerce and its Fourteenth Amendment power to provide equal protection under the law. The Court rejected both grounds.

Regarding the commerce power, the Court held in the 2000 case that Congress did not have the power to regulate noneconomic activity. Quoting from the 1995 decision, Chief Justice William H.

Rehnquist wrote that "simply because Congress may conclude that a particular activity substantially affects interstate commerce does not necessarily make it so."

But the dissenting opinion in the 2000 case argued that Congress had provided more than enough testimony and evidence, over four years of hearings, to justify finding an economic interstate interest in combating violence against women. Justice David H. Souter closed his dissent with a shot at the majority opinion: "All of this convinces me that today's ebb of the commerce power rests on error, and at the same time leads me to doubt that the majority's view will prove to be enduring law."

The Rehnquist Court's enthusiasm for state sovereignty was intended to reassert the role of state governments in the federal system. But the justices did not aggressively pursue that line of thinking through mid-2007. Instead, in two decisions in 2005 the Court invalidated state laws that interfered with the power of Congress to regulate interstate commerce. In one the Court struck down, by a 6–3 ruling, a California medical marijuana statute that legalized use of the drug for treating chronic pain when under prescription from a physician. The Court said the state's action, even though aimed only at intrastate activity, nonetheless interfered with Congress's ability to regulate the national illicit trade in the drug. In another case, the Court overturned Michigan and New York laws that discriminated between in-state and out-of-state wineries by prohibiting shipments directly to consumer from the out-of-state businesses. The Court's decision, by a 5–4 vote, rested on the grounds that the differential treatment between in- and out-of-state producers violated interstate commerce power.

Commerce, Science, and Transportation Committee, Senate

The Senate Commerce, Science, and Transportation Committee has jurisdiction over all forms of transportation, from ships to jets. It also handles legislation dealing with global climate change, communications, consumer protection, interstate commerce, ocean policy, science, technology, and space. The array of issues it handles placed it at the center of many of the most important and contentious issues of the twenty-first century.

In recent decades the committee played a central role in the deregulation of the transportation industry and overhaul of the telecommunications industry, but those actions remained controversial and were by no means settled by earlier legislative activity.

The committee spent most of the late 1970s and 1980s deregulating the airlines and the trucking industry—and then reexamining what it had done. Faith in the magic of the free market was shaken by complaints about bad service and by mergers and bankruptcies. The committee never considered undoing its work, but its members did discuss tinkering with the remains of the regulatory structure in order to regain some federal control.

In the early 1990s the committee shifted its focus to the complex and controversial task of revising regulation of the telephone, broadcast, and print industries to keep up with technological advances. The committee played a key role in passing a law in 1996 to overhaul the telecommunications industry, a law that was designed to spur competition in the burgeoning industry. It was later criticized for partially deregulating the telecommunications business while not ensuring that more competition resulted in lower prices for consumers.

At the start of the 110th Congress, in early 2007, the committee had twenty-three members, twelve Democrats and eleven Republicans.

⊙ **CLOSER LOOK**

The sweeping jurisdiction of the Senate Commerce, Science, and Transportation Committee—including transportation, global climate change, communications, consumer protection, science and technology, and more—places it at the center of many of the most important and contentious issues of the day.

History

The Commerce Committee, set up in 1816, was among the first committees created in the Senate. Its name was changed in 1961 from the Interstate and Foreign Commerce Committee to Commerce Committee. In 1977 it became the Commerce, Science, and Transportation Committee.

For more than two decades, from 1955 to 1977, the Commerce Committee was chaired by Warren G. Magnuson, a Washington Democrat who was the most senior member of the Senate when he lost his seat to a Republican in 1981. A close friend of Lyndon B. Johnson, Magnuson in the 1960s worked to implement the president's policies on consumer issues. He fought for automobile safety standards and tougher safety requirements for other consumer products. He led an unsuccessful campaign to introduce federal no-fault automobile insurance.

Nevada Democrat Howard W. Cannon served as chair from 1978 to 1981, a period of difficult negotiations between the House and Senate over deregulation of the transportation industry. Cannon quickly became known as a tough negotiator in conference who always carried enough proxies in his pocket to back up his position. Cannon lost the 1980 election to one of the Republicans who tipped control of the Senate to the Republican Party.

Republican Bob Packwood of Oregon, who chaired the committee from 1981 to 1985, tried to continue the wave of deregulation, focusing on loosening federal controls on the broadcasting industry. But his efforts failed. For the next two years, John C. Danforth, a Missouri Republican, served as chair. Skeptical of complete deregulation, he favored national licensing standards for truck and bus drivers.

When Democrats regained control of the Senate in 1987, Ernest F. Hollings, an imposing and sometimes caustic South Carolina Democrat, became chair. Under Hollings's leadership, the committee plunged into the controversial area of communications regulation. The committee achieved some success in 1992 when Congress reinstated price regulation of cable television rates. A major overhaul of the nation's antiquated telecommunications laws was slow in coming, however.

In 1995 South Dakota Republican Larry Pressler became committee chair. Pressler modified the early work on the telecommunications overhaul begun by Hollings. The massive Telecommunications Act, which ushered in a new era of competition in telephone, video, and data services, was signed into law in 1996. After Pressler was defeated for reelection, Republican John McCain of Arizona assumed the chair in 1997. McCain failed in his 1998 bid to enact legislation that would implement a major $368.5 billion settlement between tobacco companies and state attorneys general. However, before his unsuccessful run for the presidency in 2000, McCain oversaw enactment of a number of laws affecting telecommunications and transportation.

The committee later came under the leadership of Ted Stevens, a strong-willed and temperamental Alaska Republican. The ranking Democrat was Daniel K. Inouye of Hawaii. The two had many similar priorities and worked well together for many years on Commerce as well as on the Senate Appropriations Committee. The two regularly referred to each other as "co-chairmen." Inouye and Stevens switched positions in 2007 after Democrats retook control of both houses in the 2006 elections.

In the 110th Congress that began with Inouye in the chair, the committee was faced with complex and deeply controversial issues, of which major telecommunications legislation was at the top of the agenda. The committee's 1996 far-reaching telecommunications legislation was by 2007 being overtaken by real-world developments as new ways of communicating, transmitting information and entertainment, and offering varied services to consumers emerged. One key priority was to stabilize a fund that subsidizes local telephone service in rural and low-income areas through a surcharge on long-distance bills. Its revenue source was shrinking in the face of expanding e-mail, cell phones, and Internet calling plans. Other issues included rules for dealing with municipalities that wanted to negotiate contracts with companies, including the traditional Bell telephone firms, that were going into video delivery to replace their diminishing telephone business.

One central issue that the committee faced was reconciling the positions of Democrats on the panel, who generally favored governmental intervention in commerce issues, and free-market Republicans, who saw a limited role for government regulation and sought to cut back existing federal programs.

Committee Action   *See* LEGISLATIVE PROCESS.

Committee of the Whole

The House of Representatives considers almost all important bills within a parliamentary framework known as the Committee of the Whole. This is one of the most important stages in the LEGISLATIVE PROCESS and comes after the House legislative committees have studied and drafted the bills. The Committee of the Whole is not a committee as the word is usually understood; it is the House meeting under another name for the purpose of speeding action on legislation.

The committee is formally known as the Committee of the Whole House on the State of the Union and includes all 435 members of the House. The Democratic majority approved a rules change in 1993 allowing the five DELEGATES to Congress to participate also, as long as their votes did not determine the outcome of an issue. Their participation was short-lived when the rule was rescinded after Republicans took control of the House in 1995, but it was reinstated by Democrats when they took back control in 2007. Also in early 2007 the House approved legislation to allow the District of Columbia delegate to vote in all cases, not just when the vote did not matter. However, questions about the constitutionality of the measure, plus opposition from the Bush administration, left in doubt if the change would ever take effect.

Meeting on the floor of the House chamber and using special parliamentary rules, the Committee of the Whole debates and amends legislation. It cannot pass a bill. Instead, it reports the measure to the full House with whatever changes it has approved. Amendments adopted in the Committee of the Whole are then put to a second vote in the full House of Representatives. Usually this is a pro forma voice vote with all amendments considered en bloc, but separate recorded votes may be requested on closely contested amendments. The full House then may pass or reject the bill—or, on occasion, return it to the legislative committee where it originated.

Far fewer members must be on the House floor to conduct business in the Committee of the Whole than in a regular House session. This may be an advantage when busy representatives cannot be rounded up to attend a floor meeting. A quorum for doing business in the Committee of the Whole is only 100 members, in contrast to 218 in the full House. The Speaker does not preside but selects another member of the majority party to take the chair. AMENDMENTS are considered under the five-minute rule, which in theory, but not in practice, limits debate to five minutes for those who favor the amendment and five minutes for those opposed.

Until 1971 there was no record of how individual members voted on matters considered by the Committee of the Whole. That was an attraction for representatives who wanted to avoid publicity on politically difficult issues. But under rules in force today, a recorded vote must be ordered in the Committee of the Whole if twenty-five members (one-fourth of a quorum) demand it. An electronic voting system is used, and each member's vote is displayed beside his or her name on panels above the Speaker's desk. The vote is also published in the *CONGRESSIONAL RECORD*. (See VOTING IN CONGRESS.)

The Committee of the Whole has no counterpart in the Senate. The concept originated in the British House of Commons, where it was used during periods of strained relations with the king to evade the normal restrictions of a formal House of Commons session.

Committee on Committees *See* LEADERSHIP.

Committee System

Committees are Congress's workshops. The panels and their chairmen and—increasingly by the 110th Congress (2007–2009)—chairwomen have been described as gatekeepers to the House and Senate floor. Although more true of the House than the Senate, where committees are more easily circumvented, panels in both chambers form the infrastructure for Congress.

CONGRESSIONAL COMMITTEES, 110TH CONGRESS

These committees were in existence at the beginning of the 110th Congress in 2007. The table shows the committees' size and the partisan division.

House		Banking, Housing and Urban Affairs	21 (D 11; R 10)
Agriculture	46 (D 25; R 21)	Budget	23 (D 12; R 11)
Appropriations	66 (D 37; R 29)	Commerce, Science, and Transportation	23 (D 12; R 11)
Armed Services	62 (D 34; R 28)	Energy and Natural Resources	23 (D 12; R 11)
Budget	39 (D 22; R 17)	Environment and Public Works	19 (D 10; R 9)
Education and Labor	49 (D 27; R 22)	Finance	21 (D 11; R 10)
Energy and Commerce	57 (D 31; R 26)	Foreign Relations	21 (D 11; R 10)
Financial Services	70 (D 37; R 33)	Health, Education, Labor	
Foreign Affairs	50 (D 27; R 23)	and Pensions	21 (D 11; R 10)
Homeland Security	34 (D 19; R 15)	Homeland Security and	
House Administration	9 (D 6; R 3)	Governmental Affairs	17 (D 9; R 8)
Judiciary	40 (D 23; R 17)	Indian Affairs	15 (D 8; R 7)
Natural Resources	49 (D 27; R 22)	Judiciary	19 (D 10; R 9)
Oversight and Government Reform	41 (D 23; R 18)	Rules and Administration	19 (D 10; R 9)
Rules	13 (D 9; R 4)	Small Business and Entrepreneurship	19 (D 10; R 9)
Science and Technology	44 (D 24; R 20)	Veterans' Affairs	15 (D 8; R 7)
Small Business	33 (D 18; R 15)		
Standards of Official Conduct	10 (D 5; R 5)	*Senate Select and Special*	
Transportation and Infrastructure	75 (D 41; R 34)	Aging	21 (D 11; R 10)
Veterans' Affairs	29 (D 16; R 13)	Ethics	6 (D 3; R 3)
Ways and Means	41 (D 24; R 17)	Intelligence	15 (D 8; R 7)
House Select		*Joint Committees*	
Energy Independence and		Joint Economic	Senate 10 (D 6; R 4);
Global Warming	15 (D 9; R 6)		House 10 (D 6; R 4)
Intelligence	21 (D 12; R 9)	Joint Library	Senate 5 (D 3; R 2);
			House 5 (D 3; R 2)
Senate		Joint Printing	Senate 5 (D 3; R 2);
Agriculture, Nutrition, and Forestry	21 (D 11; R 10)		House 5 (D 3; R 2)
Appropriations	29 (D 15; R 14)	Joint Taxation	Senate 5 (D 3; R 2);
Armed Services	25 (D 13; R 12)		House 5 (D 3; R 2)

Committees: Big and Small

The 110th Congress starting in 2007 had more than 200 committees: twenty standing (so called because they are part of the formal rules of the chamber) and two select panels in the House; twenty in the Senate (including two select and one special panel). Their size ranged from seventy-five members to just nine. The two chambers in total had more than 175 subcommittees with some still being formed.

There are several types of committees:

- Standing committees have the power to prepare and approve legislation.
- Subcommittees are units of standing committees that handle a defined area of the full panel's jurisdiction.
- Select or special committees usually are created to study specific issues and may or may not be essentially the same as standing committees.
- Joint committees have equal numbers of Senate and House members and continuing bodies with special responsibilities such as economics and employment. There were four of them in the 110th Congress.
- Conference committees are special temporary joint committees formed to resolve differences between the Senate and House versions of a specific piece of legislation.

Committees have long been the object of criticism and many efforts to alter the powers and restrain the authority of their chairs. As the twenty-first century begins, committees possessed less clout than they once did. Nevertheless, they remain at the heart of congressional operations. The committee system of the new century has remained largely intact since the early 1920s and is—along with political parties—a central structural feature of Congress. The vast majority of members find committees essential to their careers. Both tradition and rule make it difficult to consider legislation that has not been vetted in committee.

Almost every piece of LEGISLATION introduced in the Senate or House of Representatives initially is sent to a committee for review and recommendations. Committees do not have to wait for bills to be referred to them; they often write their own bills from scratch.

Specialized subcommittees usually consider the legislation first, frequently making substantial changes before sending the bill to the full committee for action. A committee or subcommittee often holds hearings at which those who favor and those who oppose a measure have an opportunity to express their views. The committee may decide to approve the bill, with or without changes, and "report" it to the parent chamber, or it may decide to kill the measure altogether. It is difficult for a bill to reach the floor, especially in the House, without first winning committee approval, although there are exceptions. An example occurred in early 2007 when House Democratic leaders, newly empowered from the 2006 elections as a majority after twelve years in the minority, brought a number of bills to the floor directly to fulfill their campaign promises of action on a range of items during their first 100 hours of legislating. Similarly, Republicans on taking control in 1995 for the first time in forty years quickly pushed through elements of the party's "Contract with America," which had been a key part of their successful 1994 election campaign.

That type of event, however, is the exception. Normally, committees do the detailed work of crafting legislation and then also manage the debate once the measure has arrived on the floor. Later, after both the Senate and House have passed the bill, committee members from both chambers work out any differences and put the measure into final form.

In addition to their legislative role, committees conduct investigations that highlight national problems or disclose official wrongdoing. Investigations are one aspect of committee responsibility for congressional oversight of government programs and agencies. That power largely went unused between 2001 and 2007 when Republicans controlled both Congress and the White House. Democrats in 2007, back in control of both chambers, aggressively resurrected it to probe what they said were the many shortcomings of the administration of President George W. Bush. Although only four new oversight panels were created by Democrats as the 110th Congress got underway, the number of oversight hearings—by one count—more than doubled compared to the beginning of the previous Congress (under GOP control) two years earlier.

The prestige of individual committees rises and falls as national issues change. Democrats in 2007 made committee changes to emphasize the party's interest in environmental, energy independence, and global warming issues. One new select committee on the subject was created, and a number of committees either added new subcommittees or changed the names of existing panels to include the words energy, national resources, and environmental protection. The House Agriculture Committee even added a subcommittee on organic agriculture.

Still, some panels remain at the center of power. That inner circle includes House Ways and Means and Senate Finance, which are responsible for tax legislation, and House and Senate Appropriations, which have jurisdiction over federal spending. At one time one of the most influential committees in either chamber was the House Rules Committee, which controls access to the House floor for all major bills and sets the terms of floor debate. This power remains crucial to the party in the majority, but the committee's historically exalted status was largely gone by the end of the twentieth century because the leadership in both parties made it a panel fully under their control. In the decades after World War II, it was all but an autonomous fiefdom that could block legislation favored by a party's majority, but that power was gradually taken away starting with reforms in the 1970s.

Members of the House Committee on Appropriations and the Appropriations Subcommittee on the Legislative Branch discuss the proposed 2008 appropriations for the legislative branch. Subcommittee chair Debbie Wasserman-Schultz, D-Fla., is middle right, full committee chair David R. Obey, D-Wis., is at far left. Rep. Barbara Lee, D-Calif., and ranking member Zack Wamp, R-Tenn., look on.
Source: CQ Photo/Scott J. Ferrell

Many congressional committees, such as Rules, have changed dramatically in recent decades. The reforms of the 1970s significantly altered the committee system. Subcommittees took over much of the work once performed by full committees, and junior members began to share the power previously exercised by authoritarian committee chairs. Seniority was no longer the only factor in determining who would head committees. Committee STAFF expanded rapidly, so much so that some observers complained that committee aides had undue influence on legislative policy.

In time the empowerment of subcommittees led to a decentralization of power and heavier legislative workloads for members of both houses. Critics noted a slowing down of the legislative process and blamed subcommittees, in part, for the inability of Congress to act coherently on major issues. So great had been the proliferation of subcommittees that limits on their numbers were set in both chambers. Other changes were made as well. (See box, Brief History of Committee Reform, p. 116.)

Types of Committees

There are several types of congressional committees, each with its own purpose. Below the committee level are numerous subcommittees. In the 110th Congress there were more than 200 committees and subcommittees.

Standing Committees

Standing committees handle most of the legislation considered by Congress. In 2007 there were twenty-two committees in the House and twenty in the Senate. Standing committees, embodied in the standing rules of the chambers, are permanent bodies with responsibility for broad areas of legislation, such as agriculture, the environment, health, and foreign affairs. The standing committees are organized on roughly parallel lines in each chamber and generally follow the major organizational divisions of the executive branch.

Many standing committees have existed for decades, some dating back to the earliest days of Congress. The House Ways and Means Committee dates to 1802, and the Senate Foreign Relations, Finance, and Judiciary committees to 1816. The 1946 Legislative Reorganization Act substantially consolidated the standing committee structure in both houses. Further modifications occurred in the House in 1974 and 1995 and in the Senate in 1977.

The number of members varies from committee to committee. In the 110th Congress, for example, House standing committees ranged in size from seventy-five, Transportation and Infrastructure, the largest in Congress, to nine on House Administration; Senate standing committees ranged from twenty-nine on Appropriations to fifteen on both Indian Affairs and Veterans' Affairs.

Although the rules of both the Senate and House are silent on the question of party ratios on committees, the majority party in each chamber makes sure that it maintains a majority in each committee as well. In the Senate, committee membership is generally in proportion to the overall party breakdown in the chamber. The House, on the other hand, has been less inclined to do this. On some key committees—such as House Appropriations, Rules, and Ways and Means—the majority party often gives itself an extra edge so it can maintain strong control.

Subcommittees

Most standing committees have subcommittees, which provide the ultimate division of labor within the committee system. They help Congress handle its huge workload, and they permit members to develop specialized knowledge in a particular field. But they are often criticized for fragmenting responsibility and increasing the difficulty of policy review, while adding substantially to the cost of congressional operations.

Subcommittees are often less important in the Senate than in the House. Senate committees frequently take up bills without formal subcommittee action (except on Appropriations); House committees do this far less often. As in the full committees, membership is weighted toward the majority party in the parent body.

Subcommittees vary in importance from committee to committee. Some, such as the twelve subcommittees apiece of the House and Senate Appropriations committees, have great authority; much of their work is routinely endorsed by the full Appropriations committees without further review.

After the number of subcommittees skyrocketed in the wake of the 1970s reforms, both chambers took steps to reverse the trend. The House approved several reductions in the number of subcommittees most committees were allowed and also limited members' subcommittee assignments. Committees in the early years of the twenty-first century were mostly limited to five subcommittees, except for the Appropriations Committee.

Select Committees

Both chambers from time to time create select or special committees to study special problems or concerns, such as aging, hunger, or narcotics abuse, or to investigate scandals, such as the WATER-GATE SCANDAL or the IRAN-CONTRA AFFAIR.

These committees may make recommendations, but they usually are not permitted to report legislation. In most cases they remain in existence for only a few years.

There are exceptions. The Select Intelligence committees in both chambers do consider and report legislation. Indeed, they are standing committees in everything but name. Because their subject matter is narrower than that of most standing committees, the Intelligence panels were designated as select rather than standing committees. (See INTELLIGENCE COMMITTEES, HOUSE AND SENATE SELECT.)

In 2002 the House created a Select Committee on Homeland Security to write the final draft of comprehensive legislation establishing a Department of Homeland Security. The panel went out of existence when the measure was signed into law later that year. However, the committee was reconstituted at the beginning of the 108th Congress in 2003. In the 110th Congress starting in 2007 it was a separate House standing committee. In the Senate the existing Government Affairs Committee was renamed Homeland Security and Government Affairs. (See HOMELAND SECURITY COMMITTEE, HOUSE.)

Joint Committees

Joint committees are usually permanent panels composed of members drawn from both the Senate and House; their composition reflects the party ratios in each chamber. Chairmanships generally rotate from one chamber to the other every two years, at the beginning of each new Congress.

Of the four joint committees in existence in the 110th Congress, none had the authority to report legislation. The Joint Economic Committee studies economic problems and reviews fiscal and budgetary programs. The Joint Committee on Taxation performs staff work for the House Ways and Means and Senate Finance committees. Having long enjoyed a nonpartisan reputation, the taxation panel was used by the new Republican majority that took control of Congress in 1995 to develop its agenda for enacting major tax cuts. (See ECONOMIC COMMITTEE, JOINT; TAXATION COMMITTEE, JOINT.)

The two remaining joint committees—those on printing and the library—deal with administrative matters, including the GOVERNMENT PRINTING OFFICE and the LIBRARY OF CONGRESS, respectively. (See LIBRARY COMMITTEE, JOINT; PRINTING COMMITTEE, JOINT.)

Conference Committees

CONFERENCE COMMITTEES, a special kind of joint committee, are temporary bodies that have important powers. Their job is to settle differences between bills that have passed the House and Senate. They go out of business when the job is done.

Development

The congressional committee system had its roots in the British Parliament and the colonial legislatures. In the earliest days of Congress, legislative proposals were considered first on the Senate or House floor, after which a temporary committee was appointed to work out the details. The committee then reported its bill to the full chamber for further debate, amendment, and passage. Once the committee had reported, it was dissolved.

Gradually the temporary panels were replaced by permanent committees, and legislation came to be referred directly to the committees without prior consideration by the full Senate or House.

By the end of the nineteenth century these small groups had developed such great power that Congress was said to have abdicated its lawmaking function to its committees. Although committees were created by and responsible to their parent bodies, they functioned with almost total independence. The panels tended to be dominated by their chairs, whose power resulted from the rigid operation of the SENIORITY SYSTEM. Under that system the member of the majority party with the longest continuous service on a committee automatically became its chair. The formal title of a person who heads a committee is "chairman."

More on this topic:
Appropriations Committees, pp. 23, 26
Finance Committee, Senate, p. 218
Investigations, p. 292
Legislative Process, p. 344
Oversight Power, p. 404
Reform, Congressional, p. 470
Rules Committee, House, p. 478
Seniority System, p. 505
Ways and Means Committee, House, p. 603

A Brief History of Committee Reform

Congressional committees, the infrastructure where the bulk of legislative work is done, have evolved significantly in the years since 1946 when Congress undertook sweeping reorganization of its structure and operations. The most important committee changes took place in the House, but the Senate too has evolved. Committees changed from isolated principalities under the iron grip of the most senior members, largely hidden from public view, to open and accountable forums and—especially in the House—mostly under the control of party leadership. Many House reforms came about in the 1970s under pressure from frustrated younger Democrats and in the mid-1990s when Republicans took control of the chamber after forty years in the minority. Here is a summary of important mileposts on the reform road.

Congress

1946 Legislative Reorganization Act passed. Many minor committees were eliminated and functions and jurisdictions of all committees revamped and spelled out in detail. No major changes followed for nearly three decades, while additional committees were created and subcommittees proliferated. The norm of seniority hardened, allowing the committee chair to run a panel as a personal fiefdom. Many of these chairs—heavily from the South or big city urban machines—became increasingly unrepresentative of the parties as younger members were elected and often were unsympathetic to their party's program. The stage was set for major reform.

1965 Joint Committee on the Organization of Congress. This committee, headed by Sen. A.S. Mike Monroney, D-Okla., and Rep. Ray J. Madden, D-Ind., recommended wide-ranging reforms in 1966. Although not immediately embraced, the proposals kept the subject of reform on the public agenda.

1970 Legislative Reorganization Act. Drawn on Monroney-Madden recommendations, the law encouraged open committee proceedings, written rules, public disclosure of roll-call votes, radio and television coverage of hearings, and safeguards for minority party members on a committee. The most important change required recorded House teller votes, ending the practice of members being able to avoid going on record on important issues. No seniority system changes were made, but that was considered a turning point in the 1970s reform efforts that followed.

House

Unlike the 1970 Legislative Reorganization Act, which affected both chambers, the most far-reaching changes in the 1970s occurred in the House where the principal focus was on breaking the power of committee chairs. Moreover, the next step in reform became an exercise of the party caucuses and rules rather than a function of the full House, at least until 1995 when Republicans wrote many of the changes into the rules of the chamber.

1961 House Rules Committee. Major reforms in the 1970s were foreshadowed when Speaker Sam Rayburn allied himself with the incoming John F. Kennedy administration to break the absolute power of conservatives that controlled the panel, allowing them to thwart any bills they did not like, particularly those on civil rights. Rayburn enlarged the committee, allowing him to name allies of his choosing.

1969–1970 Speaker Challenged, Caucus Revived. Rep. John W. McCormack, D-Mass., an ally of the dominant committee chairs, was challenged for reelection as Speaker. Although McCormack won, the challenge signaled a new era dawning in the House, and he retired in 1970. At the same time regular meetings of the Democratic Caucus, the organization of all House Democrats, were revived in 1969. This gave moderate and liberal Democrats a vehicle to change House procedures.

1970–1975 Committee Changes. In a succession of changes during this period the Democratic Caucus ended the era of autocratic committee chairs. The most important change, fully realized by 1975, provided for a secret-ballot election of top Democrats on committees. In 1974 nominations for chairs were taken from the Ways and Means Committee, where it had long resided, and given to the party's Steering and Policy Committee, a leadership entity. (House Republicans, still then in a minority, also agreed in 1971 that the ranking GOP member on a committee would be selected by vote of the Republican conference, the organization of all House Republicans.) The Democratic Caucus in 1973 adopted a subcommittee "bill of rights," which allowed subcommittees to select their chairs, establish jurisdictions, write their rules, and to control many of their functions. In 1975 further reforms enlarged and strengthened committees' professional staffs and assured the minority of some access to staff funding. In addition, committees were ordered to have subcommittees (a few of the most powerful did not) and strengthened the authority of the Speaker in referring bills to committees. Proxy voting in committee was briefly banned but reintroduced until Republicans banned the practice for good in 1995. In addition, the previous ability of a senior member to claim multiple subcommittee positions was restricted to allow junior members more access to valuable posts.

1994   Republicans Take Control. After forty years out of power, the GOP captured House control in the 1994 elections. The new majority quickly enacted changes to the House rules—not just party rules—that firmly cemented the reforms from earlier years. Among the changes to the rules were limiting committee chairs to six years, limiting nearly all committees to five subcommittees, prohibiting proxy voting in committee, enhancing the authority of party leaders in the committee and assignment process, and reducing member assignments to two full and four subcommittee slots. When Democrats regained the majority in 2007 they retained these changes. But unlike the 1970s changes, these rules had the effect of undercutting subcommittees and further empowering the party's leadership.

Senate

The more collegial and smaller Senate experienced less pressure for change in the decades after the 1946 reorganization act. Where change did occur, the chamber moved in the same general direction as the House.

1953   Johnson Rule. Senate Minority Leader Lyndon B. Johnson proposed that all Democratic senators be given a seat on one major committee before any Democrat was assigned to a second major committee. Although a stunning blow to seniority, the rule held, and Republicans adopted it for themselves informally in 1959 and formally in 1965.

1971   Caucus Call. Majority Leader Mike Mansfield, D-Mont., announced that a meeting of the Democratic Conference of all party members would be held at the request of any senator and any senator could challenge the nomination by the Steering Committee. Republicans limited a senator to one ranking minority position on only one standing committee, a rule they applied to committee chairs when they gained a majority in 1981.

1973–1975   Seniority Limited. Republicans in 1972 required standing committee members to elect the top-ranking GOP member. In 1975 Democrats provided for a secret-ballot election of a committee chair if one-fifth of their conference requested it. This was first invoked in 1977, although no chair was rejected.

1975   Staff Help. A new rule authorized junior senators to hire up to three committee staffers. Previously staff was controlled by committee chairs.

1977   Committees Limited. A Senate reorganization consolidated a number of committees, revised some jurisdictions, set a ceiling on the number of committees and subcommittees on which a senator could serve or chair, and gave more staff to minority members. The ceiling in effect limited subcommittee proliferation.

1995   GOP Reform Package. A Republican task force recommended a reform package. Changes adopted included six-year term limits for committee chairs, six-year term limits for GOP leaders, a ban on reclaiming seniority when returning to a committee on which a senator previously served, secret-ballot elections for committee chairs, and adoption of a formal legislative agenda prior to election of committee chairs. None of these changes applied to Democrats.

The chairs often did not share the prevailing views of Congress as a whole or even of the membership of their own party. Yet their powers were so great that Woodrow Wilson in 1885 described the system as "a government by the chairmen of the standing committees of Congress."

One of the last old-time committee czars was Rep. Howard W. SMITH, a conservative Virginia Democrat who chaired the House Rules Committee from 1955 until 1967. The Rules Committee is the gateway through which major bills must pass to reach the House floor, and Smith made the most of his power to censor the legislative program of the House. He regularly blocked civil rights legislation sought by the Democratic leadership. This absolute power was clipped following the 1960 election of Democrat John F. Kennedy as president. Knowing that the Rules Committee dominated by southern Democrats would be a nearly insurmountable obstacle to the progressive program expected from Kennedy, the House's Democratic leadership, led by Speaker Sam Rayburn, D-Texas, moved in 1961 to expand the committee temporarily by three members. This allowed naming two Democrats and one Republican to the committee who were expected to be sympathetic to the Kennedy program. The change was approved by a narrow 217–212 House vote.

The expansion allowed important administration legislation to proceed through the House where it might have been blocked previously. But the precarious leadership control of the panel was not fully successful, particularly on any legislation that involved civil rights. Nevertheless, the temporary expansion was made permanent in 1963 and was the first significant move in the House that was to lead eventually to complete control of the committee by the leadership.

Congress did not take major steps to curb committee powers until the 1970s, when junior House members demanded and won fundamental changes in the way Congress, and particularly the committees, operated. Although the reformers had many complaints, the focus was on ending the iron hand of the seniority system that gave all but absolute power to the committee chairs who had risen to that position simply by staying in Congress long enough.

The changes, which peaked during the 1970s, were driven by a generational change, primarily in the House. Between 1958 and 1970, 293 Democrats entered the House. Between 1970 and 1974, another 150 Democrats were elected. A large portion of these new members were more moderate or liberal than their predecessors, and they became the core of the reform movement with the votes to effect change.

The changes diluted the authority of committee chairs and other senior members and redistributed power among their younger and less experienced colleagues. Many of these junior members became chairs of newly created subcommittees. By the 1980s the full committees had lost some of their influence to subcommittees, whose chairs became powers in their own right. The most significant of the 1970s reforms was a decision by House and Senate Democrats to allow the caucus of party members in each chamber to elect committee chairs. (See CAUCUSES, PARTY.) Although most chairs continued to be chosen on the basis of seniority, the election requirement made them accountable to their colleagues for their conduct. Its force was illustrated in 1975, when three House chairs were deposed in caucus elections. Several others lost their posts in subsequent Congresses.

Caucus election of committee chairs was only one of the changes that restricted the chairs' authority. Most House committees were required to establish subcommittees; House Democrats adopted a subcommittee "bill of rights" that transferred authority over subcommittee organization from committee chairs to subcommittee Democrats. Committees were required to have written rules, and limits were placed on the number of chairmanships members could hold. Members were given their own professional staff to help them with committee work. Committee and subcommittee staff increased.

The diffusion of committee power ended the era of autocratic committee chairs. From that time on a chair's authority depended on the support of a committee majority and his or her own personal and legislative skills. In the 1960s, during his heyday as chair of the House Ways and Means Committee, Arkansas Democrat Wilbur D. MILLS enjoyed almost unchallenged authority over his panel. But the political climate had changed by the time Oregon Democrat Al Ullman succeeded Mills in 1975.

In the Senate, seniority remained the primary path to committee chairs and ranking minority status even though leaders of both parties increasingly since the 1970s exerted more influence on decisions, and the chamber itself set out rules to limit the number of the most important panels on which a senator could serve.

In the House, however, the old power of seniority continued to decline until its potency became more advisory than binding. That occurred in 1995 when Republicans took House control for the first time in forty years and the new Speaker, Newt Gingrich from Georgia, moved aggressively to control all decisions on who would head a committee. From that point on—even when Democrats regained control in 2007—committee chairs came more fully under the influence of party leadership. The Republicans even instituted term limits on chairs, requiring them to leave their posts after six years. Democrats in 2007, with some reluctance and grumbling from the most senior party members who had regained positions held before 1995, kept in place the six-year limit, further cementing the control of the party's leadership over committees.

Power Centers

Committees vary greatly in how much power they have. A panel may be powerful because of the subjects it handles or because an aggressive chair has expanded its turf. Another may be formally classified as a "minor" committee.

Money committees are enduring centers of power. The House Ways and Means and Senate Finance committees write tax bills that govern the flow of revenues into the U.S. Treasury. They also have jurisdiction over billions of dollars in federal spending for Social Security, Medicare, welfare, unemployment, and other programs. The House and Senate Appropriations committees, which prepare annual funding bills for government agencies, oversee the full range of federal activity. Control over federal spending gives Appropriations members considerable influence with their colleagues, as well as with the executive branch. The House and Senate Budget committees exert power more subtly. They set broad spending limits that other committees are expected to observe. But the limits can be violated whenever the political will to meet them is lacking.

The power a committee wields may change with the times. Under an aggressive chair with expansionist aims, the House Energy and Commerce Committee emerged in the 1980s as a major power center and remained so in the first decade of the twenty-first century. John D. Dingell, a Michigan Democrat who chaired the committee from 1981 until the GOP takeover in 1995, oversaw the expansion of the panel's jurisdiction and its acquisition of the largest staff and budget of any House committee at that time. Dingell, the longest-serving House member, returned to that chair in 2007.

As issues fluctuate in importance, so, too, do the panels with jurisdiction over them. Beginning in the 1990s, members clamored to be assigned to the House Transportation and Infrastructure Committee, the panel with jurisdiction over the traditionally "pork"-laden bill that authorized vast numbers of transportation projects.

Rep. John D. Dingell, the longest-serving House member in 2007, has twice served as chair of the House Energy and Commerce Committee.
Source: CQ Photo/Scott J. Ferrell

Power centers of an earlier era sometimes find themselves in marked, though perhaps temporary, decline. The Senate Energy and Natural Resources Committee, for example, shone in the 1970s, when energy policy was a major economic issue, but national interest in the issue subsided. Interest in the committee was revived somewhat in 2001 when President George W. Bush called for a national energy bill, but it still was not quite as sought-after as it had been. The House Education and Labor Committee had its days in the sun in the 1960s, when Congress was enacting landmark school aid laws. Then the Education panel lost its appeal for a time, but by the 1990s education resurged as a prominent issue and seats on the committee gained in popularity. The prestigious Senate Foreign Relations Committee declined after the departure of chair J. William FULBRIGHT in 1975, but activist conservative chair Jesse Helms of North Carolina helped to revive the committee's importance in the 1990s. When Richard Lugar of Indiana took over the chairmanship in 2003, he vowed to elevate the panel's profile even more but had limited success. In 2007, however, Democrats took back control of the panel and made it a prominent forum for examination—and sharp criticism—of the continuing war in Iraq that President Bush had launched in 2003.

With authority to draft ground rules for floor debate on most major bills, the House Rules Committee can limit or bar amendments to a bill, or prevent its consideration altogether. The House seldom rejects the panel's recommendations on such matters. However, a seat on the committee became less attractive after the panel was brought increasingly under the control of the majority party leadership in the chamber. By 2007 there was so little interest in serving on the committee that the new Democratic chair, in an unprecedented move, accepted four freshmen from the party. Only four newcomers, in either party, had been assigned to the committee in the previous quarter-century.

Members' Assignments

Members' influence in Congress often is closely related to the committee or committees on which they serve. Assignment to a powerful committee virtually guarantees plentiful campaign contributions. Many members seek a particular committee because they have an interest in the panel's jurisdiction, while others stake out committee assignments according to political need. Members from large agricultural districts gravitate toward the Agriculture committees. Those whose districts have major military installations often seek out the Armed Services committees.

The political parties in each chamber assign members to committees. The assignments are then routinely approved by the full House or Senate at the beginning of each two-year Congress. The specific process varies by chamber and party.

Just wanting to be on a committee is not enough to ensure assignment to it, particularly in the House. In most cases representatives often have to lobby for assignments to the more influential panels. In the smaller Senate, however, there are more plum seats available and nearly every senator has the opportunity to serve on one of the more prestigious panels. By contrast, congressional leaders often have to seek "volunteers" to serve on less popular panels. A member's rank on a committee is determined by his or her length of service, or seniority, on the panel, and a new member, with few exceptions, must start at the bottom.

Representatives typically serve on only two committees. Senators often serve on four. Although some veteran members do switch committees, most keep their assignments throughout their careers, gradually advancing through the seniority system to the coveted position of chair (or ranking minority member, depending on which party is in power).

The organizations of the House's two political parties—the Republican Conference and Democratic Caucus—control committee assignments, chairs, and ranking minority member positions. The full House ratifies decisions made in these organizations. Both parties have rules—especially complex ones for the Democrats—to guide distribution of committee assignments to ensure a fair distribution among members. A few committees are considered exclusive panels, which means a member on them cannot service on any other committees. Both parties consider these committee as exclusive: Appropriations, Energy and Commerce, Rules, and Ways and Means. Democrats also consider Financial Services as exclusive. Most others are nonexclusive and a few are exempt; the most important of the exempt panels are Select Intelligence and Standards of Official Conduct, which is better known as the ethics committee.

Nevertheless, in the House, where from 1995 onward committee positions became largely under leadership control, assignments can be influenced by the needs of the party as well as political objectives. In the 110th Congress, which the Democrats organized in 2007 after twelve years

More on this topic:

Education and Labor Committee, House, p. 174

Energy and Commerce Committee, House, p. 187

Energy and Natural Resources Committee, Senate, p. 189

Foreign Relations Committee, Senate, p. 231

Transportation and Infrastructure Committee, House, p. 558

out of power, the leadership, and especially the Speaker, Nancy Pelosi of California, deferred almost entirely to seniority in naming chairs. But beyond that hallowed tradition, Pelosi continued an effort she began after becoming party leader in late 2002 of spreading positions of influence to freshmen and other junior members, more women and ethnic minorities, and members from all regions of the country. As the new Congress began, women chaired twenty-seven panels: four full committees and twenty-three subcommittees, which closely reflected the number of females in the Democratic caucus. (One of the women who headed a committee as the 110th Congress opened died a few months later from cancer. The post later went to a male committee member.) Blacks, Hispanics, and Asian Americans held seven committee and thirty subcommittee chairs. One result of Pelosi's efforts was to give more freshmen chairs: five were in charge of subcommittee gavels.

In the Senate both parties decided in the 1970s that seniority should not dictate the choice of committee leaders. Nevertheless, the Senate continued to adhere to the seniority tradition, and in the smaller body longtime personal relationships among senators also worked to smooth over disagreements about political ideology in selecting chairs.

Computers in Congress

When newly elected members of Congress check in for orientation, the lawmakers and their top aides almost immediately receive cell phones, laptop computers, and wireless e-mail devices—evidence of the complex and multifaceted relationship the legislative branch has with computer technology. Individual members and congressional committees maintain Web sites, tap into numerous Internet databases, and swap information via e-mail. Legislative support organizations such as the Congressional Research Service also have integrated the World Wide Web into their work. Lawmakers and their constituents also increasingly communicate with each other online—a trend that accelerated following the September 11, 2001, terrorist attacks.

While computers often are promoted as a means of revolutionizing politics, Congress generally has reacted slowly to digital innovations, according to a 2001 Congressional Research Service (CRS) report on the Internet and congressional decision making for the House Rules Committee. A computer-

Rep. Cliff Stearns, R-Fla., answers Internet bloggers' questions during a "Blog Row" sponsored by the House Republican Conference.
Source: CQ Photo/Scott J. Ferrell

ized scheduling system was in place for Senate committees by 1977. However, critical information and technology resources were not widely available for members until the 1990s. The pace of development accelerated in the mid-1990s, in part due to Speaker Newt Gingrich, R-Ga. Gingrich, soon after becoming Speaker in 1995, inaugurated an online legislative computer system operated out of the Library of Congress called THOMAS (after Thomas Jefferson, at http://www.thomas.loc.gov) that provides free and worldwide access to summaries, status, and texts of legislation, as well as committee reports and the *CONGRESSIONAL RECORD*. Such resources were previously only available to legislative insiders on Capitol Hill.

Gingrich also oversaw a modernization of the House's information system and pushed for adoption of a new House rule requiring each standing committee to make its publications available in electronic form "to the maximum extent feasible." In the Senate, an internal legislative retrieval system was established in 1997 at the prompting of the Appropriations and Rules and Administration committees. The innovations collectively had the effect of making Congress and the legislative process considerably more accessible to constituents and researchers.

Rapid advances in technology have since added even more transparency to the way Congress does its business. High-speed Internet links allow House and Senate committees to broadcast hearings over the Internet and even "stream" live video of the events. The House Education and Workforce Committee (now the House Committee on Education and Labor) in 2001 became the first committee to create a Spanish-language Web site so speakers of that language could obtain background on the Bush administration's "No Child Left Behind" initiative.

The pervasiveness of computers has changed the way some lawmakers do business. Electronic lobbying has become a way of life, as interest groups and their supporters regularly blitz congressional offices with e-mails advocating various positions prior to key votes or debates. E-mail inquiries from constituents also have surged. The total number of e-mail messages to Congress shot from 20 million in 1998 to 48 million in 2000 and has continued to grow by 1 million per month, often overwhelming offices. In response, some member offices have acquired software that can automate message sorting and the entry of e-mailers' names, addresses, and other information into the offices' databases. The software can also produce form letters, reducing staff workload and turnaround times.

Lawmakers, in turn, use computers to communicate position statements and raise money for campaigns. During a heated congressional debate on rising drug prices in 2000 and 2001, Democratic senator Debbie Stabenow of Michigan used her Web site to detail stories of senior citizens who could not afford prescription medications—a pet cause of the first-term lawmaker. Congressional Republicans three years earlier used Web sites to depict "horror stories" of overzealous Internal Revenue Service agents harassing taxpayers. Representatives and senators are banned from posting electronic communications on the Internet within ninety days of any election in which their names appear on a ballot. Political parties also use the Web to advocate their agendas and stake out their positions.

The digital connectivity of Congress and the public has raised questions about whether the federal government is doing as much as it can to promote privacy protection. The issue aroused comment and concern in 2001 after some Senate offices began using electronic files known as "cookies" that help monitor browsing habits and preferences of visitors. Though none of the cookies transmitted information to third-party sites outside of the Senate, the federal government has been moving away from the use of cookies since the Clinton administration restricted their use on executive branch Web sites in 2000. The restriction does not apply to congressional sites, and a number of House sites use them. Although the Senate has an umbrella privacy policy, it permits the collection of some information for "statistical purposes," including which sites and pages attract the most visitors and which Internet browsers are used most often. Lawmakers contend they do not use cookies to collect personal information.

New security concerns in the wake of the 2001 terrorist attacks focused attention on ways Congress could tap into the capabilities of computer technology. The sending of the potentially lethal bacterium anthrax through the U.S. mail prompted study of whether constituent mail could be digitally screened, then transmitted to members' computer networks. (See ANTHRAX ATTACK.) Soon after the Capitol complex was evacuated on September 11, 2001, House and Senate officials distributed tiny wireless keypads to lawmakers to give them an adequate way to communicate in emergencies and to receive security and logistical information. Too many lawmakers had to rely on cell phones, old-style one-way pagers, or in-person conversations to learn about floor votes, hearing cancellations, and opportunities for security briefings.

Congress operates hundreds of Web sites, and trends show more extensive use of the technology in the future, according to the CRS study. Party task forces have even been established to solidify links with the technology sector. For example, a Republican High-Tech Task Force was established in 1999 to meet with technology executives and work with figures from the sector to address such issues as high-speed Internet access and privacy.

Concurrent Resolution   *See* LEGISLATION.

Conference Committees

Conference committees play such an important part in the LEGISLATIVE PROCESS that they are sometimes called the third house of Congress. A bill cannot be sent to the president for signature until it has been approved in identical form by both the Senate and House of Representatives. Frequently, however, the two chambers pass different versions of the same bill. When neither is willing to accept the version passed by the other, the bill goes to a conference committee, a temporary Senate-House panel established solely to work out the differences between the two chambers on a particular bill. Although conferences are convened on a relatively small number of measures, these bills generally include the most important LEGISLATION before Congress.

Conference committee members are formally appointed by the Speaker of the House and the presiding officer of the Senate. In practice they are chosen by the chair and senior minority party member of the committee (or committees) that originally handled the bill. These members usually select themselves to serve on the conference committee, as well as other members of their panel. If a subcommittee has exercised major responsibility for a bill, some of its members may be chosen. Seniority, or length of service, once governed the selection of conferees, but it is quite common today for junior members in each chamber to be chosen, especially if they are particularly knowledgeable about or interested in the bill. (See SENIORITY SYSTEM.) Occasionally a member from another committee with expertise in the subject matter of the bill may be named to the conference, or one who sponsored a major amendment adopted on the floor. Both political parties are represented on the conference committee.

There need not be an equal number of conferees, known as managers, from each house, because a majority vote determines the position of each chamber's delegation on all decisions made in the conference. Conference committees vary widely in size, ranging from a minimum of six (each chamber must send three, so that the majority party will have a majority of the delegation) up into the hundreds. Clean air legislation in 1990, for example, had a conference of 149 members, and more than 250 members were appointed as conferees on a 1981 budget reconciliation bill. Such large conferences usually divide up into smaller groups to consider separate sections of the bill, and the roles of some conferees may be limited to certain sections of the bill, especially if they are not members of the main committee responsible for the bill.

Senate and House conferees vote separately on each issue, and a majority of both delegations must agree before a compromise provision is included in the final bill. Conferees are supposed to defend their own chamber's provisions even if they disagree with them. In 1993 the House adopted a rule allowing the Speaker to remove any House member from, or add additional ones to, a conference committee. The rules change effectively limited the ability of House conferees to defy the will of the majority leadership.

Conferees are not supposed to insert new material in a bill or reconsider provisions that are the same in both the House and Senate versions. In practice, however, many bills are largely rewritten in conference and new provisions added that were not in either bill. Rules changes enacted in 2007 made new provisions subject to points of order in the Senate, which was expected to curtail the practice. Conferees are not always able to compromise on all their differences; in such case they may leave final decisions on some matters to the full House and Senate. A majority of conferees from each chamber must sign the conference report containing the compromises they reached.

The Senate and House must approve the conference report and resolve any remaining differences before the compromise bill can go to the White House. Conference reports are rarely rejected and cannot be amended on the floor under ordinary procedures. The conference committee dissolves after approval by one chamber; should the conference report be rejected, a new conference could be required.

The conference system, used by Congress since 1789, had developed its modern practice by the middle of the nineteenth century. Until 1975 most conference committees met in secret, but House and Senate rules changes have broken down the secrecy and seniority that once were the norm. However, some conferences, such as those dealing with secret intelligence activities, still are closed, and others are settled by a small number of senior members negotiating behind closed doors. For example, agreement on an omnibus spending/tax/authorization bill in 1998 was reached after eight days of closed-door negotiations among the House Speaker, Senate majority leader, and a team of White House officials led by the president's chief of staff. (See REFORM, CONGRESSIONAL.)

Confirmation *See* APPOINTMENT POWER.

Conflict of Interest *See* ETHICS.

Congress

In broad usage, the term "Congress" refers to the national legislature of the United States, consisting of a Senate, with two members representing each state no matter how big or small the population, and the House of Representatives, with members elected from geographic districts determined by population. More specifically the term refers to the national legislature meeting in session during a two-year period, and numbered sequentially. The Congress that began in January 2007 was the 110th to meet since 1789. It will continue for two years, from 2007 to the beginning of 2009. The Constitution provides that a Congress meet from January 3 of an odd-numbered year to January 3 of the next odd-numbered year. Normally, a Congress holds two annual sessions, but some have had three sessions and the 67th Congress (1911–1913) had four. Any measure, not enacted before a Congress ends, expires also. Bills do not carry over automatically to the next Congress, although identical legislation can be introduced again. (See CONGRESS: STRUCTURE AND POWERS.)

Congress: Structure and Powers

Under the Constitution, Congress is charged with carrying out the legislative functions of government. The framers of the Constitution wanted the lawmaking role to be in the hands of a representative body. They considered Congress, the collective name for the Senate and House of Representatives, to be the "first branch" of the U.S. government, the primary maker of national policy. The powers, structure, and procedures of the national legislature are outlined in considerable detail in the Constitution, unlike those of the presidency and the judiciary, the other independent branches in the American system of SEPARATION OF POWERS. (See U.S. Government Organization Chart in the Appendix.)

Checks and Balances

Each branch is structured so that it may restrain the others' excesses, resulting in a form of institutionalized "checks and balances." Within Congress itself the legislative power is checked in many ways. To a degree the House and Senate are competitors, even when both are controlled by the same party. And that rivalry can be seen no matter which party is in control. Each chamber seeks to protect its own powers and prerogatives. The Constitution helps to create the competition—that is, the checks—by giving some powers to the Senate alone and others to the House. Powers reserved to the Senate include approval of treaties, confirmation of presidential nominations, and the power to try impeachments. Granted to the House alone is the authority to originate impeachments and all revenue-raising bills.

Although competition and conflict are built into the system, cooperation between House and Senate is essential because legislation must be passed in identical form by both chambers before it can be sent to the president for approval or veto. A form of checks and balances between branches comes into play once Congress has finished acting on a bill. The president may veto any bill that Congress sends him, forcing legislators to consider the chief executive's opinions and priorities. Congress, however, may override the president's action by a two-thirds vote of both chambers. (See VETOES.) The actions of both the legislative and executive branches are at least implicitly checked by the review functions of the national judiciary.

Congress by design is untidy, unwieldy, and unrestrained. But an independent, decentralized, and deliberative legislature is exactly what the framers of Article I of the Constitution had in mind.

Another form of checks and balances derives from the system of federalism, the countervailing forces of the state and federal governments. Federalism is a factor to be reckoned with in the legislative process. Because members of Congress are elected either from a state or from a congressional district within a state, local and regional interests strongly influence how the laws are drafted. This often creates tensions between the House and Senate and between Congress and the executive branch. (See STATES AND CONGRESS.)

Members in modern Congresses often have a surprising amount of independence from their national party apparatus for their election. Senators or representatives who are popular back home usually cannot be forced to heed the wishes of the president or their party's congressional leaders. This independence is a result of many modern developments, including television, direct mail, and campaign-financing trends.

The pattern of independence was seen especially in the decades after World War II as national political parties became increasingly enfeebled. That pattern started to break down in the last years of the century when Republicans in 1994 won control of the House for the first time in forty years. Emboldened with the long-sought triumph and under the direction of a tightly disciplined leadership, the GOP imposed a much tighter rein on the rank and file. When the Democrats regained House control in the 2006 elections, a similar pattern developed in the early days of the 110th Congress in 2007. But in all these years the parties were united by factors that might prove less durable in time: between 1996 and 2001 the GOP, at least in the House, was adamantly opposed to the Democratic president, Bill Clinton; from 2001 to 2007 the Republicans fell in lock-step behind their president, George W. Bush, to enact the Republican agenda; and in 2007 Democrats—replicating the GOP in the late 1990s—were united against the Bush administration, particularly on the unpopular war in Iraq.

The relative independence seen in the postwar years leading up to 1995 was a significant change from historical patterns, under which political parties and major party leaders were able to control the political conduct and votes of members.

The Senate, always a more collegial body than the House, was more or less susceptible to party discipline during all these years, depending on who the leaders were and the nature of the issues on the legislative agenda. In general, however, most senators retained substantial independence from party pressure if doing so served their interests.

Congress's Many Roles

Congress by design is untidy, unwieldy, and unrestrained. But an independent, decentralized, and deliberative legislature is exactly what the framers of Article I of the Constitution had in mind.

Members' constituents are not united on most issues most of the time, and a halting, indecisive Congress usually mirrors the public at large. The framers of the Constitution did not look upon efficiency as the primary goal in lawmaking. Sensitive to what they viewed as the denial of basic human rights under British rule, and to other failings of eighteenth-century governments, they were mainly concerned with ensuring individual rights and liberties. Within the federal government they feared the potential excesses or domination of one branch over the others, and in Congress they feared the domination of a majority over the minority.

The Constitution, then, provides the framework of a complicated system of government. Some of the complexities become quickly apparent when tracing the steps involved in the legislative process. Legislation must follow an intricate course before it can become law. Each step presents potential barriers to passage and gives legislators opportunities to kill or modify bills or provisions they oppose.

Many experts on Congress have observed that the legislative process resembles an obstacle course that favors the opponents of legislation over the proponents. There are many points at which bills can be stymied or delayed and relatively few effective tools for speeding passage through Congress, particularly when members differ strongly over issues. Although opponents have the upper hand in most situations, members also are under pressure to get legislation enacted, especially programs in the domestic field that can benefit their districts, states, or regions—a public works project, for example, or a navy ship-building contract. Therefore, bargaining, compromise, and LOGROLLING are necessary to offset the institutional bias against speedy enactment of bills.

The president "shall from time to time give to the Congress Information on the State of the Union, and recommend to their Consideration such Measures as he shall judge necessary and expedient."

Article II, section 3, of the Constitution

President as Legislative Leader

The modern president plays the principal role in setting the legislative agenda. Congress expects the White House to submit proposals for new laws dealing with the whole spectrum of foreign and domestic policy. When existing programs come up for renewal, Congress generally waits for the executive branch to present its recommendations before setting the legislative wheels in motion. Although the Constitution implies that the president should play the leading role, this was not the general practice during the nineteenth century.

The president uses a variety of vehicles and forums to present his program to Congress and the nation. Best known is the annual STATE OF THE UNION address, which is a constitutional requirement. Article II, section 3, of the Constitution directs the president periodically to "give to the Congress Information of the State of the Union, and recommend to their Consideration such

Measures as he shall judge necessary and expedient."

Equally important is the president's annual budget message, with its accompanying documents. The budget message contains many of the president's legislative goals for the coming year, as well as requests for money to run the federal government. The agenda also is shaped by periodic messages and statements proposing new measures or changes in pending bills. Even presidential veto messages may contain recommendations for future legislation.

Structure

The legislative branch is bicameral, meaning that it consists of two houses, or chambers. Representatives are elected for two-year terms; senators,

President George W. Bush delivers his 2008 State of the Union address to a joint session of Congress.
Source: CQ Photo/Scott J. Ferrell

for six-year terms. Before adoption of the Seventeenth Amendment to the Constitution in 1913, senators were elected by their state legislatures. (See DIRECT ELECTION OF SENATORS.)

Senators represent entire states, while House members represent population-based districts within the states. States that have very small populations relative to the others qualify for only one representative in the House. For these, the entire state is the congressional district and is referred to as an at-large district. In the 110th Congress (2007–2009), there were seven at-large districts: Alaska, Delaware, Montana, North Dakota, South Dakota, Vermont, and Wyoming. Congress has passed a law prohibiting House members from being elected at large in states that have more than one representative.

Traditionally House members were considered to represent the people more closely than senators because of their short terms and small constituencies. Although facing re-election every two years does tend to force representatives to view their roles somewhat differently than senators do, this distinction is fast disappearing. The major factors are the pervasive influence of television—including gavel-to-gavel coverage of both Senate and House floor debates—and other media coverage, and the ease with which members can return to their states and districts. These factors make senators and representatives equally accessible to the public and aware of the views of the citizens they represent. Earlier, senators were drawn closer to their constituents when they became subject to direct election.

The complexities of the legislative process require Congress to operate through elaborate rules as well as informal practices that have been refined, modified, and changed over the years. Except where the Constitution delineates the powers and parliamentary procedures, each chamber has developed its own set of rules from the body of traditions and precedents that developed during more than 200 years of legislating. Size alone accounts for many of the differences in the organization of the two bodies and in the rules and customs each has adopted. The House requires a more formal structure and detailed rules; the smaller Senate legislates in an informal setting and may not follow its formal rules if it prefers not to.

CLOSER LOOK

The Constitution sets only three qualifications to be in Congress, which the Supreme Court has ruled are the only three that can be applied in judging whether a person is qualified to be sworn in:

- **Minimum age:** House, twenty-five years; Senate, thirty years.
- **Citizenship:** House, a U.S. citizen for at least seven years; Senate, at least nine years.
- **Residency:** For both houses, an individual must be a resident of the state from which he or she is elected.

Qualifications

The Constitution sets minimum age, citizenship, and residency qualifications for membership in Congress. The minimum age for a House member is twenty-five years, and thirty years for a senator. A House member must have been a citizen for at least seven years, a senator, for at least nine. A representative or senator must also be a resident of the state from which he or she is elected.

Since adoption of the Twentieth Amendment in 1933, members' terms have begun on January 3 of the year following their election. That amendment also made January 3 the beginning of each new two-year term of Congress, and January 20 the date that newly elected presidents take office. The original constitutional language regulating when sessions of Congress began, and the precedents Congress followed in its first 140 years, proved inefficient for timely lawmaking and unrepresentative of the most recent general election results. Elections are held on the first Tuesday following the first Monday in November in even-numbered years. (See LAME-DUCK AMENDMENT; TERMS AND SESSIONS OF CONGRESS.)

Size

The Senate, as mandated by the Constitution, consists of two senators from each state. Senators' terms are staggered. Only thirty-three or thirty-four Senate seats—one-third of the membership— are at stake in each biennial general election. For this reason the Senate considers itself a continuing body, and its rules continue in effect from one Congress to the next. The House adopts its rules at the beginning of each Congress.

The size of the House is determined by Congress itself, within certain constitutional prescriptions. Throughout the nineteenth century the membership of the House was increased to reflect the growth of the nation's population and the addition of new states to the Union. In 1910 the size of the House was set at 435 members, where it has remained ever since, except for a brief period (1959–1963) after Alaska and Hawaii were admitted to statehood, when it was increased to 437.

The size of each state's House delegation is determined by the results of the census, which is conducted every ten years. The Constitution specifies that House seats must be reapportioned among the states after every census to reflect population growth and shifts in population from one state to another since the last census. (No reapportionment took place after the 1920 census because Congress could not agree on any plan to reapportion House seats.)

Ever since the House decided to keep its membership at 435, reapportionment has resulted in some states gaining seats at the expense of others. After the reapportionment following the 2000 census, House districts averaged about 645,000 constituents. (See REAPPORTIONMENT AND REDISTRICTING.) In addition to its 435 voting members, the House has five DELEGATES. They represent the District of Columbia, Puerto Rico, the Virgin Islands, Guam, and American Samoa. The D.C. delegate does not have full voting rights.

An effort was made in 2007 to increase the size of the House by two, with one seat going to the District of Columbia, a Democratic stronghold, and a second to Utah, a predominately Republican state. The effort, however, faced problems over whether D.C. could be considered a state in the constitutional sense, as well as opposition from the Bush administration and some Republicans who feared it eventually would lead to two senators from the District who almost certainly would be Democrats. The Senate in September voted against taking up the proposal. Although advocates promised to press for action during the 110th Congress, most observers thought the Senate action doomed the proposal until after the 2008 elections.

Powers of Congress

The many explicit powers of Congress enumerated in the Constitution reflect in part the framers' experience with the woefully weak Congress under the Articles of Confederation, the nation's original plan of government. Under the Articles, Congress was essentially powerless to protect the national interest. It could not limit encroachment on the federal government's authority by the thirteen independent states. The Constitution's detailed, precise enumeration of many of Congress's powers, principally in Article I, Section 8, reflects the fears and distrust between the various states and blocs of states at the time the document was drafted. Although these powers are extensive, most of them are shared with the other two branches, particularly the executive. Thus the Constitution established a system not of separate powers but of separate institutions sharing powers and functions.

The Tenth Amendment specifies that powers not expressly delegated to Congress or the other branches, and not prohibited by the Constitution, are reserved to the states or to the people.

Domestic Powers

Foremost among Congress's powers is the right "to lay and collect taxes, duties, imposts and excises, to pay the debts [and] ... to borrow money on the credit of the United States." Article I, section 9, stipulates that no federal funds can be spent except "in consequence of appropriations made by law." Three key powers are involved here: taxing, borrowing, and spending. They are known collectively as the power of the purse.

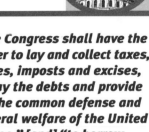

Most of the time members spend on legislative work is occupied with measures that either directly or indirectly involve these three powers. Although certain limitations are placed on how Congress can legislate under these powers, raising and spending money, or committing the federal government to spend money in the future, lie at the heart of congressional decision making.

Congress also is charged with providing for the "general welfare." These two words have provided the underpinning for the whole list of public assistance programs enacted by the modern Congress that are taken for granted today: Social Security, agricultural subsidies, workers' unemployment and disability insurance, food stamps, Medicare and Medicaid, and many other programs.

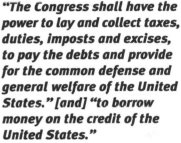

> **"The Congress shall have the power to lay and collect taxes, duties, imposts and excises, to pay the debts and provide for the common defense and general welfare of the United States." [and] "to borrow money on the credit of the United States."**
>
> Article I, section 8, of the Constitution

Also important is Congress's power to regulate foreign and domestic commerce. Since the earliest days of the republic, Congress has vigorously used the power to regulate foreign trade through tariffs, import quotas, and licenses and trade embargoes. Through its power to regulate domestic commerce, Congress has vastly expanded its powers to cope with national problems in areas never imagined by the framers of the Constitution.

The Constitution simply states that Congress shall have the power to regulate commerce with foreign countries "and among the several states." This general and rather innocuous language gave Congress the latitude it needed, beginning in the 1880s, to expand its power over commerce to meet the needs of an increasingly industrialized and urbanized society linked by rapid transportation and communication. In the early and mid-nineteenth century the Supreme Court accepted congressional regulation of interstate commerce but viewed this power narrowly. It accepted regulation of common carriers, such as the railroads, but rejected regulation of private property rights, states' rights, and most businesses, as well as legislation concerning social evils, such as child labor.

Only in the late 1930s and 1940s did the Court embrace Congress's broad interpretation of interstate commerce to include business activity even where it had only an indirect effect on interstate commerce. The power was expanded further in the 1960s to deal with racial discrimination and other social problems and in the 1970s to encompass conservation and environmental issues.

After these decades it appeared that congressional power in this area was practically limitless. Congress could set the rules conferring citizenship on foreign-born persons and regulate the admission into the country and the deportation of aliens. Congressional power extended to bank-

Congress has not exercised its power to declare war since World War II. President George W. Bush encountered few obstacles in getting Congress to approve the use of force in Afghanistan and Iraq after the September 11, 2001, terrorist attacks.
Source: AP Images/Saurabh Das

ruptcy, patent and copyright issues, regulation of the U.S. currency, the right to set standard weights and measures, and authority to establish a national postal system. But in the latter years of the twentieth century the Supreme Court issued a number of rulings that indicated the power was not without limits. As of early 2007 the rulings were seen more as a warning signal from the Court than an effort to reverse the fundamental direction of commerce jurisprudence from the 1930s and later, but they did indicate to Congress that extension of this power had to be thoroughly justified and carefully circumscribed. (See COMMERCE POWER.)

Foreign Policy Powers

Congress most clearly shares its powers with the executive branch in the area of foreign affairs. The Constitution presupposes that the two branches will maintain a delicate balance in exercising their foreign policy prerogatives. Nonetheless, both branches still debate vigorously the scope of and limits on Congress's power in the formulation of U.S. foreign and defense policies. The extent of Congress's involvement in and influence over foreign policy has varied throughout American history. Since the early years of the Vietnam War in the 1960s, Congress and the White House have actively competed with each other for control of foreign policy.

Certain specific foreign policy powers granted to Congress are not disputed. These include the power to raise, support, and regulate the armed forces; the power to declare war and, through its power of the purse, to finance or withhold financing for U.S. participation in foreign wars; and the requirement that the Senate give its consent to all treaties and executive branch nominations of diplomatic officials. Although these powers have been important in ensuring that the legislative branch remains an independent force in U.S. foreign affairs, its role in some cases has been altered or diminished by international developments since World War I.

Probably the most important change is the erosion of the power of Congress to declare war. In the nuclear age, when decisions about war had to be made in minutes, not in days or weeks, the power of the national legislature to declare war seemed impractical. Presidents since World War II have committed U.S. armed forces without first asking Congress's consent. World War II, in the 1940s, was the last in which Congress exercised its power to declare war. Since then U.S. military forces have engaged in several major armed conflicts, including those in Korea, Vietnam, and Iraq.

In 1991, however, Congress—at the request of President George H. W. Bush—debated heatedly before approving a resolution authorizing the president to use force to evict invading Iraqi troops from Kuwait. In 2001 and 2002 his son, President George W. Bush, encountered few problems in convincing Congress to approve resolutions authorizing the use of force to respond to the September 11, 2001, terrorist attacks on the nation and to defend against the threat posed by Iraq.

More on this topic:

Treaty-Making Power, p. 559

War Powers, p. 588

Reacting to its inability to curtail or, ultimately, end U.S. involvement in the Vietnam War in the 1960s and early 1970s, Congress in 1973 enacted the War Powers Resolution over President Richard NIXON's veto. This measure was an effort by Congress to reinvigorate its warmaking—or war-curtailing—power. But later presidents avoided its use, maintaining that it was an unconstitutional infringement on their powers. In battles with President Bill Clinton, some Republicans demanded advance congressional approval for U.S. deployment to Haiti and Bosnia and for any dispatch of combat forces under the United Nations flag. In 1993 some House Republicans invoked provisions of the war powers law, which they had long rejected as unconstitutional, to force expedited House action on a resolution that would have required U.S. forces to be withdrawn from Somalia more quickly than the administration had planned. In the end, Clinton survived a series of votes in the Senate over intervention abroad with his executive powers intact.

Congressional control of the purse strings also has not been effective in preventing U.S. armed intervention abroad. Once presidential decisions have been made to deploy U.S. military personnel overseas in hostile situations, it is difficult for Congress to force a halt to such operations, especially because doing so might jeopardize the lives of Americans stationed in those areas. Congress did, however, use the power of the purse to wind down the Vietnam War.

Much of this long-running dispute came together in 2003 and the next several years following the Bush administration's decision to invade the Iraq nation to topple its dictator Saddam Hussein who was believed to harbor weapons of mass destruction. Much like the Vietnam conflict, Congress gave its blessings to the administration's decision, even without formally declaring war on Iraq. Also like Vietnam, the experience went from bad to worse as the conflict dragged on without victory or end in sight. By early 2007, Democrats—back in control of both houses of Congress—were seeking legislative ways to force the Bush administration to bring an end to American troop involvement—at least combat action—in Iraq under a specific timetable. President Bush was adamantly refusing, leaving the two opposing views of controlling war efforts unresolved once again.

Another change in Congress's foreign policy powers was an increased reliance on executive agreements, which were compacts with other nations informally drawn up and agreed to by the executive branch alone, without any requirement for Senate consent. In certain areas of U.S. foreign policy, executive agreements largely replaced treaties.

Although some of Congress's formal constitutional powers in foreign affairs have decreased in importance, lawmakers' influence in this field has greatly expanded in other ways. Congressional backing is indispensable to the array of programs for foreign economic and military aid and international lending that the United States launched after World War II. These programs have expanded greatly since then, which gives Congress significant leverage over presidential policies. For example, when Congress approves such aid programs, it often writes laws giving itself a voice on how they are funded and administered and mandating what actions the White House can and cannot take.

Institutional Powers

Congress employs a wealth of institutional powers to buttress its position as an equal branch of government. In the procedure for amending the Constitution, Congress and the states act alone; the president may propose constitutional amendments but has no formal role in their ratification. Article V provides that Congress, "whenever two-thirds of both Houses shall deem it necessary, shall propose" amendments to the Constitution, which take effect when ratified by three-fourths of the states. Alternatively, the states themselves, if two-thirds agree, can call a constitutional convention to propose amendments. The latter route, however, has never been used.

The Senate alone possesses the key power to confirm or reject presidential appointments to many government positions. Most are confirmed routinely, but the few hundred top-level appointments requiring confirmation give the Senate a potent policy voice. Besides appointments at and beneath the cabinet level, the Senate's advice and consent power covers nominees for the Supreme Court and lower courts; for top-level diplomatic and military posts; and for federal regulatory agencies and boards.

The power to conduct investigations is not mentioned in the Constitution. It is an implied power, derived from the introductory clause in Article I declaring that "all legislative Powers herein granted shall be vested" in Congress. Investigations can cover the entire range of congressional activity. They are used to review the effectiveness of existing laws, to assess the need for new ones, and to probe into government waste, inefficiency, and corruption. While conducting investigations, chairs of committees sometimes use their subpoena power to compel reluctant witnesses to testify or provide information.

Questions about the right of Congress to investigate the executive branch emerged during an unprecedented lawsuit filed by the General Accounting Office (GAO), the investigative arm of Congress, against Vice President Richard CHENEY, who was leading an executive branch task force on energy policy. The GAO (which was renamed the GENERAL ACCOUNTABILITY OFFICE in 2004) sought to determine the costs of the task force's work and with whom Cheney's task force met as it wrote the administration's energy policy recommendations. A U.S. District Court judge dismissed the case in December 2002, saying in part that the GAO was not injured by the activities of the task force and therefore did not have standing to sue. However, the judge declined to decide the merits of whether the GAO should have the right to seek such information through lawsuits. "This case, in which neither a house of Congress nor any congressional committee has issued a subpoena for the disputed information or authorized this suit, is not the setting for such unprecedented judicial action," said U.S. District Judge John Bates. The GAO did not pursue the case after that decision.

Congress is also charged with making the "Rules for the Government." It can add or abolish federal agencies and departments and can even alter the size of the Supreme Court. The entire federal court structure was established by Congress. The power to admit new states into the Union also is conferred on Congress.

Several congressional powers directly affect the presidency. Congress is given the duty, now largely ceremonial, of counting the electoral votes for president and vice president after every election and formally announcing the winners. More important is the House's power to choose the president, and the Senate's power to choose the vice president, in the event that no candidate receives a clear majority of the vote. (See ELECTING THE PRESIDENT.)

The Twentieth and Twenty-fifth amendments also give Congress powers dealing with PRESIDENTIAL DISABILITY AND SUCCESSION, including the power to confirm presidential choices to fill vacancies in the vice presidency. The House and Senate share the power to impeach the president and other officials and remove them from office for treason, bribery, or other "high crimes and misdemeanors." Although rarely used, the IMPEACHMENT POWER is perhaps Congress's most formidable weapon against the executive branch. The House draws up impeachment charges; the Senate acts as judge and jury.

Finally, the Constitution declares that Congress may "make all laws which shall be necessary and proper for carrying into Execution the foregoing Powers." This catchall provision was originally intended to help Congress exercise the powers specifically enumerated in the Constitution. It was broadly defined by the Supreme Court in 1819 in the case of *McCulloch v. Maryland.* In practice, the provision has allowed Congress to extend its role and has led to far-reaching debates over the scope of congressional powers.

Congressional Accountability Act of 1995

This law—a long-sought reform by Capitol Hill activists—was one of the first changes put in place by the new Republican majority that took control of Congress in the 1994 elections, in the case of the House for the first time in four decades. The law applied eleven labor, workplace, and civil rights laws to the legislative branch. Critics of Congress had long chastised the legislative branch for applying these and many other requirements on business and other private organizations while never giving its employees the same protection. Vocal critics said this reflected the "plantation" mentality that had long governed Congress. These reforms had long been resisted by Democrats, particularly the longest-serving senior members who believed that Congress, as a political institution, needed to be free of the restraints imposed under the laws applicable to most workplaces.

The new law established procedures and remedies for legislative branch employees with grievances under these laws. The act provided an Office of Compliance to enforce the laws. The act brought to congressional employees the protections of the 1938 fair labor standards act, the 1964 civil rights act, the 1967 age discrimination act, the 1970 occupational safety and health act, the 1990 disabilities act, the 1993 medical leave act, and a number of others.

Congressional Budget and Impoundment Control Act *See* BUDGET PROCESS.

Congressional Budget Office

Congress has its own office of budget specialists and economists to provide budgetary analyses and economic forecasts. The Congressional Budget Office (CBO) is intended to give legislators nonpartisan information and set out policy options without making recommendations. CBO acts as a scorekeeper when Congress is voting on the federal budget, tracking bills to make sure they comply with overall budget goals. The agency also estimates what proposed legislation would cost over a five-year period.

CBO works most closely with the House and Senate Budget committees. All three were established in 1974 by a new congressional budget law. The intent of that law was to force Congress to consider the overall federal budget, with projected revenues, spending, and deficits. In the past legislators had made spending decisions haphazardly, rarely considering future costs or how new programs fit into the overall budget. (See BUDGET PROCESS.)

The new budget process was also an attempt to regain fiscal control that had been lost to the executive branch. Congress created CBO to give it the kind of expert budgetary support that the president receives from the White House's Office of Management and Budget.

The newly appointed director of the Congressional Budget Office, Peter Orszag, briefs the Senate Budget Committee in January 2007 on CBO's economic outlook for the coming year. The CBO director is appointed by the Speaker of the House and president pro tempore of the Senate.
Source: CQ Photo/Scott J. Ferrell

CBO sometimes gets caught between political factions that want budget figures to help make a point, not a decision. CBO directors in particular can become targets of partisan snipping.

The CBO director is appointed for a four-year term by the Speaker of the House and the president pro tempore of the Senate. Alice M. Rivlin, a Democrat, was CBO director from 1975 to 1983. She was followed by Rudolph Penner, a Republican, who left in 1987. Two acting directors, Edward M. Gramlich and James L. Blum, led CBO during a two-year period in which House and Senate budget leaders were unable to agree on a replacement for Penner. From 1989 to 1995 Robert D. Reischauer, a Democrat, was CBO director.

With the return of Republican control of Congress, June E. O'Neill ran the agency from 1995 to 1999. Daniel Crippen, a Washington lobbyist who previously had served as chief counsel to Senate Majority Leader Howard H. BAKER in the mid-1980s, became CBO director in 1999. He was succeeded in 2003 by Douglas Holtz-Eakin, an academic who was serving as the chief economist with President George W. Bush's Council of Economic Advisers at the time of his appointment. Peter R. Orszag took the position on January 17, 2007. Previously he was with the Brookings Institution in Washington, D.C. where he was a senior fellow and deputy director of economic studies. Earlier, he was with the National Economic Council and the president's Council of Economic Advisers.

The office operated with a $35 million budget for fiscal 2007 and employs about 230 persons, most of them economists or public policy analysts.

Congressional Directory

The *Congressional Directory* is the official "Who's Who" of Congress. The thick volume, published at the beginning of each two-year term of Congress, contains biographies of each senator and representative, as well as a hodgepodge of other information: lists of committees, telephone numbers, maps of congressional districts, diagrams of Capitol offices, staffs of executive agencies, and a roster of ambassadors, among other material.

The *Directory* has been published since 1821. The postmaster printed it until 1857, when the Joint Committee on Printing took over. The format of the book has changed little over the years, although it has grown larger. The 1877 edition had 160 pages; the 2002 edition had 1,200 pages. Single copies of the *Directory* can be purchased from the GOVERNMENT PRINTING OFFICE.

Republican Texas state Sen. Todd Staples shows his version of a congressional redistricting map in July 2003. The GOP-controlled Texas legislature, in an unusual and controversial move, redrew congressional district lines that had been recently established after the 2000 census.
Source: AP Images/Harry Cabluck

Congressional Districts

Districts are the geographical area represented by a single member of the House of Representatives. The Constitution provides that every state must have at least one district no matter how small the state's population. As of 2007 seven states had only one congressional district: Alaska, Delaware, Montana, North Dakota, South Dakota, Vermont, and Wyoming. The state with the largest number of districts was California, with fifty-three. After the 2001 redistricting, congressional districts averaged about 645,000 residents. But the range of sizes went from Wyoming's single district of just under 500,000 people to Montana's single district of more than 900,000 people.

The configuration of districts within a state is changed after each decennial census to ensure that the populations of each within the state are equal, as required by Supreme Court decisions on one person, one vote. On some occasions, states have redrawn district lines between the censuses, usually at the order of a court. This occurred commonly during the 1990s, mostly in the South, over the issues of minority-majority districts in a continuing effort to ensure that blacks and Hispanics were fairly represented in Congress. The major exception to either a census-driven or court-ordered redrawing of lines came in Texas in 2003 when Republicans—newly in control of the state legislature—reopened the districting plan that had been put in place by Democrats after the 2000 census. The GOP plan aimed at new lines that were expected to result in the defeat of a number of Democrats in the next election. With one exception, the plan succeeded as targeted Democrats lost, thereby tipping the Texas delegation majority from Democratic to Republican. (See REAPPORTIONMENT AND REDISTRICTING.)

Congressional Record

The *Congressional Record* is the primary source of information about what happens on the floors of the Senate and House of Representatives. The *Record,* published daily when Congress is in session, provides an officially sanctioned account of each chamber's debate and shows how individual members voted on many issues.

By law, the *Record* is supposed to provide "substantially a verbatim report of the proceedings." Exchanges among legislators during debate can be quite lively and revealing. Until recent years, senators and representatives were able to edit their remarks for the *Record* and even delete words spoken in the heat of debate. But when Republicans took control of the House in 1995, the rules for that chamber were changed to limit alterations that members might make "only to technical, grammatical and typographical corrections," which prohibited removal of remarks actually made.

Speeches not given on the floor are often included. At one time the reader had no way of knowing whether a member actually delivered a speech on the floor. But both the Senate and House have tightened their rules on "inserting remarks," as the process is known. Since 1978, inserted remarks have been indicated by a different typeface or other typographical device. And since 1995, the House has required that even material inserted into the text of actual remarks made by a member be printed in a distinctive typeface. The full texts of bills and other documents, never read aloud on the floor, are often printed in the *Record* as well.

Because much of what Congress does takes place off the House and Senate floors, reading the *Record* gives

The Congressional Record, *coming off the printing presses in the Government Printing Office, is published daily when Congress is in session. It is the official record of Congress.*
Source: Government Printing Office

only a limited sense of how Congress works. Despite these drawbacks the *Record* is an essential tool for students of Congress and for anyone following a specific issue. In addition to floor debate and vote tallies, the *Record* notes past and future committee meetings and hearings, as well as the next day's schedule for floor action. (See LEGISLATIVE PROCESS.)

The *Record* is not the official account of congressional proceedings. That is provided in each chamber's *Journal*, which reports actions taken but not the accompanying debate. But the *Record* is often used by the courts and federal agencies to determine what Congress intended when it passed a law.

The *Record* contains four sections: House proceedings, Senate proceedings, EXTENSIONS OF RE-MARKS, and the Daily Digest. An index published twice a month helps readers find their way around the gray pages, which typically have three columns of tightly spaced text. Tables and charts rarely appear. Newspaper articles are often inserted by legislators, but editorial cartoons are taboo. Since 1979 time cues have marked House floor debate to show roughly what time a particular discussion occurred; Senate proceedings have no indication of time. Speakers during debate are identified by name but not by party or by state, unless to distinguish between two legislators with the same last name.

The cost of compiling, printing, and distributing the *Record* was about $22 million a year by fiscal 2006. Printing costs alone were about $6.5 million. About 6,000 copies of each day's issue are printed. An annual subscription to the Record cost $503 in 2007. It was available for free each day on the Government Printing Office Internet Web site: http://www.gpo.gov/gpoaccess. On the Internet it also can be found on the Library of Congress's THOMAS Web site: http://thomas.loc.gov. Until 1970 a subscription cost only $1.50 a month. The *Record* is also available on microfiche. Rules require that any insert of more than two printed pages include an estimate of printing costs by the Government Printing Office, which has printed the *Record* since 1873. One of the most expensive inserts appeared in the issue of June 15, 1987, when Rep. Bill Alexander, an Arkansas Democrat, inserted 403 pages covering three and a half years of congressional debate on an amendment barring military aid to the antigovernment contra guerrillas in Nicaragua. The estimated cost of the insertion was $197,000. Republicans said they would object automatically to any future inserts costing more than $10,000.

Congressional Research
Service *See* LIBRARY OF CONGRESS.

Conkling, Roscoe

A skilled political operator, Roscoe Conkling (1829–1888) always managed to have a role in power struggles, whether in the Republican Party, Congress, or his home state of New York. Conkling seemed to relish conflict and to invite confrontation with his arrogant manner and backroom machinations. In the end, however, he pushed too far, ending his political career.

Conkling first served in the House from 1859 to 1863 and from 1865 to 1867. He then served in the Senate from 1867 to 1881. In the Senate Conkling led a Republican faction that usually controlled the Committee on Committees, rewarding supporters with valuable committee appointments. He eventually chaired the Senate Foreign Relations Committee.

Control of appointments was also the key to the New York political machine that Conkling headed. Two of his allies ran the customhouse in New York, where U.S. customs revenue was collected and where hundreds of people worked at PATRONAGE jobs. When President Rutherford B.

Hayes, a supporter of civil service reform, took office in 1877, he attempted to curb patronage abuses. Conkling's two allies refused to comply with a ban on partisan political activities by federal employees, and Hayes called for their resignations. When they refused to resign, he nominated others to replace them. The Senate declined to approve Hayes's nominees after Conkling invoked SENATORIAL COURTESY (a custom permitting senators of the party in office to control selection of local federal officials). The Senate did, however, confirm two later nominations by Hayes. (See APPOINTMENT POWER.)

When James A. Garfield was elected president in 1880, Conkling expected a return to the patronage system. But Garfield was overwhelmed by competing Republican Party factions, all demanding patronage slots. When Garfield did not accept Conkling's choices for the customhouse, Conkling tried to have the Senate reject Garfield's nominations. The effort failed. In a risky power play, Conkling resigned his Senate seat in May 1881, as did his ally and fellow New York senator, Thomas C. Platt. Conkling expected the state legislature to reelect them, thus strengthening his hand. But the legislature refused, and Conkling's political career was over.

New York politician Roscoe Conkling seemed to relish conflict and knew how to navigate the political machine.
Source: The Granger Collection, New York

Connally, Tom

Tom Connally (1877–1963), a Texas Democrat, was chair of the Senate Foreign Relations Committee from 1941 to 1953, except for two years when Republicans controlled the Senate. He entered the Senate in 1929, after serving twelve years in the House of Representatives, and remained until his retirement in 1953. He played an important role in U.S. foreign policy in the post World War II period.

Connally supported successive Democratic administrations on foreign policy. He helped Franklin D. Roosevelt plan the United Nations and was one of the eight representatives of the United States at the San Francisco Charter Conference in 1945. As a result of membership in the United Nations, the United States became a member of the International Court of Justice. Connally also played an important part in persuading the Senate to accept membership in the court.

In 1946 the Senate considered a resolution allowing the International Court jurisdiction over all matters that it did not deem purely domestic. Although President Harry S. TRUMAN urged that the Senate agree to the resolution, senators were reluctant to let the court decide what was or was not a matter under do-

Texas Democrat Tom Connally served in both the House and the Senate and assisted Franklin D. Roosevelt in plans for the United Nations.
Source: Library of Congress

mestic jurisdiction. Connally offered a compromise that became one of the most notable reservations to an international treaty. The Connally reservation provided that the Senate would decide what are matters "within the domestic jurisdiction of the United States."

Although he lost his post as chair of Foreign Relations in 1947, when Republicans gained control of the Senate, Connally helped win Senate approval of the Marshall Plan for postwar European recovery. When he regained the post two years later, he championed the North Atlantic Treaty Organization.

Conservative Coalition

The most potent congressional alliance of much of the twentieth century was the conservative coalition, which never had a staff or formal organization. Beginning in the 1930s Republicans and southern Democrats combined to exert powerful conservative influence in both the House and Senate.

Disillusioned with NEW DEAL economic policies, southern Democrats began banding together with Republicans to defeat or weaken President Franklin D. Roosevelt's proposals. The coalition dominated the House in the 1950s, and in the early 1960s it defeated many initiatives of President John F. KENNEDY. It was less powerful in the Senate but still had an important influence on legislation.

By the mid-1980s institutional changes in Congress and demographic changes in southern states had weakened the conservative coalition. Many southern Democrats had abandoned coalition politics, saying they did not expect to return to it any time soon. After Republicans won a majority in Congress in 1994, the coalition faded completely as House Republican leaders no longer needed Democratic help to pass major initiatives. In addition, there were fewer and fewer southern Democrats in Congress as most retired or were defeated by GOP candidates as the South became the base for the Republican Party. Instead of the coalition, partisan voting became more rigid.

The Changing South

For reasons that go back to the Civil War, the "solid South" evolved as a one-party region. Well into the 1960s most congressional districts in the South were overwhelmingly rural, with a one-party political system and, in the Deep South, an all-white electorate. Southern members of Congress controlled most of the important committees. Together with conservative Republicans they could often block civil rights and other social legislation proposed by the national Democratic Party.

The situation in the South began to change as early as 1948, when the Democratic Party under President Harry S. TRUMAN added civil rights for blacks to its agenda. During the next three decades, southern allegiance to the Democratic Party steadily eroded, and the Republicans gained a firm foothold in the region.

At the same time, the southern electorate became much less rural, more suburban, less poor, and more educated. As northern natives moved into the South, the region became less "southern." With the enfranchisement of black residents in the 1960s and 1970s, southern politicians of both parties became far more sensitive to civil rights and other social issues.

No longer feeling the traditional allegiance to the Democratic Party, the new South became a Republican bastion in the 1990s, changing the national balance of power between the two political parties. Propelled by their Dixie base, Republicans swept to congressional majorities in the 1994 elections and established a mostly southern leadership team. In 1995 the House elected as Speaker Newt GINGRICH of Georgia, and in 1996 the Senate picked Trent LOTT of Mississippi to be majority leader.

At the same time, the surviving southern Democrats—especially those from predominantly black congressional districts—became more liberal and more loyal to their party. Republicans made fewer attempts to promote unified positions with the southern Democrats. Instead,

Republican leaders focused their energies on wooing their moderate northeastern members, seeking to prevent them from entering a coalition with Democrats.

By the late 1990s, the conservative coalition had become moribund and few significant bills were enacted because of the votes of the coalition. Strikingly, the House showed it could take the most momentous step possible, impeachment of President Bill Clinton, with the votes of only four southern Democrats. But the Senate could not pick up a single southern Democrat to convict the president.

The decline of the conservative coalition can be seen by charting the percentage of floor votes on which a majority of southern Democrats and a majority of Republicans voted together against a majority of Democrats from outside the South. During the coalition's heyday in the 1960s and 1970s, the coalition appeared on 20 percent to 30 percent of Senate and House floor votes. In 1998 it appeared on less than 8 percent of House votes. That year, southern Democrats in the Senate left their party on only eight votes—too few to be statistically significant.

Constitutional Amendments

The framers of the Constitution gave Congress a key role in amending the nation's fundamental body of law. They wanted to ensure that the amendment process embodied the principle of checks and balances, the division of authority among the various branches of government. Thus they divided the power to amend between Congress, the lawmaking branch of government, and the states, whose ratification of the Constitution originally gave it force.

The Constitution's framers wanted to incorporate some flexibility into their document without making it too easy to change. The method of amending the Articles of Confederation, the nation's first legal charter, had proved to be impractical. Any change in that document required the consent of the Continental Congress and every one of the states. At the other extreme, the British Parliament could change England's unwritten constitution at will.

Under Article V of the Constitution, Congress plays a leading part in proposing

The Fifteenth Amendment, ratified in 1870, prohibited denial of the right to vote on the basis of race, color, or previous condition of servitude.
Source: Library of Congress

amendments. The final decision on amendments still rests with the states, but unanimity is not required. Amending the Constitution nonetheless remains difficult. The first ten amendments, known as the Bill of Rights, are considered practically a part of the original document. Aside from those, the Constitution has been amended only seventeen times in more than two hundred years.

Many Proposals, Few Changes

Even though the Constitution has been changed only twenty-seven times in more than 200 years, the drumbeat for amendments is constant. But many of the proposals sent forth in each new Congress are only repeats of failed earlier proposals, with some new ones emerging to reflect new political issues. Thus such long-standing proposals as banning abortions, requiring a balanced budget, authorizing public school prayer, limiting taxation, and establishing congressional term limits emerge in Washington as regularly as the city's famed cherry blossoms. Occasionally new ones are added such as restricting marriage to unions between a man and a woman, guaranteeing high quality health care, doing away with the electoral college, and even to prohibit presidential pardons between October 1 and January 21 of any presidential election year. Some of these are perennials and others reflect political flaps of the day, such as President Bill Clinton's issuance of several highly controversial pardons in his final days in office.

The most recent amendment, ratified in May 1992, prohibits midterm changes in congressional salaries. Proposed by James Madison and approved by the first Congress in 1789, the amendment was sent to the states as part of a package of twelve, ten of which became the Bill of Rights. Six states had ratified the pay raise amendment by 1792; a seventh state did so in 1873 and an eighth over a hundred years later in 1978. By 1992 thirty-three more states had ratified the amendment.

Widespread discontent with Congress inspired the push to ratify the Madison amendment more than two hundred years after it was proposed. Some legal scholars and members of Congress questioned its legitimacy, arguing that the ratification had taken place over too long a span of time.

Thousands of proposed amendments have not become part of the Constitution. Between 1787 and 2007, Congress had submitted only thirty-three amendments to the states; six of those were not ratified.

No fully accurate count exists of the number of proposed amendments since the first Congress. The U.S. Senate Historical Office estimated that more than 11,200 amendments had been proposed between 1789 and December 30, 2004. But the office cautioned that the number is flawed because of such factors as inadequate indexing in the early years of Congress, separate counting of amendments that were actually substitutes rather than entirely separate proposals, and the increasingly common practice of identical proposals introduced by different members of both the Senate and House.

One of the unratified proposals was the Equal Rights Amendment (ERA), which died on June 30, 1982. Although Congress extended the original 1979 deadline for ratification, the ERA fell three states short of the thirty-eight needed for ratification. The amendment, championed by women's rights advocates, stated: "Equality of rights under the law shall not be denied or abridged by the United States or by any state on account of sex." Congress had approved the proposal in 1972, forty-nine years after it was first introduced.

An amendment that would have given the District of Columbia voting representation in Congress died in 1985. Only sixteen state legislatures ratified that proposal within the seven-year deadline set by Congress.

Several proposed amendments circulated in Congress in recent decades, including measures to require a balanced federal budget, permit prayer in public schools, ban abortion, prohibit the use of busing to desegregate public schools, ban desecration of the U.S. flag, limit the terms of members of Congress, and require in most cases a two-thirds majority vote in both chambers to raise taxes. Congress repeatedly considered several versions of the most popular of these, the balanced-budget amendment, during the 1980s and 1990s, but it always backed away from approval.

Amendment Procedures

The Constitution provides two procedures for amendment, but only one has been used. The process begins with Congress, which by two-thirds majority votes of the Senate and House of Representatives may send amendments to the states for ratification. Under the second, untried method, amendments may be proposed by a constitutional convention, which Congress must convene if requested to do so by the legislatures of two-thirds (thirty-four) of the states.

In either case a proposed amendment becomes part of the Constitution if it is ratified, or approved, by three-fourths (thirty-eight) of the states. Congress can set a deadline for state ratification of proposed amendments; in recent cases, the limit has been seven years. Congress also has the

OTHER AMENDMENTS TO THE CONSTITUTION

Besides the Bill of Rights, the first ten amendments to the Constitution, seventeen other amendments have been successful.

Amendment		Year of Ratification
Eleventh	Laws against states	1795
Twelfth	Selecting president and vice president	1804
Thirteenth	Abolition of slavery	1865
Fourteenth	Civil rights, due process, support of rebellion	1868
Fifteenth	Voting rights for all races	1870
Sixteenth	Federal income tax	1913
Seventeenth	Popular election of senators	1913
Eighteenth	Outlawing intoxicating liquors (Prohibition)	1919
Nineteenth	Voting rights for women	1920
Twentieth	Terms of office (lame-duck amendment)	1933
Twenty-first	Repeal of Prohibition	1933
Twenty-second	Two-term limit for presidents	1951
Twenty-third	Presidential vote for D.C. residents	1961
Twenty-fourth	Abolition of poll taxes	1964
Twenty-fifth	Presidential succession	1967
Twenty-sixth	Voting rights for eighteen-year-olds	1971
Twenty-seventh	Ban on midterm congressional pay raises	1992

power to determine which of two procedures states must use to ratify a proposed amendment: approval by either state legislatures or state conventions. In every case but one Congress has prescribed approval by legislatures. The exception was the Twenty-first Amendment, repealing Prohibition.

The president cannot veto constitutional amendments, and governors cannot veto approval of amendments by their legislatures.

Convention Controversy

No procedures have been established for determining what is a valid state call for a constitutional convention, or for running one. As a result, no guidelines have been set for what a convention could debate, how the delegates would be selected, or who would preside. Many people fear a convention might get carried away and open the entire Constitution for amendment. Congressional moves to establish convention procedures never have become law.

Backers of a proposed constitutional amendment that has been bottled up in Congress sometimes campaign for a convention to consider their proposal. While no such campaign has yet succeeded, the effort sometimes spurs Congress to act on the proposed amendment. The Seventeenth Amendment was forced on the Senate in the early 1900s by popular pressure for a constitutional convention to take the selection of senators out of the hands of state legislatures. Fearing that such a convention might go too far, senators decided to submit a specific direct-election proposal to the states. (See DIRECT ELECTION OF SENATORS.)

Some convention campaigns have come close to success. In the 1960s thirty-three states petitioned Congress for a convention on a constitutional amendment permitting one house of a state legislature to be apportioned on some basis other than population. In the 1970s and 1980s thirty-two states petitioned for a convention on an amendment requiring a balanced federal budget.

The balanced-budget campaign illustrates the concern the prospect of a convention can arouse. Responding to a convention drive launched in 1975, Congress began considering a balanced-budget amendment while intensifying its own efforts to bring the budget under control. In 1982 the Senate passed a balanced-budget amendment by slightly more than the two-thirds majority needed for passage, but the measure failed to garner enough votes in the House. Although the state convention drive lost steam in 1984, Congress continued to debate the balanced-budget amendment issue. In 1986 the Senate rejected a balanced-budget proposal. Efforts in the House were defeated in 1990 and 1992. Both houses of Congress rejected an amendment in 1994. However, in 1995 the House, with its new Republican majority, adopted a balanced-budget measure. The Senate would defeat that amendment twice—in 1995 and 1996. The Senate rejected another proposal in 1997.

Successful Amendments

The Constitution has proved remarkably durable. Although the country has changed dramatically during its more than two-hundred-year history, only a handful of amendments have changed the document drafted in 1787.

The first ten amendments, known as the Bill of Rights, were passed almost at the beginning. Omission of a bill of rights was the principal source of dissatisfaction with the new Constitution in the state ratifying conventions held in 1788. Congress and the states moved quickly, and the amendments were approved in 1791. The Bill of Rights added explicit guarantees of fundamental civil liberties, such as freedom of speech and trial by jury, that had not been spelled out in the original document.

A Supreme Court decision and a crisis in presidential election procedures prompted the next two amendments. The Eleventh Amendment (1795) stated that the power of the federal judiciary did not extend to private suits against states. The Twelfth Amendment (1804) provided for separate balloting for president and vice president in the electoral college.

Civil War Era

The Civil War inspired three amendments. The Thirteenth Amendment (1865) abolished slavery. The Fourteenth Amendment (1868) was designed to protect the basic rights of freed slaves, most significantly by forbidding states to deprive any person of life, liberty, or property without due process of law or to deny anyone equal protection of the laws. The Fifteenth Amendment (1870) prohibited denial of the right to vote on the basis of race, color, or previous condition of servitude.

The due process and equal protection clauses of the Fourteenth Amendment have served as the basis of controversial shifts in the government's role. Until the mid-1930s the amendment was used more often to protect property rights than to safeguard individual liberties. But in the years following World War II, the Supreme Court began to use the Fourteenth Amendment to restrict state action infringing on civil and political rights. By invoking the due process clause, the Court gradually extended the guarantees of the Bill of Rights to cover actions by state governments. Relying largely on the equal protection clause, the Court brought about fundamental reforms in state policies on racial segregation and legislative malapportionment. The equal protection clause was the basis for the Court's historic 1954 decision outlawing racial segregation in public schools.

Twentieth Century

Four amendments were ratified from 1913 to 1920, largely in response to the Progressive movement. (See PROGRESSIVE ERA.) The Sixteenth Amendment (1913) gave the United States the income tax, the Seventeenth (1913) provided for direct election of senators, the Eighteenth (1919) prohibited the manufacture, sale, or transportation of alcoholic beverages, and the Nineteenth (1920) cleared the way for WOMEN'S SUFFRAGE.

Two more amendments were ratified in 1933. The Twentieth Amendment altered the dates for the beginning of a new Congress and of the president's term. The Twenty-first Amendment repealed the Eighteenth, thus ending Prohibition.

Six amendments have been added to the Constitution since World War II. The Twenty-second Amendment (1951) limited presidents to two terms in office. The Twenty-third (1961) gave citizens of the District of Columbia the right to vote in presidential elections. The Twenty-fourth Amendment (1964) outlawed poll taxes in federal elections. The Twenty-fifth (1967) set procedures for handling presidential disability, and the Twenty-sixth (1971) lowered the voting age to eighteen. (See YOUTH FRANCHISE.)

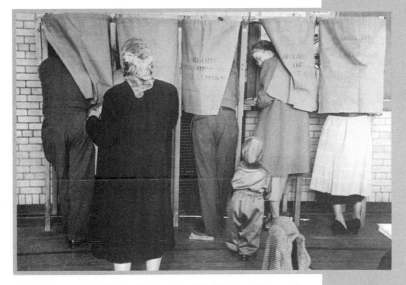

Ratified in 1920, the Nineteenth Amendment finally cleared the way for women's suffrage.
Source: U.S. Information Agency

The Twenty-seventh Amendment (1992) reads in full: "No law varying the compensation for the services of the Senators and Representatives shall take effect, until an election of Representatives shall have intervened." The ratification of this amendment more than two hundred years after it was proposed by James Madison was a result of public resentment of congressional pay raises. Earlier amendments had taken an average of about a year and a half for ratification.

Constitutional Rules and Votes

The Founders who wrote the Constitution spelled out the structure and powers of Congress in far more detail than they gave to the other two branches, reflecting their belief that the legislature was going to be the heart of the new government. In doing so they set out detailed rules that prescribe procedures for Congress.

Among the rules are these proscriptions: the House chooses its Speaker, the Senate its president pro tempore, and both houses their officers; each house requires a majority quorum to conduct business; neither house may adjourn for more than three days without the consent of the other; each house must keep a journal; the yeas and nays are ordered when supported by one-fifth of the members present; and all revenue-raising bills must originate in the House, but the Senate may propose amendments to them. Certain procedures must also be followed when the House elects a president, the Senate elects a vice president, a vacancy in the office of vice president is filled, and there is an attempt to override a presidential veto.

The Constitution also sets out specific rules on matters that require votes or voting methods, such as a two-thirds vote to override a presidential veto or propose a constitutional amendment and to expel a member. A two-thirds Senate vote is required to convict a person whom the House has impeached and to consent to ratification of treaties. But the Constitution requires only a majority vote in the House to elect a president when no candidate receives a majority of the electoral votes.

Contempt of Congress

John Conyers Jr., D-Mich., chairs a House Judiciary Committee meeting to consider citing two former White House officials, Harriet Miers and Joshua Bolton, for contempt of Congress for their refusal to comply with subpoenas issued in an investigation of the firings of nine U.S. attorneys in 2006. The committee approved the report but the full House had not by November 2007.
Source: CQ Photo/Dana Statton

A person who refuses to testify or to produce documents demanded by a congressional committee risks being cited for contempt of Congress, a criminal offense. This ability to punish for contempt reinforces the congressional INVESTIGATIONS process.

The Constitution does not specifically grant Congress the power to punish for contempt, except in the case of one of its own members. But from the beginning Congress assumed that it could jail persons who were judged in contempt. It even confined some of them in the Capitol. At first Congress imposed punishment itself, but since the 1930s contempt cases have been prosecuted in the courts.

When a committee wishes to begin criminal proceedings against an uncooperative witness, it introduces a resolution in the Senate or House citing the witness for contempt. If the full chamber approves the resolution, as it generally does, the matter is referred to a U.S. attorney for prosecution in a federal court. Contempt of Congress is a misdemeanor punishable by a fine of $100 to $1,000 and one to twelve months' imprisonment.

On rare occasions contempt citations stem from acts, such as bribery or libel, that obstruct the proper functions of Congress. Most contempt citations in modern times, however, have resulted from refusal to cooperate with congressional committees. The peak period for contempt citations came in the years following World War II. In those years the House Un-American Activities Committee zealously pursued people suspected of association with organizations that were considered subversive, such as the Communist Party. In 1950 the House voted fifty-nine contempt citations, fifty-six of them recommended by the Un-American Activities Committee. Many cases involved private persons who invoked Fifth Amendment protection against self-incrimination.

More recently, most contempt disputes have been triggered by the refusal of executive branch officials to supply documents sought by Congress. These disputes have tested the limits of EXECUTIVE PRIVILEGE to withhold confidential information. They have often been settled through compromise. That was the case in 1982 when a House committee recommended that Interior Secretary James G. Watt be cited for contempt for refusing to turn over documents sought by committee investigators. President Ronald Reagan eventually settled the dispute by giving committee members limited access to some of the documents for one day.

The House in 1983 held Anne M. Gorsuch (later Burford), head of the Environmental Protection Agency, in contempt of Congress. White House officials in 1983 agreed to meet subcommittee demands for access to some of that agency's documents, and the House subsequently canceled the contempt citation. Acting on Reagan's

CLOSER LOOK

Congress has the power to punish persons who refuse to testify or produce documents demanded by a committee. The punishment is carried out through a contempt citation, a criminal offense. However, the procedure is only rarely carried to this extent. More commonly a recalcitrant individual or executive agency reach a compromise to avoid the cost, lengthy time, and uncertainty of pursuing contempt proceedings to full criminal action.

orders, Gorsuch had refused to turn over the documents; she was the first person to be held in contempt of Congress for refusing to produce information on grounds of executive privilege.

The House Government Reform and Oversight Committee in August 1998 voted to cite Clinton administration attorney general Janet Reno with contempt of Congress for refusing to hand over internal Justice Department memos making the case for appointment of an independent counsel to investigate allegations of illegal fundraising by Democrats in the 1996 presidential campaign. The full House did not vote on the contempt charge, however. Reno was thought to be only the second attorney general cited for contempt by a congressional committee. William French Smith, Ronald Reagan's attorney general, was cited by a Senate subcommittee for failing to produce documents in 1981 pertaining to a probe of defense contractor General Dynamics Corp., but the matter was dropped.

In February 2002 Republican Dan Burton of Indiana, chair of the House Government Reform Committee, threatened to hold President George W. Bush in contempt for the Justice Department's refusal to turn over FBI records in a thirty-year-old case that led to wrongful criminal convictions. The administration handed over the documents before any action was taken.

In 2007 Democrats—now controlling Congress—and President George W. Bush were dueling over release of information about a number of activities of his administration, particularly the firing in 2006 of nine U.S. attorneys. Democrats had issued subpoenas for documents and testimony from administration officials, while the president was claiming executive privilege to shield information and individuals. As of November the administration had ignored the subpoenas and Congress had not taken contempt actions.

Continuing Resolution

A continuing resolution is a measure to keep government agencies operating when regular APPROPRIATIONS BILLS have not been enacted by the beginning of the government's FISCAL YEAR on October 1. The resolution takes its name from the fact that, if it does not become law, the agencies could not continue working because they would run out of money.

Congress has used continuing resolutions (called CRs in Capitol Hill jargon) for more than a century as a temporary expedient to buy time for completing action on regular appropriations bills. From 1954 through 2002 Congress approved at least one continuing resolution every year, except in 1988, 1994, and 1996 when lawmakers completed the appropriations bills on time. Most continued funding for a few days, weeks, or months. In the late 1970s, however, Congress began putting into continuing resolutions the entire text of appropriations bills that had not cleared. It also began to make the resolutions cover the full fiscal year. This trend reached its peak in 1986 and 1987, when Congress swept all thirteen regular appropriations measures into huge continuing resolutions that provided funding for entire fiscal years.

For decades the executive branch had shifted funds to bridge short gaps between the end of the fiscal year and the enactment of new appropriations. But in 1980 the attorney general prohibited that practice for all but essential costs; instead, agencies had to shut down if their funding lapsed. The impact of the ruling was dramatically illustrated the following year, after President Ronald Reagan vetoed a full-year continuing resolution for virtually the entire government. Federal workers were sent home, the Statue of Liberty and Washington Monument were closed, and the Constitution was lowered into a protective vault at the National Archives. Congress and the president hastily agreed on a substitute measure. Reagan vetoed continuing resolutions twice more during his presidency, shutting down the government for only a few hours each time.

By the early 1990s continuing resolutions were once again being used primarily to continue funding for a period of days or weeks. For fiscal year 1992 Congress adopted a total of four continuing resolutions, but the final one contained funding for only one of the thirteen regular appropriations bills.

A protracted battle between the 104th Congress and Democratic president Bill Clinton over Republican efforts to shrink the size and power of the federal government began in 1995 and finally concluded seven months later in April 1996, after fourteen continuing resolutions and an omnibus spending bill were enacted. (See OMNIBUS BILLS.) Two politically debilitating partial government shutdowns—November 14–19, 1995, and December 16, 1995–January 2, 1996—took much of the steam out of the so-called Republican revolution, and by the end of the process, Clinton had won at least partial funding for all of his priorities.

After passing a series of stopgap measures, Congress in 2003 once again used a continuing resolution to package together multiple funding bills for what was left of the fiscal year. Eleven fiscal 2002 appropriations bills were packed into a continuing resolution that cleared nearly five months into the fiscal year.

In 2007 Democrats, who had just taken back control of Congress from Republicans after the 2006 elections, decided to fund most of the government for fiscal 2007, ending September 30 that year, through a continuing resolution. Only two regular bills for that year had cleared, for defense and for homeland security. Democrats decided to focus on the fiscal 2008 appropriations bills rather than revisit the many conflicts and controversies in the unfinished 2007 bills.

Because of their urgency, continuing resolutions increasingly became magnets for controversial bills and amendments, or riders, that might not pass on their own. (See RIDER.)

Courts and Congress

The federal judiciary and Congress have the power to check each other's authority. Congress determines the courts' jurisdictions, confirms their members, and pays their bills. The judiciary—most particularly, the Supreme Court—defines the limits of congressional authority.

Both branches have exercised these powers with restraint. Leaving aside the frequent disagreements and heated rhetoric, there have been few instances of direct conflict between the judiciary and Congress.

Judicial System

The framers of the Constitution left much unwritten regarding the judicial branch. Unlike Articles I and II of the Constitution, which listed the powers and prerogatives of Congress and the executive, Article III simply sketched the outline of a federal judiciary. "The judicial Power of the United States shall be vested in one supreme Court, and in such inferior Courts as the Congress may from time to time ordain and establish," the Constitution states. The existence and structure of any federal courts lower than the Supreme Court were left entirely to the discretion of Congress.

Congress exercised that discretion early in its history. The Judiciary Act of 1789 established the Supreme Court, three circuit courts of appeal, and thirteen district courts. Thereafter, as the nation grew and the federal judiciary's workload increased, Congress established additional circuit and district courts. In 2007 the system consisted of thirteen circuit courts and ninety-four district and territorial courts.

Judicial Review

The Constitution is silent on the question of judicial review. It grants various powers to the judiciary but does not mention the authority to declare unconstitutional and nullify a law passed by Congress.

Many constitutional scholars agree that most of the framers intended the Supreme Court to assume the power of judicial review. Writing under the name of Publius in *The Federalist Papers*, Alexander Hamilton argued that "the courts were designed to be an intermediate body between the people and the legislature in order, among other things, to keep the latter within the limits assigned to their authority."

The question whether the Supreme Court could nullify an act of Congress was first answered in 1803. In *Marbury v. Madison,* a case that had begun as a relatively unimportant controversy over a presidential appointment, the Court laid down the principle of judicial review. Chief Justice John Marshall declared that "a law repugnant to the Constitution is void." In so doing, he firmly asserted the power of the Supreme Court to make such determinations: "It is, emphatically, the province and duty of the judicial department to say what the law is."

Despite the historic importance of the *Marbury* decision, the Court's assertion of its power to nullify a law attracted little attention at the time. More than fifty years elapsed before the power was exercised again.

Of the many thousands of acts passed by Congress in its more than two centuries, only about 160 had been declared unconstitutional by 2006. But the power of judicial review is a constant reminder to Congress that the laws it passes can be nullified by the Supreme Court if they violate the Constitution. (See LEGISLATION DECLARED UNCONSTITUTIONAL.)

> **"It is, emphatically, the province and duty of the judicial department to say what the law is."**
>
> —*Chief Justice John Marshall* in *Marbury v. Madison*, stating the principle of judicial review

Congressional Influence

Congress has several ways of influencing the judicial branch. It does so mainly through selection, confirmation, and impeachment of judges; institutional and jurisdictional changes; and direct reversal of specific decisions.

Individual Pressures

The Constitution requires that the Senate give its "advice and consent" to appointments to the federal judiciary. Through the custom of SENATORIAL COURTESY the Senate has wielded considerable influence over appointments to federal district courts. The Senate generally refuses to confirm a nomination within a particular state unless the nominee has been approved by the senators of the president's party from that state. Once a candidate is selected, the nomination usually receives a perfunctory hearing and quick approval. But there are exceptions. (See APPOINTMENT POWER.)

Indeed, the judicial nomination process has become highly politicized in recent years, as members of the party opposed to the president have sought to put the breaks on some nominees deemed too controversial. When the opposition party controls the Senate, one common tactic involves the Senate Judiciary Committee delaying hearings on a nominee. President George W. Bush suggested a new system in 2002 that would entail hearings in the committee to be followed automatically by a straight up-or-down vote on the floor of the Senate. The move would effectively remove the Judiciary panel's advisory role in the selection of judges. Congress appeared unlikely to embrace the idea.

Although the Senate has little to say in the selection of Supreme Court nominees, it does play a significant role once the nomination has been submitted for its approval. In the more than two centuries from 1789 to April 2007, the Senate confirmed 122 presidential nominees for the Court. The Senate rejected twelve nominees outright, took no action on ten others, and postponed action on three more, effectively killing their nominations. Most of these rejections occurred between 1793 and 1900. Only four nominees were rejected outright by the Senate in the twentieth century. (See table, p. 561)

Congress's IMPEACHMENT POWER is a rarely invoked power, but it has been used most often against federal judges. Federal judges made up thirteen of the seventeen officials who had been impeached by the House of Representatives by the end of 2007, and all seven of the officials convicted by the Senate. Three of the judges were convicted under Senate procedures in which a twelve-member panel heard evidence in the cases. The full Senate then voted on the recommendations of the panel.

Only one Supreme Court justice—Samuel Chase—has ever been impeached by the House, but he was acquitted in 1805 following a sensational Senate trial. Two other Supreme Court justices have faced serious threats of impeachment. William O. Douglas weathered impeachment inquiries in 1953 and 1970; Abe Fortas retired from the Court in 1969 after the House threatened an inquiry.

Congress has even used its power of the purse to show displeasure with the Court. (See PURSE, POWER OF.) In 1964, when legislation was passed authorizing federal pay increases, Supreme Court justices were given $3,000 less than the increase for other federal executives. The action was generally seen as retaliation for recent Court decisions on such issues as obscenity, school prayer, and desegregation.

Institutional Pressures

Congress sometimes tries to influence the judiciary through institutional or procedural changes, but it has considered many more proposals than it has approved.

A 1937 American newspaper cartoon illustrates President Franklin D. Roosevelt's plan to enlarge the Supreme Court to save his New Deal agencies and programs.
Source: U.S. Senate Historical Office

Congress has the power to create judgeships; politics often plays an important role in the process. In 1801, for example, the Federalist-dominated Congress created additional circuit court judgeships to be filled by a Federalist president. But when the Jeffersonians came to power in the midterm elections, the new posts were abolished.

Congress has increased or reduced the number of justices on the Supreme Court seven times. Generally, laws decreasing the number of justices have been motivated by a desire to punish the president; increases have been aimed at influencing the philosophical balance of the Court.

The size of the Supreme Court has remained at nine since passage of the Judiciary Act of 1869, but proposals to change the number of justices have occasionally been put forward. The most serious proposal in the twentieth century came not from Congress but from the president. Franklin D. Roosevelt in 1937 proposed legislation that would have made it possible to appoint six additional justices. The increase was portrayed as an effort to improve the efficiency of the Court. In reality it was designed to allow Roosevelt to appoint new justices who would support the constitutionality of his NEW DEAL programs. A series of New Deal statutes had been struck down by the existing Court. The Court packing plan was strongly opposed within and outside of

Congress and was never enacted. Nonetheless, it coincided with a change of attitude on the part of the Supreme Court. Shortly after the proposal was made public, the Court upheld revised versions of several key statutes in quick succession.

Proposals have occasionally been made to require two-thirds of the Court to concur in order to declare unconstitutional an act of Congress or a state statute. However, Congress has seldom seriously considered such proposals.

In 1802 Congress delayed a decision by abolishing a Supreme Court term altogether. Once, in *Ex parte McCardle* (1868), Congress prevented the Court from deciding a pending case by repealing its appellate jurisdiction over the subject matter of the case. Several other such attempts have been made, but they have been defeated, most of them by large margins.

Reversals of Rulings

Of all the methods of influencing the Supreme Court, Congress has had most success in reversing individual Supreme Court rulings through adoption of CONSTITUTIONAL AMENDMENTS or passage of legislation.

Four of the twenty-seven amendments to the Constitution were adopted specifically to overrule the Supreme Court's interpretation of the Constitution. The amendments reversed rulings on the ability of citizens of one state to bring suit against another state (Eleventh Amendment), the application of the Bill of Rights to the states (Fourteenth Amendment), the income tax (Sixteenth Amendment), and the extension of voting rights to eighteen-year-olds (Twenty-sixth Amendment).

Congress has frequently reversed Supreme Court rulings on statutory questions by approving amendments to the laws at issue; one scholar counted more than 120 such instances in the period between 1967 and 1990. In some cases, Congress decided that the Court interpreted a law contrary to lawmakers' intentions. In other cases, the Court answered questions left open by Congress and produced a result that lawmakers found unacceptable. In a few instances, the Court has even suggested how Congress could rewrite a law to better achieve its original purpose. Typically, the Court acquiesces in legislative overrides. On occasion, however, the Court has refused to go along with congressional efforts to void its decisions by legislation.

C-SPAN

C-SPAN is the acronym for Cable-Satellite Public Affairs Network. It provides live continuous coverage of Senate and House floor proceedings as well as televising important committee hearings in both chambers. In addition, it provides lengthy coverage of other important congressional events such as press conferences and public affairs conferences. It is sent to all congressional offices and is carried on many cable networks. The House has televised its floor proceedings since 1979 and the Senate since 1986.

According to a 2004 survey by the PEW Research Center, C-SPAN has a highly loyal audience—which C-SPAN estimates at fifty-two million Americans—with more than 60 percent saying they find it useful.

In late 2006 C-SPAN president and chief executive officer Brian Lamb asked Rep. Nancy Pelosi, D-Calif., who was soon to become House Speaker, to allow the company to use and control its own cameras on the House floor. The request was denied. (See TELEVISING CONGRESS.)

D

Daschle, Tom

A mild-mannered, popular politician who nonetheless was known for his steely determination to win and underlying partisanship, Tom Daschle (1947–) of South Dakota served as Senate majority leader during a chaotic period from mid-2001 to 2003. Daschle's Democrats regained majority status in the Senate after Vermont Republican senator Jim Jeffords decided in May 2001 to leave the GOP, become an Independent, and caucus with the Democrats. This change, which was made official on June 6, gave the Democrats control of the chamber by a margin of 50 Democrats to 49 Republicans and one Independent.

A few months later, the September 11 terrorist attacks reshaped the congressional agenda as leaders tried to determine how to improve the nation's defenses. Daschle supported the Bush administration's decision to launch a military campaign in Afghanistan and, with reservations, backed a move in 2002 to give the administration the authority to invade Iraq.

However, Daschle's hold on the Senate was tenuous, and Democratic losses in the 2002 elections handed control back to the Republicans in the 108th Congress

Tom Daschle, South Dakota senator from 1987 to 2005, served as both majority and minority leader in the Senate.
Source: CQ Photo/Scott J. Ferrell

(2003–2005). Daschle began his congressional career as an aide to South Dakota Democrat senator James G. Abourezk in the mid-1970s, before winning a seat in the House in 1978. During his service in the House from 1979 until 1987, he secured his reputation as a fierce advocate of aid to farmers. In 1987 he moved to the Senate, where he became minority leader in 1995. In that post, he negotiated a landmark power-sharing agreement with the Republicans at the beginning of the 107th Congress in 2001, when the Senate was split 50–50 and the GOP was in control because Republican vice president Richard B. CHENEY had the power to break a tie vote. That agreement gave Democrats equal representation on Senate committees and equal staff resources and office space. That all changed a few months later when Jeffords made his switch.

After his tenure as majority leader, Daschle returned to the minority leader post in 2003. Although he had been considered a formidable candidate for the Democratic presidential nomination in 2004, Daschle in early 2003 took himself out of the race. He said he wanted to remain focused on leading his party in the Senate where "my passion lies." In 2004 Republicans targeted him as a liberal Democrat in a generally conservative state. He lost his reelection race by 4,508 votes out of a total of 391,188 cast.

Debt Limit

Since 1917 Congress has set an overall debt ceiling that fixes the limit for federal government borrowing from the public. Over the years the limit has been lifted many times to accommodate increased borrowing as the federal government expanded and deficits became routine. The increase is always granted because to refuse it would prevent the government from paying its bills. But, equally, the increase exercise is invariably a vehicle for conservatives to vent their anger over what they see as proliferate government spending.

Debt-limit debates quickly become highly politicized. Many members of Congress have a love-hate relationship with bills that raise the debt limit because such bills often serve as a way to get around the regular legislative process in Congress. Congress has little choice but to pass debt-limit bills so government bills are paid. Congress must act on them quickly, and a president is likely to think twice before vetoing them.

This gives debt-ceiling measures a special urgency that makes them a natural target for unrelated amendments. (See RIDER.) Members whose pet proposals are languishing in committee frequently try to slip them through as amendments to debt-ceiling bills.

Many major proposals have become law as amendments to debt-limit measures. A 1985 debt-limit increase included a radical overhaul of the congressional BUDGET PROCESS. Known as the Gramm-Rudman-Hollings Act, the budget measure swept through Congress without committee consideration or extensive floor debate. Two years later another debt bill was used to make major repairs in the original Gramm-Rudman-Hollings law.

Conservatives often used debt-limit debates to protest high federal spending. In 1995 Republican strategists hoped to use a debt-limit bill to force President Bill Clinton to accede to their plan for balancing the federal budget in seven years. The showdown came when Congress sent Clinton legislation containing a short-term debt-limit extension along with a provision barring the juggling of accounts to put off default in the absence of a permanent debt-ceiling extension. The two provisions were designed to force Clinton either to forge a budget deal or face the prospect of the nation's first-ever federal government default, while robbing the Treasury Department of the cash management tools required to forestall a crisis. The bill also included provisions to limit death penalty appeals and to require federal agencies to conduct risk-assessment and cost-benefit analyses on new regulations. Clinton vetoed it, and Treasury undertook a series of maneuvers that

CLOSER LOOK ◉

Can Anyone Spare a Dime?

In 2006 the national debt limit was increased for the fourth time under President George W. Bush, as it had been under almost all his modern-day predecessors. The debt limit then stood at just under $9 trillion.

forestalled default and enabled the administration to resist the Republican budget demands. Congressional leaders ultimately backed down in 1996 and voted to raise the debt limit.

The next hike came during a rare time of peace in the budget wars, when the GOP Congress and Clinton came together to pass the 1997 balanced budget law. The debt limit was increased as part of the measure.

By 2002 the debt limit was a politically sensitive issue once again. But this time the parties had reversed roles. It was the Republicans who wanted an increase in the debt limit and the Democrats who hoped to use that to their advantage.

Some Democrats wanted to use the must-pass legislation to extract more discretionary spending than Republicans wanted to allow. In addition, many Democrats wanted to use the issue to inflict maximum political pain on GOP leaders, portraying them as fiscally irresponsible tax-cutters who had not planned ahead.

House Republican leaders blamed the need to raise the debt limit on the September 11, 2001, terrorist attacks and a stumbling economy. Hoping to avoid an uncomfortable up-or-down vote, they pushed to attach the debt ceiling increase to an antiterrorism supplemental spending bill. But Senate Democrats refused to go along. Meanwhile, the government bumped against the limit, forcing the Treasury to execute short-term accounting maneuvers to avert a default. Congress then finally enacted a stand-alone bill.

However, by early 2003, President George W. Bush had to ask for another increase in the debt limit as the public debt neared the $6.4 trillion cap. In 2006 the ceiling was raised once again, by $781 billion, the fourth increase since President Bush took office in 2001. The debt limit then stood at just under $9 trillion.

Deferral *See* BUDGET PROCESS; LEGISLATIVE VETO.

Deficit *See* BUDGET PROCESS.

DeLay, Tom

Tom DeLay, a Texas Republican, was one of the most powerful members of the House during the GOP's twelve years in power beginning in 1995. He was a central part of the Republican leadership, first as minority whip in 1995 and then majority leader in 2003. Rep. New Gingrich of Georgia, who served as Speaker from 1995 until his resignation at the end of 1998, was the engineer behind the ascent of House Republicans to the majority in the 1994 elections. But it was DeLay, more than any other representative in the GOP hierarchy, who was the force behind the disciplined Republican ranks that relentlessly pushed through the conservative political and economic agenda of the administration of George W. Bush. DeLay constructed and then drove an internal operation that used all the levers of power—organizations, political, and financial—that kept the GOP majority running smoothly. He became known as "the Hammer" for his aggressive tactics in lining up votes for Republican bills, and was proud of the nickname.

DeLay built a whip operation that consistently delivered the needed votes for Republican bills. By arranging for his hand-picked deputy whip, J. Dennis Hastert of Illinois, to become Speaker in 1999, DeLay saved the GOP from continuing embarrassment after Gingrich's fall from grace over his leadership style and 1998 election losses. DeLay engineered the "K Street Project," which not only compelled lobbying firms and advocacy groups to hire many more Republicans, but also gave them specific assignments for writing legislation, raising money, and delivering votes.

DeLay got much of the credit for Republican election strengths that maintained a majority after 2002. In that year, he organized a widespread get-out-the-vote drive that helped the GOP gain seats rather than losing them as historically occurs in a midterm election when a party controls the White House. The next year, to further cement a Republican majority, he was instrumental in redrawing congressional district boundaries in Texas to create more politically safe House seats for Republicans, a strategy that paid off when all but one of the GOP candidates won in the next election.

DeLay's career, however, ended ignominiously in 2006 when, on June 6, he resigned from the House after being indicted in Texas on criminal charges from alleged election violations in the state. His House career and influence had been threatened for a lengthy period before as he was tainted by a series of ethics charges and, most significantly, by his close proximity to a widening influence-peddling scandal involving an influential lobbyist named Jack Abramoff. Once a close associate of DeLay, Abramoff agreed in early 2006 to cooperate

Tom DeLay of Texas was one of the House's most powerful Republicans, rising to the position of majority leader in 2003. He resigned in 2006 when he was indicted on criminal charges from election violations.
Source: CQ Photo/Scott J. Ferrell

with federal investigators and pleaded guilty to charges of conspiracy, mail fraud, and income tax evasion. Earlier, in 2004, DeLay was admonished two times in one week by the House Committee on Official Standards, better known as the House ethics committee, for exceeding the bounds of acceptable behavior in promoting his political and legislative agenda.

During his run as the powerful House GOP leader second only to the Speaker himself, DeLay used his hardball tactics to great success, keeping fellow Republicans in line and almost entirely shutting out Democratic participation in the legislative process. One of his most famous acts—Democrats called it infamous—was a key role in 2003 in holding open a House floor vote on a controversial drug prescription program for Medicare for three hours while enough GOP votes were rounded up to pass the legislation; normally, roll-call votes are not supposed to last more than fifteen minutes. The drug vote also led the ethics committee to later admonish DeLay for using tactics to change the vote of one reluctant Republican that the panel said probably violated House rules.

By the end of 2007, DeLay legal problems remained unresolved as he awaited trial.

Delegates

In addition to its 435 voting members, the House of Representatives has five members with limited powers. They represent the District of Columbia and four islands closely linked to the United States: Puerto Rico, the Virgin Islands, Guam, and American Samoa. All are known officially as delegates, except the representative of Puerto Rico, who is called a resident commissioner. The delegates are elected to two-year terms, while the resident commissioner serves for four years. In 2007 an effort was underway in Congress to make the District of Columbia delegate a full member of the House.

The five are allowed to vote in committees and make speeches on the floor, but they may not vote on the House floor. In 1993 the House Democratic majority changed the rules to allow the five to participate in many key floor votes. Under the new rule, the delegates and the resident commissioner

Del. Eleanor Holmes Norton, D-D.C., has represented the District since 1991. The four delegates and the resident commissioner of Puerto Rico have limited voting rights in the House.
Source: CQ Photo/Scott J. Ferrell

could participate in votes taken when the House constituted itself as the COMMITTEE OF THE WHOLE, a parliamentary framework under which the full House meets to debate and amend important legislation.

The new rule outraged many House Republicans, who charged that their voting power had been diluted in violation of the Constitution. (All five of the limited members at the time were Democrats.) In response, House Democrats agreed to soften the rule by requiring an automatic revote that excluded the delegates whenever their votes determined the outcome of an issue. Republicans lost a court challenge of the rule; but when their party took control of the House in 1995, the rule was rescinded and the five lost their floor-voting privileges. Democrats restored the privilege when they retook House control in 2007.

Nonvoting positions have existed in some form or other since 1794, when the House received James White as the nonvoting delegate from the Territory South of the Ohio River, which later became the state of Tennessee. Most of the current positions date from the 1970s; Puerto Rico's position was granted in 1900.

In addition to its House delegate, the District of Columbia in 1990 elected two "shadow" senators and one "shadow" representative. The delegation, which carried no congressional recognition, public budget, or salaries, was also given the mandate of lobbying Congress for District statehood. The "shadow member" tradition dates to the early nineteenth century, when six territories sent shadow senators to Congress before their admission as states. (See DISTRICT OF COLUMBIA AND CONGRESS.)

Dies Committee   *See* INVESTIGATIONS.

Direct Election of Senators

Like members of the House, senators are chosen by a vote of the people in each state. But it has not always been that way. Only since 1913 have U.S. voters had the right to vote directly for the men or women they want to represent them in the Senate. Before 1913 senators were selected by the legislatures of each state. The voters had only an indirect voice in the choice of senators, through their right to elect members of the state legislature. It required a decades-long battle, leading to the Seventeenth Amendment to the Constitution, to establish the direct election of senators.

Under the Constitution states were given seats in the House according to the size of their population. But seats in the Senate were equally divided, with each state having two senators. The framers of the Constitution thought of the House and Senate in basically different ways. House members were to be representatives of the people, elected by the voters. Senators, by contrast, were to be representatives of the sovereign states—"ambassadors," in effect, to the federal government. As a result the framers believed that the people should not elect senators. They believed that the legislatures would be more thoughtful and responsible in selecting people qualified to represent the interests of the states in Congress.

The Constitution gave Congress the right to establish specific rules governing the election of senators by the legislatures. For more than seventy-five years, however, Senate election procedures were left up to the individual states. The election system used by most states proved to have serious flaws. Most states required candidates to win majorities in both houses of the legislature. But since members of the two houses often disagreed on candidates, the system produced many deadlocks. Frequently all other legislative business ground to a halt as members of the legislature struggled vainly to agree on a candidate. Sometimes the legislature was simply unable to elect anyone, leaving the state without full representation in the Senate.

Congress reacted to the problems by passing a Senate election law in 1866. The law required the two houses of a state legislature first to vote separately on candidates. If no candidate received a majority in both houses, then members of both chambers were to meet together and vote jointly, until one candidate received a majority of all votes.

Unfortunately, the 1866 law did little to correct the problems surrounding Senate elections. Deadlocks and election abuses continued to occur as political factions in each state fought for control of its two Senate seats. The stakes were high because senators customarily controlled much of the federal PATRONAGE—government jobs and contracts—available in the state. In many cases the election of a senator became the dominant issue in the legislature, causing other important state business to be largely ignored.

Until the early twentieth century, voters had only an indirect voice in the choice of senators, through their right to elect members of state legislatures that, according to the Constitution, had the right to select senators. The ratification of the Seventeenth Amendment in 1913 established the direct election of senators.
Source: Library of Congress

A dispute in Delaware at the end of the nineteenth century illustrates how bitter and prolonged the fights over Senate elections could be. Divisions in the Delaware legislature were so fierce that no Senate candidate was elected for four years. The Delaware legislature took 217 ballots in 1895 over the course of 114 days without agreeing on a senator. For two years, from 1901 to 1903, Delaware was left entirely without representation in the Senate because members of the legislature could not agree on candidates. Other states also went without full Senate representation during this period. In 1893 deadlocks occurred in five states, and in three states— Montana, Washington, and Wyoming—the deadlocks meant Senate seats remained vacant.

The system also encouraged corruption. Because of the importance of Senate seats, and the relatively small numbers of state legislators who controlled them, candidates frequently were tempted to use bribery and intimidation to win. Controversies over alleged election fraud often had to be resolved by the Senate.

The basic criticism of legislative elections of senators, however, was that they did not reflect the will of the people. For more than a century the American political system had gradually tended to

Blair Lee, a Maryland Democrat, was the first senator to be directly elected to the Senate after the Seventeenth Amendment took effect in 1913. Previously, state legislatures selected senators, but bitter disputes sometimes left states without full—or any—Senate representation. Delaware's legislature took 217 ballots in 1893 without agreeing on a candidate. Deadlocks in 1893 resulted in Montana, Washington, and Wyoming having open Senate seats.

give the mass of voters more power. By the early years of the twentieth century the Senate was the most conspicuous case in which the people had no direct say in choosing those who would govern them.

Reform Efforts

Efforts to establish direct election of senators followed two different strategies. One involved a constitutional amendment, which passed the House on five separate occasions. But the Senate, all of whose members had been chosen by the legislatures, was adamantly opposed to direct election. Even after the legislatures of thirty-one states petitioned for a constitutional amendment for direct election, the Senate did not consider the proposal for many years. (See CONSTITUTIONAL AMENDMENTS.)

The other approach was through changes in state laws. Although the legislatures were required by the Constitution to select senators, reformers sought ways to ensure that the will of the people would control the legislatures' choices.

Oregon, which had a strong tradition of political reform, made the most determined attempts to guarantee the popular choice of senators. In 1901 the state established a system in which voters cast ballots for Senate candidates. Although the results were not legally binding, they were supposed to guide the legislature in selecting candidates.

The system initially was unsuccessful. The first time it was used, the legislature selected a candidate who had not received any votes at all in the popular election. Soon after, however, Oregon reformers devised a system in which candidates for the legislature promised to support the popular choice for Senate regardless of their preferences. Once most members of the legislature were committed to backing the candidate who won a majority of popular votes, the legislative election became a mere formality ratifying the choice of the people.

Other states soon adopted the "Oregon plan," so that by 1910 nearly half the senators chosen by the legislatures had already been selected by popular vote.

The state reform plans put more pressure on the Senate to approve a constitutional amendment. Fearing that the states would demand a new constitutional convention, senators finally agreed in 1910 to vote on a constitutional amendment for direct election. But opposition in the Senate remained strong.

After a long and heated battle in the Senate, Congress approved the amendment on May 13, 1912. The amendment became part of the Constitution on April 8, 1913, after the required three-fourths of the states had given their approval. The direct election amendment did not have dramatic consequences. Most of the senators who had been elected by the legislatures were reelected by the people. But over the years since 1913 the selection of senators by the people has become a key part of the American political system.

The first person to be directly elected after the amendment went into effect was Blair Lee, a Democrat from Maryland. His election came on November 4, 1913, but he had to wait until January of 1914 to take his seat because the senator in the Maryland slot, William Jackson, who had been named by the legislature, challenged Lee on the grounds that Jackson had been named under the original provisions of the Constitution and therefore was entitled to serve longer. The Senate disagreed and on January 28, 1914, declared Lee duly elected.

Dirksen, Everett McKinley

Everett McKinley Dirksen (1896–1969), a Republican from Illinois, was one of the most colorful members of Congress in the twentieth century. He was known as "the Wizard of Ooze" for his florid speaking style. As minority leader of the Senate from 1959 to 1969, Dirksen proved himself to be a master of compromise and persuasion. He used his great skills as an orator and negotiator to unify and strengthen the Republican voting bloc. His remark that "the oil can is mightier than the sword" spoke both to his skill in managing his flock and his ability to bring Republican legislation before a Democratic Senate.

Dirksen began his congressional service in the House of Representatives in 1933, but in 1949 illness forced him to leave the House. Upon his recovery, in 1950 he ran successfully for the Senate, where he served until his death in 1969. During the 1950s, Dirksen endorsed all of President Dwight D. Eisenhower's major policies and was elected minority whip in 1957, at the beginning of his second Senate term. Two years later he advanced to minority leader.

Sen. Everett McKinley Dirksen once commented on the value of switching positions at critical moments: "One would be a strange creature indeed in this world of mutation if, in the face of reality, he did not change his mind." In this photo Dirksen as Senate minority leader meets with President Lyndon B. Johnson in the Oval Office in the late 1960s.
Source: Senate Historical Office

Dirksen was unpredictable, often switching positions at critical moments. He publicly opposed the Civil Rights Act of 1964 and the nuclear test ban treaty but then voted for them. He played an important role in the passage of the 1968 Civil Rights Act. "One would be a strange creature indeed in this world of mutation if, in the face of reality, he did not change his mind," the senator once said.

Dirksen was unable to persuade the Senate to approve two of his favorite legislative projects, both of which would have reversed Supreme Court decisions of the early 1960s. In the wake of the Court's "one person, one vote" decision, he worked for a constitutional convention to restructure legislative apportionment. He also repeatedly sponsored resolutions to allow voluntary school prayer.

Discharge a Committee

Both the House of Representatives and the Senate have procedures by which committees may be relieved, or discharged, of legislation under their jurisdiction. The discharge mechanism was designed as a way to keep committees from blocking action on controversial bills.

The House procedure, first adopted in 1910, works through a rarely used device called the discharge petition. If a bill has been held up by a legislative committee for at least thirty days, or if the Rules Committee refuses to clear it for floor action within seven days, any member may offer a motion to discharge the committee of the bill. (See RULES COMMITTEE, HOUSE.) The CLERK OF THE HOUSE draws up a discharge petition, and if a majority of the House (218 members, if there are no vacancies) signs on, the discharge motion goes on the Discharge CALENDAR.

The names of House members signing the petition and the order in which they sign are published in the CONGRESSIONAL RECORD on a weekly basis and made public by the clerk daily. At one time the identity of members signing a discharge petition was kept secret until the required 218 signatures had been obtained. But, in an attempt to pressure more to sign such petitions, members primarily from the Republican minority pushed through a rules change in 1993 requiring ongoing public disclosure. Ironically, the resolution to open up the process to public view was passed only after it was discharged from the Rules Committee.

Once a motion to discharge has been placed on the calendar, there is a seven-day grace period. After that, if the committee still has not acted on the bill, any member may move to call up the discharge motion on the floor. If that motion is approved, a motion to call up the bill itself follows. Discharge measures may be considered on the second and fourth Mondays of each month, except during the last six days of the session.

Discharge efforts are seldom successful, since members are reluctant to disregard a committee's judgment and the committee review process. Plus, the committee is usually working in concert with or at the direction of the leadership. (If the leadership wanted a vote on a measure, it could simply use the Rules Committee to bring it out to the floor.) Still, the threat of such a move may spur action. That happened in 1983, when the House Ways and Means Committee approved a controversial tax-withholding bill only after 218 members had signed a discharge petition to force the bill to the floor. Gun control legislation was reported from the Judiciary Committee in 1985, after 200 members signed a discharge petition; another eighteen signatures on that petition forced the Rules Committee to send a specific version of the legislation to the floor. An attempt by the Republican leadership in 1998 to block consideration of any major campaign finance legislation, particularly an important bipartisan bill, triggered a discharge effort; when the petition moved above 200 signatures, the leadership capitulated and agreed to allow floor debate on various competing proposals.

Campaign finance legislation was finally enacted in 2002, but only after House sponsors once again used a discharge petition to get their bill to the floor. The bill originally had been set to go to the floor in July 2001. But then the House Rules Committee, controlled by the GOP leadership, wrote a rule for the debate that the bill's sponsors objected to. After the rule was voted down, the Republican leadership refused to reschedule the bill. But over the next six months the bill's sponsors gathered the 218 signatures they needed on a discharge petition to bring the bill back to the floor. In February 2002 the House passed the bill. The next month the Senate agreed to it and it was signed into law.

The House has another little-used procedure, known as CALENDAR WEDNESDAY, to bring to the floor a bill that has been blocked by the Rules Committee.

Attempts to discharge a committee occur even less often in the Senate than in the House. Because the Senate allows nongermane AMENDMENTS on most legislation, it has little need for procedures to wrest bills out of reluctant committees. A member may simply offer the legislation blocked by a committee as an amendment to another measure being considered on the floor. Moreover, many members believe the discharge procedure undercuts the committee system.

The Senate discharge procedure is cumbersome and rarely effective. The motion to discharge, which is debatable and thus open to a FILIBUSTER, must be made during the MORNING HOUR. However, morning hour is rarely used in the Senate, and even if it were, opponents would have ample opportunities to delay any discharge attempt. If debate is not completed by the time morning hour ends, the motion is placed on the calendar, where it can be subjected to another series of delays. If a discharge attempt were to be successful, in virtually all cases the legislation discharged is placed on the Senate calendar. Legislation listed on the calendar can be brought up on the floor only by unanimous consent or by MOTIONS, which are debatable as well.

Disciplining Members

Congress is legally responsible for monitoring the behavior of its members. The Constitution states that Congress may "punish its Members for disorderly Behaviour and, with the Concurrence of two thirds, expel a Member." On that authority the House and Senate have sometimes voted to expel, censure, or reprimand an erring colleague. Other offenders have been stripped of chairmanships, rebuked, or fined.

Acting under the sweeping ethics codes Congress adopted in 1977 and enforced by law the following year, the permanent House and Senate ethics committees—formally known as the House Committee on Standards of Official Conduct and the Senate Select Committee on Ethics—investigate charges made against a member and recommend penalties. In some cases, the full House or Senate will act on the recommendations. Other times the ethics committees may express disapproval of a member's behavior without recommending formal sanctions by their parent chambers. (See ETHICS.)

> *Congress may "punish its Members for disorderly Behaviour and, with the Concurrence of two thirds, expel a Member."*
>
> —Article I, section 5, of the Constitution

The most serious discipline, and the rarest, has been expulsion, which under the Constitution requires support from two-thirds of those voting. Only a majority is required for a vote to censure, reprimand, or fine a member. Discipline involving a loss of chairmanship or committee membership is usually handled by the caucus of party members, which is responsible for those assignments. (See CAUCUSES, PARTY.)

Sitting in judgment of a colleague is something most members would prefer not to do. Many of those assigned to the ethics panels are reluctant conscripts serving as a favor to their party's leaders.

Sometimes the panels are spared difficult decisions on disciplining members by the timely resignations of those under fire. In 1989, for example, House Democratic leaders Jim WRIGHT of Texas and Tony Coelho of California resigned to avoid possible disciplinary action because of their financial activities. Wright, who was formally charged by the ethics panel with accepting improper gifts and using a book deal to evade House limits on outside earned income, became the first SPEAKER forced by scandal out of office in the middle of his term. Coelho, the majority whip, resigned amid controversy over his role in a "junk bond" deal and calls by an outside government watchdog group for an investigation.

Expulsion

Except for expulsions of Southerners loyal to the Confederacy during the Civil War, Congress has rarely used its powerful authority to remove a legislator from office for misconduct. The first expulsion occurred in 1797, when the Senate ousted William Blount of Tennessee for inciting members of two Native American tribes to attack Spanish Florida and Louisiana. The expulsion followed a House vote to impeach Blount—the only time the House, which originates all impeachment proceedings, has ever voted to impeach a senator or representative. The Senate headed off the impeachment proceedings by voting to expel Blount, something the House had no authority to do. (See IMPEACHMENT POWER.)

During the Civil War fourteen senators and three representatives were expelled. On a single day, July 11, 1861, the Senate expelled ten southerners for failure to appear in their seats and for participation in secession from the Union. One of the ten expulsions was rescinded after the expelled member's death.

From the Civil War through 2007, formal expulsion proceedings were instituted eleven times in the Senate and fifteen times in the House. Only twice during that time, however, have members actually been expelled. The House voted in 1980 to expel Rep. Michael J. "Ozzie" Myers, a Democrat

CASES OF EXPULSION IN THE SENATE

Year	Member	Grounds	Disposition
1797	William Blount, Ind-Tenn.	Anti-Spanish conspiracy	Expelled
1808	John Smith, D-Ohio	Disloyalty	Not expelled
1858	Henry M. Rice, D-Minn.	Corruption	Not expelled
1861	James M. Mason, D-Va.	Support of rebellion	Expelled
1861	Robert M. T. Hunter, D-Va.	Support of rebellion	Expelled
1861	Thomas L. Clingman, D-N.C.	Support of rebellion	Expelled
1861	Thomas Bragg, D-N.C.	Support of rebellion	Expelled
1861	James Chestnut Jr., States Rights-S.C.	Support of rebellion	Expelled
1861	Alfred O. P. Nicholson, D-Tenn.	Support of rebellion	Expelled
1861	William K. Sebastian, D-Ark.	Support of rebellion	Expelled[1]
1861	Charles B. Mitchel, D-Ark.	Support of rebellion	Expelled
1861	John Hemphill, State Rights D-Texas	Support of rebellion	Expelled
1861	Louis T. Wigfall, D-Texas	Support of rebellion	Not expelled[2]
1861	Louis T. Wigfall, D-Texas	Support of rebellion	Expelled
1861	John C. Breckinridge, D-Ky.	Support of rebellion	Expelled
1861	Lazarus W. Powell, D-Ky.	Support of rebellion	Not expelled
1862	Trusten Polk, D-Mo.	Support of rebellion	Expelled
1862	Jesse D. Bright, D-Ind.	Support of rebellion	Expelled
1862	Waldo P. Johnson, D-Mo.	Support of rebellion	Expelled
1862	James F. Simmons, Whig-R.I.	Corruption	Not expelled
1873	James W. Patterson, R-N.H.	Corruption	Not expelled
1893	William N. Roach, D-N.D.	Embezzlement	Not expelled
1905	John H. Mitchell, R-Ore.	Corruption	Not expelled
1907	Reed Smoot, R-Utah	Mormonism	Not expelled
1919	Robert M. La Follette, R-Wis.	Disloyalty	Not expelled
1934	John H. Overton, D-La.	Corruption	Not expelled
1934	Huey P. Long, D-La.	Corruption	Not expelled
1942	William Langer, R-N.D.	Corruption	Not expelled

SOURCE: Senate Committee on Rules and Administration, Subcommittee on Privileges and Elections, *Senate Election, Expulsion, and Censure Cases from 1793 to 1972*, compiled by Richard D. Hupman, 92d Cong., 1st sess., 1972, S Doc. 92-7; *Congress and the Nation 1981–1984*, Vol. 6. (Washington, D.C.: Congressional Quarterly, 1985); *Congress and the Nation 1993–1996*, Vol. 9 (Washington, D.C.: Congressional Quarterly, 1988).

NOTES: 1. The Senate reversed its decision on Sebastian's expulsion March 3, 1877. Sebastian had died in 1865, but his children were paid an amount equal to his Senate salary between the time of his expulsion and the date of his death. 2. The Senate took no action on an initial resolution expelling Wigfall because he represented a state that had seceded from the Union; three months later he was expelled for supporting the Confederacy.

from Pennsylvania, after he was caught in the a sting operation conducted by the Federal Bureau of Investigation (FBI) that came to be known as the Abscam scandal. Myers, who had accepted money from an FBI agent posing as an Arab sheik, was the first member of Congress ever expelled for corruption. The House in 2002 expelled Rep. James A. Traficant, a Democrat from Ohio, after he was accused of demanding kickbacks from some of his congressional aides and using his office for personal gain. A federal court jury earlier had found Traficant guilty of conspiracy to conduct bribery, seeking and accepting illegal gratuities, obstruction of justice, and filing false federal income tax returns. A subcommittee of the House ethics committee, after examining the criminal proceeding, found Traficant guilty of nine ethics counts. The full committee then recommended his expulsion.

CASES OF EXPULSION IN THE HOUSE

Year	Member	Grounds	Disposition
1798	Matthew Lyon, Anti-Fed.-Vt.	Assault on representative	Not expelled
1798	Roger Griswold, Fed.-Conn.	Assault on representative	Not expelled
1799	Matthew Lyon, Anti-Fed.-Vt.	Sedition	Not expelled
1838	William J. Graves, Whig-Ky.	Killing of representative in duel	Not expelled
1839	Alexander Duncan, Whig-Ohio	Offensive publication	Not expelled
1856	Preston S. Brooks, State Rights Dem.-S.C.	Assault on senator	Not expelled
1857	Orsamus B. Matteson, Whig-N.Y.	Corruption	Not expelled
1857	William A. Gilbert, Whig-N.Y.	Corruption	Not expelled
1857	William W. Welch, American-Conn.	Corruption	Not expelled
1857	Francis S. Edwards, American-N.Y.	Corruption	Not expelled
1858	Orsamus B. Matteson, Whig-N.Y.	Corruption	Not expelled
1861	John B. Clark, D-Mo.	Support of rebellion	Expelled
1861	Henry C. Burnett, D-Ky.	Support of rebellion	Expelled
1861	John W. Reid, D-Mo.	Support of rebellion	Expelled
1864	Alexander Long, D-Ohio	Treasonable utterance	Not expelled[1]
1864	Benjamin G. Harris, D-Md.	Treasonable utterance	Not expelled[1]
1866	Lovell H. Rousseau, R-Ky.	Assault on representative	Not expelled[1]
1870	Benjamin F. Whittemore, R-S.C.	Corruption	Not expelled[1]
1870	Roderick R. Butler, R-Tenn.	Corruption	Not expelled[1]
1873	Oakes Ames, R-Mass.	Corruption	Not expelled[1]
1873	James Brooks, D-N.Y.	Corruption	Not expelled[1]
1875	John Y. Brown, D-Ky.	Insult to representative	Not expelled[1]
1875	William S. King, R-Minn.	Corruption	Not expelled
1875	John G. Schumaker, D-N.Y.	Corruption	Not expelled
1884	William P. Kellogg, R-La.	Corruption	Not expelled
1921	Thomas L. Blanton, D-Texas	Abuse of leave to print	Not expelled[1]
1979	Charles C. Diggs Jr., D-Mich.	Misuse of clerk-hire funds	Not expelled[1]
1980	Michael J. "Ozzie" Myers, D-Pa.	Corruption	Expelled
1990	Barney Frank, D-Mass.	Discrediting House	Not expelled[2]
2002	James A. Traficant, D-Ohio	Felony convictions[3]	Expelled

SOURCE: Asher C. Hinds and Clarence Cannon, *Hinds' and Cannon's Precedents of the House of Representatives of the United States*, 11 vols. (Washington, D.C.: Government Printing Office, 1935–1941); Joint Committee on Congressional Operations, *House of Representatives Exclusion, Censure, and Expulsion Cases from 1789 to 1973*, 93d Cong., 1st sess., 1973, committee print; *Congressional Quarterly Almanac, 1980* (Washington, D.C.: Congressional Quarterly, 1981); *Congressional Quarterly Weekly Report*, selected issues.

NOTES: 1. Censured after expulsion move failed or was withdrawn. 2. Reprimanded after expulsion and censure moves failed. 3. Convicted on ten felony counts, including conspiracy to commit bribery and tax evasion.

In most other cases the House shied away from expulsion and instead opted for a lesser form of punishment. Eleven of the House expulsion cases resulted in censure or reprimand. Several members have resigned to avoid expulsion proceedings. Among them was Mario Biaggi, a New York Democrat who was twice convicted on criminal charges that included accepting bribes. Biaggi resigned in 1988 to avoid near certain expulsion from the House.

The Senate Select Committee on Ethics in 1982 recommended the expulsion of New Jersey Democrat Harrison A. Williams Jr., another Abscam target. Senate floor debate had already begun

○ CLOSER LOOK

Rep. James Traficant, an Ohio Democrat, was expelled from the House in July 2002 for ethics violations stemming from a federal conviction on charges of bribery, kickbacks, and tax evasion. His expulsion was only the fifth in House history and the first since 1980. No senator has been expelled since the Civil War, although two resigned in modern times in the face of almost certain expulsion.

James A. Traficant
Source: CQ Photo/Scott J. Ferrell

by the time Williams, realizing that a vote to expel him was likely, announced his resignation. In 1995 Republican Sen. Bob Packwood of Oregon resigned after the ethics panel recommended his expulsion on charges of sexual harassment and other misconduct. These two were among the eleven against whom expulsion proceedings were begun.

Censure

By the end of 2007, there had been nine times in the Senate and twenty-two times in the House that a majority of legislators had voted to censure a colleague for misconduct. Censure is a formal show of strong disapproval that requires a legislator to listen as the presiding officer reads aloud the condemnation of his or her actions. In the House the member must stand at the front of the chamber while being censured and, unlike the Senate, usually cannot speak in his or her defense.

CENSURE PROCEEDINGS IN THE SENATE

Year	Member	Grounds	Disposition
1811	Timothy Pickering, Fed-Mass.	Breach of confidence	Censured
1844	Benjamin Tappan, D-Ohio	Breach of confidence	Censured
1850	Thomas H. Benton, D-Mo.	Disorderly conduct	Not censured
1850	Henry S. Foote, Unionist-Miss.	Disorderly conduct	Not censured
1902	John L. McLaurin, D-S.C.	Assault	Censured
1902	Benjamin R. Tillman, D-S.C.	Assault	Censured
1929	Hiram Bingham, R-Conn.	Bringing Senate into disrepute	Condemned[1]
1954	Joseph R. McCarthy, R-Wis.	Actions "contrary to senatorial ethics and tend[ing] to bring the senate into dishonor and disrepute, to obstruct the constitutional processes of the senate"	Condemned[1]
1967	Thomas J. Dodd, D-Conn.	Financial misconduct	Censured
1979	Herman E. Talmadge, D-Ga.	Financial misconduct	Denounced[2]
1990	Dave Durenberger, R-Minn.	Financial misconduct	Denounced[3]
1991	Alan Cranston, D-Calif.	Improper conduct	Reprimanded[3]

SOURCE: Senate Committee on Rules and Administration, Subcommittee on Privileges and Elections, *Senate Election, Expulsion, and Censure Cases from 1793 to 1972*, compiled by Richard D. Hupman, 92d Cong., 1st sess., 1972, S Doc. 92-7; *Congress and the Nation 1977–1980*, Vol. 5 (Washington, D.C.: Congressional Quarterly, 1981); *Congressional Quarterly Almanac 1990* (Washington, D.C.: Congressional Quarterly, 1991); *Congressional Quarterly Almanac 1991* (Washington, D.C.: Congressional Quarterly, 1992).

NOTES: 1. The word "condemned" as used in the Bingham and McCarthy cases is regarded as the same as "censured." 2. The word "denounced" as applied to Talmadge and Durenberger is considered virtually synonymous with "censured." 3. The Ethics Committee reprimanded Cranston on behalf of the full Senate, after determining that it lacked the authority to issue a censure in the same manner. The reprimand was delivered on the Senate floor by committee leaders, but there was no vote or formal action by the full Senate. It was the first use of reprimand in the Senate.

CENSURE PROCEEDINGS IN THE HOUSE

Year	Member	Grounds	Disposition
1798	Matthew Lyon, Anti-Fed-Vt.	Assault on representative	Not censured
1798	Roger Griswold, Fed-Conn.	Assault on representative	Not censured
1832	William Stanbery, JD-Ohio	Insult to Speaker	Censured
1836	Sherrod Williams, Whig-Ky.	Insult to Speaker	Not censured
1838	Henry A. Wise, Tyler Dem.-Va.	Service as second in duel	Not censured
1839	Alexander Duncan, Whig-Ohio	Offensive publication	Not censured
1842	John Q. Adams, Whig-Mass.	Treasonable petition	Not censured
1842	Joshua R. Giddings, Whig-Ohio	Offensive paper	Censured
1856	Henry A. Edmundson, D-Va.	Complicity in assault on senator	Not censured
1856	Laurence M. Keitt, D-S.C.	Complicity in assault on senator	Censured
1860	George S. Houston, D-Ala.	Insult to representative	Not censured
1864	Alexander Long, D-Ohio	Treasonable utterance	Censured
1864	Benjamin G. Harris, D-Md.	Treasonable utterance	Censured
1866	John W. Chanler, D-N.Y.	Insult to House	Censured
1866	Lovell H. Rousseau, R-Ky.	Assault on representative	Censured
1867	John W. Hunter, Ind-N.Y.	Insult to representative	Censured
1868	Fernando Wood, D-N.Y.	Offensive utterance	Censured
1868	E. D. Holbrook, D-Idaho[1]	Offensive utterance	Censured
1870	Benjamin F. Whittemore, R-S.C.	Corruption	Censured
1870	Roderick R. Butler, R-Tenn.	Corruption	Censured
1870	John T. Deweese, D-N.C.	Corruption	Censured
1873	Oakes Ames, R-Mass.	Corruption	Censured
1873	James Brooks, D-N.Y.	Corruption	Censured
1875	John Y. Brown, D-Ky.	Insult to representative	Censured[2]
1876	James G. Blaine, R-Maine	Corruption	Not censured
1882	William D. Kelley, R-Pa.	Offensive utterance	Not censured
1882	John D. White, R-Ky.	Offensive utterance	Not censured
1883	John Van Voorhis, R-N.Y.	Offensive utterance	Not censured
1890	William D. Bynum, D-Ind.	Offensive utterance	Censured
1921	Thomas L. Blanton, D-Texas	Abuse of leave to print	Censured
1978	Edward R. Roybal, D-Calif.	Lying to House committee	Not censured[3]
1979	Charles C. Diggs Jr., D-Mich.	Misuse of clerk-hire funds	Censured
1980	Charles H. Wilson, D-Calif.	Financial misconduct	Censured
1983	Gerry E. Studds, D-Mass.	Sexual misconduct	Censured
1983	Daniel B. Crane, R-Ill.	Sexual misconduct	Censured
1990	Barney Frank, D-Mass.	Discrediting House	Not censured[3]
1997	Newt Gingrich, R-Ga.	Providing false statements to House	Not censured[4]

SOURCE: Asher C. Hinds and Clarence Cannon, *Hinds' and Cannon's Precedents of the House of Representatives of the United States,* 11 vols. (Washington, D.C.: Government Printing Office, 1935–1941); Joint Committee on Congressional Operations, *House of Representatives Exclusion, Censure, and Expulsion Cases from 1789 to 1973,* 93d Cong., 1st sess., 1973, committee print; *Congress and the Nation 1977–1980, 1981–1984, 1985–1988, 1992–1996,* Vols. 5, 6, 7, 9 (Washington, D.C.: Congressional Quarterly, 1981, 1985, 1989, 1997); *Congressional Quarterly Almanac, 1990* (Washington, D.C.: Congressional Quarterly, 1991).

NOTES: 1. Holbrook was a territorial delegate, not a representative. 2. The House later rescinded part of the censure resolution against Brown. 3. Reprimanded after censure resolution failed or was withdrawn. 4. Reprimanded and fined $300,000.

A typical censure was the wording read aloud in 1967 to Sen. Thomas J. Dodd, a Democrat from Connecticut. Dodd, who had been charged with pocketing for personal use more than $100,000 in campaign contributions, heard that his conduct was "contrary to accepted morals." The censure said Dodd's behavior "derogates from the public trust expected of a senator and tends to bring the Senate into dishonor and disrepute."

Censure has been prompted by a wide variety of actions, including treasonable utterance, a fist-fight on the Senate floor, insulting remarks made to colleagues, acceptance of stock for legislative favors, use of campaign contributions for personal expenses, and sexual misconduct. Probably the most publicized was the censure of Sen. Joseph R. MCCARTHY in 1954. Although his tactic of labeling colleagues and others as communists or communist sympathizers had long been controversial, the Senate for several years did nothing to curb the growing power of the Wisconsin Republican. Only after the nationally televised Army-McCarthy hearings, when McCarthy's arrogance and abuses were seen by the public, did the Senate act to "condemn" McCarthy, an action historians consider equal to a censure. (See INVESTIGATIONS.)

Among those censured have been the following:

Laurence M. Keitt, censured by the House in 1856 for not acting to stop an assault on a senator, even though he knew of the plan in advance and actually witnessed the attack. Keitt, a South Carolina Democrat, allowed a fellow South Carolinian, Rep. Preston S. Brooks, to strike Sen. Charles SUMNER, a Massachusetts Republican. Brooks attacked Sumner with a heavy walking stick while Sumner sat at his desk in the Senate chamber. An attempt to expel Brooks failed. Brooks resigned his seat but then was elected to fill the vacancy.

Oakes Ames, a Massachusetts Republican, and *James Brooks*, a New York Democrat, censured by the House in 1873 for their part in a financial scandal involving stock of the railroad construction company Crédit Mobilier that had been given to members of Congress in return for legislative favors.

South Carolina Democrats *Benjamin R. Tillman* and *John L. McLaurin,* censured by the Senate in 1902 for engaging in a fistfight in the Senate chamber.

Hiram Bingham, a Connecticut Republican, censured by the Senate in 1929 for placing on his staff a manufacturing association employee whose assignment was to advise on tariff legislation.

Charles C. Diggs Jr., a Michigan Democrat, censured by the House in 1979 for taking kickbacks from the salaries of his office employees.

Charles H. Wilson, a California Democrat, censured by the House in 1980 for using campaign contributions to cover personal expenses and accepting gifts from an individual with a direct interest in legislation before Congress.

Gerry E. Studds and *Daniel Crane,* censured by the House in 1983 in separate cases of sexual misconduct. Studds, a Democrat from Massachusetts, had admitted having a homosexual relationship with a teenager working as a congressional page. Crane, a Republican from Illinois, had an affair with a female page.

Of the nine members the Senate had in effect censured, the word *censure* was used against only five of them. As in the McCarthy case, historians have regarded the Senate's substitute terms as synonyms for *censure.* These have included the *condemnations* of Bingham and McCarthy and the *denouncements* of Herman Talmadge, a Georgia Democrat, in 1979, and Dave Durenberger, a Minnesota Republican, in 1990 (both for financial misconduct).

Reprimand

The reprimand was first used by the House in 1976 as a milder form of punishment than censure. A reprimanded House member is spared the indignity of standing before his or her colleagues to be chastised.

The most notable use of this punishment was the 1997 reprimand of Newt GIN-GRICH, the first SPEAKER OF THE HOUSE ever to be sanctioned. The case against Gingrich grew out of a series of televised town hall meetings and a college course the Georgia Republican had taught. They were financed through donations solicited by tax-exempt groups, an arrangement that allowed supporters to make undisclosed contributions and to claim tax write-offs as well—two benefits not available to political contributors. While the Speaker maintained that the course was nonpartisan and thus eligible for tax-exempt support, an ethics subcommittee found that it was probably tied to party politics and to Gingrich's quest to lead a Republican takeover of Congress. In a kind of plea-bargaining arrangement, Gingrich did not admit to improperly using tax-exempt groups for partisan politics but instead acknowledged that he had failed to seek legal advice in his use of foundations to finance the activities. He also conceded a more serious offense—that he had given the House ethics committee misleading information in the course of its investigation, which he publicly blamed on his lawyer. In addition to the reprimand, Gingrich was required to reimburse the ethics committee $300,000 to cover some of the costs related to sorting out the misleading information he had given the committee.

The House ethics committee first suggested a reprimand instead of censure in the 1976 case of Florida Democrat Robert L. F. Sikes. The longtime chair of the House Appropriations Subcommittee on Military Construction was reprimanded for failing to disclose stock holdings in a defense contractor and a bank on a naval base and for conflict of interest.

The House again opted for the lesser penalty in 1978, when John J. McFall, Edward R. Roybal, and Charles H. Wilson, all California Democrats, were reprimanded for their failure to report either campaign contributions or cash gifts from South Korean rice dealer Tongsun Park. In 1983 the ethics committee recommended a reprimand for Studds and Crane, but the House instead chose to censure them. George Hansen, an Idaho Republican, was reprimanded in 1984 after being convicted of violating federal financial disclosure laws. The next member to be reprimanded was Pennsylvania Democrat Austin J. Murphy in 1987; the House said Murphy had diverted government resources to his former law firm, allowed another member to vote for him on the House floor, and kept a "no show" employee on his payroll.

Rejecting calls for expulsion or censure, the House in 1990 went along with the ethics panel in reprimanding Massachusetts Democrat Barney Frank for using his office to help a male prostitute. Frank, who acknowledged in 1987 that he was homosexual, had befriended the man two years earlier.

On the Senate side, Alan Cranston, a California Democrat, was reprimanded in 1991 for improper conduct in the Keating Five Scandal. His case marked the Senate's first use of a reprimand as a form of punishment halfway between a committee rebuke and a full-Senate censure. The language used to reprimand Cranston was as severe as in a censure, but there was no formal action by the full Senate. The matter was taken to the floor and, without asking for a vote, Senate Ethics Committee leaders said the panel imposed the reprimand "on behalf of and in the name of the U.S. Senate." The Senate action differed from a House reprimand in that Cranston was present for the reprimand and gave a rebuttal and there was no vote.

Rebuke

A committee rebuke is yet another form of chastisement. The Senate Ethics Committee, for example, in 1991 rebuked four of the "Keating Five" for their role in

CLOSER LOOK

Sen. Benjamin Tillman
Source: Library of Congress

Among the more colorful episodes that led to censure came in 1902 involving South Carolina senators Benjamin Tillman and John McLaurin. According to a Senate history by Sen. Robert Dole, of Kansas, Tillman said "improper influences" changed McLaurin's vote on a treaty. McLaurin, "pale with anger," said the charge was "a willful, malicious, and deliberate lie." Dole recounted: "Tillman jumped forward and struck … McLaurin above the left eye. McLaurin returned a punch to his adversary's nose. Both men traded blows until separated by a doorkeeper and several senators. The presiding officer immediately ordered the doors closed and the galleries cleared." Both were later censured and suspended for six days.

the scandal. The panel issued a more formal rebuke in 1992 as a disciplinary action against Oregon Republican Mark O. Hatfield. The committee resolution rebuked Hatfield for violating the 1978 ethics act by neglecting to report the receipt of several expensive gifts. Most of the gifts were from a former president of the University of South Carolina, which had received a federal grant while Hatfield headed the Appropriations Committee. As in the Cranston reprimand, the committee said it was acting against Hatfield "on behalf of and in the name of" the full Senate, with no further action recommended. But the unusual floor presentation of the Cranston case was not repeated.

The Senate Ethics Committee in 2002 "severely admonished" Sen. Robert G. Torricelli, D-N.J., for improperly accepting expensive gifts from a former campaign supporter who was serving an eighteen-month prison term for making illegal contributions to Torricelli's 1996 campaign. The committee action followed a four-year Justice Department investigation of Torricelli's finances. Federal officials concluded they lacked sufficient credible evidence for an indictment but forwarded their findings to the ethics panel. Two months after the panel's rebuke, Torricelli abandoned his campaign for a second term amid plummeting poll ratings.

Sen. Robert G. Torricelli of New Jersey was "severely admonished" in 2002 for accepting gifts from a former campaign supporter. At the time, the supporter was serving a jail term for making illegal contributions to Torricelli's campaign in 1996.
Source: CQ Photo/Scott J. Ferrell

In other cases, both the House and Senate ethics committees have issued "letters of reproval" to members where more stringent action was not deemed necessary. The House committee took this path in 2001 when it formally rebuked five-term representative Earl A. Hilliard, D-Ala., following a nineteen-month probe into misuse of campaign money. The panel found Hilliard diverted campaign money for, among other things, campaign staffers doing work for businesses connected to Hilliard's family. The committee had issued a letter of reproval in 2000 to Rep. Bud Shuster, R-Pa., chair of the House Transportation and Infrastructure Committee, after a lengthy investigation of his ties to campaign donors and his business relationship with a former top aide-turned-lobbyist. The probe revealed, among other things, that Shuster received advice and scheduling services from the former aide eighteen months after she left his House office.

Loss of Chairmanship

Depriving members of chairmanships has been used as a form of punishment in the House since the 1960s.

Removal from his chairmanship was one of several disciplinary actions taken against Adam Clayton POWELL Jr., a Democratic representative from New York's Harlem district, who in the 1960s was the most prominent African American in Congress. Powell came under investigation for misuse of committee funds and other alleged abuses. He was deposed as chair of the Education and Labor Committee in a 1967 vote by the Democratic Caucus. The full House then voted to exclude Powell from the House, an action that the Supreme Court overturned two years later.

In the mid-1970s two powerful House Democrats resigned their positions as committee chairs to avoid having them taken away by the party caucus. Wilbur MILLS, a Democrat from Arkansas who chaired the House Ways and Means Committee, came under fire after publicity about his affair with an Argentine strip dancer, Fanne Foxe. Mills, who was eventually treated for alcoholism, gave up his influential position in late 1974 but served out the term to which he was reelected that year.

Two years later the spotlight was on Wayne L. Hays of Ohio, who chaired both the House Administration Committee and the Democratic Congressional Campaign Committee. Hays was accused of keeping a mistress, Elizabeth Ray, on his payroll. He was about to be stripped of both positions by the Democratic Caucus when he gave them up. Hays resigned from the House before any further disciplinary action was recommended.

Florida Democrat Robert Sikes, who was reprimanded by the House in 1976, subsequently lost his Appropriations subcommittee chair. In 1979 Diggs, who had been reelected in 1978 despite being convicted of taking kickbacks, voluntarily stepped down as chair of the House District of Columbia Committee and gave up a subcommittee chair as well. Diggs was later censured by the House.

Under rules adopted by the House Democratic Caucus in 1980 and the House Republican Conference in 1993, indicted committee and subcommittee leaders had to step aside in favor of the next ranking member if indicted for a felony punishable by two years or more in prison. If the charges were dropped or reduced or if the member was acquitted, the member could resume the committee leadership post. If the member was convicted or censured by the House, caucus members would choose a permanent replacement.

It was not long before the rules came into play. By the end of 1980, Democrats John M. Murphy of New York and Frank Thompson Jr. of New Jersey had lost full committee chairs following their indictments in the Abscam scandal, and Wilson had been stripped of his subcommittee chair after his censure. Others have been affected by the rule since then but, as of 2002, none more powerful than Ways and Means chair Dan Rostenkowski. The Illinois Democrat stepped down in 1994 after he was indicted on criminal charges stemming from an investigation of the House Post Office. Rostenkowski lost his reelection bid in 1994 and pleaded guilty to reduced charges in 1996.

When the Republican Conference adopted its rule in 1993, it exempted pending cases. As a result, Joseph M. McDade of Pennsylvania, who was under federal indictment on corruption charges, was allowed to keep his position as ranking Republican on the Appropriations Committee. However, when the Republicans took control of the House in the next Congress, McDade was ordered to step aside until the case against him was resolved, and Robert L. Livingston of Louisiana was chosen to chair Appropriations. McDade was acquitted in 1996, but Speaker Gingrich refused to accept Livingston's resignation to make way for McDade to chair the powerful committee.

Loss of Vote

When a member of Congress is convicted of a crime, the question arises whether he or she should continue to vote on the floor or in committee. To deny that right also denies representation to the people of the legislator's state or district.

Many years ago indicted senators voluntarily remained off the floor and did not vote. But in 1924 Montana Democrat Burton K. Wheeler continued to vote before he was acquitted of bribery, a charge he said was trumped up by the Warren G. Harding administration. Since then senators have kept on voting. Williams did so until he resigned in March 1982 following his Abscam conviction in May 1981.

The House in 1975 added to its rules a policy statement that members convicted of a crime for which the punishment could be two or more years in prison should refrain from participating in committee business or floor votes. The voluntary prohibition would end when they were cleared or reelected. On the latter basis, Diggs, who was convicted in October 1978 and reelected the next month, continued to vote until he resigned from Congress in 1980 and went to prison. His decision to vote, however, triggered a Republican-led effort to discipline him that eventually resulted in his censure.

Exclusion

Exclusion is a disciplinary procedure that applies to those not yet formally seated in the House or Senate. One purpose of the procedure is to resolve debate over whether just-elected legislators meet the basic constitutional qualifications for office; Congress has found some who did not. Legislators have also tried, sometimes successfully, to exclude Mormons who practiced polygamy, colleagues considered disloyal because of the Civil War, and individuals charged with misconduct.

The broad use of exclusion as a disciplinary tool was apparently ended by the Supreme Court decision in *Powell v. McCormack* (1969), which limited exclusion to cases in which constitutionally set qualifications for office were not met. Powell, who had challenged his exclusion from the House, had a flamboyant lifestyle that fueled colleagues' anger over his frequent absences, his extensive use of public funds for travel, and his payment of a congressional salary to his wife while she lived in Puerto Rico. Powell's response to the criticism was to insist that he was a victim of racism. New York Democrat Emanuel Celler, who chaired both the House Judiciary Committee and the special panel set up to investigate Powell, agreed publicly that he saw an element of racism in the vote to exclude him. In his appeal to the Supreme Court, Powell argued that Congress could refuse to seat an elected legislator only if the individual did not meet the qualifications spelled out in the Constitution: age, citizenship, and residence in the appropriate state or district. (See CONGRESS: STRUCTURE AND POWERS.)

The Supreme Court agreed with this argument and sharply limited the application of exclusion. However, the Court left up to Congress the discipline of members already seated. Powell, who had been reelected in 1968, took his seat in 1969 after the Court decision. The House then fined him $25,000 for his earlier misuse of government funds and stripped him of his seniority. After returning to Congress Powell rarely attended sessions, lost his seat in 1970, and died less than two years later.

District of Columbia and Congress

The framers of the Constitution gave Congress the exclusive right to legislate for the nation's capital. Striking a balance between federal and local interests has been difficult, however. The District's residents have continued to press a reluctant Congress for more autonomy ranging from additional voting rights in Congress to complete statehood. Some opponents of increased District self-rule argue that the drafters of the Constitution never intended the area to have the same authority as states in the union, a decision that only a constitutional amendment can change. Political and racial issues also have been important. The District is heavily Democratic and politically liberal, which has prompted many Republicans and conservatives to resist giving it more voting power in Congress. In addition, the District's population is heavily black, which in the past was depicted as creating racial overtones with a predominately white Congress that includes many members from areas of the nation where race remains a volatile issue. That was increasingly less true, however, in the early years of the twenty-first century.

Congress granted limited self-government to the District of Columbia in 1800, a situation that lasted for nearly seventy years. Then in 1874, after a brief experiment with a territorial system, Congress took back virtually all government authority over the District. For the next century Congress acted as the District's governing council while the president chose its administrators.

The Senate passed home-rule measures six times between 1949 and 1965. These were blocked in the House by the chair of the District of Columbia Committee, Democrat John L. McMillan of South Carolina, with the support of other southerners on the panel.

Pressure for home rule grew in the civil rights era. In the late 1960s President Lyndon B. JOHNSON persuaded Congress to loosen its grip on the District government, but the changes fell short of full home rule. Finally, in 1973, with McMillan and many of his supporters no longer in the House, Congress once more gave local residents limited control over their affairs.

The unusual layout of Washington, D.C., with its wide, diagonal boulevards and traffic circles is owed chiefly to architect Pierre Charles L'Enfant who modeled the city after capitals in Europe. President George Washington, however, grew exasperated with the hot-tempered L'Enfant and fired him when work fell behind schedule. Andrew Ellicott, a surveyor who worked with L'Enfant, completed this plan for the city. Ellicott's drawing was similar to the original one envisioned by L'Enfant.
Source: Library of Congress

Under the 1973 home-rule law, Congress retained veto power over legislation approved by the District's elected government, as well as control over the District budget. In the years that followed, the House and Senate continued to intervene from time to time in District affairs. The Senate abolished its standing Committee on the District of Columbia as part of a 1977 committee reorganization and placed District matters under the broad jurisdiction of the Senate Governmental Affairs Committee. The House would not do the same until 1995. Eventually, even the District subcommittees on the Appropriations Committee would disappear.

On a separate track from the home-rule debate was a drive by the District to give its residents a voice in national politics. The Twenty-third Amendment to the Constitution, ratified in 1961, permitted District residents to vote in presidential elections. The 1964 presidential election marked the first time since 1800 that citizens in the nation's capital had voted in a national election.

District residents have had a nonvoting delegate in the House since 1971. In 1990 Eleanor Holmes Norton, a civil rights lawyer and constitutional scholar, was elected to succeed Walter E. Fauntroy, who had served as the District delegate since the office was created. Norton assumed Fauntroy's leadership role in the fight for more autonomy for the District.

In 1978 Congress approved a proposed constitutional amendment that would have given the District of Columbia full voting representation in Congress—two senators and at least one House member. The proposal died, however, when it failed to win ratification by three-fourths of the states as required by the Constitution.

In the 1980s the proponents of autonomy increased their efforts to make the District a separate state. In 1990 District voters elected a nonvoting, unpaid delegation of two "shadow" senators and one "shadow" representative with a mandate to lobby Congress for statehood. One of the first senators was Jesse Jackson Jr., a nationally prominent black leader.

The House District Committee in 1992 approved legislation to transform the District into the fifty-first state, called New Columbia. Proponents of statehood argued that to deny District residents a voice in Congress amounted to taxation without representation. Opponents countered that statehood for the District would lead to similar claims from territories, such as Guam and the Virgin Islands. However, the legislation did not make it out of the committee. In 1993 a similar proposal was debated on the House floor for the first time, but it was rejected 277–153.

In 1993 Norton led the successful Democratic effort to give floor-voting privileges to the House's five nonvoting delegates when the House constituted itself as the COMMITTEE OF THE WHOLE. Their new power was completely symbolic as an automatic revote occurred that excluded them whenever their votes affected the outcome. (See DELEGATES.)

Statehood proponents suffered a setback in 1995, when the Republicans took control of Congress. On the first day of the new Congress, a rule change abolished the chamber's District of Columbia Committee, transferring its jurisdiction to the House Government Reform and Oversight Committee (which became the Government Reform Committee in 1999). The House Republicans also abolished the delegates' floor-voting privileges. They were restored in 2007 when Democrats regained House control.

In addition, in early 2007 an effort began in the House to make the D.C. delegate a full representative in Congress. The House passed legislation adding two seats to that chamber, one for the District and the other for Utah. The latter was a Republican-leaning state, which would balance the almost certain election of a Democrat in the District. The Senate in September 2007 voted not to take up the legislation. Observers thought that killed the proposal for the 110th Congress, but advocates promised they would try to persuade the Senate to try again.

Congress also enacted legislation in 1995 creating a five-member financial control board to restore order to the District's increasingly chaotic budgetary and fiscal affairs. The control board was to lose all but oversight power after the District had recorded four consecutive balanced budgets. Anthony A. Williams, a career public servant who had held managerial posts in other cities, was named the board's chief financial officer.

In passing the fiscal 1998 District of Columbia appropriations bill, Congress further altered the uneasy relationship between the District and the federal government by shifting several costly city services to the federal government. In return, the city was to forgo its annual federal payment, designed mainly to compensate the District government for property taxes not paid on federally owned or occupied real estate. The bill also stripped Mayor Marion Barry of much of his power. Many members of Congress blamed Barry for the District's precarious financial condition.

Washington residents thus were surprised by the announcement, in 1998, that the city government had posted a $185 million budget surplus for the previous fiscal year. Many commentators credited the turnaround to the self-effacing Williams. After Barry announced in 1998 that he would not seek a fifth term, Williams entered the mayoral race and easily won the Democratic primary and the general election.

The District's financial control board allowed Williams to resume control of virtually all of the city's daily operations after he was sworn in as mayor in January 1999. Under the arrangement, the heads of most city agencies reported to the new mayor through the District's chief management officer. Williams, firmly in control of the city's operations, was reelected in 2002 but retired when his term ended. By that time, the District's financial condition was significantly improved and considered on a sound foundation.

Dole, Robert

Through a combination of legislative skill and a forceful personality, Kansas Republican Robert Dole (1923–) became a formidable figure in the Senate in the 1980s and 1990s. He served as majority leader from 1985 to 1987 and again in 1995 to 1996, when he left the Senate to make a run for the White House. Having twice failed to win his party's presidential nomination (1980 and 1988), Dole won the Republican nomination in 1996 but lost in the general election to Bill Clinton.

Dole was first elected to the House in 1961 and moved to the Senate in 1969. He chaired the Republican National Committee from 1971 to 1973 and in 1976 was Gerald R. Ford's vice-presidential running mate on the losing Republican ticket. When the Republicans came to power in the Senate in 1981, Dole became chair of the Finance Committee. In that position he oversaw passage of several major bills, including President Ronald Reagan's sweeping 1981 tax-cut program.

Dole was often able—through a mixture of compromise, arm-twisting, and verbal lashing—to bring competing interests into line behind a controversial bill. He seasoned his legislative skill with a quick wit and a sharp tongue. His leadership style was in marked contrast to that of the amiable Howard H. BAKER Jr., the Tennessee Republican whom he succeeded as majority leader in 1985.

A fixture in the Senate for many years, Sen. Robert Dole served as majority leader from 1985 to 1987 and from 1995 to 1996. He also was the Republican Party's vice-presidential nominee in 1976 and presidential nominee in 1996. Here Dole as part of the Republican Congressional Leadership meets with President Ronald Reagan in the Cabinet Room at the White House in October 1985.
Source: Ronald Reagan Library

In June 1996 Dole resigned his Senate seat to run full-time for president, ending a thirty-five-year congressional career. Although Dole was an effective Senate leader comfortable with the wheeling and dealing needed to pass laws, he was a lackluster campaigner. He lost the race, taking 41 percent of the popular vote to Clinton's 49 percent. Later, the wives of the former political rivals became Senate colleagues. Elizabeth Dole was elected to the Senate as a North Carolina Republican in 2002, joining former First Lady Hillary Rodham Clinton who had been elected as a New York Democrat in 2000 and 2006.

Doorkeeper, House   *See* CLERK OF THE HOUSE; SERGEANT-AT-ARMS.

Douglas, Stephen A.

Called "the Little Giant" for his small stature and formidable talents, Stephen A. Douglas (1813–1861) was a skilled and energetic orator. He is best remembered as Abraham Lincoln's opponent in the Lincoln-Douglas debates of 1858. At the time of the debates Douglas was campaigning for his third term in the Senate, where he had served as a Democrat since 1847. He also served in the House of Representatives for two terms (1843–1847).

As chair of the Senate Committee on Territories, Douglas opposed anything that would hinder the organization of new territories or the entrance of new states into the Union. Because slavery proved to be just such a hindrance, Douglas searched for a compromise on the issue. He became an advocate of popular sovereignty, under which new states and territories could decide whether or not to allow slavery. In 1854 he sponsored the Kansas-Nebraska bill, allowing those territories to determine for themselves whether to allow slavery within their borders. The measure angered both North and South and led to violence in the territories.

In 1857 the Supreme Court handed down the Dred Scott decision *(Scott v. Sandford),* which held that Congress did not have the power to curtail the expansion of slavery. In 1858 Douglas and Lincoln, his opponent for the Senate, debated the Dred Scott decision. Douglas took the position that although the national legislature could not limit slavery, state legislatures could do so. Douglas won the election, but his position angered many southerners. In 1859, to punish him for his perceived opposition to slavery, the Senate Democratic Caucus voted to remove him as chair of the Committee on Territories.

Douglas opposed Lincoln in the presidential election of 1860 and lost in part because the Democratic ticket was split. He loyally supported the new president, and in 1861 he undertook a trip at Lincoln's request to encourage support for the government's policies. During the trip he contracted typhoid and died.

Democrat Stephen Douglas of Illinois, best remembered as Abraham Lincoln's opponent in the Lincoln-Douglas debates of 1858, was called the "Little Giant" for his stature and formidable talents. This satirical cartoon of Douglas campaigning for president in 1860 not only shows his height but also employs a double-entendre on the word "stump," referring to the colloquialism for campaigning as well as Douglas's wooden leg. Other presidential candidates in the illustration include Constitutional Union candidate John Bell of Tennessee (far left), Democratic candidate John C. Breckinridge of Kentucky (with the cane), and the eventual victor, Republican candidate Lincoln (leaning on fence).
Source: Library of Congress

Earmarks

An earmark is the practice of setting aside funds for a specific designated purpose, whether it is a use or a recipient. Members of Congress have long used earmarks to provide guaranteed funding for some purpose of significance to an individual, usually to benefit a member's district or state. Earmarks may be designated for such activities as research or demonstration projects, a park, a building or other construction project, an academic grant, or specific contracts to benefit businesses in the district or state. The earmark normally is placed in appropriations bills, but earmarks also are used to direct tax or user revenues to specific government trust funds, such as for highways.

Although spending earmarks had long been used, they became increasingly controversial in the first years of the 2000s as more of them began to appear in appropriations bills. The Congressional Research Service counted about 3,000 of them in 1996 but more than 13,000 ten years later. The growing use of earmarks became a political assault weapon for both parties as each accused the other of recklessly wasting taxpayer monies on pet projects of members, many of them of dubious value. Even disinterested experts said the use of earmarks removed the spending from a critical analysis of value, which restricted the ability of appropriations committees to make informed judgments about spending priorities and tradeoffs.

Democrats, on taking control of Congress at the beginning of the 110th Congress in 2007, promised to reduce earmarks by at least half and to require members to disclose their earmark requests and certify that the outlay did not benefit themselves or their spouses. Initially earmarks were banned, at least in part because so many came in—more than 30,000 in the House alone according to one report—that appropriators lacked time to evaluate their merit. But members soon took up a different tactics: calling agencies directly to secure funding for their favorite activities. Additional changes later in 2007 required that earmarks be publicly disclosed.

Economic Committee, Joint

Since 1946 the House and Senate have had a joint committee to monitor the nation's economy. The Joint Economic Committee has a much broader focus than most congressional committees. It tries to provide an overview of the economy and a look at long-range economic trends. Although it cannot write legislation, the Joint Economic Committee issues reports and holds hearings on a variety of topics, ranging from U.S. unemployment figures to Russian economic reforms.

Most widely known are the committee's annual March report and its midyear report, usually issued in August. The March report responds formally to the economic report issued early each year by the president's Council of Economic Advisers; both reports are mandated by the Employment Act of 1946, which set up the committee and the council. The goals of that act were "maximum employment, production, and purchasing power."

Because Democrats and Republicans have traditionally had such different expectations for the economy, the two parties have often written separate reports. During the administration of President Ronald Reagan (1981–1989), for example, Republicans usually predicted a healthy economy and Democrats forecast calamity.

Since 1967 the committee has had ten members from the Senate and ten from the House, with six majority and four minority members from each chamber. The post of committee chair rotates between the House and Senate every two years. The chair often initiates studies, directing the staff to work on a particular topic.

Two individuals put their personal stamp on the committee in the 1950s and 1960s. Rep. Wright Patman, a Texas Democrat, served as chair five times between 1957 and 1975. An outspoken critic of powerful commercial banks and the politics of the Federal Reserve Board, Patman used the Joint Economic Committee as a platform for his attacks.

On the Senate side, the chair was held three times in the 1950s and 1960s by Democrat Paul Douglas of Illinois, a prominent liberal who had been a well-regarded professor of economics at the University of Chicago.

Another longtime member of the panel was Senate Democrat William Proxmire of Wisconsin, who left Congress in 1989. He served twenty-seven years on the joint committee, including two terms as chair and two as vice chair.

In 2007 Sen. Charles E. Schumer, D-N.Y., was chair and Rep. Carolyn B. Maloney, D-N.Y., was vice chair.

Education and Labor Committee, House

The House Education and Labor Committee has responsibility for many of the programs established by the federal government to attack poverty and other social problems. Its jurisdiction includes federal education and job training programs, as well as a wide range of efforts to aid children, the poor, and the disabled.

After the Republicans took control of the House in 1995, the committee became the site of pitched battles between the parties over who should be in control of these programs—the federal government or state and local governments. The panel was known as the Education and Labor Committee during the decades of Democratic control before 1995. Republicans renamed it Education and the Workforce when they came into the majority. The name of the committee reflected the philosophic tensions between Democrats and the GOP. Organized labor, a major constituency of the Democratic Party, had long seen the panel as fertile ground for legislation it supported. Republicans, with little sympathy for labor unions, removed the term from the name and substituted "workforce," to emphasize their interest in workplace relations. In 2007 the Democrats, back in control of the panel after twelve years in the minority, put "labor" back in the name.

Philosophical differences were seen as the committee struggled with reauthorization of the Elementary and Secondary Education Act in 2001. The political parties were bitterly divided over how far the federal government should go in influencing public school policy. The committee was headed by a chair who was a conservative GOP loyalist—John A. Boehner of Ohio—and a ranking Democrat who was an ardent liberal—George Miller of California. But compromises were reached and the most ambitious overhaul to date of the 1965 law ultimately was enacted. That legislation was known as the No Child Left Behind law. It became a magnet for praise and criticism in the next five years.

Rep. George Miller, chair of the House Education and Labor Committee, House Speaker Nancy Pelosi, and Rep. Xavier Becerra discuss labor legislation at a news conference. Many saw Miller's close friendship with fellow Californian Pelosi as an advantage that drew attention to his education and labor initiatives.
Source: CQ Photo/Scott J. Ferrell

During the 1960s the committee was the originator in the House of much of the legislation sought by President Lyndon B. JOHNSON for his GREAT SOCIETY. Most important, it helped write the 1965 legislation that for the first time provided federal financial support for locally controlled elementary and secondary education. In later years the committee approved legislation that greatly expanded financial aid to college students and set up programs for health and safety in the workplace. In 1990 the panel shepherded through Congress the Americans with Disabilities Act, which prohibits job discrimination against the disabled.

The committee continues to have jurisdiction over many of those programs. But the panel's influence declined after its heyday in the 1960s, in part because the political climate in the House changed. Many House members became skeptical of the value of federal involvement in social problems. Few members favored creation of new social programs, and many advocated substantial reductions in spending on existing programs. Budget restrictions also limited the committee's ability to offer new social programs. As a result, the committee members found themselves increasingly isolated in the House and often left out of serious policy debate.

Even during President Bill Clinton's push for health care legislation in 1993–1994, the committee, which has joint jurisdiction over health care with two other committees, did not play the strong role that many of its members wanted.

During the 1990s the committee concentrated on defending existing programs. But the growing interest in education reform issues raised the committee's profile.

In 2007 the Democrats retook control of the panel and George Miller returned to the chair. A high priority for the panel in the 110th Congress was reauthorization of the No Child Left Behind law. But the panel was expected to take a careful look at it before acting. Even though Congress with bipartisan support approved the initiative of President George W. Bush in 2001, Democrats and much of the education community soon began to protest that it was underfunded and too difficult to implement.

In other areas the committee was expected to favorably consider other traditional Democratic goals, including a higher minimum wage, increases in federal student aid, reexamination of student loan terms and interest rates, and a reauthorization of the Head Start program, the early-childhood development program for low-income children.

Miller was a close ally of the new House Speaker, Nancy Pelosi, a fellow California Democrat, which was expected to help the committee push its agenda in the 100th Congress.

Electing the President

Many Americans are aware that something called the electoral college plays a role in presidential elections, but few are able to say just what it is or how it works. The framers of the Constitution conceived the electoral college system as a compromise between direct popular election of presidents and the less democratic method of election by Congress. The system they established has been a source of confusion and controversy almost from the beginning.

Voters cast their ballots for president in November of every fourth year. Their choice is not final, however, until the following January when Congress meets to count the votes of the "electors" chosen in each state. Each state has as many electors as it has senators and representatives, and the District of Columbia has three electors, for a total of 538.

Counting the electoral votes is almost always a ceremonial function. But if no candidate for president or vice president wins a majority of electoral votes, the House of Representatives must choose the president and the Senate must choose the vice president. The House has chosen a president only twice. But several campaigns have been designed deliberately to throw elections into the House, where each state has one vote and a majority of states is needed for election. The spotlight was back on the electoral college in 2000 when the outcome of the presidential election hinged on

ELECTORAL VOTES BY STATE, 2004–2010

whether George W. Bush's razor-thin popular vote advantage over Al Gore in Florida would withstand legal challenges and he would claim the state's twenty-five electoral votes.

Few decisions of the framers have received more criticism than the constitutional provisions governing the selection of the president. Thomas Jefferson called them "the most dangerous blot on our Constitution." A proposed constitutional amendment to reform the system was introduced in Congress as early as 1797. Since then hardly a session of Congress has passed without the introduction of one or more such measures.

In 1969 the House voted 338–70 for a constitutional amendment to replace the electoral college with direct popular election of the president, but the amendment was derailed in the Senate. In 1979 the Senate voted 51–48 in favor of a similar amendment—a margin far short of the two-thirds majority needed for approval of constitutional amendments. In both cases, senators from small states were among the most vocal opponents. This was not surprising, since small states have disproportionate representation in the electoral college and would pull extra weight if the House elected a president.

CLOSER LOOK

The electoral college, in existence since the Constitution was written, is an institution that has no buildings, no campus, no curriculum, no faculty, and no football team. It also never actually convenes. It has been a constant source of confusion to American voters that the Senate and House—each once—have tried to put out of business.

Electoral Vote System

The Constitution provided that each state should appoint presidential electors, known collectively as the electoral college, equal to the total number of its senators and representatives. The electors, chosen as each state legislature directs, would meet in their separate states and vote for two persons. The votes would be counted in Congress, and the candidate who received a majority of the total would become president. The candidate who received the second highest number of votes would become vice president.

If no candidate won a majority of electoral votes, the House of Representatives was to select the president; each state would have one vote, and a majority of states would be required for election. Selection of the vice president would fall to the Senate, with a majority required.

At first no distinction was made between ballots for president and vice president. This caused confusion when national political parties emerged and began to nominate party tickets for the two offices. All the electors of one party tended to vote for the two nominees of their party. But with no distinction between the presidential and vice-presidential nominees, there was the danger of a tie vote. This actually happened in 1800, leading to adoption of the Twelfth Amendment to the Constitution, which required separate votes for the two offices.

The framers of the Constitution intended that each state should choose its most distinguished citizens as electors and that they should vote as individuals. But with the development of political parties, the electors came to be chosen merely as representatives of the parties. At first some state legislatures chose electors, but by the 1830s most states chose electors by statewide, winner-take-all popular vote. Independent voting by electors disappeared almost entirely. Occasionally electors have voted for someone other than their party's candidate. These "faithless electors" never have affected the outcome of an election.

Counting the Electoral Vote

In modern practice, the electors meet in their states to cast their ballots in December following a presidential election. In most states the candidate who carried the popular vote wins all the state's electoral votes. Maine and Nebraska are exceptions, awarding electoral votes based on popular vote winners in particular districts. The ballots of all the states are opened and counted before a joint session of Congress in early January, clearing the way for inauguration of the president on January 20.

Counting electoral votes in Congress is not always just a formality. This illustration depicts a special electoral commission taking testimony on disputed electoral votes in the 1876 presidential election. Congress gave the election to Republican Rutherford B. Hayes even though Democrat Samuel J. Tilden had a majority of the popular vote.
Source: Library of Congress

The Constitution did not specify what to do if there were disputes about electors' ballots. This became a critical concern following the 1876 election. That year, for the first time, the outcome of the election had to be determined by decisions on disputed electoral votes. The 1876 campaign pitted Republican Rutherford B. Hayes against Democrat Samuel J. Tilden. Tilden led in the popular vote count by more than a quarter of a million votes but trailed by one vote in the electoral college; the votes of three southern states were in dispute. A special electoral commission, set up to settle the dispute, awarded the votes to Hayes. Democrats in the House objected but, after Republicans agreed to withdraw federal troops from the South, southern conservatives allowed the electoral count to continue and Hayes became president.

In 1887 Congress passed permanent legislation on the handling of disputed electoral votes. The 1887 Electoral Count Act, still in force, gives each state final authority to determine the legality of its choice of electors. Majorities of both the Senate and House are needed to reject any disputed electoral votes.

Election by Congress

The election of 1800 was the first in which the House of Representatives elected the president. Candidates of the Democratic-Republican faction had more electoral votes than the Federalists, but their electors unintentionally cast equal numbers of votes for Thomas Jefferson, their choice for president, and Aaron Burr, their choice for vice president. The tie vote threw the election into the House, where the losing Federalists insisted on backing Burr over Jefferson, whom they considered a dangerous radical. It took thirty-six ballots to arrive at a decision; on the final tally ten states voted for Jefferson, four for Burr. Thus Jefferson became president, and Burr automatically became vice president.

The Jefferson-Burr contest dramatized the dangers of the constitutional double-balloting system. The Twelfth Amendment, requiring separate votes for president and vice president, was proposed by Congress and quickly adopted by the states in time for the 1804 election.

The only other time the House elected a president was in 1825. There were four chief contenders in the 1824 presidential campaign: John Quincy ADAMS, Henry CLAY, William H. Crawford, and Andrew Jackson. When the electoral votes were counted, Jackson had 99; Adams, 84; Crawford, 41; and Clay, 37. Jackson led in the popular vote, but he failed to win a majority of the electoral vote. As required by the Twelfth Amendment, the names of the top three contenders—Jackson, Adams, and Crawford—were placed before the House. Clay threw his support to Adams, who narrowly won election. Adams in turn made Clay his secretary of state, lending credence to charges that Clay had agreed to support Adams in return for the appointment. Adams took office under a cloud from which his administration never recovered; he lost the presidency to Jackson four years later.

On one occasion, in 1837, the Senate was forced to decide a vice-presidential contest. That year Democrat Martin Van Buren was elected president with 170 electoral votes, while his vice-presidential running mate, Richard M. Johnson, received only 147—one short of a majority. The Senate elected him, 33–16.

No presidential election has gone to the House in modern times, but several three-way races with potential for electoral deadlock have aroused concern. The threat of House election hung over the presidential campaign of 1968, when George C. Wallace of Alabama was a serious third-party candidate. Wallace predicted that he would win a majority of the electoral votes. His backup plan was to hold the balance of power in the electoral college voting, forcing political concessions from one of the major-party candidates in exchange for the support of his electors. The election was close, and Wallace won forty-six electoral votes, but Republican Richard NIXON defeated Democrat Hubert H. HUMPHREY without help from Wallace's electors.

The possibility of House election became real to Americans again during the 1980 presidential race, when the independent candidacy of Illinois representative John B. Anderson briefly threatened to disrupt the contest between incumbent president Jimmy Carter and Republican challenger Ronald Reagan. But Reagan won in a landslide, while Anderson received less than 7 percent of the popular vote and no electoral votes.

Richard M. Johnson
Source: Library of Congress

Only two presidential elections have been decided in the House of Representatives. In the first, in 1800, Thomas Jefferson was tied with Aaron Burr in electoral votes. The House elected Jefferson after thirty-five ballots. The second came in 1824 when neither John Quincy Adams, Andrew Jackson, or two other candidates had an electoral college majority. The House elected Adams in a controversial decision. Only once did the Senate elect a vice president: in 1837 Martin Van Buren's running mate, Richard M. Johnson, was one vote short of an electoral college majority. The Senate elected him.

⊙ **CLOSER LOOK**

The election of 1824 was the second and last time a presidential election has been determined in the House. John Quincy Adams won on the first ballot.

Discussion of the electoral college and House election of the president revived once again in 1992 when the independent campaign of Texas business executive H. Ross Perot showed surprising early strength. Perot's campaign faltered, and he ended up with 19 percent of the popular vote. The winner, Democrat Bill Clinton, outpolled incumbent Republican president George H. W. Bush 43 percent to 38 percent in the popular vote. Clinton won even more decisively in the electoral college, 370–168. Although Perot received the greatest share of the popular vote for any third-party candidate since Theodore Roosevelt's run on the Progressive Party ticket in 1912, Perot did not win any electoral votes because he carried no states.

As in 1980, the specter of deadlock in 1992 brought renewed calls for abolition of the electoral college and warnings that the House was ill-prepared to elect a president. A 1980 study had pinpointed several vague areas, but Congress had done nothing to clarify them. For example, no rules existed to specify whether the old or newly elected Congress would elect the new president, whether the House vote could be televised, or what would happen if the House itself became deadlocked. Clinton's decisive electoral victory in 1992 allayed those concerns—at least for another four years.

In 1996, running against former Senate majority leader Bob DOLE, and with Perot making another presidential bid, Clinton easily won reelection with 49 percent of the popular vote and 379 electoral votes to Dole's 41 percent and 159 electoral votes. Perot polled less than half his 1992 showing and again won no electoral votes. Clinton's even more conclusive victory muted any movement in the late 1990s for electoral college reform.

⊙ **CLOSER LOOK**

Benjamin Harrison
Source: Library of Congress

Rutherford B. Hayes
Source: Library of Congress

The vote in the electoral college to select a president has often been close, as occurred in 2000 when George W. Bush won 271–266. A president is elected by winning the electoral vote not the popular vote. Eighteen presidents have been elected, either by the electoral college itself or in two elections by the House, who did not receive a majority of the popular votes cast. Four of them actually trailed their opponents in the popular vote although they were the ones to move into the White House: John Quincy Adams (1824), Rutherford B. Hayes (1876), Benjamin Harrison (1888), and Bush (2000).

The dramatic political machinations surrounding the 2000 presidential race renewed debate about the electoral college. Disputes over how votes were counted in Florida, and whether Bush actually defeated Gore, briefly raised the possibility that separate panels of electors pledged to Bush and Gore would show up at the state capitol to cast their votes. In the charged political environment, there also was the strong likelihood of one party mounting a congressional challenge to the state's vote. If the House and Senate could not agree on the validity of the challenge, the slate certified by Florida governor Jeb Bush, George W. Bush's brother, would have been counted. But there also was the prospect that Florida's electoral votes would not be counted at all if the state could not certify its final result by the time the electoral college convened, or if its slate of electors would be thrown out as part of a lawsuit. The Supreme Court's intervention in the race, by ruling the Florida Supreme Court violated the Constitution by ordering manual recounts of votes, quashed the prospect of such nightmare scenarios. Bush took all of Florida's votes and defeated Gore 271–266 (with one abstention). Democrats soon after renewed calls for electoral college reform, but none gained momentum in the following years.

Vice-Presidential Vacancies

The Twenty-fifth Amendment to the Constitution, adopted in 1967, gave Congress additional authority over vice-presidential selection. The amendment, which established procedures to be followed if the president became disabled or died, also gave directions for filling a vacancy in the office of vice president. Whenever a vice president died, resigned, or succeeded to the presidency, the president was to nominate a successor. A majority vote of the Senate and the House of Representatives was required to confirm the nominee. (See APPOINTMENT POWER; PRESIDENTIAL DISABILITY AND SUCCESSION.)

The vice-presidential selection system was used for the first time in 1973 after the resignation of Vice President Spiro T. Agnew, who was under investigation on criminal charges. President NIXON nominated Rep. Gerald R. FORD of Michigan, the House Republican leader, to succeed him. Ford was confirmed by the House and Senate in less than two months.

In 1974 the Twenty-fifth Amendment was used again, after Nixon resigned as president to avoid impeachment because of the WATERGATE SCANDAL. Ford succeeded to the presidency, thus becoming the first president in U.S. history who had not been elected either president or vice president. Ford nominated Nelson A. Rockefeller, the governor of New York, to succeed him as vice president. Rockefeller's great wealth provoked controversy, but he, too, was confirmed.

Elections, Congressional

Americans elect a new Congress on the first Tuesday after the first Monday in November of even-numbered years. Early the following January the elected representatives and senators begin their first session of that Congress. Those elected November 7, 2006, for instance, were sworn in January 4, 2007, on the opening day of the 110th Congress. They included many new faces—ten new senators (nine Democrats and one Republican) and fifty-five new representatives (forty-two Democrats and thirteen Republicans)—as occurs in each Congress.

As an institution, Congress has suffered public criticism almost since the nation's beginnings. Alexis de Tocqueville, the astute French visitor of the late 1820s, observed the "vulgar

CLOSER LOOK

Shifts Between Chambers

From the early days of Congress, members have sometimes shifted from one chamber to the other. Far fewer former senators have gone to the House than vice versa. In the 1790s nineteen former representatives became senators and three former senators moved to the House. The same pattern continued through the nineteenth century and into the twentieth. By the end of the twentieth century, it was common to find House members running for the Senate, but senators rarely, if ever, sought election to the House. Former senators were more likely to return home to pursue a race for governor, run as their party's vice-presidential candidate, or seek the office of president.

Although both chambers are equal under the law, the Senate's six-year terms offer the officeholder greater stability. That body also has larger staffs and more generous perquisites. Senators' opportunities to make their mark are undoubtedly better in a chamber of one hundred members than in the 435-member House. The Senate's role in foreign affairs may add to its luster, and senators enjoy the prestige of statewide constituencies.

Perhaps the most notable shift from the Senate to the House was Henry Clay's journey in 1811. Giving up a Senate seat from Kentucky, he entered the House and was promptly elected Speaker, a position he used to prod the country to go to war with Britain in 1812. After five terms in the House, Clay returned to the Senate in 1823. Another prominent transfer was that of John Quincy Adams of Massachusetts; he served in the Senate (1803–1808), as secretary of state (1817–1825), as president (1825–1829), and finally in the House (1831–1848).

More on this topic:

Incumbency, p. 286

Political Parties, p. 420

CLOSER LOOK

Congress in Low Regard

Congress, as an institution, has long been held in low regard by voters, reflecting a public disdain for politics and the messy process of accommodating often widely divergent opinions and needs in society. There have been periods of approval such as during the 1970s Watergate scandal when legislators challenged President Richard Nixon.

But over time public opinion polls reveal a consistent skepticism about Congress. Gallup polls show Congress ranking poorly on trust and confidence compared to the presidency and the Supreme Court. In June 2006 Gallup found that 19 percent of respondents had "a great deal" or "quite a lot" of confidence in Congress; for the presidency the response was 33 percent and for the Supreme Court 40 percent. Thirty-two percent had "very little" confidence in Congress, while the tally was 25 percent for the presidency and 15 percent for the Court.

A year later, in June 2007, a Gallup poll found that public approval ratings for Congress had never been lower in seventy-five years that Gallup had been conducted; only 14 percent of Americans expressed any confidence in the work of congressional lawmakers.

demeanor" of the House of Representatives, where often he could not detect even one "distinguished man." In contrast, as he wrote in his classic *Democracy in America*, the Senate was "composed of eloquent advocates, distinguished generals, wise magistrates, and statesmen of note, whose arguments would do honor to the most remarkable parliamentary debates of Europe." Subsequent views of the entire Congress often have been no more charitable than de Tocqueville's opinion of the House.

Nevertheless, in a paradox long noted by Congress watchers, voters generally return incumbents to office, indicating that many Americans think better of their representatives and senators than the collective group in the House and Senate. Only in years of broad-based national concerns, such as war, the economy, or congressional performance, have many incumbents faced defeat. This occurred most recently in 1994, when Republicans swept Democrats out of control of Congress, and in 2006, when Democrats did the same to the GOP.

Turnover in Membership

Congress saw high turnover rates in the nineteenth and early twentieth centuries, principally in the House. The Senate experienced more stability because its members were selected for six-year terms and because state legislatures tended to send the same people to the Senate time after time. The Senate's turnover rate began to increase only after the popular election of senators was instituted by the Seventeenth Amendment in 1913. In the middle decades of the twentieth century, congressional turnover held steady at a relatively low rate. For a quarter-century after World War II each Congress had an average of about seventy-eight new members. An increase began in the 1970s; more than one hundred new members entered Congress in 1975. Turnover remained fairly high through the early 1980s, and then came a spell of strong incumbency and relatively low turnover that lasted through the 1990 election.

Several factors contributed to the turnover rates in the 1970s and early 1980s. The elections of 1972 and 1974 were affected by redistricting that followed the 1970 census; many House veterans retired rather than face strong new opposition. Those two elections also were the first in which eighteen-year-olds could vote. Probably the chief reason for change in 1974 was the Watergate scandal, which put an end to the Nixon administration and badly damaged the Republican Party. Democrats gained forty-three seats in the House that year, and the following January seventy-five of the ninety-two freshman representatives in the Ninety-fourth Congress were Democrats.

Most of those Democrats managed to hold their seats in the 1976 elections. The upheavals in that year's voting were in Senate races. Eighteen new senators took their oath of office in January 1977, marking the Senate's largest turnover since 1959.

An even larger Senate turnover came in the 1978 elections. It resulted in a 1979 freshman class of twenty senators, the biggest since the twenty-three member class of 1947. In the House for that same election cycle a record fifty-eight seats were opened by retirement, death, primary defeat, and other causes. Moreover, nineteen incumbents fell in the general election, giving the House seventy-seven freshmen when the 96th Congress opened in January 1979.

As in the early 1970s, redistricting was an important factor in the 1982 election. The 1980 census shifted seventeen seats from the Northeast and Midwest to the Sun Belt states of the South and West. Democrats took ten of these seats despite the Sun Belt's propensity to vote for Republican presidential candidates.

In the presidential election year of 1992, voters opted to give the Democrats a chance to run both Congress and the White House by electing Democrat Bill Clinton, the former governor of Arkansas, as president.

Heading into the 1992 campaign, some observers thought that the American political system had lost its capacity for renewal—low turnover in the 1980s fostered a perception of Congress as an incumbency club, fueled by special interest cash that nearly always defeated any challengers. But 1992 redistricting as a result of the 1990 census dramatically reshaped many districts, prodding some members into retirement and forcing others to run in unfamiliar constituencies. Reports of lax management and overdrawn checks at the House Bank also contributed to a high congressional turnover.

The 1992 and 1994 elections were marked by heavy turnover in Congress. Among the incoming freshmen of 1992 was Native American Ben Nighthorse Campbell of Colorado, who won election to the Senate as Democrat. He later switched to the Republican Party in 1995.
Source: CQ Photo/Scott J. Ferrell

All this tumult resulted in 110 new members entering the House in January 1993, an influx of freshmen exceeding anything Washington had seen in more than forty years. In the postwar era, only one House freshman class was larger—the 118 newcomers to the 81st Congress in 1949. No other freshman class had so many women (twenty-five) and minorities, including sixteen African Americans, eight Hispanics, and one Korean American.

The Senate freshman class of the 103rd Congress was the largest since 1981, with nine men and five woman, including the chamber's first black woman (Democrat Carol Moseley-Braun of Illinois) and its first Native American (Democrat Ben Nighthorse Campbell of Colorado) since Charles Curtis, a Republican from Kansas who stepped down in 1929 to become vice president under Herbert Hoover.

The midterm elections of 1994 brought even more upheaval as the Republicans gained control of both the House and Senate for the first time since 1955. The Democratic loss was truly national in scope. Republicans won 37 million votes in 1994—nearly 9 million more than the party had won in the 1990 midterm elections. It was the first time since 1946 that Republican House candidates received a majority (52.3 percent) of the total House vote. Democrats in 1994 drew almost one million fewer votes than in 1990, continuing a general downward slide in their congressional voting strength that had begun in the mid-1980s.

The GOP tide of 1994 was caused by large surges in voter support for the Republicans, voter apathy for the Democrats fueled by their four-decade control of the House, and a mixed performance by President Clinton in his first two years in office.

In 1994 Republicans gained fifty-two House seats, increasing their number from 178 to 230. The Democrats dropped from 256 to 204 seats. For the Republicans, seventy-three freshmen were elected, 157 incumbents were reelected, and thirty-four incumbents were defeated.

Republicans also swept the Senate in 1994, after eight years in the minority. The Republicans captured all nine open seats and ousted two Democratic incumbents, gaining control by a margin of 52–48 seats. The incoming Senate freshman class had eleven Republicans and no Democrats.

In 1994 Rep. Olympia Snowe of Maine picked up the former Democratic seat in the Senate held by retiring majority leader George Mitchell. She was a part of the sweep that won both chambers for the Republican Party for the first time in forty years. Snowe rose to chair the Senate Committee on Small Business and Entrepreneurship beginning in 2003; in 2007 she became the ranking minority member. Here she talks to reporters after the Senate Republican policy luncheon in 2006.
Source: CQ Photo/Scott J. Ferrell

Since 1914, when the popular election of senators began, there had never been an all-GOP Senate freshman class.

The 1996 elections also ended up in the record books. Never before had voters reelected a Democratic president and at the same time entrusted both the House and the Senate to the Republican Party. Clinton, nearly written off after the disastrous 1994 midterm elections, won handily in November 1996. The Republicans also won their first back-to-back majority in the House since the 1920s. The Democrats managed, however, to cut into the GOP's numbers. Democrats gained a net of nine seats, leaving a party breakdown in the House of 227 Republicans and 207 Democrats, and Bernard Sanders of Vermont as the lone Independent.

By 1998 the turnover in the House and Senate seemed to have settled down. All but seven of the 401 House members seeking reelection were returned to office. The Democrats also regrouped in 1998—Clinton's second midterm election—and managed to close the partisan gap even further in the House. The Democrats picked up five House seats, giving the 106th Congress 223 Republicans, 211 Democrats, and one Independent. This twelve-seat majority was the slimmest majority in the House since 1955.

The Senate's partisan breakdown remained the same in 1999 with fifty-five Republicans and forty-five Democrats. Just three of the thirty-four senators up for reelection in 1998 were defeated. Eight Senate freshmen joined the 106th Congress—four Democrats and four Republicans.

The pattern continued in the 2000 elections. Although the GOP maintained control in both chambers, its margin was reduced to nine votes in the House. In the Senate, an exact tie resulted: fifty Democrats and fifty Republicans. However, the Republicans retained control because their party won back the White House, which allowed Richard Cheney, the new vice president and presiding Senate officer, to vote to break a tie. This rare arrangement was short-lived, however, as moderate Republican James Jeffords of Vermont left the GOP to become an Independent in June 2001, giving majority control of the Senate to the Democrats for the first time since 1994.

The Republicans won back the Senate and held onto the House in the 2002 elections. For only the third time in a century, and the first time since 1934, the party in control of the White House won seats in a midterm election. The GOP regained the Senate by winning two seats and expanded its majority in the House by picking up six seats.

In 2004 Republican George W. Bush was reelected president while his party picked up seats in both houses of Congress. In the Senate the GOP gained four seats to widen its majority to fifty-five versus forty-four Democrats and one Independent. In the House the GOP added three seats to increase its majority to 232 versus 202 Democrats and one Independent. Incumbents continued to be returned to Congress at a high rate. In the House 97.8 percent of those incumbents seeking reelection won.

Then, in the 2006 elections, the Republican ascendancy fell apart, at least for the 110th Congress. In a national sweep that resembled the Republican takeover of Congress in 1994, Democrats regained control of both chambers by picking up a net of thirty seats in the House and six in the Senate. The Democrats gained seats in each of the four national regions, including eleven House seats—the largest number—in the Northeast. Only one Republican survived in that part of the country, turning the once rock-solid GOP region into a Democratic bastion. In the Midwest, the Democrats picked up nine House seats, reducing the Republican majority there to a near dead-heat, 49–51. Even in the South, which by the first decade of the new century had become the core of Republican strength, the Democrats picked up six House seats, although they still trailed the GOP by a substantial margin, 57–85.

President Bush's declining popularity, reflected most significantly in popular disapproval of the intractable war in Iraq, was seen in Democratic gains in 2006 in districts carried by Bush in the 2004 presidential elections: two-thirds of Democratic gains came in states or districts that favored Bush just two years earlier. The defeat of GOP incumbents accounted for all the Senate Republican losses. In the House, Democrats picked up twenty-two Republican seats in which an incumbent was running in the general election; the other eight Democratic wins were in open seat contests. Not a single Democratic incumbent lost.

Nevertheless, incumbency remained an important bulwark for both parties in 2006. All Democratic incumbents won and all open seats previously held by a Democrat were retained by the party. On the Republican side only one in ten GOP incumbents running lost in the general election. Overall 94 percent of House incumbents won; in Senate races the figure was almost 79 percent.

Election analysts noted that most defeated Republican House candidates did not have close races in 2004 and were veteran members with at least eight years in the chamber. All of these seats were expected to be vigorously contested in the last two elections of

CLOSER LOOK

John Quincy Adams
Source: Library of Congress

Andrew Johnson
Source: Library of Congress

White House to Congress

Only two presidents have returned to Congress after serving in the White House. The first was John Quincy Adams, who was president from 1825 to 1829. He served in the Senate from 1803 to 1808. After his presidency he served in the House from 1831 until 1848.

The other president was Andrew Johnson, who came into the White House in 1865 when Abraham Lincoln was assassinated. He had served in both houses of Congress from Tennessee before he entered the White House. The Tennessee legislature sent him back to the U.S. Senate in 1875, where he served for the last five months of his life.

the decade before redistricting will occur after the 2010 census to draw new House boundaries.

Elections expert Rhodes Cook said Democrats made House gain "largely because they were able to expand the playing field, which had shrunk dramatically in recent elections. When Republicans won control of Congress in 1994, there were nearly 100 competitive House races (as measured by a winning percentage of less than 55 percent of the total vote). In 2002 that number was less than fifty, and two years ago [2004] the total of such competitive House contests fell to just thirty-two. But [in 2006] the number of sub-55 percent winners jumped to sixty-eight, the highest total in a decade. Going into the elections, the bulk of these seats were held by Republicans. But Democrats won many of them November 7, with the result that a number of marginal House seats are now held either by Democratic challengers who won narrowly or Republican incumbents who barely escaped defeat. Altogether, thirty-five Republicans won in 2006 with less than 55 percent of the vote, compared to thirty-three Democrats."

Electronic Voting

Recorded votes in the House have been taken by an electronic voting system since 1973. Quorum calls also are conducted by the electronic system. The Senate has not adopted a similar system. Its roll call votes still are conducted by individuals calling out their response.

House votes normally are limited to fifteen minutes, although they can be shortened to as little as five when several votes occur immediately after one another. But on occasions the fifteen-minute period is bent, sometimes dramatically. The most dramatic bend came in 2003 when Republicans held open a roll call on a controversial Medicare drug bill until they could round up enough votes to pass the legislation. The first came in June when the vote was held open for fifty minutes. The second came in November on the conference report on the bill when the voting was held open for two hours and fifty-three minutes before getting a majority. It was believed to be the longest recorded tally since electronic voting began in 1973.

House members vote by inserting their voting cards into one of the boxes at many locations in the chambers. While a vote is underway, a large panel above the Speaker's desk in the well of the chamber displays how each member has voted.

Ellsworth, Oliver

Oliver Ellsworth served in the Senate before becoming chief justice of the United States.
Source: Library of Congress

Although Oliver Ellsworth ranks among the most notable framers of the Constitution who went onto an important career in Congress and the judiciary, he remains one of the lesser-known figures to modern generations. He was born in Connecticut and graduated from the school that later became Princeton. He became a delegate to the Continental Congress and later the Constitutional Convention. In that role he coauthored the "Connecticut Compromise" to settle the dispute between large and small states over representation in the federal legislature.

He was elected as one of Connecticut's first two senators and served until 1796 when President George Washington nominated him as chief justice of the United States.

In Congress, Ellsworth helped write rules for the Senate and assisted in organizing the army, U.S. Post Office, and census bureau. He also was instrumental in developing the conference report on the Bill of Rights. As head of the Judiciary Committee, he was the principal drafter of the Judiciary Act of 1789, which established the federal judicial system.

Enacting Clause

"Be it enacted by the Senate and House of Representatives of the United States of America in Congress assembled…." This imposing language is the standard opening for bills introduced in either chamber. Known as the enacting clause, it gives legal force to measures once they have been approved by Congress and signed by the president.

During House floor action, opponents of a bill sometimes offer a motion to "strike the enacting clause." Such a motion, if approved, kills the measure. It is rarely successful, but it does allow for five more minutes of debate and can be used to make a political point.

Energy and Commerce Committee, House

With its sweeping jurisdiction and colorful personalities, the House Energy and Commerce Committee is a congressional hot spot. Topics such as auto emission controls, oil and gas exploration, patients' rights, generic drugs, and broadband Internet service fall under its jurisdiction. The panel attracts more than its share of lobbyists representing the many industries and environmental, medical, and consumer groups whose interests are affected by its actions. The high level of controversy means debates can be heated at times and the votes close.

The Four Corners Power Plant, one of the largest coal-fired generating stations in the United States, is located on Navajo land in northwest New Mexico, near Farmington. Overseeing energy policy is the responsibility of the House Energy and Commerce Committee.
Source: AP Images/Susan Montoya Bryan

More on this topic:

Commerce Power, p. 102

Energy and Natural Resources Committee, Senate, p. 189

An octopus of a committee, Energy and Commerce oversees energy, health, communications, consumer safety, the stock market, part of the transportation industry, and numerous regulatory agencies. The panel's authority extends to "everything that moves, is sold, or is burned," according to Michigan Democrat John D. Dingell, who was the panel's chair from 1981 to 1995 and again starting in 2007.

Although the primary Senate counterpart of the House Energy and Commerce Committee is the Energy and Natural Resources Committee, the jurisdictions of the two do not entirely coincide. The Senate Energy Committee and the House Resources Committee share responsibility for federal lands, most nuclear power matters, and most regulation of the coal industry. The environmental concerns of the House Energy and Commerce Committee, such as air pollution, are the responsibility in the Senate of its Environment and Public Works Committee. When the House Energy and Commerce Committee tackles communications policy or transportation deregulation, it deals in conference with the Senate Committee on Commerce, Science, and Transportation.

History

The Interstate and Foreign Commerce Committee, the forerunner of the House Energy and Commerce Committee, was set up in 1795. The panel's authority over interstate commerce expanded dramatically in 1887 when Congress created the Interstate Commerce Commission to regulate the railroads. Since then, federal oversight of the marketplace has become extensive, and the committee has helped create a wide variety of regulatory agencies.

The committee's visibility increased in the 1950s as it investigated several scandals. A subcommittee probe revealed that a Boston industrialist had paid hotel bills and given an expensive coat and Oriental rug to Sherman Adams, a top Eisenhower administration aide who later resigned. The panel also looked into rigged television quiz shows and "payola," or payoffs, given by the record industry to radio disk jockeys in exchange for air time.

Among the longest-running debates in the committee was one over energy pricing. In the 1970s top Democrats on the committee, including Dingell and then-chair Harley O. Staggers of West Virginia, were still resisting deregulation of natural gas and oil.

The committee's jurisdiction shifted in the mid-1970s, when the Public Works Committee (now known as the Transportation and Infrastructure Committee) was assigned responsibility for all forms of transportation except railroads, a special interest of Staggers. The reforms also gave the panel jurisdiction over health issues not related to taxes, previously a responsibility of the Ways and Means Committee.

The 1970s brought change within the committee as well. Frustrated by Staggers's low-key style, other Democrats on the panel shifted more and more authority to the subcommittees. In 1979 they voted to strip Staggers of his post as chair of the committee's investigations subcommittee. Dingell, who was chair of the Energy and Power Subcommittee, ran the full committee in all but name until he became chair.

Energy issues dominated the late 1970s, but the Interstate and Foreign Commerce Committee temporarily lost its dominance in that area when the House leadership set up an ad hoc energy panel to push through President Jimmy Carter's energy program. A second challenge to Commerce's primacy in the energy field came in 1979, when a special House committee on reorganization recommended that a permanent energy committee be established. With Dingell leading the opposition, that proposal was defeated. In 1980 the House instead renamed the committee Energy and Commerce and designated it the House's lead panel on energy issues.

Staggers retired in 1981 and Dingell moved into the chair. A tough-talking former prosecutor and powerful member of Congress, Dingell defended his committee's turf aggressively and expanded it whenever he could. As chair of the committee's Oversight and Investigations Subcommittee, Dingell presided over well-publicized investigations into government practices, increasing his power and the committee's public profile at the same time.

Throughout the 1980s Dingell battled with another forceful member of the committee, Henry A. Waxman, over auto emission controls. Dingell, a liberal on most issues, sided with the auto industry, the economic mainstay of his Detroit district and much of Michigan. Waxman, representing a mostly liberal and affluent constituency in smog-choked Los Angeles, fought Dingell for tougher air pollution controls from his power base as chair of the Subcommittee on Health and the Environment. In 1989 they reached a compromise that contributed to enactment of a new, stricter clean air law the following year.

Its vast legislative jurisdiction was only part of the reason for continued dominance of this committee in the 1980s and 1990s. Another was the work of Dingell's Oversight and Investigations Subcommittee. Staffed by a team of eager investigators, the panel focused on allegations of government wrongdoing, particularly misuse of government funds. Its investigation of practices at the Environmental Protection Agency (EPA) during the early 1980s led to the resignation of one top EPA administrator and the perjury conviction of another.

Other investigations targeted waste and corruption in defense contracting, fraud in government-financed scientific research, and misuse of federal grants by private universities. Dingell's supporters applauded his use of "whistle blowers" to gather information, his tough questioning of witnesses at hearings, and his flair for publicity. Critics charged that Dingell and his investigators frequently exceeded the bounds of propriety and fairness in their zeal to expose wrongdoing. Although Dingell lost his chair when the Republicans took control of the House in 1995, he continued to routinely issue investigatory letters in his position as the ranking Democrat—particularly after George W. Bush became president.

> **"Dingell is great when he's on your side, and he will kill you when he's not. If you are the head of an agency, you don't want him hauling you up there [before the committee]."**
>
> —***Mark Cooper,*** research director for the Consumer Federation of America

Lobbyists held Dingell in high respect. "Dingell is great when he's on your side, and he will kill you when he's not. If you are the head of an agency, you don't want him hauling you up there [before the committee]," said Mark Cooper, research director for the Consumer Federation of American.

Dingell had been replaced as chair by Republican Thomas J. Bliley of Virginia. The mild-mannered Bliley presided over a major overhaul of telecommunications laws, a bipartisan rewrite of pesticide laws, and health care insurance portability. Bliley was succeeded in 2001 by a far more energetic, ambitious, and media-savvy chair, Billy Tauzin, R-La.

With Dingell back in charge in 2007, House members and lobbyists alike expected a return to the aggressive activity that characterized Dingell's earlier period. In meeting with reporters soon after the 2006 elections Dingell mentioned numerous issues touched by the panel's jurisdiction, including health care, telecommunications, energy and environmental policy. He declined to rank his priorities or give a timeline, saying his method is to "kill the nearest snake first" and then move on to the next one.

Energy and Natural Resources Committee, Senate

Managing federal lands and setting energy policy are the main tasks of the Senate Committee on Energy and Natural Resources. The committee traditionally has been controlled by westerners whose states have vast amounts of federal parks and forests, but it also attracts senators whose

More on this topic:

Energy and Commerce Committee, House, p. 187

Energy Independence and Global Warming Committee, House Select, p. 191

Environment and Public Works Committee, Senate, p. 193

states depend on oil and gas. In addition, the committee includes advocates of wilderness and proponents of energy conservation.

In the 1970s, when there was widespread concern over U.S. oil imports, the committee focused on energy. The panel struggled to adapt price controls and other federal rules to an energy market dominated by a cartel of oil-rich Middle Eastern countries, which limited supplies and kept prices high. By the 1980s the energy situation had changed drastically; prices, imports, and overall consumption had all declined. The 1991 Persian Gulf War renewed concern over access to the world's oil, prompting the committee to craft a wide-ranging energy bill that encouraged energy efficiency and the development of alternative fuels. Comprehensive energy legislation was back on its agenda a decade later, when the Republican White House proposed a new national energy strategy that centered on increasing production of domestic oil and gas.

History

The committee was first organized in 1816 as the Committee on Public Lands. A 1977 Senate re-organization shifted jurisdiction of some environmental laws to the Environment and Public Works Committee; what was then the Interior and Insular Affairs Committee became Energy and Natural Resources.

Henry M. Jackson, a Washington Democrat, chaired the committee for eighteen years (1963–1981). His leadership had a profound effect on the panel. Jackson, who was both forceful and well liked, managed to keep the committee's concerns in the Senate limelight. Although conservative in matters of foreign policy, Jackson was a liberal on domestic issues. For years he advocated price controls on oil and gas, a position that caused no conflict in his state, which does not produce oil.

When Republicans controlled the Senate from 1981 to 1987, James A. McClure of Idaho was chair. He favored a completely free market for energy and in 1983 pushed a Reagan administration plan to remove all remaining federal controls from natural gas. Despite his opposition to controls, McClure supported federal subsidies for synthetic fuels, such as liquids made from coal. That program, announced with great fanfare in the late 1970s, died in 1985 because of budget constraints.

McClure's successor, Louisiana Democrat J. Bennett Johnston, shared his outlook, preferring a market-oriented approach to energy policy. Johnston was known for his solid grasp of the technical aspects of energy and for his ability to craft compromises. He disliked the label "oil-state senator," arguing that his decisions were not governed by the industry position on an issue. Johnston showed his willingness to compromise during work on a wide-ranging energy bill in 1992. He wanted to include provisions in the measure to allow oil drilling in Alaska's Arctic National Wildlife Refuge and to require automobile fleets to have better miles-per-gallon averages, but he dropped the provisions when they stood in the way of passing a bill.

Opening up parts of the oil-rich federal refuge in Alaska to oil drilling was one of the top goals of Frank H. Murkowski of Alaska, who became chair when the Republicans took over in 1995 and ranking member when party control of the Senate switched in 2001. But as lawmakers worked in the 107th Congress (2001–2003) on the first comprehensive energy bill since 1992, Murkowski was unable to win his Senate colleagues' support for drilling in the Alaskan refuge. The issue was one of several that blocked House-Senate agreement on a final bill. A major energy bill finally was passed, in 2005, but drilling in Alaska was blocked once again by opponents.

New Mexico Democrat Jeff Bingaman served as chair after Murkowski, and he was followed in 2003 by New Mexico Republican Pete V. Domenici. Bingaman returned to the chair in 2007 after

Democrats retook the Senate in the 2006 elections. The two New Mexico senators enjoyed a generally courteous and professional relationship while working together on nuclear and energy issues over the years. They worked together on the 2005 energy overhaul bill, even though many Democrats were critical of the legislation as tilted too much to oil and gas producers. But both men supported the spectrum of energy alternatives, from nuclear energy and fossil fuels to renewables such as solar and wind power. Domenici tended to push more for traditional fossil fuel development while Bingaman leaned more toward renewable energy. Climate policy also has attracted both senators. In 2005 Domenici decided to support Bingaman on a "sense of the Senate" amendment to the energy bill declaring that global warming needed to be addressed through mandatory controls on greenhouse gases. Although few observers expected a climate policy bill out of Congress in the immediate future following Bingaman's taking back the chair, they expected a more mainstream discussion of the subject than occurred in recent years when committees in both chambers were under the control of Republican hard-line global warming skeptics.

Senate Energy and Natural Resources Committee chair Sen. Jeff Bingaman., D-N.M., speaks at a news conference on health care reform in January 2007.
Source: CQ Photo/Scott J. Ferrell

Energy Independence and Global Warming Committee, House Select

This committee was created at the beginning of the 110th Committee in 2007 at the direction of the new House Speaker, Nancy Pelosi, D-Calif., and over the vigorous objections of Energy and Commerce Committee chair John Dingell, D-Mich., who considered it an infringement on his panel's jurisdiction.

The committee was established as a temporary one without power to report legislation. Pelosi's motivations were widely attributed to her party's interest in increasing focus on—and drawing public attention to—environmental and global warming issues. The panel had fifteen members, nine Democrats and six Republicans. Its authorizing rule specifically stated it could not act on legislation; its role was to "investigate, study, make findings and develop recommendations on policies, strategies, technologies and other innovations" to reduce U.S. dependency on foreign energy sources and reduce emissions and other activities contributing to climate change and global warming. Pelosi named Edward J. Markey, D-Mass., as its chair.

Engrossed Bill

An engrossed bill is the official copy of a measure as passed by either the Senate or House of Representatives, including changes made during floor action. It must be certified in its final form by the secretary of the Senate or the clerk of the House. (See ENROLLED BILL; LEGISLATIVE PROCESS.)

Enrolled Bill

The final official copy of a bill that has been passed in identical form by both the Senate and House of Representatives is known as an enrolled bill. It is certified as correct by either the secretary of the Senate or the clerk of the House, depending on where the bill originated, and is then sent on for the signatures of first the House Speaker, next the Senate president pro tempore, and finally the president of the United States. An enrolled bill is printed on parchment-type paper. (See EN-GROSSED BILL; LEGISLATIVE PROCESS.)

Entitlements

An entitlement is a federal program that guarantees a certain level of benefits to persons or other entities that meet requirements set by law. Some examples of entitlements are Social Security, Medicare, unemployment benefits, and federal pensions. Congress cannot refuse to provide funding for these programs.

Protesters rally against new legislation that would create Medicare part D, which many believe failed to provide adequate drug coverage. Part D was touted by President George W. Bush and the Republican Party as a way to help seniors cover prescription drug costs.
Source: Reuters/Kevin Larmarque

Since the 1970s the largest component of federal spending has gone for programs that provide payments to individuals. Many of these programs have been established as entitlements. Congress has found it almost impossible to gather the political will to reduce spending for entitlement programs. Legislators would have to make significant policy changes to reduce the cost of these programs.

In 1990 Congress took a step toward curbing new entitlements when it enacted a pay-as-you-go requirement for mandatory spending on entitlements. The law required that any new entitlements or policy changes that would increase the cost of existing entitlements had to be matched by revenue increases to pay for the new programs.

In 1996 landmark welfare reform legislation was enacted, ending the federal government's sixty-one-year-old entitlement of cash aid to poor women and children. Direct federal payments to individuals were converted into block grants to the states, which determined new eligibility requirements.

President George W. Bush vowed to make major changes to the Medicare and Social Security programs by allowing more private entities to provide benefits. He proposed a fundamental change in Social Security under which individuals would have private savings accounts that would replace or supplement reduced benefits under that New Deal program. But under sharp Democratic criticism, Congress rebuffed his proposals. However, by 2007 even staunch defenders of entitlements were beginning to acknowledge that changes were needed in the programs to ensure their long-term solvency. This was especially true of the Medicare program that provided health care for senior citizens.

Some entitlements carry permanent appropriations, while others must go through the annual appropriations process. Programs without permanent appropriations also may require a supplemental appropriation to provide the required funds to program beneficiaries.

Environment and Public Works Committee, Senate

Two markedly different responsibilities fall to the Senate Committee on Environment and Public Works: watching over the nation's environment, and building its highways, dams, and sewers.

The committee experienced a checkered history in the latter years of the twentieth century and into the twenty-first as committee chairs of different abilities came and went. Although the panel participated in many far-reaching laws, by the 110th Congress in 2007 there was growing polarization on central environmental issues, especially climate change and global warming. Although an increasing number of scientists and others were convinced that climate change was real and a great danger to the planet, many others were not persuaded. No solid consensus had emerged as had occurred in earlier decades over such environmental concerns as clean air and clean water. As a result, the ability of the panel to force through significant new laws in this area was much in doubt even as Democrats regained control of the panel after the 2006 elections.

The decade of the 1970s probably was the heyday of the committee, a time when landmark environmental laws were passed and federal money still flowed freely. In the 1980s efforts to clean up the environment were stymied by complex problems, such as toxic waste disposal and acid rain. Glamorous public works projects lost out in the federal budget squeeze and gave way to concerns about the deterioration of existing dams and bridges. The 1990s opened with a sweeping reauthorization of the 1977 Clean Air Act after more than a decade of political stalemate, but other successes on major environmental issues were rare. A decade later Congress was grappling with many of the same issues.

CLOSER LOOK

The committee's heyday was in the 1970s when major environmental laws were passed. By 2007 growing polarization on many environmental issues, especially climate change, had made the panel a battleground.

When Republicans controlled the Senate, from 1981 to 1987, Robert T. Stafford of Vermont chaired the committee. Stafford was forced to take defensive action, deflecting attacks on environmental laws by industry; he was often on the opposite side from the administration of President Ronald Reagan. Stafford also helped win extensions of water pollution controls and the "superfund" program to clean up toxic waste. He concentrated on the environment rather than highways, reflecting his years spent on the Environmental Protection Subcommittee.

Quentin N. Burdick, a North Dakota Democrat, became the committee's chair in 1987. It was his first top post after almost three decades as a senator. Never one to seek power or publicity, Burdick brought his low-key style to the Environment and Public Works Committee. He gave great latitude to active, aggressive subcommittee chairs, such as Democrats George J. MITCHELL of Maine and Frank R. Lautenberg of New Jersey.

Burdick died in 1992, and Daniel Patrick Moynihan, a well-known New York Democrat, became chair. Moynihan used his slot on the panel to address constant water shortages in his state. In 1993, when Moynihan became chair of the Senate Finance Committee, Max Baucus, a Montana Democrat, took over as chair of the Environment and Public Works panel.

When the Republicans gained control of the Senate in 1995, John H. Chafee of Rhode Island assumed the chair. While the committee under Chafee was able to pass a major water projects bill, the panel continued to be confounded by the deep split in Congress over environmental issues such as reauthorization of the endangered species and "superfund" pollution cleanup laws.

More on this topic:

Energy and Commerce Committee, House, p. 187

Energy Independence and Global Warming Committee, House Select, p. 191

Those divisions continued when Republican Robert C. Smith of New Hampshire took over the chair in 1999. Smith was able to shepherd through Congress a bipartisan bill to encourage the cleanup of less hazardous sites known as "brownfields," along with many other low-profile bills. But Smith could not gain enough support outside of the committee to tackle more ambitious legislation.

The debate became more polarized in 2001 under Jim Jeffords of Vermont, who won the gavel when he left the Republican Party to become an Independent and agreed to caucus with the Democrats. His move gave control of the Senate to the Democrats. Under Jeffords, debates over proposals to reauthorize the Clean Air Act were particularly heated. Those debates did not abate after Republican James Inhofe of Oklahoma took over the chair in 2003. Inhofe had often been outside the mainstream of environmental policy, sometimes taking a more conservative stance than his own Republican leadership. He had advocated a close and skeptical reexamination of the Clean Air Act and often dismissed the threat of climate change as a hoax, calling it a "Chicken Little" story.

Californian Barbara Boxer, chair of the Senate Environment and Public Works Committee, was expected to take on the Bush administration over its environmental policies.
Source: CQ Photo/Scott J. Ferrell

Inhofe was continually at odds with the committee's ranking Democrat, Sen. Barbara Boxer of California. The two clashed on nearly every major environmental issue. In 2007, with the Democrats back in control of the Senate, the two traded chairs, resulting in perhaps the most dramatic swing in style and priorities of any committee in the 110th Congress. Boxer, a hard-charging liberal from a generally liberal state, clashed repeatedly in her minority position with Bush administration officials about environmental and climate change issues. She called the administration's efforts to reverse global warming a farce and engaged in testy exchanges with witnesses, often scolding them for what she saw as efforts to roll back bedrock environmental safeguards.

With her record during her days in the minority, Boxer's clashes with the Bush administration as chair were expected to escalate. But observers doubted she was positioned to push through significant new legislation in the face of Bush administration opposition. In addition, her committee in 2007 included a number of moderate Democrats, as well as Republicans, with whom she needed to compromise.

Equality of the Houses

This concept is based on the idea, embedded in the Constitution's design of checks and balances, that each house has essentially equal status in the enactment of legislation and in the relations and negotiations between the two houses. There are some differences, however. The House initiates revenue and appropriations bills, which the Senate can amend. Other types of legislation can originate in either chamber. Neither house can force the other to accept or even act on its bills. Either chamber has in effect a veto over the other just by not acting, because to pass legislation must be approved by both in identical form. In addition, in conferences to resolves differences each house casts one vote. Generally, in bicameral legislatures one house has markedly greater powers than the other.

Ervin, Sam J., Jr.

Sam J. Ervin Jr. (1896–1985) served twenty years as a Democratic senator from North Carolina. He is best remembered as chair of the Senate Watergate committee, which investigated charges that led to the resignation of President Richard NIXON in 1974. (See WATERGATE SCANDAL.) During the committee's televised hearings, Ervin's knowledge of and respect for the Constitution, his courtly manner, and his pithy quotations made him an admired national figure.

Before his Senate service, Ervin practiced law in North Carolina, served in the state legislature, and sat on the bench of the criminal and supreme courts within the state. In 1946 Ervin served one year in the U.S. House of Representatives to finish the term of his brother Joseph, who died while in office.

Ervin was appointed to fill a vacant Senate seat in 1954 and was elected to full terms starting in 1956. As a freshman senator, he was a member of the select committee that recommended Senate censure of Sen. Joseph R. MCCARTHY, a Wisconsin Republican whose investigations of communism had drawn great criticism.

Ervin construed the provisions of the Constitution strictly. On the grounds of protecting states' rights, he rejected civil rights legislation and other Democratic domestic programs, such as health care for the elderly and school busing. But as a member of the Judiciary Committee he worked to strengthen the civil rights of government workers, Native Americans, and mental patients. He often criticized the government practice of gathering information on private citizens. "It is my belief that the Recording Angel drops a tear occasionally to wash out the record of our human iniquities," he said. "There is no compassion to be found in computers."

As chair of the Separation of Powers Subcommittee of the Judiciary Committee, Ervin recommended procedures to be followed in a convention held to consider CONSTITUTIONAL AMENDMENTS; although such a convention had never been held, the prospect troubled many leaders. Ervin's bill passed the Senate in 1971 and 1973, but the House did not vote on the measure.

In 1973 Ervin was chosen to head the Senate Watergate committee, formally called the Senate Select Committee on Presidential Campaign Activities. He was chosen because of his knowledge of the Constitution and also because, earlier that year, he had declined to run for reelection in 1974. He was therefore unable to benefit from the publicity generated by the committee's investigations. Quoting the Bible and Shakespeare, Ervin immediately caught the attention of the public. A self-described "old country lawyer," Ervin seemed the antithesis of the Watergate conspirators. He became a folk hero and retired in 1974 on a wave of public admiration.

Ethics

The Constitution gives Congress the power and responsibility to police itself. This is no easy task, as the record of the 1980s, 1990s, and the early years of the twenty-first century reveals.

For the first time in history a Speaker of the House—Republican Newt GINGRICH of Georgia—was formally reprimanded and another Speaker—Democrat Jim WRIGHT of Texas—was forced by scandal to resign in midterm, both after investigations into their financial affairs. In 2005 the Republican majority leader in the House, Tom DeLay of Texas, became caught up in a larger scandal involving lobbyist Jack Abramoff that ended the careers of several Republicans, including DeLay who resigned his seat in 2006.

Six House members and one senator were convicted in a bribery scheme known as the Abscam scandal in 1980; one was expelled from Congress and the others were defeated or resigned. Five senators were investigated in the Keating Five scandal in the late 1980s for allegations that they had improperly intervened against federal regulators on behalf of a campaign contributor; four were rebuked and the fifth, reprimanded. Hundreds of House members got caught up in a 1991 House bank scandal for writing bad checks. A House member convicted of criminal charges was expelled from Congress. Other members have been censured, denounced, reprimanded, rebuked, and investigated for a variety of misdeeds.

In addition, other sitting and former members of Congress were convicted of criminal wrongdoing on charges ranging from extortion to campaign finance violations to drunk driving. One of the mightiest among them to fall was the former chair of the House Ways and Means Committee, Illinois Democrat Dan Rostenkowski, who was convicted of mail fraud in a scandal involving the House Post Office, also in 1991.

A listing of ethics and criminal cases involving members might make some people wonder whether Mark Twain was right when he joked that "there is no distinctly native American criminal class except Congress."

A listing of ethics and criminal cases involving members might make some people wonder whether Mark Twain was right when he joked that "there is no distinctly native American criminal class except Congress."

But in reality the vast majority of senators and representatives are law-abiding citizens. Their ethics today are as high, perhaps higher, than at any other time in history. What has changed over the years are the standards to which they are held accountable, as well as the scrutiny to which they are subjected.

Some behavior that was accepted, winked at, or ignored in the past is no longer acceptable today. For example, Daniel WEBSTER, a respected Massachusetts leader in the nineteenth century, openly demanded money from the railroads in return for his support of a bill before the Senate. James A. Garfield, an Ohio representative who went on to become president in 1881, accepted a gift of stock from Crédit Mobilier of America, a company seeking legislative favors.

These actions, which went unpunished, certainly would be seen today as blatant conflicts of interest. They would come under scrutiny by one or more of the four groups that monitor legislators' behavior: the courts, House or Senate colleagues, the media, and the voters.

The courts handle indictments of legislators charged under federal criminal statutes. They also review violations of the 1989 Ethics Reform Act. Federal laws for campaign financing, which require public disclosure of donations and monitor use of funds, are also designed to expose, or at least discourage, corruption. Regulation is handled by the Federal Election Commission, which can fine violators, take them to court, or refer cases to the Justice Department for criminal prosecution.

The House and Senate ethics codes are the internal guidelines for how legislators behave. Personal finances must be disclosed, income earned outside Congress is restricted, and use of public funds is carefully monitored. The House Committee on Standards of Official Conduct and the Senate Select Committee on Ethics investigate allegations and make recommendations to the House and Senate, which then decide whether to discipline a legislator.

The media have played an increasingly important role in the monitoring of members' behavior. They have not only uncovered unethical behavior on the part of some members, but they have also been important in keeping the spotlight on the House and Senate ethics committees' response to allegations of illegal or improper activities by members.

One of the most powerful additions to public scrutiny has been the emergence of bloggers on the Internet, who by 2007 were increasingly reporting on conduct by members of Congress. In one example, a blogger's 2005 report of sexual activities by an Idaho senator, Larry Craig, was part of the story that broke six months later when Craig was arrested at an airport for allegedly soliciting sex in a men's restroom. Craig, who at first said he would resign his Senate seat at the end of September 2007, later said he would serve out the final year of his term and not run for reelection. (See PRESS AND CONGRESS.)

The remaining judge of representatives and senators is the electorate. Voter approval or disapproval usually means the extension or the end of an official's political life in Washington. Voters can be the toughest critics of all: they apply an unwritten set of rules and standards to an official's performance and then hand down their verdict at the polls. This was demonstrated forcefully in 1992 when the voters showed their displeasure with members involved in the House Bank scandal. Of the 269 sitting members who had overdrafts at the bank, more than one in four were defeated or chose to retire. That was a far higher casualty rate than the one for members with clean bank records, which was one in six. Another example occurred in 2002 after the Senate Ethics Committee "severely admonished" Sen. Robert G. Torricelli, D-N.J., for improperly accepting expensive gifts from a former campaign supporter. Two months later, amid plummeting poll ratings, Torricelli abandoned his campaign for a second term.

For a man such as Webster, who openly complained when payments to him for favors were late, the modern guidelines would leave little room to operate. Yet, despite these restrictions and the proper behavior of the majority, members of Congress continue to be accused of bribery, influence peddling, misuse of funds, sexual misconduct, violations of campaign disclosure laws, and breach of security. The standards for a politician's conduct are high; so are the temptations.

More on this topic:

Campaign Financing, p. 66

Disciplining Members, p. 159

Ethics Committee, Senate Select, p. 204

Financial Disclosure, p. 220

Franking Privilege, p. 237

Lobbying, p. 359

Pay and Perquisites, p. 410

Scandals, Congressional, p. 482

Standards of Official Conduct Committee, House, p. 532

Reluctance to Discipline

For most of its history, Congress operated under an unwritten ethics code, backed by the constitutional directive that Congress should "punish its Members for disorderly Behaviour, and, with the Concurrence of two thirds, expel a Member." The framers left it to the legislators to determine the rules and decide who was breaking them.

Thomas Jefferson set the tone in 1801, while he was vice president and presiding officer of the Senate. In JEFFERSON'S MANUAL he wrote, "Where the private interests of a member are concerned in a bill or question he is to withdraw." Jefferson was suggesting that a legislator avoid what is known today as a conflict of interest, when the chance for personal gain influences a decision ostensibly made for the public good. The rules of both chambers permit members not to vote on matters affecting their personal interests.

The policing of Congress has been done on an ad hoc basis. When someone complains about a colleague's behavior, the House or Senate usually investigates. But over the years members of Congress have shown a distaste for passing judgment on their colleagues. By 2003 only fifteen senators and five representatives had ever been expelled (one of those decisions was later reversed), and almost all such cases arose during the Civil War, when southerners were expelled for disloyalty.

Between 1861 and 2007 only two members were removed. Rep. Michael J. "Ozzie" Myers, a Pennsylvania Democrat, was expelled in 1980 after he took bribe money from an agent of the Federal Bureau of Investigation (FBI) who was posing as a wealthy Arab in the Abscam scandal. The House in 2002 expelled Rep. James A. Traficant Jr., D-Ohio, six days before he was sentenced and led away in handcuffs to begin an eight-year prison term for conspiracy to commit bribery, seeking and accepting illegal gratuities, racketeering, obstruction of justice, and filing false federal income tax returns. Defiant to the end, Traficant attributed the charges against him to a government vendetta and unsuccessfully ran for reelection from his prison cell, as an independent, receiving 15 percent of the vote.

Congress has turned more often—although still rarely—to another formal punishment: censure, in which a member's conduct is condemned in a formal hearing before the entire House or Senate. More recently Congress devised a milder version of censure, called a reprimand. Loss of chairmanships, rebukes, and fines have also been used as punishment. House Democratic Caucus and House Republican Conference rules require that indicted members step down from their posts as committee or subcommittee chairs for the duration of the session or until the charges are dismissed.

Congress's reluctance to discipline its members is due in part to the belief held by some members and scholars that, except in cases of illegal acts punishable by the courts, the electorate, not colleagues, must be the ultimate judge of a member's behavior. Loyalty among members, especially of the same party, and toward Congress as an institution is another factor. The difficulty of agreeing on what constitutes a conflict of interest and misuse of power has also clouded the question.

Politics, a member's personal popularity, and even the customs of the times play a part in the judgment. When one member of the House shot another to death in a duel in 1838, the House declined to expel the murderer or to censure two colleagues who had served as seconds in the duel. As another legislator noted, dueling by members had been frequent and generally had gone unnoticed by the House. Just six years earlier, when the House for the first time had formally censured a member, the reason for the censure was simply a remark. The representative had told the Speaker his eyes were "too frequently turned from the chair you occupy toward the White House."

The House and Senate have often delayed their investigations and decisions until after an election; the voters frequently will defeat the colleague under fire and thus make disciplinary action unnecessary. For example, Rep. Jay C. Kim, a California Republican, pleaded guilty in federal court in 1997 to charges of receiving illegal campaign contributions and subsequently lost his primary reelection bid. The House ethics panel concluded an investigation of Kim in 1998, finding that he had violated federal campaign laws and House rules, but took no action against him because of his electoral defeat. (Kim had the distinction of being the first sitting member of Congress to have his movements tracked by an electronic monitoring bracelet during his home detention sentence.)

Rep. Jonathan Cilley of Maine was shot to death in a duel by a fellow Rep. William J. Graves of Kentucky in 1838. Graves was not punished by Congress.
Source: Library of Congress

Members have also been spared from disciplining a colleague by that member's timely resignation. Two House members and one senator used resignation in 1980–1982 to duck their almost certain expulsion following indictments for conspiracy and bribery in the Abscam scandal. In 1988 the House ethics committee recommended expulsion of New York Democrat Mario Biaggi, who resigned after his second conviction on criminal charges. Two House Democratic leaders, Speaker Wright and Majority Whip Tony Coelho of California, left Congress in 1989 to head off punishment in separate investigations of their financial activities. Republican Bob Packwood of Oregon resigned his Senate seat in 1995 after the Senate ethics panel recommended his expulsion on charges of sexual harassment and other misconduct.

The several scandals that engulfed the congressional House Republicans in 2005 and 2006 were other cases where members resigned, sparing colleagues the painful task of passing judgment. DeLay's 2006 departure was the most newsworthy because of his position as the House GOP's powerful majority leader in the years since the party took control of the chamber in 1995. But in addition, Randy "Duke" Cunningham, R-Calif., resigned in 2005 after pleading guilty to bribery. Bob Ney, R-Ohio, who was chair of the House Administration Committee, resigned in December 2006 after pleading guilty to federal counts of conspiracy and false statements. Rep. Mark Foley, R-Fla., resigned in September 2006 over inappropriate e-mails sent to teenage male pages over several years. In 2007 Senate Republicans had to deal with the fallout when Craig's airport arrest became public knowledge. Craig blunted initial criticism by saying he would resign his seat within a month. Later he changed his mind and said he would fight the charges, finish the final year of his term, but not run for reelection.

Both Congress and the voters have tended to forgive those with personal problems and those who admit their wrongdoing and repent. Criminal misconduct and a refusal to promise better behavior tend to result in disciplinary action and/or election defeat.

Ethical Questions

Money pervades most ethical questions, but legislators have also been disciplined for insults, questions of loyalty, sexual misconduct, and other offenses. For example, Joseph R. MCCARTHY, a Wisconsin Republican who gained notoriety for his anticommunist investigations in the early 1950s, was censured by the Senate in 1954 for insulting his colleagues and obstructing the constitutional process. Two House members were censured in 1983 for sexual misconduct. Disloyalty was the charge in the many cases of censure during the Civil War; southerners had supported the Confederacy rather than the Union.

Financial Misconduct

But much more common are allegations of bribery, kickbacks, misuse of public funds, or improper campaign contributions. Scrutiny of a legislator's financial accountability has centered on income from outside sources, on campaign contributions, and on the member's access to and use of public funds and privileges.

The criminal code has long prohibited a member of Congress from acts such as soliciting or receiving a bribe in return for a vote or other favor, benefiting from a contract with a federal agency, or promising to influence an appointment in return for something of value, including a political contribution. These laws are enforced by the Justice Department, which investigates the accusation and then can indict a legislator for illegal activity.

There was little doubt that most of the House Republican problems in the 109th Congress, 2005 to 2006, fell squarely within financial misconduct. DeLay's once unshakeable command of the GOP ranks eroded over a number of issues, including an indictment in Texas over money laundering in a case that was still pending in 2007. Earlier he had already been admonished for three ethics offenses: improperly pressuring a colleague to vote for a controversial Medicare drug bill; hosting a gold fundraiser with energy executives as Congress worked on a major energy bill; and pressing the Federal Aviation Administration to use its resources to track down a group of Democratic state lawmakers who had fled Texas in 2003 rather than vote for a redistricting map engineered by DeLay.

But DeLay's crucial problem was his proximity to a widening influence-peddling case involving lobbyist Jack Abramoff. Once a close associate of DeLay, Abramoff in January 2006 agreed to cooperate with federal investigators and plead guilty to charges of conspiracy, mail fraud, and income tax evasion. Later in the year two top DeLay aides pleaded guilty in the Abramoff case. DeLay

Jack Abramoff leaves federal court in Washington, D.C., in January 2006. An influence-peddling scandal involving Abramoff resulted in several Republican representatives losing their jobs.
Source: AP Images/Gerald Herbert

was not charged in connection with the Abramoff case, but the scandals eroded his support at home and threatened to cost him his seat in the 2006 elections.

Ney, however, was directly implicated in the Abramoff scandal. DeLay's former press secretary Michael Scanlon pleaded guilty to conspiring to bribe Ney. Ney continued to insist on his innocence, but in September 2006 he did an abrupt U-turn, pleading guilty to conspiracy and false statements. He admitted receiving gifts, including expensive meals and trips worth more than $170,000 from Abramoff and his associates in exchange for trying to shape legislation and inserting statements in the *Congressional Record* for the benefit of Abramoff's clients.

Cunningham's case was similar. He was an influential Republican voice on defense and intelligence policy during his fifteen years in Congress. He admitted accepting at least $2.4 million in bribes, including about $1 million in cash as well as rugs, antiques, furniture, yacht club fees, boat repairs, moving costs, and vacation expenses in exchange for using his House Appropriations Committee seat to obtain earmarks on behalf of defense contractors. He was sentenced to eight years and four months in prison.

Although Republicans were burdened with the larger scandals, the Democrats did not avoid controversy. The House ethics committee in 2006 undertook an investigation, which continued in 2007 and 2008, into whether Rep. William J. Jefferson of Louisiana had demanded and accepted bribes in exchange for helping to arrange contracts between a U.S. telecommunications company and Nigerian officials. Jefferson, the subject of a highly publicized Justice Department investigation, maintained his innocence. In June 2007 federal officials formally charged Jefferson in a sixteen-count indictment with racketeering, money laundering, and obstruction of justice. The grand jury indictment said Jefferson had been offered and accepted bribes to support business ventures in the United States and Africa. The indictment came after Jefferson handily won reelection in 2006.

But such blatant influence peddling has been just part of the picture. Critics over the years have argued that a legislator could also be improperly influenced by receiving a generous fee for giving a speech or writing an article, a large retainer for legal services, or a handsome salary for serving on a corporate board. The question of whether to limit such income became the most controversial aspect of ethics reform, which culminated in 1978 in a formal federal code of ethics. Amended and tightened in 1989 and 1991, the ethics law banned honoraria, the last remaining source of sizable outside earnings for members of Congress.

A murkier area concerned large campaign contributions and their effect on a legislator's decisions. Concern over undue influence and the escalating costs of elections prompted several reforms of campaign finance laws, including a 2002 law banning the national parties and federal candidates from raising or using "soft money"—a type of contribution that up to that time had largely fallen outside the restrictions of federal campaign finance law. A 2007 reform bill outlawed the bundling of contributions, a practice that hid the source of campaign funds from public view.

Sex and Alcohol

Next to money, sex and/or alcohol are leading causes of ethical lapses and scandal on Capitol Hill. Behavior that might have been ignored in the past is no longer tolerated by the public or Congress itself.

The women's movement, scandals in the military, and allegations of sexual misconduct made in 1991 by Anita Hill against Clarence Thomas, whom President George H.W. Bush had nominated to be a Supreme Court justice, have sensitized the nation to sexual harassment as never before. After a number of women complained of unwanted sexual advances from Packwood, the Oregon senator apologized and began treatment for alcohol abuse. But the powerful chair of the Senate Finance Committee, who was known for his strong support of women's rights, ultimately was forced to resign to avoid being expelled.

Other noted downfalls have included that of the influential chair of the House Ways and Means Committee, Democrat Wilbur D. MILLS of Arkansas, who resigned his committee post in 1974 after a well-publicized escapade with an Argentine strip dancer, Fanne Foxe, which Mills blamed on alcoholism. Two years later came a scandal over Ohio Democrat Wayne L. Hays, another highly placed veteran representative, allegedly putting his mistress, Elizabeth Ray, on the House payroll even though, in her words, "I can't type. I can't file. I can't even answer the phone."

In the wake of the White House sex scandal that set off the 1998–1999 impeachment and trial of President Bill Clinton, members of Congress and their past indiscretions came under increased scrutiny. The greatest shock wave occurred just two days before the impeachment debate, when House Speaker-designate Robert L. Livingston confessed to having had several extramarital affairs. Although he had violated no congressional rules or laws, it came at an embarrassing time for the Republican effort against Clinton and did not bode well for party unity in the next Congress. During the impeachment debate, the Louisiana Republican, who chaired the House Appropriations Committee, announced that he would not run for Speaker when the next Congress convened and planned to resign his seat in the House. (See CLINTON IMPEACHMENT TRIAL.)

Rep. Gary A. Condit, D-Calif., endured a withering controversy over his past relationship with Washington intern Chandra Levy, who disappeared in 2001 and whose remains were later found in a Washington park. Although he was not a suspect in the murder case, he was roundly criticized for his initial unwillingness to acknowledge what he later called a "close relationship." California Democrats redrew Condit's district, and he was defeated in a 2002 primary.

The Foley case illustrated the heightened sensitivity in Congress over sexual conduct of members. Although several high-profile inquiries were launched in the House in 2006, no case was pursed with the urgency that the House ethics committee gave to the Foley matter. Although Foley resigned after some of the sexually explicit communications he sent to pages became public, technically ending the ethics committee's jurisdiction over him, the panel actively probed whether the House GOP leadership had mishandled allegations of Foley's conduct for several years. The panel in early October formed an investigative subcommittee to explore whether leaders had ignored signs of Foley's behavior. Just two months later the full committee issued a bipartisan report saying that the Speaker, J. Dennis Hastert, R-Ill., other lawmakers, and aides had violated no laws or House rules. But the report also criticized the leadership for failing "to exercise appropriate diligence and oversight" of Foley's contact with pages. But the report did not recommend disciplinary action.

Republican representative Mark Foley, R-Fla., resigned after his sexually explicit communications with House pages became public.
Source: CQ Photo/Scott J. Ferrell

A similar issue came in the Senate in 2007 involving Idaho senator Larry Craig. As soon as it became known that the events probably involved sexual conduct Senate GOP leaders quickly removed Craig from committee positions and called for a swift ethics investigation. Craig first said he would resign at the end of September 2007, but his later decision to finish out his term and fight the charges left open the question of a Senate probe in 2008.

Scandals Prompt Reforms

Congress took no effective action to establish guidelines of ethical behavior until 1958, when a scandal in the executive branch prompted its members to enact a formal code of ethics applying throughout the government. Among the activities it opposed was the dispensation or receipt of special favors. But the code had no enforcement mechanism; it was, in effect, simply advice about how to behave properly. Only after a series of scandals did Congress slowly begin to move toward a formal ethics code and a way to enforce it.

The Senate set up a permanent ethics committee in 1964; the House followed suit in 1967. Politicians found that votes in favor of ethics were a good way to quiet negative news coverage, of which there seemed to be plenty. In 1963 Bobby Baker, the powerful secretary for the Senate majority, resigned under fire after allegations that he had used his office to promote his business interests. The Senate then went through a painful examination of how Sen. Thomas J. Dodd, a Connecticut Democrat, had misused campaign contributions; Dodd was censured in 1967. The House was rocked in 1967 by its decision not to seat New York Democrat Adam Clayton POWELL Jr. because of misconduct, a decision that the Supreme Court later ruled to be unconstitutional. Largely in response to these scandals the House and Senate in 1968 separately adopted new rules intended to help prevent conflicts of interest in Congress.

Congress in 1977 adopted sweeping new codes of conduct that would ultimately affect every key employee in the three branches of government. Impetus had come from a heightened concern about integrity in government in the wake of the WATERGATE SCANDAL, as well as another round of congressional scandals. The previous year had been one of the worst for scandals. In 1976 Rep. Robert L. F. Sikes, a Florida Democrat, was reprimanded for not disclosing investments in defense-related companies while he chaired the Appropriations Subcommittee on Military Construction. That was the same year Wayne Hays resigned in the midst of an investigation into the charges that he had kept a mistress on his payroll. Congress was also stung in 1976 by a report that Gulf Oil had illegally contributed more than $5 million to the campaigns of dozens of legislators during the previous decade.

Further pressure for reforms came from two public commissions that recommended pay increases for Congress on the condition that the two chambers adopt effective codes of ethics.

Enforceable Codes

The House in mid-1976 appointed a special ethics study commission chaired by David R. Obey, a Wisconsin Democrat; the Senate then set up its own special group. Early in 1977 the House approved the Obey commission's recommendations almost intact, despite controversy over income limits and other key issues. The Senate somewhat reluctantly approved a similar code. The new codes of ethics required disclosure of substantial financial information about members and key employees, imposed new restrictions on outside income of members, ended unofficial office accounts that were financed with private contributions and were used to supplement official allowances, forbade significant gifts from lobbyists, and tightened standards for use of the FRANKING PRIVILEGE.

In 1978 Congress passed a law, the Ethics in Government Act, to enforce the financial disclosure requirements in the new House and Senate codes and to apply those requirements to top officials in the other two branches of government.

More reforms in the late 1980s followed another spate of investigations. These investigations led to the Senate disciplining Minnesota Republican Dave Durenberger and California Democrat Alan Cranston for financial misconduct. Durenberger's case involved book and real estate deals, while Cranston was one of the senators who had accepted campaign contributions from savings and loan operator Charles H. Keating Jr. in what became the Keating Five scandal. In the House, besides the Wright and Coelho resignations, there were probes that resulted in reprimands of Democrat Austin J. Murphy of Pennsylvania for misuse of his office and of Barney Frank, a Massachusetts Democrat, for disgracing the House by improperly using his office to help a male prostitute.

The Ethics Reform Act of 1989, which supplanted the landmark 1978 Ethics in Government Act, closed several loopholes that enabled members and other federal officials to skirt the older law's financial disclosure provisions. It brought all three branches of government under the same disclosure law, although each branch would continue to be responsible for its own administration of the requirements. It also included restrictions and cutbacks in perquisites, or "perks," which were intended to offset public hostility to an almost 40 percent pay raise over two years provided in the measure for the House, along with provisions for cost-of-living adjustments.

The bill's limits on outside income were by far the most controversial aspect of the 1989 ethics law. The bill included a total ban on honoraria, or fees, for speeches and articles by House members. It also barred House members from being paid for serving on boards of directors and for outside law or other professional practices. Senators were not subject to the honoraria ban in the 1989 law but had been barred from accepting fees for outside professional work since 1983.

Congress had been wrestling with the issue of outside income and honoraria since it first set honoraria limits in a 1974 campaign finance law. The objective was to reduce the number of instances in which a legislator was paid thousands of dollars for a half-hour speech to an association or industry lobbying Congress. The 1977 ethics code had tightened those limits, both by lowering the allowed amount and by broadening it to include all earned income. The allowed amount was changed several times over the years, with the Senate showing the most resistance to curtailing honoraria.

The Senate continued to resist, but after chafing under the lower pay, it voted in 1991 to give up honoraria and take the same salary as the House. Although senators, representatives, and other federal officials could no longer keep honoraria, they could request that such fees be paid in their name to charities, with a limit of $2,000 per contribution and with mandatory disclosure of the sources and amounts. The receiving charities would be identified only in confidential reports to the ethics offices.

As part of the deal under which the House agreed to the Senate pay raise, the 1991 legislation eased some of the gift rules Congress had passed less than two years earlier. Under the revised rules, members and employees of Congress could accept gifts worth up to $250 a year from any one person; gifts below $100 did not count toward the ceiling. Only certain larger gifts had to be disclosed. In 1995 both chambers changed their gift rules again. The Senate's new rule prohibited gifts that exceeded $50 and prohibited senators and staff from accepting more than $100 from the same source each year. The House adopted a rule that largely banned all gifts to members and their staff except for close personal friends or family. But the House had great difficulty implementing the rule and in 1999 revised its rule to match the Senate's. The House eased its gift rule further in 2003.

The 1989 ethics law also eliminated, beginning in 1993, a loophole that had allowed House members who had been in office at the beginning of 1980 to convert to personal use any remaining campaign funds when they left office. Senate rules had previously prohibited the practice. Other provisions of the 1989 law included new restrictions on domestic and FOREIGN TRAVEL by members, and on lobbying by government officials, including members of Congress, after they left office. The lobbying restrictions were strengthened in 2007 in the wake of the Abramoff scandals in the previous Congress.

The conduct of members is affected by other statutes as well. Major campaign financing laws and rules, for example, regulate how members finance their election campaigns. Federal labor and antidiscrimination laws govern members' treatment of their STAFF. Congress prohibited nepotism by senators and representatives under a 1967 law. Nepotism—the hiring of spouses, children, and close relatives—had given rise to criticism from the press. Over the years certain members had been accused of padding their official staffs with relatives who did little or no work for their government paychecks.

Ethics Committee, House *SEE* STANDARDS OF OFFICIAL
CONDUCT COMMITTEE, HOUSE.

Ethics Committee, Senate Select

The six members of the bipartisan Senate Select Committee on Ethics have the awkward responsibility of ensuring their colleagues behave properly. They are charged with enforcing the Senate code of ethics, a formal set of rules adopted in 1977. The three Democrats and three Republicans are expected to act collectively as investigator, prosecutor, and jury. In practice, committee members rarely conduct an official probe, preferring to handle potential problems in private before they escalate into scandals.

Most ethics questions focus on finances. Senators are required to keep separate their personal, office, and campaign funds, and they must file financial disclosure statements with the Ethics Committee. Senators must also avoid situations where they benefit personally from their official acts. Bribery is the most blatant example of this, but less obvious corruption also occurs, such as an inside financial deal with an industry seeking a legislative favor.

The committee has also had to deal with sensitive issues of harassment and other types of sexual indiscretion. In late 1992 the committee began investigating complaints lodged against Oregon Republican Bob Packwood by female staff members and lobbyists who accused the senator of having made unwanted sexual advances to them. After a bitter three-year battle, Packwood resigned in 1995 rather than face almost certain expulsion from the Senate.

Committee Actions

The Senate voted in 1964 to establish an ethics committee. By 2007 four disciplinary cases had been brought to the Senate floor for a vote. The Senate endorsed the committee's recommendation in three of the four cases. The exception was the 1982 case of New Jersey Democrat Harrison A. Williams Jr., the only senator convicted in the Abscam scandal. Debate over Williams's expulsion was cut short by his resignation. The Senate had already indicated its reluctance to handle the controversy by delaying its debate for seven months after receiving the unanimous recommendation of the Ethics Committee. In the other cases, three senators were censured or denounced for financial misconduct: Connecticut Democrat Thomas J. Dodd in 1967, Georgia Democrat Herman E. Talmadge in 1979, and Minnesota Republican Dave Durenberger in 1990.

A fifth disciplinary case went to the floor in 1991, but not for a vote. Instead, the Senate heard the committee's reprimand of California Democrat Alan Cranston for improper conduct in the Keating Five scandal. The committee used reprimand because it lacked authority to issue a censure on its own. But in other respects the reprimand was no less harsh than in the three previous cases.

The committee's last major action was an admonishment of Democrat Robert G. Torricelli of New Jersey in 2002 for improperly accepting expensive gifts from former campaign supporters. Torricelli dropped his bid for reelection soon thereafter.

Critics complain that the Ethics Committee has not aggressively policed the Senate. But committee members have said they want to prevent scandals as much as uncover them. To this end the committee published a manual containing more than 400 questions senators had asked of the Ethics Committee, along with answers compiled by the committee and its staff.

Unlike the House Committee on Standards of Official Conduct, where only members may press ethics complaints against other members, the Senate committee accepts complaints filed by outside watchdog groups and individuals. (See STANDARDS OF OFFICIAL CONDUCT COMMITTEE, HOUSE.)

If a complaint is filed against a senator, rules allow the Ethics Committee to investigate and, if no action is recommended, to keep the matter from public knowledge. In three of its cases—those of Williams, Durenberger, and the Keating Five—the committee brought in a special counsel, Robert S. Bennett, to act as prosecutor. With his aggressive manner and insistence that senators should avoid even the appearance of impropriety, Bennett went a long way toward toughening the committee's image.

History

The Ethics Committee was established in 1964 and organized in 1965. Its first chair was John C. STENNIS, a veteran Mississippi Democrat. A former judge with a reputation for fairness and integrity, Stennis chaired the panel until 1975, when Nevada Democrat Howard W. Cannon took over for two years. Adlai E. Stevenson III, an Illinois Democrat, chaired the committee from 1977 through most of 1979, the year the Senate voted to denounce Georgia Democrat Herman Talmadge. Stevenson resigned in the fall, and Democrat Howell Heflin, a freshman from Alabama, was named chair. This was the first time since 1910 that so new a member had been given a post as committee chair. A former judge, Heflin demonstrated a judicious restraint that his colleagues appreciated. Heflin was chair from 1979 to 1981 and again from 1987, when Democrats regained the Senate, to 1991.

During Republican control of the Senate from 1981–1987, the committee had two chairs. Malcolm Wallop of Wyoming, who often criticized the Senate ethics code, held the post from 1981 to 1985; Warren B. Rudman of New Hampshire took over from 1985 to 1987. North Carolina Democrat Terry Sanford succeeded Heflin as chair in 1991 and Nevada Democrat Richard Bryan became chair in 1993. With the Republicans back in control of the Senate, Kentucky Republican Mitch McConnell chaired the panel from 1995 until 1997. He was succeeded by Republican Robert

CLOSER LOOK

Harrison A. Williams Jr.
Source: AP Images/J. Scott Applewhite

Senate Disciplinary Case

Sen. Harrison A. Williams Jr., D-N.J., resigned from the Senate in 1982 as his colleagues were debating expelling him. Williams had been convicted on criminal charges in the Abscam scandal.

C. Smith of New Hampshire, who held the post until the Democrats took control of the Senate in June 2001. Democrat Harry Reid of Nevada headed the committee until 2003, when the Republicans were back on top and George V. Voinovich of Ohio became chair. In 2007 the panel was under the acting chair of Barbara Boxer, D-Calif. Tim Johnson of South Dakota was scheduled to be the chair, but on December 13, 2006, he was admitted to a Washington hospital for brain surgery. Doctors stanched bleeding on the brain from a congenital condition known as arteriovenous malformation. By December 2007 his condition had improved significantly.

A member of the minority party serves as vice chair of the Ethics Committee.

Executive Branch and Congress

The legislative and the executive are separate but interdependent branches of government. Although the Constitution vested the president with "the executive power," the president is often referred to as the "chief legislator." Congress was granted "all legislative powers," which gives it significant leverage over the executive branch through its legislative and oversight powers. (See SEPARATION OF POWERS.)

Constitutional Deliberations

No questions troubled the framers of the Constitution more than the powers to be given the executive branch and how it should be structured. How much authority and independence to give the national executive remained in dispute until the end of the Constitutional Convention.

The convention at first favored a single executive, chosen by Congress for a term of seven years, whose powers would be limited. Congress would appoint judges and ambassadors and would make treaties. This plan for legislative supremacy finally gave way to a more balanced plan, which called for a president to be chosen by electors for a four-year term without limit as to reelection. (The Twenty-second Amendment, adopted in 1951, set a two-term limit for the presidency.) The president was to make appointments and treaties, subject to Senate approval; act as commander in chief; and ensure that the laws were faithfully executed. The framers did not attempt to elaborate on how the system would actually work. The provisions on presidential power were brief and ambiguous.

President as Lawmaker

The president's role as lawmaker begins with the constitutional duty to "from time to time give to the Congress Information of the State of the Union, and recommend to their Consideration such Measures as he shall judge necessary and expedient." To these bare bones, Congress has added further requirements. For example, the president is required to submit an annual budget message and an economic report.

Other legislative powers granted by the Constitution to the president include the power to veto bills; the power to make treaties, subject to Senate consent; and the rarely used power to convene one or both houses of Congress. The president's role as lawmaker has been further increased through the authority to issue rules and regulations, proclamations, and executive orders—or administrative legislation.

The president traditionally sets forth a legislative agenda in the annual State of the Union address before a joint session of Congress. The president then sends legislative proposals to Congress in the form of draft bills.

What happens to these administration bills after they are introduced depends on a variety of factors, including who is in the White House, which party controls Congress, the times and mood of the country, and the issue itself.

The Constitution said little about how a president would go about persuading Congress to pass presidential proposals. Several tools are available to the chief executive.

Lobbying

One tool of persuasion is for the president to lobby Congress directly. Early presidents kept their lobbying discreet, either doing it themselves or entrusting it to a few helpers. In modern times, executive lobbying has become more open and more elaborate.

President Harry S. TRUMAN set up a small legislative liaison office in 1949, but the staff was inexperienced; Truman and a few top advisers still did the real lobbying. Truman's successor, Dwight D. Eisenhower, in 1953 appointed full-time, senior staff to the task. Liaison operations continued to expand and grow more sophisticated in succeeding administrations.

Lobbying of Congress took on increased urgency in the aftermath of the September 11, 2001, terrorist attacks when the George W. Bush administration aggressively sought expanded powers to monitor terror suspects and pressed Congress to authorize creation of a cabinet-level department of homeland security. The efforts generated friction with Democrats and some Republicans in Congress, who believed the White House was being excessively secretive with its plans and was not adequately consulting them on the war on terrorism.

In addition to the White House operation, all federal departments also have their own congressional liaison forces. The practice began in 1945, when the War Department created the office of assistant secretary for congressional liaison, centralizing congressional relations that had been handled separately by the military services. The services and some civilian agencies have liaison offices on Capitol Hill today.

Some legal limits have been placed on executive lobbying. A 1919 criminal statute prohibits the executive branch from spending money to influence votes in Congress.

Public Pressure

When direct appeals to Congress fail, presidents often turn to their vast constituency for help. Presidents sometimes can mobilize enormous public pressure to persuade Congress to act on legislative programs. Radio and television have been especially effective tools for shaping public opinion.

One of the most skillful users of the media was President Franklin D. Roosevelt. In 1933, at the end of his first week in office, Roosevelt went on the radio to urge support for his banking reforms. He addressed a joint session of Congress, too. His reforms were passed that very day. Similar radio messages, which became known as "fireside chats," followed.

Television gave presidents further power to influence the public. President Lyndon B. JOHNSON in 1965 made masterful use of television to win support for the most sweeping voting rights bill in ninety years. Instead of appearing before Congress at the customary hour of noon, he waited until evening, when the television audience would be greater. He then delivered what has been called his best speech as president.

CLOSER LOOK ◉

Presidents have no specific constitutional power to persuade Congress to follow their wishes. They can, however, influence outcomes through direct contact with legislators, use of patronage, veto threats, and—especially—encouraging public pressure on senators and representatives. President Franklin D. Roosevelt was highly skillful using radio through his famous "fireside chats" to influence congressional decisions. Ronald Reagan and later presidents used television to the same effect.

President Ronald Reagan enjoyed great success with his use of television. His 1981 televised appeal to Congress for passage of his budget package, accompanied by vigorous lobbying for public support of the program, was labeled by House Speaker Thomas P. O'NEILL Jr., a Massachusetts Democrat, "the greatest selling job I've ever seen."

President Bill Clinton's public portrayal of the conservative Republicans who took control of Congress after the 1994 midterm elections as "extremists" (and the Republicans' subsequent political missteps) helped the beleaguered president reinvigorate his political fortunes and consequently win reelection in 1996.

President George W. Bush helped Republicans regain control of the Senate in the 2002 elections and won congressional support for national security initiatives by publicly questioning whether some Democrats were putting special interests, such as the needs of organized labor, ahead of national security considerations. Bush effectively used the presidential bully pulpit even before the terrorist attacks by stumping nationwide for a tax cut soon after taking office. The personal appeals put pressure on lawmakers, who subsequently enacted the cut.

Patronage

Another means for exerting pressure on Congress is patronage. Over the years presidential patronage has included everything from distributing government jobs to issuing coveted invitations to the White House.

Although the civil service and postal reforms of the twentieth century dramatically reduced the president's patronage, the award of government contracts, selection of sites for federal installations, judicial appointments, and other political favors remain powerful inducements in the hands of a president.

Veto

When all else fails, there is always the veto, the president's most powerful defensive weapon. A president uses the veto to try to kill unacceptable bills and also to dramatize administration policies.

Short of an actual veto, a presidential threat to veto legislation is a powerful persuader. In 1975 both the House and Senate passed a consumer protection bill, but they dropped the measure because President Gerald R. FORD threatened to veto it. George H. W. Bush used vetoes and veto threats to force Congress to compromise on key legislation, such as gun control, civil rights, and unemployment compensation.

After the takeover of both houses of Congress by the Republican Party in 1995, Clinton also turned to veto threats and vetoes to thwart an aggressively conservative Republican legislative agenda and to reestablish the "relevance" of the presidency. During a December 1995 budget showdown with congressional Republicans led by Speaker Newt Gingrich, R-Ga., Clinton objected to Republican efforts to slash spending on his priorities. The president's refusal to compromise and his subsequent vetoes of a stopgap spending measure as well as a debt limit bill designed to force him to accept a GOP balanced budget plan led to a government shutdown that was widely blamed on GOP congressional leaders. Clinton subsequently vetoed a budget reconciliation bill that included the Republicans' balanced budget and tax cut plans. When budget talks collapsed and federal funding ran out, a second government shutdown occurred. The budget battles strengthened Clinton and tarnished the Republicans.

Like his father, President George W. Bush used the veto threat effectively in his first six years to deter Congress from actions he did not favor. But unlike his father, Bush was aided in this effort by GOP control of Congress during most of those years. With the Democrats in control of Congress in 2007, Bush not only raised his rhetoric on veto threats but also followed through by issuing six vetoes that year.

Although the Constitution permits the House and Senate to override a presidential veto by a two-thirds vote in each chamber, in reality Congress rarely overrides vetoes.

Congressional Role

Congress plays an important role in the functioning of the executive branch. Its responsibilities range from counting electoral votes, to providing funds for the executive branch, to monitoring the implementation of laws.

The Constitution provides that Congress will count electoral votes for president and VICE PRESIDENT. If no candidate wins a majority, the House chooses the president and the Senate, the vice president. Congress also bears responsibility in the related areas of PRESIDENTIAL DISABILITY AND SUCCESSION. (See ELECTING THE PRESIDENT.)

The Senate has the power to confirm executive appointments. Both the House and Senate can launch investigations into executive activities, and both chambers work together to seek the impeachment and conviction of top officials accused of wrongdoing. Through much of 1997 and all of 1998, Clinton faced investigations by various congressional committees, as well as an independent counsel, in regard to alleged wrongdoings. In December 1998, after a referral from the independent counsel, the Republican-controlled House Judiciary Committee voted along party lines to recommend to the full House that Clinton be impeached. The House subsequently impeached the president, sending the matter to trial in the Senate, where he was acquitted. (See IMPEACHMENT POWER; CLINTON IMPEACHMENT TRIAL.)

Congress also shares with the executive important war powers and responsibility for ratifying treaties. (See TREATY-MAKING POWER.) But the power that gives Congress the most influence is its power of the purse. Through its AUTHORIZATION BILLS and APPROPRIATIONS BILLS, Congress helps formulate and carry out executive policies. It may use its taxing power to raise money to run the country and to regulate government activities.

Many of these powers help Congress in performing one of its primary responsibilities: oversight. In the laws it passes, Congress often leaves much to the discretion of the president and the federal bureaucracy. Congress must, therefore, ensure that its legislative intent is being carried out and remedy the situation if it is not.

Executive Privilege

Presidents occasionally refuse congressional demands for information or for officials' testimony before committees by claiming executive privilege. The term is modern, but the practice is as old as the nation.

The Constitution does not specifically grant executive privilege, but presidents since George Washington have asserted a right to withhold information from Congress based on the constitutional separation of powers. Congress has been reluctant to seek a decisive court ruling on the validity of executive privilege. Instead, it has tried to rally public opinion in support of congressional demands for information, and occasionally it has cited executive branch officials for contempt of Congress.

Presidents have offered a variety of reasons to justify denying information to Congress. Perhaps the most common is the need for secrecy in military and diplomatic activities. Other reasons for withholding information include protecting individuals from unfavorable publicity and safeguarding the confidential exchange of ideas within an administration. Critics frequently charge that an administration's real motive for refusing to supply information is to escape criticism or to cover up wrongdoing.

The most dramatic clash over executive privilege between Congress and the White House came during an inquiry into the Watergate scandal, which brought about the resignation of President Richard M. NIXON in 1974. The Watergate affair began with a 1972 break-in at Democratic National Committee headquarters in the Watergate office building in Washington, D.C. As the scandal unfolded, it revealed administration political sabotage that went far beyond the original incident.

Presidents from George Washington to George W. Bush have asserted that they have certain rights or privileges based on constitutional separation of powers. Yet claims of executive privilege are not unchallengeable. President Richard Nixon's attempt to withhold documents and tape recordings from Congress investigating the Watergate scandal was ultimately overruled by the Supreme Court.
Source: White House

Claiming executive privilege, Nixon tried to withhold tapes and documents demanded by congressional investigators. The Supreme Court ruled unanimously in July 1974 that Nixon must give up tapes showing his involvement in the scandal. Days later the House Judiciary Committee recommended that Nixon be removed from office for, among other things, failing to comply with a committee subpoena, or demand, for the tapes. The president quickly resigned, ending the NIXON IMPEACHMENT EFFORT.

The Court's ruling on the Nixon tapes was a defeat for one president but a victory for the presidency. In its unanimous opinion in *United States v. Nixon,* the Court said that the public interest outweighed Nixon's need for confidentiality in the case of the tapes, which might contain evidence relevant to a criminal prosecution. But at the same time the Court recognized executive privilege as a legitimate, if limited, aspect of the president's authority.

In 1998 a federal district court ruled that President Bill Clinton could not invoke executive privilege to keep his White House aides from testifying in independent counsel Kenneth W. Starr's investigation of alleged criminal conduct by the president. The ruling—triggered by subpoenas from Starr's grand juries, not a congressional committee—created a new area of case law on executive privilege. Previously, negotiations between the White House and Congress and the framers' precepts of checks and balances had been sufficient to settle most disputes over its usage. The expected effect was that power had been shifted from the presidency to Congress and that future Congresses would be emboldened to issue subpoenas to future administrations. (See CLINTON IMPEACHMENT TRIAL.)

George W. Bush's administration invoked executive privilege on several sensitive matters, angering many in Congress. The Bush administration in 2002 refused to allow then-director of the Office of Homeland Security Tom Ridge to testify before Congress in support of domestic security budget requests and

More on this topic:

Contempt of Congress, p. 144

Separation of Powers, p. 508

Watergate Scandal, p. 596

other priority-setting matters, citing Ridge's role as a confidential adviser to the president. Among administration officials' concerns was the prospect of lawmakers getting Ridge to commit under oath to various spending proposals.

The administration also provoked a major showdown with the GOVERNMENT ACCOUNTABILITY OFFICE (GAO)—the investigative arm of Congress—by refusing to disclose which energy industry executives were consulted in 2001 by a task force headed by Vice President Richard CHENEY that was charged with formulating energy policy. The GAO in 2002 took the unprecedented step of suing in federal court to compel disclosure. After a U.S. district court judge ruled that the GAO could not sue for the records, the GAO in early 2003 decided not to appeal the decision.

Bush, nevertheless, benefited during most of his first six years in the White House by having Republican control of Congress. The GOP legislators rarely challenged the administration for information or actively engaged in oversight activity. But in 2007 Democrats regained control of both houses and immediately began aggressive oversight hearings, significantly increasing the chances of new clashes over executive privileges in Bush's final two years in office.

Executive Session

An executive session is a meeting of a congressional committee—or occasionally the full Senate or House of Representatives—that only its members and necessary staff may attend. Witnesses regularly appear at committee meetings in executive session. Defense Department officials, for example, testify in executive session during presentations of classified defense information. Other members of Congress may be invited, but the public and press are excluded.

The term is also used to describe those sessions in which the Senate considers a treaty or nomination. Such sessions usually are open to the public. Normally the Senate meets in legislative session.

Expulsion

Expulsion is the removal from office of a senator or representative. It is the most severe sanction against a member, and is rarely used. The Constitution requires a two-thirds vote for expulsion. Courts have ruled that it can be used only for conduct during a member's term of office, not for conduct before a member's election. (See DISCIPLINING MEMBERS.)

Extensions of Remarks

Each issue of the *CONGRESSIONAL RECORD* has a special section that serves almost as a scrapbook of the day. Legislators who want to publicize articles, newspaper stories, or other information can submit the text for a section called "Extensions of Remarks," which is located in the back pages of the *Record*. Any statement expected to take up more than two printed pages must be accompanied by an estimate of printing costs.

Senators usually prefer to have their articles or undelivered speeches printed as part of the day's floor debate, instead of in "Extensions of Remarks." The extra section is popular with House members, who often fill several pages.

Federalist Papers, The

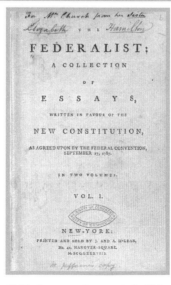

Eighty-five essays in support of ratifying the Constitution were combined into a single pamphlet in 1788, known today as **The Federalist Papers.**
Source: Library of Congress

When the Constitutional Convention adjourned on September 17, 1787, the success of the new and radical document was by no means assured. A strong faction in the nation known as the Anti-Federalists opposed adoption of the new Constitution. To overcome this opposition, three prominent members of the founding generation wrote a series of essays defending the Constitution and presenting the arguments for its ratification. These were published as newspaper articles and later brought together in pamphlet form as *The Federalist.* Today they are usually referred to as *The Federalist Papers.*

The principal authors were Alexander Hamilton and James Madison, two of the most important Founders involved in creating the Constitution. Hamilton is believed to have written fifty-one of the essays and three with Madison, who probably wrote twenty-six on his own. In addition, John Jay wrote five essays. All were published under the name Publius, a political figure of the ancient republic of Rome, and were published between October 27, 1787, and August 16, 1788.

The essays were particularly aimed at the people of New York, the home state of Hamilton and Jay, and the delegates who would be selected to vote on ratification. The fate of the

Constitution was much in doubt in New York and in some danger elsewhere. Consequently, the essays were intended also to influence opinion favorably toward ratification in all states.

Modern historians doubt that essays, with their abstract arguments about the general welfare, played a significant role in ratification; they believe economic issues and calculations of self-interest by those voting on ratification played a bigger role. Nevertheless, *The Federalist Papers* have become famous as one of the most important political and philosophical documents ever written. Throughout the eighty-five essays, the authors set out the rationale for the new government so well that Congress and the courts still cite them in efforts to interpret and understand the Constitution as it was understood by the Founders. The volume remains a central part of any curriculum for students of government even after more than two centuries.

Federal Register

The *Federal Register* is a daily government publication that provides a wide variety of information on government operations. It contains presidential proclamations; executive orders (with the exception of those that are classified and pertain to sensitive national security matters); and other executive branch documents, including rules, regulations, and notices issued by federal agencies. The *Federal Register* spells out government requirements in many fields of public concern: environmental protection, food and drug standards, and occupational health and safety, to name just a few. It also includes proposed changes in agency regulations, on which the public is invited to comment. The *Federal Register* is published by the National Archives and Records Administration and has been online (www.gpoaccess.gov/fr/index.html) since 1995.

Filibuster

The Senate has long been famous for the filibuster: the deliberate use of prolonged debate and procedural delaying tactics to block action supported by a majority of members. Filibusters have been mounted on issues ranging from peace treaties to internal Senate seating disputes. Editorial writers have condemned them, cartoonists have ridiculed them, and satirists have caricatured them. But filibusters also have admirers, who view them as a defense against hasty or ill-advised legislation and as a guarantee that minority views will be heard.

Filibusters are permitted by the Senate's tradition of unlimited debate, a characteristic that distinguishes it from the House of Representatives. The term filibuster is derived from a word for pirates or soldiers of fortune; the term originated in the House, although the modern House seldom experiences delay arising from a prolonged debate.

The Senate proudly claims to be a more deliberative body than the House. George Washington described it as the saucer where passions cool. But many people believe the modern filibuster impedes rather than encourages deliberation. Once reserved for the bitterest and most important battles—over slavery, war, civil rights—filibusters today have been trivialized, critics say.

Historically the rare filibuster provided the Senate's best theater; participants had to be ready for days or weeks of free-wheeling debate, and all other business was blocked until one side conceded or a compromise acceptable to all was found. In the modern era the number of filibusters has increased but drama is rare. Disappointment awaits visitors to the Senate gallery who expect a real-life version of actor Jimmy Stewart's climactic oration in the 1939 classic film *Mr. Smith Goes to Washington*. They are likely to

CLOSER LOOK

The filibuster—extended debate in Senate-speak—has been part of the Senate history since its earliest days, although the first true use of this device dates from 1841. It was not until the twentieth century that it became an important parliamentary device and only in the latter decades a commonly used tactic. Even into the 1950s and 1960s the filibuster was reserved for the most contentious issues, such as civil rights legislation. By 2000 it was invoked—or often just threatened—over the most mundane of issues, and not infrequently for purposes unrelated to the bill being filibustered.

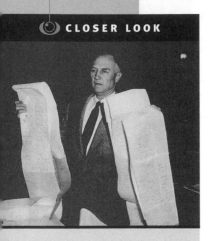

Source: Strom Thurmond Institute

The longest speech in the history of the Senate was made by Strom Thurmond of South Carolina. Thurmond, a Democrat who later became a Republican, spoke for twenty-four hours and eighteen minutes during a filibuster against passage of the Civil Rights Act of 1957. The second longest was made by Wayne Morse, who was both a Democrat and an Independent during his career, who spoke for twenty-two hours and twenty-six minutes on an oil bill in 1953.

look down on an empty floor and hear only the drone of a clerk reading absent senators' names in a mind-numbing succession of QUORUM calls. Often the filibusterers do not even have to be on the floor, nor do the bills they are opposing.

Despite the lack of drama, filibusters and threats of filibusters remain a common weapon of senators hoping to spotlight, change, delay, or kill legislation. Frequent resort to the filibuster, real or threatened, often impedes Senate action on major bills. Success is most likely near the end of a session, when a filibuster on one bill may imperil action on other, more urgent legislation. Since unanimous consent is out of the question, a filibuster can be ended by negotiating a compromise on the disputed matter or persuading a supermajority of senators to vote for a cumbersome cut-off procedure known as cloture. The two are often interrelated, as compromises win more votes for cloture.

Dramatic filibusters do still occur on occasion, as demonstrated by a 1987–1988 Republican filibuster against a campaign finance reform bill. To counter Republican obstruction, the majority leader, Democrat Robert C. BYRD of West Virginia, forced round-the-clock Senate sessions that disrupted the chamber for three days. When Republicans boycotted the sessions, Byrd resurrected a little-known power that had last been wielded in 1942: he directed the Senate SERGEANT-AT-ARMS to arrest absent members and bring them to the floor. In the resulting turmoil, Oregon Republican Bob Packwood was arrested, reinjured a broken finger, and was physically carried onto the Senate floor at 1:19 a.m. Democrats were still unable to break the filibuster, and the campaign finance bill was pulled from the floor after a record-setting eighth cloture vote failed to limit debate.

As Old as the Senate

Delaying tactics were first used in the Senate in 1789, by opponents of a bill to locate the nation's capital on the Susquehanna River. The first full-fledged filibusters occurred in 1841, when Democrats and Whigs squared off, first over the appointment of official Senate printers and then over the establishment of a national bank.

Slavery, the Civil War, Reconstruction, and blacks' voting rights in turn were the sparks for the increasingly frequent and contentious filibusters of the nineteenth century. Opponents had no weapon against them, since the only way to terminate debate was through unanimous consent, and proposed rules to restrict debate were repeatedly rejected.

Minor curbs were adopted early in the twentieth century. But they did not hinder Republican filibusterers from killing two of President Woodrow Wilson's proposals to prepare the nation for World War I: a 1915 ship-purchase bill and a 1917 bill to arm merchant ships. As a political scientist in 1882, Wilson had celebrated "the Senate's opportunities for open and unrestricted discussion." After the 1917 defeat he railed, "The Senate of the United States is the only legislative body in the world which cannot act when the majority is ready for action. A little group of willful men … have rendered the great government of the United States helpless and contemptible."

Public outrage finally forced the Senate to accept debate limitations. On March 8, 1917, it adopted a rule under which a filibuster could be halted if two-thirds of the senators present voted to do so. The framers of this first cloture rule predicted it would be little used, and for years that was the case. The first successful use of the rule, in 1919, ended debate on the Treaty of Versailles following World War I.

Nine more cloture votes were taken through 1927, and three were successful. The next successful cloture vote did not occur until 1962, when the Senate invoked cloture on a communications satellite bill.

Only sixteen cloture votes were taken between 1927 and the successful 1962 vote, most of which involved civil rights. Southern Democrats were joined by westerners and some Republicans in an anticloture coalition that successfully filibustered legislation to stop poll taxes, literacy tests, lynching, and employment discrimination.

Many filibusters turned into grueling endurance contests. Strom THURMOND of South Carolina set a record for the longest speech in the history of the Senate. Thurmond, a Democrat who later switched to the Republican Party, spoke for twenty-four hours and eighteen minutes during a 1957 filibuster of a civil rights bill. Speakers did not always confine themselves to the subject under consideration. Democrat Huey P. LONG of Louisiana entertained his colleagues during a fifteen-and-a-half-hour filibuster in 1935 with commentaries on the Constitution and recipes for southern "pot likker," turnip greens, and corn bread.

During a 1960 filibuster of a civil rights bill, eighteen southerners formed into teams of two and talked nonstop in relays. Supporters of the bill had to stay nearby for quorum calls and other procedural moves or risk losing control of the floor. Then–majority leader Lyndon B. JOHNSON, a Texas Democrat, kept the Senate going around the clock for nine days in an effort to break the filibuster. That was the longest session ever, but Johnson ultimately had to abandon the bill. Later in the year a weaker version passed.

"We slept on cots in the Old Supreme Court chamber [near the Senate floor] and came out to answer quorum calls," recalled William Proxmire, a Wisconsin Democrat who supported the bill. "It was an absolutely exhausting experience. The southerners who were doing the talking were in great shape, because they would talk for two hours and leave the floor for a couple of days."

Changing the Rule

Proponents of the right to filibuster gained a further advantage in 1949, when they won a change in the rules to require a two-thirds vote of the total Senate membership to invoke cloture, instead of just those present and voting. But the civil rights filibusters in the 1950s stimulated efforts to make it easier to invoke cloture.

The 1949 cloture rule had banned any limitation of debate on proposals to change the Senate rules, including the cloture rule itself. Since any attempt to change the cloture rule while operating under this stricture appeared hopeless, Senate liberals devised a new approach. Senate rules had always continued from one Congress to the next on the assumption that the Senate was a continuing body because only one-third of its members were elected every two years. Liberals now challenged this concept, arguing that the Senate had a right to adopt new rules by a simple majority vote at the beginning of a new Congress.

The dispute came to a head in 1959, when a bipartisan leadership group seized the initiative from the liberals and pushed through a change in the cloture rule. The new version permitted cloture to be invoked by two-thirds of those present and voting, as the original cloture rule adopted in 1917 had, and it also applied to proposals for changes in the rules.

Once cloture was invoked, further debate was limited to one hour for each senator on the bill itself and on all amendments affecting it. No new amendments could be offered except by unanimous consent. Nongermane amendments and dilatory motions (those intended to delay action) were not permitted. (See AMENDMENTS; RIDER.)

> *"The Senate of the United States is the only legislative body in the world which cannot act when the majority is ready for action. A little group of willful men ... have rendered the great government of the United States helpless and contemptible."*
>
> **—President Woodrow Wilson**

Source: Library of Congress

Although they did not address the continuing-body question directly, members added new language to the rules, stating that "the rules of the Senate shall continue from one Congress to the next unless they are changed as provided in these rules."

The Modern Filibuster: Additional Changes

In 1964 the Senate for the first time invoked cloture on a civil rights bill, thus ending the longest filibuster in history after seventy-three days of debate. Other civil rights filibusters were broken in 1965 and 1968. Liberal supporters of civil rights legislation, who had tried repeatedly to tighten controls on debate, became less eager for cloture reform in the wake of these victories. By the 1970s they themselves were doing much of the filibustering—against Vietnam War policies, defense weapons systems, and antibusing proposals.

⦿ CLOSER LOOK

Filibusters: The Nuclear Option

For much of the last decades of the twentieth century and the early years of the twenty-first few issues raised political temperatures more highly than presidential nominations to the federal judiciary, including the Supreme Court. Liberals and conservatives were locked in what they saw as a monumental struggle over the philosophical direction of the judicial system.

Because judicial nominations must receive Senate confirmation, the struggle brought forth the most significant use of the filibuster since earlier debates over civil rights legislation. In the 1990s Republicans routinely did whatever they could to slow or block President Bill Clinton's judicial appointments, which they saw as too liberal. Democrats returned the favor for President George W. Bush beginning in 2001 over nominations they saw as too conservative.

Although Bush had success with his two 2005 Supreme Court nominations, the larger fight over lower federal court nominations nearly led in 2004 and 2005 to a fundamental change in one of the Senate's most cherished institutions: the filibuster. The change, involving use of an arcane parliamentary procedure, would have allowed confirmations of judicial nominations by majority vote rather than a supermajority of sixty votes needed to invoke cloture to halt a filibuster. It was aimed only at presidential appointments to the federal judiciary, but it could have formed a precedent for changing the filibuster procedures that applied to any issue, which would have in effect turned the Senate into a chamber resembling the House. Moreover, the minority Democrats at that time warned the majority Republicans that they would use whatever tactics were necessary to tie up the Senate and prevent any legislation going forward if the change were approved. It was for these reasons that the proposed changes came to be called the "nuclear option."

Even though the changes would have given an immediate benefit to the Republicans, some in the GOP were thought to harbor reservations about so drastic a change in the Senate's filibuster traditions, knowing that someday they might need to use the privilege of extended debate when they were in the minority (which occurred in 2007). Eventually, a group of fourteen senators (seven members from each party)—who came to be known as the Gang of Fourteen—drafted a "memorandum of understanding" that defused the tension.

Under the agreement, the seven Democrats agreed to invoke cloture on three previously filibustered judicial nominations, but they made no commitments on four others. They also agreed that judicial nominations should be filibustered only under "extraordinary circumstances," although the phrase was never defined. The seven Republicans, in turn, agreed to oppose any change in Senate rules or procedures that would eliminate filibusters of judicial nominations. But they retained the right to pursue filibuster changes if Democrats mounted one in what they considered less than "extraordinary circumstances." Ironically, for Democrats, the agreement led to approval of many of the Bush judicial nominations that they had been so ardently opposing.

In 1975, however, the liberals tried again to tighten restrictions on debate. They succeeded in easing the cloture requirement from two-thirds of those present and voting (a high of sixty-seven votes, if the full Senate was there) to three-fifths of the Senate membership (a flat sixty votes, if there were no vacancies). The old requirement still applied for votes on changes in Senate rules.

The 1975 revision made it easier to invoke cloture. But the revision's success relied on the willingness of senators to abide by the spirit as well as the letter of the chamber's rules. When cloture was invoked, senators in the past had generally conceded defeat and proceeded to a vote without further delay.

But minorities soon found other ways to obstruct action on measures they opposed. The most effective tactic was the postcloture filibuster, pioneered by Alabama Democrat James B. Allen, a frequent obstructionist. In 1976, when the Senate invoked cloture on a bill he opposed, Allen demanded action on the many amendments he had filed previously. He required that each be read aloud, sought roll-call votes and quorum calls, objected to routine motions, and appealed parliamentary rulings. Other senators soon adopted Allen's tactics.

As filibusters changed in character, the Senate's enthusiasm for unlimited debate eroded. At the mere threat of a filibuster it became a routine practice to start rounding up votes for cloture—or to seek a compromise—as soon as debate began. Most of that action occurred behind the scenes. If the first cloture vote failed, more were taken. Meanwhile, leaders often shelved the disputed bill temporarily, with members' unanimous consent, so that the Senate could turn to other matters. That tactic, known as double-tracking, "kept the filibuster from becoming a real filibuster," as one senator said.

In 1979 the Senate agreed to set an absolute limit of one hundred hours on postcloture delaying tactics. The television era prompted additional restraints on debate. When live televised coverage of Senate proceedings began in 1986, members gave new thought to their public image. Senators shied away from several proposals designed to quicken the pace and sharpen the focus of their proceedings for television viewers. But they did agree to one significant change in Senate rules. They reduced to thirty hours, from one hundred, the time allowed for debate, procedural moves, and roll-call votes after the Senate had invoked cloture to end a filibuster.

In 2005 and 2006 the filibuster was used aggressively by Democrats to block judicial nominations by President George W. Bush, much as Republicans had done in the 1990s to President Bill Clinton over his judicial appointments. The use of the filibuster against Bush's nominations almost led to a fundamental revision in the filibuster rule, but in the end even the most frustrated senators backed away from change. (See box, p. 216.)

Despite these restrictions, filibusters continue to be an effective tool to obstruct Senate action. In fact, the number of filibusters has increased in recent decades. Several factors account for the increase. More issues come before the Senate, making time an even scarcer commodity than in the past. More issues are highly controversial and of intense interest to the core supporters—called the base—of each political party. This "playing to the base" and the decreasing influence of senators in the center of the political spectrum have produced increased partisanship. Constituents and special interest groups also put more pressure on members, many of whom are more increasingly likely to pursue their political goals even if it means inconveniencing colleagues.

With this increase in filibusters has come an increase in cloture votes as well. From 1961 to 2001, there were more than 500 cloture votes in the Senate, with more than one-third being successful in cutting off debate. While some senators have called for additional restrictions on filibusters, many members are reluctant to curb the hallowed Senate tradition—a tradition cherished by Democrats as well as Republicans.

During President Bill Clinton's second term, a particularly partisan period from 1997 to 2001, more than 35 percent of cloture votes were decided by a majority of seventy votes or more in favor.

This higher success rate than during previous decades suggested that cloture was being used less to close debate on far-reaching national issues, as often had been the case in the past, and more for political and legislative maneuvering. That is largely because, when invoked, cloture requires amendments to be germane to the legislation being debated. Under normal procedures, senators may offer nongermane amendments to get a vote on proposals that were blocked in committee or advocated by only a few senators. In some cases, a nongermane amendment may be aimed at advancing a political agenda or requiring senators to take a position that can be used against them in the next election. Those types of amendments can be avoided by invoking cloture even if a true filibuster is not expected. Thus, increasingly, cloture votes have come to be used by the majority party to control the Senate agenda.

Finance Committee, Senate

The most heavily lobbied committee in the Senate is the Finance Committee, which handles all federal taxation and more than 45 percent of all federal spending.

Revenue goals are set through the congressional BUDGET PROCESS, but the Finance Committee decides how the money should be raised. Because the tax code has so many special provisions, ranging from deductions for home mortgages to credits for child care, the committee has almost unlimited jurisdiction. Its responsibility for Social Security, health care for the poor and elderly, and welfare programs gives it a much larger share of the federal pie than most committees have. The Finance Committee also handles tariffs and other restraints on international trade.

"What is a [tax] loophole? That is something that benefits the other guy. If it benefits you, it is tax reform."

—*Sen. Russell B. Long,* D-La.

Source: CQ Photo

Not surprisingly, assignment to the committee is keenly sought by senators. In early 2007, the committee had twenty-one members, eleven Democrats and ten Republicans.

Because the Constitution says revenue bills must originate in the House, the House Ways and Means Committee has taken the lead on most tax bills. It usually operates under strict rules to shepherd its proposals safely through the House without major amendments. The Senate Finance Committee operates very differently: committee members' special wishes are accommodated, and other senators are allowed to add a variety of amendments on the floor. In conference the bills are rewritten again; this may take place in small, closed caucuses or in one-on-one meetings between the House and Senate committee chairs.

Although subcommittees have in many cases diluted the power of full committees, the Finance Committee has resisted such a shift. Its subcommittees do not have separate staff and have almost no role in writing legislation. That leaves the Finance chair better able than most to steer the committee toward his or her own ends. Senators often gather in an "exec room" behind the large hearing room, where they discuss privately what will happen in the public markup, or drafting, of the legislation. When the chair is ready, and not before, they take up a matter in formal session.

The federal tax code is extremely complex, riddled with tax incentives treasured by various industries. Any effort to pass new tax legislation attracts a corridor full of lobbyists. Members of the Finance Committee have often been able to accommodate favored lobbyists or even fellow senators by adding a sentence worded in a general way but carefully crafted to benefit a particular case. Russell B. LONG, the Democratic senator from Louisiana who chaired the committee from 1966 to 1981, once asked, "What is a loophole? That is something that benefits the other guy. If it benefits you, it is tax reform."

Overhauling the welfare system and changes in health care benefits for the poor and elderly are other subjects that occupied the Finance Committee in recent years. The breadth of its jurisdiction and the importance of its decisions, both financially and socially, have made the Finance Committee a most formidable group of senators. Its members are consistently among those receiving the largest donations from POLITICAL ACTION COMMITTEES.

History

Set up in 1816, the Finance Committee was among the first committees established in the Senate. Initially the committee handled all aspects of the federal budget, but it lost responsibility for spending during the Civil War, when a separate Appropriations Committee was established. With the high costs of war, the job had simply become too large for one group to handle. (See APPROPRIATIONS COMMITTEE, SENATE.)

In the late nineteenth century the Finance Committee upheld protectionism, advocating tariffs on imports at rates often exceeding 50 percent. Among its leaders at that time were Republicans John SHERMAN of Ohio (1861–1877, 1881–1897), who chaired the committee, and William B. ALLISON (1873–1908), a senior member of Finance who also chaired the Appropriations Committee.

At the turn of the century, millionaire Nelson W. ALDRICH (1881–1911), a Republican from Rhode Island, took the helm. Aldrich was one of the nation's leading conservatives and consistently supported high tariffs. Politically astute, he won crucial votes from western senators by endorsing new tariffs to protect western-based industries. Often commodities in which Aldrich had personally invested, such as sugar, benefited from the tariff structure he helped create.

After the federal income tax was enacted in 1913, the importance of tariffs and excise taxes as a source of government funds diminished. The Finance Committee's focus shifted as Congress began to write exceptions into the tax code, eventually creating a maze of rules. The pressure for special tax treatment is continual, and the Finance Committee has always been in the center of the clamor.

Two southern Democrats had long tenures as Finance chairs after World War II. Harry Flood Byrd of Virginia chaired the committee from 1955 to 1965. One of the most conservative Democrats in the Senate, Byrd used his position as Finance chair to block much of the social welfare legislation sought by presidents John F. KENNEDY and Lyndon B. JOHNSON. After Byrd's death Russell B. Long took over as chair. He proved more amenable to social programs—and also to requests for special tax treatment from business and industry, particularly the oil industry. At first, in fights with the House, Long was overshadowed by the more experienced Wilbur D. MILLS, chair of the House Ways and Means Committee. But by 1987, when Long retired after almost forty years of service, he had become a legend in the Senate, confident in his command of complex subjects and skilled at breaking up tense negotiations with a funny story.

Robert DOLE of Kansas became Finance Committee chair when Republicans gained control of the Senate in 1981. That year he helped engineer the passage of sweeping tax cuts sought by President Ronald Reagan. The following year, in a break from the usual procedure, the Finance Committee initiated a major tax bill, and the House did not vote on the measure until it emerged from a Senate-House conference.

When Dole was elected majority leader in 1985, Republican Bob Packwood of Oregon took over as chair of the Finance Committee. He served in that post for just two years, until Democrats

CLOSER LOOK

The iron grip of the seniority system was no better illustrated than in the Finance Committee, where for more than three decades—from 1955 to 1987—just two senators, Harry Flood Byrd of Virginia and Russell B. Long of Louisiana, both Democrats and both from the South, held the chairmanship. Senate Republicans in 1995 imposed a six-year term limit on committee chairmanships. The rule applies only to Republicans, however.

The chair of the Senate Finance Committee is one of the most influential figures in the Senate. Here chair Max Baucus, D-Mont (left), and ranking Republican Charles E. Grassley, R-Iowa, consult over a children's health insurance bill, eventually endorsing a bipartisan deal among the panel's members.
Source: CQ Photo/Scott J. Ferrell

won back the Senate majority. Although at first he did not support tax reform, Packwood presided over a major overhaul of the tax code. In 1987 Democrat Lloyd Bentsen of Texas became committee chair. Bentsen gave up that post in 1993 to become secretary of the Treasury under President Bill Clinton. He was succeeded by Democrat Daniel Patrick Moynihan of New York.

Packwood was able to chair the committee for most of 1995 when Republicans took over the chamber again. But when he resigned rather than face expulsion from the Senate for sexual harassment charges, Delaware Republican William V. Roth assumed the chair. During his tenure, Roth worked closely with Moynihan, the ranking Democrat.

After Roth was defeated in 2000, he was succeeded by Charles E. Grassley, R-Iowa. Grassley worked closely with ranking Democrat Max Baucus of Montana, who captured the gavel in June 2001 when Democrats assumed control of the chamber. Grassley retook the chair when the GOP again became the majority in 2003 but again surrendered it to Baucus in 2007 after Democrats regained the majority in the 2006 elections.

With his long relationship with Grassley, Baucus was one of the few Democrats that the Republicans were able to rely on for support on sensitive issues such as taxes, trade, and prescription drug coverage. In 2007 the committee, like its House counterpart, the Ways and Means Committee, faced a plethora of controversial matters including extending or scaling back George W. Bush's tax cuts, expanding government-run children's health insurance, relaxing trade constraints and expanding free trade, and dealing with the future of major and costly entitlement programs—especially Medicare and Social Security.

Senate Republicans in 1995 imposed a six-year term limit on committee chairs. The rule applies only to Republicans, however.

Financial Disclosure

> *"Congress reached the conclusion that public disclosure of political contributions, together with the names of contributors and other details, would tend to prevent the corrupt use of money to affect elections. The verity of this conclusion reasonably cannot be denied."*
>
> —U.S. Supreme Court, *Burroughs v. United States*

Financial disclosure is a key principle behind two different reforms: federal ethics codes and laws concerning campaign financing.

Top federal officials are required to report annually the sources of their income, and candidates for federal office must file detailed reports of campaign contributions and expenditures. The hope is that public scrutiny of financial records will discourage corrupt practices, which range from conflicts of interest to outright bribery.

The Supreme Court, upholding a 1925 law requiring reports on campaign spending, commented in 1934: "Congress reached the conclusion that public disclosure of political contributions, together with the names of contributors and other details, would tend to prevent the corrupt use of money to affect elections. The verity of this conclusion reasonably cannot be denied."

In actual practice, the soundness of the underlying concept made little difference. Until the reforms of the 1970s, the laws on disclosure simply did not work. President Lyndon B. Johnson, in proposing election reforms in 1967, described the campaign laws: "Inadequate in their scope when enacted, they are now obsolete. More loophole than law, they invite evasion and circumvention."

The requirements for financial disclosure, both in the ethics codes and in campaign finance laws, were greatly improved in later years, though critics still complained that they were flawed and inconsistently enforced.

The following paragraphs describe the requirements in force in 2007.

Income Disclosure

Following passage of the Ethics in Government Act in 1978, top federal officials, in Congress and in the executive and judicial branches, had to file annual financial reports that covered salaries, honoraria (fees received for giving speeches and writing articles), gifts, reimbursements, income from investments, and the value of assets and liabilities.

In the Ethics Reform Act of 1989 Congress changed some of the figures and added some new requirements, but it retained the structure and spirit of the 1978 law. The 1989 act barred, as of 1991, House members from the controversial practice of accepting honoraria, in exchange for a hefty pay hike. The Senate decided in 1991 to join in the ban on honoraria and to make Senate salaries equal to those in the House. (Members could request that charitable contributions up to $2,000 be made in their name in lieu of honoraria for speeches and appearances. Such payments had to be disclosed.)

The ethics laws did not require specific amounts to be disclosed but instead allowed officials to report within a range of figures set in the law. This gives a rather vague picture of an individual's and his or her spouse's financial situation, but it does convey a sense of their wealth and income, and of their debt and how it has increased or decreased. However, under the rules, details of certain assets and transactions, such as the value or the sale or purchase of a member's home, can be omitted. Mortgages on personal residences, car loans, and certain other consumer loans also do not have to be reported. Certain trusts are also exempted from disclosure.

Members of Congress file their reports with the CLERK OF THE HOUSE and the SECRETARY OF THE SENATE, and the House and Senate ethics committees review them and investigate complaints. If the committees find omissions or false reports, they can recommend House or Senate disciplinary action against that member. Expulsion, censure, and reprimand are among the disciplinary actions the legislators can take. Sometimes the ethics committees recommend against any punishment, even if they conclude that the legislator has broken rules.

Executive branch employees file their reports with their department or agency, while presidential appointees file their reports with the Office of Government Ethics. Judicial branch employees file with the Administrative Office of the U.S. Courts.

The 1989 amendments doubled to $10,000 the maximum civil penalty against anyone who knowingly and willfully files a false report or fails to file a report. Violators are also subject to criminal penalties under a general statute prohibiting false reporting to the federal government. Breaking that law is a felony, for which someone may be fined, imprisoned, or both.

Although various members have been investigated for not complying with the financial disclosure rules, few have been prosecuted. The first member to be convicted under the rules was George Hansen, a Republican representative from Idaho, who was found guilty in 1984 of failing to report nearly $334,000 in loans and profits. Hansen was fined and imprisoned for nearly a year. The ethics committees typically did not investigate or make recommendations while a Justice Department probe was taking place, but they did review convictions to see if congressional disciplinary action was warranted. Following Hansen's conviction, the House Committee on Standards of Official Conduct, as the House ethics panel is formally known, recommended that he be reprimanded for

More on this topic:

Campaign Financing, p. 66

Disciplining Members, p. 159

Ethics, p. 195

Political Action Committees, p. 417

Separation of Powers, p. 508

Watergate Scandal, p. 596

the false reports. The House agreed. Hansen, who declined to change his reports when given a chance by the ethics committee and who maintained his innocence, was narrowly defeated in his reelection bid in 1984.

The House ethics panel concluded in 1988 that Democrat Charlie Rose of North Carolina had violated House rules by putting campaign funds to personal use and by failing to report certain aspects of his financial affairs. The committee sent him a letter of reproval but recommended no formal punishment. The panel noted that he had voluntarily amended his financial disclosure forms and had repaid the money. The Justice Department then filed a civil suit in which it accused him of failing to disclose loans totaling more than $100,000. Rose contended that the constitutional doctrine of separation of powers protected him from prosecution because the ethics panel already had investigated and acted on the matter. But the courts rejected that argument and in 1994 Rose paid a fine to settle the lawsuit. Rose also was fined by the Federal Election Commission.

Former Democratic representatives Nicholas Mavroules of Massachusetts (1979–1993) in 1993 and Carl C. Perkins of Kentucky (1985–1993) in 1994 pleaded guilty to charges that included filing false or incomplete financial disclosure statements.

Inaccurate reports played a role in the charges that resulted in the House censure of Democrats Charles C. Diggs Jr. of Michigan in 1979 for taking kickbacks from the salaries of his office employees and Charles H. Wilson of California in 1980 for converting campaign funds to his personal use and other financial misconduct.

The Senate denouncement of Georgia Democrat Herman E. Talmadge in 1979 for misconduct related to campaign contributions and office expense vouchers also resulted from inaccurate reports, as was the case when the Senate denounced Minnesota Republican Dave Durenberger in 1990 for collecting improper Senate per diem expenses and honoraria payments. In 1992 the Senate Ethics Committee formally rebuked Oregon Republican Mark O. Hatfield for failing to disclose several expensive gifts. Ten years later, it admonished Democrat Robert G. Torricelli of New Jersey for violating Senate rules prohibiting members from accepting gifts of more than $50 in value and requiring disclosure.

Rep. Jay C. Kim, R-Calif., was one of several members of Congress charged with violating disclosure laws during the 1990s.
Source: CQ Photo/Douglas Graham

Campaign Disclosure

The use of disclosure to keep tabs on campaign financing began in 1910 and 1911, when Congress passed and then amended the Federal Corrupt Practices Act. The 1911 law required congressional candidates and political organizations operating in two or more states to file financial reports, and it set spending limits for Senate and House candidates.

Loopholes and lack of enforcement meant that the law had little effect on campaigns; neither did an overhaul of the statute approved in 1925. A major flaw allowed congressional candidates to report that they had received and spent nothing on their campaigns. They did this by maintaining that campaign committees established to elect them had been working without their "knowledge and consent." No candidate for the House or Senate was ever prosecuted under the 1925 act, although it was widely known that most candidates spent more than the act allowed and did not report all they spent. Only two persons elected to Congress—Republican senators-elect William

S. Vare of Pennsylvania and Frank L. Smith of Illinois in 1927—ever were excluded for spending in excess of the act's limits.

Not until the Federal Election Campaign Act of 1971 did Congress, for the first time, require relatively complete and timely public reports by candidates on who was financing their campaigns and how much they were spending. Less than three years later, however, investigation of the Watergate scandal revealed misuse of campaign funds. As a result, Congress in 1974 extensively rewrote the existing campaign finance law to include, among other things, a number of new disclosure and reporting procedures. Although the Supreme Court overturned several features of that law in BUCKLEY V. VALEO in 1976, the disclosure requirements remained intact.

Reporting requirements were expanded in the 1976 campaign finance law amendments that were written in the aftermath of the *Buckley* ruling. A further revision in 1978 was directed in part toward reducing the red tape associated with financial disclosure. The changes decreased the frequency of required reports, raised the minimum contribution and expenditure amount that had to be itemized, and exempted candidates who raised or spent less than $5,000.

A complex set of rules defined the various political committees that had to register and file financial reports with either the clerk of the House, the secretary of the Senate, or the Federal Election Commission (FEC). Copies of all reports were kept on file at the FEC and in the relevant state.

Rules about when reports had to be filed varied according to the type of campaign, whether an election was scheduled, and the amount of money involved.

Candidates' Reports

Each candidate designated a principal campaign committee that usually solicited and spent the bulk of his or her campaign funds. This committee had to report to the FEC if the candidate spent or received more than $5,000.

In addition to overall total receipts and expenditures, the reports had to list all contributions from party committees and political action committees (PACs) regardless of amount. The report also had to identify individuals who gave more than $200 in a year. Those who were paid more than $200 in a year by a campaign—for such things as advertisements, transportation, management, or other campaign operating expenses—had to be listed by name and address.

Other Reports

Also covered by the disclosure rules were political parties and their campaign committees. National and state party organizations that spent funds for a federal election had to register with the FEC when more than $1,000 was spent or received in a year.

Most PACs (organizations that distribute campaign contributions to candidates for Congress and other offices) also had to report to the FEC. Tighter restrictions applied to the PACs tied to parent organizations, such as corporations and labor unions. Administration of these PACs was often handled by the parent organizations, but the voluntary contributions of employees and executives were kept in what the FEC called "separate segregated accounts."

Party committees and PACs had to report all receipts from political committees regardless of the amount and identify individuals who contributed more than $200 in a year. They also had to report all contributions they made to candidates and political committees, regardless of the amount. A 2002 campaign finance law—known as the Bipartisan Campaign Reform Act but commonly called the McCain-Feingold Act—also required any entity that spent $10,000 in a calendar year on electioneering communications to file disclosure statements with the FEC within twenty-four hours of reaching the threshold, identifying the person or group spending the money.

A separate rule applied to expenditures made without consulting the candidate. Such independent expenditures, either by party committees, PACs, or individuals, had to be reported once they exceeded $200 to the same entity in a year. The significance of independent expenditures has fluctuated. Initially they were seen as a useful tactic for groups or individuals supporting or opposing candidates, but the tactic lost favor for a while when candidates came to resent this outside interference in their campaigns, even when the spending was in their favor. Independent expenditures increased after a 1996 Supreme Court decision allowed political parties to make them. The Court held that the limits in the 1974 law on party spending did not apply to spending that was not coordinated with a candidate's campaign. But then the 2002 law barred parties from making both coordinated expenditures and independent expenditures on behalf of a candidate.

Beginning in 1991, rules required national party committees to report to the FEC all "soft money" receipts and expenditures. Soft money described unlimited and largely unregulated contributions from individuals, corporations, and unions that national party committees either transferred to state parties for "party building" and grassroots activities or used for advertising campaigns that supposedly promoted issues and not candidates. Contributors of more than $200 to soft money accounts had to be identified. The 2002 overhaul banned the national parties and federal candidates from raising or spending soft money. The new law also barred organizations from using soft money for issue ads that mention specific candidates just before an election. In late 2003 the Supreme Court upheld all major sections of the 2002 law.

Disclosure Violations

The filing of false or incomplete campaign finance reports can result in FEC fines or federal prosecution, and possibly disciplinary action by Congress. Reporting violation charges often are part of broader allegations of wrongdoing. In 1995, for example, the FEC fined Texas Democrat Charles Wilson $90,000—the largest FEC fine against a congressional candidate up to that time—on charges that Wilson borrowed money from his campaign committee and never repaid it or disclosed it. Wilson was also rebuked by the House ethics committee.

Florida representative Lawrence J. Smith pleaded guilty in 1993 to charges of tax evasion and lying to the FEC. Smith had funneled campaign funds to his personal use. Former Democratic representative Mary Rose Oakar of Ohio (1977–1993) pleaded guilty in 1997 to charges of conspiracy and violation of campaign finance laws for fabricating contributor names to disguise donation sources. California Republican Jay C. Kim in 1997 pleaded guilty on behalf of his campaign committee to five felony counts of concealing illegal campaign contributions.

Financial Services Committee, House

The House Financial Services Committee is responsible for regulation of the complex U.S. financial system. The banking, securities, insurance, and housing industries fall within the panel's jurisdiction. The committee deals with a wide range of authorizing legislation, from the Export-Import Bank to rehabilitation of rental housing, and it shares responsibility for overseeing international trade.

But several high-profile issues have dominated the committee's attention in the late 1980s and after. Corporate accountability and terrorism insurance were at the top of the committee's agenda in 2001–2002, as had been an overhaul of the banking industry in the previous decade and a bailout of the savings and loan industry a few years before that.

In the late 1980s and early 1990s, as hundreds of savings and loan institutions went bankrupt under the weight of bad loans, recession, and a collapsed commercial real estate market, the committee had to craft several bills to pay for a multibillion-dollar federal bailout. The savings and loan crisis came after the committee had deliberated for years on how to respond to revolutionary changes in the financial industry.

When money-market funds began offering high interest rates in the 1970s, banks had to wait for permission to compete. New computer technologies made interstate banking attractive, but federal rules kept banks from competing across state lines. Then corporations such as Sears, Roebuck, and Co. began to take deposits and offer bank services—eroding territory banks had once had to themselves. Banks argued that they were hindered by Depression-era laws (mainly stemming from the 1933 Glass-Steagall Act) designed to insulate the banking system from the more volatile world of stock trading and land transactions. The 1933 Glass-Steagall Act erected barriers between the banking and securities industries, and the 1956 Bank Holding Company

Rep. Barney Frank, D-Mass., incoming chair of the House Financial Services Committee, discusses his 2007 priorities, which included an overhaul of mortgage lending practices.
Source: CQ Photo/Scott J. Ferrell

Act imposed barriers between banking and insurance activities. Banks wanted the rules changed so that they could compete in insurance, real estate, and securities.

After decades of failed efforts, Congress passed and President Bill Clinton signed in 2000 a historic overhaul of laws governing the financial services industry. The measure repealed laws restricting cross-ownership among banks, brokerages, and insurers. Supporters said that widespread financial collapse could be averted through less restrictive regulations; that new rules would improve customer service by allowing one-stop shopping; and that U.S. financial institutions would be better equipped to compete globally. The move to repeal the old laws had gained momentum as court and regulatory decisions eroded the barriers among industries.

In the wake of the September 11, 2001, terrorist attacks, the committee moved quickly to approve legislation to establish a federal terrorism insurance program to serve as a backstop for commercial property and casualty insurers in the event of cataclysmic terrorist acts. The committee was also the first to produce legislation addressing corporate fraud and accountability in response to the December 2001 bankruptcy of the energy giant Enron Corp.

The committee's other role, as monitor of urban affairs, has received little attention in recent years. Membership on the committee was once sought after by liberal legislators from urban districts and is still popular among representatives from New York City. It also has drawn moderates whose districts serve as regional banking centers. In 1998, after three years of efforts, Republicans pushed through legislation that overhauled the public housing system by giving more control to local housing authorities.

The banking committee was established in 1865 along with the Appropriations Committee, when the overloaded Ways and Means Committee was split into three parts. However, the financial committee has never matched the standing of the other two panels.

The committee was called Banking and Currency until 1975, when the word Housing was added. In 1977 it was renamed Banking, Finance, and Urban Affairs. Wright Patman, the Texas Democrat who chaired the panel from 1963 to 1975, was a consummate populist who used the committee as a pulpit to attack Federal Reserve Board restraints on credit. Patman ran the committee with a firm hand until age made it difficult for him to keep the fractious panel in line. In 1975, when he was eighty-two years old, Patman was one of three chairs ousted by the Democratic Caucus after a loosening of seniority rules.

The succeeding chair, Wisconsin Democrat Henry Reuss, had an almost academic interest in both banking and urban affairs; he focused attention on the latter with a special Subcommittee on the City. Reuss lacked political skills, however. He had trouble with the back-room bargaining needed to pass legislation, and he suffered some embarrassing floor defeats.

After Reuss stepped down for health reasons in 1980, the top post went to Fernand St Germain, a Rhode Island Democrat. St Germain had chaired the preeminent banking subcommittee, the subcommittee on financial institutions, since 1971. St Germain, considered to be politically shrewd, held on to the post of subcommittee chair. As committee chair, he relished being able to orchestrate the committee's every move and seldom shared his plans. Though always careful to speak for the consumer, St Germain was criticized for his close financial ties with the banking and housing industries. The House ethics panel in 1987 absolved him of allegations that he had grown rich through abuse of his office. In 1989, after fresh allegations were made, St Germain lost a re-election bid and was replaced as chair by Texas Democrat Henry B. Gonzalez, a populist who sought to focus more attention on housing issues.

With the Republican takeover of the House in 1995, the majority renamed the panel the Banking and Financial Services Committee, in part to stress the Republican desire to have the committee deal less with urban issues. Taking the chair, Jim Leach of Iowa led the effort to repeal the Glass-Steagall Act. In 2001, when Leach was forced to relinquish his position because of term limits, House Republicans redrew the jurisdiction of the committee and renamed it Financial Services. The committee was given jurisdiction over two new issues—securities and insurance, which were taken from the purview of the Commerce Committee. The jurisdictional change was made to appease a Republican, Michael G. Oxley of Ohio, who had unsuccessfully vied for the chair of the renamed Energy and Commerce Committee. Oxley took over the Financial Services panel after its authority had been expanded. Oxley was to lend his name to a 2002 landmark law, known as Sarbanes-Oxley (for Oxley and the Senate cosponsor Paul Sarbanes of Maryland), which was aimed at cracking down on corporate malfeasance.

With Democrats back in control in 2007, the chair passed to Rep. Barney Frank, of Massachusetts. He was expected to focus on better access to and funding for affordable housing programs. Oxley, who retired from Congress at the end of 2006, shared with Frank a financial pragmatism grounded in the knowledge that a hands-off approach often is the best choice when dealing with the complexities of the economy and financial markets.

Frank was interested in protecting investors and consumers from corporate excesses. The committee also wanted to examine predatory lending practices and regulation of the giant mortgage underwriters, Fannie Mae and Freddie Mac. In addition, the Sarbanes-Oxley law was back before the panel. Business groups had assailed the law after passage as an overreach by Congress and made changes a top lobbying priority.

Fiscal Year

The financial operations of the federal government are carried out in a twelve-month fiscal year that begins on October 1 and ends on September 30. The president's budget and congressional spending bills are calculated on a fiscal-year basis. (See BUDGET PROCESS.)

The fiscal year carries the date of the calendar year in which it ends. The current fiscal calendar has been in use since fiscal 1977. From fiscal 1844 through fiscal 1976 the fiscal year began July 1 and ended the following June 30.

Floor Debate   *See* LEGISLATIVE PROCESS.

Floor Manager

The floor manager of a bill is responsible for guiding a bill through floor debate and the amendment process to final vote in the House or the Senate. The chair of the committee or subcommittee that handled a bill usually acts as floor manager for its supporters. The committee's ranking member of the minority party often leads the opposition.

In both the House and Senate the floor managers operate from designated aisle seats. Staff members, who rarely come onto the floor, are allowed to sit alongside the floor manager. Regardless of their personal views on a bill, floor managers are under obligation to present the work of their committees in the most favorable light and to fend off undesirable amendments. The mark of successful floor managers is their ability to get a bill passed without substantial change.

Foley, Thomas S.

The office of SPEAKER OF THE HOUSE returned to a traditional stance above the fray of partisanship when Washington Democrat Thomas S. Foley (1929–) held the position from 1989 to 1995. Foley's judicious presence was a marked contrast to that of his hard-charging predecessor, Texas Democrat Jim WRIGHT, who quit in the middle of his term after questions arose about his personal finances.

Foley's approach resembled those of Speakers such as Sam RAYBURN and Nicholas LONGWORTH more than those of Wright or "Czar" Thomas REED. A thoughtful and articulate man, Foley was perhaps the first Speaker his Democratic colleagues felt comfortable putting in front of a television camera. With a knack for telling stories and a near-photographic memory, Foley was a superb negotiator who was on good terms with most Democrats and many Republicans. He rose to Speaker without displaying the vaunting ambition and partisanship that characterizes many other leaders.

The only Speaker from west of the Rocky Mountains, Foley came to the House in 1964 from a largely rural district in western Washington. A veteran of numerous battles against secrecy and seniority in the committee system, Foley became chair of the Democratic Caucus in 1977. He moved easily up the party's leadership ladder without major opposition, becoming majority whip in 1981 and majority leader in 1987. Foley's apprenticeship was cut short after Wright abdicated rather than face an extended inquiry into his finances. Foley's reputation for integrity and evenhandedness was an antidote to Wright's style.

Thomas S. Foley, D-Wash., became House Speaker in 1989. Foley's judicious presence represented a marked contrast to that of his highly partisan and hard-charging predecessor Jim Wright, D-Texas.
Source: CQ Photo/R. Michael Jenkins

As Speaker, Foley was able to lead Democrats on economic issues and to oppose the 1991 Persian Gulf War without opening his party to charges of a lack of patriotism. Some liberal colleagues grumbled about his distaste for fiery torch-bearing and harsh discipline. Many were dissatisfied with his handling in 1992 of a scandal involving bad checks written by members at the House's internal bank. (See SCANDALS, CONGRESSIONAL.)

With the arrival of the Democratic administration of Bill Clinton in 1993, Foley was put in the position of having to pass an ambitious presidential program with a caucus that was not united either on policy or in loyalty to the new chief executive. Effective opposition from a unified Republican minority and Clinton's political missteps, most notably on a national health care overhaul plan, contributed to the disarray within the party.

In addition to vulnerability based on his high-profile leadership post, Foley was also attacked in his district for not supporting Washington state's newly enacted term-limit law (later declared unconstitutional by the Supreme Court). Amid the national Democratic rout in 1994, Foley lost in the general election, only the third such defeat for a sitting Speaker. The last had been Galusha A. Grow, a Pennsylvania Republican, who lost in 1862; his predecessor, William Pennington of New Jersey, lost in 1860.

After his departure from Congress, Foley joined a Washington, D.C., law firm and in 1997 became ambassador to Japan. He was replaced as ambassador in 2001 by former Senate majority leader Howard H. BAKER Jr., a Tennessee Republican.

Ford, Gerald R.

Gerald R. Ford (1913–2006) is best known as the thirty-eighth president of the United States. He came to that position after twenty-four years as a Republican representative from Michigan, including nine years as House Republican leader. He also served a brief stint as vice president under President Richard NIXON.

Chief Justice Warren E. Burger (left) administers the vice-presidential oath to Michigan representative Gerald R. Ford, whose wife, Betty, holds an open Bible. At right is President Richard Nixon, who less than one year later would become the first president to resign from office, elevating Ford to the presidency.
Source: White House

Ford was the first person to assume executive office under provisions of the Twenty-fifth Amendment to the Constitution governing presidential and vice-presidential succession. In 1973 Nixon chose Ford to replace Vice President Spiro T. Agnew, who had resigned in the face of criminal charges. Ford became president in 1974 when Nixon himself resigned under threat of impeachment. Thus Ford became the only president to serve without being chosen by popular ballot for either of the two highest offices in the federal government. He had spent nearly a quarter century in Congress, longer than any other president in history, including Lyndon B. Johnson.

Ford was first elected to the House of Representatives in 1948. From the beginning he compiled a strongly conservative voting record. He consistently voted against amendments to limit defense spending and was critical of the policies of the Johnson administration during the Vietnam War. He voted against the 1973 War Powers Resolution, which sought to limit the president's war-making powers, and supported increased bombing of North Vietnam.

On domestic issues, Ford backed attempts to limit federal spending and the expansion of the federal government. He opposed the Medicare program of health care for the elderly and federal aid to education. Although he voted for the civil rights acts of the 1960s, he preferred milder substitutes.

Angry over the Senate's rejection of two of Nixon's appointees to the Supreme Court, Ford in 1970 launched an unsuccessful attack on Justice William O. Douglas. Calling for his impeachment, Ford cited Douglas's financial connections with a private foundation and his defense of civil disobedience as set forth in his book *Points of Rebellion.*

More on this topic:
Nixon Impeachment Effort, p. 396
Presidential Disability and Succession, p. 433
Watergate Scandal, p. 596

Ford's unwavering loyalty to his party led to his election as chair of the House Republican Conference in 1962. He was elected House minority leader in 1965. Ford was admired by his peers for his honesty and frankness. His popularity in Congress and loyalty to the administration made him a logical choice for vice president upon Agnew's resignation on October 10, 1973. He was confirmed by the Senate on November 27, 1973, by a vote of 92 to 3.

On August 9, 1974, Nixon resigned, and Ford assumed the office, becoming the nation's thirty-eighth president. His popularity with Congress and the country, at first high, suffered after he pardoned Nixon one month later on September 8, 1974. Ford ran for president in 1976 but was defeated by Democrat Jimmy Carter. He then largely retired from public life but would on occasion join other notable public officials in commenting on issues of the moment.

Ford died on December 26, 2006, in Rancho Mirage, California. His flag-draped coffin lay in state in the Capitol Rotunda, a rare honor for public officials.

The reviews and commentary that came at the time of his death painted a significantly different picture than the controversial one at the time of his presidency. The defining event was his pardon of Nixon, which Ford said was necessary to move the nation beyond the calamitous events of the Watergate scandal that led to Nixon's resignation. Ford later wrote: "I had to get the monkey off my back." After his death, colleagues—including both Republican allies and his Democratic critics, as well as many historians—largely agreed that Ford had successfully led the nation out of what he in his speech on being inaugurated called "our long national nightmare."

Foreign Affairs Committee, House

The House Foreign Affairs Committee has broad responsibility for legislation dealing with relations between the United States and other countries. The most important legislative topics that fall under its jurisdiction are foreign aid programs, which provide economic assistance to poor and developing countries, and military equipment and training for U.S. allies around the world. Yet, despite its seemingly significant responsibilities, the panel has had little impact on the direction of U.S. foreign policy.

The committee was known as Foreign Affairs until 1995 when the Republicans changed the name. Democrats in 2007 reverted to the previous name. It is one of the oldest in Congress, dating to its creations in 1822. Traditionally, it was overshadowed by its Senate counterpart, the Foreign Relations Committee. To a great extent, this reflects the foreign policy roles of the House and Senate as established by the Constitution. Since the Constitution gives the Senate exclusive control over international treaties and nominations, the Senate Foreign Relations Committee is frequently at the center of debate over major international issues. The House has much less authority over foreign affairs under the Constitution, so the House committee has less authority as well. (See FOREIGN RELATIONS COMMITTEE, SENATE).

CLOSER LOOK

The House Foreign Affairs Committee historically has been less prominent—and, some observers think, less influential—than its Senate counterpart. But both panels have been pushed increasingly out of the limelight by the aggressive assertion by the executive branch—primarily the White House—of complete control of foreign issues—a position that Democratic chair, Tom Lantos, D-Calif., worked to reverse before his death in 2008.

The Foreign Affairs Committee receives less public notice than the Senate committee. While Foreign Relations for many decades drew some of the best-known and most respected members of the Senate, the House committee included many obscure junior members, who quickly left for a committee of greater legislative and political importance.

The House committee was affected by the same forces that reduced the once-great power of Senate Foreign Relations. The executive branch assumed greater control over foreign issues, thus reducing the foreign policy role of Congress as a whole. In addition, other committees with overseas interests, such as the Armed Services panels, eclipsed the role of the two foreign affairs panels.

Another problem for the committee was the political weakness of foreign aid programs. Although advocates of foreign aid say it can be an effective means of advancing U.S. interests in the world, these programs have long been unpopular among the public and much of Congress. The climate for foreign aid grew even more hostile as the domestic economy declined in the 1980s and early 1990s. Foreign aid programs became so controversial that between 1980 and 2007 Congress only twice completed action on legislation authorizing foreign aid, in 1981 and 1985.

Foreign aid became more popular in the years after the 2001 terrorist attacks, but bills to authorize the programs continue to stall in one chamber or the other. Congress is required by law to authorize State Department and foreign policy activities every two years. Those authorizing bills, however, over the years became important barometers of congressional sentiment on controversial issues and therefore increasingly difficult to pass. Although Congress had authorized some specific foreign aid programs, as of early 2007 a broad stand-alone foreign aid authorization had not been enacted since the one in 1985.

As a result, the House panel rarely was able to have any legislative impact on how the programs were run, unless a provision of a foreign aid authorization bill became law separately. The inability of Congress to pass foreign aid authorization bills effectively transferred control over the shape and direction of foreign aid to the House Appropriations Committee and its Foreign Operations Subcommittee, which made many of the decisions about the programs during this period. (See APPROPRIATIONS COMMITTEE, HOUSE.) Venting his frustration, committee chair Dante B. Fascell, a Florida Democrat, complained in 1990 that the need for action by the authorizing panels "has been less and less and less. It has made our work almost irrelevant."

In 2006 Rep. Tom Lantos (left) talks with Pakistan president Pervez Musharraf at a Washington, D.C., luncheon. Lantos, ranking Democrat on the House Foreign Affairs Committee at the time, became chair in 2007 but died unexpectedly in early 2008.
Source: AP Images/Charles Dharapak

Nevertheless, the influence of the committee grew in some ways during Fascell's tenure. From 1983 to 1993, Fascell brought strong leadership to the post. In 1990 when most Democrats opposed authorizing the use of military force in the Persian Gulf War, Fascell helped organize a group of key House committee chairs to back it. The committee gained a higher profile as various committee members became more visible participants in foreign policy debates.

Significant changes in the committee's membership came in 1993. Both Fascell and several other veteran members of the committee retired. Lee H. Hamilton, a Democrat from Indiana, succeeded Fascell as chair.

Beginning in 1995, the committee was chaired by New York Republican Benjamin A. Gilman, a soft-spoken moderate. Although Gilman was not able to raise the profile of the panel, he did see one triumph. Legislation to reorganize the foreign affairs bureaucracy, a project Congress struggled with for two years, was included in the mammoth end-of-session appropriations bill in 1998.

Gilman was forced from the chair in 2001 because of a rule limiting the tenure of chairs. His successor, Republican Henry J. Hyde of Illinois, brought prestige to the position as Congress focused increasingly on foreign affairs in the wake of the 2001 terrorist attacks on the nation. Still, Hyde was repeatedly frustrated during the 107th Congress (2001–2003) when bills he steered through the House died or languished in the Democratic-controlled Senate. In 2006, however, Hyde—with the support of ranking Democrat Tom Lantos of California—won House approval of legislation that allowed President George W. Bush to make final negotiations on a nuclear cooperation treaty with India, despite concerns it might fuel an arms race and help Iran. The bill was later cleared by the Senate.

The next year, in the 110th Congress, Lantos became the chair as Democrats were again the majority. Lantos was a Hungarian-born Holocaust survivor who seldom minced words. He called the 2006 election outcome equivalent to the 1906 earthquake that devastated San Francisco. Although Lantos had drawn some Democratic criticism for his warm working relationship with Hyde as well as his vigorous support of President Bush in the Iraq invasion— although not in the aftermath—Lantos did not face a challenge to being the chair. The committee was poised under Lantos to conduct a closer examination of the Bush foreign policy, with special attention to Iraq reconstruction. Lantos also pledged to examine reconstruction efforts in Afghanistan. However, he died in February 2008 from cancer. Rep. Howard L. Berman, D-Calif., was in line to succeed him.

Foreign Relations Committee, Senate

The Senate Foreign Relations Committee oversees most aspects of the relations of the United States with other countries. Historically, it has been one of the most important forums for congressional influence in the field of international affairs.

Like its House counterpart, the Foreign Affairs Committee, the Senate Foreign Relations Committee has jurisdiction over foreign aid and legislation concerning the operations of the State Department, which is nominally charged with carrying out most U.S. foreign policies. Unlike the House committee, Foreign Relations also has the right to recommend Senate approval or rejection of foreign policy nominations and treaties submitted by the president.

Since the early nineteenth century the Foreign Relations Committee has been one of the most prestigious and powerful committees on Capitol Hill. Its members played important roles in crucial foreign policy debates. In the decades following World War II, for example, the committee helped guide U.S. policy through the cold war of the late 1940s and 1950s, the Vietnam War in the 1960s, and the Panama Canal treaties in the 1970s. The committee was widely admired as the source of a bipartisan foreign policy consensus that for many years guided U.S. actions.

More on this topic:
Foreign Affairs Committee, House, p. 229
Fulbright, J. William, p. 241
Treaty-Making Power, p. 559

By the 1980s, however, the committee had lost much of its power and influence. For a variety of reasons, the committee no longer occupied the vital role in decision making for foreign policy that it had in previous decades. But beginning in the mid-1990s the committee's chairs made a determined effort to have their voices heard once again in important policy debates.

Loss of Influence

One factor weakening the Foreign Relations Committee was the general decline in the foreign policy authority of Congress. As power shifted from Congress to the executive branch, the Foreign Relations Committee lost its role in many key international issues.

The unpopularity of foreign aid programs also hindered the committee. One of the committee's most important duties is to write a bill authorizing economic and military aid to other countries. The bill, which sets overall policy guidelines and spending limits for foreign aid programs, was once an important means for Congress to influence U.S. foreign policy. But from 1980 onward the bills approved by the committee rarely won approval from the Senate or Congress as a whole. From 1980 to 2007 only two authorization bills for foreign aid cleared Congress, although some provisions of foreign aid authorization bills became law separately.

Efforts to include the foreign aid authorization in the biennial authorization of the State Department and related agencies did not resolve matters because the State Department bill had become increasingly difficult to pass as well. In 2005, for example, the House managed to pass a foreign relations authorization that covered departmental operations and some foreign aid programs, but the Senate version, which included authorizations for many more foreign aid programs, was pulled from the floor amid a deluge of floor amendments dealing with everything from abortion to policy toward Cuba. The previous year a similar bill had been dropped from the Senate calendar out of fear that it could get bogged down in an unrelated debate over the minimum wage. From 1995 through 2006, only one stand-alone State Department authorization bill was enacted, and that was in 2002. In the absence of separate foreign affairs authorizing bills, the foreign aid authorizations were either included in or waived by appropriations bills.

The Foreign Relations Committee's loss was the Appropriations Committee's gain, as the traditional annual or biennial authorization bills for foreign aid were supplanted by provisions in appropriations bills. The committee also lost power to other congressional committees, such as the Armed Services Committee, which gained influence over arms control matters.

The political makeup of the Foreign Relations Committee also changed significantly. In its glory days, the committee was dominated by a coalition of moderate Democrats and Republicans, who usually were able to work out a common position on critical issues. But by the late 1980s the committee had become deeply divided between mostly liberal Democrats and a group of very conservative Republicans. Debates on important issues, such as war in Central America and nuclear arms control, were marked by bitter arguments between the two factions.

In an attempt to resolve some of its problems and restore the effectiveness of the panel, Democrats on the committee agreed in the early 1990s to restructure the panel to shift more power to its subcommittees.

History

The Foreign Relations Committee was created in 1816 and quickly became one of the most important committees in Congress, primarily because of its jurisdiction over treaties. All treaties, regardless of their subject matter, are referred to the committee.

The committee attracted some of the most illustrious members of the Senate, including Daniel WEBSTER, John C. Calhoun, Roscoe CONKLING, and Robert A. TAFT. Among its chairs have been Charles SUMNER, Henry Cabot LODGE, William E. BORAH, Arthur H. VANDENBERG, and J. William FULBRIGHT.

The growing importance of the United States in world politics during the twentieth century added to the importance of the Foreign Relations Committee. After World War I, for example, Lodge and other committee members helped determine whether the United States would ratify the Versailles Treaty and thus join the League of Nations. The committee helped draft limitations on the treaty that were unacceptable to President Woodrow Wilson. As a result the treaty was rejected, and the United States did not join the League of Nations.

After World War II the committee helped commit the United States to a policy of heavy involvement in world affairs and the containment of communism. Before the war Vandenberg and many other committee members had been isolationists who opposed U.S. entanglements with other countries. But Vandenberg, who chaired the committee from 1947 to 1949, became an internationalist after the war. Along with other committee members, he helped create a bipartisan consensus in favor of a strong foreign policy.

Fulbright served as chair from 1959 to 1975. The combination of television and the Vietnam War made him the committee's most famous chair. Fulbright was an outspoken critic of President Lyndon B. Johnson's policy of expanding the U.S. role in the Vietnam War. To dramatize his opposition Fulbright held nationally televised hearings on the war in the mid- and late 1960s. The hearings commanded public interest and attention and helped organize widespread opposition to Johnson's policies.

Fulbright was defeated for reelection in 1974. Most committee chairs after him lacked his ability to lead the committee aggressively. Idaho Democrat Frank Church (1979–1981) and Indiana Republican Richard G. Lugar (1985–1987) were widely seen as strong chairs able to restore the committee's influence. For example, Lugar used his position to exercise influence over the policies of President Ronald Reagan on two important foreign issues: the Philippines, where a popular movement ousted President Ferdinand E. Marcos, and South Africa, where the white minority government continued to deny basic human rights to the nation's black majority. But both Church and Lugar chaired the panel for only one Congress before a new chair came in, although Lugar would return later.

Claiborne Pell, a Democrat from Rhode Island, took over as chair in 1987. Under his leadership the panel continued to lose influence. The problems came partly from Pell's disengaged leadership style, as well as from the tactics of the ranking Republican on the committee, Jesse Helms of North Carolina, a master of parliamentary obstruction. Helms, one of the Senate's most conservative members, often differed not only with the committee's Democratic majority but also with the administration and with more moderate Republicans on the committee. The panel became recognized more for its failure to gain quorums at meetings than as a force in setting foreign policy.

The panel's loss of influence was illustrated by the 1990–1991 debate over the U.S. decision to go to war to end Iraq's occupation of Kuwait. The committee held hearings on the crisis but was even less involved than the House Foreign Affairs Committee in the congressional decision to authorize war against Iraq. The course of that debate was set largely by the Democratic leaders as well as by the chairs of the House and Senate Armed Services committees.

Frustrated by the committee's marginal role in foreign policy debates, committee Democrats, with the quiet backing of a few Republicans, in 1991 developed a plan to strengthen the panel's subcommittees and expedite legislation through the committee. Pell was persuaded to turn over much of his authority to the panel's subcommittee chairs, allowing legislation to be marked up in

CLOSER LOOK

Source: Library of Congress

The Senate Foreign Relations Committee, under J. William Fulbright, D-Ark., became of a focus in the 1960s of growing opposition to U.S. involvement in the Vietnam War. Fulbright held nationally televised hearings on the war that contributed to widespread opposition to the conflict. But the panel's influence waned after this period. Here Secretary of State Dean Rusk testifies about the war before the committee in March 1968.

subcommittee for the first time. As part of the move, the majority staff was enlarged and reorganized along subcommittee lines.

But these changes did not last for long. In 1995 Helms assumed the chair of the committee and recentralized control of the panel under a strong full committee. During Helms's tenure, the committee took stronger stands on issues from key foreign policy appointments of the Clinton administration to the Chemical Weapons Convention, a pact Helms tried unsuccessfully to defeat. In 1998 Helms achieved a key goal: reorganization of the foreign policy bureaucracy.

When control of the Senate changed hands in 2001, Democrat Joseph R. Biden Jr. of Delaware became chair of the committee. Lugar returned to head the committee in 2003, thanks to the GOP takeover of the Senate and Helms's retirement. Biden and Lugar had worked together often on major issues, such as arms control and Iraq.

The 2006 election, in which Democrats regained the majority, again switched the position of these two long-serving members, with Biden taking the chair and Lugar becoming the ranking Republican. The dominating issue as 2007 began was the war in Iraq, which started when President George W. Bush sent U.S. forces into the country in 2003 to overthrow Iraqi dictator Saddam Hussein. The Bush administration claimed Saddam was obtaining weapons of mass destruction, and that his overthrow would spread democracy to Middle Eastern nations. Neither claim proved correct. By 2007 the U.S. military remained deeply involved in the increasingly sectarian violence in Iraq between Sunnis and Shiites. Biden, with support from some Republicans—some of it open, some tacit—immediately began using his position to more vigorously challenge the Bush administration on the war and ending U.S. involvement in it.

Foreign Travel

Foreign trips by senators and representatives have been one of the most visible and controversial perquisites of serving in Congress. Defenders of foreign travel see it as a valuable way to educate legislators about world problems, particularly when many congressional votes deal with foreign affairs. But critics call the trips junkets—adventures or vacation trips at taxpayers' expense. In the past they also criticized travel paid for by corporations, nonprofits, or educational organizations, saying such trips give these groups an unfair advantage in promoting their agendas. Such free travel became even more controversial when it was revealed that top legislators had received lavish trips overseas financed by a lobbyist, Jack Abramoff, who in early 2006 pleaded guilty to federal charges of conspiracy, mail fraud, and income tax evasion. The Abramoff scandal, which mainly affected Republicans, led the 110th Congress, which started in 2007, to further restrict private foreign travel. Senators and Senate candidates and presidential candidates were required to pay charter rates for trips on private planes, and House candidates were barred from accepting trips on private planes, a prohibition already in effect for sitting House members. (See PAY AND PERQUISITES.)

Most trips are sponsored by congressional committees, but House and Senate leaders receive special travel allowances. In 1988 Jim Wright, a Texas Democrat and House Speaker at the time, caused comment by taking thirteen members and seven staff aides to Australia for a week to celebrate the centennial of that country's parliament. The excursion cost $188,266.

Winter recess is a popular time for members to go on fact-finding trips, generally in more temperate climates. In January 1998 Trent LOTT, a Republican from Mississippi who was Senate majority leader at the time, led four other senators, their wives, and staffers—twenty-three people in all—on a government-paid trip through Central America and Mexico, staying one night in the colonial capital of Guatemala at a luxury hotel built from a seventeenth-century monastery. Lott's office said the trip was to study trade and efforts to curb smuggling of drugs and immigrants.

Large delegations also go each year to meetings of the Interparliamentary Union and the North Atlantic Assembly, which bring together U.S. and foreign legislators. And congressional travel has provided a means of showing expressions of solidarity in the war against terrorism. In 2002 four House lawmakers, led by Democrat Peter Deutsch of Florida and Republican Jack Kingston of Georgia, flew with aides and a security detail to visit hospitalized Israelis and Israeli Arabs injured in the Palestinian uprising. Lawmakers initially said they were not on a diplomatic mission, were not traveling to areas controlled by Palestinians, and did not plan to meet with senior Israeli officials. After questions about the necessity of the trip surfaced, aides said meetings with Israeli officials had indeed been scheduled.

Often congressional delegations travel on military planes, accompanied by marines or other military escorts who help with baggage and act as flight attendants. Embassy personnel in each city they visit are expected to set up meetings with local officials, arrange tours, and sometimes take the visitors to see night spots. But not all trips are luxury excursions. In 1989 Rep. Mickey Leland, a Texas Democrat, was killed in a plane crash while helping deliver food and supplies to famine-ridden Ethiopia.

Many legislators traveled to Iraq in the years after the Bush administration invaded the country in 2003 to topple the regime of Saddam Hussein. Although Saddam was deposed quickly, the war continued into 2007. The seemingly endless conflict prompted members to visit Iraq to form their own estimates of conditions.

Senators and representatives have been required since the 1950s to file accounts of travel spending, but the rules have been rewritten several times since then. In 1973 Congress voted to stop requiring that travel reports be printed in the CONGRESSIONAL RECORD, but the rule was restored in 1976 after public protest. Under the rules, committees have to file quarterly travel reports with the CLERK OF THE HOUSE or the SECRETARY OF THE SENATE. Individual members, staff, or congressional groups authorized by the leadership to travel have to report within thirty days after a trip. Although information on the use of public funds for travel is once again published in the *Record*, it is still difficult at times to tell the true cost of travel. For example, when military transportation is used, the cost is not counted in.

Reports do not have to be filed on trips funded by the executive branch or by private groups, but members are required to list private trips on their annual FINANCIAL DISCLOSURE forms. In 1989 Congress declared that members could not accept trips abroad that lasted longer than seven days (excluding travel time) from private interests. Congress reiterated this limit in 1995 as part of overall tighter restrictions on gifts.

Former Members of Congress

When senators and representatives leave Congress, typically after eight or ten years, their activities are as varied as those they pursued before election. Many return to the practice of law or to business. A few take prestigious posts outside of government. Many join Washington law or lobbying firms where their congressional knowledge is in high demand. Still others simply retire, living on a congressional pension that can be quite generous and is automatically adjusted for inflation.

In 2006 the average annual pension ranged from nearly $61,000 under one retirement plan to nearly $36,000 under another. The amount in both depended on the length of service in Congress. In addition, members have participated in Social Security since 1984. (See PAY AND PERQUISITES.)

Former House members who have found prestigious jobs in the private sector include Barber B. Conable Jr., a New York Republican who became head of the World Bank in 1986, and Pennsylvania Democrat William H. Gray III, who retired from the House in 1991 to become president of the

United Negro College Fund. In 1993 Bill Gradison, Republican House member from Ohio, left Congress and the prestigious Ways and Means Committee to head the Health Insurance Association of America. In that position he spearheaded the attack on President Bill Clinton's ill-fated health care reform proposal. Richard A. Gephardt, who once was Democratic leader in the House and erstwhile but unsuccessful presidential candidate, became a Washington lobbyist after leaving Congress in 2005. He set up the Gephardt Group as his primary base, where he lobbied and consulted largely on labor relations and alternative energy. But he also worked for a large law firm, a major Wall Street investment bank, and a corporate turnaround company.

Many members left Congress but stayed in politics. As of 2007, twenty-seven of the nation's forty-three presidents served in Congress or its predecessor, the Continental Congress, and thirty-six vice presidents had served in the legislative branch.

Some former members of Congress have been appointed to the cabinet or other top posts. After serving in the House and Senate, Albert Gallatin of Pennsylvania became Treasury secretary in 1801, serving for a record thirteen years. Another veteran legislator, John C. Calhoun of South Carolina, served as secretary of war and secretary of state, as well as vice president, in the pre–Civil War period. In the 1980s President Ronald Reagan turned more than once to ex-legislators to staff his cabinet; in the White House itself, Tennessee Republican Howard H. BAKER Jr., a former Senate majority leader, served as chief of staff. In 1994 President Clinton followed suit by appointing his OMB director and former California representative Leon Panetta to be his chief of staff. Clinton also crossed party lines to appoint former Republican senator Bill Cohen of Maine to head the Department of Defense. He appointed several other ex-members of Congress to serve in his cabinet, including former representative Norman Mineta of California, at the time an aerospace industry lobbyist, who was named commerce secretary. George W. Bush turned to a number of former members of Congress as well in assembling his first cabinet, appointing John Ashcroft of Missouri to be attorney general and Spencer Abraham of Michigan to be energy secretary after each lost Senate reelection bids. Bush also crossed party lines when he named Democrat Mineta to be his transportation secretary. In 2005 he named Rob Portman, a six-term House member from Ohio, as trade representative and the following year appointed him director of the Office of Management and Budget. When Portman resigned in 2007 to return to Ohio and probably to prepare for a Senate run, Bush turned to Jim Nussle, a former GOP House member from Iowa.

Some members of Congress have given up congressional seats to accept posts in the executive branch. In the 1840s and 1850s Daniel WEBSTER, a Massachusetts Whig, twice left the Senate to become secretary of state. More recently, Sen. Edmund S. Muskie, a Democrat from Maine, left to become secretary of state in 1980. Richard B. Cheney, a Wyoming Republican, left the House in 1989 to become President George H. W. Bush's secretary of defense. Just over a decade later, Cheney returned to the executive branch as President George W. Bush's vice president and became one of the most influential persons ever to occupy that office.

Clinton picked three of his initial cabinet secretaries from the Democratic ranks of members in Congress. Senate Finance Committee chair Lloyd Bentsen of Texas became Clinton's Treasury secretary; House Armed Services Committee chair Les Aspin of Wisconsin became defense secretary; and Mike Espy of Mississippi, a member of the House Agriculture Committee, became agriculture secretary. Democrat Bill Richardson of New Mexico left the House to become U.S. ambassador to the United Nations in 1997 and then Clinton's secretary of energy in 1998.

President George W. Bush similarly coaxed members of Congress into his administration. In 2001 Asa Hutchinson, R-Ark., resigned from the House to head the federal Drug Enforcement Administration. Tony P. Hall, an Ohio Democrat, in 2002 also left the House to become United Nations ambassador. Near the end of President Bush's first term, Rep. Porter J. Goss, R-Fla., resigned in 2004 to head the Central Intelligence Agency.

Governors have often been elected to Congress, particularly to the Senate. The reverse is also true—Democrat Lawton Chiles, for example, left the Senate to become governor of Florida, as did Republican Dirk Kempthorne in Idaho and Republican Frank H. Murkowski in Alaska. Republican Henry Bellmon of Oklahoma had an unusual résumé: he served first as governor, then as a senator, and in 1986 he was elected governor again.

Still another career choice for former members has been the judiciary. Although the pattern has been rare since the 1940s, about one-third of all Supreme Court justices had previously served in Congress or the Continental Congress.

Among the most visible former members of Congress are those who stay in Washington as lobbyists, with law firms or organizations whose views they share. They stalk familiar corridors and hearing rooms to win votes from former colleagues—or, in many cases, favorable wording from staff who draft the bills. Although ex-members have lifetime privileges on the House and Senate floors, the House has a rule against LOBBYING on the floor and the practice is frowned on in the Senate. Lobbying is permitted, however, in the congressional dining rooms and gymnasiums still open to ex-members.

Often ex-member lobbyists handle the same issues they concentrated on as legislators. Arkansas Democrat J. William FULBRIGHT chaired the Senate Foreign Relations Committee for fifteen years until 1975; as a lobbyist he later had clients from Saudi Arabia and Japan, among other countries. Idaho Republican James McClure served as chair of the Senate Energy and Natural Resources Committee; he later represented several organizations with mining interests.

Some lawmakers have used lobbying as a rest stop, of sorts, in their careers. Republican senator James M. Talent of Missouri moved to a Washington lobbying firm when he left the House in 2001, after an unsuccessful run for governor. He won election to the Senate in 2002. During his lobbying stint, Talent, a former chair of the House Small Business Committee, represented small businesses and grain processors.

Ex-congressional leaders can be an especially appealing resource. Former Senate majority leader George MITCHELL, a Democrat from Maine, became a special counsel to a firm that listed aerospace and defense contractors among the companies it represented. Democrat Thomas FOLEY of Washington, a three-term Speaker of the House, became a partner in a Washington law firm with an extensive list of clients who had government-related interests. Foley was later appointed ambassador to Japan, and Mitchell served as chair of peace negotiations in Northern Ireland, head of an international committee to study the eruption of violence between the Israelis and Palestinians, and chief investigator of the use of performance-enhancing drugs in major league baseball. Robert Walker of Pennsylvania, once Republican chief deputy whip in the House, was named president of a high-profile Washington lobbying firm.

About 550 ex-members belonged to the U.S. Association of Former Members of Congress in early 2007. The group, which has a variety of educational programs, hosts a reunion every spring on Capitol Hill. Returning members meet in the House chamber, just before an official session, and have a chance once again to make a speech in the Capitol.

Sen. Frank H. Murkowski argues in favor of oil drilling in the Arctic National Wildlife Refuge in 2001.
Source: CQ Photo/Scott J. Ferrell

Although many governors have later won election to Congress—usually the Senate—in some cases the reverse occurs. In recent times, Democrat Lawton Chiles, of Florida, left the Senate to become governor of his home state, as did Republicans Dirk Kempthorne of Idaho and Frank H. Murkowski of Alaska.

Franking Privilege

Most people receive mail occasionally from their legislators. Instead of a stamp, the envelope may bear the legislator's signature in the upper right-hand corner. For senators and representatives this

The concept of the frank goes back to 1779, when the first Continental Congress enacted a law giving its members mailing privileges—permitting members of Congress to communicate directly with their constituents at government expense. This 1869 wood engraving shows bags of franked mail leaving the Washington, D.C., post office.
Source: Library of Congress

facsimile of their handwriting, called the frank, is an important privilege. It allows them to send newsletters and other mailings to their constituents at government expense. Using the franking privilege, legislators can communicate directly with their constituents to inform them of congressional decisions and pass on useful news about the federal government.

Congressional expenditures on franked mail have dropped substantially in recent years, as Congress tightened the rules on its use, but remain in the millions and are often criticized by groups that monitor federal spending. In fiscal 1997 Congress spent about $19 million on franked mail. In fiscal 2006 the total was $34.3 million, according to a Congressional Research Service analysis. One news organization that studied 2006 data said House members alone spent $20.3 million sending nearly 116 million pieces of mail. In the latter years of the 1980s, however, total franking costs had topped $100 million.

A franked envelope might contain a legislator's response to a question or request, a copy of a newsletter, a survey, a press release, a packet of voting information, government publications, or other printed matter that in some way relates to the legislator's "official duties." The frank cannot be used to solicit money or votes. Letters related to political campaigns, political parties, or personal business or friendships are not permitted. For example, a legislator cannot use the frank on a holiday greeting, a message of sympathy, an invitation to a party fund-raising event, or a request for political support.

Congress has limited use of the frank in the weeks preceding elections, but the amount of franked mail usually jumps by more than half in election years. This has prompted charges from challengers that the privilege is yet another advantage for incumbents.

Those authorized to use the frank include the vice president, members and members-elect of Congress, and certain officers of the House and Senate. Committees and subcommittees send mail under the frank of a committee member.

The franking privilege has been in effect since the first Congress, except for a few months in 1873, but the concept of the frank is older than Congress itself. The first Continental Congress in 1775 adopted the seventeenth-century British practice of giving its members mailing privileges as a way of keeping constituents fully informed. It was also a way of reminding voters back home between elections that their legislator was thinking of them. A common practice in the nineteenth century was to send home packets of seeds, courtesy of the Agriculture Department. Congress enjoyed the use of the frank almost without restriction until 1973, when the first effort at self-policing began.

Although no stamp is needed on a franked letter, such letters are not actually mailed free of charge. The U.S. Postal Service keeps track of how many franked pieces of mail it handles and how much they weigh. At the end of the year the Postal Service sends Congress what amounts to a bill; Congress then transfers the funds to the Postal Service.

The cost of the mailing privilege jumped dramatically in the 1970s and 1980s because of increases in mailing rates and the amount of mail. In 1970 Congress sent 190 million pieces of franked mail at a cost of $11.2 million; by 1988 more than 800 million letters and packages were sent under the frank at a cost of $113 million.

Congress frequently spent more than it appropriated for mailing costs; only after an election would it vote for more money to pay the final tab. But concerns about federal budget deficits and political fairness prompted Congress to reduce the flood of mail.

The Senate used improved cost accounting to control its mailings. Beginning in 1986 each senator received a budget showing his or her share of the appropriation for postage, based on population. Each senator also received reports, twice a year, on his or her mass mailings and their cost. Senators were required to disclose how much they had spent.

The power of publicity was demonstrated in 1989, when the Senate temporarily lifted its disclosure requirements. During the first five months of the year, the Senate spent $6 million on official mail; during the rest of the year, with disclosure suspended, mailing costs soared to $29 million. In 1990, once disclosure was again in force, the cost sank to $15 million.

Advantage to Incumbents

The advantage the frank gives to someone in office running for reelection has been the most controversial aspect of the traditional privilege. The debate intensified after the 1972 election campaign. Several mailings during the campaign were considered improper, since they seemed too much like advertising for members' political campaigns. Twelve cases reached the courts. One case of abuse took place in Georgia. Fletcher Thompson, a Republican representative running for the Senate, used the frank to send mail throughout the state, not just to his congressional district. The mailing, which cost taxpayers more than $200,000, became a campaign issue and a key factor in the representative's loss to Democrat Sam Nunn.

Restrictions

In response to the abuses and the threat of court intervention, Congress in 1973 passed a new law setting guidelines for use of the frank. These included tighter definitions of the types of mail eligible and a limit on mass mailings (defined as more than 500 pieces of largely identical mail) during the four weeks before an election, either a primary or a general election. To oversee use of the franking privilege, the House set up a Commission on Congressional Mailing Standards, more commonly called the Franking Commission. Later the Senate gave its Ethics Committee a similar responsibility, although its Rules and Administration Committee handles routine administration of the frank.

Additional changes in later years tightened the rules. For example, in 1977 the preelection cut-off was extended from twenty-eight to sixty days, making it harder to use the frank for political purposes. The sixty-day standard remained in effect for senators. The House, however, later required that any mass mailings had to be postmarked at least ninety days before an election. For both chambers, the rule applied to any representative or senator whose name appears on any ballot, thus covering primary as well as general elections. The growth in franking began to slow down after 1986, when the Senate made members individually and publicly responsible for their own accounts. The House resisted such disclosure until 1990. Disclosure had an effect: in 1992 the House was able to send back to the Treasury $20 million of the $80 million it had appropriated for the fiscal year.

Under a 1992 law, a representative cannot send any mass mailing outside the congressional district from which the person is elected. Representatives must obtain clearance for mass mailing from the Franking Commission.

Other changes in the 1990s included combining franking money with members' office allowances, thus giving members more flexibility in choosing between franked mailings and expenditures for such things as travel or staff. Caps on newsletters were set at one piece for each address in the state for senators and three pieces for each address in the district for representatives. Restrictions were placed on self-promotional material, such as photos of a member, in newsletters. In 1998 the House Oversight Committee removed remaining limits on franking within a member's overall allowance. Beginning in fiscal 1999, lawmakers could use any portion of their official budget for mailings. Senators have an "official mail account," which is combined with the official office expense allowance and is based on the number of addresses in a senator's state. The Senate in 1996 allowed senators to use up to $50,000 of their office expense allowance for mass mailings.

Mass mailings must include the disclaimer: "This mailing was prepared, published, and mailed at taxpayer expense." Former members may use the frank for limited purposes for ninety days after the end of their terms.

Spending under the frank inevitably increases in election years. According to the U.S. Postal Service, Congress spent $18.8 million on the frank in fiscal 1997. The House spent $15.4 million; the Senate spent $3.4 million. The 1997 figure was a decrease of about 41 percent from fiscal 1996, when Congress spent $32 million on official mail.

Frist, Bill

Tennessee Republican Bill Frist had been a senator only since 1995 and never a top leader before becoming Senate majority leader in late 2002. His catapult to power was caused by a need for Republicans to redeem themselves on the issue of civil rights. Frist succeeded Trent LOTT of Mississippi, who was forced to resign from the position after making a verbal gaffe that many perceived as racist. At a December 2002 birthday party for retiring Republican senator Strom Thurmond of South Carolina, Lott said: "I want to say this about my state. When Strom Thurmond ran for president, we voted for him. We're proud of it. And if the rest of the country had followed our lead, we wouldn't have had all these problems over all these years, either."

But Frist's fame did not last. He left the Senate in 2006 at the end of the 109th Congress. His period heading the Republicans had mixed results. After successful 2004 elections for the GOP, he shepherded important bills through the Senate, but by the end of the 109th Congress in 2006 much of the president's agenda remained in limbo.

Frist, a wealthy doctor who traveled at his own expense annually to Africa to treat patients, was favored by the White House to succeed Lott. A close ally of President George W. Bush, Frist was expected to champion the White House agenda loyally. Although his voting record largely followed the conservative party line, Frist's public demeanor and reputation were more mainstream than Lott's. Frist's credibility on health care issues also was an asset for a party that needed to demonstrate concern about domestic problems such as rising prescription drug prices.

Flanked by fellow Republicans, Senate Majority Leader Bill Frist of Tennessee announces new deficit-reducing budget policies in June 2006. A senator for only two terms, Frist served as majority leader from 2002 to 2007.
Source: CQ Photo/Scott J. Ferrell

But many colleagues saw his loyalty to the White House as a handicap. Frist, unlike many senators, was a relative newcomer to politics, starting in 1994. He portrayed himself as a citizen legislator, an outsider in the tradition-bound Senate. He did little to hide his presidential ambitions, and critics saw calculations for a White House bid in every move. But with his primary constituency at the other end of Pennsylvania Avenue, Frist had to operate under strong White House pressure without having built up the political capital with colleagues that most party leaders need in the Senate. In a body of political insiders, Frist stood out for his lack of political ability.

Critics said Frist spent too much time and energy on issues such as gay marriage and flag burning that were certain not to pass and not enough on necessary bills. By the end of the Congress, for example, only two of eleven appropriations bills had passed.

Frist also showed a questionable political touch in 2004 by campaigning for the opponent of Senate Minority Leader Tom Daschle, D-S.D., who lost his reelection bid by a small margin. This decision permanently frayed his relationships with Democrats. Daschle's successor, Harry Reid, D-Nev., made little effort to conceal his dissatisfaction with Frist. After he left Congress in 2007, Frist abandoned the idea of running for president in 2008.

Fulbright, J. William

Dean of foreign affairs in the Senate, J. William Fulbright (1905–1995) was a critic of U.S. foreign policy in the decades following World War II. From the beginning of his Senate career, Fulbright advocated the conduct of international relations based on understanding and the exchange of ideas rather than show of force. As chair of the Senate Foreign Relations Committee from 1959 to 1975, Fulbright was at the forefront of Senate opposition to U.S. involvement in Vietnam.

An Arkansas lawyer and educator, Fulbright spent several years as president of the University of Arkansas before entering the House of Representatives as a Democrat in 1943. After one term in the House, he moved to the Senate in 1945 and remained there for thirty years.

In his first year in the House, Fulbright introduced a resolution advocating the establishment of a postwar organization to maintain world peace. In 1946 he sponsored legislation to establish the educational exchange program that bears his name. In later years Fulbright saw the exchange program as his greatest contribution to international understanding.

As chair of the Senate Foreign Relations Committee, J. William Fulbright, D-Ark. (right), was at the forefront of opposition to U.S. involvement in Vietnam.
Source: LBJ Library Photo by Yoichi Okamoto

In the Senate Fulbright was best known for his opposition to the Vietnam War. He voted for the Gulf of Tonkin resolution in 1964, although he later regretted having done so. The resolution became the primary legal justification for prosecution of the war during the presidency of Lyndon B. Johnson. Fulbright criticized Johnson for his invasion of the Dominican Republic in 1965, and after this incident Fulbright had little influence over Johnson's conduct of the Vietnam War. Fulbright also was an outspoken critic of President Richard Nixon's handling of the war.

In 1973 Congress passed the WAR POWERS resolution, designed to limit the president's power to commit U.S. forces abroad without congressional approval. Fulbright had introduced the forerunner of the measure in 1967 and 1969.

Although liberal on international issues, Fulbright followed the more conservative domestic policies supported by his constituents. He opposed the Supreme Court's 1954 school desegregation decision and voted against the Civil Rights Act of 1964. In the end Fulbright's concentration on international affairs distanced him from his constituents, and he was defeated for reelection in 1974.

G

Gag Rule

This term is normally used as a pejorative for rules approved by the House Rules Committee that limit or prohibit amendments to legislation the House will consider. More broadly, critics use the term to apply to any special rule that significantly limits the ability of members to alter legislation before the House. A procedure that limits or restricts amendments usually is called a closed rule.

Gephardt, Richard A.

House Minority Leader Richard A. Gephardt, D-Mo., briefs the media in his office in the U.S. Capitol in 2001. Gephardt led the House Democrats for more than a decade.
Source: CQ Photo/Scott J. Ferrell

The consensus-building ability of Missouri Democrat Richard A. Gephardt (1941–) served him well as House majority leader (1989–1995) and minority leader (1995–2003). Adept at the detail work of moving legislation through the House, Gephardt also was a strong spokesperson for his party.

Gephardt was elected to the House in 1976 and immediately won a seat on the Ways and Means Committee with the help of his mentor Richard BOLLING, then dean of the Missouri delegation and Rules Committee chair.

Gephardt's career was characterized by political pragmatism. In 1984 he helped found the Democratic Leadership Council to move the party away from identification with traditional liberal interest groups and toward the political center. Yet in 1988 Gephardt, by then chair of the House Democratic Caucus, ran unsuccessfully for president as an angry populist outsider. Gephardt became majority leader in 1989 when Thomas S. FOLEY of Washington became Speaker. Like Foley, Gephardt was a strong negotiator but showed more aggressive partisanship than Foley.

Gephardt's role decreased significantly when the Republicans took over the House in 1995. From then until 2003, he focused on winning back control of the House for the Democrats. Despite monumental fundraising and tireless efforts, his party remained in the minority. Partly to take responsibility for additional seat losses, Gephardt stepped down as Democratic leader and was succeeded by Nancy PELOSI of California. He retired from Congress after the 2004 elections and in 2005 set up the Gephardt Group, a lobbying firm in Washington, D.C.

Germaneness *See* AMENDMENTS.

Gerrymandering

Gerrymandering—the practice of shaping voting districts to benefit a particular party, politician, or group of voters—takes its name from a salamander-shaped legislative district illustrated here that was created by the Massachusetts legislature under Gov. Elbridge Gerry in 1812.

Source: Library of Congress

Gerrymandering is the practice of manipulating the shape of legislative districts to benefit a particular politician, political party, or group of voters. The practice is almost as old as the nation. The word was coined in 1812, when the Massachusetts legislature redrew the boundaries of state legislative districts to favor the party of Governor Elbridge Gerry. One of the redrawn districts, it was pointed out, looked like a salamander, a kind of lizard. An artist added a head, wings, and claws to the district map, and a Boston newspaper published the resulting drawing, which it called a "GerryMander."

The oddly shaped district was drawn to encompass most of the state's Federalists. Governor Gerry's strategy was to let the Federalists win there and to leave his party, the Anti-Federalists, with the balance of power in all the other districts of the state. The term *gerrymandering* quickly became part of the American political vocabulary, and the practice it describes is still in use. In 1986 the Supreme Court ruled that gerrymanders are subject to federal court review. However, the Court did not rule on the constitutionality of the practice.

After the 1990 census many states redistricted according to the mandates of the 1965 Voting Rights Act, which prohibited diluting the voting power of minorities. The result was a handful of bizarrely shaped minority districts. The Supreme Court during the 1990s struck down a number of these districts as unconstitutional racial gerrymandering. The Court ruled that the strangely shaped district lines were drawn up with race as an overwhelming factor. The Court, however, avoided setting clear redistricting guidelines for states that had to redraw minority districts. Although gerrymandering to enhance the chances of minorities winning was much less pronounced in the redistricting that followed the 2000 census, the lines of many districts were as peculiarly shaped as always. Much of the meandering lines of districts came from the effort of politicians to design areas that favored reelection chances of incumbents. It was a practice followed by both Democrats and Republicans, and often in cooperation with one another. (See REAPPORTIONMENT AND REDISTRICTING.)

Gingrich, Newt

As the first Republican Speaker of the House in forty years, Newt Gingrich (1943–) of Georgia began his tenure in January 1995 with complete authority over his party. He stood as the symbol of the new Republican era on Capitol Hill. But his star burned too brightly to be sustained.

In late 1998 after a disastrous election showing for House Republicans, Gingrich faced an insurrection by many GOP lawmakers sharply critical of his management of the party's election strategy. Gingrich had predicted healthy gains for his party; instead, Democrats gained five seats, almost wiping out the House Republicans' margin of control. Gingrich announced after the election that he would step down as Speaker and resign from Congress. Still, Gingrich's move from freshman to Speaker in only sixteen years, without ever chairing a committee or subcommittee, was unprecedented in the modern era.

A former history professor, Gingrich had uncommon energy, toughness, and the ability to articulate his vision of government. As a backbencher in the 1980s, Gingrich was credited, or blamed, for escalating partisan tensions in Congress. As minority whip in 1989, Gingrich urged Republicans to confront Democrats rather than compromise in pursuit of marginal wins. It was his tenacious pursuit of Speaker Jim WRIGHT on ethics matters that led to Wright's resignation—the first in the history of that office. But, as observers noted, he

Leading his party back into control of the House of Representatives after forty years, Republican Newt Gingrich resigned from Congress after four powerful but controversial years as Speaker.
Source: CQ Photo/Douglas Graham

most resembled Wright, among modern Speakers, in his desire to use power. He was not, however, a "man of the House" as were all recent Speakers—a term that described long-service and quintessential congressional members whose loyalty and conduct was formed by respect for the chamber as an institution.

Gingrich crafted the campaign blueprint that won the Republicans control of the House in the 1994 elections, built around the "Contract with America"—a promise to bring ten issues to floor votes within the first 100 days of the new Congress. Key elements of the contract dealt with strengthening national security, cutting spending for everything else, lowering taxes, and reducing the regulation of business.

In 1995 at the start of his speakership, Gingrich not only had the votes to control the House floor, he also had the votes in the Republican Conference to decide who would chair committees—despite the rule of seniority. It was a power unrivaled since the days of Joseph CANNON early in the century. As the new Republican majority reformed the House's rules, cut spending, and approved a balanced budget constitutional amendment, Gingrich's stock could not have been higher. But his success did not last. By the end of his first term as Speaker, his leadership was marred by scandal, unrest within his party, and a level of personal unpopularity that was practically without rival in American politics.

Two partial government shutdowns during 1995–1996 added to Gingrich's poor national image. The staunchly conservative House Republicans led by Gingrich thought they could use the shutdowns to force President Bill Clinton to compromise on their balanced budget plan. But when it became clear that the Republicans were blamed by the public for the lack of some government services, the Republicans reversed course and voted to fund the government, giving Clinton a major victory.

Ethics problems also plagued Gingrich. The House ethics subcommittee found that he had used tax-exempt money for political purposes and had provided the panel with information that he should have known was "inaccurate, incomplete and unreliable." The House voted 395–28 to reprimand Gingrich and assess him a financial penalty of $300,000. It was the first time a Speaker had been punished for violating House rules.

In 1997 a small group of conservatives, believing that Gingrich had compromised too willingly on fundamental conservative principles, challenged his leadership. Gingrich emerged from an abortive coup attempt shaken, but still in control.

The final challenge came one year later, after Gingrich and his allies had failed to convict Clinton after impeaching him. After the surprising Republican loss of House seats in the 1998 elections, Appropriations chair Robert L. Livingston of Louisiana announced that he would challenge Gingrich for the speakership. A few hours after Livingston threw his hat into the ring, Gingrich stunned the nation by announcing that he would step down. Livingston later took himself out of the running to avoid scrutiny of his extramarital affairs. In what many saw as a move away from the confrontational style perfected by Gingrich, Republicans chose low-key J. Dennis HASTERT of Illinois to be the next Speaker. Gingrich turned to a career in political consulting and writing, winning a measure of admiration in Washington as a political pundit. As the 2008 presidential race got underway, Gingrich toyed with the possibility of seeking the White House, but in September 2007 he announced that he would not run.

Gore, Al

Elected as vice president with President Bill Clinton in 1992 and 1996, Al Gore (1948–) previously had served eight years in the Senate (1985–1993) and eight years in the House (1977–1985).

His bid in 2000 to succeed Clinton resulted in the most unusual presidential election of the twentieth century. Gore and his running mate, Sen. Joseph I. Lieberman of Connecticut, won the popular vote. However, problems with the voting procedures in Florida left the electoral votes in that state—and the outcome of the presidential contest—undecided for five weeks. After a series of court battles, the U.S. Supreme Court issued a controversial 5–4 ruling that decided the election in Republican George W. Bush's favor.

A Harvard graduate, Gore was an army journalist during the Vietnam War, but he never saw combat. From 1971 to 1976 he worked as a reporter for a Nashville newspaper.

With strong political roots—his father Albert Gore Sr. had represented Tennessee in the House and Senate for more than thirty years—Gore moved effortlessly into politics. In 1976 he won his father's former seat in the House of Representatives, and he was easily re-elected to the heavily Democratic district in 1978, 1980, and 1982. In 1984 he successfully jumped to the Senate—receiving more than 60 percent of the vote, despite Republican Ronald Reagan's landslide reelection as president.

During his years in Congress, the Tennessee Democrat gained a reputation as a moderately liberal, detail-oriented lawmaker. Gore became a respected voice on technology development, the environment, and defense issues. He wrote a book outlining an international plan of action on environmental issues, called *Earth in the Balance: Ecology and the Human Spirit*.

Gore ran unsuccessfully for his party's presidential nomination in 1988 and then joined the winning Clinton ticket four years later. As vice president, he became one of Clinton's closest advisers, taking on many critical assignments. He continued to champion technology and the environment and led the charge for the administration's "reinventing government" program, which was designed to streamline the federal government.

Al Gore served eight years in the House, eight years in the Senate, and eight years as vice president before losing the 2000 presidential contest. In a return to Capitol Hill in March 2007, he makes an emotional appeal before the Senate Environment and Public Works Committee for a reduction in U.S. emissions blamed for climate change. His work in raising international awareness of global warming won him the Nobel Peace Prize in 2007.
Source: CQ Photo/Scott J. Ferrell

Gore's politically clean image was tarnished slightly in 1997, by unproven charges of misconduct in his campaign fundraising for the 1996 presidential election. He also demonstrated his loyalty to Clinton by remaining steadfast in his support of the president during his impeachment investigation and trial in 1998–1999. But despite the administration's scandals, Gore was the Democratic nominee for president in 2000. The unusual contest that followed marked the first time that the outcome of a presidential election had been determined through the courts. It was also the fourth time in U.S. history that the loser of the popular vote gained the presidency.

Two years later, Gore announced that he would not seek a rematch in 2004. While some analysts predicted that Gore might attempt another campaign in 2008, Gore himself said that he "made the decision in the full awareness that that probably means I will never have another opportunity to run for president."

He continued to be mentioned as a possible dark horse throughout 2007, when the Democratic field was crowded with aspirants. But Gore's main fame in these years was his association with efforts to highlight the environmental dangers he believed the world faced from global warming. In 2006 a documentary movie titled *An Inconvenient Truth* featured Gore in his campaign to warn the world about global warming. It was an instant success, won two Academy awards in 2007 and sixteen other prizes, and received numerous nominations for other awards.

Calls for Gore to run for president swelled again in October 2007 when he shared the Nobel Peace Prize along with the UN's Intergovernmental Panel on Climate Change. With his spokespeople denying his intent to run again, Gore remained focused on his global mission in his acceptance speech in Oslo, Norway, "We, the human species, are confronting a planetary emergency—a threat to the survival of our civilization that is gathering ominous and destructive potential even as we gather here."

Government Accountability Office

The GAO seal was updated in 2004 to reflect the agency's new name.
Source: Government Accountability Office

Congress has its own agency, the Government Accountability Office (GAO), to monitor spending by the executive branch. The largest congressional support agency, the GAO had 3,260 employees in 2006 who conduct investigations, perform audits, and offer legal opinions about financial disputes. The office's basic role is to review how the executive branch spends the money Congress appropriates. Individual members of Congress, as well as committees, can ask the GAO to investigate specific programs or broad policy questions. The GAO also can act on its own initiative.

Founded in 1921, the agency was known as the Government Accounting Office until 2004. The change went into effect July 7 and included new personnel provisions that took the agency out of the federal employee pay system and allowed it to offer compensation based on performance.

When Congress revamped federal budget making in 1921, two new agencies were set up. The Bureau of the Budget (now the Office of Management and Budget) was to work with the president on proposals for how and where federal funds should be spent. The General Accounting Office, an agency of the legislative branch, was to give Congress an independent review and audit of executive branch expenditures.

During World War II almost 15,000 people worked for the GAO, handling masses of vouchers and routine claims related to the war. In 1950 the GAO was freed from performing regular audits of agencies; the agencies themselves handled the audits, as well as the routine processing of vouchers

David M. Walker has served as the GAO's comptroller general since November 1998.
Source: CQ Photo/Scott J. Ferrell

and claims. As a result, instead of concentrating on details of spending, the GAO was able to review how agencies were managed, with a focus on uncovering waste and fraud. Some people maintain that the office's reports are overly critical; others complain that it waters down its reports to avoid controversy.

The GAO's authority to investigate the executive branch became the focus of a major Washington power struggle in 2002, when Comptroller General David M. Walker sued Vice President Richard CHENEY after Cheney refused to disclose which industry executives were consulted by the National Energy Policy Development Group, the formal name for an energy task force convened to develop a new energy policy. Democrats and other administration critics contended the task force was too closely aligned with contributors to President George W. Bush's 2000 campaign.

A federal judge in late 2002 dismissed the suit, saying the court should not get involved in the separation-of-powers struggle that would result if the GAO were allowed to compel disclosure of everyone Cheney's task force met with in 2001. The judge ruled in essence that the GAO lacked standing to sue because Walker had not suffered any personal injury and that the GAO was only "an agent of Congress." Without some official endorsement, such as a subpoena from the House or Senate or a congressional committee, there was no reason to believe Congress supported the GAO's action, the judge wrote.

After the ruling the GAO reiterated that the lawsuit had been undertaken at the request of several committee and subcommittee chairs acting on behalf of their panels. But the agency decided not to appeal the decision, citing the significant time and resources it would have required.

Comptroller General

Heading the GAO is the comptroller general, who is appointed by the president and confirmed by the Senate. In 2007 the position paid $168,000 annually. The comptroller serves a fifteen-year term. Seeking a larger role in filling the position, Congress in 1980 set up a special committee to suggest nominees to the president, though the list would be nonbinding.

Walker began his term in November 1998, which was scheduled to continue through 2013.

Government Printing Office

About 2,200 people work for the Government Printing Office (GPO), which is one of the largest printing operations in the world. For Congress, the GPO prints, or contracts with commercial companies to print, thousands of publications each year. These publications include bills, public laws, committee reports, the CONGRESSIONAL RECORD and CONGRESSIONAL DIRECTORY, legislative calendars, hearing records, and franked envelopes. (See FRANKING PRIVILEGE.)

Many books, pamphlets, and reports printed by the GPO may be purchased by the public at the sixteen (as of the end of 2002) bookstores it operates throughout the country; they can also be ordered by mail or through the Internet (www.access.gpo.gov). The GPO also administers the depository library program. Selected libraries throughout the country receive from the GPO copies of important government publications, including those that by law must be made public.

Congress agreed in 1861 to establish the GPO, which has retained the old-fashioned title of public printer for its top official. To set up the printing office, buildings, equipment, and machinery were purchased from Cornelius Wendell, a private printer, for $135,000. A GPO building still stands on the site of the original plant. Oversight of the GPO is handled by the congressional Joint Committee on Printing.

The Bush administration in 2002 sought to end the century-old congressional rule requiring most federal agencies to use the printing office for products and services by seeking bids from private firms to print the fiscal

Ordering from the Government Printing Office

A wide range of information is provided in government publications. Although many are geared to a small audience and cover extremely technical matters, hundreds of publications are designed for general readers. Government publications are usually reasonably priced, and some are available free of charge. The GPO maintains an online catalog of publications at its Web site. Free printed catalogs are also available.

Questions about print publications and orders are handled by the Superintendent of Documents, Government Printing Office, Washington, DC 20402, and can be purchased in a number of ways:

- In person at the GPO Bookstore: 710 North Capitol Street N.W., Washington, DC
- Web Site: http://bookstore.gpo.gov
- Phone: 202-512-1800; toll-free: 866-512-1800
- Fax: 202-512-2104
- E-mail: contactcenter@gpo.gov
- Postal mail: Superintendent of Documents, P.O. Box 37954, Pittsburgh, PA 15250-7954

Electronic versions of documents are available at www.gpoaccess.gov.

Payment must be received before orders are shipped and can be made by credit card, check, or SOD deposit account.

Two Government Printing Office employees prepare pages of a congressional report.
Source: CQ Photo/Scott J. Ferrell

2004 budget. The move came after Congress, in a stopgap spending measure, specifically ordered the Office of Management and Budget to use the printing office. The administration said it was under no legal obligation to comply, arguing the mandate constituted an infringement on executive branch power.

The GPO operates a Web site called GPO Access (www.gpoaccess.gov), which is the primary host for online versions of congressional documents. Included is the *Congressional Record*, the *Federal Register*, versions of legislation, and public and private laws.

Gramm-Rudman-Hollings Act

Gramm-Rudman-Hollings is the common name for the law that established new budget procedures aimed at balancing the federal budget by fiscal 1991. Known formally as the Balanced Budget and Emergency Deficit Control Act of 1985, the law reflected the continuing frustration of many members of Congress about their inability to keep federal revenue and spending in balance. To achieve a balanced budget by 1991—a deadline later extended to 1993—the act set annual maximum deficit targets and mandated automatic across-the-board spending cuts, known by the unwieldy name of sequesters, by the president to enforce the limits.

The act's principal sponsors were Sens. Phil Gramm, R-Texas, Warren Rudman, R-N.H., and Ernest Hollings, D-S.C. In addition to creating the sequesters, it also extensively amended its primary budget-control predecessor, the Congressional Budget Act of 1974.

The Supreme Court in 1986 said that one key provision of the new law was unconstitutional. That provision gave the General Accounting Office—later renamed the Government Accountability Office—the power to determine the sequesters required of the president. The Court said this violated the Constitution's separation-of-powers doctrine because the GAO was a legislative branch agency. Congress in 1987 assigned the function to the Office of Management and Budget. (See BUDGET PROCESS.)

Great Society

The Great Society is the name given to the sweeping array of social programs proposed by President Lyndon B. JOHNSON and enacted by the Democratic-controlled Congress in the mid-1960s. In his 1964 speech launching the Great Society, Johnson said it rested "on abundance and liberty for all." The Great Society demanded "an end to poverty and racial injustice," but that was "only the beginning."

The Great Society was the most ambitious social agenda advanced by any president since the New Deal era in the 1930s. Great Society programs included medical care for the aged, a historic voting rights law, the first comprehensive plan of federal aid to elementary and secondary education, the War on Poverty, a Model Cities program, and housing, job training, and conservation measures.

Johnson, who became president after John F. KENNEDY was assassinated in 1963, opened his War on Poverty in 1964. But most Great Society programs were enacted in 1965, following Johnson's landslide election to a four-year term. By 1966, Johnson's Vietnam War policy had damaged the president's popularity, and Congress became increasingly reluctant to support controversial new domestic programs.

The War on Poverty was the most innovative of Johnson's Great Society initiatives. It was launched under the Economic Opportunity Act of 1964, which established an Office of Economic Opportunity to direct and coordinate a wide variety of new and expanded activities in education, employment, and training. The ten separate programs authorized by the law were designed to make a coordinated attack on the multiple causes of poverty. Together, the programs were to alleviate the combined problems of illiteracy, unemployment, and lack of public services that left one-fifth of the nation's population impoverished, according to the administration's statistics.

President Lyndon B. Johnson set forth an ambitious social agenda in a 1964 speech that became known as the Great Society program. Here he signs legislation establishing the Medicare program of health care for seniors. To the right is former President Harry S. Truman, who unsuccessfully advocated national health care when he was in the White House.
Source: LBJ Library Photo

Key sections of the law authorized a Job Corps to provide work experience and training for school dropouts, a Neighborhood Youth Corps to employ youths locally, a community action program under which the government would assist a variety of local efforts to combat poverty, an adult education program, and Volunteers in Service to America (VISTA), which was billed as a domestic Peace Corps.

The 1964 law was one of the most controversial laws of Johnson's presidency. The poverty program was plagued from the beginning by charges of "boss rule" and rule by the militant poor at the local level, of rioting and excessive costs in the Job Corps, and of excessive salaries in the Office of Economic Opportunity and at local levels.

Such reports, which distressed both conservatives and liberals, eventually led Congress to take a strong stance in molding the program. Republicans made unremitting efforts to abolish the Office of Economic Opportunity, and the agency was finally dismantled during the presidency of Johnson's successor, Republican Richard NIXON. VISTA and the Job Corps programs continued into the twenty-first century.

Hart, Philip A.

Philip A. Hart of Michigan (1912–1976) entered the Senate in 1959 as one of a class of freshman Democrats destined for prominence. Some, like Eugene McCarthy of Minnesota and Edmund S. Muskie of Maine, ran for president. Another, Robert C. Byrd of West Virginia, became Senate majority leader. Hart distinguished himself in a different way, earning the unofficial title of "conscience of the Senate."

Hart's political views were to the left of the majority, but he was revered for his honesty, fairness, and intellectual depth. A soft-spoken man who did not seek the limelight, Hart worked diligently on the details of legislation and had a talent for making his points without offending those who disagreed. Before he died of cancer in December 1976, at the end of his third term, the Senate voted to name a new office building after him. It was an honor accorded to only two other senators before him, Everett M. DIRKSEN of Illinois and Richard B. RUSSELL of Georgia.

Hart played an important role in the framing and passage of major legislation on voting rights, open housing, drug safety, and consumer credit. As chair of the Judiciary Subcommittee on Antitrust and Monopoly, he held extensive hearings on economic concentration but had difficulty moving legislation because of the opposition of conservatives on the panel. Hart prevailed in 1976 when the subcommittee released, and Congress approved, an antitrust law that authorized the states to bring class-action suits on behalf of citizens.

On the major issues of his time, Hart stood with the liberals. He advocated strict gun control, opposed capital punishment, and refused to join opponents of school busing. He took part in the Democrats' successful efforts to block two of President Richard NIXON's nominees to the Supreme

The Senate named this office building in honor of Sen. Philip A. Hart of Michigan, a measure of the high esteem accorded by his colleagues. Only two other senators, Everett M. Dirksen of Illinois and Richard B. Russell of Georgia, have Senate buildings named for them.
Source: AP Images/Harvey Georges; CQ Photo/Scott J. Ferrell

Court: Clement F. Haynsworth Jr. and G. Harrold Carswell. He fought the controversial antiballistic missile (ABM) system and opposed the war in Vietnam. His wife Jane Hart, an earlier and more militant antiwar activist, was arrested in a demonstration at the Pentagon.

Hart frequently was at odds with Mississippi Democrat James O. Eastland, chair of the Judiciary Committee and a foe of civil rights legislation. Still, Eastland later spoke warmly of Hart and described him as "a man of principle, courage, and intellectual honesty." Similar praise came from virtually the entire Senate at the end of Hart's eighteen years there. The Hart Building, opened in 1982 after many delays and revised cost estimates, was the most expensive of the six congressional office buildings, costing close to $140 million.

Hastert, J. Dennis

J. Dennis Hastert (1942–) was elected Speaker of the House in 1999, after a chaotic series of events suddenly thrust the Illinois Republican from a low-level leadership slot into the top job in the House. He remained the Speaker until 2007 when he was replaced by Nancy Pelosi, D-Calif., after Democrats recaptured the House majority in the 2006 elections. In his eight years in the post he became the longest-serving Republican Speaker in history.

He was as unlikely a prospect for Speaker as any in House history. This turn of events came about because Newt GINGRICH of Georgia, the Republican Party leader in the House who in 1994 led the GOP to a majority for the first time in forty years, announced in 1998 that he was stepping down as Speaker and would resign from Congress in the aftermath of a disappointing party showing in the midterm elections that year. The party's first choice to succeed Gingrich was Appropriations Committee chair Robert L. Livingston of Louisiana. But then Livingston unexpectedly turned down the position to avoid further scrutiny of his admitted extramarital affairs. Hastert quickly emerged as the consensus candidate of House Republicans.

Hastert was first elected to the House in 1986. Not well known outside of Capitol Hill, he had just finished his second term as chief deputy whip, an appointed post that ranked seventh on the leadership ladder. In that job, Hastert had taken the temperature of his colleagues on legislative proposals coming to the floor. An able and ambitious inside operator, Hastert was able to push the party line without making members feel they had been arm-twisted.

House Speaker J. Dennis Hastert leads a news conference in the lobby of the Republican National Committee near the U.S. Capitol in May 2006. Also speaking (from left to right) are House Majority Whip Roy Blunt, R-Mo., House Rules Committee chair David Dreier, R-Calif., and House Republican Conference chair Deborah Pryce, R-Ohio.
Source: CQ Photo/Scott J. Ferrell

A beefy former wrestling coach who once headed the National Wrestling Congress, Hastert was usually reticent in his public persona. He had picked up many of his legislating skills from his mentor, Robert H. Michel, also of Illinois, who had served as Republican leader when the party was in the minority.

Known for his ability to listen to his members and motivate a divided conference to reach agreement on contentious issues, Hastert succeeded in shepherding a number of President George W. Bush's legislative priorities through the House in the years between 2001 and 2006. With assistance from the highly persuasive majority whip, Tom DeLay of Texas—to whom Hastert had reported before he was Speaker and who suggested to GOP colleagues that Hastert be put in the Speaker's chair—the Illinois Republican pushed through the White House's tax cut, fast-track trade negotiating authority, an education bill, a GOP plan to add a prescription drug benefit to Medicare, a wide-ranging energy bill, a rewrite of the bankruptcy law, and numerous others. With the chamber narrowly divided, Hastert and other GOP leaders convinced the rank and file that they all needed to stick together on major issues or their party could face more electoral losses. He insisted on bringing to the floor only bills that he knew the majority of Republicans would support—"the majority of the majority," as he liked to put it. A testament to his ability to hold together a fractious caucus came at the start of the 108th Congress in 2003, when the Republican conference recommended purging a House rule that set an eight-year limit on the Speaker's tenure, the only term-limit rule on a House leader.

That persistence paid off. With the help of the White House, Republicans widened their margin of control in the 2002 and 2004 elections before losing control in 2006. Nearly one year after losing the Speakership, Hastert announced he would not seek reelection and resigned his office midterm on November 26, 2007.

CLOSER LOOK ◉

GOP House Speaker J. Dennis Hastert of Illinois was careful to bring to the floor only bills he knew a majority of Republicans would support. He called this "the majority of the majority" during the years the Republicans controlled the chamber.

Hayden, Carl

Carl Hayden, Arizona's first representative, holds the record for longest service in Congress—fifty-seven years.
Source: Library of Congress

Carl Hayden (1877–1972) gave up his job as a county sheriff to become Arizona's first representative in 1912; he was sworn in five days after Arizona became a state. The Arizona Democrat remained in Congress for the next fifty-seven years—a record unmatched, as of January 1, 2008, by any other member of Congress. However, Sen. Robert C. Byrd, D-W Va., who was reelected in 2006, would surpass Hayden if he served out even a portion of his term. As of January 2008, Byrd had served fifty-five years.

Hayden served fifteen years in the House before moving in 1927 to the Senate, where he served seven six-year terms. When Hayden retired in 1969, at the age of ninety-one, he was president pro tempore of the Senate and chair of the Senate Appropriations Committee, a post he had assumed when he was seventy-eight.

Hayne, Robert Y.

Almost by accident, Robert Y. Hayne (1791–1839) ended up participating in one of the Senate's most famous debates, the Webster-Hayne debate of 1830. Hayne, then a thirty-nine-year-old senator from South Carolina, spoke boldly for states' rights, arguing that a state could reject a federal law it considered unconstitutional, a concept known as nullification. His chief opponent, Daniel WEBSTER of Massachusetts, said the Union was not a compact of states but a creation of the people. The states, Webster maintained, had no authority to reject a tariff or any other federal law. The debate, which took place over a two-week period, packed the Senate galleries with spectators. Hayne gave a stirring defense of state sovereignty, a key proslavery position, but Webster, with a deep voice and a flair for drama, was more forceful in his defense of federal power over the states. (See STATES AND CONGRESS.)

Hayne had been elected to the Senate in 1823 as a Tariff Democrat, with help from fellow South Carolinian John C. Calhoun, a leading proponent of nullification. While Hayne was advocating his mentor's position on the Senate floor, Calhoun, then vice president, was presiding. As South Carolina's resistance to high tariffs intensified in 1832, the state legislature named Hayne governor, opening up the Senate seat for Calhoun, whom many considered the more effective statesman. Hayne, though ready to fight any federal troops enforcing the tariff laws, responded favorably to a congressional compromise, which Calhoun had crafted with Henry CLAY.

Before entering the Senate, Hayne served in the South Carolina state legislature and as the state's attorney general. He had only two years as governor; state rules prevented his serving an additional term. In 1834 Hayne became mayor of Charleston. He then devoted his energies to the establishment of a railroad that would link Charleston with the West.

Health, Education, Labor and Pensions Committee, Senate

As its name indicates, the Health, Education, Labor and Pensions Committee's jurisdiction covers many aspects of the Senate's social policy agenda. Its responsibilities range from biomedical research and prescription drugs to the Head Start preschool program and college education grants, from the minimum wage to private pension plans.

The committee is the key Senate panel on education and labor issues. On many health and welfare issues, however, it has been overshadowed by the Senate Finance Committee, which has jurisdiction over Medicare, Medicaid, Social Security, and the block-grant aid to families program that replaced the welfare entitlement.

Historically among the most liberal committees in the Senate, the panel—whose acronym is HELP—has been a key advocate of the federal health, welfare, and education programs it helped create in the 1960s and 1970s. Even for a time after the Republicans won control of the Senate in 1995, the chairs of the committee were among the most

The chair of the Senate Health, Education, Labor and Pensions Committee, Democrat Edward M. Kennedy of Massachusetts (right) and Republican Orrin G. Hatch of Utah talk to reporters in the Senate Daily Press Gallery in August 2007 about the children's health bill they co-sponsored that ultimately passed Congress but fell to two presidential vetos that year.
Source: CQ Photo/Scott J. Ferrell

liberal in the party. By 2003 the panel was in more conservative hands, but that was reversed in 2007 when Democrats retook Senate control and one of that chamber's most liberal members, Sen. Ted Kennedy, D-Mass., became the panel's chair.

History

The committee was set up in 1869 as the Education and Labor Committee. The 1946 Senate reorganization gave it a new title, Labor and Public Welfare. Another reform, in 1977, renamed the committee Human Resources. The new title was in effect for only two years before labor advocates convinced the Senate to call the committee Labor and Human Resources. The Senate renamed the panel in 1999 as the Committee on Health, Education, Labor and Pensions.

The legacy of the New Deal guided the committee as it pursued a gradual expansion of the federal social role. A key advocate of that view was Lister Hill, an Alabama Democrat who chaired the committee from 1955 to 1969. Although typical of southerners in his opposition to civil rights laws, Hill had a liberal view of social programs and often backed health proposals opposed by the medical establishment. He favored federal aid for medical research, hospital construction, and training of doctors and nurses. Hill's authority was enhanced because he also chaired the appropriations subcommittee that handled labor, health, and welfare spending.

In the 1970s New Jersey Democrat Harrison A. Williams Jr. chaired the committee, continuing the liberal tradition. An early proponent of safety in the workplace, Williams worked with labor leaders on various issues, not always with success. Williams's conviction on charges that included bribery and influence peddling in the Abscam scandal led to his resignation from the Senate in 1982.

During the administrations of presidents Ronald Reagan and George H. W. Bush from 1981 to 1993, the committee doggedly defended key social programs, not always successfully. Congress cut some programs and consolidated others during the 1980s.

The Republicans gained control of the Senate in 1981 with Orrin G. Hatch of Utah becoming chair of the committee. Under Hatch, the committee often deadlocked on votes, as Republicans Lowell P. Weicker Jr. of Connecticut and Robert T. Stafford of Vermont frequently voted with Democrats. Despite Hatch's reputation as a strident conservative, however, he worked with his colleagues to find acceptable compromises. He quickly learned that his more controversial proposals, such as establishment of a separate, lower minimum wage for young people, had no chance of approval.

A bigger challenge to the committee's standing and power, however, was the bleak outlook for expensive new social programs in the 1990s. Democrats regained control of the Senate in 1987, making the liberal Kennedy the committee chair. But these changes did not mean a return to the days when the committee could champion expansive and costly social programs. Major new initiatives were not possible because of the growing federal budget deficit. Even popular ideas, such as funding for day care and protection against catastrophic medical costs, were blocked by lack of tax revenue to pay for them.

CLOSER LOOK

Historically among the most liberal committees in the Senate, the panel—whose acronym is HELP—has been a key advocate of the federal health, welfare, and education programs it helped create in the 1960s and 1970s.

It was ironic and frustrating that a broader political consensus for at least some social programs had been reached at the same time federal funds were drying up. Just three decades before, Congress had vigorously debated a limited federal commitment to education and health care. By the late 1980s the situation was much different. Even Hatch and other conservatives had endorsed a federal role in providing child care. The price tag was the problem.

The election of Democrat Bill Clinton as president in 1992 raised hopes that the committee might have a more active legislative agenda. For a time, the committee did play a larger role during the failed effort in 1993–1994 to develop a plan to overhaul the nation's health care system.

Unexpectedly, incremental progress in making it easier to obtain health care insurance was achieved after the Senate reverted to GOP control in 1995. Republican Nancy Landon Kassebaum of Kansas, who chaired the committee from 1995 until 1997, along with Kennedy as the ranking Democrat, was able to push through legislation.

In 1997 Republican James M. Jeffords of Vermont became chair and requested the committee's name be changed to Health, Education, Labor and Pensions. He said the new name better reflected the committee's mission and the acronym HELP described its social policy objectives. Kennedy returned to chair the committee from 2001 to 2003, after the Democrats regained control of the Senate. The switch occurred after Jeffords left the Republican Party and became an Independent. The Democrats named Jeffords chair of the Environment and Public Works Committee.

When party control switched back to the Republicans in 2003, the chair went to Judd Gregg of New Hampshire, who favored more conservative positions than any of his recent predecessors. Still, Kennedy, as chair, and Gregg, as ranking Republican, had worked together with President George W. Bush to produce a bipartisan elementary and secondary education overhaul—called No Child Left Behind—in 2001.

That legislation was to be before the committee for renewal in 2007 with Kennedy once more in the chair. Gregg remained on the panel, but the ranking Republican was now Michael B. Enzi, of Wyoming, with whom Kennedy had worked well in the past. No Child Left Behind was expected to be one of the highest priorities of the panel. It also was likely to be one of the most controversial because the educational community and some states found aspects of its requirements burdensome and costly.

Kennedy's personal top priority was making health care available and affordable for more Americans. In 2007 he worked with Sen. Orrin G. Hatch, R-Utah, to craft a bipartisan expansion of the popular State Childrens Health Insurance Program (SCHIP) by $35 billion over five years. The bill quickly became a priority for the Democrats, newly in charge of Congress and wishing to burnish their creditials as champions for the middle and lower classes. The health insurance expansion, however, fell to vetoes by President George W. Bush in October and December 2007.

The committee also was likely to examine an overhaul of the National Institutes of Health and the Food and Drug Administration. A more contentious issue was expected in expansion of federally funded embryonic stem cell research, which was opposed by President Bush's administration. Changes to the student loan programs also were expected to be before the committee.

Hispanics in Congress

Like other underrepresented groups, such as blacks and women, Hispanic Americans have gradually won increased representation in Congress. When the 110th Congress convened in 2007, it included twenty-six members and one nonvoting delegate from Puerto Rico who identified themselves as Hispanics—people of Spanish ancestry. Three were senators and the rest representatives in the House.

The number of Hispanics in Congress has grown substantially in recent decades—but not enough to give Hispanics representation equal to their proportion of the population. People of Hispanic ancestry with roots in Mexico, Puerto Rico, Cuba, and other Latin American nations constituted an estimated 14 percent of the population in 2007, up from 12.5 percent in the 2000 census, but made up only 5 percent of the congressional membership. A variety of explanations were given for this, from the group's ethnic and economic diversity to low voter turnout caused by poverty and the language barrier.

The recent growth of Hispanic representation was in large part the result of judicial interpretations of the Voting Rights Act requiring that minorities be given maximum opportunity to elect members of their own group to Congress. After the 1990 census, congressional district maps in states with significant Hispanic populations were redrawn with the aim of sending more Hispanics to Congress. (See REAPPORTIONMENT AND REDISTRICTING.)

Including new members of the 110th Congress in 2007, forty-eight Hispanics had served in Congress: three who served only as senators, and forty-five in the House including forty-two who served only in that chamber. Three Hispanics

HISPANIC MEMBERS OF CONGRESS, 1877–2007

As of January 2008, forty-eight Hispanics had served in Congress. Of those members, forty-two served in the House only, three in the Senate only, and three—Dennis Chavez, Joseph M. Montoya, and Robert Menendez—in both chambers. Following is a list of the Hispanic members, their political affiliations and states, and the years in which they served. Not included are Hispanics who served as territorial delegates, resident commissioners of Puerto Rico, or delegates of Guam or the Virgin Islands.

Senate

Octaviano Larrazolo	1928–1929
Dennis Chavez, D N.M.	1935–1962
Joseph M. Montoya, D-N.M.	1964–1977
Mel Martinez, R-Fla.	2005–
Ken Salazar, D-Colo.	2005–
Robert Menendez, D-N.J.	2006–

House

Romualdo Pacheco, R-Calif.	1877–1878; 1879–1883
Ladislas Lazaro, D-La.	1913–1927
Benigno Cardenas Hernandez, R-N.M.	1915–1917; 1919–1921
Nestor Montoya, R-N.M.	1921–1923
Dennis Chavez, D-N.M.	1931–1935
Joachim Octave Fernandez, D-La.	1931–1941
Antonio Manuel Fernandez, D-N.M.	1943–1956
Joseph M. Montoya, D-N.M.	1957–1964
Henry B. Gonzalez, D-Texas	1961–1999
Edward R. Roybal, D-Calif.	1963–1993
E. "Kika" de la Garza II, D-Texas	1965–1997
Manuel Lujan Jr., R-N.M.	1969–1989
Herman Badillo, D-N.Y.	1971–1977
Robert Garcia, D-N.Y.	1978–1990
Anthony Lee Coelho, D-Calif.	1979–1989
Matthew G. Martinez, D-Calif.	1982–2001
Solomon P. Ortiz, D-Texas	1983–
William B. Richardson, D-N.M.	1983–1997
Esteban E. Torres, D-Calif.	1983–1999
Albert G. Bustamante, D-Texas	1985–1993
Ileana Ros-Lehtinen, R-Fla.	1989–
José E. Serrano, D-N.Y.	1990–
Ed Pastor, D-Ariz.	1991–
Xavier Becerra, D-Calif.	1993–

(continues)

HISPANIC MEMBERS OF CONGRESS, 1877–2007 (CONTINUED)

Henry Bonilla, R-Texas	1993–2007
Lincoln Diaz-Balart, R-Fla.	1993–
Luis V. Gutierrez, D-Ill.	1993–
Robert Menendez, D-N.J.	1993–2006
Lucille Roybal-Allard, D-Calif.	1993–
Frank Tejeda, D-Texas	1993–1997
Nydia M. Velázquez, D-N.Y.	1993–
Rubén Hinojosa, D-Texas	1997–
Silvestre Reyes, D-Texas	1997–
Ciro D. Rodriguez, D-Texas	1997–2005; 2007–
Loretta Sanchez, D-Calif.	1997–
Charlie Gonzalez, D-Texas	1999–
Grace Napolitano, D-Calif.	1999–
Joe Baca, D-Calif.	1999–
Hilda L. Solis, D-Calif.	2001–
Mario Diaz-Balart, D-Fla.	2003–
Rául M. Grijalva, D-Ariz.	2003–
Linda T. Sanchez, D-Calif.	2003–
John Salazar, D-Colo.	2005–
Henry Roberto Cuellar, D-Texas	2005–
Albio Sires, D-N.J.	2007–

SOURCE: *Biographical Directory of the American Congress, 1774–1996* (Alexandria, Va.: CQ Staff Directories, 1997); Congressional Hispanic Caucus; *CQ Weekly,* selected issues.

served in both houses. Several other Hispanics represented territories as non-voting delegates or resident commissioners. Until 2005 no Hispanic candidate had been elected to the Senate since 1970, when Joseph Montoya of New Mexico won his second and last term. In the 2004 election Republican Mel Martinez, a Florida Republican, and Ken Salazar, a Colorado Democrat, won their contests. In 2006 Robert Menendez, a New Jersey Democrat, was appointed to a vacant seat and won a full six-year term that fall. Earlier, Dennis Chavez, also a Democrat from New Mexico, served in the Senate from 1935 to 1962, and Octaviano Larrazolo, a New Mexico Republican, served from 1928 to 1929. (*See Hispanic Members of Congress, table, p. 259.*)

Salazar's brother, John Salazar (D-Colo.), also began serving in the House in 2005, making the brothers one of three pairs serving in Congress. A second Hispanic pair of brothers were Lincoln Diaz-Balart (R-Fla.) and Mario Diaz-Balart (R-Fla.). Two other Hispanic siblings, Linda Sanchez (D-Calif.) and Loretta Sanchez (D-Calif.) made history in 2003 when they became the first sisters ever to serve in Congress.

In the House, most of the Hispanic members come from Texas, Florida, and California.

The first Hispanic to serve in Congress was Romualdo Pacheco, a California Republican, who entered the House in 1877. After he retired in 1883, there was no Hispanic representation in Congress until Ladislas Lazaro, a Louisiana Democrat, entered the House in 1913.

Holds

A "hold" is a request by a senator to the party leadership to delay action on a matter. The intent may be to delay indefinitely or postpone action until some concern is addressed. Senators sometimes hold one bill hostage as leverage in order to force action on another measure or nomination. The leadership usually respects holds; to do otherwise would likely be self-defeating since the senator could easily block any UNANIMOUS CONSENT request to consider the measure or nomination. A hold carries an implicit threat that a FILIBUSTER will begin if the hold is not honored.

Most holds are requested simply so that the senator will be told when the bill is likely to come up. But some senators use them extensively as bargaining tools. The potency of holds increases dramatically at the end of a session, when delays can prove devastating. In the past, senators were able to place holds anonymously. In 1999 Senate leaders announced that a senator placing a hold on a matter had to identify himself or herself to the bill sponsor and the committee with jurisdiction over it within certain time limits. However, the anonymous use of holds soon resumed. Senators found a loophole in 2000, dropping their own holds before it was time to identify themselves while a like-minded colleague imposed a new hold for the next day. The hold would then be traded back and forth indefinitely.

Senators such as Ron Wyden, D-Ore., attempted in 2001 to stop such trading with a proposed rule change that would give senators a total of twenty-four hours per hold and ban multiple holds. However, that attempt failed. In January 2007 the Senate passed legislation on ethics and lobbying that required a senator who wanted to block a bill to announce his or her objection in writing in the *Congressional Record* within three days of placing the hold.

Homeland Security and Governmental Affairs Committee, Senate

The Senate Homeland Security and Governmental Affairs Committee has a vast jurisdictional canvas on which to paint. Even before the terrorist attacks in 2001, when it was known as the Government Operations Committee alone, it was charged with overseeing how the federal government operates. The panel is able to probe almost every cranny of the bureaucracy. Although it is rarely responsible for major legislation, the committee's oversight role is so broad that aggressive senators can use a seat on the committee to pursue almost any matter that interests them, from telling the Defense Department it is a poor shopper to investigating the bankruptcy of energy giant Enron Corp.

Its jurisdiction became even broader after the attacks and the creation of the sprawling Department of Homeland Security in 2004. By 2007, at the start of the 110th Congress, a significant part of its work was focused on homeland security alone.

With the broadened responsibility, the committee does not have an exact parallel to House panels. In that chamber there is a Homeland Security Committee and an Oversight and Government Reform Committee.

The Homeland Security and Governmental Affairs Committee looks at the federal government from a different perspective than most other committees. Concerns about personnel management or maintenance of buildings can make much of its agenda appear mundane. But the committee at times has focused on broader trends, such as the government's future role in health care, or launches headline-grabbing investigations, such as into campaign funds in the 1996 election.

The committee was established in 1842. It was known as the Committee on Expenditures in Executive Departments until 1952, when it was renamed Government Operations. In 1979 the title was changed to Governmental Affairs. Homeland Security was added in 2005.

The committee typically has operated without much publicity—except for its Permanent Investigations Subcommittee. Formally created in 1948, the subcommittee grew out of a special committee that then-senator Harry S TRUMAN convinced the Senate to set up in 1941. The Special Committee to Investigate the National Defense Program, known as the Truman committee, concentrated on uncovering fraud and inefficiency as defense programs multiplied during World War II. The publicity the Missouri Democrat gained on the committee helped him win his party's vice-presidential nomination in 1944. When the Senate in 1948 abolished all special committees, Vermont Republican George Aiken made the Truman committee part of his Committee on Expenditures in Executive Departments, giving it a broader mandate to investigate the management of all government agencies.

More on this topic:

Homeland Security Committee, House, p. 263

Oversight and Government Reform Committee, House, p. 403

Oversight Power, p. 404

Sen. Joseph I. Lieberman, I-Conn., returned to chair the Senate Homeland Security and Governmental Affairs Committee in 2007, replacing Susan Collins, R-Maine. The two have worked closely during their years on the committee.
Source: CQ Photo/Scott J. Ferrell

In the 1950s the subcommittee was the setting for the anticommunist INVESTIGATIONS of Joseph R. MCCARTHY. The Wisconsin Republican was chair of both the subcommittee and full committee from 1953 to 1955.

From 1949 until 1972, except during McCarthy's tenure, the full committee was chaired by Democrat John L. McClellan of Arkansas. McClellan, who was also chair of the investigations subcommittee, initiated highly publicized investigations of organized crime that focused on, among others, the Teamsters Union and its head, Jimmy Hoffa. The panel also probed white-collar crime, including the case of Texan Billy Sol Estes and his paper empire of fertilizer and federal cotton allotments. The subcommittee's chief counsel at that time was Robert F. Kennedy, brother of future president John F. KENNEDY. McClellan left the committee in 1972 to become chair of Appropriations.

Other chairs of the Governmental Affairs Committee have included Connecticut Democrat Abraham A. Ribicoff (1975–1981); Delaware Republican William V. Roth Jr. (1981–1987; 1995–1996); and Ohio Democrat John Glenn (1987–1995).

Republican Fred Thompson of Tennessee became chair in 1997. Under Thompson, the committee delved into the campaign finance irregularities of President Bill Clinton's 1996 reelection campaign. Despite an extensive effort, the committee did not find compelling evidence against the administration and the probe quietly faded.

When Democrat Joseph I. Lieberman of Connecticut won the gavel in June 2001, the focus of the panel shifted to investigations of the regulatory policies of the administration of George W. Bush. Lieberman asked Vice President Richard CHENEY to provide information on the lobbyists with whom White House officials met as they wrote President Bush's 2001 energy proposal. Similarly, Lieberman sought to gather information from other cabinet officers about meetings held with industry lobbyists who had an interest in pending regulatory issues. Lieberman showed a particular interest in the way that an Environmental Protection Agency regulation affecting clean air policy, known as "new source review," was written. However, despite his efforts, Lieberman received little enlightening information from the White House.

Republican Susan Collins of Maine became just the third woman in history to wield the gavel of a major Senate committee when she took over the panel in 2003. She developed a close working relationship with Lieberman in the role of ranking Democrat. This close cooperation continued in the 110th Congress, starting in 2007, when the roles were again reversed with Lieberman as chair. (Lieberman became an Independent in 2006 but agreed to continue to caucus with the Democrats.) He took a more aggressive stance than Collins did in overseeing the Bush administration.

Homeland Security Committee, House

Faced with the task of having to oversee the start up of a cabinet-level Department of Homeland Security and vet dozens of homeland security bills, House leaders at the start of the 108th Congress in 2003 established a Select Committee on Homeland Security.

The new panel drew some of the biggest names on Capitol Hill to its membership. Christopher Cox, a conservative Republican from southern California and chair of the House Republican Policy Committee, was chosen to chair the select committee and given two years to convert the panel into a permanent Homeland Security Committee whose jurisdiction would be taken directly from other standing committees. The panel became a standing committee in 2005.

The select committee had fifty members—twenty-seven Republicans and twenty-three Democrats—and consisted mostly of chairs or ranking members of some of the panels that had to surrender jurisdiction in order for the homeland panel to work. Many came with their own agendas and competitive egos. Some had resisted establishment of a new standing committee to deal with domestic security concerns. With the nation on edge over the threat of terrorism, Cox said his top priorities would be the prevention of terrorism and "aggressive oversight" of the new department, an amalgam of twenty-two existing federal agencies that each had a hand in counterterrorism.

The House's Homeland Security Committee is charged with the prevention of terrorism and the oversight of the new Homeland Security Department, but the committee competes with other panels in the House for jurisdiction over domestic security issues, such as port security. Here, the Coast Guard cutter Sailfish *conducts a homeland security patrol through New York Harbor on June 19, 2007.*
Source: U.S. Coast Guard photo/Petty Officer 3rd Class Annie R. Berlin

Cox and Republican leaders said they envisioned the panel playing a coordinating role on homeland security and being a "one-stop shop" for the new department, in order to help avoid jurisdictional conflict with other panels. Programmatic details of the former Immigration and Naturalization Service, for instance, were to be left to the House Judiciary Committee, but broader security issues were to be addressed by the Homeland Security panel. Cox said he even planned to invite other committees for joint hearings on topics where jurisdiction and expertise could be shared.

By the start of the 110th Congress in 2007 the jurisdictional tensions of the early days of the panel had lessened but not disappeared. The new chair was Bennie Thompson, a Mississippi Democrat, who placed a larger emphasis on oversight of the counterterrorism strategy of the George W. Bush administration. Homeland Security Secretary Michael Chertoff testified before the committee just twice in 2006. Thompson said that was insufficient. "He cannot be a stranger before the" committee, Thompson declared.

Thompson's agenda was expended to place new emphasis on rail and mass transit security, which Democrats said were vulnerable following the March 2004 bombings of commuter trains in Madrid, Spain. But the turf battles continued. In 2006 Thompson's panel, then headed by Republican Peter T. King of New York, battled with the Transportation and Infrastructure Committee for jurisdiction over port security and the Federal Emergency Management Agency. The same issues emerged early in 2007 between the two panels.

House Administration Committee

Internal operations of the House are handled by the House Administration Committee. Details of committee budgets and decisions about allocating space that affect members' quality of life give the panel significant influence. The chair in particular has considerable power to dole out or withhold favors for colleagues, for example granting a request for some extra office space or denying a plea for some new furniture. These housekeeping matters, not the politics of leadership, are the committee's business. For that reason the panel's chair is often referred to as the "mayor" of the House.

Although committee chairs are usually supreme in their own territory, the House Administration Committee holds a different view. To committee members, chairs are an annual parade of supplicants, asking for money to run their committees. Individual members, too, must deal with the committee, depending on it for office space and allowances, and approval for various expenditures.

Most spending requests are handled routinely. But the committee has the potential to be both controversial and powerful. Of little consequence outside the House, the committee looms large in the world of Capitol Hill. Ohio Democrat Wayne L. Hays, who chaired the committee from 1971 to 1976, used his authority over money and office space to reward friends and punish enemies. Even petty matters, such as orders for new telephones, were reviewed to see whether the request had come from an ally, or someone who had irritated the prickly chair. Hays's empire collapsed after revelations that he had kept a mistress, Elizabeth Ray, on the committee payroll; he resigned from the House in 1976.

Although never so manipulative as Hays, New Jersey Democrat Frank Thompson Jr. also used his authority as chair against those who crossed him. Thompson was indicted as part of the Abscam scandal, which became a major factor in his 1980 election defeat.

Frank Annunzio, an Illinois Democrat, chaired the committee from 1985 to 1991. He also gained a reputation for playing favorites among members. Annunzio was ousted in 1991 partly due to complaints about his handling of members' requests. Charlie Rose, a Democrat from North Carolina, became chair next, just as the House was rocked with allegations of wrongdoing at the House bank and post office. Drug dealing and embezzlement at the House post office led to a committee investigation, which was critical of how the bank was run and members' use of post office employees. (See SCANDALS, CONGRESSIONAL.)

In 1995 Republican Bill Thomas of California took over as chair. The new Republican majority renamed the committee House Oversight, only to change it back to House Administration in 1999. As chair, Thomas oversaw the privatization of several House services and slashed committee staffing by a third.

Republican Bob Ney of Ohio assumed control of the committee as it oversaw the construction of a CAPITOL VISITOR CENTER. Ney was forced to address new concerns about security after the terrorist attacks of September 11, 2001, and the ANTHRAX ATTACK on Capitol Hill a month later. He updated emergency procedures and oversaw the purchase of emergency equipment that would assist personnel in case of a crisis. His career, however, ended in disaster. Ney was caught in an influence-peddling case involving lobbyist Jack Abramoff. In September 2006 he admitted that he had been corrupted by golf trips, tickets, meals, and campaign donations from Abramoff and agreed to plead guilty to a pair of felonies: making false statements to federal officials and conspiracy to commit fraud. Ney admitted inserting favorable statements into the *Congressional Record* that backed Abramoff's business ventures. Ney also admitted trying to add language to the 2002 voting overhaul law that would allow a liquor distiller—an Abramoff client—based in a former Soviet republic to label its liquor as "Made in Russia." He formally entered his plea in October, after spending time in an alcohol treatment program, and he resigned from the House in November 2006. In January 2007 he was sentenced to thirty months in federal prison. He also was fined $6,000 and ordered to perform 200 hours of community service after prison.

At the start of the 110th Congress in 2007 the committee was chaired by Juanita Millender-McDonald, D-Calif. However, she died from cancer on April 22. She was replaced by Robert A. Brady, D-Pa., a month later.

The committee had a busy agenda when Democrats took over in 2007. There were two contested House elections in Florida, proposals to overhaul the federal election system before the 2008 presidential races, a review of the congressional page program, and oversight of the Capitol Visitor Center, which was significantly behind schedule and over original costs plans.

The Senate counterpart to the House Administration Committee is its Committee on Rules and Administration. The Senate committee also handles legislative matters, such as questions of committee jurisdiction or floor procedure; in the House, those matters are in the purview of the Rules Committee.

Rep. Robert A. Brady, D-Pa., became chair of the House Administration Committee upon the death of Rep. Juanita Millender-McDonald, D-Calif., in April 2007.
Source: CQ Photo/Scott J. Ferrell

House Chief Administrative Officer

The House of Representatives, home to more than 440 legislators, including five delegates, and thousands of staff members, has a variety of support services and amenities available. In 1992 revelations in the news media about mismanagement and abuses of some of these amenities—notably the House bank and post office—prompted House leaders to create a new position: a professional administrator to manage their institution in an up-to-date, nonpartisan style.

The new director of nonlegislative and financial services was given responsibility for member and staff payrolls, the computer system, internal mail, office furnishings and supplies, restaurants, telecommunications, barber and beauty shops, child-care center, photography office, tour guides, and nonlegislative functions of the House printing services, recording studio, and records office.

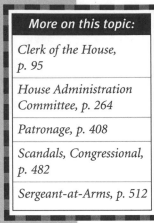
The position of House postmaster was abolished along with the controversial House post office. (The House bank had been closed earlier.) The responsibilities of the three other officers in charge of internal House business were greatly changed—the responsibilities of the Clerk of the House and the sergeant-at-arms were scaled back, and the doorkeeper position was eliminated entirely. A new, bipartisan subcommittee of the House Administration Committee was set up to oversee the position of House administrator, as it was then known.

The first person selected to fill the new position was Leonard P. Wishart III, a retired army lieutenant general who had run two large Kansas military bases. It was hoped that Wishart's administrative experience, combined with his status as a nonpartisan outsider, would bring a new professionalism to the House's internal operations and help improve its tarnished image.

Traditionally, the party in control of the House has handed out most of the institution's internal jobs as rewards for political loyalty, a practice known as patronage. The House specified that its new administrator was to "hire and fire his or her staff on the basis of competency and qualifications, not patronage." When Wishart assumed the position in the fall of 1992, however, less than half of the 600 or so patronage jobs in the House had been transferred to his control. The law that created the new position left it up to the House Administration Committee to decide if the new administrator should take on additional responsibilities—an expansion that would further reduce the number of patronage slots left in the House.

Wishart had several run-ins with House Administration Committee chair Charlie Rose, a North Carolina Democrat. The legislation creating Wishart's job included a list of tasks that he was to be in charge of, but Rose said that the law gave his panel the power to change the list and was not binding on the current Congress. Wishart abruptly quit in 1994.

When Republicans gained control of the House in 1995, they eliminated the post of director and created a new office called chief administrative officer (CAO) of the House, to be nominated by the Speaker and elected by the full House. The new position was placed directly under the Speaker, rather than the House Administration Committee; the change meant the person could be removed by the Speaker. The responsibilities of the post were more or less the same as when the administrative position was first created in 1992. The officers staff is largely administrative and technical and is organized into five units (in addition to the CAO's office: finance including financial management and processing expenses; information resources to coordinate technology and communications products and services; human resources including administering payrolls, support services such as furnishing offices and providing equipment; and procurement and purchasing.

These groups have responsibility for such varied tasks as carrying for an estimated 125,000 pieces of furniture, 7,000 BlackBerrys, 15,000 laptops, and 5,800 parking spaces.

When Democrats took control of the House in 2007 they hired Dan Beard for the position, which paid $160,000 annually. Beard had earlier worked in the office of Rep. George Miller, D-Calif., but had recently retired from a national consulting firm. Miller was a close associate of the new Speaker, Nancy Pelosi of California. Beard told a reporter that among his early marching orders was improving the energy efficiency of the House. Pelosi also told him a wait-list for a House day-care center needed to be reduced.

House Manual

The rulebook of the House of Representatives bears a formidable title: *Constitution, Jefferson's Manual, and Rules of the House of Representatives.* It is known informally simply as the House

Manual. The House Manual is prepared for each two-year term of Congress by the PARLIAMEN-TARIAN of the House. In addition to the written rules of the chamber, the document contains the text of the Constitution, portions of *JEFFERSON'S MANUAL*, and the principal rulings and precedents of the House. It also includes separate sections with provision of some laws that apply to the House and a description of various support services available to members.

House of Representatives

The 435 members of the House of Representatives share responsibility with the Senate for writing the nation's laws and overseeing operation of the federal government.

Representatives are elected every two years to represent districts of more than half a million people. Today they work full time at a job that once took only a few weeks a year. Representatives must attend committee hearings, draft legislation, keep up with floor debate, consider or offer amendments, vote on bills, and respond to constituents' problems. At the same time they must campaign, because a new election is always less than two years away.

This drawing captures a nineteenth-century House session packed with visitors.
Source: Library of Congress

The rapid rhythm of House procedures and the hubbub caused by the sheer number of representatives contrast sharply with the slower pace and quieter atmosphere of the Senate. The Senate, with one hundred members, is less than one-fourth the size of the House and prefers to operate informally. Senators' six-year terms allow them time between campaigns, a luxury House members do not enjoy.

Maintaining high visibility in their districts and raising campaign funds are part of the routine for most representatives. Most representatives travel home at least every other weekend; travel expenses are usually covered by official allowances. Meanwhile, newsletters are mailed out, letters answered, and individual problems with the federal bureaucracy handled, usually by the representatives' staffs in Washington and in the home district. Political action committees and individuals are asked to contribute campaign funds; the solicitation is often accompanied by an invitation to a cocktail party or a speech by the representative. In 2000 the average winning House candidate spent $847,000 on his or her campaign.

The House is a complex institution, having at the beginning of the 110th Congress in 2007 more than 200 committees: twenty standing (so called because they are part of the formal rules of the chamber) and two select panels. (Senate committees total twenty standing, two select, and one special.) Committee size ranged from seventy-five members to just nine. The two chambers in total had more than 175 subcommittees with some still being formed early in the year. With the array of panels decision making is broadly spread.

The leadership controls the key gateways to floor action, but participation is open and usually democratic in the first stages of the legislative process when members question witnesses at hearings or debate amendments during bill-drafting sessions. The House has been most effective under strong leaders, who face the difficult task of satisfying a large and diverse body.

More than two centuries of evolution have given the House thick volumes of rules and procedures, but the institution is far from rigid. Its decisions can turn in a matter of minutes on what Speaker Sam RAYBURN, a Texas Democrat, called "rolling waves of sentiment." The basic principle in the House is that all points of view should be heard, but that minorities should not be able to block action. Filibusters, which are common in the Senate, are not allowed in the House. The idea of delaying a vote to accommodate a single member, as the Senate sometimes does, is almost unheard of. "Senate rules are tilted toward not doing things," said Speaker Jim WRIGHT, also a Texas Democrat, in 1987. "House rules, if you know how to use them, are tilted toward allowing the majority to get its will done."

> **"Senate rules are tilted toward not doing things. House rules, if you know how to use them, are tilted toward allowing the majority to get its will done."**
>
> **—House Speaker Jim Wright,** D-Texas

Senators who have been representatives are often frustrated with the slow pace of the Senate and long for the relative orderliness of the House. "Simply to come here and work in a museum is not my idea of a modern legislative process," said Democratic senator Tom A. DASCHLE of South Dakota, who had served four terms in the House before moving to the Senate where he would hold the posts of majority leader and minority leader until his election defeat in 2004.

Despite its tight procedures, though, the House often leaves major questions unresolved for years as opposing sides scramble for votes and compromises are drafted. The lack of national consensus on an issue is sure to be reflected in the House. The most difficult choices often are put off, and the last month of a session is a blinding whirl of legislative activity and night meetings. The habit is an old one. Davy Crockett, a legendary frontiersman who served three House terms (1827–1831, 1833–1835), said, "We generally lounge or squabble the greater part of the session, and crowd into a few days of the last term three or four times the business done during as many preceding months." Barber B. Conable Jr., a New York Republican who served in the House from 1965 to 1985, was untroubled by disorderliness. He enjoyed saying that "Congress is working the way it is supposed to work, which is not very well."

When the pace of voting is particularly frenetic at the end of a session, the House is filled with legislators who mill about, gathering in groups on the floor to talk or streaming in and out of the chamber into the cloakrooms or nearby hallways. When a vote is close, representatives gather in the well of the chamber, near the rostrum, and watch the electronic voting chart, which displays how each member voted. Like spectators at a horse race, they wait expectantly for any vote switches and react with a collective gasp to any surprises. The Senate, which lacks a tally board, has no such sport.

Although many senators arrive on Capitol Hill as public figures, having served previously as representatives or governors, members of the House face the prospect of anonymity among more than 400 colleagues. New representatives, called freshmen, jockey for spots on favored committees and try to develop expertise on a subject to avoid obscurity and gain credibility in debate. Their ability to act independently is facilitated by their staff. Staff help was once reserved for senior members who ran committees, but reforms in the 1970s gave additional staff even to the most junior members. (See REFORM, CONGRESSIONAL.)

Despite the House's reputation as an open, democratic institution, House members have seen their ability to influence policy diminish over the years. Budget constraints dominated the agenda in the 1990s, and members not on the fiscal committees—Appropriations and Ways and Means—complained that they were left out of major decisions. There was almost no opportunity to initiate new programs. Floor amendments had once offered a way for individuals to influence the committee-driven system of the House. Even this opportunity had been limited beginning in the 1980s, as the Democratic leadership convinced the Rules Committee to restrict floor action.

The ascendancy of the Republican Party at the beginning of the 104th Congress (1995–1997) added a new twist. Both chambers were populated by a new cadre of lawmakers more intensely antigovernment than any other in contemporary times. The large group of conservative freshmen, especially in the House, displayed remarkable ideological cohesion and became the most influential newcomers since fallout from the Watergate scandal swept reformist Democrats into Congress in 1975. The House GOP's "Contract with America"—their election platform—became the focal point of their legislative agenda. Moreover, the House adopted new rules challenging some of its most encrusted traditions.

Newt GINGRICH of Georgia used his position to consolidate power like no Speaker since Joseph G. CANNON of Illinois in the early part of the twentieth century. Gingrich stepped in to overrule committee chairs whenever an issue was important to him or to the Republican Conference. In many cases, the chairs submerged their policy goals to the collective agenda as defined by Gingrich. Though Gingrich's involvement worked well for the Republicans as a whole, it raised questions about the ability of individual chairs to exercise the policy expertise found only at the committee and subcommittee level. It also made maintaining discipline difficult for the chairs. Furthermore, Democrats complained bitterly about legislation being rushed to passage, without careful congressional consideration.

However, the ambitions of the House were often thwarted by the Senate and the White House during this time. President Bill Clinton successfully used the bully pulpit to curb Republicans' more aggressive legislative goals. As a result, the first year of the Republican revolution closed with institutional Washington much the way the Republican majority found it: No federal departments

> *"We generally lounge or squabble the greater part of the session, and crowd into a few days of the last term three or four times the business done during as many preceding months."*
>
> **—Rep. Davy Crockett,** legendary frontiersman

were eliminated and no long-standing social policies were reshaped. Their chief demand—that Clinton agree to balance the budget in seven years on their terms—ended in humiliating defeat. Hoping to force Clinton's hand, they twice allowed much of the federal government to shut down. But the public blamed the Republicans for the mess, their message was lost in the din, Clinton refused to concede, and Senate Republicans sought to distance themselves from the House activists.

> **"Congress is working the way it is supposed to work, which is not very well."**
>
> —*Rep. Barber B. Conable Jr.*

The confrontational tactics of 1995 gave way to bipartisanship in 1996. Although Republicans went from revolutionaries to realists, they still managed to clear several major elements from their contract, including a bill making Congress live under the same laws as industry, a line-item veto empowering the president to kill specific spending items in appropriations bills (later declared unconstitutional), a modest increase in defense spending, and conservative changes in welfare.

But conservatives failed to win enough votes to clear constitutional amendments to impose term limits on members and to require a balanced budget. In 1997 Congress and Clinton agreed on a five-year balanced-budget plan. A year later, even as Republicans were preparing to impeach him, Clinton scored a significant win in the annual appropriations debate by forcing Republicans to accept higher spending for his priorities than they favored. Clinton also was able to force Republicans in Congress to at least consider issues that were not GOP priorities, such as legislation to provide managed care patients more leverage over their insurers; gun control bills; and plans to increase the minimum wage.

Gingrich's grip on the legislative process loosened considerably after he ran into ethics problems and his most ardent followers became disgruntled with his willingness to compromise. A poor showing by Republicans in the 1998 elections compelled Gingrich to step aside as Speaker and soon after to resign from Congress. The House selected Republican J. Dennis HASTERT of Illinois to be Speaker of the House at the start of the 106th Congress (1999–2001). He continued as Speaker until the Democrats regained the majority in the 2006 elections.

Hastert was a proponent of allowing the majority of the House to "work its will" on issues by allowing committees to produce bills without excessive instructions from GOP leaders. However, on high-profile issues—or, later in his tenure, on issues that were important to Republican president George W. Bush—Hastert was renowned for keeping his members publicly unified. He was careful to bring to the floor only bills he knew were favored by a majority of the GOP caucus—the "majority of the

Shown here is the rostrum of the chamber of the U.S. House of Representatives. On the left, the mace, the symbol of legislative authority, rests on its pedestal.
Source: Architect of the Capitol

The House chamber is the setting for the president's annual State of the Union address to a joint session of Congress. Here, in addition to members of Congress, administration officials, justices of the Supreme Court, and other dignitaries listen to President Ronald Reagan's speech.
Source: CQ Photo

majority," as he called it. In the 107th Congress (2001–2003), when Hastert's party maintained the narrowest margin of control over the House since 1954, he typically relied on Majority Whip Tom DeLay of Texas, who was often effective in persuading reluctant members to support the leadership's position, to deliver the votes. DeLay's influence expanded hugely in the following years until an indictment in Texas for alleged campaign finance violations forced him to relinquish the post in 2005 and resign from Congress the following year.

The twelve years of Republican control of the House, from 1995 to 2007, had two distinct parts, which reflected the different political roles the chamber could play in the modern Congress. From 1995 to 2001, the White House was occupied by a Democrat, Bill Clinton, widely acknowledged even by his opponents as a brilliant and canny politician. In those years the atmosphere was filled with confrontation, as in the budget disagreement and even more in the effort of a core of conservatives to impeach Clinton and remove him from office, an effort that did not succeed.

But in 2001 Republican Bush moved into the White House, giving the nation a unified federal government. In this situation, the House became a largely obedient servant of the presidency. This role became even more pronounced after the September 11, 2001, terrorist attacks that led to new security law, a war in Afghanistan where many terrorists were believed to be hiding, and in 2003 a war of choice when Bush ordered an invasion of Iraq. This war was presented as necessary to topple Iraq's dictator, Saddam Hussein, who was believed to have, or trying to get, weapons of mass destruction. In time that belief was proven incorrect, and the war continued into 2008 and had become an intractable controversy. Increasingly Democrats came to criticize the Bush administration over the war as well as many domestic issues, but the House Republican majority stayed loyal to the White House.

Pelosi: First Female Speaker

In the 2006 elections, Democrats retook control of the House, propelled in large measure by the plummeting popularity of Bush and rising national opposition to the long war in Iraq. The election was also notable for a historical first: the Democratic House leader, Nancy Pelosi of California, previously the minority leader, became Speaker when the new Congress organized. She thus became the highest-ranking woman ever elected in the federal government. (See PELOSI, NANCY).

Pelosi led a rejuvenated Democratic majority aggressively in the opening months of the 110th Congress, quickly passing an agenda of high-profile Democratic objectives. But only one—a minimum wage increase—had become law by midyear because all the legislation also had to go through the Senate where Democrats had a single-vote majority. Nevertheless, by midyear Pelosi was increasingly pictured as in the Gingrich mold by asserting strong centralized control of the party's operations and fortunes. This included naming committee chairs of her choosing, telling some powerful chairs that their parochial legislative interests had to be secondary to wider interests of the party and the Democratic Caucus, and guiding the legislative agenda carefully to prevent ambushes from the well-organized Republican minority.

Origins and Development

The structure of the House was a victory for the more democratic-minded framers of the Constitution. The House "was to be the grand depository of the democratic principles of the government," said George Mason of Virginia. He and his colleagues prevailed over others who wanted state legislatures to elect the House, as they did the Senate until 1913. "The people immediately should have as little to do" with electing the government as possible, argued Roger Sherman of Connecticut, because they lack information "and are constantly liable to be misled."

Although the House and Senate have equal standing on most matters, the Constitution gave each chamber certain duties and responsibilities. The House has three special powers: to originate all revenue bills, to recommend removal of federal officials through the impeachment process, and to elect a president when the electors have failed to do so.

Originally the House was a body of just sixty-five legislators, compared with twenty-six in the Senate. In the early years of the nation, the House was seen as more desirable than the Senate. Gradually, however, legislators such as Henry CLAY, John C. CALHOUN, and Daniel WEBSTER shifted to the Senate, cutting what became a well-worn path. The larger, more diverse House could not be easily swayed by an impassioned, eloquent speech. Rules, not orators, had already assumed control.

As early as 1841 the House limited debate, giving each representative an hour to speak on a bill. The rule prevails today, and the Rules Committee often curtails members' time to speak even further. That is in contrast to the Senate, where a senator's right to speak for as long as he or she wants is curbed only rarely.

The House almost from the start delegated the drafting of bills to committees. At first legislative debate took place on the House floor, and then a select committee was set up to write a specific bill based on floor discussions. The committee would return to the full House with its proposed language for a final vote. Often more than a hundred different select committees would be created in a session.

More on this topic:

Committee System, p. 111

Electing the President, p. 176

Impeachment Power, p. 280

Purse, Power of, p. 446

Rules Committee, House, p. 478

Seniority System, p. 505

Speaker of the House, p. 516

Over time the House established standing committees that had jurisdiction over particular subjects. Among the earliest were the Ways and Means Committee and the Commerce and Manufactures Committee (known today as Energy and Commerce). What is now standard House practice began in this period: committee members developed expertise in particular areas and thus gained credibility to back their positions on the House floor. The Rules Committee, created in 1789 and made a standing committee in 1880, provided further structure to the legislative process. It was responsible for deciding which legislation should reach the floor and what rules should cover floor debate. The Rules Committee today works as an agent of the leadership of the majority party, although it operated independently in the 1940s and 1950s and held up action on an array of liberal programs.

Shifting Power Centers

The center of power in the House has shifted several times during the past two centuries. Strong individuals, such as Henry Clay, Thomas Brackett REED, Joseph G. Cannon, Sam RAYBURN, and Newt GINGRICH, used their terms as House Speaker to consolidate power. At other times the House has been dominated by committee chairs, party caucuses, its Rules Committee, or voting blocs of members. For much of the twentieth century the Democratic Party was in the majority, though it was not always able to control House action.

The Speaker was the only House officer mentioned in the Constitution, which left undefined the rest of the organizational structure of the House. Only the Speaker is chosen by a formal House vote, though the Speaker is nominated and effectively chosen by the majority party. Each party votes in caucus to elect the majority and minority floor leaders. (See CAUCUSES, PARTY.) The whips, who rank next and are responsible for maintaining party loyalty, are also elected. These officials rank just below the Speaker in the House hierarchy.

The Speaker is usually chosen from among the most senior and loyal party members; since 1925 every Speaker except Hastert has first served as majority leader, minority leader, or minority whip. The post of majority leader was formally created in 1899. Before that time the chair of the Ways and Means Committee had been the floor manager and had been considered the deputy leader.

Forging a unified position is a difficult task with 435 members and the array of committees and subcommittees that are the first level of decision making in the House. Each panel competes to have its opinion heard—and its solution selected by the House. Most members serve on as many as four subcommittees; however, each can chair only one subcommittee.

Legislators must ultimately answer to the voters in their districts. Although Democrats and Republicans have tried to strengthen party ties by providing campaign funds and other support, ideological differences within each party—and the need to "keep the voters back home happy"— make it difficult to keep the party voting together, particularly on controversial questions.

The House membership, though accustomed to rules, has occasionally revolted when the power structure became too rigid and failed to respond to changing demands. Cannon's autocracy, for example, gave rise to a coalition of Republicans and Democrats who in 1910 reduced the Speaker's powers. Rules changes in the 1970s were prompted by a seniority system that had grown more rigid because of the safe seats of conservative southern Democrats. Control of the House rested in the hands of a few elderly men whose ideas about civil rights, conduct of the war in Vietnam, and other major questions were at odds with the views of a growing number of House Democrats.

By the mid-1970s a new generation of legislators, both Democrats and Republicans, had rewritten the rules to make the leadership more accountable to the Democratic Caucus and Republican Conference, the party organizations. The new members of the House, once kept meekly disciplined, suddenly had a voice in picking the leaders.

Some retrenchment was evident after the Republicans became the majority party as a result of the 1994 elections. Republican Speaker Gingrich, who quickly maximized both the formal and informal powers at his disposal, effectively named the committee chairs and imposed term limits on them. Chairs could no longer build power bases from their committees.

Hastert modified Gingrich's centralized approach. Although he preferred to let committee chairs write the legislative details of bills that required strong technical expertise, Hastert did not hesitate to insist that the caucus endorse President Bush's legislative priorities. Hastert's style was far more low-key than Gingrich's, however. Hastert was most known for his willingness to listen to all of the various factions within his conference and bring them together to reach a consensus on controversial issues.

In the early months of her position as Speaker, Pelosi appeared to be combining elements of her two predecessors with the goal of maintaining a strong centralized control over powerful chairs and an often fractious caucus while seeking out an increasingly wider array of opinion from rank and file members.

Membership

To serve in the House, a representative must have been a U.S. citizen for at least seven years and must be at least twenty-five years old. Members of the House must be residents in the state they represent, but they do not have to live in their particular district. In practice, few legislators need worry about the minimum age; the average House member in the 110th Congress (2007–2009) was fifty-six years old. Most have been citizens since birth. The overwhelming pattern remains for representatives to live in the district they serve.

Characteristics

At the beginning of the 110th Congress, the House was dominated, as it always had been, by middle-aged white men with a background in law, business, or—increasingly—prior public service and a Christian upbringing. But its membership continued to broaden to include seventy-one women, forty blacks, and twenty-three Hispanics. (In addition, the nonvoting DELEGATES for the District of Columbia and the Virgin Islands were black women and the resident commissioner for Puerto Rico was Hispanic.)

The legal profession has long been the dominant occupational background of members of Congress since its beginning. In the First Congress, more than one-third of the House members had legal training. The proportion of members with a legal background crested at 70 percent in 1840 but remained high. From 1950 to the mid-1970s it was in the 55–60 percent range.

The first significant decline in members with a law background began with the 96th Congress. In 1979 lawyers in the House made up less than a majority for the first time in at least thirty years. The situation continued through the 1990s. When the 109th Congress convened in January 2005, 178 representatives were lawyers. In 2005, for the first time, business or banking, which had long been the second most listed category by members, overtook law with 205 representatives claiming a background in these areas. Two years later, at the start of the 110th Congress, the two professional areas were nearly in balance with 162 House members listing law as a profession and 166 members putting themselves in the business/banking category.

However, another category (some members listed overlapping backgrounds) topped both law and business in 2005 and highlighted the trend toward career politicians. In the 109th Congress, 222 House members listed backgrounds in public service or politics. By 2007, that number had dropped markedly to 174 members. This reflected the composition of the large freshman Democratic class that picked up thirty seats to take back control of the House for Democrats.

More on this topic:

Blacks in Congress,
p. 42

Hispanics in Congress,
p. 259

Incumbency, p. 286

Members of Congress:
Characteristics, p. 382

Women in Congress,
p. 606

Roughly half the Democratic freshmen, nineteen of forty-two Democrats sworn in for the first time in January 2007, had never before held political office, indicating to many observers the voters' displeasure with status quo politics in Congress. Many new members stood out for their different backgrounds. The group included a social worker, a wind-turbine executive, an allergist, two college professors, a publisher of an alternative newspaper, and a former professional football quarterback. But there were hardly any political neophytes among Republican freshmen.

The number of members with military experience declined dramatically into the twenty-first century, in part a reflection of the advent of an all-volunteer army in 1973. In 2007, at the start of the 110th Congress, only 101 House members were veterans, just 23 percent. In 1969 more than 70 percent were veterans, and even by 1991 more than half claimed military service.

Representation

State legislatures redraw the lines of congressional districts every ten years, after the national census, to reflect population increases and shifts. Some states lose seats while others gain, depending on shifts in the national population. Politics plays a major role in the way the new district lines are drawn within each state. (See REAPPORTIONMENT AND REDISTRICTING.)

Under the 2000 census, eighteen states were affected by changes in the size of their congressional delegations. Power shifted from the Northeast and Midwest to the South and West. Four states won two more seats: Arizona, Florida, Georgia, and Texas. Four states gained one seat: California, Colorado, Nevada, and North Carolina. Eight states lost one seat: Connecticut, Illinois, Indiana, Michigan, Mississippi, Ohio, Oklahoma, and Wisconsin. Two states lost two: New York and Pennsylvania. Seven states with small populations were entitled to only one representative each: Alaska, Delaware, Montana, North Dakota, South Dakota, Vermont, and Wyoming. The largest House delegations were those from California (fifty-three representatives), Texas (thirty-two), and New York (twenty-nine).

Until the 1920s the House simply added seats to reflect population increases and to keep states from having the size of their delegations reduced. After a decade of dispute, Congress in 1929 agreed to 435 permanent seats, the number reached after the 1910 census. The legislators also voted in 1929 to reapportion the districts after the 1930 census, thus avoiding another lengthy protest from the states losing seats. The 1930 census eventually cost twenty-one states a total of twenty-seven seats in the House.

In addition to its full members, the House has five delegates representing the District of Columbia and four islands closely linked to the United States: Puerto Rico, Guam, the Virgin Islands, and American Samoa.

Incumbency

Although technically it becomes a new body every two years, the House in the mid-twentieth century changed only gradually, with familiar faces retaining the positions they had held for years. The situation contrasted sharply with the mid-nineteenth century. In 1869, 145 of 243 members were new to the House. Most elections after 1949 brought fewer than eighty new members to the House. Just thirty-three new members were seated in 1991, but retirements and electoral defeats caught up with the House two years later as 110 new members arrived.

Incumbents have a powerful edge in contests for House seats. Roughly three-quarters of all House members routinely win reelection with 60 percent of the vote or more. Since 1946 more than 90 percent of House members seeking reelection have retained their seats.

Incumbency during the 1990s, however, provided less protection, particularly in the House. In the 1992 and 1994 congressional elections more than eighty incumbents lost reelection bids. Voters were increasingly wary of long-service incumbents, labeled "career politicians" by their critics.

A Typical Day in the House

A typical day in the House of Representatives might go as follows:

- The chaplain delivers the opening prayer.
- The Speaker approves the Journal, the record of the previous day's proceedings. Often a member will demand a roll-call vote on its approval.
- At the request of the Speaker, a member comes forward and leads the chamber in reciting the Pledge of Allegiance.
- After some procedural activities—receiving messages from the Senate or the president and granting committees permission to file reports—members are recognized for one-minute speeches on any topic.
- The House then turns to its legislative business. Virtually every major bill is considered under a rule setting guidelines for floor action. The rule is usually approved with little opposition, but the vote may be the first test of a bill's popularity. Members who want a less restrictive rule, so they can offer amendments, often work with opponents of a bill to defeat the rule.
- After the rule is adopted, the House resolves into the Committee of the Whole to consider the bill. The Speaker relinquishes the gavel to a chair, who presides over the committee. The debate time is controlled by the managers of the bill, usually the chair and ranking minority member of the standing committee that has jurisdiction over the measure.
- After time for general debate has expired, members can offer amendments permitted under the rule. Debate on the amendments is conducted under a rule that limits each side to five minutes, unless the rule for the bill allows more time, as it usually does for major amendments. Members may obtain additional time by offering pro forma amendments to "strike the last word."
- Voting is usually by voice. Some votes are recorded electronically; members insert a plastic card into one of many voting stations on the House floor and press a button to record a vote of yea, nay, or present. Their vote is immediately recorded on a big screen on the wall above the Speaker's desk and tabulated, giving a running vote total. Most electronic votes are scheduled for fifteen minutes, though they usually are kept open as long as members are on their way to the chamber.
- After the amending process is complete, the committee "rises," and the chair reports to the Speaker on the actions taken. Acting once again as the House, the members vote on final passage of the bill, sometimes after voting on a motion by opponents to recommit the bill to its committee of origin.
- On many noncontroversial bills, the House leadership can speed up action, bypassing the Rules Committee and the Committee of the Whole. It can do that by waiving, or suspending, the rules. Bills under suspension, sometimes as many as a dozen at a time, are usually brought up early in the week. Suspensions cannot be amended. Debate is limited to forty minutes, and then members are asked to vote on whether they want to suspend the rules and pass the bill. A single vote accomplishes both steps. A two-thirds vote is needed to suspend the House rules, making it a gamble sometimes to bring up legislation under suspension. Measures that are even less controversial are placed on the consent calendar or are passed by unanimous consent.
- After the House completes its legislative business, members may speak for up to sixty minutes under special orders. They must reserve the time in advance but may speak on any topic—often to an almost deserted chamber.

In 1994 Republicans gained fifty-two House seats, increasing their number from 178 to 230. The Democrats dropped from 256 to 204 seats. For the Republicans, seventy-three freshmen were elected, 157 incumbents were reelected, and thirty-four incumbents were defeated.

At the start of the 104th Congress, Georgia representative Newt Gingrich became the first Republican Speaker of the House from the South. His ascendancy accompanied the long-anticipated realignment of the South away from Democratic dominance to a Republican majority. For the first time since the end of Reconstruction in the 1870s, Republicans won a majority of southern congressional districts.

The anti-incumbent mood of the 1990s was clearly evident when the 107th Congress convened in January 2001. Almost two-thirds of the members of the House, 65 percent, were first elected in 1992 or later. Two out of every three representatives had never served in congressional office during any of the most momentous events of the post–World War II years. They had never experienced an economic recession, had not been part of the long twilight struggle of the cold war, were not in office when the Soviet Union broke up, and did not have to vote on waging war against Iraq in the Persian Gulf. Almost half of the House in 2001—48 percent—had never served in other than a Republican-controlled Congress, an enormous reversal of the Democratic dominance of the institution during most of the period since the New Deal days.

By the end of the decade, however, the turnover had settled down; incumbents again were being reelected and Republicans were largely in control from 2001 to 2006.

Then, in the 2006 elections, the Republican ascendancy fell apart, at least for the 110th Congress. In a national sweep that resembled the Republican takeover of Congress in 1994, Democrats regained control of both chambers by picking up a net of thirty seats in the House and six in the Senate. The Democrats gained seats in each of the four national regions including eleven House seats—the largest number—in the Northeast. Only one Republican survived in that part of the country, making the once rock-solid GOP region more like a Democratic bastion. In the House, Democrats picked up twenty-two Republican seats in which an incumbent was running in the general election; the other eight Democratic wins were in open seat contests. Not a single Democratic incumbent lost. Nevertheless, incumbency remained an important bulwark for both parties. All Democratic incumbents won and all open seats previously held by a Democrat were retained by the party. On the Republican side only one in ten GOP incumbents running lost in the general election. Overall 94 percent of House incumbents won.

Humphrey, Hubert H.

The Senate career of Hubert H. Humphrey (1911–1978) spanned four decades, from 1949 until his death. The Minnesota Democrat left the Senate in 1964 to serve as vice president and ran unsuccessfully as the 1968 Democratic presidential nominee. But Humphrey ended up back on Capitol Hill in 1971, still the "happy warrior" as he was widely known, as enthusiastic and irrepressible as ever.

Perceived as too liberal and garrulous when he first arrived in the Senate, Humphrey eventually became one of the most loved and revered senators in modern history. Many of his original goals, from civil rights to medical care for the elderly, became part of mainstream politics. But Humphrey never achieved his personal dream, to become president. He was never able to overcome his identification with the unpopular war in Vietnam.

Humphrey learned his liberal politics in Minneapolis. He lost his first political race, for mayor of Minneapolis, in 1943, but then won in 1945 and 1947. The mayoral race was nonpartisan, but Humphrey was deeply involved in building the Democrat-Farmer-Labor Party. In 1947 and 1948 he and his supporters wrested control of the party from a group of leftists who had ties to the

Communist Party. Humphrey became his party's nominee for a Senate seat then held by a Republican.

Humphrey made an impression at the Democratic national convention in 1948 with his impassioned plea for a strong civil rights plank in the party platform. "The time has arrived for the Democratic Party to get out of the shadow of states' rights and walk forthrightly into the bright sunshine of human rights," he said. When the convention adopted Humphrey's tough stand on civil rights, outraged southern Democrats walked out of the hall.

Vice President Hubert H. Humphrey meets with President Lyndon B. Johnson in the Oval Office. Humphrey's term as vice president was a brief interlude during his lengthy Senate career.
Source: LBJ Library Photo

In the Senate, where southerners held the balance of power, Humphrey began his career at a disadvantage. Nonetheless, by 1961 he was majority whip, the second-ranking party leader.

The culmination of his fight for equality came in 1964, when he managed floor action on landmark civil rights legislation. He was in large part responsible for Senate ratification of the 1963 treaty banning some nuclear tests. The 1965 Medicare law built on a concept Humphrey had proposed in one of the first bills he introduced in the Senate.

In 1964 Lyndon B. JOHNSON chose Humphrey as his running mate. For Humphrey the alliance, though successful, proved unhappy. When he made his own bid for the presidency four years later, he was dragged down by his loyalty to Johnson over conduct of the Vietnam War. Still, Humphrey came close to defeating Richard Nixon, with less than a percentage point of difference in the popular vote. After that defeat, he was out of public office for the first time in more than two decades. He reentered the Senate in 1971.

> *"The time has arrived for the Democratic Party to get out of the shadow of states' rights and walk forthrightly into the bright sunshine of human rights."*
>
> *—Hubert H. Humphrey*

Humphrey made another run for the presidency in 1972. Still haunted by Vietnam, he lost the race for the Democratic nomination. Back in the Senate, in 1975 he became chair of the Joint Economic Committee, a platform ideally suited to his advocacy of full employment programs. In 1976 he was reelected to the Senate for the last time. Early in 1977 the Senate created a new post, deputy PRESIDENT PRO TEMPORE, to honor Humphrey, now gravely ill with cancer. He died January 13, 1978.

Immunity, Congressional

The Constitution shields members of Congress from lawsuits or criminal charges that relate to their legislative duties. This congressional immunity, provided by the "speech and debate" clause, was borrowed from British law. Still, questions persist about where to draw the line between official and private acts, and courts have given different interpretations of the extent to which legislators' actions are protected. By shielding lawmakers from retribution for official acts, the framers of the Constitution hoped to guarantee the independence of the legislative branch. They wanted to keep Congress free from executive or judicial scrutiny inappropriate under the SEPARATION OF POWERS. The speech and debate clause states that senators and representatives "shall in all Cases, except Treason, Felony and Breach of the Peace, be privileged from Arrest during their Attendance at the Session of their respective Houses, and in going to and returning from the same; and for any Speech or Debate in either House, they shall not be questioned in any other Place."

Limits to Immunity

The Constitution appears to give legislators immunity from being arrested while in the Capitol or handling congressional work. But the courts have decided that immunity applies only to arrests for civil, not

> **Members of Congress "shall in all Cases, except Treason, Felony and Breach of the Peace, be privileged from Arrest during their Attendance at the Session of their respective Houses, and in going to and returning from the same; and for any Speech or Debate in either House, they shall not be questioned in any other Place."**
>
> —Article I, section 6, of the Constitution

criminal, matters. This leaves the privilege with limited practical application. Members of Congress are still subject to criminal and civil charges for actions outside of Congress. Their behavior within Congress is monitored by their peers, who have authority to discipline colleagues for unethical behavior. (See DISCIPLINING MEMBERS; ETHICS.)

In 1992 the possibility arose of an important test case of whether the executive branch can punish a member for an infraction already judged by the ethics committees. A federal judge refused to dismiss a civil suit brought by the Justice Department in 1989 against North Carolina Democrat Charlie Rose for "knowingly and willfully" filing false and incomplete FINANCIAL DISCLOSURE forms. Because the House ethics committee had disciplined him for the violation in 1988, Rose and House leaders contended that the Constitution shielded him from court action. In a legal brief, the leaders said, if the court "were to allow the Justice Department to follow up congressional ethics proceedings by changing the rules and adding penalties in a second proceeding....Congress could not perform the ethics functions consigned to it by the Constitution, and members would not receive their speech-or-debate protection for their participation in ethics committee proceedings." Justice Department lawyers disagreed, saying, "Taking the [House's] argument to its logical conclusion, a congressional investigation of a member of Congress could even be used to immunize a congressman from criminal prosecution. Such a result would be patently unconstitutional." A U.S. Court of Appeals in 1994 unanimously rejected the arguments by Rose and House lawyers. Rose later paid a fine to settle the case.

Drawing the Line

The speech and debate clause has been controversial because of disputes about how to distinguish between legislative and nonlegislative actions.

As one judge noted, a lawmaker can be immune from legal problems concerning a floor speech but not immune from charges related to circulating a copy of the same speech. The rulings have not always appeared consistent. One legislator's bribery conviction was reversed because evidence against him was based on what he had done, as subcommittee chair, to prepare for an investigative hearing. The Supreme Court agreed with him that such activity was shielded by congressional immunity. In another bribery case prosecution continued because the Court found that the actions in question were not part of the legislative process.

Senators and representatives have also used congressional immunity as a shield against civil actions by private citizens. Sen. William Proxmire, a Wisconsin Democrat, was sued for libel by a researcher who said his work had been ridiculed in 1975 by one of Proxmire's Golden Fleece Awards, which claimed to spotlight wasteful government spending. The Supreme Court ruled in 1979 that congressional immunity covered Proxmire's statements on the floor of the Senate, but not his press release or newsletter. The case was eventually settled out of court.

In another 1979 case the Court held that federal employees, including members of Congress, are subject to civil suit for employment discrimination. The action grew out of a decision by Rep. Otto Passman, a Louisiana Democrat, to fire a female staff employee because he preferred a male in the position.

Impeachment Power

Impeachment is a constitutional process that the nation's founders created to provide Congress with the ultimate authority to check abuses of power. The impeachment method allows Congress to remove officials who are found guilty of serious misconduct.

Congress has invoked this severe penalty sparingly. Only seven federal officials, all judges, have been removed from office through the impeachment process in more than two centuries. Others resigned voluntarily rather than risk impeachment, and thus the purpose of the impeachment process was fulfilled, if not in the precise manner the framers of the Constitution envisioned.

Of the three presidents who have faced impeachment inquiries, Andrew Johnson and Bill Clinton were impeached by the House but acquitted by the Senate, and Richard NIXON resigned, becoming the first president in history to resign in order to avoid near certain impeachment and removal from office.

The impeachment process is similar to an indictment and trial in the criminal court system. First, the House of Representatives approves formal charges, called articles of impeachment, against an official accused of wrongdoing. House members then prosecute the case in a trial held in the Senate chamber. The Senate is judge and jury. The penalty upon conviction is removal from office. There is no appeal.

By 2007, the three most powerful officials impeached by the House were Supreme Court justice Samuel Chase in 1805, President Johnson in 1868, and President Clinton in 1998. Chase and Johnson were acquitted by the Senate after sensational trials. With the likely outcome known beforehand, Clinton was acquitted in an anticlimactic trial in 1999. The overwhelming majority of impeachment proceedings have been directed against federal judges. Because they hold lifetime appointments "during good behavior," federal judges cannot be removed by any other means.

Two tickets to impeachment: (top) ticket that allowed admittance to the Senate galleries for the impeachment trial of President Andrew Johnson in 1868; (bottom) ticket to the Senate impeachment trial of President Bill Clinton in 1999.
Source: Library of Congress; AP Images/Doug Mills

Constitutional Background

The impeachment process outlined in the Constitution had its origins in fourteenth-century England, where Parliament used the procedure to gain authority over the king's advisers. Impeachment was used against ministers and judges whom Parliament believed guilty of breaking the law or carrying out unpopular orders of the king. The king himself was considered incapable of wrongdoing and therefore could not be impeached.

The framers of the U.S. Constitution embraced impeachment "as a method of national inquest into the conduct of public men," in the words of Alexander Hamilton. Details of the process were not settled until the closing days of the Constitutional Convention in 1787, when the delegates determined that "the president, vice president, and all civil officers of the

CLOSER LOOK

Impeachment involves two steps. First the House of Representatives approves formal charges, called articles of impeachment, against an official. House members then prosecute the case in a trial held in the Senate. The Senate decides the outcome: either acquittal or removal from office. There is no appeal.

United States" should be subject to impeachment. Conviction was to be followed by "removal from office" and possibly by "disqualification to hold" office in the future.

The delegates had difficulty deciding who should try impeachments. They finally agreed to follow the pattern used by Parliament, where charges were brought by the House of Commons and tried before the House of Lords. Thus the House of Representatives was granted sole power to impeach, or charge, a federal official. The Senate was granted sole power to try impeachments.

Another difficult issue involved the definition of impeachable offenses. The language ultimately adopted was "treason, bribery, or other high crimes and misdemeanors," which left many questions unanswered. While treason and bribery have established legal definitions, the meaning of "high crimes and misdemeanors" remains in dispute to this day. As a Republican representative from Michigan, Gerald R. FORD took a sweeping view. In 1970, during an unsuccessful attempt to impeach Supreme Court justice William O. Douglas, Ford declared, "An impeachable offense is whatever a majority of the House of Representatives considers it to be at a given moment in history." However, during the trial of President Clinton, the president's defense lawyers repeatedly argued that his accused crimes, even if true, did not rise to the level of "high crimes and misdemeanors." Clinton had been charged with perjury and obstruction of justice in his bid to cover up an extramarital affair.

On one side of the dispute over what constitutes an impeachable offense are the "broad constructionists," who view impeachment as a political weapon. On the other side are "narrow constructionists," who argue that impeachment is limited to offenses for which a person may be indicted under the criminal code. During President Nixon's impeachment inquiry in 1974 on charges arising out of the Watergate scandal, staff members of the House Judiciary Committee argued for a broad interpretation of high crimes and misdemeanors, while the president's attorneys argued for a narrow view. As adopted by the committee, the first article of impeachment charged Nixon with obstruction of justice, a charge falling within the narrow definition of impeachable offenses. The second and third articles reflected the broader definition, charging Nixon with abuse of his presidential powers and contempt of Congress.

Procedures

In modern practice, impeachment proceedings begin in the House Judiciary Committee, which holds hearings and investigates charges against an accused official. If its investigation supports the charges, the committee draws up articles of impeachment stating the reasons that the official should be removed from office. (See JUDICIARY COMMITTEE, HOUSE.)

A resolution containing the articles of impeachment then goes to the full House of Representatives. The House may approve the committee's recommendations without change, or it may alter or reject them. The accused official is impeached if the House adopts the resolution of impeachment by a simple majority vote. Upon adoption of the impeachment resolution, the House selects several of its members to present the case to the Senate. For the Clinton Senate trial, the House selected thirteen Republican members of the Judiciary Committee as its managers.

The Senate trial resembles a criminal proceeding, with the House managers acting as prosecutors. Senators take a special oath promising to act impartially in the matter. If the president or the vice president is on trial, the Constitution requires the chief justice of the United States to preside. Both sides may present witnesses and evidence; the defendant is allowed counsel, the right to testify in his or her own behalf, and the right of cross-examination.

The Senate votes separately on each article of impeachment; the Constitution requires a two-thirds vote of those present for conviction. If any article receives two-thirds approval, the defendant is convicted. The Senate may also vote to disqualify the convicted person from holding federal office in the future. Only two of the seven convictions have been accompanied by disqualification, which is decided by majority vote.

In addition, the removed officer remains subject to trial in the ordinary courts. As president, Ford granted a pardon to Nixon in 1974, protecting him from possible prosecution in the wake of the impeachment inquiry.

Notable Cases

Although impeachment proceedings have been launched more than sixty times since 1789, the House has impeached only seventeen officers: two presidents, one cabinet officer, one senator, and thirteen federal judges. Sixteen cases reached the Senate. Seven resulted in acquittal, seven ended in conviction, and two were dismissed before trial because the person impeached left office. One case did not go to the Senate because the accused official had resigned.

SENATE IMPEACHMENT TRIALS, 1789–2007

Between 1789 and 2007 the Senate sat as a court of impeachment sixteen times, as follows:

Year	Official	Position	Outcome
1798–1799	William Blount	U.S. senator	charges dismissed
1804	John Pickering	district court judge	removed from office
1805	Samuel Chase	Supreme Court justice	acquitted
1830–1831	James H. Peck	district court judge	acquitted
1862	West H. Humphreys	district court judge	removed from office
1868	Andrew Johnson	president	acquitted
1876	William Belknap	secretary of war	acquitted
1905	Charles Swayne	district court judge	acquitted
1912–1913	Robert W. Archbald	commerce court judge	removed from office
1926	George W. English	district court judge	charges dismissed
1933	Harold Louderback	district court judge	acquitted
1936	Halsted L. Ritter	district court judge	removed from office
1986	Harry E. Claiborne	district court judge	removed from office
1989	Alcee L. Hastings	district court judge	removed from office
1989	Walter L. Nixon Jr.	district court judge	removed from office
1999	Bill Clinton	president	acquitted

NOTE: The House in 1873 adopted a resolution of impeachment against district judge Mark H. Delahay, but there was no Senate action because Delahay resigned before articles of impeachment were prepared.

Presidents

The first president to face a serious impeachment challenge was Andrew Johnson. In 1868 the House impeached Johnson, and the Senate came within one vote of removing him from office. The Johnson impeachment trial grew out of a power struggle between Johnson and Radical Republicans in Congress, who opposed his moderate policies toward the South after the Civil War. The president was formally charged with violating the Tenure of Office Act, which required Senate assent for removal of any official appointed through its power of advice and consent. Johnson had fired the secretary of war, a holdover from the administration of President Abraham Lincoln.

In 1974 the House Judiciary Committee recommended that President Nixon be impeached for obstruction of justice, abuse of power, and contempt of Congress. The Nixon impeachment effort

House Judiciary chair Henry Hyde (right) leads the procession of the thirteen House trial managers to the Senate to read articles of impeachment against President Bill Clinton in January 1999.
Source: CQ Photo/Douglas Graham

stemmed from a 1972 break-in at Democratic National Committee headquarters in the Watergate complex in Washington, D.C. The break-in was followed by efforts to cover up White House involvement in the burglary. Facing almost certain impeachment and conviction, Nixon relinquished the office to which he had been overwhelmingly reelected less than two years earlier. Nixon's resignation on August 9, 1974, came as the House prepared to begin debate on impeaching him. "Our long national nightmare is over," said Nixon's successor, Gerald R. Ford. "Our Constitution works."

In 1998 independent counsel Kenneth W. Starr, in a report to Congress, charged President Clinton with perjury, obstruction of justice, witness tampering, and abusing the power of his office in an effort to cover up an extramarital affair. After conducting highly partisan hearings on the charges, the House Judiciary Committee recommended four articles of impeachment to the full House in December. In a lame-duck session on December 19, 1998, the Republican-led House adopted two of the articles—those dealing with grand jury perjury and obstruction of justice. After a five-week-long trial in the Senate, on February 12, 1999, Clinton was acquitted 45–55 on perjury (with ten Republicans joining all forty-five Democrats for acquittal), and 50–50 on obstruction of justice (with five Republicans joining all Democrats). Sixty-seven votes were needed for conviction.

> "Our long national nightmare is over. Our Constitution works."
>
> —President Gerald R. Ford

More on this topic:

Appointment Power, p. 14

Clinton Impeachment Trial, p. 97

Johnson Impeachment Trial, p. 307

Nixon Impeachment Effort, p. 396

Judiciary

In 1804 the House impeached Supreme Court justice Samuel Chase, charging him with partisan behavior on the bench. The Senate trial in 1805 ended in acquittal. Chase, a Federalist, was a victim of attacks on the Supreme Court by Jeffersonian Democrats, who had planned to impeach Chief Justice John Marshall if Chase were convicted.

By 2007 seven judges of lower courts had been impeached by the House and convicted and removed from office by the Senate. The charges ranged from drunkenness to tax fraud and sometimes were politically motivated. The Senate acquitted three other judges and dismissed charges against a fourth. Federal judges also have been the subject of most of the resolutions and investigations in the House that have failed to result in impeachment.

The three impeachment trials of the 1980s followed a fifty-year period with no judicial impeachments. Judge Harry E. Claiborne of Nevada, convicted by the Senate in 1986, had refused to resign his judgeship even though he was serving a prison sentence for tax fraud. In 1989 the Senate convicted a Florida judge, Alcee L. Hastings, on charges of perjury and bribery. Later the same year Judge Walter L. Nixon Jr. of Mississippi was convicted by the Senate. He was accused of having lied to a grand jury about his role in trying to win leniency for the indicted son of a business associate.

In those three trials the Senate for the first time used a shortcut procedure authorized in 1935. The shortcut allowed a special twelve-member committee to hear witnesses and gather evidence before the full Senate convened to try the judges. This saved the Senate months of deliberation but resulted in court challenges from the judges, who claimed that their convictions were unconstitutional because the full Senate had not heard the evidence. In 1993 the Supreme Court refused to consider that argument, ruling unanimously in the case of *United States v. Nixon* that the courts could not interfere with the Senate's conduct of impeachment trials because the Constitution gave the Senate "the sole power to try all impeachments."

The Court's ruling was an important affirmation of the Senate's impeachment power, but the unique case of Hastings remained unresolved. Unlike Claiborne and Nixon, Hastings had been impeached and convicted after having been tried and acquitted of criminal charges. In 1992 he made history by winning election to the House as a Democrat from Florida, a seat he still held as of 2008. Hastings's election raised a new constitutional question: whether conviction by the Senate was sufficient to disqualify a person from holding public office, or whether disqualification required a separate Senate vote.

The Constitution states that "judgment in cases of impeachment shall not extend further than to removal from office, and disqualification to hold and enjoy any office of honor, trust or profit under the United States." In practice the Senate had treated the punishments as distinct and held separate votes on whether to block an impeached official from holding office again. In three of its seven convictions, the Senate had taken separate votes on disqualification from future office and had twice voted to do so. A disqualification vote was not taken for Hastings, and in January 1993 a federal judge rejected a lawsuit claiming that Hastings's Senate conviction disqualified him from holding office. Hastings took his seat with the rest of the 103rd Congress.

Cabinet

William W. Belknap, President Ulysses S. Grant's fourth secretary of war, is the only cabinet member ever to have been tried by the Senate. He was acquitted in 1876 of bribery charges, largely because senators questioned their authority to try Belknap, who had resigned several months before the trial.

Congress

The House has impeached only one member of Congress, Sen. William Blount of Tennessee. Blount was impeached in 1797 for having conspired with the British to launch a military expedition intended to conquer Spanish territory for Great Britain. The Senate expelled Blount and later dismissed impeachment charges for lack of jurisdiction.

Impoundment of Funds

Presidential refusal to spend money appropriated by Congress is known as impoundment. The practice has been a thorny issue throughout the nation's history. Although the Constitution gave Congress authority to appropriate federal funds, it left vague whether a president was required to spend the appropriated money or whether he could make independent judgments on the timing and need for spending. (See PURSE, POWER OF.)

CLOSER LOOK

The Constitution gives Congress the power to provide for federal spending through appropriations but left vague whether the president must actually use the money. As a result, Congress and presidents have wrestled for years over whether a president can make an independent judgment about the timing and need for spending.

Impoundments go back to the administration of Thomas Jefferson, but they became a major dispute only in the late 1960s and 1970s, when Republican president Richard NIXON refused to spend billions of dollars of appropriated funds. Nixon argued that he was withholding the money to combat inflation, but Democrats contended that the president was using impoundment primarily to enforce his spending priorities in defiance of the will of Congress.

This conflict prompted Congress in 1974 to reassert its control over the federal budget by enacting the Congressional Budget and Impoundment Control Act. In addition to creating the BUDGET PROCESS used thereafter by Congress, the 1974 law established procedures for congressional approval or disapproval of presidential impoundments.

Under this system the presidents must notify Congress if they intend to cancel spending altogether, a step called a rescission. Rescissions require positive action by Congress. Unless Congress enacts a law approving the rescission within forty-five days, the president must spend the money. In March and April 1992 President George H. W. Bush sent four rescission packages—a total of 126 rescissions worth $7.9 billion—to Capitol Hill. Congress responded by passing its own $8.2 billion package of rescissions that ignored many of the cuts recommended by Bush and instead substituted cuts in programs targeted by legislators.

A 1996 law gave the president new authority to cancel, or rescind, previously enacted spending provisions—roughly equivalent to a line-item veto. The new law, creating enhanced rescissions authority, was intended to strengthen the hand of the president in his budget dealings with Congress by making it easier to strike out individual spending items from appropriations bills and narrowly targeted provisions in tax bills. Both Presidents Ronald Reagan and Bush had called for increased rescission authority. The Supreme Court in 1998 declared the new law unconstitutional, a violation of the separation of powers doctrine. (See VETOES.)

The original 1974 budget act also permitted the president to delay spending temporarily—called a deferral—unless Congress acted to forbid the delay. Two court decisions in the 1980s restricted the use of deferrals for policy reasons. The Gramm-Rudman amendment to the 1987 debt-limit bill further clarified the matter when it limited the use of deferrals to management issues.

Incumbency

Election results show that voters generally return incumbents to office, even though public opinion polls show a consistently low opinion of Congress as an institution. This pattern is broken in some years when overriding national issues such as war, economic troubles, or political scandals result in more than the usual number of incumbents being thrown out of office. This occurred most recently in 1994, when Republicans swept Democrats out of control of Congress, and in 2006, when Democrats did the same to the GOP.

CLOSER LOOK

Even though Congress is often held in low esteem by American voters, those same voters generally return incumbents to office year after year. In most years in House races the reelection rate is greater than 90 percent. It is slightly lower in the Senate but still typically 75 percent or higher.

In the modern era the power of incumbency has remained strong with the turnover rate from deaths, resignations, and election defeats averaging about 10 percent or less, historically an exceptionally low level. In the 2006 elections, for example, 94 percent of House incumbents who ran were reelected. In the Senate, the reelection rate was 79.3 percent. Even so, the turnover record was high by recent standards. In the House the number of incumbents who lost was the highest since 1994, the year the Republicans swept into control of that chamber. In the Senate in 2006 the six incumbents who lost in the general election were the largest number in a general election since 1980, when nine were defeated. (One incumbent, Joseph Lieberman of Connecticut, lost his primary election but won in the general election when he ran as an independent.)

INCUMBENTS REELECTED, DEFEATED, OR RETIRED, 1946–2006

Year	Retired[1]	Total seeking reelection	Defeated in primaries	Defeated in general election	Total reelected	Percentage of those seeking reelection
House						
1946	32	398	18	52	328	82.4
1948	29	400	15	68	317	79.3
1950	29	400	6	32	362	90.5
1952	42	389	9	26	354	91.0
1954	24	407	6	22	379	93.1
1956	21	411	6	16	389	94.6
1958	33	396	3	37	356	89.9
1960	27	405	5	25	375	92.6
1962	24	402	12	22	368	91.5
1964	33	397	8	45	344	86.6
1966	23	411	8	41	362	88.1
1968	24	408	4	9	395	96.8
1970	30	401	10	12	379	94.5
1972	40	392	14	13	366	93.4
1974	43	391	8	40	343	87.7
1976	47	384	3	13	368	95.8
1978	49	382	5	19	358	93.7
1980	34	398	6	31	361	90.7
1982	31	387	4	29	354	91.5
1984	22	409	3	16	390	95.4
1986	38	393	2	6	385	98.0
1988	23	408	1	6	401	98.3
1990	27	407	1	15	391	96.1
1992	65	368	19	24	325	88.3
1994	48	387	4	34	349	90.2
1996	49	384	2	21	361	94.0
1998	33	402	1	6	395	98.3
2000	32	405	3	6	396	97.8
2002	35	398	8	8	382	96.0
2004	29	404	2	7	395	97.8
2006	27	404	2	22	380	94.1
Senate						
1946	9	30	6	7	17	56.7
1948	8	25	2	8	15	60.0
1950	4	32	5	5	22	68.8
1952	4	31	2	9	20	64.5
1954	6	32	2	6	24	75.0
1956	6	29	0	4	25	86.2
1958	6	28	0	10	18	64.3
1960	4	29	0	1	28	96.6
1962	4	35	1	5	29	82.9
1964	2	33	1	4	28	84.8
1966	3	32	3	1	28	87.5
1968	6	28	4	4	20	71.4
1970	4	31	1	6	24	77.4
1972	6	27	2	5	20	74.1

(continues)

INCUMBENTS REELECTED, DEFEATED, OR RETIRED, 1946–2006 (CONTINUED)

Year	Retired[1]	Total seeking reelection	Defeated in primaries	Defeated in general election	Total reelected	Percentage of those seeking reelection
1974	7	27	2	2	23	85.2
1976	8	25	0	9	16	64.0
1978	10	25	3	7	15	60.0
1980	5	29	4	9	16	55.2
1982	3	30	0	2	28	93.3
1984	4	29	0	3	26	89.7
1986	6	28	0	7	21	75.0
1988	6	27	0	4	23	85.2
1990	3	32	0	1	31	96.9
1992	7	28	1	4	23	82.1
1994	9	26	0	2	24	92.3
1996	13	21	1	1	19	90.5
1998	4	30	0	3	27	90.0
2000	5	29	0	6	23	79.3
2002	5	28	1	3	24	85.7
2004	8	26	0	1	25	96.2
2006	4	29	1	6	23	79.3

SOURCE: Norman J. Ornstein, Thomas E. Mann, and Michael J. Malbin, *Vital Statistics on Congress, 2001–2002* (Washington, D.C.: American Enterprise Institute, 2002); Harold W. Stanley and Richard G. Niemi, *Vital Statistics on American Politics 2007–2008* (Washington D.C., CQ Press, 2007); Richard Scammon, Alice McGillivray, and Rhodes Cook, *America Votes* (Washington, D.C.: CQ Press), selected editions; *CQ Weekly*, selected issues.

NOTE: 1. Does not include persons who died or resigned before the election except, in the case of deaths, for candidates whose name remained on the ballot.

An incumbent's appeal rests on more than the person's record in Congress and is significantly influenced by the public image projected through television, direct mail, telephone banks, the Internet, and other devices used in election campaigns. But projecting that image, particularly through costly television advertising, is extremely expensive, requiring any candidate to raise substantial campaign funds. Incumbents are particularly well placed to raise money from special interest groups, whether business, labor, or ideological, as a result of their service in Congress and participation in important decisions that may affect the donors' organizations. This incumbency advantage generally tilts voter recognition toward the member and away from a challenger who often will have more difficulty raising money from the interest groups.

Incumbency during the 1990s, however, provided less protection, particularly in the House. In the 1992 and 1994 congressional elections more than eighty incumbents lost reelection bids. Voters were increasingly wary of long-service incumbents, labeled "career politicians" by their critics. Many challengers ran antigovernment campaigns presenting their absence of previous elected office as a reason to be elected. Some challengers vowed to serve only a limited number of terms to avoid becoming "career politicians" out of touch with the voters, although some winners by the end of their pledged terms found reasons to stay in office.

The anti-incumbent mood of the 1990s was clearly evident when the 107th Congress convened in January 2001. Almost two-thirds of the members of the House, 65 percent, were first elected in 1992 or later. Two out of every three representatives had never served in congressional office during any of the most momentous events of the post–World War II years. They had never experienced an economic recession, had not been part of the long twilight struggle of the cold war, were not in office when the Soviet Union broke up, and did not have to vote on waging war against Iraq in the Persian Gulf. Almost half of the House in 2001—48 percent—had never served in other than a Republican-controlled Congress, an enormous reversal of the Democratic dominance of the institution during most of the period since the New Deal days. Turnover in the Senate was less dramatic during the period but significant nevertheless. As the 107th Congress began, forty-five senators had been in the chamber for six years or less, a figure not matched since 1981.

In 1994 a landmark election swept Republicans to power in both chambers. Democrats had controlled either the House or Senate, and usually both, since 1955. Since 1933, when the Great Depression realigned political power, Republicans had managed to control both houses only twice—in the Eightieth Congress (1947–1949) and the Eighty-third Congress (1953–1955). Republicans also held a Senate majority from 1981 to 1987.

In the following elections, the power of incumbency was seen again as sitting members won re-election at rates in the high 90 percent range. But as in 1994, incumbency was less a shield in 2006 when voters expressed their displeasure with—more than any other issue—the continuing and seemingly intractable war in Iraq. The poll ratings of the party's president, George W. Bush, who had launched the war in 2003, were at an all-time low. Even so, the GOP held on to many seats that were thought to be toss-ups. Moreover, some losses were expected because historically most parties that hold the White House experience losses—sometimes large losses—in the midterm elections six years into the president's term. In that light, some scholars thought the Republican Party managed relatively well in 2006.

Indian Affairs Committee, Senate

The Indian Affairs Committee was created in 1977 as a temporary select committee in the midst of a Senate reorganization that was intended to consolidate and eliminate committees, not add new ones. That beginning, against all odds, and the several reauthorizations since then that ulti-

mately led to the panel's designation as a standing committee of the Senate in 1993, reflect a recognition within Congress of Native Americans' problems. Native Americans have a unique relationship with Congress and the rest of the federal government. Although subject to federal laws and tribal regulations, those living on reservations are covered by state and local laws only when Congress gives its consent, as it has for criminal laws and in many other instances. Indian reservations have a special status under which the federal government acts as trustee.

The primary advocate of establishing the Senate select committee in 1977 was Democrat James Abourezk of South Dakota, whose mother was a Native American. After Abourezk left the Senate in 1979, Montana Democrat John Melcher persuaded the Senate to continue the select committee, and Melcher became its chair.

During a hearing of the Senate Indian Affairs Committee, John McCain, R-Ariz. (left) discusses strategy with Byron Dorgan, D-N.D. McCain chaired the committee from 2005 to 2007. Dorgan became chair in 2007 when Democrats regained control of Congress.
Source: AP Images/Susan Walsh

In 1984 the panel was made a permanent select committee and in 1993 it was redesignated as a standing committee with legislative authority. Previously the panel could only review legislation, conduct studies, and hold hearings.

Republican Ben Nighthorse Campbell of Colorado, the only Native American in the Senate, became the chair in 1997. He was replaced from mid-2001 to 2003 by Democrat Daniel K. Inouye of Hawaii, and then returned as chair in 2003 when the Republicans regained control of the Senate. Inouye became the ranking Democrat. The two worked well together and that bipartisanship would be needed if the panel's legislation was to have any chance of clearing Congress, a tough job given that the House did not have a committee devoted solely to Indian affairs.

Campbell left the Senate at the end of the 108th Congress. He was succeeded in 2005 by Sen. John McCain, R-Ariz., who brought unaccustomed attention to the committee by leading an aggressive two-year investigation into the activities of disgraced lobbyist Jack Abramoff. Abramoff and others defrauded Indian tribal clients of tens of millions of dollars.

With Democrats back in control in 2007 the chair went to Byron L. Dorgan of North Dakota. He inherited a committee in the middle of dealing with efforts to force a settlement between Native American tribes and the government in a long-running lawsuit over Interior Department mismanagement of Indian trust funds. Under Dorgan the committee also continued to examine the money trail left by Abramoff and an associate, Michael Scanlon. A committee report in June 2006 said the lobbyists schemed to get Indian tribes to hire Scanlon as a grassroots lobbyists and then "dramatically" overcharged them, keeping an "unconscionable percentage" for themselves. Abramoff pleaded guilty in January that year to conspiracy, tax evasion, and mail fraud.

Intelligence Committees, House and Senate Select

Most of the work of the House and Senate Select Intelligence committees is done in closed session, and even the legislation they report is usually kept secret. These habits reflect their role: oversight of the nation's espionage agencies.

The committees gained increased importance after the terrorist attacks of September 11, 2001, left the nation shaken.

The relationship between Congress and the agencies is uneasy. The intelligence agencies criticize Congress for leaking sensitive information and are wary of any congressional interference. The committees complain that they are not kept informed and insist on exercising their oversight responsibilities.

The dynamics between lawmakers and agency officials became particularly tense during the Intelligence committees' hearings when questions were raised as to whether the intelligence agencies had properly safeguarded the nation in the months leading up to the 2001 attacks on New York and Washington. Committee members became frustrated over their inability to get information from the intelligence agencies.

Centralizing the reporting in the two intelligence committees did not fully resolve the problem. Critics still claimed that Congress was not careful enough about keeping classified information secret, and the intelligence agencies continued to withhold information from Congress.

The IRAN-CONTRA AFFAIR, which shook President Ronald Reagan's administration in the 1980s, illustrated the problem. Congress was not fully briefed about the extent of Central Intelligence Agency (CIA) involvement in the "contra" resistance to Nicaragua's Sandinista government, and was not told about secret arms sales to Iran. After Congress banned U.S. aid to the contras, White House officials orchestrated private donations to them. When questioned by Congress, the officials denied any involvement in illegal aid to the contras. The administration also kept Congress in the dark for months about the Iranian arms sales and formally notified Congress only after the sales had become public. Administration officials later argued that they had withheld information from Congress in order to guard against leaks on Capitol Hill. They also complained about Capitol Hill interference in foreign policy.

Conflicts over intelligence matters continued in the wake of the Iran-contra affair, as the intelligence committees pressed for legislation aimed at preventing a similar scandal in the future. Attempts to set a forty-eight-hour limit on how long the president could wait before telling Congress about covert operations ended in a compromise in 1991 that did not include a specific timetable for reporting.

In 1989 a House intelligence subcommittee was refused access to detailed information on the activities of the CIA's inspector general, the agency's internal watchdog who was assigned to root out mismanagement. Congress then established an independent inspector general, subject to Senate confirmation, and mandated that the House and Senate intelligence committees should have access to that official's reports.

Leaders of the intelligence committees in 1992—Sen. David L. Boren and Rep. Dave McCurdy, both Democrats from Oklahoma—launched a high-profile attempt to restructure the nation's multiagency intelligence apparatus for the post–Cold War era. But the George H. W. Bush administration, on guard against congressional attempts to restructure executive agencies, was cool to the proposals and announced its own overhaul of the CIA and other intelligence operations.

Creation of the two special committees was prompted by revelations in the mid-1970s that intelligence agencies had run illegal covert operations, including plots to assassinate foreign leaders and surveillance of U.S. mail. The disclosures were detailed in news reports and later in investigations by two study committees set up temporarily by the House and Senate. Most notable was the fifteen-month probe headed by Sen. Frank Church, an Idaho Democrat, that chronicled a long list of intelligence abuses. Both the House and Senate decided they needed permanent intelligence committees to monitor how the United States conducted its espionage. The Senate established its permanent panel in 1976.

The House committee, set up on a temporary basis in 1975, had a shaky beginning. Its first chair was replaced after members found out he had not shared inside information about illegal CIA activities. Then in 1976 the House blocked release of the committee's final report in deference to objections from the Gerald R. Ford administration. But the report was leaked and published in the *Village Voice*, a New York City weekly newspaper, prompting an investigation by the House Committee on Standards of Official Conduct. Not until 1977 did the House set up a permanent intelligence committee. The first chair of the permanent committee was Edward P. Boland, a Massachusetts Democrat, who became a key opponent of undercover U.S. aid to the contras in Nicaragua. But the committee remained controversial. Republicans argued, without success, that the ratio of nine majority members and four minority members would make the panel too partisan. The committee gradually expanded and became less lopsided. In 2007 the panel had twelve Democrats and nine Republicans.

Membership of the House committee must include a representative from each of several committees: Appropriations, Armed Services, Foreign Affairs, and Judiciary. The House Speaker and minority leaders are nonvoting ex officio members. A member is allowed no more than eight years of service on the intelligence committee in a twelve-year period.

The Senate set up a special committee in 1975 and then voted in 1976 to create a permanent, fifteen-member panel. In 2007 the committee had eight Democrats and seven Republicans. Similar to the House, the Senate limits service on the committee, allowing a senator to serve a maximum of eight years unless granted a waiver for another two-year term. In an effort to create a bipartisan spirit, the post of vice chair is given to a member of the minority party. Membership on the committee must include two members from each of several committees: Appropriations, Armed Services, Foreign Relations, and Judiciary.

Although most special or select committees do not handle legislation, the intelligence committees do consider and report legislation. Each year they approve the spending authorization for the intelligence agencies, including the CIA, Defense Intelligence Agency, National Security Agency, intelligence branches of the armed services, and intelligence activities of the Federal Bureau of Investigation. The select committees share with other committees jurisdiction over the intelligence agencies, except for the CIA, but the select committees act first and have primary responsibility.

The Senate committee also handles the confirmation of top intelligence officials, such as the director of central intelligence. (See APPOINTMENT POWER.)

Republican Porter J. Goss of Florida, a former CIA agent, became chair of the House Intelligence Committee in 1997 and was granted a waiver to continue in the job in 2003. Goss had planned to retire at the end of the 107th Congress (2001–2003), but GOP leaders convinced him that his expertise was needed. Goss later was named by President George W. Bush as director of the CIA. But after a short and tumultuous period in office he stepped down.

John D. Rockefeller, D-W.Va., (left) and Pat Roberts, R-Kan., have both chaired the Senate Intelligence Committee. Their disputes often reflect partisan differences regarding U.S. intelligence policy.
Source: CQ Photo/Scott J. Ferrell

In 2007 the chair went to Silvestre Reyes, D-Texas, even though he was not the most senior member. That was California Democrat Jane Harman, but she and the new Speaker, Nancy Pelosi, also from California, simply did not get along. Also Harman was more conservative on national security issues than the Speaker, further harming her claim to the chair. Next in line was Alcee L. Hastings. He was passed over amid controversy over his impeachment and removal by Congress as a federal district judge in Florida in 1988 over a bribery charge that remained mired in controversy, including allegations that the FBI misrepresented evidence against him. Three years later Hasting was elected to the House.

Reyes was third in seniority, a moderate, and Latino. He was once a border patrol agent and had focused his committee work on border security. He also has encouraged more intelligence gathering by human spies as well as through sophisticated spy technology.

When the Republicans regained control of the Senate in 2003, Pat Roberts of Kansas became chair, replacing Democrat Bob Graham of Florida, who had headed the panel from mid-2001 to 2003. In 2007 the chair went to John D. Rockefeller, D-W. Va. Although Roberts and Rockefeller cooperated on some aspects of the committee's work, particularly in singling out the CIA for various failings, the two also engaged in vigorous disputes over the panel's work, reflecting a deepening partisan division about U.S. intelligence activities, much of which was rooted in investigations of information about Iraq and alleged weapons of mass destruction before the Bush administration invaded that country in 2003. (See INVESTIGATIONS.)

Investigations

Investigations are the eyes and ears of the legislative branch. They test the effectiveness of existing laws and document the need for new legislation. They inquire into the performance of government officials, including members of Congress themselves. They expose waste and corruption in government. They educate the public on great issues of the day.

Investigations have given Congress some of its finest hours, and some of its most deplorable. They have transformed minor politicians into household names and have broken the careers of important officials. Since 1948, television has permitted millions of Americans to witness some of the high drama congressional investigations can generate.

Harry S. TRUMAN and Richard NIXON both gained national fame for their leadership of congressional investigations before they attained the presidency. Truman, a Democratic senator from Missouri, won distinction during World War II for his committee's investigation of the nation's defense program. As a Republican representative from California, Nixon drew wide attention in 1948 for his zealous investigations of suspected communists in the government.

Soon afterward, Sen. Joseph R. MCCARTHY, a Republican from Wisconsin, captured the spotlight. He skillfully used speeches, press releases, and hearings to accuse—often falsely—many prominent Americans of being communists or communist sympathizers. McCarthy was widely feared, but gradually public sentiment shifted as television cameras displayed his antics during hearings in 1953 and 1954. A Senate inquiry into McCarthy's conduct led to a vote of censure by his colleagues in 1954, ending his political power. Twenty years later President Nixon was forced from office by the threat of impeachment arising from investigations into the Watergate scandal. The House Judiciary Committee recommended his impeachment in the summer of 1974, after a dramatic television debate that helped prepare the nation to accept the resignation of a president it had overwhelmingly reelected less than two years earlier.

The Senate Select Committee on Presidential Campaign Activities, known as the Watergate committee, contributed to the impeachment inquiry by exposing the efforts of the Nixon administration to cover up political sabotage and other illegal activities. Sen. Sam J. Ervin Jr., the North Carolina Democrat who chaired the panel, observed that the power to investigate is a double-edged sword in the hands of Congress. He said, "The congressional investigation can be an instrument of freedom. Or it can be freedom's scourge. A legislative inquiry can serve as the tool to pry open the barriers that hide governmental corruption. It can be the catalyst that spurs Congress and the public to support vital reforms in our nation's laws. Or it can debase our principles, invade the privacy of our citizens, and afford a platform for demagogues and the rankest partisans."

> *"The congressional investigation can be an instrument of freedom. Or it can be freedom's scourge. A legislative inquiry can serve as the tool to pry open the barriers that hide governmental corruption. It can be the catalyst that spurs Congress and the public to support vital reforms in our nation's laws. Or it can debase our principles, invade the privacy of our citizens, and afford a platform for demagogues and the rankest partisans."*
>
> **—Sen. Sam J. Ervin Jr.,** the North Carolina Democrat who chaired the Senate Watergate committee that investigated illegal activities by the Nixon administration

The Investigative Process

Investigations are not mentioned anywhere in the Constitution, but the Supreme Court has upheld Congress's power to investigate as part of the legislative process. The Court first asserted its authority to review congressional investigations in the case of *Kilbourn v. Thompson* in 1881.

From the beginning Congress has delegated investigative functions to its committees. A major investigation typically begins when the Senate or House authorizes it, often establishing a temporary committee (known as a select or special committee) to undertake the job. At other times investigations are conducted by the standing committees with jurisdiction over the subject in question.

Following a preliminary inquiry by its staff, the committee holds hearings at which people with knowledge of the matter under investigation are called to testify. At the conclusion of the investigation the committee issues a report summarizing its findings and offering recommendations for future action. Much of the information disclosed in investigations is uncovered during the staff inquiry. The formal hearings, at which witnesses appear, often become dramatic spectacles intended to educate and influence the public through the media, particularly television.

The Senate committee that investigated the Watergate scandal spent several months interviewing people, including scores of Nixon administration officials, before the televised hearings began in May 1973. Similarly, months of spadework preceded the May 1987 opening of joint Senate-House hearings on the Iran-contra affair, an investigation of undercover U.S. arms sales to Iran and the diversion of profits from those sales to the "contra" rebels in Nicaragua. Although the House and Senate each established a committee to investigate the affair, leaders of the two committees agreed to merge their investigations and hearings to avoid duplication. That was an unusual procedure for the two houses of Congress, which do not often cooperate on investigations.

Major investigations call for big staffs. At the height of the Watergate investigation, sixty-four professional staff members were working for the committee looking into the scandal. The House Judiciary Committee employed a staff of nearly a hundred, including forty-three attorneys, in its 1974 Nixon impeachment inquiry.

Sometimes people refuse to cooperate with congressional committees that request testimony or demand records and documents. In such cases, legislators can draw upon their subpoena power to force compliance. A subpoena is a legal order that requires a person to testify or to produce documents. Those who ignore subpoenas risk being punished for contempt of Congress.

Witnesses who appear before a committee may be prosecuted as criminals if they do not tell the truth. Witnesses sometimes avoid testifying by citing the Fifth Amendment to the Constitution, which says a person does not have to be a witness against himself or herself in any criminal case. Witnesses who invoke the Fifth Amendment may be required to testify if they are granted limited immunity from prosecution.

On occasion, government officials either refuse to testify or withhold information by order of the president, citing the president's executive privilege to protect sensitive information. Presidents have had considerable success in using executive privilege to refuse demands for information.

Because many congressional investigations target mismanagement or wrongdoing by the administration in power, they tend to have partisan overtones, especially if the House or Senate and the presidency are controlled by different political parties. Partisanship may be the motive for an investigation and can influence how it is conducted. Votes on areas to be investigated, witnesses to be called, and final committee recommendations may divide along party lines.

A House investigation of federal regulatory agencies in 1957–1958 is a case in point. The Democratic chair of the investigating subcommittee insisted that the inquiry was not politically motivated. But its main result was the resignation of White House assistant Sherman Adams, right-hand assistant to Republican president Dwight D. Eisenhower. Adams was accused of having interceded with federal agencies on behalf of a Boston industrialist from whom he had received gifts. Democrats used the Adams affair to embarrass the Republicans on the eve of the 1958 congressional elections.

Beginning with the 104th Congress (1995–1997), partisan politics fueled Republican-controlled investigatory and oversight committees to target suspected abuses within the Clinton administration. Congressional hearings were held on the Clintons' personal financial involvement in a failed Arkansas land deal called Whitewater, the firing of White House travel office employees, and the request for Federal Bureau of Investigation (FBI) background files on former Republican administration officials. During the 105th Congress (1997–1999), both the House and the Senate investigated Democratic fundraising violations in the 1996 presidential campaign.

In October 1998 the House Judiciary Committee began an impeachment inquiry against President Bill Clinton on numerous charges stemming from an investigation headed by independent counsel Kenneth W. Starr into Clinton's attempt to conceal an extramarital affair. The rancorous, bitterly partisan hearings resulted in the committee voting out four articles of impeachment against the president. On December 19, 1998, a lame-duck House impeached Clinton on two articles. The Senate acquitted him on February 12, 1999.

Investigative Milestones

During more than two centuries Congress has investigated scandals, wars, national security threats, and a host of other topics. Many of the earliest investigations involved charges brought against a senator or representative, but most concerned the civil and military activities of the executive branch.

Between 1880 and World War I (1914–1918) economic and social problems and government operations were the principal fields of investigation. Subversive activities—those aimed at overthrowing the government—emerged as a major investigative concern in the period between the two world wars (1918–1939). They became the dominant concern for the first decade or so after World War II. In later decades headline-making investigations focused on organized crime and abuses of power by government officials and agencies.

Who Says a Watched Pot Never Boils?

In the 1920s congressional investigations of the Teapot Dome scandal prompted several members of the administration of President Warren G. Harding to resign.
Source: Library of Congress

Wartime

The first congressional investigation focused on an Indian massacre of troops sent into the Ohio territory in 1791. A select committee established by the House in 1792 to inquire into the affair absolved Maj. Gen. Arthur St. Clair, the troops' commander, of blame for the disaster. It said the War Department was at fault.

Seventy years later Congress set up its first joint investigating committee in response to another military action, the Civil War. The Joint Committee on the Conduct of the War routinely second-guessed President Abraham Lincoln's military moves and attempted to impose its military strategy on him.

The committee was controlled by Radical Republicans who were convinced that Lincoln was not acting aggressively enough to secure a Union victory against the southern Confederacy.

Confederate general Robert E. Lee welcomed the committee's disruption of the northern war effort, observing that the panel was worth about two divisions of Confederate troops.

Aware of the excesses of the Civil War committee, the World War II–era Truman committee, formally titled the Senate Special Committee to Investigate the National Defense Program, scrupulously avoided any attempt to judge military policy or operations. Created early in 1941, the committee worked closely with the executive branch to uncover and reduce wasteful practices in the war mobilization effort. The Truman panel came to be widely regarded as one of the most effective investigating committees in the history of Congress.

Following the September 11, 2001, terrorist attacks, the House and Senate Intelligence committees held joint hearings into intelligence lapses, uncovering situations in which U.S. agents had information about increasingly belligerent terrorist threats that went unheeded. The panels found intelligence agencies lacked resources to sift through raw data acquired from satellites and agents and, in some cases, did not adequately communicate with each other. Panel members concluded that an independent commission was needed to continue to seek answers because many lawmakers would rotate off the intelligence panels at the end of the 107th Congress (2001–2003). After initially resisting the creation of an independent commission, the Bush administration, under pressure from families of September 11 victims, acquiesced.

Corruption

Other investigations have dealt with money and favors. Widespread corruption during Ulysses S. Grant's two terms in the White House (1869–1877) sparked numerous congressional investigations. One famous scandal of the time, the Crédit Mobilier affair, tarnished both the legislative and executive branches. The scandal involved wholesale corruption in the construction of the last portion of the transcontinental railroad, which had been completed in 1869 by Crédit Mobilier of America, a company related to the Union Pacific Railroad.

Attempting to head off a legislative inquiry into the affair, Rep. Oakes Ames, a Massachusetts Republican who was a principal shareholder in Crédit Mobilier, arranged to sell $33 million of stock in the company at bargain prices to members of Congress and executive branch officials.

Ames and another House member eventually were censured by the House. Others, including Vice President Schuyler Colfax and Rep. James A. Garfield, were implicated, but no action was taken against them. Garfield, an Ohio Republican, was elected to the presidency in 1880.

Another series of congressional investigations in 1922–1924 uncovered the TEAPOT DOME scandal, which ravaged the administration of President Warren G. Harding. That scandal involved the Interior Department's leasing of naval oil reserves on public lands to private oil companies. The reserves, at Elk Hills, California, and Teapot Dome, Wyoming, were natural deposits of oil that had been set aside for use by the navy. As a result of the investigations Harding's secretary of the interior, Albert B. Fall, served almost a year in prison for accepting a bribe. Two other cabinet members resigned, and other high officials resigned or were fired.

Finance and Industry

Investigations of American business practices paved the way for several major regulatory laws in the early decades of the twentieth century.

A 1912–1913 House investigation of the "money trust"—the concentration of money and credit in the United States—led to passage of the Federal Reserve Act of 1913, the Clayton Antitrust Act of 1914, and the Federal Trade Commission Act of 1914. A 1932–1934 Senate investigation of the stock exchange and Wall Street financial manipulation paved the way for the banking acts of 1933 and 1935, the Securities Act of 1933, and the Securities Exchange Act of 1934.

The munitions industry was the focus of an investigation by a special Senate committee in 1934–1936. The committee was chaired by Gerald P. Nye, a Progressive Republican from North Dakota. It set out to prove that arms makers were merchants of death who promoted conflicts throughout the world to reap enormous profits. The evidence was thin, and the inquiry produced no legislation. Still it established Nye as leader of the movement to curb the arms traffic and as the nation's most eloquent isolationist.

Lawmakers more recently have responded to news of corporate fraud with investigative hearings. Congress reacted to the December 2001 bankruptcy of Houston energy giant Enron Corp. with hearings into how the company fabricated financial results, and the role its accountants played in the

Congressional investigations often focus on the business practices of U.S. companies. After investigating the sudden and devastating bankruptcy of energy giant Enron, Congress mandated new accounting and disclosure rules for publicly traded companies.
Source: AP Images/Pat Sullivan

scheme. Though key executives refused to testify, citing their Fifth Amendment rights against self-incrimination, the hearings prompted legislation that imposed new rules on accounting firms that audit publicly traded companies, mandated new disclosure and conflict-of-interest rules for those companies, and increased penalties for securities fraud.

Subversives

After World War I members of Congress frequently pushed for inquiries into threats to national security posed by groups within the United States that were loyal to other nations. After World War II rising tensions with the Soviet Union raised fears of communist subversion, and investigations of communist activities set the stage for enactment of various antisubversive laws.

In 1938 the House established the Special Committee to Investigate Un-American Activities and Propaganda in the United States. The committee was known popularly as the Dies Committee after its first chair, Rep. Martin Dies Jr., a Texas Democrat. The committee and its successors weathered nearly four decades of controversy.

In 1945 the Dies Committee was replaced by the House Un-American Activities Committee. Like its predecessor, the new committee carried on a crusade against persons and groups it considered to be subversive. Witnesses who agreed with the committee's activities accused hundreds of citizens of being communists or communist sympathizers. The committee's aggressive style raised concerns about abuse of Congress's investigative powers and the need to safeguard the constitutional rights of those who appeared before or were investigated by the committee.

A remark made to a witness by Rep. J. Parnell Thomas, a New Jersey Republican who was chair of the House Un-American Activities Committee in 1947–1949, was a good indication of the committee's view of its power: "The rights you have are the rights given you by this committee. We will determine what rights you have and what rights you have not got before the committee."

> *"The rights you have are the rights given you by this committee. We will determine what rights you have and what rights you have not got before the committee."*
>
> —**Rep. J. Parnell Thomas**, R-N.J., chair of the House Un-American Committee to a witness appearing before the panel

In 1947 the panel trained its sights on the movie industry. Hollywood personalities, including an actor named Ronald Reagan, testified about communist efforts to infiltrate the Screen Actors Guild. It was the year of the Hollywood Ten, mostly screenwriters such as Dalton Trumbo, who defiantly challenged the panel's conduct and later went to jail for contempt of Congress. Nervous studio executives responded with a blacklist of suspected communists, who were barred from Hollywood jobs. The blacklisting practice lingered into the 1950s and beyond.

"I've said many a time that I think the Un-American Activities Committee ... was the most un-American thing in America!"

—Former President Harry S. Truman in a 1959 lecture

The Un-American Activities Committee, with Nixon playing a key role, gained the most attention in 1948 with a dramatic confrontation between Alger Hiss, a State Department official, and a man named Whittaker Chambers, who accused Hiss of having been a communist years earlier. While Hiss professed his innocence, Nixon doggedly pursued the matter. He eventually managed to refute Hiss's claim that he did not know Chambers, paving the way for Hiss to be convicted and jailed for perjury.

In the early 1950s the Un-American Activities Committee was overshadowed by Sen. Joseph McCarthy's more flamboyant hunt for communists. But McCarthy's investigation into alleged subversion in the U.S. Army, televised nationwide in 1954, ultimately convinced his Senate colleagues that he had gone too far. The Senate's 1954 vote to censure McCarthy for his tactics ended his crusade, but the Un-American Activities Committee continued its work until the House abolished it in 1975.

In 1947 the House Un-American Activities Committee investigated alleged communist influence on the movie industry.
Source: CQ Photo

Concern over how U.S. nuclear secrets are protected peaked in 1999 and 2000 following revelations of lax security at the Department of Energy's nuclear weapons laboratories. A bipartisan House committee report, released in 1999, detailed China's alleged attempts to steal highly classified information from the labs and confirmed earlier newspaper reports that China had used a network of spies, front companies, and visitors to the United States to obtain nuclear secrets and other military technology over several decades. Attention was particularly focused on Wen Ho Lee, a former scientist at the Los Alamos National Laboratory in New Mexico, who was suspected of giving nuclear weapons data to China, though he was not charged with espionage. Lee in 2000 pleaded guilty to one felony count of mishandling classified information. (Lee later sued the government and several news organizations for invasion of privacy as a result of leaks about his involvement in the affairs. In 2006 the government and news organizations jointly paid Lee $1.6 million to settle the suit.) The congressional probe led lawmakers to respond by placing the Energy Department's nuclear weapons program into a new agency, the National Nuclear Security Administration. Lawmakers took other actions, including expanding polygraph testing of Energy Department workers in sensitive jobs.

Age of Television

Televised hearings, first used spectacularly by the Un-American Activities Committee in 1948, soon were adopted by other committees as well. Although television exposed witnesses to vast, often damaging, publicity, it enabled ambitious members of Congress to make a name for themselves in national politics.

In 1950–1951 Sen. Estes KEFAUVER, a Tennessee Democrat, used televised hearings by his special investigating committee to spotlight racketeering, drug trafficking, and other organized crime. One of the highlights of the hearings was the appearance before the committee of reputed underworld king Frank Costello. Costello refused to have his face televised, so television audiences viewed only his hands.

The Kefauver hearings were followed by scores of citations for contempt of Congress and many local indictments for criminal activities. In a series of reports the committee claimed that crime syndicates were operating with the connivance and protection of law enforcement officials. Kefauver became a leading presidential candidate after the widely viewed hearings; he was the unsuccessful Democratic nominee for vice president in 1956.

In 1957 another special committee, chaired by Sen. John L. McClellan, an Arkansas Democrat, began investigating shady activities of labor unions. The panel's chief counsel was Robert F. Kennedy, brother of future president John F. KENNEDY and himself a future senator and presidential candidate. The committee focused much attention on the Teamsters union and its president, James R. Hoffa, whom it characterized as a national menace running a "hoodlum empire." During the committee's 270 days of hearings, 343 witnesses invoked their Fifth Amendment right against self-incrimination. The inquiry led to the 1959 passage of the Landrum-Griffin Act, a measure designed to fight corruption in union affairs.

Abuses of Power

The Watergate scandal prompted a 1973–1974 investigation by a Senate select committee that looked into widespread abuses of power by President Nixon and his top aides. The Senate committee was established early in 1973 to investigate White House involvement in a break-in the previous year at Democratic National Committee offices in the Watergate complex in Washington, D.C.

The committee hearings revealed a pattern of political sabotage that went far beyond the original break-in. They also brought to light administration efforts to cover up the affair. The Watergate hearings led to the disclosure of tape recordings of Nixon's White House conversations and revelations of his role in the cover-up. In summer 1974 the House Judiciary Committee capped its investigation by voting articles of impeachment against Nixon. He resigned on August 9, 1974, rather than face a House impeachment vote and probable conviction by the Senate.

Six months later a Senate select committee was established to look into charges of another form of government abuse: activities by the Central Intelligence Agency (CIA) that exceeded its legal authority. The Senate committee conducted a fifteen-month inquiry that confirmed accounts of CIA spying on U.S. citizens, assassination plots against foreign leaders, and other abuses. In the wake of the Senate's CIA investigation, and a parallel one conducted by a House special committee, both chambers created ongoing intelligence committees with oversight jurisdiction over the CIA.

The CIA also figured in 1987 hearings on the Iran-contra affair. Several witnesses testified that CIA officials had actively participated in a network of aid to the "contra" guerrillas in Nicaragua at a time when official U.S. assistance was barred by law. The Reagan administration's backing of the Nicaraguan rebels led Democrats to charge that the administration had flouted the will of Congress, endangering the constitutional system of government. In its November 1987 report, a bipartisan majority of the committee faulted the White House for "secrecy, deception, and disdain for the rule of law."

Practices at the Department of Housing and Urban Development (HUD) were the subject of congressional investigations in 1989. Three committees, with a House subcommittee on employment and housing in the lead, uncovered evidence of influence peddling and political favoritism within the agency during the Reagan administration.

Perhaps the most difficult investigations for Congress are those that involve abuses of power by its own members. In the early 1990s, the Senate took on the painful task of investigating five of its own members for actions that at least appeared unethical. After more than a year of investigation and two months of televised hearings, one senator was harshly rebuked and four others reprimanded for their actions on behalf of Charles H. Keating Jr., the powerful owner of a thrift and real estate empire.

The Democratic takeover of both the Senate and House in the 2006 elections set off a flurry of investigations as the 110th Congress unfolded in 2007. Democrats began focusing on a variety of Bush administration activities that they had long contended needed aggressive oversight and that they alleged the Republicans, when they were the majority from 2001 through 2006, were unwilling to undertake. The most volatile of the investigations in the early months of 2007 concerned activities in the Justice Department involving—Democrats alleged—firing of nine U.S. attorneys for political reasons. This investigation by June had produced subpoenas to former White House officials and a claim by Bush of executive privilege to prevent the individuals from testifying before Congress.

Partisanship

The investigation of House Speaker Jim WRIGHT on ethics charges in 1989—and his eventual resignation from Congress—set off a new era of highly partisan congressional investigations not previously seen in the modern Congress. Using tactics pioneered by backbencher Newt GINGRICH of Georgia in his pursuit of Wright, members sought to destroy rivals both personally and politically, by using investigations, demands for special prosecutors, ethics charges, or seemingly any other technique that would garner advantage. Some referred to it as "the politics of personal destruction." (See ETHICS.)

After becoming Speaker in 1995, Gingrich himself faced the ire of the Democratic minority, which filed dozens of ethics complaints against him. After admitting that he had misled one ethics investigation, Gingrich became the first Speaker to be reprimanded by the House and charged with paying a $300,000 penalty.

After taking control of Congress in 1995, the Republican majority launched numerous congressional investigations of the Democratic Clinton administration, exacerbating partisan warfare. From investigating the president and first lady's financial involvement in Whitewater to campaign finance abuses in Clinton's successful 1996 reelection effort, these investigations turned up little and cast public doubt on Republican motives. For example, during the investigations into campaign finance abuses of the 1996 presidential race, the Republicans were accused of abusing their subpoena powers to investigate campaign violations by Democrats while virtually ignoring Republicans.

Bruised in the polls by public distaste of such partisan tactics and by a poor showing in the 1998 midterm elections where the Republicans lost five seats, House Speaker J. Dennis HASTERT at the start of the 106th Congress (1999–2001) signaled that he was against funding further investigations of the Clinton administration. With the acquittal of President Clinton of two impeachment articles in February 1999, the mood of the public seemed to favor such a shift in congressional energy.

Iran-contra Affair

Debate over Congress's proper role in foreign policy was rekindled in 1986 with the startling revelation of secret U.S. arms sales to Iran. Iran was considered an enemy nation after it held Americans hostage for more than a year beginning in 1979. Moreover, some of the profits from those

The most publicized form of congressional oversight involves investigations and hearings, which often provide dramatic moments on Capitol Hill. The Iran-contra hearings in 1987 were held under the glare of television lights.
Source: CQ Photo/Ken Heinen

sales had been diverted to U.S.-backed "contra" rebels fighting the leftist government of Nicaragua. Congress had been kept in the dark about the Iranian arms sales and had banned U.S. aid to the contras.

The disclosures triggered several investigations and curtailed the political effectiveness of a very popular president, Ronald Reagan.

What Happened

Following the trails that brought two countries on opposite sides of the globe—Nicaragua and Iran—together in a U.S. foreign policy scandal was not an easy task for investigators or the American public. A bewildering array of charges, allegations, and facts emerged.

Contra Aid

U.S. involvement with the Nicaraguan contras began in the early 1980s when the Reagan administration authorized the Central Intelligence Agency (CIA) to form a paramilitary force to harass the leftist Sandinista government of Nicaragua. The amount of aid provided to the contra force grew, but a skeptical Congress began to restrict and ultimately cut off U.S. aid.

As it became clear in 1984 that Congress would block further assistance for the contras, an alternative network of aid was developed, under the direction of an aide to the president's National Security Council (NSC), Lt. Col. Oliver L. North. North raised funds for the contras from wealthy Americans, while other members of the administration solicited money from foreign allies. North, apparently working closely with CIA director William J. Casey, provided the contras with intelligence information and advice on military tactics. He also arranged for the contras to buy covert shipments of arms. Although providing regular CIA aid was illegal, CIA agents cooperated unofficially with North's private aid network.

Lt. Col. Oliver North gestures while testifying before the joint House-Senate committee investigating the Iran-contra affair in July 1987. North said he was willing to be the scapegoat if the arms diversion plan was revealed to the public.
Source: AP Images/Lana Harris

When questions about North's activities were raised on Capitol Hill, North's bosses—national security adviser Robert C. McFarlane and his successor, Vice Admiral John M. Poindexter—insisted that the administration was complying with congressional restrictions. North and Poindexter later contended to investigators that Congress had barred involvement with the contras only by the U.S. intelligence agencies, not by the NSC staff.

In early 1986 the contra operation crossed paths with another covert operation, arms sales to Iran, when some of the profits from the Iranian sales were used to help finance the contra-aid network.

Iran Initiative

Despite a U.S. policy against arms sales to Iran and deep enmity between the United States and the Iranian government, the Reagan administration in 1985 approved Israeli sales of U.S. arms to Iran. In 1986 the United States began selling arms directly to Iran. The sales were intended to help win, through Iranian intercession, the release of American hostages kidnapped in war-torn Lebanon by pro-Iranian groups.

In December 1985 Reagan signed a "finding" retroactively authorizing CIA participation in a November 1985 arms sale. In January 1986 he signed another finding, which authorized direct arms sales and contained an important and unusual provision directing that Congress not be told about it. Reagan allowed ten months to pass before he formally notified Congress, and he did so only after his secret was published in a Beirut magazine.

Congressional investigators were later told that about $3.5 million was diverted to the contras out of the profits from the Iranian arms sales.

Investigations

When the Iran-contra story broke in November 1986, investigators scrambled to find out what had happened. Conflicting recollections, contradictory statements from the White House, sloppy record keeping, a misleading chronology prepared by key participants, destruction and alteration of documents, and the illness and death of former CIA director Casey complicated their job.

An inquiry into the Iranian arms sales was made by Attorney General Edwin Meese III. Although much criticized for its investigative techniques, Meese's inquiry uncovered a memo from North that mentioned the diversion of funds to the contras. In the aftermath of that revelation, North was fired and Poindexter resigned.

Reagan then appointed a prestigious review board, headed by former senator John Tower, a Texas Republican. Other board members were former senator and secretary of state Edmund S. Muskie, a Maine Democrat, and former national security adviser and retired lieutenant general Brent Scowcroft, who later served as President George H.W. Bush's national security adviser. The Tower commission served up a damning indictment of failures by Reagan and his aides throughout the events of the Iran-contra affair. The board criticized the president's inattention to detail and the White House staff's failure to take compensating steps. It said the administration should adhere to existing structures and procedures instead of creating ad hoc means of carrying out foreign policy and should be more responsive to congressional concerns.

Congress launched other investigations. The House and Senate Intelligence committees and the House Foreign Affairs Committee held hearings. Each chamber also appointed a select investigating committee. Those committees were headed by Sen. Daniel K. Inouye of Hawaii and Rep. Lee H. Hamilton of Indiana, both Democrats.

In a strongly worded report released in late 1987, the bipartisan majority of the select committees found that the failures of the affair stemmed from White House "secrecy, deception, and disdain for the rule of law." The committees found a pervasive willingness by administration officials to use any means, legal or illegal, to accomplish the president's policy objectives. The majority charged that the administration had "violated," "disregarded," or "abused" a series of laws and executive orders.

The majority devoted a chapter of its report to a defense of the proposition that Congress and the executive branch share power over foreign policy. North and Poindexter had bluntly told the committees that Congress should stay out of foreign policy, and even Secretary of State George P. Shultz, who was considered to be one of the Reagan officials most sensitive to congressional sentiment, had complained about congressional interference in the conduct of diplomacy. (See EXECUTIVE BRANCH AND CONGRESS.)

A Republican minority of the two committees issued a heated rebuttal to the report, acknowledging that Reagan had made mistakes but claiming that most of the fault rested with Congress for interfering with the president's policies.

Independent Counsel

Shortly after the scandal broke, the Reagan administration, under political pressure, requested appointment of an independent counsel, or special prosecutor. Retired federal judge Lawrence E. Walsh, an Oklahoma Republican, was selected.

Walsh's lengthy probe resulted in indictments of Iran-contra participants both within and outside of government, but his efforts in the major cases ultimately proved unsuccessful. North and Poindexter were tried and convicted of felony charges, but their convictions were overturned on the grounds that their trials might have been tainted by their earlier immunized testimony before Congress. Six other high-ranking officials indicted or convicted in the scandal were pardoned by Bush just weeks before he left the White House. Bush said the prosecutions represented not law enforcement but "the criminalization of policy differences." Among the six was Caspar W. Weinberger, Reagan's former secretary of defense, who was awaiting trial on charges that included lying to Congress.

Walsh concluded his seven-year, approximately $38 million investigation in January 1994. In his final report, he exonerated Reagan of criminal culpability in the affair even as he bluntly accused the former president of creating a climate in which his senior aides felt free to violate the law. Unlike the congressional investigating committees that put the blame on a middle-level "cabal of zealots," Walsh said Reagan and his entire foreign policy team knowingly pursued the secret programs. Walsh also sharply disputed Bush's assertions that he had been "out of the loop" during the dealings with Iran.

Both former presidents Reagan and Bush denied wrongdoing and denounced Walsh's investigation, as did most of the other former officials named by Walsh.

J

Jefferson's Manual

Thomas Jefferson
Source: Library of Congress

The Senate's first compilation of procedures was prepared by Thomas Jefferson for his guidance when he was president of the Senate in the years of his vice presidency (1797–1801). Known as *Jefferson's Manual of Parliamentary Practice*, the work reflected English parliamentary practice of his day. *Jefferson's Manual* was adopted in part by the House of Representatives in 1837 and remains the foundation for many practices in the modern Senate and House. (See HOUSE MANUAL; SENATE MANUAL.)

Johnson, Hiram

Hiram Johnson (1866–1945), a California Republican, was an isolationist leader in the Senate in the period of World Wars I and II. Before entering the Senate in 1917, Johnson served six years as a reform governor of California. He was Theodore Roosevelt's running mate on the unsuccessful Progressive (Bull Moose) ticket in 1912. In the Senate, Johnson worked to block U.S. participation in the League of Nations and the World Court following World War I. He opposed U.S. participation in World War II and the United Nations Charter in 1945.

Johnson, Lyndon B.

Lyndon B. Johnson would often employ the "Johnson treatment"—use of his imposing six-foot, three-inch frame in very close physical encounters to persuade others. Here Johnson, as Senate majority leader, works on Theodore F. Green, chair of the Senate Foreign Relations Committee, in 1957.
Source: George Tames/*New York Times*/Redux

Lyndon B. Johnson (1908–1973) is considered by many scholars as one of the most important political leaders, and presidents, in the nation's history. More than three decades after his death, he remains a controversial figure whose record, both in Congress and the White House, continues to be debated.

He succeeded to the presidency after the assassination of John F. KENNEDY in 1963. After being elected to a term of his own in 1964, he pressed Congress to enact his GREAT SOCIETY programs, which were designed to fight poverty, ignorance, disease, and other social problems. By 1968, however, his expansion of U.S. involvement in the Vietnam War had weakened his popularity, and he declined to run for another term.

Schooled in politics on Capitol Hill, the Texas Democrat used that expertise when he became president. He built a working relationship with Congress considered the best of any president in modern times until the public's growing discontent with the war ruined his influence and forced him to disavow seeking another term.

Johnson first came to Washington in December 1931 to work for a House member from his home state. When a Texas representative died in 1937, Johnson won a special election to fill the vacancy. But he was impatient with the slow pace of the House, where power accrued gradually through the SENIORITY SYSTEM. When a Texas senator died in 1941 Johnson, then thirty-two, ran in a special election to fill the seat. He lost narrowly, despite support from President Franklin D. Roosevelt.

He succeeded on his second try in 1948, winning the primary by a margin of eighty-seven votes—and earning the nickname "Landslide Lyndon." Johnson's experience on the House Naval Affairs Committee helped win him a seat on the Senate Armed Services Committee, then chaired by Georgia Democrat Richard B. RUSSELL. One of the most powerful members of the Senate, Russell led a coalition of Republicans and southern Democrats known as the CONSERVATIVE COALITION. Johnson was friendly with Russell, but he avoided a close alignment with the southern bloc. This decision later made it possible for him to work with both southern and northern Democrats.

An ambitious man with a huge ego to match, Johnson worked hard throughout his career but also—while a senator—benefited from a void in the top Democratic leadership ranks caused by election losses. In 1950 both the Democratic floor leader and whip were defeated. Johnson was still a freshman senator, but with Russell's support he was elected whip. He was elected minority floor leader in 1952, when the top post again fell vacant after an election that also cost the Democrats their majority in Congress. In 1954 the Democrats regained control of the Senate, and Johnson was elected majority leader, a job that had not tempted more senior colleagues away from their committee chairmanships. As Senate Democratic leader in the 1950s, Johnson transformed the job into a powerful, prestigious post.

Johnson had long been adept at building a network of loyal supporters. With committee assignments, campaign contributions, and a variety of other favors at his disposal, the new majority leader wove a tapestry of alliances with his colleagues. Johnson also had an extraordinary ability to persuade others, in one-on-one encounters, through sheer force of will. The "Johnson treatment" became famous. To make a convert he might urge, threaten, beg, or cajole. "The only power available to the leader is the power of persuasion," he once said. "There is no patronage; no power to discipline; no authority to fire senators like a president can fire members of his cabinet."

Johnson was often described as crude and sometimes as cruel, but even his detractors had to acknowledge his talent for Senate leadership. As minority leader he worked to maintain amicable relations between President Dwight D. Eisenhower and Senate Democrats. He convinced the Democratic caucus in 1953 to give each senator, regardless of seniority, a seat on a major committee. This move, known as the "Johnson rule," presaged the congressional reform of the 1970s. In 1957 Johnson engineered passage of the first civil rights bill since Reconstruction. A testimony to Johnson's skill as majority leader, it passed without a filibuster and without causing a rift in the Democratic Party.

Building on his six years of success as majority leader, Johnson ran for the presidency in 1960. After an intense battle for the Democratic nomination, he surprised many by agreeing to run for vice president on a ticket headed by Kennedy. Like other vice presidents, Johnson was never comfortable in the role. He also differed markedly in style and background from Kennedy and his top aides.

Kennedy's assassination on November 22, 1963, elevated Johnson to the presidency. In 1964 he won election to a full term in a landslide victory over Republican Barry Goldwater. Johnson took advantage of an overwhelmingly Democratic Congress to complete action on Kennedy's legislative program and then to win passage of his own Great Society bills and civil rights legislation that many historians consider his most important legacy. Of the supportive Congress he remarked that it "could be better, but not this side of heaven." Johnson still suffered, however, from the feeling that he remained in Kennedy's shadow. "They say Jack Kennedy had style, but I'm the one who's got the bills passed," Johnson told a group of senators in 1966.

Johnson's good relationship with Congress did not last. The 1966 midterm elections brought forty-seven additional Republicans to the House and three to the Senate. Concerned about the escalating war in Vietnam, the country's economic problems, and urban rioting, Congress and the public expressed growing dissatisfaction with the administration. On March 31, 1968, Johnson announced that he would not seek reelection. At the end of his term he retired to his Texas ranch, where he died of a heart attack on January 22, 1973.

Johnson Impeachment Trial

During the first 210 years of the presidency, only one chief executive of the United States stood trial on impeachment charges: President Andrew Johnson, who in 1868 escaped removal from office by a single Senate vote. This changed in December 1998 when the Republican-led House of Representatives impeached President Bill Clinton, who was acquitted in the Senate in 1999.

The impeachment power granted by the Constitution permits Congress to remove federal officials it finds guilty of grave misconduct. The process requires two steps. An accused official must first

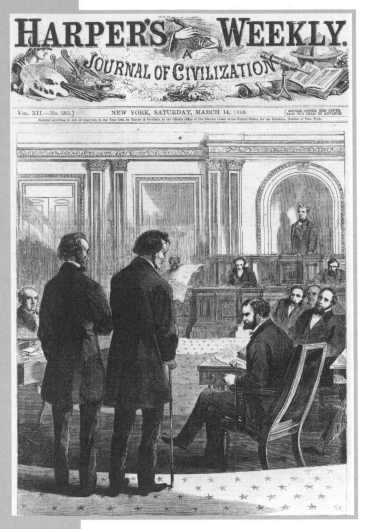

HARPER'S WEEKLY.

JOURNAL OF CIVILIZATION

Vol. XII.—No. 585.]   NEW YORK, SATURDAY, MARCH 14, 1868.   [SINGLE COPIES, TEN CENTS.
$4.00 PER YEAR IN ADVANCE.

Andrew Johnson was the first U.S. president to stand trial in the Senate on impeachment charges. In this illustration Rep. Thaddeus Stevens (left) and Rep. John A Bingham appear before the Senate to read the charges. Johnson escaped removal from office in 1968 by a single Senate vote.
Source: Library of Congress

be formally charged, or impeached, by the House of Representatives. The official is then tried in the Senate, where a two-thirds majority is required for conviction.

Johnson was charged with having dismissed the secretary of war in violation of the Tenure of Office Act. But his impeachment was part of a larger political struggle with a hostile Congress. A Tennessee Democrat who had remained loyal to the Union at the outbreak of the Civil War, Johnson was chosen as Republican Abraham Lincoln's vice-presidential running mate in 1864 on the Union ticket—an attempt to unify the nation as the war wound to a close. Johnson became president upon Lincoln's assassination the following year. Johnson tried to pursue Lincoln's moderate approach to the South, but this brought him into conflict with the Republican-controlled Congress—particularly the Radical Republicans, who favored harsh treatment of the defeated Confederacy.

On their first attempt to impeach Johnson, in 1867, the Radical Republicans suffered a crushing defeat. The House Judiciary Committee recommended impeachment on general charges, but the full House of Representatives rejected an impeachment resolution by a vote of 108 to 57.

A second impeachment effort was triggered early in 1868 when Johnson dismissed Secretary of War Edwin M. Stanton, a holdover from the Lincoln administration who had close ties to the Radical Republicans. In dismissing Stanton, Johnson defied the Tenure of Office Act, which required Senate approval for removal of government

officials who had been appointed with Senate consent. The tenure law had been enacted over Johnson's veto in 1867. Its purpose was to protect Republican officeholders from executive retaliation if they did not support the president. Johnson's action infuriated Congress, which moved swiftly to impeach him. The House Committee on Reconstruction, headed by Rep. Thaddeus STEVENS of Pennsylvania, one of the Radical Republican leaders, reported an impeachment resolution on February 22, 1868. The full House approved the measure two days later by a 126–47 vote that divided along party lines.

In early March the House approved specific charges, called articles of impeachment, against Johnson and chose seven of its members to prosecute the charges before the Senate. There were eleven articles in all, the main one concerning Johnson's removal of Stanton.

The Senate trial ran from March 30 to May 26. Chief Justice Salmon P. Chase presided, as required by the Constitution in a presidential impeachment trial. The president himself did not appear. He was represented by a team of lawyers headed by Henry Stanbery, who had resigned as attorney general to lead the defense.

After weeks of argument and testimony, the Senate on May 16 voted on a catchall charge considered most likely to result in a vote for conviction. The drama of the vote has become legendary. With thirty-six votes needed for conviction, the final count was guilty, thirty-five, and not guilty, nineteen. Seven Republicans joined twelve Democrats in supporting Johnson. Votes on two further charges were taken May 26, and again the tally was one short of conviction, 35–19. The trial was abruptly ended to save Johnson's opponents from further defeats.

One reason why several Republicans voted to acquit Johnson may have been their distaste for the next-in-line for the presidency—Benjamin F. Wade of Ohio, the president pro tempore of the Senate. Wade was an uncompromising Radical who offended many moderate and conservative Republicans. Another possible reason was the impending end of Johnson's term. With less than one year to go, Johnson was politically hamstrung by a veto-proof Republican majority. The Republicans who voted against conviction wanted General Ulysses S. Grant to be their party's presidential candidate. If Wade were to succeed Johnson, this was less likely to happen.

Grant became the Republican candidate and won the 1868 election. The Tenure of Office Act was weakened early in his administration because Republicans had regained control of the appointment power. The act was eventually repealed in 1887. In 1926 the Supreme Court declared that the tenure act had been unconstitutional.

After he left the White House in 1869, Johnson returned to Tennessee, where the state legislature elected him to the Senate in 1874. Johnson became the first and only ex-president to serve in the Senate. He died five months into his term in 1875.

More on this topic:
Clinton Impeachment Trial, p. 97
Impeachment Power, p. 280
Removal Power, p. 474

Joint Committee

Most congressional committees are established separately in either the House or the Senate, although nearly all have roughly parallel responsibilities with their counterparts in the other chamber. But a few committees are established as joint panels with members selected from each house. The functions of most joint committees involve investigation, research, or oversight of agencies closely related to Congress. Permanent joint committees, created by statute, are sometimes called standing joint committees. At one time they were numerous but in 2007—as for most recent years before that—there were just four: Joint Economic, Joint Taxation, Joint Library, and Joint Printing. None has authority to report legislation.

Sometimes Congress will establish temporary joint committees by concurrent resolution. Technically, all conference committees—created to resolve differences between Senate and House versions of bills—are temporary joint committees, but they are never called by that name.

Usually, the Senate and House have equal representation of committees, although that is not true of conference committees. Chairs of a joint committee usually rotate between the houses from Congress to Congress.

Joint Resolution

Congress uses joint resolutions for purposes other than general legislation. It is similar to a bill in that it has the force of law when passed by both houses and signed by the president, or passed over a presidential veto. The measures are designated H.J. Res if originating in the House or S.J. Res if in the Senate.

Usually joint resolutions are employed to deal with relatively limited matters such as correcting errors in existing law, making continuing appropriations or a single appropriation, or establishing a permanent joint committee. Unlike bills, however, joint resolutions also are used to propose constitutional amendments. In this case the measures do not need the president's approval. They become effective only when ratified by three-fourths of the states. In addition, preambles are sometimes included in joint resolutions. Preambles are not used in a bill, but they may be used in a joint resolution to set out events or facts that prompted the measure. A declaration of war is a prominent example. (See LEGISLATION.)

Joint Session; Joint Meeting

A combined meeting of the Senate and House of Representatives is called a joint session or a joint meeting of Congress, depending on what arrangements are made.

Joint sessions require adoption of a concurrent resolution by each chamber. Joint meetings are held when each chamber merely agrees to recess to meet with the other body.

A combined meeting to hear the U.S. president is called a joint session of Congress. Such sessions are always held in the House chamber, which has a larger seating capacity than the Senate chamber. A joint session usually is held early each year to hear the president's STATE OF THE UNION address. The president may address joint sessions at other times as well.

Important visiting foreign leaders occasionally speak before a joint session of the House and Senate. Here Mexican president Vicente Fox addresses a joint session of Congress in 2001.
Source: CQ Photo/Scott J. Ferrell

From time to time foreign leaders are invited to address joint meetings of Congress. Strictly speaking, such occasions are not joint sessions. The first foreign leader to address Congress was the Marquis de Lafayette, the French hero of the American Revolution, in 1824. This event has historically been called the first joint meeting of Congress. But the House and Senate Journals of the time indicate that Lafayette actually addressed the House of Representatives with a few senators present as guests of House members. Since then nearly 100 foreign dignitaries had addressed joint meetings by early 2007. Congress turned down a proposed address by Soviet leader Mikhail S. Gorbachev in 1987; it was said that such appearances should be reserved for world leaders who were friends of democracy.

The Constitution requires that Congress meet jointly every four years to count electoral votes for president and vice president. These meetings are called joint sessions. If no candidate receives a majority of the electoral vote, the House and Senate must vote separately to decide the outcome: The House chooses the president, the Senate the vice president. (See ELECTING THE PRESIDENT.)

Journal

A Journal is the official record of House or Senate actions. It includes every motion offered, every vote cast, amendment agreed to, quorum call, and many other details of daily congressional activity. It does not, unlike the *Congressional Record*, provide a record of speeches, debates, statements, and similar activity.

The Constitution requires each house to maintain a journal and publish it periodically. The House keeps a single journal while the Senate keeps four: one for its legislative sessions; a second titled Executive Proceedings in the Senate, for its executive business sessions; a third for confidential legislative proceedings; and the fourth for proceedings when it sits as a court of impeachment.

Judiciary Committee, House

Legislation on many controversial issues, such as abortion, civil rights, and gun control must begin its path through the House in the Judiciary Committee. Because the committee deals with such highly politicized issues, some of the most partisan representatives in the House gravitate to the panel. Perhaps the committee's greatest notoriety results from its jurisdiction over impeachment. Articles of impeachment against two presidents—Richard NIXON in 1974 and Bill Clinton in 1998— originated there. The first attempt to impeach President Andrew Johnson in 1867 came out of the committee. It failed but a different panel tried again the following year. The House approved that effort but the Senate did not convict Johnson.

During a 2007 hearing on the Bush administration's controversial dismissal of U.S. attorney generals, John Conyers Jr., D-Mich., chair of the House Judiciary Committee, consults with Linda T. Sanchez, D-Calif., chair of the House Judiciary Commercial and Administrative Law Subcommittee.
Source: CQ Photo/Scott J. Ferrell

While most committees concentrate on programs or dollars and cents, the Judiciary Committee often deals with raw emotion. Under liberal leadership in the 1960s, the panel gave civil rights legislation a boost; in the 1970s and 1980s the same liberal advantage foiled conservatives seeking constitutional amendments to outlaw abortion and busing and to permit school prayer. Critics called the Judiciary Committee a legislative mortuary.

The Judiciary Committee helped draft a variety of laws in the 1980s and early 1990s. Voting rights laws were extended, anticrime and antidrug programs were passed, and the nation's immigration laws were overhauled. When Republicans took control of the House in 1995, the committee took a sharp turn to the right. The panel was the starting point for key portions of the House Republicans' "Contract with America"—from constitutional amendments to balance the federal budget to tough anticrime measures.

CLOSER LOOK

The Judiciary Committee often deals with raw, emotional issues. In the 1960s it gave civil rights a boost. In the 1970s and 1980s it foiled conservative efforts to outlaw abortion and school busing and to permit school prayer. Critics have called the panel a legislative mortuary.

History

One of the first standing committees created by the House, the Judiciary panel was made permanent in 1813. Because of its responsibility for handling constitutional amendments, the committee has participated in a large share of Congress's most difficult and important decisions over the years.

Between the mid-1950s and the late 1980s, the committee had only two chairs: Democrats Emanuel Celler of New York and Peter W. Rodino Jr. of New Jersey. No other House committee could make that claim.

Celler first chaired the panel from 1949 until Republicans gained the House majority in 1953. Then Celler again served as chair from 1955 to 1973. Under his leadership the committee in the 1950s focused on antitrust violations and monopolies, then shifted to civil rights legislation in the 1960s. Celler's support of civil rights was crucial because the Senate Judiciary Committee was led by an ardent opponent of the legislation. Celler also was a key advocate of immigration reform, passed in 1965, and gun control. Considered an autocratic chair, he shared little authority with subcommittees. At age eighty-four, he lost a bid for renomination in 1972.

Rodino took over in 1973 and had been chair for barely a year when the Watergate scandal put the committee in the national spotlight. At first criticized for moving slowly, Rodino was later praised for his evenhandedness in the inquiry. By avoiding a partisan approach, he was able to pick up impeachment votes from Republicans. In late July 1974 the Judiciary Committee voted three articles of impeachment against President Nixon, who resigned in early August before the House could act on the articles.

Rodino continued the tradition of liberal politics and, like Celler, kept action under his control in the full committee. Cautious and deliberate, he usually focused on just a few issues in each Congress. Although a more philosophical, aggressive chair might have served as a visible counterpoint to the conservative social agenda of President Ronald Reagan, Rodino preferred to be a relatively quiet obstructionist. But he still knew how to save faltering legislation; he did so in 1986 on immigration reform, when he successfully pressured key negotiators to keep talking.

During the late 1980s the committee handled the impeachment of several federal judges. Judge Harry E. Claiborne was the first official in fifty years to be removed from office by impeachment and the fifth in the history of the country. The panel then recommended the impeachment of federal judges Walter L. Nixon Jr. and Alcee L. Hastings. Both were impeached by the full House and convicted and removed from office by the Senate. Hastings later won election to the House in 1992.

Texas Democrat Jack Brooks became chair of the committee in 1989. An irascible partisan, though no liberal, Brooks made his mark immediately by pushing a vertical price-fixing bill and a civil rights measure through Congress.

In 1995, when Illinois Republican Henry J. Hyde became the chair, the committee quickly refocused on social issues troubling to conservatives—including illegal immigration, same-gender marriages, and domestic terrorism. A longtime antiabortion advocate, Hyde's committee pushed a ban of the controversial late-term "partial-birth" abortion method. Hyde's name had become a household word in the 1970s because of a series of "Hyde amendments," barring federal funding of abortion affixed to various appropriations bills. Hyde was not the original author of the amendment idea, but he was the most energetic proponent of its use.

In fall 1998 the eyes of the nation again became riveted on the Judiciary Committee as it held hearings on the impeachment charges brought by independent counsel Kenneth W. Starr against President Clinton. Although regarded as thoughtful and fair-minded, Hyde had difficulty presiding over the often rancorous, bitterly partisan hearings on whether Clinton illegally tried to cover up an extramarital affair. Abandoning any pretense of bipartisanship, the Republican majority pushed on with the inquiry in the face of strenuous Democratic complaints of unfairness and unwavering public opinion against impeachment. Along strict party lines, the House Judiciary Committee recommended four articles of impeachment to the full House, which adopted two of them in December 1998. The Senate acquitted the president in February 1999.

Under the leadership of Wisconsin Republican James Sensenbrenner, who took over as chair in 2001, the committee approved major legislation following the September 11, 2001, terrorist attacks in New York and Washington. Despite misgivings of some lawmakers over the possible impact on civil liberties, Congress overwhelmingly agreed to legislation that gave the Bush administration sweeping new authority to track, arrest, and prosecute suspected terrorists. President George W. Bush had requested the powers. The House Judiciary Committee had laboriously marked up a bipartisan bill, but after the White House voiced its opposition, Sensenbrenner worked with the House leadership and White House negotiators to produce legislation closer to the administration's position.

The following year, Sensenbrenner's committee participated in drafting the legislation creating an agency of homeland security. The panel assisted in reaching agreement on provisions to abolish the Immigration and Naturalization Service (INS) and replace it with two separate bureaus—one to handle immigration services, and another to protect the borders and keep out illegal immigrants. Both bureaus were to become components of the newly created Department of Homeland Security.

Sensenbrenner continued as chair until the Democrats regained the majority in the 110th Congress in 2007. He was replaced by John Conyers Jr. of Michigan. The most evident result of the change was the disappearance from the agenda of various proposals—some constitutional amendments, some legislation—that Republicans previously had served up to fortify their base of conservative partisans. Gone were proposals to bar gay marriage and flag burning, to strip federal courts of jurisdiction over social issues such as the Pledge of Allegiance, and to provide still mandatory minimum prison sentences.

Democrats instead focused on the expansive claims of President George W. Bush's administration about executive power such as a controversial warrantless surveillance program. Democrats on the committee also revisited a law from the last Congress that governed interrogations and trial of terrorist detainees. Another deeply divisive issue under the jurisdiction of the committee, reform of the nation's immigration system, fell off the committee's agenda in 2007 when an immigration overhaul bill died in the Senate. The issue was not likely to surface again until after the 2008 elections.

Judiciary Committee, Senate

Ideological issues dominate the Senate Judiciary Committee, making it a volatile panel that attracts activists from both ends of the political spectrum. Although committee members manage to compromise on some issues, they also have bitter fights, and the nation's disputes about sensitive issues are often played out in the committee.

Dating from 1816, the Judiciary Committee is one of the oldest Senate committees but has never ranked among the most powerful. Its jurisdiction encompasses constitutional amendments, the federal judiciary, immigration, antitrust laws, and civil liberties. An important duty is recommending to the Senate whether to confirm presidential nominations to the Supreme Court, an increasingly controversial

Senior members of the Senate Judiciary Committee, (left to right) Orrin Hatch, R-Utah, Arlen Specter, R-Penn., and Patrick Leahy, D-Vt., listen to chief justice nominee John Roberts (back to camera) at his 2005 confirmation hearing.
Source: Reuters/Jonathan Ernst

undertaking. Nominations to lower federal courts also can generate great controversy within the committee and on the Senate floor—if they get that far.

History

For more than two decades, from 1956 to 1979, the Judiciary Committee was chaired by James O. Eastland, a conservative Democrat from Mississippi known for his fervent obstruction of civil rights legislation. When the Senate leadership began setting deadlines for committee action on voting rights and other bills in the mid-1960s, Eastland called the rules "legislative lynching." He never wavered in his support of conservative causes, endorsing school prayer, opposing the ban on poll taxes, arguing against immigration reform, and voting against gun control. He once claimed in a Senate address that the Supreme Court was biased in favor of communism. As committee chair, however, Eastland mellowed over the years. Autocratic and protective of his power at first, Eastland was pressured into letting subcommittees have more authority. He eventually developed a reputation for evenhandedness.

After Eastland's retirement, Massachusetts Democrat Edward M. KENNEDY served two years as chair, from 1979 to 1981. Distracted by his campaign for president, he never took advantage of the post to promote the liberal causes he supported. Kennedy won credit for working well with Republican Strom THURMOND of South Carolina when the latter became chair in 1981. Thurmond was in a position to become chair because he had opted in 1977 for the top minority spot on the Judiciary Committee instead of the Armed Services Committee. That prevented the Judiciary Committee post from going to Charles McC. Mathias Jr. of Maryland, whose liberal leanings made Republican leaders nervous. When Republicans took over the Senate and Thurmond became chair, he went so far as to abolish an antitrust subcommittee that Mathias was in line to head.

Thurmond served as chair from 1981 to 1987, while his party controlled the Senate. During that period the committee pushed through the Senate two bills high on the conservative agenda. But the measures, one to reestablish the federal death penalty and one to add a balanced budget amendment to the Constitution, died in the House and had little chance of resurrection when the Democrats took control of the Senate in 1987 and Joseph R. Biden Jr. of Delaware became chair of the Judiciary Committee.

Democrats on the Judiciary panel brought their ideological differences with the administration of President Ronald Reagan to the fore in 1987 when they recommended against the confirmation of one Supreme Court nominee, Robert H. Bork—who was rejected by the full Senate—and forced the withdrawal of a second, Douglas H. Ginsburg. But the panel was widely criticized in 1991, during the confirmation hearings of a Supreme Court appointment made by President George H. W. Bush.

Bush had nominated Clarence Thomas, a conservative African American judge, to a vacancy on the Court created by the retirement of black justice Thurgood Marshall. Although his nomination was controversial among groups

More on this topic:
Appointment Power, p. 14
Constitutional Amendments, p. 139
Judiciary Committee, House, p. 311

that opposed his judicial philosophy, Thomas was expected to be confirmed by the Senate. But as the committee hearings concluded, allegations were reported in newspapers that a former employee of Thomas had accused him of sexual harassment. Hearings were reconvened, during which University of Oklahoma law professor Anita Hill, who had worked for Thomas at the Department of Education and the Equal Employment Opportunity Commission, testified that Thomas had repeatedly sexually harassed her. The Thomas-Hill hearings, nationally televised, were sensational. Thomas denied the allegations, and a split Senate later confirmed him by the closest margin in more than a century.

The episode was a huge embarrassment for the Judiciary Committee. Biden's leadership came under strong criticism because of the committee's handling of the Thomas nomination hearings. The panel was harshly and widely criticized for not acting on the allegations as soon as it had heard them, which had been early in the committee's deliberation on the appointment. The committee was also criticized for the leak of information about the charges to the press. The episode embarrassed the full Senate as well, which was lambasted for lack of sensitivity to the issue of sexual harassment. Finally, it also drew attention to the all-male membership of the committee at that time, a situation that motivated several women to run for the Senate in 1992.

Despite such partisan disagreements, the Senate Judiciary Committee managed to compromise on many issues. In the 1980s both a major revision of the criminal code and an overhaul of the nation's immigration laws reflected cooperation between Republicans and Democrats.

When Republicans recaptured the Senate in 1995, Orrin Hatch of Utah became chair. Under Hatch, the committee pursued a conservative agenda including a balanced budget constitutional amendment and a ban on late-term "partial-birth" abortions.

Patrick J. Leahy of Vermont was given the gavel in June 2001, when control of the Senate switched to the Democrats. But Leahy had little time to promote Democratic legislation before the September 11, 2001, terrorist attacks in New York and Washington shook the nation. Despite misgivings of some lawmakers—particularly Democrats—over the possible impact on civil liberties, Congress overwhelmingly agreed to legislation that gave the administration of George W. Bush sweeping new authority to track, arrest, and prosecute suspected terrorists.

The following year, Leahy's committee participated in drafting the legislation creating an agency of homeland security. The panel assisted in reaching agreement on provisions to abolish the Immigration and Naturalization Service (INS) and replace it with two separate bureaus—one to handle immigration services, and another to protect the borders and keep out illegal immigrants. Both bureaus were to become components of the newly created Department of Homeland Security.

Leahy and Hatch, who served as the ranking Republican from 2001 to 2003, battled over the pace of action on judicial nominees. Republicans argued that Democrats were deliberately slowing the process, while Democrats said that they were moving as quickly as Republicans had done during the Clinton administration. The confirmation battles continued when the Republicans regained control of the Senate in 2003 and reflected a lengthy effort by conservatives, dating at least to the years that Ronald Reagan was in the White House in the 1980s, to reorient the judicial philosophy of the federal judiciary.

Leahy, a dedicated liberal and one-time state prosecutor, returned to the chair in 2007 as Democrats organized the 110th Congress. Judicial nominations were still on the agenda including a number of appellate judgeship left over from the last Congress. The committee increased oversight of the Bush's administration's counterterrorism efforts including the warrantless surveillance program that was on the agenda of the House Judiciary Committee. The panel was interested in increased oversight of the Justice Department as well, especially after a group of federal prosecutors were fired by the administration. Evidence began to emerge that some were dismissed for political reasons, as opposed to performance, which violate federal law.

In 2007 the committee took up immigration reform, a high priority for President Bush. Democratic leaders on the committee crafted a compromise measure to not only beef up border security and crack down on the hiring of illegal immigrants but also provide a pathway to citizenship for the estimated 12 million illegal immigrants in the country. But the measure was highly divisive, especially within the GOP where it pitted business interests against social conservatives, and it died in the full Senate in June 2007.

Junkets *See* FOREIGN TRAVEL.

Jurisdiction

Jurisdiction is the word used to denote a congressional committee's area of legislative responsibility. Committee jurisdictions are spelled out in each chamber's rules or other documents. They guide the assignment of bills to committees for preliminary consideration in the House and Senate. Most referrals are routine matters handled by the PARLIAMENTARIAN of each chamber. But sometimes jurisdictional matters are not quite so clear.

Many bills do not fall within the subject area of a single committee; in that case, they may be referred to two or more committees before going to the floor—a practice known as multiple referrals.

In the Senate, a bill could be referred to two or more panels simultaneously or sequentially, or it could be split up among the panels.

On the House side, to avoid the jurisdictional battles that sometimes had erupted during the period of Democratic rule, Republicans in 1995 abolished the referral of a bill to several committees at the same time and instead required the Speaker to designate one committee as having primary responsibility for the legislation. The bill could be referred to other committees after that. It also could be split up among several committees.

Because jurisdictional boundaries are not always precise, committees sometimes compete for referral of an important bill. Or one committee may try to usurp legislative territory that another committee considers its own.

K

Kefauver, Estes

Estes Kefauver (1903–1963) was an independent-minded Tennessee Democrat who served in the House of Representatives from 1939 to 1949 and in the Senate from 1949 until his death. Kefauver was known for his populist rhetoric and liberal voting behavior; his political trademark was a coonskin cap. He rose to national prominence as chair of a Senate committee investigating organized crime. (See INVESTIGATIONS.) The resulting publicity fueled Kefauver's presidential ambitions. He was an unsuccessful aspirant to the presidency in 1952 and 1956.

Kefauver won his House seat in a special election in 1939. As a representative, his particular interest was legislative reorganization; he presented his case for re-

Sen. Estes Kefauver (second from left) gained national notice by his televised special investigating committee hearings on organized crime in 1950 and 1951.
Source: AP Images/Bill Chaplis

form in his popular book *A Twentieth-Century Congress,* published in 1947. The Legislative Reorganization Act of 1946 contained several reforms espoused by Kefauver, including regulation of LOBBYING and expansion of congressional STAFF. (See REFORM, CONGRESSIONAL.)

Kefauver won his Senate seat in 1948 by defeating the powerful Crump machine of Memphis. As a senator, he championed civil liberties—he was one of only seven senators to vote against the Internal Security Act of 1950—and concerned himself with antitrust issues. He urged the Senate to investigate organized crime and in 1950 became chair of the Special Committee to Investigate Organized Crime in Interstate Commerce. The committee heard testimony from Mafia figures and well-known criminals. Hearings were held all around the country, many of them televised. Although the investigation highlighted crime problems, little legislation resulted.

Kefauver did well in the 1952 presidential primaries and was considered the most popular Democratic contender. Still, he lost the nomination to Adlai E. Stevenson at the national convention; his independence appealed to voters, but not to his party. Republican Dwight D. Eisenhower won the presidency that year. Kefauver again entered the primaries for the 1956 election, but he withdrew to support Stevenson's nomination. He was chosen to be Stevenson's running mate after a hard-fought contest with Sen. John F. KENNEDY of Massachusetts.

Kefauver returned to the Senate after Eisenhower's landslide win in 1956. There he played a critical role in the adoption of the Twenty-fourth Amendment to the Constitution, which banned poll taxes. He continued to head congressional investigations, most notably into antitrust violations.

Kennedy, Edward M.

With nearly forty-six years in the Senate at the beginning of 2008, Edward M. Kennedy (1932–) was the third longest-serving senator. He has remained one of the nation's leading liberals, and his defense of old Democratic values has helped score some big legislative victories even while his party was in the minority. The earnestness of his support for labor protections and a social safety net has won the Massachusetts Democrat grudging respect even from colleagues who differ with him on the issues.

Although the Reagan-era caricature of Kennedy as a big government liberal stuck, he consistently has been able to form alliances with Republican senators to advance legislation. From his position as the ranking minority member of the Labor and Human Resources Committee, Kennedy joined with committee chair Nancy Landon Kassebaum, R-Kan., to push through a bill in the 104th Congress (1995–1997) that mandated health insurance portability, guaranteeing that individuals who lose or leave their jobs can keep their coverage. In 1997 Kennedy joined with Orrin G. Hatch, R-Utah, to pass legislation that created a program to help uninsured children receive health coverage. Kennedy also won accolades from Republicans for teaming up with President George W. Bush in 2001 to pass comprehensive education legislation, known as the No Child Left Behind bill.

Sen. Edward M. Kennedy, D-Mass., announces legislation that would allow the FDA to regulate tobacco products in 2006. He is flanked by bill cosponsors Sen. Mike DeWine, R-Ohio, (left) and Rep. Thomas M. Davis III, R-Va.
Source: CQ Photo/Scott J. Ferrell

Yet Kennedy's legislative acuity does not seem to carry over into his personal life. His image was probably shattered for all time in 1969 when he drove his car off a bridge in Chappaquiddick, Massachusetts, and his companion, Mary Jo Kopechne, drowned.

Kennedy had been elected majority whip earlier in 1969, beating Finance chair Russell B. LONG of Louisiana. But after Chappaquiddick, Kennedy's leadership fortunes fell, and when Senate Democrats elected their leaders in 1971, they chose Robert C. BYRD of West Virginia for whip, 31–24.

Despite his personal troubles, many Democrats looked to Kennedy to follow his brothers' aspirations and run for president. In 1980 he challenged President Jimmy Carter for his party's nomination but was unsuccessful. His stirring Democratic convention speech, however, with its liberal affirmation that "the work goes on, the cause endures, the hope still lives, and the dream shall never die," helped restore some of Kennedy's lost luster.

Kennedy was first elected to the Senate in 1962 to fill the vacancy left by the resignation of his brother, John F. KENNEDY, in 1960. Edward Kennedy chaired the Senate Judiciary Committee from 1979 to 1981, Labor and Human Resources Committee from 1987 to 1995, and Health, Education, Labor, and Pensions (HELP) Committee from mid-2001 to 2003.

In 2007 he was back in the chair of the HELP committee, as it was known, as a result of Democrats reclaiming control of the Senate in the 2006 elections. In that role he would revisit the 2001 education legislation, which was up for renewal. The reauthorization effort was difficult because educators and state officials had become increasingly critical of the law's testing and teacher-quality mandates.

Kennedy also focused on another of his favorite topics: the cost and availability of health care in the United States. In 2007 Kennedy teamed with Hatch again to reauthorize and expand the popular State Childrens Health Insurance Program (SCHIP) that they created in 1997. While the program was reauthorized that year, its $35 billion expansion to cover an additional 3 to 4 million uninsured children fell to two George W. Bush vetoes in October and December.

Kennedy, John F.

John F. Kennedy's (1917–1963) congressional career has been overshadowed by his term as president. Kennedy, a Massachusetts Democrat, served in the House of Representatives from 1947 to 1953 and in the Senate from 1953 to 1960. Much of his career in Congress was spent building a legislative record that would serve him well when he sought higher office. He was elected to the presidency in 1960 and served from 1961 until his assassination on November 22, 1963.

Kennedy was a World War II hero and a member of a powerful political Democratic family. After a brief career as a journalist, he ran for the House in 1946. An indefatigable campaigner, he won handily and was returned twice to that office. During his tenure in the House he was preoccupied with serving the needs of his Massachusetts constituents. Liberal in his defense of labor and support of low-cost housing and other domestic issues, he was more conservative when voting on foreign policy measures. He sharply criticized the administration of President Harry S. Truman for allowing communist rule in China and gave only grudging support to foreign aid proposals.

In 1952 Kennedy made a successful bid for the Senate seat held by Henry Cabot LODGE Jr. Although Dwight D. Eisenhower carried the state in that year's presidential election, Kennedy captured the Senate seat from the Republican incumbent with little difficulty. Once in the Senate, Kennedy began to emphasize national issues over northeastern concerns. In 1954 he voted for the St. Lawrence Seaway, a project that his general constituency opposed. He gained a seat on the Foreign Relations Committee in 1957, and this gave him a base from which to criticize the foreign policy of the Dwight D. Eisenhower administration. During his Senate tenure, while convalescing from a grave operation, Kennedy wrote *Profiles in Courage,* sketches of senators who had followed their consciences over the wishes of their constituents.

Kennedy was denied the Democratic nomination for vice president in 1956 in a floor fight at the party's national convention. In 1960 his party nominated him for president, and he defeated Republican Richard NIXON by a slim margin, 49.7 percent to 49.5 percent in the popular vote (303

"*Let the word go forth from this time and place, to friend and foe alike, that the torch has passed to a new generation of Americans— born in this century, tempered by war, disciplined by a hard and bitter peace, proud of our ancient heritage—and unwilling to witness or permit the slow undoing of those human rights to which this nation has always been committed, and to which we are committed today at home and abroad.*

Let every nation know, whether it wishes us well or ill, that we shall pay any price, bear any burden, meet any hardship, support any friend, oppose any foe to assure the survival and the success of liberty....

And so, my fellow Americans: ask not what your country can do for you—ask what you can do for your country...."

—*John F. Kennedy's* inaugural address January 20, 1961

Source: John F. Kennedy Presidential Library and Museum

to 219 in the electoral vote). As president, his most notable achievements were in the area of foreign affairs; his domestic program was planned but not fully implemented during his lifetime. He was assassinated while visiting Dallas, Texas.

Two of John Kennedy's brothers served in Congress after his death. Robert F. Kennedy, who had been attorney general in his brother's administration, was a senator from 1965 until his own death on June 6, 1968; he was assassinated while campaigning for the Democratic presidential nomination. Edward M. KENNEDY entered the Senate in 1962; despite a strong effort to win the Democratic presidential nomination in 1980, he was unable to capture the prize.

La Follette, Robert M., Sr.

In one of the longest individual filibusters in Senate history, Sen. Robert La Follette, R-Wisc., in 1908 held the floor for eighteen hours and twenty-three minutes. He was opposing a currency bill supported by Sen. Nelson W. Aldrich, R-R.I.
Source: Library of Congress

Robert M. La Follette Sr. (1855–1925) was one of the founders of the progressive wing of the Republican Party. Progressivism's basic themes of regulation of business, conservation, and dislike of machine politics surfaced in the late nineteenth century.

La Follette was elected to the House of Representatives as a Republican from Wisconsin in 1884. During his years in the House he was not distinguished for the independence and enthusiasm for reform that he later showed. In 1890 La Follette lost his bid for reelection in a wave of Republican defeats, and he resumed practicing law in Wisconsin.

In the decade after his defeat, La Follette formulated a series of reform proposals. Elected governor of Wisconsin in 1901, he worked to implement his proposals. He believed that businesses should bear a heavier burden of taxation consistent with that borne by other sectors. To challenge machine-ruled political conventions, he supported political primaries. La Follette also supported increased regulation and oversight of the railroads. These proposals were eventually accepted by the state legislature; known as the "Wisconsin Idea," they were eventually copied by other states.

La Follette left the statehouse to become a U.S. senator in 1906. His brand of Republicanism was very different from that of the conservative ruling clique led by Nelson W. ALDRICH of Rhode Island. He opposed Aldrich on several occasions, including a filibuster on an Aldrich currency bill in 1908. La Follette held the floor for eighteen hours and twenty-three minutes, one of the longest individual filibusters in the history of the Senate.

As a senator, La Follette championed public ownership of the railroads. He once inserted a 365-page speech on railroad rates in the *Congressional Record.* Known as an "insurgent," La Follette so angered the "stalwart" faction of Senate Republicans that on one occasion they voted to elect a Democratic representative as chair of the Interstate Commerce Committee rather than have La Follette assume that position. However, the Senate refused to expel him for sedition in 1917 when petitioned to do so by the Minneapolis Public Safety Commission. La Follette had given a speech in St. Paul criticizing U.S. involvement in World War I.

Twice an unsuccessful candidate for the Republican nomination for president, in 1908 and 1912, La Follette ran on the Progressive ticket in 1924. He lost the election but garnered 16 percent of the popular vote.

La Follette died in office in June 1925. Two months later he was succeeded by his son, Robert M. La Follette Jr. ("Young Bob"), who served in the Senate until 1947.

Lame-Duck Amendment

The Twentieth Amendment to the Constitution, ratified in 1933, is known as the Lame-Duck Amendment. It established the beginning date and frequency of sessions of Congress. The amendment requires the House and Senate to meet at least once a year, and it specifies January 3 as the opening date for each congressional session unless members select another date. Members' terms begin and end on January 3. (See TERMS AND SESSIONS OF CONGRESS.)

The amendment also sets the date for the inauguration every four years of the president and vice president: January 20 of the year following the election. Previously, both presidential and congressional terms had begun and ended on March 4. Other sections of the amendment outline Congress's authority in certain cases involving the death of a president-elect.

The Lame-Duck Amendment was added to the Constitution after a decade-long struggle by its chief sponsor, Sen. George W. NORRIS, a Nebraska Republican. It received its nickname because it was an attack on the long-standing practice of "lame duck" sessions of Congress. In congressional jargon, a lame duck is a member who serves out the balance of his or her term after being defeated or not seeking reelection.

From its earliest days, Congress followed a lopsided schedule that gave ample opportunity for lame ducks to wield considerable influence long after they had been rejected by their constituents. Under the traditional practice, which lasted more than 140 years, the first session of each two-year-long Congress began in December of odd-numbered years. That session, which opened more than a year after the election, customarily lasted for six months or so. The second, "short" session of a Congress typically began in December of the even-numbered years. That session, which ran until March 4 of the following year, was known as the lame-duck session because it was conducted after the election for the succeeding Congress had already been held. As a result, many of the members who served were lame ducks.

The traditional schedule had many drawbacks and was widely criticized. The long delay in beginning each Congress slowed the government's response to public opinion as expressed through the elections. It also allowed presidents to make recess appointments and other moves without any interference from Congress. (See APPOINTMENT POWER.)

In addition to allowing defeated members to retain power for a few more months, the short sessions were rarely productive. The fixed adjournment date was an invitation to a FILIBUSTER, and members frequently took advantage of it as the session drew to a close. Merely by talking long enough, members could kill a bill by blocking action until the current Congress expired.

The short session survived for so long because it was advantageous to congressional leaders, particularly in the House. House leaders liked the short session because its automatic termination strengthened their ability to control the legislative output of the House. The House Republican leadership was the strongest opponent of the proposed Twentieth Amendment during more than ten years of congressional debate.

History

The practice of long and short sessions began early in Congress's history. The First Congress opened on March 4, 1789, and soon decided that congressional terms would begin and end on that date each year. But the Constitution directed that Congress should meet each year early in December. The congressional schedule soon accommodated both requirements by use of long and short sessions.

Later Congresses sometimes were called into special session by the president, and often they fixed earlier dates for meeting. But the basic pattern of long and short sessions did not change much.

Dissatisfaction with lame-duck sessions grew more intense in the early twentieth century. The use of the filibuster was seen by reformers as a major obstacle to legislative progress. During the administration of President Woodrow Wilson (1913–1921), each of four second sessions of Congress ended with a Senate filibuster and the loss of important legislation.

Norris advocated revision of the congressional schedule to abolish lame-duck sessions as a way of undermining use of the filibuster. His plan was in the form of a constitutional amendment because the Constitution specifically mentioned the first week in December as the opening date for a congressional session. Norris's amendment ended the gap between the start of congressional terms and the opening day of annual sessions by putting both in early January.

The Norris amendment was popular in the Senate, which was searching at this time for ways to control the legislative havoc created by filibusters. The amendment was first passed by the Senate in 1923, on a 63–6 vote that far exceeded the two-thirds majority needed for approval. However, the plan soon ran into trouble in the House. The Senate joint resolution was approved by the House

Sen. George W. Norris. R-Neb., was the primary sponsor of the Lame-Duck Amendment.
Source: Library of Congress

Election Committee and won the support of a majority of members of the Rules Committee, whose approval was necessary for floor consideration of the measure. But the Rules Committee chair, Philip P. Campbell, a Kansas Republican who was himself a lame duck, refused to act on the resolution, and the proposal died for that session.

Consideration of the Norris amendment followed the same pattern for many years. The Senate approved the amendment six times before it finally won House approval. In the Sixty-eighth Congress (1923–1925), the Senate-passed measure was again blocked in the Rules Committee, causing Norris to charge that his amendment was "being held up because machine politicians can get more out of this [legislative] jam than the people's representatives can get." When the Norris amendment finally reached the House floor in 1928, a majority of members supported it. But the 209–157 vote for the proposal was short of the two-thirds majority required under the Constitution.

In 1931 the House passed an amended version of the Norris plan, but the House and Senate could not agree on a final version, and it died once again. The Democratic takeover of the House in 1931 cleared the way for final approval of the amendment. The Senate adopted the joint resolution on January 6, 1932, and the House followed the next month with a 335–56 vote. The amendment became part of the Constitution less than a year later, when it had been ratified by three-quarters of the states. (See CONSTITUTIONAL AMENDMENTS.)

The amendment helped reduce the dangers of delay in postponing a new president's assumption of office for four months after the November elections. It did so by moving the inauguration date to January 20, from March 4. The dangers of that long delay were shown by the inauguration that took place while the amendment was still in the process of being ratified. After the 1932 election, president-elect Franklin D. Roosevelt was not able to take over from defeated incumbent Herbert Hoover for four months. During that period the nearly leaderless nation, in the throes of the Great Depression, veered to the edge of economic catastrophe. (See NEW DEAL.)

Lame-Duck Session

A lame-duck session of Congress is one held after a successor Congress has been elected in November of an even-numbered year but before it is sworn in the following January. Senators and representatives who have been rejected at the polls can vote in a postelection session, as can those who are about to retire from Congress by choice. Such members are known as lame ducks.

Lame-duck sessions are not noted for legislative accomplishments. They frequently bog down in partisan bickering, especially if party control of one or both chambers is about to shift in the new Congress.

Before adoption of the Twentieth Amendment to the Constitution in 1933, the so-called LAME-DUCK AMENDMENT, postelection sessions were a regular feature of the congressional calendar. The amendment advanced the starting date of a new Congress to January from March. The first time Congress held a lame-duck session after the amendment's ratification was in 1941, and then it was on a standby basis. President Franklin D. Roosevelt called Congress into special session—technically, the third session of the 76th Congress—to deal with the threat of war in Europe. From that time through 2006 Congress has met in lame-duck sessions sixteen times.

To the chagrin of some lawmakers, lame-duck sessions became more common starting in the late 1990s as partisan bickering stalled action in the closely divided legislative bodies. End-of-the-year sessions were required in 1998, 2000, 2002, 2004, and 2006.

The most significant of these was the 1998 lame-duck session, when the House of Representatives alone reconvened and voted to impeach President Bill Clinton. (See CLINTON IMPEACHMENT TRIAL.)

Battles over budget priorities forced lawmakers to lumber into a lame-duck session in 2000. In 2002, after Democrats lost control of the Senate and surrendered House seats in the election, lawmakers returned to complete action on a comprehensive bill creating a Department of Homeland Security. But they could not reach agreement on almost all of the annual appropriations bills and instead passed a continuing resolution to push off the budget debate until 2003.

Other lame-duck sessions since World War II include the one in 1950, when Congress met in a marathon session to act on a "must" agenda presented by President Harry S. TRUMAN; the session ended only a few hours before the new Congress took over. In 1954 the Senate reconvened and voted to censure Sen. Joseph R. MCCARTHY, a Wisconsin Republican whose anticommunist investigations had rocked the nation. In a 1974 lame-duck session Congress approved the nomination of Nelson A. Rockefeller as vice president under President Gerald R. FORD and passed several major bills. During the 1994 lame-duck session, Congress approved legislation implementing a major trade agreement; a powerful Senate opponent of the pact—Commerce Committee chair Ernest F. Hollings, a South Carolina Democrat—had forced the delay until after the 1994 elections.

Laws

Each bill that is passed and signed by the president, or passed over the presidential veto, becomes a law. Eventually the law is incorporated into the *U.S. Code,* which is organized according to subject matter and divided into titles, chapters, and sections. The *Code* is updated annually by the House Office of the Law Revision Counsel, and a new set of bound volumes is published every six years. (See LEGISLATION.)

Laws are also given numbers separate from their designation in the *U.S. Code.* A new series of numbers is assigned at the beginning of each two-year term of Congress; thus, the first public law passed in the 108th Congress (2003–2005) was labeled Public Law 108-1, or PL 108-1. Private laws, which deal with individuals and not the general public, have a separate numbering system (Private Law 108-1, etc.). Laws are also referred to by their formal titles, such as the Legislative Reorganization Act of 1946 or the Ethics in Government Act of 1978.

Although a bill technically becomes an act as soon as it has been passed by one chamber of Congress, the term *act* is generally reserved for measures that have become law. *Statute* is used interchangeably with *law.*

At the end of each session of Congress, all the public and private laws, as well as concurrent resolutions, are compiled and published as *United States Statutes at Large* by the Office of the Federal Register, which is part of the National Archives and Records Administration. Throughout the year, the same office publishes "slip laws," which are single sheets or pamphlets containing the text of a bill as enacted and a summary of its legislative history. In the margin, alongside the legal language, are notes that identify a section as dealing with a particular subject.

Leadership

Leadership is the term used to describe, collectively, the Democratic and Republican leaders in Congress and their lieutenants. These leaders play a dual role: they attempt to win support in Congress for their party's goals, and they are responsible for operating Congress as an institution. The party that commands a majority in a chamber has primary direction of its operations.

Congressional leaders have thrived in the modern era of hostile partisan division that characterized the 1990s and the early years of the new century. In the ongoing partisan warfare leaders increasingly were central power brokers in the interdependent arts of lawmaking, fundraising, and campaigning. Out of this convergence has risen a remarkably consolidated power structure in the

With Democrats in control of both chambers at the start of the 110th Congress in January 2007, the top positions of power went to Senate Majority Leader Harry Reid of Nevada and House Speaker Nancy Pelosi of California.
Source: CQ Photo/Scott J. Ferrell

House in which most lawmakers owe their spot on the ballot, their campaign war chest, their favorable district lines, their committee assignments, their television appearances, their foreign travel, and even their late-night dinner to elected party leaders.

The Senate, by comparison, remains a bastion of individualism, although the election of numerous former representatives to Senate seats has contributed to a partisan dynamic that reflects their previous lives in the highly partisan House.

In both the House and Senate, the organizations of party members, known as conferences or caucuses, vote on top leaders at the start of each two-year term of Congress. The elected leaders then make several key appointments to complete the leadership structure of each party. Committee chairs, always from the majority party or—if elected as an independent—sympathetic to the majority, are also part of the leadership. Nominated by party leadership groups, often but not always on the basis of seniority, they must win approval from the party caucuses.

Control over legislative activity is a powerful tool for leaders of the majority party. If they oppose a bill, they can usually keep it from coming to the floor, while a measure they favor receives top priority. Depending on the minority party's numbers and its degree of unity, minority leaders also can help, or hurt, the progress of legislation.

In the House strict rules govern floor action of legislation, giving leaders powerful leverage over rank-and-file members Strong leaders are able to orchestrate how the rules are applied and enforced to benefit party-backed legislation. In the Senate the rights of minority members are protected by tradition; they can bottle up legislative work with prolonged debate (known as a FILIBUSTER) and other delaying tactics. As a result, Senate majority leaders, in the hope of avoiding such obstructions, are usually more sensitive to the minority's viewpoint than are House majority leaders.

The structure and practices of congressional leadership have evolved. The Constitution established a presiding officer for each chamber, but other leaders have little written authority for their roles. Their positions and duties are based on tradition within the parties rather than on formal rules that apply to Congress as a whole.

In acknowledgment of their special duties, top party leaders receive additional pay, enjoy spacious offices in the Capitol, and are allotted extra funds to hire staff.

CLOSER LOOK

The leadership normally refers collectively to the Democratic and Republican leaders in Congress and their lieutenants. More narrowly, it means the majority and minority leaders of the Senate or the Speaker and minority leader of the House. These leaders play a dual role: they attempt to win support in Congress for their party's goals, and they are responsible for operating Congress as an institution.

More on this topic:

Caucuses, Party, p. 85

Committee System, p. 111

Filibuster, p. 213

Presiding Officer, p. 437

Reform, Congressional, p. 470

Rules Committee, House, p. 478

Seniority System, p. 505

Speaker of the House, p. 516

House

Speaker

The most visible and prestigious officer within Congress is the Speaker of the House. The Constitution made the Speaker the presiding officer of the House; custom has made the Speaker also the leader of the majority party in the House.

The Speaker is formally elected by the House at the start of each two-year term of Congress. The House chooses between candidates selected by the party caucuses, and the vote follows party lines. The majority's candidate becomes Speaker, and the minority's candidate becomes minority leader.

The modern Speaker is often the chief spokesperson for the party nationally (when the party does not control the White House), as well as the leader of its members in the House. Most of the time the Speaker does not actually preside over floor debates but delegates that role to another member of the same party. In practice, the Speaker takes the chair primarily when important matters are before the House. Then the Speaker's authority to recognize members, resolve disputes over rules, and oversee roll-call votes may be used to partisan advantage.

The Speaker traditionally gives up seats on legislative committees and rarely votes except to break a tie.

In the 1800s the Speaker was often a forceful orator, elected because of the ability to command attention and articulate ideas. Seniority, or length of service, which later became an important factor, was hardly considered. For example, Henry CLAY was elected Speaker the day he entered the House in 1811. In contrast, all but two Speakers since 1925 have first served as majority or minority leader. (Republican Newt GINGRICH of Georgia, Speaker from 1995–1999, previously had served as minority whip. Republican J. Dennis HASTERT of Illinois, who was Speaker from 1999 until 2007 when Democrats were again the majority, had been chief deputy whip.) This was true also of Nancy Pelosi, D-Calif., who became Speaker in 2007; she had been minority leader since 2003.

Before the two political parties became dominant, the candidates' stands on certain issues often turned the contest. The issue of slavery, in particular, had a role. The 1855 race was so bitterly divided by the slavery question that resolving it took two months—and 133 ballots. By the twentieth century, with the Democratic and Republican Parties well established, topical issues were rarely a factor in the contests. Instead, the Speaker was chosen from the most senior and most loyal party members.

Several times in the twentieth century the Speaker's role underwent significant changes. In 1910 the House revolted against the autocratic rule of Speaker Joseph G. CANNON and sharply curtailed the Speaker's powers. Power shifted to committee chairs and the Rules Committee, which had been freed from the Speaker's domination. In the 1970s the Speaker regained some of the authority that had been lost some sixty years earlier. By the mid-1990s, Gingrich seemed to be exercising the kind of control that had been unseen since Cannon's days, but during his four years as Speaker, he discovered there were, indeed, limits on his power. At the end of the century, with the selection of Hastert to succeed Gingrich, the House appeared to be returning to a more collegial style of Speaker. But the impression was not fully accurate. The collegiality extended largely to Republicans; Hastert's chief deputies, particularly majority leader Tom DeLay of Texas, ran the chamber with an iron hand, keeping GOP troops fully in line and largely excluding Democratic members from meaningful participation in legislative activity. There was no more collegiality between the parties during Hastert's period as Speaker than there had been during Gingrich's. The sharp division was not exclusive to the Republicans, however. Democratic Speakers preceding Gingrich tended to marginalize the Republican minority much of the time.

Top Republican leaders in the 110th Congress were House Minority Leader John A. Boehner of Ohio (left) and Senate Minority Leader Mitch McConnell of Kentucky.
Source: Reuters/Jason Reed

Although in the post–World War II era the Speaker was largely a well-respected individual, there were occasions when the office came under a cloud. This occurred first in the 1980s, when its occupant, Texas Democrat Jim WRIGHT, became embroiled in an ethics scandal. Wright became the first House Speaker in history to be forced by scandal to leave the office in the middle of his term. Gingrich, in 1997, became the first Speaker to be formally sanctioned by the House because of ethics problems. His tenure also was marked by a free-wheeling style in which he exercised his well-acknowledged authority—for having led the GOP to the majority for the first time in forty years—was often unfocused and lacking the discipline some rank-and-file members thought necessary to lead the party successfully.

The year 2007 was a historic occasion for the House and the office of the Speaker. Pelosi, the minority leader for four years, became the first woman to take the Speaker's chair. She also became the highest-ranking woman ever elected to the federal government. But with this honor came the entirely different challenge of leading the often fractious Democratic caucus in a coherent and effective manner to counteract the continuing Republican control of the White House under George W. Bush. One year into the job, she was receiving guarded good reviews from neutral observers. Many noted that she stumbled a number of times early in the year, especially supporting a candidate for majority leader not favored by the rank and file who lost convincingly and by sticking with a small—and critics said, closed—circle of advisers. But, like Gingrich and Hastert before her, she exerted strong control over party discipline and decisions, including committee assignments, and by midyear was broadening her circle of advisors and taking firm, often difficult, stances on party issues, even when it meant opposing some of the most senior and powerful committee chairs. Her most difficult challenge remained directing the Democratic response to Bush's handling of the war in Iraq, a task complicated by significantly diverse party views about U.S. involvement in the conflict.

Floor Leaders

The floor leaders for each party are responsible for handling legislation once it reaches the full House; they oversee debate, amendments, and voting.

The majority leader is the number two official in the House. The post was formally created in 1899. Until then, the chair of the Ways and Means Committee had served so often as floor manager that he was considered the deputy leader. The Speaker chose the majority leader until Democrats gained control of the House in 1911, when that authority was shifted to the Democratic Caucus. Similarly, since 1923, the Republican Conference has selected the leader when its party held the majority. In most cases the majority leader has continued to be the Speaker's chief lieutenant, rather than a rival.

The minority leader is the minority party's top official. Ever since the post first became identifiable in the 1880s, the minority leader has been that party's nominee for Speaker. The minority leader monitors floor activity but can only try to influence scheduling, lacking direct control over it. The minority leader also speaks for the minority party in the House and performs other duties that the Speaker handles for the majority party.

HOUSE FLOOR LEADERS, 1899–2007

Congress		Majority	Minority
56th	(1899–1901)	Sereno E. Payne, R-N.Y.	James D. Richardson, D-Tenn.
57th	(1901–1903)	Payne	Richardson
58th	(1903–1905)	Payne	John Sharp Williams, D-Miss.
59th	(1905–1907)	Payne	Williams
60th	(1907–1909)	Payne	Williams/Champ Clark, D-Mo.[1]
61st	(1909–1911)	Payne	Clark
62nd	(1911–1913)	Oscar W. Underwood, D-Ala.	James R. Mann, R-Ill.
63rd	(1913–1915)	Underwood	Mann
64th	(1915–1917)	Claude Kitchin, D-N.C.	Mann
65th	(1917–1919)	Kitchin	Mann
66th	(1919–1921)	Franklin W. Mondell, R-Wyo.	Clark
67th	(1921–1923)	Mondell	Claude Kitchin, D-N.C.
68th	(1923–1925)	Nicholas Longworth, R-Ohio	Finis J. Garrett, D-Tenn.
69th	(1925–1927)	John Q. Tilson, R-Conn.	Garrett
70th	(1927–1929)	Tilson	Garrett
71st	(1929–1931)	Tilson	John N. Garner, D-Texas
72nd	(1931–1933)	Henry T. Rainey, D-Ill.	Bertrand H. Snell, R-N.Y.
73rd	(1933–1935)	Joseph W. Byrns, D-Tenn.	Snell
74th	(1935–1937)	William B. Bankhead, D-Ala.[2]	Snell
75th	(1937–1939)	Sam Rayburn, D-Texas	Snell
76th	(1939–1941)	Rayburn/John W. McCormack, D-Mass.[3]	Joseph W. Martin Jr., R-Mass.
77th	(1941–1943)	McCormack	Martin
78th	(1943–1945)	McCormack	Martin
79th	(1945–1947)	McCormack	Martin
80th	(1947–1949)	Charles A. Halleck, R-Ind.	Sam Rayburn, D-Texas
81st	(1949–1951)	McCormack	Martin
82nd	(1951–1953)	McCormack	Martin
83rd	(1953–1955)	Halleck	Rayburn
84th	(1955–1957)	McCormack	Martin
85th	(1957–1959)	McCormack	Martin
86th	(1959–1961)	McCormack	Charles A. Halleck, R-Ind.
87th	(1961–1963)	McCormack/Carl Albert, D-Okla.[4]	Halleck
88th	(1963–1965)	Albert	Halleck
89th	(1965–1967)	Albert	Gerald R. Ford, R-Mich.
90th	(1967–1969)	Albert	Ford
91st	(1969–1971)	Albert	Ford
92nd	(1971–1973)	Hale Boggs, D-La.	Ford
93rd	(1973–1975)	Thomas P. O'Neill Jr., D-Mass.	Ford/John J. Rhodes, R-Ariz.[5]
94th	(1975–1977)	O'Neill	Rhodes
95th	(1977–1979)	Jim Wright, D-Texas	Rhodes
96th	(1979–1981)	Wright	Rhodes
97th	(1981–1983)	Wright	Robert H. Michel, R-Ill.
98th	(1983–1985)	Wright	Michel
99th	(1985–1987)	Wright	Michel
100th	(1987–1989)	Thomas S. Foley, D-Wash.	Michel
101st	(1989–1991)	Foley/Richard A. Gephardt, D-Mo.[6]	Michel

(continues)

HOUSE FLOOR LEADERS, 1899–2007 (CONTINUED)

Congress		Majority	Minority
102nd	(1991–1993)	Gephardt	Michel
103rd	(1993–1995)	Gephardt	Michel
104th	(1995–1997)	Dick Armey, R-Texas	Richard A. Gephardt, D-Mo.
105th	(1997–1999)	Armey	Gephardt
106th	(1999–2001)	Armey	Gephardt
107th	(2001–2003)	Armey	Gephardt
108th	(2003–2005)	Tom DeLay, R-Texas	Nancy Pelosi, D-Calif.
109th	(2005–2007)	Delay/Roy Blunt, R-Mo./John A. Boehner, R-Ohio[7]	Pelosi
110th	(2007–2009)	Steny H. Hoyer, D-Md.	John A. Boehner, R-Ohio

SOURCE: Randall B. Ripley, *Party Leaders in the House of Representatives* (Washington, D.C.: Brookings Institution, 1967); *Biographical Directory of the American Congress, 1774–1996* (Alexandria, Va.: CQ Staff Directories, 1997); *CQ Weekly,* selected issues.

NOTES: 1. Clark became minority leader in 1908.

2. Bankhead became Speaker on June 4, 1936. The post of majority leader remained vacant until the next Congress.

3. McCormack became majority leader on September 26, 1940, filling the vacancy caused by the elevation of Rayburn to the post of Speaker on September 16, 1940.

4. Albert became majority leader on January 10, 1962, filling the vacancy caused by the elevation of McCormack to the post of Speaker on January 10, 1962.

5. Rhodes became minority leader on December 7, 1973, filling the vacancy caused by the resignation of Ford on December 6, 1973, to become vice president.

6. Gephardt became majority leader on June 14, 1989, filling the vacancy created when Foley succeeded Wright as Speaker on June 6, 1989.

7. DeLay was required by GOP Conference rules to temporarily vacate the position after being indicted in Texas on September 28, 2005, on campaign finance charges. Speaker J. Dennis Hastert named Blunt to act as majority leader for the remainder of the session. When DeLay resigned from the House on June 9, 2006, Republicans elected Boehner as majority leader.

Whips

Ranking after the majority and minority leaders are the whips, House or Senate members who try to persuade party colleagues to follow the leadership's program. The title *whip* was borrowed from the British Parliament and first used in the U.S. Congress in 1897. The term comes from the fox-hunting term *whipper in,* the person assigned to keep hunting dogs in a pack.

The whips handle the mechanics of polling members on their views on issues and their stands on specific floor votes. They inform members about upcoming floor action and make sure members are present for tight votes. Whips and their assistants sometimes stand at the door of the House chamber, signaling the leadership's position on a vote by holding their thumbs up or down.

Whips are elected by each party. House Republicans have always elected their whip. The Democratic whip was chosen by the Speaker and majority leader until 1987, when the Democratic Caucus began electing the whip. One reason for the change was that the whip often moved up to majority leader and Speaker; junior members wanted a say in who got the inside track.

Each party designates numerous members as assistants to the whips. The number of whips in any Congress is difficult to determine because a whip organization early in the session remains an evolving part of the leadership structure. But the scope of whip operations could be seen at the beginning of the 110th Congress. By one count, Democrats had a senior chief deputy whip, six chief deputy whips, twelve deputy whips, and ninety-four regional or at-large whips. Republicans had a chief deputy whip, seventeen deputy whips, and forty-nine assistant whips. In addition, the titles for different level of the organization are often inconsistent.

Whips are less prominent in the smaller and less formal Senate, although they are important to the parties. An early count in the 110th Congress shows Senate Democrats with one chief deputy whip and three deputy whips; Republicans had one chief deputy whip and seven deputy whips.

Party Committees

House Republicans have a Steering Committee, which makes committee assignments. The panel, dominated by House Republican leaders, is chaired by the Speaker when the GOP is in the majority, or the minority leader when it is not. Top party leaders also serve, along with other party members, on a Policy Committee, which advises on party action and policy. House Democrats have a Steering Committee to handle committee assignments and a Policy Committee to study and propose legislation and make public the party's policy positions.

Both parties also have congressional campaign committees that provide campaign money and advice to party candidates. In the House, these are the Democratic Congressional Campaign Committee and the National Republican Congressional Committee. The campaign committees help identify potential candidates, brief them on issues, and assist them with all phases of campaigning. The committees also raise and disburse campaign funds to candidates for Congress. (See CAMPAIGN FINANCING.)

Senate

Presiding Officers

No post comparable to that of Speaker exists in the Senate. The Constitution designated the vice president as the "president of the Senate" and authorized him or her to vote in case of a tie. But the vice president, who is elected as a member of the executive branch, is the president's choice; the vice president's party affiliation may differ from that of the Senate majority. In modern practice, the vice president seldom visits the Capitol and presides over the Senate only occasionally, for example, when it appears that the vice president's vote might be needed to break a tie.

SENATE FLOOR LEADERS, 1911–2007

Congress		Majority	Minority
62nd	(1911–1913)	Shelby M. Cullom, R-Ill.	Thomas S. Martin, D-Va.
63rd	(1913–1915)	John W. Kern, D-Ind.	Jacob H. Gallinger, R-N.H.
64th	(1915–1917)	Kern	Gallinger
65th	(1917–1919)	Thomas S. Martin, D-Va.	Gallinger/Henry Cabot Lodge, R-Mass.[1]
66th	(1919–1921)	Henry Cabot Lodge, R-Mass.	Martin/Oscar W. Underwood, D-Ala.[2]
67th	(1921–1923)	Lodge	Underwood
68th	(1923–1925)	Lodge/Charles Curtis, R-Kan.[3]	Joseph T. Robinson, D-Ark.
69th	(1925–1927)	Curtis	Robinson
70th	(1927–1929)	Curtis	Robinson
71st	(1929–1931)	James E. Watson, R-Ind.	Robinson
72nd	(1931–1933)	Watson	Robinson
73rd	(1933–1935)	Joseph T. Robinson, D-Ark.	Charles L. McNary, R-Ore.
74th	(1935–1937)	Robinson	McNary
75th	(1937–1939)	Robinson/Alben W. Barkley, D-Ky.[4]	McNary
76th	(1939–1941)	Barkley	McNary
77th	(1941–1943)	Barkley	McNary
78th	(1943–1945)	Barkley	McNary
79th	(1945–1947)	Barkley	Wallace H. White Jr., R-Maine

(continues)

SENATE FLOOR LEADERS, 1911–2007 (CONTINUED)

Congress		Majority	Minority
80th	(1947–1949)	Wallace H. White Jr., R-Maine	Alben W. Barkley, D-Ky.
81st	(1949–1951)	Scott W. Lucas, D-Ill.	Kenneth S. Wherry, R-Neb.
82nd	(1951–1953)	Ernest W. McFarland, D-Ariz.	Wherry/Styles Bridges, R-N.H.[5]
83rd	(1953–1955)	Robert A. Taft, R-Ohio/	Lyndon B. Johnson, D-Texas
		William F. Knowland, R-Calif.[6]	
84th	(1955–1957)	Lyndon B. Johnson, D-Texas	William F. Knowland, R-Calif.
85th	(1957–1959)	Johnson	Knowland
86th	(1959–1961)	Johnson	Everett McKinley Dirksen, R-Ill.
87th	(1961–1963)	Mike Mansfield, D-Mont.	Dirksen
88th	(1963–1965)	Mansfield	Dirksen
89th	(1965–1967)	Mansfield	Dirksen
90th	(1967–1969)	Mansfield	Dirksen
91st	(1969–1971)	Mansfield	Dirksen/Hugh Scott, R-Pa.[7]
92nd	(1971–1973)	Mansfield	Scott
93rd	(1973–1975)	Mansfield	Scott
94th	(1975–1977)	Mansfield	Scott
95th	(1977–1979)	Robert C. Byrd, D-W.Va.	Howard H. Baker Jr., R-Tenn.
96th	(1979–1981)	Byrd	Baker
97th	(1981–1983)	Howard H. Baker Jr., R-Tenn.	Robert C. Byrd, D-W.Va.
98th	(1983–1985)	Baker	Byrd
99th	(1985–1987)	Bob Dole, R-Kan.	Byrd
100th	(1987–1989)	Byrd	Bob Dole, R-Kan.
101st	(1989–1991)	George J. Mitchell, D-Maine	Dole
102nd	(1991–1993)	Mitchell	Dole
103rd	(1993–1995)	Mitchell	Dole
104th	(1995–1997)	Bob Dole, R-Kan./Trent Lott, R Miss.[8]	Tom Daschle, D-S.D.
105th	(1997–1999)	Lott	Daschle
106th	(1999–2001)	Lott	Daschle
107th	(2001–2003)	Lott/Daschle[9]	Daschle/Lott
108th	(2003–2005)	Bill Frist, R-Tenn.	Daschle
109th	(2005–2007)	Frist	Harry Reid, D-Nev.
110th	(2007–2009)	Harry Reid, D-Nev.	Mitch McConnell, R-Ky.

SOURCE: *Biographical Directory of the American Congress, 1774–1996* (Alexandria, Va.: CQ Staff Directories, 1997); *Majority and Minority Leaders of the Senate,* comp. Floyd M. Riddick, 94th Cong., 1st sess., 1975, S Doc 66; *CQ Weekly,* selected issues.

NOTES: 1. Lodge became minority leader on August 24, 1918, filling the vacancy caused by the death of Gallinger on August 17, 1918.

2. Underwood became minority leader on April 27, 1920, filling the vacancy caused by the death of Martin on November 12, 1919. Gilbert M. Hitchcock, D-Neb., served as acting minority leader in the interim.

3. Curtis became majority leader on November 28, 1924, filling the vacancy caused by the death of Lodge on November. 9, 1924.

4. Barkley became majority leader on July 22, 1937, filling the vacancy caused by the death of Robinson on July 14, 1937.

5. Bridges became minority leader on January 8, 1952, filling the vacancy caused by the death of Wherry on November 29, 1951.

6. Knowland became majority leader on August 4, 1953, filling the vacancy caused by the death of Taft on July 31, 1953. Taft's vacant seat was filled by Democrat Thomas Burke on November 10, 1953. The division of the Senate changed to 48 Democrats, 47 Republicans, and 1 Independent, thus giving control of the Senate to the Democrats. However, Knowland remained as majority leader until the end of the 83rd Congress.

7. Scott became minority leader on September 24, 1969, filling the vacancy caused by the death of Dirksen on September 7, 1969.

8. Lott became majority leader on June 12, 1996, following the resignation of Dole on June 11.

9. The 2000 elections resulted in an even party split between Democrats and Republicans, fifty members on each side. With Republican vice president Richard B. Cheney acting as the nominal Senate leader, the GOP retained technical control of the Senate, allowing party members to be in the primary leadership roles even though the two parties worked out a power-sharing arrangement on committees. When James M. Jeffords, R-Vt., announced he would become an Independent and caucus with the Democrats, on June 6 the Democrats achieved a 50-49 majority as a result, allowing them to take control of the majority positions in the leadership and on all committees.

The Constitution also directed the Senate to elect a PRESIDENT PRO TEMPORE to handle the vice president's duties in his or her absence. *Pro tempore* is a Latin phrase meaning "for the time [being]"; the title is commonly shortened to president pro tem. The Senate has not given much parliamentary authority to the post, but the president pro tem does preside over or select a substitute to oversee floor debate. Until 1890 the post was filled, on a temporary basis, only when the vice president was absent. After that, the Senate allowed the president pro tem to serve until the Senate decided otherwise. Since 1945 custom has given the job to the member of the majority party with the longest record of Senate service. (The one exception was Arthur H. Vandenberg of Michigan, who was the second-ranking Republican when elected president pro tem in 1947.)

Floor Leaders, Whips

Both Democrats and Republicans had developed a centralized leadership structure by the late 1890s. The position of floor leader probably emerged around 1911, though the official titles of leader or floor leader apparently were not used until the 1920s. The position of whip was established by Democrats in 1913 and by Republicans in 1915.

Duties and roles are less institutionalized than they are in the House. The leadership's authority has been hampered by the Senate tradition of giving strong rights to individual senators, instead of to any group. The majority leader schedules floor action in consultation with the minority leader, and much of the Senate's business is conducted by UNANIMOUS CONSENT of the members. This bipartisan cooperation is in sharp contrast to the House, where scheduling is solely a responsibility of a majority party that has the ability to enforce its decisions by majority vote.

Party Committees

The Senate parties each have a Policy Committee and a panel that makes committee assignments (the Republican Committee on Committees and the Democratic Steering and Coordination Committee). Democrats also have a Technology and Communications Committee to assist Democratic senators in informing the public about policies. The Republicans elect senators other than their top leader to chair their party committees and conference. The Democratic leader chairs the party conference and cochairs its Policy Committee.

As in the House, both parties also have campaign committees, known as the National Republican Senatorial Committee and the Democratic Senatorial Campaign Committee, to aid their candidates.

Leadership Tactics

Congressional leaders must juggle a number of different tasks and roles. Leaders organize each

At a January 2007 news conference, the top hierarchy of the Democratic House leadership (left to right), House Majority Whip James E. Clyburn of South Carolina, House Democratic Caucus vice chair John B. Larson of Connecticut, House Majority Leader Steny Hoyer of Maryland, and House Democratic Caucus chair Rahm Emanuel of Illinois, discuss the legislative activity of first "one hundred hours" of the 110th Congress.
Source: CQ Photo/Scott J. Ferrell

chamber and each party within the chamber, setting and reviewing committee jurisdictions and assignments and institutional and party rules. They schedule bills for floor action. Deciding what will come to the floor when, under what conditions, and in what order may be the majority leadership's most important institutional task, and it is a forceful tool in realizing a party's policy agenda. Leaders must build winning coalitions within their respective chambers, and they must negotiate with the executive branch as well.

Congressional leaders often serve as national party spokespersons, publicizing their party's programs and achievements. Their role becomes especially visible when the president is of the opposing party. They also play an important part in helping their party's members raise campaign money and win reelection.

Advancing a party's programs through Congress is a formidable job. House Republicans after winning control in 1994 imposed exceptionally tight control over the membership under the direction of DeLay, who was famous for keeping troops in line and delivering the votes to pass the Republican agenda from the White House. But modern senators and even many representatives chafe at following their leaders blindly. Senators in particular take pride in their independence, and some representatives will stray from party dictates, although at risk of losing influence in the party and even having their careers derailed. To encourage a strong party alliance, party leaders can use several kinds of rewards—and a few punishments. A legislator who votes with his or her party might be rewarded with a better committee assignment or a visit by party leaders to his or her district at campaign time. A pet program could be handled sympathetically by a committee or attached to an important bill heading for the floor.

Leaders are also aware of the local slant on everyday congressional business; they can steer to loyal members what their district or state needs, whether a tax break for a key industry, a new flood control project, or an exemption from clean air rules. Campaign appearances and funds are also distributed judiciously to encourage loyalty.

Punishment for disloyal behavior can be subtle. A member's bid for a local dam or scheme to revamp national education grants could languish in an unresponsive committee. A request to switch committees, add another staff member, or move to a bigger office could be denied. Sometimes the threat of punishment may be enough to induce a member to fall into step. In the 104th Congress, for example, Gingrich threatened to refuse to appoint members to a conference committee and to deny permission for foreign travel as a penalty for supporting a former member who was running in a primary against a Republican incumbent. In rare cases, legislators have been stripped of committee seniority or a committee post for repeatedly betraying the party position. Democratic leaders removed then-representative Phil Gramm of Texas from his seat on the House Budget Committee in 1983, after Gramm masterminded enactment of budgets proposed by Republican Ronald Reagan. Gramm resigned his House seat, won reelection as a Republican, and soon rejoined the committee as a Republican member. In the 109th Congress, GOP leaders named Jerry Lewis of California as Appropriations Committee chair, skipping over two others in a three-way race—one of whom had more seniority. Lewis had shown iron-clad loyalty to the leadership over the years while the other two often had not.

Senate Democrats rewarded GOP defector James M. Jeffords of Vermont in 2001 when he switched his party affiliation from Republican to Independent, thereby handing control of the chamber to Democrats, by ap-

Republicans lost control of the Senate when Sen. James Jeffords of Vermont switched his affiliation to Independent in 2001. Democrats subsequently appointed Jeffords as chair of the Environment and Public Works Committee, which was seen as a reward for his facilitating the switch in power.
Source: CQ Photo/Scott J. Ferrell

pointing him the chair of the Environment and Public Works Committee. The new majority whip, Nevada Democrat Harry Reid, relinquished his right to head the committee to reward Jeffords.

The need to satisfy diverse groups within their party has kept congressional leaders near the center of their party. They usually occupy the middle ground as the various factions of the party try to draft legislative compromises that the party and Congress will accept. But ideological perceptions can be deceiving and the ideological center of a party can shift rapidly. For example, Gingrich, who had been branded as a right-wing extremist by Democrats and even by some moderate Republicans when the party was a minority in the House, later was criticized as too centrist by some of the conservatives he helped elect in 1994. In 1998 Senate Majority Leader Trent LOTT of Mississippi, who might have been considered on the far right of his party just a few years earlier, made a comfortable fit early in his tenure with the Republican Conference that had moved toward him politically and added many like-minded legislators. Lott was even criticized by his former conservative allies in 2001 for making too many deals with Democrats, particularly on the unprecedented power-sharing agreement that Lott reached with Democrats when the Senate was divided equally in the five months prior to Jeffords's switch. The demands of institutional leadership and majority responsibility changed these leaders as well, along with their approach to politics.

Styles

Personal style can contribute to or detract from a leader's effectiveness. In his ten years as House Speaker (1977–1987), Massachusetts Democrat Thomas P. O'NEILL Jr. depended on close personal relationships and a warm, friendly manner to win support. A game of golf with colleagues was O'Neill's way of building close ties. But his reluctance to temper both his liberal beliefs and his partisanship made coalition-building, even within his party, difficult at times.

Jim WRIGHT, who became Speaker in 1987, was a backslapper with a broad grin and confident manner. But in his pursuit of an activist agenda, Wright caused resentment by acting without first consulting other party leaders or the rank and file. That exclusion, coupled with his aggressive and sometimes abrasive style, left him politically vulnerable when the challenge to his personal ethics arose.

Wright's successor, Thomas S. FOLEY, was known as a consensus builder. He was thought to be well equipped to help the Democrats and the House put the divisions of the Wright era behind them, when he became Speaker in 1989. But Foley's hands-off leadership style sparked criticism from some rank-and-file Democrats in 1992, when the chamber was rocked by scandals involving the House bank and post office. Some critics wanted the leadership to move more aggressively and decisively to contain the volatile situation. Foley, however, survived the criticism and seemed well-positioned for a long career as Speaker. But he lost his seat in Congress in the 1994 elections. (See SCANDALS, CONGRESSIONAL.)

Gingrich became Speaker when the Republicans took control of Congress in 1995. After a House career as a conservative backbencher and rabble-rouser, Gingrich became the most powerful Speaker since the days of Cannon, inspiring enormous loyalty from his fellow Republicans, who credited him with their return to majority control after forty years. He enjoyed remarkable success initially in passing legislation and in shaping a national debate over his party's agenda. But his interest in bold visions rather than legislative details caused difficulties for his speakership in the long run. Moreover, his assertive style was often perceived by the public as arrogance, and polls began to show him as a highly disliked political figure. By 1997 Gingrich was employing a less confrontational approach toward the White House and Democrats in Congress. But his leadership style remained erratic, consultative at times and autocratic at other times, involved and then aloof. Gingrich survived an ethics reprimand, a close vote for a second term as Speaker, and an abortive coup attempt within his party. But following unanticipated Republican losses in the 1998 midterm elections, his support eroded further and he decided not to seek reelection as Speaker and to resign from the House.

Hastert, Gingrich's successor, was seen as a "healer" and a behind-the-scenes consensus-builder, which many thought was exactly what the House needed after the confrontational style of Gingrich and the partisan breakdown in civility that occurred during the 1998–1999 impeachment and trial of President Bill Clinton. He left the more difficult and often brass-knuckle work of lining up votes and imposing party discipline to his deputies, particularly DeLay. For his hard-edged tactics to keep the GOP rank and file in line, DeLay became known as "The Hammer." (See CLINTON IMPEACHMENT TRIAL.)

As Senate majority leader from 1955 to 1961, Lyndon B. JOHNSON was known for his extraordinary ability to persuade colleagues to support him. In one-on-one encounters Johnson applied "the treatment," cajoling, touching an arm or shoulder for emphasis, leaning closer to make a point. By all accounts, Johnson was the most effective leader the Senate had ever seen, if not always the most liked. Johnson was a protégé of another forceful personality, fellow Texan and Democrat Sam RAYBURN, who served a record seventeen years as Speaker (plus four years as minority leader) between 1940 and 1961. Like Johnson, Rayburn demanded loyalty and responded ruthlessly to disobedience. He skillfully mixed political and personal relations, gathering favorite colleagues in a hideaway Capitol office to share a drink and stories. This "board of education" carried on a tradition begun by another House Speaker, Republican Nicholas LONGWORTH of Ohio, who ran the House from 1925 to 1931.

Johnson's successor, Democrat Mike MANSFIELD of Montana, could not have provided a greater contrast in leadership styles. Known as the "gentle persuader," Mansfield, who served longer than any other majority leader in Senate history (1961–1977), was a permissive, at times even passive, leader.

West Virginian Robert C. BYRD served as Democratic majority leader from 1977 to 1981 and again from 1987 to 1989, and as the minority leader in the intervening years. He built a solid political base with diligence, loyalty to allies, and unsurpassed knowledge of the Senate's arcane rules and procedures. Most senators were indebted to him for practical reasons: for years, Byrd meticulously accommodated his colleagues' personal and political needs. Although some criticized him for being more interested in procedure than substance, Byrd could use his knowledge as a powerful weapon to disadvantage or circumvent legislative opponents.

In contrast to the strong-willed Byrd, his successor Democrat George J. MITCHELL of Maine brought a more accommodating, consensus-oriented style to the leadership. His collegial approach was evident at the outset when, unlike his Democratic predecessors, he chose to share the responsibilities of the party committees. Mitchell retired from the Senate in 1995. Control of the Senate reverted to the Republicans that year and remained in GOP hands until mid-2001. After Jeffords left the Republican Party and the Democrats regained control, Tom DASCHLE of South Dakota led the Senate until 2003. Under Daschle's quiet, easy-going demeanor was a strong partisanship and willingness to battle for his party's priorities in the acrimonious atmosphere that prevailed after the Senate changed hands. But the tensions between the parties soon gave way to a bipartisan response to the September 11, 2001, terrorist attacks on New York and Washington. The need to be supportive of the Republican White House in the aftermath of the attacks, while still leading the Democratic charge against other parts of the GOP agenda, made Daschle's tenure as majority leader a challenging one.

Among Senate Republicans, Howard H. BAKER Jr. of Tennessee brought an open personal style to the majority leader's job, which he held from 1981 to 1985. He had served the previous four years as minority leader. His steady, low-key performance stood in sharp contrast to that of his father-in-law, Republican Everett DIRKSEN of Illinois, who was minority leader from 1959 to 1969. Dirksen's florid style and distinctive bass voice caused him to be called the "Wizard of Ooze."

After four years of Baker's easygoing stewardship, Republican senators opted for a leader who could restore some discipline and sense of purpose to a chamber increasingly bogged down in procedural chaos: Robert DOLE of Kansas. In addition to his image as a decisive leader, Dole was known as a superb negotiator able to find compromises where others had failed. Dole, who was the longest-serving Republican leader in history (1985–1996), was relegated to minority leader in 1987 but returned as an aggressive majority leader in 1995. He stayed in the post until the spring of 1996, when he resigned from Congress to run for president.

Lott, Dole's successor as Senate majority leader, had been considered a sharp-edged ideologue during his days as House minority whip. But Lott did not use the Senate post, as some thought he would, to transform the chamber into an engine of conservative activism similar to Gingrich's House. Instead, he took a more pragmatic approach and adapted to the consensus-building demands of his job. In fact, Lott was criticized by some conservative senators in 2001 when he accepted a power-sharing agreement that many in his party considered too generous to the Democrats. Lott attempted to smooth over tensions through his affable, confident demeanor.

However, none of those personal attributes could save Lott nearly two years later when a verbal gaffe reinforced negative impressions of his conservative beliefs. Lott's leadership suffered a deep blow when he made a statement that was widely perceived as racist. At a one-hundredth birthday party on December 5, 2002, for retiring senator Strom Thurmond, R-S.C., Lott said: "I want to say this about my state. When Strom Thurmond ran for president, we voted for him. We're proud of it. And if the rest of the country had followed our lead, we wouldn't have had all these problems over all these years, either."

Although Lott did not mention it, Thurmond's 1948 Dixiecrat campaign had focused on promoting racial segregation. Lott's stature was diminished even more when it was revealed that he had uttered similar words two decades earlier. That revelation prompted many to examine his ties to conservative organizations in the South that promoted the preservation of the white race.

As the firestorm over his remarks intensified, Republicans who had been seeking to broaden the political appeal of the party to minorities and suburban voters feared that the GOP's public image was being tainted. President George W. Bush publicly chastised Lott, saying that "any suggestion that the segregated past was acceptable or positive is offensive and it is wrong."

Lott announced on December 20 that he was stepping down from his position as minority leader. At the beginning of the 110th Congress in 2007, Lott returned to a leadership post as minority whip, second in line to Republican minority leader Mitch McConnell of Kentucky. In December 2007, however, Lott resigned his seat to return to private life.

Bill FRIST of Tennessee was approved as his replacement by GOP senators in a conference call on December 23, 2002. Although Frist also was a southerner whose voting record was nearly as conservative as Lott's, his public image was far more moderate than Lott's. As the Senate's only trained physician, Frist had focused on health care and educational issues that appealed to suburbanites since his election to the Senate in 1994. Politically astute and a close ally of President Bush, Frist had won accolades for his service as the National Republican Senatorial Committee chair, a position that allowed him to raise millions for candidates in his party. The strong showing by Republicans in the 2002 elections had only bolstered Frist's image. Frist's tenure as majority leader, however, was a mixed success. Many observers thought he was a weak leader who could not get as much of the president's agenda enacted as he should have. The 109th Congress, 2005–2007, was particularly disappointing. To a considerable extent, this resulted from the increasing divisions in Congress and the nation over the intractable war in Iraq that Bush had launched in 2003. By the end of the session, few major pieces of legislation had passed, including immigration policy, a framework for the administration's warrantless electronic surveillance program, repeal of the estate tax, an overhaul of the telecommunications law, or a revamping of lobby laws in the face of a number of high-profile influence-peddling scandals. Moreover, Congress did not complete action on nine of the eleven appropriations bills for fiscal 2007. Frist retired from Congress in 2007 and abandoned plans to run for president in 2008.

In 2007, with Democrats in control again, the leadership returned to a quintessential Senate insider, Harry REID, of Nevada. He was a moderate Democrat from a swing state who built a constituency within the chamber as a backroom deal-cutter on the Appropriations Committee and spent many hours on the floor developing a keen sense of parliamentary procedure. He proved a good vote counter and was trusted by colleagues on both sides of the isle. But, like Pelosi's in the House, his early tenure as majority leader in the 110th Congress was enveloped by controversy over the war in Iraq and the significant split in the party—both in and out of Congress—about the U.S. participation in it. He also on occasion spoke with a candor that caused fellow Democrats to cringe. For example, he called George W. Bush a "loser" in 2005 when the president was abroad, violating a long-standing tradition against criticizing the chief executive when the person was abroad. In 2007 he declared the Iraq war "is lost," going farther than many Democrats preferred.

Challenges

Today the job of leading Congress is perhaps more challenging than ever before. A series of reforms and developments both inside and outside Congress has changed it markedly from the seniority-driven, hierarchical institution of the 1950s, when Rayburn and Johnson exercised legendary control over their chambers.

Widespread turnover has brought into both chambers younger members, less bound by tradition, who object to being closed out of the process. New rules and procedures have made the institution more democratic. Power that had resided almost exclusively with committee chairs has been parceled out to subcommittees, and the iron grip of the old seniority system has disappeared. At the same time election law reforms, the advent of television campaigning, and the role of political action committees in financing campaigns have made individual members of Congress much less dependent on the political party apparatus for their electoral survival.

Leaders today must take care to lead in the direction the rank and file wants to go and to involve members in the decision-making process along the way. Failure to do this could mean stalemate or humiliating defeat. A widely publicized example of this was the budget debacle in 1990, when House Democratic and Republican leaders agreed to a budget deal with the White House, but neither party was able to deliver its share of the votes. The agreement was defeated. An unwieldy omnibus appropriations bill negotiated by a small group of congressional leaders and senior White House aides late in the 1998 session outraged many Republicans and contributed to Speaker Gingrich's fall from power.

In 2002 the Republican leadership in the House, having delayed action on campaign finance legislation, agreed to bring it to the floor when a small but growing number of Republican rebels joined with Democrats to force the action. The event was a replay of similar action in 1998. However, in 2002 the bill had already passed the Senate during the previous year. GOP leaders could not prevent it from becoming law.

That same year, a disagreement between conservatives and moderates essentially prevented GOP leaders from enacting eleven appropriations bills. Republican leaders could not broker an effective compromise between the two groups that would allow the measures to pass and the process stalled, leaving the legislation unresolved until 2003.

Personalities and styles of leaders may vary and party control may change, but ultimately leadership power today is still the power to persuade others to follow. In 2007 the new House Speaker, Nancy Pelosi, faced difficult challenges in her new role. Democrats had won House control in 2006 in large part because of growing national angst over the intractable war in Iraq. Once in power, the war became the defining issue for Democrats, but the House caucus had a array of opinions ranging from members who wanted to force an immediate U.S. troop withdrawal to others who were reluctant to end military funding—the primary leverage Congress possessed—while fighting was going on and troops were in danger. Bridging these differences and presenting a clear Democratic face on the issue to the public was proving, by the end of 2007, a daunting task for the new Speaker.

Legislation

Legislation is a bill or resolution that Congress uses as a vehicle to create a law or state a policy. It may be broad enough to affect the entire nation or so narrow it affects only one person. It may be done in conjunction with the executive branch or it may be a matter within Congress or just one chamber of Congress.

Congress uses various types of legislation to differentiate how the thousands of bills and resolutions introduced each term are handled by the committees and scheduled for floor action. Different types of legislation receive different treatment. (See LEGISLATIVE PROCESS.)

Both chambers use four types of legislation. Two of these, bills and joint resolutions, become law if passed in identical form by both houses and signed by the president (or passed over a presidential veto). In the House of Representatives, these measures are labeled "HR" for a bill and "H J Res" for a joint resolution. In the Senate "S" denotes a bill, and "S J Res," a joint resolution.

Every legislative proposal is given a number that reflects the order in which it is introduced during each two-year congressional term (HR 1, HR 2, HR 3, etc.; S 1, S 2, S 3, etc.). If passed and signed by the president, a bill that is public in nature receives another designation, a public law (PL) number. Public law numbers also include the Congress in which they are enacted; thus, "PL 110 1" identifies the first public law enacted in the 110th Congress, which began in 2007. (See LAWS.)

The vast majority of legislative proposals—recommendations dealing with either domestic or foreign issues and programs affecting the U.S. government or the population generally—are drafted in the form of bills. These include authorization bills and appropriations bills.

Joint resolutions—the other form of legislation that can become law—have a more limited focus, though occasionally they may be used for omnibus legislation, measures that combine provisions from several disparate subjects into a single bill. Proposed constitutional amendments also are drafted in the form of joint resolutions, as are some emergency and catchall appropriations measures. In addition, routine measures making technical or minor changes in existing law or correcting errors in newly enacted legislation may be drafted as joint resolutions.

There are no significant differences in consideration of joint resolutions and bills. Both must be passed in identical form by the House and Senate and signed by the president (or passed over a veto) to become law. There is one major exception, however: joint resolutions embodying proposed constitutional amendments are not sent to the president for signature after they have been approved by Congress (by a two-thirds vote in each house). Instead, they are forwarded directly to the fifty states for ratification, which requires approval by a three-fourths majority (thirty-eight states).

One other form of legislation can be enacted into law: private bills (also labeled either "HR" or "S"). If enacted, these bills have a separately numbered system of laws. Private bills deal primarily with matters for the relief of individuals or private parties and are not of a general nature affecting the nation. Immigration cases and grievances or claims against the United States constitute the largest categories of private bills today.

The other two forms of legislation are concurrent resolutions and, simply, resolutions. These are labeled "H Con Res" and "H Res" in the House, "S Con Res" and "S Res" in the Senate. Unlike bills and joint resolutions, concurrent resolutions and resolutions are not signed by the president, do not become law,

---

CLOSER LOOK

Legislation is a bill or resolution by which Congress creates a law or states a policy. It may affect the entire nation or only one person. It may be done in conjunction with the executive branch or it may be a matter solely within Congress or just one chamber of Congress.

More on this topic:

Appropriations Bills, p. 22

Authorization Bills, p. 33

Constitutional Amendments, p. 139

Legislative Process, p. 344

Omnibus Bills, p. 401

Rules Committee, House, p. 478

Treaty-Making Power, p. 559

and thus do not receive PL numbers. Concurrent resolutions are internal measures of Congress and are considered by both the House and the Senate. Simple resolutions are considered only by the chamber in which they are introduced.

House and Senate concurrent resolutions address matters involving Congress itself as well as some wider issues that do not require the president's signature. Examples of the first category are the resolution that fixes the time of adjournment of a Congress and the so-called sense of Congress resolutions, which are expressions of congressional sentiment that do not have the force of law. Of potentially greater impact is the second category of concurrent resolutions, such as the annual congressional budget resolutions setting Congress's revenue and spending goals for the coming fiscal year. These are drafted as concurrent resolutions because they are not binding on the federal government and thus do not have to become law. Instead, they are statements of congressional intent or expressions of Congress's budgetary priorities.

House and Senate resolutions deal with internal matters of each chamber, often of a house-keeping nature. For example, resolutions are used periodically to set the spending levels for the various legislative committees or to revise the standing rules of each chamber. In the House, resolutions also embody the rules granted by the Rules Committee setting the guidelines for floor debate on each bill.

Introducing Bills

Legislation can be introduced only by senators and representatives and only when Congress is in session. All bills must be printed and made available to the public as well as to members of Congress. There is no limit on the number of cosponsors a bill or resolution may have or on the number of bills a member may introduce. Once it has been introduced, assigned a number, and printed, a bill almost always is referred to the appropriate legislative committee.

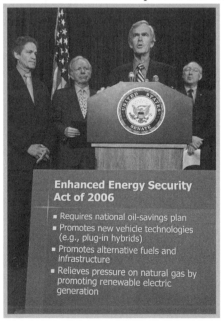

Enhanced Energy Security Act of 2006

- Requires national oil-savings plan
- Promotes new vehicle technologies (e.g., plug-in hybrids)
- Promotes alternative fuels and infrastructure
- Relieves pressure on natural gas by promoting renewable electric generation

Legislators can only introduce bills and resolutions while Congress is in session. Here, Sen. Jeff Bingaman, D-N.M., unveils a bipartisan plan, the Enhanced Energy Security Act of 2006. It was designed to spur energy conservation and reduce oil demand through greater fuel efficiency and to moderate natural gas demand by promoting renewable electricity production.

Source: CQ Photo/Scott J. Ferrell

Frequently, identical legislation is introduced in both houses. So-called companion bills are employed primarily to speed the legislation through Congress by encouraging both houses to consider the measure simultaneously. Sponsors of companion bills also may hope to dramatize the importance or urgency of the issue and show broad support for the legislation.

Major legislation undergoes changes in nomenclature as it works its way through the legislative process. When a measure is introduced and first printed, it is officially referred to as a bill and is so labeled. When the bill has been passed by one chamber and sent to the other body, it is reprinted and officially labeled an act (although it generally still is referred to as a bill). If cleared by Congress and signed by the president or enacted over a veto, it becomes a law (and also may still be referred to as an act).

When legislation is heavily amended in committee, all the changes, deletions, and additions, together with whatever is left of the original bill, may be organized into a new bill. Such measures, which are reintroduced and given a new bill number, are referred to as clean bills. For parliamentary reasons, this procedure is a timesaver once the bill reaches the floor of either house. If the original bill, with all the changes, is considered by the House or Senate, those changes must be considered and voted on by the chamber. In a clean bill, all the changes made in committee become part of the new bill, so that only one vote is needed to approve it, unless additional amendments are introduced from the floor. This not only saves time but reduces the opportunities for House members to raise challenges that additions to the bill are not germane, or relevant, to the original bill.

Treaties

In the Senate a unique type of resolution, known as a resolution of ratification, is used for consideration of treaties. These resolutions have their own "treaty document" number, which indicates the Congress and the order in which treaties are submitted to the Senate. For example, "Treaty Doc 108-1" would indicate the first treaty to be submitted in the 108th Congress. Before the 97th Congress (1981–1983), resolutions of ratification were listed in alphabetical order along with the Congress and the session in which they were submitted (Exec [for Executive] A, 96th Cong., 1st sess.).

Of all the varieties of legislation used by Congress, resolutions of ratification are the only ones that do not lapse at the end of the Congress in which they are introduced. If not acted upon by the Senate, these resolutions are held by the Senate Foreign Relations Committee and may be brought before the Senate during any future Congress. (The Senate also can show its lack of enthusiasm for a treaty by voting to return it to the president.) Approval of resolutions of ratification requires a two-thirds vote of senators present. The House does not participate in the ratification process, although it does play an equal role in passing legislation to implement a treaty.

Legislation Declared Unconstitutional

The Supreme Court early in its history asserted the power to review laws passed by Congress and to invalidate any laws found to violate the Constitution. Over time the doctrine of judicial review has become an established part of the U.S. system of separation of powers. It serves as a constant reminder to Congress that the laws it passes will be measured against the provisions of the Constitution and nullified if found in conflict.

While Congress has passed thousands of statutes over more than two centuries, the Court had exercised its power to rule laws or portions of laws unconstitutional at least 161 times by the mid-2000s. The congressional statutes invalidated have included many relatively minor laws, but also such major enactments as the Missouri Compromise, a federal income tax, child labor laws, New Deal economic recovery acts, the post-Watergate campaign finance law, statutes to curb pornography on the Internet, efforts permitting victims of gender-motivated violence to sue their attackers in federal court for compensatory damages, amendments to a landmark age discrimination law, and the line-item veto.

The Court invalidated only two statutes before the end of the Civil War. But as Congress broadened the scope of federal regulation in the late nineteenth century, the number of federal laws declared unconstitutional increased. Dominated by economic conservatives, the Court often blocked laws Congress enacted to protect workers and consumers. The conflicts peaked from 1918 to 1936. The Court threw out twenty-nine laws during that period, including several statutes of President Franklin D. Roosevelt's NEW DEAL program.

Roosevelt changed the Court's ideological composition during his second and third terms, appointing justices who supported broad federal powers in economic affairs while taking a more expansive view of civil liberties. In succeeding decades, the Court often used its power to strike down laws as infringements of individual freedoms, in particular freedom of speech. Under Chief Justice

Major Congressional Statutes Held Unconstitutional

The following lists the Supreme Court case, date, and law or provision held unconstitutional:

Marbury v. Madison (1803) Judiciary Act of 1789 provision giving Supreme Court power to issue writs of mandamus in cases originating at the Court. Established the Court's power of judicial review of legislation.

Scott v. Sandford (1857) Missouri Compromise provision (known as the Dred Scott case) barring slavery in the northern part of the Louisiana Territory; overturned by Fourteenth Amendment. Intensified the debate over slavery, which led soon to the Civil War.

Ex parte Garland (1867) Test oath for former Confederate supporters, invalidating an 1865 law that required attorneys, as a condition to practice in federal courts, to declare they never supported the southern rebellion against the Union. Suggested, with other cases, the Court would not be sympathetic to Reconstruction era laws.

Hepburn v. Griswold (1870) "Legal tender clauses" making paper money legal tender for all debts; overruled in 1871 (*Knox v. Lee*).

Civil Rights Cases (1883) 1875 civil rights act barring racial discrimination in public accommodations; five cases overturning Reconstruction-era civil rights provisions.

Pollock v. Farmers' Loan & Trust Co (1895) Income tax provisions of the tariff act of 1894; overturned by Sixteenth Amendment.

The Employers' Liability Cases (1908) 1906 act imposing liability on railroads for injuries to employees.

Adair v. United States (1908) Law that prohibited "yellow-dog contracts," which required employees to agree not to join a union as a condition of employment. In 1930 the Court sanctioned a federal law guaranteeing collective bargaining rights for railway employees.

Hammer v. Dagenhart (1918) Original child labor law barring products made with child labor from interstate commerce; overruled in 1941 (*United States v. Darby Lumber Co.*).

Newberry v. United States (1921) Federal Corrupt Practice Act of 1911 provision limiting spending by senatorial candidates in party primary; overruled in 1941 (*United States v. Classic*).

Bailey v. Drexel Furniture Co. (Child Labor Tax Cases) (1922) Child Labor Tax Act imposing 10 percent excise tax on goods manufactured with child labor; overruled in 1941 (*United States v. Darby Lumber Co.*).

Adkins v. Children's Hospital (1923) District of Columbia minimum wage law for women; overruled in 1937 (*West Coast Hotel Co. v. Parrish*).

Myers v. United States (1926) 1876 law requiring "the advice and consent of the Senate" for removal of postmasters.

Panama Refining Co. v. Ryan (1935) National Industrial Recovery Act's "hot oil" provision penalizing interstate transportation of petroleum in excess of state production controls.

Schechter Poultry Corp. v. United States (1935) National Industrial Recovery Act provision for industry-written codes of fair competition; most important of several rulings striking down New Deal economic recovery legislation.

United States v. Butler (1936) Agricultural Adjustment Act providing for processing taxes on agricultural commodities and benefit payments to farmers.

Carter v. Carter Coal Co. (1936) Bituminous Coal Conservation Act of 1935 regulating prices and labor relations in the coal industry and levying tax on coal to finance regulation scheme.

Bolling v. Sharpe (1954) 1862 statute establishing segregated schools in the District of Columbia (companion case to *Brown v. Board of Education of Topeka*).

United States v. Brown (1965) Labor-Management Reporting and Disclosure Act of 1959 provision barring current or former communists from labor union office.

Shapiro v. Thompson (1969) District of Columbia law establishing one-year residency requirement for welfare benefits.

Oregon v. Mitchell (1970) Voting rights for eighteen-year-olds; overturned by Twenty-sixth Amendment.

Frontiero v. Richardson (1973) Gender-based benefits provision for members of the armed forces; first of several sex discrimination rulings in benefits cases.

Buckley v. Valeo (1976) Federal Election Campaign Act of 1974 provisions limiting spending by political candidates and establishing Federal Election Commission with congressionally appointed members.

National League of Cities v. Usery (1976) Fair Labor Standards Act provisions extending wage and hour coverage to state and local government workers; overturned in 1985 *(Garcia v. San Antonio Metropolitan Transit Authority)*.

Immigration and Naturalization Service v. Chadha (1983) Legislative veto provisions of Immigration and Nationality Act; ruling deemed to apply to similar provisions in as many as 200 statutes.

United States v. Eichman (1990) 1989 flag desecration statute.

United States v. Lopez (1995) Gun Free Schools Zone Act.

Printz v. United States (1997) Brady Act provision for background checks on prospective gun purchasers.

Reno v. American Civil Liberties Union (1997) Communications Decency Act aimed at limiting access by minors to sexually oriented material on the Internet.

Clinton v. City of New York (1998) Line-Item Veto Act.

Alden v. Maine (1999) Fair Labor Standards Act provision for damage suits against state governments; extended to suits under Age Discrimination Act *(Kimel v. Florida Board of Regents,* 2000), Americans with Disabilities Act *(Board of Trustees of Univ. of Alabama v. Garrett,* 2001).

United States v. Morrison (2000) Violence Against Women Act.

William H. Rehnquist, the Court in the 1990s continued to invoke the First Amendment to strike down some laws passed by Congress. At the same time, the Court also took a stricter view of congressional powers vis-à-vis the states, nullifying several laws on grounds they infringed states' rights.

Judicial Review

The Constitution makes no mention of judicial review, but the framers seem to have intended that the Supreme Court would have the power to determine whether acts of Congress conformed to its provisions. The Court first dealt with the question in 1803 in a rather minor political controversy over a presidential appointment. The dispute produced what many regard as the most important decision in the Supreme Court's history: *Marbury v. Madison.* (See COURTS AND CONGRESS.)

Democratic-Republican Thomas Jefferson defeated Federalist John Adams in his quest for re-election to the presidency in 1800. Before the Democratic-Republican took office, Adams nominated several Federalists to judicial posts created by legislation passed by the lame-duck Federalist Congress. The nominations were confirmed by the Senate and the commissions signed by Adams, but not all the commissions were delivered before Jefferson entered office. Jefferson promptly ordered that these commissions be withheld. William Marbury, who had been named justice of the peace for the District of Columbia, asked the Supreme Court to order Jefferson's secretary of state, James MADISON, to deliver his commission. Marbury filed suit under the Judiciary Act of 1789, which empowered the Court to issue writs of mandamus compelling federal officials to perform their duties.

It is "the province and duty of the judicial department to say what the law is."

—*Chief Justice John Marshall*
in *Marbury v. Madison* (1803)

The Supreme Court, led by Chief Justice John Marshall, held that Marbury should have received his commission but that the Court lacked the power to order that the commission be delivered. The Court ruled that the provision of the Judiciary Act empowering the Court to issue such an order was unconstitutional because Congress had no power to enlarge the Court's original jurisdiction. In the course of his opinion, Marshall stated emphatically that it was "the province and duty of the judicial department to say what the law is." The Court has repeated that assertion countless times since to justify its decisions to find laws passed by Congress contrary to the Constitution.

Legislative Day

In congressional usage, a legislative day extends from the time either chamber of Congress meets after an ADJOURNMENT until the time it next adjourns. The rules in each chamber call for certain routine business at the beginning of each legislative day. (See MORNING HOUR.)

The House normally adjourns at the end of a daily session, so its legislative days usually correspond to calendar days. The Senate, however, frequently goes days and sometimes weeks or even months without an adjournment; instead, it recesses. By recessing, it continues the same legislative day and avoids interrupting unfinished business.

Legislative Obstruction   *See* FILIBUSTER.

Legislative Process

The procedures Congress uses to write the laws of the land are collectively known as the legislative process. Through this process the ideas of presidents, members of Congress, political parties, interest groups, and individual citizens are transformed into national policy. The lawmaking function as set forth by the Constitution is complicated and time-consuming. It is governed by detailed rules and procedures, as well as more than 200 years of customs and traditions.

To become law a proposal must be approved in identical form by both the Senate and the House of Representatives and signed by the president—or else, infrequently, approved by Congress over the president's veto or allowed to become law without his signature during a session of Congress. Legislative proposals usually follow parallel paths through the two chambers of Congress. Bills are referred to committees for preliminary consideration, then debated, amended, and passed (or rejected) by the full House or Senate. The process is repeated in the other chamber. When the House and Senate pass different versions of a major bill, a temporary Senate-House conference committee normally is appointed to work out a compromise. Both chambers must approve the conferees' changes before the bill can be sent to the president for signature.

Not surprisingly, relatively few bills make it through this complex process. In the 109th Congress (2005–2006) about 10,500 bills and joint resolutions were introduced, but only 482 public laws were enacted.

Bills that are not passed die at the end of the two-year term of Congress in which they are introduced. They may be reintroduced in a later Congress.

A typical bill that survives the many roadblocks to enactment generally travels the route described in the remainder of this article.

Introducing Legislation

All legislation must be formally introduced by members of Congress, although members themselves do not originate most bills. Much of the legislation considered by Congress originates in the executive branch—the White House and federal agencies. This is especially true if Congress and the president are of the same political party. Special-interest organizations, such as trade unions or business associations, are another fertile source of legislation. There are many other sources as well, including Congress itself, state and local government officials, and ordinary citizens.

Legislation is drafted in various forms. Bills originating in the House are designated "HR," and resolutions are labeled "H J Res," "H Con Res," or "H Res," depending on the type of resolution. Senate measures are designated "S," "S J Res," "S Con Res," or "S Res." Each measure carries a number showing the order in which it was introduced: "HR 1" or "S 1" would be the first bill introduced at the beginning of a new Congress. Many bills fall into one of two categories:

Authorization bills, which establish or continue government programs or policies and set limits on how much money may be spent on them, and appropriations bills, which provide the actual funds to carry out authorized programs or policies or provide funds to operate government agencies.

Authorization bills may be valid for several years, but appropriations bills generally are valid for only one year.

Committee Action

Once a bill has been introduced by a member, it is almost always referred to a committee that has specialized knowledge of the subject matter. Bills that involve more than one subject may be referred to two or more committees, a practice known as multiple referral. Senators and representatives are far too busy to follow every bill that comes before Congress, and they cannot be experts in all the different subjects bills cover. They must rely on the committees to screen most of this legislation.

A bill usually faces the sharpest scrutiny in committee. It is here that most deliberation and rewriting are done. This is especially true in the House; in the Senate deliberation and revision by the full chamber sometimes are equally important in determining a measure's final form.

Bills may be considered by the full committee initially or by a subcommittee. Sometimes the major review of a bill takes place at the subcommittee level, and the full committee simply endorses the subcommittee's recommendations. But frequently the full committee will propose additional amendments to alter the proposal.

The committee or subcommittee generally holds hearings on legislation before taking further action on it. Comment is requested from administration officials and from federal bureaucrats who run the programs that might be affected by the bill. Heads of cabinet-level departments of the government testify on the most important proposals. Scholars and technical experts also

The legislative process sets off committee debates and often requires long rewrite periods. Here, Rep. Greg Walden, R-Ore., waves a copy of a bill during the House Energy Committee's markup of children's health insurance legislation.
Source: CQ Photo/Scott J. Ferrell

The legislative process typically involves these steps in Congress:

1. A bill is introduced. This must be done by a member of Congress and can occur in either the House or Senate. But the text of bills often is written in federal agencies, the White House, lobbying group offices, and elsewhere.

2. Committee action occurs in which hearings usually are held by a legislative committee. Individuals interested in a bill will testify and often urge approval, rejection, or modification of a proposal.

3. The legislative committee then decides whether or not to proceed with the legislation. If it goes ahead, the committee may alter or completely rewrite the original text. It then approves the bill and sends it to the full chamber, the House or Senate, for debate. Most of the work on bills is done in committees.

4. The bill is then scheduled for floor action under procedures that differ significantly between the Senate and the House. Once a bill is taken up it is debated and often altered through amendment. It then is passed, or sometimes rejected, by the chamber. If passed it is sent on to the other chamber for consideration.

5. The other chamber in Congress goes through similar steps. In the case of major proposals the Senate and House are often working on versions of a bill at the same time.

6. Once a bill is passed by both chambers, almost always in different form, it must go to a conference committee made up of a few members from the Senate and House who were involved in the legislation. If possible they resolve differences to get a single piece of legislation that each chamber then usually approves.

7. Once a single bill is approved by Congress it is sent to the president. The president may sign the bill into law or, on occasion, veto the measure and return it to Congress. Presidents usually spell out their objections when returning vetoed bills. Congress then has the opportunity to override the veto. If it does so the bill will become law.

may appear at hearings. Lobbying groups and private citizens may testify for or against the legislation.

Committee hearings help set the legislative agenda and shape its political tone. They are one of the most important forums for finding out what the public thinks about national problems and how to solve them. Hearings also may have an educational function. Members of Congress need political support for the actions they take, especially when controversial issues or remedies are involved. Hearings assist Congress in developing a consensus on proposed legislation.

After the hearings, committee members may meet to consider the provisions of the legislation in detail, a process known as marking up the bill. Sometimes bills are heavily amended—that is, revised—or entirely redrafted in committee. Votes may be taken on controversial amendments and, finally, on whether to approve the bill and recommend that the full House or Senate pass the measure.

When committee action has been completed, the panel prepares a written report describing the bill and its amendments, and explaining why the measure should become law. Both the members supporting the bill and those opposed may include their views in the report, which is filed with the parent chamber. At this point a bill is said to be reported to the House or Senate.

The fate of most bills is sealed in committee. Bills that gain committee approval do not always win consideration by the parent chamber, but those that do are likely to pass—although they may be revised on the floor. Most bills simply die in committee. Procedures to remove a bill from an unsympathetic committee seldom succeed.

Scheduling Floor Debate

House

The House Rules Committee functions as a sort of traffic cop for bills reported from the legislative committees. Its power is considerable, and its role in the legislative process is crucial. The power of the Rules Committee comes from its authority to control the flow of legislation from the legislative committees to the full House and to set the terms of debate for almost every major bill that reaches the floor of the House. Generally, it acts on behalf of the Speaker in facilitating and promoting the majority party's program.

The chair of the Rules Committee, who is the Speaker's personal choice for the post, has wide discretion in arranging the panel's agenda. The decision to schedule, or not to schedule, a hearing on a bill will usually determine whether the measure ever comes before the House for debate. Under regular House rules, bills must be brought up and debated in the order in which they are reported from the committees. The large volume of bills vying for action makes it necessary to have some system of setting priorities. In the modern Congress there is just not enough time to act on all the legislation working its way through the legislative process.

Once the Rules Committee has given a bill the go-ahead for floor debate, it drafts a special RULE FOR HOUSE DEBATE, which is custom-made for each bill. The committee decides how many hours the House may have to debate the bill and whether all amendments, some amendments, or no amendments may be introduced from the floor. Although it has no authority to amend bills that come before it from other committees, the Rules Committee can strike bargains on proposed amendments desired by various members in return for granting the rule.

Until the 1980s the vast majority of rules were open, allowing any germane amendment to be offered on the floor at the appropriate time. Closed rules, barring all but committee amendments, generally were reserved for tax bills and other measures too complicated or technical to be tampered with on the House floor. But as the number of amendments increased substantially and the leadership seemed to be losing control of the amendment process, the Rules Committee began to draft an increasing number of modified rules, specifying which amendments could be offered and often stipulating in what order they would be considered. The modified rules varied considerably. They could, for example, allow amendments only to specific sections of a bill, or permit only amendments that had been drafted and printed in the *CONGRESSIONAL RECORD* in advance of the debate. After the Republicans took control of the House in 1995, they claimed a return to more open rules, but, predictably, the Democrats disputed their statistics and definition of "openness."

The drafting of legislation in the modern Congress is complicated. In many cases, more than one committee works on a bill before it goes to the full House. Frequently the committees' work involves fragile compromises, which lead to demands to keep these bills intact. Modified rules help to avoid hasty and sometimes ill-advised writing of legislation on the House floor. There also are political benefits for the leadership in controlling the amending process on the most controversial elements of a major bill. In the 1980s the Republican minority in the House skillfully used the amending process to frustrate the Democratic leadership's floor strategy. Modified rules can often be used to head off embarrassing defeats or surprises during debates. The Rules Committee has become increasingly innovative in designing rules to keep floor debate under control and achieve the objectives of the leadership.

The rule from the Rules Committee also may waive points of order—that is, objections raised during the debate because something in the bill or a procedure used to bring the bill to the floor violates a House rule. A POINT OF ORDER is often used by a bill's opponents when they do not have enough votes to defeat the bill outright, in order to delay action and perhaps win concessions from the sponsors of the legislation. The Rules Committee can set aside temporarily any rule of House procedure—except those ordered by the Constitution—in order to facilitate action.

Like the bill to which it is attached, the rule for full House action requires the approval of a simple majority of the House. It is possible to amend the rule on the floor, but this happens infrequently. Rules are seldom rejected. Once the rule is adopted, the bill itself can be debated.

There are special procedures for bringing up measures stymied in legislative committees or in the Rules Committee: the discharge petition and CALENDAR WEDNESDAY. In addition, the Rules Committee has a special power to draft rules dislodging bills from balky legislative committees. These procedures are seldom used.

There also are procedural shortcuts for bringing routine legislation to the floor. Most legislation is passed this way. The SUSPENSION OF THE RULES procedure is the most frequently used. Bills debated under this shortcut can be passed quickly if they can garner a two-thirds majority vote.

"I believe in friendly compromise. I said over in the Senate hearings that truth is the glue that holds government together. Compromise is the oil that makes governments go."

—Rep. Gerald R. Ford in remarks before a House committee on his nomination by President Richard M. Nixon to become vice president, filling the vacancy in that office

Senate

Scheduling legislation for debate in the Senate is a more informal process than in the House. Although the Senate has an elaborate framework of parliamentary machinery to guide its deliberations, in practice its procedures are far more flexible than those of the House. Almost anything can be done by UNANIMOUS CONSENT. But that flexibility also means that only one senator can delay or threaten to delay action on a bill until a compromise is struck.

Almost all noncontroversial matters, including minor legislation, private bills, and presidential nominations, are called up by a simple unanimous consent request. Generally these matters are cleared with the leadership beforehand.

For major legislation, the Senate often legislates through what is called a UNANIMOUS CONSENT AGREEMENT. This informal agreement geared to a particular bill is the functional equivalent of a rule issued by the House Rules Committee. Such an agreement may limit debate time on a bill and on proposed amendments and may specify what amendments can be introduced and by whom. It may set a time and date to consider the bill and, leaving nothing to chance, may even set a time for a final vote.

Frequently the agreement stipulates that any amendments offered must be germane, that is, they must pertain to the subject of the bill. Unlike the House, the Senate does not have a germaneness rule; unless there has been prior agreement to exclude extraneous policy provisions, there is nothing to prevent a senator from offering a measure concerning, say, water quality or civil rights as a RIDER to a health bill.

Unlike a House rule, a unanimous consent agreement is drawn up privately, without committee hearings, by the majority and minority leadership and other interested senators. Because a unanimous consent agreement cannot take effect if any senator objects, the drafters must be sensitive to the rights of all one hundred members of the Senate. In contrast to the House, where scheduling is solely a majority party responsibility, Senate scheduling requires bipartisan cooperation.

Once an agreement has been struck, the measure is brought to the floor at the prearranged time. Bringing up controversial legislation by any other method—for instance, by offering a motion to do so—is risky, since most Senate motions are debatable. Any senator may engage in unlimited debate on the motion, so that a time-consuming attempt to cut off this "debate" may be necessary even before the bill is formally before the Senate.

Like the House, the Senate has several ways of bringing to the floor legislation stalled in committee or never considered in committee: bypassing the committee stage and placing the bill on the legislative calendar; suspending Senate rules; discharging the bill from the committee blocking it; or attaching the bill as a rider to another already on the floor. Of these, only the last is generally effective.

Floor Action

There are marked differences in how the two chambers debate and dispose of legislation. This stage in the legislative process is called floor action. The House, because of its size, must adhere strictly to detailed procedures designed to expedite legislative business. The SPEAKER OF THE HOUSE controls the agenda and is easily the most powerful member in either chamber. The smaller Senate operates more informally. Power is less centralized, and no Senate leader wields the power the Speaker of the House possesses. Scheduling in the Senate traditionally has been the joint work of the majority and minority leaders.

The philosophy behind the rules of the two chambers also is different. Senate procedures are intended to give great weight to the minority, even at the expense of legislative efficiency, while House rules emphasize majority rights.

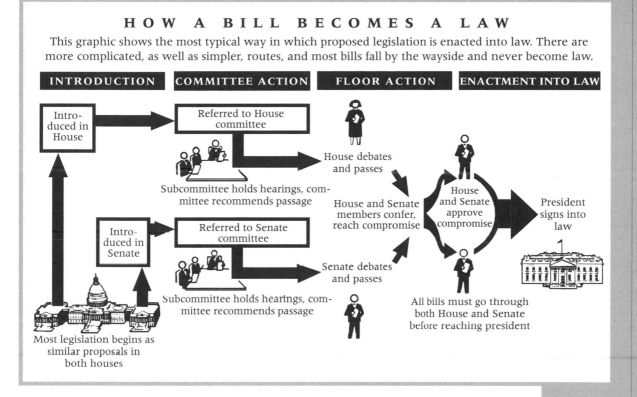

HOW A BILL BECOMES A LAW

This graphic shows the most typical way in which proposed legislation is enacted into law. There are more complicated, as well as simpler, routes, and most bills fall by the wayside and never become law.

| INTRODUCTION | COMMITTEE ACTION | FLOOR ACTION | ENACTMENT INTO LAW |

Introduced in House → Referred to House committee

Subcommittee holds hearings, committee recommends passage

House debates and passes

House and Senate members confer, reach compromise

House and Senate approve compromise

Introduced in Senate → Referred to Senate committee

Subcommittee holds hearings, committee recommends passage

Senate debates and passes

President signs into law

Most legislation begins as similar proposals in both houses

All bills must go through both House and Senate before reaching president

Approval of bills and amendments in either chamber requires a majority of the members voting. Thus a tie vote spells defeat. In the Senate the VICE PRESIDENT of the United States, who under the Constitution is the Senate's PRESIDING OFFICER, may vote to break a tie. But this is the only circumstance in which the vice president may vote. In the House the Speaker traditionally votes only to break a tie, although as an elected member of that chamber the Speaker may vote at any time on any proposal.

House

Most bills are debated and disposed of in the House in one afternoon, although some bills take two or three days. Rarely is action drawn out over many days or even weeks, as occurs in the Senate. House rules make filibusters and most other stalling tactics impractical. The House uses a parliamentary tool known as the PREVIOUS QUESTION to close debate and guarantee that a bill will come to a final vote.

House parliamentary procedures are the same for most major bills, except those handled under shortcut methods. The rule, presented in a resolution reported by the Rules Committee, is debated and adopted. The House debates most legislation in the Committee of the Whole House on the State of the Union, or more simply, the COMMITTEE OF THE WHOLE. This is nothing more than the House sitting in another form. When functioning as the Committee of the Whole, the House uses special rules designed to speed up floor action. On each bill there is a period for general debate, as regulated by the Rules Committee's rule, and separate debate and votes on all amendments introduced and allowed under the rule.

General debate is controlled by floor managers for the majority and minority parties, who often are the chair and ranking minority member of the committee or subcommittee with jurisdiction over the bill. (See FLOOR MANAGER.)

General debate usually lasts one hour, although more time may be allowed for controversial measures. The bill then is read section by section for amendment. The House considers amendments under guidelines that give both the proponents and opponents at least five minutes to discuss each one. But a legislator can gain extra time by employing certain parliamentary MOTIONS.

Since the majority party sets the agenda, the minority party underlines its policy differences by trying to amend the bill. Amendments publicize the minority's positions even if there is little chance they will be adopted. Amendments also may be used as part of a strategy to defeat a bill. Opponents may attempt to weigh down the legislation with so many amendments that the bill will lose support. Some members, particularly on the minority side, develop great parliamentary expertise and act as self-appointed watchdogs of the rules and tactics of the majority.

Some votes in the House are taken by methods that make it impossible to tell how individual members voted. Others are taken by an electronic system that provides a public record of each member's vote on an issue. The Constitution spells out certain instances when votes must be individually recorded.

When all amendments have been disposed of, the Committee of the Whole dissolves and the bill is reconsidered by the members, now sitting as the House of Representatives. The House then proceeds through a series of parliamentary motions and votes that give opponents a final opportunity to influence the outcome while guaranteeing that the proponents—assuming they are in the majority—will be able to pass the bill. Unlike the situation in the Senate, a determined House majority can always be expected to prevail on a particular bill.

Bills that reach a final passage vote are seldom defeated outright. By that time the support or opposition has been clearly established, while attempts to revise the legislation have already been made during floor debate.

Senate

In the Senate much of what goes on has been planned in advance. Senators read speeches on legislation written by their staffs, and action on bills and amendments is by prior arrangement under unanimous consent agreements. Spontaneous debate is the exception. Normally there are few senators on the floor, except when crucial votes occur. Nevertheless, floor debate and procedural strategies are important in the Senate. One reason is that Senate rules make the legislative outcome less certain than in the House. The play of personalities and political influence affects the result to a much greater extent.

Floor action bears little resemblance to the procedures outlined in the formal rules. Scheduling is quite flexible. Debate is unstructured; for example, no period is reserved for general debate. The Senate often conducts its business by setting aside its rules and operating through unanimous consent agreements. All senators can participate in scheduling. If there is broad backing for a bill, the Senate can act quickly. But if a political consensus is lacking, Senate action can be held up almost indefinitely.

On controversial bills for which agreements cannot be reached ahead of time, the majority leader may put the Senate on a track system. Tracking permits the Senate to have two or more bills pending simultaneously, with a specific time of the day designated for each bill. If one bill is being filibustered, the Senate can turn to another and thus not hold up all floor action.

The majority leader's greatest influence comes from control of the legislative agenda. The majority leader can schedule bills to suit certain senators or the White House and can hold votes at times that benefit a bill's supporters or minimize the opposition's strength. The minority leadership, however, must be consulted.

The Senate mostly relies on two types of votes, voice votes and roll calls. The roll sometimes is called slowly to give absent senators time to hustle to the floor from their offices in nearby buildings. Senators have a second chance to vote when the roll call is repeated. Much legislation is passed by unanimous consent. Even measures on which the Senate is closely divided may be passed without a roll call because the controversial issues already have been resolved, either by approval or rejection of key amendments or by procedural votes that reflect the Senate's positions before the bill itself is voted on.

The Senate does not use such House parliamentary tools as the previous question to end debate. Since unanimous consent is impossible, debate can be cut off only by informal compromise or by cloture; for most legislation a vote of three-fifths of the entire Senate, or sixty members if there are no vacancies, is needed to end debate by cloture. Even without the filibuster, senators have many devices at their disposal for sidetracking legislation. Certain rules may delay consideration of a bill after it has been reported by a committee, and an informal practice allows senators to place "HOLDS" on bills for varying lengths of time.

Action in Second Chamber

After a bill has been passed by one chamber it is sent to the other. At this point several parliamentary options are available. The normal practice for all but the most routine legislation is for the measure to go to committee, where there will be more hearings, followed by markup, a vote to approve the bill, and the drafting of a committee report. (In most cases, the other chamber has already begun action on its own version of a bill.) It may then go to the floor and be passed.

Differences between the House and Senate versions must be resolved before the bill can be sent to the president. On many noncontroversial measures, the second chamber may simply agree to the version passed by the first chamber. When that happens, no further legislative action is required, and the bill can be submitted to the president.

On virtually all major legislation, however, the second chamber approves a version that differs, sometimes radically, from the measure adopted by the first chamber. Often members and staff of the House and Senate committees with jurisdiction over the bill informally work out a compromise that the two chambers agree to. But some bills will require a House-Senate conference committee to negotiate a compromise.

Conference Action

The House-Senate conference is a critical juncture. Everything the bill's sponsors have worked for may be won or lost during these negotiations, and all the effort exerted by the executive branch and private interests to help pass or defeat it may have been in vain.

Either chamber may request a conference with the other to resolve the differences between the versions passed by the House and Senate. Conferees are appointed from each chamber. They are generally chosen by the chair and highest-ranking minority member of the committee or subcommittee in which the bill originated.

Before House and Senate conferees begin their negotiations, each delegation may meet separately to work out its positions on the key differences. The conferees decide what they are willing to sacrifice and what provisions they will not bargain away.

Conferences are more informal than regular committee bill-drafting sessions. The staffs play a more obvious role in the final bargaining. Spokespersons for the administration usually are present, and lobbyists try to influence proposed compromises during breaks in the meetings. In theory,

Conference committees are for House and Senate negotiators to work out the final shape of legislation, resolving differences between the two chambers.
Source: CQ Photo

conferees must observe certain rules: they may not amend or delete any section of the bill that is not in dispute, and they may not introduce new provisions not relevant to the differences already in the bills. In practice, however, many bills are largely rewritten in conference.

If there are disagreements among House conferees or among Senate conferees, such disputes must be settled by majority vote. The size of conference delegations varies, but each side votes as a unit on each provision in disagreement. The political influence and skill of conference leaders play an important part in the outcome.

After conferees have agreed to a compromise bill, they write a conference report, explaining specific changes they have made. The legislative intent of certain provisions may be written into the conference report rather than into the bill itself. The report becomes official once a majority of conferees from each chamber has signed it.

Finally, after the report has been printed, the two houses vote on the compromise. Under legislative rules, bills that have been approved in conference are not supposed to be further amended by the House or Senate. But if conferees have been unable to agree on any of the amendments in disagreement, separate votes are taken in both houses to resolve the disputed provision. The House also may vote separately on nongermane provisions added by the Senate; this practice, however, was largely abandoned under the Republican leadership in the 1990s. Sometimes bills are sent back to conference for further compromise efforts. The final version is rarely defeated, although this happens on occasion when wholesale changes are made in a long, controversial conference. Once the compromise has been approved, the bill is sent to the White House for the president's review.

President's Role

When a bill reaches the White House, the president has three choices:

- Sign it, thus enacting the measure into law.
- Veto it and return it to Congress with a statement giving the administration's objections. Congress may override the veto by a two-thirds majority vote of those present and voting in both chambers. The bill then becomes a law without the president's approval.
- Take no action, in which case the bill will become law without the president's signature after ten days excluding Sundays—provided Congress does not adjourn for the year during that period. Should Congress adjourn, however, the legislation does not become law. This is known as a pocket veto.

Legislative Veto

Congress lost one of its most useful oversight devices in 1983, when the Supreme Court ruled that most legislative vetoes were unconstitutional. Congress had used the legislative veto with increasing frequency in the 1970s and early 1980s. The device allowed either one house or both houses of Congress, and in some instances even legislative committees, to reject regulations and policies recommended by the president or various federal departments and independent agencies.

In its 1983 decision the Court held that most legislative vetoes were unconstitutional because they barred the president from having any role in Congress's veto process. The Court ruled that the Constitution requires final legislative decisions to be approved by both houses of Congress and presented to the president for signature or veto. Congress's self-styled veto was criticized as a backhanded, even careless way of legislating that was outside the bounds of legitimate legislative procedures. The Court held that the legislative veto violated the constitutional separation of powers by expanding Congress's powers from lawmaking and oversight to "shared administration" of the laws.

Nevertheless, the legislative veto served many useful purposes from the point of view of both lawmakers and presidents. Although presidents since Herbert Hoover had denounced the procedure as an infringement on executive powers, they had accepted it to gain additional authority and flexibility in administering certain laws. As a result, Congress and federal agencies developed several informal methods that allow Congress to continue to veto proposed agency actions.

Background

The legislative veto was first written into law in 1932, when Congress passed legislation that gave President Hoover the authority to reorganize U.S. government departments. That legislation allowed either house of Congress, by majority vote, to "veto" the president's recommendations for reorganization. Just a year later the House exercised that veto, blocking Hoover's plan. Hoover later vetoed an emergency appropriations bill that would have allowed a single committee—the Joint Committee on Taxation—to exercise a veto over certain tax legislation.

Hoover's initial acquiescence in and later opposition to the legislative veto set the pattern for future presidential views on the issue. Presidents after Hoover voiced strong objections to it, but most of them chose not to confront the issue directly. An exception was President Gerald R. FORD, who in 1976 dramatized his opposition by vetoing an environmental bill because it contained a veto provision. As a candidate for president in 1980, Ronald Reagan gave some support to Congress's use of the legislative veto, but once in office he reversed his position. In 1982 Reagan's solicitor general urged the Supreme Court to declare the veto unconstitutional.

The legislative veto was seldom used until the early 1940s, when lawmakers saw it as an effective way to check the vast war-making and emergency powers Congress had granted the Roosevelt administration during World War II. Its use then declined in the 1950s and 1960s.

In the 1970s Congress began adding legislative veto provisions to a wide range of legislation, especially in foreign policy and defense, energy, and environment. This trend was fueled by the Democratic Congress's growing distrust of President Richard NIXON's actions and by public criticism of excessive federal regulation.

The Vietnam War and the Watergate scandal weakened the presidency and led to a more assertive Congress. Some of the most important laws of the period contained legislative vetoes, including the 1973 War Powers Act, the 1974 Congressional Budget and Impoundment Control Act, and the 1974 Federal Election Campaign Act. By the time the Reagan administration took office in 1981, there were well over 200 laws containing legislative veto provisions. Of these, more than one-third had been enacted since the mid-1970s.

Types of Legislative Vetoes

Over the years Congress devised several types of legislative vetoes. Most of them had one feature in common: they allowed Congress, by one method or another, to block executive branch actions without the president having the opportunity to reverse the vetoes. Usually Congress gave itself thirty to sixty days in which to consider and approve a veto. In some cases lawmakers were free to apply the veto at any time.

Probably the most common form of the veto procedure was the two-house veto, which required a majority vote in both the House and Senate to block an executive branch policy. Concurrent resolutions were used to approve two-house vetoes because they were not sent to the president for signature or disapproval. (Some two-house vetoes were provided in bills requiring the president's signature.)

Congress also used one-house legislative vetoes. These allowed either chamber to block a regulation of a government department or independent agency by adopting a simple resolution of disapproval. A variation permitted either chamber to veto a federal regulation unless the other chamber overturned the action of the first chamber within a specified period. Still another form of the veto gave certain House and Senate committees the power to block or delay a department's regulation.

All these veto procedures allowed federal departments or agencies to implement certain rules or programs unless Congress intervened to block them. However, another variation of the veto blocked or delayed certain regulations from taking effect unless lawmakers took the initiative and voted to approve them. This in effect constituted a veto in advance, which could be reversed only if one or both houses voted to let stand a proposed regulation or policy.

Yet another option is for Congress to invoke the 1996 Congressional Review Act, which allows Congress to overturn a major regulation within a certain time limit if both houses pass a joint resolution of disapproval by a simple majority vote. The law limits debate and amendments, and also prohibits the administration from writing a new rule in "substantially the same form" as the one Congress rejected. Congressional Republicans in 2001 successfully used the 1996 law to overturn ergonomics regulations designed to reduce workplace injuries that the Clinton administration published in the fall of 2000. The business community had strenuously opposed the regulations. In 2002 the principal sponsors of a new campaign finance law attempted to use the 1996 law to challenge

Federal Election Commission rules to carry out a ban on donations of "soft money" to national political parties. But no action was taken on their resolutions to disapprove the regulations.

Supreme Court Ruling

The Supreme Court reached its decision in *Immigration and Naturalization Service v. Chadha* on June 23, 1983. In that ruling and in follow-up decisions soon thereafter, the Court held that all forms of the legislative veto that did not give the president the opportunity to respond to Congress's action were unconstitutional. The Court said the legislative process outlined in the Constitution demanded that all acts of Congress must include the president's participation, through his approval or veto, to be enforceable. Thus, if Congress gives federal departments and agencies the authority to issue certain regulations or make policy decisions, it "must abide by its delegation of authority until that delegation is legislatively altered or revoked." In the majority decision in *Chadha*, Chief Justice Warren E. Burger said it was beyond doubt "that lawmaking was a power to be shared by both houses [of Congress] and the president."

The only type of veto not affected by the Court's rulings was the two-house veto by joint resolution, which must be sent to the president for signature or disapproval. This procedure essentially is the same as passing a new law. (See LEGISLATION.)

Congress has taken steps to conform to the Supreme Court's decisions by repealing some legislative vetoes and amending others. But many legislative vetoes are still incorporated in current law despite their doubtful constitutionality. In many other cases federal agencies find it politically prudent to agree to informal legislative review—and implicit rejection—of their activities.

Library Committee, Joint

The Joint Library Committee oversees the LIBRARY OF CONGRESS, dealing primarily with legal matters and general questions of policy. More detailed oversight of the library's budget and operations is handled by House and Senate appropriations subcommittees. The Joint Library Committee also rules on proposals to erect statues or other memorials on the Capitol grounds. The committee consists of five members of the House Administration Committee and five members of the Senate Rules and Administration Committee; the post of chair rotates between the House and Senate every two years. The Library Committee usually meets only once or twice in each two-year term of Congress, although members are frequently polled between meetings. Nominations for librarian of Congress are handled solely by the Senate Rules and Administration Committee, since that is a Senate duty.

Library of Congress

The Library of Congress has the dual role of assisting Congress and serving as the nation's library. With more than 120 million items in its collection, the library is one of the largest in the world. The collection grows each year, usually by more than 2 million new items.

The librarian of Congress oversees the library and its staff of about 4,000 people. The librarian is a presidential appointee, confirmed by the Senate, but reports to Congress, which has a ten-member Joint Committee on the Library. The thirteenth librarian of Congress, historian James H. Billington, was appointed in 1987. (See LIBRARY COMMITTEE, JOINT.)

Members of Congress are privileged users of the library. Their requests for books or background information are handled by a separate division, the Congressional Research Service (CRS). It has about 700 employees whose duties range from answering simple queries to spending several

In 1897, after the demand for space became overwhelming, the Library of Congress moved out of the Capitol and into its own building across the street.
Source: Library of Congress

months on a complicated analysis. CRS answered more than 700,000 inquiries from Congress in fiscal 2001.

The library is housed in three sprawling buildings on Capitol Hill. Its holdings include one of three known perfect copies of the Gutenberg Bible (which is on display), a set of stringed instruments made by Antonio Stradivari, Thomas Jefferson's rough draft of the Declaration of Independence, a nearly complete set of Matthew Brady's photographs of the Civil War, and the personal papers of twenty-three presidents, from Washington through Coolidge.

The earliest known motion picture, *Fred Ott's Sneeze,* copyrighted in 1893 by Thomas Edison, is part of the library's collection, as is the world's smallest book, *Ant,* which is 1.4 millimeters square.

Not every book published in the United States enters the library's collection. Although the library buys books and subscribes to periodicals, its collection also benefits from copyright laws. Authors seeking U.S. copyright protection for books, music, photographs, art, movies, or other work must deposit one, and sometimes two, copies at the Library of Congress. The library does not keep every copyrighted work, but it adds to its collection thousands of the more than half a million items that are copyrighted each year.

Works in more than 450 different languages are included in the library's holdings; about two-thirds of its books are not in English.

A major library service is cataloging books published in the United States and abroad. U.S. libraries buy catalog cards, computer tapes, and other materials from the Library of Congress. The Library of Congress gives a catalog number to every book published in the United States (and many published abroad) that reflects the book's subject matter. The library also maintains the Dewey Decimal Classification System, which is used by most public libraries.

The library produces books in Braille and records books on tape for distribution to 136 cooperating libraries that provide services to nearly 700,000 blind or partially sighted people. About

2,500 book titles and a variety of music scores are selected each year for Braille transcription or for recording.

Scholars from all over the world are attracted to the Library of Congress and its extensive holdings. Their appreciation of its resources was given a rare public display in 1986, when more than one hundred researchers protested early closing hours. Some protesters refused to leave the main reading room at the new closing time of 5:30 p.m., and several were eventually arrested. Others marched in front of the building. A public relations success, the protest prompted Congress to provide additional funds and earmark them for operating the library during evening hours. (Many parts of the library close to the public at 5 p.m., but a number of the reading rooms remain open until 9:30 p.m., generally on Mondays, Wednesdays, and Thursdays. Visitors should check with the library's Web site (www. loc.gov/visit/hours.html) or call 202-707-8000.

Jefferson's Library

When Congress decided in 1800 to transfer the U.S. government to Washington, D.C., the legislators set aside $5,000 to buy books

The Great Hall of the Library of Congress. After Congress's original library books burned with the sack of the Capital by the British in 1812, Thomas Jefferson's collection of 6,000 books formed the nucleus of the new library.
Source: Library of Congress

and set up a congressional library. After a Joint Committee on the Library made a list, London booksellers supplied 152 works in 740 volumes. The new Library of Congress was given a room in the north wing of the Capitol. Most of the library's books were burned or pillaged in 1814 when British troops attacked Washington.

After the war Thomas Jefferson, then in retirement at Monticello, offered to sell Congress his distinguished collection of more than 6,000 volumes. Despite some grumbling from critics of Jefferson, the legislators agreed to pay about $24,000 for the library, pricing each book by size and format.

Congress further boosted the library's status in 1815 by appointing George Watterston as librarian. He was the first person to hold the post on a full-time basis. The library suffered from another major fire in 1851, when 35,000 of its 55,000 books were lost. After the Civil War the library

Using the Library of Congress

The main building of the Library of Congress is across from the Capitol on First Street, S.E. Two additional buildings are nearby. Approximately 1 million people visit the library each year, and tours are available through a visitors' center. The library also hosts concerts, poetry readings, and lectures.

Anyone over high school age is allowed to use the library's materials; high school students may do so if their principal writes that other searches for material have been unsuccessful. Anyone wishing to use one of the library's reading rooms must first register and present a photo identification to receive free of charge a "reader identification card."

The Library of Congress usually does not loan out its books. Instead, users request materials, and staff then retrieve them from the stacks. As a last resort, books can be checked out through interlibrary loan. This means the Library of Congress will lend a book, through another library, if it cannot be found anywhere else.

Visitors often wait for their books in the main reading room, an ornate, domed chamber decorated with stained glass, enormous pillars, and elaborate statues. The old central card catalog (covering books and documents published from the nineteenth century through 1980) is housed there—and spills into other nearby areas. Also available are computer terminals the public can use for searching records that the library has computerized since 1980.

The Library of Congress has several other reading rooms for particular subjects or collections; these are scattered throughout the library and are also open to the public. Library hours vary; each reading room has a separate schedule.

benefited from a new, stronger copyright law, passed in 1865. It required anyone applying for a copyright to deposit a copy of the publication in the library.

A major advocate of that law was Ainsworth R. Spofford, who in 1864 began thirty-two years of service as the librarian of Congress. A bookseller, publisher, and writer, Spofford had been assistant librarian. Under his tenure, the number of books and pamphlets the library owned grew from about 100,000 to more than 1 million. He was one of three librarians to serve more than three decades; the others were John S. Meehan (1829–1861), a newspaper publisher, and Herbert Putnam (1899–1939), librarian of the Boston Public Library and member of a family of book publishers. The twelfth librarian of Congress, Daniel J. Boorstin, a historian, was appointed in 1975 and served until 1987, when Billington was named to the post.

Source: Library of Congress

Whose Library Is It?

The name should make it clear, but not everyone realizes that the Library of Congress is Congress's library. Take the gentleman who became incensed when told a member was using a book he wanted.

"A congressman!" the man fumed. "Why is a congressman using it? I thought Congress had its own library!"

"You may believe it," the reference librarian replied. "They do. And you're in it."

Three Library Buildings

In 1886, while Spofford was librarian, Congress agreed to construct a separate building for the library. The collection was moved in 1897 from crowded quarters in the Capitol to the new $6.36 million facility, modeled after the Paris Opera in the Italian Renaissance style and located across the street from the Capitol to the east. It has been called the Jefferson Building since 1980. An annex was authorized by Congress in 1930 and occupied in 1939. The white marble building, which cost $9 million, is behind the main library. Originally it was called the Jefferson Building; Congress in 1980 renamed it the John Adams Building. The third building, called the Madison Building, received congressional approval in 1965, but Congress for years postponed appropriating the money to build it. Construction was finally completed in 1982 at a cost of more than $130 million, substantially more than the original estimate of $75 million. About 1.5 million square feet in size, the Madison Building is one of the largest in Washington. About 70 percent of the library's employees work in the building, which stands across Independence Avenue from the Jefferson Building.

The library at times has had to cope with budget cuts and increased security concerns. Lawmakers have proposed combining its independent police force with those of the Government Printing Office and the Capitol Police. The library suffered financially following the September 11, 2001, terrorist attacks and subsequent anthrax attacks in the U.S. mail when about 600,000 pieces of mail sent to the library were delayed because they had to be irradiated and screened. Many contained checks for royalties and copyright registration. Fiscal 2007 funding for the library, which was still pending early in calendar 2007, were about $575 million. In fiscal 2003, Congress funded the library at $374 million, a $67 million increase over the previous year's appropriations.

Line Item Veto Act

Congress in 1996 passed a law that gave the president authority known as enhanced rescission. It allowed the president to cancel amounts of discretionary appropriations (as opposed to those that had to be made by law), new items of direct spending, or certain limited tax benefits. With these powers, the procedure was known as the line-item veto, an authority that presidents for years had been urging Congress to grant. Many members of Congress, primarily fiscal conservatives who believe government spending was uncontrollable by fellow legislators, agree with the concept. But the law lasted fewer than eighteen months, from January 1997 to mid-1998. The Supreme Court ruled the law unconstitutional under Article I, Section 7, which requires all bills passed by Congress to be "presented" to the president for approval or rejection. (See VETOES.)

Lobbying

A retiree buttonholes her representative at a Fourth of July picnic to complain about Medicare. A hiker writes his senator urging an end to logging in national forests. A teacher sends her dues to the National Education Association, which then fights cuts in federal education funds. A lawyer phones an old friend newly elected to the House and makes a pitch for a corporate client's military aircraft. An aide to the president drops in on a committee meeting to suggest new wording for an amendment. A senior citizen responding to a suggestion from the AARP, once known by its full name of the American Association of Retired Persons, sends an e-mail opposing Medicare cuts to her member of Congress.

All these people are lobbying Congress, trying to win support for a certain point of view. Thousands of voices compete for congressional attention as laws are written and money provided for everything from health care to weapons. Individuals, organizations, corporations, and even governments can influence the way laws are made and carried out.

The term *lobbying* comes from England, where in the mid-seventeenth century citizens would wait in an anteroom, or lobby, near the House of Commons to see members of Parliament. It was first widely recognized in Washington during the administration of Ulysses S. Grant, who escaped the pressures of the Oval Office to enjoy brandy and cigars in the lobby of the nearby Willard Hotel. Influence-peddlers and the day's power brokers frequently approached him there to plea special causes, prompting Grant to refer to them as lobbyists. Lobbying is sanctioned by the Constitution. The First Amendment protects the right of the people to "petition the government for redress of grievances."

CLOSER LOOK

The term *lobbying* comes from England, where in the mid-seventeenth century citizens would wait in an anteroom, or lobby, near the House of Commons to see members of Parliament. It was first widely recognized in Washington during the administration of Ulysses S. Grant. It is sanctioned by the Constitution's First Amendment that guarantees citizens the right to "petition the government for redress of grievances."

Since the nineteenth century, lobbyists have been known collectively as the Third House of Congress. Shown here is the lobby of the House of Representatives during passage of the 1866 civil rights bill.
Source: Library of Congress

Central to a democratic society is the freedom to ask questions, make suggestions, and debate results. Lobbying is an element of such widespread political participation. It allows competing points of view to be heard and provides information to those making decisions. It is how the wronged and needy, as well as the greedy, call attention to their cause. But there is no guarantee that all the voices will be heeded, or even heard.

How Lobbyists Work

Unlike voters, who each get one ballot, lobbyists are not equal: some are clearly more influential than others. The most visible lobbyists are those who work full time in Washington. Their employers include trade or professional associations, law firms, public relations firms, large corporations, organizations with particular interests, and other groups. Political insiders populate the field; many lobbyists once held jobs on congressional staffs or in federal agencies. Former members of Congress frequently find jobs as lobbyists or "rainmakers" and are valued by law firms because they attract clients eager for inside contacts.

Some lobbyists focus on esoteric details of specific laws, while others concentrate on broader policy changes. Many handle a range of issues and a variety of clients, while others specialize in a single area. Whatever their approach, lobbyists are important players in the legislative process.

Although representatives and senators still bristle at the notion of being "in someone's pocket," most would count a lobbyist or two in their circle of close advisers.

Often a lobbyist's best technique is simply to provide accurate information, either directly to a legislator or at a committee hearing. The credibility gained then gives the lobbyist more influence when arguing his or her point of view. A record of reliability can win a quick hearing if a lobbyist should find a minor clause that is damaging to a client. Information packets, drafts of bills, and scenarios of how a bill would affect an industry are among the ways lobbyists approach legislators and their staffs.

Nevertheless, lobbying has an unsavory reputation. A century ago lobbyists were widely portrayed as unscrupulous characters, hanging out in the halls and lobbies of the Capitol. That reputation was reinforced whenever bribery and other improper practices were exposed. Industry's apparently excessive influence on the Senate was a major factor in the push for direct election of senators; until 1913, senators were chosen by state legislatures, where moneyed interests reigned supreme.

Among the most colorful lobbyists of the past was the self-described "King of the Lobby," Samuel Ward, whose legislative successes in the mid-1800s were so dazzling that Congress decided to investigate him. When the investigating committee asked Ward about the well-known elegant dinners he hosted for politicians, he replied, "At good dinners people do not talk shop, but they give people a right, perhaps, to ask a gentleman a civil question and get a civil answer."

At dinners and cocktail parties, at plush resorts where legislators combine speech making and vacationing, well-heeled lobbyists continue to use Ward's methods. Less prosperous groups emphasize letter writing, telephone calls, and e-mail. In the White House, the president can use the prestige of his office to impress legislators. Federal agencies have their own professionals assigned to monitor Congress.

Senators and representatives still find lobbyists waiting for them as they step off elevators, heading for votes on the Senate or House floor. Thumbs pointing up or down, to signal a yes or no vote, were once very common and can sometimes still be seen. But most lobbying is done long before a bill reaches the floor.

In addition to direct lobbying contacts, organizations can influence legislators by giving money to their political campaigns. Although campaign financing laws restrict donations made to candidates' campaign committees, powerful lobbies make certain that responsive legislators receive sizable contributions. Lobbyists often direct fundraising efforts for members they support. While corporations and labor unions are not allowed to make campaign contributions directly to congressional candidates, their employees and members can form political action committees (PACs), which then channel their donations to candidates. Trade associations and membership groups also form PACs.

During the 2006 campaign, corporate and labor PACs combined for a total of $177 million in contributions—$123 million by corporate-sponsored PACs and $54 million by labor-sponsored PACs. When associations and ideological groups are included, PACs provided $340 million for congressional campaigns. PACs also can spend as much as they want independently to help candidates—for example, with heavy television advertising—as long as they do not coordinate their actions with the candidates' campaigns. But many candidates do not appreciate outside interference—well intentioned or not—in their campaigns. PACs devoted about $37 million to independent expenditures in the 2006 congressional elections.

Beginning in the 1980s "soft money" became an important and highly controversial source of campaign funding. Soft money contributions were made directly to the political parties and, in theory at least, were to be used only for party-building activities, not for direct campaign support.

More on this topic:

Campaign Financing, p. 66

Direct Election of Senators, p. 154

Legislative Process, p. 344

Political Action Committees, p. 417

What made this form of political money so controversial was that there was no limit on how much an organization could give; further, corporations, unions, and other organizations could give directly from their treasuries without using a PAC. For lobbyists and clients willing and able to play a high-stakes game, these advantages could be enormous. But a 2002 campaign finance law barred national party committees and congressional candidates from raising or spending soft money after the 2002 election. However, lobbyists already were finding other means to add to favored lawmakers' coffers, including contributing to tax-free foundations set up to advocate a particular cause or political point of view.

In addition to providing campaign financing to members of Congress, lobbyists sought to gain favor by plying legislators and key staff members with meals, entertainment, and gifts. An evening at the theater preceded by a fine dinner "on the company or association" was standard fare. One major association made a great show of rolling a gift-laden cart down House and Senate hallways each Christmas season. A senior lobbyist swooped up gifts from the cart and ducked into offices to distribute the holiday cheer.

An even more valued "perk" for members, and some senior staff, was an all-expense-paid trip to a posh resort in order to make a speech to a trade association gathering. Frequently the member was handed a sizable honorarium before returning to Washington.

Much of this has changed since the late 1980s. Honoraria for lawmakers have been abolished, and the House and Senate have each established rules that prohibit accepting all but nominal gifts. Travel expenses for attending meetings and conventions may be accepted, but these must be for "widely attended" events that are related to the legislator's "official" activities. Both chambers barred members from accepting free travel to charity events where members and lobbyists golfed and skied together to raise money for charities. The House, however, in 2003 loosened its rule to allow charitable groups to pay for members to attend such events. The House stirred further controversy by changing its gift rule to allow lobbyists to cater meals in the House.

Too close a relationship with a lobbyist can be dangerous for a politician. In 1989, for example, House Speaker Jim WRIGHT, a Texas Democrat, and Democratic whip Tony Coelho of California both resigned because of questions about whether their personal finances had become intertwined with favor-seeking private interests. In the same year the Senate opened a sweeping investigation into the favors that five of its members had done for a wealthy savings-and-loan operator, Charles H. Keating Jr., who had contributed heavily to their political causes. (See SCANDALS, CONGRESSIONAL.) In 1995 Speaker Newt GINGRICH of Georgia was rebuked (though not formally found guilty) by the House Committee on Standards of Official Conduct for entering into a highly suspect book deal with a company owned by Rupert Murdoch. At the time of the deal, Murdoch had substantial issues pending before Congress. In 2000 the House ethics committee rebuked Republican Bud Shuster of Pennsylvania, chair of the House Transportation and Infrastructure Committee, for violations of House rules that included having significant official contact with a former staffer-turned-lobbyist during the year after she left his staff, when such contact was prohibited, and accepting a trip to Puerto Rico for himself and his family from a lobbyist.

A new round of congressional soul-searching about lobbying activities and rules came in the last years of Republican control of Congress before the 2006 elections returned Democrats to power. In early 2006 a prominent lobbyist named Jack Abramoff pleaded guilty to conspiracy, mail fraud, tax evasion, and bribery charges in a continually expanding influence-peddling scandal that involved lobbying members of Congress with, among other things, expensive free trips abroad. Late in 2006 Congress acted on—but in the end did not pass—proposals to limit congressional junkets paid for by private interests, set new prohibitions on gifts from lobbyists, and strengthen disclosure and conflict of interest laws.

Under Democratic leadership, Congress in early 2007 returned to the subject, with the House putting new lobbying strictures in its official rules. Separately the Senate worked on legislation to strengthen lobby disclosure laws and, like the House, put new limitations in place.

In August Congress passed the Honest Leadership and Open Government Act of 2007, which President George W. Bush signed the into law in September. Among the sweeping changes in lobbying reform law were these: lobbyist activity reports had to be filed quarterly (rather than semi-annually) and put into an Internet-searchable database; campaign committees had to file reports listing lobbyists who had supplied $15,000 or more in aggregated, or bundled, contributions over a six month period; senators and senatorial candidates and presidential candidates had to pay charter rates

Staff, press, and lobbyists fill the room where the House Energy and Commerce Committee is "marking up" an Internet commerce bill. Lobbyists used to signal their intent to receptive members of Congress with their thumbs up or down. Now, however, most lobbyists do their work behind the scenes.
Source: CQ Photo/Scott J. Ferrell

for trips on private planes and House candidates were barred from trips on private planes (sitting members already were barred); and senators were prohibited from lobbying colleagues for two years after leaving office. Senior Senate staffers were barred for one year, and similar but weaker prohibitions were applied to House staff members. The existing House restriction—which was not changed—barred members from lobbying for one year after leaving office.

Lobby Regulation: Constitutional Challenges

Lobbying is a constitutionally protected activity, but the combination of special interests is not always for the public good. Woodrow Wilson, when campaigning for president in 1912, said, "The government of the United States is a foster child of the special interests. It is not allowed to have a will of its own."

Congress has found it difficult to regulate lobbying without infringing on the right to free speech. Rules on domestic lobbying were considered in every Congress after 1911 but were not approved until 1946, when Congress passed the Federal Regulation of Lobbying Act. The principle behind the 1946 law was disclosure, not regulation. The law simply required lobbyists for corporations and organizations to register their names and subjects of interest, along with how much they had spent. But the law left loopholes, so that not all individuals and groups were listed and financial reports did not accurately reflect expenditures.

The Supreme Court in 1954 upheld the constitutionality of the 1946 law, but its narrow interpretation made the statute less effective. The Court ruled that the law applied only to funds directly solicited for lobbying, thereby exempting organizations that used general funds for lobbying purposes. Another ruling required registration only for individuals whose primary job was contact with Congress—a definition that allowed many lobbyists to avoid registering. Only contacts with members of Congress counted; lobbying staff aides did not count. Court interpretations made enforcement of the law almost impossible. There were only six prosecutions between 1946 and 1980.

Critics of the 1946 law fought for new rules. They came close in 1976 when both the House and Senate passed revision bills, but senators and representatives could not resolve their differences.

Finally, in 1995 Congress approved a number of important changes to the law. The definition of lobbying was broadened to include contacts with congressional staff and executive branch policymakers. Registration requirements were amended to cover anyone who spends 20 percent or more of his or her time lobbying during a given six-month period, though individuals who earn less than $5,000 and organizations that spend less than $20,000 during the reporting period are exempted from the registration requirement. Also exempted are grassroots lobbying campaigns and tax-exempt organizations such as churches.

The 1995 act tightened reporting requirements for lobbying by foreign interests. It makes clear that foreign entities with substantial interests in lobbying organizations and their clients must register. This provision eliminates the prior-existing exemption for U.S. subsidiaries of foreign corporations.

> *"No one will take a bagel without a ruling from a lawyer."*
> —Rep. Emanuel Cleaver II, D-Mo.

Many efforts over the following decades focused on expanding disclosure of lobbying activities and the men and women who do the work. The Honest Leadership and Open Government Act of 2007 increased penalties for breaking the law. The new rules prompted members, and staff, to carefully look over their shoulders lest they run afoul of prohibitions. One member, Emanuel Cleaver II, a Missouri Democrat, said, "No one will take a bagel without a ruling from a lawyer." While Cleaver's comment was exaggerated, there was an underlying truth to it. For example, two organizations employing lobbyists proposed to send gifts to House offices. One considered sending stuffed toy ducks, its widely known business mascot, and the other—a nursery group—considered complimentary poinsettias at the Christmas holidays. The duck would be legal, the plant not because it exceeded a $10 limit on gifts to House offices. Lobbyists reported many similar conundrums as they sort through allowed and prohibited activities.

Powerful Voices

The first step of the legislative process is committee hearings. The hearings are familiar turf for lobbyists. A trade association often sends its president or an executive from a member company to testify instead of its Washington-based legislative representative, on the assumption that someone with "hands-on" experience has more credibility. The witness spells out the organization's view of the legislation, and that position becomes the lobbyist's theme as he or she follows the bill through subcommittee or committee, onto the House or Senate floor, to a conference between the two houses, and then back to each house again for final passage. If necessary, the lobbyist may then try to convince the executive branch to sign or veto the bill.

In a parallel move, an interest group may ask its members to write directly to their states' leg-

AARP Executive Director and CEO Bill Novelli, left, and AARP President James Parkel speak about AARP's support of a Medicare bill in Washington in 2003. With more than 35 million members, the AARP is one of the nation's largest and most influential lobbying groups—it even has its own ZIP code in Washington, D.C.
Source: AP Images/Susan Walsh

islators. This grassroots lobbying can be extremely effective. Often an association, in its newsletter or a separate mailing, provides a sample letter or even a stamped postcard for members to sign and mail. A technology-age variation on this theme has been the use of e-mail. Telephone patch-through systems are yet another lobby tool made possible by modern communications technology. These allow lobby groups to connect their members with targeted offices free of charge.

The huge membership of some associations can result in formidable amounts of mail and calls to legislators. For example, one of the largest associations is the AARP, which has more than 35 million members. Because of the amount of mail that it receives, it even has its own postal ZIP code in Washington, D.C.

Just as a huge membership gives an organization credibility, so does a group's economic power. For example, the Business Roundtable, which consists of the chief executive officers of major corporations, always receives a respectful hearing on Capitol Hill. Other groups, lacking such ready access, may resort to dramatic demonstrations to draw attention to their cause. For example, an estimated 200,000 people massed before the Lincoln Memorial in August 1963 in support of civil rights legislation pending in Congress. Marchers gathered in November 1969 to press for an end to the war in Vietnam. Just a few months later, in April 1970, environmentalists held the first Earth Day to galvanize support for laws to clean up the air and water. Antiabortion groups have skirmished on the steps of the Supreme Court each January 22 to mark the anniversary of the court's 1973 *Roe v. Wade* decision that legalized abortion.

Industry Groups

Certain groups have become legendary for their lobbying influence. One such is the National Rifle Association (NRA), with more than 4 million members by mid-2005. The NRA has such a strong

The enormous influence of the big business lobby on Congress is illustrated by this 1889 cartoon by Joseph Keppler.
Source: Library of Congress

grassroots organization that going against the NRA position may cost a politician votes. Those with pro-NRA records receive big campaign contributions from the organization's richly endowed political action committee; those who favor any form of gun control find themselves the targets of hard-hitting advertisements.

The U.S. Chamber of Commerce follows a long list of business issues before Congress and backs up its position with an extensive network of local chambers. Geographically scattered membership is an important advantage for the Chamber, as it is for organizations of doctors, pharmacists, insurance agents, teachers, and homebuilders, among others. The same large groups, however, may be handicapped by the need to satisfy a diverse membership. Trying to reach a consensus so as to speak with one voice in Washington can hinder an organization's effectiveness. Even within an industry, certain groups become more adept than others at presenting their point of view. The Independent Petroleum Association of America, for example, has often effectively opposed stands taken by the major oil companies.

Because of the billions spent on defense by the federal government, the weapons industry has an array of Washington representatives who make up an extremely powerful group. Simple geography helps make the American Trucking Association influential: the group's legislative headquarters near Capitol Hill has rooms readily available for campaign fundraising events. Knowing how to throw a good party is a special talent of some groups: the International Ice Cream Association throws a lavish ice cream party every June to which many members of Congress bring their children.

Some groups develop a cozy relationship with a congressional committee or subcommittee and an executive agency or department. This set of lobbyists, legislators, and bureaucrats was once called an "iron triangle," providing three-sided protection against budget cuts or program changes advocated by "outsiders." Veterans' groups, for example, have always had a close relationship with key congressional committees, such as the House Veterans' Affairs Committee, and with the Department of Veterans Affairs. Few such triangles are so tightly knit, however, and complex issues combined with increasing media and public interest group scrutiny have helped to keep most relationships fluid. Most close observers of Washington lobbying today believe the "iron triangle" label gave a misleadingly simple picture of the complex work of organizations representing a myriad of interests before Congress.

Labor Unions

Labor unions once had enough clout to influence union members at election time. But in the last decades of the twentieth century and into the next many unions continued to lose members, making it more difficult to deliver voting blocs, and hence to have an impact on Capitol Hill. Union membership declined from 35 percent of the workforce in the 1950s to 16 percent in the 1990s. In 2006 just 12 percent of wage and salary workers—15.4 million workers—were union members. In the 1980s and early 1990s labor piled up defeats under Republican administrations. Even President Bill Clinton rebuffed the largest union in the country, the AFL-CIO, by supporting the North American Free Trade Agreement. Labor did show muscle by convincing some members of the Democratic congressional leadership to hold firm against Clinton's efforts.

But they have continued to be tested by Republican Congresses and administrations. Unions and their congressional allies won a 2001 showdown with President George W. Bush over an airline bailout bill, when a majority of lawmakers supported language requiring airport security screeners to be government employees, not contractors. However, the White House prevailed at the end of the 107th Congress (2001–2003) by persuading lawmakers to create a homeland security department with personnel rules that operate outside of the normal civil service system. The law, as written, allowed the administration to exempt some federal workers from union representation on national security grounds, ostensibly so the workers could not jeopardize public safety by striking. Unions contended the move was a smokescreen to gut collective bargaining protections.

Nevertheless, organized labor remained a potent—if diminished—force in American politics, especially when Democrats controlled Congress or the White House. Some unions, in fact, were expanding, primarily in governmental and service sectors of the economy—strengthening their voice in Congress.

Forming Coalitions

Lobbyists have learned to form coalitions among themselves. As Congress prepared in the 1970s and 1980s to eliminate tax incentives for companies that produce products in Puerto Rico, a diverse group of manufacturers joined with the government of Puerto Rico to form a lobby group directed to maintaining the incentives. Although the member-groups did not agree on every point, they compromised on major areas and together presented their case to Congress. Their united front helped convince Congress to preserve the incentive package, though its provisions were made less "generous."

Government Organizations

Governments have become lobbyists, too. The National Governors' Association, the National League of Cities, and the U.S. Conference of Mayors are among the leading groups. States and cities also have their own representatives in Washington, many housed together in the Hall of the States just a few blocks from the Capitol. Though at first preoccupied with getting a bigger share of the federal budget, the government associations have become sophisticated lobbyists on a variety of issues. In 1988, for example, Democratic governor Bill Clinton of Arkansas and Republican governor Michael N. Castle of Delaware went door-to-door on Capitol Hill to promote a welfare reform plan hammered out a year earlier by the National Governors' Association. The group's emphasis on work and training programs bridged a liberal-conservative gulf and provided the impetus for the most significant overhaul of the welfare system in half a century.

Foreign governments usually are most effective when U.S.-based groups argue their position for them. Israel, Greece, and Ireland have loyal friends in Congress in part because Americans of those heritages belong to strong, well-financed associations with political influence, such as the American Israel Public Affairs Committee.

Former Officials

Congress has attempted to weaken the influence of former insiders. In 1978 former executive branch officials were barred from lobbying their ex-associates for a year after leaving government. But this prohibition did not seem to deter Michael K. Deaver, former deputy chief of staff for President Ronald Reagan and confidant of Nancy Reagan. He moved so quickly to set up his public relations firm and take on clients that he was convicted in 1987 of perjury for having lied to investigators about his activities. In 1988 one-year limits were placed on former military officers, and in 1989 similar limits were put on former members of Congress and top staff aides, prohibitions that were tightened in 2007.

Citizens' Groups

Broad-based citizens' groups sprang up in the 1970s that claimed to give the public the same lobbying sophistication as big business and unions. Common Cause, founded in 1970 by John Gardner, a former cabinet secretary, concentrated on "good government" issues, such as campaign finance and ethics. Public Citizen was founded in 1971 by lawyer-activist Ralph Nader to work on consumer and safety issues. These groups combined grassroots activism with publicity seeking and traditional lobbying but avoided campaign contributions and election endorsements. By the 1990s about 2,500 organizations were calling themselves "public interest" groups.

The President as Lobbyist

Standing above all other lobbyists is the president himself. The White House has its own legislative agenda and its own "congressional liaison" staff, a euphemism for lobbyists. Representatives and senators feel the pull when invited to the White House for a chat with the nation's most powerful politician.

The president possesses a powerful tool that other lobbyists can only dream of: the veto. By threatening to veto a bill he does not like, the president can quickly get the attention of the House and Senate and may win changes in the measure. Most presidents use the veto as a last resort, relying instead on their ability—like other lobbyists—to persuade legislators to support their agenda. (See VETOES.)

The most successful presidential lobbyist was Franklin D. Roosevelt, whose legislative victories in the 1930s were the basis of the NEW DEAL. Another sweeping domestic program, the GREAT SOCIETY, was enacted in the 1960s at the behest of President Lyndon B. JOHNSON. Johnson had worked at the Capitol for thirty-two years—as a congressional aide, member of the House, senator, Senate minority leader, majority leader, and vice president. With President Johnson lobbying vigorously for his agenda, Congress endorsed new federal programs on poverty, voting rights, and health care for the aged. Ronald Reagan, who came to Washington as an "outsider," became a master lobbyist–public relations specialist in moving his 1981 supply-side tax cuts through Congress. Not since FDR had a president so mastered the art of going "over the heads of Congress" to the public to build support for his program.

Less successful at lobbying was President George H. W. Bush, a former member of the House who retained many personal friends on Capitol Hill. In spite of his experience and contacts, Bush was able to get little legislation enacted during his four years in office, after promising to put out his hand in openness to a Democratic Congress.

President Clinton achieved mixed results. He successfully lobbied for the North American Free Trade Agreement (NAFTA), a major crime bill, and tax and budget packages, but his health care reform measure never came close to passage.

President George W. Bush prevailed in several high-profile showdowns early in his administration over taxes, education, and national security matters but also showed a tendency to anger senior members of Congress for failing to adequately consult with lawmakers on his agenda. By 2007, when he began his last two years in office, his influence was eroding rapidly—even within his party. Democrats had won control of Congress in 2006, and the growing opposition to the five-year-old war in Iraq greatly limited his ability to influence legislators. This was vividly demonstrated in Congress's rejection of a wide-ranging immigration reform bill that Bush aggressively lobbied members to pass. Even with considerable support from Democrats the legislation went down to defeat in the Senate in June 2007.

Congressional Reform

A series of congressional reforms in the 1970s opened up the legislative process with the intention of freeing Congress from the hidden influence of powerful groups. Steps such as making committee meetings public and recording individual votes allowed voters to see more, but they hardly squelched lobbying. As power was decentralized throughout the Capitol, there were more people to persuade, and consequently the ranks of lobbyists swelled.

Members of Congress found that they were often uncomfortable publicly taking an action that would antagonize powerful interests. After the changes, the House Appropriations Committee, traditionally known as a bastion of anonymous skinflints, became a magnet for ingratiating lobbyists. In writing the 1986 tax overhaul, the House Ways and Means Committee voted repeatedly to close its doors in order to make tough choices between competing industries. "Members ought to have the courage to look the lobbyists right in the eyes and go against them," said committee member Don J. Pease, an Ohio Democrat who supported open meetings. "But as a practical matter, that's hard to do."

Group Against Group

A lobbying story can be found behind every major bill that goes through Congress. Most intriguing are those that pit powerful groups against one another.

Steamships and Railroads

In the late 1850s Commodore Vanderbilt, the steamship king, found his lucrative contracts with the post office challenged by the railroads. Directing the lobbying effort himself, Vanderbilt successfully fought off the railroads, who wanted major help from Congress in building the transcontinental railroad. The railroad was put off until after the Civil War; by then Vanderbilt had sold his steamships and gotten into the railroad business, which Congress embraced with generous land grants and special financial treatment.

Prohibitionists and the Liquor Industry

Convincing Congress to act on a controversial subject can take years, as the Anti-Saloon League found during its campaign for a national ban on alcoholic beverages. Impatient with the milder tactics of the Woman's Christian Temperance Union, the Anti-Saloon League in the 1890s beefed up its efforts and began to raise money, make campaign contributions, and rally local leaders. Eventually the league dispatched field organizers across the country to develop local groups. Opposing the league was the well-financed liquor industry, for which the fight against prohibition appeared to be a matter of survival. The league's persistence finally paid off in 1919, when its supporters won ratification of a constitutional amendment banning the sale of alcoholic beverages. (The Eighteenth Amendment remained in effect until 1932, when another constitutional amendment repealing Prohibition was ratified.)

NRA and the Police

The National Rifle Association for years fought a rear-guard action against gun control laws enacted in 1968 as a response to political assassinations. On several occasions the NRA had to contend with opposing police organizations, which brought state and local police officers in full-dress uniform to the Capitol to stand as silent witnesses—thus skirting rules against demonstrations inside the building. The NRA, using its millions of members and hard-ball election tactics, was able to win some key victories: relaxation of the 1968 laws (1986); sidetracking of proposals to ban high-powered "assault weapons" (1990); and death of a crime bill that would have required a waiting period for handgun purchases (1992).

But in 1993 gun control advocates finally scored a major victory over the NRA when Congress and the president approved the Brady Law, which requires a five-day waiting period for gun purchases. The next year the NRA suffered yet another loss when a ban on semi-automatic "assault" weapons became law. The law was later allowed to expire. Despite the takeover of Congress in 1995 by Republicans, who generally were more sympathetic to their cause, the NRA and other pro-gun groups had to spend a significant amount of time and effort playing defense against new gun restrictions supported by the Clinton administration and Democrats, particularly in the Senate. Still, although a series of deadly shootings in 1999 sparked impassioned gun control debates in Congress, lawmakers failed to clear any gun control legislation in the 107th Congress. The worst domestic shooting occurred on the campus of Virginia Tech University in 2007 when a student methodically killed thirty-two students and staff before killing himself. Yet even this event produced few outcries for tougher gun laws. Democrats, newly back in control of Congress and long the focus of NRA attacks, made no move in the weeks after the shootings to change gun law.

Environmentalists and the Auto Industry

A fashionable and broad-based movement to protect the environment waged a battle against a mainstay of the U.S. economy, the auto industry, which had close ties to the American way of life. At first environmentalists had the upper hand. The Clean Air Act of 1970 led to auto emission tests in most states, and the Energy Policy Act of 1975 set minimum standards for gas mileage that auto manufacturers had to meet. But concern over the nation's energy crisis came to be overshadowed by the economic problems of the manufacturing sector, which only worsened by 2007. As a result, the auto industry was able to hold its own in the 1990 rewrite of the Clean Air Act and the 1992 energy strategy law. In 2002 the auto industry again prevailed during consideration of an omnibus energy bill, arguing higher fuel efficiency standards would lead to smaller, lighter, and more dangerous cars—and fewer jobs for automakers. By 2007, however, increasing concerns about global warming from, among other sources, auto exhaust was creating new pressures on car makers to provide cleaner and more fuel efficient engines. In 2007 Congress approved higher fuel efficiency standards.

Lodge, Henry Cabot

An influential leader of the Senate, Henry Cabot Lodge mobilized opposition to the post–World War I Treaty of Versailles.
Source: Senate Historical Office

Henry Cabot Lodge (1850–1924) played an important role in the conduct of U.S. foreign policy from the Spanish-American War through World War I. An influential member of the Senate (1893–1924), Lodge was an intimate of Theodore Roosevelt and an enthusiastic imperialist. He believed that military strength, not law or moral suasion, was the determining factor in the conduct of international affairs. As chair of the Foreign Relations Committee and as Senate majority leader (1919–1924), he mobilized opposition to the post–World War I Treaty of Versailles, which contained the Covenant of the League of Nations.

Lodge received the first Ph.D. in political science granted by Harvard University. He then wrote several historical works and taught. Turning from theory to practice, he entered state politics and was elected to the U.S. House of Representatives in 1887. He served as a Republican representative from Massachusetts until 1893, when he entered the Senate.

As a representative, Lodge played an important role in support of the so-called "Force Bill" in 1890–1891. The bill would have promoted black suffrage by authorizing the presence of federal officers at polling places from which blacks might be excluded during national elections.

Lodge supported Roosevelt's domestic reforms, although without much enthusiasm. His real interest was in the conduct of foreign affairs. His support of the Spanish-American War in 1898 led him to advocate the annexation of all of Spain's colonial holdings.

In 1919 Lodge gained international notoriety as the most powerful congressional opponent of the League of Nations. As chair of the Senate Foreign Relations Committee, Lodge wrote the majority report on the committee's consideration of the Treaty of Versailles. In it he endorsed ratification, but only with the addition of four reservations and forty-five amendments. The changes Lodge proposed strongly rejected any infringement on the sovereignty of the United States. Under his leadership the Senate rejected the treaty and membership in the League of Nations in 1919 and 1920.

Lodge's grandson and namesake, Henry Cabot Lodge Jr., served in the Senate in the World War II era (1937–1944, 1947–1953). He was an unsuccessful Republican vice-presidential candidate in 1960.

Logrolling

Members of Congress often trade their votes so that each may attain his or her goal. Senators and representatives eager for passage of a bill win votes from colleagues by promising them support on future legislation. Such mutual aid, known as logrolling, has been practiced in Congress since the early days of the republic. The term originated in the nineteenth century, when neighbors used to help each other roll logs into a pile for burning.

A classic example of logrolling occurred in 1964, when northern Democrats convinced southern Democrats to vote for a permanent food-stamp program. In return the northern Democrats agreed to vote for a bill providing price support for wheat and cotton, which was sought by the southern Democrats. Republicans, who opposed the food-stamp bill, were not able to break up the Democratic coalition.

In the 1980s, when efforts to reduce the federal budget deficit held a high priority, members bargained with each other to distribute the effects of spending cuts. In this case logrolling was a way to share burdens rather than win rewards. But when budget surpluses returned in the late 1990s, members struck deals to boost spending for Democratic-backed social programs while simultaneously meeting the conservative goal of cutting taxes. Logrolling is probably most common on legislation that benefits particular districts. The practice is also more common when party discipline is weak, as legislators cross party lines to cast votes they believe are—or promise to be—of particular benefit to their home districts or states.

Long, Huey P.

Huey P. Long (1893–1935) was governor of Louisiana when he was elected to the Senate in 1930. Determined to prevent his lieutenant governor, whom he disliked, from taking over, Long delayed entering the Senate until 1932, after his preferred successor had been elected governor. This determination to control politics in Louisiana was typical of "the Kingfish," as Long was called.

Long was a Democrat and a populist. He began his political career in 1918 as a member and later commissioner of Louisiana's railroad (or public service) commission, where he argued the consumers' case against the utilities. Unsuccessful in his first run for the governor's seat, he ran again and was elected in 1928. As governor, Long built roads and bridges, eliminated the poll tax, and provided free textbooks for schoolchildren. He also built a strong state organization through what many said was a combination of coercion and political favors. Even after he entered the U.S. Senate, Long continued to dominate Louisiana politics and government.

Championing the poor against the interests of big business and the wealthy, Long had a strong appeal for a populace battered by the Depression. He supported the campaign of Franklin D. Roosevelt but later opposed the president's NEW DEAL, believing that it was not radical enough.

Instead, in 1934 he proposed a Share Our Wealth Society that would have put a limit on personal wealth and guaranteed a minimum income and homesteading allowance.

Regarded in Washington as an eccentric (he reportedly wore green pajamas to greet formal callers), Long was famous for his lengthy and colorful Senate filibusters.

Furious with Roosevelt for withholding patronage prizes, Long threatened to leave the Democratic Party, and in August 1935 he declared his candidacy for president. Before his campaign got under way, Long was assassinated on September 8, 1935, in the Louisiana state capitol in Baton Rouge. His son, Russell B. LONG, served in the Senate from 1948 to 1987.

Serving as Louisiana's Democratic governor and senator, Huey P. Long was one of the most flamboyant figures in American politics in the 1920s and 1930s.
Source: Senate Historical Office

Long, Russell B.

When Russell B. Long (1918–2003) entered politics in 1948, he was following in the steps of other members of the Long family of Louisiana. His father was Huey P. LONG, a flamboyant governor and senator, who was assassinated in 1935. One uncle and a cousin were members of the House of Representatives, and another uncle was governor of Louisiana. Unlike his father, an ardent champion of the poor, Long spent much of his career aiding home-state businesses—specifically oil and gas producers—through the Internal Revenue Code. But he saw himself also as a populist, rather in the mold of his father, and backed many proposals to help the less wealthy. He promoted the earned income tax credit, which over the years became an important program benefiting low-income workers. He also was identified with legislation to allow employee stock-option programs, which he saw as allowing worker ownership of corporations.

In his thirty-five years on the Senate Finance Committee, including many as chair, Long became a master of the tax code and oversaw its numerous revisions. He had a sardonic understanding of voters' ambivalence toward taxation. A favorite quote was: "Don't tax me, don't tax thee, tax that man behind the tree." He also described a tax loophole as "something that benefits the other guy. If it benefits you, it is tax reform."

"Don't tax me, don't tax thee, tax that man behind the tree."

—Sen. Russell B. Long, D-La., who was for many years chair of the Senate Finance Committee, had a sardonic understanding of voters' ambivalence toward taxes

A Democrat, Long was elected to fill a vacant Senate seat in 1948 shortly before his thirtieth birthday. He joined the Finance Committee in 1953 and was its chair from 1965 to 1981. The committee has jurisdiction over almost half of the federal government's spending, including Social Security and many social programs, as well as jurisdiction over the federal tax code. (See FINANCE COMMITTEE, SENATE.)

His style of committee leadership was based on rewards. In exchange for members' support of legislation, Long allowed them to add provisions benefiting interests in their states. Critics complained that this led to unwieldy legislation that was not always the best. But Long had few critics within the Senate. Wily, candid, and generous with fundraising help, Long was well liked by colleagues. But their affection for him did not blind them to his shortcomings. Elected majority whip in 1965, Long was judged unreliable in that post and was removed in 1969. He retired from the Senate in 1987.

Longworth, Nicholas

Nicholas Longworth (1869–1931) served as a Republican representative from Ohio from 1903 to 1913 and from 1915 to 1931. He was a conservative rather than a progressive Republican. In 1912 he supported the presidential candidacy of William Howard Taft over that of his own father-in-law, Theodore Roosevelt. This contributed to Longworth's defeat in the 1912 elections. Longworth had little sympathy for partisan squabbles, believing that order and a spirit of cooperation were essential for the smooth running of the House of Representatives. Elected SPEAKER OF THE HOUSE in 1925, Longworth restored much of the power of that office, which had been greatly reduced when the House in 1910 revolted against the dictatorial rule of Joseph G. CANNON.

A lawyer by training, Longworth became involved in politics first in Cincinnati and then at the state level. In the U.S. House he was one of Speaker Cannon's trusted lieutenants, a member of Cannon's inner circle and poker group. Longworth became majority leader in 1923 and was elected Speaker two years later.

As Speaker, Longworth was determined to centralize authority in his office. One of his first acts was to demote thirteen progressive Republicans to the bottom of committee rosters. The loss of seniority was punishment for their votes in favor of a progressive candidate for Speaker and against a rules change that Longworth favored. Longworth bypassed the party steering committee and, like Cannon, relied on a few trusted colleagues to control the House. Unlike Cannon, however, Longworth did not rule through arbitrary interpretation of House rules but through persuasion and mediation. He prized and achieved the efficient and dignified conduct of the House.

Lott, Trent

When Trent Lott (1941–) became Senate majority leader in 1996, many wondered if the Republican from Mississippi would transform the Senate into a bastion of sharp-edged conservatism. Lott first entered Congress in the House (1973–1989), in the vanguard of a younger generation of confrontational conservatives. After moving to the Senate and ascending its leadership ladder to become majority leader, however, he took a more pragmatic approach and adapted to the consensus-building demands of his job.

However, his conservative background came back to haunt him in 2002. Lott was forced to give up his leadership post after uttering a statement that many perceived as racist. At a December 2002 birthday party for retiring senator Strom Thurmond, R-S.C., Lott said: "When Strom Thurmond ran for president, we (in Mississippi) voted for him. We're proud of it. And if the rest of the country had followed our lead, we wouldn't have had all these problems over all these years, either." Since Thurmond's platform at the time largely centered on maintaining

Trent Lott, R-Miss., held several leadership positions during his time in the Senate, including majority leader.
Source: CQ Photo/Scott J. Ferrell

racial segregation, Lott was sharply criticized, although he apologized and said he was "winging" his off-the-cuff comments. The uproar grew when critics noted that he had used eerily similar words to praise Thurmond two decades earlier.

During his eight terms in the House, Lott was a key GOP strategist as minority whip. The first Deep South Republican to serve as whip, Lott held the post from 1981 until he moved to the Senate in 1989. In the Senate Lott quickly moved up in the leadership, becoming conference secretary in 1993. After Republicans won Senate control in 1994, Lott defeated incumbent whip Alan K. Simpson of Wyoming for the majority whip position. When Kansas Republican Robert DOLE left the Senate in June 1996 to focus on his presidential campaign, Lott and his Mississippi colleague, Sen. Thad Cochran, vied to succeed Dole. Lott cast the race as a chance for a more aggressive style of leadership, and he won by a lopsided vote.

As majority leader he showed his practical side. Lott helped shepherd through legislation overhauling welfare, protecting people from losing health insurance, and improving the nation's drinking water systems. Despite his willingness to deal with the Democrats, Lott suffered some high-profile defeats, including the Senate's failure by one vote in 1997 to pass a constitutional amendment requiring a balanced federal budget.

Even without the constitutional amendment, Lott negotiated a balanced budget agreement with President Bill Clinton in 1997. When Clinton's impeachment trial—only the second of a president in U.S. history—landed in the Senate in January 1999, Lott strove to avoid the rancorous partisanship that characterized the impeachment proceedings in the House, and Clinton was acquitted. (See CLINTON IMPEACHMENT TRIAL.)

In 2007, when Republicans were again in the minority following the 2006 election, Lott returned to the leadership ranks as the GOP whip in the Senate. He held that post for less than a year, however, as he resigned his seat on December 18, 2007. "It's time … to do something else," Lott said at the news conference announcing his departure. In 2008 Lott opened a lobbying firm with former Democratic senator John Breaux of Louisiana.

McCarthy, Joseph R.

Joseph R. McCarthy (1908–1957), a Republican senator from Wisconsin from 1947 to 1957, was Congress's most notorious anticommunist investigator of the post–World War II period. He gave his name to the atmosphere of fear and intimidation that pervaded American politics in the 1950s.

As chair of the Senate Permanent Investigations Subcommittee in 1953–1954, McCarthy conducted a series of wide-ranging and controversial investigations; the State Department and the armed services were primary targets.

The hearings were the high-water mark of the "McCarthy era." National television exposure of the senator's abrasive and aggressive character, particularly during the Army-McCarthy hearings, began to turn public sentiment against McCarthyism. McCarthy's behavior led to his censure by the Senate in 1954.

McCarthy's Tactics

In February 1950 McCarthy gave a speech in Wheeling, West Virginia, in which he claimed many government officials were communists. He followed up this charge with six hours of accusations on the Senate floor. McCarthy charged that fifty-seven people, "known to the secretary of state as being communists," were still working and shaping policy at the State Department.

Democrats, forced to respond to attacks on a Democratic administration, set up a special subcommittee of the Foreign Affairs Committee to investigate. During the panel's thirty-one

> **More on this topic:**
>
> *Disciplining Members, p. 159*
>
> *Investigations, p. 292*

In the eyes of many in Congress, Sen. Joseph McCarthy's anticommunist investigations went too far. Here he is sworn in on May 5, 1954, during a Senate hearing on his tactics; the Senate censured McCarthy by the end of that year.
Source: AP Images

days of hearings, McCarthy charged ten people by name with varying degrees of communist activities. He claimed he was hampered by President Harry S. TRUMAN's refusal to release the confidential personnel files of federal workers. However, the investigating panel, chaired by Maryland Democrat Millard E. Tydings, found most of McCarthy's charges to be false and rejected others because the person charged had never worked for the government. In its report the panel said, "We have seen how, through repetition and shifting untruths, it is possible to delude great numbers of people." In response, the Republican Policy Committee said the report was "of a purely political nature and is derogatory and insulting to Senator McCarthy."

The investigation, one of the most bitterly controversial in the history of Congress, became an important issue in the 1950 elections. Charges of "softness" toward communism were a major factor in Tydings's defeat and in several other campaigns. McCarthy, who took an active role in the Tydings race, was criticized in a later Senate investigation that called it a "despicable, back-street type of campaign." In 1951 and 1952 investigations of alleged communism were carried out by both the House Un-American Activities Committee and the newly formed Senate Judiciary Subcommittee on Internal Security. In 1953, when Republicans gained control of Congress, McCarthy launched his own investigations and hearings as chair of a third "anticommunist" panel, the Government Operations Permanent Subcommittee on Investigations.

McCarthy, who had just been reelected, focused on a wide range of topics, questioning the Voice of America, the condition of State Department personnel files, trade with China, the loyalty of a Harvard University professor, and army operations in New Jersey. His aides toured Europe, checking out the holdings of State Department libraries, which they complained included thousands of books written by communists or "communist sympathizers." In its year-end report, the subcommittee included among its accomplishments several resignations from the government of what it called "Fifth Amendment communists."

Army-McCarthy Hearings

The subcommittee was continuing its probe of possible spies in the army in 1954 when McCarthy hit an unexpected roadblock. McCarthy had told a brigadier general he was questioning that the general was "not fit to wear that uniform" and did not have "the brains of a five-year-old." Army Secretary Robert T. Stevens announced he would appear in the officer's place. Stevens said he was "unwilling to have so fine an officer…run the risk of further abuse." Eventually the army charged that McCarthy and his staff had used improper means to seek preferential treatment for a private, G. David Schine, who had been a consultant to the subcommittee and a friend of committee counsel Roy M. Cohn. McCarthy, in turn, claimed the charges were an attempt to force the subcommittee to call off its probe of the army. The result was an investigation by the subcommittee of both sets of charges. McCarthy temporarily resigned his chairmanship. The thirty-five days of televised hearings offered an unprecedented look at the phenomenon, which by then was widely known as McCarthyism.

In charges and countercharges Stevens, army counsel John G. Adams, McCarthy, Cohn, and several other witnesses told their stories, often contradicting one another. McCarthy, who managed to convince his fellow Republicans that he personally was innocent, made a poor impression on the television audience and on the Senate as a whole. The committee's report said that McCarthy should have kept better control of his staff, especially Cohn, who was "unduly aggressive and persistent." Democrats, in a minority report, said McCarthy "fully acquiesced in and condoned" the "improper actions" of Cohn.

Censure by the Senate

By the time the reports were issued, McCarthy was already the subject of a censure resolution. Sen. Ralph E. Flanders, a Vermont Republican, had introduced the resolution charging McCarthy with, among other things, "personal contempt" of the Senate for refusing to answer questions and "habitual contempt of people." On August 31, the same day the investigations subcommittee filed its report, two weeks of censure hearings began before a special bipartisan committee. The special committee recommended censure on two counts: McCarthy's conduct during the investigation of the Tydings election and his treatment of the brigadier general in early 1954. The Senate, voting after the November elections, accepted the first charge but rewrote the second to focus on McCarthy's conduct during the censure hearings. The vote to censure McCarthy was 67–22.

With the return of the Senate to Democratic control in 1955, McCarthy lost his subcommittee chair. His influence and his ability to command publicity had already been curbed by the Senate censure. McCarthy died of a liver ailment on May 2, 1957.

McCormack, John W.

Seventy years old when he became SPEAKER OF THE HOUSE in 1962, Massachusetts Democrat John W. McCormack (1891–1980) never managed to get the House running smoothly. Frustrated liberal Democrats tried to oust him in 1969. Their attempt failed, but such an attack on a sitting Speaker was unprecedented. McCormack retired the next year, after forty-three years in the House. He was the first casualty of an increasingly impatient crowd of young Democrats who went on to reform House procedures in the 1970s. (See REFORM, CONGRESSIONAL.)

McCormack, a Boston native, never attended high school, but he read law books at the law firm where he worked as an office boy. At the age of twenty-one, McCormack passed the bar. After a stint in the state legislature, he lost his first bid for Congress in 1926 but then, after the incumbent died, won the seat in 1928.

Becoming Speaker in 1962 at the age of seventy, Democrat John W. McCormack had trouble running the House. Here Speaker McCormack (right) meets with the bipartisan congressional leadership in the Cabinet Room at the White House in 1965 to discuss the Vietnam War.
Source: LBJ Library Photo

McCormack was an early ally of Texas Democrat Sam RAYBURN, who was elected majority leader in 1936. McCormack became secretary and then chair of the House Democratic Caucus. When Rayburn became Speaker, he backed McCormack as majority leader, a key factor in McCormack's victory.

McCormack's poor reputation as Speaker overshadowed his more effective performance in the number-two Democratic post. Rayburn decided when to bring legislation to the floor and how to craft it for the best chance of success; McCormack did the legwork, rounding up votes and speaking for the Democratic leadership during the debate.

McCormack was comfortable on the floor. "I believe in fighting hard, but I don't like personal fights," he once said. "I go down on the floor of the House and take on my Republican friends." Although he consistently backed liberal positions on domestic issues, McCormack was never passionate about his beliefs. Not naturally forceful, he had little chance to act independently while Rayburn was in charge.

When Rayburn died in November 1961, McCormack was heir-apparent and succeeded him without challenge. But McCormack was seen as a weak leader by the increasingly active liberal Democrats who were frustrated by the CONSERVATIVE COALITION of southern Democrats and Republicans. When Republican gains in the 1966 elections reduced the Democratic majority, McCormack drew even more criticism for not bringing southern Democrats into line. His enthusiastic support of the war in Vietnam also put him out of step with many younger members.

In 1969 Rep. Morris Udall, an Arizona Democrat in his forties, ran for Speaker against McCormack. Although Udall received only fifty-seven votes, the challenge was a sign of how the Speaker's authority had declined. McCormack did not run for reelection in 1970.

Mace, House

The most treasured possession of the House of Representatives is the mace, a traditional symbol of legislative authority. The concept, borrowed from the British House of Commons, had its origin in republican Rome, where the fasces—an ax bound in a bundle of rods—symbolized the power of the magistrates.

The mace was adopted by the House in its first session in 1789 as a symbol of office for the SERGEANT-AT-ARMS, who is responsible for preserving order on the House floor. The first mace was destroyed when the British burned the Capitol in 1814, and for the next twenty-seven years a mace of painted wood was used.

The present mace, in use since 1841, is a replica of the original mace of 1789. It consists of a bundle of thirteen ebony rods bound in silver, terminating in a silver globe topped by a silver eagle with outstretched

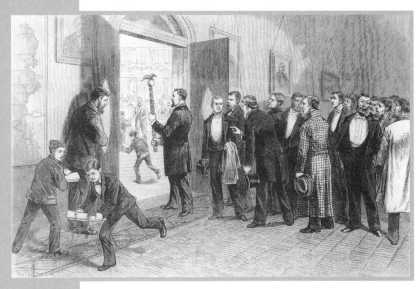

The mace was adopted by the House of Representatives in its first session in 1789 as a symbol of office for the sergeant-at-arms, who is responsible for preserving order on the House floor.
Source: Library of Congress

wings. It is forty-six inches high and was made by William Adams, a New York silversmith, for the sum of $400.

On several occasions in the history of the House the sergeant-at-arms, on order of the Speaker, has lifted the mace from its pedestal and "presented" it before an unruly member. On each such occasion, order is said to have been promptly restored. At other times the sergeant-at-arms, bearing the mace, has passed up and down the aisles to quell boisterous behavior in the chamber.

When the House is in regular session, the mace rests on a tall pedestal beside the Speaker's desk. When the House is sitting as the COMMITTEE OF THE WHOLE, the mace is moved to a low pedestal nearby. Thus it is possible to tell at a glance whether the House is meeting in regular session or as the Committee of the Whole.

Madison, James

When James Madison (1751–1836) was in his mid-twenties he suffered from melancholia, leading him to conclude that he was fated to die young and that, faced with eternity, earthly matters had little importance. When he died at age eighty-five, he could look back on a life distinguished by extraordinary service to his country. Wide reading and observation combined with concern for the needs of the United States led him to formulate many of the precepts later set forth in the Constitution.

As a young man, Madison was caught up in the political affairs of Virginia. In 1776 he was a delegate to Virginia's Revolutionary Convention, serving on the committee responsible for the drafting of Virginia's constitution and bill of rights. In 1780 he was elected to the Continental Congress, where he became a leader of those who favored the interests of national government over state sovereignty. Returning to Virginia, Madison entered the Virginia legislature in 1784.

Convinced that the Articles of Confederation were inadequate, Madison called for a convention to resolve problems plaguing the union of states. He played a leading role in the Constitutional Convention held in Philadelphia in 1787.

James Madison, one of the key framers of the Constitution, served four terms in the House, where he introduced the Bill of Rights. He also served as the nation's fourth president from 1809 to 1817.
Source: Library of Congress

Madison was one of the authors of the "Virginia Plan," which proposed a tripartite national government, reflecting his belief that the governing power should be shared among three separate but dependent branches of government. Madison also advocated representation in Congress on the basis of state population, the right of the government to raise revenue, and the popular election of national legislators and executives. He kept a detailed diary of the proceedings of the convention, published in 1840 as the *Journal of the Federal Convention*. With Alexander Hamilton and John Jay, he wrote *The Federalist Papers*, a series of commentaries on the Constitution aimed at building support for its ratification. (See FEDERALIST PAPERS.)

In 1789 Madison entered the new U.S. House of Representatives, where he served four terms. He introduced the Bill of Rights, fought for revenue legislation, and took part in shaping the executive branch. Angry over John Jay's 1796 treaty with Great Britain, Madison left Congress in 1797.

Madison served as secretary of state under President Thomas Jefferson and was elected to succeed him in 1808. Madison's presidency was plagued by political dissension and his inability to organize the country and armed forces for the War of 1812. After ratification of the Treaty of Ghent in 1815, Madison turned his attention to domestic problems and retired in 1817 with his popularity restored.

Majority and Minority Leaders

In both the House and Senate, each party elects leaders who become the party's chief spokespeople. They are sometimes referred to as the floor leaders. These leaders are elected by their party caucuses.

In the House, the Speaker is the highest-ranking person and is often the public face of the majority. However, the majority party in the House also has a majority leader who is the Speaker's deputy, helps plan the floor agenda and the party's legislative strategy, and usually speaks for the party leadership in debate. In the Senate the majority leader also develops the party's political and procedural strategy, often in collaboration with other party officials and committee chairs. This cooperative approach often extends to some extent to the minority leader, reflecting the accommodative mores of the Senate. The majority leader will negotiate the Senate's schedule with the minority leader but remains largely in charge of the chamber's agenda.

In both houses, the minority party also has its leaders. In the House, with its highly controlled procedures directed by the majority, the minority leader's influence is significantly affected by a personal relationship, if any, with the Speaker, the size of the minority party relative to the majority, and the presence of factions from either party that can be pulled together to affect the House agenda. The Speaker's consultation with the minority leader is often a courtesy rather than a necessity.

Senate rules, however, allow the minority party wide latitude to obstruct proceedings. As a result, the majority leader in the Senate often negotiates with the minority leader about the legislative schedule. (See LEADERSHIP.)

Majority Party Control   *See* LEADERSHIP.

Mansfield, Mike

Mike Mansfield (1903–2001), a Montana Democrat who followed Lyndon B. JOHNSON as majority leader of the Senate, exercised a permissive style of leadership that contrasted sharply with Johnson's methods. A representative for ten years and a senator for nearly twenty-five, Mansfield brought a wealth of congressional experience to the leadership post. His sixteen-year tenure as leader (1961–1977) was the longest in Senate history. After Mansfield retired, President Jimmy Carter named him to be U.S. ambassador to Japan; the Japanese respected Mansfield so highly that President Ronald Reagan kept him in the post throughout his administration.

Mansfield left a career as a professor of Latin American and Asian history to run for a House seat. Unsuccessful in 1940, he won in 1942. He gained a seat on the Foreign Affairs Committee, and in 1944 President Franklin D. Roosevelt sent him to China on a fact-finding mission.

Moving to the Senate in 1953, Mansfield was given a seat on the Foreign Relations Committee. He was one of the first two freshman senators to benefit from Johnson's decision to place newcomers on key committees. In the Senate as in the House, Mansfield compiled a liberal voting record on domestic and foreign issues.

A taciturn man, Mansfield often answered questions simply with "yep" or "nope." But his sparseness with words did not keep him from the leadership track. In 1957 he became majority whip under Johnson. When Johnson moved to the vice presidency in 1961, Mansfield took over the majority leader's post. Johnson had been assertive, powerful, and manipulative; Mansfield was known as "the gentle persuader" because he held that each senator should conduct his affairs with minimal pressure from the leadership. Besides, he said, "Sooner or later they'd just tell you to go to hell and do what they wanted to anyway."

Mansfield held the respect of his colleagues, but he was not an aggressive leader. Under him the Johnson system of rewards and punishment gave way to a collegial pattern in which the Democratic Policy Committee and the legislative committees played important roles. He was one of the first Democrats to differ openly with Johnson on the Vietnam War. Later he was a leader of efforts to cut off funds for the war and thus force President Richard NIXON into negotiations to end it.

Mansfield died in 2001 at age ninety-eight.

Mike Mansfield's sixteen-year tenure as majority leader was the longest in Senate history. Here Mansfield (left) talks with President Lyndon B. Johnson in November 1968 shortly before Johnson left office.
Source: LBJ Library Photo

Marbury v. Madison   *See* COURTS AND CONGRESS.

Markup   *See* LEGISLATIVE PROCESS.

Martin, Joseph W., Jr.

A representative from Massachusetts for forty-two years, Joseph W. Martin Jr. (1884–1968) was leader of the House Republicans from 1939 to 1959. For most of those twenty years he was minority leader. But in the two Congresses in which the Republicans controlled the House (1947–1949, 1953–1955), Martin served as Speaker. He was the only Republican SPEAKER OF THE HOUSE between 1931 and 1995, when Newt GINGRICH became Speaker after the Republicans regained majority status following forty years in the minority. Martin also served as chair of the Republican National Committee from 1940 to 1942.

Martin was a newspaper publisher in North Attleboro before he became involved in Republican politics in Massachusetts. After six terms in the state legislature, in 1925 he entered the U.S. House, where he remained until 1967. He served on the Foreign Affairs Committee and later the Rules Committee. Martin's name is not associated with any major legislation, and he was not known as an orator. A consummate politician, he was mainly interested in the day-to-day workings of the House.

In 1933 Martin became minority whip. In this position and later as minority leader and Speaker, Martin worked to defeat the domestic initiatives of Franklin D. Roosevelt and Harry S. TRUMAN. To this end he helped form an alliance of southern Democrats and Republicans, known as the CONSERVATIVE COALITION, which proved both durable and powerful. His efforts to defeat the NEW DEAL, together with the opposition of New York Republicans Bruce Barton and Hamilton Fish Jr., so enraged Roosevelt that during his 1940 presidential campaign he referred sarcastically to the three men as "that historic trio ... Martin, Barton, and Fish."

If Martin's relations with Democratic presidents were bad, his understanding with House Democratic leader Sam RAYBURN of Texas was good—too good for many House Republicans. Martin had an amicable and cooperative relationship with Rayburn, who both preceded and succeeded him as Speaker.

In 1959 Republicans took the unusual step of ousting Martin as party leader, complaining that he was too old for the post and too conciliatory to the Democratic leadership. They replaced him with Charles A. Halleck of Indiana, an outspoken conservative.

Members of Congress: Characteristics

Congress has been dominated from the beginning by middle-aged white men with backgrounds in law or business. But the institution's group portrait gradually has acquired more diversity, and the freshman classes who have entered the House and Senate in recent years have altered it further.

Minorities and women, shut out of Congress for decades, are now well integrated into Congress. The 110th Congress, when it convened in January 2007, had eighty-seven women members, forty-one African Americans, and twenty-six Hispanics. Although these numbers were still disproportionate to the population, they marked dramatic increases over the congressional makeup as recent as the early 1990s. During the 102nd Congress (1991–1993), for example, there were only thirty-one women, twenty-six African Americans, and eleven Hispanics.

Asians and Pacific Islanders also have gained increased representation. Including Democratic senators Daniel K. Inouye and Daniel K. Akaka of Hawaii, there were six members of Asian or Pacific Island descent in the 110th Congress. There was one lawmaker of Native American descent, House Republican Tom Cole of Oklahoma.

The average age of members of Congress increased substantially between the post–Civil War period and the 1950s. It has fluctuated since then, but—with only a few exceptions—it has been on the rise in recent decades. The average age rose from forty-seven years in 1983 to fifty-three in 1993 to just above fifty-seven at the start of the 110th Congress in 2007.

The legal profession was long the dominant occupational background of members of Congress. In the First Congress, more than one-third of the House members had legal training. The proportion of members with a legal background crested at 70 percent in 1840 but remained high. From 1950 to the mid-1970s it was in the 55–60 percent range.

The first significant decline in members with a law background began with the 96th Congress. Although sixty-five of the one hundred senators were lawyers in 1979, lawyers in the House made up less than a majority for the first time in at least thirty years. The situation continued through the 1990s. When the 109th Congress convened in January 2005, 178 representatives and sixty-four senators were lawyers, or about 45 percent of both chambers. In 2005, for the first time, business or banking, which had long been the second-most-listed category by members, overtook law. In the 109th

Congress, 205 representatives and forty senators claimed a business or banking background, or nearly 46 percent. Two years later, at the start of the 110th Congress, the rankings reversed again. In January 2007, 162 House members and fifty-nine senators listed law as a profession, a little above 41 percent of the membership. However, 166 House members and twenty-seven senators placed themselves in the business/banking category, dropping the overall ratio to 36 percent of all members.

However, another category (some members listed overlapping backgrounds) topped law and business in 2005 and highlighted the trend toward career politicians. In the 109th Congress, 254 members, or 47 percent, listed backgrounds in public service or politics. By 2007, that number had dropped markedly to 206 members, 38.5 percent, who listed public service or politics as an occupation. This reflected the composition of the large freshman Democratic class that picked up thirty seats to take back control of the House for Democrats. Roughly half the Democratic freshmen, nineteen of forty-two Democrats sworn in for the first time in January 2007, had never before held political office, indicating to many observers the voters' displeasure with status quo politics in Congress. Many new members stood out for their different backgrounds. The group included a social worker, a wind-turbine executive, an allergist, two college professors, a publisher of an alternative newspaper, and a former professional football quarterback. There were hardly any political neophytes among Republican freshmen.

David T. Canon, a political scientist who studies Congress, said the preponderance of Democrats without a political background and Republicans with those credentials was consistent with historical patterns. If an election goes strongly for one party, as it did for Democrats in 2006, persons elected for the first time often have included many political amateurs. He noted that the Republican freshman class of 1994, when the GOP unexpectedly swept into control of the House, also had a large contingent of amateurs.

But even with the occasional large class of amateurs with little political background, the long-term trend of a new breed of legislator that emerged in the 1970s remained true: the career politician whose primary earnings had always come from political office at the local, state, or federal level. This trend became possible because states and localities had begun to think of political positions as full-time jobs and had raised salaries accordingly. In addition, the demands of modern political campaigns left less time for the pursuit of other careers. This trend continued through the following decades. In the 109th Congress, 72 percent of new House members and 88 percent of new senators had held prior office. The Senate class included several experienced former House members. A few years earlier, in the 107th Congress, only 64 percent of new senators had held previous office. Even in the 110th Congress, the "amateur" group was confined to the House; all ten of the freshman senators held other political offices, including three who earlier were in the House.

The number of members with military experience declined dramatically into the twenty-first century, in part a reflection of the advent of an all-volunteer army in 1973. At the start of the 91st Congress in 1969, 73 percent of members were military veterans. By 1991 the percentage of veterans in Congress dropped to 52 percent. At the start of the 109th Congress in 2005, only 140, or 26 percent, cited military service.

In 2007, at the start of the 110th Congress, only 24 percent of members were veterans: 101 in the House and twenty-nine in the Senate. Still, there were two notable freshmen: Democratic representatives Joe Sestak, a retired Navy vice admiral who was the highest-ranking military officer ever to serve in Congress, and Patrick J. Murphy, the only Iraq war veteran in Congress.

Protestantism has been the most common religious affiliation for legislators. In the 110th Congress in 2007, Baptists were most numerous (sixty-seven), followed

More on this topic:

Blacks in Congress, p. 42

Hispanics in Congress, p. 259

Reapportionment and Redistricting, p. 456

Women in Congress, p. 606

by Methodists (sixty-three), Presbyterians (forty-four), Episcopalians (thirty-eight), and Lutherans (nineteen). There were forty-three Jewish members. In all, members listed affiliations with some twenty religious groups. Forty-seven simply listed "Protestant," and only six did not specify a religious preference.

Although the House and Senate in many ways do not mirror the electorate, the House does reflect geographic shifts in the nation's population. After each ten-year census, the 435 districts are reapportioned, with a few states gaining or losing representatives. Under the 2000 census, eighteen states were affected by changes in the size of their congressional delegations. Power shifted from the Northeast and Midwest to the South and West. Four states won two more seats: Arizona, Florida, Georgia, and Texas. Four states gained one seat: California, Colorado, Nevada, and North Carolina. Eight states lost one seat: Connecticut, Illinois, Indiana, Michigan, Mississippi, Ohio, Oklahoma, and Wisconsin. Two states lost two seats: New York and Pennsylvania.

Most elections return a large proportion of incumbents to office. This pattern is broken in some years when overriding national issues such as war, economic troubles, or political scandals result in more than the usual number of incumbents being thrown out of office. This occurred most recently in 1994, when Republicans swept Democrats out of control of Congress, and in 2006, when Democrats did the same to the GOP.

In the modern era the power of incumbency has remained strong with the turnover rate from deaths, resignations, and election defeats averaging about 10 percent or less, historically an exceptionally low level. In the 2006 elections, for example, 94 percent of House incumbents who ran were reelected. In the Senate, the reelection rate was 79.3 percent. Even so, the turnover rate was high by recent standards. In the House the number of incumbents who lost was the highest since 1994. In the Senate in 2006 the six incumbents who lost in the general election were the largest number in a general election since 1980, when nine were defeated. (One Democratic incumbent, Joseph I. Lieberman of Connecticut, lost his primary election but won in the general election when he ran as an Independent.)

Members: Service Records

On average, senators and representatives spend about ten years in Congress. As of January 2008 the longest congressional career was that of Carl HAYDEN, an Arizona Democrat who served in the House (1912–1927) and Senate (1927–1969) for a total of fifty-seven years.

The runner-up, however, was still in Congress: Sen. Robert C. BYRD, D-W.Va, who had served fifty-five years. If he served out even part of his six-year term, to which he was elected in 2006, he would pass Hayden for the all-time record. Behind Byrd was Democrat Jamie L. Whitten of Mississippi, who served in the House for fifty-three years until 1995.

At the start of 2007, six members had served at least fifty years, including Byrd and John D. Dingell, D-Mich., who continued to represent the Detroit area in the House. In addition, another sixteen persons had served at least forty years, including three still in Congress.

Service in the House often is a prelude to election to the Senate. In the 110th Congress in 2007 nearly half the Senate—forty-nine members—had previously been in the House. Some observers believed that this heavy representation of former House members contributed to the rising partisanship in Congress and to an increasing emphasis on constituent service. Both characteristics were often prevalent in the House where politics is more divisive and rough and tumble and constituent service essential to reelection.

Some members of Congress come from state houses. In the 110th Congress, nine members— eight senators and one representative—were former governors. State legislatures, and regional and

---

○ **CLOSER LOOK**

Even in election years with large numbers of incumbents leaving office—either by retirement or defeat—incumbency still rules. In 2006, when Democrats recaptured both houses of Congress, 94 percent of House incumbents who ran were reelected. In the Senate, the reelection rate was 79.3 percent.

LONGEST SERVICE IN CONGRESS

Member	Years of service	Total years[1]
Carl T. Hayden, D-Ariz.	1912–1927 (H), 1927–1969 (S)	57
Robert C. Byrd, D-W.Va.	1953–1959 (H), 1959– (S)	55
Jamie L. Whitten, D-Miss.	1941–1995 (H)	53
John D. Dingell, D-Mich.	1955– (H)	53
Carl Vinson, D-Ga.	1914–1965 (H)	50
Emanuel Celler, D-N.Y.	1923–1973 (H)	50
Daniel K. Inouye, D-Hawaii	1959–1963 (H) 1963– (S)	49
Sam Rayburn, D-Texas	1913–1961 (H)	49
Strom Thurmond, R-S.C.	1955–1956 (S), 1957–2003 (S)	48
Wright Patman, D-Texas	1929–1976 (H)	47
Joseph G. Cannon, R-Ill.	1873–1891 (H), 1893–1913 (H), 1915–1923 (H)	46
Adolph J. Sabath, D-Ill.	1907–1952 (H)	46
Edward M. Kennedy, D-Mass.	1962– (S)	45
Lister Hill, D-Ala.	1923–1938 (H), 1938–1969 (S)	45
George H. Mahon, D-Texas.	1935–1979 (H)	44
Warren G. Magnuson, D-Wash.	1937–1944 (H), 1944–1981 (S)	44
Justin S. Morrill, R-Vt.	1855–1867 (H), 1867–1898 (S)	44
Melvin Price, D-Ill.	1945–1988 (H)	44
William B. Allison, R-Iowa	1863–1871 (H), 1873–1908 (S)	44
John Conyers, Jr., D-Mich.	1965– (H)	43
Henry M. Jackson, D-Wash.	1941–1953 (H), 1953–1983 (S)	43
John C. Stennis, D-Miss.	1947–1989 (S)	41

SOURCE: Congressional Research Service; Congressional Quarterly.

NOTES: H = House; S = Senate.

1. Dates are the service record as of January 2008. Totals, based on exact dates of service, are rounded to nearest year. Minor differences in days or months of service determine rankings of members with the same total of years. Byrd and Kennedy were reelected in 2006 for six-year terms; Inouye was reelected in 2004 for six years; Dingell and Conyers were reelected in 2006 for two-year terms.

local governments also function as training grounds for future members. In the 110th Congress 273 members were former state legislators, 162 were former local and regional elected officials, and forty-one were previously state officials elected statewide. Members also have been drawn from courts. In the 110th Congress, twenty-one members were previously judges at various levels in state and local judicial systems.

Mills, Wilbur D.

An expert on U.S. tax law, Wilbur D. Mills (1909–1992) skillfully used his knowledge and political savvy during seventeen years as chair of the House Ways and Means Committee (1958–1975). Mills's preeminent position made his fall in 1974 even more dramatic. After well-publicized escapades with a striptease dancer, he announced that he would resign as chair at the end of the Congress and entered a hospital for treatment of alcoholism. Mills served the term he had just won and then retired in 1977.

Mills was a judge in White County, Arkansas, when he first ran for Congress in 1938. Friendship with Democratic leader Sam RAYBURN of Texas won Mills a seat in 1943 on the Ways and Means Committee, a coveted spot usually reserved for more senior members. Mills studied the tax code and by the time he became chair was well known for his grasp of even minor details. Colleagues were awed by his ability to speak, without notes, in favor of his committee's work.

An authoritarian chair, Mills kept control over all tax measures by bringing them before the whole committee and refusing to establish subcommittees to consider different issues. Mills consolidated his power by accurately sensing what the House would support and drafting legislation accordingly. He took tax bills to the floor under ground rules that barred floor amendments, and the full House regularly passed the measures by wide margins.

Mills's personal prestige was enhanced by his role as chair of the Democratic Committee on Committees. Since 1910 the chair of the Ways and Means Committee, along with the panel's Democratic members, had made Democratic committee assignments. Mills was the last chair to have the double responsibility; the Democratic Caucus in 1974 shifted committee assignments to the Democratic Steering and Policy Committee. The caucus also tried to dilute the authority of the chair of the Ways and Means Committee by expanding the panel from twenty-five to thirty-seven members. (See CAUCUSES, PARTY.)

Conservative in his politics, Mills still managed to work with Presidents John F. KENNEDY and Lyndon B. JOHNSON, though not on every issue. Opposition from Mills was enough to kill a bill; his resistance to Medicare stalled the legislation for several years.

By the 1970s Mills was a target of Democratic reformers, who considered his accumulation of power improper and a roadblock to a more democratic House. His personal indiscretions simply bolstered their position.

Mill's congressional career effectively ended ignominiously in 1974 when police stopped his car near the Tidal Basin, a shallow part of the Potomac River not far from the Washington Monument. One of the passengers was Annabelle Battistella, later identified by her better known name as stripteaser Fanne Foxe, the "Argentine Firecracker." She jumped from the car and ended up in the water. Several weeks later Mills appeared briefly on stage with Foxe in Boston.

Although he had just been reelected, Mill's standing in Congress was never the same after the Tidal Basin incident. After his retirement in 1977 Mills stayed in Washington working for a law firm, Shea and Gould, and lobbying his former colleagues.

Mitchell, George J.

George J. Mitchell's (1933–) election as Senate majority leader in the late 1980s surprised those who thought his thoughtful, low-key manner and liberal views would disqualify him. A Democrat from Maine, Mitchell was respected during his six years in the post for his effective Democratic leadership, his command of legislative detail, and his skill at forging consensus.

Mitchell began his career in politics as an assistant to Democratic senator Edmund S. Muskie of Maine. Mitchell was named U.S. attorney for Maine in 1977 and two years later became a federal judge. He left that position after only a few months to fill the Senate seat vacated in 1980 when Muskie became President Jimmy Carter's secretary of state.

In the Senate Mitchell quickly caught the attention of his colleagues with his keen memory for detail and his command of facts, particularly on environmental and health care issues. He further impressed his fellow senators with his political skills when he came from behind to win election to a full term in 1982 with 61 percent of the vote. Chosen to chair the Democratic Senatorial Campaign Committee for the critical 1986 elections,

Former senator George Mitchell (left) smiles as he receives the Presidential Medal of Freedom from President Bill Clinton at the White House in March 1999. Mitchell received the award for his work in the Irish peace process.
Source: AP Images/Susan Walsh

Mitchell was instrumental in helping his party regain control of the Senate. As a reward, he was made deputy president pro tempore, a post created for Hubert H. HUMPHREY in 1977 and not occupied after that.

Appointed in 1986 to the Senate committee investigating the IRAN-CONTRA AFFAIR, Mitchell proved himself to be an able performer before national television cameras, a factor considered crucial to his election as majority leader.

Becoming majority leader in 1989, Mitchell often played the role of adversary in opposition to Republican president George H. W. Bush during his first four years in the position. He managed to kill a capital gains tax proposal favored by Bush, and he spoke eloquently against Bush's use of military force in the Persian Gulf. Mitchell proved an effective negotiator as well, working out a compromise with Republicans that contributed to enactment of a major clean air bill.

The election of Democrat Bill Clinton as president in 1992 for the first time put Mitchell in a position to cooperate with an administration on legislative goals. He helped pass several key Democratic measures, including Clinton's massive deficit-reduction bill and the North American Free Trade Agreement, during his final two years as majority leader.

Mitchell retired from the Senate in 1995 and became President Clinton's economic adviser on Ireland. He was then asked by the president to chair the Northern Ireland peace talks. Mitchell helped to broker the deal with leaders of the Irish political parties that led to the April 10, 1998, Good Friday peace accord. The peace agreement was later approved by the Irish people in a referendum vote.

Mitchell was appointed by Clinton in 2000 to head an international committee to study the eruption of violence between the Israelis and Palestinians. The group issued its report in 2001, and the George W. Bush administration urged that its recommendations be implemented.

Morning Business *See* MORNING HOUR.

Morning Hour

The morning hour is a time set aside by the Senate at the beginning of a daily session for transaction of routine business. Under Senate rules the morning "hour" may actually extend for up to two hours. During that period members conduct what is known as morning business—introducing bills, filing committee reports, and receiving messages from the House of Representatives and the president. Senators may make brief speeches by unanimous consent. A senator also may move to consider any bill on the CALENDAR, but such motions must be decided without debate and therefore are immune from FILIBUSTERS. This tactic is rarely used.

The Senate's rules do not call for a morning hour every day. The Senate holds a morning hour only if its previous session ended in ADJOURNMENT, as distinguished from a recess. Even then the morning hour may be limited or dropped by unanimous consent. Between adjournments the Senate conducts morning business by unanimous consent. (See LEGISLATIVE DAY.)

Although House rules also provide for a morning hour, the arrangement is almost never used there.

Motions

Motions play as important a role as voting in Congress. In fact, without the use of motions members could never reach the voting stage. Virtually every step in the LEGISLATIVE PROCESS is initiated and completed by motions of one type or another. Put another way, motions enable senators and representatives to consider and dispose of legislation in a deliberate and orderly manner. Certain motions are especially important to the opponents of a bill, giving the minority side on any issue an opportunity to be heard and to present its policy choices.

Motions have specific functions, and their use is governed by the parliamentary situation. Among others, there are motions to adjourn, recess, postpone debate, end debate, withdraw other motions, proceed to the consideration of a bill or conference report, table (kill) a bill, reconsider a bill, strike out and insert substitute provisions in a bill, recommit a bill to a committee, discharge a committee from consideration of a bill, move the previous question to bring a measure to a vote, suspend the rules, and make a point of order. A few are used only in one chamber.

Under normal circumstances members can offer motions or initiate other legislative business only when they are recognized by the chair (the presiding officer). Once a member who has the floor offers, or "moves," a motion or introduces an amendment, he or she gives up the floor.

The standing rules of each house recognize certain motions as having precedence, or PRIVILEGE, over others. A formal hierarchy is necessary to avoid confusion and disputes when several members desire to offer different, and sometimes conflicting, motions at the same time. A tabling motion supersedes a motion to reconsider a previous vote on a bill. A vote therefore would be held on the tabling motion first; if adopted, the motion to reconsider would be nullified. A motion to adjourn in either house takes precedence over all others.

Some motions are more important than others to the everyday operations of the House and Senate, and some are indispensable. Others are clearly intended as delaying tactics. Some are offered merely to gain extra debate time when the House is sitting as the COMMITTEE OF THE WHOLE and debate on amendments is limited to five minutes for each side. A pro forma amendment moving to "strike the last word" or a motion "to strike the enacting clause" of a bill gives proponents and opponents each five additional minutes to debate an amendment. However, delays cannot go on indefinitely. Members who think debate is dilatory can always offer their own motion to end debate immediately or at a specified time. This procedure for ending debate does not apply in the Senate, where cloture needs to be invoked to end debate. (See FILIBUSTER).

Must-Pass Bill

This is the common term applied to critically important legislation that must be passed. It often involves authorization or funding to continue the operations of the federal government, pay the government's obligations, or protect its credit. As a result, such legislation often becomes a fly paper for completely unrelated attachments, usually offered in the Senate, that sponsors have found no other way to get passed.

Presidents usually are reluctant to veto must-pass legislation. Often, however, a president will threaten to do so if the must-pass bill becomes laden with amendments that the president likely would veto separately. Sometimes a veto does occur. This happened in the 1990s when a Republican majority under the leadership of House Speaker Newt Gingrich of Georgia sought to impose its views of government spending on President Bill Clinton. Clinton vetoed the GOP efforts on several bills, leading to an embarrassing shutdown of federal offices; most of the blame for the debacle was laid on the Republicans.

The last major must-pass bill of a session, sometimes called the "last train out of the station," invariably attracts many riders. As a result, such bills are sometimes called "Christmas tree bills," with riders as ornaments.

> **More on this topic:**
>
> *Christmas Tree Bill, p. 93*
>
> *Legislative Process, p. 344*

N

Natural Resources Committee, House

The House Natural Resources Committee oversees federal lands, carrying out the decades-old philosophy that some land should be set aside and managed by the government for the good of all. Conflicts between preserving the land as wilderness and using it for logging, grazing, and mining often fall to the committee, and then Congress, to resolve. Legislators from the West, where most federal land is located, dominate the committee, particularly on the Republican side. The Natural Resources Committee also oversees the federal water projects that subsidize irrigation of arid western areas and make large-scale agriculture possible there.

Among the oldest House committees, the panel was

The House Natural Resources Committee oversees federal lands including the national parks, such as Montana's Glacier National Park shown here.
Source: Jon Preimesberger

established in 1805 as the Public Lands Committee; its title was changed in 1951 to Interior and Insular Affairs. It became the Natural Resources Committee in 1993. Republicans shortened it further to Resources Committee in 1995, but the Democrats returned "Natural" to the name when they retook control of the House in 2007. Although the Resources Committee is not considered a major committee, it is still crucial to representatives from the West.

Many environmental issues, such as clean air and water, lie outside the committee's jurisdiction. Even federal lands are not entirely within its purview; it shares management of oversight of forestry with the Agriculture Committee. The Resources Committee handles some aspects of energy policy, such as regulation of nuclear power and restrictions on the strip mining of coal, but the Energy and Commerce Committee is the primary House energy panel.

History

Under Morris K. Udall, the Arizona Democrat who chaired the committee from 1979 to 1991, the committee was a strong advocate of protecting public lands. Although many committee members still wanted to accommodate the timber and mineral industries, that attitude did not dominate the committee in the late 1970s and 1980s as it had earlier under the lengthy chairmanship (1959–1973) of Colorado Democrat Wayne N. Aspinall. Although Stewart Udall, interior secretary from 1961 to 1969 and Morris Udall's brother, had won support from the Senate to close certain federal lands to commercial use, the proposals had faced opposition from Aspinall and the House. Congress eventually passed the 1964 Wilderness Act, a landmark bill that also included concessions to mineral leasing and other activities.

More than a decade later the House, not the Senate, was the lead player on preservation issues. When Congress was considering what parks, forests, and energy development were appropriate on the millions of acres of federally owned land in Alaska, the Senate pushed for less protection and more development. In contrast, the committee won House passage of a conservation-oriented bill. Eventually enacted in 1980, the measure concerning Alaska lands fell short of House goals, but it did reflect earlier concessions by the Senate to the committee's proposals.

In the early 1980s James Watt, President Ronald Reagan's secretary of the interior, launched an aggressive campaign to allow private industry to develop wilderness areas before a 1984 deadline would close them to commercial use. That legacy from Aspinall's era had permitted an additional twenty years of development in areas designated as wilderness in 1964. Never were the ideological differences between the Democrats and Republicans more apparent than during those early years of Reagan's presidency. But eventually, even Republicans on the Resources panel objected to Watt's plans, and Congress blocked him from acting. On many other issues, the committee took positions more favorable to conservation than did the Republican-controlled Senate Energy and Natural Resources Committee, which handled most public land questions.

The Resources Committee had a mixed record in one area: water projects. The committee oversees the Bureau of Reclamation, which since 1902 has provided water in the West at subsidized rates. Although sensitive to environmentalists' complaints in most areas, even Udall was a staunch defender of dams and waterworks, particularly the massive Central Arizona Project, which promised to bring water to the arid cities of Tucson and Phoenix in his district.

George Miller, a California Democrat, ushered in a more combative style when he became committee chair in 1991. Sparks flew almost immediately, with western members opposed to Miller's environmentalist agenda. He sought to limit big farms' use of federally subsidized water and divert it instead to restore damaged breeding areas for fish and wildlife.

The friction continued when Republican Don Young of Alaska took the chair in 1995 and tried to advance conservative rewrites of key environmental laws, such as the 1973 Endangered Species Act. Though he did not succeed, his committee was the scene of many pitched battles between the parties over environmental policies. The panel was able to win passage of measures authorizing water projects and establishing national parks.

Following Young's model was James V. Hansen of Utah, who chaired the panel from 2001 until his retirement two years later. Like Young, Hansen was a classic western Republican who favored less federal intervention in land issues and more access to public lands. Hansen oversaw committee action on part of a comprehensive energy bill that died in conference during the 107th Congress.

California Republican Richard W. Pombo succeeded Hansen as chair in 2003 and continued in the position through 2006. He was selected over four more senior committee members, thanks to his staunch conservatism and his success at fundraising, two things that made him a favorite with the House leadership. A fourth-generation rancher, Pombo adopted an antiregulatory agenda, particularly regarding property issues important to his fellow westerners. He long had advocated a rewrite of the Endangered Species Act, which he said did not save species but instead infringed on commercial and residential property rights. Pombo lost his reelection bid in 2006, along with many other Republicans that cost the GOP control of the House.

In 2007 Nick J. Rahall II, a West Virginia Democrat, took the chair, ushering in an entirely different tone on the panel. Unlike Pombo, who advocated boosting production of fossil fuels on publics lands, including vast areas in Alaska, Rahall urged new legislation to focus on energy sources beyond fossil fuels. Past efforts to rewrite the Endangered Species Act also were not expected to move forward under the Democrats. Rahall, however, represented a West Virginia area in which coal mining was an important part of the economy. This forced him to balance pressures from both environmentalists and coal interests. He said he would seek to push clean-coal technology and to redirect fees paid by coal companies to cover health care costs of some retired miners and to accelerate cleanup of abandoned mine sites.

New Deal

New York City residents stand in line at a soup kitchen in 1931. One major goal of the New Deal was to relieve the nation's overwhelming poverty.
Source: The Granger Collection, New York

The period in U.S. history encompassing the New Deal took in the first two terms (1933–1941) of President Franklin D. Roosevelt. Made up of hundreds of individual programs, the New Deal was designed to rescue the United States from the greatest economic depression in its history. The recovery programs of the Roosevelt administration in turn brought about major changes in American society, economic relationships, and government.

Roosevelt coined the term *New Deal* in his acceptance speech at the 1932 Democratic National Convention in Chicago. Breaking with tradition by attending the convention in person to accept the presidential nomination, Roosevelt pledged "a new deal for the American people." He was the overwhelming winner in 1932 against President Herbert Hoover. The election also gave Roosevelt large Democratic majorities in both houses of Congress—a clear mandate to initiate his recovery programs.

Roosevelt vowed in his presidential inaugural speech "to treat the task as we would treat the emergency of a war."

Philosophy

Roosevelt's governing philosophy called for a dynamic role for the federal government, including the responsibility to relieve the nation's poverty and unemployment. His New Deal called for action in many different areas:

- Massive changes in agriculture to improve the lot of the farmer through a variety of assistance programs
- Conservation and development of the nation's resources for the widest benefit of the population
- New protections for working people and reform of labor-management relations
- Rehabilitation of U.S. industry to establish a more productive as well as a more humane economy
- Wholesale changes in the nation's financial system, including tighter federal regulation of banking and securities exchanges
- Lower tariffs and reciprocal trade agreements with foreign nations to stimulate business activity

Many innovative domestic programs and reforms are associated with the New Deal. Roosevelt, however, did not assume office with an overall plan to remake the U.S. economy or institute a welfare state. Instead the New Deal began with a series of stopgap relief measures aimed at revitalizing free enterprise, which was near collapse after four years of massive economic dislocation.

Pragmatic rather than doctrinaire, Roosevelt drew on the ideas of experts in many fields in and out of government. Many of his proposals originated in the Progressive Era and in the Wilson administration's experience in mobilizing the country in World War I. But the New Deal went far beyond any earlier U.S. government involvement in the affairs of its citizens.

More on this topic:
Commerce Power, p. 102
Conservative Coalition, p. 138
Courts and Congress, p. 146
Progressive Era, p. 443

Strategy

Immediately upon taking office, Roosevelt convened a special session of Congress—the famous "Hundred Days" session—to deal with the economic emergency. Congress, acting with breathless speed and virtually without debate, enacted some fifteen landmark bills proposed by the administration, most of them highly controversial. The president himself delivered ten major speeches. He assumed the role of a bipartisan leader reaching out to all groups and interests in a time of crisis. That strategy could not last indefinitely. Within a few years the New Deal concentrated on fundamental long-term reforms and programs directed at groups and economic interests that threatened its success. Conservative southern Democrats as well as northern industrialists, whom the president called "economic royalists," increasingly felt uncomfortable and insecure. By early 1935 the more innovative New Deal laws were being challenged directly by the Supreme Court. In the next year and a half, the Court overturned six of the New Deal's most sweeping laws.

In his second term Roosevelt began to focus the New Deal on structural reform and was more outwardly supportive of organized labor, the unemployed and the rural poor, the aged, and small business. At the same time he called for more stringent federal regulation of big business and higher taxation of the more affluent. He tried to meet the Supreme Court challenge head-on by introducing his so-called Court-packing plan. Having just won reelection in the greatest presidential landslide in U.S. history, Roosevelt early in 1937 called for increasing the Court's size as a way to dilute the influence of several old, conservative justices on the nine-member bench. By pushing

The New Deal was designed to lift the United States out of the greatest economic depression in its history by implementing massive changes and reforms. Here a figure of Uncle Sam carries a wheel whose spokes contain facts and figures on New Deal legislation.
Source: Library of Congress

this proposal the president suffered one of his most humiliating defeats in Congress. He miscalculated public reaction, and the plan divided the ranks of the New Deal coalition.

Although he lost the battle, Roosevelt won the war. Even before Congress debated the controversial proposal, the Court began to show a willingness to accept New Deal policies. Newly passed legislation similar to that declared unconstitutional just a year or two earlier was now upheld. The president also made changes in the membership of the Supreme Court, beginning in August 1937 with the appointment of Hugo Black, to ensure that a majority of the justices would be sympathetic to the expansive legislation of the New Deal.

Between March 1937 and February 1941 the Court upheld revised versions of virtually all the legislation it had declared unconstitutional in Roosevelt's first term. In doing so, it reversed many of the doctrines it had espoused in curtailing state and federal power over economic matters. The Court's new direction culminated in a 1941 decision upholding the Fair Labor Standards Act of 1935, commonly known as the Wagner Act. That law prohibited child labor, set a maximum forty-hour workweek, and established the first national minimum wage (forty cents an hour) for workers engaged in, or producing goods for, interstate commerce. Child labor was prohibited, and severe limits were placed on teenage employment in hazardous occupations.

Nevertheless, the political costs of Roosevelt's defeat on the Court-packing bill had lasting effects on the New Deal. After 1938 a conservative coalition of southern Democrats and Republicans repeatedly blocked administration initiatives. At the same time the administration was forced to turn its attention to mobilization for war. Still, as late as 1939 Roosevelt could point to enactment of an impressive list of administrative reforms for controlling the expanded federal bureaucracy.

Legislation

The National Industrial Recovery Act (NIRA) was the centerpiece of the New Deal recovery plan. Enacted in 1933, the measure established a National Recovery Administration that encouraged cooperation among industry trade groups under exemption from antitrust laws. It also set maximum daily working hours and minimum wage rates, and it guaranteed workers the right to join a labor union and bargain collectively. Other provisions of the law established a Public Works Administration to organize and supervise a network of public works projects. This landmark law was overturned by the Supreme Court in 1935, only to be replaced by the even stronger Wagner Act.

The NIRA was only one of the major New Deal bills. Another was the Agricultural Adjustment Act, which aimed to increase farm income by holding down production. The Wagner-Steagall Act established the Federal Housing Authority and authorized several billion dollars—an unheard-of amount in those days—to supervise and pay for slum clearance and construction of low-income housing. The Home Owners' Loan Act set up the Home Owners' Loan Corporation to help avert foreclosures by refinancing home mortgages at very low interest rates.

The Glass-Steagall Act, part of the Banking Act of 1933, barred commercial banks from operating in the investment banking business. (This legislation was repealed in 1999 as part of a sweeping overhaul of U.S. financial services laws, reflecting vast changes that had occurred in the banking business since 1933.) Other provisions of the Banking Act of 1933 established the Federal Deposit Insurance Corporation. The Securities Exchange Act established a commission to fight fraud and misrepresentation in the securities business. Probably the best-known and most lasting New Deal accomplishment was federal old age and unemployment insurance: the Social Security Act of 1935.

Nixon, Richard

The stormy career of Richard Nixon (1913–1994) reached heights and fell to lows remarkable in U.S. political history. First elected to the House in 1946 as a Republican representative from California, he served two terms before moving to the Senate. Before he could complete his first Senate term, he was put on the Republican ticket with Dwight D. Eisenhower in 1952 and became the second-youngest vice president in the nation's history.

In 1960 Nixon lost a close race for the presidency to John F. KENNEDY. Two years later he lost a bid for the California governorship and bade a bitter farewell to politics. "You won't have Nixon to kick around anymore," he told members of the press, which he blamed for his two losses. Six years later Nixon was elected president; he was reelected in 1972. Midway through his second term he was forced to resign in the wake of the WATERGATE SCANDAL.

Nixon viewed his career in terms of crises and setbacks; he wrote *Six Crises*, a political memoir, in 1962. His rise to high political office was swift, impelled by political leaders who chose him as a candidate before, it seemed, he had declared himself. Nixon was a lieutenant in the navy in 1946 when a California Republican group asked him to run for the House

The front page of the **New York Times**, on August 9, 1974, reports on President Richard Nixon's decision to resign from office. Nixon faced near-certain impeachment.
Source: The Granger Collection, New York

of Representatives. He accepted and was successful; in his campaign he accused his opponent Jerry Voorhis, a New Deal Democrat, of communist sympathies.

As a freshman representative, Nixon served on the Education and Labor Committee, where he helped to draft the Taft-Hartley Act of 1947, a landmark labor law. His career in the House is most notable for his activities on the House Un-American Activities Committee. Over the objections of some committee members, Nixon persuaded the committee chair to allow him to reopen an investigation into charges that Alger Hiss, a former State Department official, had communist affiliations. The investigation led to Hiss's indictment for perjury, the first indictment to result from the committee's investigation into communist activities. The case brought Nixon national recognition and, as he himself acknowledged in *Six Crises,* "it also left a residue of hatred and hostility toward me" that was to wax and wane throughout his public career. (See INVESTIGATIONS.)

Nixon used the country's fear of communism to his advantage in his 1950 Senate bid, linking the voting record of his Democratic opponent, incumbent Helen Gahagan Douglas, with that of an allegedly procommunist representative. Nixon won handily, but many observers called his campaign the dirtiest on record. Nixon's later reputation as a ruthless campaigner stemmed from his conduct in that campaign.

Nixon had been a senator for less than two years when he caught the eye of New York governor Thomas E. Dewey, who was promoting Eisenhower's 1952 bid for the presidency. Soon Dewey also was promoting Nixon for the vice presidency. Nixon came close to being forced off the ticket when charges surfaced that he had used the proceeds of a secret campaign fund to supplement his Senate salary. On September 23, 1952, he went on national television in an emotional defense of his actions. In what came to be known as the "Checkers speech," he vowed to keep a gift cocker spaniel by that name and referred to his wife's "respectable Republican cloth coat" as evidence of their modest lifestyle. The appeal worked. Thousands of viewers telegraphed their support, and Eisenhower kept Nixon as his running mate for two terms.

Nixon's presidency was notable for his achievements in foreign relations, particularly improved relations with the Soviet Union and China and the ending of the war in Vietnam. His domestic programs, however, suffered gravely from poor relations with the Democratic Congress. Then came the 1972 break-in at the Democratic National Committee headquarters in the Watergate complex. Revelation of White House involvement in the burglary and its cover-up fatally injured Nixon's administration. In the face of almost certain impeachment and removal from office for obstruction of justice, Nixon left the White House on August 9, 1974, the first American president to resign the office. (See NIXON IMPEACHMENT EFFORT.)

Nixon Impeachment Effort

Dusting off a rarely used piece of constitutional machinery, Congress in 1974 began impeachment proceedings against President Richard NIXON for his role in the Watergate scandal. Nixon's resignation from the presidency cut short the effort, sparing him almost certain impeachment and removal from office.

Under the IMPEACHMENT POWER granted by the Constitution, Congress may remove the president and other officials for "Treason, Bribery, or other high Crimes and Misdemeanors." The process requires two steps. An accused official must first be formally charged, or impeached, by the House of Representatives. The official must then be convicted on those charges in a Senate trial. Only one president before Nixon had faced a serious impeachment threat: Andrew Johnson, who was acquitted by the Senate in 1868. In 1999 Bill Clinton became the second president to be acquitted of impeachment charges by the Senate.

The House Judiciary Committee adopted three charges, called articles of impeachment, against Nixon in late July 1974. The articles charged him with abuse of his presidential powers, obstruction of justice, and contempt of Congress. The full House never voted on these articles because Nixon resigned on August 9. Republican House and Senate leaders had told him that the evidence against him virtually ensured that he would be impeached, convicted, and removed from office.

The chain of events that ended in Nixon's resignation began with a 1972 break-in at Democratic National Committee headquarters in the Watergate complex in Washington, D.C. A national scandal unfolded with discovery of White House involvement in the burglary and other political sabotage, as well as cover-up efforts. The extent of White House activities was spelled out in 1973 hearings before a special Senate committee headed by Sen. Sam J. ERVIN Jr., a North Carolina Democrat noted for his knowledge of the Constitution.

A House impeachment inquiry was triggered in October 1973 when Nixon fired a special prosecutor who had been appointed to investigate the Watergate affair. The prosecutor, Archibald Cox, had tried to force Nixon to release tape recordings of conversations concerning Watergate. In July 1974 the Supreme Court ordered Nixon to release the tapes, which made clear that the president had participated in efforts to cover up White House involvement in the burglary. The Supreme Court action came as the House Judiciary Committee was preparing to vote on impeachment charges against Nixon.

The Senate Watergate Committee's televised hearings exposed a web of political scandals in the Nixon administration. The committee's chair was Democrat Sam J. Ervin (center) of North Carolina, and the ranking Republican was Howard Baker (left) of Tennessee.
Source: Senate Historical Office

The Judiciary Committee approved three articles of impeachment in a series of votes, July 27–30. The first, adopted 27–11, charged Nixon with obstruction of justice. The second, adopted 28–10, charged him with abuse of power. The third, adopted 21–17, charged him with contempt of Congress.

House debate on impeachment was set to begin August 19. Adoption of the charges was considered a certainty, and the Senate began preparing for a trial. It was at this point that Republican congressional leaders told Nixon the evidence against him almost guaranteed that he would be impeached, convicted, and removed from office. On August 8 Nixon appeared on television to announce that he would resign. The following day his resignation became effective, and Nixon left the White House.

The House Judiciary Committee continued to prepare its report recommending Nixon's impeachment, and the report was later filed in the House. But the impeachment proceedings themselves went no further. Vice President Gerald R. FORD succeeded Nixon as president. A month after taking office, Ford granted his predecessor a "full, free and absolute pardon … for all offenses against the United States which he … has committed or may have committed" during his years as president.

More on this topic:

Clinton Impeachment Trial, p. 97

Johnson Impeachment Trial, p. 307

Watergate Scandal, p. 596

Nominations *See* APPOINTMENT POWER.

Norris, George W.

George W. Norris (1861–1944) entered Congress as a Republican from Nebraska, became a Progressive Republican, and ended his congressional career as an Independent Republican. No matter what his party label, Norris was and remained a reformer. His zeal led him to advocate changes in the House of Representatives, the electoral system, the ownership of utilities, and the resolution of labor disputes.

Sen. George W. Norris, author of the Lame-Duck Amendment, also sponsored legislation that established the Tennessee Valley Authority.
Source: Senate Historical Office

Norris entered the House in 1903. He joined with Democrats in 1908 to try to curtail the powers of the Speaker of the House that had been so abused by Joseph G. CANNON, a Republican. The attempt was unsuccessful, and Norris was reelected by a margin of just twenty-two votes. Norris and his Democratic allies eventually won their goal, however, and in 1910 the post of Speaker was stripped of much of its power.

Norris moved to the Senate in 1913, the year the Seventeenth Amendment, calling for direct election of senators, was ratified. Norris had backed the amendment, and he continued to push for presidential primaries and the abolition of the electoral college. He supported President Woodrow Wilson's domestic policies but was one of six senators to vote against entry into World War I. He voted against the Treaty of Versailles, which ended the war and created the League of Nations.

Concerned by filibusters that slowed the proceedings of the Senate, Norris proposed doing away with the LAME-DUCK SESSION at the end of every Congress (held after a new Congress was elected but before it began on March 4). The Senate was most vulnerable to filibuster during the short session. Norris wrote the Twentieth Amendment to the Constitution, ratified in 1933, which abolished the short session by advancing the first day of a Congress to January.

A supporter of organized labor, Norris sponsored legislation restricting the use of federal injunctions against striking workers. He believed that hydroelectric power should be publicly owned, and he sponsored the legislation establishing the Tennessee Valley Authority.

Never one to take party ties too seriously, Norris endorsed the candidacy of Franklin D. Roosevelt in 1932 and later elections. Norris was defeated for reelection in 1942.

> **More on this topic:**
>
> Direct Election of Senators, p. 154
>
> Lame-Duck Amendment, p. 322
>
> Speaker of the House, p. 516

Oath of Office

House Speaker Nancy Pelosi administers the oath of office to Rep. Keith Ellison, D-Minn., the first Muslim member of Congress, in January 2007. Ellison's wife Kim holds Thomas Jefferson's Quran, which was provided by the Library of Congress for the occasion.
Source: AP Images/Lawrence Jackson

Article VI of the Constitution states that senators and representatives, as well as the president and other public officers, "shall be bound by Oath or Affirmation, to support this Constitution; but no religious Test shall ever be required as a Qualification to any Office or public Trust under the United States." The form of the oath of office was established by law: "I, A B, do solemnly swear (or affirm) that I will support and defend the Constitution of the United States against all enemies, foreign and domestic; that I will bear true faith and allegiance to the same; that I take this obligation freely, without any mental reservation or purpose of evasion, and that I will well and faithfully discharge the duties of the office on which I am about to enter. So help me God."

The oath of office is administered to newly elected members at the start of each new Congress in January of odd-numbered years. Because the entire House is up for election every two years, all representatives take the oath each time. Members first elect their chief presiding officer, the SPEAKER OF THE HOUSE, who is sworn in by the chamber's longest-serving member, known as the dean of the House of Representatives. The Speaker then administers the oath to all other members as they stand together in the chamber. In the Senate, one-third of whose members are elected every two years, the VICE PRESIDENT administers the oath to senators-elect as they come to the front of the chamber in small groups.

Office Buildings, Capitol Hill

Capitol Hill in Washington, D.C., located about a mile from the White House at the opposite end of Pennsylvania Avenue, is home to more than a dozen buildings that serve the legislative and judicial branches of government. The centerpiece is the United States Capitol with the Senate in one wing, on the north side, and the House in the other. It includes offices, cloakrooms for legislators, press rooms, and the National Statuary Hall and the Rotunda that thrill tourists when they first encounter them.

An aerial view of Capitol Hill shows the Madison, Jefferson, and Adams buildings of the Library of Congress behind the Cannon House Office Building.
Source: Library of Congress

The area is accessible by subway (Washington's Metro system), bus, taxi, and car, although public parking is limited. Union Station on the north side of the Capitol is one location where space usually can be found. The Metro station closest to the Capitol itself and House office buildings is Capitol South; the station closest to Senate offices is Union Station.

The larger area, known as Jenkins Hill at the time Washington streets were laid out by Pierre L'Enfant in the 1790s, has many other large and generally imposing structures. Each house maintains its own office buildings where legislators have their offices and most committees meet to do their work. The major structures for the House are the Cannon, Longworth, and Rayburn buildings, all named after notable House members, each of whom served as Speaker of the House during their careers. In addition, the House has the O'Neill and Ford office buildings. The Senate has the Russell, Dirksen, and Hart office buildings, named for distinguished senators. The primary office buildings are connected to the Capitol by underground passages and subways.

Capitol Hill also is the location of the Supreme Court building and three buildings for the Library of Congress, all of which are located on the east side of the Capitol and named for early presidents: Jefferson, Madison, and Adams. All are connected by underground walkways. (The west side of the Capitol has an unobstructed view of Pennsylvania Avenue.)

While the area was once a must-see tourist destination where visitors could roam freely, today greatly enhanced security requirements have restricted movement. Many streets are blocked from traffic. Congress in 2008 was nearing completion of a vast underground center to accommodate visitors.

In recent years many trade, law, and lobbying groups have purchased Capitol Hill townhouses for their operations. Real estate prices, always high in the area, have been pushed even higher by this trend.

More on this topic:
Capitol Building, p. 76
Capitol Hill, map, p. 82
Capitol Visitor Center, p. 83
House of Representatives, p. 267
Library of Congress, p. 355
Senate, p. 494

Omnibus Bills

A noteworthy feature of the modern Congress has been its tendency to package many, often unrelated, proposals in a single, long piece of legislation, called an omnibus bill. Although such bills have been used throughout the nation's history, they assumed new importance after Congress adopted its BUDGET PROCESS in 1974. Using that process, each year the Senate and House of Representatives adopt a budget resolution setting an overall plan for government spending and revenues. In many years, the chambers have followed up with an omnibus measure revising government programs to conform to the overall plan.

It became common practice in the 1980s for Congress to provide funding for most or all government departments and agencies in a single omnibus bill known as a CONTINUING RESOLUTION. This type of resolution was usually used for stopgap funding, and in the 1990s Congress began to back away from its use as an omnibus funding bill.

But this did not mean an end to other types of omnibus bills. In 1996, for example, Congress took a funding bill for one department and turned it into an omnibus bill containing all or part of five unfinished fiscal 1996 annual appropriations bills. Indeed, during Bill Clinton's administration, it was rare for the annual spending bills to move on their own rather than in an omnibus bill carrying at least two or more bills. In 2003, in the George W. Bush presidency, a continuing resolution was used once again, this time as the vehicle for eleven of the thirteen annual appropriations bills.

Critics complained that individual provisions of omnibus bills often receive little debate, and members are forced to vote on the mammoth measures without fully understanding or supporting what is in them. Others defended the omnibus approach, however, arguing that members benefit from the broad overview of government activities it provides. Some noted that many politically unpopular actions, however necessary, might be impossible unless they were buried in an omnibus bill. Omnibus budget bills often enjoy special protections from floor amendments or filibusters.

O'Neill, Thomas P., Jr.

As Speaker of the House from 1977 until his retirement in 1987, Thomas P. O'Neill Jr. (1912–1994) found himself playing a new role. Before becoming Speaker, "Tip" O'Neill spent twenty-four years as a Democratic representative from Massachusetts. As a representative, O'Neill practiced insider politics, talking over strategy with close friends during games of poker or golf. The post of Speaker in those years was similarly an inside office. O'Neill's three predecessors all sought to win key showdowns on the House floor by quietly building coalitions within the chamber. O'Neill became Speaker, however, just as House members began to put more stock in independence, rather than party loyalty, and to take their cues from constituencies outside the chamber. O'Neill soon found that he could win more votes by influencing public opinion than by twisting arms. As the one visible Democratic officeholder at the national level during the first six years of the Reagan administration, from 1981 to 1987, O'Neill inevitably became the party symbol to the national press.

Thomas P. "Tip" O'Neill Jr. of Massachusetts served for twenty-four years in the House before becoming Speaker. During the first six years of the administration of Republican president Ronald Reagan, O'Neill used his speakership as a national platform for the Democratic Party. Here O'Neill speaks to reporters in April 1981 in front of a portrait of President George Washington.
Source: AP Images/John Duricka

O'Neill came to the House in 1953, a cigar-smoking, poker-playing Red Sox fan from Cambridge, proud of his great success in state politics, where he had been his party's first Speaker of the Massachusetts house in the twentieth century. In Congress O'Neill joined the Public Works Committee to make sure that Massachusetts received its share of federal jobs and projects. In his second term he moved to the Rules Committee, which controls access to the floor for major legislation. O'Neill nearly always supported the Speaker during his eighteen years on the Rules panel. He also was viewed more as a loyal soldier than as a potential House leader. Two events, however, helped change that perception.

In late 1967 O'Neill broke with President Lyndon B. JOHNSON and publicly opposed the war in Vietnam, thus drawing the attention of younger House liberals. Three years later he worked with many of these same liberals to pass a major reform of House procedures. In 1971 he won a place on the leadership ladder as majority whip, and in 1973 he became majority leader. Democrats chose O'Neill by acclamation to succeed Speaker Carl B. ALBERT, who retired in 1977.

Strongly partisan, more interested in the politics of the House than the content of legislation, O'Neill carried the Democratic

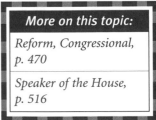

More on this topic:

Reform, Congressional, p. 470

Speaker of the House, p. 516

banner during the administrations of Democrat Jimmy Carter and Republican Ronald Reagan. Although he had no particular enthusiasm for Carter's programs, O'Neill worked hard to pass them through Congress. He pushed through tough ethics legislation and speedily delivered House approval of Carter's massive energy package. But by the end of Carter's term in 1981 O'Neill was having a difficult time, often unable to break up a united Republican front or to prevent Democratic defections.

With the election in 1980 of a Republican president and a Republican-controlled Senate, O'Neill fell victim to the rising partisan tension on the House floor. He was unable to block House approval of Reagan's economic package. Democrats regained effective control of the House in the 1982 elections. In his final years as Speaker, O'Neill nearly always had the votes to prevail when he wanted.

> **"All politics is local."**
>
> —*Speaker Thomas P. O'Neill*

When he retired, O'Neill published his memoirs (coauthored with William Novak), *Man of the House: The Life and Political Memoirs of Speaker Tip O'Neill.*

Oversight and Government Reform Committee, House

The House Oversight and Government Reform Committee, like its counterpart in the Senate— the Senate Homeland and Security Governmental Affairs Committee—focuses primarily on how the federal government functions. Its sweeping jurisdiction over the entire federal government permits an aggressive chair to pursue almost any issue of interest from homeland security to health care. But the committee is mostly detail-minded, tackling such subjects as computer security and the government's financial management.

Established in 1816, the committee was originally called the Committee on Expenditures in Executive Departments. It became Government Operations in 1952. Republicans changed its name to House Government Reform and Oversight when they took control of the House in 1995. It was shortened to Government Reform in 1999. In 2007 Democrats—newly back in the majority—returned "oversight" to the name, but they put it at the beginning, reflecting the party's widely publicized plan to closely examine all aspects of administrative policies and programs of President George W. Bush. Democrats had sharply criticized Republicans for giving Bush a pass on many issues when they controlled the House during his first six years in the White House.

The committee originates little legislation. Bills handled by the committee include proposals for government reorganization, including new agencies or departments, and intergovernmental relations as well as the entire federal civil service. Subcommittees often concentrate on investigations; exposure of waste and fraud is a theme that runs through many reports. The committee has at times focused on procurement—what and how the government buys from private industry.

Long considered a congressional backwater, the committee gained a new image when Texas Democrat Jack Brooks became chair in 1975. Brooks quickly turned it into an aggressive investigatory arm that touched many federal agencies. John Conyers Jr., a Michigan Democrat, took over the panel in 1989 when Brooks moved to Judiciary. Conyers showed that he intended to keep up the watchdog role. The committee investigated corporate defense-contracting improprieties and allegations of wrongdoing by the Internal Revenue Service.

With the Republican takeover of the House in 1995, Dan Burton of Indiana became chair. Burton's reputation as a fierce partisan was affirmed by his investigation into allegations of political

CLOSER LOOK

The House Oversight and Government Reform Committee focuses primarily on how the federal government functions. Democrats in 2007 added "Oversight" at the front of the panel's name, reflecting the party's widely publicized plan to investigate policies and programs of the Bush administration.

More on this topic:

District of Columbia and Congress, p. 168

Homeland Security and Governmental Affairs Committee, Senate, p. 261

fundraising irregularities in the 1996 presidential election, particularly alleged abuses by the Clinton-Gore campaign. Burton's committee, unlike the Senate Governmental Affairs Committee that was also investigating the matter, was heavily criticized for its high-handed methods and one-sided inquiry. Like the Senate, the House found no compelling evidence of wrongdoing by the Clinton administration.

Burton was barred by GOP term limits from staying on as chair in the 108th Congress (2003–2005), and the committee chair went to Thomas M. Davis III, a more moderate Republican whose Northern Virginia district was home to many federal workers and contractors. Davis—who as chair of the National Republican Congressional Committee engineered the House GOP gains in the 2002 elections—was chosen by the leadership-dominated GOP Steering Committee over more senior Republicans on the panel.

In 2007, as the 100th Congress began, the panel came under the chairmanship of Henry A. Waxman, an aggressive and tenacious Democrat from California. Even when in the minority Waxman pursued the White House on Iraq contracting, the recovery from hurricanes Katrina and Rita, Vice President Richard Cheney's energy tax force, prescription drug issues, and irregularities in elections. But in the minority he had limited leverage to force information out of the administration or compel witnesses to come before the panel. As the chairman, with the backing of committee colleagues and—most importantly—the support of Speaker Nancy Pelosi, a fellow Californian, plus the power to issue subpoenas, Waxman aggressively pursued investigations of the Bush administration.

On legislation, the committee enjoyed one important success early in the 110th Congress when the House passed a bill from the panel to grant the District of Columbia a full voting-rights seat in the House. It would replace the existing delegate seat under which a person elected from D.C. can vote in committee and under certain parliamentary procedures on the floor so long as the vote did not alter the outcome on a roll call. The measure also would give an additional House seat to Utah. The proposal was not enacted during the 110th Congress.

Oversight Power

Congress has delegated to the executive branch broad authority over agencies and programs it has created. Its oversight power helps ensure that the executive branch performs as Congress intends.

Hearings and investigations, the most publicized form of oversight, provide some of the most colorful and dramatic moments on Capitol Hill, as was seen in the Watergate scandal, the Iran-contra affair, and the impeachment of President Bill Clinton.

Other examples included probes by the 104th Congress (1995–1997) of personnel firings at the White House travel office and access by Clinton administration officials to Federal Bureau of Investigation (FBI) files on former Republican White House staffers, and hearings by the 105th Congress (1997–1999) on allegations of CAMPAIGN FINANCING violations in the 1996 election and of Internal Revenue Service (IRS) abuses of taxpayers' rights. In the 107th Congress (2001–2003), hearings were held to look into intelligence failures prior to the September 11, 2001, terrorist attacks. In the 110th Congress in 2007 with Democrats newly back in power, committees began vigorous oversight investigations of Bush administration actions. The most dramatic, still unfolding in mid-year, was an investigation of the firing of nine federal attorneys for allegedly political—rather than performance—reasons.

Members of Congress have been known to use the subpoena power of a committee to compel executive branch officials to testify or to produce documents. The 2007 probe of the attorney firing had by July already produced subpoenas to witnesses who had worked in the administration, which Bush officials immediately sought to shield by asserting executive privilege. That claim and Democrats' determination to push ahead set the stage for a major constitutional showdown between the two branches.

Oversight takes less dramatic forms as well. The most effective may stem from the power of the purse. Because Congress controls the federal purse strings, it is able to review agency performance and demand changes before providing the money needed to operate programs. House and Senate Appropriations committees make searching inquiries into agency activities before voting annual appropriations. Other committees review agency performance as they consider renewal of authorizations, without which programs cannot be funded. (See APPROPRIATIONS BILLS; AUTHORIZATION BILLS; PURSE, POWER OF.)

During confirmation hearings, senators may seek to establish a record of a nominee's views to which the person may be held accountable later. (See APPOINTMENT POWER.)

Lawmakers also exercise their oversight function through informal contacts with executive officials, as well as statements made in committee and conference reports and during hearings and floor debate. Staffs of individual members of Congress conduct ongoing oversight through casework—the handling of constituent questions and problems regarding agency actions.

The Government Accountability Office and other support agencies help Congress keep tabs on the executive branch. Congress also receives reports from the offices of inspectors general, independent "watchdogs" created by Congress within every executive department and major agency to investigate and audit management and performance. In addition, many agencies are required to report to Congress on their activities. However, because of complaints that Congress was trying to "micromanage" administrative details, the 104th Congress passed legislation to reduce the number of reports required.

The Supreme Court in 1983 ruled unconstitutional another widely used oversight device: the LEGISLATIVE VETO. The veto had allowed one or both houses of Congress—or sometimes even a committee—to overrule executive actions. The Supreme Court decision, in the case of *Immigration and Naturalization Service v. Chadha*, was a major defeat for Congress, whose attorneys had argued that the legislative veto was a useful and necessary modern invention that enabled Congress to delegate authority without abdicating responsibility. Congress had included legislative veto provisions in more than 200 laws since 1932. Some of these provisions continue to exist in statutes, however, and can occasionally still be used under the rules of each chamber to make a political point, even though they no longer have legal effect. Other statutes have been rewritten to pass constitutional muster.

Congress has used a 1996 law known as the Congressional Review Act to overturn regulations that it opposed. The law required agencies to submit reports on regulations to Congress, which has sixty days to pass by simple majorities a joint resolution of disapproval. Once cleared by Congress, the resolution of disapproval must be sent to the president for signature or veto. Congress successfully used the untested law in 2001, when congressional Republicans persuaded a handful of centrist Democrats to join them in dismantling workplace ergonomics regulations issued under the Clinton administration. Key to their victory was a provision specifying that when a rule was submitted near the end of a Congress or after it adjourned, the sixty-day clock would begin ticking again on the fifteenth day of the new session. Under most circumstances, the president could be expected to veto the resolution, but with a change of administrations, Republicans had a president who was ready to sign.

More on this topic:

Investigations, p. 292

Iran-contra Affair, p. 301

Legislative Veto, p. 353

Subpoena Power, p. 545

Watergate Scandal, p. 596

P

Pages

Visitors to the Capitol often see young people in dark blue suits hurrying through the corridors with messages or handing out documents on the House or Senate floor. Called pages, the boys and girls must be high school juniors and at least sixteen years of age. They attend school early in the morning and then run errands for Congress the rest of the day. About 100 serve at any one time: approximately seventy for the House and thirty for the Senate. Pages are patronage appointees. Those nominated by the more senior representatives and senators have the best chance of being selected. Pages serve for at least one semester; some stay for a full year. There is also a summer program for pages. Pages do not work directly for those who appoint them but instead report to the House clerk and the Senate sergeant-at-arms.

In 2006 the House paid pages at an annual rate of $18,817, of which $400 was deducted each month for room and board. The Senate paid pages at an annual rate of $20,491, and deducted $600 for room and board. Pages are responsible for transportation to and from Washington and are required to follow a dress code. A House description of the page program, noting the extensive walking required on the job, says, "We cannot stress enough that pages bring well broken-in, comfortable shoes."

Congress revamped the page program in the early 1980s after criticism that pages were poorly supervised and schooled. Housing for pages was set up in 1983. Congress also agreed that only juniors in high school should serve as pages; previously pages had ranged in age from fourteen to eighteen, making it difficult to provide an appropriate curriculum. Each chamber has its own school for pages, offering an accredited academic program.

Scandals shook the page program in the early 1980s and again in 2006. In news reports in 1982, two unidentified pages told of sexual misconduct on the part of House members. Later they recanted their stories; a House investigation concluded that most of the allegations "were the product of teenage exaggeration, gossip, or even out-and-out fabrication." More painful for the House was its 1983 censure of two representatives who had had sexual relationships with pages. Daniel B. Crane, an Illinois Republican with a wife and six children, admitted that he had had an affair in 1980 with a seventeen-year-old female page. Gerry E. Studds, a Massachusetts Democrat, was found to have had a homosexual relationship in 1973 with a seventeen-year-old male page.

Congress employed boys as pages as early as 1827. The first girl page was not appointed until 1970. Here Vice President Thomas R. Marshall poses with Senate pages in the early 1900s.
Source: Library of Congress

In the 109th Congress (2005–2007) reports emerged that a House member, Florida Republican Mark Foley, had sent inappropriate e-mail messages with sexual content to male House pages. After the messages became public Foley resigned from the House, on September 29, 2006. This removed him from the jurisdiction of the Ethics Committee, but the panel continued to examine whether House leaders knew of his behavior earlier and did not act, and whether the pages were generally receiving proper supervision. In a lengthy report late in the year, the panel concluded that the GOP leadership had not violated laws or House rules. But at the same time the report took them to task for not doing all they could to protect pages from what some lawmakers said appeared to be homosexual advances by Foley. The page investigation was one of a number of scandals involving Republicans in the last two years of their control of Congress that were instrumental—along with growing public anger over the continuing Iraq war—in helping Democrats win the 2006 elections.

Records as early as 1827 show that boys worked as messengers. The name *pages* came into use a decade later. The first Senate page, Grafton Dulany Hanson, was appointed at the age of nine by Sen. Daniel Webster. Webster's second page served the Senate in various capacities from 1831 to 1895. In the 1800s pages augmented their pay by collecting autographs from members and by arranging for printing and sale of major speeches. Sen. Jacob K. Javits, a New York Republican, broke the color barrier when he appointed the first black page in 1965. Javits also appointed the first female page in 1970, but her employment was delayed until the following May, when the Senate voted to permit girls as pages. Some pages have returned to the halls of Congress as legislators. Rep. John D. Dingell of Michigan and Sen. David Pryor of Arkansas, both Democrats, were once pages. In the 110th Congress eight House members and two senators were once pages.

More on this topic:

Clerk of the House, p. 95

Disciplining Members, p. 159

Patronage, p. 408

Sergeant-at-Arms, p. 512

Parliamentarian

Two of the most powerful employees of Congress are the Senate and House parliamentarians. These officials are the arbiters of legislative practice in each chamber. Their interpretations of the body's rules and precedents can have a profound impact on the shape of legislation and the course of floor action. The parliamentarian or an assistant is always on the floor during House and Senate sessions, whispering advice to the PRESIDING OFFICER.

The parliamentarians do not officially make rulings. But presiding officers rarely ignore their advice, especially in the Senate, where freshman senators traditionally take the chair. The parliamentarians can often anticipate the points of order and parliamentary inquiries likely to be raised. When they cannot do so, they must be able to offer authoritative on-the-spot advice to the presiding officers. (See POINT OF ORDER.)

Parliamentarians also play an important role behind the scenes. As masters of the procedural and technical skills that are the backbone of successful legislating, they are consulted by members of both parties and their staffs. They are acknowledged experts in suggesting ways to route legislation to a sympathetic committee, prepare it for floor debate, and protect it from opposition attacks. The parliamentarians customarily are responsible for referring bills to the committees with appropriate jurisdiction. They also prepare and maintain compilations of the precedents in each chamber.

House parliamentarians build on the work of two House members, Asher Hinds, a Maine Republican who served from 1911 to 1917, and Clarence A. CANNON, a Missouri Democrat who served from 1923 to 1964. Senate precedents were compiled by Floyd M. Riddick, Senate parliamentarian from 1965 to 1974.

Parliamentarians are chosen by the leadership of the House and Senate. In the House the parliamentarian is named by the Speaker. Lewis Deschler, parliamentarian from 1928 to 1974, was a member of the "Board of Education," a group of House friends of Speaker Sam RAYBURN who met with the Texas Democrat at sundown for drinks and strategy talks. In the Senate, where power is more diffused, parliamentarians have occupied a less central position. The person is named by the secretary of the Senate, but always with the approval of the majority leader.

The House formally recognized the position in 1927, but the Senate not until 1937. In 1977 the House established an office of the parliamentarian and directed that it be managed, supervised, and administered by a nonpartisan parliamentarian appointed by the Speaker. Unofficial parliamentarians advised the presiding officers during most of the nineteenth and early twentieth centuries.

Party Discipline *See* LEADERSHIP.

Patronage

Patronage is the term for the use of political power to place favored individuals in jobs. Members of Congress once pulled the political strings on thousands of jobs, but the practice has declined to virtually nothing today. On Capitol Hill today the only jobs remaining under patronage are those that do not require specialized skills or technical knowledge, such as doorkeepers and elevator operators. Unlike many of the other vanishing perks, the loss of patronage has not been particularly lamented; many legislators regarded it as a nuisance that was little help in strengthening their political positions or rewarding campaign supporters back home.

The practice of patronage—considering political loyalty when filling jobs—began with George Washington. At one time Congress controlled a huge number of patronage jobs, extending even to the choice of rural mail carriers.
Source: U.S. Postal Service

All members of Congress hire their own office staff, and committee and subcommittee chairs have even more slots to fill. These legislative jobs are not considered to be patronage.

The majority party in the House or Senate fills most patronage slots, although the minority party staffs its own cloakroom and other posts that have a party designation. When control of the House or Senate changes hands, to either a new leader or a new party, the tradition has been to let those in patronage jobs stay on.

The practice of considering political loyalty when filling jobs began with President George Washington. President Andrew Jackson was the first to provoke public criticism by his aggressive use of the "spoils system."

The civil service system was established to insulate most federal employees from political pressures. It was created after the 1881 assassination of President James A. Garfield by a disappointed job seeker.

In 1969 President Richard NIXON removed from congressional influence 63,000 postmaster and rural carrier jobs, leaving only a few Capitol Hill posts for members to control. Congress itself eliminated patronage from most jobs that required skill and training, such as the Capitol Hill police force.

Patronage employees were hired on the word of senior members. Their supervisors could not fire them without checking with their sponsor, but they could lose their jobs at a moment's notice if their sponsor wanted to give the post to someone else.

In the House patronage dwindled to insignificance after the House in 1992 gave up most of its members' direct control over these positions. The House turned over control of its workforce to a professional administrative officer following a series of embarrassing incidents in the House's own bank and post office involving patronage employees.

A Republican report said the post office was greatly overstaffed, with some functionally illiterate workers incapable of sorting mail, and promotions and pay depending on political favoritism. The whole operation was "more akin to a feudal system than a modern business," the report said.

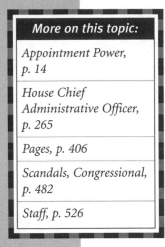

More on this topic:

Appointment Power,
p. 14

House Chief
Administrative Officer,
p. 265

Pages, p. 406

Scandals, Congressional,
p. 482

Staff, p. 526

At the time, there were roughly 600 patronage jobs (of which about fifty were allocated to Republicans, who were in the minority then), mostly for low-level postal clerks, mailroom workers, door attendants, pages, and elevator operators. They were hired by the Democratic Personnel Committee at the recommendation of senior Democrats, and worked for the doorkeeper, clerk, sergeant-at-arms, and postmaster—elected officers whose own jobs were dependent on personal ties and party loyalty.

Under the 1992 overhaul, the new House administrator, as the person was called when the post was established, was to supervise the financial and management operations of the House officers. About 200 jobs that had previously been filled through patronage were placed under his control, now to be filled on the basis of competency and qualifications. But the new administrator struggled with the House Administration Committee over what tasks he was in charge of and after two years in the post abruptly resigned. When the Republicans took over in 1995, they changed the position to a chief administrative officer, who initially reported to the House Speaker and later to the House Administration panel once again. But the goal of the office remained essentially the same: to professionalize the administrative functions of the House.

In the Senate the arrangement for patronage employees has been less formal, with the two party leaders and their staffs allocating the patronage among fellow senators. Although seniority is a factor, party leaders can also make patronage slots available to colleagues in return for favors, such as crucial votes on legislation. Most Senate patronage posts were supervised by the Senate sergeant-at-arms. The sergeant-at-arms testified at a hearing in 1997 that the office developed an approach toward patronage that would preserve senators' ability to appoint short-term employees while complying with the 1995 Congressional Accountability Act, a law that extended eleven federal labor and workplace laws to Congress and its related offices.

One remnant of the patronage system was members' ability to make appointments to the Military Academy, the Naval Academy, and the Air Force Academy. About three-fourths of these academies' combined enrollments came through members of Congress. Although candidates were required to meet minimum academic and physical standards, members had great latitude in deciding how to select their nominees.

Other patronage appointees included elevator operators. Senate officials contended the operators, whose numbers had so dwindled nationwide that the Labor Department no longer even tracked them, still performed essential functions in the Senate, including efficient running of elevators and crowd control.

Pay and Perquisites

Senators and representatives earn the same amount: $165,200 at the beginning of the 110th Congress in 2007, with automatic cost-of-living increases set for the future to keep pace with inflation. The pay was the same as in 2006 because Congress voted to forgo a scheduled 1.7 percent pay hike for 2007—a 2006 campaign promise—until the lawmakers voted an increase in the minimum wage. That increase did occur in 2007, but a number of months into the session. By summer, however, lawmakers were poised to accept a cost-of-living increase in 2008, an amount that was expected to be in the range of $4,400.

Although members can earn other money from investments, they cannot hold outside jobs or earn significant income in most ways. Federal law and congressional rules have many provisions to prevent members from capitalizing on their office or pocketing money from special interests.

The Constitution gave Congress the task of setting its own salaries, a built-in conflict of interest that has caused recurrent political headaches. Members generally have earned less than people who reach the top in other professions, but far more than their constituents. Whenever members of Congress have raised their salaries, they have been accused of lining their pockets; sometimes a member has lost a seat in the next election because of public outcry.

In addition to their salaries, members have other benefits and perquisites, such as free travel and an excellent pension program. The exact value of those benefits is difficult to calculate.

A Political Football

Disputes over pay levels have been a feature of congressional politics since the First Congress. The Constitution settled one key question concerning pay by decreeing that members would be paid by the federal government, rather than by the states they represented. But the Constitution left up to members themselves the delicate question of the level of pay. Members have raised their pay many times over the past two centuries but often have suffered politically at the hands of the electorate as a result.

The first pay raise, in 1815, was a 60 percent hike from $6 a day to $1,500 a year in 1815. It had to be repealed the next year after scores of members were defeated for reelection. Congress did not regain an annual salary until 1855.

In the past, economic and political problems have sometimes led Congress to reduce pay levels, or to pay one chamber more than the other, or to leave salaries alone for years as inflation gnawed at purchasing power. Members had no pay raise from 1969 to 1975 while the cost of living rose by nearly 50 percent. Members have tried to avoid political retaliation by devising automatic mechanisms for pay increases, such as independent commissions to recommend pay levels or presidential responsibility for congressional pay raises. But more often than not these mechanisms failed, since there was no way to prevent Congress from voting on the issue. In early 1989 Speaker Jim WRIGHT's maneuvers to prevent the House from voting to block a recommended pay raise provoked severe public criticism. His attempt failed; it also undercut support for Wright's leadership and contributed to his resignation five months later.

CONGRESSIONAL PAY

Year	Salary
1789–1795	$6 per diem
1795–1796	$6 per diem (House)
	$7 per diem (Senate)
1796–1815	$6 per diem
1815–1817	$1,500 per year
1817–1855	$8 per diem
1855–1865	$3,000 per year
1865–1871	$5,000 per year
1871–1874	$7,500 per year
1874–1907	$5,000 per year
1907–1925	$7,500 per year
1925–1932	$10,000 per year
1932–1933	$9,000 per year
1933–1934	$8,500 per year
February–July 1934	$9,000 per year
July 1934–1935	$9,500 per year
1935–1947	$10,000 per year
1947–1955	$12,500 per year
1955–1965	$22,500 per year
1965–1969	$30,000 per year
1969–1975	$42,500 per year
1975–1977	$44,600 per year
1977–1979	$57,500 per year
1979–1982	$60,662.50 per year[1]
1984	$72,600 per year
1985–1986	$75,100 per year
January 1987	$77,400 per year
February 1987–1990	$89,500 per year
1990	$96,600 per year (House)
1990	$98,400 per year (Senate)
January 1991–1992	$125,100 per year (House)
	$101,900 per year (Senate)
August 1991–1992	$125,100 per year (Senate)
1992	$129,500 per year
1993–1997	$133,600 per year
1998–1999	$136,700 per year
2000	$141,300 per year
2001	$145,100 per year
2002	$150,000 per year
2003	$154,700 per year
2004	$158,100 per year
2005	$162,100 per year
2006	$165,200 per year
2007[2]	$165,200 per year

SOURCE: Congressional Research Service.

NOTES: The top six leaders of Congress—the Speaker of the House, the Senate president pro tempore, and the majority and minority leaders of both chambers—receive additional pay. As of January 2007 the Speaker received $212,100 and the others $183,500.

1. Percentage increases in congressional salaries generally are rounded to the nearest $100. The 1979 increase was not rounded because of specific language in the enacting legislation.

2. Congress voted to forgo a scheduled 1.7 percent pay increase for 2007.

Under the Constitution, Congress sets its own salaries, a built-in conflict of interest that has caused recurrent political headaches. Whenever members specifically vote to raise their salaries, a political storm follows as critics accuse them of lining their pockets; sometimes a member has lost a seat in the next election because of public outcry. As a result, Congress now gets automatic pay increases in line with other government cost-of-living pay hikes unless members specifically vote to forgo a raise, as they did in 2006.

Slightly more successful have been annual cost-of-living increases for members, linked to those for all federal employees. Congress in 1989 set these adjustments a little under the rate of inflation. But the increases could still be challenged by floor votes.

The Twenty-seventh Amendment forbade a pay raise from taking effect until a congressional election had taken place. The amendment was first proposed by James Madison in 1789 as part of the group of amendments that became the Bill of Rights. It was originally ratified by six states, was ratified by a seventh in 1873, and then lay dormant until Wyoming picked it up in 1978. Other states followed, and after the large pay raises of 1989 and 1991, enough states ratified it by 1992 to make it official. Despite lingering questions about whether the early ratifications were still valid, Congress declined to interfere with such a popular proposal. The last time Congress specifically voted to increase pay was in 1989 and 1991, both of which would have come under the Madison amendment. The automatic cost-of-living increases do not.

The terms of debate over congressional pay have not changed much over the years. Supporters of higher pay stress the importance of paying enough to attract talented people to run for Congress. Without adequate pay, only the rich would be able to afford to serve in Congress. Although in comparison with most workers members of Congress seem to be well paid, they argue that they are hard pressed to meet their needs. They must support two residences, one in Washington, D.C.—one of the highest cost-of-living areas in the nation—and one in their home state, on salaries that are often much lower than what they could earn as lawyers or business executives. Often they find themselves being wooed by lobbyists who are paid much more than they are.

Opponents of pay raises traditionally have argued that it is wrong for members to be able to act to raise their own pay. Congressional salaries normally are several times the average wage earner's income and should suffice to attract qualified people. Opponents also contend that members should not be able to protect themselves during times of economic difficulties, while their constituents must struggle with inflation or unemployment.

In 1997 Congress allowed the first pay raise for members in five years. The raise had been blocked every year since fiscal 1993, usually after a member—often one in a tight reelection race—introduced an amendment to the Treasury–Postal Service appropriations bill blocking the cost-of-living increase for that year. Lawmakers in 1998, an election year, again blocked the cost-of-living increase that was to take effect in 1999. In the following years, until 2007, Congress received the scheduled cost-of-living pay hike.

More on this topic:
Financial Disclosure, p. 220
Foreign Travel, p. 234
Franking Privilege, p. 237

Outside Income

Traditionally, service in Congress was a part-time job. Members attended sessions for a few months each year and then returned to their regular jobs, from which they earned most of their income. In modern times, however, Congress has tended to meet for most of the year. The demands of legislation and constituent service make it difficult for members to hold other jobs.

Until 1992, however, many members still received a significant portion of their income from private interests. The principal vehicle for this was the system of honoraria, in which members could keep fees for speeches, writings, or appearances for businesses, labor unions, and trade associations. There were no limits on such payments until 1975, and prominent members sometimes earned more from honoraria than they received as their salaries. The restrictions placed limits on the amount members could keep in total and for any single speech or article. At first the limit per speech or article was $1,000; after 1976 it was raised to $2,000. Members could accept more and give the rest to charity. In 1990 Rep. Dan Rostenkowski, chair of the House Ways and Means Committee, reported that he had received $310,000 in honoraria, of which he had kept the maximum allowed, $26,850.

Common Cause, the self-styled citizens' lobby, and other government watchdog groups argued for years that the payments were little more than the purchase of influence by special interests. Gradually members began to refuse honoraria because of the questions they raised. This was especially the case after Speaker Wright was brought down in 1989 by ethics charges stemming from a book deal that seemed designed to evade honoraria limits. Late that year the House banned honoraria as of 1991. The Senate, which tended to be more supportive of honoraria because its better known members booked more speaking engagements, held on to the system until 1991, when it banned honoraria in return for a 23 percent pay raise that brought it up to the House level.

Over the years Congress has also placed restrictions on members' ability to earn income from outside work. They are limited in how much they can make and from what sources. Book royalties, the cause of Wright's trouble, have been limited to conventional arrangements with established publishers. An attempt was made in 1995 to limit House members' book royalties after Republican Newt GINGRICH of Georgia accepted a $4.5 million book advance just two weeks before he was to be sworn in as Speaker. When critics accused him of cashing in on his office, Gingrich returned the lucrative advance and agreed to accept a $1 advance, plus royalties—15 percent for each hardcover book sold and 10 percent for each paperback and audiocassette sold.

Members have long been prohibited from earning income from professional services such as real estate, insurance, the practice of law or medicine, and service as an officer or board member of an organization. Earnings from other types of outside work can be no more than 15 percent of a member's congressional pay. However, a member may serve without pay as an officer or board member, but these activities must be reported on the individual's financial disclosure form. Some doctors in Congress provide medical care for free such as participating during recesses in programs such as Doctors Without Frontiers.

Congress has never placed restrictions on how much unearned income—such as that from stocks and bonds—members can receive. However, members are required to file annual financial disclosure statements reporting their income from various sources.

Other Benefits

The list of other financial benefits available to members of Congress is a long one. For example, senators and representatives participate in a federal pension program that provides generous benefits, such as automatic increases for inflation, in contrast with private pensions, which are usually fixed.

Members have participated in Social Security since 1984. Before that, members—along with other federal civil service employees—were not eligible for this program. Instead, they were covered by the Civil Service Retirement System (CSRS), which predated Social Security; the two programs were not designed to coordinate with one another. In 1983 legislation was passed requiring all members to pay into Social Security and calling for the creation of a new retirement system for federal employees. The new program, the Federal Employees' Retirement System (FERS), has automatically provided coverage for members elected since 1984, unless they opt out. Members already covered by CSRS could stay there, switch to FERS, or participate in a combined plan.

Members' pensions vest after five years; the amount of pension payment varies based on length of service and is influenced by a combination of employer and payroll contributions. According to the Congressional Research Service, in 2006 retired members receiving a pension under CSRS had an average of twenty years of federal service and received an annuity of $60,972. Members retired under FERS had an average annuity of $35,952 (not including Social Security) in 2006, with an average 16.3 years of service.

Members of Congress receive many other benefits. These include health and life insurance, access to health and recreation facilities, and free parking on Capitol Hill and at Washington, D.C., area airports. Some benefits are of minor importance. For example, senators' offices are "loaned" six potted plants a year; representatives received free plants until 1990 when the House canceled this perquisite.

Another type of congressional benefit is related more closely to members' performance at their jobs. Members receive allowances to pay the salaries of their STAFF and to cover the expenses of offices in Washington and their home districts. They can send postage-free mail to constituents, a practice known as the franking privilege. The government pays for their travel home, and they can engage in foreign travel at government expense.

Although such benefits are intended to help members carry out their duties, they also aid members personally. Most galling to critics is the fact that members can use their staff and travel allowances to build up their political strength at home, thus improving their chances of reelection.

Pay-as-You-Go (PAYGO)

Pay-as-You-Go—or PAYGO, as it is usually called—was designed in the early 1990s, when it was enacted to control congressional actions that had an impact on the federal deficit. PAYGO required that revenue legislation and bills on entitlement or other mandatory programs should not add to the budget deficit, or decrease a surplus. If new legislation required increased spending, those increases had to be offset by expenditure cuts elsewhere or new taxes or other revenue increases. Because its provisions limited the cherished practice of legislators to pass new programs or cut taxes without concern for the impact of the federal deficit, it was never wildly popular, and it was allowed to expire under Republican control of Congress starting in 1995. However, Democrats, on regaining the majority in 2007, reinstituted the requirement.

Pelosi, Nancy

A major event in House history occurred in 2007 when California Democrat Nancy Pelosi (1940–) was elevated to Speaker, becoming the highest-ranking woman ever elected in the U.S. government. As Speaker, Pelosi was second in line for the presidency, after the vice president. Earlier, in 2003, she became the first woman to serve as a party leader in either chamber when she was elected House minority leader at the beginning of the 108th Congress.

Pelosi learned politics from her father, Thomas D'Alesandro Jr., a New Deal–era House member who went on to be Baltimore mayor. In the working-class enclave near downtown called Little Italy, the D'Alesandro rowhouse on Albemarle Street was open to people who needed food, some wood for heat, or a job on the city payroll. With her five brothers, "Little Nancy" took turns at the desk near the door, keeping a "favor file" to be consulted at reelection time. Copies of the daily *Congressional Record* were stacked beneath her bed. Pelosi's mother, Annunciata, balanced caring for the kids with political organizing, a model her daughter would adopt.

Pelosi graduated from Trinity College, an all-female Catholic school in Washington, D.C., and worked briefly in 1963 as a receptionist for Sen. Daniel B. Brewster of Maryland before leaving the job after a few months to marry college sweetheart Paul Pelosi. The couple moved to his native San Francisco, where he became a successful investment banker and she became a stay-at-home mother of five, albeit a wealthy one with live-in help.

Even as a full-time mother, Pelosi was honing political skills. She developed into an impressive Democratic fundraiser by keeping lists, memorizing names and faces, and meticulously hand-writing thank you notes to donors. Her five children served food at political events, stuffed envelopes, and canvassed door-to-door as soon as they could walk. In the 1980s Pelosi rose to chair the California Democratic Party. But she waited until she was forty-seven, and her youngest was in high school, to run for office herself. When San Francisco's main House seat came open with the death of Democrat Sala Burton, Pelosi used her insider's contacts to capture the nomination, which was tantamount to election in one of the nation's most Democratic districts. She won re-election easily after that.

Pelosi's congressional career up the ladder took a key step in 2001 when she was elected party whip over Steny H. Hoyer of Maryland, 118–95. From 2003 to 2007 she served as minority leader, building support among the Democratic troops by giving favors to allies and allowing junior members new opportunities, especially on committees. She was especially interested in broadening the party's structure in the House to open doors for more women, Hispanics, African Americans, and—significantly—party moderates. The latter was noteworthy because of her reputation—encouraged at every turn by Republicans—that she was an old-time liberal. She was, in fact, from the liberal wing of the party—once joining the Progressive Caucus, which she left as she became a party leader—and her home of San Francisco was one of most left-leaning jurisdictions in the nation.

But even though her personal politics matched the reputation, in her leadership activities she more resembled a ward boss, an approach she got from her father, who maintained power as Baltimore mayor with an old-fashioned system of favors and patronage jobs. As the 2006 elections approached, Pelosi worked tirelessly, flying to several cities in a week and ultimately raising $50 million.

Republicans already knew that Pelosi was a tough opponent, in spite of her ready smile and studied graciousness. She possessed a steely determination, demanded discipline from the ranks, and punished those who crossed her. Should a member resist her entreaties on a difficult vote with the common plea, "I'm sorry, but I can't be with you this time," Pelosi's response typically was, "Then we can't be with you." During her triumphant march to deliver a Democratic majority control of the House in 2006, she told the *Los Angeles Times,* "I'm fighting a battle here. I'm not getting my hair done."

Her demands for loyalty sometimes backfired, most notably after the 2006 elections in a contest for majority leader between Hoyer, the minority whip who had earned the respect of many Democrats with his hard work and generous fundraising during the campaign to win the House, and a long-time ally of Pelosi, John P. Murtha of Pennsylvania. She made it clear Murtha was her choice, but Hoyer already had lined up the votes and won easily, 149–86. Pelosi congratulated him and declared, "Let the healing begin."

In 2007 Pelosi moved swiftly to set a House agenda reflecting the new Democratic majority. She launched a "first 100 hours" of legislation that focused on long-held party goals: an increase in the federal minimum wage; a cut in student loan rates to make college more affordable; authority for the government to negotiate directly with pharmaceutical companies for Medicare prescription drug discounts; and implementation of many recommendations from a commission that studied the terrorist attacks of September 11, 2001, a report that Republicans had ignored. Many of the items on the "first 100 hours" agenda quickly passed the House, although far fewer had passed the Senate by the end of the year.

CLOSER LOOK

Nancy Pelosi
Source: AP Images

In 2007 after the Democrats returned to majority in the House, the Speakership went to Nancy Pelosi of California. As Speaker, Pelosi became the highest-ranking woman ever in U.S. government and second in line for the presidency, after the vice president.

More on this topic:

House of Representatives, p. 267

Leadership, p. 325

Majority and Minority Leaders, p. 380

Members of Congress: Characteristics, p. 382

Women in Congress, p. 606

The most notable achievement of her first year, the Fair Minimum Wage Act of 2007 raising the minimum wage, was signed into law by President Bush in May. By the end of 2007, she had received good reviews for her control over the party hierarchy and the powerful committee chairs. Her most daunting challenge continued to be uniting her party, with its diverse views about U.S. involvement in Iraq, into strong Democratic opposition to the president's management of the war there.

Permanent Appropriation, Authorization

A permanent appropriation is one that remains continuously available, without action or renewal by Congress, under a previous enactment. A major example is payment of interest on the public debt. Another covers salaries for members of Congress. Similarly, a permanent authorization is one without a time limit. Usually it does not specify a limit on funds that may be appropriated for an agency, program, or activity that the authorization covers. Instead, decisions on amounts are left to the Appropriations committees and the two houses.

Petition

In May 2006 Ben Smilowitz of the Campaign for America's Future leads students and parents through the Longworth House Office Building to deliver a petition in support of increasing federal college aid.
Source: CQ Photo/Scott J. Ferrell

The First Amendment to the Constitution guarantees the right of the people "to petition the Government for a redress of grievances." This language forms the basis of the modern concept of LOBBYING, in which individuals and groups plead special cases to Congress and seek to influence lawmakers' votes.

Organizations and private citizens' groups from time to time exercise their right to submit a formal petition to one or both houses of Congress to ask for support of particular legislation or favorable consideration of a matter not yet receiving congressional attention. Petitions are referred to committees with legislative jurisdiction over the subject matter.

More broadly, organizations and individuals use less formal techniques such as demonstrations, advertising campaigns, and mass e-mailings to lawmakers' offices to attract attention to a cause and demand action.

Point of Order

If a member of the Senate or House of Representatives believes that the chamber is violating rules governing its conduct of business, he or she may enter an objection. This action, known as raising a point of order, usually stops all parliamentary proceedings, except a recorded vote, until the chair sustains or overrules the member's objection. Before ruling, the chair often allows debate on the point of order, giving both sides the opportunity to explain their position. The chair's rulings are subject to APPEAL and may be overturned by the chamber's membership. This occurs more frequently in the Senate than in the House. Some House bills go to the floor under ground rules that prohibit points of order.

When a member in either chamber raises a point of order that a QUORUM—the minimum number of members required to conduct business—is not present, no further legislative activity can take place until enough absent members have been rounded up.

Policy Committee *See* LEADERSHIP.

Political Action Committees (PACs)

Political action committees (PACs) are organizations that raise and distribute campaign contributions to candidates for Congress and other offices. Their rapid growth during the 1970s and 1980s made them for a time one of the most controversial aspects of the campaign financing system. However, in the late 1990s, they were all but eclipsed by the hot issues of "soft money" contributions and issue advocacy advertising, two types of political spending that ultimately were restricted by a 2002 federal campaign finance law.

Organizations commonly thought of as PACs fall into two main categories: those that are connected to either a labor organization or incorporated entity and those that are not. The first category—the largest—includes the PACs of corporations, labor unions, trade and health associations, and membership organizations. The nonconnected category includes ideological and single-issue groups.

The latter also includes a small but influential group of PACs within Congress called "leadership PACs" or politicians' PACs. These PACs, which are separate from members' campaign committees, are set up by members to raise money for political goals other than reelection to Congress. These goals might include election to a leadership position, appointment to a prestigious committee, support for the party leadership, earning a favor from another member, or backing for a run for the presidency. Money raised by the leadership PACs may be used not only for direct contributions to other candidates but also to cover a variety of expenses, such as polling, direct mail, overhead, and travel by the sponsoring member.

Sometimes the term "political action committee" is used more broadly to refer to other political groups formed to influence elections. Such groups—nicknamed

TOP PAC CONTRIBUTORS TO CONGRESSIONAL CANDIDATES, 2005–2006 ELECTION CYCLE

National Association of Realtors PAC	$3.8 million
National Beer Wholesalers Association PAC	$2.9 million
BUILD-PAC of the National Association of Home Builders	$2.9 million
Dealers Election Action Committee of the National Automotive Dealers Association	$2.8 million
International Brotherhood of Electrical Workers Committee on Political Education	$2.8 million
American Bankers Association PAC (BANKPAC)	$2.6 million
American Association for Justice PAC (AAJ PAC)	$2.6 million
Credit Union Legislative Action Council of CUNA	$2.4 million
Laborers' Political League-Laborers' International Union of North America	$2.3 million
United Parcel Service Inc. PAC	$2.3 million

SOURCE: CQ MoneyLine.
NOTE: Figures have been rounded.

More on this topic:

Campaign Financing, p. 66

"stealth PACs"—were set up under Section 527 of the tax code and initially were not subject to regulation under federal campaign finance law. Legislation requiring that these groups register with the Internal Revenue Service and disclose most of their receipts and expenditures was enacted in 2000.

PAC Contributions

Business PACs for years distributed their contributions relatively evenly between the two political parties. However, in the 1980s business PACs began taking a more pragmatic approach as they shifted more and more of their contributions to the majority party in Congress. Shifts in corporate PAC giving were again seen in the wake of the 1994 and 2006 elections when control of Congress switched parties. Labor PACs, on the other hand, give overwhelmingly to Democrats, whether they are in power or not. Among other types of PACs, recipients vary. The National Rifle Association's PAC, for example, gives more to the Republicans, while EMILY's (an acronym for Early Money Is Like Yeast) List, an abortion-rights PAC, contributes exclusively to Democratic women candidates.

Corporate PACs gave more than $123 million to congressional candidates in the 2006 campaign, of which about 66 percent went to Republicans. Association PACs gave nearly $96 million, with about 62 percent going to Republican candidates. Labor PACs gave more than $54 million, with 88 percent going to Democrats. Ideological PACs gave more than $67 million, with almost 62 percent going to Republicans.

Under federal law most PACs are permitted to contribute $5,000 per candidate, per election. (Primary, general, runoff, and special elections are considered to be separate elections, each with a $5,000 limit for qualified PACs.) There is no limit on the total amount they can give to all candidates. The National Association of Realtors PAC, for example, gave $3.8 million to federal candidates in the 2005–2006 election cycle. (See table, p. 417.)

PACs also can spend as much as they want independently to help candidates—for example, with heavy television advertising—as long as they do not coordinate their actions with the candidates' campaigns. But many candidates do not appreciate outside interference—well intentioned or not—in their campaigns. PACs devoted about $37 million to independent expenditures in the 2006 congressional elections—$22 million for congressional candidates and almost $15 million against. This marked an increase over previous election cycles, but it was still a small part of overall PAC giving.

Although PACs date back to the 1940s, their significance in political campaigns began with the passage in 1971 and 1974 of laws to reform campaign financing. These laws, along with later Federal Election Commission and Supreme Court rulings and a general waning of political party influence at the time, allowed PACs to become a major factor in the financing of congressional elections. In 1974 only about 600 PACs were registered, and they gave about $12.5 million to congressional candidates. By mid-2007 registered PACs numbered more than 4,000, and PACs gave nearly $349 million to congressional candidates in the 2005–2006 election cycle.

Over the years PACs have provided a significant share of congressional candidates' funds. In the 2006 election cycle, almost one-fourth of their receipts came from PACs. PAC contributions are particularly important in House races—nearly a third of House candidates' funds in 2006 came from PACs. Senate candidates usually are less reliant on PACs—about 12 percent of receipts in 2006 came from PACs.

With the exception of the leadership PACs of candidates, PACs have little involvement in presidential elections. They provide only a small share of funds needed by candidates seeking their party's presidential nomination, and they are barred from contributing to publicly financed general election campaigns.

Critics and Defenders

Many people are sharply critical of the role played by PACs, arguing that they allow well-financed interest groups to gain too much political influence. By accepting contributions from PACs, critics say, members of Congress become dependent on them. That may make the members reluctant to vote against the interests of the PAC, either from fear of losing the PAC's contributions or from fear of having the PAC help finance their political opponents. PACs also have been criticized for increasing their clout by "bundling" together checks from individual contributors and other PACs and then passing them on to candidates. EMILY's List has perfected the practice of bundling.

Critics also have argued that PACs have a bias toward incumbents that reduces competition in elections. Campaign contribution statistics show that PACs have a strong preference for incumbent legislators who are running for reelection, regardless of party affiliation. PACs give most often to incumbents because they are in a position to support PAC interests when legislation is drafted as well as when it comes to a vote. This is particularly true for committee chairs and party leaders, who have more power than other members to see that legislation is approved. Many of these leaders also have leadership PACs and solicit for party accounts as well. Challengers represent a gamble for PACs because only a few defeat incumbents in any election. By contributing to a challenger, PACs risk alienating a successful incumbent. Of the almost $349 million that 2006 congressional candidates reported receiving from PACs during the campaign, nearly $280 million went to incumbents, about $34 million to challengers, and $32 million to candidates for open seats. But the argument that PACs perpetuate a "permanent" Congress with little turnover lost much of its force when Congress changed hands after the 1994 elections and again after the 2006 elections.

Defenders of PACs argue that the groups provide a legitimate means by which citizens can join together to support candidates. PACs encourage people to participate in politics, they say, and offer the most efficient method for channeling campaign contributions. PACs say they are seeking not to buy votes but to gain access to members of Congress, so that their views will be heard on legislative decisions affecting them.

Proposals to curb the influence of PACs have been debated by Congress. Some called for banning PAC contributions altogether, some would have reduced the amount a PAC could contribute to a candidate, and others would have imposed an overall limit on the amount of PAC money a candidate could accept. Some members of the House called for weakening PACs by providing public funds for congressional campaigns, as the federal government has done for presidential campaigns since 1976. But no such proposal has become law. Legislation that included public financing and limits on PACs was vetoed by President George H. W. Bush in 1992 and effectively delayed to death in the next Congress. Efforts in the next several Congresses never reached the president's desk.

By the late 1990s the PAC issue had been taken off the table, overshadowed by growing controversy over campaign money that fell outside the reach of federal campaign finance law. PAC contributions—limited by law and well-disclosed—paled in significance when compared to the unrestricted flow of soft money ostensibly for nonfederal political party activities and the rapid growth of "issue" advertising that critics said were thinly veiled campaign ads supporting or opposing specific candidates. PAC-related provisions were not included in the campaign finance legislation enacted in 2002 that restricted both soft money and issue ads.

Congress did clear an ethics and lobbying bill in 2007 that included a provision to shine light on the bundling activities of lobbyists. Congressional and presidential candidates were required to report when donations bundled by a lobbyist totaled $15,000 during a six-month period.

Political Parties

Political parties are vital elements in the life and work of Congress and its members. Although not specifically mentioned in the Constitution, political parties have been important in Congress almost since its creation. An important function of parties is to help select and then elect candidates for Congress, through the electoral process, and to organize and distribute power within the institution. The party that holds a majority of seats in each chamber normally controls all key positions of authority.

In the broadest sense, a political party is a coalition of people who join together to try to win governmental power by winning elections. They are organizations seeking to gain control of government to further their social, economic, or ideological goals. Members of a party supposedly share a loosely defined set of common beliefs, although members of the same party often hold different opinions and outlooks. Citizens rely on political parties to define issues, to support or oppose candidates on the basis of those issues, and to carry out the agreed-upon policies when the party is in power.

There have been only two major political parties in Congress, the Democratic and the Republican, since the mid-nineteenth century. Almost all members of Congress have belonged to one of these two coalitions. But it has not always been that way. In the nineteenth century several different parties were significant in Congress. Only after the Civil War did the Democrats and Republicans begin to share complete control of Congress between them. Even since then, however, members of other parties—the Progressive Party in the early 1900s, for example—occasionally have been elected. Sometimes a member declines to join either major party and is called an independent.

The Democrats and Republicans have been dominant at different times during the history of Congress. For much of the period between the Civil War and the Great Depression of the 1930s, Republicans held majorities in both the House of Representatives and the Senate. From 1932 through 1994, Democrats usually controlled both chambers. They were particularly strong in the House, where for decades they held a majority solid enough to withstand periodic Republican gains that resulted from that party's frequent and often landslide presidential victories. Control of Congress remained closely divided as the twenty-first century began, with the GOP appearing to have a slight advantage as the nation's political trends moved in a conservative direction and redistricting generally benefited Republicans. However, in the 2006 elections Democrats made a stunning comeback by winning a solid majority in the House and squeaking out a one-vote majority in the Senate. In the House, in particular, Democrats picked up a number of seats that normally would have gone to the GOP, including districts that voted heavily for Republican president George W. Bush in 2000 and 2004. Whether Democrats could hold those gains was expected to be a crucial test of which party would be in control in 2008 and the near-term years to follow. Most analysts agreed that the Democratic surge in 2006 was rooted in national dissatisfaction over the continuing war in Iraq that Bush launched in 2003.

CLOSER LOOK

Political parties are not mentioned in the Constitution, but they play a vital role in Congress. In the broadest sense, a political party is a coalition of people who join together to try to win governmental power by winning elections. Once in power they seek to further their social, economic, or ideological goals. Party influence in Congress has waxed and waned, but since the mid-1990s it has been vital to advancing—or thwarting—the objectives of Republicans or Democratic majorities.

More on this topic:

Campaign Financing, p. 66

Caucuses, Party, p. 85

Caucuses, Special, p. 88

Leadership, p. 325

Legislative Process, p. 344

Political Action Committees, p. 417

President Pro Tempore, p. 435

Reform, Congressional, p. 470

Seniority System, p. 505

Speaker of the House, p. 516

Congressional Elections

Party affiliation is often a crucial factor in whether a candidate wins or loses a political race. Normally, a Democrat running in a traditionally Democratic area will more than likely win, just as a Republican has the advantage in a predominantly Republican region.

Political parties provide a mechanism for choosing and supporting congressional candidates. Without the parties, a congressional election could be a confusing process in which many individual candidates sought votes with the aid of their friends and personal connections alone. Through primary elections held by the parties, the choice is narrowed to two candidates instead of a multi-candidate free-for-all.

Primaries were introduced early in the twentieth century to reduce the power of corrupt "party bosses" by giving the choice of the party nominee to party members as a whole. Primaries have had the unintended effect of weakening the parties. Because party leaders no longer control who runs for office on the party ticket, congressional candidates can bypass the established party leadership in their area and appeal directly to voters in primary races. They can generate their own support instead of being recruited and groomed by party leaders. The increasing importance of interest groups and abundance of campaign financing sources, plus the emergence of new avenues of reaching voters such as Internet sites and blogs, have made it easier for candidates to campaign independently of the party structure.

During the general election campaigns, parties do provide important campaign assistance and services to their candidates. In addition to traditional campaigning by local party regulars, both parties in the House and Senate have campaign committees. The committees help party candidates in a variety of ways, the most important being financial assistance. The Republicans were first to develop their campaign committees into sophisticated, high-tech operations, but Democrats showed they were rapidly catching up when they successfully orchestrated campaigns to recapture the House and Senate in 2006.

Direct campaign contributions by the parties to congressional campaigns are small when compared to the

Descending the steps of the U.S. Capitol to a rally celebrating the Democratic takeover of the Senate after the 2006 congressional elections (left to right) are Sens. Charles E. Schumer of New York, Harry Reid of Nevada, and Richard J. Durbin of Illinois. Schumer led the Democratic Senatorial Campaign Committee that supported party candidates running for the Senate that year.
Source: CQ Photo/Scott J. Ferrell

money that pours in from individuals and the political action committees of labor, business, and interest groups. But parties provide valuable assistance through spending that is coordinated with the campaigns on such essentials as polls, fundraising, and advertising. The party committees' ability to make independent expenditures for or against candidates has given them significant clout, especially in targeting money to competitive races late in a campaign. After years of playing a diminishing role in congressional campaigns, the political parties are proving how vital their role is in winning seats in Congress.

For a time, especially from the 1996 election through the 2002 election, the parties dramatically increased their clout by taking in large amounts of so-called soft money contributions and using that money to finance issue ad campaigns. Soft money was the term used to describe money raised and spent outside the limits and prohibitions of federal campaign finance law. Parties were allowed to accept unlimited amounts of soft money for "party-building" activities and generic party costs supposedly unrelated to federal candidates. Ads paid for with soft money also fell outside federal regulation because ostensibly they did not expressly advocate the election or defeat of a particular candidate, a contention sharply disputed by critics. A new campaign finance law was enacted in 2002 barring the national party committees and federal candidates from raising or using soft money and barring others from using it for issue ads in the weeks before an election. In an attempt to mollify the parties, Congress raised the limit on contributions to the political parties. The law was immediately challenged in the courts. A lower federal court found parts of the law to be unconstitutional in a May 2003 ruling. Its decision was then appealed to the Supreme Court.

In a 5–4 decision in *McConnell v. Federal Election Commission,* the Supreme Court in 2003 upheld the major provisions of the 2002 law, including its ban on soft money and its restrictions on issue advertising. The Court, however, struck down other provisions. In that decision the Court ruled that the issue ad provision was not on its face overbroad and unconstitutional, but in another case that soon followed the provision was challenged as it applied to a specific set of ads a Wisconsin nonprofit corporation had wanted to run before the 2004 election. In 2007 the Court—with two new justices on the bench—ruled 5–4 in *Federal Election Commission v. Wisconsin Right to Life, Inc.,* that three of the issue ads constituted "grassroots lobbying advertisements" and therefore the law's restrictions as applied to those ads were unconstitutional.

Organizing Congress

Parties play an important role in the internal organization of Congress. Without structures for bringing together like-minded members for common action, Congress might find itself in constant chaos, as 100 senators and 435 representatives each fought solely for his or her individual agenda. Instead, the parties help to create a system in which leaders and followers can work together in pursuit of policy goals.

Leadership positions are allocated according to party. The party that holds a majority in each chamber has the votes to select leaders, such as the Speaker of the House and the president pro tempore and the majority leader in the Senate. All committee and subcommittee chairs are members of the majority party.

Senators and representatives who are affiliated with a political party, as most are, belong to party caucuses or conferences. The caucus as a whole votes on party and committee leaders and committee assignments. Caucuses provide forums for debating substantive legislative issues. They can have a major impact on the procedures of their chambers as well. This was the case in the 1970s when the House Democratic Caucus led the way on reforms that dramatically loosened the hold of the seniority system, which had awarded positions of authority on the basis of length of service. Having given itself the power to elect committee chairs, the House Democratic Caucus used that power several times to oust chairs who were thought to be out of step with the party mainstream.

Committees within the party caucuses advise on policy, make committee assignments, and provide campaign support for their party's candidates. Hopes that the policy committees would evolve into effective policy-making bodies have not been realized. Powerful committee chairs were unwilling to give up the control they had over their policy areas, and the diversity within each party made it hard to achieve policy consensus.

Majority party committees set their chamber's legislative schedule. In the House this is done in conjunction with the Rules Committee. In the Senate the majority party committee sets the schedule in consultation with the minority party leaders and any other member who wants a say as to when a bill comes to the floor.

Party Unity

Once members are united under their party banners, do they stay together? Sometimes—but not consistently and definitely not easily. Their cohesion depends in important measure on the political calculus of the day, particularly which party controls the White House and Congress.

In the early part of the twentieth century, parties often exercised significant control over all aspects of Congress, but this is no longer always the rule. The parties of the modern Congress cannot arbitrarily dictate party policy and expect their members to fall into line. Now party leaders must work to persuade members to support party positions and to put together coalitions on specific issues.

This is no easy task. Members who have an electoral base independent of their party do not automatically support party positions or obey party leaders. They know that their constituents, not the party, gave them their seat in Congress and that those same constituents can take it away in the next election. Outside interest groups also compete with the parties for members' attention and support on votes.

The distribution of power within Congress further complicates attempts at party unity. Powerful committees and their chairs are always on the lookout for any encroachment on their turf by rival power centers, including their parties. The reforms of the 1970s decentralized Congress, and as a result leaders have to build a consensus within a much broader constituency. The party is further fragmented when members join subgroups representing parochial interests or philosophical factions within their parties.

Yet, with all this working against them, parties still display considerable unity when congressional votes are tabulated. In fact, party affiliation appears to be the most important factor in members' voting decisions. In an annual study of party votes that began in the 1950s, Congressional Quarterly has identified the votes on which a majority of Republicans opposed a majority of Democrats and calculates the percentage of times members voted with their party. Throughout the 1990s, the level of partisanship in Congress was high compared to earlier decades. In 1995 it reached record levels. The partisanship has ebbed a bit since then, although in late 1998 when the House was considering articles of impeachment against President Bill Clinton, all but five of the 228 Republicans voted in favor of Article I (which accused the president of perjury before a grand jury), while all but five of 206 Democrats voted against the article. (See CLINTON IMPEACHMENT TRIAL.) In 2002 some of the most partisan congressional battles never made it to a floor vote, making the House and Senate appear, statistically speaking, much more bipartisan than they really were. In the two Congresses that followed, still under Republican control, party unity voting remained high.

Members vote with their party for several reasons. For one thing, many of them come from more or less similar districts and share certain goals. In addition, it is much easier for them to vote with their party than to oppose it. Leaders may have a weak hold over party members, but they still have tools to reward or punish party members. Incentives for members to support party positions include desirable committee assignments, campaign assistance, and help with members' bills or amendments and—especially—local projects and appropriations to impress constituents come reelection time. Leaders are also assisted by whip organizations, which gather intelligence, conduct polls, and count and cajole votes.

Party unity has also been enhanced by changes in the parties themselves. Party mavericks are far fewer than they once were. Many conservative southern Democrats have been replaced by Republicans, or in some cases moderate Democrats, and many liberal northern Republicans have been replaced by Democrats. In the 2006 election only a single House Republican in the northeast was reelected while Democrats picked up eleven seats. A region that was once reliably Republican now was a Democratic stronghold. The CONSERVATIVE COALITION, a voting bloc of Republicans and southern Democrats that held a place in American politics for half a century, declined as the twentieth century ended and became extinct thereafter because a key part of the coalition—the conservative Democrats—had all but left Congress.

Even before the Clinton administration (1993 to 2001), partisanship was building on Capitol Hill during the administrations of Ronald Reagan (1981–1989) and George H. W. Bush (1989–1993). Republicans rallied behind Republican White House proposals, and Democrats, rallied against them. The situation was reversed when Democrat Clinton was in the White House and partisanship was especially heightened after the Republican takeover of Congress in 1995. Bush's son, George W. Bush, began his presidency in 2001 with Republicans in control of Congress, but midway through his first year in the White House, Democrats resumed control of the closely divided Senate, thanks to the defection of one GOP senator. The razor-thin split in the Senate increased the pressures to conform to party wishes. When the GOP won control of both houses in the 2002 election, many of the GOP-favored initiatives flowing from the White House were warmly endorsed by congressional Republicans and generally denounced by Democrats.

This latter factor—the political givens of any particular period—is crucial in understanding party unity and the ability, or inability, of party leaders to keep their troops in line in spite of the many factors allowing members a measure of independence. In 1995 Republicans regained House control under the leadership of Newt Gingrich of Georgia. That alone gave the leadership the stature to demand loyalty, which was reinforced by GOP opposition to the Clinton-led White House. In 2001, briefly and then again after the 2002 elections, Republicans were in firm control of both the presidency and the White House. This gave the GOP, and the great majority of its members, the incentive to stick together to enact a Republican program that had been thwarted for decades by divided government in Washington. The incentive was further strengthened by the increasing homogeneity of the Republican Party, which was by then dominated by conservatives with few moderates and even fewer liberals. These factors made it easier, predominately in the House, for a highly disciplined leadership to insist on party loyalty on key issues and votes. Its most visible enforcer was Rep. Tom DeLay of Texas, known as "the Hammer" for his arm-twisting abili-

On January 4, 1995, during the opening session of the 104th Congress, House Minority Leader Richard A. Gephardt, D-Mo., hands the gavel to House Speaker Newt Gingrich, R-Ga. Gephardt had been majority leader the previous year, while the incoming majority Republicans had elected Gingrich Speaker.
Source: AP Images/Joe Marquette

ties. A similar situation emerged in 2007 when House Democrats were back in the majority under a disciplined Speaker, Nancy Pelosi of California, who was working actively to keep the often-fractious Democratic caucus on message in opposition to the Bush White House and in support of a legislative program she and her lieutenants hoped would be well received by voters in the next election.

The House is by tradition a more partisan body than the Senate. House rules are designed to let the majority party get things done, and the wishes of the minority party may well be ignored in that large, impersonal chamber. In contrast, the Senate emphasizes individualism and accommodation with the minority party. The bitter partisan battles that are frequently seen in the House are less common in the Senate, although during George W. Bush's years there were more instances of it, particularly controversies over contentious social issues and the naming of federal judges.

Development of the Party System

The framers of the Constitution never envisioned the importance that political parties would develop in Congress and the nation. The framers had little understanding of the functions of political parties; they were ambivalent, if not hostile, to the new party system as it developed in the early years of the republic. "If I could not go to heaven but with a party, I would not go there at all," said Thomas Jefferson in 1789.

The Constitution did not mention parties, either to authorize them or prohibit them. It made possible a permanent role for parties, however, by giving citizens civil liberties and the right to organize. At the same time it erected safeguards against partisan excesses by creating a system of checks and balances within the government.

Parties emerged soon after the adoption of the Constitution. Those who favored the strong central government embodied in the Constitution came to be called Federalists. Led by Treasury Secretary Alexander Hamilton, they were drawn mostly from merchants and bankers of the Northeast, who favored strong government action to prevent money from losing its value through inflation. They were opposed by a group that later became known as the Democratic-Republicans. Led by Jefferson and James Madison, the Democratic-Republicans were largely southern and western farmers, who opposed a strong central government and sought government policies to make it easier to borrow money.

Party lines were fluid in the early Congresses, with members drifting between one loose coalition and the other. By the mid-1790s, however, the factions had hardened enough for one senator to observe that "the existence of two parties in Congress is apparent." Federalists generally held the upper hand in these early years, controlling the Senate and contending equally for power with the Democratic-Republicans in the House. By 1800 Jefferson's supporters had become a majority. Their control of Congress continued to tighten in the ensuing years. The 1816 elections signaled the effective end of the Federalist Party, whose representation in Congress dropped off to a small minority.

Along with the dominance of the Democratic-Republicans, the first twenty years of the nineteenth century saw growth in the power of the party caucus over Congress's operations. Important decisions were made in private meetings of the Democratic-Republicans, and members were pressed to follow the party's position. The power of the party caucus was increased by its role as presidential nominating committee. Party members

---

CLOSER LOOK

Party Name Confusion

The nomenclature used to define political parties in the early years of the nation has perplexed students ever since because of the reuse of a few common labels. The Democratic-Republican Party developed in the early 1790s as the group opposed to the Federalists and as successor to the Anti-Federalists, a loose coalition of individuals opposed to ratification of the Constitution. This new party, led by Thomas Jefferson, also called themselves Republicans, which became the name used in most areas, but others referred to the group as Jeffersonian Republicans, Jeffersonian Democrats, and National Republicans. Historians tend to use Democratic-Republicans to distinguish the Jeffersonians from the modern Republican Party, which emerged in 1854.

The Jeffersonian party that dominated in the first two decades of the nineteenth century unraveled by the end of the 1820s, with many of its members moving to form what became known as the Whig Party that lasted until it too dissolved by the time of the Civil War. Nevertheless, the Democratic-Republican Party is seen as the forerunner of the modern-day Democratic Party, which became a recognizable entity with the election of Andrew Jackson as president in 1828, defeating incumbent John Quincy Adams, the son of Federalist president John Adams. Jackson is seen as the first president to represent the "Democratic Party," which has maintained that name ever since.

> *"If I could not go to heaven but with a party, I would not go there at all."*
>
> —*Thomas Jefferson*

in the House and Senate had the authority to name the Democratic-Republican presidential candidate, who at that time was virtually assured of being elected. Caucus nominations continued through 1824.

The size and power of the Democratic-Republican Party soon led to the development of internal factions, as different regional groups struggled for influence within the only national political organization. By the mid-1820s two groups had emerged: the National Republicans and the Democrats. The National Republicans favored internal economic development projects and a protective tariff against foreign goods. The Democrats, who represented agrarian interests from the South and West, held that the common people, not the rich, should have the dominant voice in government. The Democrats captured control of Congress in 1826.

The Democrats, who took over the White House in 1828 with the election of Andrew Jackson, remained the dominant party in Congress for the next three decades. The National Republicans, who soon took the name of Whigs, twice won the presidency and always held many seats in Congress. But the Whigs were able to capture a majority of either body on only a few occasions.

The Whigs faded rapidly during the 1850s and ceased to exist in 1856. In their place arose the Republican Party of today, which was initially composed of Democrats and Whigs who opposed the extension of slavery. The Republicans won control of the House in 1854, lost it in 1856, and then regained it in 1858. They were not able to muster a majority in the Senate until 1860, on the eve of the Civil War. The young party held a solid majority throughout the war. The Democratic presence in Congress was sharply reduced after its many members from the South quit to join the Confederacy.

Party Dominance

The Republican Party controlled Congress and the presidency for most of the next seventy years. Democrats sometimes were able to win a majority of House seats, and on occasion they won a Senate majority. But the Republicans, who soon gained the nickname of "Grand Old Party" (GOP), dominated the era. They were backed by eastern business interests and favored high tariffs and tight controls of the amount of money in the economy. The Democrats were the party of the South and of disaffected agricultural interests from the West. They generally sought low tariffs and liberal credit.

The role of the parties became much more important during this period. While the Congress of the pre–Civil War period tended to be dominated by brilliant individuals, the postwar Senate and House were the arenas of powerful party leaders. This trend was particularly apparent in the Senate, where many of the members were party bosses who had gained power through political organizations in their states. These men placed a high value on party loyalty and the need for party discipline. They were often ready to compromise their ideals to maintain harmony within the party.

The first attempt at developing a strong party structure came in the 1870s, when New York Republican Roscoe CONKLING organized a faction that controlled the Senate on procedural matters. Conkling's group had little effect on legislation, however, and the Senate returned to individualistic ways after Conkling left.

The true birth of modern party discipline came in the 1890s. Republican senators William B. ALLISON of Iowa and Nelson W. ALDRICH of Rhode Island organized an informal group of senators, who at first met only for poker and relaxation. After Allison was elected chair of the Republican Caucus in 1897, the group assumed control of the Senate. Allison used his office to consolidate his control of his party, and the party's control of the Senate. "Both in the committees and in the offices, we should use the machinery for our own benefit and not let other men have it," Allison said.

The Republican elephant made its first appearance in a Thomas Nast illustration for Harper's Weekly *on November 7, 1874.*
Source: Library of Congress

Allison controlled the Steering Committee, which directed floor proceedings, and the Committee on Committees, which made committee assignments. Although chairmanship of committees was determined solely by seniority, Allison had great leeway to assign committee positions to members who would follow his wishes. Access to positions of influence soon depended on the favor and support of the party leaders.

Republicans used the caucus to work out party positions in private and then to speak with a unified voice on the Senate floor. Although they were not bound to obey the party position, members who ignored it risked losing most of their power in the Senate. The Democrats soon followed the Republicans by organizing their own internal power structure. In the House, majority party control was consolidated under two powerful Republican Speakers: Thomas Brackett REED and Joseph G. CANNON.

By the end of the nineteenth century, the two major political parties had assumed a decisive role in the legislative process. The parties named the committees that initially considered legislation and determined what bills would be brought to the floor. Party members worked out their differences in caucus meetings, then went forth in disciplined ranks to ratify caucus decisions on the floor.

The system of strict party control was not popular among many people outside of Congress, who saw it as violating the principles of representative democracy. Some members of Congress also criticized the system, including the Liberal Republicans of the 1870s and the "Mugwump"

CLOSER LOOK

The true birth of modern party discipline came in the 1890s when Republican senators William B. Allison of Iowa and Nelson W. Aldrich of Rhode Island organized an informal group of senators, who at first met only for poker and relaxation. After Allison was elected chair of the Republican Caucus in 1897 he used his office to consolidate his control of his party, and the party's control of the Senate. "Both in the committees and in the offices, we should use the machinery for our own benefit and not let other men have it," Allison said.

antileadership Republicans of the 1880s. Representatives of third parties also attacked the system.

The most important third party was the Populist Party, an agrarian reform movement based in the Midwest. The Populists won three Senate seats and eleven House seats in 1892. They reached their peak in the crucial election of 1896, when they and their allies won seven Senate seats and thirty House seats. Much of their program, which stressed loosening of controls on the amount of money circulating in the economy, was adopted by the Democrats, and the Populists soon faded from the scene.

The cause of reform was soon picked up by the progressives. This movement sought both economic changes, such as antitrust legislation and introduction of the income tax, and political measures aimed at opening up the system to public pressure, such as direct election of senators and laws against corrupt election practices. The progressives included reformist Republicans and members of the separate Progressive Party. The Bull Moose–Progressives, as they were called in honor of their leader, former president Theodore Roosevelt, elected seventeen House members in 1912. The progressives played a key role in the congressional reform movement of the early 1900s, working to reduce the autocratic power of House Speaker Cannon and pushing through the Senate curbs on the filibuster and a proposal for direct election.

The system of party control of Congress that had grown up in the last decades of the nineteenth century developed into a formal institution in the first two decades of the twentieth century. In 1911 Senate Democrats elected a single member to serve both as chair of the party caucus and as floor leader (although the title of floor leader apparently was not used until 1920). Republicans soon followed suit, and by 1915 the majority and minority leaders were the acknowledged spokespersons for their parties in the Senate. In the House the revolt against the power of the Speaker led to a great increase in the power of the party caucuses. The Democrats, who controlled the House from 1911 to 1919, worked out most legislative decisions within the "King Caucus." Members were obliged to vote for the party position if endorsed by a two-thirds majority. The dominant force in the chamber was Democratic majority leader (and Ways and Means Committee chair) Oscar W. UNDERWOOD of Alabama, who had far more power than Speaker James B. "Champ" CLARK of Missouri.

Republicans regained control of both houses of Congress in 1918, and they maintained their power until the early years of the Great Depression a decade later. However, the party was torn by deep divisions between regular forces and the progressives, who often cooperated with the Democrats in pushing legislation favorable to the economic interests of western farmers. Progressive Republicans who tried to challenge their party leadership were quickly punished by the loss of seats on important committees.

More on this topic:

Direct Election of Senators, p. 154

Filibuster, p. 213

Progressive Era, p. 443

Democratic Dominance

The Republicans lost their exclusive control of Congress in 1930, when Democrats gained a narrow majority in the House. That election foreshadowed the avalanche that was to follow. The 1932 elections were a watershed in the history of partisan divisions in Congress. Led by presidential candidate Franklin D. Roosevelt, who promised relief from the economic disaster that had befallen the nation, the Democrats gained commanding majorities in both House and Senate. By the 1936 elections the Republicans had been reduced to a small minority.

The Democrats remained in control of Congress for most of the next six decades. Between the 1930s and the early 1990s, they lost their House majority only twice, in the 1946 and 1952 elections. Senate Republicans had brief interludes in power as a result of the same elections, as well as a more significant period of ascendancy in the 1980s. The Republicans controlled the Senate during the first six years of President Reagan's administration (1981–1987). However, Democrats regained a sizable majority in the 1986 elections.

Remarkably, the Democrats long remained the majority party in Congress even when popular sentiment was shifting to the Republicans, as shown by decisive Republican presidential victories. Several reasons have been cited for the Democrats' long-term dominance of Congress. Among them was the fact that, quite simply, the electorate favored Democratic candidates over Republicans by a small but consistent margin in congressional races. Once in office, members of Congress had the advantage over challengers. Aside from missteps by an incumbent or major scandals that spawn anti-incumbent sentiment, it has been difficult to defeat a sitting member of Congress. Incumbents work hard to stay in office. They campaign constantly, assist and communicate regularly with their constituents, have access to media coverage, and attract campaign money.

"A LIVE JACKASS KICKING A DEAD LION."

And such a Lion! and such a Jackass!

Thomas Nast's illustration for **Harper's Weekly** *on January 15, 1870, helped to popularize the donkey as a symbol for the Democratic Party.*
Source: Library of Congress

Republicans Gain, Then Lose, the Majority

Still, the Democrats' long-running congressional majority was not a permanent one. In the 1994 midterm elections, they lost both chambers. New district lines drawn at the beginning of the decade tended to help the Republicans. So did missteps by the Clinton administration, climaxed by the failure of an ambitious health care plan the president proposed in 1993. The Republicans were boosted as well by a basic perception of arrogance that surrounded the Democratic Congress, highlighted by the House banking scandal in 1991. It all added up to a powerful mood for change that swept the Republicans into power on Capitol Hill. (See SCANDALS, CONGRESSIONAL.)

Pointing to the "Contract with America" on which many of their candidates had campaigned, Republicans claimed a mandate. But their honeymoon did not last long. A series of Republican missteps, culminating in two partial shutdowns of the federal government, helped President Clinton regain the upper hand and go on to win a second term. At the start of the 106th Congress (1999–2001) the Republican Party maintained control of both houses. However, the party's trouble in consolidating its majorities in Congress was exemplified by its surprising loss of five House seats in the 1998 midterm elections.

The 2000 elections resulted in a narrow GOP majority in the House and an evenly divided Senate. With Republican vice president Richard B. CHENEY in the presiding chair of the Senate, as provided in the Constitution, the GOP was positioned to break tie votes in its favor. This did not occur often but became moot in June 2001 when Republican senator James M. Jeffords of Vermont left his party to become an Independent, giving the Democrats power to organize the Senate and committees and take control of the agenda. Democratic control lasted only until the end of the Congress. In the 2002 elections the Republicans won back control of the Senate with a majority, albeit narrow, that did not rely on a vice-presidential vote.

Republicans retained the majority in both chambers for the next two Congresses, 2003 through 2006, allowing them to enact much of the long-stalled legislative program of the GOP. But in 2006 the pendulum swung back as the nation—weary of the ongoing Iraq war and repelled by a series of scandals involving Republicans—voted heavily for Democrats. In the House, the Democrats gained a net of thirty seats and a solid majority. In the Senate they gained six seats, just enough to give them a one-vote majority. Thus in 2007 Washington returned to the divided government it had known for much of the half-century after World War II.

The congressional parties showed remarkable discipline in the latter years of this long period, far more than in the earlier decades. But members still enjoyed vastly wider latitude than their forbearers a century earlier, which required party leaders to work diligently to keep members in line and to form winning coalitions.

Pork-Barrel Politics

Since the earliest days of Congress, local concerns have played an important role in decision making on Capitol Hill. Legislators from farm states agitate for price supports, while those from the arid West press for water reclamation projects. The drafting of trade and tax laws is complicated by the efforts of lawmakers to attach provisions that will benefit industries and businesses in their districts or states. When federal funds go to a particular local project or entity, and when the decision is based primarily on political clout rather than on an objective assessment of need, pork-barrel politics is at work.

Using a giant pig to symbolize pork-barrel spending in Congress, protesters from Americans for Prosperity, an economic policy organization, urge taxpayer scrutiny of lawmakers' pet projects at a news conference.
Source: AP Images/*Wausau Daily Herald*, Rob Orcutt

The term *pork-barrel* has been traced to the pre–Civil War practice of distributing salt pork to hungry slaves, who were said to clamber over one another in a mad rush to grab as much as they could from a barrel of pork. Whatever its exact origin, the phrase was applied to congressional practices early in the twentieth century, and it stuck—so has the practice. Few legislators can resist taking credit for a new park, post office, dam, or sewage treatment plant in their district. Since much of their work in Congress involves broad national issues, senators and representatives are eager to accomplish something concrete for their constituents. In securing the construction of a dam or a defense contract for a local company, a lawmaker contributes directly to the livelihood of his or her constituents—and earns their gratitude. The member with a reputation for "bringing home the bacon" is hard to beat.

In addition to allowing members to boost their image with constituents, pork-barrel politics helps committee chairs and other influential members to enhance their power within Congress. For example, Rep. Jim WRIGHT of Texas for many years used his position on the Public Works

Committee to help congressional colleagues obtain federal projects for their districts. The favors were returned in 1976, when Wright was elected Democratic majority leader.

Traditionally, "pork" has been identified with public works projects, such as roads, bridges, dams, and harbors. But contemporary lawmakers seek many other benefits for their constituents, including university research grants, corporate tax breaks, and environmental cleanup projects. APPROPRIATIONS BILLS have long been a favorite vehicle for pork-barrel projects. A member who gets a project included in an appropriations bill is bound to support the whole bill. As efforts to trim federal spending intensified during the 1980s and into the 1990s, less money was available for traditional pork-barrel spending. The list of projects became shorter, and the fight to get an item included grew more intense. Members who lacked influence within Congress often found their requests ignored. "Those with the clout use the clout to get what they want, and merit selection never enters into the thinking," complained Republican representative Robert S. Walker of Pennsylvania in 1987.

By then, members of the Appropriations committees, once able to accommodate favored colleagues, had little left to share after the needs of top legislators were met. Appropriations legislation, which once passed with ease, became the focus of intense legislative disputes. In 1992 George E. Brown Jr. of California, chair of the House Science, Space, and Technology Committee for the 103rd Congress, won an unusual victory on the House floor when he moved to cut $95 million from an energy and water appropriations bill. The funds, earmarked for university building projects, had been added to the final version of the bill during the House-Senate conference and benefited the home states of some of the conferees. Brown argued that the funds should be authorized only after a competitive selection process. After the House voted to delete the funds, supporters of the projects had them added to a defense appropriations bill despite Brown's objections. "We always try to help as many members as we can," said John P. Murtha of Pennsylvania, then chair of the House Appropriations subcommittee that wrote the bill.

More recently, *after* hammering out an agreement on the omnibus appropriations bill for fiscal year 1999, Republican whip Tom DeLay of Texas announced that the process of including funding for pet projects would continue until "the members are happy." But not all members were happy. DeLay's Murtha-like sentiment was not appreciated by many of his Republican allies: "How can a fiscal conservative vote for this?" fumed South Carolina representative Mark Sanford. Veteran Democrat Lee Hamilton of Indiana called the process "an abomination."

With all of this understood, most legislators see their efforts to distribute federal funds back home as a legitimate aspect of their jobs; they apply the term *pork-barrel* to the pet projects of other members, if they use it at all. But critics complain that Congress is overly influenced by parochial concerns and should be more attuned to national needs. Republican senator John McCain of Arizona in recent years has waged a populist fight against earmarks in appropriations bills, loudly deriding spending items he deemed pork during floor debate on the measures. However, McCain's amendments to strip questionable spending items out of the bills almost always have gone down to defeat.

In the late 1990s and into the 2000s the practice of earmarks emerged as a highly controversial way of locking in special benefits for congressional districts and states. A representative or senator would arrange for a funding bill to include a specific amount designated for a specific use such as

CLOSER LOOK

As this New York Herald *1918 cartoon shows, critics have long been deriding Congress for spending money on "pork-barrel" projects.*
Source: Library of Congress

The term "pork-barrel politics"—almost always used disparagingly— describes the practice of legislators obtaining funding or other narrowly focused benefits for their constituents, such as a new office building, a water project, a road or bridge, or a tax break. Although widely condemned— outside the halls of Congress, at least—few legislators can resist taking credit for securing federal funding for their districts or states.

a highway or park in a member's district. The number of earmarks under both Democrats and Republicans, however, quickly grew into the thousands. Public outrage forced Congress to cut back on them or at least to require every one to get closer examination before approval.

Presidents, given their national constituencies, are more likely to evaluate federal budgets and spending measures from a broader perspective than are members of Congress. President Jimmy Carter sought the elimination or modification of five water projects on grounds that they were wasteful or damaging to the environment. Congress rejected most of his suggestions, and the episode soured Carter's relations with Capitol Hill and weakened his presidency.

Carter's successor, Ronald Reagan, also tangled with Congress over pork-barrel spending. Despite Reagan's enormous popularity, even some top Republican leaders in Congress voted to override the president's 1987 veto of an authorization bill for highways and mass transit. A classic pork-barrel bill, the measure set up more than 120 special "demonstration" projects for which members could claim credit back home.

President George H. W. Bush continued Reagan's attacks on congressional spending, calling on Congress to vote on specific "items of pork" instead of concealing them within huge multibillion-dollar appropriations bills. "Funds for local parking garages, $100,000 for asparagus-yield declines, meat research, prickly pear research," Bush complained in 1992, "the examples would be funny if the effect weren't so serious."

> *"All of us go begging to the Appropriations Committee for water projects or different things we want in our district.... It isn't easy to vote to cut one of these bills because a lot of times you're fearful that the next time you go asking for something, the door will be slammed in your face."*
>
> **—Rep. Douglas H. Bosco,** D-Calif.

Presidential opposition may count for something, but it is Congress that determines how much will be spent, where, and for what purpose. This means that local politics and divvying up the pork will always play a role in federal spending decisions. While serving as a Democratic representative from California, Douglas H. Bosco captured the legislative perspective: "All of us go begging to the Appropriations Committee for water projects or different things we want in our district.... It isn't easy to vote to cut one of these bills because a lot of times you're fearful that the next time you go asking for something, the door will be slammed in your face."

In the 1980s and 1990s, many Republicans, including Reagan and Bush, touted the presidential line-item veto as the answer to curbing pork-barrel politics. The Republican-led 104th Congress passed the Line Item Veto Act in 1996—but it failed in its short run to check the congressional appetite for pork. Not much more than a year after passing the historic act, Congress overrode President Bill Clinton's "veto" of thirty-eight military construction projects with a combined price tag of $287 million. Clinton used the "veto" on eight additional appropriations bills. But these were much more modest cuts, totaling less than $200 million, and were not overridden. The Supreme Court found the line-item veto unconstitutional in 1998. (See VETOES.)

Powell, Adam Clayton, Jr.

Rep. Adam Clayton Powell Jr. (1908–1972), a flamboyant Democrat from New York, provoked a storm of controversy over congressional powers and ethics in the 1960s. A House vote to exclude Powell from Congress because of misconduct led to a Supreme Court decision prohibiting Congress from adding to the constitutional qualifications for membership. The Powell case was also a key factor in the development of congressional codes of ETHICS.

Powell was pastor of the Abyssinian Baptist Church in Harlem, New York, one of the largest congregations in the country, when he was first elected to Congress in 1944. He rose in seniority to become the chair of the House Education and Labor Committee in 1961 and was considered by many to be the most powerful African American in the United States.

But Powell came under fire on a variety of issues: his involvement in court cases concerning income tax evasion and libel, his numerous well-publicized trips at government expense, and his employment of his wife as a member of his congressional staff while she lived in Puerto Rico.

His downfall began in 1966 as a result of a revolt in his committee over legislative business. When his long absences delayed passage of antipoverty legislation in 1966, the committee adopted new rules that limited his power as chair.

Rep. Adam Clayton Powell, D-N.Y., holds news conference on March 30, 1966. Considered by many to be the most powerful African American in Washington at the time, Powell was excluded from the 90th Congress for misconduct. He was later reelected to Congress, and the Supreme Court declared his exclusion unconstitutional.
Source: AP Images/Charles Gorry

Following an investigation into Powell's use of committee funds, he was stripped of his committee chairmanship in 1967 and temporarily denied a seat in the House. In March 1967 the House, rejecting the recommendations of a select committee that Powell be punished but seated, excluded Powell from the 90th Congress. (See DISCIPLINING MEMBERS.)

Powell was reelected in a special election in April 1967 but did not attempt to claim the seat in that Congress. After winning again in 1968, he was seated in January 1969, although he lost his seniority and was fined. Following his swearing in, Powell told a press conference: "I'll behave as I always have."

The Supreme Court in 1969 ruled in *Powell v. McCormack* that the House had acted unconstitutionally in excluding Powell. The Harlem Democrat was defeated in a primary election in 1970 and died in 1972.

CLOSER LOOK ◉

Efforts in Congress to exclude Adam Clayton Powell from being seated led to a major Supreme Court decision that prevented legislators from adding to the simple list of requirements in the Constitution for membership: age, citizenship, and state residency.

President and Congress *See* EXECUTIVE BRANCH AND CONGRESS.

Presidential Disability and Succession

Congress has broad responsibility for maintaining the continuity of the presidency. The Constitution provides (Article II, Section 1) that Congress should decide who is to succeed to the presidency if both the president and vice president die, resign, or become disabled. Congress enacted a presidential succession law as early as 1792. But for nearly 200 years legislators avoided the question of presidential disability because they were unable to decide what constituted disability

President Gerald R. Ford (left) and Vice President Nelson A. Rockefeller owed their jobs to the passage of the Twenty-fifth Amendment that outlined how vacancies in the presidency or vice presidency were to be filled in the modern era.
Source: White House

or who would be the judge of it. Those questions were not resolved until adoption of the Twenty-fifth Amendment to the Constitution in 1967.

At least two presidents who served before the amendment was adopted became disabled while in office. James A. Garfield was shot in 1881 and was confined to his bed until his death two and a half months after the shooting. Woodrow Wilson suffered a severe stroke in 1919 but remained in office until his term ended in 1921. In each case the vice president did not assume any of the duties of the presidency for fear of appearing to usurp the power of that office. The result was uncertainty about who was in charge, especially in Wilson's case. A 1947 law clearly spells out the order of succession; following the vice president, the Speaker of the House and then the president pro tempore of the Senate would succeed to the presidency, followed by the secretary of state and then other cabinet officers in a specific order.

The Twenty-fifth Amendment permits the vice president to become acting president under either of two circumstances. If the president informs Congress that he is unable to perform his duties, the vice president becomes acting president until the president says he is able to take over again. The vice president also can become acting president if he and a majority of the cabinet (or another body designated by Congress) decide that the president is disabled. The vice president then is to remain acting president until the president informs Congress that he is able to resume his duties; however, Congress can overrule the president's declaration that he is no longer disabled by a two-thirds vote of both the Senate and the House of Representatives.

Another section of the Twenty-fifth Amendment spells out what will happen if the vice president dies, resigns, or succeeds to the presidency. In such a case the president is to nominate a replacement, who then must be confirmed by a majority vote of both the Senate and House.

More on this topic:

Electing the President, p. 176

President Pro Tempore, p. 435

Speaker of the House, p. 516

Vice President, p. 576

The presidential disability procedures first came into play in 1985 when President Ronald Reagan underwent cancer surgery. Responding to criticism that he had not invoked the Twenty-fifth Amendment in 1981 when he was seriously wounded in an assassination attempt, Reagan transferred his powers to Vice President George H. W. Bush just before receiving anesthesia and signed papers reclaiming them less than eight hours later. The president did not formally invoke the Twenty-fifth Amendment, however. A bipartisan advisory commission, in a 1988 report, criticized Reagan's reluctance to do so; it urged routine use of the disability mechanism in such cases. President George W. Bush transferred power to his vice president, Richard B. Cheney, on two occasions, in 2002 and 2007. Both resulted from voluntary colonoscopy exams, which require use of anesthesia. Nonmalignant polyps had been discovered in Bush's colon when he was Texas governor, which made him a prime candidate for regular colon screening. Bush did invoke the amendment.

The first vice president to be confirmed under the Twenty-fifth Amendment was Gerald R. FORD, who was nominated by President Richard NIXON in 1973; Ford succeeded Spiro T. Agnew, who had resigned as a result of political corruption charges. The second was Nelson A. Rockefeller, whom Ford nominated in 1974 after he replaced Nixon in the White House.

President of the Senate

The president of the Senate is the vice president of the United States, serving in the constitutional role as presiding officer of the Senate. The Constitution allows the vice president to vote in the Senate only to break a tie, but does not require the vice president to do so. Senators address the vice president, or surrogates sitting in for him, as "Mr. President." In modern practice vice presidents rarely preside, usually filling their role only when their vote may be needed, on ceremonial occasions, or to rule on some crucial procedural questions. In the absence of the vice president, the president pro tempore or a senator designated by that person presides over the Senate. (See PRESIDING OFFICER.)

President Pro Tempore

Officially the highest ranking senator, the president pro tempore (a Latin term meaning the president "for the time [being]," often shortened to "president pro tem") is in practice a largely ceremonial leader. By tradition, the post goes automatically to the senator in the majority party with the longest service record. Because of seniority, the president pro tempore usually chairs a committee and is counted among the top decision makers in the Senate. However, the position carries far less influence than the party floor leaders. There is no Senate post comparable to the House Speaker.

The Constitution calls for the president pro tempore to preside when the VICE PRESIDENT, the constitutional president of the Senate, is absent. The post of president pro tempore has never become a politically powerful position, in part because the vice president at any point is able to take the chair, unseating the president pro tempore. One ceremonial task of the president pro tempore is to sign, along with the House Speaker, the final version of legislation passed by Congress. The president pro tem is third in line, behind the vice president and the Speaker, to succeed to the presidency.

In the nineteenth century the post was filled on a temporary basis, whenever the vice president was not present. But the Senate never let the vice president be an active participant in its affairs; often the vice president was of a political party different from that of most senators. As the vice president spent less time in the Senate chamber, the post of president pro tempore evolved into a long-term position. In 1890 the Senate decided that the president pro tempore should serve until "the Senate otherwise ordered." In effect, it gave tenure to the person elected.

More on this topic:

Leadership, p. 325

Speaker of the House, p. 516

The practice of electing the most senior member of the majority party in terms of Senate service as president pro tempore has been followed since 1945, with the exception of Arthur H. Vandenberg of Michigan, who was the second-ranking Republican when elected president pro tem in 1947.

Although the president pro tempore occasionally presides over the Senate, the day-to-day routine often is handled by more junior members of the majority party who rotate as PRESIDING OFFICER.

Republican Ted Stevens of Alaska, who was appointed to fill a vacancy in the Senate in December 1968 and subsequently won his first Senate election in 1970, became president pro tem at the beginning of the 108th Congress in 2003. He replaced Republican Strom THURMOND of

South Carolina who retired at the end of the previous Congress. At the start of the 110th Congress in 2007, the president pro tem was Robert C. BYRD of West Virginia, by then the longest-serving senator in history.

Presidents Who Served in Congress

More than half of the nation's presidents have followed a well-trodden career path by serving first in Congress. Of the nation's forty-three presidents, twenty-four sat in one or both chambers before becoming chief executive: nine served in the House of Representatives, six in the Senate, and nine in both. In addition to the nine presidents who sat in the House before assuming the presidency, one served there after leaving it. Another ex-president returned briefly to the Senate, where he had served before becoming president.

The move from Congress to the White House began early. James MADISON, the fourth president, served in the House; his successor, James Monroe, was in the Senate. Both Madison and Monroe also had been members of the Continental Congress, as had their predecessors George Washing-

Few presidents have moved directly from Congress to the White House. John F. Kennedy made that leap in 1961, as James A. Garfield and Warren G. Harding had done earlier. Here Senator Kennedy, catcher, plays softball in 1954 with Senate colleagues Henry M. Jackson, batter, and Mike Mansfield, umpire.
Source: Senate Historical Office

ton, John ADAMS, and Thomas Jefferson. Few have moved directly from Congress to the White House. John F. KENNEDY made that leap in 1961, as James A. Garfield and Warren G. Harding had before him.

Others advanced through the vice presidency. John Tyler, Millard Fillmore, Andrew Johnson, Harry S. TRUMAN, and Lyndon B. JOHNSON all succeeded presidents who had died in office. Martin Van Buren was vice president when he ran for president, as was George H. W. Bush. Gerald R. FORD, Richard Nixon's vice president, became president when Nixon resigned.

Others held intervening posts in government: Madison, Monroe, and John Quincy ADAMS were secretaries of state, for example, while James K. Polk, William McKinley, and Rutherford B. Hayes were governors. Bush took on a variety of jobs, including ambassador to the United Nations, chair of the Republican Party, chief envoy to China, and director of the Central Intelligence Agency.

Success in one branch of the government has not always been matched by success in the other. Lyndon B. Johnson, a Senate majority leader of legendary skill, was a powerful and effective chief executive until his presidency foundered on the Vietnam War. Abraham Lincoln's single term in the House did not foreshadow his immense stature as president, while Ford's years of House leadership did not translate into White House triumphs. More consistent was the performance of Harding, an ineffectual senator who became an ineffectual president.

The two presidents who served in Congress after leaving the White House were John Quincy Adams and Andrew Johnson. Adams pursued a seventeen-year career in the House of Representatives; earlier in life he had served in the Senate. Johnson, with a background of service in both chambers, returned to the Senate for five months before his death.

Countless members of Congress have sought the presidency in vain. Aaron Burr, Henry CLAY, Stephen A. DOUGLAS, James G. BLAINE, William Jennings Bryan, Robert A. TAFT, Hubert H. HUMPHREY, Barry Goldwater, George McGovern, Walter F. Mondale, Robert DOLE, and Al GORE are among the many who have tried and failed to win the highest office.

Congress is not the only popular route to the White House. A growing number have come to the presidency from the governor's mansion. Texas governor George W. Bush's election in 2000 brought to twenty the number of former governors of states, colonies, or territories who later served as the nation's chief executive. Bush succeeded Bill Clinton, who had been governor of Arkansas.

CLOSER LOOK

President George H. W. Bush
Source: George Bush Presidential Library and Museum

Over the nation's history, more than half of the presidents had served in Congress. But that was becoming less common in the latter decades of the twentieth century. After 1976 only one of five presidents—as of 2007—had been in either chamber: George H. W. Bush. More typically, recent presidents had previously been state governors.

Presiding Officer

Members of the Senate and House of Representatives take turns presiding over floor debate, a job that is viewed by some as drudgery, by others as an honor requiring finesse and skill. Members may speak on the floor only if the presiding officer permits, or "recognizes," them. The presiding officer also rules on points of order and delivers other pronouncements that regulate floor debate. The script is usually written by the PARLIAMENTARIAN, who cannot directly address the chamber but can prompt the member in the chair. Members may APPEAL, or challenge, the presiding officer's decisions, and, in the House, the rulings can be overturned by majority vote. Some rulings in the Senate require sixty votes to overturn.

In the Senate it once was common for the vice president, its constitutionally designated president, to preside over floor debates. In the modern Senate the vice president seldom is called in unless the vote might be needed to break a tie. In 1979 Vice President Walter F. Mondale, who previously had served for twelve years in the Senate, took the chair to help Democratic majority leader Robert C. BYRD of West Virginia quash a filibuster on a natural gas deregulation bill by issuing a series of controversial rulings. But that was a rare departure from the normal practice.

The president pro tempore, usually the senior member of the majority party in the Senate, may preside in the absence of the vice president, but generally the Senate puts a freshman member in the chair. That relieves senior members of a time-consuming task and gives newcomers experience in Senate rules and procedures. Not surprisingly, new senators are heavily dependent on the parliamentarian for advice.

The House puts no premium on giving new members experience in the chair. Its formal presiding officer is the Speaker of the House, the leader of the majority party in the chamber. But the Speaker must appoint other representatives to preside when the House is considering bills for amendment in the Committee of the Whole. When sensitive bills are under consideration, the Speaker turns to senior members who are skilled parliamentarians or who are close to the leadership.

While many senators tend to view presiding as drudgery, some welcome the task. Some House members also actively seek the duty. In an institution as large as the House, it is one way for members to increase their visibility.

In both the House and Senate only members of the majority party preside. Until 1977 members of each party took turns presiding in the Senate. The practice was abandoned following an incident in which the presiding officer, a member of the minority party, broke with Senate custom by denying recognition to the majority leader.

But an exception occurred, albeit temporarily, early in the 107th Congress (2001–2003) when the Senate was divided equally between fifty Democrats and fifty Republicans. Under an unprecedented power-sharing agreement, the parties took turns presiding. That structure lasted until June 2001 when Sen. James M. Jeffords of Vermont changed his party affiliation from Republican to Independent, giving Democrats a one-seat majority.

Press and Congress

The media have never been more important—or as divisive—on Capitol Hill than today. On the one hand, legislators vie for attention for their pet issues or bills in an increasingly diversified news and entertainment landscape. At the same time, senators and representatives must cope with constant and sometimes critical scrutiny by newspapers, magazines, and radio, television, and cable networks. Meanwhile, the Internet and emerging digital technologies have leveled the playing field and made it possible for everyone from lowly congressional staffers and citizen journalists to party machines and powerful senators to report on the activities of Congress.

A series of dramatic changes in the media landscape have provided the public with many more outlets for news from Capitol Hill today. The deregulation of the cable television industry in the 1980s brought about an explosion in news organizations, including CNN, MSNBC, Fox News, and the cable industry–financed Cable Satellite Public Affairs Network, known as C-SPAN, which operates channels featuring live coverage of the House of Representatives and Senate. The advent of the Internet at the turn of the century led to the creation of Web sites for every existing news organization in addition to new online-only publications and a plethora of political-oriented blogs of all stripes, from Wonkette to the Huffington Post to RedState.org. A Pew Research Center survey after the 2006 midterm elections showed that the number of Americans who received most of their information about the campaign from the Internet had doubled since 2002, to 15 from 7 percent.

Digital technologies have changed the traditional news cycle and forced different types of media to compete now on some of the same platforms when covering Congress. News outlets—from traditional daily newspapers such as the *New York Times* and the *Washington Post* to weekly journals focused on Congress, such as *Congressional Quarterly* and the *National Journal*—now update their Web sites frequently throughout the day and send out alerts and reports via e-mail.

Lawmakers and staff members are no longer passive participants just feeding information to reporters and waiting to see how events will be covered in the news. Some staffers and even members of Congress write blogs. Key staffers and lawmakers are now frequent guests on the numerous cable TV and Sunday morning talk shows. Campaign staffs submit camcorder clips— sometimes unflattering tapes of rivals—to video-oriented Web sites, such as YouTube.com. These clips, often e-mailed around the nation, are sometimes seen by more Americans than the nightly network newscasts.

Washington investigative reporting, largely born as a result of the Watergate scandal in the 1970s, has been criticized by some in recent years for not being as alert for official misconduct in Congress and the White House as it was in past years. During Bill Clinton's tenure as president, the press gave great attention to alleged extramarital affairs and other aspects of office-holders' and candidates' private lives. But at the dawn of the twenty-first century, investigative reporting took on more substantive issues. Reporting on powerful Washington lobbyist Jack Abramoff led to not only his conviction on fraud and corruption charges but also legal proceedings against Rep. Bob Ney, R-Ohio. In 2006 the Web site of ABC News reported that a former congressional page had received suggestive e-mails from Rep. Mark Foley, R-Fla. After other reports surfaced, Foley resigned.

With greater partisanship evident in both Congress and the public discourse following the divisive terms of presidents Bill Clinton and George W. Bush, news coverage focused more on political disputes in Congress, often couching battles in terms of winners and losers. This was true with the debate over health care during the 1990s, but even more so in the wake of the Iraq war in the early 2000s. The image of Congress as an institution, often as reflected through the media, has plummeted. In a survey a year before the 2006 midterm elections, in which Democrats regained control of both houses for the first time in twelve years, an NBC News/*Wall Street Journal* poll found that only 33 percent of respondents approved of the job Congress was doing. A Gallup poll in June 2007 found that public-approval ratings for Congress have never been

The press has covered Congress since its first meeting in 1789. Here a congressional reporter uses a dictaphone in 1908. Over the years press coverage has greatly evolved, from the early newspaper reports that were a little more than a record of floor speeches to the modern-day analytical, behind-the-scenes reporting that reaches the public through a variety of ways—newspapers, radio, television, cable, and Web sites and blogs.
Source: Library of Congress

In September 2007 Senate Minority Leader Mitch McConnell speaks with reporters after a Senate Republican policy luncheon. Members of Congress must cope with constant and sometimes critical scrutiny by members of the media.
Source: CQ Photo/Scott J. Ferrell

lower in the seventy-five years that the Gallup Poll has been conducted; only 14 percent of Americans expressed any confidence in the work of congressional lawmakers.

As the media environment has grown much larger and more fragmented, and politics has become more divisive, lawmakers have had more difficulty passing legislation. To counter this, members have increasingly worked together in public relations efforts, with party leaders providing "talking points" so that the party presents a unified message to the public at home. Political scientists lament that members of Congress—and the president—are today conducting a "permanent campaign," confusing governing with the constant clamor for public support, much of that being waged through the media. The lawmakers' argument is that by presenting a united message they can cut through the overwhelming glut of information that the public receives, while critics contend they are striving to control that information.

Today about seven thousand journalists, photographers, and technicians are accredited to the House and Senate press galleries—an increase of 40 percent since the late 1980s. Many members of this group work for specialized publications that focus on particular issues. Three newspapers, *The Hill, Roll Call,* and *The Politico,* cover nonlegislative actions of Congress in depth, targeting an audience of lawmakers, staff aides, and lobbyists. Yet most Americans are informed of only a few of the events that occur on Capitol Hill: of the dozens of hearings, meetings, and debates that occur in Congress each day, only one or two are likely to receive attention in most newspapers or in radio and television broadcasts.

Reforms enacted in the 1970s opened more of congressional activities than ever before to both the press and the public. Almost all House and Senate committees conduct much of their work in public sessions. Reporters and lobbyists often crowd around while conference committees hammer out final decisions on compromise legislation. Both the House and the Senate record members' votes on most questions during floor debate on legislation, and floor action is transmitted to millions of households via C-SPAN.

Despite the greater openness in Congress, reporters must still cultivate senators, representatives, and their staffs to discover what goes on backstage and to be able to explain the subtle pressures that shape the legislative process. Legislators, in turn, use contact with the media as an opportunity to seek favorable coverage in the hope of not only improving their image among their constituents but also increasing their influence among Washington colleagues.

Members of Congress use a variety of methods to attract favorable press coverage. The number of press releases has increased, according to press secretaries, because they are so easily distributed via e-mail, instead of fax or costly paper mail, and reporters can sign up for distribution lists via the Internet. Lawmakers also appear on television or radio shows, grant personal interviews to reporters, give floor speeches on major issues, and hold press conferences and briefings for journalists. Increasingly, they also blog on the Internet, and their staff members alert TV and cable media of satellite video feeds featuring important speeches or statements. During election times, campaign committees increasingly submit video clips of lawmakers running for election to Internet video sites, in addition to instructing staffers to follow around campaign rivals with handheld video cameras, recording their every speech.

Occasionally, a member may draw widespread attention by conducting a highly publicized hearing or investigation. Members of Congress are particularly adept in the use of television. In 2005 Rep. Tom Davis, R-Va., held widely publicized hearings into allegations of steroid use in Major League Baseball, which included testimony from the league's all-time single-season home-run leader Mark McGwire, among other players, who declined to answer questions at the hearing about whether he had ever used steroids. The testimony resulted in a flurry of headlines and lawmakers took center stage. "These people are not above the law," Davis said in an appearance on NBC's *Meet the Press* in the midst of the hearings. "You know, they may fly in private planes and make millions of dollars and be on baseball cards, but a subpoena is exactly what it says it is."

As recently as the 1950s, few senators and virtually no representatives formally designated staff members as press secretaries. Today nearly all lawmakers employ press officers, often former journalists, to handle relations with reporters and press strategy. Congressional committees also hire press secretaries and may even set up separate press information offices to communicate the majority and minority viewpoints. Press secretaries steer journalists to knowledgeable staff members, set up interviews with members of Congress, and provide much of the background information that reporters use to write Capitol Hill stories. Press secretaries are accorded so much power that, often, the quotes ascribed to lawmakers were in fact written by press secretaries and may never even have been uttered by the members.

Previous Question

The previous question motion is one of the fundamental rules of general parliamentary procedure. Its use is indispensable to the legislative process in the House of Representatives because it is the only way to bring debate to a formal close.

The previous question is adopted, or "ordered," by a majority vote. Adoption of a motion ordering the previous question brings the House to a direct vote on the pending question. The motion itself is not debatable but must be put to a vote immediately. The motion is used not only to bring debate to a close, but also to foreclose the opportunity to revise, or amend, the question or legislation pending before the House. The previous question is used only when members are sitting as the House; it is not permitted in the Committee of the Whole where other debate limitations apply. When the Rules Committee grants a special rule for floor debate on a bill, it routinely adds language "ordering the previous question."

The motion normally is offered by the floor manager of the bill. Adoption of the previous question means essentially that the House thinks the legislation or parliamentary question has been debated adequately and that members are ready to vote. If the House defeats the previous question, debate continues and amendments are in order. In addition, control of the debate passes to those who successfully opposed adoption of the previous question.

Use of the previous question motion in the House distinguishes its debates from those in the Senate. Since it is a debate-limiting device, the previous question is not permitted in the Senate, which cherishes "extended debate." Senate debate can be restricted or shut off by unanimous consent (an impossibility in the face of a filibuster) or by a three-fifths vote of the Senate membership to invoke cloture.

An example of the importance of ordering the previous question occurred in 1981 on the eve of debate on a $35 billion package of budget cuts that had been proposed by President Ronald Reagan and House Republicans. The rule supported by

More on this topic:
Committee of the Whole, p. 110
Filibuster, p. 213
Floor Manager, p. 227
Legislative Process, p. 344

the House Democratic leadership would have forced the House to vote separately on each proposed cut, making it difficult for the Republicans to sustain their budget package. But the procedural vote ordering the previous question on the rule, which would have cleared the way for the Democrats' ground rules, failed on a vote of 210–217. That vote opened the rule to amendment, and the Republicans then rewrote the rule to allow a single vote on the entire package of budget cuts; their version was adopted 216–212.

Printing Committee, Joint

Although it rarely meets, the Joint Printing Committee is responsible for monitoring the printing operations of the entire federal government. Unlike most congressional committees, which oversee the operations of executive agencies and their implementation of congressional mandates, the Joint Printing Committee has been given authority to actually approve or disapprove specific agency decisions about printing.

But the executive branch has increasingly challenged that far-reaching jurisdiction. Since the Supreme Court in 1983 declared Congress's use of LEGISLATIVE VETOES unconstitutional, executive agencies have pushed for greater independence in making printing decisions.

Federal law requires that government documents go through the GOVERNMENT PRINTING OFFICE (GPO), but the Joint Printing Committee has authorized a number of printing plants outside of GPO to print government publications, and in 2002 the printing office was subcontracting 84 percent of the jobs to private printers. Still, the committee kept business coming to the GPO that many agencies preferred to handle themselves or buy from private companies. Critics said GPO rates and schedules for completing work were not competitive. Congress created the GPO to handle congressional publications, but the Joint Printing Committee operated on the premise that the GPO should also be used for other federal printing. The struggle between the two branches escalated in 2002 when the Bush administration's Office of Management and Budget ordered federal agencies to use private printers if they could do the jobs faster and more cheaply.

The Joint Printing Committee's other duties include responsibility for the style and format of the *CONGRESSIONAL RECORD* and for the contents of the *CONGRESSIONAL DIRECTORY*. When the House and Senate each decided to mark in the *Record* those speeches that were not actually delivered, the Joint Committee chose the mechanism for making that distinction.

Private Bill

A private bill applies to one or more specified persons, corporations, institutions, or other entities. Usually the legislation is intended to grant relief when no other legal remedy is available. Many private bills deal with claims against the federal government, immigration and naturalization cases, and land titles. The title of a private bill usually begins, "For the relief of...." Private bills once proliferated in Congress but that was significantly reduced by the end of the twentieth century by delegated authority to executive agencies to settle cases. *See* LEGISLATION.

Privilege

Privilege relates to the rights of members of Congress and to the relative priority of motions and actions in their respective chambers.

"Questions of privilege" concern members of Congress collectively or individually, and they take precedence over almost all other proceedings. Matters affecting the rights, safety, dignity, and integrity of proceedings of the House or Senate as a whole are questions of privilege in both chambers. Questions involving individual members are called "questions of personal privilege."

"Privileged questions" deal with legislative business. The order in which bills, motions, and other legislative measures are considered on the floor of the Senate and House is governed by strict priorities. A motion to table, for instance, is more privileged than a motion to recommit, so it would be voted on first. A motion to adjourn is considered "of the highest privilege" and would have to be considered before virtually any other motion. (See MOTIONS.) Certain types of legislation, such as budget resolutions, House-Senate conference reports, and bills vetoed by the president, are considered privileged and can be brought up for consideration on the floor sooner than other bills.

Progressive Era

The Progressive Era flourished from about 1900 to 1917, when Americans concluded that the governmental and economic affairs of the country were being run by unscrupulous politicians and powerful corporate interests. Much legislation enacted by Congress was designed to further the influence and financial advantage of these interlocking groups.

The national economy was largely the province of the railroads, manufacturing and mining corporations, and the large banks and financial institutions. In addition to the collusion between big business and the federal government, almost all state governments and large cities had fallen under the control of these same economic interests.

One goal of the Progressive movement was to curb oppressive child labor. In the political arena, progressives sought the popular election of senators, the secret ballot, and the initiative, referendum, and recall.
Source: Library of Congress

CLOSER LOOK

Historians date the Progressive Era to the first two decades of the twentieth century when legislators—backed by activists and large parts of the American society—sought to break the vast political influence that business interests, including railroads, manufacturing and mining corporations, and large financial institutions, had gained over economic conditions in the nation. Its roots were in the rural populist protests of the Midwest at the end of the previous century. Although some of the Progressives' initiatives were thwarted by entry into World War I and the different political climate of the 1920s, many core progressive ideas were incorporated into the nation's political and economic fabric by the New Deal under President Franklin D. Roosevelt in the 1930s.

The Progressive movement was basically a revolt against this conspiracy of politics and economic power. Its roots were in the rural populist protests of the Midwest during the final third of the nineteenth century. Concerned citizens feared that democratic government and the basic well-being of vast numbers of Americans were threatened by this concentration of wealth and political power in a privileged few. Exploitation of the underprivileged, women, and children was widespread. The Progressive Era, therefore, was both a culmination of reform pressures that had been building since the 1880s and the beginning of a new political activism directed at bringing government and economic institutions under genuine popular control. The Progressives sought reform of existing structures rather than revolutionary change.

Progressive Agenda

The Progressives became an influential force at various levels of American society. Their initial targets were the injustices and political corruption in the cities. Cleaning up the cities required wresting power from bosses of political machines. This led to campaigns to capture control of state governments, because reformers found that in most cases the big-city machines were tied into statewide political networks. Inevitably, the reform pressures affected the two national political parties.

At the local level the Progressive movement sought to relieve problems, such as the substandard living and health conditions in urban areas, unemployment, child labor, exploitation of women and immigrant workers, and the high incidence of industrial accidents. At the state level it tried to break the stranglehold on economic life of the giant trusts and corporations, such as the railroads; to end the exploitation and abuse of natural resources by business interests; and to reform state constitutions.

At the national level the Progressives' concerns centered on the need for a fairer distribution of the country's wealth and an end to social and class divisions along economic lines. Specific proposals included direct election of senators; direct primaries; the Australian, or secret, ballot; the initiative, referendum, and recall to give voters more direct control over government; the graduated income tax; postal savings banks; protective labor laws; and regulation of economic power generally.

The quest for social justice, urban rehabilitation, and the health and welfare of working people and the disadvantaged did not always center on economic, political, or administrative solutions. The Eighteenth Amendment to the Constitution, outlawing the sale or manufacture of alcoholic beverages, was in part a Progressive concern.

More on this topic:
Direct Election of Senators, p. 154
Legislative Process, p. 344
New Deal, p. 392
Women's Suffrage, p. 613

Progressivism in Politics

The influence of the Progressives in Congress began with attempts to open up the LEGISLATIVE PROCESS. Politically, the Progressives were an insurgent element within the Republican Party. For a few years before U.S. entry into World War I, they held the balance of power. Joining forces with a majority of Democrats in the House, they were able in 1910 to strip the autocratic and conservative Speaker, Illinois Republican Joseph G. CANNON, of most of his power. The revolt against "Cannonism," led by Progressives George W. NORRIS of Nebraska and John M. Nelson of

Wisconsin and by Democrats James B. "Champ" CLARK of Missouri and Oscar W. UNDERWOOD of Alabama, was consolidated in 1911. That year House Democrats returned to power and won approval of meaningful reforms in the rules that made it easier to bring to the floor for debate legislation that had been blocked by the conservative leadership. Clark was elected Speaker, but Underwood became the real leader of the House.

Speaker Cannon had opposed much of the Progressive agenda sought by President Theodore Roosevelt (1901–1909). Roosevelt's reputation as a Progressive rested on his policies toward "trust busting," railroad regulation, conservation, his Square Deal for labor, and other efforts. His administration took the first tentative steps nationally to grapple with the complex social and economic problems of a modern industrial nation.

In the Senate the Progressives were led by Robert M. LA FOLLETTE Sr. of Wisconsin, Albert J. BEVERIDGE of Indiana, and Albert B. Cummins and Jonathan P. Dolliver of Iowa, and by Norris and Underwood, both of whom went from the House to the Senate.

A split in Republican ranks between the Progressives and the conservative backers of President William Howard Taft led Roosevelt in 1912 to form the Progressive (Bull Moose) Party. The division among Republicans gave Democrat Woodrow Wilson a landslide victory in that year's presidential election. Wilson, who initially had championed traditional free enterprise and rejected the activist government role advocated by Roosevelt, eventually supported a dynamic federal role to solve the nation's social and economic problems. By 1916 Wilson had won enactment of most of the demands the rural populists and Progressives had advocated.

Progressives' Accomplishments

The Progressives achieved an impressive record of social, economic, and political reforms. But many of these programs were disrupted by U.S. entry into World War I, by the disillusionment that followed the failed peace settlement, and later by Supreme Court rulings and the conservative presidential administrations of the 1920s. Many of the changes the Progressives had fought for had to be won anew in the 1930s. To an important degree the philosophical and political foundations of the New Deal had their origin in the Progressive Era.

A few of the landmark initiatives identified with the Progressives and enacted during the Wilson administration were the Federal Reserve Act, Federal Trade Commission Act, Clayton Antitrust Act, and Rayburn Securities Act. Others included the Adamson Act, which created the first eight-hour workday on interstate railroads, and the first federal law regulating child labor. Although not ratified until 1920, the Nineteenth Amendment, granting suffrage to women, also was a consequence of the Progressive Era.

Proxy Voting

Proxy voting is the practice of permitting a member of Congress to cast the vote of an absent colleague in addition to his or her own vote. Proxy voting is prohibited on the floor of both the Senate and House. It also has been prohibited in House committees since 1995. However, a House rule change adopted at the outset of the 108th Congress in 2003 by the Republican leadership allowed committee chairs to postpone votes on a variety of substantive matters. The effect of this change, Democrats claimed at the time, was essentially the same as allowing proxies, because chairs could simply wait for favorable majorities to appear and thereby conclude business to their advantage. Nevertheless, the Democrats retained the rule when they took control of the House in January 2007.

The Senate permits its committees to authorize proxy voting, which reflects the much smaller size of the chamber and inability of senators who may serve on several committees to attend sessions held at the same time. Proxy voting is used by both senators and representatives in conference committees.

Purse, Power of

The Constitution entrusted to Congress the power to tax and spend. For more than two centuries this power of the purse has given the legislative branch paramount authority to command national resources and direct them to federal purposes. No other congressional prerogative confers so much control over the goals of government, or so much influence on the nation's well-being.

Since the 1930s Congress has made broad use of its taxing, spending, and borrowing powers to vastly enlarge the government and expand its influence over the U.S. economy. The way the government spends its money—and raises it through taxes or borrowing—carries enormous consequences for the nation's economic performance and its political and social balance. Under congressional direction, the federal government provides aid to education and health care to the elderly, builds highways and taxes gasoline, encourages economic development with subsidies and tax advantages, and pays for weapons and the soldiers to operate them.

Through the years the House and Senate have jealously guarded most congressional powers to finance the machinery of government. But Congress has had trouble using its taxing and spending powers to shape a coherent federal budget policy. The result was mounting gaps between spending and revenues and constant battling between Congress and successive presidents for final authority to set budget policy.

Much as it wanted to control the purse strings, Congress rarely bothered until the mid-1970s to tie its separate legislation to tax and spending totals. (Since 1921 the executive branch had drawn up yearly federal budgets setting forth revenue, spending, and deficit or surplus targets.) But in the early 1970s a heavily Democratic Congress fiercely resisted when Republican President Richard NIXON refused to spend billions of dollars already appropriated to federal agencies, a practice known as impoundment of funds.

Congress responded in 1974 by setting up its own elaborate budget process, which forced it to weigh spending against expected government revenues and to establish limits for each. Lawmakers continue to make decisions on spending and revenues through separate legislation, written by different House and Senate committees. Budget committees in each chamber draw up overall budget plans, but the actual spending bills are written by the House and Senate Appropriations committees within limits set by authorization bills that have been drafted by various other committees. The House Ways and Means and Senate Finance committees control the complicated process of writing tax legislation.

More on this topic:

Appropriations Bills,
p. 22

Appropriations Committee, House,
p. 23

Appropriations Committee, Senate,
p. 26

Authorization Bills,
p. 33

Budget Process, p. 54

Finance Committee, Senate, p. 218

Impoundment of Funds,
p. 285

Ways and Means Committee, House,
p. 603

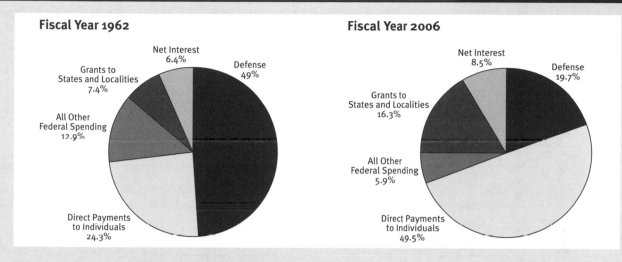

Fiscal Year 1962

Net Interest
6.4%

Grants to
States and Localities
7.4%

Defense
49%

All Other
Federal Spending
12.9%

Direct Payments
to Individuals
24.3%

Fiscal Year 2006

Net Interest
8.5%

Defense
19.7%

Grants to
States and Localities
16.3%

All Other
Federal Spending
5.9%

Direct Payments
to Individuals
49.5%

Federal Spending: Where the Money Goes

An analysis of federal spending from the early 1960s to the mid-2000s shows striking changes in federal priorities. Increases in spending can be seen across the board, but growth in mandatory or entitlement spending is the most dramatic.

Entitlement spending is often called uncontrollable spending. These federal programs—such as Social Security, Medicare, Supplemental Security Income, and child nutrition programs—provide benefits to which the recipients have a legally enforceable right. As long as a person meets the program criteria, the government must pay these programs' bills and appropriate more if money runs out during a fiscal year. Some of the programs, such as Social Security and Medicare, have permanent funding and do not have to go through the annual appropriations process.

The charts provide information on changing budget priorities from fiscal 1962 to fiscal 2006.

Defense: President Ronald Reagan's military buildup in the 1980s provided only a temporary rise in defense spending as a percentage of total federal outlays. Defense outlays, which accounted for 49 percent of all spending in fiscal 1962, fell to 22.8 percent under President Jimmy Carter in 1978, peaked at 28.1 percent under Reagan in 1987, and then declined to a historic low of 16.1 percent under President Bill Clinton in 1999. Following the September 11, 2001, terrorist attacks and start of the war in Iraq in 2003, defense spending surged under President George W. Bush but still amounted to just 19.7 percent of total outlays in fiscal 2000.

Direct Benefits to Individuals: The creation of Great Society social programs during the Lyndon B. Johnson administration and an ever expanding population of older Americans made direct benefit payments to individuals—accounting for most entitlement—the fastest growing part of the federal budget. In fiscal year 1962, direct benefits to individuals accounted for 24.3 percent of federal spending; by the mid-1990s, these payments were about half of all spending and the fiscal 2006 figure was 49.5 percent. Medicare, which was added to the Social Security program in 1965, accounted for a large part of the growth in direct benefits, while spending on veterans' benefits significantly declined.

Net Interest: The federal debt soared because of periods of record budget deficits in the 1980s, and as interest rates also rose interest payments on that debt as a percentage of federal spending more than doubled from fiscal 1962 (6.4 percent) to fiscal 1996 (15.4 percent). As budget deficits gave way to surpluses in the late 1990s and interest rates declined, so did interest payments. But a period of new record deficits in the mid-2000s caused interest payments to rise again, and they amounted to 8.5 percent of all outlays in fiscal 2005.

Grants to State and Local Governments: At first glance, the federal government seems to have been generous with the states over the years. Grants to state and local governments were 7.4 percent of all outlays in fiscal 1962 and more than doubled to 16.3 percent in fiscal 2006. A closer look, however, reveals that the increase was almost entirely the result of federal payments to states for social programs, such as Medicaid. Federal grants for capital investment have remained steady for decades. (During the late 1970s, federal spending for capital investment grew as a share of all spending, but funding was curtailed during the Reagan administration and has grown little since.)

All Other Federal Spending: Out of the remaining funds, the federal government must run all government programs related to agriculture, education, foreign aid and diplomacy, the environment, the judiciary, and hundreds more.

Power to Tax

Without sufficient revenues, no government could function effectively. The Constitution granted Congress the right to enact almost any type of tax, except for duties on exports. The power to tax was enlarged in 1913 by adoption of the Sixteenth Amendment to the Constitution, authorizing a federal tax on incomes.

Tariffs

During the nineteenth century the federal government derived the bulk of its revenues from tariffs on imports and other customs duties. Limited funds were also provided by estate or excise taxes.

Disputes over tariff policy were common. At times the nation was divided by region: protective tariffs were popular in the North and East, where manufacturing was important to the economy, and unpopular in the agricultural West and South. Critics were so upset by duties imposed in 1828 that they called the law the "tariff of abominations." In the last part of the nineteenth century, tariff policy split the major political parties; Republicans generally favored high tariffs, while Democrats supported low tariffs.

Customs duties provided a smaller share of federal revenue after taxation of incomes began, but the political debate continued. Thinking that higher tariffs would boost the badly ailing domestic economy, Congress in 1930 passed the Smoot-Hawley Tariff Act, which raised duties to the highest levels in U.S. history. Most analysts agree that the higher tariffs worsened the Great Depression. The misguided effort was repealed in 1934.

Congress delegated authority to reduce some tariffs to the president, beginning with the Reciprocal Trade Agreements Act of 1934. By then individual and corporate income taxes had begun replacing customs receipts as the main source of government revenues. In 1910 customs duties still brought in more than 49 percent of federal revenues; by fiscal 2006 they contributed only 1 percent, even though customs receipts totaled almost $25 billion.

Income Tax

Congress first passed taxes on income to finance the Civil War, but the levy expired in 1872. The income tax was renewed in 1894, with the rate set at 2 percent on personal incomes in excess of $3,000. The next year, however, the Supreme Court ruled the tax unconstitutional, stating that it violated a requirement that direct taxes be apportioned among states according to population.

That roadblock was removed by the Sixteenth Amendment, and a new income tax system was established in 1913. Congress exempted families with low incomes from the income tax; over the years a complicated sliding scale evolved that set higher tax rates on higher incomes. Tax deductions, allowed from the start, encouraged specific activities; among the best known is the deduction for interest on home mortgages, a subsidy to encourage home ownership that nearly 33 million taxpayers took advantage of in 2000.

Congress had no constitutional difficulty with the corporate income tax it first levied in 1909. The Supreme Court let the tax stand as an excise on the privilege of doing business as a corporation. An outright corporate income tax was enacted in 1913.

Federal taxes on individual incomes made up about 43 percent of all federal revenues in fiscal 2006, $1.04 trillion. Corporate income taxes amounted to 15 percent of revenues, $353.9 billion. Together they totaled 58 percent of the $2.41 trillion in federal revenue for that fiscal year.

Excise, Other Taxes

The power of Congress to tax in other areas is well established. Excise taxes (taxes on the sale of products or services) have always been a part of the federal tax system. The excises levied after ratification of the Constitution included taxes on carriages, liquor, snuff, sugar, and auction sales. Modern excise taxes extend to telephone service and diesel fuel. Another important area of taxation is payroll taxes, which support the Social Security and Medicare programs. Payroll taxes are the second largest source of government revenues, amounting to nearly 38 percent of revenues in fiscal 2006.

Power to Spend

The Constitution gave Congress the basic authority to decide how the government should spend the money it collects. It set few specific limits on the spending power.

By authorizing Congress to collect taxes "to pay the debts and provide for the common defense and general welfare of the United States," the Constitution opened the way for an expansive interpretation of the spending power. The new national government spent $5 million in fiscal 1792, its fourth year in operation. Peacetime spending grew slowly until the 1930s, when President Franklin D. Roosevelt and Congress launched federal programs to pull the economy out of the Great Depression. During World War II federal spending grew tenfold, reaching $92.7 billion in fiscal 1945. Spending dropped off after the war ended, only to rise again during the Korean War. It continued upward in an almost uninterrupted path for the next three decades.

Federal spending amounted to about $2.7 trillion in fiscal 2006, accounting for nearly a fifth of the nation's total output of goods and services. As recently as the late 1980s, about half that amount was spent annually. A combination of factors swelled the federal budget and kept spending at high levels even when revenues, though also increasing, fell behind. Annual deficits, the gap between revenues and spending, first exceeded $200 billion in 1983. After enactment of the Gramm-Rudman-Hollings legislation, deficits dipped below the $200 billion mark for a few years in the late 1980s. By 1992 the deficit had reached more than $290 billion despite the enactment of a major deficit-reduction package in 1990. That legislation, however, in combination with the 1993 reconciliation bill resulted in a turnaround. Annual deficits began to decline drastically, to the point that in 1998 the federal government announced a budget surplus of $70 billion. However, by fiscal 2002 deficits had returned, reaching $158 billion that year.

Since the 1970s the largest portion of spending has been for payments to individuals: retirement benefits, welfare, disability insurance, and other programs. When inflation in the 1970s made fixed benefits seem unfairly small, Congress provided automatic cost-of-living increases for many programs, a process known as indexing. That increased the government's costs, as did the growing ranks of participants. Many benefit programs were established as ENTITLEMENTS, which required payments to everyone who met legal requirements. Once these programs were in place, Congress found it politically difficult to dismantle or overhaul them. Payments to individuals—some of which are direct payments while others are made through grants to state and local governments—made up 55.7 percent of federal spending in fiscal 2006, far outstripping defense spending, which accounted for more than 19.6 percent, according to the Office of Management and Budget. Interest on the national debt was an uncontrollable element of the budget, consuming about 8.5 percent of spending.

Only about a third of federal spending remained under direct congressional control through the annual appropriations process. Reducing those programs by substantial amounts proved very difficult for the House and Senate. The bureaucracy that operated the programs, and the groups that benefited from them, created a powerful block against budget cuts.

Power to Borrow

No constitutional restriction exists on the government's power to borrow money on the nation's credit. Congress by statute has set a DEBT LIMIT since 1917, but it has regularly raised the limit, though often with political difficulty. Funds to pay interest on the debt have been permanently appropriated since 1847. Congress protected that obligation from political uncertainty, thus strengthening the nation's credibility as a borrower.

The federal government has incurred debt when it has had to spend more than it collected in taxes and other forms of revenue. The deficit must be made up by borrowing.

During most of the nation's history, government has tried to ensure that revenues were sufficient to meet spending requirements. This philosophy, which dictated an approximate balance between revenues and spending, was generally accepted until the early 1930s. But then Congress approved major federal projects to stimulate economic recovery. In the process the government began following an economic philosophy, developed by British economist John Maynard Keynes, that justified peacetime deficits to ensure stable economic growth.

As a result, the government abandoned its former insistence on balancing revenues and spending. The practice of using the federal budget to help solve national economic problems was increasingly accepted. Budget deficits and a rapidly increasing national debt were the result. In fiscal 1998 the federal government recorded its first budget surplus since 1969, and the surpluses continued for four straight years, until fiscal 2001. The election of George W. Bush in 2000 put the budget back on a different path. Tax cutting became a top priority of his administration. The first came in 2001, reducing revenue by $1.4 trillion over ten years. Additional tax cuts followed in 2002 and 2003. The terrorists attacks in 2001, a recession, and the cost of fighting wars in Afghanistan and Iraq quickly wiped out surpluses during all of Bush's first six years. The era of deficit spending had returned, leading to a record $412.1 billion shortfall in fiscal 2004. Although the sea of red ink receded some in the immediately following years, it still was $248.2 billion in fiscal 2006 and was projected at $244.2 billion for fiscal 2007. No surpluses were in sight in the near future.

Budget deficits must be financed. The federal government does so by borrowing, a power granted under the Constitution. Modern day debt of the government first became significant from the World War II years; in 1945 the debt of the U.S. government stood at $260.1 billion, requiring interest payments of $3.1 billion. By 2006 the gross debt was $8.5 trillion with interest payments of $226.6 billion. It was expected to reach $9 trillion in fiscal 2007.

Qualification of Members

Before launching her 2000 bid for an open Senate seat in New York, First Lady Hillary Rodham Clinton and President Bill Clinton purchased this home in Chappaqua in late 1999 in order to attain needed residency in the state. The Clintons had never lived in New York before that time.
Source: AP Images/Stephen Chernin

Qualifications for service in Congress are spelled out in the Constitution and are simple. Members of the House must be twenty-five years of age at the time their terms begin. They must have been citizens of the United States for seven years before that date and, when elected, must be "Inhabitant[s]" of the state from which they were elected. There is no constitutional requirement that they reside in the district they represent.

Senators are required to be thirty years of age at the time their terms begin. They must have been citizens for nine years before that date and, when elected, must be "Inhabitant[s]" of the state in which they were elected.

The "Inhabitant" qualification is broadly interpreted, and in modern times a candidate's declaration of state residence has generally been accepted as meeting the constitutional requirement.

None of the other qualifications have been an important issue in modern times. Nearly all members are significantly over the minimum age, and most have been citizens from birth. However, in the late 1960s the House refused to seat a duly elected member—Rep. Adam Clayton Powell Jr., D-N.Y.—over charges of misconduct. He was reelected and eventually reseated. More important, the Supreme Court in a case arising from the exclusion ruled that Congress could not add to the constitutional requirements for membership, all of which Powell met. (See POWELL, ADAM CLAYTON, JR. ; DISCIPLINING MEMBERS.)

Quorum

A quorum is the minimum number of members who must be present for the transaction of business. In both chambers of Congress it is a majority of the total membership: fifty-one in the Senate and 218 in the House of Representatives, provided there are no vacant seats. Only 100 members are required when the House is sitting as the COMMITTEE OF THE WHOLE, the parliamentary framework it adopts when it considers bills for amendment.

A quorum is assumed to be present, even when only a few members are on the floor, unless a member suggests otherwise. In that case the roll is called, and absentees quickly stream into the chamber to make up a quorum. Quorum calls are frequently used in the Senate to kill time while groups of senators informally negotiate legislative or procedural disputes or to give a senator time to reach the floor to speak or offer an amendment. Once the quorum call's purpose has been accomplished, the call can be dispensed with by unanimous consent.

Randolph, John

John Randolph (1773–1833) represented Virginia in the House of Representatives intermittently from 1799 to 1833. His tenure there was interrupted four times, once to allow service in the Senate from 1825 to 1827. Randolph was a States Rights Democrat who opposed legislation that he believed would strengthen the national government at the cost of state sovereignty. He had a difficult personality, but many in Congress were in awe of his brilliant oratory and his uncompromising beliefs. Henry Adams described Randolph standing to speak to the House "with the halo of youth, courage, and genius around his head—a sort of Virginian Saint Michael, almost terrible in his contempt for whatever seemed to him base or untrue."

Randolph entered Congress as a supporter of Thomas Jefferson and almost immediately became chair of the Ways and Means Committee. He supported Jefferson's purchase of the Louisiana territory but later broke with the president over his attempts to acquire Florida.

A constitutional purist, Randolph refused to bow to necessity if it conflicted with principle. He opposed protective tariffs, roads built by the national government, the chartering of the Bank of the United States, and federal interference in the issue of slavery.

Randolph also was a prominent opponent of the Missouri Compromise of 1820. Ill feeling over this issue between Randolph and Henry CLAY, another great orator, went beyond words in 1826. That year, the two men fought a duel over Randolph's denunciation of Clay's support for John Quincy ADAMS's selection as president. Neither man was harmed. Clay had been a losing candidate for the presidency in the 1824 election, which had been decided by the House of Representatives. (See ELECTING THE PRESIDENT.)

In 1830 Randolph traveled to St. Petersburg as Andrew Jackson's minister to Russia. He became ill and was forced to leave shortly after his arrival. Having been in ill health for most of his life, Randolph died in 1833 after periods of dementia, alcoholism, and opium use.

Rankin, Jeannette

The first woman to serve in Congress, Jeannette Rankin entered the House in 1917, four years before ratification of the Nineteenth Amendment guaranteeing women the right to vote. Rankin voted against U.S. entry into World War I and II.
Source: AP Images

Jeannette Rankin (1880–1973) was the first woman to serve in Congress. A suffragist and pacifist, she ran for the House at a time when only a handful of states allowed women to vote and as the nation was about to enter World War I. (See WOMEN IN CONGRESS.)

Born into a family that believed in education for women and political activism, Rankin graduated from the University of Montana and went on to study social work at the New York School of Philanthropy. She then returned west and lobbied for the enfranchisement of women in the states of Washington, California, and Montana.

Rankin ran as a Republican for one of Montana's House seats in 1916 on a platform favoring Prohibition, women's rights, and federal suffrage. (The Nineteenth Amendment giving women the right to vote was not ratified until 1920.) When elected, Rankin said: "I knew the women would stand behind me. I am deeply conscious of the responsibility. I will not only represent the women of Montana, but also the women of the country, and I have plenty of work cut out for me."

In the House Rankin worked to further the cause of women. She introduced legislation to grant women citizenship independent of their husbands and sponsored a bill providing for federally supported maternal and infant health instruction. She helped set up a House committee on women's suffrage and tried to ensure that employment generated by legislation would include women.

In 1917 the House voted on the entry of the United States into World War I. With forty-nine other representatives Rankin voted no, saying, "I want to stand by my country but I cannot vote for war." Her vote brought national notoriety for her, but not for her forty-nine male colleagues.

After her first term in the House, Rankin ran unsuccessfully for the Senate. Out of office, she continued to work for women's rights, and in 1940 she was reelected to the House. Once again she was faced with a vote on U.S. involvement in a war. Rankin was the only member to vote against entry into

"I knew the women would stand behind me. I am deeply conscious of the responsibility. I will not only represent the women of Montana, but also the women of the country, and I have plenty of work cut out for me."

—*Jeannette Rankin* on her election as the first woman in Congress

World War II. Few people shared the view of Kansas newspaper editor William Allen White, who said of her pacifist stand: "It was a brave thing! And its bravery somehow discounted its folly." After the vote, she was forced to lock herself in a phone booth to escape from the curious and angry crowds.

In 1968, when she was in her late eighties, Jeannette Rankin led a Jeannette Rankin Brigade to the Capitol to protest the war in Vietnam. She died at the age of ninety-two.

Ratification

In congressional usage, ratification has two meanings. In one, it is the president's formal act of promulgating a treaty after the Senate has approved it. The resolution of ratification agreed to by the Senate is the procedural vehicle by which the Senate gives its consent to ratification. (See LEGISLATION.)

The second meaning applies to a state legislature's act in approving a proposed constitutional amendment. An amendment becomes effective when ratified by three-fourths of the states.

Rayburn, Sam

Sam Rayburn (1882–1961) served as SPEAKER OF THE HOUSE longer than any other member in history. He wielded great authority through a combination of personal prestige, persuasiveness, and an almost uncanny sense of the nature of the institution and how it worked.

A Texan and a Democrat "without prefix, without suffix, and without apology," Rayburn entered the House in 1913. In 1931 he became chair of the Interstate and Foreign Commerce Committee, where he managed the regulatory measures of the New Deal. In 1937 he became majority leader, and in 1940, Speaker. Except for stints as minority leader in 1947–1949 and 1953–1955, he retained the post of Speaker until his death.

Rayburn's advice to younger members has often been quoted: "To get along, you've got to go along." The comment reflected a House in which it was no longer

Speaker of the House for seventeen years until his death in 1961, Sam Rayburn held the post longer than any other member in history. This portrait was printed by Douglas Chandor in 1941.
Source: The Granger Collection, New York

Political scientist Richard Fenno pioneered the study of style among members of Congress have two styles: a "home style" for consumption in their districts or states, and a "Hill style" for their official work in Washington. A prime example of split styles was House Speaker Sam Rayburn, Democrat from Texas, who wore tailored suits, rode in a chauffeured limousine, and moved easily in Washington's high society. Back home in Bonham, Rayburn became a plain dirt farmer, wearing old khakis, driving a battered pickup, and spitting from a wad of tobacco that he never seemed to chew in the capital.

possible to exercise the kind of power earlier Speakers had enjoyed. "You cannot lead people in order to drive them," he said. "Persuasion and reason are the only ways to lead them. In that way the Speaker has influence and power in the House."

Rayburn used all the power available to him. He gave out good committee assignments as a reward to members who were sympathetic to the goals of the Democratic Party. In 1961 he gave way to the pressure of party liberals and orchestrated the expansion of the Rules Committee to ease the passage of liberal legislation. Occasionally he could be autocratic. In 1941, for example, he was "suspected of wielding a quick gavel" to prevent reconsideration of a military draft extension that had passed by a 203–202 vote. But mainly Rayburn ruled behind the scenes through conciliation and compromise. Although plagued by a CONSERVATIVE COALITION of southern Democrats and Republicans that stymied much Democratic domestic legislation, Rayburn was generally successful in getting legislation through the House. He oversaw the passage of the civil rights acts of 1957 and 1960 and was able to gain approval for much foreign affairs legislation.

"You cannot lead people in order to drive them. Persuasion and reason are the only ways to lead them. In that way the Speaker has influence and power in the House."

—Rep. Sam Rayburn, who was House Speaker for seventeen years, longer than any other person

Readings of Bills

House and Senate rules require that all bills be read three times before passage, in accordance with traditional parliamentary procedure. The original purpose was to make sure legislators knew what they were voting on, but in modern practice usually only the title of the bill is actually read.

Senate rules require bills and resolutions to be read twice, on different legislative days, before they are referred to committee. The third and final reading follows floor debate and voting on amendments.

In the House the first reading occurs when the bill is introduced and printed by number and title in the *Congressional Record*. The second reading takes place when floor consideration begins; often the bill is read section by section for amendment. The third reading comes just before the vote on final passage.

Reapportionment and Redistricting

Reapportionment and redistricting are the two processes that allocate the 435 seats in the House of Representatives. As such, they are central to the American political system. They help to determine whether Democrats or Republicans, liberals or conservatives, will dominate the House—and whether racial or ethnic minorities will receive fair representation.

Reapportionment is the redistribution of House seats among the states to reflect shifts in population as indicated by the national census, which is conducted every ten years. States whose populations have grown quickly over the previous decade are given additional House seats, while those that have lost population or have grown more slowly than the national average have seats taken away.

Redistricting means that the boundaries of congressional districts within each state are redrawn, based on the number of House seats allotted to the state and population changes within the state. Most House members represent a specific area, or district, within a state, although seven states with sparse populations have only one House member for the entire state. Redistricting usually occurs in the two years following reapportionment; the governor and legislature of the state normally control the process. In the latter years of the twentieth century, maps were often challenged in court, often over allegations that minorities—African Americans in particular—were not receiving representation required under civil rights laws. This was less prevalent after the 2000 census and redistricting but still occurred frequently. In these cases, courts frequently ordered additional redistricting in the middle of a decade, and on occasion even drew new district maps on their own.

Reapportionment and redistricting have been subjects of debate throughout U.S. history because the Constitution did not specify how they should be done. The framers of the Constitution decreed that House seats would be divided among the states on the basis of population, and that House members would be elected by the people. Beyond that, the Constitution gave little guidance on these subjects, leaving Congress, the courts, and state governments to wrestle with them.

After many decades of debate, the basic goal of reapportionment and redistricting was settled by Supreme Court rulings in the 1960s. The guiding principle of the two processes is "one person, one vote." Under this principle, fairness requires that each citizen must have approximately the same representation in the House. This means that each of the congressional districts within a state should be as close to equal in population as possible. Many other questions about reapportionment and redistricting have yet to be settled. Most important, the courts have not decided definitively whether the Constitution permits gerrymandering, the practice of states drawing the boundaries of House districts so as to favor one party or group.

In contrast to the House, the Senate never undergoes reapportionment or redistricting. The Constitution gave each state two Senate seats, and senators are always chosen on a statewide basis.

Reapportionment

Reapportionment determines the relative strength of states and regions in the House according to a mathematical formula that distributes House seats to states on the basis of population. It has not been easy to pick the best formula for distributing House seats. Congress has tried different methods over the years, but none, including the one currently in use, has worked perfectly. Many experts believe it is impossible to devise a method of allocating House seats that does not give some states more or less representation than they deserve.

The cause of the difficulty is simple: no state can have a fraction of a representative. Each state must have a whole number of House members, from one (the seven states with populations so small they are entitled to a only single representative under the Constitution) to as many as fifty-three (California) in the early 2000s. Even with the complex reapportionment formula now in use, there are variations in the amount of representation states receive based on their populations.

The framers settled the difficult question of distribution of House seats for the first Congresses by specifically listing the number of seats each of the thirteen original states would have. This was necessary because at that time there were no accurate statistics on the populations of the states. After the first census in 1790,

CLOSER LOOK

Reapportionment is the redistribution of House seats among the states to reflect shifts in population. Redistricting occurs when the boundaries of congressional districts within each state are redrawn to accommodate the number of seats a state is allotted under reapportionment and to reflect shifts in population within the state. Court decisions have required that districts have equal population. Shifting populations within a state plus the gain or loss of seats from reapportionment can mean minor or significant changes in the geographical areas the make up districts. Reapportionment occurs every ten years after a national census. Normally redistricting also occurs after the decennial reapportionment, but occasionally states voluntarily or under court order change district lines between censuses.

More on this topic:

Blacks in Congress, p. 42

Gerrymandering, p. 244

Hispanics in Congress, p. 259

the Constitution directed that each congressional district should have at least 30,000 residents. An exception was made for small states, which were guaranteed at least one representative no matter what their population. In a compromise between the slave-owning South and the rest of the country, the Constitution provided that each slave would be counted as three-fifths of a person.

At first Congress followed the Constitution in basing representation on an ideal population size of a congressional district. As a result, the total number of House members at any time varied widely. In 1832, for example, the standard size of a congressional district was set at 47,700 people, producing a House of 240 members. None of the different allocation methods used in those days could solve the problem of fractional representation, so congressional districts varied widely.

The early reapportionment methods also failed to deal with the rapid growth in the nation's population. No matter what method was used, there seemed to be unanticipated effects that went against common sense. One method was subject to the "population paradox," in which an increase in the total population led to a decrease in the size of the House. Another technique produced the "Alabama paradox," which at times decreased the size of a state's delegation even as the total number of House seats went up.

Finally, around 1850, Congress settled on a method that seemed to solve many reapportionment problems. The size of the House was supposed to be fixed, although Congress regularly voted to add more members as new states entered the Union. The addition of members allowed the House to side step the difficult task of cutting back on the representation of existing states to make room for new ones. By the beginning of the twentieth century, however, the process threatened to make the House too large to be a workable legislative body. In 1911 Congress fixed the size of the House at 435, where it has remained as of early 2007 except for a brief period (1959–1963) when the admission of Alaska and Hawaii raised the total temporarily to 437.

The decision to freeze the size of the House set the stage for the reapportionment battles of the 1920s. The 1920 census was a landmark event in the nation's history because it showed that for the first time there were more Americans living in cities than in rural areas. States with large cities thus were entitled to many more representatives, while rural states faced sharp cutbacks in their House representation.

Arguing that people who lived on farms and in small towns were the heart and soul of America, rural representatives fought hard to prevent their loss of power. They managed to block reapportionment throughout the 1920s. Redistribution of House seats did not take place until after the 1930 census. That reapportionment led to drastic shifts in power, with California nearly doubling its House delegation, from eleven to twenty, while twenty-one other states lost a total of twenty-seven seats.

The current method of reapportionment, called "the method of equal proportions," was adopted in 1950 and made retroactive to 1941. It allocates House seats according to a complicated mathematical formula designed to minimize population variation among districts. Its adoption put an end to most controversy over reapportionment until the early 1990s, when two states mounted legal challenges. Both succeeded in the lower courts but were rejected by the Supreme Court in 1992.

Massachusetts argued that it deserved one more seat than it received because the census had counted overseas military personnel inaccurately. Montana, which had lost one of its two seats in the 1990 reapportionment, challenged the reapportionment formula on grounds that it was unfair to less populous states. The Supreme Court's refusal to support either claim reflected its traditional reluctance to interfere in the politically explosive issue of reapportionment.

Reapportionment every ten years has continued to exert major influence on political strength in the House. Because Americans move so often, the populations of many states change substantially in ten years. The political strength of those states in the House can change considerably as well.

The most important change in state populations in the latter decades of the twentieth century was the shift of people away from the older, industrial states of the Northeast and Midwest to the newly developing states along the nation's southern tier, from Florida to California (the Sun Belt). As a result of the 1980 census, seventeen House seats shifted from the Northeast and Midwest to the Sun Belt. The state that benefited most was Florida, which picked up four seats, followed by Texas with three and California with two. New York, on the other hand, lost five seats—the sharpest drop in House representation for any state since 1840. Illinois, Ohio, and Pennsylvania lost two seats each.

The 1990 census and 2000 census showed that the trend had continued. After the 1990 census, California picked up seven seats, reflecting a dramatic westward population shift, while Florida gained another four seats and Texas gained three. New York once again was the big loser, dropping three seats. Illinois, Ohio, and Pennsylvania again lost two seats each, as did Michigan.

Under the 2000 census, eighteen state delegations changed. Power continued to shift from the Northeast and Midwest to the South and West. Four states won two more seats: Arizona, Florida, Georgia, and Texas. Four states gained one seat: California, Colorado, Nevada, and North Carolina. Eight states lost one seat: Connecticut, Illinois, Indiana, Michigan, Mississippi, Ohio, Oklahoma, and Wisconsin. Two states continued to lose more than other states: New York and Pennsylvania lost two more seats.

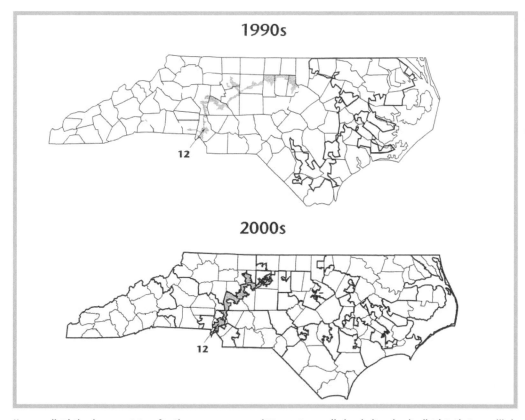

House redistricting in some states after the 1990 census sought to create so-called majority-minority districts that were likely to elect a person from a minority group, usually an African American. The effort resulted in unusually shaped districts such as North Carolina's 12th. The Supreme Court in a series of rulings cast doubt on these configurations and mapmakers after the 2000 census focused on other concerns, particularly protection of incumbents. Nevertheless, North Carolina's 12th District in 2002 (above, bottom) looked similar to the 1990s version (above, top). States with large minority populations continued efforts after the 2000 count to ensure district configurations provided representation in the House for minority groups.

Many political analysts predicted that the 1980 reapportionment would alter the political makeup of the House. Most of the states that lost seats tended to favor liberal Democrats, while the states that gained seats were more likely to favor Republicans or conservative Democrats. In part because of Democratic successes in the state redistricting battles that followed reapportionment, Republicans were disappointed in their hopes to substantially reduce the Democrats' majorities in Congress after the 1992 election, the first to reflect reapportionment following the 1990 census. But the shift of House seats to more conservative areas in the South and West did play a part in Republicans taking control of the House in the 1994 election, and holding a majority in the chamber for the rest of the 1990s and through the first few years of the twenty-first century. Reapportionment was credited as one key factor in the 2002 midterm elections when Democrats lost seats. But the theory took a beating in 2006 when Democrats roared back to gain thirty seats and control of the House; many of the seats were in districts thought to be solidly Republican.

Redistricting

Redistricting has become a subject of intense dispute in recent decades as a result of Supreme Court decisions in the 1960s, major population shifts within states, and the development of computer-based technology. The national Republican and Democratic parties devote immense resources to the effort to persuade state legislatures and the courts to approve state district plans favorable to their own candidates.

The early years of debate over redistricting were dominated by the question of whether there needed to be congressional districts within states at all. The Constitution does not say so, and several states favored at-large elections in which all the voters in the state chose all the state's House members. Use of the system declined because it did not encourage the close ties between representatives and citizens that developed when a member of Congress represented a specific area.

Congress banned at-large House elections in 1842, except in one-member states, although the ban frequently was violated until the 1960s. The 1842 law also established the basic principle that House districts should be contiguous—that is, a single, connected area rather than several separate areas scattered across a state.

For a hundred years redistricting questions received little attention. State legislatures had to draw new district lines when reapportionment cost the state House seats, and occasionally a heated dispute arose over a single congressional district. But state legislatures usually ignored the question of redistricting and rarely acted to change district lines. As a result, cities did not gain additional representatives as their populations grew. Partisan fights over district lines were rare, however, and there was little pressure for major alterations in the shape of most districts.

The situation changed radically when the Supreme Court began to consider redistricting issues in the 1960s, after refusing for decades to become involved in the matter. By the time the Court began to act, there was clear evidence that something was wrong with the way legislative districts were drawn. Particularly in state legislatures, rural areas were vastly overrepresented, while cities did not have nearly as much representation as their populations warranted. In every state the most populous state legislative district had more than twice as many people as the least populous district. The discrepancy was not as pronounced in congressional districts, but wide differences between rural and urban representation remained. For example, in Texas one urban district had four times as many people as one lightly populated rural district.

The state legislatures, which were dominated by members from rural areas, refused to change the existing districts. Frustrated urban dwellers turned to the courts, arguing that they were being denied fair representation by the legislatures. In its historic decision in *Baker v. Carr* (1962), the Supreme Court ruled that the districts used in the Tennessee state legislature were unconstitutional because they violated the principle of one person, one vote. One year later, in *Gray v. Sanders,* a

Georgia elections case, Justice William O. Douglas set out the Court's "one person, one vote" belief. "The conception of political equality from the Declaration of Independence, to Lincoln's Gettysburg address, to the Fifteenth, Seventeenth, and Nineteenth Amendments can mean only one thing—one person, one vote."

In 1964 the Court extended that doctrine to the House in the case of *Wesberry v. Sanders,* which concerned congressional districts in Georgia. That decision stated that congressional districts should be as nearly equal in population "as is practicable."

Since then, the Court has continued to tighten the requirement that congressional districts should have equal populations. In *Kirkpatrick v. Preisler* (1969) the Court struck down the district plan of Missouri, where the largest district had a population only 3.1 percent larger than that of the smallest district. Any population difference, "no matter how small," the Court declared, was unacceptable in all but a few cases. The Court set an even more rigorous standard in *Karcher v. Daggett* (1983). In that case the Court overturned New Jersey's congressional map because the difference between the most populated and the least populated districts was 0.69 percent.

Although the principle of one person, one vote is now widely accepted in American politics, some political experts are critical of the strict standard of population equality set by the Court. For one thing, the census figures for district populations are not entirely accurate, and they usually are out of date within a year or two after the census has been taken. The 1990 census was especially controversial because studies showed that certain urban and minority populations were seriously undercounted.

Moreover, districts that are drawn to ensure equal population often cross traditional political boundaries, such as cities, counties, or regions, that help voters develop a sense of identification with and interest in their congressional district. Finally, critics have pointed out that the Court's standard can be satisfied by a district plan that is a grossly unfair case of political gerrymandering, as long as each district has the same number of people.

The issue of gerrymandering has been at the center of recent debate over redistricting. The subject is complex, but it is centered on one basic idea: certain areas within each state show a long-term preference for one party over the other. In each election the majority in these areas votes for the candidate of one party, regardless of who is running or what issues are being debated. An area with many working-class people and African Americans, for example, tends to favor Democratic candidates year after year. A wealthy area in the suburbs, on the other hand, may support Republicans in almost every election.

Because these voting habits are well known to political experts in each state, it is possible to create districts that are almost certain to favor candidates of one

The Supreme Court's rulings in the 1960s that congressional districts within a state had to be of near equal size in population, or "one person, one vote," resulted in a reduction of rural districts and an increase in urban ones.
Source: Gene Basset

> "The conception of political equality from the Declaration of Independence, to Lincoln's Gettysburg address, to the Fifteenth, Seventeenth, and Nineteenth Amendments can mean only one thing—one person, one vote."
>
> —*Justice William O. Douglas* in *Gray v. Sanders,* a central case in the Supreme Court's collection of decisions in the 1960s prohibiting state legislative and congressional districts with vastly different populations

party. A district composed solely of blue-collar and inner-city neighborhoods will almost always elect a Democrat, while one made up entirely of well-to-do suburbanites will be a "safe" Republican seat.

State legislators and party strategists have learned over the years to play even more subtle redistricting games. If an incumbent barely survives a tough reelection fight, the state legislature might agree to redraw that legislator's district to include areas filled with voters who favor that candidate's party, while taking out some neighborhoods that usually vote against the party. On a larger scale, "party A" might try to dilute the voting strength of "party B" by spreading B voters among several districts, preventing B candidates from winning a majority in any one district. Or else A strategists might concentrate all possible B voters in one district, creating a safe district for party B but making all the other districts in the state favorable to A candidates.

Another potential kind of gerrymandering involves racial or ethnic groups. By dividing up African Americans or other minority voters among several districts, a legislature might be able to ensure that members of a minority group make up no more than half the voters in a district and so prevent election of a minority representative. When blacks in the South began to vote in large numbers in the 1960s, civil rights groups feared that they might be subjected to racial gerrymandering by white-dominated legislatures. To prevent this, Congress added provisions to the 1965 Voting Rights Act barring redistricting plans that dilute the voting strength of blacks.

The law required states with histories of racial discrimination to submit their redistricting plans to the U.S. Justice Department to ensure that African American voters were being treated fairly. Other minorities, including Hispanics, Asian Americans, and Native Americans, were later included in the law's protection. The department and the courts have required changes in redistricting plans in several states to ensure that minority candidates have a chance of being elected. The department required fourteen states to submit their redistricting plans for approval after the 1990 census.

In the *Thornburg v. Gingles* (1986) ruling on districts in North Carolina, the Supreme Court said that gerrymandering that deliberately diluted minority voting strength was illegal. The burden of proof shifted from minorities, who had been required to show that lines were being drawn to dilute their voting strength, to lawmakers, who had to show that they had done all they could to maximize minority voting strength.

The expansion of minority rights sparked by *Gingles* and later court rulings changed redistricting dramatically. Republicans, many of whom originally had opposed the creation of "majority-minority" districts, became promoters of the trend when they saw how it might benefit them. Since minorities usually vote Democratic, concentrating them in one district leaves surrounding districts more favorable to Republican candidates.

"A congressional district map that groups people "who may have little in common with one another but the color of their skin bears an uncomfortable resemblance to political apartheid."

—Justice Sandra Day O'Connor in *Shaw v. Reno*

In 1992 Republicans in several states expected to profit from legislative or judicial efforts to draw new districts to benefit minority voters—but their hopes were disappointed. Although Republicans failed to make significant gains, the new district maps resulted in record numbers of Hispanics and African Americans being elected to Congress in 1992. Maps drawn for the 1990s that went to extreme lengths to elect minorities came quickly under scrutiny by the Supreme Court. In the *Shaw v. Reno* (1993) ruling on districts in North Carolina, Justice Sandra Day O'Connor wrote for the Court majority that any map that groups people "who may have little in common with one another but the color of their skin bears an uncomfortable resemblance to political apartheid." In a case involving districts in Georgia, *Miller v. Jackson* (1995), the Court further ruled that using race as "the predominant factor" in drawing districts is presumed to be unconstitutional, unless it serves a compelling government interest.

Those two rulings represented a speedy swing of the judicial pendulum away from the 1986 *Gingles* doctrine of maximizing minority-voting strength in redistricting. As the 1990s unfolded, the constitutionality of majority-minority districts was widely challenged, and eventually, federal courts ordered a number of states—including North Carolina, Georgia, Florida, Louisiana, New York, Texas, and Virginia—to redraw districts that were adjudged to be unconstitutional racial gerrymanders. However, in Illinois, a majority-minority district was allowed to stand after the state argued successfully that it had a "compelling state interest" in giving Chicago's large Hispanic population the opportunity to elect one representative of its own. Although numerous majority-minority districts were redrawn in the mid- and late 1990s to reduce their minority populations, nearly all those districts remained in the hands of minority-group representatives beyond the decade's end.

Unresolved Question: Partisan Gerrymandering

The constitutionality of partisan gerrymandering remained in 2007 an important unresolved question in American politics. By one argument it is unconstitutional because it deprives voters in a gerrymandered district of the right to make an effective choice between candidates of both parties. If a district is set up to make election of a Democrat virtually inevitable, then Republicans in the district have lost the right to cast anything more than a symbolic vote for their candidate. The Supreme Court has been reluctant to address partisan gerrymandering directly. The Court has viewed the issue as a political question outside its jurisdiction. As long as districts are sufficiently similar in population, the Court has not been willing to judge whether they were unfairly gerrymandered—except in cases where racial discrimination is at issue.

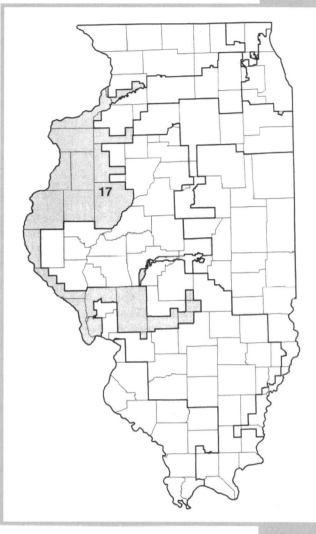

Following the 2000 census, Democrats and Republicans were particularly interested in drawing new House districts that protected incumbents and were less concerned about creating new districts that benefited their party—although a good deal of that went on as well. One of the most striking examples of a bizarrely shaped district that was drawn to ensure the re-election of an incumbent was the 17th District in Illinois. The 17th covered nine full counties and parts of fourteen others.

The emphasis on one person, one vote was clear when the Supreme Court in the *Karcher* 1983 decision overturned New Jersey's congressional map because of the 0.69 percent population variation. But in separate dissents Justices Lewis F. Powell Jr. and John Paul Stevens broadly hinted that they were willing to hear constitutional challenges to instances of partisan gerrymandering. "A legislator cannot represent his constituents properly—nor can voters from a fragmented district exercise the ballot intelligently—when a voting district is nothing more than an artificial unit

divorced from, and indeed often in conflict with, the various communities established in the State," wrote Powell.

In 1986 the Court handed down a significant decision on gerrymandering. In a case involving Indiana's state legislative districts, the Court ruled that political gerrymanders were subject to constitutional challenges for unfairly discriminating against political parties. The case was expected to open the door for many other challenges to allegedly gerrymandered district plans. But in 1989 the Court declined to become involved in the gerrymandering question when it reaffirmed without comment a lower court's decision to uphold California's congressional map, widely recognized as a classic example of a partisan gerrymander.

> **"A legislator cannot represent his constituents properly—nor can voters from a fragmented district exercise the ballot intelligently—when a voting district is nothing more than an artificial unit divorced from, and indeed often in conflict with, the various communities established in the State."**
>
> **—Justices Lewis F. Powell Jr. and John Paul Stevens**

Nevertheless, with the law largely settled on population and racial issues in redistricting, partisan gerrymandering appeared at the beginning of the twenty-first century to be the next frontier. The 1983 decision, with its exceptionally difficult standard to prove a partisan drawing of lines, still was the controlling law and remained so when the Court in 2004 rejected a claim under it to districts in Pennsylvania that Democrats said were constitutionally invalid (*Vieth v. Jubelirer*). In that case the swing vote on the Court came from Justice Anthony Kennedy, who agreed that the Pennsylvania Democrats had not shown enough to meet the framework for partisan gerrymandering set out in earlier decisions. But Kennedy also said that because no adequate standard to measure partisan gerrymandering had yet emerged did not mean that it would never evolve in the future. The more conservative justices on the Court wanted to sweep away all previous hints from decisions that political gerrymandering might be constitutionally challengeable.

Two instances of partisan gerrymandering were prominent after the 2000 census. In Colorado, Republicans sought to tweak district lines to enhance the reelection chances of an incumbent who barely won in 2002. The state supreme court on December 1, 2003, ruled a second redistricting in the decade was impermissible under the state's constitution. The U.S. Supreme Court in June 2004 declined to review the decision.

In Texas, however, Republicans orchestrated a major redrawing of some district lines with the goal of defeating as many as seven incumbents who had won in 2002 under a court-ordered district plan. Six of the seven lost in 2004. Democrats charged the redrawing was unconstitutional, but courts did not accept their contention except in one instance that involved a violation of a civil rights law.

Recess *See* ADJOURNMENT.

Recess Appointment *See* APPOINTMENT POWER.

Recommittal Motion

Motions to recommit a bill to the committee that reported it are used often in the House of Representatives, seldom in the Senate. These motions are offered for purposes ranging from killing a bill outright to significantly altering it before final passage to obtaining a recorded vote on a proposal.

There are two kinds of recommittal motions. A simple motion to recommit, if adopted, kills the bill for all practical purposes. The second type of motion is to recommit "with instructions." The latter often contains language instructing the committee to report the bill back "forthwith" with certain amendments (or sometimes after a study is completed or by a certain date). If the motion to report back forthwith is adopted, the bill is not actually returned to the committee. Rather, the floor manager announces that the committee has reported the bill back to the House with the amendments contained in the instructions and the floor action continues.

The motion to recommit is a standard parliamentary procedure occurring just before the vote on final passage of a bill in the full House. It is not used during consideration of a bill for amendment in the Committee of the Whole. It is a privileged motion and the right to offer it is guaranteed by the rules of the House. Opponents must be given preference in offering the motion, and only one such motion is permitted on each bill. If made with instructions to add or amend certain provisions, recommittal motions give opponents of a bill a final opportunity to revise the legislation. The motions are an important strategic and policy tool of the minority, especially on bills considered under ground rules that bar floor amendments. Few controversial recommittal motions, however, are ever adopted in the House.

They are, however, sometimes used in the ongoing guerilla warfare between the majority and minority parties. Republicans in 2007, newly in the minority, began using recommittal motions aggressively—sometimes to alter legislation but often to force Democrats from marginal districts—which included a large number of freshmen who had in 2006 captured normally GOP districts—to make tough choices. Moreover, Democrats had changed House rules at the start of the new Congress to reinstate a pay-as-you-go requirement, called PAYGO, that required finding ways to pay for new spending, such as cutting other spending or increasing revenue through taxes. But on at least one occasion when Democrats did include, a small tax, Republicans seized the opportunity to add a controversial and unrelated amendment on gun control. That was possible because the tax provision opened the bill to amendments that otherwise would be disallowed.

In the Senate recommittal motions are unnecessary because opponents have many other ways to defeat or amend legislation. Occasionally the Senate will vote to recommit legislation with certain instructions to be reported back to the Senate within a specified period of time.

From time to time the Senate entangles itself in such a parliamentary morass that it uses the recommittal motion to extricate itself. That happened in 1982 when the Senate was considering a bill to raise the national debt limit. Majority Leader Howard H. BAKER Jr., a Tennessee Republican, had promised senators for months that they could offer their pet proposals as amendments to the debt bill. But when the measure reached the floor, it became bogged down in a debate on controversial amendments dealing with abortion and school prayer. After five weeks, and with more than 1,400 amendments still pending, the Senate recommitted the measure to the Finance Committee, which immediately stripped it of all but the debt limit provisions and returned it to the floor for a final vote.

Motions to recommit also may be offered to resolutions, House-Senate conference reports, and, in the House, amendments added by the Senate to legislation.

More on this topic:
Committee of the Whole, p. 110
Legislative Process, p. 344
Pay-as-You-Go, p. 414
Privilege, p. 442

Reconciliation   *See* BUDGET PROCESS.

Reconsider, Motion to

The motion to reconsider a vote is a necessary procedure for the final disposition of legislation in both the Senate and House of Representatives. It is a principle of parliamentary law that floor action on bills and amendments is not conclusive until there has been an opportunity to reconsider the vote by which the question was approved or rejected.

The motion to reconsider usually is followed immediately by a motion to table the motion to reconsider. Once the motion to reconsider has been tabled, the earlier action on the bill or amendment is final; the act of tabling blocks any future attempt to reverse the result. (See TABLE, MOTION TO.)

In the House, the Speaker usually makes the tabling motion by stating that "without objection a motion to reconsider is laid on the table." Under the rules of both houses, a motion to reconsider can be made only by a member on the prevailing side of the original vote approving or rejecting the bill or amendment (or, in the Senate, by someone who did not vote at all).

The rules in both houses set a time limit for entering motions to reconsider, and the parliamentary situation determines when such motions are in order. For example, a motion to reconsider a vote rejecting an amendment after the bill itself has been passed would come too late.

Reconstruction Era

The period immediately following the Civil War is known as the Reconstruction Era. The name refers to the policies implemented by the victorious Union government in its effort to "reconstruct" the eleven war-torn and economically devastated Confederate states. But Reconstruction, which lasted from 1865 to about 1877, connotes more than merely a sectional administrative matter. It also represents a period of unprecedented radical national leadership dominated by Congress at the expense of the presidency and the judiciary.

Lincoln's Leniency

Even before the Civil War ended, President Abraham Lincoln had outlined a policy for dealing with the Southern states once they capitulated to the Union armies. As early as 1862 he began appointing military governors in areas that had fallen to the Union. He first outlined his Reconstruction policy in December 1863 and eloquently reiterated his views in his last public address, on April 11, 1865. Lincoln's primary goal was to return the seceded states to the Union as quickly and painlessly as possible. Amnesty and restoration of property rights were to be granted to everyone who gave an oath of loyalty to the Union, except for a relatively few Confederate civilian and military leaders. Whenever 10 percent of the electorate of any state made such a pledge, a state government could be established. Once each new state government ratified the Thirteenth Amendment—thereby nullifying its previous secession, repudiating the debts of its Confederate government, and abolishing slavery—the president was prepared to recognize that state as once again a loyal part of the United States. The states of Louisiana and Arkansas promptly accepted Lincoln's terms and adopted new constitutions abolishing slavery even before the president was assassinated.

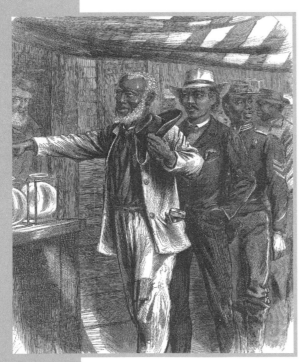

The collapse of the Confederacy resulted in the emancipation of about four million slaves. The Radical Republicans' aim was to use the former slaves' votes to ensure Republican domination in state governments in the South and the representation of those states in Congress.
Source: Library of Congress

Such magnanimous treatment of the South was at odds with the will of Congress, which during and after the war was controlled by the Republicans, the most influential of whom were radical abolitionists. They made little attempt to disguise their hatred of southerners and southern institutions, and they refused to accept the validity of Lincoln's terms. In their view Reconstruction was solely the jurisdiction of Congress. When the two readmitted southern states sent their newly elected representatives to Washington, Congress refused to seat them.

Radical Reconstruction

To the Radical Republicans, the southerners remained traitors and rebels, who could not be restored to citizenship of a country they had rejected without first undergoing rigid tests of loyalty. They devised a punitive plan of their own for implementing Reconstruction. Embodied in the Wade-Davis bill—named for Sen. Benjamin F. Wade of Ohio and Rep. Henry W. Davis of Maryland—the plan required that a majority of the electorate in a state, rather than 10 percent, swear their allegiance to the federal government before the state could be readmitted to the Union.

The Radicals' amnesty excluded even common Confederate soldiers from holding federal office. Such a policy had the effect of excluding the natural leaders and experienced statesmen of the region from participation in its new civilian governments. But that was just the beginning. Underlying all the invective and passion, the Radicals' real goal was to force upon the South the immediate, full equality of all former slaves and to use black votes to ensure Republican domination in Southern state governments and in Congress. The collapse of the Confederacy had resulted in the emancipation of about 4 million slaves.

But Lincoln was convinced that leniency was the only way to build loyalty to the Union and establish intersectional peace. Although he pocket-vetoed the Wade-Davis bill, the bill's authors issued the legislation as a manifesto of congressional sentiment and intent. "The president ... must understand that the authority of Congress is paramount and must be respected ... and if he wishes our support he must confine himself to his executive duties—to obey and execute, not to make the laws—to suppress by arms any armed rebellion, and leave political reorganization of the South to Congress." Confrontation between the legislative and executive branches over Reconstruction now was inevitable.

After Lincoln's assassination his successor, Andrew Johnson, lacking Lincoln's political astuteness, played into the hands of the Radicals. Johnson had the disadvantage of being the nominal leader of a party in which he was not a member. A War Democrat added to the Republican ticket in 1864 to emphasize unity, he had no personal following in either the North or the South. After a brief period of vindictiveness that appeased the Radicals, Johnson reversed positions and adopted Lincoln's mild policies.

The conflict between the two branches was not resolved until Johnson had been impeached (but not removed from office), harsh and constitutionally questionable Reconstruction laws enacted, and the Constitution itself amended to suit the Radicals' purposes.

Committee of Fifteen

The Radicals were led by Rep. Thaddeus STEVENS of Pennsylvania. Stevens's policies were based less on sympathy for blacks than on a desire for political advantage and a cold hatred of the southern gentry.

Although he was not its chair, Stevens dominated a joint committee of the House and Senate, the Joint Committee of Fifteen. This committee was the outgrowth of the Committee on the Conduct of the War that had tried to force its views on Lincoln. The joint committee officially investigated and reported on the credentials of southern members-elect to Congress. In reality, it also wielded the real power in Congress at the time. The Radicals' Reconstruction policies and the tactics used against the president were formulated by this group.

The Radicals' leader in the Senate was Charles SUMNER of Massachusetts. He was not on the Committee of Fifteen, but next to Stevens he was the most powerful figure in the Reconstruction policy. He too believed the Confederate states had committed political suicide and that Congress had exclusive jurisdiction over postwar administration of these outlaw states. As an idealist, lacking any personal knowledge of the slaves' condition, Sumner insisted on giving the freed slaves immediate equality. He lent the Radical cause a tinge of idealism and respectability.

In 1866 Johnson vetoed the first of two Freedmen's Bureau bills, designed to provide services for and protect the rights of the ex-slaves. The Radicals were unable to override that veto, but soon thereafter they did manage to override the veto of a civil rights bill as unconstitutional. Even Radicals had doubts about the bill's constitutionality, however. To allay any doubts they drafted the Fourteenth Amendment, which among other things guaranteed the civil rights of blacks against state interference, reduced the Southern states' representation in Congress in proportion to their denial of black suffrage, and disqualified from holding federal or state office ex-Confederates who had formerly held such offices. But the most important provision was the first clause: "No State shall make or enforce any law which shall abridge the privileges or immunities of citizens of the United States; nor shall any State deprive any person of life, liberty, or property, without due process of law; nor deny to any person within its jurisdiction the equal protection of the laws."

The congressional elections of 1866, in which the Radicals were reelected, proved critical to the direction of Reconstruction policy. Using the results as vindication of their policy, the Radicals pushed through Congress a series of punitive laws, including the First Reconstruction Act of 1867. This law declared that no legal governments existed in the Southern states (except in Tennessee) and divided the South into five military districts supervised by Union officers. There followed a harsh military occupation of some 20,000 soldiers, including a force of black militia. The military commanders' primary tasks were to create new electorates and establish new state governments. In Alabama, Florida, Mississippi, Louisiana, and South Carolina, black voters outnumbered whites. New constitutions were drafted enfranchising blacks, disenfranchising ex-Confederate leaders, and guaranteeing civil and political equality to the freedmen.

The threat of reduced representation in the House, included in the Fourteenth Amendment, failed to prompt Southern states to extend the franchise to blacks. As a result, Congress in 1869 submitted to the states the Fifteenth Amendment, which prohibited denial of the right to vote on the basis of race, color, or previous condition of servitude. The amendment was ratified the following year. Congress also passed legislation designed to make the amendment effective, but parts of that law were later held unconstitutional.

Separation of Powers

The Reconstruction policies threatened more than the South. The Radicals' goal was ultimately to establish a government dominated by Congress and, within Congress, by the Radical Republicans themselves. With pliant executive and judicial branches, the constitutional principle of separation of powers was in jeopardy. This was the inescapable implication of passage, over Johnson's veto, of the First Reconstruction Act of 1867, as well as two other laws passed at the same time.

The first, the Command of the Army Act, barred the executive from exercising any control over the army by requiring the president to issue all military orders through the general of the army. The president could not fire or suspend this officer.

The second, the Tenure of Office Act, prevented the president from removing civilians in the executive branch, including members of his cabinet, without the consent of the Senate. This made it impossible for a president to control his own administration. Johnson refused to recognize the constitutionality of the law and dismissed his secretary of war, Edwin M. Stanton. This action provided the Radicals with the excuse they needed to attempt to remove Johnson from office through the impeachment process. The House impeached Johnson, but in a Senate trial the president escaped removal by a single vote. If the Radicals' effort had succeeded, the presidency would have gone to Senator Wade, because the vice presidency was vacant and, under the law at that time, the Senate president pro tempore—the post held by Wade—was next in the line of succession.

Congressional Republicans remained in control of most of the reconstructed states well into the 1870s. Control was maintained by an alliance of blacks and Radical Republicans. The latter were of two types: "carpetbaggers," northerners who came to the South for political and economic profit; and "scalawags," southern white renegades. This situation led to a dreadful record of misrule, political corruption, human exploitation, and economic dislocation, including staggering budget deficits.

By the early 1870s the Radicals' drastic policies toward the South had lost most of their popular appeal. In 1874 Democrats gained control of the House of Representatives, and the policy of Reconstruction was finally rejected. The last Union troops were withdrawn from South Carolina and Louisiana in 1877 by order of President Rutherford B. Hayes.

More on this topic:
Impeachment Power, p. 280
Johnson Impeachment Trial, p. 307
Separation of Powers, p. 508

Reed, Thomas Brackett

Thomas Brackett Reed (1839–1902) of Maine, known as "Czar" Reed, was one of the most powerful Speakers in House history. Determined to put an end to the obstructionist tactics of the minority party, Reed made a series of rulings from the chair that allowed the Republican majority to conduct the business of the House without hindrance. His biting wit, determination, and physical presence made Reed impressive and aided him in forming a Republican voting bloc. (See SPEAKER OF THE HOUSE.)

After practicing law in Portland, Maine, and serving in city and state offices (including the state legislature), Reed was elected to the House of Representatives in 1876. In 1882 he was appointed to the Rules Committee, where he acquired power and the respect of fellow members of his party. When Republicans assumed control of the House in 1889, they elected Reed Speaker. He led Republicans when they were out of power from 1891 to 1895 and resumed the job of Speaker from 1895 to 1899.

The House of which Reed took control was plagued by filibusters that slowed the conduct of business. Democratic representatives

THOMAS BRACKETT REED,
Member of
Congress and
Speaker of the
House
Author of
"Reed's Rules"
and Editor of
"Modern Eloquence"

This drawing by
Thomas Nast
was presented to the
Authors Club
by
Frederic Rowland Marvin

Thomas Brackett Reed, illustrated here in a Thomas Nast drawing, was one of the most powerful Speakers in House history. Known as "Czar" Reed, he established the "Reed Rules" to curb Democratic obstructionism in the 1890s.
Source: National Portrait Gallery, Smithsonian Institution

Thomas Brackett Reed of Maine was one of the most powerful Speakers in House history. He also was one of the most acerbic. Replying to a colleague who said he would rather be right than be president, Reed said: "The gentleman need not be disturbed, he never will be either." On another occasion, referring to two of his House colleagues, he said: "They never open their mouths without subtracting from the sum of human knowledge."

refused to answer quorum calls (even when they were present on the House floor) and introduced a flurry of delaying motions to harry their opponents and lengthen the passage of legislation. Reed's insistence that all members present—whether answering or not—be counted toward a quorum caused pandemonium on the floor. Members tried to hide and were prevented from leaving by the sergeant-at-arms, who was ordered to lock the door. Reed ruled further that the chair would not entertain motions whose purpose was to delay business. These and other "Reed Rules" were formally incorporated into the rules of the House in 1890.

The rules revisions and Czar Reed's exercise of power allowed the House to pass an unprecedented number of bills during the so-called Billion-dollar Congress of 1889–1891. Although resented for his assumption of power, Reed was admired as a wit, albeit an acerbic one. When a member, Rep. William McK. Springer, said, "As for me, I would rather be right than be president," Reed replied, "The gentleman need not be disturbed, he never will be either." On another occasion, referring to two of his House colleagues, he said, "They never open their mouths without subtracting from the sum of human knowledge."

Reed was an unsuccessful candidate for the Republican presidential nomination in 1896. He resigned from Congress in 1899 in protest over U.S. involvement in the Philippines and Hawaii.

Reform, Congressional

Making Congress work better is a never-ending process that has preoccupied senators and representatives ever since reformers turned the Continental Congress into the House of Representatives and Senate. Once institutional reforms are in place, they may turn out to be ineffective or cause new, unexpected problems—prompting yet another set of institutional reforms.

Reforms are changes that have been made deliberately, but changes in the House and Senate also happen gradually, as the institutions adapt to new circumstances and new members. The story of the evolving Congress encompasses far more than reorganizations and formal revisions of rules.

Changing the Rules

Like many institutions, Congress is biased toward maintaining the status quo. Reform does not come easily, and it frequently threatens the existing power structure. In 1910 the House ended the autocratic rule of Speaker Joseph G. CANNON, a conservative Illinois Republican, but only after a two-year struggle by Democrats and insurgent Republicans. They finally succeeded in stripping the Speaker of his power base on the Rules Committee and removing his authority to appoint House committee members and their chairs.

The Rules Committee, which controls access to the House floor for major bills, has been the focus of lengthy reform efforts. For many years the committee was dominated by a coalition of conservative Democrats and Republicans who repeatedly blocked or delayed liberal legislation. In 1959 Speaker Sam RAYBURN, a Texas Democrat, headed off a liberal effort to curb the Rules panel by giving his "personal assurance" that civil rights and other social legislation "would not be bottled up in the committee." Rayburn often was unable to deliver on his promise, however, and two years later the House voted to add three additional members to the committee, thus diluting the power of its conservative members. The dramatic 217–212 House vote in January 1961 was an early signal of the wave of reform that came in the next decade.

In the 1970s the party caucuses in each chamber voted institutional reforms that enabled junior members to share power held by their older and more experienced colleagues. Among the changes was a sweeping attack on the seniority system, which used length of service to determine committee chairmanships. Democrats and Republicans in both chambers agreed to elect their committee leaders, using secret ballots in most cases. The most vivid evidence of the new system at work came in 1975, when House Democrats deposed three chairs. Seniority nonetheless remained a major factor in choosing leaders. (See CAUCUSES, PARTY.)

The House rejected proposals for wholesale reorganization of its committee structure, but the Senate approved substantial changes in its committee system in 1977. Several of the most important Senate reforms centered on the FILIBUSTER, the use of unlimited debate to block the will of the majority. The reforms aimed to strengthen Senate restrictions on the filibuster, which were first adopted in 1917.

Reformers of the 1970s also sought to increase members' accountability by opening to the public and press the inner workings of Congress. The House began gavel-to-gavel television broadcasts of its floor proceedings in 1979; the Senate followed suit in 1986.

Statutory Changes

Other major reforms have been achieved by statute. The Legislative Reorganization Act of 1946 streamlined the committee structure, reduced and redistributed the workload of Congress, and improved staff assistance. Budget control provisions included in the act soon proved unworkable and were dropped. A section on lobby regulation was too weak to be effective. Although fewer committees were provided for under the new structure, subcommittees proliferated.

Another legislative reorganization act, this one in 1970, opened Congress to more public scrutiny and curbed the power of committee chairs. Among other things, the law changed House VOTING procedures to allow for recorded votes on amendments offered on the House floor, required public disclosure of all committee roll calls, authorized radio and television broadcasts of committee hearings, made it more difficult for committees to meet in closed sessions, and required committees to have written rules. The 1970 law authorized additional staff, strengthened Congress's research and information sources, and required the administration to provide Congress with more information about the federal budget. The act also included changes in Senate rules that limited the ability of the most senior members to monopolize choice committee assignments.

The Congressional Budget and Impoundment Control Act of 1974 established a process that for the first time forced lawmakers to coordinate their spending and revenue decisions in a single budget package. It also curbed presidential impoundment of funds appropriated by Congress. The 1974 act was less effective than its sponsors had hoped; in 1985 and again in 1990, as budget deficits rose to alarming levels, lawmakers made substantial changes in the BUDGET PROCESS. They also revised laws dealing with campaign financing and ethics.

Two important twentieth-century reforms were achieved through constitutional amendments. The Seventeenth Amendment, ratified in 1913, provided for direct election of senators; previously, senators had been chosen by state legislatures. The Twentieth Amendment, ratified in 1933, advanced to January from March the date for beginning a new Congress. The change ended the regular practice of LAME-DUCK SESSIONS that ran from the December after an election until the new Congress convened the following March.

Push for Further Reforms

Despite these reforms, legislators in the 1980s became increasingly dissatisfied with the way Congress worked. By the early 1990s Congress appeared ready to tackle reform once again. Congress in 1992 created a Joint Committee on the Organization of Congress to develop a bipartisan plan for improving legislative operations.

Although partisan differences arose, many members on both sides shared views about what was wrong with Congress. One of the most common complaints was that the committee system was an unwieldy anachronism. Critics said the system—troubled by turf battles, overlapping jurisdiction, and outdated delineations of issues—was a significant obstacle to prompt consideration of legislation. For example, a clean air bill in 1990 was handled by seven committees in the House, and that chamber sent 140 members to the conference with the Senate. Major contemporary issues, such as health and international economics, were split among several committees in the House and Senate.

Critics also complained that the Democratic and Republican party leadership in Congress had trouble offering a cohesive legislative agenda because of its weak hold on rank-and-file party members. In 1990, for example, Republican and Democratic leaders agreed to a budget deal with the White House, but neither party was able to deliver its share of the votes in the House. Majority party leaders faced an additional problem, because many powerful committee chairs did not feel compelled to answer to party leaders.

Congressional floor debate was also cited as a problem. The House was criticized for being too restrictive in its rules for limiting amendments; the Senate was criticized for not being restrictive enough. Both were faulted for giving too much time to political sideshows.

Others wanted changes in the legislative and budget processes. Most policy questions had to be addressed in three processes: the budget process, which set general spending priorities; authorization bills, which set policy; and appropriation bills, which provided year-by-year financing for government programs. Critics charged that procedures were complex, redundant, and ill suited to addressing long-term problems, such as the budget deficit, health care, and international competition.

Some saw these problems as arising from the last round of reforms. The drive to break up the power of committee chairs in the 1970s complicated the job of party leaders. Until then, majority party leaders had been able to cut deals with only a handful of power brokers; after the reforms, they had to build consensus within a much broader constituency. Opening Congress to greater public scrutiny made members more accountable, but it also made debate more partisan, unruly, and beholden to special interests. Efforts to give Congress a stronger hand in budgeting ended up obscuring responsibility for fiscal decisions.

Despite the common complaints members had regarding Congress's operations, the joint committee's reform effort ran aground, the victim of partisan bickering and opposition from senior members who stood to lose power. Tensions between the Senate and House ran so high that the two chambers ended up reporting separate recommendations. With little public pressure in evidence, most of the proposals never got to the floor of either chamber.

Congressional reform was one of the planks of the "Contract with America" that the Republican Party campaigned successfully on in 1994 to win control of Congress. Back in power after forty years, House Republicans in 1995 reorganized the administration of the House, privatizing several House services and, with Democratic support, ending workplace law exemptions for congressional employees. The Republican majority also revised House rules, eliminating three committees, reducing staff size by one-third, ending the practice of proxy voting, and imposing term limits on the Speaker and committee chairs, among other changes.

More on this topic:

Appropriation Bills, p. 22

Authorization Bills, p. 33

Leadership, p. 325

Legislative Process, p. 344

Political Parties, p. 420

After these initial reforms, however, House Republicans quickly embraced many of the same Democratic rules and procedures they had so long criticized while in the minority.

A number of Republicans complained when the new term limits rule on chairs took effect at the start of the 107th Congress in January 2001. House Republicans elected thirteen new full committee chairs, largely as a result of those limits. Appropriations subcommittee "cardinals" were shuffled as well, as five came up against term limits and two retired. However, many of the chairs moved on to head other powerful committees or subcommittees.

Also in 2001, the House moved all financial services issues—including banking, insurance, securities, housing, and community development issues—from the Energy and Commerce Committee to the renamed Financial Services Committee. (See ENERGY AND COMMERCE COMMITTEE, HOUSE; FINANCIAL SERVICES COMMITTEE, HOUSE.)

By 2003 the GOP ardor for some of the institutional changes the party initiated in 1995 had diminished, and Republicans pushed through rules changes easing some of them. An eight-year term limit on the Speaker was repealed because Republicans had come to realize that a lame-duck Speaker's powers of persuasion could be sharply curtailed. Speaker J. Dennis HASTERT of Illinois would have been forced to step aside at the beginning of 2007 under the old rule, but he had to step down anyway when Democrats gained thirty seats in the 2006 election to regain the majority. Another change allowed committee chairs to postpone committee votes. Democrats claimed this change would allow chairs to block the minority party's amendments in much the same way chairs had frustrated such amendments when proxy votes were allowed. Nevertheless, Democrats retained most of the GOP changes, including committee chair term limits, when they resumed control in 2007.

Reid, Harry

The 2006 midterm elections that brought Democrats back in control of Congress made Harry Reid, a Nevada Democrat, the most powerful member of the Senate. Previously the party's minority leader, he became in 2007 the new majority leader. But unlike the new House Speaker, Nancy Pelosi of California, Reid had just a one-vote majority in a chamber (one Independent caucused with the Democrats) where almost any senator can create insurmountable obstacles to legislating. Moreover, Reid faced a Republican president, George W. Bush, who made clear he would veto bills not to his liking. With sixty votes to break a filibuster or sixty-seven votes to override a veto beyond his reach, Reid's ascension to power did not mean he could easily advance a Democratic agenda.

In the first year of the new Congress, Reid and the Senate in fact accomplished little other than passing a handful of proposals that had GOP support or no chance

At the start of the 110th Congress in 2007, Sen. Harry Reid of Nevada became majority leader. Reid often took conservative stances on issues such as abortion and environmental reform.
Source: AP Images/Caleb Jones

of getting Bush's approval. To a significant extent, this unimpressive record reflected the focus in both chambers on Democratic efforts—supported by some Republicans—to wrest full control of the intractable Iraq war away from Bush, or at least to set the United States on a clear path to end its combat involvement. By the end of the year, that effort remained unfulfilled.

Nevertheless, no one in either party doubted Reid's determination and skill at directing the Senate toward Democratic objectives, one of the most important of which was putting pressure on the Republicans who had to face reelection challenges in 2008.

Outwardly, Reid lacked modern political panache. He could be taciturn, even dour on television, without the personal charisma of the several presidential hopefuls in the Senate. He preferred reading books to hosting fundraising dinners, and he shunned the continual self-promotion typical of many lawmakers. But the Democratic colleagues who put him on the leadership track knew the side of Reid that was a scrappy former amateur boxer, a wily parliamentarian, and an effective behind-the-scenes operator who could count votes. Though he promoted basic Democratic issues, Reid often consulted conservatives with whom he shared some beliefs on social issues. A practicing Mormon, Reid often voted with Republicans in favor of restrictions on abortion. A defender of his state's economically important mining industry, he could be skeptical of new environmental controls.

Before being elected leader, Reid was the party's second-in-command as the whip for six years under Tom Daschle, the former Senate minority leader. When Daschle was defeated for reelection in 2004, Reid quickly got commitments to become the party's leader.

Reid grew up in a cabin without plumbing in the tiny mining town of Searchlight, Nevada, on the edge of the Mojave Desert. His mother was a high school dropout who took in laundry to support the family; his father was an alcoholic miner who killed himself at fifty-eight. As a young man, Reid was an amateur middleweight who sometimes sparred with pros in exhibition fights.

Reid boarded with families forty miles away in Henderson to attend high school, where he became student body president. He later attended Utah State University and earned a law degree at George Washington University in Washington, D.C., while moonlighting as a U.S. Capitol police officer.

Reid returned to the West and served in the Nevada Assembly and later as lieutenant governor. In 1982 Reid won the first of two terms in the U.S. House. He lost a 1974 bid for the Senate, but in 1986 he tried again and won with 50 percent of the vote.

It was not his only close call. In his 1998 campaign Reid won by only 428 votes over Republican John Ensign, a House member from Las Vegas, in a bitter contest. Reid called Ensign "an embarrassment to the state," and Ensign described Reid as an "old card shark." After Ensign was elected in 2000 to the state's other Senate seat, the two reconciled. In 2004 Reid easily defeated Republican Richard Ziser, an activist against same-sex marriage, for a fourth term.

Removal Power

The Senate can approve or reject presidential nominations through its APPOINTMENT POWER, but the congressional role in removing individuals from office is limited. The Constitution does not mention removal except for the impeachment provisions of Article II, Section 4. Presidents have resisted numerous efforts by Congress to restrict their ability to dismiss officials.

The debate over the Senate's role in the removal of government officers dates back to the First Congress, when the Senate narrowly agreed to legislation that implied recognition of the president's exclusive power of removal under the Constitution.

Early presidents exercised great restraint in their use of the removal power. But in the 1830s Congress resisted President Andrew Jackson's partisan use of the removal power and his insistence on political loyalty as a requirement for government jobs, a practice known as PATRONAGE. The Senate passed a series of resolutions requesting Jackson to inform it of his reasons for removing various officials.

The legislative and executive branches clashed again over removal power during the administration of Andrew Johnson, who sought to control the post–Civil War Reconstruction effort by giving key posts to his followers. The result was the Tenure of Office Act, passed over Johnson's veto in 1867. The act stated that officials appointed by the president and confirmed by the Senate could not be removed without the consent of the Senate. Johnson's defiance of the act led to his impeachment by the House in 1868. (See JOHNSON IMPEACHMENT TRIAL.)

The Tenure of Office Act was weakened in 1869 and repealed in 1887, ending Congress's most aggressive effort to curb the president's removal power. The Senate also has attempted to force removal of officials, but without much success.

The courts have upheld the president's right to remove government officials without the approval of Congress, except in certain cases. After nearly 140 years of controversy over the issue, the Supreme Court in 1926 ruled that the Constitution gives the president unrestricted power of removal. The Court modified this position in a 1935 decision, *Humphrey's Executor v. United States,* which allowed Congress to restrict the president's authority to remove officials from independent regulatory agencies. The Court extended the *Humphrey* doctrine in a 1958 decision, *Wiener v. United States,* by limiting the president's power to remove quasi-judicial officers without cause, even if Congress had not specified the terms of their removal.

Report   *See* LEGISLATIVE PROCESS.

Reprimand   *See* DISCIPLINING MEMBERS.

Rescission   *See* IMPOUNDMENT OF FUNDS.

Resident Commissioner   *See* DELEGATES.

Resolution   *See* LEGISLATION.

Rider

An amendment that is not germane, or pertinent, to the subject matter of a bill is called a rider. Riders are most frequently used in the Senate, where nongermane amendments are considered fair play. But they also turn up in the House of Representatives, even though House rules prohibit them.

A rider is often a proposal that would be unlikely to become law as a separate bill, either because one chamber would not pass it or because the president would veto it.

Riders are more likely to be accepted if they are attached to urgent legislation, such as bills providing funds to operate the federal government. Emergency funding bills, called continuing resolutions, have become magnets for unrelated amendments because they must be passed quickly to keep government agencies from shutting down. For example, a continuing resolution

More on this topic:

Christmas Tree Bill, p. 93

Continuing Resolution, p. 145

Legislation, p. 339

Omnibus Bills, p. 401

approved in 1984 included, almost as a footnote, a sweeping revision of federal criminal law. Omnibus bills passed at the end of a session when regular government funding bills have stalled also have attracted riders. The massive one Congress approved in 1998 included an array of unrelated measures ranging from a tax moratorium on Internet commerce to a plan to expand the number of U.S. visas for foreign computer workers to an extension of the duck-hunting season in Mississippi.

Sometimes a rider is used as a "sweetener" to win the president's approval of a measure he opposes. A tax bill that President Ronald Reagan had vowed to veto became law in 1983 after Congress attached to the measure a trade plan favored by the president. Other riders have been used to rescue bills that had become stalled in hostile committees. A notable example occurred in 1960 when Senate Majority Leader Lyndon B. JOHNSON made good on a promise to act on civil rights legislation. When the Senate Judiciary Committee failed to produce such legislation, Johnson called up a minor bill that had been passed by the House, and invited senators to offer civil rights amendments to it. A landmark civil rights measure was enacted several months later.

Riders may also obstruct the passage of a bill. In 1997 President Bill Clinton vetoed an emergency disaster relief bill because it contained several controversial riders he opposed, including one that sought to change the way the 2000 census would be conducted and another that would have given Congress more leverage in future budget negotiations with the White House. Congress succumbed to public pressure and passed the bill without the extraneous provisions.

Tax legislation is frequently subject to riders. The Constitution says tax bills must originate in the House, but the Senate Finance Committee has learned how to initiate major tax proposals by attaching them to minor bills passed by the House. That happened with a far-reaching tax increase in 1982.

The Senate also has a fondness for loading tax or trade bills with nongermane amendments that benefit special interests. Such a measure is known as a CHRISTMAS TREE BILL.

Even though House rules prohibit nongermane amendments, members have found ways to get around the restrictions. Antiabortion riders have been a regular feature of annual government appropriations bills since the 1970s. They have met the House germaneness standard because they have been worded to restrict the use of federal funds for abortions. The House may also waive—or ignore—its germaneness rule, a practice that sometimes makes for strange legislative bedfellows. A 1980 House bill, for example, simultaneously set new nutritional requirements for infant formulas and increased federal penalties for marijuana trafficking. A House bill enacted into law in 1991 included not only its original provisions on the trading status of Czechoslovakia and Hungary but also provisions expanding unemployment benefits and imposing sanctions to limit the spread of chemical and biological weapons. House insistence on a rider restoring some Medicare fees to doctors scuttled attempts in late 2002 to reach agreement on legislation extending unemployment benefits.

Rule for House Debate

Most major legislation that reaches the House floor is debated and amended under a resolution, known as a rule, that governs floor consideration of the measure. The rule establishes time limits for debate and determines what amendments, if any, may be offered; it may include other provisions as well. A bill goes to the Rules Committee after it has been reported by a legislative committee. The Rules Committee then writes the rule and presents it to the full House. House approval of the rule precedes floor debate and amendments. (See LEGISLATIVE PROCESS; RULES COMMITTEE, HOUSE.)

In devising rules for floor consideration, the Rules Committee works closely with the House leadership. Before the 1975 reforms, the committee frequently was able to frustrate leadership goals.

Rules, House and Senate *See* LEGISLATIVE PROCESS.

Rules and Administration Committee, Senate

The task of overseeing Senate operations is handled by the Senate Rules and Administration Committee. Its focus is usually on the details of running the Senate: committee budgets, assignment of office space, and other housekeeping matters. The panel also has jurisdiction over election law, including restrictions on campaign financing, corrupt practices, presidential succession, and contested elections. Although the committee is responsible for Senate rules and organization, most efforts to reform Senate procedures have been handled by special temporary committees. The rules committee, central to the Senate establishment, has had little enthusiasm for change.

> **"Here we are, technologically the most sophisticated nation on Earth, and voting was more reliable when we had old technology."**
>
> **—Sen. Dianne Feinstein** after the 2006 elections on continuing problems with voting systems

The committee has two House counterparts, the House Administration Committee and Rules Committee. Although rarely in the limelight, the Senate rules committee has had a role in several key decisions. In the 1950s, reacting to Sen. Joseph R. MCCARTHY'S abusive treatment of witnesses before his subcommittee, the rules panel pushed committees to adopt safeguards giving witnesses a chance for rebuttal. A 1960s investigation into misconduct by Bobby Baker, secretary of the Senate from 1955 to 1963, was handled by the rules committee. Republicans on the panel said Democrats limited their probe to protect Lyndon B. JOHNSON, who had hired Baker while he was the Democratic leader.

Various reforms went through the rules committee in the 1970s, though it often did not originate the changes. The panel endorsed opening the Senate chamber to television cameras in the early 1980s; the rest of the Senate went along in 1986.

When the committee was called into action on a Senate election challenge after the 1996 election in Louisiana, the panel took eleven months to decide that alleged voting irregularities did not warrant overturning the state-certified victory of Democrat Mary L. Landrieu.

In the 108th Congress (2003–2005), members continued to oversee the general operations of the Senate, the construction of a Capitol visitors center, and Capitol security—issues with new urgency since the terrorist attacks of September 11, 2001.

While Republicans controlled the Senate from 1981 to 1987, Charles McC. Mathias Jr. of Maryland chaired the committee. Wendell H. Ford of Kentucky assumed the post when the Democrats took control of the Senate in 1987. With the return of Republican control in 1995, John W. Warner of Virginia assumed the chair. When Warner became chair of the Armed Services

More on this topic:
Campaign Financing, p. 66
House Administration Committee, p. 264
Reform, Congressional, p. 470
Rules Committee, House, p. 478
Televising Congress, p. 554

At the beginning of the 110th Congress in 2007 the chair of the Senate Rules Committee went to Dianne Feinstein, a three-term California Democrat.
Source: CQ Photo/Scott J. Ferrell

Committee in 1999, Mitch McConnell of Kentucky became chair of the committee. Democrat Christopher J. Dodd of Connecticut headed the committee from mid-2001 until Republican Trent LOTT of Mississippi took the helm in 2003.

The chair passed to California Democrat Dianne Feinstein in 2007 at the beginning of the 110th Congress after Democrats won back the majority by a narrow two-vote margin in 2006. The panel faced many contentious issues including campaign finance changes and lobbying reforms in the wake of several influence-peddling scandals in the previous Congress. The committee also faced continuing concerns about the national election system's reliability and accuracy. On balloting Feinstein said after the 2006 elections: "Here we are, technologically the most sophisticated nation on Earth, and voting was more reliable when we had old technology."

Feinstein was a well-regarded member whose collegial style and proven skill at bridging party divides was expected to benefit her in leading the committee through issues that quickly could become highly partisan.

Rules Committee, House

The House Rules Committee occupies a unique place in the congressional committee system. Almost all major legislation that is debated on the floor of the House of Representatives must first win the committee's blessing. Its opposition can kill a bill that another House committee spent months preparing.

The Rules Committee is frequently described as a traffic cop for the House: it determines which bills get to the floor, which amendments—if any—can be considered, and in what order they will come up. By controlling the amendment procedure, the Rules Committee is able to influence the substance of legislation. In addition, the panel has broad jurisdiction over House rules of procedure and House reorganization issues.

The committee is strictly partisan. It is an agent of the Speaker of the House, who is both the presiding officer of the House and the overall leader of the majority party in the chamber. Members of the majority party are appointed by the Speaker, and with rare exceptions, they do as the Speaker directs. In 2007 the panel ratio was nine Democrats to four Republicans—giving the dramatically outnumbered Republicans little say in most matters.

Granting a Rule

All but the most routine legislation passes through the Rules Committee. A bill goes to the panel after it has been considered and approved by a legislative committee. During a hearing before the Rules Committee the legislative committee's chair, senior minority party member, and others explain the content of the bill and how they want it to be handled on the floor.

After the hearing the Rules Committee generally approves a resolution, known as a rule, that sets time limits for general debate on the entire bill and establishes ground rules for considering amendments to it. Some rules permit any germane, or relevant, amendment to be offered from the

⊙ CLOSER LOOK

All but the most routine legislation passes through the Rules Committee, which sets the terms for a bill's consideration by the full House. At one time the committee was an independent power onto itself, but starting in the early 1960s the panel has been brought under the control of the majority party leadership.

floor. These are known as open rules. Others, called closed rules, prohibit all floor amendments. Frequently, bills are given modified rules that allow only specified amendments to be introduced or permit floor amendments only to certain sections of the bill.

The committee became increasingly creative in devising rules to meet the leadership's objectives, keep debate under control, and ensure that members are given an opportunity to debate the major amendments and alternatives to a particular bill. In the early 1990s Republicans complained that the increase in restrictive rules prohibited them from offering amendments that might win on the floor, but their attitude changed after they took control of the committee in 1995 and found themselves in the position of supporting similarly restrictive rules.

The rule must be adopted on the House floor before the bill is debated. Occasionally rules are amended or defeated when they reach the floor, but most receive routine approval. (See LEGISLATIVE PROCESS.)

Shifting Role

The Rules Committee was established on a temporary basis in 1789, but originally it had jurisdiction only over House rules. Its influence over legislation did not develop until after the Speaker was made a member of the panel in 1858. The panel became a standing committee in 1880 and began issuing rules for floor debate in 1883. Until 1910 the committee worked closely with the House leadership in deciding what legislation could come to the floor. It was made independent of the leadership in the 1910–1911 Progressive revolt against the arbitrary reign of Speaker Joseph G. CANNON, a Republican from Illinois.

A coalition of conservative Democrats and Republicans took control of the committee in the late 1930s and frustrated the Democratic leadership for decades. Under the twelve-year chairmanship of Virginia Democrat Howard W. SMITH (1955–1967), the panel repeatedly blocked or delayed civil rights measures sought by the Democratic majority. Because the committee had no regular meeting day and could be called together only by the chair, it was frequently unable to clear any bills for floor action during the final days of a session when Smith simply "disappeared" to his Virginia farm.

The first attempt to restrict this absolute power followed the 1960 election of Democratic president John F. KENNEDY. Knowing that the southern-dominated Rules Committee would likely block the progressive program expected from Kennedy, the House's Democratic leadership, led by Speaker Sam RAYBURN, D-Texas, moved in 1961 to expand the committee temporarily by three members. This allowed naming two Democrats and one Republican to the committee who were expected to be sympathetic to the Kennedy program. The change allowed important administration legislation to proceed through the House where it might have been blocked previously. But the precarious leadership control of the panel was not fully successful, particularly on any legislation that involved civil rights issues. Nevertheless the temporary expansion was made permanent in 1963 and was the first significant move in the House that was to lead eventually to complete control of the committee by the leadership.

Finally in 1975 the House Democratic Caucus gave the Speaker the power to name all Democratic members of the panel, subject to caucus approval. The Rules Committee thus returned to leadership control. A seat on the Rules Committee at one time was considered an important post. It was at times a springboard to House leadership. Rules Committee member Thomas P. O'NEILL Jr. earned a place on the leadership ladder for his role in a House reorganization effort advanced by the Rules Committee in 1970. O'Neill, a Massachusetts Democrat, went on to become Speaker in 1977.

More on this topic:
Caucuses, Party, p. 85
Committee System, p. 111
House of Representatives, p. 267
Reform, Congressional, p. 470
Speaker of the House, p. 516

Rules Committee members also had an opportunity to leave their imprint on bills that came before them. The committee often would require changes in a measure as the price of granting a rule; it might bar or require a floor amendment that would transform another measure. Legislative committees sometimes wooed votes for their bills in the Rules Committee by appealing to the interests of individual members of the panel—adding a flood control project in one member's district, perhaps, or revising a foreign policy provision opposed by another.

For these reasons, among others, Rules Committee assignments historically were highly prized. But this began to break down in the 1990s when the Republican majority beginning in 1995 moved to cement the panel under the control of the Speaker. The GOP leaders, particularly the Speaker, increasingly gave the committee its marching orders, leaving members with little room to influence legislation and shape policy. Moreover, the committee was considered an "exclusive" panel, which meant members could not take other committee assignments. The panel also was subject to harsh working conditions, with meetings often on short notice and lasting past midnight. Morale got bad enough by 2005 that four majority Republicans quit to join legislative committees.

As a result, by 2007 the panel had become so unambiguously a tool of the leadership that the new chair, Louise M. Slaughter of New York, decided to take on four Democratic freshmen. It was a stunning change; only four newcomers, in either party, had been assigned to the committee in the previous quarter century. But to get them to join and to keep other senior members, Slaughter and the House's Democratic leadership backed an even more important break with precedent: the Rules Committee effectively dropped its long-standing status as an exclusive committee to permit members—other than Slaughter, the chair—to sit on other committees as well.

Others chairs of the committee have included Joe Moakley, a Democrat from Massachusetts, who became chair in 1989 after the death of Florida Democrat Claude Pepper. Pepper had taken over the committee in 1983 when Richard BOLLING, a Democrat from Missouri, retired. As chair, Bolling had done much to transform the internal operations of the committee as well as its role in the House. During his tenure, two standing subcommittees were created, the committee's staff and budget were increased, and the committee's legislative initiatives were expanded. In 1995 Republican Gerald B. H. Solomon of New York became chair and served until his retirement in 1999, when Republican David Dreier of California took over. Dreier became the ranking minority member in 2007.

Russell, Richard B.

Richard B. Russell (1897–1971) was at the heart of the Senate power structure for most of his long career (1933–1971). Even before seniority made him chair of two top committees, Armed Services and then Appropriations, the Georgia Democrat was leader of a tightly knit bloc of southern conservatives who dominated the Senate for years. He also worked closely with Lyndon B. JOHNSON, who had been a freshman senator when Russell backed him for the Democratic leadership in the early 1950s. For his leadership role, Russell preferred working behind the scenes and on the Democratic policy and steering committees, where he usually held sway.

Patrician in his demeanor and gracious in his dealings with others, Russell built his reputation on what he called "doing homework." His byword was caution. "When I am in doubt about a question, I always vote no," Russell once said. His assessment of leadership was straightforward: "Any man who dares to vote independently is a leader … and any man who can persuade three or four men to vote with him is a power."

Russell was an opponent of civil rights legislation, but he avoided racist statements, invoking instead the traditional states' rights arguments against federal interference. His politics, though generally conservative, could not be neatly categorized; for example, Russell opposed U.S. involvement in Vietnam from the beginning.

As chair of the Armed Services Committee (1951–1953, 1955–1969), Russell never took as gospel the military policies proposed by the executive branch; he questioned and criticized without hesitation. Russell also learned how to steer defense contracts toward Georgia, which became a major center of the military industry. Russell chaired the Appropriations Subcommittee on Defense in the 1960s, which gave him a powerful dual role of controlling first the authorization of military programs and then the actual spending.

Born and raised in Winder, Georgia, Russell was the fourth of thir-

Sen. Richard B. Russell was leader of a tightly knit bloc of southern conservatives who dominated the Senate for years. Here, Russell participates in a White House meeting in April 1968.
Source: LBJ Library Photo/Frank Wolfe

teen children. His father, who had made unsuccessful bids for governor and senator, served as chief justice of the Georgia supreme court. Russell, who practiced law in Winder, was elected in 1921 to the Georgia legislature; in six years he was chosen Speaker. The next step for the young politician was the governor's mansion; he won a two-year term as governor in 1930. When he took office in 1931 at the age of thirty-four, he was the youngest chief executive in the state's history. But his tenure was brief. When a Georgia senator died, Russell was selected to fill the unexpired term, and he joined the Senate in January 1933. Except for a bid for the Democratic presidential nomination in 1952, which he lost on the third ballot, Russell focused his life on the Senate for the next thirty-eight years.

Russell became the most senior senator in 1969, a standing that gave him the title president pro tempore. His health by that time was poor, and he died in 1971. The following year his colleagues marked their affection and respect by naming one of two existing Senate office buildings in his honor.

> "Any man who dares to vote independently is a leader ... and any man who can persuade three or four men to vote with him is a power."
>
> —*Richard B. Russell*, D-Ga.

Scandals, Congressional

Over its long history of more than 200 years, Congress has many times encountered misconduct by members. Sometimes members acted at the bidding of individuals or corporations that stood to gain financially by their actions. Other times the conduct was more individual, involving narrow monetary misdeeds or, not uncommonly, sexual conduct and alcohol abuse. Sometimes the conduct of members involved criminal activities that led to prosecution and jail, and at other times questionable ethical activity that each chamber had to deal with internally by disciplining members.

Many incidents over the decades were more personal than institutional scandals, but members' constituents were unlikely to make a distinction, an important reason that Congress often is held in low esteem by voters. In the modern Congress, dating from the end of World War II in the mid-1940s, a number of institutional scandals have rocked the Senate and House, leading to writing—and rewriting—codes of conduct and creation of ethics committees to investi-

More on this topic:

Campaign Financing, p. 66

Disciplining Members, p. 159

Ethics, p. 195

Ethics Committee, Senate Select, p. 204

Franking Privilege, p. 237

House Chief Administrative Officer, p. 265

Investigations, p. 292

Standards of Official Conduct Committee, House, p. 532

gate conduct. The most noteworthy of these scandals, detailed below, involve a sting operation involving bribes called Abscam, activities of several senators at the time of the collapse of the savings and loan business in the 1980s, House "bank" and post office operations, and a series of lobbying and other events that damaged the Republican majority after 2000.

Abscam Scandal

An undercover operation by the Federal Bureau of Investigation (FBI) in 1980 implicated seven members of Congress in criminal wrongdoing. Called Abscam (a combination of "Arab" and "scam"), the operation was a "sting" that used FBI agents posing as wealthy Arabs to offer bribes to an undisclosed number of legislators.

By May 1981 seven who took the bait—six House members and one senator—had been convicted, and by the following March all seven were gone from Congress, one of them having been expelled. Some of the members had been asked if they could use their positions to help the "Arabs" obtain U.S. residency. Others were offered money to use their influence in obtaining gambling licenses or federal grants, or in arranging real estate deals.

A hidden videotape captures Rep. Michael Myers, second from left, receiving an envelope containing $50,000 from undercover FBI agent Anthony Amoroso, left. Meyers was one of seven members of Congress convicted in the sting operation known as Abscam.
Source: AP Images

Four of the House members convicted in the affair were videotaped accepting money. They were Republican Richard Kelly of Florida and Democrats Raymond F. Lederer and Michael J. "Ozzie" Myers, both of Pennsylvania, and Frank Thompson Jr. of New Jersey. John W. Jenrette Jr., a South Carolina Democrat, was recorded on tape saying he had been given the cash by an associate. John M. Murphy, a New York Democrat, allegedly told an associate to take the cash. A seventh House member, Pennsylvania Democrat John P. Murtha, was named as an unindicted coconspirator. He later was cleared by the House ethics committee.

The only senator caught in the sting was New Jersey Democrat Harrison A. Williams Jr. Although Williams turned down a cash bribe, he was convicted on charges that included accepting a secret share of a titanium mine owned by several of his friends in return for a promise to help the enterprise get government contracts. Undercover FBI agents promised a sizable loan to the venture. Williams maintained that the government "manufactured" the crimes of which he was accused.

All seven of the convicted members served prison sentences. On October 2, 1980, the House expelled Myers. He was only the fourth representative to be expelled up to that time and the first since the Civil War. Myers remained the only member of Congress to be expelled for corruption until Rep. James A. Traficant Jr., D-Ohio, was expelled in July 2002 following his conviction in federal court on bribery, racketeering, and tax evasion charges. Kelly, Murphy, and Thompson were defeated for reelection before their convictions, thereby escaping House disciplinary action. Jenrette, Lederer, and Williams resigned. By leaving the Senate voluntarily in 1982, Williams avoided becoming the first senator to be expelled since the Civil War and the first ever ejected on grounds other than treason or disloyalty.

CLOSER LOOK

Abscam was a sting operation that used FBI agents posing as wealthy Arabs to offer bribes to a number of members of Congress. The name came from a combination of "Arab" and "scam."

House Bank and Post Office Scandals

The House was buffeted in the 1990s by major scandals involving the House bank and the House post office. Seeking to avert future scandals and improve the chamber's day-to-day financial management, the House created a new position, administrative officer, to oversee day-to-day operations. The position was reconstituted as chief administrative officer in 1995, but the responsibilities remained basically the same.

House Bank Scandal

Few if any other congressional abuses of privilege have exploded with the fury of the House of Representatives bank scandal in 1991. Disclosures that more than 60 percent of House members had overdrawn their House bank accounts without penalty shook the House for months and fueled the anti-incumbent mood of the public. Congress's Government Accountability Office (GAO)—known then as the General Accounting Office—reported that in one twelve-month period 8,331 bad checks had been written, all of them honored by the House bank.

An investigation was launched and the bank closed down, but this did little to calm outraged voters worried about their own bank balances amid a persistent recession. Many vowed to take revenge at the polls, and they did.

The so-called House bank was not a true bank but a checking service provided by the SERGEANT-AT-ARMS. Representatives pooled their money by depositing their paychecks. When they wrote checks, if they were overdrawn, the shortage could be covered by the remaining deposits. The worthless checks thus floated from when they were cashed until they were covered by the writer's next paycheck. Regulated banks would have bounced the checks or provided overdraft protection at extra cost. By honoring the checks, the House bank in effect gave members interest-free loans.

GAO auditors frowned on the long-standing practice and had urged tighter restrictions. Some warnings were issued, and a few checks were bounced. But most of the reforms affected nonmember users, such as journalists, who could cash small checks. Among House members, the problem of floating checks became worse.

After the situation was exposed in the press in September 1991, Speaker Thomas S. Foley, D-Wash., and Minority Leader Robert H. Michel, a Republican from Illinois, took to the floor to scold members and announce that the bank would no longer honor their bad checks. But when the scandal did not subside, the House voted to authorize an inquiry by the House Committee on Standards of Official Conduct (the ethics committee) and close the bank.

After a five-month investigation, the ethics committee proposed revealing the names of only the worst offenders. Republicans called for full disclosure of the members involved, but the Democratic leadership strongly backed limited disclosure. Foley, however, relented under pressure from rank-and-file Democrats who either favored full disclosure or saw the fight as a sure loser.

In April 1992 the ethics committee published two lists. The first contained the names of twenty-two current and former members—eighteen Democrats and four Republicans—whom the committee identified as the most serious abusers of their privileges at the House bank. The second list had an additional 303 names of current or former members—188 Democrats, 114 Republicans, and one independent—who had overdrawn their bank accounts. The number of overdrafts listed for individual members in a thirty-nine-month period ranged from one to nearly 1,000.

In the 1992 congressional elections, the overdrafts proved troublesome to incumbents. Of 269 sitting members with overdrafts, seventy-seven members or one in four, retired or were defeated for reelection or election to another office. Incumbents with clean bank records did much better, losing only one in six of their number.

◉ CLOSER LOOK

The House bank scandal involved overdrawn accounts in that chamber, even though the bank was not a true bank but a checking service provided as a convenience to members. The post office scandal initially involved embezzling and drug dealing by employees but escalated to criminal activity by representatives who were getting cash for fraudulent activities.

A Justice Department investigation of House bank records resulted in the prosecution of several former members and staffers on various charges. The first to be convicted was former sergeant-at-arms Jack Russ, who had resigned his post in the midst of the scandal. In 1993 Russ pleaded guilty in federal court to three felony counts, including writing bad checks at the House bank. In another case stemming from the investigation, former representative Mary Rose Oakar, Democrat of Ohio, pleaded guilty in 1997 to a misdemeanor conspiracy charge and a misdemeanor campaign finance violation, but a charge of writing a $16,000 overdraft check at the House bank was thrown out because there was no House rule prohibiting it.

House Post Office

The bank affair had barely dropped out of the headlines when the House was rocked by another scandal, this one from the members' post office. The affair began as an investigation of embezzling and drug dealing by employees but escalated to criminal activity by representatives. Two members ended up going to prison, including the powerful chair of the House Ways and Means Committee, Democrat Dan Rostenkowski of Illinois.

The House post office ran its postal operations under contract with the U.S. Postal Service; it was headed by a postmaster who was an elected House official. In mid-1991 the U.S. attorney for the District of Columbia began looking into accusations that stamp clerks had been stealing funds from the House post office and dealing drugs there. Several post office employees eventually pleaded guilty to various charges. Investigations depicted a sloppily run operation where cash and stamps were treated casually and where workers were beholden to political sponsors, not to professional managers. Its status as a House office was ended and its operations turned over to the Postal Service in 1992.

The investigation took a dramatic turn when a post office supervisor reportedly told the grand jury that he had helped House members get thousands of dollars in cash through false transactions disguised as stamp purchases. Public records indicated several members with large amounts of stamp purchases, which was puzzling since members could send virtually all public business for free using the franking privilege.

In 1993 the former House postmaster, Robert V. Rota, pleaded guilty to three misdemeanors— one count of conspiracy to embezzle and two of aiding and abetting members identified only as Congressman A and Congressman B "in willfully and knowingly embezzling" U.S. funds. Related documents detailed certain stamp purchases as fake. The alleged sham purchases matched stamp purchases attributed in House public records to Rostenkowski and Rep. Joe Kolter, Democrat of Pennsylvania. Rota told prosecutors that he had been supplying members of Congress with cash in exchange for vouchers, stamps, and campaign and political action committee checks since shortly after he became postmaster in 1972. Reforms implemented in 1977–1978 were supposed to have ended all such "cash-outs."

Rostenkowski, who had been defeated for reelection in 1994, pleaded guilty in 1996 to two counts of felony mail fraud stemming from his misuse of public funds to purchase gifts and to pay employees who did little or no official work. Federal prosecutors dropped eleven other corruption charges in a plea agreement worked out with Rostenkowski. Kolter, who had been defeated in a 1992 primary, pleaded guilty in a 1996 plea bargain to one count of conspiring to steal thousands of dollars in taxpayers' money by converting stamps into cash. Both members were fined and sentenced to prison.

Keating Five Scandal

With the reprimand of one senator, the Senate Ethics Committee in 1991 completed a sweeping investigation of possible wrongdoing by five senators in behalf of a failed California savings and loan (S&L) institution. The S&L was headed by Charles H. Keating Jr., and the investigated senators thus came to be known as the Keating Five.

The five senators were Democrats Alan Cranston of California, Dennis DeConcini of Arizona, John Glenn of Ohio, and Donald W. Riegle Jr. of Michigan, and Republican John McCain of Arizona. All had received help from Keating, who had contributed or raised some $1.5 million for their campaigns or favorite political causes. The committee investigated to determine whether the senators, in exchange, had intervened against federal regulators in a vain effort to save Keating's ailing thrift, Lincoln Savings and Loan Association. Lincoln Savings had collapsed in 1989 at a cost to taxpayers of $2 billion.

Reprimand for Cranston

After weeks of televised hearings and thirty-three hours of closed deliberations, the Ethics Committee concluded that all five senators had shown poor judgment in dealing with Keating, but that only Cranston's official actions were "substantially linked" to his fundraising. In February 1991 the committee issued written statements criticizing the other four senators for poor judgment. DeConcini and Riegle also were chided for giving the appearance of acting improperly. But the panel left Cranston's fate undecided.

Months passed as the members of the bipartisan committee debated the issue. Republicans favored a full Senate censure—next to expulsion, the harshest available penalty—and Democrats attempted to avoid a floor vote. With one Republican abstaining, the committee on November 19, 1991, voted 5–0 for a compromise, halfway between a committee rebuke and a Senate censure. The following day on the Senate floor the committee, without asking for a vote, announced its reprimand of Cranston "in the name of the Senate" for "an impermissible pattern of conduct in which fundraising and official activities were substantially linked."

Cranston, who was seventy-seven years old and suffering from prostate cancer, accepted the rebuke but then derided the committee and said other members had done what he had done or worse. He in turn was criticized by the committee vice chair, New Hampshire Republican Warren B. Rudman. Rudman said Cranston's statement was "arrogant, unrepentant, and a smear on this institution. Everybody does *not* do it." The committee listed as "extenuating circumstances" Cranston's poor health and his decision not to seek reelection.

Pressure for Reform

Keating and his associates had begun seeking help from legislators in 1984–1986. They hoped to stop federal regulators from limiting direct ownership of real estate and other assets by savings and loans, which made possible the thrifts' expansion into deals much more profitable than their traditional role as mortgage lenders. The collapse of real estate values in some parts of the country later triggered the failure of many federally insured S&Ls. Twice the Keating Five senators (except Riegle in one case) met privately with officials of the Federal Home Loan Bank Board in April 1987. Much of the Ethics Committee hearings dealt with those meetings and the efforts of special counsel Robert S. Bennett to determine whether the senators had acted improperly in behalf of Keating. All denied any wrongdoing, saying their efforts in behalf of Keating were no more than any member of Congress would do to help a constituent having problems with a federal agency.

Keating, who did not testify at the hearings, was convicted of securities fraud under California law in 1991 and on racketeering and securities fraud charges in federal court in 1993. He spent five years in prison before both convictions were overturned. In 1999 to avoid a retrial, Keating admitted to wrongdoing in a plea bargain.

The Keating Five investigation fueled demands for reform of existing campaign financing laws. Keating had used a technique called bundling—raising money for a candidate, generally from associates, members of an organization, or employees, and then forwarding the checks in a bundle to a candidate—to circumvent limits on individual contributions. Although direct corporate payments to candidates were prohibited, Keating had channeled some $850,000 in such money to nonprofit voter registration organizations affiliated with Cranston.

Financial, Sexual Scandals Continue

Between 2005 and 2007 a series of high-profile scandals engulfed Republicans and one Democrat. Most of the events involved House members and came to light in the 109th Congress, 2005 to 2006,

although their roots went back a number of years earlier. Most fell squarely within financial misconduct, but two involved sexual activity.

In 2005 the Republican majority leader in the House, Tom DeLay of Texas, became caught up in a larger scandal involving lobbyist Jack Abramoff that ended the career of several Republicans including DeLay, who resigned his seat in 2006. DeLay's once unshakeable command of the GOP ranks eroded over a number of issues, including an indictment in Texas over money laundering in a case that was still pending in early 2008. Earlier he had already been admonished for ethics offenses involving undue pressure on a colleague to vote for controversial legislation, fundraising activities, and improperly trying to influence a federal agency.

But DeLay's crucial problem was his proximity to a widening influence-peddling case involving lobbyist Abramoff. Once a close

In 2005 and 2006 the Republican Party struggled with multiple scandals, including those dealing with Majority Leader Tom DeLay and House Administration Committee chair Bob Ney, which many felt contributed to their party's loss of the majority in Congress in the 2006 elections.
Source: © 2006 RJ Matson, the *St. Louis Post-Dispatch* and PoliticalCartoons.com

associate of DeLay, Abramoff in January 2006 agreed to cooperate with federal investigators and plead guilty to charges of conspiracy, mail fraud, and income tax evasion. Later in the year two top DeLay aides pleaded guilty in the Abramoff case. DeLay was not charged in connection with the Abramoff case, but the scandals eroded his support at home and threatened to cost him his seat in the 2006 elections.

But Rep. Bob Ney, R-Ohio, who was chair of the House Administration Committee, was directly implicated in the Abramoff scandal. A former press secretary to DeLay pleaded guilty to conspiring to bribe Ney, who at first continued to insist on his innocence. But in September 2006 Ney did an abrupt U-turn, pleading guilty to conspiracy and false statements. He admitted receiving gifts, including expensive meals and trips worth more than $170,000, from Abramoff and his associates in exchange for trying to shape legislation and inserting statements in the *Congressional Record* for the benefit of Abramoff's clients. Ney resigned in December 2006.

Another case involved Rep. Randy "Duke" Cunningham, R-Calif., who resigned in 2005 after pleading guilty to bribery. Cunningham's case was similar to Ney's. He was an influential Republican voice on defense and intelligence policy during his fifteen years in Congress. He admitted accepting at least $2.4 million in bribes, including about $1 million in cash as well as rugs, antiques, furniture, yacht club fees, boat repairs, moving costs, and vacation expenses in exchange for using his House Appropriations Committee seat to obtain earmarks on behalf of defense contractors. He was subsequently sentenced to eight years and four months in prison.

Although Republicans were burdened with the larger scandals, the Democrats did not avoid controversy. The House ethics committee in 2006 undertook an investigation, which continued in 2007, into whether Rep. William J. Jefferson of Louisiana had demanded and accepted bribes in exchange for helping to arrange contracts between a U.S. telecommunications company and Nigerian officials. Jefferson was the subject of a highly publicized Justice Department investigation, but maintained his innocence. In June 2007 federal officials formally charged Jefferson in a sixteen-count indictment with racketeering, money laundering, and obstruction of justice. The grand jury indictment said Jefferson had offered money and accepted to support business ventures in the United States and Africa. The indictment came after Jefferson handily won reelection in 2006. The case was awaiting trial in early 2008.

A different type of scandal, involving sexual conduct, also hit the GOP during this period. It illustrated the heightened sensitivity in Congress over sexual conduct of members. Rep. Mark Foley, R-Fla., resigned in September 2006 over inappropriate e-mails sent to teenage male pages over several years. No case was pursed with the urgency that the House ethics committee gave to the Foley matter. Although Foley resigned, technically ending the ethics committee's jurisdiction over him, the panel actively probed whether the House GOP leadership had mishandled allegations of Foley's conduct for several years. The committee, within two months, issued a bipartisan report saying that the Speaker, J. Dennis Hastert, R-Ill., other lawmakers, and aides had violated no laws or House rules. The report, however, criticized the leadership for failing "to exercise appropriate diligence and oversight" of Foley's contact with pages. The report did not recommend disciplinary action.

A similar issue came in the Senate in 2007 involving Idaho's senator Larry Craig. Craig was arrested at an airport in Minnesota for allegedly soliciting sex in a men's restroom. As soon as it became known that the events probably involved sexual conduct Senate GOP leaders removed Craig from committee positions and called for a swift ethics investigation. Craig had pleated guilty to a misdemeanor charge in the case and said he would resign his seat at the end of September. He soon had second thoughts and initiated proceedings to reverse the guilty plea and announced that he would serve out his term (which ended in January 2009) but would not run for reelection.

Science and Technology Committee, House

Energy, astronautics, civil aviation, and environment are among the research topics within the House Science and Technology Committee's jurisdiction. It also reviews overall government science policy and serves as a clearinghouse of information. It has jurisdiction over such prestigious and well-known agencies as the National Science Foundation, the National Institute of Standards and Technology, the National Weather Service, and—the largest of all—the National Aeronautics and Space Administration (NASA).

The panel has focused on a wide array of government research and development programs that included such topics as renewable energy, the nation's voting systems, the security of the water supply infrastructure, and nanotechnology. In the wake of the destruction of the space shuttle *Columbia* in early 2003, the panel was part of Congress's review not only of NASA's safety record and funding but also of the agency's overall mission and the future of America's space program.

Still, House members have tended not to take the science panel seriously because it had less influence than many other committees. Legislation written by the committee often became part of a broader measure that other committees had helped draft. In floor action on major bills, the science panel became a junior partner of a more aggressive committee that dominated the debate. The Energy and Commerce Committee remained the primary authorizing panel on energy, health, and telecommunications policy, while the Appropriations Committee made funding decisions that determined the direction of agencies such as NASA and the National Science Foundation.

Within its own territory—research and space—the science panel began showing more independence by the late 1980s. The committee was often lobbied by aerospace, energy, and high-tech companies competing

Although the House Science and Technology Committee's jurisdiction has expanded beyond its original focus on space exploration, its oversight of the National Aeronautics and Space Administration (NASA) remains a significant part of its work. Here NASA's Mars Exploration Rover Spirit moves its robotic arm in August 2007.
Source: NASA/JPL-Caltech/Cornell

for government support. Committee members sought to keep research compatible with overall government science policy. They even began to engage in critical questioning of NASA, although the panel traditionally was an enthusiastic backer of the agency. After the GOP takeover of the House in 1995, the committee assumed a more skeptical attitude toward science projects and space spending. Relations between Republican F. James Sensenbrenner Jr. of Wisconsin, who chaired the panel from 1997 to 2001, and the NASA administrator were strained.

Sensenbrenner came up against chairmanship term limits in 2001, and Sherwood L. Boehlert of New York, a staunch environmentalist, took over the committee. In 2007 Democrat Bart Gordon of Tennessee took the chair. Although he was generally supportive of President George W. Bush's proposal to return astronauts to the moon in preparation for a future mission to Mars, Gordon also criticized the spending blueprint that he said would shift money away from NASA's aeronautics and science research programs.

The Science and Technology Committee was established in 1958 as the Select Committee on Astronautics and Space Exploration. In 1959 it became the Science and Astronautics Committee. When reorganization proposals became commonplace as part of reform efforts in the 1970s, the science panel at first seemed vulnerable to efforts to streamline committee jurisdictions. Instead, the committee ended up with a broader mandate, a move that gave it higher standing within the House. It was renamed the Science and Technology Committee in

CLOSER LOOK

A seat on the House Science and Technology Committee has seldom been a first choice of members even though it reviews overall government science policy and has jurisdiction over well-known government activities, including the weather service and space program.

1975 and the Science, Space and Technology Committee in 1987. In 1995 Republicans shortened the committee's name to Science. Democrats in 2007 changed it back to Science and Technology.

Seating Disputes

The Constitution authorized each house of Congress to judge the fairness of the elections of its members. Under that authority the Senate and House of Representatives have settled hundreds of contested elections. Defeated candidates have challenged election results after close tallies or apparent voting irregularities. Although Congress has tried to give a judicial tone to its decisions, the result usually is partisan: the party in power gives the seat to its candidate.

The House is governed by the Federal Contested Election Act of 1969. No comparable law guides the Senate, but it handles far fewer elections and thus fewer disputes. The entire membership of the House, but only a third of the Senate, is elected every two years, so that the House oversees 435 elections every other November, while the Senate oversees only about thirty-three. The Senate has been elected by popular vote since 1913. Previously, senators were chosen by state legislatures. (See DIRECT ELECTION OF SENATORS.)

CLOSER LOOK

In 1974 a New Hampshire Senate contest was so close that an initial tally showed only two votes separating the candidates. The Senate wrangled for months over the outcome, casting forty-one roll-call votes on the question of who won. Finally the seat was declared vacant and a second election held with the Democratic candidate winning by a clear margin.

The closest Senate election since 1913 was a 1974 New Hampshire contest that ultimately was settled by a new election. The initial tally was so close that one count showed only two votes separating the contenders. Senators spent seven months wrangling over the results. After forty-one roll-call votes on the question, John A. Durkin, the Democratic candidate, asked for a new election. The Senate declared the seat vacant and set the second election for September 1975. It was the first time senators had ever declared a vacancy because they could not make up their minds. Durkin handily defeated Republican Louis C. Wyman the second time around.

The closest House contest of the twentieth century was resolved in 1985 by a vote along party lines. The decision, which came after an acrimonious four-month struggle, made Republicans so angry they walked out of the House chamber in protest. For the next several days they used parliamentary tactics to disrupt proceedings on the House floor. The dispute centered on Democratic incumbent Frank McCloskey, who appeared to have narrowly lost his Indiana House seat in November 1984 to Republican Richard D. McIntyre. After a recount of votes McCloskey claimed the seat. The House in early 1985 declared the seat vacant and called for an investigation. A special investigating committee then declared McCloskey the winner by four votes. The House, dominated by Democrats, voted to accept the committee recommendation, triggering the Republican walkout. In a 1986 rematch, McCloskey beat McIntyre by a comfortable margin.

The 105th Congress (1997–1999) provided two examples of just how divisive disputes over congressional seats can be, although in these cases the majority party's candidates did not win. Louisiana Democrat Mary L. Landrieu narrowly defeated Republican Louis "Woody" Jenkins by 5,788 votes out of 1.7 million cast in their 1996 race for the Senate. Jenkins, who had the strong backing of Republican conservatives, alleged that systematic illegality—including vote buying, multiple voting, and fraudulent voter registration—marred the contest. He took his case to the Senate Rules and Administration Committee, which hired two outside counsels to investigate the charges. When the two independent lawyers recommended a limited probe, the panel, on a party-line vote, instead chose to pursue an aggressive investigation that lasted for nearly six months and was marked by partisan fits and starts. But in the end, eleven months after the election, the committee decided unanimously that there was no evidence of widespread malfeasance to warrant unseating Landrieu.

The House had its share as well of bitter partisan wrangling over the outcome of a 1996 race. After California Democrat Loretta Sanchez defeated Republican Robert K. Dornan by 984 votes, Dornan, a fiery conservative who had served eighteen years in the House, claimed Sanchez won because of a rash of illegal voting by noncitizens. Sanchez, who was Hispanic, contended Dornan's charges were racially motivated. A task force of the House Oversight Committee spent most of 1997 embroiled in an investigation of the election. Several times the probe spilled onto the House floor, where Democrats brought action to a halt with a series of privileged motions to end the inquiry. In early 1998 the

Rep. Loretta Sanchez, D-Calif., celebrates in February 1998 after a Republican-led committee ended its fourteen-month investigation of alleged voter fraud in the 1996 election in which she won her seat.
Source: CQ Photo/Douglas Graham

House agreed to drop the investigation but the partisan fighting continued until the end as Democrats disputed the task force's finding that 748 votes had been illegally cast. They were, however, unsuccessful in their attempt to have most of the task force's conclusions stripped from the resolution ending the probe. Sanchez soundly defeated Dornan in their 1998 rematch.

A disputed House race in Florida, which a Republican won by a few hundred votes, was contested in 2007 by the loser. However, the Republican was seated while the Democrat's claims worked their way through both a House examination and a court case in Florida.

Secretary of the Senate

The secretary of the Senate is the chief legislative officer of the Senate. The secretary's responsibilities are similar to those of the CLERK OF THE HOUSE: certifying passage of bills, keeping the Senate *Journal*, and making periodic reports. Like the House clerk, the secretary of the Senate is elected by the majority party in the chamber and generally continues in the post as long as that party maintains its majority.

Security: Capitol Building

The Capitol was believed to be a probable target in the September 11, 2001, terrorist attacks. After terrorists seized three commercial jetliners and piloted them into the World Trade Center's twin towers in New York and the Pentagon, a fourth hijacked plane—United Flight 93—was on a course toward Washington but crashed in rural Pennsylvania when passengers resisted the hijackers. Two fugitives linked to the terrorist group al Qaeda reportedly told a correspondent for the Arabic satellite network Al Jazeera in a June 2002 interview that the Capitol was the target. Vice President Richard B. CHENEY said five days after

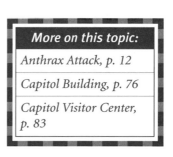

More on this topic:

Anthrax Attack, p. 12

Capitol Building, p. 76

Capitol Visitor Center, p. 83

As threats to the Capitol have increased so has security for the building itself. Visitors can no longer walk straight into the Capitol as they could do in the 1990s. Here a Capitol Police officer keeps an eye on the visitors waiting for a guided tour of the Capitol. By the end of 2008 a new Capitol visitor center with enhanced security was to be completed.
Source: AP Images/Manuel Balce Ceneta

CLOSER LOOK

A little more than a month after the September 11, 2001, terrorist attacks on New York and Washington, D.C., Congress experienced terrorism firsthand when letters containing deadly anthrax bacteria were mailed to Senate leaders. The first, addressed to Majority Leader Tom Daschle, D-S.D., was opened in the Hart Office Building. Lawmakers and staffers in the vicinity were offered the antibiotic Cipro, and eventually 3,000 people were tested for exposure and nearly 1,200 were put on the antibiotic. Investigators later found a letter addressed to Senate Judiciary Committee chair Patrick J. Leahy, D-Vt., similar to the one sent to Daschle. That letter was opened in a sealed and controlled environment to avoid releasing deadly anthrax spores into the air. Traces of the finely milled substance turned up elsewhere in the Hart building, in the Dirksen Senate Office Building mailroom that handled the Daschle letter, in several members' offices in the Longworth House Office Building, and in a mail processing center in the Ford House Office Building. Most of the congressional office buildings were closed only temporarily, but it would be ninety-six days before the Hart building reopened.

the attack that the Capitol "probably" was United Flight 93's intended destination.

The evacuation of the Capitol during the terrorist attacks and subsequent anthrax attack in the U.S. mails dramatically changed security in the vast Capitol complex. The most obvious change was the increase in the number of uniformed U.S. Capitol Police on patrol. Car traffic on half a dozen streets around the Capitol complex was halted and most commercial truck traffic was prohibited around the perimeter of the campus in an attempt to minimize the risk of a car bomb. Bicyclists also were required to dismount before entering the Capitol plaza.

While the Capitol building eventually was reopened to visitors, tourists were no longer allowed to roam the halls unescorted but instead had to be chaperoned by a congressional staffer. Tourists, lobbyists, and other guests also had to pass through enhanced security screening once they got past the pedestrian barricades that lined sidewalks around the Capitol. Lobbyists complained about the long waits they had to endure to get into the Capitol and that they could no longer ride the subway cars to House and Senate office buildings unless accompanied by a congressional aide or a lawmaker.

Construction of a new visitor center under the East Front of the Capitol was accelerated following the attacks. The long-postponed project was expected to open in late 2008 at an estimated cost of $600 million. The complex would move tourists several hundred feet from the Capitol itself.

Tighter security could lead to more innovations, such as technology tested in a House pilot project to convert constituent mail into digital images that could be sent to a congressional computer. After potentially deadly anthrax bacteria were sent in letters to several members' offices, mail was irradiated off-campus to protect against pathogens, although this raised concerns about the health effects of handling irradiated mail.

The enhanced security placed stress on many denizens of Capitol Hill. The Capitol Police, faced with extra security demands that required many officers to work overtime, struggled to retain members of the force, who were tempted by better paying jobs at other federal law enforcement agencies. To improve retention, lawmakers provided a 9.1 percent pay increase as well as recruitment and retention bonuses in a fiscal 2003 appropriations bill.

Safety lapses continued to exist more than a year after the attacks. A November 2002 report by the congressional Office of Compliance concluded that while emergency readiness significantly improved, numerous flaws continued to exist at the Capitol, including inaudible fire alarms and public address messages, lack of emergency evacuation planning in parts of the complex, inadequate safety equipment, and information on the health effects of irradiated mail.

Past Acts of Violence

The events of 2001 were not the first time that security became a major issue in the life of Congress. Violence has visited the Capitol numerous times over the years. Here is a partial list of incidents:

- Attempt on President Jackson. On January 30, 1835, Richard Lawrence fired two pistols at Andrew Jackson as the president stood in the Rotunda. Both pistols misfired. Lawrence, seized immediately, was found to be insane.
- Beating of Sumner. Wielding a heavy cane, Rep. Preston S. Brooks of South Carolina repcatedly struck Sen. Charles Sumner of Massachusetts in the Senate chamber on May 22, 1856. The attack occurred two days after Sumner had publicly denounced Brooks's uncle, Sen. A. P. Butler of South Carolina. Sumner was beaten senseless and was not able to resume his official duties for more than three years. Brooks, censured, quit his House seat but was reelected.
- Killing of Taulbee. On February 28, 1890, Charles E. Kinkead, a reporter for the *Louisville Times,* shot former representative William P. Taulbee of Kentucky on a House stairway. The shooting was prompted by *Times* stories about a scandal involving Taulbee. Taulbee died of his wounds on March 11, 1890.
- Bricker Shooting. On July 12, 1947, Sen. John W. Bricker of Ohio was fired at twice—both shots missed—as he entered the Senate subway. The gunman was a former Capitol policeman who had lost money when an Ohio building and loan firm failed fifteen years earlier.
- Puerto Rican Attack. On March 1, 1954, five representatives were wounded on the House floor by pistol shots. The three assailants, members of Puerto Rico's Nationalist Party, fired about thirty bullets from a visitors gallery into a crowd of about two hundred representatives. The gunmen, plus a fourth member of the group captured later, received prison sentences.
- Vietnam Era Bomb Blast. An explosion in the Capitol on March 1, 1971, caused heavy structural damage but no injuries. Coming at a time of rising protest against U.S. involvement in the Vietnam War, the blast led to tighter security for the Capitol and nearby congressional office buildings. Electronic surveillance devices were installed throughout the Capitol complex, and X-ray machines appeared at building entrances to scan incoming packages and briefcases. At the same time, the Capitol Police force was substantially expanded. The perpetrators of the 1971 explosion never were found.
- Bombing, Senate wing. Even with the enhanced security measures, another Capitol bombing occurred on November 7, 1983. Shortly before 11 p.m. a powerful device

Senate Bomb

Extensive damage but no injuries occurred when a bomb went off on July 2, 1915, behind a telephone switchboard in a Senate reception room. Police soon arrested a man named Frank Holt, a one-time Cornell German instructor, in connection with an attempt to murder financier J. P. Morgan Jr., whose company was Great Britain's U.S. purchasing agent for World War I munitions. Holt had written a number of similar letters to newspapers about his actions, and one to President Woodrow Wilson to "call attention to the murders being done in Europe by American ammunition." Colleagues described Holt as "decidedly pro-German." Confessing to the Senate bombing, Holt noted that he walked the corridors looking for a spot where the bomb would not hurt anyone. Soon after his arrest Holt committed suicide; later it was discovered that he was actually Erich Muenter, a Harvard German professor who had disappeared nine years earlier.

exploded in a second-floor alcove about thirty feet from the Senate chamber. The blast blew out a wall partition and shattered the windows of the Republican cloakroom. There were no injuries or structural damage. A group calling itself the Armed Resistance Unit claimed responsibility. In 1998 seven persons were indicted for conspiring to carry out the bombing. Three pleaded guilty, and charges against the others were dropped.

- Capitol Police Slayings. On July 24, 1998, a gunman barged through a security checkpoint at the Capitol and fatally shot two Capitol Police officers, Jacob J. Chestnut and John M. Gibson, and wounded a tourist. The suspected assailant, also wounded in the attack, had been diagnosed as a paranoid schizophrenic and was judged mentally incompetent to stand trial. The flag-draped coffins of Chestnut and Gibson lay in state July 28 in the Capitol Rotunda, a tribute normally reserved for presidents, generals, and lawmakers of unusual distinction.

The 1998 shootings sparked fresh efforts to upgrade security in the Capitol area. Several months after the shootings Congress increased spending for the Capitol Police and authorized funds for additional security improvements at the Capitol, including $100 million to start to build the underground visitors center where people could be screened before entering the "People's House."

Senate

Although the Constitution says the two chambers of Congress are equal, senators rarely leave the Senate to run for the House of Representatives. Representatives, however, often decide to run for the Senate.

More on this topic:

Appointment Power, p. 14

Congress: Structure and Powers, p. 124

Direct Election of Senators, p. 154

Electing the President, p. 176

Filibuster, p. 213

House of Representatives, p. 267

Impeachment Power, p. 280

Legislative Process, p. 344

Purse: Power of, p. 446

Treaty-Making Power, p. 559

The two chambers share the tasks of legislating, overseeing the federal government, and representing their constituencies. But striking differences exist between the two legislative bodies and how they go about their work. The Senate, once known as the "world's most exclusive club," projects an image of influence and prestige that the House does not match. The Senate has 100 members—two from each state—while the House as of the beginning of the 110th Congress in 2007 has 435 members, allocated among the states according to population. Senators are elected for six years, House members for two. Senators have a broad, statewide constituency, while most House members represent districts within states. These differences have shaped the practices and procedures of the two chambers.

Thanks to its small size, the Senate is informal and flexible, in contrast to the highly structured House. It is also more individualistic, with power more evenly distributed among its members. The Senate shares certain executive powers with the president, which contributes to the chamber's prestige. With fewer members to share the limelight, senators enjoy more attention. But, by the same token, there are fewer members to share the workload, which is as heavy in the Senate as in the House. As a result, senators tend to be policy generalists, while representatives develop specialties. The Senate takes longer to consider legislation, in part because it sees its chief role as one of deliberation.

Matthew Brady's photograph of the sixty-eight members of the Senate in 1859.
Source: Library of Congress

A TYPICAL DAY IN THE SENATE

A typical day in the Senate might run as follows:

- The Senate is called to order by the presiding officer. The constitutional presiding officer, the vice president, is seldom in attendance. Usually the president pro tempore presides over the opening minutes of the Senate session. During the course of the day, other members of the majority party take turns presiding for an hour at a time.

- The Senate chaplain delivers the opening prayer.

- The majority leader and the minority leader are recognized for opening remarks. The majority leader usually announces the plan for the day's business, which is developed in consultation with the minority leadership.

- Senators who have requested time in advance are recognized for special orders; they may speak about any topic for five minutes.

- After special orders, the Senate usually conducts morning business. During morning business—which need not take place in the morning, in spite of its name—members receive reports from committees and messages from the president.

- After morning business, the Senate considers legislative or executive matters. If the majority leader wants the Senate to begin work on a piece of legislation, he or she normally asks for unanimous consent to call up the measure. If any member objects, the leader may make a debatable motion that the Senate take up the bill. The debatable motion gives opponents the opportunity to launch a filibuster, or extended debate, even before the Senate officially begins considering the bill. A few measures, such as budget resolutions and reports from Senate-House conference committees, are privileged, and a motion to consider them is not debatable.

- After the Senate begins work on a bill, floor debate is generally handled by managers, usually the chair and ranking minority member of the committee that has jurisdiction over the measure. Some measures are considered under a time agreement in which the Senate unanimously agrees to limit debate and to divide the time in some prearranged fashion. In the absence of a time agreement, any senator may seek recognition from the chair and, once recognized, may speak for as long as he or she wishes. Unless the Senate has unanimously agreed to limit amendments, senators may offer as many as they wish. Generally, amendments need not be germane, or directly related, to the bill. Most bills are passed by a voice vote with only a handful of senators present.

- Any member can request a roll call, or recorded vote, on an amendment or on final passage of a measure. Senate roll calls are casual affairs. Few members answer the clerk as their names are called. Instead, senators stroll in from the cloakroom or their offices and congregate in the well (the area in the front of the chamber). When they are ready to vote, senators catch the eye of the clerk and vote, often by indicating thumbs up or thumbs down. Roll-call votes are supposed to last fifteen minutes, but some have dragged on for more than an hour.

- Often, near the end of the day, the majority leader and the minority leader quickly move through a wrap-up period, during which minor bills that have been cleared by all members are passed by unanimous consent.

- Just before the Senate finishes its work for the day, the majority leader seeks unanimous consent for the agenda for the next session: when the Senate will convene, which senators will be given special orders, and sometimes specific time agreements for consideration of legislation.

Representatives who move to the Senate feel a sort of political "culture shock" in their new environment. They welcome the Senate's tradition of deference to individual senators. But some look back with nostalgia on the efficient procedures of the House. Many miss the camaraderie of the House, though few wish to return to it. "Rules and tradition make it possible for every member of the Senate to play a significant role in legislating," said Colorado Republican William L. Armstrong, who was elected to the Senate in 1978 after six years in the House. "It's possible even for a brand new member to jump right in."

"A senator has greater access to virtually anyone inside or outside of government," remarked Paul Simon, an Illinois Democrat who moved from the House to the

"This is a Senate, a Senate of equals, of men of individual honor and personal character, and of absolute independence. We know no masters, we acknowledge no dictators."

—Daniel Webster

Senate in 1985. "There are very few people who won't return a phone call from a U.S. senator."

Origins

The differences between the two chambers were not an accident of history but the result of a carefully crafted plan of the framers of the Constitution in 1787. The Senate was born of compromise—one so significant it was called the "Great Compromise" of the Constitutional Convention. Without it, the convention would have collapsed. When it was decided that representation in the House would be proportional to a state's population, the small states sounded the alarm. Fearful of domination by the more populous states, they insisted that states have equal representation in the Senate. The large states resisted until agreement was reached that, in return for equality of state representation in the Senate, the House would be given sole power to originate money bills, which the Senate could accept or reject but could not modify. This last provision was changed in the final draft to allow the Senate to alter or amend revenue bills.

The convention also decided that voters would elect House members but that the Senate should be insulated from popular sentiments. To this end, the convention directed that senators be elected by the state legislatures and for six-year terms. James MADISON explained the delegates' thinking: "The use of the Senate is to consist in its proceeding with more coolness, with more system, and with more wisdom, than the popular branch."

State legislatures no longer select senators because the Seventeenth Amendment to the Constitution provided for direct election of senators. Despite their long terms, senators today devote considerable time and energy to running for re-election, making them no longer insulated from public opinion. Some observers would also question whether the Senate has stayed aloof from popular legislative battles.

Nonetheless, the framers' views can still be heard two centuries later. During a 1986 debate over whether to televise Senate proceedings, the discussion was laced with references to the differences between the two chambers, with the Senate depicted as the voice of reason and the House as the more impulsive voice of popular demands. The Senate ultimately voted to allow television cameras into the chamber, as the House had done earlier.

Powers

Contrasting views of the roles of the Senate and House were apparent in the Constitutional Convention's debates over congressional powers. For the most part, the two chambers were given equal powers, but there were several important exceptions.

Power of the Purse

One of the most significant instances in which one chamber was given precedence over the other was in the exercise of the power of the purse. The Constitution required that the House originate tax legislation. The convention's debate over the question of whether the Senate should be allowed to amend the House tax bills reflected the contrasting views of the Senate as likely to be either the most responsible branch or the most aristocratic one, to be strengthened or checked accordingly.

The question eventually was resolved in favor of the Senate's right to amend. This is a right the Senate does not hesitate to use, particularly toward the end of a session. Because the Senate has few

CLOSER LOOK ⊙

The small size of the Senate—less than a quarter of the House membership—contributes to its informality and flexibility. The House, by contrast, is highly structured. The Senate is more individualistic, with power more widely and evenly distributed among its members. The Senate shares certain executive powers with the president, which contributes to the chamber's prestige. With fewer members to share the limelight, senators enjoy more attention. But unlike House members, who can become highly specialized in policy areas, senators tend to be policy generalists.

"A senator has greater access to virtually anyone inside or outside of government. There are very few people who won't return a phone call from a U.S. senator."

—*Sen. Paul Simon,* D-Ill., who moved from the House to the Senate in 1985

procedures or rules to ward off amendments, the Senate often has turned a tax measure into a Christmas tree bill by attaching to it amendments that bestow benefits on various economic interests.

The Senate has even on occasion circumvented the constitutional stricture on originating tax bills. In 1982 it wrote what was at the time the largest peacetime tax increase in the nation's history by attaching the plan to a minor tax bill passed by the House that went straight to a House-Senate conference committee.

Power of Confirmation

Counterbalancing the House's precedence in money matters are the Senate's executive powers, which it shares with the president. These are the powers of confirmation of appointments and treaty ratification.

The Constitution requires that the president appoint government officials with the advice and consent of the Senate. The vast majority of nominations receive routine confirmation, but those for top positions in the federal government and judiciary are closely scrutinized by Senate committees and sometimes hotly debated on the Senate floor.

For example, grueling battles were waged over President Ronald Reagan's Supreme Court nominations in 1987. One nominee was defeated, and a second withdrew under intense Senate scrutiny before a third finally received Senate approval. One of President George H. W. Bush's cabinet nominees was rejected, becoming only the ninth cabinet nominee in history to be turned down by the Senate. President Bill Clinton faced severe attacks from conservatives for some of his nominees, and President George W. Bush in turn was criticized fiercely by Democrats for some of his.

Treaty Power

The Constitution requires that the Senate give its advice and consent to a treaty. A two-thirds vote of the senators present is necessary for treaty ratification. The Senate's voting record on treaties has been overwhelmingly favorable. Outright rejection is rare. In 1920, however, after prolonged debate the Treaty of Versailles was ultimately rejected. The Treaty of Versailles was the World War I treaty of peace with Germany and also covered U.S. membership in the League of Nations.

Congressional involvement in the treaty process reached an unprecedented level in modern times during negotiation in the late 1970s of an arms agreement with the Soviet Union and during consideration of the Panama Canal treaties and related legislation. The Panama Canal treaties were eventually approved by the Senate, but the arms agreement was shelved after the Soviet invasion of Afghanistan.

Impeachment Power

The Senate and House share the power to impeach high federal officials. The House conducts the investigation, brings charges (called articles of impeachment) against an official, and argues for removal from office during a trial conducted in the Senate. The final decision is the Senate's. The Constitution requires a two-thirds vote of the senators present to convict on any article of impeachment. Between 1789 and 2007 the Senate sat as a court of impeachment sixteen times. Seven cases ended in conviction and seven in acquittal. In two cases the Senate dismissed the charges.

Election Power

Both chambers have the responsibility of counting the electoral votes for president and vice president. If no candidate for the presidency has a majority of the electoral votes, the House chooses the president. If no vice-presidential candidate has a majority, the Senate makes the choice.

Only once has the Senate resolved a vice-presidential contest. In 1837, when Martin Van Buren was elected president, his running mate, Richard M. Johnson, was one vote short of a majority because Van Buren electors from Virginia had boycotted Johnson. The Senate elected Johnson vice president.

Development

The framers of the Constitution assumed that the House would be the preeminent chamber, with the Senate functioning as a revisory body and a restraining influence. Initially the House did overshadow the Senate. It was reported that, in the First Congress (1789–1791), the Senate often adjourned its tedious sessions so that its twenty-six members could go listen to the livelier floor debates in the House.

The Senate's influence was soon felt. The importance of its treaty and appointment powers, in which the House had no share, was a factor; in addition, membership in the smaller Senate became more desirable than election to the rapidly expanding House. The Senate's longer term and more stable membership also made it more attractive.

The Senate's legislative importance increased gradually. In the early years the House dominated the great debates, such as those surrounding the War of 1812. But the Senate took the lead in the struggle over the Missouri Compromise of 1820, involving the extension of slavery to new territories, and succeeded in imposing on the House an amendment barring slavery in future northern states. In the years leading up to the Civil War, the Senate became the chief forum for the great antislavery debates. Illustrious figures, such as Daniel WEBSTER of Massachusetts, Henry CLAY of Kentucky, and John C. CALHOUN of South Carolina, dominated this "golden age" of the Senate.

Alexis de Tocqueville, French aristocrat, scholar, and astute observer of American life, wrote in 1834 that "the Senate is composed of eloquent advocates, distinguished generals, wise magistrates, and statesmen of note, whose arguments would do honor to the most remarkable parliamentary debates of Europe." He had harsher words for the House of Representatives: "One is struck by the vulgar demeanor of that great assembly. Often there is not a distinguished man in the whole number."

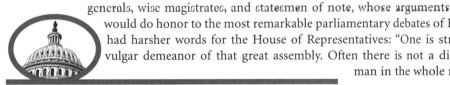

"The Senate is composed of eloquent advocates, distinguished generals, wise magistrates, and statesmen of note, whose arguments would do honor to the most remarkable parliamentary debates of Europe." But in the House: "One is struck by the vulgar demeanor of that great assembly. Often there is not a distinguished man in the whole number."

—*Alexis de Tocqueville*

Senate Giants

Some of the most well-known and illustrious senators included the following:

- Henry Clay, of Kentucky, known as the "Great Compromiser" for his efforts to heal bitter regional differences over slavery
- Daniel Webster of Massachusetts, an outstanding orator who, like Clay, fought to preserve the Union
- John C. Calhoun of South Carolina, champion of states' rights and gifted spokesperson for the South before the Civil War
- Robert M. La Follette Sr. of Wisconsin, a progressive Republican leader who advocated public ownership of railroads in the early twentieth century
- Robert A. Taft Sr. of Ohio, known as "Mr. Republican" for his party leadership and conservative policies in the 1940s and early 1950s

Legislative Process

Courtesy, dignity, and informality marked the proceedings of the early Senate. Sometimes on a chilly morning members would leave their seats and gather around the fireplace to conduct Senate business. An elaborate procedure or a formal division of labor was not needed because there was not much labor to divide. As the duties of Congress grew and as legislation increased in volume and complexity, however, a discernible legislative process began to evolve. "Rules are never observed in this body; they are only made to be broken. We are a law unto ourselves," claimed Republican senator John J. Ingalls of Kansas in 1876. In the smaller, more individualistic Senate, rules have been far less important than in the larger House.

The Senate today operates largely by UNANIMOUS CONSENT, suspending or adjusting its rules as needed. Because the early Senate saw its primary function as deliberation, no restrictions were placed on debate, and thus was born the Senate's cherished tradition of unlimited debate. There was little obstruction in the early Senate, but the filibuster—the practice by which a minority employs extended debate and delaying tactics to put off or block action on a bill—became increasingly common in the nineteenth century. A virtual epidemic of filibusters occurred in the 1880s and 1890s. A rule to cut off filibusters was finally adopted in 1917 and was first used several years later during the seemingly interminable debates on the Treaty of Versailles. Further reforms to curtail obstructionism in the Senate were adopted over the years. For many decades the filibuster was used primarily in debates on the most significant issues of the day, but in the modern Congress dozens of filibusters occur over even the most minor matters, and often just the threat of a filibuster can significantly affect the chamber's operation. The filibuster is one of the most potent weapon in the hands of determined senators.

The Senate originally conducted most of its deliberations in its chamber. Senators would consider questions brought before them and indicate the line of action to be followed before appointing a temporary committee to work out the details of proposed legislation. Ad hoc select committees soon grew to an unmanageable number (nearly one hundred in the 1815–1816 session), and the Senate established permanent legislative committees.

Committees developed into powerful, autonomous institutions during the nineteenth century. The important practice of having the majority party's most senior member of a committee serve as chair was begun at this time. These committee chairs often served as floor managers of bills until formal floor leaders were established.

The Constitution mentioned only two Senate officers: the vice president of the United States was to serve as the president of the Senate, and a president pro tempore was to act in his absence.

CLOSER LOOK

Alben Barkley, pictured in the center of a delegation visiting Nazi concentration camp Buchenwald in April 1942, had a lengthy Senate career. After serving in the House, he entered the Senate in 1927 and became majority leader in 1937. Holding the post for ten years, he became minority leader in 1947 when party control of the Senate switched hands.

Source: USHMM, courtesy of National Archives and Records Administration

Leading the Majority

Alben Barkley, having won the majority leadership by only one vote over Pat Harrison, a Southern Democrat, was initially perceived as a mere spokesperson for President Roosevelt. Barkley drew resentment over his support of the president's Court-packing plan and other domestic policies that divided his own party. Over time, however, Barkley gained credibility as a leader of the Senate and eventually garnered support for crucial foreign policies prior to the U.S. involvement in World War II; he fought for the repeal of the Neutrality Act, and in 1941 he successfully sponsored the Lend-Lease Act. In a dramatic turn, he opposed Roosevelt when he vetoed a tax relief bill in 1944, calling the president's action "a calculated and deliberate assault upon the legitimate integrity of every member of Congress." Barkley resigned as majority leader but was unanimously reelected the following day. A group of Barkley's colleagues rushed to notify him of the vote as Senator Tom Connally of Texas shouted, "Make way for liberty!" Barkley subsequently served as minority leader in the 80th Congress and as vice president under Harry Truman.

But neither officer was given any real power, and as a result neither has done much more than preside over the Senate.

Eventually the Senate developed a formal leadership hierarchy, but it did not build a tradition of strong leadership like that in the House. As Webster put it in 1830, "This is a Senate, a Senate of equals, of men of individual honor and personal character, and of absolute independence. We know no masters, we acknowledge no dictators."

Leadership was provided by powerful individuals or groups until political parties began to dominate. Modern party discipline made its appearance in the Senate in the 1890s, and formally designated majority and minority floor leaders followed in the early 1900s. These leaders came to play an important role in organizing the Senate to carry out their parties' programs. Senators reached top leadership positions after years of spending time on the floor, mastering parliamentary rules, and constantly doing favors for other members.

No Senate leader in modern times has rivaled the effectiveness of Lyndon B. JOHNSON, a Texas Democrat who served as minority leader in 1953–1954 and as majority leader from 1955 until 1961, when he resigned to become John F. KENNEDY's vice president.

Johnson's influence was the accumulation of hundreds of intense one-to-one relationships. He got his way by subjecting senators to his legendary "treatment"—cajoling, accusing, threatening, and promising—until he had won.

Johnson's power was not something that could be passed on to successors, partly because it was uniquely his but also because the climate in the Senate was changing. Organizational and procedural changes in the 1970s enabled less senior members of the Senate to gain power at the expense of older and more experienced legislators. With more staff, more money, and more power, individual senators were able to maintain their independence from party leaders and more easily pursue their own interests and legislative goals.

The Modern Senate

By the 1980s members were increasingly frustrated by the legislative system and the Senate's bouts of legislative paralysis. A few highly publicized retirements focused attention on the problems of the modern Senate. "We are legislators. Like baseball players who like to play nine innings, like farmers who like to plant all of their fields, we like to pass laws," said South Dakota Democrat Thomas A. DASCHLE, who in 1987 moved from the House to the Senate, where in time he served as both minority and majority leader. "In an era of fast moving, globalized issues, the possibility that the world could pass the Senate by increases immeasurably."

Complaints about the Senate's cumbersome processes are as old as the institution itself. Because of its privileges of unlimited debate and virtually unlimited amending powers, the Senate may well spend days considering a measure that the House debated and passed in one afternoon.

To keep business moving, the Senate in the early 1970s began operating on a two-track system, with a certain period of time reserved daily for particularly controversial bills. It was hoped that in this way a much-debated bill would not interfere with other business. Nonetheless, delays and obstructionism continued to increase.

Filibusters, which a couple of generations ago were reserved for civil rights and a handful of other divisive issues, came to be used on dozens of less important subjects. A few intransigent senators—just one, if he or she was sufficiently determined—could block action on any bill that did not have the sixty votes required to end a filibuster. Probably no one voiced the growing frustration felt by many senators better than Barry Goldwater, who retired in 1987

"We are legislators. Like baseball players who like to play nine innings, like farmers who like to plant all of their fields, we like to pass laws. In an era of fast moving, globalized issues, the possibility that the world could pass the Senate by increases immeasurably."

—Sen. Thomas A. Daschle of South Dakota in 1987. He served as both minority and majority leader.

after thirty years as a Republican senator from Arizona. "If this is the world's greatest deliberative body," he told a colleague one day in 1982, "I'd hate to see the world's worst."

Efforts to streamline procedures were made in the 1980s. Yet, in an institution as traditional as the Senate, those seeking changes in procedures and organization inevitably faced a battle. Senior members jealously guarded their power bases. Others resisted change because they thought the Senate's constitutional role and its identity as a "deliberative" body were inextricably linked to its inefficiency. They feared that changes would weaken the power of the minority party—and even individual senators—to affect the outcome of legislation. The burden of proof rested heavily on those seeking procedural revisions.

The leadership in the 100th Congress (1987–1989) inaugurated a new system to answer one frustration of senators: the chamber's erratic schedule. The new plan called for the Senate to be in session for three five-day work weeks and then off for a week. Until then, the Senate generally had had floor business four days a week. Members had complained that the unpredictable schedule interfered with family events, meetings with constituents, and campaign fundraising events. But the Senate quickly returned to four-day weeks and unpredictable schedules. Majority Leader Robert C. BYRD, a West Virginia Democrat, had cautioned against expecting too much. "There is no magic solution that will automatically make the Senate a 9-to-5 job," Byrd said in 1987. "We could make it a 9-to-5 job but it would no longer be the United States Senate."

Byrd's successor as majority leader, Democrat George J. MITCHELL of Maine, was more successful in improving senators' working conditions. He resumed the three-weeks-on, one-week-off legislative schedule and held few late-night sessions. Republican Majority Leader Trent LOTT of Mississippi, who held the position from 1996 until 2001, generally sought to avoid late-night votes until the intense workload at the end of the year required a more frenetic schedule.

Lott directed the Senate during the historic 107th Congress, which was evenly split between fifty Democrats and fifty Republicans. Lott oversaw an unprecedented power-sharing agreement between the two parties that lasted only five months in 2001. The agreement gave each party equal representation on committees. If a panel tied on a vote, the full Senate could move the issue to the floor, where GOP vice president Richard CHENEY could break the tie.

However, the deal was short-lived. In June, Republican James M. Jeffords of Vermont left his party to become an Independent, handing control of the chamber to the Democrats. After the Democrats lost seats in the 2002 elections, control reverted to the Republicans in 2003.

Republicans regained the majority in the 2002 elections and came under the leadership of Bill FRIST of Tennessee. Although the Republican Congress—the GOP had the majority in the House also—was able to pass large parts of President George W. Bush's agenda and supported him in launching a war in Iraq—his most significant action if office—Frist's leadership was given mixed reviews by both senators and outside observers.

In addition, by the end of 2006 some senators had grown weary of a long period of internecine warfare that had gripped the chamber for years, much of it over the approval of presidential appointments—both from Clinton and Bush—to the federal judiciary. When Frist and supporters threatened to alter the cherished filibuster rule to allow a majority vote to confirm such appointments—a plan that became known as the nuclear option because of its probable effect on all Senate traditions and comity among members—a group of cooler heads struck a compromise that deflected the danger. However, the Senate was closely divided in 2007, with the Democrats having only a one-vote margin. With Democrats firmly in control of the House, the Senate became the Republican bulwark to block legislation the GOP administration of George W. Bush did not want.

This set the stage for many confrontations in the 110th Congress, including unresolved fights over immigration reform and the course of the war in Iraq.

In addition, the historic congeniality of the Senate was changing in the first decade of the new century with the influx of more former House members who were steeped in the highly partisan conduct common to that chamber. Many of these former representatives had served in the House only in the latter years of the twentieth century when both parties—but the Republicans in particular after reclaiming the majority in 1994 for the first time in a half century—engaged in protracted political and legislative warfare that polarized both political parties. Newly elected senators fresh from the House often brought with them the combative mind-set of their House years, adding to the difficulty of reaching compromises that had been easier in previous decades in the Senate.

Elections

Senators were elected by state legislatures until the early twentieth century. But in the PROGRESSIVE ERA with its movement toward more democratic control of government, public opinion increasingly favored popular election of senators. Eventually the Senate was forced to participate in its own reform. The Seventeenth Amendment, approved by Congress in 1912 and ratified by the states the following year, provided for the direct election of senators.

The modern Senate Chamber.
Source: U.S. Senate Commission on Art and Antiquities

The six-year terms of senators are staggered so that one-third of the Senate seats are up for election every two years, instead of all the seats being open at one time. In the event of a vacancy, a state governor may make a temporary appointment until the vacancy can be filled by a special election.

The length of a senator's term has always been considered a real advantage, especially by House members who face elections every two years. Historically, senators were able to act as statesmen for the first half of their terms and deal with politics in the last few years. But Senate seats today are not so secure as they once were, and senators increasingly have become—by the end of the twentieth century—permanent candidates, like their House colleagues. Senate races are not only more competitive but also more costly, with multimillion-dollar campaigns common. According to former majority leader Byrd, one of his biggest problems as leader was accommodating the senators' need for time away from the floor to raise campaign money. (See CAMPAIGN FINANCING.)

Qualifications

To serve in the U.S. Senate, the Constitution requires that a person be at least thirty years of age, have been a citizen of the United States for not less than nine years, and live in the state he or she is to represent.

Characteristics

Few senators in modern times have found the age requirement to be a problem. The average senator at the start of the 110th Congress in 2007 was 61.2 years, up from 59.7 years in 2003. The youngest was forty-two-year-old John E. Sununu, a Republican from New Hampshire. Six of the 100 senators had served more than half their lives in Congress.

The Senate in 2007 counted sixteen women among its ranks, including two from each of three states: California, Maine, and Washington. These small numbers were hardly surprising, given that only thirty-three women had been elected or appointed to the Senate since its beginning. (Of these, one served just a day and another never was sworn in because Congress was not in session.) Only three African Americans had served in the Senate before Carol Moseley-Braun, the first black woman senator, was elected by Illinois in 1992. But Moseley-Braun lost her seat in the 1998 elections. Only one African American sat in the Senate in 2007, Barack Obama, also of Illinois.

One telling statistic from the 110th Congress was the number of former representatives serving in the Senate: fifty, exactly half the membership. Although representatives tend to bristle when the House is referred to as the "lower chamber," they recognize the incentives to make a run for the Senate: the Senate's greater prestige and publicity; its longer term, larger staff, and more generous perquisites; the opportunity for increased effectiveness; a greater role in foreign affairs; and the challenge of dealing with a statewide constituency.

More than half of the senators (fifty-nine) at the start of the 110th Congress in 2007 listed law as their occupation. This was a much higher percentage than the 162 House members who cited a legal profession that year.

Only one former senator sat in the House in recent years. This was Florida Democrat Claude Pepper who, after serving as a senator from 1936 through 1951, became a House member in 1963 and served until his death in 1989. Even after Pepper's several decades in the House, people still called him by his more prestigious title, "Senator Pepper."

More on this topic:

Blacks in Congress, p. 42

Members of Congress: Characteristics, p. 382

Women in Congress, p. 606

Senate Manual

The Senate Manual is a handbook of rules and other requirements for Senate operations, comparable to the HOUSE MANUAL in the House of Representatives. Its formal name is the *Senate Manual Containing the Standing Rules, Orders, Laws, and Resolutions Affecting the Business of the United States Senate.* In the back of the document, which is printed biennially, is an appendix that includes charts of electoral votes and lists of every senator, cabinet secretary, and Supreme Court justice who has ever served.

Senatorial Courtesy

The Senate has derived from its role in the APPOINTMENT POWER a custom, called senatorial courtesy, that gives senators additional influence over presidential nominations to federal positions within their own states. According to the custom the full Senate usually goes along when a senator from the president's party objects to a nominee in his or her state. The custom primarily affects nominations of judges to federal district courts and certain other courts, U.S. attorneys, federal marshals, and other federal officials based locally.

The custom of senatorial courtesy dates from 1789, when President George Washington replaced his nominee for a post in Georgia with the candidate endorsed by the state's two senators. Among the most aggressive advocates of senatorial courtesy was Roscoe CONKLING, a New York Republican who served in the Senate from 1867 to 1881. The importance of senatorial courtesy diminished as positions once filled by PATRONAGE were brought into the civil service.

Another aspect of senatorial courtesy is the "hold" a senator can place on a nomination. A hold, considered a temporary delay, is possible even when a job has national significance. Usually the leadership of a senator's party will honor the hold, delaying the vote on the nomination. The senator may be waiting for written answers to questions or other information; when the information is received, the hold is released. A hold may also be used when a senator wants to pressure the administration to change its position on an issue. Like other aspects of senatorial courtesy, the hold is not always honored by a senator's colleagues. (See HOLDS.)

Seniority System

For many decades positions of authority in Congress were routinely given to the members who had served in the institution the longest. The practice of reserving power to the most veteran senators and representatives is known as the seniority system. It defines a long-standing set of customary practices voluntarily observed by members, rather than binding requirements.

The seniority system still exists in Congress today but in a more informal and less iron-clad way than prevailed earlier. Leadership positions, elected by each party's members, often go to the more senior members. Chairs of House committees—although largely under the control of party leaders—usually follow seniority, but not always. In 2007, for example, the new Speaker, Nancy Pelosi, D-Calif., bypassed Jane Harman, a fellow Californian, and Alcee L. Hastings of Florida for the chair of the Select Intelligence Committee; by seniority both were next in line. Pelosi and Harman did not get along personally and Hasting was still plagued by his impeachment and removal as a federal judge in 1989. In the Senate the leadership asserted some influence on chairmanship but mostly at the margins; seniority still determined nearly all moves up the committee ladder.

The seniority system has been a unique aspect of Congress's internal organization. In no other major legislative body in the world has sheer length of service determined which members will

CLOSER LOOK

For decades the congressional seniority system promoted long-serving members to positions of enormous influence. By simply getting reelected time after time they rose to the top committee positions where they remained until defeat, retirement, or death. From those positions they controlled the flow of legislation. By the end of the twentieth century, however, the iron grip of seniority had been broken, although it still guided the rise of members up the committee ladder.

have power and influence. Even when it was followed most closely in Congress, the seniority system was not a formal law or rule of the House of Representatives or Senate.

There are three types of seniority. The first is seniority within the House or Senate as a whole. This type of seniority has limited significance, but it helps determine who has access to the most desirable office space and a few other privileges. The other types are seniority within a political party in the chamber and seniority on a committee. These last two are linked because members are chosen for service on committees by the political parties and are listed in order of seniority only with others from the same party. Members elected to a committee at the same time are then ranked in order of their full chamber seniority.

Seniority has little effect on the top leadership of Congress. The most senior member of the majority party in the Senate does hold the post of president pro tempore, but it is a virtually powerless position. The most important positions—Speaker of the House and majority and minority leaders in each chamber—have never been filled on the basis of seniority.

The seniority system has had its greatest impact within committees. Seniority on a committee is determined by the time that a member joined that committee, not when he or she became a member of Congress. During its heyday the seniority system ensured that the member with the longest service on each committee became the chair. Other veteran members of the committee automatically became subcommittee chairs.

Congress did not always follow the seniority system. The practice of awarding committee chairmanships solely on the basis of length of service evolved slowly in the late nineteenth and early twentieth centuries. It reached its peak after World War II, when the Democrats enjoyed decades of almost unbroken dominance in Congress.

The revolt against the seniority system began in the early 1970s. Many younger House members, who resented the power of a handful of veteran members, pushed through a series of reforms that greatly weakened the importance of seniority. For example, the decision was made to choose committee chairs without regard to seniority and to allow members of the majority party to choose committee chairs on a secret-ballot vote.

The reforms did not obliterate the seniority system entirely. Today the most senior member of the majority party on a committee or subcommittee usually will be chosen chair, unless there is strong political or personal opposition to that individual. Seniority still is normally followed in positioning members on committees and in filling vacancies; new members are ranked at the bottom of their committees. If members, even senior members, transfer from one committee to another, they are ranked, with rare exception, at the bottom in seniority on their new committees.

Efforts to change the seniority system have provoked heated debate. One argument for the system is simple: experience counts. It often takes many years for members to master the difficult subjects before their committees. The most experienced members often have more of the political skills needed to provide strong leadership for a committee. Moreover, the practice of automatically awarding posts according to seniority prevents periodic internal battles for power.

Critics of seniority view it as a rigid, inefficient system that deprives vigorous younger members of influence while reserving power to a small group of senior members. In some cases the system produced elderly chairs whose talents and intellect had faded with the years. In others it encouraged chairs to run their committees in an arrogant, autocratic manner, ignoring the wishes of other members.

Several factors led to the development of the seniority system. One was the trend toward longer congressional careers that became evident in the early twentieth century. In earlier times, when most members served for only a few terms, seniority meant little. But the arrival on Capitol Hill of members who viewed Congress as a lifetime job tended to emphasize the importance of seniority.

The seniority system also developed as a result of conflicts between leaders and the congressional rank and file. In the late nineteenth century, all-powerful leaders—the House Speaker and the chair of the majority party caucus in the Senate—controlled committee assignments and chairmanships. The revolt against that system led to the use of seniority to fill key posts.

The Legislative Reorganization Act of 1946 solidified the rule of seniority. The act consolidated many committees into a smaller number of panels, thus giving a few seniority-selected chairs wide power over every aspect of congressional activity.

A key consequence of the seniority system was to give an unusual amount of power to members who were easily reelected—those holding safe seats in the South and in predominantly urban areas often dominated by party machines. These men grew increasingly unrepresentative of the party as younger members were elected in the political landslides of 1958 and 1964, many of whom advocated new social programs and civil rights, and, later, opposed the Vietnam War.

Members who were out of step with their party's program or with the mood of the country, because of advanced age, ideology, or both, chaired important committees thanks to seniority. For example, James O. Eastland, a Mississippi Democrat who chaired the Senate Judiciary Committee from 1956 to 1978, was notorious for bottling up civil rights bills sought by party leaders.

The rule of the veteran members caused intense frustration on the part of less senior members. By the 1970s most committee chairs were above age sixty-five and had decades of service. That left many middle-aged members, who might otherwise have been at the peak of their careers, with little more power than the most junior members.

The revolt against the seniority system was a major element in the reform movement that transformed Congress in the 1970s. The key battleground for this movement was the House Democratic Caucus, which over the course of a few years took a series of actions that greatly reduced the importance of seniority in allocating power. As the minority party, the Republicans had far less power to allocate, but they also took steps to reduce the dominance of seniority. The Senate also acted to reduce the iron-clad rule of seniority at about this time, although the changes there were less marked than in the House.

The changes approved by the House Democratic Caucus during the 1970s made it possible for party members to reject, by secret ballot, committee chairs, as well as subcommittee chairs of the Appropriations Committee. (In the early 1990s subcommittee chairs of the Ways and Means Committee also became subject to a caucus vote.) Another change barred members from chairing more than one subcommittee, thus opening up the posts to more junior members.

As a result of the changes made in the 1970s, senior members are no longer guaranteed chairmanships if they have angered their colleagues for some reason. A key development in this movement came in 1975, when House Democrats defeated the autocratic chairs of the Agriculture, Armed Services, and Banking committees—W. R. Poage of Texas, F. Edward Hébert of Louisiana, and Wright Patman of Texas, respectively. Ten years later House Democrats deposed eighty-year-old Melvin Price of Illinois, who was considered too old and infirm to provide adequate leadership for the

More on this topic:

Appropriations Committee, House, p. 23

Caucuses, Party, p. 85

Reform, Congressional, p. 470

Ways and Means Committee, House, p. 603

CLOSER LOOK

The seniority system concentrated substantial power in the hands of easily reelected members, often from the South or urban areas dominated by party machines. The revolt against seniority, which focused on Democrats in the House because they were the entrenched party for most of the years between 1932 and 1994, was a major part of the reform efforts of the 1970s. The key battleground was the House Democratic Caucus, and the central reforms allowed party members to reject, by secret ballot, committee chairs, as well as subcommittee chairs of the Appropriations Committee. In the early 1990s subcommittee chairs of the Ways and Means Committee also became subject to a caucus vote. Another change barred members from chairing more than one subcommittee, thus opening up the posts to more junior members.

Armed Services Committee. He was replaced by the panel's seventh-ranking Democrat, Les Aspin of Wisconsin. Two chairs regarded as weak, ineffective leaders—Public Works Committee chair Glenn M. Anderson of California and House Administration Committee chair Frank Annunzio of Illinois—were deposed when House Democrats organized for the 102nd Congress (1991–1993). Later in that Congress, aged and ailing Appropriations Committee chair Jamie L. Whitten of Mississippi was pressured to relinquish most of the public duties of his chairmanship, a move that was formalized in the next Congress when Democrats replaced him with William H. Natcher of Kentucky. When Natcher became terminally ill, the panel's fifth-ranking member, David Obey of Wisconsin, became "acting chair" and then chair upon Natcher's death. Obey returned as committee chair in the 110th Congress in 2007 after the twelve-year GOP majority was ended in the 2006 elections.

Upon taking control of Congress in 1995, the Republicans immediately demonstrated they could easily override seniority, too. House Speaker Newt GINGRICH of Georgia hand-picked the chairs of the Appropriations, Commerce, and Judiciary committees, bypassing senior members.

There have been other inroads on the seniority system. When organizing for the 103rd Congress (1993–1995), House Democrats voted to allow their Steering and Policy Committee at any time to declare the chairmanship of a committee or a subcommittee vacant, and the matter then would go to the full caucus for a vote. House Republicans prohibited anyone in their caucus from holding any committee's top post for more than six consecutive years. The decision represented a fundamental shift for Republicans, who even more than Democrats usually gave their top committee posts to each panel's most senior member.

In the Republican-controlled 104th Congress (1995–1997), the House adopted a new rule limiting committee and subcommittee chairs to a maximum service of three consecutive terms. In 1995 Senate Republicans adopted a party rule, effective in 1997, to limit committee chairs to a six-year term limit. The House rule was tested for the first time in 2001, when Republicans had to elect thirteen new committee chairs, largely as a result of term limits. Five of the thirteen House Appropriations subcommittee chairs, or "cardinals," also were subject to the rule and had to rotate to the chairmanship of another subcommittee.

Separation of Powers

The Constitution established a national government divided into three independent branches: legislative, executive, and judicial. Each has distinct functions and powers derived directly from the Constitution. The resulting arrangement is generally referred to as the separation of powers.

Having experienced forms of arbitrary rule under both the British monarchy and various state legislatures under the Articles of Confederation, the framers of the Constitution were preoccupied with ways of avoiding a repetition of either executive or legislative tyranny. They feared despotism by an elected legislature almost as much as by an autocracy. By dividing the powers of government among three separate bodies, the framers believed that no one branch would be able to dominate the government. Such an arrangement has its price, however, because to some extent government efficiency and speed are sacrificed to protect individual liberties.

One famous description of the concept was made by Supreme Court Justice Louis D. Brandeis in 1926, although in a dissent to a case. Brandeis said: "The doctrine of separation of power was adopted by the [Constitutional] Convention in 1787, not to promote efficiency but to preclude the exercise of arbitrary power. The purpose was, not to avoid friction, but, by means of the inevitable friction incident to the distribution of the governmental powers among three departments, to save the people from autocracy."

The Constitution delineates the separation of powers between the three branches of the federal government. This painting from a book published by Huntington and Hopkins in 1823 shows George Washington standing before the delegates to the Constitutional Convention of 1787.
Source: Library of Congress

Constitutional Structure

Article I of the Constitution outlines in detail the powers and limitations of the legislative branch, which is divided into two chambers, the HOUSE OF REPRESENTATIVES and the SENATE. Of the three branches of government, the framers of the Constitution were most familiar with the legislature, and its importance is reflected in the attention given it. Almost half of the Constitution is devoted to the operation and powers of Congress. The framers viewed Congress as the "first branch" of the government because they believed strongly in the need for a representative body to formulate national policy.

Article II outlines the powers of the executive branch, headed by the president. The organization and powers of the presidency are not described in nearly as much detail as those of the legislature. The ambiguities have helped give the modern president great latitude in running the executive branch, particularly in foreign affairs.

The authors of the Constitution had serious reservations about establishing a strong executive. At the same time, they realized that the lack of a strong national executive under the Articles of Confederation was the primary reason that the nation's first experiment in representative government

had failed. Under the Confederation there was no independent presidency; the legislature controlled and directed executive functions. At the Constitutional Convention in 1787, the delegates gradually were won over to the necessity of a stronger chief executive, though the extent of the president's powers remained a matter of dispute until the final days of the Convention.

"The doctrine of separation of power was adopted by the [Constitutional] Convention in 1787, not to promote efficiency but to preclude the exercise of arbitrary power. The purpose was, not to avoid friction, but, by means of the inevitable friction incident to the distribution of the governmental powers among three departments, to save the people from autocracy."

—**Supreme Court Justice Louis D. Brandeis** in Myers v. United States

Article III describes the powers and organization of the national judiciary, including the Supreme Court. Constitutional scholars have noted that the judiciary article is even less detailed than the article for the executive branch.

The other articles of the Constitution confer additional powers on the legislative and executive branches and spell out various government procedures and guarantees.

Sharing of Powers

The American system is based on separation of powers, but those powers are not neatly divided. In many instances executive, legislative, and judicial powers overlap. Mixing the various powers of government among the three branches was another way of checking arbitrary rule. Thus the framers saw a network of checks and balances as an essential corollary to the separation of powers.

Separation of powers, to be effective as a governing doctrine, requires officials of all three branches, particularly legislators and the president, to work together in making national policy. From time to time in the nation's history, executive-legislative cooperation has broken down. Particularly divisive eras, such as the periods immediately before and after the Civil War, resulted in the near collapse of this necessary cooperation.

Given that no one branch or political party can govern alone under this system, senators and representatives of the two major political parties must work out compromises with each other as well as with the executive branch. The president must become involved in the legislative process by formulating a legislative agenda and working hard for its enactment. Since the early years of the twentieth century, and particularly since the administration of Franklin D. Roosevelt from 1933 until his death in 1945, the president has in large part set the legislative agenda. Congress generally reacts to presidential initiatives. Still, the president depends on members of Congress to help promote and pass his legislative program.

Division of Powers

The Constitution grants many powers and responsibilities to one branch exclusively. All appointed and elected officials of the U.S. government are prohibited from serving in more than one branch simultaneously. The vice president is an exception: as second in command, the vice president is next in line of succession as the nation's chief executive, but the vice president also serves as president of the Senate.

The Supreme Court periodically has to resolve issues involving the separation of powers. For example, a provision of the 1985 deficit-reduction law known as Gramm-Rudman-Hollings was declared unconstitutional by the Supreme Court in 1986 on grounds that it violated the separation of powers. The Court struck down the law's provision for automatic spending cuts because it assigned certain executive powers and duties to the General Accounting Office, an agency controlled by the legislative branch. The separation of powers figured in a 1983 Supreme Court decision declaring Congress's use of the legislative veto unconstitutional. In a 1976 decision the Supreme Court declared that congressional appointment of Federal Election Commission officials who exercised executive powers violated the constitutional clauses concerning separation of powers and appointments. The Supreme Court in 1998 upheld a lower court ruling affirming the unconstitutionality of the line-item veto because it permitted the president to rewrite bills he had already signed into law. In a concurring opinion to that decision, Justice Anthony M. Kennedy wrote, "Separation of powers was designed to implement a fundamental insight: Concentration of power in the hands of a single branch is a threat to liberty."

Checks and Balances

As an additional safeguard against the exercise of arbitrary power, the framers incorporated in the Constitution provisions in which the legislative, executive, and judicial branches were checked by overlapping functions of one or both of the other branches. For example, the president wields two important legislative functions: formulation of a legislative agenda, and thus the ability to set national priorities; and the veto power that allows the president to block legislation he opposes, subject to the congressional power to override such vetoes. The president also exerts influence on the judicial branch through the power to appoint judges and Supreme Court justices, subject to confirmation by the Senate.

Many powers granted to Congress infringe upon executive branch functions, including the power to declare war and to organize and maintain the armed forces. Congress was given the power to impeach (in the House) and to try impeachments (in the Senate) of executive and judicial branch officials, including the president and federal judges. Congress exerts influence on the other two branches through its power to confirm appointments. Legislators also are granted, in Article III, the power to establish lower courts—the district and appeals courts—and to reorganize the federal court system. The judicial branch has the ultimate check on Congress. Soon after the new republic was established, the Supreme Court declared and exercised the right to decide the constitutionality of laws passed by Congress.

Problems

Throughout the nation's history, the separation of powers has worked well in protecting against arbitrary rule and domination by any branch of government. Whether separation of powers provides effective government in an increasingly complex age is controversial. Some political scientists believe the present system fails to provide enough concentrated authority and harmony to ensure decisive governmental action. They also argue that a system of fragmented powers does not clearly identify responsibility for setting government policies or make officials accountable for their actions. For example, in such a system, how can the nation's voters apportion responsibility between the executive and legislative branches for staggering budget deficits?

However, other students of Congress note that the voters do exercise considerable judgment on responsibility for the most important issues of any period. The most recent example was the 2006 elections in which—most observers believed—the voters passed judgment on the conduct of the war in Iraq that a Republican president, George W. Bush, and a Republican-led Congress (albeit with the support of many Democrats) launched in 2003 and were still pursing on election day. The result was that voters gave control of Congress to the Democrats. Similarly, the GOP takeover of Congress in the 1994 elections was seen by many observers as a long-overdue judgment on the Democratic Party's forty years in power. These two important elections were seen as persuasive rejoinders to the arguments that divided power left no one accountable.

The U.S. system of two-year House terms, a four-year presidential term, and six-year Senate terms is another form of checks and balances, one that tends to diffuse power and responsibility.

Divided government also complicates matters. Divided government occurs when one political party controls the White House and the opposing party controls one or both houses of Congress, as happened during the Republican administrations of Ronald Reagan and George H. W. Bush. For two of the eight years of Reagan's administration, the Democratic Party controlled both houses of Congress; the House of Representatives was in Democratic hands for all eight years. Both houses were controlled by the Democrats during Bush's four years in office. Conflict between the executive and legislative branches resulted in deadlocks in policy making and confusion about the role of the two branches in foreign policy. The problem inherent in divided government came into stark relief following the 1994 elections, when Republicans gained the majority in both houses of Congress during the Democratic administration of Bill Clinton. As led by the Republican Party, Congress became an institution more active, more partisan, and more willing to defy the president than ever before in the post–World War II period. That resistance to White House priorities faded under George W. Bush, who presided over a GOP-controlled House and a closely divided Senate whose control rotated between the parties in the 107th Congress (2001–2003) and then returned to GOP control in the 108th Congress and continued through 2006.

With Democrats back in the majority in 2007 the national government returned to division with at least the potential for inaction and indecision. In the past divided government often meant gridlock on vital issues that needed attention. In earlier eras divided government, although always an impediment to a consensual approach to legislative action, was worked around by cooperative efforts of the two major parties to compromise on common ground. It helped that both parties usually included a variety of members from liberal to conservative, and with many in the middle, a spectrum of opinions that was increasingly absent as each party became more captive of their conservative or liberal bases. While compromise and accommodation still occurred in the latter decades of the twentieth century, the increasingly partisan tone of American politics—expressed most vividly in the national arena—often prevented opposing parties from coming together.

Sequestration *See* BUDGET PROCESS.

Sergeant-at-Arms

The House and Senate sergeants-at-arms are the police officers of their respective chambers. They attend all sessions and are responsible for enforcing rules and maintaining decorum, ensuring the security of buildings and visitors, and supervising the Capitol police force.

The House sergeant-at-arms is in charge of the mace, the symbol of legislative power and authority, and carries it when enforcing order in the House chamber.

Sergeants-at-arms are also responsible for rounding up members for floor votes. This authority, unused since 1942, became an issue during a 1988 filibuster in which Republican senators boycotted votes on campaign finance legislation. Senate majority leader Robert C. BYRD, a West Virginia Democrat, directed the sergeant-at-arms to arrest absent members and bring them to the Senate floor. Carrying out this order, sergeant-at-arms Henry K. Giugni tracked down Bob Packwood, an Oregon Republican, who was arrested and carried feet first into the Senate chamber. Packwood, whose broken finger was reinjured in the escapade, took his arrest in good humor, although other Republicans spoke bitterly of the incident.

Sessions of Congress *See* TERMS AND SESSIONS OF CONGRESS.

Sherman, John

John Sherman (1823–1900) became a fixture of the Republican Party in the nineteenth century, serving both in Congress and in the executive branch. As an influential member, and later chair, of the Senate Finance Committee, the Ohio Republican played a major role in formulating national financial policies. Later in his Senate career he sponsored antitrust legislation that carries his name to this day.

Sherman was elected to the House of Representatives in 1854 as part of the wave of antislavery sentiment that had led to the founding of the Republican Party that year. In 1859 he was involved in a hotly contested race for House Speaker. Sherman led in the early voting, but he was abhorred by the proslavery camp. The Republicans finally concluded he could not be elected, and he withdrew on the thirty-ninth ballot. Sherman became chair of the House Ways and Means Committee instead.

When he moved to the Senate in 1861, he was assigned to the Senate Finance Committee and became its chair in 1867. From this base, Sherman played an important role in the nation's finances during the Civil War and in the Reconstruction period. He supported wartime legislation authorizing paper money, or "greenbacks," and helped plan a new national banking system. In the postwar period he backed legislation calling for the redemption of paper money in gold.

Sherman's efforts were rewarded when he was named secretary of the Treasury in 1877. He failed to win the Republican presidential nomination in 1880 (and again in 1884 and 1888) and returned to the Senate in 1881. His legislative achievements included the Sherman Antitrust Act of 1890, a basic antitrust statute that is still on the books, and the Sherman Silver Purchase Act of 1890. He was named president pro tempore of the Senate in 1886, the year he also became chair of the Senate Foreign Relations Committee.

Sherman left the Senate to become President William McKinley's secretary of state in 1897. Ineffectual in the role, Sherman resigned the next year in protest against the Spanish-American War. He died two years later.

Small Business Committees, House and Senate

Popular with legislators, whose districts always include small businesses, the House and Senate small business committees have survived several attempts to reorganize them out of existence. Usually bipartisan in their actions, the two committees often serve as advocates, reminding other congressional panels of the special problems of small businesses. The panels have slightly different names. In the Senate it is called Small Business and Entrepreneurship; in the House it is simply Small Business.

The committees' main focus in the 1980s was preserving the Small Business Administration, which the Reagan administration wanted to make part of the Commerce Department. Another concern was to guarantee the participation of small businesses in federal procurement and government contracts.

The Senate committee was set up in 1950 as a select committee. It gained standing committee status in 1981. The panel's name was changed to the Small Business and Entrepreneurship Committee in 2001.

Alabama Democrat John J. Sparkman was the Senate panel's first chair and had a long tenure in the post (1950–1953, 1955–1967). Connecticut Republican Lowell P. Weicker Jr. chaired the committee from 1981 to 1987, when Arkansas Democrat Dale Bumpers took over. With the

Republican takeover of the Senate in 1995, Christopher S. Bond of Missouri became chair. Massachusetts Democrat John Kerry took the helm in mid-2001 when the Democrats won control of the Senate. Olympia J. Snowe of Maine became chair when the Senate reverted to the Republicans in 2003.

Snowe planned to use her post to encourage women entrepreneurs and pursue a wide-ranging legislative agenda. Roughly 97 percent of her home state's employers were small businesses with fewer than twenty employees. Snowe was the last GOP chair before Democrats won the 2006 election. She was succeeded in 2007 by Kerry. The change was not likely to make much difference because the panel had long been highly bipartisan. Snowe and Kerry had worked closely together in the past. Like the House committee, Kerry's panel was expected to place emphasis on the cost of health care for small businesses.

The House committee was set up in 1947 as the Select Committee to Conduct a Study and Investigation of the Problems of Small Business. Two representatives served several terms as chair: Texas Democrat Wright Patman (1949–1953, 1955–1963) and Tennessee Democrat Joe L. Evins (1963–1979). The panel became the Small Business Committee in a 1974 reorganization. Democrat John J. LaFalce of New York took over as chair in 1987.

With Republican control of the House in 1995, Jan Meyers of Kansas assumed the chair. After she retired in 1997, James M. Talent of Missouri became chair. Talent, who left the House in 2001 after a failed bid to win the seat of governor, was succeeded by Donald Manzullo of Illinois. Manzullo fought to reduce tax and regulatory burdens of small businesses and to discourage the government's practice of bundling together contracts to the disadvantage of small bidders. The Bush administration announced in 2002 that it would encourage agencies to avoid bundling. Manzullo also sought to pass broader legislation on the issue in the 108th Congress (2003–2005). The panel had approved a bipartisan bill to reduce bundling in the previous Congress, but the bill never made it to the floor.

In 2007 Democrat Nydia M. Velazquez became chair. She pledged to make health insurance overhaul for small businesses a top priority along with tax code overhaul. However, both topics are under the legislative authority of other committees.

Smith, Howard W.

Howard W. Smith (1883–1976) served as a representative from Virginia from 1931 to 1967. A leader of the conservative southern Democrats, or "Dixiecrats," and chair of the Rules Committee, Smith often was called the second most powerful member of the House of Representatives.

Smith began his career as a lawyer and went on to become a circuit judge and a banker. He became a foe of Franklin D. Roosevelt's New Deal and opposed social welfare programs throughout his career. Smith also spoke out against legislation aiding organized labor and voted against the 1935 National Labor Relations Act. He sponsored a bill in 1939 that called for the imprisonment of resident foreigners who recommended changes in the U.S. system of government. In 1940 he authored the Smith Act, which made it a crime to be a communist. The act was later struck down by the Supreme Court.

Roosevelt called Smith "the greatest obstructionist in Congress," and it was as a dissenter that Smith made his career. From his seat on the Rules Committee, Smith harried opponents from both political parties. By forming an alliance with conservative Democrats and Republicans on the committee, Smith was able to bottle up legislation, which had to move through the Rules panel before going to the House floor. In 1939 this CONSERVATIVE COALITION began demanding changes in bills before it would approve a rule. Dominated by these conservatives, the committee often flouted the wishes of the Democratic Speaker.

Smith became chair of the Rules Committee in 1955. He once held up consideration of legislation for days by disappearing to Virginia because, he said, his barn had burned down and it had taken a while to repair. The committee could meet only when convened by the chair.

In 1958 liberals sought to restructure the Rules Committee, but the proposal was rejected by Speaker Sam RAYBURN, who promised that the committee would not hold up civil rights and welfare legislation. In 1961 Rayburn himself recognized the need to reorganize the committee and supported a successful attempt to increase its membership. The addition of loyal Democrats to the committee diminished Smith's authority. He was defeated for reelection in 1966.

Howard W. Smith of Virginia, leader of the southern Democrats in the House, was considered by President Franklin D. Roosevelt to be "the greatest obstructionist in Congress."
Source: AP Images/Henry Griffin

Smith, Margaret Chase

Margaret Chase Smith (1897–1995), a Maine Republican, entered the House of Representatives in 1940 after the death of her husband, Rep. Clyde H. Smith. In 1948 she was elected to the Senate, where she served until 1973. An independent-minded Republican, Smith was the first of her party to denounce Sen. Joseph R. MCCARTHY on the Senate floor for his virulent anticommunist activities.

Before her marriage, Smith worked as a teacher and then as an executive with a newspaper and a woolen mill. After her husband entered Congress, she worked as his assistant in his congressional office. He encouraged her to run for his House seat after he suffered a heart attack in 1940. He died later that year, and she was elected to the seat in a special election.

In the House Smith served on the Naval Affairs Committee, where she was a strong advocate of military preparedness. Her reputation as a "hawk" was borne out by her 1961 speech in the Senate criticizing President John F. KENNEDY's seeming reluctance to use nuclear weapons. She charged that this reluctance put the United States at a disadvantage with the Soviet

Margaret Chase Smith was a firm supporter of the military. Here Smith and two other women help two boy scouts unload tin-ware collected for war use in front of the Capitol building in 1941.
Source: Library of Congress

Union. The speech prompted Nikita S. Khrushchev, then Soviet premier, to call her "the devil in the disguise of a woman."

In 1950 Smith presented a "declaration of conscience" on the Senate floor. The declaration, supported by six other Republican senators, criticized McCarthy's anticommunist campaign. She said, "I am not proud of the way we spear outsiders from the floor of the Senate.... I do not want to see the party ride to political victory on the Four Horsemen of Calumny—fear, ignorance, bigotry, and smear."

Smith was proud of her congressional attendance record and late in her career introduced measures to regulate senators' attendance on the floor. From June 1955 to July 1968 she never missed a Senate roll-call vote. Smith was defeated for reelection in 1972.

Soft Money *See* CAMPAIGN FINANCING.

Speaker of the House

The Speaker is both the presiding officer of the House of Representatives and the overall leader of the majority party in the chamber. The Constitution says that the House shall choose its Speaker, but it does not describe the Speaker's duties. The role has developed over more than two centuries of parliamentary give-and-take. Today the Speaker is widely regarded as the most powerful figure in Congress.

The formal duties of the Speaker are broad. The Speaker officially has authority to refer bills to committees for preliminary consideration and to schedule legislation for House floor action. When presiding over the House, the Speaker has the power to recognize members wishing to speak, subject to certain limitations spelled out in the House rules. With the advice of the parliamentarian, the Speaker also may decide points of order, objections raised by members who think House rules have been violated. The Speaker chooses members to chair the Committee of the Whole, a parliamentary framework the House adopts when it considers bills for amendment. The Speaker appoints members to various special House committees, as well as to conference committees, which work out the differences between bills passed by the House and Senate.

These are usually routine tasks, governed by House customs and rules that limit the Speaker's options. Skillful Speakers nonetheless find ways to make the rules work to their advantage.

The Speaker's formal powers are less critical than political mastery in determining the Speaker's influence in the House. A successful Speaker enjoys personal prestige as head of the party leadership structure and commands a high degree of party loyalty. Such a Speaker combines a deep understanding of the legislative process with strong persuasive skills. The Speaker's formidable political tools include proposing the slate of committee chairs for party approval and chairing the panel that makes the majority party's committee assignments—in effect, selecting the chairs for all committees and essentially controlling the assignment of members to committees. The Speaker also appoints the majority party's members of the House Rules Committee. The powerful committee works in concert with the majority leadership to control the flow of legislation to the floor and set the terms of floor debate.

The Constitution does not specify that a Speaker must be a member of the House, but no nonmember has ever been elected to the post. Speakers are chosen by the caucus of the majority party's members, whose decision is confirmed by the full House at

The Speaker—who is mentioned in the Constitution—is both the presiding officer of the House of Representatives and the overall leader of the majority party in the chamber. But the person's formal powers are far less significant than his or her understanding of the legislative process and reputation among colleagues. The person must possess strong persuasive skills and a tough political skin.

the beginning of each new Congress. (See CAUCUSES, PARTY.) In the twentieth century only senior members were chosen; since 1925 every Speaker except Republicans Newt GINGRICH of Georgia and J. Dennis HASTERT of Illinois has advanced from the position of either majority or minority leader. Gingrich had been minority whip prior to becoming Speaker and Hastert, chief deputy whip. Hastert, moreover, was the first person since 1925 to preside over the House without a prior elected leadership post.

All but one Speaker retained the post as long as their party held a majority in the House or until their retirement. The exception was Jim WRIGHT, who became embroiled in an ethics scandal and in 1989 became the first Speaker to be forced to resign in midterm. (Gingrich voluntarily stepped down as Speaker after Republicans suffered surprising setbacks in the 1998 midterm elections. Gingrich also said he would resign his seat at the start of the 106th Congress in January 1999, even though he won reelection. Gingrich, however, did complete his term as Speaker through the 105th Congress.)

Under rules adopted by the Republican-led House in 1995, Speakers were to be limited to no more than four consecutive two-year terms. However, at the beginning of the 108th Congress in 2003, that term limit was repealed. House Republicans concluded that a lame-duck Speaker's clout could be sharply curtailed. Under the old rule, Hastert's term as Speaker would have been up in 2007 but it would have made no difference anyway because Republicans lost their majority in the 2006 elections.

Like any other member, the Speaker may participate in debate and vote. Modern Speakers occasionally speak from the floor; they rarely vote except to break a tie. They do not serve on legislative committees.

Under the Presidential Succession Act of 1947, the Speaker follows the vice president in the line of presidential succession.

More on this topic:
Committee of the Whole, p. 110
Committee System, p. 111
Leadership, p. 325
Legislation, p. 339
Legislative Process, p. 344
Parliamentarian, p. 408
Presiding Officer, p. 437
Rules Committee, House, p. 478

Historical Highlights

In the early years of Congress the Speaker was largely a figurehead. The first Speaker, Frederick A. C. Muhlenberg of Pennsylvania, was necessarily a nonpartisan presiding officer because political parties had not yet formed when he assumed the post in 1789.

The authority of the office ebbed and flowed during the nineteenth century, but by the 1880s the Speaker had become the dominant leader of the House. The office reached its peak of power in the early 1900s under a series of autocratic Speakers, but their arbitrary use of that power led to a 1910 "revolt" that stripped the Speaker of most formal authority. Power was concentrated in the hands of committee chairs until the reforms of the 1970s restored many of the Speaker's powers. But even then Speakers found that to lead the House they had to rely chiefly on their persuasive arts.

Clay

The first really influential Speaker of the House was Henry CLAY, a popular Kentuckian who was elected to the post six

LONGEST-SERVING HOUSE SPEAKERS

Name	Years
Sam Rayburn	17
Henry Clay	10
Thomas P. O'Neill Jr.	10
John W. McCormack	9
J. Dennis Hastert	8
Joseph G. Cannon	8
James B. "Champ" Clark	8
Andrew Stevenson	7
Carl Albert	6
James G. Blaine	6
John G. Carlisle	6
Schuyler Colfax	6
Frederick H. Gillett	6
Nicholas Longworth	6
Nathaniel Macon	6
Thomas Brackett Reed	6

NOTE: Figures have been rounded to the nearest year.

SPEAKERS OF THE HOUSE OF REPRESENTATIVES, 1789–2008

Congress	Years	Speaker
1st	(1789–1791)	Frederick A. C. Muhlenberg, Pa.
2nd	(1791–1793)	Jonathan Trumbull, F-Conn.
3rd	(1793–1795)	Muhlenberg
4th	(1795–1797)	Jonathan Dayton, F-N.J.
5th	(1797–1799)	Dayton
6th	(1799–1801)	Theodore Sedgwick, F-Mass.
7th	(1801–1803)	Nathaniel Macon, D-N.C.
8th	(1803–1805)	Macon
9th	(1805–1807)	Macon
10th	(1807–1809)	Joseph B. Varnum, Mass.
11th	(1809–1811)	Varnum
12th	(1811–1813)	Henry Clay, R-Ky.
13th	(1813–1814)	Clay
	(1814–1815)	Langdon Cheves, D-S.C.
14th	(1815–1817)	Clay
15th	(1817–1819)	Clay
16th	(1819–1820)	Clay
	(1820–1821)	John W. Taylor, D-N.Y.
17th	(1821–1823)	Philip P. Barbour, D-Va.
18th	(1823–1825)	Clay
19th	(1825–1827)	Taylor
20th	(1827–1829)	Andrew Stevenson, D-Va.
21st	(1829–1831)	Stevenson
22nd	(1831–1833)	Stevenson
23rd	(1833–1834)	Stevenson
	(1834–1835)	John Bell, W-Tenn.
24th	(1835–1837)	James K. Polk, D-Tenn.
25th	(1837–1839)	Polk
26th	(1839–1841)	Robert M. T. Hunter, D-Va.
27th	(1841–1843)	John White, W-Ky.
28th	(1843–1845)	John W. Jones, D-Va.
29th	(1845–1847)	John W. Davis, D-Ind.
30th	(1847–1849)	Robert C. Winthrop, W-Mass.
31st	(1849–1851)	Howell Cobb, D-Ga.
32nd	(1851–1853)	Linn Boyd, D-Ky.
33rd	(1853–1855)	Boyd
34th	(1855–1857)	Nathaniel P. Banks, R-Mass.
35th	(1857–1859)	James L. Orr, D-S.C.
36th	(1859–1861)	William Pennington, R-N.J.
37th	(1861–1863)	Galusha A. Grow, R-Pa.
38th	(1863–1865)	Schuyler Colfax, R-Ind.
39th	(1865–1867)	Colfax
40th	(1867–1868)	Colfax
	(1868–1869)	Theodore M. Pomeroy, R-N.Y.
41st	(1869–1871)	James G. Blaine, R-Maine
42nd	(1871–1873)	Blaine

Congress	Years	Speaker
43rd	(1873–1875)	Blaine
44th	(1875–1876)	Michael C. Kerr, D-Ind.
	(1876–1877)	Samuel J. Randall, D-Pa.
45th	(1877–1879)	Randall
46th	(1879–1881)	Randall
47th	(1881–1883)	Joseph Warren Keifer, R-Ohio
48th	(1883–1885)	John G. Carlisle, D-Ky.
49th	(1885–1887)	Carlisle
50th	(1887–1889)	Carlisle
51st	(1889–1891)	Thomas Brackett Reed, R-Maine
52nd	(1891–1893)	Charles F. Crisp, D-Ga.
53rd	(1893–1895)	Crisp
54th	(1895–1897)	Reed
55th	(1897–1899)	Reed
56th	(1899–1901)	David B. Henderson, R-Iowa
57th	(1901–1903)	Henderson
58th	(1903–1905)	Joseph G. Cannon, R-Ill.
59th	(1905–1907)	Cannon
60th	(1907–1909)	Cannon
61st	(1909–1911)	Cannon
62nd	(1911–1913)	James B. "Champ" Clark, D-Mo.
63rd	(1913–1915)	Clark
64th	(1915–1917)	Clark
65th	(1917–1919)	Clark
66th	(1919–1921)	Frederick H. Gillett, R-Mass.
67th	(1921–1923)	Gillett
68th	(1923–1925)	Gillett
69th	(1925–1927)	Nicholas Longworth, R-Ohio
70th	(1927–1929)	Longworth
71st	(1929–1931)	Longworth
72nd	(1931–1933)	John Nance Garner, D-Texas
73rd	(1933–1934)	Henry T. Rainey, D-Ill.[1]
74th	(1935–1936)	Joseph W. Byrns, D-Tenn.
	(1936–1937)	William B. Bankhead, D-Ala.
75th	(1937–1939)	Bankhead
76th	(1939–1940)	Bankhead
	(1940–1941)	Sam Rayburn, D-Texas
77th	(1941–1943)	Rayburn
78th	(1943–1945)	Rayburn
79th	(1945–1947)	Rayburn
80th	(1947–1949)	Joseph W. Martin Jr., R-Mass.
81st	(1949–1951)	Rayburn
82nd	(1951–1953)	Rayburn
83rd	(1953–1955)	Martin
84th	(1955–1957)	Rayburn
85th	(1957–1959)	Rayburn
86th	(1959–1961)	Rayburn

(continues)

SPEAKERS OF THE HOUSE OF REPRESENTATIVES, 1789–2008 (CONTINUED)

Congress	Years	Speaker
87th	(1961)	Rayburn
	(1962–1963)	John W. McCormack, D-Mass.
88th	(1963–1965)	McCormack
89th	(1965–1967)	McCormack
90th	(1967–1969)	McCormack
91st	(1969–1971)	McCormack
92nd	(1971–1973)	Carl Albert, D-Okla.
93rd	(1973–1975)	Albert
94th	(1975–1977)	Albert
95th	(1977–1979)	Thomas P. O'Neill Jr., D-Mass.
96th	(1979–1981)	O'Neill
97th	(1981–1983)	O'Neill
98th	(1983–1985)	O'Neill
99th	(1985–1987)	O'Neill
100th	(1987–1989)	Jim Wright, D-Texas
101st	(1989)	Wright[2]
	(1989–1991)	Thomas S. Foley, D-Wash.
102nd	(1991–1993)	Foley
103rd	(1993–1995)	Foley
104th	(1995–1997)	Newt Gingrich, R-Ga.
105th	(1997–1999)	Gingrich
106th	(1999–2001)	J. Dennis Hastert, R-Ill.
107th	(2001–2003)	Hastert
108th	(2003–2005)	Hastert
109th	(2005–2007)	Hastert
110th	(2007–)	Nancy Pelosi, D-Calif.

SOURCE: *1991–1992 Congressional Directory, 102nd Congress* (Washington, D.C.: Government Printing Office, 1991); *CQ Weekly*, selected issues.

NOTES: Key to abbreviations: D—Democrat; F—Federalist; R—Republican; W—Whig.
1. Rainey died in 1934 but was not replaced until the next Congress.
2. Wright resigned and was succeeded by Foley on June 6, 1989.

times between 1811 and 1825. The six Speakers before him had presided over the House only ceremonially; Clay was the first to lead it.

Clay was elected Speaker the day he arrived in the House at age thirty-four. He promptly set out to assert the supremacy of Congress over the other branches of government and of the Speaker over the affairs of the House. Clay owed his election as Speaker to a faction of young representatives known as the War Hawks, and he used the influence of his office to push the nation into the War of 1812. He stacked key House committees with supporters of his war policy, exploited House rules to reinforce his control of the chamber, and used his great oratorical skills to pressure President James Madison into declaring war against England.

Reed

The next great expansion of the Speaker's power came under Thomas Brackett REED, who won the nickname "Czar Reed" for his efforts. Reed, a Maine Republican, served as Speaker in 1889–1891

and 1895–1899. When he assumed the post, delaying tactics by the Democratic minority often prevented the majority from working its will. Through a succession of floor rulings, Reed firmly established the right of the majority to control the legislative process.

The minority's chief stalling tactic was the "disappearing" or "silent" quorum. A majority of the chamber's members, known as a quorum, was required to transact business. But when the roll was called to establish the presence of a quorum, minority members who were present in the chamber refused to answer to their names. Thus the vote fell short of the number required. Reed solved the problem of the disappearing quorum by counting all the members who were present, not just those who answered the roll. The Democrats were furious, but the Speaker held firm. Asked to explain the function of the minority, Reed is said to have replied: "The right of the minority is to draw its salary, and its function is to make a quorum."

Reed's rulings later became part of a new set of House rules, which was drafted by the Rules Committee under his chairmanship. Speakers had been members of and chaired the Rules Committee since 1858, and much of their power resulted from that arrangement.

> **"The right of the minority is to draw its salary, and its function is to make a quorum."**
>
> **—Thomas Brackett Reed,** R-Maine, who as Speaker in the late nineteenth century was famous for rulings that ended delaying tactics by the then-minority Democrats and that firmly established the majority's right to control the legislative process

Perhaps the most powerful Speaker in history, Joseph G. Cannon addresses the House of Representatives. Cannon served as Speaker from 1903 to 1910, when Republicans and Democrats rebelled against his arbitrary rule.
Source: Library of Congress

Cannon

The power of the Speaker reached its peak when Illinois Republican Joseph G. CANNON held the post from 1903 to 1911. Although "Uncle Joe" Cannon instituted few parliamentary changes in the House, he used fully those made by his predecessors. Cannon's use, or misuse, of the Rules Committee to control floor action proved to be particularly offensive to his colleagues. His dictatorial rule ended in 1910 when insurgent Republicans joined Democrats in a revolt against him, stripping the Speaker of the authority to chair—or even to serve on—the Rules Committee.

The Speaker was further weakened the following year, when the new Democratic majority transferred the power to make Democratic committee assignments from the Speaker to the Ways and Means Committee, where it resided until the mid-1970s.

Longworth

During his tenure from 1925 to 1931, Nicholas LONGWORTH, an Ohio Republican, tried to restore the centralized authority of the Speaker that had been lost in the revolt against Cannon and under his successors. Aided by a small group of trusted associates, Longworth personally assumed control of the House. He was able to achieve through persuasion what Cannon had done by arbitrary interpretation of the rules.

Rayburn

Legend surrounds the tenure of Speaker Sam RAYBURN, who served in the post from 1940 until his death in 1961, except for two short stints as minority leader when the Republicans controlled the House in 1947–1949 and 1953–1955. Rayburn exerted such influence as Speaker that the Texas Democrat was said to run the House out of his hip pocket.

Confronted after World War II with a party badly split over civil rights and other domestic issues, Rayburn found he could minimize disunity by making party decisions himself and bargaining with individuals rather than with the party as a whole. "To get along, you've got to go along," he routinely advised House freshmen, and they generally complied.

Rayburn's leadership style demonstrated the profound changes that had occurred in Congress since Cannon's reign. As party discipline declined, the Speaker found he had to rely on his personal style to achieve his goals. "The old day of pounding on the desk and giving people hell is gone," Rayburn said as early as 1950. "A man's got to lead by persuasion and kindness and the best reason—that's the only way he can lead people."

> *The old day of pounding on the desk and giving people hell is gone. A man's got to lead by persuasion and kindness and the best reason—that's the only way he can lead people."*
>
> —*Sam Rayburn*, R-Texas, who was House Speaker for most of the period from 1940 to 1961

O'Neill

Despite reforms of the 1970s that granted new powers to the Speaker, Thomas P. "Tip" O'NEILL Jr., a Massachusetts Democrat who was Speaker from 1977 until his retirement in 1987, had trouble capitalizing on them. A continuing decline in party discipline weakened his leadership. O'Neill himself was known for his party loyalty and partisanship, but younger and generally more liberal Democrats criticized him for failing to crack down on conservative members who voted against positions supported by a majority of the party. O'Neill maintained that the party's diversity made it nearly impossible to discipline or even threaten to discipline disloyal members.

On one of the rare occasions when discipline was attempted, it backfired. Texas Democrat Phil Gramm was removed from his seat on the Budget Committee in 1983, in reprisal for his two-year collaboration with the White House on President Ronald Reagan's budget. Gramm promptly resigned his House seat, won reelection as a Republican, and returned to the Budget Committee. Gramm was elected to the Senate in 1984.

O'Neill eventually warmed to the role thrust upon him in 1981 by Republican control of the White House: that of the chief national spokesperson for Democratic positions.

Wright

Controversy surrounded Jim Wright, the flamboyant Texas Democrat who succeeded O'Neill in 1987. As Speaker, Wright was determined to give House Democrats the policy leadership many of them had found O'Neill to lack. But in pursuing his ambitious agenda for the House, Wright may have overstepped the limits of the Speaker's powers at that time.

Wright was criticized for his aggressive tactics in getting legislation passed; Republicans considered him a match for Cannon in his treatment of the minority. Although Wright's Democratic colleagues took pride in the legislative achievements, many resented Wright's failure to include them in the process of achieving them. Wright, sometimes dubbed the "Lone Ranger," had a record of springing major decisions without consulting key colleagues.

As allegations of financial misconduct developed into a full-blown investigation, Wright found that Democrats who were willing to support him when he—and they—were winning were not as willing to back him on a question of personal ethics. Wright became the first Speaker to be forced from office at midterm, when he resigned the post of Speaker and his House seat in June 1989. The House Democratic leadership was further shaken at this time by the resignation of Democratic whip Tony Coelho of California, who gave up his House seat in the face of allegations of financial irregularities.

Foley

Democrat Thomas S. FOLEY of Washington was chosen to succeed Wright. Known for his low-key, nonconfrontational style, Foley was a striking contrast to the hard-charging Wright. The new Speaker received a great deal of credit for restoring stability to the House after the resignations of Wright and Coelho. Even Republicans who had been extremely critical of Wright praised Foley for his civil manner and attempts at bipartisanship.

Foley was a cautious, careful political navigator. He preferred to let the legislative process work, however slowly, than to impose his views or push specific legislation. But some Democrats occasionally found Foley too accommodating and lacking the aggression they thought was necessary to push their agenda. Such criticism surfaced in 1992 when the House was torn by scandals involving the House bank and post office. (See SCANDALS, CONGRESSIONAL.)

Foley seemed especially ill-suited to confront the accelerating guerrilla warfare against Democrats, and against the institution of Congress itself, led by Minority Whip Gingrich. After the 1992 election of Democrat Bill Clinton as president, Foley was put in the position of having to pass an ambitious presidential program with a caucus membership that was not united either on policy or in loyalty to the new chief executive.

Amid the national Democratic rout in 1994, Foley lost his seat in Congress, only the third such defeat for a sitting Speaker. The last had been Galusha A. Grow, a Pennsylvania Republican, who lost in 1862; his predecessor, Republican William Pennington of New Jersey, had lost in 1860.

Gingrich

Newt Gingrich took over as Speaker in 1995, the first Republican to hold the position in forty years. His move from freshman to Speaker in only sixteen years was unprecedented in the modern era. Gingrich's fall from power and abrupt decision to resign at the end of the 106th Congress (1997–1999) was equally striking.

Gingrich was clearly a new breed of legislative leader, although his role combined recognizable elements from predecessors of both parties. Among modern Speakers, Gingrich most resembled

Wright in his desire to use power. But his control of his party, at least initially, gave him a power unrivaled since the days of Cannon.

He was in no sense a congressional insider, as so many of his predecessors had been. Indeed, a substantial part of his "apprenticeship" for the speakership consisted of demonizing Congress.

Gingrich began his speakership with a loyal following, eager to enact the ten-point "Contract with America" platform Republicans had rallied around in the 1994 campaign. Gingrich enjoyed remarkable success in his first year in passing legislation through the House and in shaping a national debate over issues based on the Republicans' message of less government, more tax cuts, and a return of power to the states. He was far less successful in reaping political credit for himself or for the Republican Party. He and his followers took a beating in the polls in late 1995, when they were blamed for the government shutdowns in the stand-off between the White House and Congress over appropriations bills.

Gingrich's public image suffered more in December 1996 when he admitted, after two years of repeated denials, that he had failed to properly manage the financing of his political activities through charitable foundations and that he had given the ethics committee misleading information. On January 21, 1997, the House voted, 395–28, to reprimand Gingrich, the first formal sanction ever taken against a Speaker.

After the reprimand, Gingrich's speakership followed a turbulent course. He led Republicans to their crowning achievement, a deal with Clinton to balance the budget in five years. But in other ways his leadership was unraveling. Unhappiness with the Speaker culminated in 1997 in an ill-conceived coup attempt plotted by a band of disgruntled House Republicans. The Speaker survived and in the aftermath began to involve himself in the day-to-day concerns of fellow Republicans. He strove to become what he likely had never thought he would be, a traditional Speaker.

But ill will erupted again in 1998 when the leadership negotiated with the White House an unwieldy omnibus appropriations bill that outraged some Republicans. In the wake of Republican losses in the 1998 elections—only the second time since the Civil War that the party not in control of the White House lost seats in a midterm election—Gingrich resigned the speakership and his seat in Congress.

Gingrich's decision to resign came only hours after he drew a challenge from a candidate with the stature to beat him—Appropriations Committee chair Robert L. Livingston of Louisiana. The Republican Conference selected Livingston as Gingrich's successor in November 1998. But just two days before the House was to debate the impeachment of President Clinton in December, Livingston revealed that he had engaged in adulterous affairs. He made the stunning announcement that he would not run for Speaker and planned to resign from Congress. (See CLINTON IMPEACHMENT TRIAL.)

Hastert

Republicans then turned to J. Dennis Hastert, an affable and respected Illinois representative known for his relaxed style and low profile. As the party's chief deputy whip for the previous four years, Hastert had skillfully counted votes for the party. He also had chaired a subcommittee and several Republican task forces.

Almost universally, his fellow Republicans referred to him as a "healer." In rallying behind him, Republicans signaled their interest in a new type of leader who would not follow the confrontational style of Gingrich, but instead focus on behind-the-scenes consensus building.

During his tenure, Hastert was credited for his ability to find compromise among members of a party that was often splintered. Although Republicans held only a razor-thin majority until the 2002 elections provided a slightly more comfortable margin, Hastert was able to keep his members largely unified. He succeeded in shepherding through the House many of President George W. Bush's legislative priorities, including a $145 trillion tax cut in 2001.

On June 1, 2006, Hastert became the longest-serving Republican Speaker in history, exceeding the record set by Joseph Cannon of Missouri in the early years of the twentieth century.

Pelosi

Nancy Pelosi, a California Democrat, on January 4, 2007, became the first woman in history to serve as Speaker. She had been her party's minority leader for the four years before that—

Rep. J. Dennis Hastert of Illinois is sworn in as House Speaker 1999. In June 2006 he became the longest-serving Republican Speaker in U.S. history.
Source: CQ Photo/Douglas Graham

also a first for a woman—when the Republicans controlled the House. That changed in the 2006 elections when Democrats won back control for the first time in twelve years.

Pelosi was a highly focused party leader who had kept a sometimes fractious Democratic caucus in line as minority leader to challenge the GOP majority and President George W. Bush, particularly on the continuing and costly war in Iraq. Pelosi was determined to marshal her party to retain a majority in the 2008 elections. She forced through a number of measures she promised would be enacted in the "first 100 hours" of Democratic rule, although a number had not become law by the end of 2007. Her long-term success at keeping the Democrats in the majority was seen by many observers as not a given, an outcome that was expected to be influenced heavily by her ability to bridge the sometimes wide cap between the party liberals and conservatives.

Special Orders

Legislators who want to address the House or Senate on a topic that is not necessarily part of the day's legislative agenda can reserve a block of time in advance. This is called a special order.

In the House members who have requested special orders are allowed to speak for up to sixty minutes at the end of the day's session—before the House adjourns but after legislative business has been completed. (There are also limits on the total time available to each party for such speeches.) Television cameras record the speeches, which often are made to an almost empty chamber. (See TELEVISING CONGRESS.)

Controversy about the routine practice erupted in 1984, after Republicans repeatedly used special orders for speeches attacking the Democratic leadership. Infuriated, Speaker Thomas P. O'NEILL Jr. ordered the television cameras to pan the House chamber, showing viewers how few members were present to hear the emotional speakers. The practice has been continued; periodically during the time reserved for special orders, the cameras show the House chamber—and its rows of empty seats.

In the Senate members are recognized for special orders at the beginning of a day's session; they may speak for five minutes. Fifteen-minute speeches were permitted until 1986, when Senate sessions began to be televised and requests for special orders increased. Some senators ask for special-order time almost every day.

The term *special order* also refers to the resolution approved by the House Rules Committee setting guidelines for floor consideration of a bill. The resolution is more commonly known as a rule. (See LEGISLATIVE PROCESS; RULE FOR HOUSE DEBATE; RULES COMMITTEE, HOUSE.)

Speech or Debate Clause   *See* IMMUNITY, CONGRESSIONAL.

Staff

Thousands of people work for Congress, and its elected members depend heavily on these employees. Staff members cannot vote, but their imprint is on every other step in getting a bill passed. They draft legislation, listen to and consult lobbyists, and plot strategy for floor action. The influence of congressional staff is vast. Critics complain that the staff exercises too much power and costs too much money. But others argue that legislators are asked to debate and vote on a wide range of complex issues, and that they need staff to provide the expertise that one person alone simply could not master.

Five sisters, all employed as secretaries by five different members of Congress, enjoy a lunch break in 1924. The majority of House and Senate staff members today are female.
Source: Library of Congress

The congressional bureaucracy is well entrenched with more staff members than any other national legislature. In 2005 about 10,700 aides worked directly for its 540 voting and nonvoting members, including Puerto Rico, the District of Columbia, America Samoa, Guam, and the Virgin Islands. Another 8,300 or so congressional employees make up support staff in the Library of Congress, Government Accountability Office, Congressional Budget Office, and other agencies of the legislative branch. Staff size—and costs—increased steadily from 1947 when a major congressional reorganization occurred. By 2006 the cost of running Congress was more than $3.8 billion. In 1960 the cost, when adjusted to the value of 2006 dollars, was $667 million. About one-half of the 2006 total was devoted to House and Senate operations, with the largest share going for staff salaries.

Growth in Staff Size

The size of House and Senate staff has grown enormously since World War II, although growth has slowed from about 1990 on because of cuts in committee staff. In 1947 there were 399 aides on House and Senate committees; by 2005 the number reached 2,229. (The high point in committee staff came in the mid- to late 1980s when it was around 3,000.) In addition, in 2005 there were more than 10,700 House and Senate personal aides. The size of committee staffs had actually dropped nearly a thousand between 1990 and 2005. In response to criticism about their administration of Congress, Democrats had cut committee staffs in the House and the Senate by about 10 percent in 1993. But committee staffing cuts in 1995 were greater: House Republicans cut committee staff by one-third as part of their "Contract with America." Senate Republicans also made cuts in committee staff, although their efforts were less bold.

Still, the significant growth in the number of people employed by Congress changed the fabric of life on Capitol Hill. It crowded existing offices, spurred construction of large new office buildings for the House and Senate, and prompted expansion into "annex" buildings formerly used as hotels or apartments. The presence of so many employees made Capitol Hill more and more like a small city, bustling with restaurants, barbershops, stationery stores, gymnasiums, and its own subways linking office buildings to the Capitol.

The congressional staff explosion came about for a variety of reasons. After World War II, and again in the 1960s and 1970s, the federal government expanded rapidly and became more complex. Congress wanted its own sources of information, independent of the executive branch and interest groups, so it added staff. Changes within Congress also spurred the hiring of more people. In the 1970s the erosion of the seniority system shifted new authority to junior and minority members; they wanted aides to help with their new responsibilities. Subcommittees were given higher status, and by the late 1970s as many people worked for subcommittees as had worked for full committees in the 1960s.

Congress also became the last resort for those dealing with the federal bureaucracy. Each legislator usually had several employees whose sole job was handling voters' requests and complaints, a task known as casework or constituent services. Casework is usually the primary function of district and state offices. A measure of its importance is that in 2005 about 39 percent of senators' personal staffs worked outside of Washington and about 51 percent of representatives' staffs.

The dramatic growth in staff leveled off in the 1980s and early 1990s as Congress, trying to cut overall federal spending, responded to criticism about increases in its budget. Staffing was one of the issues on the agenda of the Joint Committee on the Organization of Congress, a special committee set up in 1992 to study and recommend reforms in congressional operations. The committee recommended tighter limits on committee assignments and, specifically, smaller committee sizes. These proposals, along with the other reform initiatives recommended by the panel, went nowhere during the Democratic-controlled 103rd Congress (1993–1995). After the Republicans took control of Congress in 1995, party leaders unveiled the most sweeping reforms of House operations in decades—including cuts in committee staff. Personal staff for individual members of Congress are evenly distributed among members regardless of party, so cuts in committee aides allowed Republicans to claim credit for what looked like a significant staff reduction while minimizing damage to individual lawmakers and to the majority's agenda. Because Democrats were

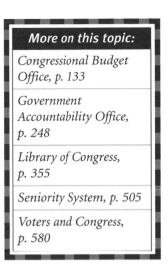

More on this topic:

Congressional Budget Office, p. 133
Government Accountability Office, p. 248
Library of Congress, p. 355
Seniority System, p. 505
Voters and Congress, p. 580

CLOSER LOOK

Congressional staff members, numbering in the thousands, work in obscurity, but they have vast influence. The elected representatives and senators depend heavily on these employees—in both Washington and in home districts and states. Congressional staffs draft legislation, listen to and consult with lobbyists, and plot strategy for their bosses.

Maryland senator John Marshall Butler and staff pose in the 1950s.
Source: Senate Historical Office

moving into the minority, most of the committee staff cuts would affect them, and not the Republicans. (See REFORM, CONGRESSIONAL.)

Partisanship

Congressional employees are drawn from a mix of backgrounds, but most are young and well educated. According to the Congressional Management Foundation, a nonprofit group that works to promote fair labor practices in Congress, the majority of House and Senate personal staffers are female. Campaign workers may end up on a legislator's payroll, but jobs also go to others who have no ties to the politician or the district. An economist might be hired for a committee post, for example. Some congressional employees outlast the legislator who originally hired them; they simply find a job with someone else. Nevertheless, in recent years staff experience has declined. A 2004 study found that more than 60 percent of House staff had two or fewer years of experience in their current position. The average tenure for a Senate aide was about 5.3 years. A similar study in 1998 found a significant decline in years served compared to early in the decade. For example, personal staff members in the House had an average of 2.7 years of experience in their current jobs, a decline of 27 percent from 1992.

Sometimes staff members become politicians themselves. President Lyndon B. JOHNSON began his career as a congressional aide; later he was elected to Congress and served twenty-four years in the House and Senate, including six years as Senate majority leader. In the 110th Congress, fifteen senators, sixty-six representatives, and one delegate had previously served as staff members.

◉ CLOSER LOOK

Congressional aides come from a mix of backgrounds but are largely young and well educated. Personal staffers are predominately female. Some employees outlast the legislator who originally hired them; they simply find a job with someone else. In recent years, however, the length of service of staff has decreased.

Traditionally, many nonlegislative posts have been PATRONAGE jobs. The chauffeur, the elevator operator, the parking garage attendant, and even jobs closer to legislative action, such as the House clerk or secretary of the Senate, have been controlled by party leaders and their top aides. But the system began to erode in the 1960s, when secretary of the Senate Bobby Baker, a Johnson protégé, was convicted of using his office—and his control of numerous Senate jobs—for personal gain. Since then the number of patronage jobs has been drastically reduced. Further reductions came about in the wake of scandals involving the House bank and post office in 1991. However, no significant reductions occurred until 1995 when the Republicans took control of the House.

In 1992 the House voted to bring its nonlegislative functions under the control of a professional, nonpartisan administrative officer and to prohibit patronage for positions controlled by the new official. (See SCANDALS, CONGRESSIONAL.) In 1995 Republicans eliminated the 1992 post and created a new office called the HOUSE CHIEF ADMINISTRATIVE OFFICER whose goal was to professionalize the administrative functions of the House. Many of the functions of the 1992 job were carried over to the new post in 1995.

Although merit, not friendship with a legislator, is usually the basis for being hired today, the political parties still maintain control over numerous jobs. The top leaders of both parties have their own staff. Party affiliation is usually a factor when legislators hire their personal aides. Committee hiring is also partisan, with the majority usually responsible for about two-thirds of the jobs and the minority for about one-third. In reality, however, other qualifications often take precedence over party allegiance.

Despite partisanship in hiring, a line is drawn between congressional work and campaign work. Congressional aides are supposed to keep from working on a reelection campaign during their official hours at work, but in reality, the work is difficult to distinguish. Sometimes House and Senate staff members take a leave from their congressional posts to become campaign workers, paid by the campaign. Another practice is to divide duties, with a staff member's congressional pay reduced to reflect time spent on the campaign.

Personal Staff

Clerks were hired by Congress even in its earliest years, for jobs such as recording floor debate and handling committee paperwork. But authority—and funding—for a member's personal staff was not provided until 1885 in the Senate and 1893 in the House. By 1919 a ceiling had been placed on the number of personal staff members each legislator could hire. (Committee staffs were handled separately.) In 1946 a House member could hire a maximum of five people, and a senator, six. In 2007 a House member could hire up to eighteen permanent and four other staff, such as paid interns. The maximum House personal staff salary was $159,828. On average, House members hired fourteen full-time staff members. In the Senate, a member has an administrative and clerical assistance allowance that varies with the size of the senator's state. There was no limit on the number of staff that a senator may hire within his or her allowance. Depending on a state's population, a senator might hire thirty to fifty staff members, and sometimes more for large states. The average was about thirty-four full-time employees. In addition, in 2007 senators were authorized to hire three legislative assistants. The maximum staff salary in a senator's office in 2006, the latest year for which a figure was available, was $157,559.

Legislators divide their personal staff between their Washington and local offices. Representatives usually have at least one office in their district; senators often have three or more spread across their state.

For their Washington office, most legislators hire an administrative assistant (AA) responsible for overall operations, including casework, and a legislative assistant (LA) who concentrates on committee action, floor votes, and a member's political agenda. Often a press secretary handles questions from reporters and writes newsletters. Other employees report to these top aides. Hiring policies, job descriptions, pay scales, and vacations differ from office to office.

Committee Staff

Each committee, like each legislator, sets its hiring policies. Most have a professional staff and a clerical staff, with staff director, chief counsel, and, for appropriations subcommittees, chief clerk among the top posts. Reporting to them are legislative aides and counsels, researchers, investigators, press assistants, computer specialists, and paraprofessional staff. Members' Washington staff concentrate on legislation and legislative correspondence. They meet with national and home-based interest representatives and local officials as well as constituent visitors to Washington. They also work on scheduling. The chief of staff in Washington and sometimes another staff member also deal with office administration. Members' state and district staffs concentrate on casework, outreach, grants, and other constituent-oriented work. Committee staff members must work on committee activities.

Authority for hiring full-time committee staff existed by 1900 (a few committees had staff even earlier), but the Legislative Reorganization Act of 1946 authorized the funding for each committee to hire a roster of aides. In the 1970s the size of the committee staffs was greatly increased. The House in 1974 tripled the size of each committee's professional staff, from six to eighteen, and doubled the clerical staff, from six to twelve. This brought the total number of permanent staff on most committees to thirty, where it remained as part of the rules. However, most committees have found ways around the restriction, and few have had as few as thirty since the late 1970s. No strict limits apply in the Senate, where committees may employ forty or more people. In 1975 the Senate gave each member authority to hire three legislative aides to help with committee work.

In addition to permanent staff, House and Senate committees also hire on temporary contract basis investigative aides, consultants, and persons detailed from congressional and executive agencies.

Employment Practices

For all the power that many Capitol Hill employees possess, for decades they were not covered by most federal workplace laws. Members of Congress argued that their employment practices should not be regulated like the private sector's because of the political nature of Congress; members must be free, they said, to choose employees who will be loyal to them. Many members also insisted that the principle of separation of powers would be violated if the executive branch had the power to enforce employment laws in the legislature.

The exemptions to workplace laws eventually became a target of reformers both inside and outside Congress, who attacked the practice as a failure by Congress to live under the laws it passed. After Democratic legislation that would have subjected Congress to the same labor laws that governed private-sector companies stalled due to Republican opposition in 1994, the Democratic-led House changed its rules to make the House subject to the compliance requirements. At the start of the 104th Congress in 1995, Congress with full Democratic and Republican support passed the Congressional Accountability Act that extended eleven federal labor and antidiscrimination laws to all congressional employees in Congress and its related offices. The legislation, which specifically allowed members to discriminate based on party affiliation or "political compatibility," replaced the haphazard mix of internal protections. (See box, p. 531.)

Some of the statutes included in the legislation were the Civil Rights Act of 1964, which prohibited discrimination in employment on the basis of race, color, religion, sex, or nationality; the Occupational Safety and Health Act of 1970, which set safety regulations for workplaces; the Rehabilitation Act of 1973, which provided federal aid for a variety of programs for disabled work-

Congress and Workplace Compliance

The first bill enacted by the Republican-led 104th Congress (1995–1997) was S 2, which amended eleven federal labor and antidiscrimination laws to apply specifically to Congress and its related offices. Among other things, the Congressional Accountability Act allowed congressional employees to take claims to federal court after an initial mediation and counseling stage. The amended laws were:

1. Civil Rights Act of 1964—prohibited discrimination in employment on the basis of race, color, religion, sex, or nationality.
2. Occupational Safety and Health Act of 1970—set safety regulations for workplaces.
3. Age Discrimination in Employment Act of 1967—prohibited workplace discrimination against people age forty and older.
4. Rehabilitation Act of 1973—provided federal aid for a variety of programs for disabled workers and for the training of personnel to work with the disabled.
5. Americans with Disabilities Act of 1990—prohibited workplace discrimination against people with disabilities.
6. Family and Medical Leave Act of 1993—set criteria for unpaid parental and medical leave for employees seeking to spend time with children or ailing family members.
7. Fair Labor Standards Act of 1938—dealt with minimum wage and mandatory overtime or compensation for employees who worked more than forty hours per week, as updated in 1989. (The minimum wage was increased again in 1996 and 2007.)
8. Employee Polygraph Protection Act of 1988—restricted the use of polygraph tests of employees by employers. The use of legal lie detector tests by the Capitol police was not affected by application of this law.
9. Worker Adjustment and Retraining Notification Act of 1988—required a sixty-day advance notice of a plant closing or large layoffs of permanent workers.
10. Veterans Re-employment Act of 1994—required employers to rehire for the same or similar position returning veterans who left their jobs after being called into military service.
11. Labor-Management Dispute Procedures—a part of the *United States Code* (Chapter 71 of Title V) that established procedures for resolving federal labor-management disputes.

Congressional offices and officers covered by the 1995 Congressional Accountability Act were:

- Each office of the House and Senate, including each office of a member and each committee
- Each joint committee
- Capitol police
- Congressional Budget Office
- Office of the Architect of the Capitol
- Senate and House restaurants and gift shops
- Botanic Garden
- Office of the attending physician
- Capitol Guide Service
- Office of Compliance

ers and for the training of personnel to work with the disabled; and the Age Discrimination in Employment Act of 1967, a law that prohibited workplace discrimination against people age forty and older. Other statutes were more recently enacted, such as the Family and Medical Leave Act of 1993, which allowed unpaid parental and medical leave for employees who want to spend time with children or sick family members; the Veterans Re-employment Act of 1994, which required employers to rehire returning veterans who left their jobs after being called into military service; and the Americans with Disabilities Act of 1990, a law prohibiting workplace discrimination against people with disabilities.

The 1995 workplace compliance law also created a new Office of Compliance for the legislative branch to enforce the labor and antidiscrimination statutes in different offices, act on complaints filed by employees, and provide counseling. Although Congress had procedures for staff to bring complaints against members—the Ethics Committee in the Senate and the Office of Fair Employment Practices in the House—critics had argued that these procedures were poorly understood and little used.

Another avenue for settling congressional employee grievances has been the court system. The Supreme Court ruled in 1979 that congressional employees have the right to sue for damages if they believe they are victims of job discrimination. In that case, the plaintiff can make a Constitution-based claim. However, if aggrieved employees have a complaint based on one of the eleven statutes under the Congressional Accountability Act, they must go through the Office of Compliance for counseling and mediation before taking their claim to federal or district court.

Congress also has specific rules against hiring relatives, a practice known as nepotism. The ban on nepotism was slipped into a House bill in 1967 and, once under consideration, was politically impossible to oppose. A senator or representative can still recommend a relative for employment in another office, and a legislator's relatives can still work in his or her office, but without pay. For example, Heather Foley for years was a top, unpaid assistant to her husband, Speaker of the House Thomas S. FOLEY.

Standards of Official Conduct Committee, House

Commonly known as the House ethics committee, the Committee on Standards of Official Conduct investigates representatives charged with ethical misconduct, such as misuse of campaign funds, failure to disclose personal finances, or improper acceptance of gratuities. The committee then reports to the full House and in some cases recommends punishment, such as reprimand, censure, or, in rare cases, expulsion from the House. The Senate has a Select Ethics Committee that monitors senators' conduct.

The committee is not a popular one for members, many of whom try to avoid serving on it. The difficulty arises from having to pass judgment on fellow members. In addition, the highly partisan conditions that characterized the House in the last decades of the twentieth century and the early years of the next tended to bolster a range of claims about the conduct of members. Often the charges arose from aggressive advocacy groups outside Congress. Sorting out the well-grounded claims from the politically frivolous was not a job enjoyed by many members of the House.

More on this topic:

Disciplining Members,
p. 159

Ethics, p. 195

Ethics Committee,
Senate Select, p. 204

Financial Disclosure,
p. 220

Scandals, Congressional,
p. 482

Unlike most House committees, where the majority party dominates, the ethics panel is bipartisan, with five members from each party. The chair is from the majority party. The committee has its own investigative staff and counsel but has hired outside attorneys. For example, former Watergate special prosecutor Leon Jaworski handled allegations of influence peddling by Korean business executives in the late 1970s.

Committee investigations are usually triggered by complaints from colleagues or from news stories. The committee also gives advice to members who are confused about ethics rules. The committee has published an ethics manual for members and staff, including its advisory opinions on some of the most frequently asked questions about gifts, outside income, and allowances. It also has issued separate publications on gifts and travel and on campaign activity.

Wright and Gingrich Investigations

In 1988 the committee investigated charges, brought by Republicans, that the Speaker of the House, Texas Democrat Jim WRIGHT, had abused his office to enrich himself. The committee vote to undertake the investigation was unanimous.

To consider the six major allegations against Wright, the committee instituted a new two-part procedure. First came a "preliminary investigation" to hear witnesses, including Wright; this resembled a grand jury procedure. Next came a staff report and recommendations, followed by a hearing, resembling a trial, to decide whether to discipline the accused. Chicago lawyer Richard A. Phelan was hired as special counsel to head the investigation.

Ten months later the committee formally charged Wright with the acceptance of improper gifts, use of book royalties to circumvent limits on earned income, and numerous other violations of House rules. But in 1989, before the disciplinary hearing took place, Wright resigned from Congress, making him the first Speaker forced from office at midterm.

The Wright case was a prelude to another controversial and lengthy case against a sitting Speaker—Republican Newt GINGRICH of Georgia. After a lengthy, two-year investigation, the committee found Gingrich guilty of mismanaging the finances of his political activities through charitable foundations. Gingrich was formally reprimanded by the House in 1997.

The two-year battle over Gingrich nearly destroyed the ethics committee. The House revised its ethics rules in 1997 and made provision for additional members to help in the investigation phase to ease the burden on ethics members.

History

The committee was established in 1967 in response to public outrage over a series of congressional scandals. The first chair was Illinois Democrat Melvin Price. The House gave the panel only a limited mission at first: to write a code of conduct. Approved in 1968, the code expanded the committee's responsibility, giving it authority to enforce the new rules.

But the code was couched in general terms, and financial disclosure was confined to sources, not amounts, of income. The House and Senate revised their codes in 1977, and in 1978 Congress applied ethics codes to the entire federal government. In 1989 the ethics law was revised and strengthened, increasing the size of the House committee to fourteen members, from twelve. The committee's membership was set at ten in 1999. Service on the committee is seen by most members as a thankless task.

Critics complain that the committee is too lenient, reporting violations and then recommending no punishment. But California Democrat Julian C. Dixon, chair from 1985 to 1991, said, "I think the committee does a good job of, one, being nonpartisan and, two, investigating facts, evaluating facts, and taking appropriate action. But is the committee on a constant search for improprieties by members of Congress? The answer is no. I think the members of Congress have a right to feel the committee is not on a witch hunt."

Although the House usually goes along with the recommendations of the ethics committee, it has acted independently. In 1983 the committee recommended that Massachusetts Democrat Gerry E. Studds and Illinois Republican Daniel B. Crane be reprimanded because of improper relationships with teenage pages; the House opted for the stiffer penalty of censure. Seven years later the House went along with the committee in reprimanding Massachusetts Democrat Barney Frank for improperly using his office to help a male prostitute, despite widespread criticism that the penalty was too lenient.

CLOSER LOOK

The House Ethics Committee—formally known as the Standards of Official Conduct Committee—is not a panel on which representatives are eager to serve. Those who do have the awkward responsibility of passing judgment on colleagues' behavior. In addition, highly partisan conflicts in recent years tended to bolster a range of claims about members' conduct.

Since the committee was created more than a dozen members have received the House's harshest punishments of censure, reprimand, or, in two cases, expulsion.

A recent high-profile case involved a lengthy probe into powerful Transportation and Infrastructure Committee chair Bud Shuster, a Republican from Pennsylvania. The House ethics committee sent a letter of reproval in 2000 to Shuster, saying he "engaged in serious official misconduct" and "committed substantial violations" of House rules. The rebuke, which stemmed from a 1997 complaint filed by the Congressional Accountability Project, was approved unanimously by the committee and did not require action by the full House. It was part of a negotiated settlement to end the probe that began with questions about his relationship with a former staffer-turned-lobbyist but was broadened to include questionable campaign expenses and his acceptance of gifts. Shuster demanded and received limited immunity before he provided certain documents to the committee. It was believed to be the first time a sitting member of Congress had received immunity from the committee. However, the limited type of immunity granted and the apparent lack of significant information the evidence provided could make the immunity of little practical consequence. Shuster subsequently resigned from Congress in 2001, citing health reasons, and his son, Republican Bill Shuster of Pennsylvania, was elected to succeed him.

Democrat James A. Traficant Jr. of Ohio was the target of the next highly publicized probe. The nine-term representative was accused of demanding kickbacks from some of his congressional aides and using his position for personal gain. The ethics panel recommended the expulsion of Traficant in 2002 after his conviction on federal felony counts that included bribery and racketeering. He was expelled from the House of Representatives on a vote of 420–1. He was only the fifth House member expelled in congressional history, and only the second since the Civil War. Traficant, defiant to the end, ran for reelection from his prison cell in 2002, as an independent, and received 15 percent of the vote.

The committee was inactive for much of the 109th Congress (2005–2007) but finished the year ending one of the most intense and politically charged investigations in its history with a report critically of the way House leaders responded to behavior of Mark Foley, R-Fla. The investigation started over inappropriate e-mails and instant messages that Foley allegedly sent over several years to current and former teenage male pages, some under eighteen years of age. Foley resigned from the House on September 29, 2006, after the contents of many messages—some sexually explicit—were revealed. His resignation removed him from the jurisdiction of the committee, but the panel continued to look into whether the GOP leadership knew about Foley's conduct and took appropriate action. After a nine-week probe, the committee reported that Speaker J. Dennis Hastert of Illinois and other GOP leaders violated no laws or House rules in handling allegations against Foley. But at the same time the panel took Hastert and other Republican officials to task for not doing all they could to protect pages from conduct that some lawmakers said appeared to be homosexual advances by Foley.

In 2007 Stephanie Tubbs Jones, D-Ohio., who had been on the panel for six years, took over as chair. The ranking minority member was Doc Hastings, R-Wash., also a committee veteran. The panel had carried over from 2006 two potentially controversial cases. One was an investigation into whether Rep. William J. Jefferson, D-La., had demanded and accepted bribes in exchange for helping arrange contracts between a U.S. telecommunications company and Nigerian officials. The investigation was complicated because a criminal investigation by the Justice Department about Jefferson's activities was underway at the same time. A second preliminary inquiry carried over to 2007 looked into whether House members and aides may have been involved in a bribery scandal that ended the career of Rep. Randy "Duke" Cunningham, R-Calif. He pleaded guilty in 2005 to accepting at least $2.4 million in bribes from defense contractors. He resigned from Congress and faced a lengthy prison term.

State of the Union

Early each year the president addresses a joint session of Congress, spelling out his or her legislative program and goals for the year in a State of the Union message. Since early in the twentieth century, the annual address has been the way that presidents comply with a constitutional directive to "from time to time give to the Congress Information of the State of the Union and recommend to their Consideration such Measures as he shall judge necessary and expedient." It has become a primary method for presidents to influence the national agenda.

The evening session of Congress, usually in late January, brings a rare mood of pageantry to the House chamber, which is seldom so full. Seated in the front rows are the Supreme Court justices and members of the president's cabinet. Nearby are foreign diplomats. Galleries are packed with family members, visitors, and reporters. A special escort committee, dispatched by the Speaker of the House, greets the president and accompanies him down the aisle.

The president's speech is usually interrupted several times with applause. On rare occasions members of an opposing party groan to indicate their disagreement with a statement. More typical is the reaction of the Democratic-controlled Congress to Republican president Ronald Reagan in 1988. Even when he was criticizing Congress for its catchall spending bills, and hefting a forty-three-pound stack of documents in demonstration, the legislators reacted with applause and cheers.

The nation's first two presidents, George Washington and John Adams, delivered their annual messages as speeches to Congress. The third president, Thomas Jefferson, chose in 1801 to avoid

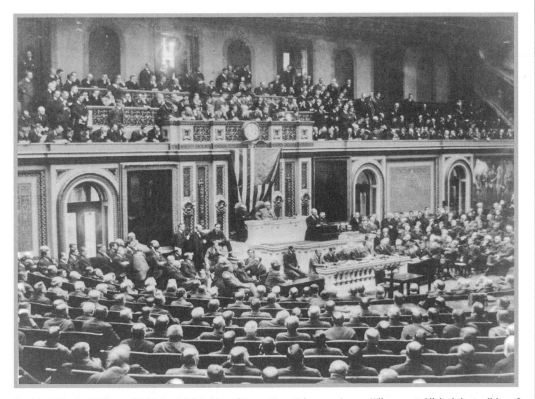

President Woodrow Wilson addresses a joint session of Congress on February 26, 1917. Wilson reestablished the tradition of presidents going before Congress to give their State of the Union speeches.
Source: Library of Congress

CLOSER LOOK

The Constitution requires the president to "from time to time give to the Congress Information of the State of the Union." This requirement has evolved into the annual State of the Union address that presidents deliver in the House chamber early in each year, usually in January. The State of the Union address allows presidents to set forth their agenda and—because the speeches are televised nationally—to influence public opinion.

CLOSER LOOK

A little-known fact is that one cabinet member is always designated to be absent during the State of the Union address. Otherwise, with the entire line of succession in one room, a disaster could leave the nation without a president. Since 2003, Congress has designated two members of each house, representing both parties, to also be absent from the Capitol during the President's speech. This ensures continuity of government.

what was an elaborate, formal ceremony, complete with a chair called "the president's throne." Instead he had his private secretary carry the message to Capitol Hill.

No president addressed Congress again until 1913 when Woodrow Wilson renewed the custom of delivering the message in person, a decision that was quite controversial. He eventually appeared before Congress twenty-six times, a record that still held in the early 2000s. Since Wilson's time, only President Herbert Hoover has declined to visit Capitol Hill at all.

President Lyndon B. JOHNSON in 1965 shifted the time of the State of the Union address from midday to evening, a move designed to attract the large prime time television audience. The next year Republicans received a half-hour slot from each network to offer their assessment of national affairs. By 1976 television time was available to the opposing party immediately following the State of the Union broadcast.

In 1986 the State of the Union address was postponed for the first time. On the morning of President Reagan's scheduled January 28 address to Congress, the space shuttle *Challenger* exploded, killing all seven crew members. Reagan delayed the speech until February 4.

There was tension surrounding President Bill Clinton's 1998 and 1999 addresses. Six days before his January 1998 address, the news media broke the story about the president's extramarital affair with a twenty-two-year-old White House intern, Monica Lewinsky, and possible illegal attempts in covering it up. Defying the political analysts who predicted that he would have to leave office, Clinton ignored the controversy and confidently delivered a message of peace, prosperity, and moderation—striking an overwhelmingly responsive chord with the national audience and reversing temporarily his abrupt political decline.

In January 1999, in the midst of the Senate impeachment trial that was considering the same Lewinsky matter, Clinton once again defied conventional wisdom and the pundits by going ahead with his address. Paying no heed to the fact that a House majority had impeached him or that the Senate was about to sit in judgment about whether he should remain in office, Clinton delivered another impressive, well-received speech that outlined an extensive legislative agenda for the coming year. The Senate acquitted him on the impeachment charges three weeks later. (See CLINTON IMPEACHMENT TRIAL.)

War themes dominated President George W. Bush's first two State of the Union addresses. His 2002 address, coming just months after the September 11, 2001, terrorist attacks on the nation, focused on the war on terrorism and homeland security. In its boldest passage, Bush singled out Iraq, Iran, and North Korea as part of an "axis of evil." By the time he delivered his 2003 address, he was preparing the nation for war with Iraq. His subsequent addresses in the following years repeated familiar themes, with an emphasis on combating terrorists and defending the U.S. invasion of Iraq and its aftermath.

States and Congress

The states and Congress have never fully agreed on how to share—or divide—responsibility for governing the nation. For more than two centuries the states have protested acts of Congress that in the states' opinion have undermined their autonomy and independence. That conflict erupted once into the Civil War and has spawned numerous other political disputes.

Certain areas, such as national defense, clearly lie in the federal domain. But the Constitution was unclear in many gray areas as to which level of government was in charge. Often the Supreme Court has been forced to referee disputes, deciding whether the federal government or the states are ultimately responsible.

The sharing of responsibility for governing is called federalism. In the United States federalism means that a national government, fifty state governments, and thousands of local governments all operate at different levels, and citizens have a connection to each of them. By the twenty-first century, the federal government clearly dominated the relationship; several Supreme Court decisions had enhanced federal authority, as had the enormous flow of federal money to state and local governments.

The Van Wyck Expressway in New York in 1951. While often battling Congress over jurisdictional issues, state and local governments look to Congress to provide highway funding.
Source: Library of Congress

State and local officials found it almost impossible to refuse their share of tax dollars, even when the money came with rules and regulations that encroached on their autonomy. Congress, for its part, became accustomed in the 1960s and 1970s to setting national goals and giving other governments money to use in reaching those goals.

By the early 1990s constraints on the federal budget had made the pattern increasingly difficult to sustain. Expensive new activities were out of the question, and existing program were at risk. Congress continued to set national goals but could no longer be counted on to accompany the rules with the "carrot" of federal money for state and local governments to use in carrying out the rules. Governors and mayors, who began lobbying Washington heavily in the 1970s and 1980s, called these policies "mandates without money." They were asked to spend their state or local governments' money to implement federal goals. Even worse, from their point of view, was the use of the federal "stick"—potential loss of federal funds in other areas if they failed to comply with new national policies. Clean air laws, for example, called for cuts in federal highway funds for states that failed to meet national goals.

A once beneficial relationship with the federal government suddenly became less attractive to state and local governments, and they began to resist federal demands. Old arguments about states' rights had a new appeal, several centuries after the Constitution tried to divide local and national responsibilities.

Constitutional Responsibilities

The Constitution enumerated several powers of Congress, including authority over the federal purse, interstate commerce, taxes and tariffs, and war. But it left untouched a wide area for the states to handle, such as education, property transactions, marriage, inheritance, contracts, and maintenance of domestic order, called the "police power."

CLOSER LOOK

The United States has a system of sharing responsibility for governing that is called federalism. It means that the national government, fifty state governments, and thousands of local governments share some level of responsibility for the functions of government. How the responsibilities are parceled out has been an enduring issue for more than 200 years. National defense and foreign relations, for example, are clearly federal matters, while education and crime fighting have primarily been state and local tasks. But dozens of other activities fall within a gray area.

The Tenth Amendment addressed the division of state and federal authority: "The powers not delegated to the United States by the Constitution, nor prohibited by it to the states, are reserved to the states respectively, or to the people."

Federal authority had an early test in Maryland, where opponents of the national bank tried to tax it into ruin. The Supreme Court in an 1819 decision, *McCulloch v. Maryland,* sided with the federal government, saying its law prevailed over any conflicting state laws or constitutions because of the "supremacy clause" of the Constitution.

But numerous Court decisions after that gave the upper hand to the states. Not until 1937, in a landmark case upholding the Social Security system *(Helvering v. Davis),* did the Court elaborate on the power of the "general welfare" clause. That was followed by other decisions endorsing a broad application of the interstate commerce clause, opening the door to broad federal regulations. Since then, federal authority has rarely been checked.

In setting up the national government, the Constitution protected state interests in several ways. Each state was to be represented in Congress by two senators and one or more representatives. States were to govern the election of presidents and vice presidents through the electoral college. No changes could be made in the Constitution itself without the approval of three-fourths of the states.

The Constitution left voter qualifications up to the states, but it has been amended five times to overrule state restrictions on voting rights. Congress and the Supreme Court have also acted against state attempts to limit voting. Males without property, African Americans, women, and young people were among those benefiting from the changes.

Three constitutional amendments ratified after the Civil War were designed to guarantee individual rights, even against action by states. The Thirteenth, Fourteenth, and Fifteenth Amendments, respectively, outlawed slavery; affirmed that voting was a right regardless of race, color, or previous condition of servitude; and promised due process and equal protection to all citizens. Not until the 1960s, however, did Supreme Court decisions and congressional action on civil rights laws put the full authority of the federal government behind the concept of equal rights.

States' Rights

The philosophical debate over states' rights influenced the drafting of the nation's first documents. Statesmen such as Alexander Hamilton, who favored a strong national government, and Thomas Jefferson, who favored the states, continued the dialogue even after the Constitution appeared to resolve many issues.

Virginia and Kentucky Resolutions

The discussion was rekindled in 1798, when the Federalist Congress enacted the Alien and Sedition Acts, which were thinly disguised attempts to weaken the Republicans. Under the Sedition Act, the most vigorously enforced of four new laws, twenty-five people, including Republican newspaper editors, were arrested for publishing articles criticizing Federalist policies. Virginia and Kentucky reacted to the restrictive law by writing resolutions asserting the right of states to resist laws they considered unconstitutional. James MADISON drafted the Virginia Resolution; Jefferson, the Kentucky Resolution.

Seven northern states protested the resolutions, particularly Kentucky's advocacy of the theory of nullification. Under that theory, a state—as opposed to the Supreme Court—could declare null and void any federal law it found to violate constitutional rights. In 1814 Massachusetts,

Connecticut, and Rhode Island borrowed the theory when they met at the Hartford Convention to consider secession as a protest against the War of 1812.

Nullification

The concept of nullification was revived in the late 1820s and used to support the proslavery argument of the southern states. South Carolinian John C. CALHOUN was an eloquent advocate of states' rights. He resigned the vice presidency in 1832 and returned to the Senate to defend the nullification doctrine. South Carolina that year voted to nullify a new federal tariff act and to prohibit its enforcement in the state. Southern opposition to protective tariffs, and to the national bank, was connected to the slavery issue; if the southern states could assert their rights on tariffs, they might also be able to nullify any federal law banning slavery.

President Andrew Jackson responded by denouncing nullification, contending that states had surrendered a part of their sovereignty to the federal government. "Disunion by armed force is treason," Jackson said. A compromise on the tariff averted a direct confrontation, but the debate continued. Georgia in the 1830s tried to nullify a Supreme Court decision favoring the Cherokee Indians in its western territories.

Civil War

The southern states took their concept of states' rights to its ultimate test in 1860 and 1861 when eleven states voted to secede from the Union. Their action was triggered by the election of Abraham Lincoln as president; he opposed slavery and argued that the states, by joining the Union, had given up certain rights.

The victory of the Union in 1865 made the national government supreme and settled the argument about secession. But other aspects of the debate remained in dispute. The concept of states' rights continued to be identified with those reluctant to end racial discrimination.

Dixiecrats and Desegregation

Champions of states' rights renewed their battle in the late 1940s and 1950s, as federal efforts to end racial discrimination intensified. When the Democratic National Convention in 1948 adopted a pro–civil rights platform, disgruntled southerners from thirteen states established a States' Rights, or Dixiecrat, Party. They nominated for president Strom THURMOND, the South Carolina governor; Thurmond eventually won in Alabama, Louisiana, Mississippi, and South Carolina. (Thurmond went on to enter the Senate as a Democrat in 1954 and became a Republican in 1964.)

The ultimate conflict between the states and the federal government resulted in the Civil War, illustrated here by the bombardment of Fort Sumter by the Confederate forces of the Southern states. Those states ultimately lost the war and the argument over which government, state or federal, was supreme.
Source: Library of Congress

Southern states also rallied around the states' rights cry in 1954, when the Supreme Court outlawed racially segregated public schools. For the next decade, congressional opponents of civil rights laws often made the claim that states had constitutional rights to resist federal policy. A 1956 "manifesto" signed by 101 southern members of Congress declared, "We commend the motives of those states which have declared the intention to resist forced integration by any lawful means." In 1957 President Dwight D. Eisenhower sent federal troops to enforce civil rights in Little Rock, Arkansas, where black students enrolled at the previously all-white Central High School.

Grants-in-Aid

The debate over states' rights has at times been deeply philosophical, but a more powerful factor in the federal-state relationship has little to do with philosophy. Federal grants-in-aid to state and local governments steadily increased in the twentieth century, particularly in the mid-1960s and after. Such grants escalated from 4.7 percent of total federal outlays in fiscal 1955 to 17.7 percent in fiscal 2004. Conditions on use of this money gave the federal government increasing control over local matters.

The patchwork of grant programs developed piecemeal, as Congress responded to various problems. Conditions were devised haphazardly and have grown increasingly complex. To be eligible for federal health funds, for example, states must have overall plans for how health care is delivered. Federally insured mortgages are available only to states with flood control programs. Highway grants come with a host of rules about how roads and bridges must be built as well as with links to other federal policies, such as the minimum legal age for drinking alcoholic beverages.

Applicable to all grants are several "cross-cutting" rules on civil rights, affirmative action, environmental impact, labor, and accessibility for the handicapped.

Land Grants

The earliest federal grants consisted of land; as western territories were divided, a portion of every parcel, often one-sixteenth of each township, was set aside, with proceeds used to support local education. Application of the same approach to roads and canals met resistance. Several presidents, from Madison to Andrew Jackson, opposed as improper a federal role in "internal improvements," despite the idea's popularity in Congress.

Land grants were sometimes controversial. President Franklin Pierce in 1854 vetoed Congress's plan to provide land to states for facilities aiding the mentally handicapped. In 1859 President James Buchanan vetoed a congressional attempt to fund agricultural colleges. Both presidents argued that such federal funding was unconstitutional. Lincoln supported a stronger federal role and in 1862 signed the Morrill Act, which provided grants of federal land to establish agricultural colleges.

Highways

A new era began in 1916 with federal highway legislation. Matching grants and formulas for distributing funds were among the procedures devised then, which became standard practice for decades afterward. To qualify for the aid, states were required to establish a highway department; by 1917 every state had managed to do so. It was no coincidence that the highway bill was passed just three years after enactment of a federal income tax, which for the first time guaranteed a steady flow of funds into federal coffers.

The New Deal and the 1950s

Coping with economic upheaval during the Depression of the 1930s, President Franklin D. Roosevelt proposed an array of federal programs, many of which were based on grants to states and also to cities. The most sweeping new law was the Social Security Act, which set up programs to benefit dependent children, the blind, and the elderly; these were administered by the states. Annual federal grants quadrupled between 1932 and 1940. By 1950 $2.3 billion was being spent on grants-in-aid.

Although the NEW DEAL clearly changed the framework of federal-state relations, debate about the proper federal role had not ended. In the 1950s Congress spent several years arguing about federal aid to elementary and secondary education, which had traditionally been handled by state and local governments. Some critics fought any federal aid, while churches insisted that funds should also be channeled to parochial schools. The deadlock was broken by the Soviet Union's launching of the first artificial satellite in 1957. In an effort to catch up with and surpass Soviet technology, Congress approved the National Defense Education Act the following year.

The Great Society

Democratic presidents John F. KENNEDY and Lyndon B. JOHNSON led Congress in a sweeping expansion of federal welfare programs that required state and local governments to handle billions of additional federal dollars—according to federal rules. "This administration today here and now declares unconditional war on poverty in America," Johnson proclaimed in 1964. Food stamps, urban housing programs, community development, health care for the poor (Medicaid), health care for the elderly (Medicare), and education programs for disadvantaged children (such as Head Start) were among the bills passed in the 1960s and 1970s. Johnson called his policy "creative federalism." (See GREAT SOCIETY.)

The New Federalism

President Richard NIXON pushed a "new federalism" that would return responsibility to the state and local levels. He wanted to accompany that with an infusion of federal money, which he called "revenue sharing." Congress in 1972 approved the revenue-sharing program, which provided virtually unrestricted grants to state and local governments. However, it resisted Nixon's efforts to combine most "categorical grant" programs, aimed at specific problems, into "block grants," a move designed to give more flexibility to local administrators.

The Reagan Years

The 1980s brought another attempt at "new federalism," this time by President Ronald Reagan, who argued that "our nation of sovereign states has come dangerously close to becoming one great national government." Reagan saw block grants as the first step in the redirection of money and power to state and local governments. But Congress, anxious to have national policy carried out uniformly in every state and city, resisted major shifts of responsibility back to the local level. As part of his program, Reagan sought sweeping cuts in federal payments to states and cities; Congress cut funding, though not so deeply as Reagan proposed in each annual budget request.

The Reagan years also brought an end to revenue sharing, which between 1973 and 1986 transferred more than $80 billion to state and local governments with few strings attached. More than 39,000 local governments benefited from the program; states did not receive revenue-sharing funds after 1980. Revenue-sharing money was used to pay police and fire personnel, provide health care to residents, buy library books, build and repair highways, support education, and meet dozens of other needs.

Clinton and GOP Congress

Republicans, who became the majority in Congress as a result of the 1994 elections, sought to reduce the size of the federal government and to transfer power to the states. President Bill Clinton in 1995 signed into law a bill to curb unfunded federal mandates—those requirements that

Congress and federal agencies imposed on state and local governments without providing the money to pay for them. The legislation was a watered-down version of a plank in the Republican Party's "Contract with America." Clinton in 1996 signed a landmark welfare reform measure that ended a sixty-one-year-old entitlement to cash benefits for poor women and children. Under the new law, federal funds would be sent to the states in lump sums, and states would have broad leeway over eligibility and benefits. It was the first time the federal government had transformed a major individual entitlement program into block grants to the states. The law did impose some federal restrictions, such as requiring recipients to work within two years of receiving funds and limiting aid to five years.

Compromises between Clinton and Republicans resulted in a number of joint federal-state programs that were created in the late 1990s. For example, lawmakers in 1997 created a federal grant program aimed at expanding health insurance for children. In 2000 Congress created a six-year, $12 billion discretionary fund for state and federal public land programs. In addition, compromise was often the result of budget debates between GOP congressional leaders and Clinton over whether directed grants or block grants would best improve the quality of schools.

Bush's Mixed Record

Similar to his Republican predecessors, President George W. Bush sought to shift power from the federal government to the states. He succeeded in some ways through the budget process by creating new federally funded block grant programs throughout various agencies and consolidating other directed grants into larger block grants.

However, at the same time, Bush also supported legislation that concentrated power at the federal level. Examples included elements of Bush's comprehensive education bill—known as the "No Child Left Behind" program, which contained some programs allowing states more flexibility but also added a number of mandates on states, including a requirement that states test their students on an annual basis. By the time the law came up for renewal in 2007, many state and local officials were sharply critical of the mandates and standards in the original legislation, saying that they improperly encroached on local prerogatives in education.

Bush also supported the creation of a new homeland security agency to direct state and local efforts to combat terrorism. In 2002 Bush signed legislation that set broad national standards for the conduct of federal elections—a first for an issue on which the details always had been handled by state and local governments. The result was a mixed record: while Bush favored local control, early in his presidency he often supported legislation that had the opposite effect.

Steering and Policy Committee *See* LEADERSHIP.

Stennis, John C.

By the time he announced his retirement in 1988, Mississippi Democrat John C. Stennis (1901–1995) had become an anachronistic figure in the Senate, a link to another era. But his physical frailty never diminished the dignity and rectitude that marked more than forty years of Senate service. His colleagues always held him in high esteem, as they demonstrated with the displays of public affection that greeted him when, barely a month after he lost a leg to cancer in late 1984, Stennis returned to the Senate floor in a wheelchair.

Born in 1901 on a Mississippi cotton and cattle farm, Stennis served in the state legislature and as a prosecuting attorney. He then spent ten years on the bench as a circuit judge. Stennis was

Sen. John C. Stennis of Mississippi served in Congress for more than four decades, always held in high esteem by his colleagues. The USS John C. Stennis, a U.S. Navy aircraft carrier, was commissioned shortly after his death in 1995. Pictured here, a Sea Hawk helicopter hovers in front of the carrier off the coast of Guam in February 2007.
Source: U.S. Department of Defense/MC3 Ron Reeves

elected to the Senate in 1947 after the death of Sen. Theodore G. Bilbo, a race-baiting demagogue. Two of the five candidates in the special election copied Bilbo's white supremacist style; Stennis, while ready to preserve "the southern way of life," did not make race the center of his campaign.

Stennis brought a judicial bearing to the Senate. A member of the committee that investigated the conduct of Sen. Joseph R. MCCARTHY in 1954, Stennis was the first Democrat to take the Senate floor to denounce him, charging that McCarthy had poured "slush and slime" on the Senate.

When the Senate Ethics Committee was established in 1965, Stennis was immediately chosen to chair the panel, even though he had not advocated establishing it. He chaired the committee until 1975. In 1973 Stennis suffered critical gunshot wounds during a holdup in front of his Washington, D.C., home. He was absent from the Senate for several months.

Stennis voted as a southern Democrat, advocating fiscal conservatism and opposing civil rights legislation. But he was overshadowed by more aggressive southern senators. Most of Stennis's career was focused on the Armed Services Committee, which he chaired from 1969 to 1981. He was also able to promote defense spending on the Appropriations Committee, where he chaired the Defense Subcommittee.

Stennis usually supported presidents in their military policies, even when his Democratic colleagues did not. But he also defended congressional prerogatives. In 1971 Stennis introduced WAR

POWERS legislation to require congressional approval of sustained military action, and he supported the law enacted two years later over President Richard NIXON's veto.

When Democrats regained control of the Senate in 1987, Stennis, as the party's senior senator, became PRESIDENT PRO TEMPORE. He also became chair of the Appropriations Committee. "I want to plow a straight furrow," he once said, "right down to the end of my row."

Stevens, Thaddeus

Thaddeus Stevens (1792–1868) served in the House of Representatives as a Whig (1849–1853) and as a Republican (1859–1868) from Pennsylvania. An accomplished orator, Stevens held several important committee chairmanships, and on occasion his power surpassed that of the Speaker. Above all, Stevens hated slavery, and his career was devoted to its eradication and to the punishment of the rebellious southern states.

Before entering national politics, Stevens practiced law, owned a forge, and served in the Pennsylvania state legislature. Once in Congress he allied himself with the Free Soilers, who opposed the spread of slavery to western states. Stevens spoke and voted against the Compromise of

An accomplished orator of the nineteenth century, Thaddeus Stevens in this illustration makes his case for the impeachment of President Andrew Johnson in 1868.
Source: Library of Congress

1850 because it failed to prohibit slavery in the territories of Utah and New Mexico. He also opposed the Fugitive Slave Act, which required the return of fugitive slaves to their owners. An uncompromising man, Stevens left Congress in 1853 to protest what he considered to be his party's indecisive stand on slavery.

Returning to the House in 1859, Stevens served as chair of the Ways and Means Committee from 1861 until he became chair of the new Appropriations Committee in 1865. During the Civil War Stevens controlled the House, unchecked by a weak Republican Speaker.

Stevens often spoke of the South with bitterness and vindictiveness. He objected to President Abraham Lincoln's plans for Reconstruction, declaring that the South had put itself beyond the protection of the Constitution. Stevens hoped to reduce the South to territorial status, thereby preventing an influx of southern representatives who would almost certainly be Democrats. (See RECONSTRUCTION ERA.)

When President Andrew Johnson pursued Lincoln's plan for Reconstruction, conservative and radical Republicans joined together to impeach him on the grounds that his firing of Secretary of War Edwin M. Stanton violated the Tenure of Office Act. Stevens was a manager of the case against Johnson. Suffering from ill health and disappointed by Johnson's acquittal, Stevens died in 1868. (See JOHNSON IMPEACHMENT TRIAL.)

He was buried in a biracial cemetery; the inscription on his tombstone states that he chose to be buried there "that I might illustrate in my death the principles which I advocated through a long life—Equality of Man before his Creator."

Subpoena Power

The power to issue subpoenas enables congressional committees to compel the cooperation of reluctant witnesses. A subpoena is a legal order that requires a witness to testify or to produce documents upon demand of a committee. A witness who refuses may be cited for CONTEMPT OF CONGRESS and prosecuted in the courts. Committees of both the Senate and the House of Representatives routinely issue subpoenas as part of their INVESTIGATIONS.

The Supreme Court has upheld Congress's subpoena power. "Issuance of subpoenas ... has long been held to be a legitimate use by Congress of its power to investigate," the Court wrote in 1927. "Experience has taught that mere requests for ... information often are unavailing."

Substitute

When a motion or amendment is pending in the House or Senate, legislators can offer a substitute proposal dealing with the same subject. Under parliamentary rules, if a substitute is accepted, it supplants the original amendment, thus killing it. Also possible is an "amendment in the nature of a substitute," which usually seeks to replace the entire text of a bill with a new version.

Substitute bills are used more often in the House, where major legislation is often handled by more than one committee. The separate House committees work out their differences and draft a compromise bill, which is offered on the floor as a substitute. (See LEGISLATIVE PROCESS.)

Sumner, Charles

Charles Sumner (1811–1874) served as a senator from Massachusetts at the time of the Civil War. His energies were directed toward the outlawing of slavery and later the radical Reconstruction of the South. Like his Radical Republican colleagues, Sumner supported the impeachment of President Andrew Johnson. (See RECONSTRUCTION ERA.)

Sumner was a practicing lawyer when Massachusetts Democrats and Free Soilers proposed him as a candidate for the Senate. He entered the Senate in 1851. Sumner remained a Democrat until 1857, when he became a Republican. As a new senator, Sumner began speaking out against slavery. His assertion that he would not comply with the Fugitive Slave Act, which required the return of escaped slaves to their owners, provoked an unsuccessful Senate petition to expel him.

Debates in the Senate on matters pertaining to slavery were fiery and personal. In 1856, while addressing the status of Kansas, Sumner vilified many individuals, including Illinois senator Stephen A. DOUGLAS, a Popular Sovereignty Democrat, whom he called a "noisome, squat and nameless animal." Two days after the speech, while Sumner was sitting at his desk on the Senate floor, he was bludgeoned by Rep. Preston S. Brooks, a States Rights Democrat from South Carolina, whose uncle Sumner had criticized. It took Sumner three years to recover from the injuries Brooks inflicted using a walking stick.

Sumner's hatred of slavery also led him into vindictiveness against the South. He believed that the Confederates had relinquished their right to constitutional protections. Disliking the more moderate Reconstruction program of Abraham Lincoln and Andrew Johnson, Sumner advocated complete congressional control over the process. He played a major role in the impeachment of Johnson, saying that if he could, he would vote on the charges, "Guilty of all and infinitely more." (See JOHNSON IMPEACHMENT TRIAL.)

In 1861 Sumner was made chair of the Foreign Relations Committee. As such, he was involved in the *Trent* affair, in which Confederate agents were seized from a British ship. Later Sumner was so upset by President Ulysses S. Grant's plan to annex Santo Domingo that he was removed as chair of the committee. Republicans felt they needed a chair who was at least speaking to the president and the secretary of state.

Sumner died in 1874 while still a member of the Senate.

Sunset Legislation

Many laws that authorizes federal agencies or programs have provisions that automatically end the activity at a specified date. A primary purpose is to encourage the authorizing committees to examine the activities and results of the agency or program to determine if they should be continued. A sunset provision is often included in controversial bills that allows the legislation to pass but ensures a reexamination of the program.

Supreme Court

The Supreme Court is the most powerful court the world has ever known. It can override the will of the majority by declaring acts of Congress unconstitutional. It can remind presidents that in the United States all persons are subject to the rule of law. It can require the states to redistribute political power. It also can persuade the nation's citizens that society must move in new directions.

The Supreme Court can do all this because it functions as both the nation's highest court of appeals and the ultimate interpreter of the Constitution. Many important parts of the Constitution are vague or ambiguous, even contradictory, leaving room for the Court to set limits on the proper exercise of power by Congress, the president, and the states. As a result, the Court has sometimes surpassed the executive and legislative branches in shaping the course of American politics. The

Supreme Court's landmark ruling in *Brown v. Board of Education* (1954) forced racial integration in public schools. Its controversial ruling in *Roe v. Wade* (1973) legalized abortion in most instances. Its "one person, one vote" reapportionment rulings in the 1960s ensured proportional representation for growing urban areas in state legislatures and continue to limit states' discretion in drawing lines for congressional and state legislative districts.

Supreme Court justices are appointed by the president and confirmed by the Senate. Justices are appointed for life. Most justices have had prior judicial experience on federal or state courts before their appointments, although

The "Guardian or Authority of Law" sculpture, created by James Earle Frasier in the 1930s, sits in front of the facade of the Supreme Court building.
Source: CQ Photo/Scott J. Ferrell

there is no requirement to that effect. Twenty-eight justices served in Congress before their appointments, including three chief justices (John Marshall, Salmon P. Chase, and Edward D. White). The Court in 2007 included no former members of Congress: the last justice with congressional experience was Hugo L. Black, a former Democratic senator from Alabama who served on the Court from 1937 to 1971.

The Court at Work

The number of justices on the Supreme Court is fixed by Congress, not the Constitution. Under the Judiciary Act of 1789, Congress created a six-member Court. Congress later changed the Court's size from time to time, but since 1869 the Court has consisted of a chief justice and eight associate justices. In early 1937 President Franklin D. Roosevelt proposed that Congress add as many as six justices to the Court, in an effort to obtain more favorable rulings on the constitutionality of NEW DEAL legislation, but his attempt to "pack" the Court failed. (See COURTS AND CONGRESS.)

Cases come before the Supreme Court in three ways: as "original" cases filed directly with the Court; as appeals that the Court is required to hear; or on "petitions for certiorari" that the Court has complete discretion in deciding whether to review.

The Constitution designates two classes of cases as being in the Court's "original" jurisdiction—that is, eligible for hearing without prior review by a lower court: cases in which a state is a party and those involving senior foreign diplomats. There are very few such cases; the most common example is a boundary dispute between two states.

In the past, Congress established a right of appeal to the Supreme Court in certain kinds of cases—for example, rulings by state courts or lower federal courts holding a federal law or treaty invalid. Over time, Congress has reduced the Court's so-called mandatory jurisdiction. A judicial reform act passed by Congress in 1988 left only one major category of cases within the Court's mandatory jurisdiction: disputes under the federal Voting Rights Act. Since then, however, Congress has passed several laws specifying that the Supreme Court hear anticipated constitutional challenges to new laws—for example, the 1996 Line Item Veto Act and the 2002 Bipartisan Campaign Reform Act.

Almost all of the cases now heard by the Court stem from petitions for certiorari filed in cases decided by state courts or lower federal courts. In seeking a writ of certiorari, a litigant who has lost a case in a lower court petitions the Supreme Court to review the case, setting forth the reasons why review should be granted. The Supreme Court, under its rules, may grant a writ of certiorari by a vote of at least four justices.

The Court grants review in a very small fraction of the cases—in recent years, fewer than 100 cases a year out of more than 7,000 petitions for certiorari filed. The Court's rules specify that it will grant certiorari only when there are "special and important reasons" for it to hear a case. The rules describe three circumstances the Court will consider in deciding whether to accept a case for review: a conflict on an issue of federal law between lower federal courts or state courts; a ruling that "departs from the accepted and usual course of judicial proceedings"; or a ruling by a state court or federal appeals court on "an important question of federal law" that should be settled by the Court.

Rarely does the Court get involved in political disputes. The most notable exception was in December 2000, when justices, in a controversial 5–4 decision, ended the presidential election recount in Florida and, in effect, decided the race for Republican George W. Bush over Democrat Al GORE. The Court heard an appeal of the Florida Supreme Court's ruling that mandated recounts of ballots in several counties. Justices found differing methods used by the counties to determine what constituted a vote violated the Constitution's Equal Protection Clause. The case had major repercussions for Congress, which historically handled contested elections. Many scholars believed the Court, in agreeing to hear the case, effectively stated it was a better forum than the legislative branch for deciding such questions. Another significant exception was a series of cases beginning in the 1960s that addressed malapportionment in state legislatures, and eventually Congress, and that produced the concept of "one person, one vote." (See REAPPORTIONMENT AND REDISTRICTING.)

The Supreme Court convenes on the first Monday in October of each year. Its normal schedule calls for arguments to be heard during seven two-week periods during the year, three days in each week (Monday, Tuesday, and Wednesday). The Court usually recesses in late June until the following autumn.

The justices meet in conference on Wednesday afternoon and Friday of a week of argument to consider cases ready for decision and petitions for certiorari. The justices themselves are the only persons in the conference; no staff members or law clerks are present. After a vote on a case, one of the justices is assigned to write the opinion for the Court. If the chief justice votes with the majority, the chief justice assigns the writing of the majority opinion. If the chief justice is in the minority, the senior associate justice voting with the majority makes the assignment.

During its argument schedule, the Court announces any completed decisions on Tuesdays or Wednesdays. It releases its "orders list"—listing its actions on petitions for certiorari—on Mondays. The Court's last arguments are heard in April. Then, as the Court finishes its work for its term in May and June, decisions are announced on Mondays and, in the final weeks, on additional days. Typically, a dozen or more decisions may be announced in the last week.

The Court's Quarters

Of the federal government's three branches, the Supreme Court has the newest home. Its building in the classical Greek style at One First Street, N.E., faces the Capitol to the west and the Library of Congress's main Jefferson Building to the south. The building was opened in 1935.

Before 1935 the Court held its sessions in about a dozen different places. Some of its early courtrooms were shared with other tribunals. After the federal government moved to Washington in

1801, the Court sat in various rooms of the Capitol—and, some sources say, in two local taverns as well.

Because the wing of the Capitol where the Court was initially housed needed renovation, the Court in 1808 moved into a library formerly occupied by the House of Representatives. According to Capitol architect Benjamin H. Latrobe, the Court's 1809 sessions took place at Long's Tavern, where the main building of the Library of Congress now stands. The following year, the Court returned to the Capitol and met in a room designed for it, beneath the Senate chamber.

There the Court remained until the Capitol was burned by the British on August 24, 1814, during the War of 1812. The justices then moved to the temporary "Brick Capitol" at the site of the present Supreme Court building and then—during the two years when the Capitol was being restored—to a rented house that later became Bell Tavern. The Court returned to the Capitol for its February 1817 term and occupied an undamaged section in the north wing until 1819, when its regular quarters beneath the Senate were ready to be occupied again.

In 1860, with the Civil War imminent, the Court moved from the basement to the old Senate chamber on the first floor of the Capitol. The new courtroom was situated on the east side of the main corridor between the Rotunda and the current Senate chamber. The large room, with a dozen anterooms for office space and storage, was by far the roomiest and most pleasing space the Court had occupied. Still, none of the justices had individual office space in the Capitol.

President William Howard Taft began promoting the idea of a separate building for the Supreme Court about 1912. Taft continued his campaign when he became chief justice of the United States in 1921. At his urging, Congress finally agreed in 1929 and authorized funds for the construction of a permanent home for the Court.

Suspension of the Rules

Suspension of the rules is a convenient shortcut procedure that the House uses for floor action on noncontroversial legislation. By avoiding the regular, time-consuming parliamentary procedures, bills—even major ones—facing little or no opposition can be approved quickly.

Debate on legislation considered under suspension of the rules is limited to forty minutes. Floor amendments are prohibited—another reason why this shortcut is so effective. Only one vote to simultaneously suspend the rules and pass the bill is in order; a two-thirds majority of members voting is required.

Suspension of the rules is in order on Mondays and Tuesdays of every week and during the last six days of the session, when there is usually a large backlog of legislation awaiting action. The SPEAKER OF THE HOUSE has control over the procedure because of the authority to recognize members. Members make arrangements in advance to receive recognition to offer a suspension motion.

The Speaker has the authority to postpone recorded votes until all the bills have been debated, and then to vote on them at one time, cutting voting time on each bill to as little as five minutes. A bill that fails to pass under suspension of the rules may be considered later under the regular parliamentary rules used in the House. (See LEGISLATIVE PROCESS.)

In the late 1970s, after Republicans accused the Democrats of using the procedure for some complex and controversial legislation, the House Democratic Caucus set guidelines for its use. When the Republicans took control of the House in 1995, they continued to use the suspension procedure much as the Democrats had. Major legislation, however, is still passed under suspension, either because there is substantial bipartisan support for it or because an emergency situation warrants suspension.

In the Senate, motions to suspend the rules are rare because they are debatable and thus open to filibusters and other delaying tactics. The shortcut procedure also is considered an affront to the committee system. As in the House, a two-thirds vote is needed in the Senate to suspend one or more rules. But in the Senate the vote is just on the motion to suspend and not at the same time to pass a measure. Suspension motions are occasionally used in the Senate to lift the rule banning policy, or legislative, amendments to appropriations bills.

Floor action can also be expedited by UNANIMOUS CONSENT.

Table, Motion to

Motions to table, or to "lay on the table," are used to block or kill a pending proposition. When approved, a tabling motion is considered the final disposition of that issue. One of the most widely used parliamentary procedures, the motion to table is not debatable, and adoption requires a simple majority vote.

Motions to table are used regularly with motions to reconsider. (See RECONSIDER, MOTION TO.) The tabling of a motion to reconsider makes final a previous legislative action, whether approval or rejection of a bill, amendment, or other parliamentary question. (See LEGISLATIVE PROCESS.)

Members of Congress often prefer procedural votes, particularly the motion to table, over direct votes for or against a substantive proposal. By voting to table, they can avoid being recorded directly on a controversial bill or politically sensitive issue. The motion to table often will win more support than a vote to defeat the issue.

Motions to table are not used when the House of Representatives considers and amends bills in the COMMITTEE OF THE WHOLE; they are used only after the Committee of the Whole has been dissolved and the legislation returned to the full House.

In the Senate, tabling motions on amendments are effective devices to end debate.

Taft, Robert A.

Robert A. Taft (1889–1953), an Ohio Republican, entered the Senate in 1939. A leader of the conservative wing of the Republican Party, Taft generally opposed President Franklin D. Roosevelt's NEW

Ohio Republican Robert A. Taft, standing, was a leader of the conservative wing of the GOP. He served in the Senate from 1939 to 1953 and was identified with "America first" isolationism until the Japanese attack on Pearl Harbor in 1941.
Source: AP Images/John Lindsay

DEAL programs. Before the Japanese attack on Pearl Harbor in 1941, he advocated "America first" isolationism.

Taft was extremely intelligent and hardworking, although he lacked charisma. In power and authority he was the leading Republican in the Senate from the 1940s to his death. Not until 1953, the year he died, however, did Taft officially lead his Senate colleagues as majority leader.

As the son of President William Howard Taft, Robert Taft was no stranger to politics. He practiced law in Cincinnati and in 1919 went to Paris to help Herbert Hoover (then head of the Food Administration) oversee the distribution of postwar aid to Europe. Shortly after his return, he entered the state legislature, where he stayed until he was elected to the U.S. Senate.

As a senator, Taft approved of only some elements of the New Deal, such as Social Security and public housing. He opposed generous farm subsidies and, until he reversed positions in 1946, federal involvement in education. Taft thought the power of organized labor had become excessive; in 1947 he cosponsored the Taft-Hartley Act, which restricted the right of unions to strike.

Taft felt that Europe's problems were its own and spoke out against the lend-lease program, through which the United States helped supply the Allies during World War II. He believed that the only organization capable of promoting world peace would be an international court buttressed by a body of strong international laws. He put little faith in the United Nations and objected to the North Atlantic Treaty Organization (NATO). He thought NATO would only antagonize the Soviet Union, which, he believed, had no interest in hegemony over Western Europe.

Earnest and well-briefed, Taft earned the respect of his colleagues. His power was centered in the Senate Policy Committee, which he headed from its establishment in 1947. He was a candidate for the Republican presidential nomination in 1940, 1948, and 1952. In 1952 he lost to Dwight D. Eisenhower, to whom he gave his support (after Eisenhower agreed to some general conservative conditions) and his unconditional friendship.

Tax and Tariff Powers *See* PURSE, POWER OF.

Taxation Committee, Joint

The principal function of the Joint Taxation Committee is to provide a neutral home for the non-partisan tax experts who advise both the House Ways and Means and Senate Finance committees. The staff in 2007 had fifty-nine lawyers, economists, accountants, and other tax specialists and supporting staff. The joint committee of five senators and five representatives is headed by the chairs of the two tax panels, who rotate as chair and vice chair. (See FINANCE COMMITTEE, SENATE; WAYS AND MEANS COMMITTEE, HOUSE.)

Established in 1926, today the Joint Taxation Committee rarely meets. It has no legislative authority, but it does from time to time conduct investigations. One of the most notable was a probe of President Richard NIXON's taxes, undertaken at his request. In 2002 the committee investigated the Enron Corp., the Houston-based energy giant that went bankrupt in late 2001. The panel focused on Enron's use of tax shelters and other entities, as well as the compensation arrangements of Enron employees.

The committee is also responsible for approving any tax refunds of more than $2,000,000, a task that involves committee staff reviewing decisions made by the Internal Revenue Service.

Teapot Dome

Teapot Dome is the enduring legacy of Warren G. Harding's presidency, a code name for scandal in government. After the disclosures of a long congressional investigation, one member of the president's cabinet, Interior Secretary Albert B. Fall, went to prison for accepting bribes to lease government-owned oil land to favored persons. Teapot Dome was the most prominent of several shady activities that left a taint of corruption on the Harding administration in the 1920s.

The name Teapot Dome comes from a sandstone formation, faintly resembling a teapot, that rises above the plains of north-central Wyoming. Deep below the rock outcropping is a reservoir of oil in the shape of a dome. This underground oil and the land above it make up a tiny portion of the vast federal holdings in the West.

In 1915 President Woodrow Wilson assigned control of Teapot Dome to the Navy Department as a reserve source of fuel for U.S. warships. It was designated Reserve No. 3; two other oil sites, Elk Hills and Buena Vista in California, already had been selected as Reserve Nos. 1 and 2. The U.S. Navy, spurred by the outbreak of World War I in Europe, was converting its fleet from the use of coal to oil. The nation's petroleum supply turned out to be far bigger than geologists had envisioned at the war's onset, and Teapot Dome did not have to be tapped.

Teapot Dome was coveted by America's fast-growing oil industry. The industry had strong support from western lawmakers who clung to the frontier belief in exploitation of natural resources. Fall, a rancher and lawyer who had represented New Mexico in the Senate, was outspoken in that view. As head of the Interior Department under Harding, Fall quickly won agreement to bring the naval reserve oil lands under the Interior Department's control. In 1922 the department

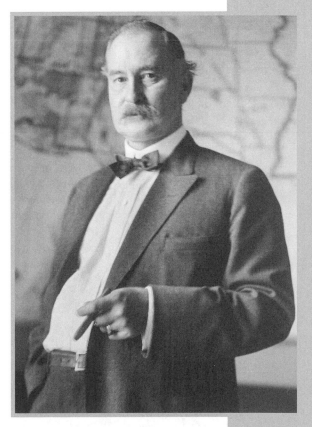

Albert B. Fall, secretary of the interior under President Warren Harding, was the first cabinet member ever convicted of a felony; he secretly leased federal oil reserves to oil magnates Henry Sinclair and Edward Doheny. Fall received $400,000, which he argued was a loan not a bribe.
Source: Library of Congress

leased the Elk Hills reserve to Edward L. Doheny of the Pan-American Petroleum and Transport Co., and the Teapot Dome reserve to Harry F. Sinclair's Mammoth Oil Co.

Pressure soon grew for a congressional investigation of the transactions. Republican control blocked action in the House. But Senate Democrats and insurgent Republicans managed to push through a resolution that authorized the Senate Committee on Public Lands and Surveys (later re-named Interior and Insular Affairs, Energy and Natural Resources, Resources and, by 2007, ENERGY AND NATURAL RESOURCES) to investigate the leases. The committee was headed by a series of Republican chairs, but a Democrat on the panel, Thomas J. Walsh of Montana, took charge of the inquiry.

When the hearings opened in October 1923, they concentrated at first on the legality of the two leases. Then Walsh learned that Fall had accepted bribes from Doheny and Sinclair. The commit-tee's evidence revealed that Doheny had given Fall at least $100,000 and Sinclair had given the in-terior secretary at least $300,000. Fall, who had meanwhile resigned his cabinet post, protested that he had received only "gifts and loans."

Fall eventually was convicted of having accepted a bribe from Doheny in connection with the Elk Hills lease. However, in a separate trial Doheny was acquitted on charges of having made the bribe. Fall entered prison in June 1931 and served eleven months. Sinclair went to jail twice: first for three months for contempt of Congress over his refusal to answer questions, and then for six months for contempt of court for attempting to bribe a juror at his bribery trial. He ultimately was acquitted of those charges.

The memory of Teapot Dome lived on, a reminder of the potential for corruption in high places. "It is the dome we live under here at the Interior Department," Interior Secretary Stewart Udall told a congressional committee in 1967, assuring the panel that department officials recalled the lessons of the past.

Televising Congress

Once Congress worried that live televised coverage of its daily proceedings would prompt grand-standing or erode the dignity of its operations. Now that televised floor coverage is commonplace, those fears have virtually disappeared. The gavel-to-gavel broadcasts of floor action have not caused significant changes in the way Congress works. For many members, television coverage has proven politically expedient, allowing them to gain public ex-posure when national and local news pro-grams air excerpts from floor debates. The broadcasts are also convenient, allowing members to follow floor action from their offices or review a debate they missed.

The House was first to open its cham-ber to television, in 1979. The Senate held out against the television era until 1986. Even senators who once opposed television applauded the results a year later. "It seems to be an unalloyed success at this point.... Our fears were unfounded," said Sen. J. Bennett Johnston, a Louisiana Democrat who had been a vocal opponent. The

Beginning in 1979, House floor proceedings have been televised. The Senate did not allow television coverage until 1986.
Source: C-SPAN

Senate painted the walls of its chamber a new color after Kansas Republican Robert Dole complained that the old backdrop made senators on television "look like they're standing in split-pea soup."

Long before broadcasts of floor debate, television had captured dramatic events on Capitol Hill. Presidential State of the Union messages were televised from the packed House chamber. Senate committee hearings were opened to cameras several times, enabling viewers to watch the KEFAUVER probe of organized crime and the Army-MCCARTHY investigation in the 1950s, testimony on the Vietnam War in the 1960s, and the hearings in the Watergate scandal in 1973. The House banned cameras from committee sessions until 1970; in 1974 it won a large national audience for committee sessions on impeachment of President Richard NIXON.

Representatives and senators have learned to exploit television by consenting to interviews, appearing on news programs, and crafting "photo opportunities" with constituents. Legislators have used the press to lobby internally. "If you want to reach your colleagues, sometimes the best way is to let them see you on TV or read your name in the paper," said Thomas J. Downey, a Democratic representative from New York. Some legislators have even devised a video version of the press release, a prepackaged statement that can be shipped, or beamed via satellite, back to local stations.

Both the House and Senate have special studios, equipped with technicians and cameras, that legislators can use for interviews or statements. The vast new Capitol Visitor Center still under construction at the start of 2008 included a state-of-the-art television center, complete with makeup facilities, for the Senate. The existing studios could not be used for political advertisements. The Democratic and Republican parties also operate separate Capitol Hill studios that legislators can use without restrictions; political campaign spots are often made there.

Lawmakers also are adapting to the increased use of video transmissions on the Internet. A number of congressional committees now "stream" hearings live on the Internet, though the quality and speed of the transmissions vary.

More on this topic:
Capitol Visitor Center, p. 83
C-SPAN, p. 149
Nixon Impeachment Effort, p. 396
State of the Union, p. 535
Watergate Scandal, p. 596

Floor Proceedings

Recordings of House and Senate floor action are not edited. Each chamber does, however, keep close control over its broadcasts, using cameras owned by Congress and operated by congressional staff. The coverage provides only a limited view of floor action, usually focusing on the rostrum or on the member who is speaking. The cameras are operated by remote control from basement studios beneath each chamber. Senators speak from their desks; representatives go to one of two lecterns in the House well or use the tables on each side of the central aisle. When votes are in progress, the cameras show the full chamber, with information about the vote superimposed on the screen. Recordings of House and Senate floor action cannot be used for political or commercial purposes.

Although networks and local television stations use excerpts from the recordings, the only gavel-to-gavel coverage is on a cable network, Cable Satellite Public Affairs Network (C-SPAN). In addition to its floor coverage, C-SPAN selectively broadcasts other major congressional events, such as committee hearings, press conferences, and the like.

Entering the TV Era

The House first allowed cameras in its chamber in 1947 to record its opening session. For the next three decades television coverage was permitted only for special joint sessions. A key opponent of broadcasts was Speaker Sam RAYBURN, who in 1952 banned cameras even from House committee sessions, a dictum that later Speakers left in place.

Televising House and Senate proceedings—as well as committee meetings—did not come to Congress easily. Older members, including legendary Speaker Sam RAYBURN, were adamant in their opposition. By the 1970s, however, the House included a new generation of members who were comfortable with television and eager for coverage of floor debate. Many senators, however, still saw their chamber as a slow, deliberative body whose decorum would be compromised by the unblinking eye of the TV camera. But a few years after the House began televising sessions, senators tiptoed into the modern age and soon were comfortable with it.

Reforms of overall legislative procedure in 1970 included a new ruling that let each committee decide whether to televise its sessions. By the time Thomas P. O'NEILL Jr. became Speaker in 1977, the House included a new generation of members who were comfortable with television and eager for coverage of floor debate. Tennessee representative Al GORE led the campaign for televising House floor proceedings. Members agreed to a test of a closed-circuit system.

The 1977 test, which lasted seven months, was considered successful, and by a lopsided vote later that year the House endorsed gavel-to-gavel coverage. In 1978 the House agreed to let broadcasters tap into its audio system. By early 1979 the House had invested $1.2 million in modern cameras, microphones, and lighting. Efforts by the networks to win access to the chamber for their own cameras failed. The first live House coverage occurred briefly on March 19, 1979. C-SPAN coverage began on April 3.

Controversy about the broadcasts has been rare. In 1984, however, O'Neill angered a group of militant House Republicans when he ordered cameras to pan the chamber, revealing to the television audience that the fiery Republican speakers were addressing an empty House. O'Neill could do this because House rules give the Speaker control of the broadcast system. In the late 1990s, however, Republicans and Democrats agreed to keep the cameras focused on the member speaking during debates and SPECIAL ORDERS, a period at the end of each day's session when legislators may address the often-deserted chamber.

Television cameras were first allowed in the Senate chamber in December 1974, when Nelson A. Rockefeller was sworn in as vice president. In 1978 the Senate permitted radio broadcasts of its debate on the Panama Canal treaty.

Despite support from top Democratic and Republican leaders, the Senate spent several more years arguing about broadcasts. Opponents, who threatened to filibuster, argued that television would erode the Senate's historic role as the slower, more deliberative body. But proponents of television—including Gore who was now a senator—prevailed, and a two-month experiment began June 2, 1986. At the end of July, the Senate voted by a four-to-one margin to keep the television cameras rolling permanently.

Television had become so pervasive that even the 1999 Senate impeachment trial of President Bill Clinton—an event so bound by 130-year-old rules that senators were not permitted to speak during the proceedings—was kept open to the cameras. Senators did hold their final deliberations in secret—mandated by the same antiquated rules—despite the effort of some senators and the pleas of news organizations to allow TV cameras. A two-thirds majority (sixty-seven senators) was required to change the rules, and only fifty-nine senators (forty-five Democrats and fourteen Republicans) voted to open the final debate.

Terms and Sessions of Congress

The meetings of Congress are divided into two-year cycles coinciding with the two-year period for which representatives are elected. The system is based on constitutional requirements that members of the House of Representatives must be elected "every second year" and that Congress must meet at least once each year.

A new term of Congress begins at noon on January 3 in odd-numbered years, following the election the previous November. The term expires, and the next term begins, on January 3 two years later. Each two-year term is known as a "Congress." The Congress that convened in January 2007 was the 110th Congress because it was the 110th to convene since the ratification of the Constitution. It would last until January 2009, when the 111th Congress would begin.

Each Congress has two regular sessions. The first begins in January of the odd-numbered year, and members elected the previous November are sworn in at that time. Because they are elected for two-year terms, all representatives must be sworn in at the beginning of each new Congress. Senators are elected for staggered six-year terms, and only about a third of the Senate is sworn in every two years. The second regular session of a Congress begins in January of the even-numbered year and may run until a new Congress takes office the following year.

Bills introduced in the first year of a Congress remain alive until that Congress ends; legislative action carries over from session to session. Unfinished measures die at the end of a Congress and may be begun again in the next.

The modern schedule of terms and sessions was established in 1933 by the Twentieth Amendment to the Constitution. Until then members of Congress took office on March 4, and Congress met annually in December. When it met in December of an even-numbered year, following the election of its successor, it could remain in session until March 4 of the next year, when the term of the new Congress began. Members who had been defeated for reelection could vote in this short lame-duck session, which was characterized by filibusters and other efforts to stall legislative action.

The Twentieth Amendment, known as the lame-duck amendment, established January 3 as the day on which the term of members of Congress would begin. It also provided that members of Congress should meet annually on January 3 "unless they shall by law appoint a different day." Congress frequently takes advantage of that option and convenes later in the month. The Twentieth Amendment failed to eliminate post-election sessions. Sixteen were held between 1935 and January 2007. They were called either by Congress itself or by the president, who has authority under the Constitution to convene special sessions of Congress.

> **More on this topic:**
>
> Adjournment, p. 2
>
> House of Representatives, p. 267
>
> Lame-Duck Session, p. 324
>
> Legislative Process, p. 344
>
> Senate, p. 494

Thurmond, Strom

On May 25, 1997, Strom Thurmond (1902– 2003) strode past a remarkable milestone, becoming the longest-serving member in Senate history to that time. He had served forty-seven years and little more than five months, according to the Senate historian. When he retired from the Senate at the beginning of 2003, he was one hundred years old. But the service record held for not quite a decade. On June 12, 2006, Robert C. BYRD became the longest-serving senator in American history.

In his last few years of service, Thurmond was hardly an active participant in Senate debates. His frailty forced him to give up the chairmanship of the Armed Services Committee to Republican John Warner of Virginia in 1999.

After starting out in 1929 as superintendent of education in the town of Edgefield, Thurmond moved up to the state Senate during the Depression years. In 1946, after returning from World War II, he was elected governor.

South Carolina Republican Strom Thurmond retired at the end of the 107th Congress in January 2003, after forty-seven years of service—at that time the longest-serving member in Senate history.
Source: CQ Photo/Scott J. Ferrell

Thurmond's long political career was punctuated with turns and reversals, but he always seemed to carry his South Carolina constituents with him. They supported him in 1948 when, during his second term as governor, he bolted the Democratic Party to run as a third-party candidate for president against Harry S. TRUMAN. The Democratic National Convention had adopted a strong civil rights plank, and Thurmond offered himself as a regional candidate on the States' Rights Democratic ticket. He carried South Carolina, Alabama, Mississippi, and Louisiana. Years later, as Thurmond was retiring, praise for Thurmond's presidential bid cost Senate Majority Leader Trent LOTT, a Republican from Mississippi, his leadership job.

Thurmond entered the Senate in 1954, winning a special election as a write-in candidate—the first and only senator to be elected that way so far. Keeping a promise made during the campaign, he resigned in 1956 and ran for reelection without benefit of incumbency. No one filed against him. In 1957 Thurmond set a record, filibustering for over twenty-four hours on a fair housing bill with civil rights implications. As a senator in 1964 he announced that he was joining the Republican Party because the Democrats were "leading the evolution of our nation to a socialistic dictatorship." Despite the state's historical partisan leanings, he easily won reelection two years later and in every election until his retirement.

Thurmond died on June 26, 2003, just months after leaving the Senate.

Tie Votes *See* VOTING IN CONGRESS.

Transportation and Infrastructure Committee, House

The federal government has spent billions of dollars building roads, airports, dams, and subways—and the House Transportation and Infrastructure Committee has had a say in most of those decisions. Even the politics of tight federal budgets has not dimmed the panel's enthusiasm for road building and channel dredging.

From 1975 to 1995, the committee was known as the Public Works and Transportation Committee; the Republicans changed its name when they took control of the House in 1995 and the Democrats kept the new name when they won back the chamber in 2006.

Labels like pork-barrel are not welcome in the committee. Although less sought after than high-profile committees such Ways and Means and Appropriations, the transportation panel has always been popular with legislators eager to show evidence of their work. The committee had seventy-five members in 2003, making it the largest House panel. When the committee is choosing special projects, those located in the districts of committee members usually receive top priority. But the committee also accommodates other members on a bipartisan basis by including dams or roads for those who comply with the unwritten rule: Give full support to bills that contain something for your district. (See PORK-BARREL POLITICS.)

Despite budget constraints in the latter years of the twentieth century and after 2000, the committee chalked up some notable successes. In 1991 Congress cleared a six-year, $151 billion authorization measure for federal highway and mass transit programs. Even the new Republican leadership in the mid-1990s could not contain the committee's enthusiasm for new roads. After furious debate, Congress in 1998 cleared a $218 billion, six-year roads bill, the work of Republican committee chair Bud Shuster of Pennsylvania.

The Transportation and Infrastructure Committee is also responsible for the aviation, railroad, and trucking industries. It played a key role in ending regulation of airlines in 1978 and of trucking in 1980. (Railroad deregulation was handled by the Energy and Commerce Committee.)

The committee has been criticized for its commitment to capital improvements. The 1991 surface transportation measure, for example, was said to be laden with pork projects. But Robert A. Roe, the New Jersey Democrat who chaired the committee from 1991 to 1993, expressed the sentiments of all those to chair the panel in recent times. "With this bill we are rebuilding America," he said. Roe and his successors never objected to pork-barrel charges, contending that the projects were vital for the states' economies and helped create jobs.

In the 110th Congress starting in 2007, the chair went to James L. Oberstar, a Minnesota Democrat who had been on the panel for a decade. Like his predecessors Oberstar believed the federal government should provide generous financial support for the nation's transportation and infrastructure needs. He also was known for support of environmental protection proposals.

Treaty-Making Power

Under the Constitution, the president and the Senate share the power to make treaties with other countries. Although the precise division of labor is ambiguous, the treaty clause has been interpreted to give the president the sole authority to conduct negotiations with foreign governments on treaties and other international agreements. The Senate has the power to approve, amend, or reject treaties once they have been formally submitted to it by the president. The House of Representatives has no authority over treaties, although efforts are sometimes made there to block or change a treaty by withholding the funds needed to fulfill its terms.

The Senate's treaty powers have been a major source of congressional influence over foreign affairs. Beginning with the first treaty it approved—the Jay Treaty with Great Britain in 1795—the Senate has used its approval power to force changes in international agreements. On a few occasions the Senate has rejected major treaties. The most notable example was the 1919 Treaty of Versailles, which formally concluded World War I and established the League of Nations.

There has been ample evidence over the decades that the Senate's treaty power continues to be a potent tool for affecting foreign policy. Members of the Senate participated directly in negotiations with Panama over conditions attached to the Panama Canal treaties in 1978. In 1988 the Senate held up approval of an arms control treaty until negotiators had clarified several issues. Opponents of a treaty banning chemical weapons delayed Senate floor action on the treaty in 1996 and forced some major concessions by the Clinton administration on collateral issues—including a reorganization of the foreign policy bureaucracy and agreement to seek Senate approval of revisions in several major treaties—before its approval in 1997. Legislation to implement the pact in the United States was not cleared until 1998, as Republicans sought to force Clinton to agree to economic sanctions on overseas companies and research labs, primarily in Russia, that provided missile technology to Iran. The chemical weapons bill was eventually added to an omnibus fiscal 1999 spending package. Proponents remained troubled by some of the law's provisions, including restrictions giving the president the right to block surprise inspections on national security grounds as well as require that no chemical samples leave the United States for testing.

Senate Republicans in 1998 tried to pass legislation that would have repudiated Clinton's plan to wait until 2000 before deciding whether to deploy a national antimissile defense system.

CLOSER LOOK ◉

The president and the Senate, under the Constitution, share the power to make treaties with other nations. This gives the Senate an important influence over foreign affairs. The House of Representatives has no authority over treaties, although it sometimes attempts to block or change a treaty by withholding the funds needed to fulfill its terms. The precise division between the president and Senate is ambiguous, but historically the president has taken full authority to negotiate treaties and other international agreements, and the Senate has the authority approve, amend, or reject them.

Republicans wanted to move faster, but the administration and many Democrats in Congress had shied away from rushing a decision partly because they feared it could violate the 1972 treaty limiting antiballistic missile (ABM) weapons and could poison relations with Russia. While Republicans did not make any specific reference to the treaty, Democratic filibusters twice blocked debate on the bill. But the next administration brushed aside complaints about violating the treaty, arguing that it was an obstacle to development of a missile defense system that would provide the new technology to deter possible attacks. In late 2001 Republican president George W. Bush announced his intention to withdraw from the pact, and the administration officially abandoned the treaty in June 2002.

The Senate in 1999 rejected a treaty that would have expanded an existing ban on atmospheric nuclear testing to include underground tests and those for peaceful purposes. The treaty was signed by President Clinton in 1996 and was a top foreign policy goal of his administration. But Republican critics charged the pact would be difficult to implement, would weaken U.S. defenses, and would give nations outside of the pact an unfair nuclear advantage. When Senate Democrats stepped up demands that the treaty be considered, Republican Majority Leader Trent LOTT of Mississippi surprised them by scheduling a vote after a minimal number of hearings and debate. The resolution to approve the treaty was rejected, 48–51.

Ratification Process

Senate consideration of a treaty is open to presidential discretion at several points. The president may refuse to submit a treaty, may withdraw it after it has been submitted, or may refuse to ratify it even after the Senate has given its consent.

Once the president has submitted a treaty to the Senate, it remains before the Senate until it is approved or rejected or until the president requests its return and the Senate agrees to withdraw it. The Senate also may take the initiative to return a treaty to the president.

The Senate Foreign Relations Committee has jurisdiction over all treaties, even if an agreement covers a subject that is not under the committee's usual jurisdiction. After treaties have been reported by the committee, they are considered by the full Senate.

Contrary to a widespread misconception, the Senate does not have the power under the Constitution to ratify treaties. Ratification means the formal acceptance of a treaty by the government and is a power of the president. But the Constitution provides that the president can take that step only with the approval of two-thirds of the senators present and voting. Technically speaking, what the Senate actually votes on is not the text of a treaty but rather a resolution approving ratification by the president.

Once approved by the Senate and ratified by the president, the terms of a treaty become the law of the land, as legally valid as any legislation.

From the founding of the Republic through 2002, the full Senate rejected outright only twenty-one treaties. The most recent was the nuclear test ban treaty in 1999.

The Senate also uses means other than rejection to thwart treaties. It can leave a treaty languishing on the Foreign Relations Committee calendar for decades and thus delay it to death. (The approval in 1986 of a treaty on genocide nearly thirty-seven years after it was submitted to the Senate, however, does offer some hope for lingering old treaties.)

The Senate may make changes that either the president or other signatories find unacceptable. Although there are no provisions in the Constitution pertaining to treaty amendments, the Senate has claimed the authority since 1795, when it consented to ratification of the Jay Treaty only on condition that an additional article be negotiated. Since then many treaties have been subjected to

---

○ **CLOSER LOOK**

The Senate does not have the power to ratify treaties, although there is a widespread misconception that it does. The Senate approves a resolution approving ratification, which means the formal acceptance of a treaty by the government. The ratification power is reserved to the president.

TREATIES KILLED BY THE SENATE
(Through 2007)

Date of Vote	Country	Yea-Nay	Vote Subject
March 9, 1825	Colombia	0–40	Suppression of African Slave Trade
June 11, 1836	Switzerland	14–23	Personal and Property Rights
June 8, 1844	Texas	16–35	Annexation
June 15, 1844	German Zollverein	26–18	Reciprocity
May 31, 1860	Mexico	18–27	Transit and Commercial Rights
June 27, 1860	Spain	26–17	Cuban Claims Commission
April 13, 1869	Great Britain	1–54	Arbitration of Claims
June 1, 1870	Hawaii	20–19	Reciprocity
June 30, 1870	Dominican Republic	28–28	Annexation
January 29, 1885	Nicaragua	32–23	Interoceanic Canal
April 20, 1886	Mexico	32–26	Mining Claims
August 21, 1888	Great Britain	27–30	Fishing Rights
February 1, 1889	Great Britain	15–38	Extradition
May 5, 1897	Great Britain	43–26	Arbitration
March 19, 1920	Multilateral	49–35	Treaty of Versailles
January 18, 1927	Turkey	50–34	Commercial Rights
March 14, 1934	Canada	46–42	St. Lawrence Seaway
January 29, 1935	Multilateral	52–36	World Court
May 26, 1960	Multilateral	49–30	Law of the Sea Convention
March 8, 1983	Multilateral	50–42	Montreal Aviation Protocol
October 13, 1999	Multilateral	48–51	Comprehensive Nuclear Test Ban

SOURCE: Compiled by Senate Historical Office from W. Stull Holt, *Treaties Defeated by the Senate* (Baltimore: Johns Hopkins University Press, 1933); and from *Senate Executive Journal*.

NOTE: A two-thirds majority vote is required for Senate consent to the ratification of treaties. In many cases, treaties were blocked in committee or withdrawn before ever coming to a vote in the Senate.

amendments, reservations, conditions, and qualifications, some of which have been added at the request of the president.

A Senate amendment to a treaty, if it is accepted by the president and the other parties to the treaty, changes it for all parties. Instead of amending a treaty, the Senate may add a reservation, which limits only the treaty obligation of the United States. A reservation, however, may be so significant that the other parties to the treaty may file similar reservations or refuse to ratify the treaty.

In many cases the Senate adds relatively minor understandings, or subtle interpretations of treaty language, which usually do not significantly affect the substance of the treaty and do not require any additional negotiations with the other parties to the treaty. Sometimes declarations are attached; these are statements of intent or policy that are not directly related to provisions of the treaty itself.

Reservations, understandings, and declarations are used more frequently than amendments. But the differences among these various conditions have become blurred over the years. Amendments to a treaty automatically require the concurrence of the other parties to the accord if it is to take effect. But the substance of reservations and understandings dictates whether the conditions must be formally communicated to the other parties and whether they must be agreed to before the treaty can take effect.

The Senate's assertion of its treaty authority sometimes is criticized by those who see it as representing excessive interference in the president's foreign policy powers. Efforts have been made over the years to amend the Constitution to reduce the two-thirds vote required for ratification to a simple majority or to include the House in the ratification process. None of these attempts has succeeded.

In the 1950s Sen. John W. Bricker, an Ohio Republican, led an effort with the opposite aim: to curb the president's powers to make treaties and other international agreements. Bricker's proposed constitutional amendment would have provided that the provisions of a treaty or other international agreement take effect only when implemented through separate legislation passed by Congress. The amendment provoked heated debate during President Dwight D. Eisenhower's first term. A revised version, requiring congressional action on agreements other than treaties, was rejected by the Senate by a one-vote margin in 1954.

History

The division of authority over treaties was a subject of considerable debate during the Constitutional Convention, but the delegates finally reached agreement. Spelling out presidential authority, Article II, Section 2, Clause 2 declares that the president "shall have Power, by and with the Advice and Consent of the Senate, to make Treaties, provided two-thirds of the Senators present concur."

Most treaties submitted to the Senate are approved. One notable exception was the defeat of President Woodrow Wilson's Treaty of Versailles, which included the League of Nations provision. This 1921 cartoon entitled "Triumphant Entry into Normalcy" by Rollin Kirby illustrates the successful Senate battle against the treaty led by Sens. Henry Cabot Lodge and Philander Chase Knox.
Source: The Granger Collection, New York

The ambiguity of the compromise language set the stage for several disputes over the treaty-making authority. The Senate established almost immediately its authority to amend treaties. But was it entitled to offer the president advice during the course of treaty negotiations? Could the Senate initiate treaty talks? Did it have the right to confirm, and thus to some extent control, negotiators appointed by the president?

In general, these and similar issues have been resolved in favor of the president. The Senate's role is basically limited to considering treaties submitted by the president. However, twentieth-century presidents often found it politically advisable to consult with key senators during the course of treaty negotiations to try to ensure that the prospective agreement had broad support in the Senate.

Disputes between the president and Congress over foreign policy issues were often played out during debates on treaties. Perhaps the most dramatic example was the Senate's rejection of the Treaty of Versailles, ending World War I. The treaty, worked out by President Woodrow Wilson and the leaders of the other nations that had defeated Germany, included provisions establishing a League of Nations for the resolution of international disputes. A faction of the Senate, led by Foreign Relations Committee chair Henry Cabot LODGE, a Massachusetts Republican, strongly opposed the part of the treaty providing for U.S. membership in the league. Lodge proposed "reservations" making clear that membership in the league would not lead to encroachment on the sovereignty of the United States or the powers of Congress. Wilson was adamantly opposed to any changes, however, and the failure of his administration to reach a compromise with key groups of senators led to the final defeat of the treaty.

Partly as a result of the rejection of the Treaty of Versailles and partly because foreign affairs were becoming more complicated, presidents began to rely on the executive agreement to conduct business with other countries. Executive agreements are understandings with other countries that are not subject to Senate approval. Although most executive agreements cover routine matters, such as regulation of fishing rights, some have had an important impact on U.S. foreign policy. President Franklin D. Roosevelt in 1940 used an executive agreement to avoid the treaty process when he provided the British with destroyers to defend against German submarines in exchange for the right to lease several British naval bases in the Western Hemisphere. The United States was still officially neutral at the time and the predominantly isolationist Senate would not have approved a lend-lease treaty. Other examples include the World War II summit agreements reached by Allied leaders at Cairo, Tehran, Yalta, and Potsdam.

Some lawmakers have been alarmed at the use of executive agreements, seeing them as presidential usurpation of the Senate's treaty power. However, the treaty power has continued to play a significant role in major foreign policy issues, particularly in shaping the debate on arms control agreements.

Truman, Harry S.

Unpretentious and unassuming, Harry S. Truman (1884–1972) represented Missouri in the Senate from 1935 to 1945. Truman's diligence and honesty as the head of a Senate investigation of defense programs drew national attention and led to his selection as President Franklin D. Roosevelt's running mate in 1944. Truman had served as vice president for less than four months when Roosevelt died and Truman assumed the presidency.

Truman's career began in Missouri's local Democratic politics. After working for years as a farmer and serving in the military in World War I, Truman was elected to a county court judgeship. The job was nonjudicial; he was responsible for the maintenance of county roads and buildings. Truman owed his election in part to Kansas City's corrupt political machine, which was run by Thomas Pendergast. It was Pendergast who in 1934 persuaded Truman not to run for the House of Representatives but to try instead for a Senate seat. Pendergast's support was a mixed blessing. While it made Truman's political career possible, it also alienated many supporters.

Sen. Harry S. Truman (center) meets with some of his colleagues in 1942, just a few years before becoming president. They are, left to right, Senators Homer Ferguson, Harold Hitz Burton, Thomas Terry Connally, and Ralph Owen Brewster.
Source: Library of Congress

After joining the Senate in 1935, Truman served on the Appropriations and Interstate Commerce committees and compiled a voting record supporting the NEW DEAL. In 1941 he traveled around the country to visit defense companies and concluded that there were abuses in defense contracting and in the location of defense plants. He succeeded in setting up the Senate Special Committee to Investigate the National Defense Program with himself as chair. Known as the Truman Committee, the panel set about uncovering and correcting waste and abuse in defense preparations for World War II. Truman's role on the committee earned him national prominence and the gratitude of Roosevelt. In later years Truman said he was genuinely surprised to be selected as Roosevelt's running mate in 1944.

Truman served nearly two full terms as president, winning election in his own right in 1948 when nearly all political observers had written him off as a certain loser to New York governor Thomas Dewey. Truman presided over the early years of the Cold War that became a half-century struggle with the United States and its Western allies on one side and the Soviet Union and its allies on the other. He pushed through the vast economic aid packages, particularly the Marshall Plan, that brought devastated Europe back from the ruins of World War II. Although Truman left office in 1952 as one of the least popular presidents in history, due to a stalemated war in Korea, various scandals in his administration, and growing industrial labor disputes, historians by the end of the century assessed him as one of America's most significant presidents.

Un-American Activities Committee

See INVESTIGATIONS.

Unanimous Consent

Proceedings of the House and Senate and action on legislation often take place upon the unanimous consent of the chamber. A unanimous consent request, as its name implies, can be blocked by a single objection.

Almost anything can be accomplished by unanimous consent. Both chambers use it to expedite floor action. Besides considering noncontroversial matters by unanimous consent, the Senate also uses a complex device called a UNANIMOUS CONSENT AGREEMENT to govern the consideration of most major legislation.

Minor matters in both chambers also are frequently handled by unanimous consent. A senator or representative will say, "I ask unanimous consent that…" and make a request. A legislator might ask to add additional material to the *CONGRESSIONAL RECORD* or seek permission to have a staff aide on the floor during debate. Such requests are handled routinely, and objections are extremely rare.

Unanimous Consent Agreement

The Senate has no procedure equivalent to the formal House rule that governs floor consideration of legislation, but senators often agree to set the order in which matters will be considered, impose time limits for debate, schedule votes for specific times, and require that amendments be germane to the bill. The device they use to expedite business is called a unanimous consent agreement. Senate leaders and interested senators from both parties privately work out such agreements, which are then formally proposed on the Senate floor. Because a single objection from a senator can prevent unanimous consent, the leaders are careful to accommodate even minor objections. Once reached, an agreement is binding on senators unless it is changed by unanimous consent. For major legislation the details of a proposed agreement, which can be quite specific, are printed and circulated to members in advance. (See LEADERSHIP; LEGISLATIVE PROCESS; RULE FOR HOUSE DEBATE.)

Underwood, Oscar W.

Oscar W. Underwood (1862–1929), an Alabama Democrat, served in the House of Representatives from 1895 to 1915, except for one brief interlude in 1896–1897. In 1915 he moved to the Senate, where he served until 1927. Underwood benefited from a House revolt in 1910 against the autocratic rule of Speaker Joseph G. CANNON, an Illinois Republican. When rules changes weakened the Speaker's authority, Underwood became the de facto ruler of the House.

In 1910 Oscar Underwood, an Alabama Democrat, became the de facto leader of the House, after a revolt against the autocratic rule of Speaker Joseph G. Cannon. Underwood also served twelve years in the Senate, where be rose to become floor leader.
Source: Library of Congress

Underwood was practicing law in Birmingham, Alabama, when he first ran for the House in 1894. He won but served only until June 1896, when he was replaced by his 1894 opponent who had successfully contested the election. Undaunted, Underwood ran again that year and won.

Underwood's particular legislative interest was tariffs. The Underwood Tariff Act of 1913 reduced protective tariffs on most imported goods; it also established the modern income tax system.

In 1910, after years of suffering under Speaker Cannon's despotic rule, a coalition of Democrats and Republicans changed House rules to strip the Speaker of much of his power. The elections of that year gave the Democrats a majority in the House. Anxious to organize into a voting bloc but unwilling to risk giving power to their own Speaker, the Democrats vested new authority in the chair of the Ways and Means Committee and in the majority leader. At the same time, they elected Underwood to both positions. (See WAYS AND MEANS COMMITTEE, HOUSE.)

As chair of Ways and Means, Underwood had the power to make committee assignments. He also controlled the Democratic caucus, which at that time had the power to tell members how to vote on the floor and in committee. The House Speaker, Missouri Democrat James B. "Champ" CLARK, was only a figurehead.

In the Senate, Underwood served as Democratic floor leader from 1921 to 1923. He resigned from the Senate after two terms. Twice, in 1912 and in 1924, Underwood was considered a candidate for the presidency. In 1924 he took a courageous stand against the popular Ku Klux Klan, a move that killed any presidential hopes he may have harbored.

V

Vandenberg, Arthur H.

Sen. Arthur Vandenberg (right), in an informal moment, pauses with his friend Jim Preston.
Source: Library of Congress

Arthur H. Vandenberg (1884–1951) was a Republican senator from Michigan from 1928 until his death. Vandenberg was an isolationist turned internationalist; his influential position in the Senate allowed him to play a critical role in the conduct of international relations in the years following World War II.

After a long career as editor of the Grand Rapids *Herald*, Vandenberg entered the Senate in 1928 to finish an unexpired term. He also was elected to a full term in the elections of the same year. In 1929, at the beginning of his first full term, Vandenberg joined the Senate Foreign Relations Committee. Vandenberg made his mark in the Senate as a member and later as chair of this committee.

Vandenberg supported ratification of the Treaty of Versailles and League of Nations covenant following World War I. Later he became an outspoken isolationist. During the 1930s he supported legislation that would keep the United

States free of foreign entanglements. During World War II, however, Vandenberg underwent a dramatic change of heart, in part because of his distrust of the Soviet Union.

Vandenberg took part in the planning of the United Nations and was one of eight U.S. representatives at the San Francisco Conference that drafted the United Nations Charter. Later he played a critical role in planning and implementing the Marshall Plan (economic aid to war-torn European countries) and Truman Doctrine (aid to Turkey and Greece). He sponsored the Vandenberg Resolution of 1948, which formed the basis of U.S. participation in the North Atlantic Treaty Organization. A bipartisan spirit characterized all his efforts in the field of foreign affairs.

Vandenberg was a colorful and emotional speaker. He enjoyed the national attention paid to him in 1947–1949, when Republicans controlled the Senate and he became chair of the Foreign Relations Committee, as well as president pro tempore of the Senate. Vandenberg wielded an unusual amount of power in the largely ceremonial post of president pro tempore; he participated in planning the legislative program and involved himself in debate while he was presiding over the chamber.

Veterans' Affairs Committees, House and Senate

Federal programs for veterans, ranging from health care to job counseling, are the responsibility of the House and Senate Veterans' Affairs committees. Both committees act within Congress as advocates of improved veterans' benefits.

The House committee, set up in 1946, for many years was dominated by conservative southerners with close ties to traditional veterans' lobbying groups, such as the American Legion and Veterans of Foreign Wars. The Senate created its committee in 1971, bucking a movement to eliminate committees with narrow jurisdictions. Its leaders were considered more sympathetic than their House counterparts toward Vietnam-era veterans. But by the late 1980s, the House committee had begun to shift its outlook, as younger members began questioning the panel's traditional orientation. At the same time the conflict between old-line veterans' lobbying groups and those representing Vietnam veterans eased. Despite budget constraints, the Veterans' Affairs committees' legislative successes included a new version of the education benefits under the GI Bill of Rights, first provided after World War II.

Texas Democrat Olin E. Teague, a decorated World War II veteran, spent almost two decades as chair of the House committee (1955–1973). He was followed by Mississippi Democrat G. V. "Sonny" Montgomery in 1981. When Republicans took control of the House in 1995, Bob Stump of Arizona became chair. Succeeding Stump in 2001 was Republican Christopher H. Smith of New Jersey. In 2007 the chair went to Bob Filner, a California Democrat.

The gavel changed hands far more often in the Senate panel. California Democrat Alan Cranston chaired the Senate committee from 1977 to 1981 and took over again from 1987 to 1993 when Democrats regained control of the Senate. In the intervening years, Wyoming Republican Alan Simpson led the committee from 1981 to 1985 and Alaska Republican Frank H. Murkowski from 1985 to 1987. Democrat John D. Rockefeller IV of West Virginia was chair from 1993 to 1995, when Simpson—and Republican control—returned. Republican Arlen Specter of Pennsylvania took over in 1997 and held the chairmanship until control of the Senate switched to the Democrats in mid-2001 and Rockefeller returned. The Republicans returned to power and Specter returned to the chair in 2003. In 2007, with Democrats back in control, the chair went to Daniel K. Akaka, a Hawaii Democrat.

The health care of troops returning from Iraq and Afghanistan is a chief concern of the House and Senate Veterans' Affairs committees. Iraq veteran Josh Dobblestein, photographed with some of his old military uniforms in March 2006, received care for posttraumatic stress disorder at a VA Hospital outside Chicago.
AP Images/Charles Rex Arbogast

Despite the frequent changes at the top, the Senate panel tended to operate free of partisanship. Smith and Lane Evans, the top Democrat on the House panel, worked closely as well.

In the 110th Congress starting in 2007, both panels faced similar issues of providing care for more soldiers returning from combat in Iraq and Afghanistan and improving the Veteran Affairs (VA) Department's catastrophic brain-injury and posttraumatic stress disorder care. The committees also were to examine VA budget problems. The agency suffered a nearly $3 billion shortfall in health care funding in 2005.

Vetoes

Perhaps the president's most potent power in dealing with Congress is the ability to veto legislation. A chief executive may use the veto as a negative weapon for blocking legislation he opposes, or he may use the threat of a veto to persuade Congress to approve the administration's legislative program or at least to compromise on key issues.

Article I, section 7 of the Constitution requires the president to approve or disapprove all legislation passed by Congress. If the president opposes a bill, he vetoes it and returns the legislation to Congress, together with a message giving his reasons for disapproving it.

The president's veto power is not absolute. Article I, section 7 gives Congress an opportunity to enact vetoed bills into law by again passing them by a two-thirds majority vote in each house. Congress, however, sustains far more vetoes than it overrides.

Veto Procedure

After both houses of Congress have passed a bill in identical form, the measure is sent to the White House. The president has ten days, excluding Sundays, in which to sign or veto it; the ten-day period begins at midnight on the day the bill is received. If the president takes no action on

A child protests President George W. Bush's veto of a children's health bill in October 2007. The House of Representatives was unable to override the decision, which Bush said was to prevent the State Childrens Health Insurance Program (SCHIP) from becoming too large in scope.

Source: AP Images/LM Otero

the measure within ten days, and Congress is in session, the bill automatically becomes law without the president's signature. However, if Congress has already adjourned and the president does not sign it within the ten-day period, the measure is killed, or "pocket-vetoed."

The Constitution specifies that the president shall return a rejected bill along with his objections to the house that originated the legislation. There is no deadline by which Congress must try to override the veto. It may act at any time during the Congress in which the bill is vetoed. Override attempts usually are made within weeks or even days of the veto. If the leadership decides Congress is unlikely to override the veto, it may decide not to schedule a vote. Or it may return the vetoed bill to the committee that had considered it. Occasionally, when the political climate is favorable, the committee will quickly draft a new version of the vetoed bill that satisfies the president's objections.

To override a veto, a quorum must be present, and the bill must be supported by two-thirds of the members voting in each chamber. If the first chamber to vote does not muster a two-thirds majority, the bill is dead and no further action is taken. If there is a two-thirds majority, the bill goes to the other chamber; a two-thirds vote there enacts the measure into law. (All legislation not enacted into law dies at the end of the Congress in which it was introduced.)

In the Senate, the question whether to override a presidential veto is debatable (and it may be filibustered, although this is rarely tried). A vetoed bill may not be amended. Only one vote to override is permitted. The Constitution requires recorded votes in each house on override attempts.

Historical Use

In the early years of the nation, the veto was seldom used. President George Washington issued the first veto, in 1792; the legislation was a congressional reapportionment bill. Until the administration of Andrew Jackson, presidents usually vetoed bills only if they believed the legislation was unconstitutional or defective in some manner. Three of the first six presidents did not veto a single bill. That pattern changed under Jackson, who vetoed twelve bills, more than the combined total of all his predecessors. More important, Jackson was the first chief executive to use the veto as a political weapon to further his legislative agenda and to kill bills he personally opposed.

After Jackson's administration, members of Congress saw the veto as a powerful weapon in the president's hands. The first attempt to impeach a president, John Tyler, resulted from his veto of a tariff bill. Proposals were introduced at the time to allow Congress to override vetoes by a simple majority rather than by a two-thirds vote. Nothing came of those attempts. President Andrew Johnson's post–Civil War struggle with the Radical Republicans in Congress led him to veto twenty-nine bills, a record up to that time. Congress responded with the first successful effort to override a veto on a major legislative issue.

President Grover Cleveland used the veto 584 times, a record that stood until the administration of Franklin D. Roosevelt. Many of Cleveland's vetoes were directed at preventing corruption that had mounted through the abuse of private pension bills.

Roosevelt vetoed 635 bills during his twelve years in office. All types of bills were targeted, including, for the first time, a revenue bill. Until that time it had been assumed that by precedent tax bills were immune from the presidential veto. Roosevelt dramatized his disapproval of one bill by personally delivering his veto message to a joint session of Congress.

Recent Use

Most presidents since World War II have made extensive use of the veto power. President Harry S. TRUMAN used it effectively to protect organized labor until the Republicans took control of Congress in the late 1940s, making it likely that his vetoes would be overridden. Republican president Dwight D. Eisenhower used the veto to block or limit new social welfare programs promoted by the Democrats when they controlled Congress during his final six years in office. Eisenhower's threat to use the veto power was just as important as the veto itself in stopping legislation he opposed.

> **CLOSER LOOK**
>
> The veto is considered the most potent weapon used by presidents in dealing with Congress because it gives them power to reject legislation. Although Congress can override a veto, the bar is high because a two-thirds majority in each house is required. The veto was used sparingly in the early days of the nation but became common after the mid-1800s. Most presidents since World War II have made extensive use of the veto power.

VETOES ISSUED AND OVERRIDDEN, 1789–2007

President	All bills vetoed	Regular vetoes	Pocket vetoes	Vetoes overridden
Washington	2	2	0	0
J. Adams	0	0	0	0
Jefferson	0	0	0	0
Madison	7	5	2	0
Monroe	1	1	0	0
J. Q. Adams	0	0	0	0
Jackson	12	5	7	0
Van Buren	1	0	1	
W. H. Harrison	0	0	0	0
Tyler	10	6	4	1
Polk	3	2	1	0
Taylor	0	0	0	0
Fillmore	0	0	0	0
Pierce	9	9	0	5
Buchanan	7	4	3	0
Lincoln	7	2	5	0
A. Johnson	29	21	8	15
Grant	93[1]	45	48[1]	4
Hayes	13	12	1	1
Garfield	0	0	0	0

(continues)

VETOES ISSUED AND OVERRIDDEN, 1789–2007 (CONTINUED)

President	All bills vetoed	Regular vetoes	Pocket vetoes	Vetoes overridden
Arthur	12	4	8	1
Cleveland (first term)	414	304	110	2
B. Harrison	44	19	25	1
Cleveland (second term)	170	42	128	5
McKinley	42	6	36	0
T. Roosevelt	82	42	40	1
Taft	39	30	9	1
Wilson	44	33	11	6
Harding	6	5	1	0
Coolidge	50	20	30	4
Hoover	37	21	16	3
F. D. Roosevelt	635	372	263	9
Truman	250	180	70	12
Eisenhower	181	73	108	2
Kennedy	21	12	9	0
L. Johnson	30	16	14	0
Nixon	43[2]	26	17[2]	7
Ford	66	48	18	12
Carter	31	13	18	2
Reagan	78	39	39	9
G. H. W. Bush	44[3]	29	15	1
Clinton	37	36	1	2
G. W. Bush[4]	8	7	1	1

SOURCE: Senate Historical Office.

NOTES:

1. Veto total listed for Grant does not include a pocket veto of a bill that apparently never was placed before him for his signature.
2. Includes Nixon's pocket veto of a bill during the 1970 congressional Christmas recess that was later ruled invalid by the District Court for the District of Columbia and the U.S. Court of Appeals for the District of Columbia.
3. Bush's total number of vetoes, listed here as 44, is controversial. Two additional actions by Bush, involving the pocket-veto procedure, have been described as vetoes. Bush asserted that he had issued pocket vetoes of HJ Res 390, involving thrift bailout rules, on August 16, 1989, and S 1176, involving a foundation named for former Rep. Morris K. Udall, on December 20, 1991. The first came during a congressional recess and the second following adjournment of the first session of the 102nd Congress. Senate experts say Bush's claim that these measures were pocket-vetoed would not stand constitutional scrutiny. The Constitution's veto provisions and Supreme Court cases on the power have established for many constitutional scholars that a true pocket veto can occur only after final adjournment of a Congress and not during recesses or between first and second sessions if Congress has taken certain steps allowing it to receive any veto message the president might send. This view is widely held in Congress but has been challenged by a number of presidents, including Bush. On the two Bush actions in question, HJ Res 390 and S 1176, congressional leaders believe that the measures became law without the president's signature, as occurs under the Constitution if a president takes no action on legislation sent to him before Congress's final adjournment. The issue is further muddied in the case of S 1176 because Congress later repealed it with a new bill, S 2184, which Bush signed while at the same time asserting that although he agreed with the measure he did not accept the congressional disclaimer that S 2184 repealed S 1176.
4. Through December 31, 2007.

Presidents John F. KENNEDY and Lyndon B. JOHNSON vetoed few bills; Johnson in particular had a large Democratic majority in Congress that favored his activist legislative agenda. Republican presidents Richard NIXON and Gerald R. FORD, however, followed Eisenhower's example in frequently vetoing social programs passed by Democratic-controlled Congresses. One of Nixon's most controversial vetoes was the 1973 War Powers Resolution, which Congress passed near the end of the Vietnam War in an effort to limit the president's flexibility to commit U.S. forces in battle zones overseas without congressional approval. Nixon argued that the bill was unconstitutional, claiming it infringed upon the president's powers as commander in chief. But with Nixon weakened politically by an unpopular war and the Watergate scandal, the House and Senate were able to override his veto.

Ford's use of the veto demonstrated its effectiveness. Despite large Democratic gains in the 1974 congressional elections, Ford was sustained on thirteen of the seventeen bills he vetoed in 1975. Another major bill was never sent to him because he had threatened to veto it.

Jimmy Carter was the first president since Truman to have a veto overridden by a Congress controlled by the president's own party. He suffered two such ignominious defeats in 1980.

Republican presidents Ronald Reagan and George H. W. Bush both used the veto and veto threat to great advantage. Faced with sizable Democratic majorities in both chambers, Bush made the veto and the veto threat the cornerstone of his legislative strategy. Bush was overridden only once, just before the end of the 1992 session, on a bill regulating cable television that was popular among consumers and both parties. Before that he had prevailed on thirty-five vetoes, often by shifting his position enough to win the support he needed. In 1991, for example, when recession deepened enough to make a second veto of extended unemployment benefits politically unwise, he negotiated a compromise.

Democratic president Bill Clinton did not veto a single bill during the 103rd Congress (1993–1995), in substantial part because his party controlled both houses of Congress. After Republicans took power in 1995, however, Clinton began to use the veto and the threat to veto to counter what the Democrats called an overly conservative Republican legislative agenda. In 1995, for example, Clinton vetoed a budget bill because he strongly disagreed with its proposed funding cuts. The impasse resulted in two shutdowns of the federal government, which turned into a public relations debacle for the inexperienced Republican leadership. The shutdowns also gave Clinton's faltering political career new life and greatly aided his reelection in 1996.

During his eight years in office, Clinton vetoed thirty-seven bills, seventeen in his first term and twenty in his second. Clinton was overridden only twice during his tenure, and one of those was to restore line-item vetoes he struck from a military construction bill. Clinton used the pocket veto only once, and that occurred in December 2000 during his last days in office. He did not use the pocket veto at all during his first term, making him the first president since Franklin Pierce (1853–1857) to serve an entire term without using the device. (See "Line-Item Veto," below.)

President George W. Bush used the veto sparingly. He did not veto any bills in his first five and one-half years in office. In mid-2006 he issued his first veto—a bill to expand stem cell research; it was upheld by Congress. Seven additional vetoes came in 2007 as Democrats, now in control of Congress, challenged the president on many issues. Bush continued to use the threat of a veto aggressively to warn Congress off actions he did not favor. This was an easy task when the GOP controlled both houses from 2001 to 2007, but with Democrats back in the majority in 2007 the tactic lost much of its potency.

Importance of Veto Power

The veto is a powerful tool because most presidents most of the time can muster the necessary support to defeat override attempts in Congress. Presidents need the support of only one-third plus one member in either house to sustain a veto. Those odds give the chief executive a great advantage. Even when Congress is controlled by the opposition political party, presidents who mobilizes all the LOB-BYING and public relations resources at their disposal usually can find the needed votes. President Woodrow Wilson once said the veto power made the president "a third branch of the legislature."

At each stage of the legislative process, senators and representatives, their staffs, and lobbyists for special interests must weigh the risk of a presidential veto if provisions opposed by the president are retained in legislation pending before Congress. Normally, most members of Congress would rather compromise with the president to gain presidential support than have a bill vetoed and face the task of trying to rally a two-thirds majority in each house to override the veto.

Decisions to veto legislation are scarcely made in a vacuum. Presidents receive advice from all sides of the issue. In the end, a president's veto decision is a collective one involving the White House staff, the heads of interested federal departments, the director of the Office of Management and Budget, key legislators of the president's party in Congress—and, when their interests are seriously affected, state and local officials, special interest groups, and influential private citizens. Some presidential vetoes are cast on principle, because the legislation is diametrically opposed to the president's policies or political philosophy. This was particularly true of the seven vetoes cast by President Bush in 2007. Many others are close calls, in which the president and his advisers must balance the provisions of the bill they support against those they oppose.

Congressional Leverage

The power to override is not the only leverage Congress can exert over presidential vetoes. Lawmakers have devised several ways to frustrate attempts by presidents to veto bills. The Senate often attaches riders to legislation regarded as essential or highly desirable by the White House, forcing the president to approve provisions he strongly opposes because they are part of bills he "must" sign. Essential legislation includes appropriations bill to maintain and run the federal departments, measures to raise the national debt limit, authorization bills for programs or activities actively promoted by the president, and various emergency measures.

In the 1980s Congress relied heavily on the continuing resolution. This is legislation incorporating many or all of the thirteen annual appropriations bills needed to run the federal government into one giant money bill, passed near the end of a session of Congress. The president must either sign the bill or veto it and watch the U.S. government run out of money and be forced to shut down temporarily. In such situations Congress often can disregard many of the president's recommendations and enact much of its own spending agenda. In 1988 President Reagan used his State of the Union address to denounce such practices.

Congress occasionally uses the presidential veto as a foil for its legislative goals. Particularly when the legislature is controlled by one party and the executive by the other, lawmakers who oppose the president may pass legislation with the expectation that it will be vetoed, or they may add amendments that they know will force the president to veto a particular bill. If it is an election year, they can then go home to their constituents and portray the president as heartless, indifferent, or out of touch with the public interest.

Presidents, of course, can do the same thing, by denouncing lawmakers or members of the opposition party as big spenders or the ones wanting to raise voters' taxes.

Pocket Veto Dispute

If the president does not act on a bill within the ten-day period specified in the Constitution, and Congress has adjourned, the bill is pocket-vetoed. The measure dies because the president is prevented from returning the legislation to Congress so that lawmakers can consider the vetoed bill. James MADISON was the first president to pocket-veto a bill, in 1812.

The pocket-veto provision continues to raise controversy. Nowhere in the veto provision is the meaning of adjournment spelled out. Presidents have interpreted it loosely, as covering short recesses and interim adjournments within a session. Congress has applied a very narrow definition, so that the word means only the final adjournment of a two-year Congress.

Twentieth-century presidents routinely pocket-vetoed bills during congressional recesses and adjournments of varying lengths. The practice unleashed a major controversy in the late 1920s when President Calvin Coolidge's pocket veto of a bill during a four-month recess was challenged. The case went all the way to the Supreme Court, which decided in favor of the president. The Court at that time broadly interpreted the president's power, holding that the president could pocket-veto bills any time a congressional recess or adjournment prevented the return of a vetoed bill to Congress within the ten-day period specified in the Constitution. Another Supreme Court decision nine years later limited this interpretation somewhat, but the issue remained murky.

In the early 1970s the question came up again. A pocket-veto controversy between Nixon and the Congress in 1973 was decided by a U.S. court of appeals in favor of the lawmakers' position. The court ruled that Nixon had acted improperly in pocket-vetoing a bill during a six-day congressional recess. A second case decided by the same court in 1976 broadened the ruling to prohibit the president from pocket-vetoing a bill during adjournments between sessions of the same Congress.

Despite these rulings, the pocket veto remains a contentious issue between the executive and legislative branches. In 1981 and 1983 Reagan pocket-vetoed bills between the first and second sessions of the 97th and 98th Congresses. In August 1985 a U.S. appeals court ruled that the president's veto between sessions of Congress was unconstitutional. Reagan was not prevented from returning the bill to Congress, the court ruled, because the House and Senate had appointed agents to receive the president's veto messages in the interim.

The first President Bush challenged these rulings by pocket-vetoing measures while Congress was in recess. Congress sometimes responded by passing compromise versions of the measures that included a repeal of the original legislation. Bush also claimed to have pocket-vetoed measures that he returned to Congress with a message explaining his objections. In those cases, Congress responded as if the rejection were a direct veto. Congress still insists that a pocket veto is valid only when a Congress has adjourned sine die. It seems likely that a definitive ruling on the issue will have to await action by the Supreme Court.

Line-Item Veto

Reagan and George H. W. Bush were strong proponents of giving presidents line-item veto authority over appropriations bills—empowering chief executives to reject the funding level approved by Congress for specific programs in an appropriations bill without being forced to veto the entire legislation. As in a regular veto, Congress could override the president's line-item veto by a two-thirds majority vote in each house.

Republicans, and some Democrats, contended that the president could use the line-item veto as a tool to control the federal budget. They maintained that it would give presidents an effective way to eliminate wasteful pork-barrel spending projects that members slip into the yearly appropriations bills. Opponents argued that the veto might usurp the powers of Congress and give presidents a club to use on members to pressure them to vote his way on legislation. They claimed it would also achieve limited fiscal results since some of the biggest federal spending would be beyond its reach, including programs for which spending was required by law. (See BUDGET PROCESS; PORK-BARREL POLITICS.)

In February 1992 the Senate rejected a Republican-sponsored amendment that would have given the president a line-item veto. A milder compromise was adopted by the House in October 1992, but it died when Congress adjourned.

The Republican-controlled Congress finally passed the Line Item Veto Act in 1996. President Clinton, between January 1997 and June 1998, used the law to cancel eighty-two provisions in

eleven laws. Congress overrode thirty-eight of the cancellations, all of them contained in one military construction bill. The president's use of the law was estimated to have saved some $869 million in spending and in tax breaks.

But court suits were filed quickly after Clinton first used the new veto power. On June 25, 1998, a six-member majority of the Supreme Court declared the law unconstitutional. In the majority opinion, Justice John Paul Stevens wrote that the line-item veto was "the functional equivalent of partial repeal of acts of Congress," even though "there is no provision in the Constitution that authorizes the president to enact, to amend, or to repeal statutes."

> *The line-item veto was "the functional equivalent of partial repeal of acts of Congress," even though "there is no provision in the Constitution that authorizes the president to enact, to amend, or to repeal statutes."*
>
> —*Justice John Paul Stevens* in the majority Supreme Court opinion in 1998 overturning the line-item veto law

Vice President

In addition to the role of presidential understudy, the vice president of the United States serves as the president of the Senate. Because the framers of the Constitution gave the position no real authority and the Senate has been disinclined to delegate power to an outsider, it is for the most part a ceremonial position.

The vice president does not participate in debates, unless permitted by a majority of the Senate, and votes only to break a tie. The vice president rarely presides over the chamber; the job usually falls to the PRESIDENT PRO TEMPORE.

When the vice president does preside, it is often by design. If close votes on administration bills are expected, the vice president is on hand to break the tie in favor of the president's position. The vice president occasionally uses the role of president of the Senate to issue parliamentary rulings that advance party floor strategy and to assist in the administration's legislative liaison efforts.

Origins and Development

The framers of the Constitution decided to give the vice president the Senate position to provide a job for the runner-up in the electoral vote and to give the Senate an impartial presiding officer without depriving any state of one of its two votes. Some objections to this arrangement were raised when the proposal was debated at the Constitutional Convention. George Mason complained that "it mixed too much the Legislative and the Executive." Elbridge Gerry thought it tantamount to putting the president himself at the head of the Senate because of "the close intimacy that must subsist between the president and the vice president." But Roger Sherman pointed out that "if the Vice President were not to be President of the Senate, he would be without employment."

Although the framers solved the problem of a job for the runner-up, the vice president was powerless to supply effective legislative leadership. Precedent was set by the first vice president, John Adams. Although he was clearly in general agreement with the majority of the Senate during his term as vice president, Adams perceived his role as simply that of presiding officer and made little effort to guide Senate action.

His successor, Democratic-Republican Thomas Jefferson, could not have steered the Federalist-controlled Senate if he had wanted to, but he did make an important contribution by compiling a manual of parliamentary procedure. (See *JEFFERSON'S MANUAL*.)

The next vice president, Aaron Burr, was so impartial that he even cost the Jefferson administration a victory or two in the Senate.

Other vice presidents were not content to sit on the sidelines. John C. CALHOUN, for example, was a commanding figure as vice president, and his influence was felt in the

CLOSER LOOK

The vice president of the United States serves as the president of the Senate as well as the presidential understudy. It has historically been a ceremonial position because the Constitution gives it no significant authority and the Senate has been disinclined to delegate power to an outsider. But some vice presidents, such as Al GORE and Richard CHENEY—have become powerful influences in the executive branch.

Senate before he resigned in 1832 to become a senator himself. Examples in the twentieth century included Charles Dawes, Calvin Coolidge's vice president, who campaigned actively though unsuccessfully against Senate rules allowing the FILIBUSTER and often openly supported legislation opposed by Coolidge. John Nance Garner, a former Speaker of the House, helped win congressional votes for New Deal legislation in Franklin D. Roosevelt's first term, although the two became estranged when Garner opposed the pace and scope of later proposals.

The most blatant power play in modern times occurred when Lyndon B. JOHNSON, a legendary Senate majority leader, sought to preside over Senate Democratic caucus meetings even after he became John F. KENNEDY's vice president. The proposal was rejected.

Vice President Thomas R. Marshall draws a capsule during a draft held under new selective service law in 1918.
Source: Library of Congress

Presiding Officers

Vice presidents have been given certain powers as presiding officers. For the most part, these powers can be overridden by the chamber. The duties include recognizing members seeking the floor; deciding points of order, subject to appeal to the full Senate; appointing senators to House-Senate conference committees (though the presiding officer usually appoints senators recommended by the floor manager of the bill); enforcing decorum; administering oaths; and appointing members to special committees.

Vice presidents occasionally become involved in parliamentary struggles while presiding over the Senate. In 1987, for example, Vice President George H. W. Bush became embroiled in a confrontation over an energy standards bill and some fairly obscure points of order under Senate rules. When the Democratic leadership began to take up the bill, which the Republicans hoped to delay, Bush rushed over from the White House to assist the Republican minority. After the Republicans had succeeded in their tactics to block immediate action, Bush was chastised by Senate Majority Leader Robert C. BYRD of West Virginia for a ruling that facilitated the delay. Bush insisted that he had done nothing wrong.

Ten years earlier, Byrd had delivered a similar rebuke to a vice president from his party, Walter F. Mondale, who presided over the Senate in 1977 during a prolonged battle over natural gas legislation. In a stinging, lengthy public lecture to Mondale, Byrd upbraided the vice president for trying to recognize Carter administration allies ahead of Minority Leader Howard H. BAKER Jr., a Tennessee Republican. Byrd reminded the vice president in cold, clear terms that Senate custom dictated that party leaders always be recognized when they sought the

CLOSER LOOK

Vice President Thomas R. Marshall frequently told a story about two brothers: "One ran away to sea; the other was elected vice president. And nothing was ever heard of either again." Marshall was vice president to Woodrow Wilson from 1913 to 1921. His view prevailed throughout much of the twentieth century; Franklin D. Roosevelt's first vice president, John Nance "Cactus Jack" Garner, described the office as "not worth a bucket of warm spit." But by recent decades and into the twenty-first century the veep position had increased significantly in importance. Al Gore, President Bill Clinton's vice president for eight years in the 1990s, played an important role in the administration. President George W. Bush's vice president, Dick Cheney, is widely considered the most important and influential person ever to hold the office.

floor. Less than two weeks later Mondale demonstrated how useful a vice president can be, when he and Byrd teamed up to bring to a halt a filibuster-by-amendment on that same gas bill. Mondale, reading from a typed script given him by Byrd, ruled a series of amendments out of order, while ignoring senators seeking to exercise their right to appeal his rulings.

Tie Votes

The vice president's constitutional authority to vote in the Senate in the event of a tie is a rarely used power, but a vital one when administration proposals are at stake. (See table, below.)

By the end of August 2007, vice presidents had cast 243 votes in the Senate. Some of these votes were recorded against questions that would have failed even if the vice president had not voted, because a question on which the Senate is evenly divided automatically dies. In such cases the vice president's negative vote is superfluous. Its only purpose is to make known the vice president's opposition to the proposal. No records are available showing how many of the tie-breaking votes cast by vice presidents were in the affirmative and thus decisive.

SENATE VOTES CAST BY VICE PRESIDENTS

Following is a list of the number of votes cast by each vice president.

Period	Vice president	Votes cast	Period	Vice president	Votes cast
1789–1797	John Adams	29	1901	Theodore Roosevelt	0
1797–1801	Thomas JeVerson	3	1905–1909	Charles W. Fairbanks	0
1801–1805	Aaron Burr	3	1909–1912	James S. Sherman	4
1805–1812	George Clinton	12	1913–1921	Thomas R. Marshall	8
1813–1814	Elbridge Gerry	6	1921–1923	Calvin Coolidge	0
1817–1825	Daniel D. Tompkins	3	1925–1929	Charles G. Dawes	2
1825–1832	John C. Calhoun	28	1929–1933	Charles Curtis	3
1833–1837	Martin Van Buren	4	1933–1941	John N. Garner	3
1837–1841	Richard M. Johnson	17	1941–1945	Henry A. Wallace	4
1841	John Tyler	0	1945	Harry S. Truman	1
1845–1849	George M. Dallas	19	1949–1953	Alben W. Barkley	7
1849–1850	Millard Fillmorc	3	1953–1961	Richard M. Nixon	8
1853	William R. King	0	1961–1963	Lyndon B. Johnson	0
1857–1861	John C. Breckinridge	9	1965–1969	Hubert H. Humphrey	4
1861–1865	Hannibal Hamlin	7	1969–1973	Spiro T. Agnew	2
1865	Andrew Johnson	0	1973–1974	Gerald R. Ford	0
1869–1873	Schuyler Colfax	17	1974–1977	Nelson A. Rockefeller	0
1873–1875	Henry Wilson	1	1977–1981	Walter F. Mondale	1
1877–1881	William A. Wheeler	6	1981–1989	George H. W. Bush	7
1881	Chester A. Arthur	3	1989–1993	Dan Quayle	0
1885	Thomas A. Hendricks	0	1993–2001	Al Gore	4
1889–1893	Levi P. Morton	4	2001–	Richard B. Cheney	7
1893–1897	Adlai E. Stevenson	2			
1897–1899	Garret A. Hobart	1	**Total**		**243**

SOURCE: Compiled by the Senate Historical Office from various sources. The Historical Office notes that the list may not include every occasion on which a vice president has voted to break a tie.
NOTE: Through January 31, 2008.

One crucial vote by a vice president was cast in 1846 when George M. Dallas broke a tie in favor of a Polk administration bill for tariff reform. Among other important vice-presidential votes were two cast by Woodrow Wilson's vice president, Thomas R. Marshall, on foreign policy issues. In 1916 his vote carried an amendment on a bill pledging full independence to the Philippines by March 4, 1921. (The amendment later was modified in conference.) In 1919 Marshall cast the deciding vote to table a resolution calling for withdrawal of U.S. troops from Russia.

In the 1980s Vice President George H. W. Bush used his vote to stave off attacks on Reagan administration defense programs, including chemical weapons, the MX missile, and the Strategic Defense Initiative. Altogether Bush was called upon seven times to break tie votes. Bush's vice president, Dan Quayle, never had to cast a tie-breaking vote. Al GORE, who served as vice president during the Clinton administration, voted only four times during his eight-year tenure—twice in 1993 on a budget reconciliation bill and once in 1994 on ethanol use and in 1999 on gun control legislation.

Richard B. CHENEY, who served as vice president during the George W. Bush administration, had cast seven tie-breaking votes by January 2008. He voted twice on a budget resolution in 2001 to break ties on amendments on Medicare and the "marriage penalty" tax, and once in 2002 on a trade bill amendment to provide loans for mortgage payments for displaced workers. In 2003, with the Senate under Republican control but closely divided, Cheney's vote was important to advance the tax reduction agenda of President George W. Bush. In April he broke a tie on a budget resolution crafted to allow a tax reduction of up to $550 billion. In May he cast two votes on the actual tax cut: one to exempt 50 percent of dividend payments from taxation in 2003, increasing to 100 percent in 2004 through 2006, and later on final approval of an overall tax reduction totaling $320 billion. The size of the tax cuts and the dividend and other sections were vigorously opposed by Democrats and some moderate Republicans.

Legislative Liaison

Many vice presidents have been well suited to the job of lobbying on behalf of their administration's policies—and of carrying back to the president advice and information from members of Congress. As of 2003, thirty-three of forty-five vice presidents previously had served in either the House or Senate, or both.

Yet only in recent decades have vice presidents been formally assigned liaison duties. Earlier vice presidents were considered to be legislative officers who could not be assigned executive duties without violating the SEPARATION OF POWERS doctrine. This view was held as recently as the 1940s and 1950s, although vice presidents were used in behind-the-scenes lobbying efforts.

Mondale, operating out of offices in the Capitol and a Senate office building, proved to be an effective spokesperson for the Carter White House on numerous occasions, as did Bush later for the Reagan administration. However, some argued that Gore played a more central role at the White House, not only in policy discussions and administration responsibilities, but also in the critical sector of media politics. Cheney was rarely used as the public spokesperson for Bush administration policies but worked behind the scenes on some of the administration's top legislative priorities, such as tax cuts and energy legislation. At the beginning of the administration, Republicans honored Cheney by offering him two congressional offices—the traditional ceremonial space for the vice president on the Senate side of the Capitol as well as a new office on the House side. By 2007 Cheney was increasingly described by journalists and scholars as the most powerful—and secretive—vice president in history. Reports continued to emerge about Cheney's operations that pictured him as a power-center in his own right, even while retaining the full support of President Bush.

Voters and Congress

Members of Congress play a dual role. As legislators, they pass laws and oversee the federal government's implementation of laws. As representatives, they listen to the views of voters back home and give voice to those views in Washington.

Members have attempted to balance the needs of the country as a whole against local concerns since the First Congress in 1789. The job has become even more challenging as the country and its national government have grown. Serving in Congress has become a full-time, year-round job. Constituencies have grown in size, diversity, and sophistication.

The president, congressional leaders, and national lobbyists all compete to win the support of legislators. But the home constituents hold the ultimate power. By definition, senators and representatives are successful politicians whose skills brought them to Congress in the first place. Not surprisingly, most are adept at courting public favor in their home states and districts.

Walter Faulkner, candidate for election to the House, speaks to a farmer in Tennessee in 1938.
Source: Library of Congress

Legislators keep themselves before the voters' eyes by making frequent trips back home, helping constituents with particular problems, sending out newsletters, and keeping a high profile in the local news. Paying attention to the voters back home has become even more important as the grass-roots influence of the political parties has waned in the decades since World War II.

Members also defend their electoral bases by playing the time-honored game of PORK-BARREL POLITICS, the effort to obtain federal projects and grants to benefit the home state or district. In addition to doling out the public works projects and other benefits traditionally known as pork, Congress makes countless decisions that can help or hurt a member's constituents—from the closing of a military base to the inclusion of a particular provision in the tax code. Legislators often attempt to influence decisions in their constituents' favor, especially if the constituents are individuals, corporations, or institutions powerful enough to influence the outcome of an election.

Pork and constituent service are among the many advantages incumbents enjoy in congressional elections. Name recognition, a staff paid from public coffers, and media access are others. But in spite of these advantages most lawmakers feel anything but secure and campaign almost continuously. This is especially true of House members whose terms are only two years. This insecurity intensified in the early 1990s as a wave of anti-incumbent sentiment swept the nation and incumbents began to do less well at the polls. By the 1994 elections this trend had become inflamed by scandals in the House and unpopular policies of Democratic president Bill Clinton. Thirty-four House incumbents, all of them Democrats, lost their seats. This, together with a ten-seat shift in the Senate, resulted in the first Republican Congress in forty years.

Four years later in 1998 voter attitudes had changed again. During the midterm elections that year voters did none of what they were anticipated to do; they refused to turn against Clinton for his scandal involving a White House intern, and they ignored electoral precedent by increasing the number of seats the president's party held in Congress. Democrats picked up five seats in the House.

The 2002 midterm elections provided an affirmation of President George W. Bush's popularity in the aftermath of the September 11, 2001, terrorist attacks. Bush's aggressive campaigning on behalf of Senate and House candidates and his showcasing of national security issues allowed Republicans to retake control of the Senate in the 108th Congress (2003–2005) and also expand their majority in the House.

But in 2006, much the same voter backlash as had occurred in 1994 came once again, this time throwing Republicans out of control of both the House and Senate. Republicans lost a number of seats normally safe for the GOP. The turnaround came as the nation became increasingly weary with the war in Iraq that Bush launched in 2003, and following a series of scandals in 2005 and 2006 that largely affected GOP incumbents in Congress.

In the Senate the six-year term provides at least a modest shelter from outside pressures, allowing a senator to concentrate on national issues, free from political distractions, during the first part of his or her term. Yet it remains true that reelection rates for senators run behind those for House members in most election years. Since the end of World War II Senate reelection rates have averaged less than 80 percent; House rates have generally exceeded 90 percent. While there is no firm explanation for lower Senate return rates, most researchers believe that more high-profile campaigns, and stronger, better-known, and adequately financed challengers, make Senate races more competitive than most House races.

"You send me to Washington to represent you in the Senate. But you do not send me there because you are interested in grave questions of national or international policy. When I come back to Arizona, you never ask me any questions about such policies; instead you ask me: 'What about my pension?' or 'What about that job for my son?' I am not in Washington as a statesman. I am there as a very well paid messenger boy doing your errands."

—Attributed to Sen. Henry Fountain Ashurst, an Arizona Democrat who served from 1912 to 1941, by Thomas C. Donnelly in *Rocky Mountain Politics* (1940)

CLOSER LOOK

Why Members Leave Congress

Congress has often been derided by critics of the institution as a gravy train—six-figure incomes, plentiful perks, and life-long employment—for the winners that voters send to Congress. Members of Congress increasingly do not see it that way.

Although once true that election to Congress amounted to secure employment in public life, increasingly in recent decades even members with safe seats, ample campaign funds, and influential positions decide not to seek voter approval for another term. Members themselves cite a variety of reasons for this declining commitment to lengthy careers in Congress.

Work in the modern Congress invokes a relentless schedule of meetings, pressure from lobbyists of special interest groups, endless campaign fund raising, and constant travel between Washington and home districts and states. This workload extracts a significant toll on member's personal and family life. Cost also is a frequently cited consideration, with members maintaining two residences and, for younger members, wrestling with such parental issues as the cost of college education for children. Other members cite the nasty partisanship that has characterized congressional politics in recent decades combined with the negative campaigning that for many goes on year-round. Members also bemoan the absence of time to carefully consider complex issues to gain enough knowledge to vote intelligently, rather than merely responding to endless entreaties of lobbyists. Recent imposition of term limits on committee and subcommittee chairs forced members from positions of influence after waiting patiently for years to achieve that influence. The consistently low opinion of Congress and politicians generally held by Americans also has helped persuade some members to find another line of work.

Scholars and other long-time observers of Congress also have noted a decline in interest in public service. Some observers believe this is related to growing cynicism about government and work in the public arena. Others suggest that turnover reflects changes in the way all workers today see their careers as many of them hold a number of jobs in their lifetimes.

Constituent Casework

Members court constituents by helping them deal with the federal government, an activity known as casework. Congressional caseworkers help constituents obtain Social Security and veterans' benefits, apply for passports and patents, interpret immigration laws, make unemployment claims, and resolve disputes with the Internal Revenue Service.

The number of services performed for constituents has skyrocketed as the federal government has expanded into many areas directly affecting the private lives of individuals. The lawmaker's STAFF handles most casework; more and more of it is being done in district and state offices. Because of the volume of constituent problems, federal agencies and the military services have special liaison offices to assist members. The Department of Veterans Affairs, military services, and Office of Personnel Management maintain offices on Capitol Hill.

Many "cases" are simply requests for information about legislation, government programs and regulations, or tourist information about Washington, D.C. Schools and other organizations often ask for an American flag that has flown over the CAPITOL BUILDING. Many members willingly supply such flags, which are hoisted over the Capitol on a flagpole put up especially for this constituent service.

Constituent Communications

Successful members of Congress communicate frequently and effectively with their constituents. They rely on constituent mail (including electronic mail or e-mail), surveys, polls, district office reports, and trips home to monitor voters' sentiments. They keep constituents informed about their activities through mass mailings, computer technology, radio and television appearances, and meetings. These contacts are financed at least in part by special allowances to incumbent members of Congress.

At one time a single clerk could handle a member's mail, but mail now consumes a large share of congressional staff time. E-mail has compounded the problem. Annual e-mail messages to Congress had exceeded 48 million by 2000 and were increasing at a rate of 1 million per month. Despite the high volume, letters and e-mails are an imprecise measure of voter sentiment, since few Americans ever write to their representatives and senators. Much legislative mail—along with telegrams and telephone calls—is inspired by pressure groups through well-organized grassroots lobbying campaigns. Outgoing mail also has continued to mushroom. One of members' most valuable perquisites is the franking privilege, which allows them to mail letters and packages under their signatures without being charged for postage. Members use the franking privilege to mail public documents, such as bill texts and committee reports, as well as copies of speeches and articles reprinted in the *Congressional Record*.

Legislators also use the frank to send out newsletters, express concern about state and district problems, and ask for constituents' views on particular issues.

Controversy surrounding the frank led Congress to restrict the kinds of mail that can be sent out free and to prohibit mass mailings in the period just prior to elections (sixty days for senators and ninety days for representatives). Despite these restrictions, there are more mailings in election years.

Effective members make good use of the news media to communicate with their constituents. The party organizations in the House and Senate operate radio and television facilities that members use to prepare programs for broadcast back home at a fraction of the cost of private taping facilities. Some members tape periodic reports to constituents that are broadcast courtesy of local radio and television stations. Members often respond to breaking news by taping a short commentary that can be incorporated into local newscasts. The profusion of all-news cable television channels and talk radio programs has only added outlets for willing members to promote their views or comment on national and international events.

Most members and their staffs also go out of their way to accommodate the newspapers back home. Members cultivate good relations with Washington-based reporters for local papers, make themselves available for interviews, and offer reporters a steady stream of press releases touting their accomplishments in Congress.

Benefiting from the technological revolution in communications, congressional offices use sophisticated telephone services, fax machines, and e-mail attachments to disseminate press releases and stay in touch with constituents. Members use computers to print and address their mail and to target mailings to constituents who have indicated an interest in a particular issue. Virtually all legislators now maintain Web sites to inform constituents of their positions and latest activities, and to facilitate communications. By 2007, e-mail rather than postal mail was widely used for communications between members and constituents.

High-tech communications aside, members know the importance of meeting with their constituents in person, both in Washington and back home. Most constituents who visit Capitol Hill are tourists hoping to pose for a photograph with their representative, shake hands, or perhaps receive passes to the House or Senate visitors' gallery. Members and their staffs usually are eager to welcome these visitors, aware that good impressions are remembered at election time.

But the number of constituents who visit Washington is limited, and a member of Congress must return home frequently to stay in touch. Only a few decades ago, most members remained in Washington for the duration of the legislative session. Jets now make it possible to go home every weekend, even when home is as far away as Hawaii. Most junior House members can be seen in their districts at least two weekends a month. Senators and representatives are permitted to take an unlimited number of trips home and to spend as much as they wish within their official expense accounts.

Legislative business is scheduled to accommodate members' travel. Most weeks the House operates on a Tuesday-through-Thursday work schedule, allowing members to spend four-day "weekends" in their home districts. Frequent "district work periods" permit longer stays. The Senate, which previously had a four-day working week, established a new schedule in 1988 that generally called for three full five-day workweeks followed by one week off. The new schedule was designed to allow senators to plan for their visits home and to stay longer once they got there. But the Senate's schedule has continued to fluctuate under different leaders.

More on this topic:

Computers in Congress, p. 121

Congressional Record, p. 135

Franking Privilege, p. 237

Lobbying, p. 359

Pay and Perquisites, p. 410

CLOSER LOOK ◉

Most members of Congress keep in touch with constituents by providing services and information they hope will encourage voters to re-elect them. But on rare occasions a member—sometimes reflecting the frustrations of colleagues with constituent demands—will be more blunt. Rep. John Steven McGroarty, a California Democrat who served in the House from 1935 to 1939, voiced this frustration (as quoted in John F. Kennedy's *Profiles in Courage*): "One of the endless drawbacks of being in Congress is that I am compelled to receive impertinent letters from a jackass like you in which you say I promised to have the Sierra Madre reforested and I have been in Congress two months and haven't done it. Will you please take two running jumps and go to hell."

On trips home, members sandwich in speeches, civic meetings, ribbon cuttings, fundraising events, district office hours, political consultations, coffee hours, breakfasts, luncheons, dinners, and picnics. While making the rounds, members are presenting what has been called their "home styles" to convince voters to trust them.

A classic example of "home style" is provided by former House Speaker Sam RAYBURN. A powerful Democrat who served as Speaker during the 1940s and 1950s, Rayburn became a plain dirt farmer when he returned home to his east Texas district. His drawl thickened, his attire changed from a business suit to khakis and a slouch hat, and he traveled in an old pickup truck rather than a limousine.

Members maintain offices in their home districts or states and sometimes even have mobile offices to make themselves more accessible to voters. The offices are funded by members' allowances. With the aid of computer technology, legislators have been shifting some constituent services—such as answering letters and casework—away from Washington and back to their local offices.

Voting in Congress

Every law must be voted on by the House and Senate. Although many votes are taken informally, with verbal yeas and nays and no record of individual positions, senators and representatives cast formal floor votes at least several hundred times a year. On those votes, each individual position is recorded in the *CONGRESSIONAL RECORD*. Months and sometimes years of work in committees come to fruition, or fail, as the House and Senate vote.

The House and Senate have each developed their own procedures for voting. Guiding them in many cases are voting rules spelled out in the Constitution. Most specific are requirements for roll-call votes, or what the Constitution calls the "yeas and nays." One rule is aimed at preventing secret ballots: "The yeas and nays of the members of either house on any question shall, at the desire of one fifth of those present, be entered on the Journal." For votes to override presidential vetoes, the Constitution is even more specific: "In all such cases the votes of both houses shall be determined by yeas and nays, and the names of persons voting for and against the bill shall be entered on the Journal."

Members vote on legislation on the House floor using one of these electronic voting devices. In the Senate voting is done by either voice or roll-call votes.
Source: CQ Photo/Scott J. Ferrell

The ritual of voting is interesting to watch even when the question is minor, and votes on major issues can be quite dramatic. When a vote is pending, a system of bells and lights is used to summon senators and representatives from their offices to the Capitol.

House members stream into their chamber through several different entrances. They pull from their pockets white plastic cards, which they insert into one of more than forty voting boxes mounted on the backs of chairs along the aisles. Each member punches a button to indicate his or her position, and a giant electronic board behind the Speaker's desk immediately flashes green for yes and red for no next to the member's name. For those who are more cautious, yellow signals a vote of present, usually changed later to reflect support or opposition. On close votes, tension builds as the fifteen minutes allowed for the vote run out. Boisterous members sometimes shout when the tally for their side hits the number needed for victory.

The House seems a bastion of high technology when compared with the Senate, where there is no electronic voting. When the Senate takes a roll-call vote, a clerk goes through the alphabet, reading each name aloud and pausing for an answer. Most senators miss the name call; when they enter the chamber, the clerk calls their name again, and they vote. On major questions the chamber fills with senators staying to hear the final result. Although party leaders keep a tally, the official vote is not announced until voting has been completed. In contrast to the rowdier House, the noise level is kept low by the gavel of the presiding officer, who must be able to hear the clerk and the senators' replies.

Voting has been a frequent target of reformers on Capitol Hill. In response to House members' complaints that all too often they must interrupt other business to come to the floor for votes, party leaders have tried to schedule several votes together and discourage members from seeking votes on unimportant questions, or those on which they have little chance of victory. Senators have had similar complaints about time-consuming votes, which often have taken more than the fifteen minutes set aside, because party leaders waited for late arrivals. In recent years the Senate leadership has tried to be stricter about keeping votes within the time limit.

Voting records are not a perfect measure of a member's politics. Controversial questions are often resolved without a clear vote. The language of amendments is often complicated, leaving members confused about what position to take. Local considerations can prompt a member to reject a bill that he or she supports philosophically. Party leaders sometimes intentionally avoid a vote to protect members from having to take an unpopular stand. As a result of these shortcomings, voting records are inevitably incomplete, but they are still the best available yardstick of members' views. The records also provide a way to measure how far Congress supports the president and whether parties or regions are voting together.

House Voting

Three types of votes are used regularly in the House: voice; standing, or division; and votes recorded by the name of the member ("yeas and nays" or "recorded vote"). The vast majority of House votes are cast when the House sits as the Committee of the Whole, a type of session used often for amending legislation because rules governing it are less restrictive than those that apply to the full House.

Voice Vote

The quickest method of voting is by voice vote. Even on controversial questions, voice votes may be held first, followed by more complex voting methods. The presiding officer calls first for the ayes and then for the noes. A chorus of members shouts in response to each question. The chair determines the results. If the chair is in doubt, or if a single member requests a further test, a standing vote is in order.

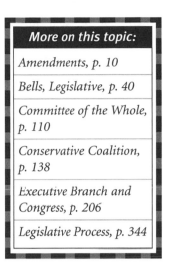

More on this topic:

Amendments, p. 10

Bells, Legislative, p. 40

Committee of the Whole, p. 110

Conservative Coalition, p. 138

Executive Branch and Congress, p. 206

Legislative Process, p. 344

CLOSER LOOK

Every law must be voted on by the House and Senate. Over the years Congress has become increasingly open about recording the votes of members in order that voters— as well as others, such as lobbyists—know where a senator or representative stands on an issue. Until the 1970s the House was particularly evasive by using voting techniques that made it difficult to impossible to track individual member's votes. Since reforms in that decade, votes on crucial issues usually are on the record. Even so, controversial questions may not be resolved by a clear vote. Often the language of an amendment is complicated or unclear, or parliamentary procedures are used to cloak members' views on a subject.

Standing or Division Vote

In a standing, or division, vote those in favor and then those opposed to the question stand while a head count is taken by the chair. Only the total vote on each side is announced; there is no record of how individual members voted. Few issues are resolved at this stage. If the issue was important enough for members to seek a standing vote, then the losing side, hoping to reverse the outcome, usually will ask for a vote in which members are recorded by name. This third type of vote draws many more members to the chamber.

Recorded Vote

A vote in which members are recorded by name is called the "yeas and nays" or a "recorded vote" depending on the circumstances in which it is taken, but the result is identical.

These votes are tallied through an electronic voting system. Votes are recorded individually as members insert their voting cards in the voting boxes in the chamber. A vote may be ordered upon demand of one-fourth of a quorum (twenty-five) when the House is meeting as the Committee of the Whole. One-fifth of a quorum (forty-four) is required when the House is meeting in regular session.

Until 1971 the "yeas and nays," provided for by the Constitution, were the only votes on which House members were individually recorded. Votes in the Committee of the Whole were taken by methods that did not reveal the stands of individual members. Many questions were decided by teller votes; the chair appointed tellers representing opposite sides on a vote and directed members to pass between them up the center aisle to be counted—first the ayes, then the nays.

Only vote totals were announced on traditional teller votes, but the Legislative Reorganization Act of 1970 opened the way for "tellers with clerks," or recorded teller votes. This procedure made it possible to record the votes of individual members for the first time in the Committee of the Whole. After the electronic voting system was installed in 1973, the recorded teller vote became known simply as a recorded vote.

Old-style teller votes in which members walked by stations where the numbers for and against a question were counted were abolished in 1993 on the grounds that they wasted time.

Use of the electronic system has blurred the distinction between yeas and nays and other recorded votes. Before the electronic voting system was installed, yeas and nays were taken by calling the roll, a time-consuming process in the 435-member House; each roll call took about half an hour. The Speaker still retains the

---

Hotlining Bills

Although most voting in the Senate on bills and amendments occurs in the chamber and is usually recorded in a roll call, an alternative device has been in use in recent years. By 2007 this alternative voting procedure was drawing increasing attention and controversy.

The procedure is called hotlining, a term that defined both a process and a mechanism. It is intended as a quick and efficient way to clear noncontroversial or less controversial bills for floor action—in effect, passage by unanimous consent, which has long been a traditional mechanism to approve bills that have little opposition. The procedure involves special phones installed in each senator's office. The leadership of both parties, having agreed on legislation or routine procedural motions that are sufficiently noncontroversial to pass by unanimous consent, separately send a phone message to members of their party saying that a bill, or a procedural motion, will be brought up for approval by unanimous consent at a certain time. The messages also say that if no objection is heard from the senator in a specified time period—sometimes as short as fifteen to thirty minutes—the leadership would assume the senator approves of, or at least has no objections to, the bill or motion.

Controversy over the procedure's use became more pronounced in 2007, even though some senators had voiced concerns earlier. Critics said the procedure was being used to push through many bills, some involving expenditures into the millions of dollars, without sufficient review or debate, or even giving senators an opportunity to review the proposal. The criticism came particularly from conservative senators who pointed to substantial expenditures required by some bills that were hotlined. Even some critics outside Congress, however, said the process detracted from congressional transparency and accountability.

right to call the roll rather than use the electronic system. The old-fashioned method is used when the electronic system breaks down, as it does from time to time.

Senate Voting

Only two types of votes are in everyday use in the Senate: voice votes and roll-call votes ("yeas and nays"). Standing, or division, votes are seldom employed. The Senate does not use the teller vote and has no electronic voting system.

As in the House, the most common method of deciding issues is by voice vote. The presiding officer determines the outcome. To obtain a roll-call vote, the backing of one-fifth of the senators present on the floor is needed.

The Senate usually allows fifteen minutes for a roll-call vote, although UNANIMOUS CONSENT requests may shorten the voting time in specific situations. The fifteen-minute period also may be extended to accommodate late-arriving senators.

Pairs, House and Senate

Both the House and Senate permit their members to "pair" on recorded votes as a way of canceling out the effect of absences. A member who expects to be absent for a vote pairs off with someone on the opposite side of the issue in question, and both agree not to vote. Pairs are voluntary, informal arrangements. They are not counted in tabulating the final results and have no official standing. However, members pairing are identified in the *Congressional Record,* along with their positions on such votes.

There are two types of pairs in current use:

• A *live pair* involves a member who is present for a vote and another who is absent. The member in attendance votes and then withdraws the vote, announcing that he or she has a live pair with a certain colleague and stating how the two members would have voted, one in favor, the other opposed. (If a two-thirds majority is required, there need to be two votes on one side and one on the other.) A live pair may affect the outcome of a closely contested vote, since it subtracts one yea or one nay vote from the final tally. In modern practice, live pairs appear from time to time in the Senate but are extremely rare in the House.

• A *specific pair,* used only in the Senate, does not affect the vote. When a senator anticipates being absent, he or she may ask to be paired with another absent member on the opposite side of the issue. Party staff develop the pairings, and then the opposing stands of the two senators are identified and printed in the *Record.* (A member also can ask unanimous consent to insert a statement in the *Record* directly after a vote indicating how he or she would have voted, which is common practice.) The House voted to abolish specific pairs at the beginning of the 106th Congress in 1999.

Informal Votes

Not all legislative or parliamentary questions are decided by formal votes. Uncontested bills, amendments, and motions, such as quorum calls, may be disposed of quickly if no one voices an objection. The terms used on the floor are "without objection" and "unanimous consent."

W

War Powers

Article I, section 8 of the Constitution assigns several different powers to Congress. Among these are the so-called war powers, which include the authority to declare war, raise and support an army, provide and maintain a navy, and make rules regulating the armed forces. At the same time, the Constitution in Article II, section 2 designates the president to be the commander in chief of the military. How these powers of the legislative and executive branches mesh—or conflict—is the subject of a debate that dates back to the Constitutional Convention.

Constitutional Background

During the drafting of the Constitution in Philadelphia in summer 1787, the framers debated whether to give the war-making power to Congress or the executive branch. Notes of the convention reflect how the framers struggled with the issue. At that time the war-making power in all other countries was vested in the executive. Because the excesses of the British monarchy were still fresh in the delegates' minds, they decided to split the responsibility. Congress was given the power to "declare" war, while the president was assigned the responsibility for conducting wars. James MADISON expressed the majority view at the Constitutional Convention when he said that government officials who wage wars are not the best judges of "whether a war ought to be commenced." The Convention delegates recognized, however, that if Congress declared war, the president as commander in chief should conduct it without interference. The delegates agreed that the president should have the flexibility to repel an armed attack or a sudden invasion without first seeking a declaration of war from Congress.

Congress's War Powers

Despite this explicit division of the powers to declare and conduct war, the roles of the legislative and executive branches have not evolved as the framers of the Constitution envisioned. Throughout history the chief executive has been the dominant force in decisions of war and peace, while Congress has played a secondary role.

Since the nation's founding, American armed forces have engaged in numerous major and minor conflicts overseas. Estimates of the number of times military forces have been used abroad vary, ranging from more than one hundred to several hundred. But Congress has formally declared war on only five occasions, and in only one of these, the War of 1812, did Congress debate the merits of committing the nation to war. In the 1846 war with Mexico, and in the first and second world wars, the president committed the nation to war, and

CLOSER LOOK ◎

The Constitution assigns Congress the power to declare war and raise and fund armed forces. The Constitution, however, designates the president as commander in chief of the military. These intertwining sources of power have never been fully resolved, but the president over the years has become the dominant force in taking the nation to war. On some occasions that has occurred with approval of Congress. Most wars, however, have not been explicitly declared, and Congress has never found a fully satisfactory way to influence military actions—short of cutting off funding, which it has not done.

In December 1941 President Franklin D. Roosevelt asked Congress to declare war on Japan following the Japanese attack on the U.S. naval base at Pearl Harbor on December 7, pictured here.
Source: Franklin D. Roosevelt Library

Congress merely ratified his decision. In the Spanish-American War in 1898, a strongly expansionist Congress forced a declaration of war on President William McKinley. Only with America's entry into World War II, in response to Japan's bombing of Pearl Harbor, could it be said that the president took military action in the face of a sudden armed attack on the United States.

In the Civil War, the Union insisted that it was putting down a rebellion in the Southern states and, technically, not waging a war with the Confederacy. By that reasoning, a declaration of war could not be considered. No declaration was made or requested in the Naval War with France (1798–1800), the First Barbary War (1801–1805), the Second Barbary War (1815), or the various Mexican-American clashes of 1914–1917.

Similarly, in modern times there was no formal declaration of war in the full-scale wars in Korea (1950–1953), Vietnam (1961–1973), the Persian Gulf (1991), and Iraq (2003). In a few instances, however, Congress passed a policy resolution supporting a presidential decision to use force. The Persian Gulf resolution of 1991, in which Congress supported the use of force if needed to oust Iraqi invading forces from Kuwait, was regarded by many as the functional equivalent of a declaration of war. Eleven years later few questions were raised about Congress's intent when lopsided majorities voted to give the executive unprecedented authority to wage a preemptive war against Iraq. There was no such consensus on claims by President Lyndon B. JOHNSON's administration that a 1964 resolution, known as the Tonkin Gulf resolution, authorized the executive to wage war in Vietnam.

Funding Powers

Besides its constitutional power to declare war, Congress also has the power to raise and support the armed forces of the United States. Through the use of its power of the purse, Congress provides appropriations to fund the military establishment.

The funding power can be a potent weapon. Congress has used it to influence foreign policies dealing with, among other things, economic and military aid and arms control. For example, in the 1980s, over President Ronald Reagan's objections, Congress refused to continue funding the efforts by Nicaraguan rebels (known as "contras") to overthrow Nicaragua's leftist Sandinista government. Administration officials' attempts to circumvent the congressional restrictions led to the Iran-contra affair.

Congress has rarely used this power to shut off funds for ongoing military operations abroad. Despite congressional complaints in recent years that the president has committed U.S. forces to trouble spots overseas without consulting Congress, lawmakers repeatedly have refused to use their power over appropriations as a way of forcing the chief executive to reverse policy. Once U.S. forces are engaged in hostilities, the last thing members of Congress want to do is to expose themselves to accusations that they are jeopardizing national security or the lives of Americans. Even during the unpopular war in Vietnam, Congress repeatedly voted funds to carry on the fighting. The Johnson and Nixon administrations cited those military appropriations bills, along with legislation to extend the military draft, to justify waging the war. Congress in 1970 barred the use of ground forces—but not aircraft—in Cambodia, but the vote came months after U.S. troops had been withdrawn. Only after the United States had pulled out of Vietnam but was continuing to bomb Cambodia and Laos did Congress in 1973 vote to bar funds for further combat activity in Indochina.

More recently, Congress in 1993 pressured President Bill Clinton to set a specific deadline for withdrawal of U.S. troops from Somalia after a U.S. humanitarian mission to that country turned into a bloody military operation under United Nations command. Congress then wrote into law a ban on any funding for the operation beyond that date without congressional authorization. In 1994 Congress barred funds for U.S. military participation in hostilities in Rwanda, but all U.S. troops had departed by the time the legislation was enacted.

Other Powers

Congress also retains authority to regulate the size and makeup of the armed forces. Through legislation it limits the number of personnel in the various military services.

The Constitution places an important qualification on the legislature's power to raise and support the armed forces. Congress is prohibited from appropriating such funds for more than two years, ensuring that its decisions will be debated and reviewed periodically. In actual practice, Congress today appropriates annually the money to maintain the armed forces.

Children run alongside a U.S. Marine M-1 Abrams tank during an armored patrol in north Mogadishu, Somalia. In 1993 Congress, displeased with U.S. peacekeeping presence in Somalia, threatened to cut off funding to pressure President Bill Clinton to set a troop withdrawal date.
Source: AP Images/Mark Duncan

Presidential War Powers

Presidential assertion of the war powers has drastically eroded Congress's prerogatives. Presidents have not hesitated to use their power as commander in chief to the fullest. Since the early days of the nation, presidents have sent armed forces into battle without first consulting Congress, much less asking for a declaration of war.

Presidential exercise of war powers has increased since World War II. In addition to the wars in Korea, Vietnam, the Persian Gulf, and Iraq, the United States has been involved in lesser fights on land, sea, and in the air—none under a declaration of war. The list includes Marine landings in Lebanon, air strikes against Libya and Iraq, the taking of the island of Grenada, the overthrow of the Panamanian government, combat action in Somalia, the occupation of Haiti, military initiatives in Bosnia and Kosovo, and war-on-terrorism operations against the Taliban regime and al Qaeda terrorists in Afghanistan. There have been harbor minings, Persian Gulf patrols, a blockade of Cuba, interdictions of shipping, seizures at sea, and combat in the sky. Beyond that were various surrogate wars fought with U.S. encouragement and equipment on three continents.

Justifications for Actions

Presidents have justified their use of the armed forces abroad on a variety of grounds, including their position as commander in chief; their sworn duty to preserve, protect, and defend the Constitution; their responsibility to protect the United States against invasion or surprise attack and to protect American citizens and interests; their claims to inherent and exclusive powers as the nation's chief executive; and United Nations and North Atlantic Treaty Organization (NATO) obligations.

The president's responsibility to defend the country and protect American citizens has been invoked to explain U.S. participation in wars and limited armed actions in which the United States was not threatened by imminent invasion or attack. The word *security* has acquired a much broader meaning than was understood by the framers of the Constitution. Modern presidents have come to view major economic dislocations and international terrorism as posing as much of a threat to U.S. security as military attacks.

With a large standing military force and an annual defense budget in the hundreds of billions of dollars, the president has been able to make military commitments without first requesting additional funds from Congress.

Congressional Role

Congress itself has been a party to this expansion of the president's war powers. When U.S. troops entered combat in Korea and in Vietnam, Congress did not make a serious effort to debate the merits of declaring war or to encourage the president to seek its approval. In neither war did the chief executive acknowledge that a declaration of war was warranted or required by the Constitution. In Korea, U.S. troops were sent to battle under the auspices of the United Nations; in Vietnam, Congress approved the controversial Gulf of Tonkin resolution, which President Lyndon JOHNSON later insisted was equivalent to a declaration of war. Congress repealed the resolution in 1970.

A somber and historic debate preceded passage of the 1991 Persian Gulf resolution, but underlying it was a sense that the legislative branch had acted too late to have any real choice except to back President George H. W. Bush in his showdown with Iraq. By the time Congress finally debated the authorization for war, months of feuding with the White House over the constitutional role of the two branches seemed beside the point.

After three days of debate in the House and five in the Senate, Congress in 2002 voted overwhelmingly to give President George W. Bush sweeping authority to launch a preemptive strike against Iraq. Although war with Iraq was still a few months away, with that vote Congress essentially relegated itself to the sidelines. Debate over war continued to rage in the United Nations and in capitals around the globe. Administration officials moved ahead with their war plans, while lawmakers during those intervening months found themselves in the frustrating position of pleading for administration briefings on Iraq and information about the war's cost—all to little or no avail.

In the years following 2002, Congress—under GOP control—exercised little oversight of the conduct of the Iraq war. But Democrats and a few Republicans became increasingly vocal in criticism of the Bush administration's handling of the conflict. This discontent was raised to a new level in 2007 when Democrats returned to power in both chambers after the 2006 election, which most analysts said occurred chiefly because of voter discontent with the war. Ending the U.S. participation in Iraq became the signature issue for Democrats as they struggled in 2007 to find a way to change the Bush administration's conduct of the conflict. But their inability to do so—Bush vetoed bills seeking to force a change and was backed up by enough Senate GOP votes to block veto overrides—once again highlighted the difficulties Congress faces in maintaining an equal footing on war powers with an administration determined to go its own way.

Congress has passed other joint resolutions authorizing or approving the president's determination to use armed forces as he deemed necessary to repel armed attacks or threats against certain nations or geographical areas, including Taiwan (Formosa), the Middle East, Cuba, and Berlin. Congress also has enacted numerous open-ended authorizations, as well as laws conferring emergency powers on the president. Congress has always proved more adept at giving than taking away authority to wage war.

Changing World

Presidential war powers have also been enhanced by a rapidly changing world. The framers wrote the Constitution with a much different world in mind. In the eighteenth century, battles usually came only after formal declarations of war. For the most part, professional armies were affected, not the general population. War was clearly defined and separate from other forms of international relations. After 1945 the United States emerged as a superpower, with major and minor interests and commitments in every part of the world. In the prewar period, diplomacy and defense had been distinct and separate entities. In the postwar world, the military establishment began to play an integral, and at some levels even a dominant, role in the foreign policy process. The Cold War between Western and Soviet-bloc nations, involving a state of tension just short of armed conflict, helped to merge traditional foreign policy concerns and defense issues.

The decades following World War II brought a massive arms race, United Nations "police actions" and peacekeeping forces, worldwide terrorism, round-the-clock surveillance against Soviet nuclear attack, and sophisticated intelligence gathering. Such a state of defense preparedness blurred the distinction between war and peace. Unlike the prewar period, the United States now had a large armed force, global treaty obligations, and numerous foreign assistance programs. One example of how these developments contributed to the erosion of Congress's war power was the network of military alliances that grew up to contain the Soviet Union. A provision of the treaty establishing NATO stated that an attack on any member nation was considered an attack on all the members, committing the United States to war in the defense of all other member states.

Some observers argued that the traditional view embodied in the Constitution—that Congress was in the best position to make decisions about war and peace—no longer was valid in the nuclear age. They held that the process the framers of the Constitution envisioned of Congress carefully weighing and debating decisions of whether to go to war over days or perhaps even weeks had become obsolete in modern times. Through advances in communications and transportation, and especially through military technology and the nature of modern warfare, the world had become much smaller. Geographic remoteness no longer ensured security. If war became imminent, the decision of whether to counterattack with nuclear missiles might have to be made in a matter of minutes, possibly even seconds. There would be no time to consult Congress, they argued, and few members of Congress would insist on consultation in such a situation.

Defenders of congressional prerogatives agreed that the world had changed dramatically. But, because of the high stakes involved in modern warfare, they insisted the decision to go to war should not be made by the president alone. On the contrary, they argued, there should be more, not less, consultation with Congress.

The end to the Cold War in the early 1990s did not quell the debate. No longer facing a clearly defined military threat such as the Soviet Union had posed, the United States found itself increasingly involved in United Nations and NATO peacekeeping deployments as regional conflicts proliferated.

The September 11, 2001, terrorist attacks against the United States and resulting focus on homeland security again shifted war-making power back in the president's favor. Within a week of the attacks, Congress had approved and President George W. Bush had signed into law a resolution authorizing the use of force to track down and punish those responsible. A little more than a year later Congress approved the resolution authorizing the use of force against Iraq. The 2002 resolution marked the first time that lawmakers gave the commander-in-chief open-ended authority to launch preemptive strikes on a sovereign nation that intelligence reports indicated was amassing weapons of mass destruction.

1973 War Powers Act

Efforts to redress the imbalance in war powers between the two branches began in the late 1960s as the Vietnam War was expanded despite repeated promises by both the Johnson and Nixon administrations to bring the conflict quickly to an end. At the height of U.S. involvement in the late 1960s, more than 500,000 U.S. troops were in southeast Asia. As the fighting dragged on, death tallies rose, and the antiwar movement gained momentum, members of Congress increasingly challenged the executive branch's prosecution of the war. Hearings on the Vietnam conflict conducted by the Senate Foreign Relations Committee helped galvanize opposition to the war. The Senate adopted a succession of antiwar amendments, but most were weakened by the House.

In 1969 the Senate adopted a resolution expressing the sense of the Senate that national commitments involving armed forces result only from actions taken by both the legislative and executive branches through treaties, statutes, or concurrent resolutions. However, the House did not consider the measure, and it was not binding on the president. Richard NIXON, in fact, ignored the resolution less than a year later when he ordered U.S. troops into Cambodia.

Frustrated by its ineffective role in the Indochina war, Congress in 1973 passed the War Powers Resolution over the veto of President Nixon. Through this law, Congress sought to check the president's war-making powers. It required the president "in every possible instance" to consult Congress before committing U.S. forces to ongoing or imminent hostilities. If the president undertook to commit military personnel to a combat situation, he had to report to Congress on the action within forty-eight hours. U.S. forces had to be withdrawn from such operations within sixty (sometimes ninety) days unless Congress declared war or otherwise authorized the operation to continue, extended the withdrawal deadline, or was unable to act because of an armed attack on the United States.

Under the original law Congress could pass a concurrent resolution at any time directing the president to withdraw U.S. forces from a foreign mission. However, this use of a concurrent resolution, which does not require the signature of the president, became constitutionally suspect in 1983 when the Supreme Court declared the so-called LEGISLATIVE VETO unconstitutional.

Presidential Opposition

Every president from Nixon through George W. Bush has refused to acknowledge the constitutionality of the War Powers Resolution. Presidents have contended that no act of Congress can curtail or modify their constitutional powers as commander in chief to take such actions as they alone think necessary to protect national security or the lives of Americans. Further, the chief executives have been careful to avoid taking any action that implied Congress had the authority, under the act, to control or delay any military or quasi-military action taken by the president. In informing Congress about military actions, presidents usually have stated that their reports were "consistent with the War Powers Resolution." To say that a report was being filed "pursuant to" or "under" the resolution would have been interpreted as acknowledging the constitutionality of the act.

Exceptions have been rare. In the more than one hundred reports submitted to Congress by mid-2007 as a result of the War Powers Resolution, only one—submitted by President Gerald R. FORD in 1975 when the United States rescued a U.S. freighter seized by Cambodian forces—mentioned a section of the act that would have triggered a time limit on the action. But the operation was over by the time it was reported to Congress.

In 1983 Reagan reluctantly agreed to a compromise with Congress and signed into law a time limit for the deployment of U.S. Marines in Lebanon. However, he insisted that the war powers act was not valid.

Both the 1991 and 2002 resolutions authorizing action against Iraq stated that they were intended to constitute specific statutory authority for using force within the meaning of the war powers act. But both Presidents George H. W. Bush and George W. Bush insisted that their requests for congressional action and signing of the resolution did not constitute any change in the long-standing executive position on the president's constitutional authority to use U.S. forces to defend vital U.S. interests or the constitutionality of the war powers act.

From the White House point of view, Congress has only one legitimate means of controlling the deployment of military forces overseas: by refusing to appropriate funds to support a foreign military operation.

A Divided Congress

Congress itself is divided on the desirability and the constitutionality of the war powers act. There is disagreement about how much power and flexibility the president should have to run the military and defend the country.

Some members think the act has served as a restraint on the executive branch. Others say it is inadequate and have proposed amendments to strengthen the congressional role in decisions to use force. Still others agree with many executive branch officials that the law is an unconstitutional and impractical restraint on the president.

Because there has been no consensus, Congress has neither struck the law from the books nor made good on its threats to invoke the resolution to force changes in administration policy in any number of trouble spots.

The diverse views were apparent in the debate over Reagan's 1987 decision to provide U.S. Navy escorts for Kuwaiti-owned oil tankers in the Persian Gulf. Reagan had refused to invoke the war powers law when he adopted the policy, despite a series of armed confrontations with Iran. Attempts in the Senate to initiate war powers procedures failed in 1987 and 1988. A lawsuit to force the president to initiate the procedures, brought by 111 House members, was dismissed by the federal courts. Reagan thus was essentially free to commit the navy to the operation.

Little had changed a decade later when U.S. troops were used to help implement a peace agreement in Bosnia. Although Congress had urged Clinton to seek advanced authorization for any deployment, congressional efforts to keep U.S. troops out of Bosnia quickly collapsed once a peace agreement was reached. Before the initial deployment in 1995, the House rejected, albeit narrowly, an effort to deny funds for the mission. In 1997 Congress allowed Clinton to extend the mission as long as he told Congress why and for how long. In 1998 the House defeated an attempt to make the Bosnia deployment a test case of the constitutionality of the War Powers Resolution.

Also in 1998, a House-approved provision to require the president to obtain congressional authorization before sending U.S. forces on an offensive military operation was dropped from the final version of a defense appropriations bill. President Clinton had threatened to veto the bill because of the provision.

Another flare-up over presidential authorization of combat activity occurred in 1999, when Clinton notified Congress he had begun air strikes against Yugoslavia in response to its repression of ethnic Albanians in the province of Kosovo. Congressional Republicans tried to use the War Powers Resolution to overturn the president's actions, and they later attempted to withhold funding for the operation, but their efforts were unsuccessful. Eighteen members of Congress even sued Clinton in federal district court in Washington, alleging his actions violated the act. The suit was dismissed after the judge ruled that the lawmakers lacked legal standing to bring the suit. The U.S. Court of Appeals for the District of Columbia Circuit upheld the ruling, and the Supreme Court refused to hear the lawmakers' subsequent appeal.

Politics of War Powers

The exercise of the war powers by the executive and legislative branches is governed by many factors besides the formal constitutional provisions. In the end, the effectiveness of Congress in exercising its powers, whether they are derived from the Constitution or from legislation, such as the war powers act and other laws, depends on political factors. When Congress favors presidential policies involving the deployment of forces abroad, there is little concern about constitutional or legal niceties. If there is substantial opposition by lawmakers, demands are quickly raised about the need to assert Congress's prerogatives.

Many factors may influence how and when the war power is used: the party composition of Congress; the influence, prestige, and popularity of the president; foreign policy successes and failures; the nature and length of a military operation; the views of U.S. allies; and international developments, among others.

Watergate Scandal

The word *Watergate* has a permanent place in the American political lexicon as the name of a tangle of scandals that destroyed the presidency of Richard NIXON and dwarfed all other scandals in U.S. political history.

The Watergate is a posh apartment-office complex in Washington, D.C., where the Democratic National Committee had its headquarters in spring 1972, as the presidential election of that year got under way. On June 17 a break-in at the Democrats' office was committed by five men connected to the Republican campaign committee. The break-in touched off the revelations of wrongdoing that toppled the Nixon administration and profoundly shook public confidence in government.

The break-in appeared insignificant at first. But the evidence of lawbreaking that emerged in the following months led directly to the White House, implicating the president himself. Facing impeachment charges in Congress, Nixon became the first president ever to resign from office. His departure from the White House on August 9, 1974, ended a constitutional crisis brought on by the president's defiance of Congress and the courts.

Nixon was spared the possibility of criminal prosecution when he received a pardon from his successor, Gerald R. FORD. But nearly a score of others in the government and in Nixon's 1972 reelection campaign, including several of his close associates, drew prison sentences. Still others paid fines or went to prison for Watergate-related activities, such as making illegal campaign contributions and attempting to sabotage Nixon's political "enemies."

EXHIBIT #3
CRIM 1827-72
WATERGATE
EXHIBITS INTRODUCED DURING FIRST
TRIAL OF LIDDY, HUNT, MCCORD,
BARKER, MARTINEZ, STURGIS &
GONZALEZ)

This photograph of the Watergate complex in 1972 was introduced during the first trial of the "burglars" accused of breaking into the Democratic National Committee's headquarters located there.
Source: National Archives and Records Administration

The Break-In

The break-in that set the scandal in motion took place at the Democrats' headquarters on the sixth floor of the Watergate building, not far from the White House. In the early morning hours of June 17, 1972, District of Columbia police caught and arrested five men who had forced their way into the office. The intruders wore surgical gloves and carried walkie-talkies and photographic and electronic eavesdropping equipment. It was later disclosed that, among other things, they intended to replace a faulty tap on the telephone of the Democratic Party's national chair, Lawrence F. O'Brien. Later insiders said they believed that the burglars were looking for information they suspected the Democrats might have gathered to embarrass Nixon during the campaign.

Four of the five burglars became known as "the Cubans." They were Bernard L. Barker, Virgilio R. Gonzalez, Eugenio R. Martinez, and Frank Sturgis—all from Miami and identified with Cuban groups bitterly opposed to Fidel Castro. They had ties to the Central Intelligence Agency (CIA), as did the fifth man, James W.

More on this topic:
Executive Privilege, p. 209
Impeachment Power, p. 280
Nixon Impeachment Effort, p. 396

McCord Jr. He had been a former agent of the CIA and the Federal Bureau of Investigation (FBI) before becoming director of security for the Committee for the Re-Election of the President, an organization sometimes known by the initials CRP or CREEP.

O'Brien called the break-in "an incredible act of political espionage" and on June 20 filed a $1 million civil lawsuit against the Nixon reelection committee. The suit eventually was settled out of court, but O'Brien did not accept the word of spokespersons for Nixon who insisted that the Republicans had had nothing to do with the break-in. The day after the break-in, John N. Mitchell, a former attorney general in the Nixon administration who was now running the president's reelection campaign, stated flatly that "McCord and the other four men arrested in Democratic headquarters Saturday were not operating on our behalf or with our consent in the alleged bugging." Ronald L. Ziegler, the White House press secretary, characterized the break-in as a "third-rate burglary" and nothing more. Nixon reinforced that view at a news conference on June 22, saying: "This kind of activity … has no place in the electoral process. And, as Mr. Ziegler has stated, the White House has no involvement whatever in this particular incident."

Despite these denials, the top echelon at the White House was busy devising a cover-up strategy. White House aides pressured the CIA to ask the FBI to call off its investigation of the case by falsely warning that intelligence operations in Mexico would be jeopardized. The Watergate schemers feared, among other things, that money "laundered" through a Mexican bank to pay the burglars would be traced to its source, the Nixon campaign headquarters. All of this and much more came to light over the next two years.

Nixon's direct participation in the cover-up was not known with certainty until his final days in office. Once his denials had been refuted, his presidency was doomed. Until then, the Watergate drama was played out in the courts, in congressional committees, in the headlines, and before the television cameras.

Without the aggressive reporting of several newspapers and magazines, the full story might never have come out. The *Washington Post* took the lead in breaching the administration's "stonewalling," as the Watergate principals called their concealment effort. The paper's reporting team of Carl Bernstein and Bob Woodward was especially adept at obtaining Watergate information from anonymous sources, including a celebrated executive branch official identified only as "Deep Throat." For its Watergate coverage, the *Post* endured the administration's wrath and won the Pulitzer Prize for "meritorious service." In 2005 "Deep Throat" was revealed to be W. Mark Felt, the assistant director of the FBI during the Nixon administration. Felt was ninety-one years old when he came forward, having spent decades denying his involvement.

During summer 1972, Rep. Wright Patman, a Texas Democrat who chaired the House Banking and Currency Committee, began inquiring into news reports of money laundering by the Nixon campaign. But the White House convinced friendly members of Patman's committee to abort his investigation. The public showed little interest in the allegations of scandal: Americans went to the polls on November 7 and reelected Nixon in a landslide.

The Hearings and the Trial

But Watergate would not go away. At the beginning of the new 93rd Congress in January 1973, the Senate unanimously approved a resolution by Majority Leader Mike MANSFIELD, a Montana Democrat, to create a seven-member, bipartisan investigating committee. Called the Select Committee on Presidential Campaign Activities, it was generally known as the Watergate Committee. Its chair was Sam J. ERVIN Jr., an elderly North Carolina Democrat serving out his last Senate term. Ervin, a former judge and a trial lawyer, became a folk hero when the committee's televised hearings displayed his courtly manners, wry humor, and penchant for quoting the Bible.

Also in January 1973, in a federal courtroom near the Capitol, the five break-in defendants and two others went on trial. The two added defendants were E. Howard Hunt and G. Gordon Liddy. Hunt was an ex-CIA agent and writer of spy novels who was then serving as a consultant to White House aide Charles W. Colson. Liddy was a former FBI agent who had subsequently worked for John D. Ehrlichman, Nixon's chief domestic adviser, and then moved on to Nixon's reelection campaign—first under Mitchell and then under Maurice H. Stans, the former secretary of commerce, who was directing fundraising.

Liddy, Hunt, and McCord belonged to a secret White House group set up to take on administration projects that might require unorthodox tactics. They called themselves "the plumbers" because their original purpose had been to stop news leaks. Headed by White House aide Egil Krogh Jr., the plumbers carried out numerous acts of political sabotage, including the Watergate break-in and another break-in the previous year at the office of a psychiatrist who had treated a man Nixon considered an enemy, Daniel Ellsberg. The plumbers were seeking derogatory information about Ellsberg, who had given the press the so-called Pentagon Papers, an official but hitherto secret study of U.S. involvement in the Vietnam War.

In federal court before Judge John J. Sirica, the Cubans and Hunt pleaded guilty. McCord and Liddy underwent a jury trial and were convicted January 30, 1973, on charges stemming from the break-in. Judge Sirica delayed sentencing until March 23, when he stunned the court by reading a letter from McCord saying that others had been involved in the break-in but that the defendants had been under political pressure to remain silent. Moreover, McCord wrote, perjury had been committed during the trial. McCord was intensely loyal to his former employer, the CIA, and expressed fear that the White House might try to portray the Watergate break-in as the agency's work.

During the trial Judge Sirica had often complained that he was not getting the full story about the case. Hoping to convince the defendants to tell more of what they knew to a sitting federal grand jury or to the Senate Watergate Committee, he provisionally handed out maximum terms of up to forty years. "Should you decide to speak freely," he said, "I would have to weigh that factor in appraising what sentence will be finally imposed."

McCord, whose sentencing was delayed indefinitely, told the Senate committee that Mitchell, Colson, John W. Dean III, and Jeb Stuart Magruder had known in advance about the break-in. Magruder was deputy director of the reelection committee; Dean was the White House counsel. Fearful of what lay ahead, Dean and Magruder agreed to tell the committee what they knew in return for partial immunity ("use" immunity) from prosecution. Several other Watergate figures followed suit. Judge Sirica's pivotal role in unraveling the Watergate cover-up

Judge John J. Sirica played a key role in helping to unravel the Watergate cover-up.
Source: AP Images

> **CLOSER LOOK** ◉
>
> The Senate named a special committee to investigate the Watergate issue. It was headed by Sen. Sam J. Ervin Jr. of North Carolina. Ervin, a former judge who was serving out his final Senate term, became a folk hero as televised hearings showed his courtly manners, wry humor, and penchant for quoting the Bible.

IN THE UNITED STATES DISTRICT COURT
FOR THE DISTRICT OF COLUMBIA

SENATE SELECT COMMITTEE ON PRESIDENTIAL
CAMPAIGN ACTIVITIES, suing in its own
name and in the name of the UNITED
STATES,

and

SAM J. ERVIN, JR.; HOWARD H. BAKER, JR.;
HERMAN E. TALMADGE; DANIEL K. INOUYE;
JOSEPH M. MONTOYA; EDWARD J. GURNEY;
and LOWELL P. WEICKER, JR., as United
States Senators who are members of the
Senate Select Committee on Presidential
Campaign Activities.

United States Senate
Washington, D.C. 20510

Plaintiffs

v.

RICHARD M. NIXON, individually and as
President of the United States.

The White House
Washington, D.C. 20500

Defendant

Civil
Action
No.

COMPLAINT FOR DECLARATORY JUDGMENT,
MANDATORY INJUNCTION AND MANDAMUS

Respectfully submitted,

Samuel Dash
Chief Counsel

Fred D. Thompson
Minority Counsel

Rufus Edmisten
Deputy Counsel

James Hamilton
Assistant Chief Counsel

Sherman Cohn
Eugene Gressman
Jerome A. Barron
    Washington, D. C.
Of Counsel

William T. Mayton
Assistant Counsel

Ronald D. Rotunda
Assistant Counsel

Arthur S. Miller
    Chief Consultant to
    the Select Committee
    Washington, D. C.
Of Counsel

United States Senate
Washington, D. C.   20510
Telephone Number 225-0531

The first and last pages of the complaint filed in federal court in Washington, D.C., by the Senate Watergate Committee, Thursday, Aug. 9, 1973. In the complaint Richard M. Nixon was named as defendant, individually and as President of the United States.
Source: AP Images

brought him prominence after an undistinguished earlier career. *Time* magazine selected him as its "man of the year" in 1973.

Nixon's problems continued to grow. At the Senate Judiciary Committee's confirmation hearings on the nomination of L. Patrick Gray as FBI director, Gray implicated several administration officials in the effort to thwart the FBI's investigation of Watergate. Gray's testimony doomed his nomination and prompted Ehrlichman to tell Dean, "Well, I think we ought to let him hang there. Let him twist slowly, slowly in the wind." Gray, abandoned by the White House, withdrew his nomination and resigned as acting FBI director in early April.

At a brief news conference on April 17, Nixon said he had begun "intensive new inquiries" into the Watergate affair "as a result of serious charges which came to my attention." On April 30, 1973, the president announced Dean's firing and the resignations of White House chief of staff H. R. Haldeman, chief domestic affairs adviser Ehrlichman, and Attorney General Richard G. Kleindienst. The last three, all implicated in the Watergate scandal through news leaks, said they could no longer carry out their duties amid the Watergate controversies. In a television address that night, Nixon took full responsibility for any improper activities in his 1972 presidential campaign. He pledged that justice would be pursued "fairly, fully, and impartially, no matter who is involved." The president named Elliot L. Richardson as the new attorney general, placing him in charge of the administration's investigation and giving him authority to appoint a special prosecutor in the case. Richardson chose Archibald Cox, a Harvard law professor who had served as solicitor general under presidents John F. KENNEDY and Lyndon B. JOHNSON.

The nationally televised Senate Watergate hearings opened on May 17, 1973, in the ornate Caucus Room of the Old Senate Office Building. The room had been the site of earlier famous hearings, including Sen. Joseph

R. MCCARTHY's inquiries into alleged communist subversion in the early 1950s and the investigation of the TEAPOT DOME oil-leasing scandal of the Harding administration. McCord, the first witness, took the stand on May 18 and told of White House pressure on him to remain silent and plead guilty to break-in charges in return for a promise of executive clemency.

As the hearings continued throughout the summer and into the fall, the committee's ranking Republican, Sen. Howard H. BAKER Jr. of Tennessee, asked repeatedly: "How much did the president know, and when did he know it?" Dean, who took the witness stand for five days beginning on June 25, became the first witness publicly to accuse the president of direct involvement in the cover-up. But it was Dean's word against the president's until tapes of some of the disputed conversations became available. In mid-July, the committee was startled to learn—almost by accident—that the president had secretly recorded many of the relevant Oval Office conversations.

The Tapes

From that time on, the Watergate struggle focused on the investigators' attempts to gain control of the tapes and Nixon's claim that the doctrine of EXECUTIVE PRIVILEGE allowed him to withhold them. After Nixon had refused to obey subpoenas from Cox and the Watergate Committee to produce more of the tapes, Judge Sirica ruled on August 29, 1973, that the president should let him review them privately to decide whether the claim of executive privilege was justified. Nixon appealed, and while the case was on the way to the Supreme Court for a historic constitutional test, he offered to prepare summaries of nine tapes Cox sought and to let John C. STENNIS, a Mississippi Democrat and Senate elder known for his integrity, check their accuracy against the tapes themselves. Cox, in turn, would have to agree to request no more tapes.

When Cox rejected the deal, Nixon ordered Richardson to fire him. Richardson refused and resigned, as did deputy attorney general William D. Ruckelshaus. Robert H. Bork, elevated to the post of acting attorney general, complied with the order to fire Cox. This dramatic chain of events, announced on Saturday evening, October 20, 1973, quickly became known as "the Saturday night massacre." It provoked, in the words of the new White House chief of staff, Gen. Alexander M. Haig Jr., "a firestorm" of public outrage. According to a Gallup poll, Nixon's popularity among the American people dropped to a low of 27 percent, a plunge of forty points during the year.

The nation's confidence in its president had also been damaged by the forced resignation of Vice President Spiro T. Agnew and by reports that Nixon had paid only nominal federal income taxes during most of his first term. He later settled the tax matter by paying $476,561 in back taxes and interest. Agnew resigned on October 10, 1973, and on the same day pleaded no contest to a charge of tax evasion. He was sentenced to three years of unsupervised probation and fined $10,000. The charge, which was the result of an investigation into Agnew's political activities as Baltimore County executive and Maryland governor, was not directly related to Watergate. But Agnew's downfall reflected on the president's judgment of people and the moral climate of the Nixon administration. Nixon named Ford, the House minority leader, as the new vice president. Ford was confirmed by the House and Senate without difficulty and sworn into office December 6, 1973.

Impeachment Drive

Shaken by the erosion of his public support, Nixon on October 23, 1973, agreed to surrender the tapes to Judge Sirica for review. His reversal came too late; the NIXON IMPEACHMENT EFFORT had begun. That day forty-four Watergate bills were introduced in Congress, many of them calling for impeachment. Rep. Peter W. Rodino Jr., a New Jersey Democrat who chaired the Judiciary Committee, said on October 24 that he would proceed "full steam ahead" with an impeachment investigation. With only four dissenting votes, the House on February 6, 1974, formally authorized the committee to investigate whether Nixon should be impeached.

In the meantime, Nixon's lawyers had told Judge Sirica that two long-sought tapes did not exist and that an eighteen-minute segment of conversation had been erased from another tape—eliminating evidence that was thought to be damning to Nixon. Leon Jaworski, a former president of the American Bar Association who had been named the new special prosecutor, demanded more tapes. Nixon refused to release them, and as Jaworski awaited a Supreme Court ruling on the tapes, his staff prepared evidence for the Watergate grand jury.

On March 1, 1974, the grand jury indicted Mitchell, Haldeman, Ehrlichman, and Colson for their roles in covering up the truth about the break-in. They were later convicted in federal district court and, after a long appeals process, went to prison. (At the time of the indictments, Mitchell and Stans were being tried in federal court in New York on charges of interfering with a government investigation of Robert L. Vesco, an international financier, in return for a $200,000 contribution to the Nixon campaign. Mitchell and Stans were acquitted; Vesco fled the country and never was tried.) The same grand jury that indicted Mitchell, Haldeman, and Ehrlichman named Nixon a coconspirator but at Jaworski's request did not indict him. The prosecutor explained later that an indictment would have resulted in a trial interfering with and probably delaying the impeachment proceedings.

On April 30, 1974, hoping to end the dispute over the tapes, Nixon released heavily edited transcripts of forty-six tapes of Watergate discussions between himself and his advisers. The transcripts failed to satisfy the demands of Watergate investigators, but the unflattering details they revealed—Nixon's frequent use of obscenity, his suspicion of outsiders, his political cynicism—did him further damage.

Hours before the House Judiciary Committee began its public debate on impeachment, on July 24, 1974, the Supreme Court ruled unanimously against the president's refusal to submit sixty-four tapes to Judge Sirica. Three in particular contained incriminating material, but the White House did not release them until August 5—after the committee had voted on impeachment. The contents of the three tapes ended any remaining hopes Nixon and his few congressional supporters harbored of turning back the impeachment effort. Recorded on June 23, 1972, six days after the Watergate break-in, the tapes clearly contradicted the president's earlier claims that he was not involved in the cover-up.

On July 27, 29, and 30, the House Judiciary Committee approved three of five proposed articles of impeachment: for obstruction of justice, abuse of presidential power, and contempt of Congress. Ten of the seventeen Republicans on the thirty-eight-member committee voted against all five articles. But the release of the tapes on August 5 ended all doubt about Nixon's involvement, and each of the ten called for his resignation or impeachment.

The president chose resignation, which came on August 9 in a tearful, televised farewell at the White House. Nixon acknowledged no wrongdoing but attributed his departure to loss of political support in Congress. Ford immediately was sworn in as the nation's thirty-eighth president. In his brief inaugural address, Ford said: "My fellow Americans, our long national nightmare is over. Our Constitution works. Our great republic is a government of laws and not of men. Here, the people rule."

Most Americans shared Ford's sense of relief. But speculation and debate continued over whether Nixon would or should be indicted for his role in the Watergate cover-up. Ford put an end to that a month after the resignation, on September 8, when he granted Nixon a "full, free and absolute" pardon for federal offenses he may have committed during his presidency. Ford argued that Nixon had suffered enough, and that the pardon would spare the nation the painful spectacle of a former president brought to trial. The pardon set off a storm of controversy. Some critics charged that Ford had agreed to pardon Nixon in exchange for his resignation, an accusation that was never substantiated. Ford denied the accusation in an unprecedented appearance before the House Judiciary Committee.

Judge Sirica later lamented that while Nixon's associates went to prison, the former president "received a large government pension and retired to his lovely home in San Clemente [California]." The judge said he believed Nixon should have faced a criminal trial after his resignation and, if convicted by a jury, should have gone to prison.

Many of Nixon's Watergate associates did go to prison, but they spent relatively little time behind bars. Liddy served the longest term, fifty-two months. Several, including Liddy, were greeted on their release by lucrative contracts and a ready audience for their books and lectures. Others found new career opportunities in business and, in the case of Colson and Magruder, the ministry.

In retirement, Nixon wrote extensively about his years in office and about world affairs. But he never admitted that he had broken the law as president. In May 1977, in a television interview with David Frost, Nixon said: "I have let the American people down. And I have to carry that burden with me the rest of my life." Twenty years after the break-in, Sen. William S. Cohen of Maine, one of the Republicans on the House Judiciary Committee who had voted for impeachment, asked a question that continued to haunt many Americans: "Why didn't Nixon ever come before the American people, condemn the break-in, explain his involvement and ask to be forgiven?" Cohen said he believed that Nixon might well have saved his presidency with such a statement, even as late as spring 1974.

Ways and Means Committee, House

The House Ways and Means Committee has a pivotal role in Congress. Charged with raising revenues to run the government, the committee is also responsible for disbursing about half of the federal budget. The range of the panel's authority is vast. Overall, in 2007 the panel had jurisdiction over revenue, debt, customs, trade, Social Security, and Medicare legislation. It had six subcommittees with jurisdiction over health, income security and family support, oversight, select revenue measures, Social Security, and trade legislation. But the full committee still considered basic tax law proposals.

The importance of the Ways and Means Committee was somewhat reduced in the reforms of the 1970s, but it is still one of the most powerful committees in the House. Because the House originates most tax legislation, the Ways and Means Committee usually sets the agenda; the Senate Finance Committee then reacts to House proposals. But sometimes a Senate plan prevails, as in 1990 when a "soak the rich" plan of the Ways and Means Committee that was vehemently opposed by President George H. W. Bush was superseded by the Senate's bill.

Made a permanent committee in 1802, the Ways and Means Committee handled all aspects of federal finances until the mid-1860s, when the Appropriations Committee was set up to oversee spending. At that time the Senate also split an appropriations panel away from the Finance Committee. After Social Security was set up in the 1930s, both taxing panels saw their plates fill with spending questions as Congress created welfare,

At the start of the 110th Congress in 2007 the chair of the powerful House Ways and Means Committee was New Yorker Charles B. Rangel. Here Rangel addresses delegates at the Democratic National Convention in Boston in 2004.
Source: AP Images/Stephen Savoia

health, and retirement programs financed by special federal levies. Funding of these programs has been kept separate from the regular appropriations process.

In the nineteenth century the Ways and Means Committee focused on tariffs. But since then its source of revenues has been taxes. Congress has spent decades manipulating tax laws, with breaks and loopholes for an endless list of causes that range from oil production to home ownership. The tax code affects every business and individual; no lobbyist can afford not to know what the Ways and Means Committee is doing.

In the modern era after the Great Depression and World War II, the most important chair of the committee, most observers believed, was Wilbur D. Mills, D-Ark, an expert on U.S. tax law. He skillfully used his knowledge and political savvy during seventeen years as chair of the panel from 1958 to 1975 to control—almost single-handily—the major elements of tax and welfare law. He was well known for his grasp of even minor details of the tax code. Colleagues were awed by his ability to speak, without notes, in favor of his committee's work. But he also was an authoritarian chair, keeping control over all tax measures by bringing them before the whole committee and refusing to establish subcommittees. Mills consolidated his power by accurately sensing what the House would support and drafting legislation accordingly. He took tax bills to the floor under ground rules that barred floor amendments, and the full House regularly passed the measures by wide margins.

Oregon Democrat Al Ullman served as chair from 1974 to 1981. Ullman was more timid politically, and competing factions on the panel rarely worked in harmony during his chairmanship. Dan Rostenkowski, a Chicago Democrat who entered the House in 1959, became chair of the Ways and Means Committee in 1981. His background as a skillful insider in House politics was expected to help bring the chaotic committee into line. But Rostenkowski's first major tax bill was rejected by the House, which instead took a substitute measure backed by President Ronald Reagan and House Republicans. That loss was eventually overshadowed by the 1986 tax reform bill, which Rostenkowski helped engineer. The measure eliminated many special tax breaks and lowered tax rates.

Florida Democrat Sam Gibbons became acting chair of the committee in mid-1994, after Rostenkowski was indicted on criminal charges. (See SCANDALS, CONGRESSIONAL.) The Republicans assumed control of the House in 1995 and Bill Archer of Texas became chair. In 1997 Archer helped push through a tax-cutting bill for the first time in sixteen years and a major triumph for majority Republicans. In the face of strenuous opposition from the administration of President Bill Clinton, the measure did not become law, however.

When the White House changed from the Democrats to the Republicans in 2001, the prospects for tax cuts brightened considerably. Under the oversight of California Republican Bill Thomas, who assumed control of the panel upon Archer's retirement in 2001, the committee produced a broad tax cut in 2001. The committee bill formed the basis for a $1.4 trillion tax cut that President George W. Bush signed into law that year. The committee remained a central player in the largely successful efforts of the Bush administration to enact far-reaching tax reductions during the president's first term. Democrats derided the cuts as sops to the richest Americans at the expense of the middle class, but the tightly focused Republican leadership in Congress forced them through nevertheless.

In 2007 the committee had forty-one members, just seventeen of whom were Republicans. That favorable ratio continued the pattern used by both parties in the past to ensure complete control of the committee. The ratio was a legacy of a Democratic caucus vote in 1974 to expand the committee, which previously had only twenty-five members split almost evenly between Democrats and Republicans. The smaller group had been cohesive, at least publicly, and had promoted its tax work as being too complex for outsiders to understand. Mills put a premium on consensus, keeping the members in closed meetings until they hashed out a bipartisan approach.

In 2007 committee leadership passed to Charles B. Rangel, D-N.Y., an unapologetic but pragmatic liberal. Democrats, back in control of both chambers, talked expansively about rolling back the Bush tax cuts, but the chances of success were limited with the Senate narrowly divided although in Democratic hands. Instead, Rangel wanted to examine other issues including restructuring the alternative minimum income tax, which was originally designed to ensure everyone—especially the very rich—paid some income tax. Because the alternative minimum income tax was not indexed for inflation, the law was increasingly snarling middle-income taxpayers. Both parties agreed it needed to be fixed, but a long-term change was estimated to cost a trillion dollars over ten years. Congress was able to pass a temporary fix for tax year 2007, but a long-term solution remained elusive.

Rangel, as with most others in his party, was firmly opposed to Bush's proposals to restructure Social Security and Medicare programs. However, Rangel said that he was open to exploring changes to entitlement programs to ensure their long-term stability.

Between 1910 and 1974 Democrats on the Ways and Means Committee had a special role in the party leadership. They were given responsibility for making Democratic committee assignments after a 1910 revolt by House members stripped that authority from the autocratic Speaker, Joseph G. CANNON. At the time, Majority Leader Oscar W. UNDERWOOD of Alabama was also chair of the tax-writing panel. Controlling committee assignments gave Democratic members of the Ways and Means Committee extra clout to win votes for tax bills and made them key players in House politics.

Later critics saw the House as a closed system, dominated by older, senior members. They wanted those making committee assignments to be more accountable to the party. In 1974 these reformers convinced Democrats to shift the task to the Democratic Steering and Policy Committee, a group of about thirty members, including top party leaders and a dozen members elected by region. (See LEADERSHIP.)

Webster, Daniel

Daniel Webster (1782–1852) was a lawyer, a member of the House of Representatives and Senate, and twice secretary of state. Above all, however, he was an orator in an era of American politics when oratory was a high art. Webster used his skill as a debater to protect the commercial interests of his constituency, to benefit his legal clients, and to sway the emotions of crowds. He is best remembered for his eloquence when, putting aside special interests, he analyzed the nature of the Union and pleaded for its preservation in the years leading up to the Civil War.

Before entering the House of Representatives from his native state of New Hampshire in 1813, Webster practiced law, pamphleteering, and occasional oratory. Once in Congress, he spoke out against the War of 1812 and protective tariffs. He continued to practice law and was retained to plead before the Supreme Court in several well-known cases. He left the House in 1817 and moved to Boston to pursue his lucrative legal career. In 1823 he again entered the House as a Federalist, although this time as a representative from Boston. He remained a member of the Federalist Party until 1845, when he became a Whig. In the House Webster continued his legal career and was made chair of the Judiciary Committee. Reflecting the commercial interests of his constituents, he supported protective tariffs and continued to do so throughout the remainder of his career.

Daniel Webster was a skilled orator in the era when oratory was a high art. The best known of his speeches was his 1830 rebuttal to Sen. Robert Y. Hayne of South Carolina in opposition to nullification and in support of the Union.
Source: Library of Congress

In 1827 he entered the Senate, where he stayed until 1850, leaving to serve as secretary of state in 1841–1843 and again in 1850–1852. The best known of his speeches and an example of Webster at his finest was his 1830 reply to South Carolina senator Robert Y. HAYNE on the subject of nullification, or the right of a state to nullify an act of the federal government. Above all, Webster believed in the sanctity of the Union; he ended his oration with the words, "Liberty *and* Union, now and forever, one and inseparable!"

It was his belief in the importance of maintaining the union of states that led Webster to criticize both the South and the North on the issue of slavery. He angered both sides by urging compromise on the western expansion of slavery.

An extravagant man, Webster was often in financial difficulties despite his large legal fees. The Bank of the United States paid him a retainer while he was a senator, and eastern business interests supplemented his congressional salary to keep him in Washington. These financial arrangements did not enhance his reputation, but his devotion to the union of states and his extraordinary eloquence made him one of the most notable members in a Senate that also included Henry CLAY, John C. CALHOUN, and Thomas Hart BENTON.

Wesberry v. Sanders *See* REAPPORTIONMENT AND REDISTRICTING.

Whips *See* LEADERSHIP; ZONE OR REGIONAL WHIPS.

Women in Congress

Women always have been underrepresented in Congress. From the time the first woman joined Congress in 1917 through early 2008, only 241 women had been elected. Of those, 238 actually served. (See table, p. 609.)

Jeannette RANKIN was elected in 1916 as a Republican representative from Montana. Her state gave women the vote before the Nineteenth Amendment to the Constitution was ratified in 1920, extending the franchise to all female citizens of the United States.

Rebecca L. Felton, the first woman to serve in the Senate, did so for only one day. The Georgia Democrat, appointed in 1922 to fill a vacancy, stepped aside one day after she was sworn in to make way for a man who had been elected to fill the vacancy.

The number of women in the male-dominated Senate and House grew slowly. But women have made steady gains in recent decades.

More than eighty-five years after Rankin took her seat in the House, the 110th Congress (2007–2009) opened with an all-time high of eighty-seven women. There were seventy-one women in the House—not including nonvoting delegates—and sixteen in the Senate. No less important than the numbers, Rep. Nancy Pelosi, D-Calif., became the first female Speaker of the House. She had made history earlier also, in 2002, when Democrats elected her as the first woman to become the top leader of any party in either chamber. She won overwhelmingly in the race to become Democratic minority leader during the 108th Congress. She had been elected Democratic whip in the previous Congress.

These seven women were members of the 79th Congress (1929–1931): Pearl P. Oldfield, Edith N. Rogers, Ruth S.B. Pratt, Ruth H. McCormick, Ruth B. Owen, Mary T. Norton, and Florence P. Kahn.
Source: Library of Congress

Many women got their start in Congress by way of the "widow's mandate." According to this custom, widows were appointed to replace their husbands who had died in office. This practice allowed state leaders extra time to choose a successor or hold a special election. Sometimes a widow was chosen by her late husband's party to run for his seat on the theory that a strong sympathy vote would sweep her into office.

Whatever the motive, the widow's mandate marked the beginning of long careers in Congress for several women. Margaret Chase SMITH, a Maine Republican, filled her late husband's House seat after his death in 1940 and then went on to serve four terms in the Senate. Edith Nourse Rogers, a Massachusetts Republican, entered the House after her husband's death in 1925 and remained there for thirty-five years, until her own death in 1960. Hattie W. Caraway, an Arkansas Democrat, took her late husband's Senate seat after his death in 1931 and continued to serve until 1945. Democrat Corinne "Lindy" Boggs of Louisiana, widow of House Democratic leader Thomas Hale Boggs, took over her late husband's seat in 1973 and held it until she retired in 1991. In spring 1998 Republican Mary Bono won the California district that had been represented by her husband, former pop singer Sonny Bono, who had died in a skiing accident. She won reelection easily in November 1998 and subsequent elections.

WOMEN IN CONGRESS, 1947–2007

Congress	Senate	House
80th (1947–1949)	1	7
81st (1949–1951)	1	9
82nd (1951–1953)	1	10
83rd (1953–1955)	1	12
84th (1955–1957)	1	17
85th (1957–1959)	1	15
86th (1959–1961)	1	17
87th (1961–1963)	2	18
88th (1963–1965)	2	12
89th (1965–1967)	2	11
90th (1967–1969)	1	10
91st (1969–1971)	1	10
92nd (1971–1973)	1	13
93rd (1973–1975)	1	16
94th (1975–1977)	0	17
95th (1977–1979)	2	18
96th (1979–1981)	1	16
97th (1981–1983)	2	19
98th (1983–1985)	2	22
99th (1985–1987)	2	22
100th (1987–1989)	2	23
101st (1989–1991)	2	28
102nd (1991–1993)	3	29
103rd (1993–1995)	7	48
104th (1995–1997)	8	48
105th (1997–1999)	9	51
106th (1999–2001)	9	56
107th (2001–2003)	13	61
108th (2003–2005)	14	60
109th (2005–2007)	14	65
110th (2007–2009)	16	71

NOTE: House totals reflect the number of members at the start of each Congress and exclude nonvoting delegates. Figures for the 110th Congress are as of January 2007.

Not all widows have enjoyed a long tenure. Democrat Jean Carnahan of Missouri faced the unusual prospect of being appointed in 2001 to fill the seat of her husband, Gov. Mel Carnahan, who was killed in a plane crash weeks before the November 2000 election while campaigning for the seat. Despite his death, voters elected the late governor as a sign of support for his platform. Carnahan narrowly lost her 2002 bid for election to complete the remaining four years of the term.

As women became more active in politics, they began to initiate independent campaigns for office. In 1978 Republican Nancy Landon Kassebaum of Kansas became the first woman ever elected to the Senate without being preceded by her husband. She and Democrat Barbara Mikulski of Maryland, elected to the Senate in 1987, were joined in 1993 by four new women for a record total of six women senators.

Those women were elected in what became known as "the year of the woman" because the 1992 elections featured record numbers of women running for and being elected to Congress. The 103rd Congress, which opened in 1993, included forty-seven women in the House, an increase of nineteen from the previous year, and six in the Senate, an increase of four.

Several factors contributed to the success of women candidates in 1992. Many capitalized on an unusually large number of retirements to run in open seats. They also benefited from reapportionment, which created dozens of opportunities for newcomers in the South and West. Another factor was public dissatisfaction with Congress, which allowed women to portray themselves positively as outsiders. The 1991 confirmation hearings of Supreme Court nominee Clarence Thomas also had an impact. The televised image of an all-male Senate Judiciary panel sharply questioning a woman, law professor Anita F. Hill, about sexual harassment charges she had made against Thomas brought home dramatically to many women their lack of representation in Congress. (See APPOINTMENT POWER.)

The field of women elected in 1992 included Democrat Carol Moseley-Braun of Illinois, the first African American woman elected to the Senate. California Democrats Barbara Boxer, a former House member, and Dianne Feinstein, who had served as mayor of San Francisco, made their state the first to send two women to the Senate at one time.

CLOSER LOOK

Nancy Landon Kassenbaum of Kansas became the first woman ever elected to the Senate without being preceded by her husband. She served from 1978 to 1997. She also became the first woman to chair a major Senate committee, the Labor and Human Resources Committee.

More on this topic:

Delegates, p. 153

Pelosi, Nancy, p. 414

Women's Suffrage, p. 613

WOMEN MEMBERS OF CONGRESS, 1917–2007

As of February 2008, a total of 241 women had been elected or appointed to Congress. Of the 238 women who actually served in Congress (two others were elected to fill vacancies when Congress was not in session and may never have been sworn in, and another resigned her seat the day after she was sworn in), 205 served in the House only, twenty-six in the Senate only, and seven—Maine Republicans Margaret Chase Smith and Olympia Snowe, Maryland Democrat Barbara Mikulski, California Democrat Barbara Boxer, Arkansas Democrat Blanche Lincoln, Washington Democrat Maria Cantwell, and Michigan Democrat Debbie Stabenow—in both chambers. Following is a list of the women members, their political affiliations and states, and the years in which they served. In the table, a single year without a dash indicates the person's term began and ended within that year. In addition, women have served as nonvoting delegates, including Mary E. Farrington, R-Hawaii (1954–1957), Eleanor Holmes Norton, D-D.C. (1991–), Donna Christensen, D-V.I. (1997–), and Madeleine Z. Bordallo, D-Guam (2004–).

Senate

Rebecca L. Felton, Ind. D-Ga.[1]	1922	Barbara Boxer, D-Calif.	1993–
Hattie W. Caraway, D-Ark.	1931–1945	Kay Bailey Hutchison, R-Texas	1993–
Rose McConnell Long, D-La.	1936–1937	Carol Moseley-Braun, D-Ill.	1993–1999
Dixie Bibb Graves, D-Ala.	1937–1938	Patty L. Murray, D-Wash.	1993–
Gladys Pyle, R-S.D.[2]	1938–1939	Olympia J. Snowe, R-Maine	1995–
Vera C. Bushfield, R-S.D.	1948	Sheila Frahm, R-Kan.	1996
Margaret Chase Smith, R-Maine	1949–1973	Susan Collins, R-Maine	1997–
Hazel H. Abel, R-Neb.	1954	Mary L. Landrieu, D-La.	1997–
Eva K. Bowring, R-Neb.	1954	Blanche Lincoln, D-Ark.	1999–
Maurine B. Neuberger, D-Ore.	1960–1967	Maria Cantwell, D-Wash.	2001–
Elaine S. Edwards, D-La.	1972	Jean Carnahan, D-Mo.	2001–2002
Maryon Pittman Allen, D-Ala.	1978	Hillary Rodham Clinton, D-N.Y.	2001–
Muriel Buck Humphrey, D-Minn.	1978	Debbie Stabenow, D-Mich.	2001–
Nancy Landon Kassebaum, R-Kan.	1978–1997	Lisa Murkowski, R-Alaska	2002–
Paula Hawkins, R-Fla.	1981–1987	Elizabeth Dole, R-N.C.	2003–
Barbara Mikulski, D-Md.	1987–	Amy Klobuchar, D-Minn.	2007–
Jocelyn B. Burdick, D-N.D.	1992	Claire McCaskill, D-Mo.	2007–
Dianne Feinstein, D-Calif.	1992–		

House

Jeannette Rankin, R-Mont.	1917–1919; 1941–1943	Effiegene Locke Wingo, D-Ark.	1930–1933
		Willa M. B. Eslick, D-Tenn.	1932–1933
Alice M. Robertson, R-Okla.	1921–1923	Marian W. Clarke, R-N.Y.	1933–1935
Winnifred S. M. Huck, R-Ill.	1922–1923	Virginia E. Jenckes, D-Ind.	1933–1939
Mae E. Nolan, R-Calif.	1923–1925	Kathryn O'Loughlin McCarthy, D-Kan.	1933–1935
Florence P. Kahn, R-Calif.	1925–1937	Isabella S. Greenway, D-Ariz.	1933–1937
Mary T. Norton, D-N.J.	1925–1951	Caroline L. G. O'Day, D-N.Y.	1935–1943
Edith N. Rogers, R-Mass.	1925–1960	Nan W. Honeyman, D-Ore.	1937–1939
Katherine G. Langley, R-Ky.	1927–1931	Elizabeth H. Gasque, D-S.C.[2]	1938–1939
Ruth H. McCormick, R-Ill.	1929–1931	Clara G. McMillan, D-S.C.	1939–1941
Pearl P. Oldfield, D-Ark.	1929–1931	Jessie Sumner, R-Ill.	1939–1947
Ruth B. Owen, D-Fla.	1929–1933	Frances P. Bolton, R-Ohio	1940–1969
Ruth S. B. Pratt, R-N.Y.	1929–1933	Florence R. Gibbs, D-Ga.	1940–1941

(continues)

WOMEN MEMBERS OF CONGRESS, 1917–2007 (CONTINUED)

House

Margaret Chase Smith, R-Maine	1940–1949	Louise Day Hicks, D-Mass.	1971–1973
Katherine E. Byron, D-Md.	1941–1943	Elizabeth B. Andrews, D-Ala.	1972–1973
Veronica G. Boland, D-Pa.	1942–1943	Yvonne B. Burke, D-Calif.	1973–1979
Clare Boothe Luce, R-Conn.	1943–1947	Marjorie Sewell Holt, R-Md.	1973–1987
Winifred C. Stanley, R-N.Y.	1943–1945	Elizabeth Holtzman, D-N.Y.	1973–1981
Willa L. Fulmer, D-S.C.	1944–1945	Barbara C. Jordan, D-Texas	1973–1979
Emily Taft Douglas, D-Ill.	1945–1947	Patricia Schroeder, D-Colo.	1973–1997
Helen G. Douglas, D-Calif.	1945–1951	Corinne "Lindy" Boggs, D-La.	1973–1991
Chase G. Woodhouse, D-Conn.	1945–1947; 1949–1951	Cardiss R. Collins, D-Ill.	1973–1997
Helen D. Mankin, D-Ga.	1946–1947	Marilyn Lloyd, D-Tenn.	1975–1995
Eliza J. Pratt, D-N.C.	1946–1947	Millicent Fenwick, R-N.J.	1975–1983
Georgia L. Lusk, D-N.M.	1947–1949	Martha E. Keys, D-Kan.	1975–1979
Katharine P. C. St. George, R-N.Y.	1947–1965	Helen S. Meyner, D-N.J.	1975–1979
Reva Z. B. Bosone, D-Utah	1949–1953	Virginia Smith, R-Neb.	1975–1991
Cecil M. Harden, R-Ind.	1949–1959	Gladys Noon Spellman, D-Md.	1975–1981
Edna F. Kelly, D-N.Y.	1949–1969	Shirley N. Pettis, R-Calif.	1975–1979
Vera D. Buchanan, D-Pa.	1951–1955	Barbara A. Mikulski, D-Md.	1977–1987
Marguerite S. Church, R-Ill.	1951–1963	Mary Rose Oakar, D-Ohio	1977–1993
Maude E. Kee, D-W.Va.	1951–1965	Beverly Byron, D-Md.	1979–1993
Ruth Thompson, R-Mich.	1951–1957	Geraldine Ferraro, D-N.Y.	1979–1985
Gracie B. Pfost, D-Idaho	1953–1963	Olympia J. Snowe, R-Maine	1979–1995
Leonor K. Sullivan, D-Mo.	1953–1977	Bobbi Fiedler, R-Calif.	1981–1987
Iris F. Blitch, D-Ga.	1955–1963	Lynn M. Martin, R-Ill.	1981–1991
Edith Starrett Green, D-Ore.	1955–1975	Marge Roukema, R-N.J.	1981–2003
Martha W. Griffiths, D-Mich.	1955–1974	Claudine Schneider, R-R.I.	1981–1991
Coya G. Knutson, DFL-Minn.	1955–1959	Jean Spencer Ashbrook, R-Ohio	1982–1983
Kathryn E. Granahan, D-Pa.	1956–1963	Barbara B. Kennelly, D-Conn.	1982–1999
Florence P. Dwyer, R-N.J.	1957–1973	Katie Beatrice Hall, D-Ind.	1982–1985
Catherine D. May, R-Wash.	1959–1971	Sala Burton, D-Calif.	1983–1987
Edna O. Simpson, R-Ill.	1959–1961	Barbara Boxer, D-Calif.	1983–1993
Jessica McCullough Weis, R-N.Y.	1959–1963	Nancy L. Johnson, R-Conn.	1983–2007
Julia B. Hansen, D-Wash.	1960–1974	Marcy Kaptur, D-Ohio	1983–
Catherine D. Norrell, D-Ark.	1961–1963	Barbara Farrell Vucanovich, R-Nev.	1983–1997
Louise G. Reece, R-Tenn.	1961–1963	Helen Delich Bentley, R-Md.	1985–1995
Corinne B. Riley, D-S.C.	1962–1963	Jan Meyers, R-Kan.	1985–1997
Charlotte T. Reid, R-Ill.	1963–1971	Cathy Long, D-La.	1985–1987
Irene B. Baker, R-Tenn.	1964–1965	Constance A. Morella, R-Md.	1987–2003
Patsy T. Mink, D-Hawaii	1965–1977; 1990–2002	Elizabeth J. Patterson, D-S.C.	1987–1993
Lera M. Thomas, D-Texas	1966–1967	Patricia Saiki, R-Hawaii	1987–1991
Margaret M. Heckler, R-Mass.	1967–1983	Louise M. Slaughter, D-N.Y.	1987–
Shirley A. Chisholm, D-N.Y.	1969–1983	Nancy Pelosi, D-Calif.	1987–
Bella S. Abzug, D-N.Y.	1971–1977	Nita M. Lowey, D-N.Y.	1989–
Ella T. Grasso, D-Conn.	1971–1975	Jolene Unsoeld, D-Wash.	1989–1995
		Jill L. Long, D-Ind.	1989–1995
		Ileana Ros-Lehtinen, R-Fla.	1989–

House

Susan Molinari, R-N.Y.	1990–1997	Darlene Hooley, D-Ore.	1997–
Barbara-Rose Collins, D-Mich.	1991–1997	Carolyn Cheeks Kilpatrick, D-Mich.	1997–
Rosa DeLauro, D-Conn.	1991–	Carolyn McCarthy, D-N.Y.	1997–
Joan Kelly Horn, D-Mo.	1991–1993	Anne M. Northup, R-Ky.	1997–2007
Maxine Waters, D-Calif.	1991–	Loretta Sanchez, D-Calif.	1997–
Eva M. Clayton, D-N.C.	1992–2003	Debbie Stabenow, D-Mich.	1997–2001
Corrine Brown, D-Fla.	1993–	Ellen O. Tauscher, D-Calif.	1997–
Leslie L. Byrne, D-Va.	1993–1995	Mary Bono, R-Calif.	1998–
Maria Cantwell, D-Wash.	1993–1995	Lois Capps, D-Calif.	1998–
Pat Danner, D-Mo.	1993–2001	Barbara Lee, D-Calif.	1998–
Jennifer B. Dunn, R-Wash.	1993–2005	Heather Wilson, R-N.M.	1998–
Karan English, D-Ariz.	1993–1995	Tammy Baldwin, D-Wis.	1999–
Anna G. Eshoo, D-Calif.	1993–	Shelley Berkley, D-Nev.	1999–
Tillie Fowler, R-Fla.	1993–2001	Judy Biggert, R-Ill.	1999–
Elizabeth Furse, D-Ore.	1993–1999	Stephanie Tubbs Jones, D-Ohio	1999–
Jane F. Harman, D-Calif.	1993–1999;	Grace F. Napolitano, D-Calif.	1999–
	2001–	Jan Schakowsky, D-Ill.	1999–
Eddie Bernice Johnson, D-Texas	1993–	Jo Ann Davis, R-Va.	2001–2007
Blanche Lincoln, D-Ark.	1993–1997	Shelley Moore Capito, R-W.Va.	2001–
Carolyn B. Maloney, D-N.Y.	1993–	Susan A. Davis, D-Calif.	2001–
Cynthia Ann McKinney, D-Ga.	1993–2003;	Betty McCollum, D-Minn.	2001–
	2005–2007	Hilda Solis, D-Calif.	2001–
Carrie P. Meek, D-Fla.	1993–2003	Debbie Watson, D-Calif.	2001–
Marjorie Margolies-Mezvinsky, D-Pa.	1993–1995	Melissa Hart, R-Pa.	2001–2007
Deborah D. Pryce, R-Ohio	1993–	Marsha Blackburn, R-Tenn.	2003–
Lucille Roybal-Allard, D-Calif.	1993–	Virginia Brown-Waite, R-Fla.	2003–
Lynn Schenk, D-Calif.	1993–1995	Candice S. Miller, R-Mich.	2003–
Karen Shepherd, D-Utah	1993–1995	Marilyn Musgrave, R-Colo.	2003–
Karen L. Thurman, D-Fla.	1993–2003	Linda T. Sanchez, D-Calif.	2003–
Nydia M. Velazquez, D-N.Y.	1993–	Denise L. Majette, D-Ga.	2003–2005
Lynn Woolsey, D-Calif.	1993–	Katherine Harris, R-Fla.	2003–2007
Helen Chenoweth-Hage, R-Idaho	1995–2001	Stephanie Herseth, D-S.D.	2004–
Barbara Cubin, R-Wyo.	1995–	Thelma Drake, R-W.Va.	2005–
Sheila Jackson-Lee, D-Texas	1995–	Virginia Foxx, R-N.C.	2005–
Sue W. Kelly, R-N.Y.	1995–2007	Doris Matsui, D-Calif.	2005–
Zoe Lofgren, D-Calif.	1995–	Melissa Bean, D-Ill.	2005–
Karen McCarthy, D-Mo.	1995–2005	Jean Schmidt, R-Ohio	2005–
Sue Myrick, R-N.C.	1995–	Cathy McMorris, R-Wash.	2005–
Lynn N. Rivers, D-Mich.	1995–2003	Gwen Moore, D-Wis.	2005–
Andrea Seastrand, R-Calif.	1995–1997	Allyson Schwartz, D-Pa.	2005–
Linda Smith, R-Wash.	1995–1999	Debbie Wasserman-Schultz, D-Fla.	2005–
Enid Greene Waldholtz, R-Utah	1995–1997	Shelley Sekula Gibbs, R-Texas	2006–2007
Juanita Millender-McDonald, D-Calif.	1996–2007	Michelle Maria Bachmann, R-Minn.	2007–
Jo Ann Emerson, R-Mo.	1996–	Nancy E. Boyda, D-Kan.	2007–
Julia Carson, D-Ind.	1997–2007	Kathy Castor, D-Fla.	2007–
Diana DeGette, D-Colo.	1997–	Yvette D. Clarke, D-N.Y.	2007–
Kay Granger, R-Texas	1997–		

(continues)

WOMEN MEMBERS OF CONGRESS, 1917–2007 (CONTINUED)

House

Gabrielle Giffords, D-Ariz.	2007–	Carol Shea-Porter, D-N.H.	2007–
Mary Fallin, R-Okla.	2007–	Betty Sue Sutton, D-Ohio	2007–
Kirsten E. Gillibrand, D-N.Y.	2007–	Laura Richardson, D-Calif.	2007–
Mazie K. Hirono, D-Hawaii	2007–	Niki Tsongas, D-Mass.	2007–

SOURCE: Commission on the Bicentenary of the U.S. House of Representatives, *Women in Congress, 1917–1990* (Washington, D.C.: Government Printing Office, 1991); *Biographical Directory of the American Congress, 1774–1996* (Alexandria, Va.: CQ Staff Directories, 1997); *CQ Weekly*, selected issues; Biographical Directory of the United States Congress (http://bioguide.congress.gov/biosearch/biosearch.asp); United States Senate (http://www.senate.gov/artandhistory/history/common/briefing/women_senators.htm).

NOTES:

1. Rebecca L. Felton was sworn in November 21, 1922, to fill the vacancy created by the death of Thomas E. Watson, D. The next day she gave up her seat to Walter F. George, D, the elected candidate for the vacancy.

2. The *Biographical Directory of the United States Congress* reports that Gladys Pyle was elected November 8, 1938, to fill a vacancy caused by a death, and served from November 9, 1938, until January 3, 1939. However, Congress was not in session between the election and the expiration of her term on January 3, which has led other sources to say she was never sworn in. The directory lists Elizabeth H. Gasque as elected to fill a vacancy but does not indicate that she actually served.

In 1996 Maine joined California and also sent two women to the Senate—Republicans Olympia Snowe, a former member of the House who was first elected to the Senate in 1994, and Susan Collins, elected in 1996 to replace her former boss, Republican senator William S. Cohen. And in 2001 the state of Washington did the same when incoming Democratic senator Maria Cantwell, a former member of the House and Internet executive, joined Democrat Patty L. Murray, a self-described "mom in tennis shoes" who had served in her state legislature before being elected to the Senate in 1992. All six were still in the Senate in 2007.

Also joining the Senate in 2001 was former first lady Hillary Rodham CLINTON, a lawyer elected as a Democratic senator from New York. Clinton's win made history—she was the only first lady to be elected to public office. In 2007 she was the leading candidate to win the 2008 nomination for president. The 2002 election of Republican Elizabeth Dole, a former cabinet secretary and former president of the Red Cross, as a senator from North Carolina made for an interesting reunion among Senate spouses. Democrat Bill Clinton had defeated Republican Robert DOLE in the 1996 presidential race.

Many of the women who have been elected to Congress in recent

In February 2003 fourteen women senators gather at a "power coffee" hosted by Senators Barbara Mikulski, D-Md., and Kay Bailey Hutchison, R-Texas. Seated left to right are Olympia J. Snowe, R-Maine, Blanche L. Lincoln, D-Ark., Barbara Boxer, D-Calif., Susan M. Collins, R-Maine, Dianne Feinstein, D-Calif., Maria Cantwell, D-Wash. Standing left to right are Mary Landrieu, D-La., Hillary Rodham Clinton, D-N.Y., Elizabeth Dole, R-N.C., Hutchison, Mikulski, Lisa Murkowski, R-Alaska, Debbie Stabenow, D-Mich., and Patty Murray, D-Wash.
Source: CQ Photo/Scott J. Ferrell

years have also had experience in state legislatures, city councils, and other local government positions. For example, Florida Republican Ginny Brown-Waite had served in the Florida Senate for a decade and served as its president pro tempore before being elected to the U.S. House in 2002.

As the number of women in Congress increased, so did the leadership experience of female lawmakers. In 1995 Kassebaum became the first woman to chair a major Senate committee, Labor and Human Resources. She was joined in the House by fellow Kansas Republican Jan Meyers, who chaired the Small Business Committee. Before Meyers, no woman had chaired a full House committee since 1977, when Merchant Marine Committee chair Leonor K. Sullivan of Missouri left Congress. Mae Ella Nolan, a California Republican who served from 1923 to 1925, was the first woman to chair a congressional committee; she headed the House Committee on Expenditures in the Post Office Department. In 2003 two more women joined their ranks. Sen. Collins of Maine assumed the chairmanship of the Governmental Affairs Committee and her Maine colleague, Sen. Snowe, took the gavel of the Small Business and Entrepreneurship Committee.

Deborah Pryce of Ohio won the GOP Conference chairmanship, becoming the fourth-ranked member of her party's leadership in 2003. She was the first woman to reach such a lofty position in the Republican Party since Sen. Margaret Chase Smith of Maine held a similar post three decades earlier.

In the Senate, two women held party leadership positions as of 2003. Republican senator Kay Bailey Hutchison of Texas had been elected vice chair of her caucus in 2001, and Democratic senator Mikulski of Maryland had been elected secretary of hers in 1994.

By the beginning of the 110th Congress in 2007, women had gained even more committee authority, chairing four panels in the House and two in the Senate. In the House they were Juanita Millender-McDonald (Administration); Louise M. Slaughter (Rules); Nydia M. Velazquez (Small Business); and Stephanie Tubbs Jones (Standards of Official Conduct). Millender-McDonald, however, died from cancer a few months after the session began. In addition, women chaired a number of subcommittees including three panels on the powerful Appropriations Committee. In the Senate they were Barbara Boxer (Environment and Public Works) and Dianne Feinstein (Rules and Administration). As in the House, women chaired a number of subcommittees including four on the Appropriations panel.

Congress has been a starting point for several women who have sought national office. Shirley Chisholm, a Democratic representative from New York, made a bid for her party's presidential nomination in 1972, and Geraldine Ferraro, another New York Democrat who served in the House, was her party's vice-presidential nominee in 1984. In 2007 Sen. Clinton launched her campaign for the presidency. But Sen. Dole reversed the order: she campaigned for the GOP presidential nomination in 2000, two years before she was elected to the Senate.

Women's Suffrage

Although several states gave women the right to vote in the nineteenth century, full voting rights were not extended to all American women until 1920, when the Nineteenth Amendment to the Constitution was ratified. That year, for the first time, women in every state had the right to participate in the November election.

The amendment states: "The right of citizens of the United States to vote shall not be denied or abridged by the United States or by any State on account of sex."

The decades-long effort for women's suffrage was under way as early as the 1830s. Women working to abolish slavery were struck by the similarity of their

> **"The right of citizens of the United States to vote shall not be denied or abridged by the United States or by any State on account of sex."**
>
> —Nineteenth Amendment to the Constitution that gave women full voting rights

For decades before the passage of the Nineteenth Amendment in 1920, suffragists battled to win the right to vote, even when it meant picketing the White House in the dead of winter.
Source: Library of Congress

lot, under law, to that of slaves. A key event was the 1848 Women's Rights Convention at Seneca Falls, New York, where women passed a Declaration of Principles, a broad manifesto that included a call for the vote.

After the Civil War, some women contended they were granted equal rights, including voting privileges, by the Fourteenth Amendment, which freed slaves. Susan B. Anthony urged women to claim their right to vote at the polls; she did so in Rochester, New York, in 1872. Anthony was arrested and later convicted of "voting without having a lawful right to vote." Anthony and her followers pressed Congress for a constitutional amendment granting the franchise to women, but in 1887 the Senate rejected the proposal, 16–34.

The suffragists then turned to the states, where they were more successful. By the turn of the century, four western states had extended the franchise to women: Wyoming, Colorado, Utah, and Idaho. Then, as the Progressive movement gained influence, additional states gave women the vote: Washington in 1910; California in 1911; Arizona, Kansas, and Oregon in 1912; Montana and Nevada in 1914; New York in 1917; and Michigan, South Dakota, and Oklahoma in 1918.

Arguments for and against the vote included extravagant claims; some said women's enfranchisement would end corruption in American politics, while others cautioned that it would lead to free love. By 1914 some advocates of women's suffrage, led by Alice Paul, were using more militant tactics. They opposed every Democratic candidate in the eleven states where women could vote, regardless of the candidate's position on women's suffrage. They reasoned that the majority party should be held responsible for the failure of Congress to endorse a constitutional amendment. More than half of the forty-three Democrats running in those states were defeated.

Many suffragists saw President Woodrow Wilson as a major obstacle to their movement. Wilson, who endorsed women's suffrage, preferred to let the states

More on this topic:

Progressive Era, p. 443

Women in Congress, p. 606

handle voting qualifications and opposed a constitutional amendment. Women responded by demonstrating in Washington, and thousands were arrested and jailed.

In January 1918 Wilson finally announced his support for the proposed amendment. The House agreed the next day. Only after a new Congress met in 1919, however, did the Senate join the House in mustering the two-thirds majority required to send the amendment to the states for ratification. The amendment took effect in August 1920, when three-fourths of the states consented to ratification.

For much of the next half century, men voted at a higher rate than women. But in every presidential and midterm election from 1984 through 2000, according to U.S. census data, women voted at a higher rate than men.

It was also in the 1980s that the "gender gap" began to appear, a marked disparity in partisan preference between the sexes. In every presidential election from 1980 through 2000, according to the Gallup Poll, the Democratic presidential candidate ran better among women than men. It was a trend that culminated in 1996, when President Bill Clinton owed his reelection to the votes of women. He ran about even with Republican Bob DOLE among male voters.

In 2003 at the start of the 108th Congress, more than 200 women had served as senators and representatives. The first woman in Congress was Jeannette RANKIN, a Montana Republican (1917–1919, 1941–1943). When Rankin first ran for the House of Representatives in 1916, only a handful of states permitted women to vote. Although women outnumber men in the nation's voting-age population, they still held less than 14 percent of the seats in Congress in 2003.

Wright, Jim

Jim Wright (1922–) became in 1989 the first House Speaker in history to be forced by scandal to leave the office in the middle of a term. Only two years before, barely into his first term leading the House, the Texas Democrat had been hailed as one of the strongest leaders of the postwar Congress. "Let me give you back this job you gave me as a propitiation for all of this season of bad will that has grown up among us," Wright said in a dramatic hour-long speech on the House floor in May 1989 announcing his impending resignation. He portrayed himself as a victim of "mindless cannibalism" on the part of Republicans and an overzealous official investigator.

Wright's problem was his personal finances. After months of newspaper stories about them, the House ethics committee in 1988 opened an investigation headed by an outside attorney to look into suggestions that Wright had used a book contract to circumvent House rules limiting outside income and had received improper favors from a Texas developer.

Under an ethics cloud in 1989, House Speaker Jim Wright, D-Texas, announces his resignation of the speakership. He was succeeded at Speaker by Rep. Thomas S. Foley, D-Wash. (to the left).
Source: CQ Photo/R. Michael Jenkins

More on this topic:

Leadership, p. 325

Speaker of the House, p. 516

Standards of Official Conduct Committee, House, p. 532

In April 1989 the panel dropped a bombshell, announcing on the basis of the investigator's report that it would look into sixty-nine instances in which Wright might have violated House rules. The prospect of open hearings was not appealing to Democrats, particularly since their third-ranking House leader, whip Tony Coelho, had resigned in May rather than face an ethics investigation of his financial affairs.

Wright's hard-charging style was that of a political loner who governed more by fear than by respect. It left him with few friends, and he quit rather than drag out a demise that appeared inevitable.

Wright's one full Congress as Speaker, the 100th (1987–1989), was one of the most legislatively productive terms in a generation. Wright himself was at the center of it all. He began by calling for higher taxes to cut the deficit; by the end of the year President Ronald Reagan had dropped his opposition and signed a modest tax increase into law. Wright's lone-wolf drive for conciliation in Nicaragua, many Democrats believed, contributed as much to the eventual downfall of an anti-American leftist regime as did the Reagan administration's support of armed rebellion.

The 100th Congress enacted landmark welfare, health, and trade laws. It also featured an unusual vote that sealed Republican enmity to Wright. The Speaker kept a close vote on a cherished budget bill open ten minutes longer than usual, announced it closed, and then let a Texas colleague—brought to the floor by one of Wright's assistants—change his vote for a 206–205 victory.

Wright, who entered the House in 1955, built his power base on the Public Works Committee. He gave attention to his colleagues' needs, making sure there was a dam here or a highway there, a courtesy that paid off later when he began his climb up the ladder of the Democratic leadership.

When Wright ran for majority leader in 1976, he offered himself as an alternative to the bitterly antagonistic front-runners, Richard BOLLING of Missouri and Phillip Burton of California. He eliminated Bolling by three votes on the second ballot and Burton by one vote on the third. In 1985, no sooner had Speaker Thomas P. "Tip" O'NEIL Jr. announced he would retire at the end of the term than Wright declared, two years before the vote, that he had the support to win the post. The preemptive strike was effective; Wright had no challengers.

Wright resigned his speakership on June 6, 1989, and was succeeded by Thomas A. FOLEY of Washington. Wright left Congress at the end of that month.

Y

Yeas and Nays *See* VOTING IN CONGRESS.

Yielding

When a member of Congress has been recognized to speak, no other member may speak unless he or she obtains permission from the person recognized. Permission usually is requested in this form: "Will the gentleman [or gentlewoman, or senator] yield?" A legislator who has the floor, perhaps for a specified period of time to make the case for a bill or amendment, may yield some of that time to supporters who also want to speak: "I yield two minutes to the gentlewoman [from Illinois, Maryland, and so on]." The rules, which are enforced by the presiding officer, protect the legislator who has the floor.

Youth Franchise

The Twenty-sixth Amendment to the Constitution, ratified in 1971, extended voting rights to citizens eighteen years of age or older. Until then, most states had required voters to be at least twenty-one years old.

The key argument for the amendment linked voting rights to the military draft, which was then in effect for males aged eighteen to twenty-six, many of whom were sent to Vietnam. The same rationale had prompted Georgia in 1943 to lower its voting age to eighteen. The war-inspired slogan was: "Old enough to fight, old enough to vote." But few other states extended the franchise. Kentucky lowered its voting age to eighteen in 1955; Alaska and Hawaii, which became states in 1959, adopted minimum voting ages of nineteen and twenty, respectively.

In 1954 President Dwight D. Eisenhower proposed a constitutional amendment lowering the voting age to eighteen, but it was rejected by the Senate.

With the Vietnam War raging, Congress passed the Voting Rights Act of 1970, which lowered the voting age to eighteen years. The Supreme Court, in a quick test of the provision's constitutionality, ruled late that year that Congress could set qualifications by law only for federal elections; a constitutional amendment was needed to regulate voting in state and local elections.

By March 1971 Congress had sent the Twenty-sixth Amendment to the states for ratification. Moving more quickly than ever before on a proposed amendment, the states endorsed the change; the required three-fourths (thirty-eight) of the states ratified the amendment by the end of June.

The youth franchise amendment was the fourth constitutional amendment to enlarge the electorate since the Constitution was adopted in 1789:

- The Fifteenth Amendment gave the vote to African Americans, although additional civil rights laws were necessary to guarantee against discrimination.
- The Nineteenth Amendment provided for women's suffrage.
- The Twenty-third Amendment gave citizens in the District of Columbia the right to vote for president.

More than 11 million people were given the franchise by the Twenty-sixth Amendment. However, since being given the right to vote, the eighteen- to twenty-year-old age group has had the poorest record of voting participation of any age group. In no election since 1972, according to U.S. census surveys, have a majority of the nation's youngest voters participated. In the presidential election of 2000, less than one-third of young voters age eighteen to twenty-four cast ballots. In the midterm election of 1998, their rate of turnout was just under 17 percent.

The Census Bureau, however, reported that young adults in the eighteen- to twenty-four year-old-range showed a substantial increase in both registration and voting between the 2000 and 2004 national elections. Its voter survey showed the registration rate increased 7 percentage points and the voting rate increased 11 percentage points between those two elections.

Despite their poor participation rates, young voters—often broadly defined as those under thirty—have become a significant voting bloc, especially in presidential races. Republican presidents Ronald Reagan and George H. W. Bush lured a majority of these voters away from their traditional loyalty to the Democrats in 1984 and 1988, but Bill Clinton, the Democrat who was elected president in 1992, brought them back.

A nineteen-year-old New Mexico University student registers to vote in September 2004. Registration among young adults increased substantially between 2000 and 2004, according to the National Census Bureau.
Source: AP Images/Las Cruces Sun-News, Norm Dettlaff

Clinton, who wooed young voters with appearances on college campuses and late-night television, achieved an advantage of 3 percentage points over Bush with voters under thirty, according to the Gallup Poll. In 1996 Clinton's advantage among younger voters swelled to 24 points—his best showing, by far, among any age group. Figures for the 2000 presidential election showed young voters split evenly between Democrat Al GORE and Republican George W. Bush.

Zone or Regional Whips

Zone whip is another name for regional whip. Party leaders in the 435-member House of Representatives need layers of assistant leaders to help them ride herd on their members. Regional whips, the lowest level of the Democratic LEADERSHIP structure, keep in touch with party members from a particular area of the country. Regional whips at one time were known only as zone whips. Later they came to be called regional whips, but the older term is still often used along with other names.

Whips are elected by their party caucuses. They are near the top of the party leadership ladder; only the floor leaders are above them. Whips are assisted by other party members variously called deputy whips, assistant whips, and at-large whips, as well as regional or zone whips. A key role they play is advising the leadership on how their colleagues intend to vote on the floor and to be sure they show up to cast their votes.

Reference Material

The Government of the United States

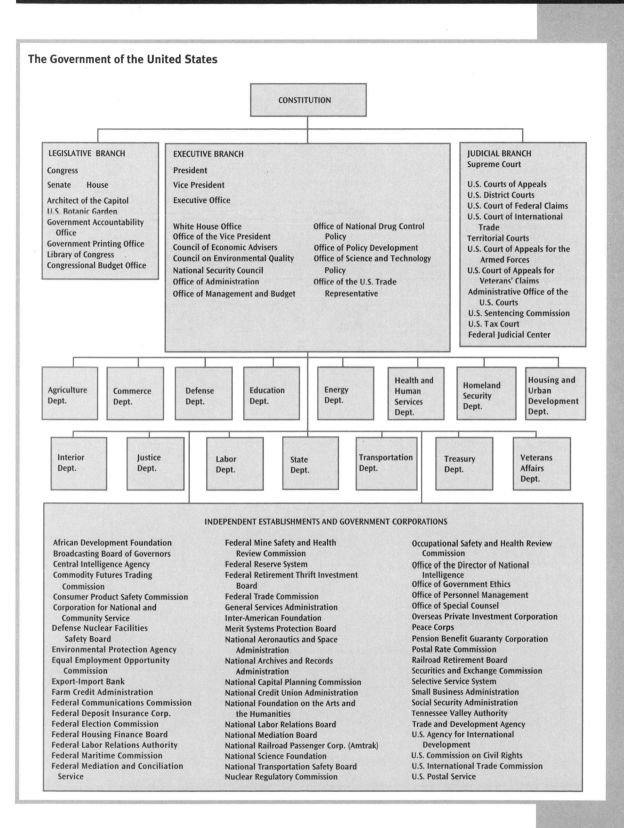

CONSTITUTION

LEGISLATIVE BRANCH

Congress

Senate   House

Architect of the Capitol
U.S. Botanic Garden
Government Accountability
  Office
Government Printing Office
Library of Congress
Congressional Budget Office

EXECUTIVE BRANCH

President

Vice President

Executive Office

White House Office
Office of the Vice President
Council of Economic Advisers
Council on Environmental Quality
National Security Council
Office of Administration
Office of Management and Budget

Office of National Drug Control
  Policy
Office of Policy Development
Office of Science and Technology
  Policy
Office of the U.S. Trade
  Representative

JUDICIAL BRANCH

Supreme Court

U.S. Courts of Appeals
U.S. District Courts
U.S. Court of Federal Claims
U.S. Court of International
  Trade
Territorial Courts
U.S. Court of Appeals for the
  Armed Forces
U.S. Court of Appeals for
  Veterans' Claims
Administrative Office of the
  U.S. Courts
U.S. Sentencing Commission
U.S. Tax Court
Federal Judicial Center

Agriculture Dept.

Commerce Dept.

Defense Dept.

Education Dept.

Energy Dept.

Health and Human Services Dept.

Homeland Security Dept.

Housing and Urban Development Dept.

Interior Dept.

Justice Dept.

Labor Dept.

State Dept.

Transportation Dept.

Treasury Dept.

Veterans Affairs Dept.

INDEPENDENT ESTABLISHMENTS AND GOVERNMENT CORPORATIONS

African Development Foundation
Broadcasting Board of Governors
Central Intelligence Agency
Commodity Futures Trading
  Commission
Consumer Product Safety Commission
Corporation for National and
  Community Service
Defense Nuclear Facilities
  Safety Board
Environmental Protection Agency
Equal Employment Opportunity
  Commission
Export-Import Bank
Farm Credit Administration
Federal Communications Commission
Federal Deposit Insurance Corp.
Federal Election Commission
Federal Housing Finance Board
Federal Labor Relations Authority
Federal Maritime Commission
Federal Mediation and Conciliation
  Service

Federal Mine Safety and Health
  Review Commission
Federal Reserve System
Federal Retirement Thrift Investment
  Board
Federal Trade Commission
General Services Administration
Inter-American Foundation
Merit Systems Protection Board
National Aeronautics and Space
  Administration
National Archives and Records
  Administration
National Capital Planning Commission
National Credit Union Administration
National Foundation on the Arts and
  the Humanities
National Labor Relations Board
National Mediation Board
National Railroad Passenger Corp. (Amtrak)
National Science Foundation
National Transportation Safety Board
Nuclear Regulatory Commission

Occupational Safety and Health Review
  Commission
Office of the Director of National
  Intelligence
Office of Government Ethics
Office of Personnel Management
Office of Special Counsel
Overseas Private Investment Corporation
Peace Corps
Pension Benefit Guaranty Corporation
Postal Rate Commission
Railroad Retirement Board
Securities and Exchange Commission
Selective Service System
Small Business Administration
Social Security Administration
Tennessee Valley Authority
Trade and Development Agency
U.S. Agency for International
  Development
U.S. Commission on Civil Rights
U.S. International Trade Commission
U.S. Postal Service

U.S. House of Representatives

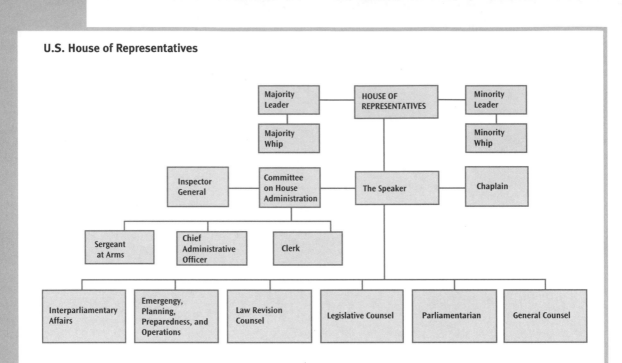

U.S. Senate

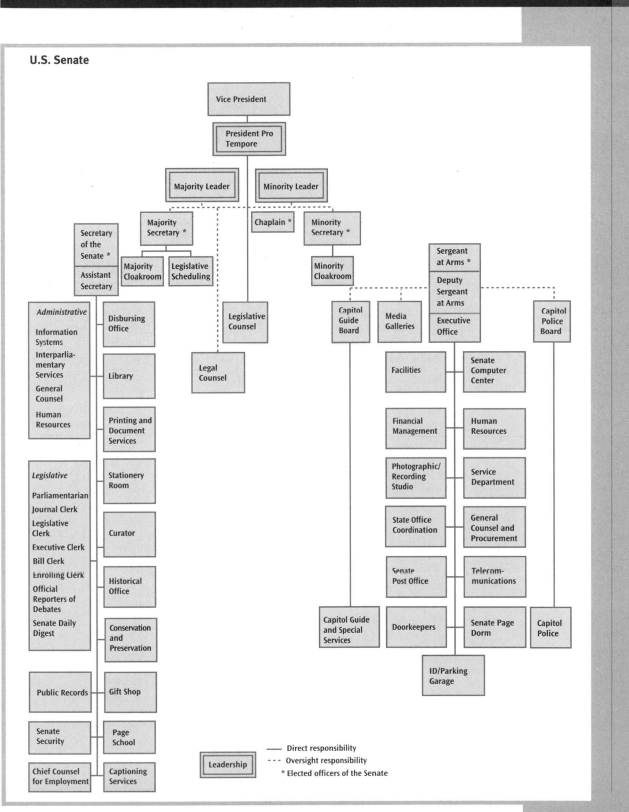

U.S. Presidents and Vice Presidents

President and political party	Born	Died	President's term of service	Vice president	Vice president's term of service
George Washington (F)	1732	1799	April 30, 1789–March 4, 1793	John Adams	April 30, 1789–March 4, 1793
George Washington (F)			March 4, 1793–March 4, 1797	John Adams	March 4, 1793–March 4, 1797
John Adams (F)	1735	1826	March 4, 1797–March 4, 1801	Thomas Jefferson	March 4, 1797–March 4, 1801
Thomas Jefferson (DR)	1743	1826	March 4, 1801–March 4, 1805	Aaron Burr	March 4, 1801–March 4, 1805
Thomas Jefferson (DR)			March 4, 1805–March 4, 1809	George Clinton	March 4, 1805–March 4, 1809
James Madison (DR)	1751	1836	March 4, 1809–March 4, 1813	George Clinton[1]	March 4, 1809–April 12, 1812
James Madison (DR)			March 4, 1813–March 4, 1817	Elbridge Gerry[1]	March 4, 1813–Nov. 23, 1814
James Monroe (DR)	1758	1831	March 4, 1817–March 4, 1821	Daniel D. Tompkins	March 4, 1817–March 4, 1821
James Monroe (DR)			March 4, 1821–March 4, 1825	Daniel D. Tompkins	March 4, 1821–March 4, 1825
John Q. Adams (DR)	1767	1848	March 4, 1825–March 4, 1829	John C. Calhoun	March 4, 1825–March 4, 1829
Andrew Jackson (D)	1767	1845	March 4, 1829–March 4, 1833	John C. Calhoun[2]	March 4, 1829–Dec. 28, 1832
Andrew Jackson (D)			March 4, 1833–March 4, 1837	Martin Van Buren	March 4, 1833–March 4, 1837
Martin Van Buren (D)	1782	1862	March 4, 1837–March 4, 1841	Richard M. Johnson	March 4, 1837–March 4, 1841
W. H. Harrison[1] (W)	1773	1841	March 4, 1841–April 4, 1841	John Tyler[3]	March 4, 1841–April 6, 1841
John Tyler (W)	1790	1862	April 6, 1841–March 4, 1845		
James K. Polk (D)	1795	1849	March 4, 1845–March 4, 1849	George M. Dallas	March 4, 1845–March 4, 1849
Zachary Taylor[1] (W)	1784	1850	March 4, 1849–July 9, 1850	Millard Fillmore[3]	March 4, 1849–July 10, 1850
Millard Fillmore (W)	1800	1874	July 10, 1850–March 4, 1853		
Franklin Pierce (D)	1804	1869	March 4, 1853–March 4, 1857	William R. King[1]	March 4, 1853–April 18, 1853
James Buchanan (D)	1791	1868	March 4, 1857–March 4, 1861	John C. Breckinridge	March 4, 1857–March 4, 1861
Abraham Lincoln (R)	1809	1865	March 4, 1861–March 4, 1865	Hannibal Hamlin	March 4, 1861–March 4, 1865
Abraham Lincoln[1] (R)			March 4, 1865–April 15, 1865	Andrew Johnson[3]	March 4, 1865–April 15, 1865
Andrew Johnson (R)	1808	1875	April 15, 1865–March 4, 1869		
Ulysses S. Grant (R)	1822	1885	March 4, 1869–March 4, 1873	Schuyler Colfax	March 4, 1869–March 4, 1873
Ulysses S. Grant (R)			March 4, 1873–March 4, 1877	Henry Wilson[1]	March 4, 1873–Nov. 22, 1875
Rutherford B. Hayes (R)	1822	1893	March 4, 1877–March 4, 1881	William A. Wheeler	March 4, 1877–March 4, 1881
James A. Garfield[1] (R)	1831	1881	March 4, 1881–Sept. 19, 1881	Chester A. Arthur[3]	March 4, 1881–Sept. 20, 1881
Chester A. Arthur (R)	1830	1886	Sept. 20, 1881–March 4, 1885		
Grover Cleveland (D)	1837	1908	March 4, 1885–March 4, 1889	Thomas A. Hendricks[1]	March 4, 1885–Nov. 25, 1885
Benjamin Harrison (R)	1833	1901	March 4, 1889–March 4, 1893	Levi P. Morton	March 4, 1889–March 4, 1893
Grover Cleveland (D)	1837	1908	March 4, 1893–March 4, 1897	Adlai E. Stevenson	March 4, 1893–March 4, 1897
William McKinley (R)	1843	1901	March 4, 1897–March 4, 1901	Garret A. Hobart[1]	March 4, 1897–Nov. 21, 1899
William McKinley[1] (R)			March 4, 1901–Sept. 14, 1901	Theodore Roosevelt[3]	March 4, 1901–Sept. 14, 1901
Theodore Roosevelt (R)	1858	1919	Sept. 14, 1901–March 4, 1905		
Theodore Roosevelt (R)			March 4, 1905–March 4, 1909	Charles W. Fairbanks	March 4, 1905–March 4, 1909
William H. Taft (R)	1857	1930	March 4, 1909–March 4, 1913	James S. Sherman[1]	March 4, 1909–Oct. 30, 1912
Woodrow Wilson (D)	1856	1924	March 4, 1913–March 4, 1917	Thomas R. Marshall	March 4, 1913–March 4, 1917
Woodrow Wilson (D)			March 4, 1917–March 4, 1921	Thomas R. Marshall	March 4, 1917–March 4, 1921
Warren G. Harding[1] (R)	1865	1923	March 4, 1921–Aug. 2, 1923	Calvin Coolidge[3]	March 4, 1921–Aug. 3, 1923
Calvin Coolidge (R)	1872	1933	Aug. 3, 1923–March 4, 1925		
Calvin Coolidge (R)			March 4, 1925–March 4, 1929	Charles G. Dawes	March 4, 1925–March 4, 1929
Herbert Hoover (R)	1874	1964	March 4, 1929–March 4, 1933	Charles Curtis	March 4, 1929–March 4, 1933

President and political party	Born	Died	President's term of service	Vice president	Vice president's term of service
Franklin D. Roosevelt (D)	1882	1945	March 4, 1933–Jan. 20, 1937	John N. Garner	March 4, 1933–Jan. 20, 1937
Franklin D. Roosevelt (D)			Jan. 20, 1937–Jan. 20, 1941	John N. Garner	Jan. 20, 1937–Jan. 20, 1941
Franklin D. Roosevelt (D)			Jan. 20, 1941–Jan. 20, 1945	Henry A. Wallace	Jan. 20, 1941–Jan. 20, 1945
Franklin D. Roosevelt[1] (D)			Jan. 20, 1945–April 12, 1945	Harry S. Truman[3]	Jan. 20, 1945–April 12, 1945
Harry S. Truman (D)	1884	1972	April 12, 1945–Jan. 20, 1949		
Harry S. Truman (D)			Jan. 20, 1949–Jan. 20, 1953	Alben W. Barkley	Jan. 20, 1949–Jan. 20, 1953
Dwight D. Eisenhower (R)	1890	1969	Jan. 20, 1953–Jan. 20, 1957	Richard Nixon	Jan. 20, 1953–Jan. 20, 1957
Dwight D. Eisenhower (R)			Jan. 20, 1957–Jan. 20, 1961	Richard Nixon	Jan. 20, 1957–Jan. 20, 1961
John F. Kennedy[1] (D)	1917	1963	Jan. 20, 1961–Nov. 22, 1963	Lyndon B. Johnson[3]	Jan. 20, 1961–Nov. 22, 1963
Lyndon B. Johnson (D)	1908	1973	Nov. 22, 1963–Jan. 20, 1965		
Lyndon B. Johnson (D)			Jan. 20, 1965–Jan. 20, 1969	Hubert H. Humphrey	Jan. 20, 1965–Jan. 20, 1969
Richard Nixon (R)	1913	1994	Jan. 20, 1969–Jan. 20, 1973	Spiro T. Agnew	Jan. 20, 1969–Jan. 20, 1973
Richard Nixon[2] (R)			Jan. 20, 1973–Aug. 9, 1974	Spiro T. Agnew[2]	Jan. 20, 1973–Oct. 10, 1973
				Gerald R. Ford[4]	Dec. 6, 1973–Aug. 9, 1974
Gerald R. Ford (R)	1913	2006	Aug. 9, 1974–Jan. 20, 1977	Nelson A. Rockefeller[4]	Dec. 19, 1974–Jan. 20, 1977
Jimmy Carter (D)	1924		Jan. 20, 1977–Jan. 20, 1981	Walter F. Mondale	Jan. 20, 1977–Jan. 20, 1981
Ronald Reagan (R)	1911	2004	Jan. 20, 1981–Jan. 20, 1985	George Bush	Jan. 20, 1981–Jan. 20, 1985
Ronald Reagan (R)			Jan. 20, 1985–Jan. 20, 1989	George Bush	Jan. 20, 1985–Jan. 20, 1989
George Bush (R)	1924		Jan. 20, 1989–Jan. 20, 1993	Dan Quayle	Jan. 20, 1989–Jan. 20, 1993
Bill Clinton (D)	1946		Jan. 20, 1993–Jan. 20, 1997	Albert Gore Jr.	Jan. 20, 1993–Jan. 20, 1997
Bill Clinton (D)			Jan. 20, 1997–Jan. 20, 2001	Albert Gore Jr.	Jan. 20, 1997–Jan. 20, 2001
George W. Bush (R)	1946		Jan. 20, 2001–Jan. 20, 2005	Richard B. Cheney	Jan. 20, 2001–Jan. 20, 2005
George W. Bush (R)			Jan. 20, 2005–	Richard B. Cheney	Jan. 20, 2005–

SOURCE: *Guide to the Presidency,* 2nd ed., ed. Michael Nelson (Washington, D.C.: Congressional Quarterly, 1996), 1631. Updated by the editor.

NOTES: D—Democrat; DR—Democratic-Republican; F—Federalist; R—Republican; W—Whig.

1. Died in office.
2. Resigned.
3. Assumed presidency.
4. The Twenty-fifth amendment to the Constitution, ratified in 1967, provided a method to fill a vacancy in the vice-presidency. The amendment provided that the president would nominate a vice president who would take office on confirmation by majority votes of both the Senate and House. When Vice President Spiro Agnew resigned in 1973 in connection with an investigation into alleged criminal conduct before becoming vice president, Richard Nixon named Ford to the office. When Nixon resigned in 1974 in connection with the Watergate scandal, Ford became president and nominated Rockefeller as his vice president. Both Ford and Rockefeller were approved quickly by Congress. As of January 2008, Ford and Rockefeller were the only two persons to hold the offices who were not elected by the voters.

Sessions of the U.S. Congress, 1789–2007

Congress	Session	Date of beginning[1]	Date of adjournment[2]	Length in days	President pro tempore of the Senate[3]	Speaker of the House
1st	1	Mar. 4, 1789	Sept. 29, 1789	210	John Langdon of New Hampshire[4]	Frederick A. C. Muhlenberg of Pennsylvania
	2	Jan. 4, 1790	Aug. 12, 1790	221		
	3	Dec. 6, 1790	Mar. 3, 1791	88		
2nd	1	Oct. 24, 1791	May 8, 1792	197	Richard Henry Lee of Virginia	Jonathan Trumbull of Connecticut
	2	Nov. 5, 1792	Mar. 2, 1793	119	John Langdon of New Hampshire	
3rd	1	Dec. 2, 1793	June 9, 1794	190	Langdon Ralph Izard of South Carolina	Frederick A. C. Muhlenberg of Pennsylvania
	2	Nov. 3, 1794	Mar. 3, 1795	121	Henry Tazewell of Virginia	
4th	1	Dec. 7, 1795	June 1, 1796	177	Tazewell Samuel Livermore of New Hampshire	Jonathan Dayton of New Jersey
	2	Dec. 5, 1796	Mar. 3, 1797	89	William Bingham of Pennsylvania	
5th	1	May 15, 1797	July 10, 1797	57	William Bradford of Rhode Island	Dayton
	2	Nov. 13, 1797	July 16, 1798	246	Jacob Read of South Carolina Theodore Sedgwick of Massachusetts	George Dent of Maryland[5]
	3	Dec. 3, 1798	Mar. 3, 1799	91	John Laurence of New York James Ross of Pennsylvania	
6th	1	Dec. 2, 1799	May 14, 1800	164	Samuel Livermore of New Hampshire Uriah Tracy of Connecticut	Theodore Sedgwick of Massachusetts
	2	Nov. 17, 1800	Mar. 3, 1801	107	John E. Howard of Maryland James Hillhouse of Connecticut	
7th	1	Dec. 7, 1801	May 3, 1802	148	Abraham Baldwin of Georgia	Nathaniel Macon of North Carolina
	2	Dec. 6, 1802	Mar. 3, 1803	88	Stephen R. Bradley of Vermont	
8th	1	Oct. 17, 1803	Mar. 27, 1804	163	John Brown of Kentucky Jesse Franklin of North Carolina	Macon
	2	Nov. 5, 1804	Mar. 3, 1805	119	Joseph Anderson of Tennessee	
9th	1	Dec. 2, 1805	Apr. 21, 1806	141	Samuel Smith of Maryland	Macon
	2	Dec. 1, 1806	Mar. 3, 1807	93	Smith	
10th	1	Oct. 26, 1807	Apr. 25, 1808	182	Smith	Joseph B. Varnum of Massachusetts

Congress	Session	Date of beginning[1]	Date of adjournment[2]	Length in days	President pro tempore of the Senate[3]	Speaker of the House
	2	Nov. 7, 1808	Mar. 3, 1809	117	Stephen R. Bradley of Vermont	
					John Milledge of Georgia	
11th	1	May 22, 1809	June 28, 1809	38	Andrew Gregg of Pennsylvania	Varnum
	2	Nov. 27, 1809	May 1, 1810	156	John Gaillard of South Carolina	
	3	Dec. 3, 1810	Mar. 3, 1811	91	John Pope of Kentucky	
12th	1	Nov. 4, 1811	July 6, 1812	245	William H. Crawford of Georgia	Henry Clay of Kentucky
	2	Nov. 2, 1812	Mar. 3, 1813	122	Crawford	
13th	1	May 24, 1813	Aug. 2, 1813	71	Crawford	Clay
	2	Dec. 6, 1813	Apr. 18, 1814	134	Joseph B. Varnum of Massachusetts	
	3	Sept. 19, 1814	Mar. 3, 1815	166	John Gaillard of South Carolina	Langdon Cheves of South Carolina[6]
14th	1	Dec. 4, 1815	Apr. 30, 1816	148	Gaillard	Henry Clay of Kentucky
	2	Dec. 2, 1816	Mar. 3, 1817	92	Gaillard	
15th	1	Dec. 1, 1817	Apr. 20, 1818	141	Gaillard	Clay
	2	Nov. 16, 1818	Mar. 3, 1819	108	James Barbour of Virginia	
16th	1	Dec. 6, 1819	May 15, 1820	162	John Gaillard of South Carolina	Clay
	2	Nov. 13, 1820	Mar. 3, 1821	111	Gaillard	John W. Taylor of New York[7]
17th	1	Dec. 3, 1821	May 8, 1822	157	Gaillard	Philip P. Barbour of Virginia
	2	Dec. 2, 1822	Mar. 3, 1823	92	Gaillard	
18th	1	Dec. 1, 1823	May 27, 1824	178	Gaillard	Henry Clay of Kentucky
	2	Dec. 6, 1824	Mar. 3, 1825	88	Gaillard	
19th	1	Dec. 5, 1825	May 22, 1826	169	Nathaniel Macon of North Carolina	John W. Taylor of New York
	2	Dec. 4, 1826	Mar. 3, 1827	90	Macon	
20th	1	Dec. 3, 1827	May 26, 1828	175	Samuel Smith of Maryland	Andrew Stevenson of Virginia
	2	Dec. 1, 1828	Mar. 3, 1829	93	Smith	
21st	1	Dec. 7, 1829	May 31, 1830	176	Smith	Stevenson
	2	Dec. 6, 1830	Mar. 3, 1831	88	Littleton Waller Tazewell of Virginia	
22nd	1	Dec. 5, 1831	July 16, 1832	225	Tazewell	Stevenson
	2	Dec. 3, 1832	Mar. 2, 1833	91	Hugh Lawson White of Tennessee	
23rd	1	Dec. 2, 1833	June 30, 1834	211	George Poindexter of Mississippi	Stevenson
	2	Dec. 1, 1834	Mar. 3, 1835	93	John Tyler of Virginia	John Bell of Tennessee[8]
24th	1	Dec. 7, 1835	July 4, 1836	211	William R. King of Alabama	James K. Polk of Tennessee
	2	Dec. 5, 1836	Mar. 3, 1837	89	King	
25th	1	Sept. 4, 1837	Oct. 16, 1837	43	King	Polk
	2	Dec. 4, 1837	July 9, 1838	218	King	
	3	Dec. 3, 1838	Mar. 3, 1839	91	King	

(continued)

Sessions of the U.S. Congress, 1789–2007 (CONTINUED)

Congress	Session	Date of beginning[1]	Date of adjournment[2]	Length in days	President pro tempore of the Senate[3]	Speaker of the House
26th	1	Dec. 2, 1839	July 21, 1840	233	King	Robert M. T. Hunter of Virginia
	2	Dec. 7, 1840	Mar. 3, 1841	87	King	
27th	1	May 31, 1841	Sept. 13, 1841	106	Samuel L. Southard of New Jersey	John White of Kentucky
	2	Dec. 6, 1841	Aug. 31, 1842	269	Willie P. Mangum of North Carolina	
	3	Dec. 5, 1842	Mar. 3, 1843	89	Mangum	
28th	1	Dec. 4, 1843	June 17, 1844	196	Mangum	John W. Jones of Virginia
	2	Dec. 2, 1844	Mar. 3, 1845	92	Mangum	
29th	1	Dec. 1, 1845	Aug. 10, 1846	253	David R. Atchison of Missouri	John W. Davis of Indiana
	2	Dec. 7, 1846	Mar. 3, 1847	87	Atchison	
30th	1	Dec. 6, 1847	Aug. 14, 1848	254	Atchison	Robert C. Winthrop of Massachusetts
	2	Dec. 4, 1848	Mar. 3, 1849	90	Atchison	
31st	1	Dec. 3, 1849	Sept. 30, 1850	302	William R. King of Alabama	Howell Cobb of Georgia
	2	Dec. 2, 1850	Mar. 3, 1851	92	King	
32nd	1	Dec. 1, 1851	Aug. 31, 1852	275	King	Linn Boyd of Kentucky
	2	Dec. 6, 1852	Mar. 3, 1853	88	David R. Atchison of Missouri	
33rd	1	Dec. 5, 1853	Aug. 7, 1854	246	Atchison	Boyd
	2	Dec. 4, 1854	Mar. 3, 1855	90	Jesse D. Bright of Indiana Lewis Cass of Michigan	
34th	1	Dec. 3, 1855	Aug. 18, 1856	260	Jesse D. Bright of Indiana	Nathaniel P. Banks of Massachusetts
	2	Aug. 21, 1856	Aug. 30, 1856	10	Bright	
	3	Dec. 1, 1856	Mar. 3, 1857	93	James M. Mason of Virginia Thomas J. Rusk of Texas	
35th	1	Dec. 7, 1857	June 14, 1858	189	Benjamin Fitzpatrick of Alabama	James L. Orr of South Carolina
	2	Dec. 6, 1858	Mar. 3, 1859	88	Fitzpatrick	
36th	1	Dec. 5, 1859	June 25, 1860	202	Fitzpatrick Jesse D. Bright of Indiana	William Pennington of New Jersey
	2	Dec. 3, 1860	Mar. 3, 1861	93	Solomon Foot of Vermont	
37th	1	July 4, 1861	Aug. 6, 1861	34	Foot	Galusha A. Grow of Pennsylvania
	2	Dec. 2, 1861	July 17, 1862	228	Foot	
	3	Dec. 1, 1862	Mar. 3, 1863	93	Foot	
38th	1	Dec. 7, 1863	July 4, 1864	209	Foot Daniel Clark of New Hampshire	Schuyler Colfax of Indiana
	2	Dec. 5, 1864	Mar. 3, 1865	89	Clark	
39th	1	Dec. 4, 1865	July 28, 1866	237	Lafayette S. Foster of Connecticut	Colfax
	2	Dec. 3, 1866	Mar. 3, 1867	91	Benjamin F. Wade of Ohio	
40th	1	Mar. 4, 1867[9]	Dec. 2, 1867	274	Wade	Colfax
	2	Dec. 2, 1867[10]	Nov. 10, 1868	345	Wade	

Congress	Session	Date of beginning[1]	Date of adjournment[2]	Length in days	President pro tempore of the Senate[3]	Speaker of the House
	3	Dec. 7, 1868	Mar. 3, 1869	87	Wade	Theodore M. Pomeroy of New York[11]
41st	1	Mar. 4, 1869	Apr. 10, 1869	38	Henry B. Anthony of Rhode Island	James G. Blaine of Maine
	2	Dec. 6, 1869	July 15, 1870	222	Anthony	
	3	Dec. 5, 1870	Mar. 3, 1871	89	Anthony	
42nd	1	Mar. 4, 1871	Apr. 20, 1871	48	Anthony	Blaine
	2	Dec. 4, 1871	June 10, 1872	190	Anthony	
	3	Dec. 2, 1872	Mar. 3, 1873	92	Anthony	
43rd	1	Dec. 1, 1873	June 23, 1874	204	Matthew H. Carpenter of Wisconsin	Blaine
	2	Dec. 7, 1874	Mar. 3, 1875	87	Carpenter Henry B. Anthony of Rhode Island	
44th	1	Dec. 6, 1875	Aug. 15, 1876	254	Thomas W. Ferry of Michigan	Michael C. Kerr of Indiana[12] Samuel S. Cox of New York, pro tempore[13] Milton Sayler of Ohio, pro tempore[14]
	2	Dec. 4, 1876	Mar. 3, 1877	90	Ferry	Samuel J. Randall of Pennsylvania
45th	1	Oct. 15, 1877	Dec. 3, 1877	50	Ferry	Randall
	2	Dec. 3, 1877	June 20, 1878	200	Ferry	
	3	Dec. 2, 1878	Mar. 3, 1879	92	Ferry	
46th	1	Mar. 18, 1879	July 1, 1879	106	Allen G. Thurman of Ohio	Randall
	2	Dec. 1, 1879	June 16, 1880	199	Thurman	
	3	Dec. 6, 1880	Mar. 3, 1881	88	Thurman	
47th	1	Dec. 5, 1881	Aug. 8, 1882	247	Thomas F. Bayard of Delaware David Davis of Illinois	J. Warren Keifer of Ohio
	2	Dec. 4, 1882	Mar. 3, 1883	90	George F. Edmunds of Vermont	
48th	1	Dec. 3, 1883	July 7, 1884	218	Edmunds	John G. Carlisle of Kentucky
	2	Dec. 1, 1884	Mar. 3, 1885	93	Edmunds	
49th	1	Dec. 7, 1885	Aug. 5, 1886	242	John Sherman of Ohio	Carlisle
	2	Dec. 6, 1886	Mar. 3, 1887	88	John J. Ingalls of Kansas	
50th	1	Dec. 5, 1887	Oct. 20, 1888	321	Ingalls	Carlisle
	2	Dec. 3, 1888	Mar. 3, 1889	91	Ingalls	
51st	1	Dec. 2, 1889	Oct. 1, 1890	304	Ingalls	Thomas B. Reed of Maine
	2	Dec. 1, 1890	Mar. 3, 1891	93	Charles F. Manderson of Nebraska	
52nd	1	Dec. 7, 1891	Aug. 5, 1892	251	Manderson	Charles F. Crisp of Georgia
	2	Dec. 5, 1892	Mar. 3, 1893	89	Isham G. Harris of Tennessee	
53rd	1	Aug. 7, 1893	Nov. 3, 1893	89	Harris	Crisp
	2	Dec. 4, 1893	Aug. 28, 1894	268	Harris	
	3	Dec. 3, 1894	Mar. 3, 1895	97	Matt W. Ransom of North Carolina Isham G. Harris of Tennessee	

(continued)

Sessions of the U.S. Congress, 1789–2007 (CONTINUED)

Congress	Session	Date of beginning[1]	Date of adjournment[2]	Length in days	President pro tempore of the Senate[3]	Speaker of the House
54th	1	Dec. 2, 1895	June 11, 1896	193	William P. Frye of Maine	Thomas B. Reed of Maine
	2	Dec. 7, 1896	Mar. 3, 1897	87	Frye	
55th	1	Mar. 15, 1897	July 24, 1897	131	Frye	Reed
	2	Dec. 6, 1897	July 8, 1898	215	Frye	
	3	Dec. 5, 1898	Mar. 3, 1899	89	Frye	
56th	1	Dec. 4, 1899	June 7, 1900	186	Frye	David B. Henderson of Iowa
	2	Dec. 3, 1900	Mar. 3, 1901	91	Frye	
57th	1	Dec. 2, 1901	July 1, 1902	212	Frye	Henderson
	2	Dec. 1, 1902	Mar. 3, 1903	93	Frye	
58th	1	Nov. 9, 1903	Dec. 7, 1903	29	Frye	Joseph G. Cannon of Illinois
	2	Dec. 7, 1903	Apr. 28, 1904	144	Frye	
	3	Dec. 5, 1904	Mar. 3, 1905	89	Frye	
59th	1	Dec. 4, 1905	June 30, 1906	209	Frye	Cannon
	2	Dec. 3, 1906	Mar. 3, 1907	91	Frye	
60th	1	Dec. 2, 1907	May 30, 1908	181	Frye	Cannon
	2	Dec. 7, 1908	Mar. 3, 1909	87	Frye	
61st	1	Mar. 15, 1909	Aug. 5, 1909	144	Frye	Cannon
	2	Dec. 6, 1909	June 25, 1910	202	Frye	
	3	Dec. 5, 1910	Mar. 3, 1911	89	Frye	
62nd	1	Apr. 4, 1911	Aug. 22, 1911	141	Frye[15]	Champ Clark of Missouri
	2	Dec. 4, 1911	Aug. 26, 1912	267	Augustus O. Bacon of Georgia[16] Frank B. Brandegee of Connecticut[17] Charles Curtis of Kansas[18] Jacob H. Gallinger of New Hampshire[19] Henry Cabot Lodge of Massachusetts[20]	
	3	Dec. 2, 1912	Mar. 3, 1913	92	Bacon;[21] Gallinger[22]	
63rd	1	Apr. 7, 1913	Dec. 1, 1913	239	James P. Clarke of Arkansas	Clark
	2	Dec. 1, 1913	Oct. 24, 1914	328	Clarke	
	3	Dec. 7, 1914	Mar. 3, 1915	87	Clarke	
64th	1	Dec. 6, 1915	Sept. 8, 1916	278	Clarke[23]	Clark
	2	Dec. 4, 1916	Mar. 3, 1917	90	Willard Saulsbury of Delaware	
65th	1	Apr. 2, 1917	Oct. 6, 1917	188	Saulsbury	Clark
	2	Dec. 3, 1917	Nov. 21, 1918	354	Saulsbury	
	3	Dec. 2, 1918	Mar. 3, 1919	92	Saulsbury	
66th	1	May 19, 1919	Nov. 19, 1919	185	Albert B. Cummins of Iowa	Frederick H. Gillett of Massachusetts
	2	Dec. 1, 1919	June 5, 1920	188	Cummins	
	3	Dec. 6, 1920	Mar. 3, 1921	88	Cummins	
67th	1	Apr. 11, 1921	Nov. 23, 1921	227	Cummins	Gillett
	2	Dec. 5, 1921	Sept. 22, 1922	292	Cummins	
	3	Nov. 20, 1922	Dec. 4, 1922	15	Cummins	
	4	Dec. 4, 1922	Mar. 3, 1923	90	Cummins	
68th	1	Dec. 3, 1923	June 7, 1924	188	Cummins	Gillett
	2	Dec. 1, 1924	Mar. 3, 1925	93	Cummins	

Congress	Session	Date of beginning[1]	Date of adjournment[2]	Length in days	President pro tempore of the Senate[3]	Speaker of the House
69th	1	Dec. 7, 1925	July 3, 1926	209	George H. Moses of New Hampshire	Nicholas Longworth of Ohio
	2	Dec. 6, 1926	Mar. 3, 1927	88	Moses	
70th	1	Dec. 5, 1927	May 29, 1928	177	Moses	Longworth
	2	Dec. 3, 1928	Mar. 3, 1929	91	Moses	
71st	1	Apr. 15, 1929	Nov. 22, 1929	222	Moses	Longworth
	2	Dec. 2, 1929	July 3, 1930	214	Moses	
	3	Dec. 1, 1930	Mar. 3, 1931	93	Moses	
72nd	1	Dec. 7, 1931	July 16, 1932	223	Moses	John N. Garner of Texas
	2	Dec. 5, 1932	Mar. 3, 1933	89	Moses	
73rd	1	Mar. 9, 1933	June 15, 1933	99	Key Pittman of Nevada	Henry T. Rainey of Illinois[24]
	2	Jan. 3, 1934	June 18, 1934	167	Pittman	
74th	1	Jan. 3, 1935	Aug. 26, 1935	236	Pittman	Joseph W. Byrns of Tennessee[25]
	2	Jan. 3, 1936	June 20, 1936	170	Pittman	William B. Bankhead of Alabama[26]
75th	1	Jan. 5, 1937	Aug. 21, 1937	229	Pittman	Bankhead
	2	Nov. 15, 1937	Dec. 21, 1937	37	Pittman	
	3	Jan. 3, 1938	June 16, 1938	165	Pittman	
76th	1	Jan. 3, 1939	Aug. 5, 1939	215	Pittman	Bankhead[27]
	2	Sept. 21, 1939	Nov. 3, 1939	44	Pittman	
	3	Jan. 3, 1940	Jan. 3, 1941	367	Pittman[28] William H. King of Utah[30]	Sam Rayburn of Texas[29]
77th	1	Jan. 3, 1941	Jan. 2, 1942	365	Pat Harrison of Mississippi[31] Carter Glass of Virginia[32]	Rayburn
	2	Jan. 5, 1942	Dec. 16, 1942	346		
78th	1	Jan. 6, 1943[33]	Dec. 21, 1943	350	Glass	Rayburn
	2	Jan. 10, 1944[34]	Dec. 19, 1944	345	Glass	
79th	1	Jan. 3, 1945[35]	Dec. 21, 1945	353	Kenneth McKellar of Tennessee	Rayburn
	2	Jan. 14, 1946[36]	Aug. 2, 1946	201	McKellar	
80th	1	Jan. 3, 1947[37]	Dec. 19, 1947	351	Arthur H. Vandenberg of Michigan	Joseph W. Martin Jr. of Massachusetts
	2	Jan. 6, 1948[38]	Dec. 31, 1948	361	Vandenberg	
81st	1	Jan. 3, 1949	Oct. 19, 1949	290	Kenneth McKellar of Tennessee	Sam Rayburn of Texas
	2	Jan. 3, 1950[39]	Jan. 2, 1951	365	McKellar	
82nd	1	Jan. 3, 1951[40]	Oct. 20, 1951	291	McKellar	Rayburn
	2	Jan. 8, 1952[41]	July 7, 1952	182	McKellar	
83rd	1	Jan. 3, 1953[42]	Aug. 3, 1953	213	Styles Bridges of New Hampshire	Joseph W. Martin Jr. of Massachusetts
	2	Jan. 6, 1954[43]	Dec. 2, 1954	331	Bridges	
84th	1	Jan. 5, 1955[44]	Aug. 2, 1955	210	Walter F. George of Georgia	Sam Rayburn of Texas
	2	Jan. 3, 1956[45]	July 27, 1956	207	George	
85th	1	Jan. 3, 1957[46]	Aug. 30, 1957	239	Carl Hayden of Arizona	Rayburn
	2	Jan. 7, 1958[47]	Aug. 24, 1958	230	Hayden	

(continued)

Sessions of the U.S. Congress, 1789–2007 (CONTINUED)

Congress	Session	Date of beginning[1]	Date of adjournment[2]	Length in days	President pro tempore of the Senate[3]	Speaker of the House
86th	1	Jan. 7, 1959[48]	Sept. 15, 1959	252	Hayden	Rayburn
	2	Jan. 6, 1960[49]	Sept. 1, 1960	240	Hayden	
87th	1	Jan. 3, 1961[50]	Sept. 27, 1961	268	Hayden	Rayburn[51]
	2	Jan. 10, 1962[52]	Oct. 13, 1962	277	Hayden	John W. McCormack of Massachusetts[53]
88th	1	Jan. 9, 1963[54]	Dec. 30, 1963	356	Hayden	McCormack
	2	Jan. 7, 1964[55]	Oct. 3, 1964	270	Hayden	
89th	1	Jan. 4, 1965	Oct. 23, 1965	293	Hayden	McCormack
	2	Jan. 10, 1966[56]	Oct. 22, 1966	286	Hayden	
90th	1	Jan. 10, 1967[57]	Dec. 15, 1967	340	Hayden	McCormack
	2	Jan. 15, 1968[58]	Oct. 14, 1968	274	Hayden	
91st	1	Jan. 3, 1969[59]	Dec. 23, 1969	355	Richard B. Russell of Georgia	McCormack
	2	Jan. 19, 1970[60]	Jan. 2, 1971	349	Russell	
92nd	1	Jan. 21, 1971[61]	Dec. 17, 1971	331	Russell[62] Allen J. Ellender of Louisiana[63]	Carl Albert of Oklahoma
	2	Jan. 18, 1972[64]	Oct. 18, 1972	275	Ellender[65] James O. Eastland of Mississippi[66]	
93rd	1	Jan. 3, 1973[67]	Dec. 22, 1973	354	Eastland	Albert
	2	Jan. 21, 1974[68]	Dec. 20, 1974	334	Eastland	
94th	1	Jan. 14, 1975[69]	Dec. 19, 1975	340	Eastland	Albert
	2	Jan. 19, 1976[70]	Oct. 1, 1976	257	Eastland	
95th	1	Jan. 4, 1977[71]	Dec. 15, 1977	346	Eastland	Thomas P. O'Neill Jr. of Massachusetts
	2	Jan. 19, 1978[72]	Oct. 15, 1978	270	Eastland	
96th	1	Jan. 15, 1979[73]	Jan. 3, 1980	354	Warren G. Magnuson of Washington	O'Neill
	2	Jan. 3, 1980[74]	Dec. 16, 1980	349	Magnuson	
97th	1	Jan. 5, 1981[75]	Dec. 16, 1981	347	Strom Thurmond of South Carolina	O'Neill
	2	Jan. 25, 1982[76]	Dec. 23, 1982	333	Thurmond	
98th	1	Jan. 3, 1983[77]	Nov. 18, 1983	320	Thurmond	O'Neill
	2	Jan. 23, 1984[78]	Oct. 12, 1984	264	Thurmond	
99th	1	Jan. 3, 1985[79]	Dec. 20, 1985	352	Thurmond	O'Neill
	2	Jan. 21, 1986[80]	Oct. 18, 1986	278	Thurmond	
100th	1	Jan. 6, 1987[81]	Dec. 22, 1987	351	John C. Stennis of Mississippi	Jim Wright of Texas
	2	Jan. 25, 1988[82]	Oct. 22, 1988	272	Stennis	
101st	1	Jan. 3, 1989[83]	Nov. 22, 1989	324	Robert C. Byrd of West Virginia	Wright; Thomas S. Foley of Washington[84]
	2	Jan. 23, 1990[85]	Oct. 28, 1990	260	Byrd	Foley
102nd	1	Jan. 3, 1991[86]	Jan. 3, 1992	366	Byrd	Foley
	2	Jan. 3, 1992[87]	Oct. 9, 1992	281	Byrd	
103rd	1	Jan. 5, 1993[88]	Nov. 26, 1993	326	Byrd	Foley
	2	Jan. 25, 1994[89]	Dec. 1, 1994	311	Byrd	

Congress	Session	Date of beginning[1]	Date of adjournment[2]	Length in days	President pro tempore of the Senate[3]	Speaker of the House
104th	1	Jan. 4, 1995[90]	Jan. 3, 1996	365	Strom Thurmond of South Carolina	Newt Gingrich of Georgia
	2	Jan. 3, 1996[91]	Oct. 4, 1996	276	Thurmond	
105th	1	Jan. 7, 1997[92]	Nov. 13, 1997	311	Thurmond	Gingrich
	2	Jan. 27, 1998[93]	Dec. 19, 1998	327	Thurmond	
106th	1	Jan. 6, 1999[94]	Nov. 22, 1999	321	Thurmond	J. Dennis Hastert of Illinois
	2	Jan. 24, 2000[95]	Dec. 15, 2000	326	Thurmond	Hastert
107th	1	Jan. 3, 2001[96]	Dec. 20, 2001	352	Robert C. Byrd of West Virginia; Strom Thurmond of South Carolina; Robert C. Byrd of West Virginia[97]	Hastert
	2	Jan. 23, 2002[98]	Nov. 22, 2002	304	Byrd	Hastert
108th	1	Jan. 7, 2003[99]	Dec. 9, 2003	336	Ted Stevens of Alaska	Hastert
	2	Jan. 20, 2004[100]	Dec. 8, 2004	323	Stevens	Hastert
109th	1	Jan. 4, 2005[101]	Dec. 22, 2005	353	Stevens	Hastert
	2	Jan. 3, 2006[102]	Dec. 8, 2006	339	Stevens	Hastert
110th	1	Jan. 7, 2007			Robert C. Byrd of West Virginia	Nancy Pelosi of California

NOTES: 1. The U.S. Constitution (Article I, Section 4) provided that "The Congress shall assemble at least once in every year … on the first Monday in December, unless they shall by law appoint a different day." Pursuant to a resolution of the Continental Congress, the first session of the First Congress convened Mar. 4, 1789. Up to and including May 20, 1820, eighteen acts were passed providing for the meeting of Congress on other days in the year. After 1820 Congress met regularly on the first Monday in December until 1934, when the Twentieth Amendment to the Constitution became effective changing the meeting date to Jan. 3. (Until then, brief special sessions of the Senate were held only at the beginning of each presidential term to confirm cabinet and other nominations—and occasionally at other times for other purposes. The Senate last met in special session from Mar. 4 to Mar. 6, 1933.) The first and second sessions of the First Congress were held in New York City. Subsequently, including the first session of the Sixth Congress, Philadelphia was the meeting place. Since then, Congress has convened in Washington, D.C.

2. Until adoption of the Twentieth Amendment, the deadline for adjournment of Congress in odd-numbered years was Mar. 3. However, the expiring Congress often extended the legislative day of Mar. 3 up to noon of Mar. 4, when the new Congress came officially into being. After ratification of the Twentieth Amendment, the deadline for adjournment of Congress in odd-numbered years was noon on Jan. 3.

3. At one time, the appointment or election of a president pro tempore was considered by the Senate to be for the occasion only, so that more than one would appear in several sessions, and in others none was chosen. Since Mar. 12, 1890, they have served until "the Senate otherwise ordered."

4. Elected to count the vote for president and vice president, which was done Apr. 6, 1789, because there was a quorum of the Senate for the first time. John Adams, vice president, appeared Apr. 21, 1789, and took his seat as president of the Senate.

5. Elected Speaker pro tempore for Apr. 20, 1798, and again for May 28, 1798.

6. Elected Speaker Jan. 19, 1814, to succeed Henry Clay, who resigned Jan. 19, 1814.

7. Elected Speaker Nov. 15, 1820, to succeed Henry Clay, who resigned Oct. 28, 1820.

8. Elected Speaker June 2, 1834, to succeed Andrew Stevenson of Virginia, who resigned.

9. There were recesses in this session from Saturday, Mar. 30 to Wednesday, July 1; and from Saturday, July 20 to Thursday, Nov. 21, 1867.

10. There were recesses in this session from Monday, July 27 to Monday, Sept. 21; from Monday, Sept. 21 to Friday, Oct. 16 and from Friday, Oct. 16 to Tuesday, Nov. 10, 1868. No business was transacted subsequent to July 27.

11. Elected Speaker Mar. 3, 1869, and served one day.

12. Died Aug. 19, 1876.

13. Appointed Speaker pro tempore Feb. 17, May 12, and June 19, 1876.

14. Appointed Speaker pro tempore June 4, 1876.

15. Resigned as president pro tempore Apr. 27, 1911.

16. Elected to serve Jan. 11–17, Mar. 11–12, Apr. 8, May 10, May 30–June 1, June 3, June 13–July 5, Aug. 1–10, and Aug. 27–Dec. 15, 1912.

17. Elected to serve May 25, 1912.

18. Elected to serve Dec. 4–12, 1911.

(continued)

Sessions of the U.S. Congress, 1789–2007 (CONTINUED)

19. Elected to serve Feb. 12–14, Apr. 26–27, May 7, July 6–31, and Aug. 12–26, 1912.

20. Elected to serve Mar. 25–26, 1912.

21. Elected to serve Aug. 27–Dec. 15, 1912, Jan. 5–18, and Feb. 2–15, 1913.

22. Elected to serve Dec. 16, 1912–Jan. 4, 1913, Jan. 19–Feb. 1, and Feb. 16–Mar. 3, 1913.

23. Died Oct. 1, 1916.

24. Died Aug. 19, 1934.

25. Died June 4, 1936.

26. Elected June 4, 1936.

27. Died Sept. 15, 1940.

28. Died Nov. 10, 1940.

29. Elected Sept. 16, 1940.

30. Elected Nov. 19, 1940.

31. Elected Jan. 6, 1941; died June 22, 1941.

32. Elected July 10, 1941.

33. There was a recess in this session from Thursday, July 8 to Tuesday, Sept. 14, 1943.

34. There were recesses in this session from Saturday, Apr. 1 to Wednesday, Apr. 12; from Friday, June 23 to Tuesday, Aug. 1; and from Thursday, Sept. 21 to Tuesday, Nov. 14, 1944.

35. The House was in recess in this session from Saturday, July 21 to Wednesday, Sept. 5, 1945, and the Senate from Wednesday, Aug. 1, to Wednesday, Sept. 5, 1945.

36. The House was in recess in this session from Thursday, Apr. 18 to Tuesday, Apr. 30, 1946.

37. There was a recess in this session from Sunday, July 27 to Monday, Nov. 17, 1947.

38. There were recesses in this session from Sunday, June 20 to Monday, July 26; and from Saturday, Aug. 7 to Friday, Dec. 31, 1948.

39. The House was in recess in this session from Thursday, Apr. 6 to Tuesday, Apr. 18, 1950, and both the Senate and the House were in recess from Saturday, Sept. 23 to Monday, Nov. 27, 1950.

40. The House was in recess in this session from Thursday, Mar. 22 to Monday, Apr. 2; and from Thursday, Aug. 23 to Wednesday, Sept. 12, 1951.

41. The House was in recess in this session from Thursday, Apr. 10 to Tuesday, Apr. 22, 1952.

42. The House was in recess in this session from Thursday, Apr. 2 to Monday, Apr. 13, 1953.

43. The House was in recess in this session from Thursday, Apr. 15 to Monday, Apr. 26, 1954, and adjourned sine die Aug. 20, 1954. The Senate was in recess in this session from Friday, Aug. 20 to Monday, Nov. 8; and from Thursday, Nov. 18 to Monday, Nov. 29, 1954, and adjourned sine die Dec. 2, 1954.

44. There was a recess in this session from Monday, Apr. 4 to Wednesday, Apr. 13, 1955.

45. There was a recess in this session from Thursday, Mar. 29 to Monday, Apr. 9, 1956.

46. There was a recess in this session from Thursday, Apr. 18 to Monday, Apr. 29, 1957.

47. There was a recess in this session from Thursday, Apr. 3 to Monday, Apr. 14, 1958.

48. There was a recess in this session from Thursday, Mar. 26 to Tuesday, Apr. 7, 1959.

49. The Senate was in recess in this session from Thursday, Apr. 14 to Monday, Apr. 18; from Friday, May 27 to Tuesday, May 31; and from Sunday, July 3 to Monday, Aug. 8, 1960. The House was in recess in this session from Thursday, Apr. 14 to Monday, Apr. 18; from Friday, May 27 to Tuesday, May 31; and from Sunday, July 3 to Monday, Aug. 15, 1960.

50. The House was in recess in this session from Thursday, Mar. 30 to Monday, Apr. 10, 1961.

51. Died Nov. 16, 1961.

52. The House was in recess in this session from Thursday, Apr. 19 to Monday, Apr. 30, 1962.

53. Elected Jan. 10, 1962.

54. The House was in recess in this session from Thursday, Apr. 11 to Monday, Apr. 22, 1963.

55. The House was in recess in this session from Thursday, Mar. 26 to Monday, Apr. 6; from Thursday, July 2 to Monday, July 20; and from Friday, Aug. 21 to Monday, Aug. 31, 1964. The Senate was in recess in this session from Friday, July 10 to Monday, July 20; and from Friday, Aug. 21 to Monday, Aug. 31, 1964.

56. The House was in recess in this session from Thursday, Apr. 7 to Monday, Apr. 18; and from Thursday, June 30 to Monday, July 11, 1966. The Senate was in recess in this session from Thursday, Apr. 7 to Wednesday, Apr. 13; and from Thursday, June 30 to Monday, July 11, 1966.

57. There was a recess in this session from Thursday, Mar. 23 to Monday, Apr. 3; from Thursday, June 29 to Monday, July 10,; from Thursday, Aug. 31 to Monday, Sept. 11; and from Wednesday, Nov. 22 to Monday, Nov. 27, 1967.

58. The House was in recess this session from Thursday, Apr. 11 to Monday, Apr. 22; from Wednesday, May 29 to Monday, June 3; from Wednesday, July 3 to Monday, July 8; and from Friday, Aug. 2 to Wednesday, Sept. 4, 1968. The Senate was in recess this session from Thursday, Apr. 11 to Wednesday, Apr. 17; from Wednesday, May 29 to Monday, June 3; from Wednesday, July 3 to Monday, July 8; and from Friday, Aug. 2 to Wednesday, Sept. 4, 1968.

59. The House was in recess this session from Friday, Feb. 7 to Monday, Feb. 17; from Thursday, Apr. 3 to Monday, Apr. 14; from Wednesday, May 28 to Monday, June 2; from Wednesday, July 2 to Monday, July 7; from Wednesday, Aug. 13 to Wednesday, Sept. 3; from Thursday, Nov. 6 to Wednesday, Nov. 12; and from Wednesday, Nov. 26, to Monday, Dec. 1, 1969. The Senate was in recess this session from Friday, Feb. 7 to Monday, Feb. 17; from Thursday, Apr. 3 to Monday, Apr. 14; from Wednesday, July 2 to Monday, July 7; from Wednesday, Aug. 13 to Wednesday, Sept. 3; and from Wednesday, Nov. 26 to Monday, Dec. 1, 1969.

60. The House was in recess this session from Tuesday, Feb. 10 to Monday, Feb. 16; from Thursday, Mar. 26 to Tuesday, Mar. 31; from Wednesday, May 27 to Monday, June 1; from Wednesday, July 1 to Monday, July 6; from Friday, Aug. 14 to Wednesday, Sept. 9; from Wednesday, Oct. 14 to Monday, Nov. 16; from Wednesday, Nov. 25, to Monday, Nov. 30; and from Tuesday, Dec. 22 to Tuesday, Dec. 29, 1970. The Senate was in recess this session from Tuesday, Feb. 10 to Monday, Feb. 16; from Thursday, Mar. 26 to Tuesday, Mar. 31; from Wednesday, Sept. 2, to Tuesday, Sept. 8; from Wednesday, Oct. 14, to Monday, Nov. 16; from Wednesday, Nov. 25 to Monday, Nov. 30; and from Tuesday, Dec. 22 to Monday, Dec. 28, 1970.

61. The House was in recess this session from Wednesday, Feb. 10 to Wednesday, Feb. 17; from Wednesday, Apr. 7 to Monday, Apr. 19; from Thursday, May 27 to Tuesday, June 1; from Thursday, July 1to Tuesday, July 6; from Friday, Aug. 6 to Wednesday, Sept. 8; from Thursday, Oct. 7 to Tuesday, Oct. 12; from Thursday, Oct. 21 to Tuesday, Oct. 26; and from Friday, Nov. 19 to Monday, Nov. 29, 1971. The Senate was in recess this session from Thursday, Feb. 11 to Wednesday, Feb. 17; from Wednesday, Apr. 7 to Wednesday, Apr. 14; from Wednesday, May 26 to Tuesday, June 1; from Wednesday, June 30 to Tuesday, July 6; from Friday, Aug. 6 to Wednesday, Sept. 8; from Thursday, Oct. 21 to Tuesday, Oct. 26; and from Wednesday, Nov. 24 to Monday, Nov. 29, 1971.

62. Died Jan. 21, 1971.

63. Elected Jan. 22, 1971.

64. The House was in recess this session from Wednesday, Feb. 9 to Wednesday, Feb. 16; from Wednesday, Mar. 29 to Monday, Apr. 10; from Wednesday, May 24 to Tuesday, May 30; from Friday, June 30 to Monday, July 17; and from Friday, Aug. 18 to Tuesday, Sept. 5, 1972. The Senate was in recess this session from Wednesday, Feb. 9 to Monday, Feb. 14; from Thursday, Mar. 30 to Tuesday, Apr. 4; from Thursday, May 25 to Tuesday, May 30; from Friday, June 30 to Monday, July 17; and from Friday, Aug. 18 to Tuesday, Sept. 5, 1972.

65. Died July 27, 1972.

66. Elected July 28, 1972.

67. The House was in recess this session from Thursday, Feb. 8 to Monday, Feb. 19; from Thursday, Apr. 19 to Monday, Apr. 30; from Thursday, May 24 to Tuesday, May 29; from Saturday, June 30 to Tuesday, July 10; from Friday, Aug. 3 to Wednesday, Sept. 5; from Thursday, Oct. 4 to Tuesday, Oct. 9; from Thursday, Oct. 18 to Tuesday, Oct. 23; and from Thursday, Nov. 15 to Monday, Nov. 26, 1973. The Senate was in recess this session from Thursday, Feb. 8 to Thursday, Feb. 15; from Wednesday, Apr. 18 to Monday, Apr. 30; from Wednesday, May 23 to Tuesday, May 29; from Saturday, June 30 to Monday, July 9; from Friday, Aug. 3 to Wednesday, Sept. 5; from Thursday, Oct. 18 to Tuesday, Oct. 23; and from Wednesday, Nov. 21 to Monday, Nov. 26, 1973.

68. The House was in recess this session from Thursday, Feb. 7 to Wednesday, Feb. 13; from Thursday, Apr. 11 to Monday, Apr. 22; from Thursday, May 23 to Tuesday, May 28; from Thursday, Aug. 22 to Wednesday, Sept. 11; from Thursday, Oct. 17 to Monday, Nov. 18; and from Tuesday, Nov. 26 to Tuesday, Dec. 3, 1974. The Senate was in recess this session from Friday, Feb. 8 to Monday, Feb. 18; from Wednesday, Mar. 13 to Tuesday, Mar. 19; from Thursday, Apr. 11 to Monday, Apr. 22; from Wednesday, May 23 to Tuesday, May 28; from Thursday, Aug. 22 to Wednesday, Sept. 4; from Thursday, Oct. 17 to Monday, Nov. 18; and from Tuesday, Nov. 26 to Monday, Dec. 2, 1974.

69. The House was in recess this session from Wednesday, Mar. 26 to Monday, Apr. 7; from Thursday, May 22 to Monday, June 2; from Thursday, June 26 to Tuesday, July 8; from Friday, Aug. 1 to Wednesday, Sept. 3; from Thursday, Oct. 9 to Monday, Oct. 20; from Thursday, Oct. 23 to Tuesday, Oct. 28; and from Thursday, Nov. 20 to Monday, Dec. 1, 1975. The Senate was in recess this session from Wednesday, Mar. 26 to Monday, Apr. 7; from Thursday, May 22 to Monday, June 2; from Friday, June 27 to Monday, July 7; from Friday, Aug. 1 to Wednesday, Sept. 3; from Thursday, Oct. 9 to Monday, Oct. 20; from Thursday, Oct. 23 to Tuesday, Oct. 28; and from Thursday, Nov. 20 to Monday, Dec. 1, 1975.

70. The House was in recess this session from Wednesday, Feb. 11 to Monday, Feb. 16; from Wednesday, Apr. 14 to Monday, Apr. 26; from Thursday, May 27 to Tuesday, June 1; from Friday, July 2 to Monday, July 19; from Tuesday, Aug. 10 to Monday, Aug. 23; and from Thursday, Sept. 2 to Wednesday, Sept. 8, 1976. The Senate was in recess this session from Friday, Feb. 6 to Monday, Feb. 16; from Wednesday, Apr. 14 to Monday, Apr. 26; from Friday, May 28 to Wednesday, June 2; from Friday, July 2 to Monday, July 19; from Tuesday, Aug. 10 to Monday, Aug. 23; and from Wednesday, Sept. 1 to Tuesday, Sept. 7, 1976.

71. The House was in recess this session from Wednesday, Feb. 9 to Wednesday, Feb. 16; from Wednesday, Apr. 6 to Monday, Apr. 18; from Thursday, May 26 to Wednesday, June 1; from Thursday, June 30 to Monday, July 11; from Friday, Aug. 5 to Wednesday, Sept. 7; and from Thursday, Oct. 6 to Tuesday, Oct. 11, 1977. The Senate was in recess this session from Friday, Feb. 11 to Monday, Feb. 21; from Thursday, Apr. 7 to Monday, Apr. 18; from Friday, May 27 to Monday, June 6; from Friday, July 1 to Monday, July 11; and from Saturday, Aug. 6 to Wednesday, Sept. 7, 1977.

72. The House was in recess this session from Wednesday, Feb. 9 to Tuesday, Feb. 14; from Wednesday, Mar. 22 to Monday, Apr. 3; from Thursday, May 25 to Wednesday, May 31; from Thursday, June 29 to Monday, July 10; and from Thursday, Aug. 17 to Wednesday, Sept. 6, 1978. The Senate was in recess this session from Friday, Feb. 10 to Monday, Feb. 20; from Thursday, Mar. 23 to Monday, Apr. 3; from Friday, May 26 to Monday, June 5; from Thursday, June 29 to Monday, July 10; and from Friday, Aug. 25 to Wednesday, Sept. 6, 1978.

73. The House was in recess this session from Thursday, Feb. 8 to Tuesday, Feb. 13; from Tuesday, Apr. 10 to Monday, Apr. 23; from Thursday, May 24 to Wednesday, May 30; from Friday, June 29 to Monday, July 9; from Thursday, Aug. 2 to Wednesday, Sept. 5; and from Tuesday, Nov. 20 to Monday, Nov. 26, 1979. The Senate was in recess this session from Friday, Feb. 9 to Monday, Feb. 19; from Tuesday, Apr. 10 to Monday, Apr. 23; from Friday, May 25 to Monday, June 4; from Friday, Aug. 3 to Wednesday, Sept. 5; and from Tuesday, Nov. 20 to Monday, Nov. 26, 1979.

74. The House was in recess this session from Wednesday, Feb. 13 to Tuesday, Feb. 19; from Wednesday, Apr. 2 to Tuesday, Apr. 15; from Thursday, May 22 to Wednesday, May 28; from Wednesday, July 2 to Monday, July 21; from Friday, Aug. 1 to Monday, Aug. 18; and from Thursday, Aug. 28 to Wednesday, Sept. 13, 1980. The Senate was in recess this session from Monday, Feb. 11 to Thursday, Feb. 14; from Thursday, Apr. 3 to Tuesday, Apr. 15; from Thursday, May 22 to Wednesday, May 28; from Wednesday, July 2 to Monday, July 21; from Wednesday, Aug. 6 to Monday, Aug. 18; from Wednesday, Aug. 27 to Wednesday, Sept. 3; from Wednesday, Oct. 1 to Wednesday, Nov. 12; and from Monday, Nov. 24 to Monday, Dec. 1, 1980.

75. The House was in recess this session from Friday, Feb. 6 to Tuesday, Feb. 17; from Friday, Apr. 10 to Monday, Apr. 27; from Friday, June 26 to Wednesday, July 8; from Tuesday, Aug. 4 to Wednesday, Sept. 9; from Wednesday, Oct. 7 to Tuesday, Oct. 13; and from Monday, Nov. 23 to Monday, Nov. 30, 1981. The Senate was in recess this session from Friday, Feb. 6 to Monday, Feb. 16; from Friday, Apr. 10 to Monday, Apr. 27; from Thursday, June 25 to Wednesday, July 8; from Monday, Aug. 3 to Wednesday, Sept. 9; from Wednesday, Oct. 7 to Wednesday, Oct. 14; and from Tuesday, Nov. 24 to Monday, Nov. 30, 1981.

76. The House was in recess this session from Wednesday, Feb. 10 to Monday, Feb. 22; from Tuesday, Apr. 6 to Tuesday, Apr. 20; from Thursday, May 27 to Wednesday, June 2; from Thursday, July 1 to Monday, July 12; from Friday, Aug. 20 to Wednesday, Sept. 8; and from Friday, Oct. 1 to Monday, Nov. 29, 1982. The Senate was in recess this session from Thursday, Feb. 11to Monday, Feb. 22; from Thursday, Apr. 1 to Tuesday, Apr. 13; from Thursday, May 27 to Tuesday, June 8; from Thursday, July 1 to Monday, July 12; from Friday, Aug. 20 to Wednesday, Sept. 8; and from Friday, Oct. 1 to Monday, Nov. 29, 1982.

(continued)

Sessions of the U.S. Congress, 1789–2007 (CONTINUED)

77. The House adjourned for recess this session from Friday, Jan. 7 to Tuesday, Jan. 25; from Thursday, Feb. 17 to Tuesday, Feb. 22; from Thursday, Mar. 24 to Tuesday, Apr. 5; from Thursday, May 26 to Wednesday, June 1; from Thursday, June 30 to Monday, July 11; from Friday, Aug. 5 to Monday, Sept. 12; and from Friday, Oct. 7 to Monday, Oct. 17, 1983. The Senate adjourned for recess this session from Monday, Jan. 3 to Tuesday, Jan. 25; from Friday, Feb. 4 to Monday, Feb. 14; from Friday, Mar. 25 to Tuesday, Apr. 5; from Friday, May 27 to Monday, June 6; from Friday, July 1 to Monday, July 11; from Friday, Aug. 5 to Monday, Sept. 12; and from Monday Oct. 10 to Monday, Oct. 17, 1983.

78. The House adjourned for recess this session from Thursday, Feb. 9 to Tuesday, Feb. 21; from Friday, Apr. 13 to Tuesday, Apr. 24; from Friday, May 25 to Wednesday, May 30; from Friday, June 29 to Monday, July 23; and from Friday, Aug. 10 to Wednesday, Sept. 5, 1984. The Senate adjourned for recess this session from Friday, Feb. 10 to Monday, Feb. 20; from Friday, Apr. 13 to Tuesday, Apr. 24; from Friday, May 25 to Thursday, May 31; from Friday, June 29 to Monday, July 23; and from Friday, Aug. 10 to Wednesday, Sept. 5, 1984.

79. The House adjourned for recess this session from Monday, Jan. 7 to Monday, Jan. 21; from Thursday, Feb. 7 to Tuesday, Feb. 19; from Thursday, Mar. 7 to Tuesday, Mar. 19; from Thursday, Apr. 4 to Monday, Apr. 15; from Thursday, May 23 to Monday, June 3; from Thursday, June 27 to Monday, July 8; from Thursday, Aug. 1 to Wednesday, Sept. 4; and Thursday, Nov. 21 to Monday, Dec. 2, 1985. The Senate adjourned for recess this session from Monday, Jan. 7 to Monday, Jan. 21; from Thursday, Feb. 7 to Monday, Feb. 18; from Tuesday, Mar. 12 to Thursday, Mar. 14; from Thursday, Apr. 4 to Monday, Apr. 15; from Friday, May 24 to Monday, June 3; from Thursday, June 27 to Monday, July 8; from Thursday, Aug. 1 to Monday, Sept. 9; and from Saturday, Nov. 23 to Monday, Dec. 2, 1985.

80. The House adjourned for recess this session from Tuesday, Jan. 7 to Tuesday, Jan. 21; from Friday, Feb. 7 to Tuesday, Feb. 18; from Tuesday, Mar. 25 to Tuesday, Apr. 8; from Thursday, May 22 to Tuesday, June 3; from Thursday, June 26 to Monday, July 14; and from Friday, Aug. 15 to Monday, Sept. 8, 1986. The Senate adjourned for recess this session from Tuesday, Jan. 7 to Tuesday, Jan. 21; from Friday, Feb. 7 to Monday, Feb. 17; from Thursday, Mar. 27 to Tuesday, Apr. 8; from Wednesday, May 21 to Monday, June 2; from Thursday, June 26 to Monday, July 14; and from Friday, Aug. 15 to Monday, Sept. 8, 1986.

81. The House adjourned for recess this session from Thursday, Jan. 8 to Tuesday, Jan. 20; from Wednesday, Feb. 11 to Wednesday, Feb. 18; from Thursday, Apr. 9 to Tuesday, Apr. 21; from Thursday, May 21 to Wednesday, May 27; from Wednesday, July 1 to Tuesday, July 7; from Wednesday, July 15 to Monday, July 20; from Friday, Aug. 7 to Wednesday, Sept. 9; from Tuesday, Nov. 10 to Monday, Nov. 16; and from Friday, Nov. 20 to Monday, Nov. 30, 1987. The Senate adjourned for recess this session from Tuesday, Jan. 6 to Monday, Jan. 12; from Thursday, Feb. 5 to Monday, Feb. 16; from Friday, Apr. 10 to Tuesday, Apr. 21; from Thursday, May 21 to Wednesday, May 27; from Wednesday, July 1 to Tuesday, July 7; from Friday, Aug. 7 to Wednesday, Sept. 9; and from Friday, Nov. 20 to Monday, Nov. 30, 1987.

82. The House adjourned for recess this session from Tuesday, Feb. 9 to Tuesday, Feb. 16; from Thursday, Mar. 31 to Monday, Apr. 11; from Thursday, May 26 to Wednesday, June 1; from Thursday, June 30 to Thursday, July 7; from Thursday, July 14 to Tuesday, July 26; and from Thursday, Aug. 11 to Wednesday, Sept. 7, 1988. The Senate adjourned for recess this session from Thursday, Feb. 4 to Monday, Feb. 15; and from Friday, Mar. 4 to Monday, Mar. 14, 1988; from Thursday, Mar. 31 to Monday, Apr. 11; from Friday, Apr. 29 to Monday, May 9; from Friday, May 27 to Monday, June 6; from Wednesday, June 29 to Wednesday, July 6; from Thursday, July 14 to Monday, July 25, and from Thursday, Aug. 11 to Wednesday, Sept. 7, 1988.

83. The House adjourned for recess this session from Wednesday, Jan. 4 to Thursday, Jan. 19; from Thursday, Feb. 9 to Tuesday, Feb. 21; from Thursday, Mar. 23 to Monday, Apr. 3; from Tuesday, Apr. 18 to Tuesday, Apr. 25; from Thursday, May 25 to Wednesday, May 31; from Thursday, June 29 to Monday, July 10; and from Saturday, Aug. 5 to Wednesday, Sept. 6, 1989. The Senate adjourned for recess this session from Wednesday, Jan. 4 to Friday, Jan. 20; from Friday, Jan. 20 to Wednesday, Jan. 25; from Thursday, Feb. 9 to Tuesday, Feb. 21; from Friday, Mar. 17 to Tuesday, Apr. 4; from Wednesday, Apr. 19 to Monday, May 1; from Thursday, May 18 to Wednesday, May 31; from Friday, June 23 to Tuesday, July 11; and from Friday, Aug. 4 to Wednesday, Sept. 6, 1989.

84. Elected Speaker June 6, 1989, to succeed Jim Wright, who resigned the speakership that day.

85. The House adjourned for recess this session from Wednesday, Feb. 7 to Tuesday, Feb. 20; from Wednesday, Apr. 4 to Wednesday, Apr. 18; from Friday, May 25 to Tuesday, June 5; from Thursday, June 28 to Tuesday, July 10; and from Saturday, Aug. 4 to Wednesday, Sept. 5, 1990. The Senate adjourned for recess this session from Thursday, Feb. 8 to Tuesday, Feb. 20; from Friday, Mar. 9 to Tuesday, Mar. 20; from Thursday, Apr. 5 to Wednesday, Apr. 18; from Thursday, May 24 to Tuesday, June 5; from Thursday, June 28 to Tuesday, July 10; and from Saturday, Aug. 4 to Monday, Sept. 10, 1990.

86. The House adjourned for recess this session from Wednesday, Feb. 6 to Tuesday, Feb. 19; from Friday, Mar. 22 to Tuesday, Apr. 9; from Thursday, June 27 to Tuesday, July 9; and from Friday, Aug. 2 to Wednesday, Sept. 11, 1991. The Senate adjourned for recess this session from Wednesday, Feb. 6 to Tuesday, Feb. 19; from Friday, Mar. 22 to Tuesday, Apr. 9; from Thursday, Apr. 25 to Monday, May 6; from Friday, May 24 to Monday, June 3; from Friday, June 28 to Monday, July 8; and from Friday, Aug. 2 to Tuesday, Sept. 10, 1991.

87. The House adjourned for recess this session from Friday, Jan. 3 to Wednesday, Jan. 22; from Friday, Apr. 10 to Tuesday, Apr. 28; from Thursday, July 2 to Tuesday, July 7; from Friday, July 9 to Tuesday, July 21; and from Wednesday, Aug. 12 to Wednesday, Sept. 9, 1992. The Senate adjourned for recess this session from Monday, Jan. 6 to Monday, Jan. 20; from Monday, Feb. 10 to Monday, Feb. 17; from Monday, Apr. 13 to Friday, Apr. 24; from Monday, May 25 to Friday, May 29; from Monday, July 6 to Friday, July 17; and from Thursday, Aug. 13 to Monday, Sept. 7, 1992.

88. The House adjourned for recess this session from Thursday, Jan. 7 to Tuesday, Jan. 19; from Friday, Feb. 5 to Monday, Feb. 15; from Thursday, Apr. 8 to Sunday, Apr. 18; from Friday, May 28 to Monday, June 7; from Friday, July 2 to Monday, July 12; and from Saturday, Aug. 7 to Tuesday, Sept. 7, 1993. The Senate adjourned for recess this session from Friday, Jan. 8 to Tuesday, Jan. 19; from Friday, Feb. 5 to Monday, Feb. 15; from Monday, Apr. 5 to Friday, Apr. 16; from Monday, May 31 to Friday, June 4; from Friday, July 2 to Friday, July 9; from Monday, Aug. 9 to Monday, Sept. 6; from Friday, Oct. 8 to Tuesday, Oct. 12; and from Friday, Nov. 12 to Monday Nov. 15, 1993.

89. The House adjourned for recess this session from Thursday, Jan. 27 to Monday, Jan. 31; from Saturday, Feb. 12 to Monday, Feb. 21; from Friday, Mar. 25 to Monday, Apr. 11; from Friday, May 27 to Tuesday, June 7; from Friday, July 1 to Monday, July 11; and from Saturday, Aug. 27 to Sunday, Sept. 11, 1994. The Senate adjourned for recess this session from Monday, Feb. 14 to Monday, Feb. 21; from Monday, Mar. 28 to Friday, Apr. 8; from Monday, May 30 to Monday, June 6; from Monday, July 4 to Friday, July 8; and from Friday, Aug. 26 to Friday, Sept. 9, 1994.

90. The House adjourned for recess this session from Saturday, Apr. 8 to Sunday, Apr. 30; from Friday, May 26 to Monday, June 5; from Saturday, July 1 to Sunday, July 9; from Saturday, Aug. 5 to Tuesday, Sept. 5; and from Saturday, Sept. 30 to Thursday, Oct. 5, 1995. The Senate adjourned for recess this session from Friday, Feb. 17 to Tuesday, Feb. 21; from Saturday, Apr. 8 to Sunday, Apr. 23; from Saturday, May 27 to Sunday, June 4; from Saturday, July 1 to Sunday, July 9; from Saturday, Aug. 12 to Monday, Sept. 4; from Sunday, Oct. 1to Monday, Oct. 9; and from Saturday, Nov. 21 to Sunday, Nov. 26, 1995.

91. The House adjourned for recess this session from Wednesday, Jan. 10 to Sunday, Jan. 21; from Saturday, Mar. 30 to Sunday, Apr. 14; from Saturday, June 29 to Sunday, July 7; and from Saturday, Aug. 3 to Tuesday, Sept. 3, 1996. The Senate adjourned for recess this session from Thursday, Jan. 11 to Sunday, Jan. 21; from Saturday, Mar. 30 to Saturday, Apr. 14; from Saturday, May 25 to Sunday, June 2; from Saturday, June 29 to Sunday, July 7; and from Saturday, Aug. 3 to Monday, Sept. 2, 1996.

92. The House adjourned for recess this session Friday, Jan. 10 to Sunday, Jan. 19; from Wednesday, Jan. 22 to Monday, Feb. 3; from Friday, Feb. 14 to Monday, Feb. 24; from Saturday, Mar. 22 to Monday, Apr. 7; from Friday, June 27 to Monday, July 7; from Saturday, Aug. 2 to Tuesday, Sept. 2; and from Friday, Oct. 10 to Monday, Oct. 20, 1997. The Senate adjourned for recess this session from Friday, Jan. 10 to Monday, Jan. 20; from Friday, Feb. 14 to Sunday, Feb. 23; from Saturday, Mar. 22 to Sunday, Apr. 6; from Saturday, May 24 to Sunday, June 1; from Saturday, June 28 to Sunday, July 6; from Saturday, Aug. 2 to Monday, Sept. 1; and from Friday, Oct. 10 to Sunday, Oct. 19, 1997.

93. The House adjourned for recess this session from Friday, Feb. 13 to Monday, Feb. 23; from Thursday, Apr. 2 to Monday, Apr. 20; from Saturday, May 23 to Tuesday, June 2; from Friday, June 26 to Monday, July 13; and from Saturday, Aug. 8 to Tuesday, Sept. 8, 1998. The House adjourned Oct. 21, 1998, and was called back by the Speaker for a resumption of the second session from Thursday, Dec. 17 to Saturday, Dec. 19, 1998. The Senate adjourned for recess this session from Thursday, Jan. 1 to Monday, Jan. 26; from Saturday, Feb. 14 to Sunday, Feb. 22; from Saturday, Apr. 4 to Sunday, Apr. 19; from Saturday, May 23 to Sunday, May 31; from Saturday, June 27 to Sunday, July 5; from Saturday, Aug. 1 to Sunday, Aug. 30; and from Saturday, Sept. 5 to Monday, Sept. 7, 1998.

94. The House adjourned for recess this session from Wednesday, Jan. 6 to Tuesday, Jan. 19; from Tuesday, Jan. 19 to Tuesday, Feb. 2; from Friday, Feb. 12 to Tuesday, Feb. 23; from Thursday, Mar. 25 to Monday, Apr. 12; from Thursday, May 27 to Monday, June 7; from Saturday, July 3 to Sunday, July 11; and from Saturday, Aug. 7 to Tuesday, Sept. 7, 1999. The Senate adjourned for recess this session from Friday, Feb. 12 to Monday, Feb. 22; from Thursday, Mar. 25 to Monday, Apr. 12; from Thursday, May 27 to Monday, June 7; from Saturday, July 3 to Sunday, July 11; from Saturday, Aug. 7 to Tuesday, Sept. 7; and from Saturday, Oct. 9 to Monday, Oct. 11, 1999.

95. The House adjourned for recess this session from Wednesday, Feb. 16 to Tuesday, Feb. 29; from Thursday, Apr. 13 to Tuesday, May 2; from Thursday, May 25 to Tuesday, June 6; from Friday, June 30 to Monday, July 10; from Thursday, July 27 to Wednesday, Sept. 6; from Friday, Nov. 3 to Wednesday, Nov. 13; and from Thursday, Nov. 14 to Wednesday, Dec. 4, 2000. The Senate adjourned for recess this session from Thursday, Feb. 10 to Tuesday, Feb. 22; from Thursday, Mar. 9 to Monday, Mar. 20; from Thursday, Apr. 13 to Tuesday, Apr. 25; from Thursday, May 25 to Tuesday, June 6; from Friday, June 30 to Monday, July 10; from Thursday, July 27 to Tuesday, Sept. 5; from Thursday, Nov. 2 to Tuesday, Nov. 14; and from Tuesday, Nov. 14 to Tuesday, Dec. 5, 2000.

96. The House adjourned for recess this session from Saturday, Jan. 6 to Saturday, Jan. 20; from Saturday, Jan. 20 to Tuesday, Jan. 30; from Wednesday, Jan. 31 to Tuesday, Feb. 6; from Wednesday, Feb. 14 to Monday, Feb. 26; from Tuesday, Apr. 3 to Tuesday, Apr. 24; from Saturday, May 26 to Tuesday, June 5; from Thursday, June 28 to Tuesday, July 10; from Thursday, Aug. 2 to Thursday, Sept. 6,; and from Monday, Nov. 19, 2001, to Tuesday, Nov. 27, 2001. The Senate adjourned for recess this session from Monday, Jan. 8 to Saturday, Jan. 20; from Thursday, Feb. 15 to Monday, Feb. 26; from Friday, Apr. 6 to Monday, Apr. 23; from Saturday, May 26 to Tuesday, June 5; from Friday, June 29 to Monday, July 9; from Friday, Aug. 3 to Tuesday, Sept. 4; and from Friday, Nov. 16, 2001, to Tuesday, Nov. 27, 2001.

97. The 2000 election produced a 50–50 split in the Senate between Republicans and Democrats. From the day the 107th Congress convened on Jan. 3, 2001, until inauguration day on Jan. 20, 2001, Vice President Al Gore, a Democrat, tipped the scale to a Democratic majority. Thus, Robert C. Byrd served as president pro tempore during this period. When Vice President Dick Cheney took office on Jan. 20, 2001, the Republicans became the majority party, and Strom Thurmond was elected president pro tempore. On June 6, 2001, Republican Sen. James M. Jeffords of Vermont declared himself an Independent, creating a Democratic majority. Robert C. Byrd was elected president pro tempore on that day.

98. The House adjourned for recess this session from Tuesday, Jan. 29 to Monday, Feb. 4; from Friday, Feb. 14 to Tuesday, Feb. 26; from Friday, Mar. 20 to Tuesday, Apr. 9; from Thursday, May 24 to Tuesday, June 4; from Friday, June 28to Monday, July 8; from Saturday, July 27 to Wednesday, Sept. 4, 2002. The Senate adjourned for recess this session from Tuesday, Jan. 29 to Monday, Feb. 4; from Friday, Feb. 15 to Monday, Feb. 25; from Friday, Mar. 22 to Monday, Apr. 8; from Thursday, May 23 to Monday, June 3; from Friday, June 28 to Monday, July 8; and from Thursday, August 1 to Tuesday, Sept. 3, 2002.

99. The House adjourned for recess this session from Wednesday, Jan. 8 to Monday, Jan. 27; from Thursday, Feb. 13 to Tuesday, Feb. 25; from Saturday, Apr. 12 to Tuesday, Apr. 29; from Friday, May 23 to Monday, June 2; from Thursday, June 26 to Monday, July 7; from Friday, July 25 to Wednesday, Sept. 3; and from Friday, Nov. 21 to Monday, Dec. 8, 2003. The Senate adjourned for recess this session from Friday, Feb. 14 to Monday, Feb. 24; from Friday, Apr. 11 to Tuesday, Apr. 29; from Friday, May 23 to Monday, June 2; from Friday, June 27 to Monday, July 7; from Friday, Aug. 1 to Tuesday, Sept. 2; from Friday, Oct. 3 to Tuesday, Oct. 14; and from Tuesday, Nov. 25 to Tuesday, Dec. 9, 2003.

100. The House adjourned for recess this session from Wednesday, Feb. 11 to Tuesday, Feb. 24; from Friday, Apr. 2 to Tuesday, Apr. 20; Tuesday, May 20 to Tuesday, June 1; from Friday, June 25 to Tuesday, July 6; from Thursday, July 22 to Tuesday, Sept. 7; from Saturday, Oct. 9 to Tuesday, Nov. 16; and from Friday, Nov. 19 to Monday, Dec. 6, 2004. The Senate adjourned for recess this session from Thursday, Feb. 12 to Monday, Feb. 23; from Friday, Mar. 12 to Monday, Mar. 22; from Tuesday, Apr. 8 to Monday, Apr. 19; from Friday, May 21 to Tuesday, June 1; from Friday, June 25 to Tuesday, July 6; from Thursday, July 22 to Tuesday, Sept. 7; from Monday, Oct. 11 to Tuesday, Nov. 16; and from Wednesday, Nov. 24 to Tuesday, Dec. 7, 2004.

101. The House adjourned for recess this session from Thursday, Jan. 6 to Thursday, Jan. 20; from Wednesday, Jan. 26 to Tuesday, Feb. 1; from Thursday, Feb. 17 to Tuesday, Mar. 1; from Monday, Mar. 21 to Tuesday, Apr. 5; from Thursday, May 26 to Tuesday, June 7; from Thursday, June 30 to Monday, July 11; from Friday, July 29 to Friday, Sept. 2; from Friday, Oct. 7 to Monday, Oct. 17; and from Friday, Nov. 18 to Tuesday, Dec. 6, 2005. The Senate adjourned for recess this session from Thursday, Jan. 6 to Thursday, Jan. 20; from Friday, Feb. 18 to Monday, Feb. 28; from Sunday, Mar. 20 to Monday, Apr. 4; from Friday, Apr. 29 to Monday, May 9; from Thursday, May 26 to Monday, June 6; from Friday, July 1 to Monday, July 11; from Friday, July 29 to Thursday, Sept. 1; from Friday, Oct. 7 to Monday, Oct. 17; and Friday, Nov. 18 to Monday, Dec. 12, 2005.

102. The House adjourned for recess this session from Tuesday, Jan. 3 to Tuesday, Jan. 31; from Thursday, Feb. 16 to Monday, Feb. 27; from Thursday, Mar. 16 to Tuesday, Mar. 28; from Thursday, Apr. 6 to Tuesday, Apr. 25; from Thursday, May 25 to Tuesday, June 6; from Thursday, June 29 to Monday, July 10; from Wednesday, Aug. 2 to Thursday, Sept. 7; from Friday, Sept. 29 to Monday, Nov. 13; and from Thursday, Nov. 16 to Tuesday, Dec. 5, 2006. The Senate adjourned for recess this session from Tuesday, Jan. 3 to Wednesday, Jan. 18; from Friday, Feb. 17 to Monday, Feb. 27; from Thursday, Mar. 16 to Monday, Mar. 27; from Friday, Apr. 7 to Monday, Apr. 24; from Friday, May 26 to Monday, June 5; from Friday, June 30 to Monday, July 10; from Thursday, Aug. 3 to Tuesday, Sept. 5; from Friday, Sept. 29 to Monday, Nov. 13; and from Thursday, Nov. 16 to Tuesday, Dec. 5, 2006.

SOURCES: For 1789–1990, *Official Congressional Directory*. For 1991–2007, Calendars of the U.S. House of Representatives and the U.S. Senate.

Political Party Affiliations in Congress and the Presidency, 1789–2007

(Affiliations are as of the beginning of the Congress.)

Year	Congress	House Majority party	House Principal minority party	Senate Majority party	Senate Principal minority party	President
1789–1791	1st	AD-38	Op-26	AD-17	Op-9	F (Washington)
1791–1793	2nd	F-37	DR-33	F-16	DR-13	F (Washington)
1793–1795	3rd	DR-57	F-48	F-17	DR-13	F (Washington)
1795–1797	4th	F-54	DR-52	F-19	DR-13	F (Washington)
1797–1799	5th	F-58	DR-48	F-20	DR-12	F (J. Adams)
1799–1801	6th	F-64	DR-42	F-19	DR-13	F (J. Adams)
1801–1803	7th	DR-69	F-36	DR-18	F-13	DR (Jefferson)
1803–1805	8th	DR-102	F-39	DR-25	F-9	DR (Jefferson)
1805–1807	9th	DR-116	F-25	DR-27	F-7	DR (Jefferson)
1807–1809	10th	DR-118	F-24	DR-28	F-6	DR (Jefferson)
1809–1811	11th	DR-94	F-48	DR-28	F-6	DR (Madison)
1811–1813	12th	DR-108	F-36	DR-30	F-6	DR (Madison)
1813–1815	13th	DR-112	F-68	DR-27	F-9	DR (Madison)
1815–1817	14th	DR-117	F-65	DR-25	F-11	DR (Madison)
1817–1819	15th	DR-141	F-42	DR-34	F-10	DR (Monroe)
1819–1821	16th	DR-156	F-27	DR-35	F-7	DR (Monroe)
1821–1823	17th	DR-158	F-25	DR-44	F-4	DR (Monroe)
1823–1825	18th	DR-187	F-26	DR-44	F-4	DR (Monroe)
1825–1827	19th	AD-105	J-97	AD-26	J-20	DR (J.Q. Adams)
1827–1829	20th	J-119	AD-94	J-28	AD-20	DR (J.Q. Adams)
1829–1831	21st	D-139	NR-74	D-26	NR-22	DR (Jackson)
1831–1833	22nd	D-141	NR-58	D-25	NR-21	D (Jackson)
1833–1835	23rd	D-147	AM-53	D-20	NR-20	D (Jackson)
1835–1837	24th	D-145	W-98	D-27	W-25	D (Jackson)
1837–1839	25th	D-108	W-107	D-30	W-18	D (Van Buren)
1839–1841	26th	D-124	W-118	D-28	W-22	D (Van Buren)
1841–1843	27th	W-133	D-102	W-28	D-22	W (W.H. Harrison) / W (Tyler)
1843–1845	28th	D-142	W-79	W-28	D-25	W (Tyler)
1845–1847	29th	D-143	W-77	D-31	W-25	D (Polk)
1847–1849	30th	W-115	D-108	D-36	W-21	D (Polk)
1849–1851	31st	D-112	W-109	D-35	W-25	W (Taylor) / W (Fillmore)
1851–1853	32nd	D-140	W-88	D-35	W-24	W (Fillmore)
1853–1855	33rd	D-159	W-71	D-38	W-22	D (Pierce)
1855–1857	34th	R-108	D-83	D-40	R-15	D (Pierce)
1857–1859	35th	D-118	R-92	D-36	R-20	D (Buchanan)
1859–1861	36th	R-114	D-92	D-36	R-26	D (Buchanan)
1861–1863	37th	R-105	D-43	R-31	D-10	R (Lincoln)
1863–1865	38th	R-102	D-75	R-36	D-9	R (Lincoln)
1865–1867	39th	U-149	D-42	U-42	D-10	R (Lincoln) / R (A. Johnson)
1867–1869	40th	R-143	D-49	R-42	D-11	R (A. Johnson)

		House		Senate		
Year	Congress	Majority party	Principal minority party	Majority party	Principal minority party	President
1869–1871	41st	R-149	D-63	R-56	D-11	R (Grant)
1871–1873	42nd	R-134	D-104	R-52	D-17	R (Grant)
1873–1875	43rd	R-194	D-92	R-49	D-19	R (Grant)
1875–1877	44th	D-169	R-109	R-45	D-29	R (Grant)
1877–1879	45th	D-153	R-140	R-39	D-36	R (Hayes)
1879–1881	46th	D-149	R-130	D-42	R-33	R (Hayes)
1881–1883	47th	R-147	D-135	R-37	D-37	R (Garfield)
						R (Arthur)
1883–1885	48th	D-197	R-118	R-38	D-36	R (Arthur)
1885–1887	49th	D-183	R-140	R-43	D-34	D (Cleveland)
1887–1889	50th	D-169	R-152	R-39	D-37	D (Cleveland)
1889–1891	51st	R-166	D-159	R-39	D-37	R (B. Harrison)
1891–1893	52nd	D-235	R-88	R-47	D-39	R (B. Harrison)
1893–1895	53rd	D-218	R-127	D-44	R-38	D (Cleveland)
1895–1897	54th	R-244	D-105	R-43	D-39	D (Cleveland)
1897–1899	55th	R-204	D-113	R-47	D-34	R (McKinley)
1899–1901	56th	R-185	D-163	R-53	D-26	R (McKinley)
1901–1903	57th	R-197	D-151	R-55	D-31	R (McKinley)
						R (T. Roosevelt)
1903–1905	58th	R-208	D-178	R-57	D-33	R (T. Roosevelt)
1905–1907	59th	R-250	D-136	R-57	D-33	R (T. Roosevelt)
1907–1909	60th	R-222	D-164	R-61	D-31	R (T. Roosevelt)
1909–1911	61st	R-219	D-172	R-61	D-32	R (Taft)
1911–1913	62nd	D-228	R-161	R-51	D-41	R (Taft)
1913–1915	63rd	D-291	R-127	D-51	R-44	D (Wilson)
1915–1917	64th	D-230	R-196	D-56	R-40	D (Wilson)
1917–1919	65th	D-216	R-210	D-53	R-42	D (Wilson)
1919–1921	66th	R-240	D-190	R-49	D-47	D (Wilson)
1921–1923	67th	R-301	D-131	R-59	D-37	R (Harding)
1923–1925	68th	R-225	D-205	R-51	D-43	R (Coolidge)
1925–1927	69th	R-247	D-183	R-56	D-39	R (Coolidge)
1927–1929	70th	R-237	D-195	R-49	D-46	R (Coolidge)
1929–1931	71st	R-267	D-167	R-56	D-39	R (Hoover)
1931–1933	72nd	D-220	R-214	R-48	D-47	R (Hoover)
1933–1935	73rd	D-310	R-117	D-60	R-35	D (F. D. Roosevelt)
1935–1937	74th	D-319	R-103	D-69	R-25	D (F. D. Roosevelt)
1937–1939	75th	D-331	R-89	D-76	R-16	D (F. D. Roosevelt)
1939–1941	76th	D-261	R-164	D-69	R-23	D (F. D. Roosevelt)
1941–1943	77th	D-268	R-162	D-66	R-28	D (F. D. Roosevelt)
1943–1945	78th	D-218	R-208	D-58	R-37	D (F. D. Roosevelt)
1945–1947	79th	D-242	R-190	D-56	R-38	D (F. D. Roosevelt)
						D (Truman)
1947–1949	80th	R-245	D-188	R-51	D-45	D (Truman)
1949–1951	81st	D-263	R-171	D-54	R-42	D (Truman)
1951–1953	82nd	D-234	R-199	D-49	R-47	D (Truman)

(continued)

Political Party Affiliations in Congress and the Presidency, 1789–2007 (CONTINUED)

Year	Congress	House Majority party	House Principal minority party	Senate Majority party	Senate Principal minority party	President
1953–1955	83rd	R-221	D-211	R-48	D-47	R (Eisenhower)
1955–1957	84th	D-232	R-203	D-48	R-47	R (Eisenhower)
1957–1959	85th	D-233	R-200	D-49	R-47	R (Eisenhower)
1959–1961	86th	D-283	R-153	D-64	R-34	R (Eisenhower)
1961–1963	87th	D-263	R-174	D-65	R-35	D (Kennedy)
1963–1965	88th	D-258	R-177	D-67	R-33	D (Kennedy)
						D (L.B. Johnson)
1965–1967	89th	D-295	R-140	D-68	R-32	D (L.B. Johnson)
1967–1969	90th	D-247	R-187	D-64	R-36	D (L.B. Johnson)
1969–1971	91st	D-243	R-192	D-57	R-43	R (Nixon)
1971–1973	92nd	D-254	R-180	D-54	R-44	R (Nixon)
1973–1975	93rd	D-239	R-192	D-56	R-42	R (Nixon)
						R (Ford)
1975–1977	94th	D-291	R-144	D-60	R-37	R (Ford)
1977–1979	95th	D-292	R-143	D-61	R-38	D (Carter)
1979–1981	96th	D-276	R-157	D-58	R-41	D (Carter)
1981–1983	97th	D-243	R-192	R-53	D-46	R (Reagan)
1983–1985	98th	D-269	R-165	R-54	D-46	R (Reagan)
1985–1987	99th	D-252	R-182	R-53	D-47	R (Reagan)
1987–1989	100th	D-258	R-177	D-55	R-45	R (Reagan)
1989–1991	101st	D-259	R-174	D-55	R-45	R (G.H.W. Bush)
1991–1993	102nd	D-267	R-167	D-56	R-44	R (G.H.W. Bush)
1993–1995	103rd	D-258	R-176	D-57	R-43	D (Clinton)
1995–1997	104th	R-230	D-204	R-53	D-47	D (Clinton)
1997–1999	105th	R-227	D-207	R-55	D-45	D (Clinton)
1999–2001	106th	R-222	D-211	R-55	D-45	D (Clinton)
2001–2003	107th	R-221	D-212	R-50	D-50	R (G.W. Bush)
2003–2005	108th	R-229	D-205	R-51	D-48	R (G.W. Bush)
2005–2007	109th	R-232	D-202	R-55	D-44	R (G.W. Bush)
2007–2009	110th	D-233	R-202	D-49[1]	R-49	R (G.W. Bush)

SOURCE: U.S. Bureau of the Census, *Historical Statistics of the United States: Colonial Times to 1970* (Washington, D.C.: Government Printing Office, 1975); U.S. Congress, Joint Committee on Printing, *Official Congressional Directory* (Washington, D.C.: Government Printing Office, 1967–); and *CQ Weekly,* selected issues.

NOTES: Figures are for the beginning of the first session of each Congress. Key to abbreviations: AD—Administration; AM—AntiMasonic; D—Democratic; DR—Democratic-Republican; F—Federalist; J—Jacksonian; NR—National Republican; Op—Opposition; R—Republican; U—Unionist; W—Whig.
1. The 110th Congress included two Independent senators who typically caucused and voted with the Democrats, giving that party a 51–49 margin of control.

Party Leadership in Congress, 1977–2007

95th Congress (1977–1979)

Senate
President Pro Tempore—James O. Eastland—D-Miss.
Deputy President Pro Tempore—Hubert H. Humphrey—D-Minn.
Majority Leader—Robert C. Byrd—D-W.Va.
Majority Whip—Alan Cranston—D-Calif.
Minority Leader—Howard H. Baker Jr.—R-Tenn.
Minority Whip—Ted Stevens—R-Alaska

House
Speaker—Thomas P. O'Neill Jr.—D-Mass.
Majority Leader—Jim Wright—D-Texas
Majority Whip—John Brademas—D-Ind.
Minority Leader—John J. Rhodes—R-Ariz.
Minority Whip—Robert H. Michel—R-Ill.

96th Congress (1979–1981)

Senate
President Pro Tempore—Warren G. Magnuson—D-Wash.
Majority Leader—Robert C. Byrd—D-W.Va.
Majority Whip—Alan Cranston—D-Calif.
Minority Leader—Howard H. Baker Jr.—R-Tenn.
Minority Whip—Ted Stevens—R-Alaska

House
Speaker—Thomas P. O'Neill Jr.—D-Mass.
Majority Leader—Jim Wright—D-Texas
Majority Whip—John Brademas—D-Ind.
Minority Leader—John J. Rhodes—R-Ariz.
Minority Whip—Robert H. Michel—R-Ill.

97th Congress (1981–1983)

Senate
President Pro Tempore—Strom Thurmond—R-S.C.
Majority Leader—Howard H. Baker Jr.—R-Tenn.
Majority Whip—Ted Stevens—R-Alaska
Minority Leader—Robert C. Byrd—D-W.Va.
Minority Whip—Alan Cranston—D-Calif.

House
Speaker—Thomas P. O'Neill Jr.—D-Mass.
Majority Leader—Jim Wright—D-Texas
Majority Whip—Thomas S. Foley—D-Wash.
Minority Leader—Robert H. Michel—R-Ill.
Minority Whip—Trent Lott—R-Miss.

98th Congress (1983–1985)

Senate
President Pro Tempore—Strom Thurmond—R-S.C.
Majority Leader—Howard H. Baker Jr.—R-Tenn.
Majority Whip—Ted Stevens—R-Alaska
Minority Leader—Robert C. Byrd—D-W.Va.
Minority Whip—Alan Cranston—D-Calif.

House
Speaker—Thomas P. O'Neill Jr.—D-Mass.
Majority Leader—Jim Wright—D-Texas
Majority Whip—Thomas S. Foley—D-Wash.
Minority Leader—Robert H. Michel—R-Ill.
Minority Whip—Trent Lott—R-Miss.

99th Congress (1985–1987)

Senate
President Pro Tempore—Strom Thurmond—R-S.C.
Majority Leader—Robert Dole—R-Kan.
Assistant Majority Leader—Alan K. Simpson—R-Wyo.
Minority Leader—Robert C. Byrd—D-W.Va.
Minority Whip—Alan Cranston—D-Calif.

House
Speaker—Thomas P. O'Neill Jr.—D-Mass.
Majority Leader—Jim Wright—D-Texas
Majority Whip—Thomas S. Foley—D-Wash.
Minority Leader—Robert H. Michel—R-Ill.
Minority Whip—Trent Lott—R-Miss.

100th Congress (1987–1989)

Senate
President Pro Tempore—John C. Stennis—D-Miss.
Majority Leader—Robert C. Byrd—D-W.Va.
Majority Whip—Alan Cranston—D-Calif.
Minority Leader—Robert Dole—R-Kan.
Assistant Minority Leader—Alan K. Simpson—R-Wyo.

House
Speaker—Jim Wright—D-Texas
Majority Leader—Thomas S. Foley—D-Wash.
Majority Whip—Tony Coelho—D-Calif.
Minority Leader—Robert H. Michel—R-Ill.
Minority Whip—Trent Lott—R-Miss.

101st Congress (1989–1991)

Senate
President Pro Tempore—Robert C. Byrd—D-W.Va.
Majority Leader—George J. Mitchell—D-Maine
Majority Whip—Alan Cranston—D-Calif.
Minority Leader—Robert Dole—R-Kan.
Assistant Minority Leader—Alan K. Simpson—R-Wyo.

House
Speaker—Jim Wright—D-Texas/Thomas S. Foley—D-Wash.[1]
Majority Leader—Foley/Richard A. Gephardt—D-Mo.[2]
Majority Whip—Tony Coelho—D-Calif./William H. Gray III—D-Pa.[3]
Minority Leader—Robert H. Michel—R-Ill.
Minority Whip—Richard B. Cheney—R-Wyo./
    Newt Gingrich—R-Ga.[4]

(continued)

Party Leadership in Congress, 1977–2007 (CONTINUED)

102d Congress (1991–1993)

Senate
President Pro Tempore—Robert C. Byrd—D-W.Va.
Majority Leader—George J. Mitchell—D-Maine
Majority Whip—Wendell H. Ford—D-Ky.
Minority Leader—Robert Dole—R-Kan.
Assistant Minority Leader—Alan K. Simpson—R-Wyo.

House
Speaker—Thomas S. Foley—D-Wash.
Majority Leader—Richard A. Gephardt—D-Mo.
Majority Whip—William H. Gray III—D-Pa./
    David E. Bonior—D-Mich.[5]
Minority Leader—Robert H. Michel—R-Ill.
Minority Whip—Newt Gingrich—R-Ga.

103d Congress (1993–1995)

Senate
President Pro Tempore—Robert C. Byrd—D-W.Va.
Majority Leader—George J. Mitchell—D-Maine
Majority Whip—Wendell H. Ford—D-Ky.
Minority Leader—Robert Dole—R-Kan.
Assistant Minority Leader—Alan K. Simpson—R-Wyo.

House
Speaker—Thomas S. Foley—D-Wash.
Majority Leader—Richard A. Gephardt—D-Mo.
Majority Whip—David E. Bonior—D-Mich.
Minority Leader—Robert H. Michel—R-Ill.
Minority Whip—Newt Gingrich—R-Ga.

104th Congress (1995–1997)

Senate
President Pro Tempore—Strom Thurmond—R-S.C.
Majority Leader—Robert Dole—R-Kan./Trent Lott—R-Miss.[6]
Majority Whip—Trent Lott—R-Miss./Don Nickles—R-Okla.[7]
Minority Leader—Tom Daschle—D-S.D.
Assistant Minority Leader—Wendell H. Ford—D-Ky.

House
Speaker—Newt Gingrich—R-Ga.
Majority Leader—Dick Armey—R-Texas
Majority Whip—Tom DeLay—R-Texas
Minority Leader—Richard A. Gephardt—D-Mo.
Minority Whip—David E. Bonior—D-Mich.

105th Congress (1997–1999)

Senate
President Pro Tempore—Strom Thurmond—R-S.C.
Majority Leader—Trent Lott—R-Miss.
Majority Whip—Don Nickles—R-Okla.
Minority Leader—Tom Daschle—D-S.D.
Assistant Minority Leader—Wendell H. Ford—D-Ky.

House
Speaker—Newt Gingrich—R-Ga.
Majority Leader—Dick Armey—R-Texas
Majority Whip—Tom DeLay—R-Texas
Minority Leader—Richard A. Gephardt—D-Mo.
Minority Whip—David E. Bonior—D-Mich.

106th Congress (1999–2001)

Senate
President Pro Tempore—Strom Thurmond—R-S.C.
Majority Leader—Trent Lott—R-Miss.
Majority Whip—Don Nickles—R-Okla.
Minority Leader—Tom Daschle—D-S.D.
Assistant Minority Leader—Harry Reid—D-Nev.

House
Speaker—J. Dennis Hastert—R-Ill.
Majority Leader—Dick Armey—R-Texas
Majority Whip—Tom DeLay—R-Texas
Minority Leader—Richard A. Gephardt—D-Mo.
Minority Whip—David E. Bonior—D-Mich.

107th Congress (2001–2003)

Senate (January 3, 2001–June 5, 2001[8])
President Pro Tempore—Strom Thurmond—R-S.C.
Majority Leader—Trent Lott—R-Miss.
Majority Whip—Don Nickles—R-Okla.
Minority Leader—Tom Daschle—D-S.D.
Assistant Minority Leader—Harry Reid—D-Nev.

Senate (June 6, 2001–2003)
President Pro Tempore—Robert C. Byrd—D-W. Va.
Majority Leader—Tom Daschle—D-S.D.
Majority Whip—Harry Reid—D-Nev.
Minority Leader—Trent Lott—R-Miss.
Assistant Minority Leader—Don Nickles—R-Okla.

House
Speaker—J. Dennis Hastert—R-Ill.
Majority Leader—Dick Armey—R-Texas
Majority Whip—Tom DeLay—R-Texas
Minority Leader—Richard A. Gephardt—D-Mo.
Minority Whip—David E. Bonior—D-Mich./
    Nancy Pelosi—D-Calif.[9]

108th Congress (2003–2005)

Senate
President Pro Tempore—Ted Stevens—R-Alaska
Majority Leader—Bill Frist—R-Tenn.
Majority Whip—Mitch McConnell—R-Ky.
Minority Leader—Tom Daschle—D-S.D.
Assistant Minority Leader—Harry Reid—D-Nev.

House
Speaker—J. Dennis Hastert—R-Ill.
Majority Leader—Tom DeLay—R-Texas
Majority Whip—Roy Blunt—R-Mo.
Minority Leader—Nancy Pelosi—D-Calif.
Minority Whip—Steny H. Hoyer—D-Md.

109th Congress (2005–2007)

Senate
President Pro Tempore—Ted Stevens—R-Alaska
Majority Leader—Bill Frist—R-Tenn.
Majority Whip—Mitch McConnell—R-Ky.
Minority Leader—Harry Reid—D-Nev.
Assistant Minority Leader—Richard J. Durbin—D-Ill.

House
Speaker—J. Dennis Hastert—R-Ill.
Majority Leader—Tom DeLay—R-Texas/Roy Blunt—R-Mo./
   John A. Boehner—R-Ohio[10]

Majority Whip—Roy Blunt—R-Mo.
Minority Leader—Nancy Pelosi—D-Calif.
Minority Whip—Steny H. Hoyer—D-Md.

110th Congress (2007–2009)

Senate
President Pro Tempore—Robert C. Byrd—D-W.Va.
Majority Leader—Harry Reid—D-Nev.
Majority Whip—Richard J. Durbin—D-Ill.
Minority Leader—Mitch McConnell—R-Ky.
Assistant Minority Leader—Trent Lott—R-Miss./Jon Kyl—R-Ariz.[11]

House
Speaker—Nancy Pelosi—D-Calif.
Majority Leader—Steny H. Hoyer—D-Md.
Majority Whip—James E. Clyburn—D-S.C.
Minority Leader—John A. Boehner—R-Ohio
Minority Whip—Roy Blunt—R-Mo.

SOURCE: *Congressional Quarterly Almanac,* selected years.

NOTES:
    1. Wright resigned as Speaker and was succeeded by Foley on June 6, 1989.
    2. Gephardt became majority leader on June 14, 1989, filling the vacancy created when Foley succeeded Wright as Speaker of the House on June 6, 1989.
    3. Gray became majority whip on June 14, 1989, filling the vacancy caused by Coelho's resignation.
    4. Gingrich became minority whip on March 23, 1989, filling the vacancy caused by the resignation of Cheney on March 17, 1989, to become secretary of defense.
    5. Bonior became majority whip on September 11, 1991, filling the vacancy caused by Gray's resignation from Congress on the same day.
    6. Lott became majority leader on June 12, 1996, filling the vacancy caused by the resignation of Dole on June 11.
    7. Nickles became majority whip on June 12, 1996, filling the vacancy caused by Lott becoming majority leader.
    8. The 2000 elections resulted in an even party split between Democrats and Republicans, fifty members on each side. With Republican Vice President Richard B. Cheney acting as the nominal Senate leader, the GOP retained technical control of the Senate, allowing party members to be in the primary leadership roles even though the two parties had worked out a power sharing arrangement on committees. On May 24, 2001, Republican James M. Jeffords of Vermont announced he was leaving the party to become an Independent, and would caucus with the Democrats. He officially switched on June 5. On June 6, the Democrats achieved a 50–49 majority as a result, allowing them to take control of the majority positions in the leadership and on all committees.
    9. Pelosi became minority whip January 15, 2002, when Bonior stepped down.
    10. DeLay was required by GOP Conference rules to temporarily vacate the position after being indicted in Texas on September 28, 2005, on campaign finance charges. Speaker J. Dennis Hastert, R-Ill., named Blunt to act as majority leader for the remainder of the session. On January 7, 2006, DeLay announced he would not seek to reclaim the position. He resigned from the House on June 9. Republicans elected Boehner as majority leader.
    11. Lott resigned from the Senate on December 18, 2007. Kyl was named as replacement.

Congressional Committee Chairs since 1947

Following is a list of House and Senate standing committee chairs from January 1947 through February 2008. The years listed reflect the tenure of the committee chairs. The 107th Congress (2001–2003) presented a special case. The 2000 elections produced a 50–50 split in the Senate between Republicans and Democrats. From the day the 107th Congress convened on January 3, 2001, until inauguration day on January 20, 2001, Democrat Al Gore, who as vice president was president of the Senate, tipped the scale to a Democratic majority. When Republican Dick Cheney became vice president on January 20, 2001, the GOP became the majority party. Then, on June 6, 2001, Republican James M. Jeffords of Vermont declared himself an Independent, who caucused and voted with Democrats to give them a 51–49 majority to control the chamber.

As committee names have changed through the years, the committees are listed by their names as of September 2007; former committee names are listed as well. This list also includes chairs of committees that were disbanded during the period.

House

Agriculture
Clifford R. Hope (R-Kan. 1947–1949)
Harold D. Cooley (D-N.C. 1949–1953)
Clifford R. Hope (R-Kan. 1953–1955)
Harold D. Cooley (D-N.C. 1955–1967)
W. R. Poage (D-Texas 1967–1975)
Thomas S. Foley (D-Wash. 1975–1981)
E. "Kika" de la Garza (D-Texas 1981–1995)
Pat Roberts (R-Kan. 1995–1997)
Bob Smith (R-Ore. 1997–1999)
Larry Combest (R-Texas 1999–2003)
Robert W. Goodlatte (R-Va. 2003–2007)
Collin C. Peterson (D-Minn. 2007–)

Appropriations
John Taber (R-N.Y. 1947–1949)
Clarence Cannon (D-Mo. 1949–1953)
John Taber (R-N.Y. 1953–1955)
Clarence Cannon (D-Mo. 1955–1964)
George H. Mahon (D-Texas 1964–1979)
Jamie L. Whitten (D-Miss. 1979–1993)
William H. Natcher (D-Ky. 1993–1994)
David Obey (D-Wis. 1994–1995)
Robert L. Livingston (R-La. 1995–1999)
C. W. "Bill" Young (R-Fla. 1999–2005)
Jerry Lewis (R-Calif. 2005–2007)
David R. Obey (D-Wis. 2007–)

Armed Services
(formerly Armed Services, 1947–1995; National Security, 1995–1998)
Walter G. Andrews (R-N.Y. 1947–1949)
Carl Vinson (D-Ga. 1949–1953)
Dewey Short (R-Mo. 1953–1955)
Carl Vinson (D-Ga. 1955–1965)
L. Mendel Rivers (D-S.C. 1965–1971)
F. Edward Hébert (D-La. 1971–1975)

Melvin Price (D-Ill. 1975–1985)
Les Aspin (D-Wis. 1985–1993)
Ronald V. Dellums (D-Calif. 1993–1995)
Floyd D. Spence (R-S.C. 1995–20013)
Bob Stump (R-Ariz. 2001–2003)
Duncan Hunter (R-Calif. 2003–2007)
Ike Skelton (D-Mo. 2007–)

Budget
Brock Adams (D-Wash. 1975–1977)
Robert N. Giaimo (D-Conn. 1977–1981)
James R. Jones (D-Okla. 1981–1985)
William H. Gray III (D-Pa. 1985–1989)
Leon E. Panetta (D-Calif. 1989–1993)
Martin Olav Sabo (D-Minn. 1993–1995)
John R. Kasich (R-Ohio 1995–2001)
Jim Nussle (R-Iowa 2001–2007)
John M. Spratt Jr. (D-S.C. 2007–)

District of Columbia
Everett McKinley Dirksen (R-Ill. 1947–1949)
John L. McMillan (D-S.C. 1949–1953)
Sidney Elmer Simpson (R-Ill. 1953–1955)
John L. McMillan (D-S.C. 1955–1973)
Charles C. Diggs Jr. (D-Mich. 1973–1979)
Ronald V. Dellums (D-Calif. 1979–1993)
Pete Stark (D-Calif. 1993–1995)
(Reorganized as a subcommittee of the Government Reform and Oversight in 1995)

Education and Labor
(formerly Education and Labor, 1947–1995; Economic and Educational Opportunities, 1995–1997; Education and the Workforce, 1997–2007)
Fred A. Hartley Jr. (R-N.J. 1947–1949)
John Lesinski (D-Mich. 1949–1950)
Graham A. Barden (D-N.C. 1950–1953)
Samuel K. McConnell Jr. (R-Pa. 1953–1955)
Graham A. Barden (D-N.C. 1955–1961)
Adam Clayton Powell Jr. (D-N.Y. 1961–1967)

Carl D. Perkins (D-Ky. 1967–1984)
Augustus F. Hawkins (D-Calif. 1984–1991)
William D. Ford (D-Mich. 1991–1995)
Bill Goodling (R-Pa. 1995–2001)
John A. Boehner (R-Ohio 2001–2006)
Howard P. ""Buck"" McKeon (R-Calif. 2006–2007)
George Miller (D-Calif. 2007–)

Energy and Commerce
(formerly Interstate and Foreign Commerce, 1947–1981; Energy and Commerce, 1981–1995; Commerce, 1995–2001)
Charles A. Wolverton (R-N.J. 1947–1949)
Robert Crosser (D-Ohio 1949–1953)
Charles A. Wolverton (R-N.J. 1953–1955)
J. Percy Priest (D-Tenn. 1955–1957)
Oren Harris (D-Ark. 1957–1966)
Harley O. Staggers (D-W.Va. 1966–1981)
John D. Dingell (D-Mich. 1981–1995)
Thomas J. Bliley Jr. (R-Va. 1995–2001)
W. J. "Billy" Tauzin (R-La. 2001–2005)
Joe L. Barton (R-Texas 2005–2007)
John D. Dingell (D-Mich. 2007–)

Energy Independence and Global Warming, Select Committee on
Edward J. Markey (D-Mass. 2007–)

Financial Services
(formerly Banking and Currency, 1947–1975; Banking, Currency and Housing, 1975–1977; Banking, Finance and Urban Affairs, 1977–1995; Banking and Financial Services, 1995–2001)
Jesse P. Wolcott (R-Mich. 1947–1949)
Brent Spence (D-Ky. 1949–1953)
Jesse P. Wolcott (R-Mich. 1953–1955)
Brent Spence (D-Ky. 1955–1963)
Wright Patman (D-Texas 1963–1975)
Henry S. Reuss (D-Wis. 1975–1981)
Fernand J. St Germain (D-R.I. 1981–1989)
Henry B. Gonzalez (D-Texas 1989–1995)
Jim Leach (R-Iowa 1995–2001)
Michael G. Oxley (R-Ohio 2001–2007)
Barney Frank (D-Mass. 2007–)

Foreign Affairs
(formerly Foreign Affairs, 1947–1975; International Relations, 1975–1979; Foreign Affairs, 1979–1995; International Relations, 1995–2007)
Charles A. Eaton (R-N.J. 1947–1949)
John Kee (D-W.Va. 1949–1951)
James P. Richards (D-S.C. 1951–1953)
Robert B. Chiperfield (R-Ill. 1953–1955)

James P. Richards (D-S.C. 1955–1957)
Thomas S. Gordon (D-Ill. 1957–1959)
Thomas E. Morgan (D-Pa. 1959–1977)
Clement J. Zablocki (D-Wis. 1977–1983)
Dante B. Fascell (D-Fla. 1984–1993)
Lee H. Hamilton (D-Ind. 1993–1995)
Benjamin A. Gilman (R-N.Y. 1995–2001)
Henry J. Hyde (R-Ill. 2001–2007)
Tom Lantos (D-Calif. 2007–2008)
Howard L. Berman (D-Calif. 2008–)

Homeland Security
(formerly Select Committee on Homeland Security, 2002–2005)
Christopher Cox (R-Calif. 2003–2005)
Peter T. King (R-N.Y. 2005–2007)
Bennie Thompson (D-Miss. 2007–)

House Administration
(formerly House Administration, 1947–1995; House Oversight, 1995–1998)
Karl M. LeCompte (R-Iowa 1947–1949)
Mary T. Norton (D-N.J. 1949–1951)
Thomas B. Stanley (D-Va. 1951–1953)
Karl M. LeCompte (R-Iowa 1953–1955)
Omar Burleson (D-Texas 1955–1968)
Samuel N. Friedel (D-Md. 1968–1971)
Wayne L. Hays (D-Ohio 1971–1976)
Frank Thompson Jr. (D-N.J. 1976–1980)
Augustus F. Hawkins (D-Calif. 1981–1984)
Frank Annunzio (D-Ill. 1985–1991)
Charlie Rose (D-N.C. 1991–1995)
Bill Thomas (R-Calif. 1995–2001)
Bob Ney (R-Ohio 2001–2006)
Vernon J. Ehlers (R-Mich. 2006–2007)
Juanita Millender-McDonald (D-Calif. 2007)
Robert A. Brady (D-Pa. 2007–)

Intelligence, Permanent Select Committee on
(formerly Select Committee on Intelligence, 1975–1976)
Lucien N. Nedzi (D-Mich. 1975)
Otis G. Pike (D-N.Y. 1975–1976)
Edward P. Boland (D-Mass. 1977–1985)
Lee H. Hamilton (D-Ind. 1985–1987)
Louis Stokes (D-Ohio 1987–1989)
Anthony C. Beilenson (D-Calif. 1989–1991)
Dave McCurdy (D-Okla. 1991–1993)
Dan Glickman (D-Kan. 1993–1995)
Larry Combest (R-Texas 1995–1997)
Porter J. Goss (R-Fla. 1997–2004)
Peter Hoekstra (R-Mich. 2004–2007)
Silvestre Reyes (D-Texas 2007–)

Congressional Committee Chairs since 1947 (CONTINUED)

Internal Security
(formerly Un-American Activities, 1947–1969)
J. Parnell Thomas (R-N.J. 1947–1949)
John S. Wood (D-Ga. 1949–1953)
Harold H. Velde (R-Ill. 1953–1955)
Francis E. Walter (D-Pa. 1955–1963)
Edwin E. Willis (D-La. 1963–1969)
Richard H. Ichord (D-Mo. 1969–1975)
(The panel was abolished in 1975)

Judiciary
Earl C. Michener (R-Mich. 1947–1949)
Emanuel Celler (D-N.Y. 1949–1953)
Chauncey W. Reed (R-Ill. 1953–1955)
Emanuel Celler (D-N.Y. 1955–1973)
Peter W. Rodino Jr. (D-N.J. 1973–1989)
Jack Brooks (D-Texas 1989–1995)
Henry J. Hyde (R-Ill. 1995–2001)
F. James Sensenbrenner Jr. (R-Wis. 2001–2007)
John Conyers Jr. (D-Mich. 2007–)

Merchant Marine and Fisheries
Fred Bradley (R-Mich. 1947)
Alvin F. Weichel (R-Ohio 1947–1949)
Schuyler Otis Bland (D-Va. 1949–1950)
Edward J. Hart (D-N.J. 1950–1953)
Alvin F. Weichel (R-Ohio 1953–1955)
Herbert C. Bonner (D-N.C. 1955–1965)
Edward A. Garmatz (D-Md. 1966–1973)
Leonor K. Sullivan (D-Mo. 1973–1977)
John M. Murphy (D-N.Y. 1977–1981)
Walter B. Jones (D-N.C. 1981–1992)
Gerry E. Studds (D-Mass. 1992–1993)
George Miller (D-Calif. 1993–1995)
(Reorganized as a subcommittee of Transportation and Infrastructure in 1995.)

Natural Resources
(formerly Public Lands, 1947–1951; Interior and Insular Affairs, 1951–1992; Natural Resources, 1993–1995; Resources, 1995–2007)
Richard J. Welch (R-Calif. 1947–1949)
Andrew L. Somers (D-N.Y. 1949)
J. Hardin Peterson (D-Fla. 1949–1951)
John R. Murdock (D-Ariz. 1951–1953)
A.L. Miller (R-Neb. 1953–1955)
Claire Engle (D-Calif. 1955–1959)
Wayne N. Aspinall (D-Colo. 1959–1973)
James A. Haley (D-Fla. 1973–1977)
Morris K. Udall (D-Ariz. 1977–1991)
George Miller (D-Calif. 1991–1995)

Don Young (R-Alaska, 1995–2001)
James V. Hansen (R-Utah 2001–2003)
Richard W. Pombo (R-Calif. 2003–2007)
Nick J. Rahall II (D-W.Va. 2007–)

Oversight and Government Reform
(formerly Expenditures in the Executive Departments, 1947–1952; Government Operations, 1952–1995; Government Reform and Oversight, 1995–1998; Government Reform, 1999–2007)
Clare E. Hoffman (R-Mich. 1947–1949)
William L. Dawson (D-Ill. 1949–1953)
Clare E. Hoffman (R-Mich. 1953–1955)
William L. Dawson (D-Ill. 1955–1971)
Chet Holifield (D-Calif. 1971–1975)
Jack Brooks (D-Texas 1975–1989)
John Conyers (D-Mich. 1989–1995)
William F. Clinger (R-Pa. 1995–1997)
Dan Burton (R-Ind. 1997–2003)
Thomas M. Davis III (R-Va. 2003–2007)
Henry A. Waxman (D-Calif. 2007–)

Post Office and Civil Service
Edward H. Rees (R-Kan. 1947–1949)
Tom Murray (D-Tenn. 1949–1953)
Edward H. Rees (R-Kan. 1953–1955)
Tom Murray (D-Tenn. 1955–1967)
Thaddeus J. Dulski (D-N.Y. 1967–1975)
David N. Henderson (D-N.C. 1975–1977)
Robert N.C. Nix Sr. (D-Pa. 1977–1979)
James M. Hanley (D-N.Y. 1979–1981)
William D. Ford (D-Mich. 1981–1991)
William L. Clay (D-Mo. 1991–1995)
(Reorganized as a subcommittee of Government Reform and Oversight in 1995.)

Rules
Leo E. Allen (R-Ill. 1947–1949)
Adolph J. Sabath (D-Ill. 1949–1953)
Leo E. Allen (R-Ill. 1953–1955)
Howard W. Smith (D-Va. 1955–1967)
William M. Colmer (D-Miss. 1967–1973)
Ray J. Madden (D-Ind. 1973–1977)
James J. Delaney (D-N.Y. 1977–1978)
Richard Bolling (D-Mo. 1979–1983)
Claude Pepper (D-Fla. 1983–1989)
Joe Moakley (D-Mass. 1989–1995)
Gerald B.H. Solomon (R-N.Y. 1995–1999)
David Dreier (R-Calif. 1999–2007)
Louise M. Slaughter (D-N.Y. 2007–)

Science and Technology

(formerly Science and Astronautics, 1959–1975; Science and Technology, 1975–1987; Science, Space and Technology, 1987–1995; Science, 1995–2007)

Overton Brooks (D-La. 1959–1961)
George P. Miller (D-Calif. 1961–1973)
Olin E. Teague (D-Texas 1973–1979)
Don Fuqua (D-Fla. 1979–1987)
Robert A. Roe (D-N.J. 1987–1991)
George E. Brown Jr. (D-Calif. 1991–1995)
Robert S. Walker (R-Pa. 1995–1997)
F. James Sensenbrenner Jr. (R-Wis. 1997–2001)
Sherwood Boehlert (R-N.Y. 2001–2007)
Bart Gordon (D-Tenn. 2007–)

Small Business

(formerly Select Committee on Small Business, 1947–1975)

Walter C. Ploeser (R-Mo. 1947–1949)
Wright Patman (D-Texas 1949–1953)
William S. Hill (R-Colo. 1953–1955)
Wright Patman (D-Texas 1955–1963)
Joe L. Ervins (D-Tenn. 1963–1977)
Neal Smith (D-Iowa 1977–1981)
Parren J. Mitchell (D-Md. 1981–1987)
John J. LaFalce (D-N.Y. 1987–1995)
Jan Meyers (R-Kan. 1995–1997)
James M. Talent (R-Mo. 1997–2001)
Donald Manzullo (R-Ill. 2001–2007)
Nydia M. Velázquez (D-N.Y. 2007–)

Standards of Official Conduct

Melvin Price (D-Ill. 1969–1975)
John J. Flynt Jr. (D-Ga. 1975–1977)
Charles E. Bennett (D-Fla. 1977–1981)
Louis Stokes (D-Ohio 1981–1985)
Julian C. Dixon (D-Calif. 1985–1991)
Louis Stokes (D-Ohio 1991–1993)
Jim McDermott (D-Wash. 1993–1995)
Nancy L. Johnson (R-Conn. 1995–1997)
James V. Hansen (R-Utah 1997–1999)
Lamar Smith (R-Texas 1999–2001)
Joel Hefley (R-Colo. 2001–2005)
Doc Hastings (R-Wash. 2005–2007)
Stephanie Tubbs Jones (D-Ohio 2007–)

Transportation and Infrastructure

(formerly Public Works, 1947–1975; Public Works and Transportation, 1975–1995)

George A. Dondero (R-Mich. 1947–1949)
William M. Whittington (D-Miss. 1949–1951)
Charles A. Buckley (D-N.Y. 1951–1953)
George A. Dondero (R-Mich. 1953–1955)

Charles A. Buckley (D-N.Y. 1955–1965)
George H. Fallon (D-Md. 1965–1971)
John A. Blatnik (D-Minn. 1971–1975)
Robert E. Jones Jr. (D-Ala. 1975–1977)
Harold T. Johnson (D-Calif. 1977–1981)
James J. Howard (D-N.J. 1981–1988)
Glenn M. Anderson (D-Calif. 1988–1991)
Robert A. Roe (D-N.J. 1991–1993)
Norman Y. Mineta (D-Calif. 1993–1995)
Bud Shuster (R-Pa. 1995–2001)
Don Young (R-Alaska 2001–2007)
James L. Oberstar (D-Minn. 2007–)

Veterans' Affairs

Edith Nourse Rogers (R-Mass. 1947–1949)
John E. Rankin (D-Miss. 1949–1953)
Edith Nourse Rogers (R-Mass. 1953–1955)
Olin E. Teague (D-Texas 1955–1973)
William Jennings Bryan Dorn (D-S.C. 1973–1975)
Ray Roberts (D-Texas 1975–1981)
G. V. "Sonny" Montgomery (D-Miss. 1981–1995)
Bob Stump (R-Ariz. 1995–2001)
Christopher H. Smith (R-N.J. 2001–2005)
Steve Buyer (R-Ind. 2005–2007)
Bob Filner (D-Calif. 2007–)

Ways and Means

Harold Knutson (R-Minn. 1947–1949)
Robert L. Doughton (D-N.C. 1949–1953)
Daniel A. Reed (R-N.Y. 1953–1955)
Jere Cooper (D-Tenn. 1955–1957)
Wilbur D. Mills (D-Ark. 1958–1975)
Al Ullman (D-Ore. 1975–1981)
Dan Rostenkowski (D-Ill. 1981–1994)
Sam M. Gibbons (D-Fla. 1994–1995)
Bill Archer (R-Texas 1995–2001)
Bill Thomas (R-Calif. 2001–2007)
Charles B. Rangel (D-N.Y. 2007–)

Senate

Aeronautical and Space Sciences

Lyndon B. Johnson (D-Texas 1958–1961)
Robert S. Kerr (D-Okla. 1961–1963)
Clinton P. Anderson (D-N.M. 1963–1973)
Frank E. Moss (D-Utah 1973–1977)
(Abolished in 1977, when its jurisdiction was consolidated under Commerce.)

Agriculture, Nutrition, and Forestry

(formerly Agriculture and Forestry, 1947–1977)

Arthur Capper (R-Kan. 1947–1949)

Congressional Committee Chairs since 1947 (CONTINUED)

Elmer Thomas (D-Okla. 1949–1951)
Allen J. Ellender (D-La. 1951–1953)
George D. Aiken (R-Vt. 1953–1955)
Allen J. Ellender (D-La. 1955–1971)
Herman E. Talmadge (D-Ga. 1971–1981)
Jesse Helms (R-N.C. 1981–1987)
Patrick J. Leahy (D-Vt. 1987–1995)
Richard G. Lugar (R-Ind. 1995–2001)
Tom Harkin (D-Iowa January 2001)
Richard G. Lugar (R-Ind. January–June 2001)
Tom Harkin (D-Iowa June 2001–2003)
Thad Cochran (R-Miss. 2003–2005)
Saxby Chambliss (R-Ga. 2005–2007)
Tom Harkin (D-Iowa 2007–)

Appropriations

Styles Bridges (R-N.H. 1947–1949)
Kenneth McKellar (D-Tenn. 1949–1953)
Styles Bridges (R-N.H. 1953–1955)
Carl Hayden (D-Ariz. 1955–1969)
Richard B. Russell (D-Ga. 1969–1971)
Allen J. Ellender (D-La. 1971–1972)
John L. McClellan (D-Ark. 1972–1977)
Warren G. Magnuson (D-Wash. 1978–1981)
Mark O. Hatfield (R-Ore. 1981–1987)
John C. Stennis (D-Miss. 1987–1989)
Robert C. Byrd (D-W.Va. 1989–1995)
Mark O. Hatfield (R-Ore. 1995–1997)
Ted Stevens (R-Alaska 1997–2001)
Robert C. Byrd (D-W.Va. January 2001)
Ted Stevens (R-Alaska January–June 2001)
Robert C. Byrd (D-W.Va. June 2001–2003)
Ted Stevens (R-Alaska 2003–2005)
Thad Cochran (R-Miss. 2005–2007)
Robert C. Byrd (D-W.Va. 2007–)

Armed Services

Chan Gurney (R-S.D. 1947–1949)
Millard E. Tydings (D-Md. 1949–1951)
Richard B. Russell (D-Ga. 1951–1953)
Leverett Saltonstall (R-Mass. 1953–1955)
Richard B. Russell (D-Ga. 1955–1969)
John C. Stennis (D-Miss. 1969–1981)
John Tower (R-Texas 1981–1985)
Barry Goldwater (R-Ariz. 1985–1987)
Sam Nunn (D-Ga. 1987–1995)
Strom Thurmond (R-S.C. 1995–1999)
John W. Warner (R-Va. 1999–2001)
Carl Levin (D-Mich. January 2001)
John W. Warner (R-Va. January–June 2001)

Carl Levin (D-Mich. June 2001–2003)
John W. Warner (R-Va. 2003–2007)
Carl Levin (D-Mich. 2007–)

Banking, Housing, and Urban Affairs
(formerly Banking and Currency, 1947–1971)

Charles W. Tobey (R-N.H. 1947–1949)
Burnet R. Maybank (D-S.C. 1949–1953)
Homer E. Capehart (R-Ind. 1953–1955)
J. W. Fulbright (D-Ark. 1955–1959)
A. Willis Robertson (D-Va. 1959–1967)
John J. Sparkman (D-Ala. 1967–1975)
William Proxmire (D-Wis. 1975–1981)
Jake Garn (R-Utah 1981–1987)
William Proxmire (D-Wis. 1987–1989)
Donald W. Riegle Jr. (D-Mich. 1989–1995)
Alfonse M. D'Amato (R-N.Y. 1995–1999)
Phil Gramm (R-Texas 1999–2001)
Paul S. Sarbanes (D-Md. January 2001)
Phil Gramm (R-Texas January–June 2001)
Paul S. Sarbanes (D-Md. June 2001–2003)
Richard C. Shelby (R-Ala. 2003–2007)
Christopher J. Dodd (D-Conn. 2007–)

Budget

Edmund S. Muskie (D-Maine 1975–1979)
Ernest F. Hollings (D-S.C. 1979–1981)
Pete V. Domenici (R-N.M. 1981–1987)
Lawton Chiles Jr. (D-Fla. 1987–1989)
Jim Sasser (D-Tenn. 1989–1995)
Pete V. Domenici (R-N.M. 1995–2001)
Kent Conrad (D-N.D. January 2001)
Pete V. Domenici (R-N.H. January–June 2001)
Kent Conrad (D-N.D. June 2001–2003)
Don Nickles (R-Okla. 2003–2005)
Judd Gregg (R-N.H. 2005–2007)
Kent Conrad (D-N.D. 2007–)

Commerce, Science, and Transportation
(formerly Interstate and Foreign Commerce, 1947–1961; Commerce, 1961–1977)

Wallace H. White (R-Maine 1947–1949)
Edwin C. Johnson (D-Colo. 1949–1953)
Charles W. Tobey (R-N.H. 1953)
John W. Bricker (R-Ohio 1953–1955)
Warren G. Magnuson (D-Wash. 1955–1978)
Howard W. Cannon (D-Nev. 1978–1981)
Bob Packwood (R-Ore. 1981–1985)
John C. Danforth (R-Mo. 1985–1987)
Ernest F. Hollings (D-S.C. 1987–1995)

Larry Pressler (R-S.D. 1995–1997)
John McCain (R-Ariz. 1997–2001)
Ernest F. Hollings (D-S.C. January 2001)
John McCain (R-Ariz. January–June 2001)
Ernest F. Hollings (D-S.C. June 2001–2003)
John McCain (R-Ariz. 2003–2005)
Ted Stevens (R-Alaska 2005–2007)
Daniel K. Inouye (D-Hawaii 2007–)

District of Columbia
C. Douglass Buck (R-Del. 1947–1949)
J. Howard McGrath (D-R.I. 1949–1951)
Matthew M. Neely (D-W.Va. 1951–1953)
Francis Case (R-S.D. 1953–1955)
Matthew M. Neely (D-W.Va. 1955–1959)
Alan Bible (D-Nev. 1959–1969)
Joseph D. Tydings (D-Md. 1969–1971)
Thomas Eagleton (D-Mo. 1971–1977)
(Abolished in 1977 and its responsibilities transferred to Governmental Affairs.)

Energy and Natural Resources
Henry M. Jackson (D-Wash. 1977–1981)
James A. McClure (R-Idaho 1981–1987)
J. Bennett Johnston (D-La. 1987–1995)
Frank H. Murkowski (R-Alaska 1995–2001)
Jeff Bingaman (D-N.M. January 2001)
Frank H. Murkowski (R-Alaska January–June 2001)
Jeff Bingaman (D-N.M. June 2001–2003)
Pete V. Domenici (R-N.M. 2003–2007)
Jeff Bingaman (D-N.M. 2007–)

Environment and Public Works
(formerly Public Works, 1947–1977)
Chapman Revercomb (R-W.Va. 1947–1949)
Dennis Chavez (D-N.M. 1949–1953)
Edward Martin (R-Pa. 1953–1955)
Dennis Chavez (D-N.M. 1955–1962)
Pat McNamara (D-Mich. 1963–1966)
Jennings Randolph (D-W.Va. 1966–1981)
Robert T. Stafford (R-Vt. 1981–1987)
Quentin N. Burdick (D-N.D. 1987–1992)
Daniel Patrick Moynihan (D-N.Y. 1992)
Max Baucus (D-Mont. 1993–1995)
John H. Chafee (R-R.I. 1995–1999)
Robert C. Smith (R-N.H. 1999–2001)
Harry Reid (D-Nev. January 2001)
Robert C. Smith (R-N.H. January–June 2001)
James M. Jeffords (I-Vt. June 2001–2003)
James M. Inhofe (R-Okla. 2003–2007)
Barbara Boxer (D-Calif. 2007–)

Ethics, Select Committee on
(formerly the Select Committee on Standards and Conduct, 1966–1977)
John C. Stennis (D-Miss. 1966–1975)
Howard W. Cannon (D-Nev. 1975–1977)
Adlai Ewing Stevenson III (D-Ill. 1977–1981)
Malcolm Wallop (R-Wyo. 1981–1983)
Ted Stevens (R-Alaska 1983–1985)
Warren B. Rudman (R-N.H. 1985–1987)
Howell Heflin (D-Ala. 1987–1991)
Terry Sanford (D-N.C. 1991–1993)
Richard H. Bryan (D-Nev. 1993–1995)
Mitch McConnell (R Ky. 1995–1997)
Robert C. Smith (R-N.H. 1997–2001)
Robert C. Smith (R-N.H. 1997–1999)
Pat Roberts (R-Kan. 1999–2001)
Harry Reid (D-Nev. January 2001)
Pat Roberts (R-Kan. January–June 2001)
Harry Reid (D-Nev. June 2001–2003)
Harry Reid (D-Nev. January 2001–2003)
Pat Roberts (R-Kan. January–June 2001)
Harry Reid (D-Nev. June 2001–2003)
George V. Voinovich (R-Ohio 2003–2007)
Tim Johnson (D-S.D. 2007–)

Finance
Eugene D. Millikin (R-Colo. 1947–1949)
Walter F. George (D Ga. 1949 1953)
Eugene D. Millikin (R-Colo. 1953–1955)
Harry Flood Byrd (D-Va. 1955–1965)
Russell B. Long (D-La. 1965–1981)
Robert Dole (R-Kan. 1981–1985)
Bob Packwood (R-Ore. 1985–1987)
Lloyd Bentsen (D-Texas 1987–1993)
Daniel Patrick Moynihan (D-N.Y. 1993–1995)
Bob Packwood (R-Ore. 1995)
William V. Roth Jr. (R-Del. 1995–2001)
Max Baucus (D-Mont. January 2001)
Charles E. Grassley (R-Iowa January–June 2001)
Max Baucus (D-Mont. June 2001–2003)
Charles E. Grassley (R-Iowa 2003–2007)
Max Baucus (D-Mont. 2007–)

Foreign Relations
Arthur H. Vandenberg (R-Mich. 1947–1949)
Tom Connally (D-Texas 1949–1953)
Alexander Wiley (R-Wis. 1953–1955)
Walter F. George (D-Ga. 1955–1957)
Theodore Francis Green (D-R.I. 1957–1959)
J.W. Fulbright (D-Ark. 1959–1975)
John J. Sparkman (D-Ala. 1975–1979)

Congressional Committee Chairs since 1947 (CONTINUED)

Frank Church (D-Idaho 1979–1981)
Charles Percy (R-Ill. 1981–1985)
Richard G. Lugar (R-Ind. 1985–1987)
Claiborne Pell (D-R.I. 1987–1995)
Jesse Helms (R-N.C. 1995–2001)
Joseph R. Biden Jr. (D-Del. January 2001)
Jesse Helms (R-N.C. January–June 2001)
Joseph R. Biden Jr. (D-Del. June 2001–2003)
Richard G. Lugar (R-Ind. 2003–2007)
Joseph R. Biden Jr. (D-Del. 2007–)

Health, Education, Labor and Pensions
(formerly Labor and Public Welfare, 1947–1977; Human Resources, 1977–1979; Labor and Human Resources, 1979–1999)
Robert A. Taft (R-Ohio 1947–1949)
Elbert D. Thomas (D-Utah 1949–1951)
James E. Murray (D-Mont. 1951–1953)
H. Alexander Smith (R-N.J. 1953–1955)
Lister Hill (D-Ala. 1955–1969)
Ralph W. Yarborough (D-Texas 1969–1971)
Harrison A. Williams Jr. (D-N.J. 1971–1981)
Orrin G. Hatch (R-Utah 1981–1987)
Edward M. Kennedy (D-Mass. 1987–1995)
Nancy Landon Kassebaum (R-Kan. 1995–1997)
James M. Jeffords (R-Vt. 1997–2001)
Edward M. Kennedy (D-Mass. January 2001)
James M. Jeffords (R-Vt. January–June 2001)
Edward M. Kennedy (D-Mass. June 2001–2003)
Judd Gregg (R-N.H. 2003–2005)
Michael B. Enzi, (R-Wyo. 2005–2007)
Edward M. Kennedy (D-Mass. 2007–)

Homeland Security and Governmental Affairs
(formerly Expenditures in Executive Departments, 1947–1952; Government Operations, 1952–1977; Governmental Affairs, 1997–2004)
George D. Aiken (R-Vt. 1947–1949)
John L. McClellan (D-Ark. 1949–1953)
Joseph R. McCarthy (R-Wis. 1953–1955)
John L. McClellan (D-Ark. 1955–1972)
Sam J. Ervin Jr. (D-N.C. 1972–1974)
Abraham A. Ribicoff (D-Conn. 1975–1981)
William V. Roth Jr. (R-Del. 1981–1987)
John Glenn (D-Ohio 1987–1995)
William V. Roth Jr. (R-Del. 1995–1996)
Ted Stevens (R-Alaska 1996–1997)
Fred Thompson (R-Tenn. 1997–2001)
Joseph I. Lieberman (D-Conn. January 2001)

Fred Thompson (R-Tenn. January–June 2001)
Joseph I. Lieberman (D-Conn. June 2001–2003)
Susan Collins (R-Maine 2003–2007)
Joseph I. Lieberman (I-Conn. 2007–)

Indian Affairs
(formerly a temporary select committee; redesignated as a permanent committee in 1993.)
Daniel K. Inouye (D-Hawaii 1993–1995)
John McCain (R-Ariz. 1995–1997)
Ben Nighthorse Campbell (R-Colo. 1997–2001)
Daniel K.Inouye (D-Hawaii January 2001)
Ben Nighthorse Campbell (R-Colo. January– June 2001)
Daniel K. Inouye (D-Hawaii June 2001–2003)
Ben Nighthorse Campbell (R-Colo. 2003–2005)
John McCain (R-Ariz. 2005–2007)
Byron L. Dorgan (D-N.D. 2007–)

Intelligence, Select Committee on
Daniel K. Inouye (D-Hawaii 1976–1978)
Birch Bayh (D-Ind. 1978–1981)
Barry Goldwater (R-Ariz. 1981–1985)
Dave Durenberger (R-Minn. 1985–1987)
David L. Boren (D-Okla. 1987–1993)
Dennis DeConcini (D-Ariz. 1993–1995)
Arlen Specter (R-Pa. 1995–1997)
Richard C. Shelby (R-Ala. 1997–2001)
Bob Graham (D-Fla. January 2001)
Richard C. Shelby (R-Ala. January–June 2001)
Bob Graham (D-Fla. June 2001–2003)
Pat Roberts (R-Kan. 2003–2007)
John D. Rockefeller IV (D-W.Va. 2007–)

Interior and Insular Affairs
(formerly Public Lands, 1947–1948)
Hugh Butler (R-Neb. 1947–1949)
Joseph C. O'Mahoney (D-Wyo. 1949–1953)
Hugh Butler (R-Neb. 1953–1954)
Guy Gordon (R-Ore. 1954–1955)
James E. Murray (D-Mont. 1955–1961)
Clinton P. Anderson (D-N.M. 1961–1963)
Henry M. Jackson (D-Wash. 1963–1977)
(Most of its jurisdiction transferred to Energy and Natural Resources in 1977.)

Judiciary
Alexander Wiley (R-Wis. 1947–1949)
Pat McCarran (D-Nev. 1949–1953)
William Langer (R-N.D. 1953–1955)
Harley M. Kilgore (D-W.Va. 1955–1956)

James O. Eastland (D-Miss. 1956–1978)
Edward M. Kennedy (D-Mass. 1979–1981)
Strom Thurmond (R-S.C. 1981–1987)
Joseph R. Biden Jr. (D-Del. 1987–1995)
Orrin G. Hatch (R-Utah 1995–2001)
Patrick J. Leahy (D-Vt. January 2001)
Orrin G. Hatch (R-Utah January–June 2001)
Patrick J. Leahy (D-Vt. June 2001–2003)
Orrin G. Hatch (R-Utah 2003–2005)
Arlen Specter (R-Pa. 2005–2007)
Patrick J. Leahy (D-Vt. 2007–)

Post Office and Civil Service
William Langer (R-N.D. 1947–1949)
Olin D. Johnston (D-S.C. 1949–1953)
Frank Carlson (R-Kan. 1953–1955)
Olin D. Johnston (D-S.C. 1955–1965)
A. S. Mike Monroney (D-Okla. 1965–1969)
Gale W. McGee (D-Wyo. 1969–1977)
(Abolished in 1977 and its jurisdiction transferred to Governmental Affairs.)

Rules and Administration
C. Wayland Brooks (R-Ill. 1947–1949)
Carl Hayden (D-Ariz. 1949–1953)
William E. Jenner (R-Ind. 1953–1955)
Theodore Francis Green (D-R.I. 1955–1957)
Thomas C. Hennings Jr. (D-Mo. 1957–1960)
Mike Mansfield (D-Mont. 1961–1963)
B. Everett Jordan (D-N.C. 1963–1972)
Howard W. Cannon (D-Nev. 1973–1977)
Claiborne Pell (D-R.I. 1978–1981)
Charles McC. Mathias Jr. (R-Md. 1981–1987)
Wendell H. Ford (D-Ky. 1987–1995)
Ted Stevens (R-Alaska 1995–1996)
John Warner (R-Va. 1996–1999)
Mitch McConnell (R-Ky. 1999–2001)
Christopher J. Dodd (D-Conn. January 2001)

Mitch McConnell (R-Ky. January–June 2001)
Christopher J. Dodd (D-Conn. June 2001–2003)
Trent Lott (R-Miss. 2003–2007)
Dianne Feinstein (D-Calif. 2007–)

Small Business and Entrepeneurship
(formerly the Select Committee on Small Business, 1950–1981; Small Business, 1981–2001)
John J. Sparkman (D-Ala. 1950–1953)
Edward J. Thye (R-Minn. 1953–1955)
John J. Sparkman (D-Ala. 1955–1967)
George A. Smathers (D-Fla. 1967–1969)
Alan Bible (D-Nev. 1969–1975)
Gaylord Nelson (D-Wis. 1975–1981)
Lowell P. Weicker Jr. (R-Conn. 1981–1987)
Dale Bumpers (D-Ark. 1987–1995)
Christopher S. Bond (R-Mo. 1995–2001)
John Kerry (D-Mass. January 2001)
Christopher S. Bond (R-Mo. January–June 2001)
John Kerry (D-Mass. June 2001–2003)
Olympia J. Snowe (R-Maine 2003–2007)
John Kerry (D-Mass. 2007–)

Veterans' Affairs
Vance Hartke (D-Ind. 1971–1977)
Alan Cranston (D-Calif. 1977–1981)
Alan K. Simpson (R-Wyo. 1981–1985)
Frank H. Murkowski (R-Alaska 1985–1987)
Alan Cranston (D-Calif. 1987–1993)
John D. Rockefeller IV (D-W.Va. 1993–1995)
Alan K. Simpson (R-Wyo. 1995–1997)
Arlen Specter (R-Pa. 1997–2001)
John D. Rockefeller (D-W.Va. January 2001)
Arlen Specter (R-Pa. January–June 2001)
John D. Rockefeller (D-W.Va. June 2001–2003)
Arlen Specter (R-Pa. 2003–2005)
Larry E. Craig (R-Idaho 2005–2007)
Daniel K. Akaka (D-Hawaii 2007–)

Extraordinary Sessions of Congress since 1797

Article II, section 3, of the Constitution provides that the president "may, on extraordinary Occasions, convene both Houses, or either of them."

This procedure occurs only if Congress is convened by presidential proclamation; it does not include the many special sessions of the Senate called primarily to confirm nominations prior to the Twentieth Amendment.

Congress	Session	Date convened	Date of proclamation	Reason	President
5th	1st	May 15, 1797	March 25, 1797	Suspension of Relations with France	Adams
8th	1st	October 17, 1803	July 16, 1803	Louisiana Cession/Purchase	Jefferson
10th	1st	October 26, 1807	July 30, 1807	Relations with Great Britain	Jefferson
12th	1st	November 4, 1811	July 24, 1811	Relations with Great Britain	Jefferson
13th	3rd	September 19, 1814	August 8, 1814	War with Great Britain	Madison
25th	1st	September 4, 1837	May 15, 1837	Suspension of Species Payment	Van Buren
27th	1st	May 31, 1841	March 17, 1841	Condition of Finances and Revenue	Harrison
34th	2nd	August 21, 1856	August 18, 1856	Army Appropriations	Pierce
37th	1st	July 4, 1861	April 17, 1861	Insurrection of Southern States	Lincoln
45th	1st	October 15, 1877	May 5, 1877	Army Appropriations	Hayes
46th	1st	March 18, 1879	March 4, 1879	Appropriations	Hayes
53rd	1st	August 7, 1893	June 30, 1893	Repeal Silver Purchase Act	Cleveland
55th	1st	March 15, 1897	March 6, 1897	Dingley Tariff	McKinley
58th	1st	November 9, 1903	October 20, 1903	Cuban Reciprocity Treaty	Roosevelt
61st	1st	March 15, 1909	March 6, 1909	Payne-Aldrich Tariff	Taft
62nd	1st	April 4, 1911	March 4, 1911	Canadian Reciprocity	Taft
63rd	1st	April 7, 1913	March 17, 1913	Federal Reserve Act	Wilson
65th	1st	April 2, 1917	March 17, 1917	World War I	Wilson
66th	1st	May 19, 1919	May 7, 1919	High Cost of Living	Wilson
67th	1st	April 11, 1921	March 22, 1921	Emergency Agricultural Tariff	Harding
67th	3rd	November 20, 1922	November 9, 1922	Independent Merchant Marine	Harding
71st	1st	April 15, 1929	March 7, 1929	Smoot-Hawley Tariff	Hoover
73rd	1st	March 9, 1933	March 5, 1933	Recovery Legislation	Roosevelt
75th	2nd	November 15, 1937	October 12, 1937	Wages and Hours Act	Roosevelt
76th	2nd	September 21, 1939	September 13, 1939	Neutrality Legislation	Roosevelt
80th	1st	November 17, 1947	October 23, 1947	Domestic Legislation	Truman
80th	2nd	July 26, 1948	July 15, 1948	Domestic Legislation	Truman

SOURCE: Senate Historical Office.
NOTE: As of February 2008.

How a Bill Becomes a Law

This graphic shows the most typical way in which proposed legislation is enacted into law. There are more complicated, as well as simpler, routes, and most bills never become law. The process is illustrated with two hypothetical bills, House bill No. 1 (HR 1) *and Senate bill No. 2 (S 2). Bills must be passed by both houses in identical form before they can be sent to the president. The path of HR 1 is traced by a gray line, that of S 2 by a black line. In practice, most bills begin as similar proposals in both Houses.*

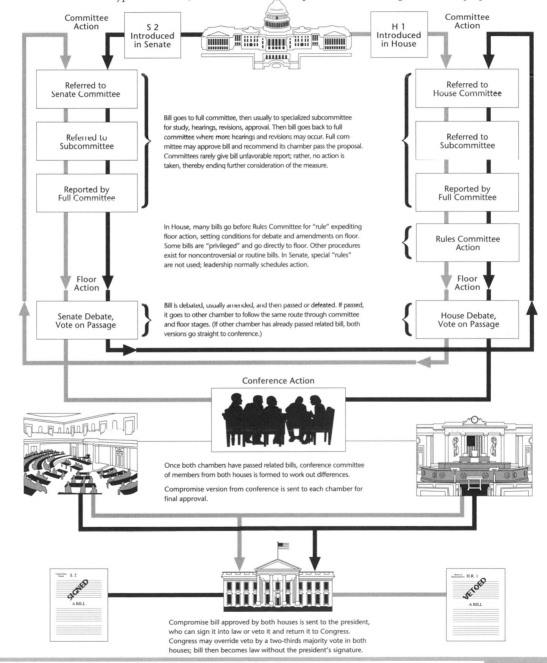

Committee Action

S 2 Introduced in Senate

H 1 Introduced in House

Committee Action

Referred to Senate Committee

Referred to Subcommittee

Reported by Full Committee

Referred to House Committee

Referred to Subcommittee

Reported by Full Committee

Bill goes to full committee, then usually to specialized subcommittee for study, hearings, revisions, approval. Then bill goes back to full committee where more hearings and revisions may occur. Full committee may approve bill and recommend its chamber pass the proposal. Committees rarely give bill unfavorable report; rather, no action is taken, thereby ending further consideration of the measure.

Rules Committee Action

In House, many bills go before Rules Committee for "rule" expediting floor action, setting conditions for debate and amendments on floor. Some bills are "privileged" and go directly to floor. Other procedures exist for noncontroversial or routine bills. In Senate, special "rules" are not used; leadership normally schedules action.

Floor Action

Floor Action

Senate Debate, Vote on Passage

Bill is debated, usually amended, and then passed or defeated. If passed, it goes to other chamber to follow the same route through committee and floor stages. (If other chamber has already passed related bill, both versions go straight to conference.)

House Debate, Vote on Passage

Conference Action

Once both chambers have passed related bills, conference committee of members from both houses is formed to work out differences.

Compromise version from conference is sent to each chamber for final approval.

S 2 — SIGNED — A BILL

H.R. 1 — VETOED — A BILL

Compromise bill approved by both houses is sent to the president, who can sign it into law or veto it and return it to Congress. Congress may override veto by a two-thirds majority vote in both houses; bill then becomes law without the president's signature.

Writing to a Member of Congress

Citizens with complaints, suggestions, comments, and requests about government can voice their views directly to Congress. You may want to support or oppose specific legislative proposals, comment more generally about public affairs, or simply seek help in dealing with government agencies.

In the past written communication with members was largely by postal mail but today the widespread use of e-mail has given voters a new and faster way to contact representatives and senators. However you decide to contact a member a few useful rules will make your voice more effective. The following hints about writing a member of Congress were suggested by congressional sources and the League of Women Voters.

- Write to your own senators or representative. Letters sent to other members will either be ignored or simply forwarded to your home state members.
- Use your own words and stationery. Avoid sending form letters, which a member quickly sees as an organized campaign and is more likely to ignore.
- Write at the proper time, when a bill is being discussed in committee or on the floor.
- Whenever possible, identify bills by their number and include pertinent editorials from local papers.
- Be constructive. If a bill deals with a problem you admit exists but you believe the bill is the wrong approach, suggest a better approach. If you have expert knowledge or wide experience in particular areas, share it with the member.
- Write to members when they do something of which you approve. A note of appreciation will make them remember you more favorably the next time.
- Feel free to write when you have a question or problem dealing with procedures of government departments. Constituent service is one of the most important jobs of elected officials.
- Be brief, write legibly, and be sure to use the proper form of address.

Suggested Form for Letters

Senator

Honorable _____
United States Senate
Washington, DC 20510
Dear Senator _____:
Sincerely yours,

Representative

Honorable _____
House of Representatives
Washington, DC 20515
Dear Representative _____:
Sincerely yours,

Sending E-Mail to a Member of Congress

Electronic mail (e-mail) is increasingly being used by constituents to convey their opinions to their senators and representatives. In sending an e-mail to members of Congress, the same letter-writing guidelines basically apply. Although an e-mail is considered less formal than a traditional letter, you should still address members of Congress formally. If you do not provide your street address within your e-mail, you most likely will only receive an e-mail response stating that your message was received. If you provide your street address, members of Congress may respond with a formal letter, as they generally do with every piece of regular mail they receive from constituents.

Although e-mail can be looked at as just another means of communication, it can provide better access for individuals and smaller groups cut off from the participatory process. E-mail has the greatest impact when it is brief and to the point and when it concerns matters currently being debated in Congress. E-mail also allows members of Congress to gauge instantaneously the response to their speeches and votes.

The members' e-mail directories are readily available at the House of Representatives and the Senate Web sites (http://www.house.gov and http://www.senate.gov).

Map of Capitol Hill

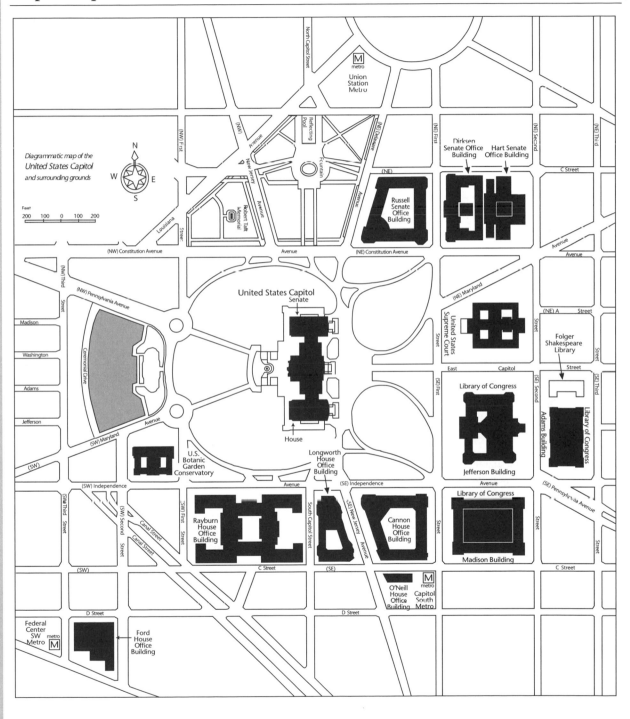

Diagrammatic map of the
United States Capitol
and surrounding grounds

Feet
200 100 0 100 200

N
W   E
S

North Capitol Street

(NW) First

(NW) Avenue

New Jersey Avenue

Reflecting Pool

M metro
Union
Station
Metro

Robert Taft Memorial

Louisiana Street

(NW) Constitution Avenue

(NE) Delaware

Fountain

(NE) Avenue

(NE) First

(NE) Second

(NE) Third

Dirksen
Senate Office
Building

Hart Senate
Office Building

C Street

(NE)

Russell
Senate
Office
Building

Avenue

Avenue

Avenue

(NE) Constitution Avenue

(NW) Third Street

(NW) Pennsylvania Avenue

Centennial Drive

Madison

Washington

Adams

Jefferson

(SW)

(NE) Maryland

United States
Supreme Court

(NE) A   Street

Folger
Shakespeare
Library

Street

United States Capitol
Senate

East   Capitol   Street

(SE) First

(SE) Second

(SE) Third

Library of Congress

House

Adams Building

Library of Congress

Jefferson Building

(SW) Maryland   Avenue

U.S.
Botanic
Garden
Conservatory

(SW) Independence

Longworth
House
Office
Building

(SE) Independence

Avenue

Library of Congress

(SE) Pennsylvania Avenue

(SW Third Street

(SW) Second Street

(SW) First Street

Canal Street

Canal Street

Rayburn
House
Office
Building

South Capitol Street

(SE) New Jersey Avenue

Cannon
House
Office
Building

Street

Madison Building

Street

C Street

(SW)   C Street   (SE)

O'Neill
House
Office
Building

M metro
Capitol
South Metro

D Street   D Street

Federal
Center
SW metro
Metro M

Ford
House
Office
Building

Capital Attractions

Many of Washington's foremost sightseeing attractions are clustered around the Mall, the grassy strip that stretches from the Capitol west to the Lincoln Memorial.

Tourmobile shuttle buses provide narrated sightseeing service to twenty-five sites in the Mall area along Pennsylvania Avenue and in nearby Arlington National Cemetery. Passengers pay a single daily fee; they may board and reboard the buses as often as they like. For information, call (202) 554-5100 or (888) 868-7707. Tourmobile Web site: www.tourmobile.com. For information on METRO bus and subway service in the Washington area, call (202) 637-7000. Washington Area Transit Authority Web site: www.wmata.com.

Listed below are major sites in the Capital area, with contact information.

Capitol

(202) 224-3121 (Capitol switchboard),
(202) 225-6827 (Capitol Guide Service, tour information: www.aoc.gov)

North Side of the Mall

National Gallery of Art
Constitution Avenue at Fourth Street, NW
(202) 737-4215; www.nga.gov

National Archives
Constitution Avenue at Eighth Street, NW
(866) 272-6272; www.archives.gov.

Washington Monument
Constitution Avenue at Fifteenth Street, NW
(202) 426-6841; www.npa.gov/wamo

Vietnam Veterans Memorial
Constitution Avenue at Twenty-first Street, NW
(202) 426-6841; www.nps.gov/vive

Lincoln Memorial
Constitution Avenue at Twenty-third Street, NW
(202) 426-6841; www.nps.gov/linc

Smithsonian Institution

Smithsonian museums line both sides of the Mall from Third to Fourteenth Streets between Constitution Avenue and Independence Avenue. General information: (202) 633-1000; Smithsonian Web site, with links to individual museums: www.si.edu.

National Museum of Natural History
Constitution Avenue at Tenth Street, NW

National Museum of American History
Constitution Avenue at Fourteenth Street, NW

South Side of the Mall

U.S. Botanic Garden Conservatory
100 Maryland Avenue, SW

National Air and Space Museum
Independence Avenue at Sixth Street, SW

Hirshhorn Museum and Sculpture Garden
Independence Avenue at Seventh Street, SW

Arts and Industries Building
900 Jefferson Drive, SW

Smithsonian Castle
1000 Jefferson Drive, SW

National Museum of African Art
950 Independence Avenue, SW

Arthur M. Sackler Gallery
1050 Independence Avenue, SW

Freer Gallery of Art
Jefferson Drive at Twelfth Street, SW

Korean War Veterans Memorial
Independence Avenue at Twenty-first Street
(202) 426-6841; www.nps.gov/kowa

Beyond the Mall

White House
1600 Pennsylvania Avenue
Open Tuesday–Saturday
(202) 456-7041; (202) 208-1631 (White House Visitor Center); www.nps.gov/whho. (Public tours of the White House were suspended following the September 11, 2001, terrorists attacks. Private tours with groups of ten or more can be arranged by contacting a member of Congress at least six months before a visit.)

Jefferson Memorial
Tidal Basin, SW
(202) 426-6841; www.nps.gov/thje

Franklin Delano Roosevelt Memorial
1850 West Basin Drive, SW (Tidal Basin)
(202) 426-6841; (202) 376-6704; www.nps.gov/frde

Library of Congress
10 First Street, SE
(202) 707-5000 (general information);
(202) 707-8000 (visitors' information); www.loc.gov

Ford's Theatre
511 Tenth Street, NW
Museum/tours: (202) 426-6924; www.nps.gov/foth

Arlington National Cemetery
Arlington, Virginia
(703) 607-8000; www.arlingtoncemetery.org

National Zoological Park (Smithsonian)
3001 Connecticut Avenue, NW
(202) 673-4800; www.natzoo.si.edu

American Art Museum's Renwick Gallery (Smithsonian)
Pennsylvania Avenue at 17th Street, NW
(202) 633-7970; www.americanart.si.edu

Anacostia Museum and Center for African American History and Culture (Smithsonian)
1901 Fort Place, SE
(202) 633-4820; www.anacostia.si.edu

National Portrait Gallery (Smithsonian)
Eighth and F Streets, NW
(202) 633-8300; www.npg.si.edu

National Postal Museum (Smithsonian)
2 Massachusetts Avenue, NE
(202) 633-5555; www.si.edu/postal

Folger Shakespeare Library
201 East Capitol Street, SE

Congressional Information on the Internet

A huge array of congressional information is available for free at Internet sites operated by the federal government, colleges and universities, and commercial firms. The sites offer the full text of bills introduced in the House and Senate, voting records, campaign finance information, transcripts of selected congressional hearings, investigative reports, and much more.

THOMAS

The most important site for congressional information is THOMAS *(http://thomas.loc.gov)*, which is named for Thomas Jefferson and operated by the Library of Congress. THOMAS's highlight is its databases containing the full text of all bills introduced in Congress since 1989 (101st Congress), the full text of the *Congressional Record* since 1989, and the status and summary information for all bills introduced since 1973 (93rd Congress).

THOMAS also offers special links to bills that have received or are expected to receive floor action during the current week and newsworthy bills that are pending or that have recently been approved. Finally, THOMAS has selected committee reports, answers to frequently asked questions about accessing congressional information, publications titled *How Our Laws Are Made* and *Enactment of a Law,* and links to many other congressional Web sites.

House of Representatives

The U.S. House of Representatives site *(http://www.house.gov)* offers the schedule of bills, resolutions, and other legislative issues the House is to consider in the current week. It also has updates about current proceedings on the House floor and a list of the next day's meeting of House committees. Other highlights include a database that helps users identify their representative, a directory of House members and committees, the House ethics manual, links to Web pages maintained by House members and committees, a calendar of congressional primary dates and candidate-filing deadlines for ballot access, the full text of all amendments to the U.S. Constitution that have been ratified and those that have been proposed but not ratified, and information about Washington, D.C., for visitors.

Another key House site is the Office of the Clerk On-line Information Center *(http://clerk.house.gov)*, which has records of all roll-call votes taken since 1990 (101st Congress). The votes are recorded by bill. The site also has lists of committee assignments, a telephone directory for members and committees, mailing label templates for members and committees, rules of the current Congress, election statistics from 1920 to the present, biographies of Speakers of the House, biographies of women who have served since 1917, information on public disclosure, and a virtual tour of the House chamber.

The site operated by the House Committee on Rules *(http://www.rules. house.gov)* has posted dozens of Congressional Research Service reports about the legislative process. Some of the available titles include *Legislative Research in Congressional Offices: A Primer; Hearings in the House of Representatives: A Guide for Preparation and Conduct; How Measures Are Brought to the House Floor: A Brief Introduction; House and Senate Rules of Procedure: A Comparison;* and *Presidential Vetoes 1789–1996: A Summary Overview*

The office of the Law Revision Counsel operates a site *(http://uscode.house.gov)* that has a searchable version of the U.S. Code, which contains the text of public laws enacted by Congress, and a tutorial for searching the Code.

Senate

The Senate's main Web site *(http://www.senate.gov)* has records of all roll-call votes taken since 1989 (101st Congress, arranged by bill), brief descriptions of all bills and joint resolutions introduced in the Senate during the past week, and a calendar of upcoming committee hearings. The site also provides the standing rules of the Senate, a directory of senators and their committee assignments, lists of nominations that the president has submitted to the Senate for approval, links to Web pages operated by senators and committees, information on the history and art of the Senate, and a virtual tour of the Senate.

General Reference

Information about the membership, jurisdiction, and rules of each congressional committee is available at the U.S. Government Printing Office site *(http://www.gpoaccess.gov/congress/index.html)*. It also has transcripts of selected congressional hearings, the full text of selected House and Senate reports, and the House and Senate rules manuals.

The U.S. Government Accountability Office (GAO, which changed its name in 2004 from General Accounting Office), the investigative arm of Congress, operates a site *(http://www.gao.gov)* that provides the full text of its reports from October 1995 to the present. The reports cover a wide range of topics: aviation safety, combating terrorism, counternarcotics efforts in Mexico, defense contracting, electronic warfare, food assistance programs, hurricane preparedness, health insurance, illegal aliens, information technology, long-term care, mass transit, Medicare, military readiness, money laundering, national parks, nuclear waste, organ donation, student loan defaults, and prescription drugs, among others.

GAO e-mail updates are excellent current awareness tools. Electronic mailing lists distribute daily and monthly lists of reports and testimony released by the GAO. Subscriptions are available by filling out a form and identifying topic interests at *http://www.gao.gov/subtest/subscribe.php.*

Current budget and economic projections are provided at the Congressional Budget Office (CBO) Web site *(http://www.cbo.gov)*. The site also has reports about the economic and budget outlook for the next decade, the president's budget proposals, federal civilian employment, Social Security privatization, cost analyses of war operations, tax reform, water use conflicts in the west, marriage and the federal income tax, and the role of foreign aid in development, among other topics. Additional highlights include monthly budget updates, historical budget data, cost estimates for bills reported by congressional committees, and transcripts of congressional testimony by CBO officials.

The congressional Office of Technology Assessment (OTA) was eliminated in 1995, but every report it ever issued is available at The OTA Legacy *(http://www.wws.princeton.edu:80/~ota)*, a site operated by the Woodrow Wilson School of Public and International Affairs at Princeton University. The site has more than 100,000 pages of detailed reports about aging, agricultural technology, arms control, biological research, cancer, computer security, defense technology, economic development, education, environmental protection, health and health technology, information technology, space, transportation, and many other subjects. The reports are organized in alphabetical, chronological, and topical lists.

Campaign Finance

Several Internet sites provide detailed campaign finance data for congressional elections. The official site is operated by the Federal Election Commission *(FEC, http://www.fec.gov)*, which regulates political spending. The site's highlight is its database of campaign reports filed from May 1996 to the present by House and presidential candidates, political action committees, and political party committees. Senate reports are not included because they are filed with the secretary of the Senate. The reports in the FEC's database are scanned images of paper reports filed with the commission.

The FEC site also has summary financial data for House and Senate candidates in the current election cycle, abstracts of court decisions pertaining to federal election law from 1976 to 2007, and a directory of national and state agencies that are responsible for releasing information about campaign financing, candidates on the ballot, election results, lobbying, and other issues. Another useful feature is a collection of brochures about federal election law, public funding of presidential elections, the ban on contributions by foreign nationals, independent expenditures supporting or opposing a candidate for federal office, contribution limits, filing a complaint, researching public records at the FEC, and other topics. Finally, the site provides the FEC's legislative recommendations, its annual report, a report about its first thirty years in existence, the FEC's monthly newsletter, several reports about voter registration, election results for the most recent presidential and congressional elections, and campaign guides for corporations and labor organizations, congressional candidates and committees, political party committees, and nonconnected committees.

Another online source for campaign finance data is CQ Money Line (*http://moneyline.cq.com*, formerly politicalmoneyline.com and FECinfo.com) from Congressional Quarterly. Its searchable databases provide extensive itemized information about receipts and expenditures by federal candidates and political action committees from 1980 to the present. The detailed data are obtained from the FEC. For example, candidates contributions can be searched by Zip code. The site also has data on soft-money contributions, lists of the top political action committees in various categories, lists of the top contributors from each state, and much more.

More campaign finance data are available from the Center for Responsive Politics *(http://www.opensecrets.org)*, a public interest organization. The center provides a list of all soft-money donations to political parties of $100,000 or more in the current election cycle and data about leadership political action committees associated with individual politicians. Other databases at the site provide information about travel expenses that House members received from private sources for attending meetings and other events, activities of registered federal lobbyists, and activities of foreign agents who are registered in the United States.

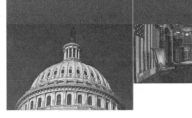

Selected Bibliography

Appointment Power

Bronner, Ethan. *Battle for Justice: How the Bork Nomination Shook America.* New York: Norton, 1989.

Carter, Stephen L. *The Confirmation Mess: Cleaning Up the Federal Appointments Process.* New York: Basic Books, 1994.

Epstein, Lee, and Jeffrey A. Segal. *Advice and Consent: The Politics of Judicial Appointments.* New York: Oxford University Press, 2005.

Harris, Joseph P. *The Advice and Consent of the Senate: A Study of the Confirmation of Appointments by the United States Senate.* Westport, Conn.: Greenwood, 1968.

Mackenzie, G. Calvin, ed. *In-and-Outers: Presidential Appointees and Transient Government in Washington.* Baltimore: Johns Hopkins University Press, 1987.

Simon, Paul. *Advice & Consent: Clarence Thomas, Robert Bork, and the Intriguing History of the Supreme Court's Nomination Battles.* Washington, D.C.: National Press Books, 1992.

Twentieth Century Fund. *Obstacle Course: The Report of the Twentieth Century Fund Task Force on the Presidential Appointment Process.* New York: Twentieth Century Fund Press, 1996.

Campaign Financing

Cigler, Allan J., and Burdett A. Loomis, eds. *Interest Group Politics.* 7th ed. Washington, D.C.: CQ Press, 2006.

Corrado, Anthony, Thomas E. Mann, Daniel R. Ortiz, and Trevor Potter. *The New Campaign Finance Sourcebook.* Washington, D.C.: Brookings Institution Press, 2005.

Magleby, David B., Anthony Corrado, and Kelly D. Patterson, eds. *Financing the 2004 Election.* Washington, D.C.: Brookings Institution Press, 2006.

Malbin, Michael J., ed. *The Election After Reform: Money, Politics, and the Bipartisan Campaign Reform Act.* Lanham, Md.: Rowman & Littlefield, 2006.

Capitol Building

Allen, William C. *History of the United States Capitol: A Chronicle of Design, Construction, and Politics.* gov/congress/senate/capitol/index.html. Washington, D.C.: Government Printing Office, 2001.

Brown, Glenn. *History of the U.S. Capitol.* 2 vols. Washington, D.C.: Government Printing Office, 1903. Reprint. New York: Da Capo Press, 1970.

Capitol Historical Society. *We the People: The Story of the United States Capitol.* 15th ed. Washington, D.C.: United States Capitol Historical Society, 2002.

Koempel, Michael L., and Judy Schneider. *Congressional Deskbook*. 5th ed. Alexandria, Va.: TheCapitol.Net, 2007.

Commerce Power

Baum, Lawrence. *The Supreme Court*. 9th ed. Washington, D.C.: CQ Press, 2006.

Benson, Paul R., Jr. *The Supreme Court and the Commerce Clause, 1937–1970*. New York: Dunellen, 1970.

Epstein, Lee, and Thomas G. Walker. *Constitutional Law for a Changing America: Institutional Powers and Constraints*. 4th ed. Washington, D.C.: CQ Press, 2007.

Gavit, Bernard C. *Commerce Clause of the United States Constitution*. New York: AMS Press, 1970.

Lofgren, Charles A. "'To Regulate Commerce': Federal Power under the Constitution," in *This Constitution: Our Enduring Legacy*. Washington, D.C.: Congressional Quarterly, 1986.

Committee System

Baughman, John. *Common Ground: Committee Politics in the U.S. House of Representatives*. Stanford, Calif.: Stanford University Press, 2006.

Cox, Gary W., and Mathew D. McCubbins. *Setting the Agenda: Responsible Party Government in the U.S. House of Representatives*. New York: Cambridge University Press, 2005.

Davidson, Roger J., and Walter J. Oleszek. *Congress and Its Members*. 10th ed. Washington, D.C.: CQ Press, 2006.

Deering, Christopher J., and Steven S. Smith. *Committees in Congress*. 3d ed. Washington, D.C.: CQ Press, 1997.

Fenno, Richard F., Jr. *Congressmen in Committees*. Boston: Little, Brown, 1973.

Frisch, Scott A., and Dean Q. Kelly. *Committee Assignment Politics in the U.S. House of Representatives*. Norman: University of Oklahoma Press, 2006.

Goodwin, George, Jr. *The Little Legislatures: Committees of Congress*. Amherst: University of Massachusetts Press, 1970.

Koempel, Michael L., and Judy Schneider, *Congressional Deskbook*. 5th ed. Alexandria, Va.: TheCapitol.Net, 2007.

Maltzman, Forrest. *Competing Principals: Committees, Parties, and the Organization of Congress*. Ann Arbor: University of Michigan Press, 1997.

Oleszek, Walter J. *Congressional Procedures and the Policy Process*. 7th ed. Washington, D.C.: CQ Press, 2007.

Unekis, Joseph K., and Leroy N. Rieselbach. *Congressional Committee Politics: Continuity and Change*. New York: Greenwood, 1984.

Conference Committees

Longley, Lawrence D., and Walter J. Oleszek. *Bicameral Politics: Conference Committees in Congress*. New Haven, Conn.: Yale University Press, 1989.

Oleszek, Walter J. *Congressional Procedures and the Policy Process*. 7th ed. Washington, D.C.: CQ Press, 2007.

Volger, David J. *The Third House: Conference Committees in the United States Congress*. Evanston, Ill.: Northwestern University Press, 1971.

Congress: Structure and Powers

Congressional Quarterly. *Guide to Congress*. 6th ed. Washington, D.C.: CQ Press, 2007.

Davidson, Roger J., and Walter J. Oleszek. *Congress and Its Members*. 10th ed. Washington, D.C.: CQ Press, 2006.

Jones, Charles O. *Separate but Equal Branches: Congress and the Presidency*. New York: Chatham House, 1999.

Josephy, Alvin M., Jr. *On the Hill: A History of the American Congress*. New York: Simon and Schuster, 1980.

Koempel, Michael L., and Judy Schneider, *Congressional Deskbook*. 5th ed. Alexandria, Va.: TheCapitol.Net, 2007.

Wilson, Woodrow. *Congressional Government: A Study in American Politics*. Boston: Houghton Mifflin, 1885. Reprint. Cleveland: Meridian Books, 1956.

Constitutional Amendments

Burns, James MacGregor, Jack W. Peltason, Thomas E. Cronin, and David B. Magleby. *Government by the People*. 19th ed. Upper Saddle River, N.J.: Prentice Hall, 2001.

Epps, Garrett. *Democracy Reborn: The Fourteenth Amendment and the Fight for Equal Rights in Post–Civil War America*. New York: Holt, 2006.

Epstein, Lee, and Thomas G. Walker. *Constitutional Law for a Changing America: Institutional Powers and Constraints*. 4th ed. Washington, D.C.: CQ Press, 2007.

Katz, William L. *Constitutional Amendments.* New York: Franklin Watts, 1974.

Labunski, Richard E. *James Madison and the Struggle for the Bill of Rights.* New York: Oxford University Press, 2006.

Mansbridge, Jane J. *Why We Lost the ERA.* Chicago: University of Chicago Press, 1986.

Nelson, Michael, ed. *Guide to the Presidency.* 2 vols. 4th ed. Washington, D.C.: CQ Press, 2007.

Newman, Roger K., ed. *The Constitution and Its Amendments.* 4 vols. New York: Macmillan, 1999.

Vile, John R. *A Companion to the United States Constitution and Its Amendments.* 4th ed. Westport, Conn.: Praeger, 2006.

Courts and Congress

Baum, Lawrence. *The Supreme Court.* 9th ed. Washington, D.C.: CQ Press, 2006.

Berger, Raoul. *Congress v. the Supreme Court.* Cambridge, Mass.: Harvard University Press, 1969.

Epstein, Lee, and Jeffrey Segal. *Advice and Consent: The Politics of Judicial Appointments.* New York: Oxford University Press, 2005.

Epstein, Lee, and Thomas G. Walker. *Constitutional Law for a Changing America: Institutional Powers and Constraints.* 6th ed. Washington, D.C.: CQ Press, 2007.

Geyh, Charles G. *When Courts and Congress Collide: The Struggle for Control of America's Judicial System.* Ann Arbor: University of Michigan Press, 2006.

O'Brien, David M. *Storm Center: The Supreme Court in American Politics.* 5th ed. New York: Norton, 2000.

Savage, David, ed. *Guide to the U.S. Supreme Court.* 2 vols. 4th ed. Washington, D.C.: Congressional Quarterly, 2004.

Electing the President

Congressional Quarterly. *Presidential Elections 1789–1996.* Washington, D.C.: Congressional Quarterly, 1997.

Bennett, Robert W. *Taming the Electoral College.* Stanford, Calif.: Stanford Law and Politics, 2006.

Best, Judith. *The Case Against Direct Election of the President: A Defense of the Electoral College.* Ithaca, N.Y.: Cornell University Press, 1975.

———. *The Choice of the People: Debating the Electoral College.* Lanham, Md.: Rowman and Littlefield, 1996.

Glennon, Michael J. *When No Majority Rules: The Electoral College and Presidential Succession.* Washington, D.C.: CQ Press, 1993.

Heard, Alexander, and Michael Nelson, eds. *Presidential Selection.* Durham, N.C.: Duke University Press, 1987.

Longley, Lawrence D., and Neal R. Peirce. *The Electoral College Primer 2000.* New Haven, Conn.: Yale University Press, 1999.

Nelson, Michael, ed. *Guide to the Presidency.* 2 vols. 4th ed. Washington, D.C.: CQ Press, 2007.

Schumaker, Paul, and Burdett A. Loomis, eds. *Choosing a President: The Electoral College and Beyond.* New York: Chatham House, 2002.

Ethics

Amer, Mildred. *House Committee on Standards of Official Conduct: A Brief History of Its Evolution and Jurisdiction.* Washington, D.C.: Library of Congress, Congressional Research Service, 1997.

Garment, Suzanne. *Scandal: The Culture of Mistrust in American Politics.* New York: Anchor Books, 1992.

Koempel, Michael L., and Judy Schneider. *Congressional Deskbook.* 5th ed. Alexandria, Va.: TheCapitol.Net, 2007.

Maskell, Jack. *Expulsion and Censure Actions Taken by the Full Senate Against Members.* Washington, D.C.: Library of Congress, Congressional Research Service, 1993.

Simon, Paul. *The Glass House: Politics and Morality in the Nation's Capital.* New York: Continuum, 1984.

Thompson, Dennis F. *Ethics in Congress: From Individual to Institutional Corruption.* Washington, D.C.: Brookings Institution Press, 1995.

———. *Political Ethics and Public Office.* Boston: Harvard University Press, 1990.

Executive Branch and Congress

Davidson, Roger J., and Walter J. Oleszek. *Congress and Its Members.* 10th ed. Washington, D.C.: CQ Press, 2006.

Fisher, Louis. *The Politics of Shared Power: Congress and the Executive.* 4th ed. College Station: Texas A&M University Press, 1998.

———. *Constitutional Conflicts Between Congress and the President.* 4th ed. Lawrence: University Press of Kansas, 1997.

Foley, Michael, and John E. Owens. *Congress and the Presidency: Institutional Politics in a Separate*

System. Manchester, England: Manchester University Press/St. Martin's Press, 1996.

Harriger, Katy J., ed. *Separation of Powers: Documents and Commentary*. Washington, D.C.: CQ Press, 2003.

Jones, Charles O. *Separate but Equal Branches: Congress and the Presidency*. 2d ed. New York: Chatham House, 1999.

Kelley, Donald R., ed. *Divided Power: The Presidency, Congress, and the Formation of American Foreign Policy*. Fayetteville: University of Arkansas Press, 2005.

Thurber, James A., ed. *Rivals for Power: Presidential-Congressional Relations*. 3d ed. Lanham, Md.: Rowman & Littlefield, 2006.

Filibuster

Binder, Sarah A. *Stalemate: Causes and Consequences of Legislative Gridlock*. Washington, D.C.: Brookings Institution Press, 2003.

Binder, Sarah A., and Steven S. Smith. *Politics or Principle? Filibustering in the United States*. Washington, D.C.: Brookings Institution Press, 1997.

Brady, David W. *Party, Process, and Political Change in Congress: New Perspectives on the History of Congress*. Stanford, Calif.: Stanford University Press, 2002.

Burdette, Franklin L. *Filibustering in the Senate*. Princeton, N.J.: Princeton University Press, 1940.

Caro, Robert A. *Master of the Senate: The Years of Lyndon Johnson*. New York: Knopf, 2002.

Dodd, Lawrence C., and Bruce I. Oppenheimer, eds. *Congress Reconsidered*. 8th ed. Washington, D.C.: CQ Press, 2005.

Koempel, Michael L., and Judy Schneider. *Congressional Deskbook*. 5th ed. Alexandria, Va.: TheCapitol.Net, 2007.

Oleszek, Walter J. *Congressional Procedures and the Policy Process*. 7th ed. Washington, D.C.: CQ Press, 2007.

Reid, T. R. *Congressional Odyssey: The Saga of a Senate Bill*. New York: Freeman, 1980.

Wawro, Gregory J., and Eric Schickler. *Filibuster: Obstruction and Lawmaking in the U.S. Senate*. Princeton, N.J.; Princeton University Press, 2006.

Whalen, Charles, and Barbara Whalen. *The Longest Debate: A Legislative History of the 1964 Civil Rights Act*. Washington, D.C.: Seven Locks Press, 1985.

House of Representatives

Baker, Ross K. *House and Senate*. 3d ed. New York: W.W. Norton, 2001.

Davidson, Roger J., and Walter J. Oleszek. *Congress and Its Members*. 10th ed. Washington, D.C.: CQ Press, 2006.

Dodd, Lawrence C., and Bruce I. Oppenheimer, eds. *Congress Reconsidered*. 8th ed. Washington, D.C.: CQ Press, 2005.

Fenno, Richard F., Jr. *Home Style: House Members in Their Districts*. Boston: Little, Brown, 1978.

Galloway, George B. *History of the House of Representatives*. 2d ed. New York: Crowell, 1976.

Koempel, Michael L., and Judy Schneider. *Congressional Deskbook*. 5th ed. Alexandria, Va.: TheCapitol.Net, 2007.

MacNeil, Neil. *Forge of Democracy: The House of Representatives*. New York: David McKay, 1963.

Sinclair, Barbara. *Legislators, Leaders, and Lawmaking: The U.S. House of Representatives in the Post-reform Era*. Baltimore: Johns Hopkins University Press, 1995.

Impeachment

Berger, Raoul. *Impeachment: The Constitutional Problems*. Cambridge, Mass.: Harvard University Press, 1973.

Black, Charles L. *Impeachment: A Handbook*. New Haven, Conn.: Yale University Press, 1974.

Gerhardt, Michael J. *The Federal Impeachment Process: A Constitutional and Historical Analysis*. Rev. ed. Durham, N.C.: Duke University Press, 2003.

Jeffrey, Harry P., and Thomas Maxwell-Long, eds. *Watergate and the Resignation of Richard Nixon: Impact of a Constitutional Crisis*. Washington, D.C.: CQ Press, 2004.

Labovitz, John R. *Presidential Impeachment*. New Haven, Conn.: Yale University Press, 1978.

McLoughlin, Merrill, ed. *The Impeachment and Trial of President Clinton: The Official Transcripts, from the House Judiciary Committee Hearings to the Senate Trial*. New York: Times Books, 1999.

Nichols, John. *The Genius of Impeachment: The Founders' Cure for Royalism*. New York: New Press/Norton, 2006.

Van Tassel, Emily Field, and Paul Finkelman. *Impeachable Offenses*. Washington, D.C.: CQ Press, 1999.

Witt, Elder, ed. *Watergate: Chronology of a Crisis*. 1974. Reprint. Washington, D.C.: Congressional Quarterly, 1999.

Investigations

Berger, Raoul. *Executive Privilege: An Executive Myth*. Cambridge, Mass.: Harvard University Press, 1974.

Ginsberg, Benjamin, and Martin Shefter. *Politics by Other Means: Politicians, Prosecutors, and the Press from Watergate to Whitewater*. 3d. ed. New York: Norton, 2002.

Hamilton, James. *The Power to Probe: A Study of Congressional Investigations*. New York: Random House, 1976.

Harriger, Katy J. *The Special Prosecutor in American Politics*. 2d ed. Lawrence: University Press of Kansas, 2002.

Jeffrey, Harry P., and Thomas Maxwell-Long, eds. *Watergate and the Resignation of Richard Nixon: Impact of a Constitutional Crisis*. Washington, D.C. CQ Press, 2004.

Johnson, Charles A., and Danette Brickman. *Independent Counsel: The Law and the Investigations*. Washington, D.C.: CQ Press, 2001.

Kean, Thomas H., Lee H. Hamilton, and Benjamin Rhodes. *Without Precedent: The Inside Story of the 9/11 Commission*. New York: Knopf, 2006.

Mayhew, David R. *Divided We Govern: Party Control, Lawmaking, and Investigations, 1946-2002*. 2d ed. New Haven, Conn.: Yale University Press, 2005.

McGeary, M. Nelson. *The Development of Congressional Investigative Power*. New York: Octagon Books, 1973.

Riddle, Donald H. *The Truman Committee: A Study in Congressional Responsibility*. New Brunswick, N.J.: Rutgers University Press, 1964.

Schlesinger, Arthur M., Jr., and Roger Burns, eds. *Congress Investigates: A Documentary History, 1792–1974*. 5 vols. New York: Bowker, 1975.

Leadership

Baker, Richard A., and Roger H. Davidson, eds. *First Among Equals: Outstanding Senate Leaders of the Twentieth Century*. Washington, D.C.: CQ Press, 1991.

Caro, Robert A. *Master of the Senate: The Years of Lyndon Johnson*. New York: Knopf, 2002.

Davidson, Roger H., Susan Webb Hammond, and Raymond W. Smock, eds. *Masters of the House: Congressional Leadership over Two Centuries*. Boulder, Colo.: Westview Press, 1998.

Davidson, Roger J., and Walter J. Oleszek. *Congress and Its Members*. 10th ed. Washington, D.C.: CQ Press, 2006.

Dodd, Lawrence C., and Bruce I. Oppenheimer, eds. *Congress Reconsidered*. 8th ed. Washington, D.C.: CQ Press, 2005.

Follette, Mary P. *The Speaker of the House of Representatives*. New York: Longmans, Green, 1896.

Reprint. New York: Burt Franklin Reprints, 1974.

Hardeman, D. B., and Donald C. Bacon. *Rayburn: A Biography*. Austin: Texas Monthly Press, 1987.

Koempel, Michael L., and Judy Schneider. *Congressional Deskbook*. 5th ed. Alexandria, Va.: TheCapitol.Net, 2007.

Kornacki, John J., ed. *Leading Congress: New Styles, New Strategies*. Washington, D.C.: CQ Press, 1990.

Mann, Thomas E., and Norman J. Ornstein, eds. *The Broken Branch: How Congress Is Failing America and How to Get It Back on Track*. New York: Oxford University Press, 2006.

Mayhew, David R. *Divided We Govern: Party Control, Lawmaking, and Investigations, 1946–2002*. 2d ed. New Haven, Conn.: Yale University Press, 2005.

Peters, Ronald M., Jr. *The American Speakership: The Office in Historical Perspective*. 2d ed. Baltimore: Johns Hopkins University Press, 1997.

Sinclair, Barbara. *Legislators, Leaders, and Lawmaking: The U.S. House of Representatives in the Postreform Era*. Baltimore: Johns Hopkins University Press, 1995.

———. *Party Wars: Polarization and the Politics of National Policy Making*. Norman: University of Oklahoma Press, 2006.

Stonecash, Jeffrey M., Mark D. Brewer, and Mack D. Mariani. *Diverging Parties: Social Change, Realignment, and Party Polarization*. Boulder, Colo.: Westview Press, 2003.

Legislative Process

Binder, Sarah A. *Stalemate: Causes and Consequences of Legislative Gridlock*. Washington, D.C.: Brookings Institution Press, 2003.

Birnbaum, Jeffrey H., and Alan S. Murray. *Showdown at Gucci Gulch*. New York. Random House, 1987.

Brady, David W. *Party, Process, and Political Change in Congress: New Perspectives on the History of Congress*. Stanford, Calif.: Stanford University Press, 2002.

Davidson, Roger J., and Walter J. Oleszek. *Congress and Its Members*. 10th ed. Washington, D.C.: CQ Press, 2006.

Dodd, Lawrence C., and Bruce I. Oppenheimer, eds. *Congress Reconsidered*. 8th ed. Washington, D.C.: CQ Press, 2005.

Elving, Ronald D. *Conflict and Compromise: How Congress Makes the Law*. New York: Simon & Schuster, 1995.

Koempel, Michael L., and Judy Schneider. *Congressional Deskbook*. 5th ed. Alexandria, Va.: TheCapitol.Net, 2007.

Oleszek, Walter J. *Congressional Procedures and the Policy Process.* 7th ed. Washington, D.C.: CQ Press, 2007.

Redman, Eric. *The Dance of Legislation.* Reprint. Seattle: University of Washington Press, 2001.

Reid, T. R. *Congressional Odyssey: The Saga of a Senate Bill.* New York: Freeman, 1980.

Sinclair, Barbara. *Unorthodox Lawmaking: New Legislative Processes in the U.S. Congress.* 2d ed. Washington, D.C.: CQ Press, 2000.

Smith, Steven S. *Call to Order: Floor Politics in the House and Senate.* Washington, D.C.: Brookings Institution Press, 1989.

Legislative Veto

Fisher, Louis. *Constitutional Dialogues.* Princeton, N.J.: Princeton University Press, 1988.

Lobbying

Berry, Jeffrey M. *The New Liberalism: The Rising Power of Citizen Groups.* Washington, D.C.: Brookings Institution Press, 2000.

Birnbaum, Jeffrey H., and Alan S. Murray. *Showdown at Gucci Gulch: Lawmakers, Lobbyists, and the Unlikely Triumph of Tax Reform.* New York: Random House, 1987.

Cigler, Allan J., and Burdett A. Loomis. *Interest Group Politics.* 7th ed. Washington, D.C.: CQ Press, 2007.

Hernson, Paul S., Ronald G. Shaiko, and Clyde Wilcox, eds. *The Interest Group Connection: Electioneering, Lobbying, and Policymaking in Washington.* 2d ed. Washington, D.C.: CQ Press, 2005.

Hula, Kevin. *Lobbying Together: Interest Group Coalitions in Legislative Politics.* Washington, D.C.: Georgetown University Press, 1999.

Koempel, Michael L., and Judy Schneider. *Congressional Deskbook.* 5th ed. Alexandria, Va.: TheCapitol.Net, 2007.

Kollman, Ken. *Outside Lobbying: Public Opinion and Interest Group Strategies.* Princeton, N.J.: Princeton University Press, 1998.

Rozell, Mark J., Clyde Wilcox, and David Madland. *Interest Groups in American Campaigns.* 2d ed. Washington, D.C.: CQ Press, 2006.

Skinner, Richard M. *More Than Money: Interest Group Action in Congressional Elections.* Lanham, Md.: Rowman & Littlefield, 2007.

Wolpe, Bruce C., and Bertram J. Levine. *Lobbying Congress: How the System Works.* 2d ed. Washington, D.C.: CQ Press, 1996.

Political Action Committees (PACs)

Cigler, Allan J., and Burdett A. Loomis, eds. *Interest Group Politics.* 7th ed. Washington, D.C.: CQ Press, 2006.

Corrado, Anthony, Thomas E. Mann, Daniel R. Ortiz, and Trevor Potter. *The New Campaign Finance Sourcebook.* Washington, D.C.: Brookings Institution Press, 2005.

Herrnson, Paul S. *Congressional Elections: Campaigning at Home and in Washington.* 4th ed. Washington, D.C.: CQ Press, 2004.

Political Parties

Aldrich, John H. *Why Parties? The Origins and Transformation of Party Politics in America.* Chicago: University of Chicago Press, 1995.

Bibby, John F., and Brian F. Shaffner. *Politics, Parties, and Elections in America.* 6th ed. Boston, Mass.: Thomas-Wadsworth, 2007.

Bond, Jon R., and Richard Fleisher, eds. *Polarized Politics: Congress and the President in a Partisan Era.* Washington, D.C.: CQ Press, 2000.

Davidson, Roger J., and Walter J. Oleszek. *Congress and Its Members.* 10th ed. Washington, D.C.: CQ Press, 2006.

Green, John C., and Daniel J. Coffey. *The State of the Parties: The Changing Role of Contemporary American Parties.* 5th ed. Lanham, Md.: Rowan and Littlefield, 2007.

Keefe, William J., and Marc Hetherington. *Parties, Politics, and Public Policy in America.* 10th ed. Washington, D.C.: CQ Press, 2007

Sabato, Larry, and Bruce A. Larson. *The Party's Just Begun: Shaping Political Parties for America's Future.* 2d ed. New York: Longman, 2001.

Power of the Purse

Birnbaum, Jeffrey A., and Alan S. Murray. *Showdown at Gucci Gulch: Lawmakers, Lobbyists, and the Unlikely Triumph of Tax Reform.* New York: Random House, 1987.

Fenno, Richard F., Jr. *The Power of the Purse: Appropriation Politics in Congress.* Boston: Little, Brown, 1973.

LeLoup, Lance T. *Parties, Rules, and the Evolution of Congressional Budgeting.* Pullman: Washington State University, 2005.

Munson, Richard. *The Cardinals of Capitol Hill: The Men and Women Who Control Federal Spending.* New York: Grove Press, 1993.

Palazzolo, Daniel J. *The Speaker and the Budget: Leadership in the Post-Reform House of Representatives.* Pittsburgh: University of Pittsburgh Press, 1992.

Rivlin, Alice M., and Isabel Sawhill, eds. *Restoring Fiscal Sanity, 2005: Meeting the Long-Run Challenge.* Washington, D.C.: Brookings Institutions Press, 2005.

Schick, Allen, and Felix LoStracco. *The Federal Budget: Politics, Policy, Process.* Rev. ed. Washington, D.C.: Brookings Institution Press, 2000.

Press and Congress

Arnold, R. Douglas. *Congress, the Press, and Political Accountability.* Princeton, N.J.: Princeton University Press, 2006.

Cook, Timothy E. *Governing with the News: The News Media as a Political Institution.* 2d ed. Chicago: University of Chicago Press, 2005.

Davidson, Roger J., and Walter J. Oleszek. *Congress and Its Members.* 10th ed. Washington, D.C.: CQ Press, 2006.

Fenno, Richard F., Jr. *Home Style: House Members in Their Districts.* Boston: Little, Brown, 1978.

Graber, Doris A. *Mass Media and American Politics.* 7th ed. Washington, D.C.: CQ Press, 2006.

———, ed. *Media Power in Politics.* 5th ed. Washington, D.C.: CQ Press, 2007.

Hess, Stephen. *Live from Capitol Hill! Studies of Congress and the Media.* Washington, D.C.: Brookings Institution Press, 1991.

Mann, Thomas E., and Norman J. Ornstein. *Congress, the Press, and the Public.* Brookings Institution Press, 1994.

Overholser, Geneva, and Kathleen H. Jamieson, eds. *The Press.* New York: Oxford University Press, 2005.

Perloff, Richard M. *Political Communication: Politics, Press, and Public in America.* Mahwah, N.J.: Lawrence Erlbaum, 1998.

Reapportionment and Redistricting

Congressional Districts in the 1990s: A Portrait of America. Washington, D.C.: CQ Press, 1993.

Congressional Districts in the 2000s: A Portrait of America. Washington, D.C.: CQ Press, 2003.

Reform, Congressional

Adler, E. Scott. *Why Congressional Reforms Fail: Reelection and the House Committee System.* Chicago: University of Chicago Press, 2002.

Davidson, Roger H., and Walter J. Oleszek. *Congress against Itself.* Bloomington: Indiana University Press, 1977.

Dodd, Lawrence C., and Bruce I. Oppenheimer, eds. *Congress Reconsidered.* 8th ed. Washington, D.C.: CQ Press, 2005.

Evans, C. Lawrence, and Walter J. Oleszek. *Congress under Fire: Reform Politics and the Republican Majority.* Boston: Houghton Mifflin, 1997.

Hinckley, Barbara. *Stability and Change in Congress.* 4th ed. New York: Harper and Row, 1988.

Mann, Thomas E., and Norman J. Ornstein, eds. *The Broken Branch: How Congress Is Failing America and How to Get It Back on Track.* New York: Oxford University Press, 2006.

Oleszek, Walter J. *Congressional Procedures and the Policy Process.* 7th ed. Washington, D.C.: CQ Press, 2007.

Ornstein, Norman J., ed. *Congress in Change: Evolution and Reform.* New York: Praeger, 1975.

Rieselbach, Leroy N. *Congressional Reform.* Washington, D.C.: CQ Press, 1986.

Sinclair, Barbara. *Legislators, Leaders, and Lawmaking: The U.S. House of Representatives in the Postreform Era.* Baltimore: Johns Hopkins University Press, 1995.

Senate

Baker, Richard A., and Roger H. Davidson, eds. *First Among Equals: Outstanding Senate Leaders of the Twentieth Century.* Washington, D.C.: CQ Press, 1991.

Binder, Sarah A., and Steven S. Smith. *Politics or Principle? Filibustering in the United States Senate.* Washington, D.C.: Brookings Institution Press, 1997.

Byrd, Robert C. *The Senate 1789–1989.* 4 vols. Washington, D.C.: Government Printing Office, 1988–1994.

Caro, Robert A. *Master of the Senate: The Years of Lyndon Johnson.* New York: Alfred A. Knopf, 2002.

Davidson, Roger J., and Walter J. Oleszek. *Congress and Its Members.* 10th ed. Washington, D.C.: CQ Press, 2006.

Fenno, Richard F., Jr. *Senators on the Campaign Trail: The Politics of Representation.* Norman: University of Oklahoma Press, 1998.

———. *Congressmen in Committees.* Boston: Little, Brown, 1974.

Haynes, George H. *The Senate of the United States: Its History and Practice.* 2 vols. Boston: Houghton Mifflin, 1938.

Loomis, Burdett, ed. *Esteemed Colleagues: Civility and Deliberation in the U.S. Senate.* Washington, D.C.: Brookings Institution Press, 2000.

Kessler, Alexander P., ed. *The United States Senate: Chronology and Institutional Bibliography.* New York: Novinka Books, 2006.

Koempel, Michael L., and Judy Schneider. *Congressional Deskbook.* 5th ed. Alexandria, Va.: TheCapitol.Net, 2007.

Oleszek, Walter J. *Majority and Minority Whips of the Senate: History and Development of the Party Whip System in the United States Senate.* Washington, D.C.: Government Printing Office, 1985.

Oppenheimer, Bruce I. *U.S. Senate Exceptionalism.* Columbus: Ohio State University Press, 2002.

Sinclair, Barbara. *The Transformation of the U.S. Senate.* Baltimore: Johns Hopkins University Press, 1989.

Wirls, Daniel, and Stephen Wirls. *The Invention of the United States Senate.* Baltimore: Johns Hopkins University Press, 2004.

Speaker of the House

Davidson, Roger H., Susan Webb Hammond, and Raymond W. Smock, eds. *Masters of the House: Congressional Leaders over Two Centuries.* Boulder, Colo.: Westview Press, 1998.

Follette, Mary P. *The Speaker of the House of Representatives.* New York: Longmans, Green, 1896. Reprint. New York: Burt Franklin Reprints, 1974.

Hardeman, D. B., and Donald C. Bacon. *Rayburn: A Biography.* Austin: Texas Monthly Press, 1987.

Koempel, Michael L., and Judy Schneider. *Congressional Deskbook.* 5th ed. Alexandria, Va.: TheCapitol.Net, 2007.

Palazzolo, Daniel J. *The Speaker and the Budget: Leadership in the Post-Reform House of Representatives.* Pittsburgh: University of Pittsburgh Press, 1992.

Peters, Ronald M., Jr. *The American Speakership: The Office in Historical Perspective.* 2d ed. Baltimore: Johns Hopkins University Press, 1997.

———, ed. *The Speaker: Leadership in the U.S. House of Representatives.* Washington, D.C.: CQ Press, 1994.

Sinclair, Barbara. *Legislators, Leaders, and Lawmaking: The U.S. House of Representatives in the Postreform Era.* Baltimore: Johns Hopkins University Press, 1995.

O'Neill, Thomas P., Jr., with William Novak. *Man of the House: The Life and Political Memoirs of Speaker Tip O'Neill.* New York: Random House, 1987.

Staff

Bisnow, Mark. *In the Shadow of the Dome: Chronicles of a Capitol Hill Aide.* New York: William Morrow, 1990.

Davidson, Roger J., and Walter J. Oleszek. *Congress and Its Members.* 10th ed. Washington, D.C.: CQ Press, 2006.

Deering, Christopher J., and Steven S. Smith. *Committees in Congress.* 3d ed. Washington, D.C.: CQ Press, 1997.

Fox, Harrison W., Jr., and Susan Webb Hammond. *Congressional Staffs: The Invisible Force in American Lawmaking.* New York: Free Press, 1977.

Malbin, Michael J. *Unelected Representatives: Congressional Staffs and the Future of Representative Government.* New York: Basic Books, 1980.

Struglinski, Suzanne, ed. *The Almanac of the Unelected, 2007: Staff of the U.S. Congress.* 20th ed. Lanham, Md.: Bernan Press, 2007.

States and Congress

Conlon, Timothy. *From New Federalism to Devolution: Twenty-Five Years of Intergovernmental Reform.* Washington, D.C.: Brookings Institution Press, 1998.

Derthick, Martha. *Keeping the Compound Republic: Essays on American Federalism.* Washington, D.C.: Brookings Institution Press, 2001.

Treaty-Making Power

Crabb, Cecil V., Jr., and Pat M. Holt. *Invitation to Struggle: Congress, the President, and Foreign Policy.* 4th ed. Washington, D.C.: CQ Press, 1992.

Fisher, Louis. *Constitutional Conflicts between Congress and the President.* 4th ed. Lawrence: University Press of Kansas, 1997.

Hamilton, Lee, and Jordan Tama. *A Creative Tension: The Foreign Policy Roles of the President and Congress.* Washington, D.C.: Woodrow Wilson Center Press, 2002.

Hersman, Rebecca K. C. *Friends and Foes: How Congress and the President Really Make Foreign Policy.* Washington, D.C.: Brookings Institution Press, 2000.

Jentleson, Bruce W. *American Foreign Policy: The Dynamics of Choice in the 21st Century.* 2d ed. New York: Norton, 2004.

Johnson, Loch K. *The Making of International Agreements: Congress Confronts the Executive.* New York: New York University Press, 1984.

Kelley, Donald R., ed. *Divided Power: The Presidency, Congress, and the Formation of American Foreign Policy.* Fayetteville: University of Arkansas Press, 2005.

Papp, Daniel S., Loch Johnson, and John Endicott. *American Foreign Policy: History Politics, and Policy.* New York: Pearson Longman, 2005.

Silverstein, Gordon. *Imbalance of Powers: Constitutional Interpretation and the Making of American Foreign Policy.* New York: Oxford University Press, 1997.

Vice President

Hayes, Stephen F. *Cheney: The Untold Story of America's Most Powerful and Controversial Vice President.* New York: HarperCollins, 2007.

Light, Paul C. *Vice-Presidential Power: Advice and Influence in the White House.* Baltimore: Johns Hopkins University Press, 1984.

Nelson, Michael. *A Heartbeat Away.* New York: Unwin Hyman, 1988.

Walch, Timothy, ed. *At the President's Side: The Vice Presidency in the Twentieth Century.* Columbia: University of Missouri Press, 1997.

Voters and Congress

Bianco, William T. *Trust: Representatives and Constituents.* Ann Arbor: University of Michigan Press, 1994.

Davidson, Roger J., and Walter J. Oleszek. *Congress and Its Members.* 10th ed. Washington, D.C.: CQ Press, 2006.

Fenno, Richard F., Jr. *Home Style: House Members in Their Districts.* Boston: Little, Brown, 1978.

———. *Senators on the Campaign Trail: The Politics of Representation.* Norman: University of Oklahoma Press, 1998.

———. *Congress at the Grassroots: Representational Change in the South, 1970-1998.* Chapel Hill: University of North Carolina Press, 2000.

Fiorina, Morris P., Samuel J. Abrams, and Jeremy C. Pope. *Culture War? The Myth of a Polarized America.* 2d ed. New York: Pearson Longman, 2006.

Herrnson, Paul S. *Congressional Elections: Campaigning at Home and in Washington.* 4th ed. Washington, D.C.: CQ Press, 2004.

Johannes, John R. *To Serve the People: Congress and Constituency Service.* Lincoln: University of Nebraska Press, 1984.

War Powers

Eagleton, Thomas F. *War and Presidential Power.* New York: Liveright, 1974.

Fisher, Louis. *Presidential War Power.* Lawrence: University Press of Kansas, 1995.

———. *Congressional Abdication on War and Spending.* College Station: Texas A&M University Press, 2000.

Haass, Richard N. *Intervention: The Use of American Military Force in the Post-Cold War World.* Rev. ed. Washington, D.C.: Brookings Institution Press, 1999.

Holt, Pat M. *The War Powers Resolution: The Role of Congress in U.S. Armed Intervention.* Washington, D.C.: American Enterprise Institute, 1978.

Reveley, W. Taylor III. *War Powers of the President and Congress: Who Holds the Arrows and Olive Branch?* Charlottesville: University Press of Virginia, 1981.

Smyrl, Marc E. *Conflict or Codetermination? Congress, the President, and the Power to Make War.* Cambridge, Mass.: Ballinger, 1988.

Westerfield, Donald L. *War Powers: The President, the Congress, and the Question of War.* Westport, Conn.: Greenwood, 1996.

Wormuth, Francis D., and Edwin B. Firmage. *To Chain the Dog of War: The War Power of Congress in History and Law.* 2d ed. Urbana: University of Illinois Press, 1989.

Yoo, John. *The Power of War and Peace: The Constitution and Foreign Affairs after 9/11.* Chicago: University of Chicago Press, 2005.

Watergate Scandal

Berger, Raoul. *Impeachment: The Constitutional Problems.* Cambridge, Mass.: Harvard University Press, 1973.

———. *Executive Privilege: An Executive Myth.* Cambridge, Mass.: Harvard University Press, 1974.

Black, Charles L. *Impeachment: A Handbook.* New Haven, Conn.: Yale University Press, 1974.

Hamilton, James. *The Power to Probe: A Study of Congressional Investigations.* New York: Random House, 1976.

Gerhardt, Michael J. *The Federal Impeachment Process: A Constitutional and Historical Analysis.* Rev. ed. Durham, N.C.: Duke University Press, 2003.

Jeffrey, Harry P., and Thomas Maxwell-Long, eds. *Watergate and the Resignation of Richard Nixon: Impact of a Constitutional Crisis.* Washington, D.C. CQ Press, 2004.

Kutler, Stanley. *The Wars of Watergate: The Last Crisis of Richard Nixon.* New York: Norton, 1992.

Lukas, J. Anthony. *Nightmare: The Underside of the Nixon Years.* New York: Viking, 1976.

Nichols, John. *The Genius of Impeachment: The Founders' Cure for Royalism.* New York: New Press/Norton, 2006.

Schlesinger, Arthur M., Jr. *The Imperial Presidency.* Boston: Houghton Mifflin, 1989.

Schudson, Michael. *Watergate in American Memory.* New York: Basic Books, 1992.

White, Theodore. *Breach of Faith: The Fall of Richard Nixon.* New York: Atheneum, 1975.

Witt, Elder, ed. *Watergate: Chronology of a Crisis.* 1974. Reprint. Washington, D.C.: Congressional Quarterly, 1999.

Woodward, Bob, and Carl Bernstein. *All the President's Men.* New York: Touchtone, 1989.

———. *The Final Days.* New York: Touchtone, 1987.

Index

Page numbers in italics indicate illustrations or photographs.